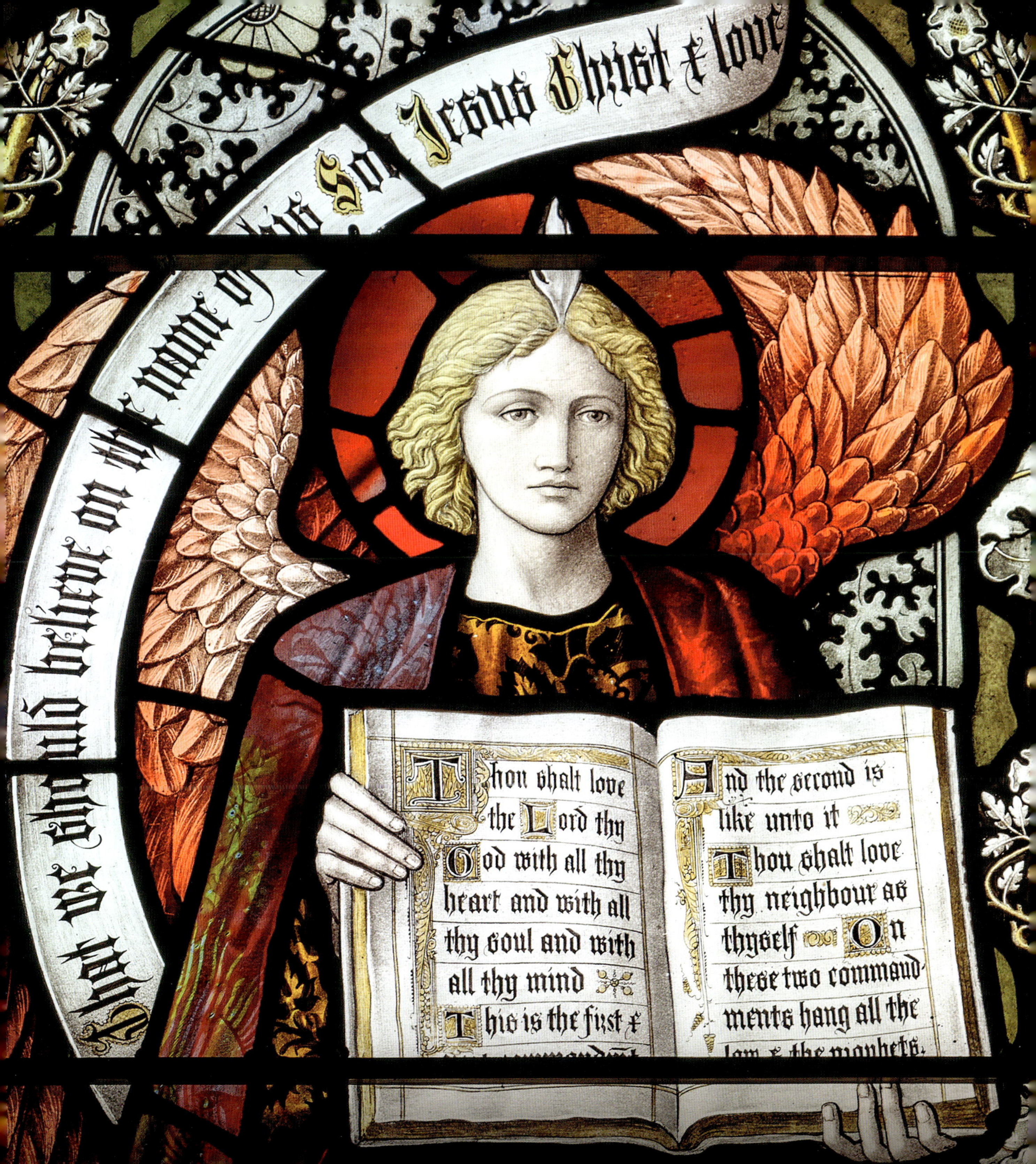

Stained Glass

from Welsh Churches

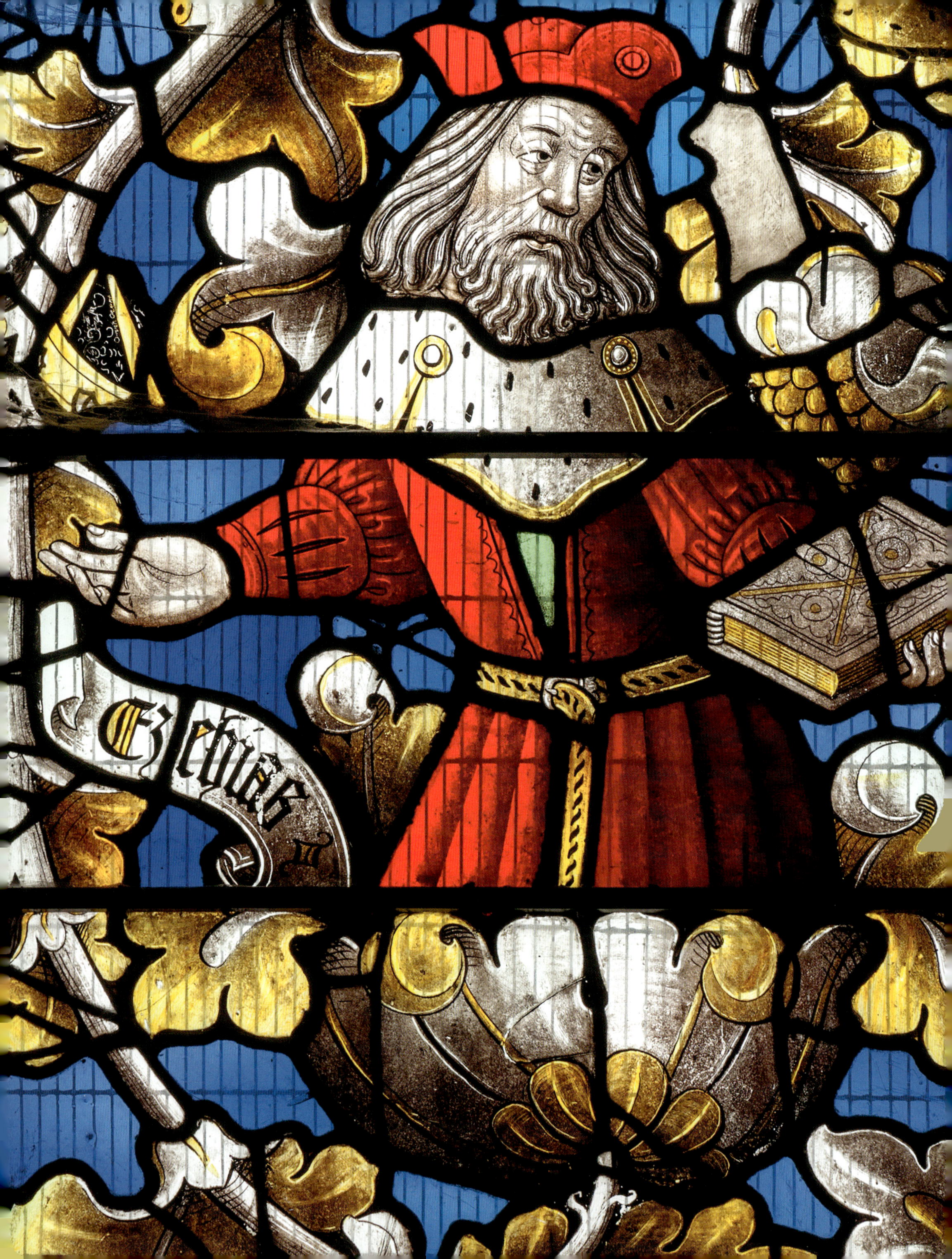

Stained Glass from Welsh Churches

Martin Crampin

y Lolfa

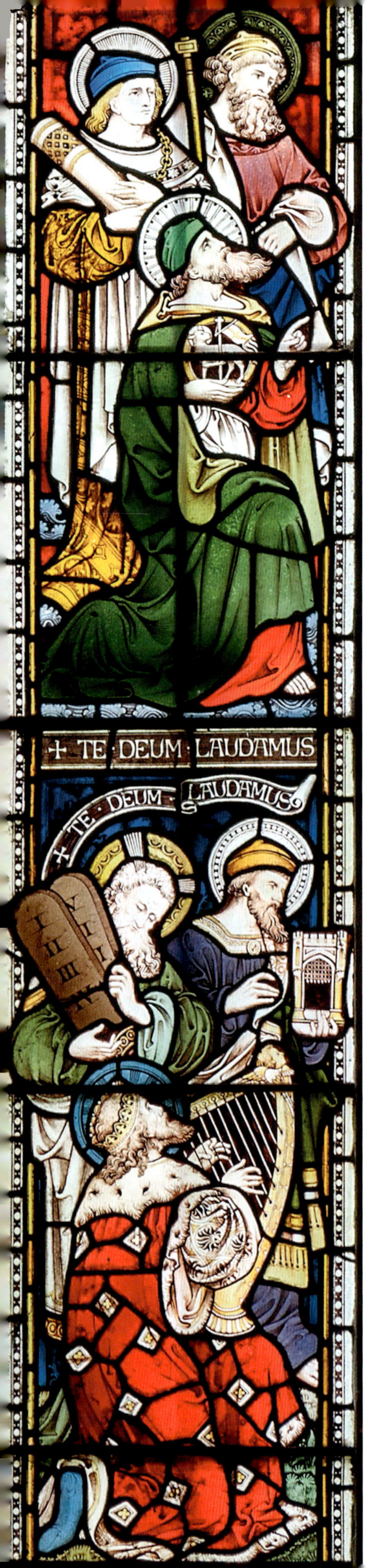

First impression: 2014

The publishers wish to acknowledge the support of
The Welsh Books Council
The Marc Fitch Fund

Design: Martin Crampin

ISBN: 978 184771 825 9

Published and printed in Wales
on paper from well-maintained forests by
Y Lolfa Cyf., Talybont, Ceredigion SY24 5HE
website www.ylolfa.com
e-mail ylolfa@ylolfa.com
tel 01970 832 304
fax 832 782

title page:
Shrigley & Hunt, Angel Holding the Commandments, 1898, Church of St Peter, Llanbedr Dyffryn Clwyd, nave

frontispiece:
Ezechias (Hezekiah), from the The Tree of Jesse, 1533, Church of St Dyfnog, Llanrhaeadr-yng-Nghinmeirch, north chancel

left:
Clayton & Bell, figures from the 'Te Deum', *c.* 1877, Church of All Saints, Llanelli, east window

opposite:
Geoffrey Robinson, Virgin and Child, 1982, Church of St Mary, Llanfair Cilgoed, east window

p. vi:
Alan Younger, detail of north aisle window, 1994, Church of St Arvan, St Arvans

Contents

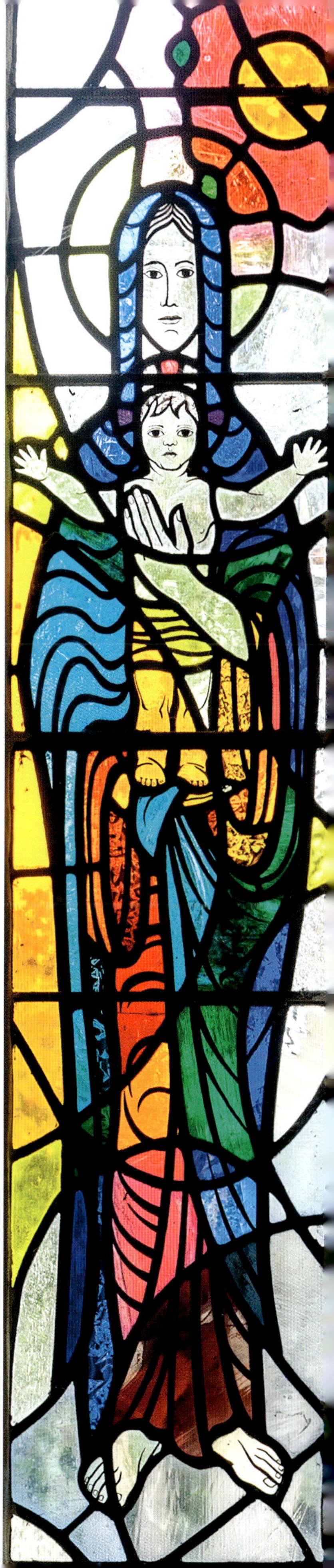

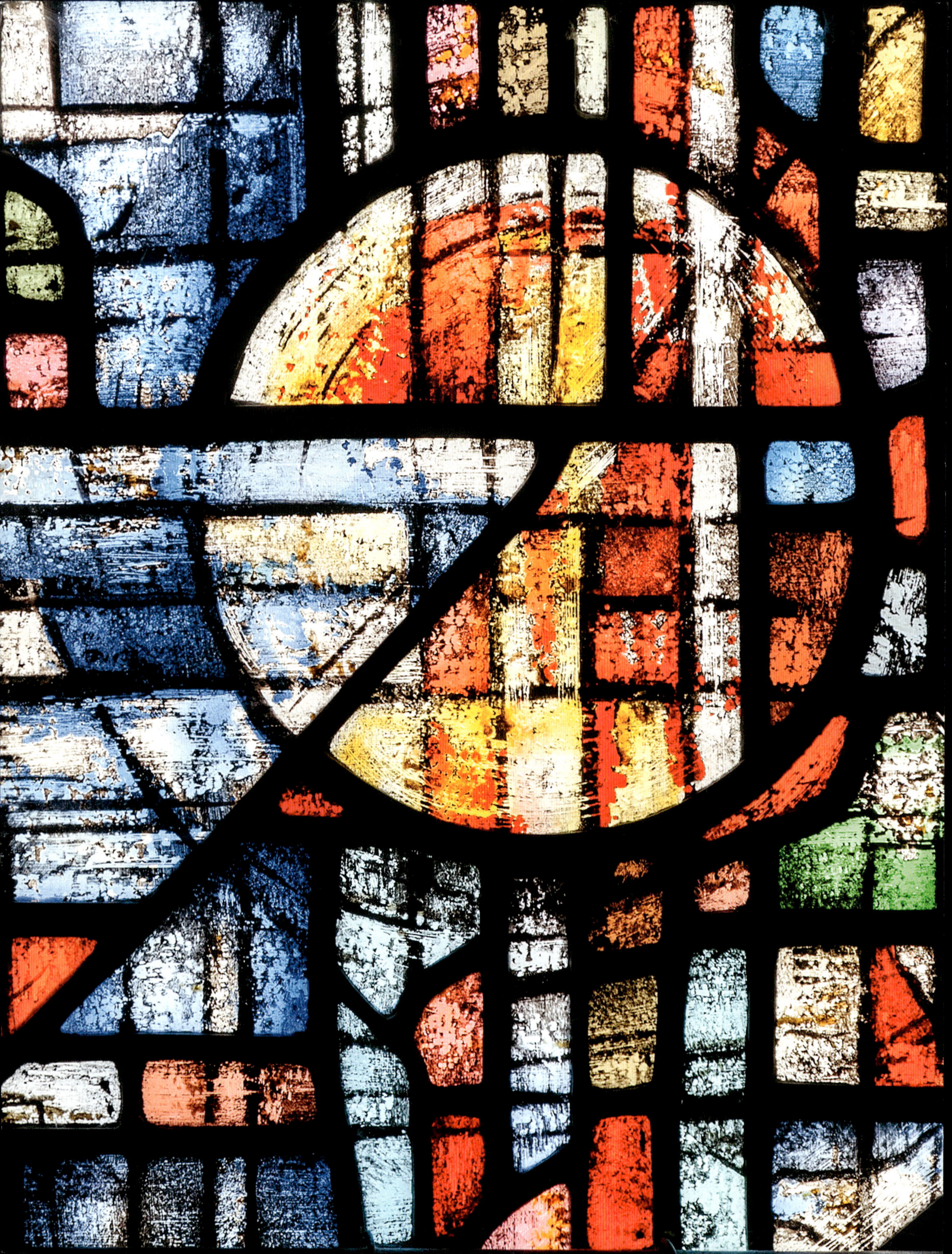

Introduction

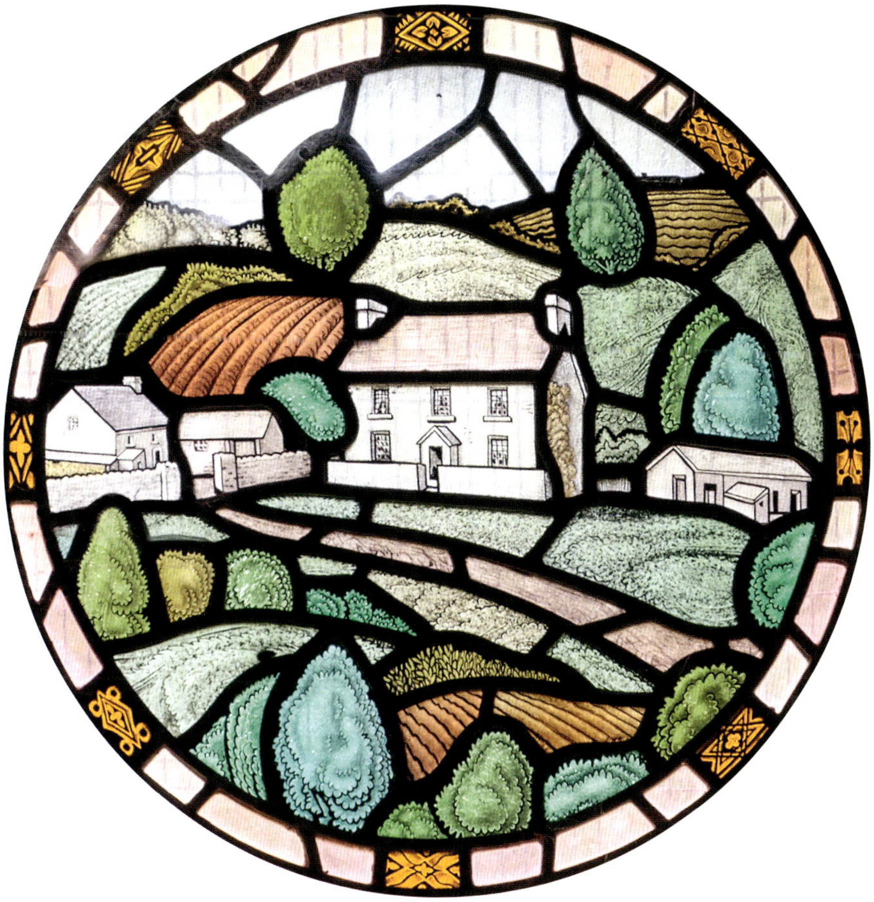

Popular use of the term stained glass often tends to include any coloured window glass, with or without imagery. The proper use of the term refers to the application of silver nitrate or oxide to stain white glass in order to produce a range of yellows and oranges after the glass is fired. The technique was used from the fourteenth century to add colour and painted detail without reducing the translucency of the glass, and it was especially prevalent in the fifteenth and sixteenth centuries.[1] But the strict definition of stained glass excludes the magnificent twelfth- and thirteenth-century windows in the great cathedrals of Chartres, Le Mans and Canterbury; eighteenth and early nineteenth-century windows painted in enamels; and also twentieth-century and contemporary works that, although not always using silver stain, nevertheless draw on the tradition of decorative and pictorial window glass extending back to the eleventh century and have become part of that tradition.

Window glass could only be made in fairly small pieces in the Middle Ages, and it had to be joined together with grooved strips of lead (cames or calmes). Often, glass was cut into diamond or rectangular shapes known as quarries, and decorated with black or brown glass paint made from iron or copper oxide, ground glass, gum Arabic and a liquid binder. These pieces of glass were then leaded up, and patterned glass of this kind is known as grisaille glass, from the French term for painting in monochrome. Pictorial windows were more expensive, requiring skilled designers, painters and glaziers, and the additional costs of manufacturing coloured glass. Lead lines could provide an outline for the design, joining pieces of clear and coloured glass, but additional detail was provided by glass paint and silver stain. Glass paint can be applied as lines or washes in a variety of thicknesses with a range of brushes and sharp tools, and can similarly be removed to restore highlights.

Coloured glass was made by adding metal oxides to clear molten glass, producing 'pot-metal' glass. Copper, for example, can produce both red and green glass, cobalt is used for blue and sodium for yellow. These deep colours darkened windows significantly, especially red (often known as ruby) and blue glass. Since the express purpose of windows

1 For more detailed histories of stained glass production and the development of techniques, see the opening chapters of general surveys such as Sarah Brown, *Stained Glass: An Illustrated History* (London: Bracken Books, 1992), and Virginia Chieffo Raguin, *The History of Stained Glass: The Art of Light Medieval to Contemporary* (London: Thames & Hudson, 2008). These books and many others on stained glass contain a glossary of terms, but others are available online, see for example <http://www.cvma.ac.uk/resources/glossary.html>.

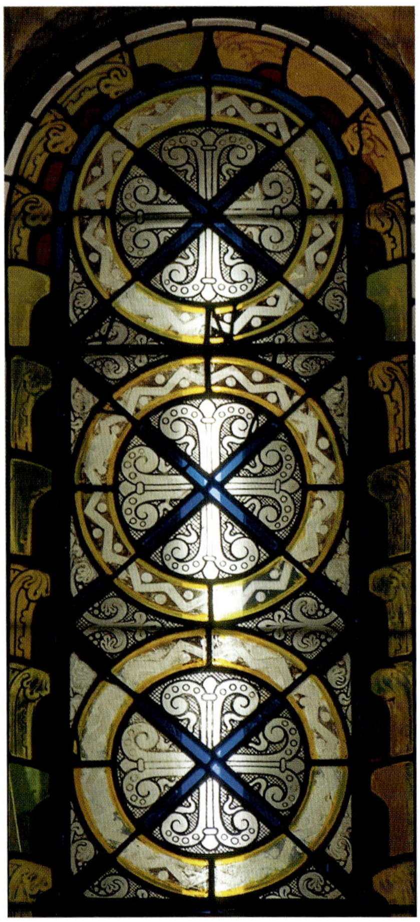

2. Patterned Glass, medieval, restored with new glass in the nineteenth century, Priory Church of St Mary, Usk, chancel

1. (Title page) Celtic Studios, Roundel from nave windo
1954, Church of St Elidyr, Crunwe

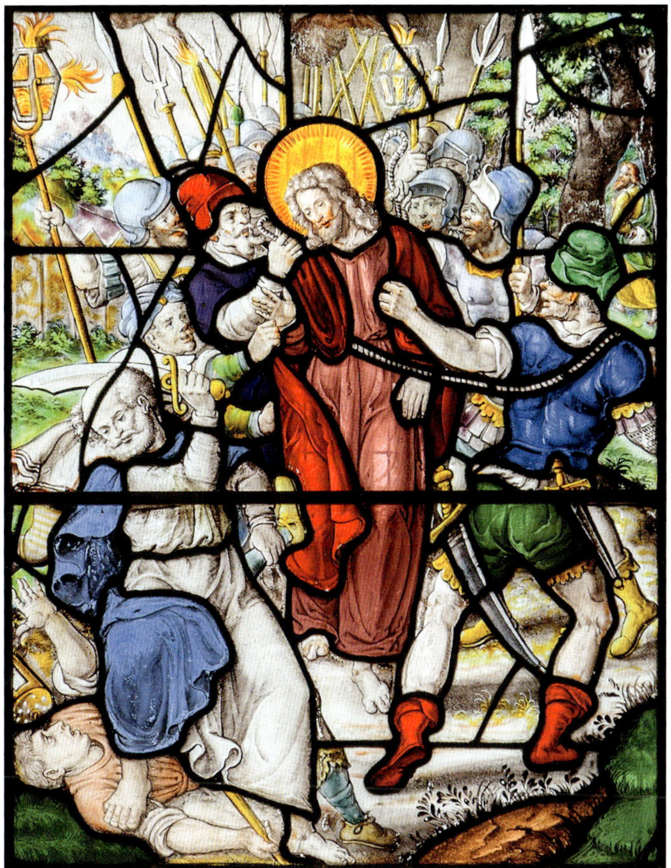

3. The Arrest of Christ, probably late sixteenth century, Church of St Gwenllwyfo, Llanwenllwyfo, east window

is to admit light, the technique of 'flashing' glass, whereby a thin layer of colour could be added onto the surface of white glass, produced more translucent colours. By the thirteenth century there is evidence that this coloured layer was sometimes abraded back to the white glass, making it possible to have white as well as another colour on a single piece of glass. The application of silver stain created the potential to make further colours on a single piece of glass, and during the course of the sixteenth century enamel colours revolutionised glass painting.[2] Red enamel pigments were available in the fifteenth century, but are seen mainly from the following century, and the introduction of blue and green enamels liberated glaziers from the necessity of leading together small pieces of different coloured glass, which was especially useful for detailed heraldic designs.

The emulation of the techniques of oil painting on glass using coloured enamels and washes made the lead line redundant as a determinant of the design, and subdued the amount of light passing through the window. The concern of admitting light and colour through the windows of the church, aligned with the dominant medievalism of the nineteenth century, brought about a decisive return to medieval techniques during the second quarter of the nineteenth century, and by 1850 Gothic was assuredly in the ascendant.[3] With the full force of Victorian industrialisation at their disposal, stained glass firms refined and perfected medieval techniques, exploiting the availability of better quality glass in a wider range of colours. The use of streaky and opalescent glass from the end of the nineteenth century extended the possibilities for artists working in stained glass, although the use of lead remained central to the construction of decorative and pictorial windows. The vocabulary of techniques for making stained glass was extended considerably during the twentieth century. The mid-twentieth century saw the use of thick chunks of glass set in concrete or resin, known by the French term *dalle de verre*, and the term architectural

2 Silver stain could also be painted on blue glass to make it appear green once fired, and if applied to blue flashed glass, parts of which had been abraded, blue, green, yellow and white could be achieved on a single piece of glass.

3 For early Gothic Revival glass in Wales see chapter three of this volume.

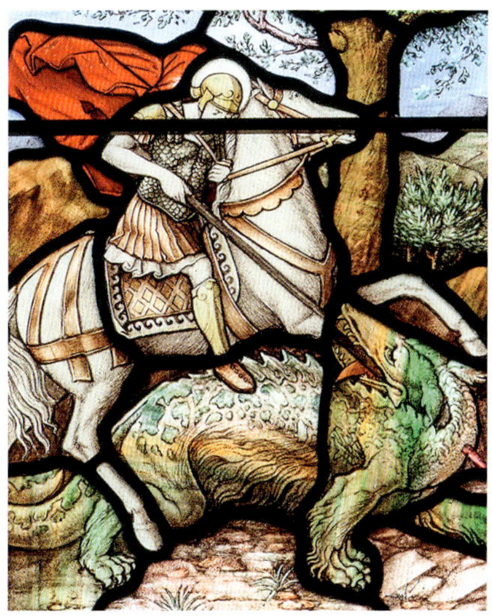

4. Shrigley & Hunt, St George and the Dragon, 1926, Church of St Peter, Carmarthen, south aisle

glass is more useful in encompassing this technique along with windows and screens that have been laminated, bonded, fused, acid-etched or polished, sandblasted and engraved – as well as the traditional techniques of making leaded mosaic windows.

Stained glass windows are more constrained than other works of visual art, as they are usually required to fulfil several functions as well as beautifying the interior. Above all they must exclude the weather and provide light, but in churches they also provide a didactic or sacred purpose.[4] Windows must be fired correctly, use materials resistant to water and changes in temperature, and must be installed with sufficient support for the weight of the glass. Designers also need to accommodate the architectural context for which their windows are made. In particular, the shape of the window constrains the design, which must often be broken up into two or more sections by the vertical mullions dividing the window lights.

The appreciation of stained glass has suffered in a culture that values innovation over tradition in the visual arts. The importance of originality has consistently pervaded art criticism in recent decades and little praise is extended to work that successfully conforms with tradition. Freedom of artistic expression in ecclesiastical stained glass has sometimes been limited by its dependence on conservative patrons and, in the twentieth century, Diocesan Advisory Committees have occasionally been a source of frustration for artists.[5]

Negotiating these constraints requires artists working with stained glass to deal with problems that rarely troubled the most celebrated artists of our age, most of whom worked independently with paint and canvas. Christopher Whall warned against striving to be original and encouraged apprentices to 'follow your master patiently ... echo his habits as Botticelli echoed Fillippo Lippi's, but improve upon them; add something to them if you can.'[6] The stained glass artists who responded to modernity in the 1950s and 60s held a deep respect for both medieval design and the idea of craftsmanship as espoused by the pioneers of the Arts and Crafts Movement.[7] The move towards abstraction was an

4 Heraldic stained glass also provided a social function in churches by denoting the status of particular families, the practice finally waning in the twentieth century. Stained glass could also modulate the light entering churches. For example, the window commissioned as a memorial and thanksgiving for the end of the Second World War at the Church of St Agnes, Port Talbot, was in part a remedy for the morning sun, which sometimes shone 'embarrassingly on the congregation'. National Library of Wales, Records of the Church in Wales: Diocese of Llandaff, uncatalogued papers, faculty 1949/66.

5 The 'various advisory committees and the different authorities', were criticised as early as 1935 for 'gradually strangling the profession' by William Morris, 'The Suitability of Stained Glass as a Means of Decoration of Churches', *Journal of the British Society of Master Glass-Painters*, vol. vi, no. 1 (April 1935), p. 31. The writer had his own stained glass studio but is not to be confused with the nineteenth-century poet, designer and socialist of the same name. The Diocesan Advisory Committees of the Church in Wales have also been responsible for censuring and improving windows designed by lesser artists, and have done their best to ensure that appropriate work of good quality has been installed in churches. Their views have however been criticised by artists, congregations and clergy, and sometimes successfully ignored with both good and unfortunate results.

5. Lavers, Westlake & Co., The Annunciation, *c.* 1911, Church of St Mary, Wenvoe, nave

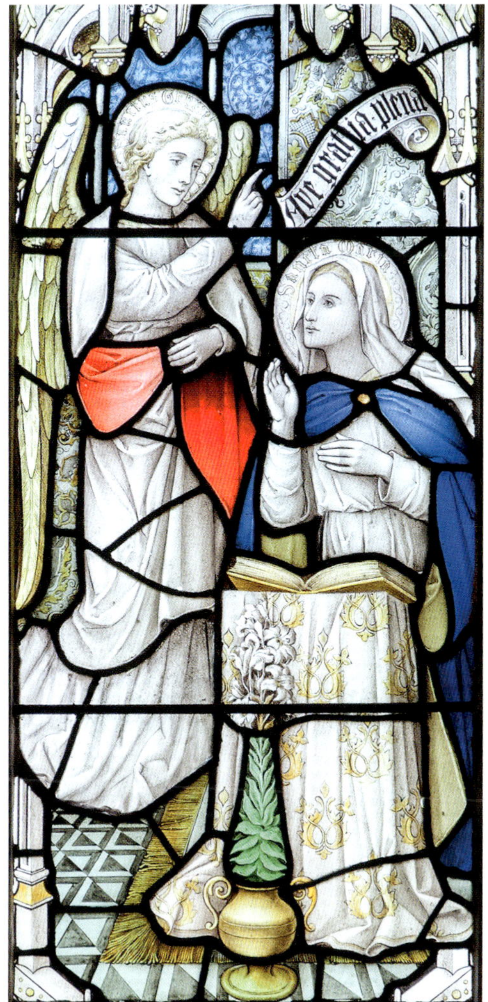

emphatic rejection of the Gothic Revival, but it did not abandon the past as avant-garde movements did in other branches of the visual arts, notably painting and sculpture, and architecture. John Piper drew and studied medieval glass, just as his Victorian predecessors C.E. Kempe and Nathaniel Westlake had done.

The reputation of Victorian stained glass in particular has suffered over the last century. Stained glass of the 1850s and 60s was regarded as unfashionable in design and poor in execution after only a few decades. It was sometimes replaced in the 1890s and into the first half of the twentieth century when it was destroyed or moved to a less prominent position. As the Luftwaffe swept across Britain in 1941, the News and Notes section in the *Journal of the British Society of Master Glass-Painters* noted that 'glass, painted in the last century, has gone. No one can regret the disappearance of some of it'.[8] Such disdain accelerated in the post-war period. Lawrence Lee, one of the most influential designers and teachers of stained glass, dismissed the Gothic Revival 'trade' windows of the nineteenth century as 'lifeless, stereotyped, utterly without conviction'.[9]

Victorian art as a whole only began to recover its reputation in the 1970s, and the stained glass of the period still trails some way behind the esteem of Pre-Raphaelite painting in the public imagination. Nineteenth-century stained glass is often sentimental, conventionalised and formulaic, but the huge number of windows made by firms such as William Wailes; Ward & Hughes; Clayton & Bell; Lavers, Barraud & Westlake and Heaton, Butler & Bayne could be far better than others. These studios employed a large staff and there is a marked difference between the numerous mundane windows and those, fewer in number, that follow an inspired design by one of their best artists, then interpreted by one of their better cartoonists, and painted by their chief glass-painter on a good day.

The finest windows often depend on the selection of the best colours of glass and the ability of a maker to treat each piece with time-consuming techniques such as the application of numerous layers of glass paint or

6 C.W. Whall, *Stained Glass Work: A text book for students and workers in glass* (Bristol: Morris & Juliet Venables, 1999, first published 1905), p. 297.

7 Peter Cormack has described Christopher Whall's *Stained Glass Work* (1905), as 'a manifesto for modern art informed by knowledge of and respect for its antecedents', *The Journal of Stained Glass*, vol. xxvi (2002), p. 7.

8 *Journal of the British Society of Master Glass-Painters*, vol. viii, no. 3 (April 1941), p. 88.

9 Lawrence Lee, *The Appreciation of Stained Glass* (London: Oxford University Press, 1977), p. 89.

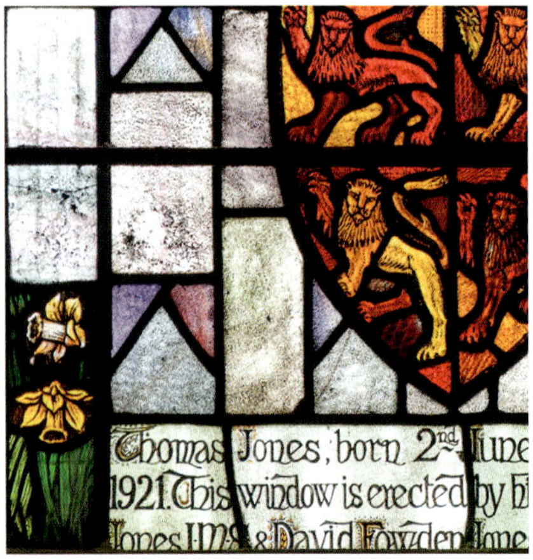

6. Christopher Whall, Detail of a panel with coat of arms beneath St David, *c.* 1922, Church of St Gwyndaf, Llanwnda, north transept

acid-etching and plating. Christopher Whall advised that 'each little bit of glass should look "cared for" and thought of, as a piece of fine jewellery is put together in its setting'.[10] The ingenuity of a skilled artist can do much with little, but while sacrifices of profit might be made for art, the best glass is expensive. It is easy to criticise the quality and design of lesser stained glass windows of the nineteenth and twentieth centuries, although it might be fairer to admit that they are cheap windows. The use of old designs, plain backgrounds or restricted colours may reflect economy on behalf of the patron, rather than lack of skill or imagination on the part of the designer or maker. Similarly, the continuing use of Gothic Revival styles, even after the Second World War, by studios such as Burlison & Grylls and that of Christopher Charles Powell can sometimes reflect sensitivity to surrounding windows and architecture, and not just a medievalist conservatism.

The neglect of stained glass, even in its poorer manifestations, by historians of visual culture has been a failure to understand its impact on congregations and communities and ignore its ubiquity right across urban and rural Wales. Remarkable examples of visual art are often little known outside of the locality, and sometimes ignored even by the worshipping communities. Where novelty of form or treatment of the subject is lacking, particularly in Victorian and Edwardian stained glass, quality of craftsmanship and excellence in glass painting can still be

10 C.W. Whall, *Stained Glass Work: A text book for students and workers in glass* (Bristol: Morris & Juliet Venables, 1999, first published 1905), pp. 323–4.

7. (below) Jones & Willis, The Crucifixion with the Virgin Mary and St John, 1936, Church of St Ffinan, Llanffinan, east window

8. (below centre) Jones & Willis, An Angel Greets the Three Marys at the Empty Tomb, 1937, Church of St Cynon, Fairbourne, chancel

9. (below right) Burlison & Grylls, St Matthew, 1949, Church of St James, Cardiff, south aisle

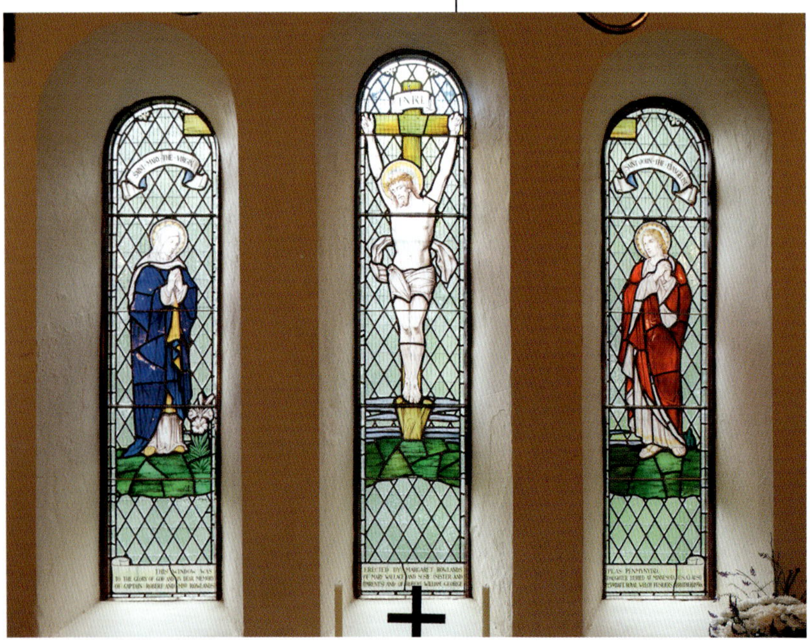

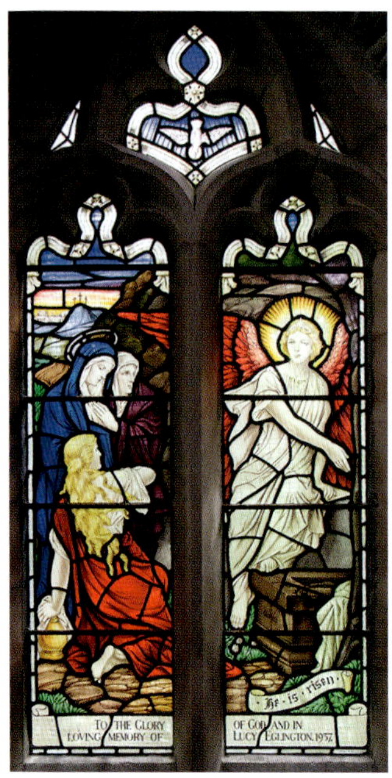

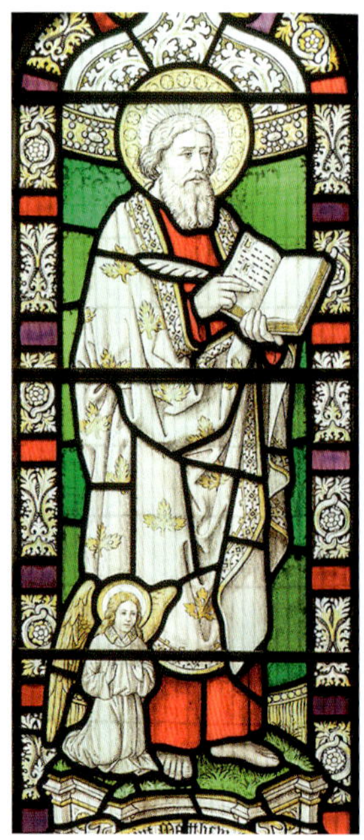

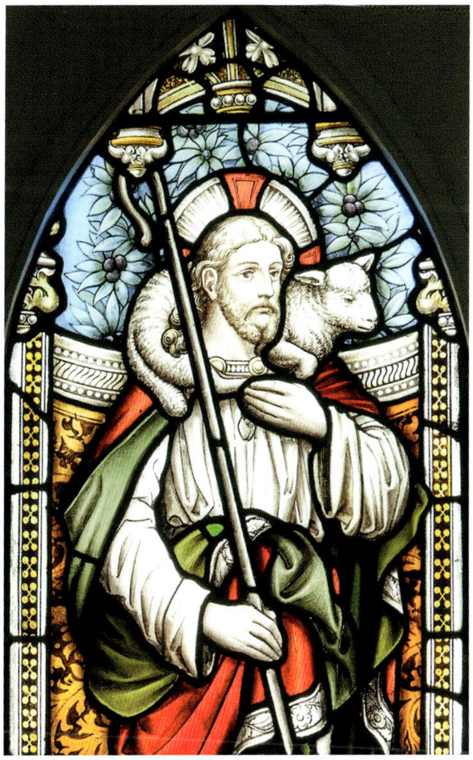

10. E.R. Suffling, The Good Shepherd, 1898, Church of All Saints, Cwmffrwdoer, nave

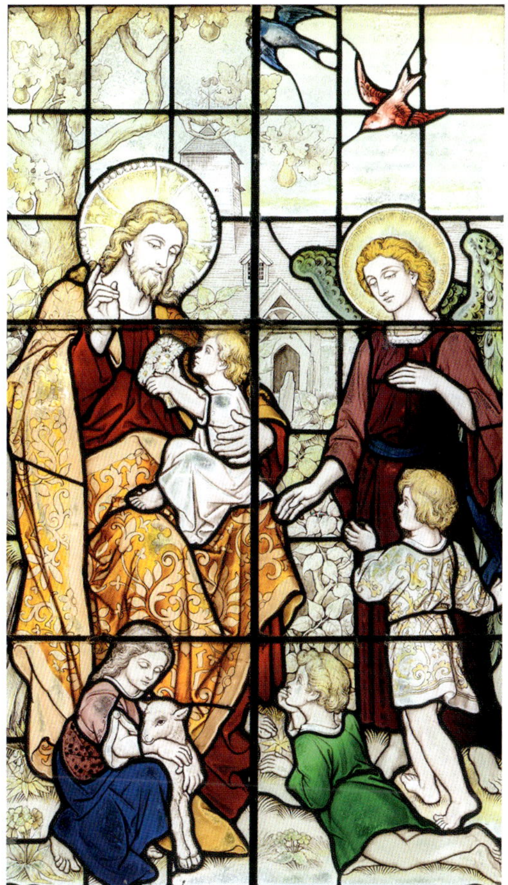

11. Christ with Children, probably 1920s, Church of St Tydecho, Mallwyd, nave

found, sometimes allied with a theological sophistication now utterly foreign to a contemporary audience. Where subjects and designs have been repeated, local detail and portraits of donors were sometimes added to individualise the windows. Welsh saints and historical figures were commemorated and in recent years the local landscape and industrial heritage have frequently been drawn on for windows in church and chapel.

This survey of stained glass in Welsh churches follows a broadly chronological course through the emergence of certain themes. Navigating a history through many hundreds of windows inevitably leaves out many interesting and unique works. Some readers in Wales will protest that there are windows in their own churches worthier of inclusion than some of the more mundane examples that have been illustrated in this study in an attempt to offer a more rounded overview. However, the windows described and illustrated here are augmented by many more on the online Stained Glass in Wales Catalogue, <http://stainedglass.llgc.org.uk>. The online catalogue can only ever be a work in progress, and it is to be hoped that it continues to grow in the future and provide further examples of windows whose artists, subjects and locations are mentioned in this book. All of these windows have their own histories, although the circumstances of their commissioning, the choices of imagery and associated texts, the techniques of manufacture, and the names of those who designed and worked on them are mostly unknown or survive only in the memories of those who were involved. In a few cases some of these pieces of information have been added in this book as footnotes for the interest of stained glass historians, church historians, architectural historians, theologians or those with a broader interest in art in Wales and local history.[11]

11 These footnotes also provide some of the sources for the information provided, but adding all of these sources, which are occasionally contradictory, for every window would overload the footnotes to an even greater extent. Further biographical notes, lists of further reading and additional bibliographical references that lie behind some of the dating and attributions used in the book can also be found on the online Stained Glass in Wales Catalogue, <http://stainedglass.llgc.org.uk>.

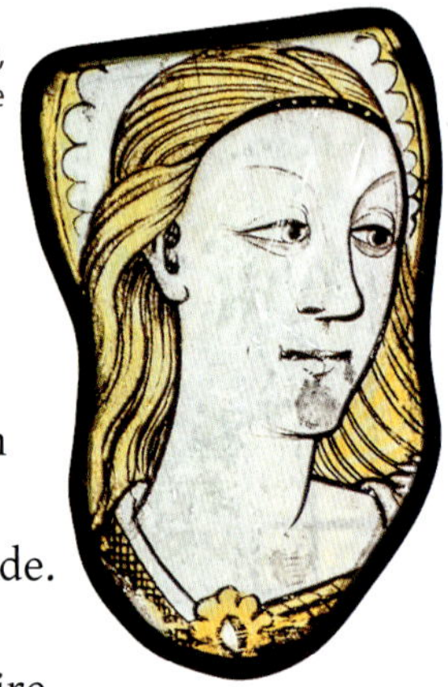

12. Female Head, perhaps *c.* 1500, Church of St Michael, Abergele, nave

Little stained glass is known to have been made in Wales until after the Second World War. Late fifteenth and early sixteenth-century glass is relatively rich in north-east Wales, but it is not known where it was made. Archaeological evidence of a medieval glasshouse was discovered in Delamere Forest in neighbouring Cheshire, and there is archival evidence of glass painters and glaziers working in Chester from the late fourteenth century up to at least the sixteenth century.[12] Geographical distribution of similar medieval stained glass also supports the possibility that the city was a centre for the production of stained glass. For example, some of the glass at the Church of St Mary, Treuddyn, is similar to figures from the 1330s at the Church of St Wilfred, Grappenhall, and further south at the Church of St Mary and All Saints, Checkley, in Staffordshire. The image of a girl's head at Grappenhall from about 1500 is also very similar to another at the Church of St Michael, Abergele, and Chester is conveniently located between these locations. The far-reaching influence of York glaziers is evident in mid-fifteenth century glass found in Welsh churches at Llanrhychwyn, Tremeirchion, Llantysilio and Caerwys, as well as at Over Peover in Cheshire, which has been attributed to a Chester workshop.[13] In the sixteenth century, some of the heads of the figures making up the Tree of Jesse at the Church of St Dyfnog, Llanrhaeadr-yng-Nghinmeirch, dated 1533, have close parallels with two fine bearded heads at the Church of St Helen, Sefton, north of Chester in Lancashire, dated to the early 1540s.[14] A half-figure of Mary at the Church of St Mary, Disley, on the eastern edge of Cheshire, is similar in design to the figures of Mary at the side of the crucified Christ at the Church of St Asaph and St Cynderyn, Llanasa, and the Church of St Mary, Cilcain, where the glass formerly had a date of 1546.[15]

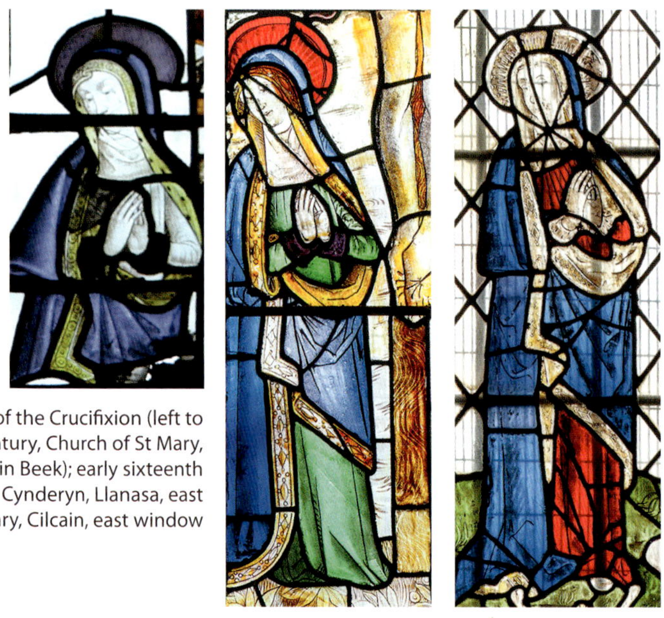

13–15. Figures of Mary from scenes of the Crucifixion (left to right): probably early sixteenth century, Church of St Mary, Disley, clerestory (photo © Martin Beek); early sixteenth century, Church of St Asaph and St Cynderyn, Llanasa, east window; 1546, Church of St Mary, Cilcain, east window

12 Christopher Woodforde, 'Glass-Painters in England before the Reformation', *Journal of the British Society of Master Glass-Painters*, vol. vi, no. 2 (October 1935), pp. 67–9; Penny Hebgin-Barnes, *The Medieval Stained Glass of Cheshire* (Oxford: Oxford University Press, 2010), pp. lxviii, lxxx.

13 Penny Hebgin-Barnes, *The Medieval Stained Glass of Cheshire*, p. clxiii. A further York-type figure survives at Chester Cathedral, and at the Church of St Mary-on-the Hill, Chester, the only two sites in Chester where medieval stained glass has survived.

14 Penny Hebgin-Barnes, *The Medieval Stained Glass of Cheshire*, pp. clxxvi–ii.

15 The date of the glass at Cilcain is given in S.R. Glynne, 'Notes on the older churches in the four Welsh dioceses', *Archaeologia Cambrensis*, fifth series, vol. i (1884), p. 182. The differences in execution, and perhaps of date, could instead suggest a common source rather than a common workshop. A further similar version, although reversed, survives at Beaumaris, see p. 35 of this volume.

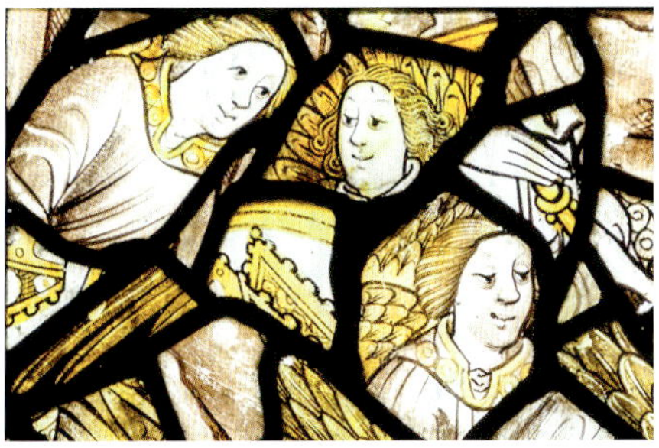

16. (left) Detail of Fragments with Angels, late fifteenth century or early sixteenth century, Church of St Tyrnog, Llandyrnog, east window

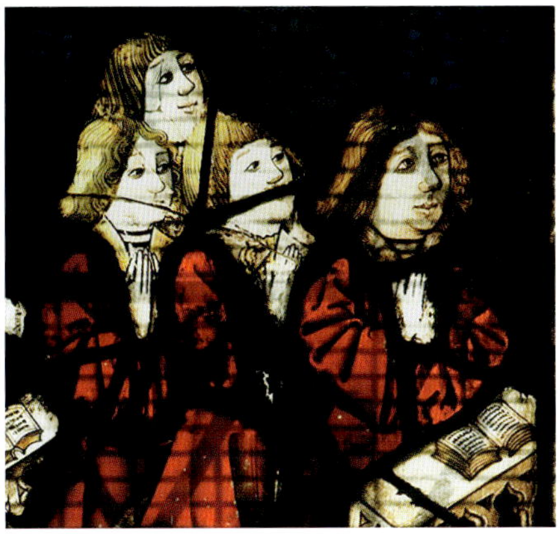

17. (below left) The Children of Sir Thomas Ashton, *c.* 1497–1512, Church of St Michael and All Angels, Ashton-under-Lyne, south aisle (photo © Gordon Plumb)

Back in the late thirteenth century an Englishman, William the Glazier, settled near Holywell and Basingwerk, but nothing is known of his career.[16] While little glass of a late-medieval date survives in Cheshire, it must remain a possibility that the workshop responsible for the glass of 1498–1510 at the Church of All Saints, Gresford – which contains far more medieval glass than any other church in Wales – and surrounding Flintshire and Denbighshire churches at Hope, Llandyrnog and Dyserth, was located nearer the centre of the surviving distribution rather than in Chester. Nevertheless, a little further north, donor figures from churches at Ashton-under-Lyne and Middleton, and scenes of the life of Helen at Ashton-under-Lyne, suggest a very similar hand to that found in the contemporary late fifteenth and early sixteenth-century work at Gresford and Llandyrnog.[17]

Patterned quarries could be produced without the need for a skilled glass painter, as simple patterns could be mass-produced using only a few stock designs. A distinctive style of painted quarries found in north-east Wales makes it likely that a workshop produced them in the vicinity of Ruthin in the Vale of Clwyd from the late fifteenth century.[18] The capabilities of such a workshop could have extended to simple heraldic motifs or pictorial work on occasion if exemplars could be found to copy.

From the mid-nineteenth century there is evidence of glass painters in Wales among gentry households and clergy, such as Sarah Salusbury at Llanwern, the Lloyd sisters of Rhagatt near Corwen, and the Revd J.E. Troughton, curate of the Church of St John the Baptist, Pentrobin (near Penymynydd).[19] Troughton also carved and painted decoration for the church and other members of the clergy made wooden furnishings for their churches. Herbert Davies-Evans' studio in his house at

16 Melville Richards, 'The Population of the Welsh Border', *Transactions of the Honourable Society of Cymmrodorion*, 1970, part 1 (1971), p. 85.

17 The church at Gresford provides a further link with Chester as the donor of a window on in the south wall was a former mayor of the city. D.R. Thomas, *The History of the Diocese of St Asaph* (Oswestry: Caxton Press, 1913), vol. iii, p. 247.

18 Mostyn Lewis, *Stained Glass in North Wales up to 1850* (Altrincham: John Sherratt and Son Ltd, 1970), pp. 12–13.

19 For J.E. Troughton see chapter four of this volume.

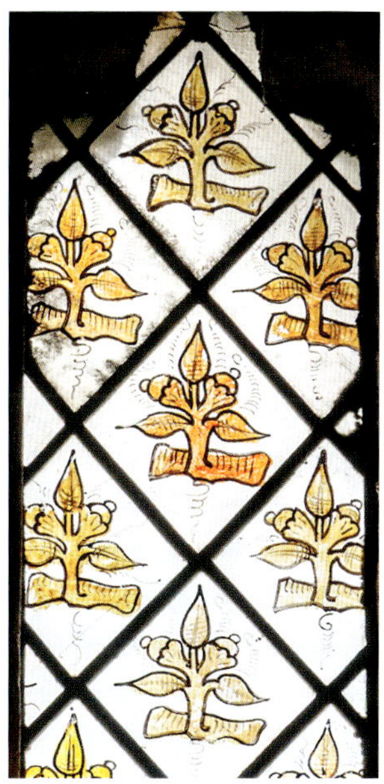

18. Painted Quarries, probably early sixteenth century, Church of St Asaph and St Cynderyn, Llanasa, east window

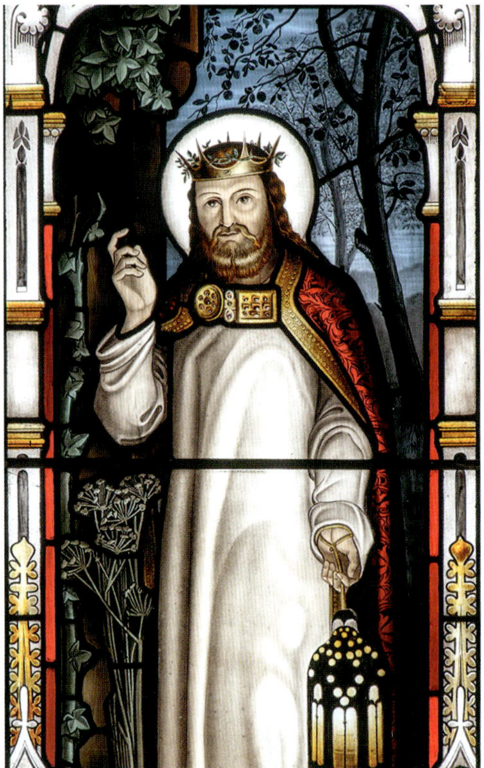

19. W. Davis & Son, Christ the Light of the World (after William Holman Hunt), late nineteenth century or probably early twentieth century, former Ebenezer Welsh Independent Chapel, Cardiff, side wall

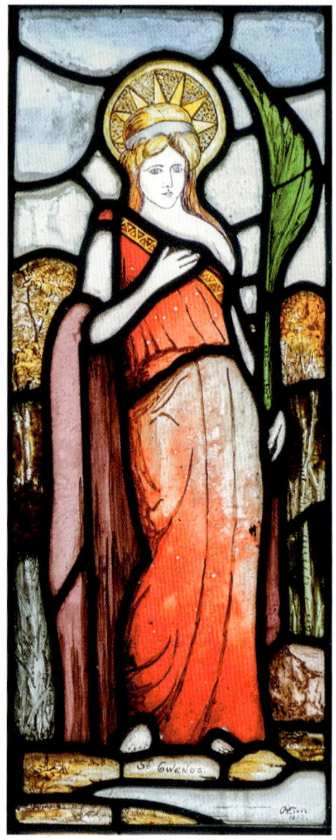

20. Herbert Davies-Evans, St Gwenog, *c.* 1895, Church of St Gwenog, Llanwenog, west wall

Highmead made the carved screen and bench ends for the Church of St Gwenog at Llanwenog, some of which was carved by Joseph Reubens, a Belgian refugee artist, during the First World War. As well as carving the rood screen, Herbert Davies-Evans' skills also extended to stained glass, and his signature is found on the west window of the church, which includes the faintly sultry figure of Gwenog, the patron of the church.

Despite the number of studios and firms that were established across England in the nineteenth century, no known commercial firms producing pictorial stained glass were established in Wales. Evidence for a possible exception to this is the window at Ebenezer Welsh Independent Chapel in central Cardiff, which is signed W. Davis & Son, Cardiff. Unfortunately the window is not dated and has the Gothic Revival character typical of the later nineteenth century that continued to be imitated well into the twentieth century. The establishment of commercial stained glass firms in Wales was perhaps also inhibited by a range of makers located in Bristol, Worcester, Shrewsbury, the West Midlands, Manchester and Liverpool, and distance proved no obstacle for the numerous London firms, William Wailes and Atkinson Brothers in Newcastle, or James Ballantine & Son in Edinburgh.

Some English makers were popular in certain parts of Wales. Windows from the studio of the London designer Robert Newbery can be found across south Wales from Monmouthshire to Pembrokeshire, with outliers in mid-Powys, such as at the country churches at Llanfihangel Rhydithon and St Harmon. However his work has not been recorded either in north Wales or in the English counties of the southern marches, or in Somerset and Wiltshire, suggesting that Newbery's family contacts in Pembrokeshire and patrons such as Sir W.T. Lewis created an unusual concentration of his work in Wales.[20] A smaller group of windows by another London maker, A. Savell, has been

20 For the work of Robert Newbery see chapter six of this volume. I am grateful to Alan Brooks for confirming the lack of work attributed to Robert Newbery in the west of England. Only seventeen windows are attributed to Newbery in the whole of the south-east of England according to an online survey at <http://www.stainedglassrecords.org>, accessed 12 February 2014, whereas there are well over a hundred in south Wales. Even though further attributions in England should be expected (as I have been doing in Wales), and his work is sometimes confused with that of Burlison & Grylls, the amount of work by the London firm in south Wales is exceptional.

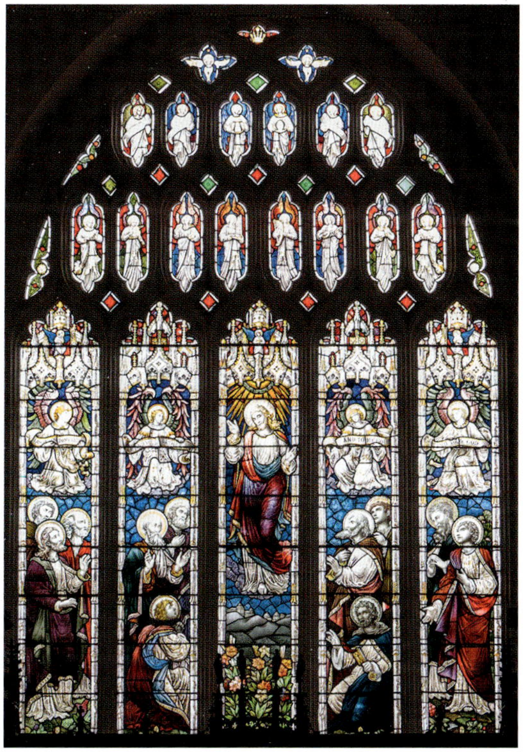

21. A. Savell, The Ascension, 1891, Church of St Mark, Newport, east window

identified by John Newman in the south-east corner of Wales, and only one other window by the firm has been identified elsewhere in Wales.[21]

A short-lived stained glass studio was established by the talented artist Dom. Theodore Baily among the monastic community on Caldey Island, near Tenby, in the 1920s. He made several windows for the island's churches and monastic buildings before the community moved to Prinknash in 1928.[22] In 1909 William Grant Murray was appointed headmaster of the Municipal School of Art and Crafts in Swansea and tried repeatedly to establish a course to teach stained glass design and manufacture, complaining that 'it was an insult to the nation that no stained glass was made in Wales'.[23] In the early 1930s Hubert Thomas made the first stained glass panel at the School and his cousin Howard Martin was invited to teach a part-time evening class at the School in 1935. Together they produced a number of windows for a variety of patrons and settings in the Swansea area during the 1930s.[24] Their window depicting Cecilia and Francis at the Church of St Michael, Llanfihangel Rhydithon, is full of the promise that was to be realised after the Second World War with the formation of Celtic Studios in Swansea.

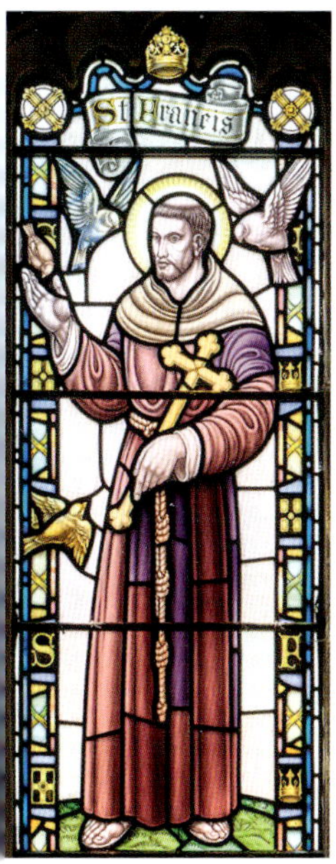

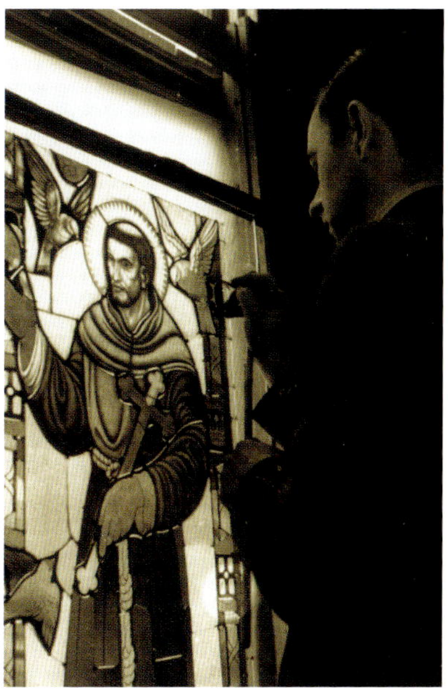

22. (far left) Howard Martin & Hubert Thomas, St Francis, 1939, Church of St Michael, Llanfihangel Rhydithon, nave

23. (left) Howard Martin, *c.* 1938, photo by Ivor Davies (reproduced courtesy estate of Ivor Davies)

21 John Newman identifies seven churches with windows by the firm in Newport, Bassaleg, Marshfield, Abertillery, Llanwonno and Peterston-super-Ely, while the outlier is at Dale, in Pembrokeshire. John Newman, *The Buildings of Wales: Gwent/Monmouthshire* (London/Cardiff: 2000), pp. 112, 115, 381, 431, 433; John Newman, *The Buildings of Wales: Glamorgan* (London/Cardiff: 1995), pp. 413, 515; Thomas Lloyd, Julian Orbach and Robert Scourfield, *The Buildings of Wales: Pembrokeshire* (New Haven/London: Yale University Press, 2004), p. 178.

22 For the work of Theodore Baily see chapter seven of this volume.

23 Maurice Broady, 'A Vision Fulfilled: The Start of the Welsh Stained Glass Tradition', *The Journal of Stained Glass*, vol. xix, no. 2 (1991–3), p. 199.

24 For the early work of Martin & Thomas see chapter 2 of Maurice Broady, *A Vision Fulfilled: The story of Celtic Studios and Swansea's architectural glass tradition* (Swansea: West Glamorgan Archive Service, 2010). Both Howard Martin and Hubert Thomas sought to identify themselves with the ideals of the Arts and Crafts Movement at the outset of their new firm Celtic Studios in 1948. Their aim was 'to produce that which is best in design and workmanship' and they had 'no stock designs', with each window specifically designed for individual settings. Maurice Broady, *A Vision Fulfilled*, p. 24. These ideals proved impossible to maintain.

25 See chapters ten and eleven of this volume.

26 National Library of Wales, Records of the Church in Wales: Diocese of Monmouth DM/P6, Faculty 398.

27 *South Wales Echo*, 17 February 1960, p. 4.

28 Bristow Wadley & Co. were asked by the Diocesan Advisory Committee where the windows for Bedlinog would be made, and replied that they were to be designed and painted by Ivor Davies at Swansea and 'fired in our electric kiln at our Swansea Studios.' National Library of Wales, Records of the Church in Wales: Diocese of Llandaff, uncatalogued papers, faculty 1952/4, letter dated 6 October 1952. From the early 1950s Ivor Davies worked at Celtic Studios as a craftsman, and was perhaps freelancing as a designer and glass painter for Bristow Wadley, but using the facilities at Celtic Studios in Swansea. However Maurice Broady includes the windows of Cadoc and Brychan at Bedlinog in his list of windows by Celtic Studios, together with an earlier window of 1951. Maurice Broady, *A Vision Fulfilled: The story of Celtic Studios and Swansea's architectural glass tradition* (Swansea: West Glamorgan Archive Service, 2010), p. 107. The Bedlinog windows are no longer extant, but Maurice Broady's own annotated list of windows by Celtic Studios describes the three figures at Bedlinog as Howard Martin's 'style at its best', suggesting either that they were not by Ivor Davies, or perhaps confirming (as suggested by the figures at Sully) that Davies' style was similar to that of his friend Howard Martin.

From the 1940s several stained glass artists retired to Wales, such as Edward Woore and Henry Gustave Hiller, while others brought their studios to Wales, such as Joan Howson (a native of Flintshire) and Harcourt Doyle. Since the 1960s a steadily increasing number of independent artists based in Wales made stained glass in their workshops, sheds and on their kitchen tables. Celtic Studios, established by Howard Martin and Hubert Thomas in 1948, together with the stained glass course under the direction of Howard Martin at Swansea School of Art, were both instrumental in establishing the rich tradition of architectural glass in the Swansea area that emerged in the 1970s.[25]

In addition to Celtic Studios, other commercial glaziers in Wales supplied some stained glass for places of worship, either made in their studios or by others. The Cardiff decorating firm Bristow Wadley & Co. was founded in 1909 and by 1960 had nine branches across south Wales and at Hereford. As well as supplying paint and wallpaper it had a stained glass department in Mill Lane, Cardiff, and a window at the Church of St Michael, Abertillery, was designed and made in their studio in 1939–40.[26] After the war the studio reassembled the stained glass that had been removed for safekeeping at Llandaff Cathedral.[27] The designer of the window at Abertillery is unknown. A simple leaded window with coloured glass made by Bristow Wadley & Co. for the Church of St Isan, Llanishen (Cardiff) in 1945 was designed by a Mr Hesp, and Ivor Davies, who had trained at Swansea, designed commissions for the firm at the Church of St Catwg, Bedlinog, in 1952 and the Church of St John the Baptist, Sully, in 1953.[28] Bristow Wadley & Co. restored figures of saints for the Church of St Barnabas, Gilfach Goch, in 1954, and also made the scene of Christ being baptised in the Jordan, which is signed by

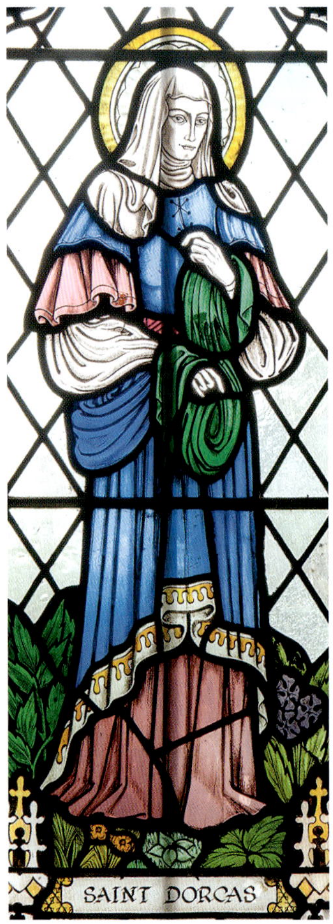

24. Bristow, Wadley & Co., Dorcas, 1953, designed by Ivor Davies, Church of St John the Baptist, Sully, chancel

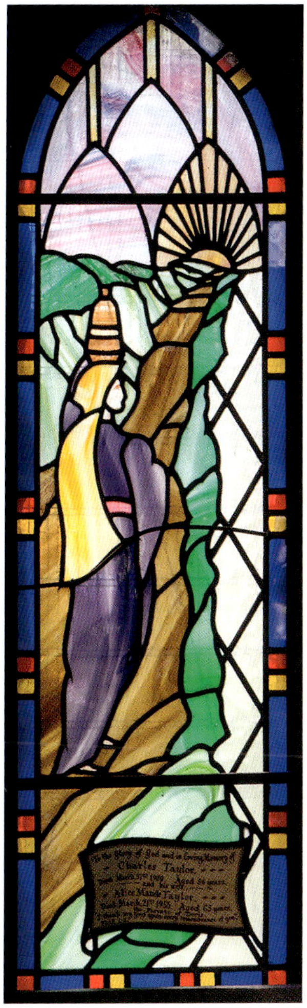

25. Farrow Brothers, *Woman Climbing the Road of Life Towards Dawn of New Day*, 1958, Church of St Paul, Newbridge, south aisle

the firm at Tredegarville English Baptist Church, Cardiff.[29] Neither of the windows at Sully or Tredegarville are distinguished, and the Diocesan Advisory Committee found the design of the figures at Sully 'unduly heavy' and requested a sample of the blue glass to be used, suggesting their unease about the quality of the design and workmanship of Bristow Wadley & Co.[30] By the mid-1960s Bristow Wadley & Co. were subcontracting painted panels to Celtic Studios to fulfil their own commissions, and more research is needed to establish the extent of their capabilities as makers of pictorial stained glass windows.[31]

Other glazing firms made and installed leaded lights and undertook less sophisticated commissions for churches, such as Ashdown's of Cardiff, who were established in 1889. Decorative or even simple figurative windows using coloured glass delineated by lead lines enabled glaziers without any expertise in glass painting to make pictorial windows. One such commission for the Church of St Paul, Newbridge, was made by Farrow Brothers, plumbers and glaziers in Newport, where it is the only window not made by the Exeter firm J. Wippell & Co.[32] Local artists may also have tried their hand at stained glass, although the striking set of abstracted figures painted by a local artist in 1965 on the window behind the altar at the Church of St Timothy, Caerau, only imitate stained glass, by bounding the fairly flat colours with a black edge.

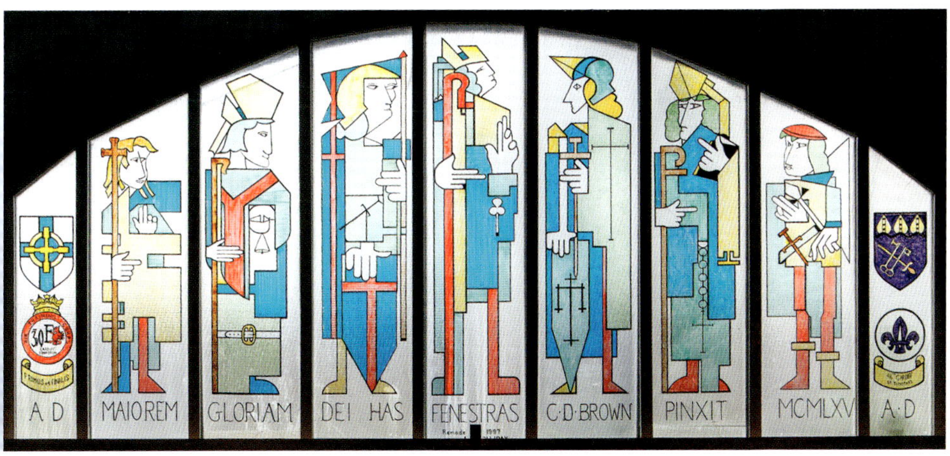

26. C.D. Brown, Saints and Symbols, 1965, Church of St Timothy, Caerau, Cardiff, sanctuary window

29 The figures of the saints David and Luke at Gilfach Goch were initially made in 1935 by C.C. Powell. National Library of Wales, Records of the Church in Wales: Diocese of Llandaff, uncatalogued papers, faculty 1954/19. The window at Tredegarville was made in 1962 and is a copy of E. Goodwyn Lewis' painting of the Baptism of Christ, probably inspired by the superior version at Tabernacl Welsh Baptist Church, also in the city.

30 National Library of Wales, Records of the Church in Wales: Diocese of Llandaff, uncatalogued papers, faculty 1953/36.

31 For example, a figure of Paul was supplied by Celtic Studios in 1966, presumably for a place of worship, and they also made a figure and industrial scenes for a three-light window at the Church of St Elli, Llanelly Hill, unmistakably the work of Celtic Studios. The figures in the outer lights were omitted to reduce the cost of the window. Correspondence regarding these commissions is held at West Glamorgan Archive Service, D/D CEL/20/802, 804 & 1201.

32 National Library of Wales, Records of the Church in Wales: Diocese of Monmouth, uncatalogued papers, faculty 535. The date from the faculty is useful as the window is hard to date stylistically and records the death of Charles Taylor, who died in 1980. Usually this could be assumed to be the earliest date for the window, but in this case the window had been commissioned in memory of his wife Alice, who had died in 1955, and the inscription changed to include his name in 1981. National Library of Wales, Records of the Church in Wales: Diocese of Monmouth, uncatalogued papers, faculty 1949.

The lack of writing about stained glass, particularly that of the modern period, presents an obstacle to the greater understanding and appreciation of stained glass in Welsh churches. Detailed studies of most of the major English firms and their principal artists are lacking, and a history of British twentieth-century stained glass has yet to be published.[33] The literature on key artists of the Arts and Crafts Movement and successive artists in this tradition, as well as those closer to the tradition of Ninian Comper, is limited to a handful of monographs and journal articles.[34] In Wales the medieval glass of north Wales was comprehensively described by Mostyn Lewis in his *Stained Glass in North Wales up to 1850*, published in 1970 (for full details of the following see the select bibliography on pp. 24–6). This was recently supplemented by Andrew Renton's list of pre-1700 stained glass in south Wales and very few examples of early glass are omitted from these surveys. Mostyn Lewis brought his survey up to 1850 and Malcolm Seaborne's work on Victorian and later glass, albeit restricted to the county of Flintshire, provides valuable detail for comparative work.[35] Maurice Broady published several articles relevant to post-war work in the Swansea area, notably on Celtic Studios, and his excellent study of the firm considerably lightened the burden on chapters nine and ten of this book.

The best guide to the stained glass of all periods across Wales has been the seven volumes of the *Buildings of Wales* series, even though some important works are omitted or, in a few instances, post-date the publication.[36] It is certainly hard to imagine attempting to write a book such as this without the help of the series, and this makes Painton Cowen's pages on Wales in his *A Guide to Stained Glass in Britain*, published in 1985, all the more impressive, even if his choice of windows is occasionally mystifying. The lists of windows made by members of the British Society of Master Glass-Painters, published between 1930 and 1972 by the Society and as a complete volume by Morris and Juliet Venables in 2003 provide further guidance for twentieth-century makers. In addition to these surveys, lists of the work of particular artists or firms have begun to appear over the last forty years. The largest and most exhaustive is A.C. Sewter's two-volume work on the stained glass of Morris & Co., and this has been followed by others including the corpus of C.E. Kempe's

33 The most readily available information on artists of the Arts and Crafts Movement includes a series of articles and lists of windows by Gordon Lawson and published on Wikipedia and as *The Arts & Crafts stained glass of Christopher Whall and his followers* (PediaPress, 2013).

34 A comprehensive summary of the known makers of stained glass is found in the NADFAS guide to stained glass marks and monograms, compiled by Joyce Little (see the select bibliography). The listing of artists and architects by John Allen on the website of Sussex Parish Churches: < http://www.sussexparishchurches.org> is also an invaluable resource for the study of nineteenth and twentieth-century stained glass.

35 Malcolm Seaborne also prepared guides to the stained glass at other churches in the region, such as the Church of St Giles, Wrexham.

36 The selection of windows for inclusion is sometimes coloured by the authors' views on stained glass, and occasionally lightened by terse descriptions such as 'Strong colours, limp gestures' (John Newman, *The Buildings of Wales: Glamorgan* [London/Cardiff: 1995], p. 550), or 'brash Modernist' (Thomas Lloyd, Julian Orbach and Robert Scourfield, *The Buildings of Wales: Pembrokeshire* [New Haven/London: Yale University Press, 2004], p. 183). The introductions of the volumes also contain useful summaries of the stained glass in each county or region.

firm and the handlist of windows by James Powell & Sons, together with gazetteers in books and attached to articles in the *Journal of Stained Glass*.[37]

The usefulness of these listings can only be realised by visiting churches and photographing windows for reference. These visits usually serve as reminders that perhaps as much as half of the stained glass in Welsh churches is not listed in any of these published sources, and speculative visits to churches that happened to be open have revealed further unrecorded work. Many of the windows illustrated in this book were discovered when either looking for something else or when not looking for anything in particular. Fieldwork yields further information from church guides, plaques associated with windows, and sometimes signatures and dates discreetly placed in the lower corners of windows.[38]

Information on stained glass in Welsh churches can also be gleaned from archival sources. Lists and photographs of fittings at most Church in Wales places of worship can be consulted in the Log Book and Terriers at the head office of the Church in Wales in Cardiff. Parish archives, as well as archives from Nonconformist chapels, can be found in County Record Offices, while diocesan archives, including the faculties, which formally give permission for the installation of new stained glass, are held at the National Library of Wales in Aberystwyth. These sources sometimes provide information on lost works, and a few never brought to fruition. For example, the faculty for a two-light window at the Church of St John the Evangelist, Maindee, Newport, includes a design for the window by the firm of Heaton, Butler & Bayne. The window was approved on the faculty dated 7 March 1930, but if installed it was either a casualty of the bomb that fell nearby in 1941, or the fire of 1951.[39] For an idea of the appearance of the window, we can compare an earlier window of the same subject by the same firm at Pontfaen in Pembrokeshire, where the main scene is to the same design.

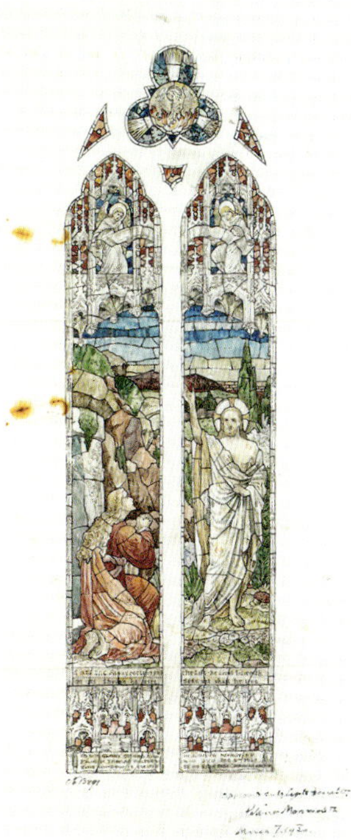

27. (right) Heaton, Butler & Bayne, The Risen Christ Appearing to Mary Magdalene, 1930, design for the Church of St John the Evangelist
National Library of Wales, Records of the Church in Wales: Diocese of Monmouth DM/P6/152, Box 48 (image courtesy of the National Library of Wales)

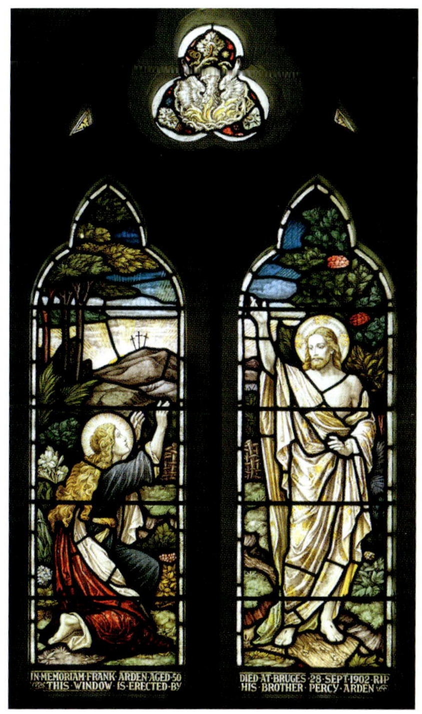

28. (far right) Heaton, Butler & Bayne, The Risen Christ Appearing to Mary Magdalene, *c.* 1903, Church of St Brynach, Pontfaen, north transept

37 Philip Collins, *The Corpus of Kempe Stained Glass in the UK and Ireland* (Kempe Trust, 2000). A list of work by James Powell & Sons (Whitefriars) Ltd was compiled by Dennis Hadley from their Order and Cash Books, available from the NADFAS website: <http://www.nadfas.org.uk/what-we-do/church-recording/stained-glass>.

38 Church guides occasionally provide useful information on stained glass, but vary from those that are based on observation and archival work to those reliant on speculation and hearsay. A few church historians have taken the trouble to add information on stained glass windows in their work, notably Geoffrey Orrin who has written numerous books and articles on Glamorgan churches.

39 Remarkably, the east windows survived the fire as they had been removed and were undergoing conservation following the bomb damage to the church.

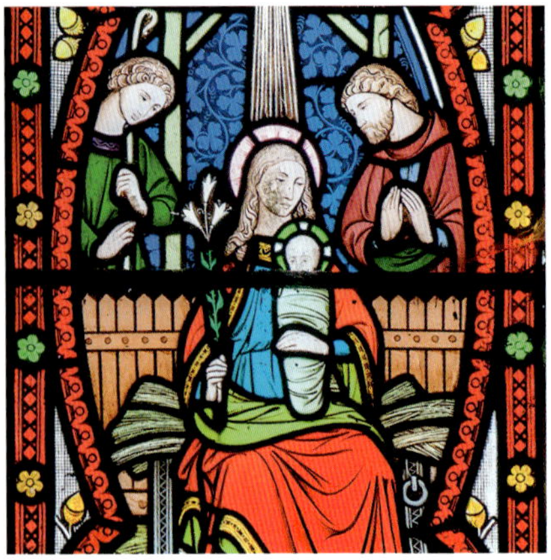

29. Probably Clayton & Bell, Virgin and Child with Shepherd and St Joseph, *c.* 1861, Church of St John the Baptist, Ysbyty Ifan, east window

30. C.E. Kempe, Maker's Mark, 1901, Church of St John, Pembroke Dock, south aisle

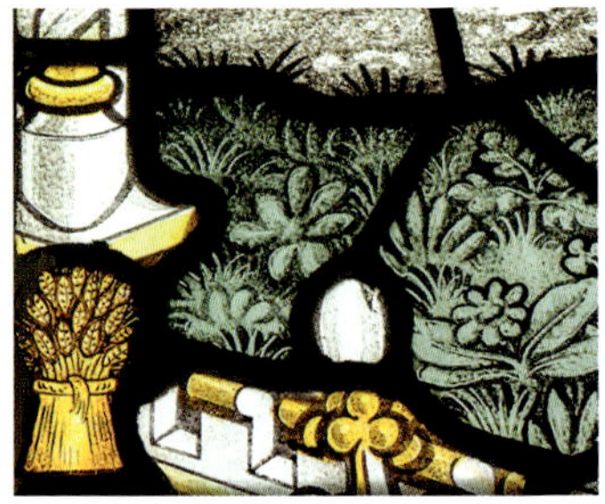

31–2. T.F. Curtis, Ward & Hughes, Decorative Panels, *c.* 1893 (below), 1898 (bottom), Church of St Sadwrn, Henllan (Denbighshire), nave

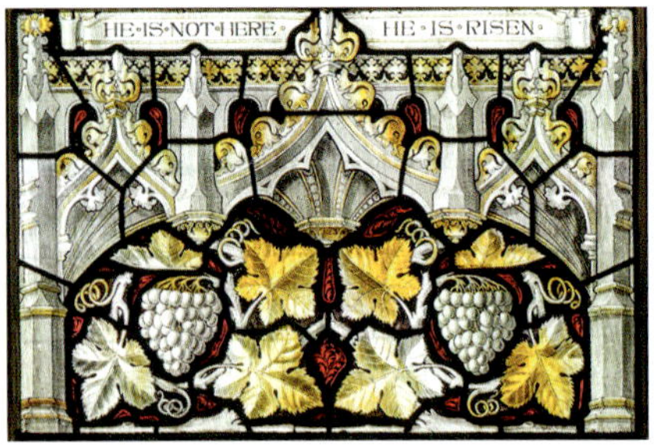

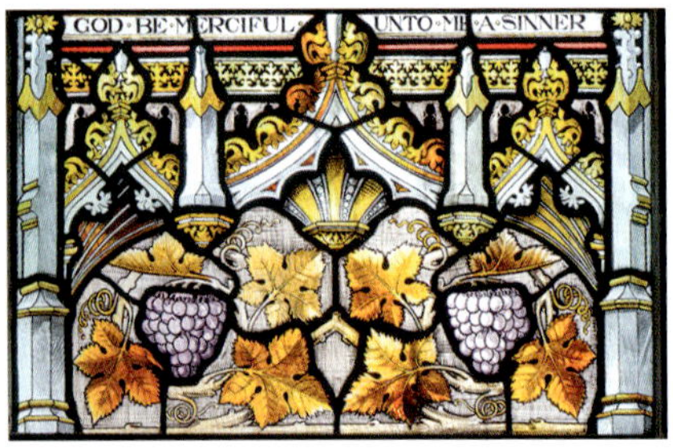

40 Designers sometimes took this a stage further by establishing their own studio with assistants who made their windows. The identification of the work of individual designers in large firms requires detailed research into surviving designs, cartoons and archives, and historians such as Peter Cormack, Dennis Hadley, Martin Harrison and William Waters have all made significant progress in unpicking the designers who worked for large firms such as James Powell & Sons; Clayton & Bell; Heaton, Butler & Bayne and Lavers, Barraud & Westlake.

The reuse of designs and uniformity of style in the work of many studios is helpful for attributing the many unsigned windows in churches. Firms such as Ward & Hughes and C.E. Kempe were more likely to sign their windows, especially from the 1880s, although their style is often recognisable. Similarly, it is often possible to identify windows by Clayton & Bell and Burlison & Grylls, who rarely signed their windows, by their design and style of glass painting. The maintenance of a recognisable style is remarkable given the many hundreds of windows made by the large firms who employed numerous cartoonists and glass painters over the years. Designers and glass painters also moved between firms and took their styles with them, while long-lived studios changed their style as designers left or retired and fashions moved on.

For example, a marked change in style can be seen in windows by Ward & Hughes after the death of Henry Hughes in 1883, when the firm was taken over by T.F. Curtis. Many of their windows were designed by George Parlby, who also provided designs for James Powell & Sons, and his design for the east window of the chancel at the Church of St Machraeth, Llanfachraeth (Anglesey), is suggestive of his more ubiquitous work for T.F. Curtis, Ward & Hughes, but executed in a manner more in keeping with other work by Powell's. The painterly style of the work of T.F. Curtis, Ward & Hughes was also adopted by Cox, Sons, Buckley & Co., after they were taken over by T.F. Curtis in 1893. Similarities in the painting of their work can be seen before and after this date, both in stained glass and, at the Church of St Edward, Knighton, in murals.

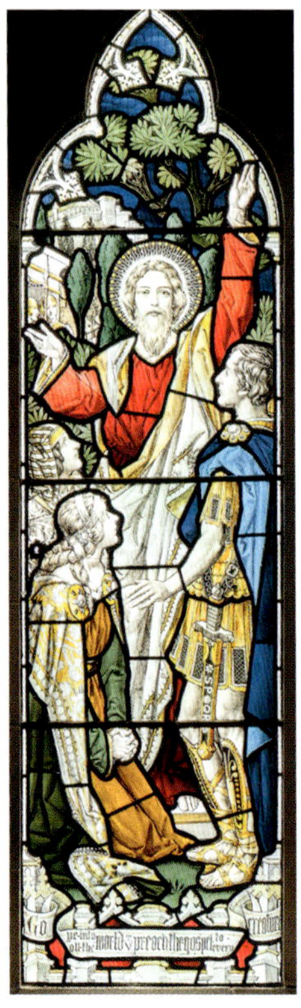

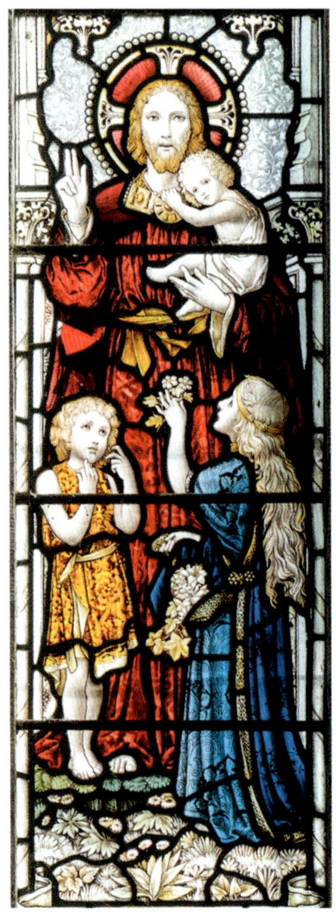

33. (right) T.F. Curtis, Ward & Hughes, St Paul Preaching, *c.* 1901, designed by George Parlby, Church of St Edward, Knighton, south aisle

34. (far right) James Powell & Sons, Christ with Children, 1909, designed by George Parlby, Church of St Machraeth, Llanfachraeth, east window

35. (right) Cox, Sons, Buckley & Co., Angels from Jacob's Dream, 1897, Church of All Saints, Glasbury, nave

36. (centre right) T.F. Curtis, Ward & Hughes, Angel, 1900, Church of St Edward, Knighton, chancel

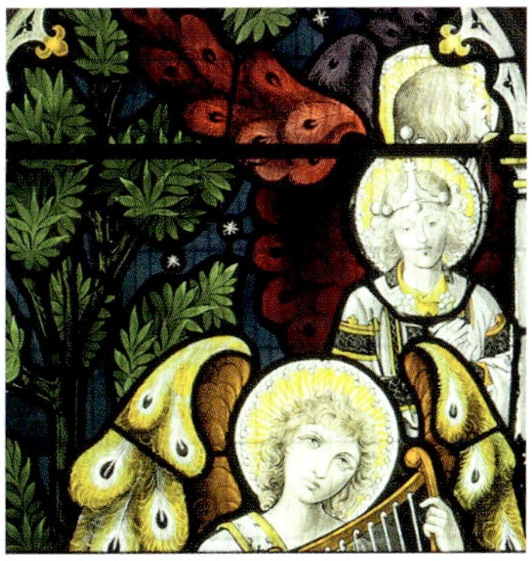

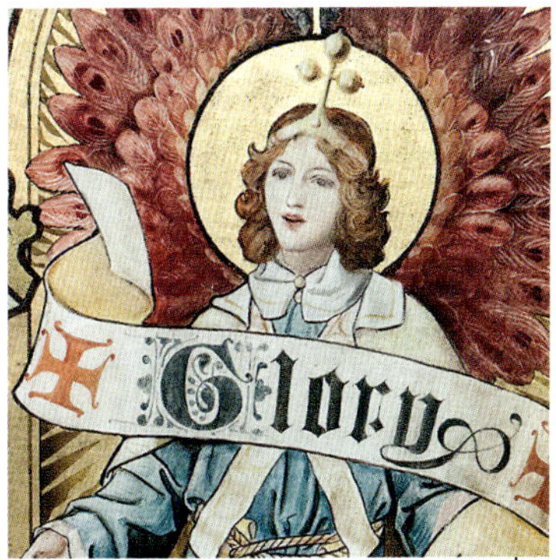

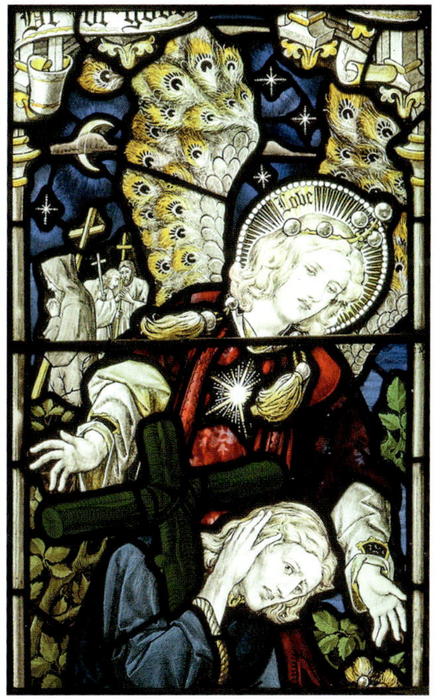

37. T.F. Curtis, Ward & Hughes, Angel with Figures Bearing Crosses, 1898, designed by George Parlby, Church of St Mary, Ruabon, north aisle

In this book I have tended to attribute windows to their makers or studios, and to add the names of designers where known. Windows signed by firms rarely acknowledge their designers and it is important to remember that the making of stained glass windows has nearly always been a collaborative process. Dennis Hadley's invaluable handlist of windows by James Powell & Sons is illustrative of this. Although the names of designers are often associated with windows made by the firm, these designs have to be interpreted by the cartoonist who prepares the full-size drawing for the glass painter and glazier. Similarly, designers combined old cartoons, sometimes based on the work of earlier designers, in new compositions for windows of different sizes and in churches of a different character. Free from their original context and the intent of the original designer, these earlier cartoons might be interpreted in a new way to suit the building, the patron and the times. Such windows are not the work of a single artist or designer, but are the product of a studio. In other cases designers were more proactive in supervising the execution of their work, whether by a studio or by a single craftsman or craftswoman working for them.[40]

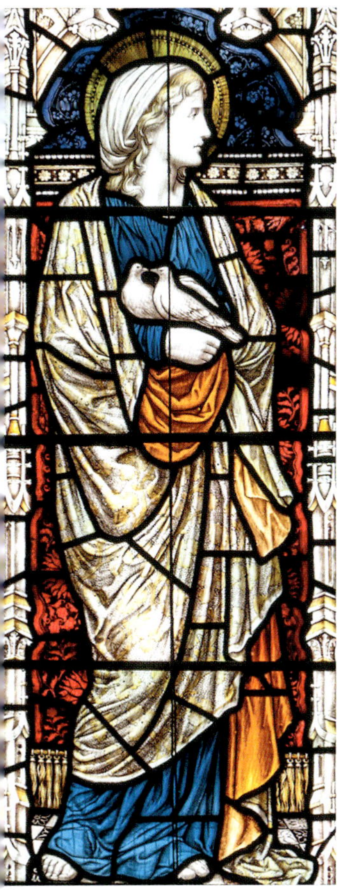

Some windows were designed on the basis of a rough initial sketch made by another artist or, when windows were installed as part of a restoration or new building, by an architect. In these cases artists and architects have sometimes been attributed as designers of windows, although they were totally removed from the execution of the windows by a stained glass studio. This was the case for windows 'designed' by architects such as William Butterfield, J.P. Seddon and G.F. Bodley. In the twentieth century, the east window of the

38. James Powell & Sons, The Virgin Mary, from the Presentation in the Temple, *c.* 1890, figure designed by Henry Holiday, Church of St Peter, Pwllheli, south aisle

39. Lavers & Barraud, Christ Raising the Son of the Widow of Nain, 1862, designed by J.P. Seddon, Church of St Peter, Dixton, nave

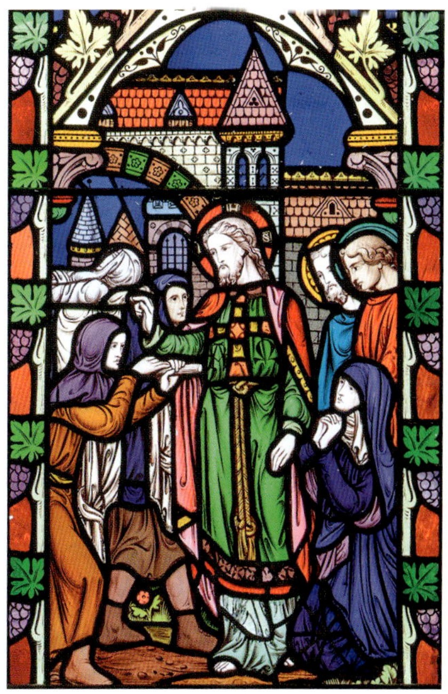

40. (right) Muriel Minter, East Window, 1939, designed by Mildred Eldridge, Church of Five Saints, Llanpumsaint

41. (far right) Abbott & Co., The Holy Family with Saints, 1933, designed by Isaac Williams, Church of St John the Baptist, Sully, nave

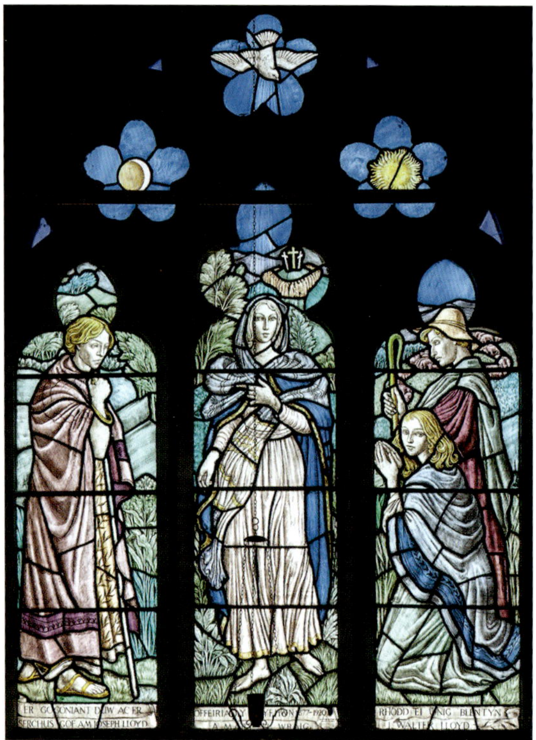

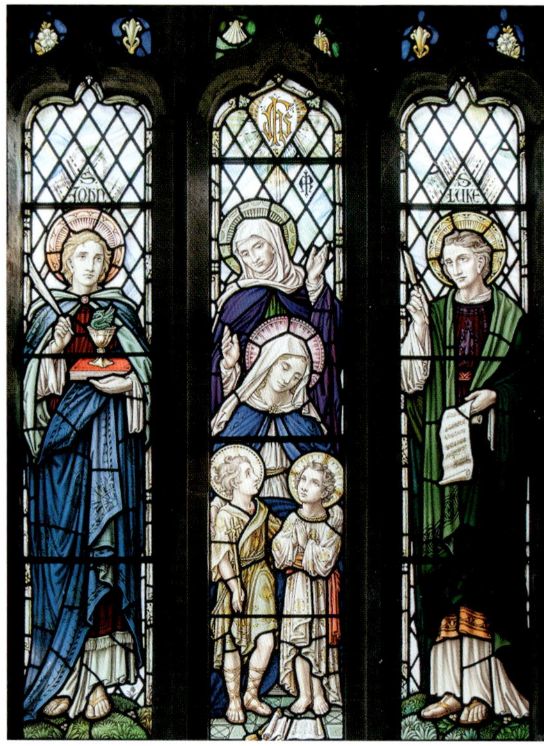

41 R.S. Thomas was a curate at Chirk at the time. The couple remained in Wales but no other windows designed by Mildred Eldridge are known. For her work see Peter Lord, 'Parallel Lives?', *Planet*, vol. 129 (June/July 1998), pp. 17–26.

42 The window was given in memory of his wife Annie (neé Summers) who died in 1932.

Church of Five Saints, Llanpumpsaint, was based on drawings by the artist Mildred Elsie Eldridge, shortly after she moved to Wales in 1937 and before she married the poet R.S. Thomas in 1940.[41] Her work was interpreted by Muriel Minter, who she had probably met in London when studying at the Royal College of Art in the early 1930s.

Patrons have occasionally been identified as designers, perhaps after providing the idea for the subject or a sketch for the window that has been interpreted by others. A window of 1933 by the Lancaster firm Abbott & Co. at the Church of St John the Baptist, Sully, was designed by its donor Isaac Williams, who also carved woodwork for the church, and was the Keeper of Art at the National Museum of Wales at the time.[42] The design for the east window of the Church of St David, Nefyn, was attributed to the Revd Jonathan Jones in the church Log Book, although the five-light window by Celtic Studios is virtually of the same design as a near contemporary window at the Church of St David, Tumble, with different local saints in the outer lights.

This survey of stained glass in Wales is limited to churches, although a fuller survey of the medium in its widest sense would encompass work in civic and public buildings, hotels, shops and

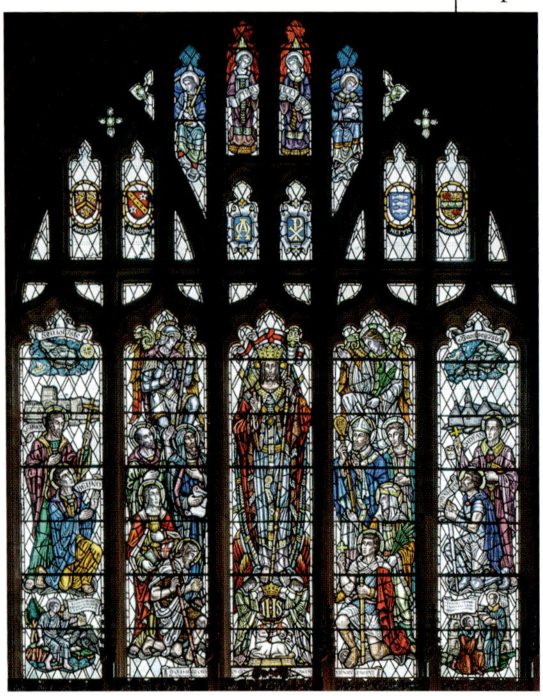

42. Celtic Studios, Christ in Majesty with Saints and Angels, 1958, Church of St David, Nefyn, east window

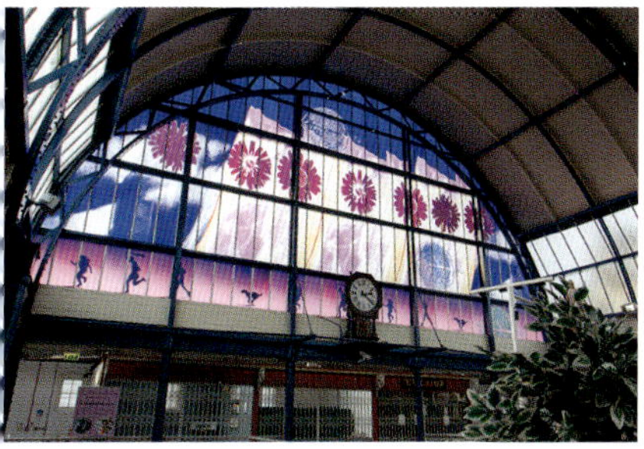

43. Catrin Jones, Window for Newport Market, 2003, made by Proto Studios Ltd

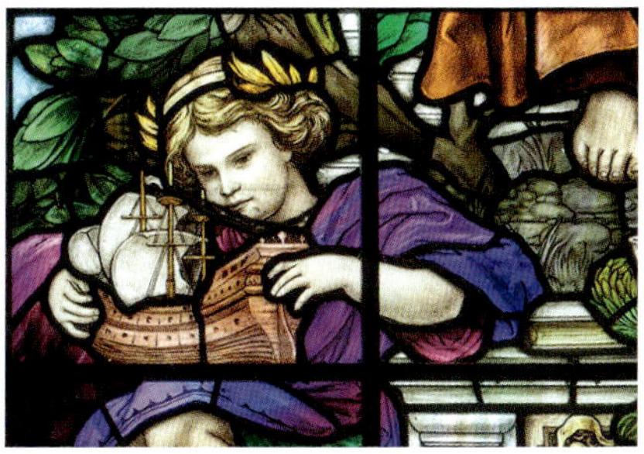

44. J. Dudley Forsyth, Child Holding a Sailing Ship, detail of a window representing Architecture, *c.* 1907, Bangor University

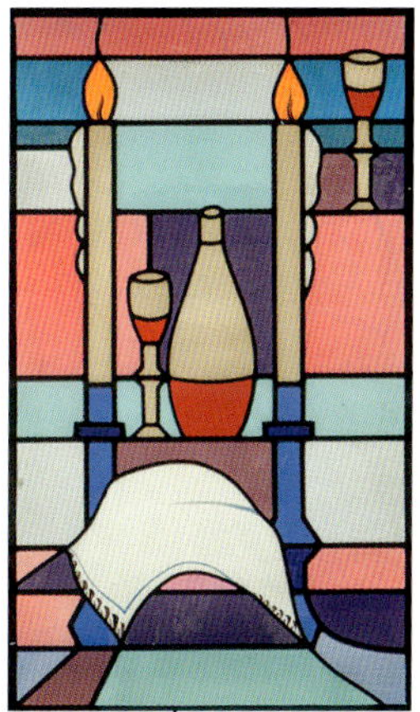

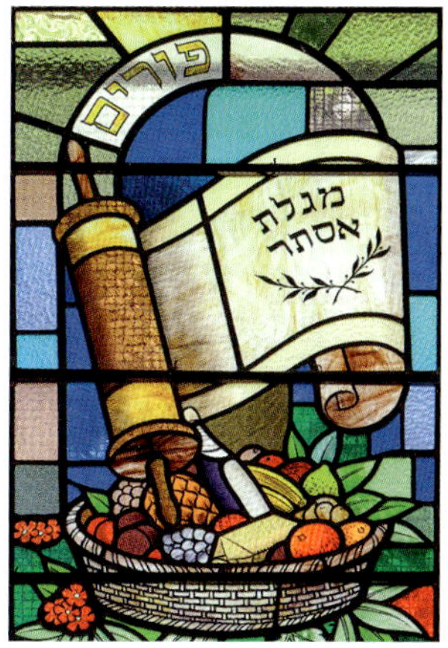

45. (above left) Francis Rapport, Shabbat, *c.* 1992, made by Bryn Young, Cardiff Reform Synagogue (gallery)

46. (above right) Purim, mid-twentieth century, Swansea Synagogue, sanctuary

private houses. From the 1980s the most innovative architectural glass was increasingly the result of commissions from public buildings such as hospitals, schools, theatres and corporate offices. Nevertheless the medium is most commonly associated with Anglican churches, although it is often found in Roman Catholic churches, which are fewer in number. Nonconformist chapels contain stained glass with pictorial scenes, although they are less common, together with a wide variety of abstract decorative panels.[43] Stained glass can also be found in the Greek Orthodox Church in Butetown, Cardiff, albeit eclipsed by the colour of the interior murals. Some private Christian spaces such as the chapels in gentry homes employ stained glass, as do the buildings of monastic houses (in addition to their churches). Stained and coloured glass can also be seen in cemetery chapels and in the various buildings and chapels in crematoria. Panels depicting the tribes of Israel and Jewish festivals, subjects that avoided the use of the human figure, were made for synagogues in Swansea and Cardiff in the second half of the twentieth century.

43 Many stained glass panels are found internally in chapels, usually opposite the main entrance in the foyer, which are impossible to see from outside, and this has aided the assumption that there is little stained glass in chapels. Current research by Alun Adams has confirmed that a significant amount of stained glass in Nonconformist chapels in Wales has gone unnoticed.

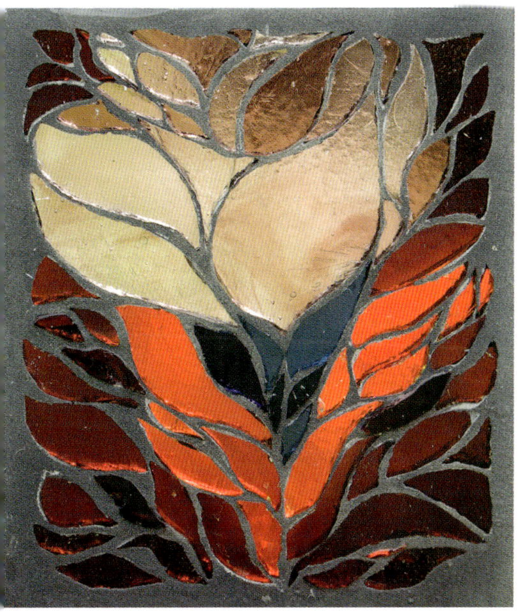

47. Susan Glyn, The Rose of St Dorothy, *c.* 2000, Tymawr Convent, Lydart

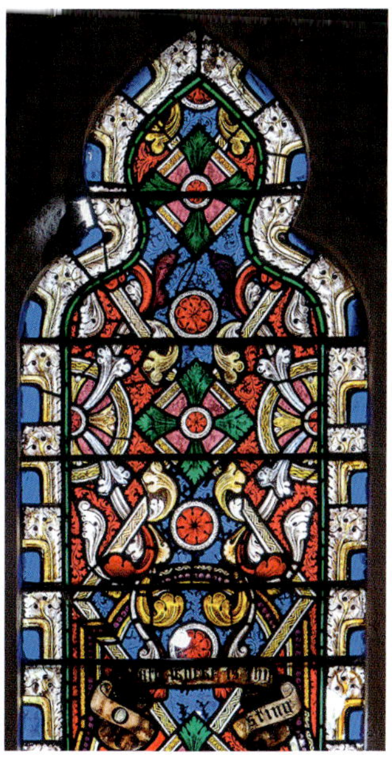

48. David Evans, East Window, *c.* 1846, Cemetery Chapel, Tenby

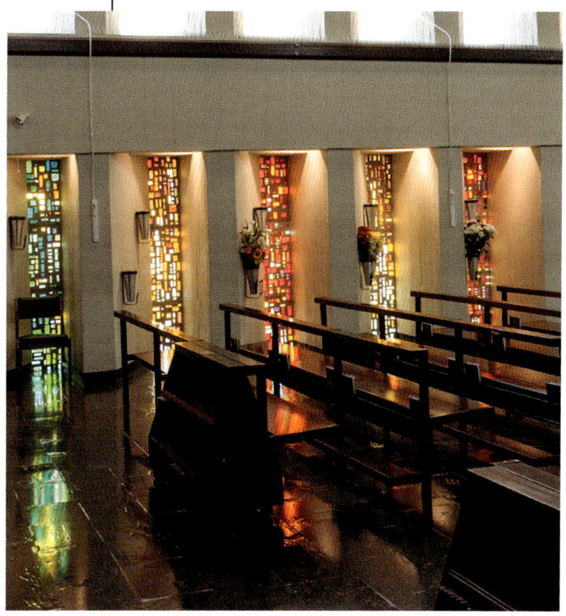

49. Powell & Sons, Windows for Margam Crematorium, 1968, designed by Pierre Fourmaintraux

44 Charles Winston, *An Inquiry into the Difference of Style Observable in Ancient Glass Paintings* (Oxford: John Henry Parker, 1847), part i, p. vi.

45 Lawrence Lee, *The Appreciation of Stained Glass* (London: Oxford University Press, 1977), p. 15.

Writing in 1847, Charles Winston noted that 'The difficulty of producing in a plate the *effect* of painted glass, has never yet been overcome, even in engravings of large size' and that the reproduction of entire windows was less effective than the reproduction of smaller details.[44] Despite the recent advances in photography and printing processes, photographs in printed books cannot match the contrast accommodated by the human eye or reproduce the saturated colours, particularly blues and purples, of coloured glass. Details still reproduce better than large windows but do not illustrate either the window's overall design, or its scale and context. Neither do photographs satisfactorily convey the effect of stained glass on interiors or the changing light at different times of the day, something that an experienced designer and maker will always take into consideration.

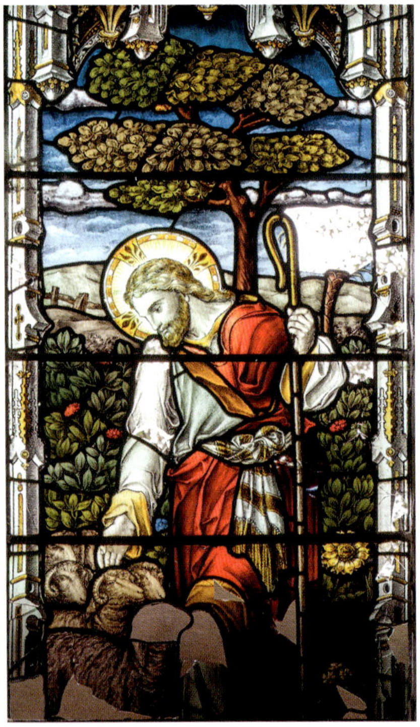

50. Jones & Willis, The Good Shepherd, probably *c.* 1900, Church of St John, Dowlais, transept

Many of the windows described and illustrated in this volume may be found in churches that are thriving and open for visitors. Others are behind locked doors in buildings that are difficult to access, as well as in churches that have closed. Once closed, some of these church buildings take on new uses that have preserved the stained glass in situ, while in other instances windows have been sold, destroyed, or remain in disused buildings and subjected to vandalism. Since medieval times, stained glass was allowed to disappear gradually from Welsh churches through neglect and failure of the lead structure as well as deliberate action. Stained glass continues to be lost today, including windows installed within the last thirty years, and many of them, old and new, will be mourned by few.

Lawrence Lee wrote of 'the special atmosphere' of a church that dulls our perceptions so that we 'come away with impressions of windows ... blurred by sentiment or prejudice to the extent that we are quite unable to fix clearly in the mind how good or bad a window was'.[45] This book is an attempt to refocus our attention on a few details, the subjects of the windows, and the artists that made them, and to bring about a better understanding of the stained glass in our churches.

The idea for this book emerged towards the end of an Arts and Humanities Research Council funded research project based at the University of Wales, Lampeter. While working on this project, 'Imaging the Bible in Wales' (2005–8), I visited many places of worship recording biblical art, and it was not long before I became struck by the power of the medium, and began to record stained glass more comprehensively. Prior to this project I was fortunate to work with Peter Lord on the 'Visual Culture of Wales' project at the University of Wales Centre for Advanced Welsh and Celtic Studies in Aberystwyth, and his approach to art history was fundamental to both the research on the visual culture of the Bible in Wales, and the methodology behind the present volume.

After the end of the 'Imaging the Bible in Wales' project I made attempts to develop this work as a broader study of stained glass in Wales at the Centre for Advanced Welsh and Celtic Studies. Although this did not receive the funding as I had hoped, a grant from the University of Wales Welsh Industries Fund made a more modest project possible, and the 'Imaging the Bible in Wales' database was developed as a new online Catalogue of Stained Glass in Wales. This funding was supplemented in 2011 by grants from the Pilgrim Trust, the Garfield Weston Foundation, and the trustees of the Friends of Friendless Churches, which enabled further work cataloguing stained glass on the database, and some additional photography. A further small grant was received from the Glaziers Trust.

I would like to take this opportunity to thank those who were involved in these projects, particularly Martin O'Kane, the director of the 'Imaging the Bible in Wales' project, Dafydd Johnston, director of the Centre for Advanced Welsh and Celtic Studies, and friends and colleagues at the Centre for their encouragement. John Morgan-Guy accompanied me on many visits to churches while we were working on the 'Visual Culture of Wales' and 'Imaging the Bible in Wales' projects, and his expertise did much to open my eyes to what we saw. I would also like to thank Nigel Callaghan for his excellent work developing the online database, and the National Library of Wales for hosting the database and its two websites on their servers.

The 'Stained Glass in Wales' project came to an end in 2011, and I am grateful to Lefi Gruffudd, Dafydd Johnston, Martin O'Kane, Matthew Saunders and Anna Eavis for supporting funding applications to assist with the publication of this book. A grant from the Welsh Books Council and a loan from the Marc Fitch Fund have provided assistance with printing costs.

Many practising artists agreed to be interviewed during the course of my research, including Rodney Bender, Anna Bessant, Chris Bird-Jones, Barry Brady, Lisa Burkl, John Edwards, Amber Hiscott, Catrin Jones, Tim Lewis, Jamie Moore, Gareth Morgan, Rachel Phillips and Christian Ryan. That so little of the information that they provided is included here has made me all the more aware of the need for a more comprehensive history of the makers based in Wales over the last fifty years. Nevertheless, I am very grateful for their help and encouragement as well as numerous others who have corresponded with me and made me aware of windows that they were familiar with, or provided dates and attributions. Some of these people are acknowledged in the footnotes and in the online Catalogue, but I would particularly like to thank Peter Jones for his corrections and additions to the online resource. Julian Orbach kindly let me have a copy of his extensive listings of stained glass in Wales, and Elspeth Broady provided me with Maurice Broady's detailed notes on the windows of Celtic Studios. Kirstine Dunthorne, Marilyn Griffiths and Gill Fildes also helped with details regarding artists who worked at Swansea College of Art in the 1960s and 70s. I am also grateful to Robert Evans and Michael Pearson at the National Library of Wales for their assistance with locating faculties among the records of the Church in Wales.

John Morgan-Guy and Alun Adams, director of the Architectural Glass Centre at Swansea Metropolitan University, deserve particular thanks for their help in the preparation of this book. Without their unwavering encouragement this book might not have been written and they have both been generous with their expertise, as well as with their notes and libraries. They have also made many suggestions and corrected my draft chapters. The text has been further edited by Sara Elin Roberts, one of a number of friends who has also offered hospitality on my many visits to the various corners of the country. Charlene Crampin helped root out errors in drafts and forestalled many others when compiling the index, and I am indebted to Eirian Jones at Y Lolfa whose attention to detail further refined the text. I would also like to thank Rhiannon and Dafydd Ifans for their advice.

Particular thanks are due to those who have met me at churches, or whose time stewarding ensures that churches are open at least some of the time. There are also numerous others who open their churches daily for visitors and pilgrims during the summer months or throughout the year, facilitating many chance discoveries that I might not otherwise have made.

Finally, I would like to thank my wife Charlene, who has also assisted me on many visits to churches. I should also apologise to her and to our children, whose day trips and holidays have been routinely hijacked by visits to churches, occasionally made more comfortable by a welcoming children's corner with books and toys.

Notes:

Descriptive titles have been used throughout the book for windows, but in a few cases windows were given titles by the artists who made them, or recorded in archival material associated with their commissioning. In these instances titles are given in italics. Some titles are given in inverted commas when a title has been taken from an inscription on a window.

Some Welsh placenames are frequently found in different forms in contemporary and historical sources. Often 'correct' forms are not those which are commonly used today, and in some cases usage continues to change as Welsh forms gradually become more predominant. As far as possible, the spelling of placenames in this volume attempts to follow the most common current English usage. In the case of personal names, Welsh spelling has been used in this volume for the names of saints, such as Cadog and Illtud, although the correct form for the churches that are dedicated to them are sometimes variants such as Cattwg, Cadoc or Illtyd. Where English and Welsh names for saints are different, the English name has been used, for example, Winifred and David rather than Gwenfrewy and Dewi.

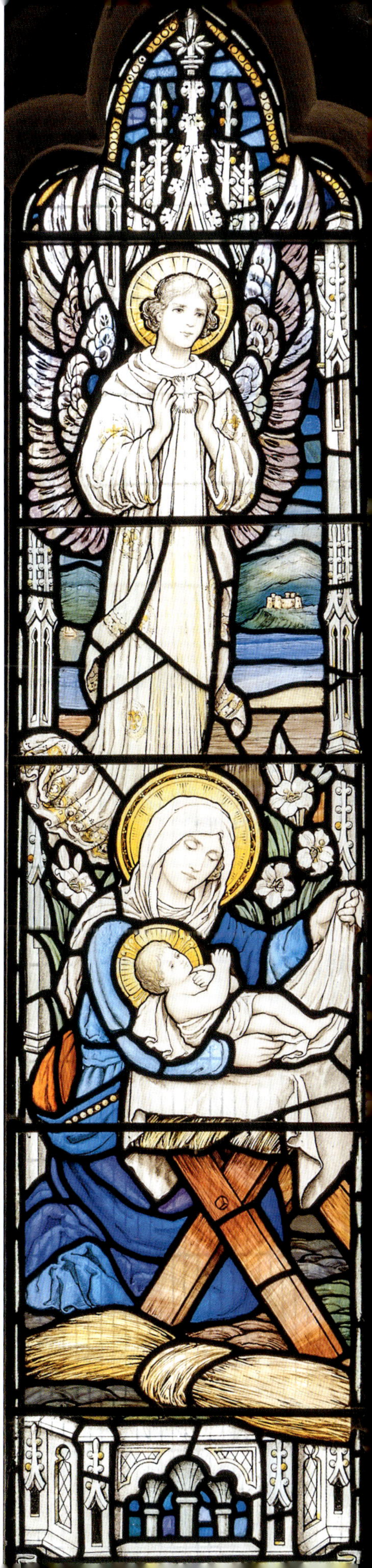

51. W. Pearce & E. Cutler, Virgin and Child with an Angel, from the Adoration of the Shepherds, 1928, Church of St Tysilio, Llantysilio, chancel

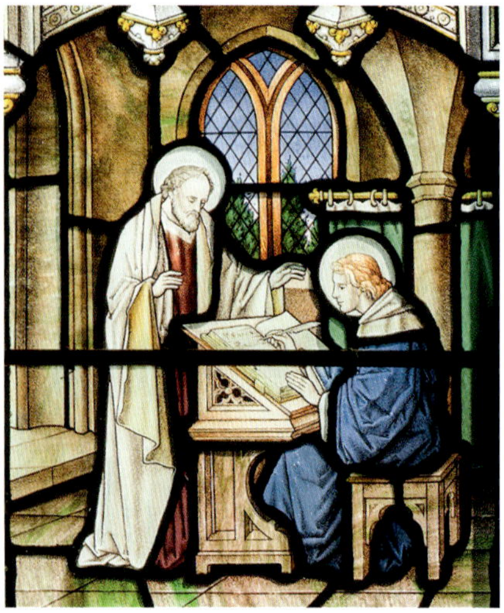

52. Shrigley & Hunt, St Mark the Evangelist Writing His Gospel with St Peter, 1936, Church of St Chad, Hanmer, east window

Select Bibliography

Armitage, E. Liddall, *Stained Glass: History, Technology and Practice* (London: Leonard Hill, 1960).

Armstrong, Barrie and Wendy, *The Arts and Crafts Movement in the North West of England* (Wetherby: Oblong, 2005).

Stained Glass Windows and Master Glass Painters 1930–1972 (The British Society of Master Glass-Painters Directories Reprinted) (Bristol: Morris & Juliet Venables, 2003).

British Society of Master Glass-Painters, *The Journal of Stained Glass* (1924–).

Broady, Maurice, *A Vision Fulfilled: The story of Celtic Studios and Swansea's architectural glass tradition* (Swansea: West Glamorgan Archive Service, 2010).

Brown, Sarah, *Stained Glass: An Illustrated History* (London: Bracken Books, 1992).

Cheshire, Jim, *Stained glass and the Victorian Gothic Revival* (Manchester: Manchester University Press, 2004).

Cowen, Painton, *A Guide to Stained Glass in Britain* (London: Michael Joseph, 1985).

Crampin, Martin and John Morgan-Guy, *Imaging the Bible in Wales* (DVD-ROM) (Sheffield: Sheffield Phoenix Press, 2010).

Harrison, Martin, *Victorian Stained Glass* (London: Barrie & Jenkins, 1980).

Haslam, Richard, Julian Orbach and Adam Voelcker, *The Buildings of Wales: Gwynedd* (New Haven/London: Yale University Press, 2009).

Haward, Birkin, *Nineteenth Century Suffolk Stained Glass* (Woodbridge: The Boydell Press, 1989).

Hebgin-Barnes, Penny, *The Medieval Stained Glass of Cheshire* (Oxford: Oxford University Press, 2010).

Hubbard, Edward, *The Buildings of Wales: Clwyd* (Harmondsworth/Cardiff: Penguin/University of Wales Press, 1986).

Lee, Lawrence, *The Appreciation of Stained Glass* (London: Oxford University Press, 1977).

Lewis, Mostyn, *Stained Glass in North Wales up to 1850* (Altrincham: John Sherratt and Son Ltd, 1970).

Little, Joyce (compiler), Angela Goedicke and Margaret Washbourn (eds.) *Stained Glass Marks and Monograms* (London: National Association of Decorative and Fine Art Societies, 2002).

Lloyd, Thomas, Julian Orbach and Robert Scourfield, *The Buildings of Wales: Pembrokeshire* (New Haven/London: Yale University Press, 2004).

Lloyd, Thomas, Julian Orbach and Robert Scourfield, *The Buildings of Wales: Carmarthenshire and Ceredigion* (New Haven/London: Yale University Press, 2006).

Lord, Peter, *The Visual Culture of Wales: Medieval Vision* (Cardiff: University of Wales Press, 2003).

Lord, Peter, *The Visual Culture of Wales: Medieval Vision* (CD-ROM) (Cardiff: University of Wales Press, 2004).

Marks, Richard, *Stained Glass in England during the Middle Ages* (London: Routledge, 1993).

Neiswander, Judith and Caroline Swash, *Stained and Art Glass. A Unique History of Glass Design and Making* (London: The Intelligent Layman, 2005).

Newman, John, *The Buildings of Wales: Glamorgan* (London: Penguin Books, 1995).

Newman, John, *The Buildings of Wales: Gwent/Monmouthshire* (London: Penguin Books, 2000).

O'Kane, Martin and John Morgan-Guy (eds.), *Biblical Art from Wales* (Sheffield: Sheffield Phoenix Press, 2010).

Osborne, June, Stained Glass in England (London: Frederick Muller, 1981).

Piper, John, *Stained Glass: Art or Anti-Art* (London: Studio Vista, 1968).

Raguin, Virginia Chieffo, *The History of Stained Glass: The Art of Light Medieval to Contemporary* (London: Thames & Hudson, 2008).

Renton, Andrew, 'Discovering Pre-1700 Stained Glass in South Wales' in *Vidimus*, vol. 34 (November 2009), http://vidimus.org/issues/issue-34/feature.

Reyntiens, Patrick, *The Beauty of Stained* Glass (London: The Herbert Press, 1990).

Scourfield, Robert and Richard Haslam, *The Buildings of Wales: Powys* (New Haven/London: Yale University Press, 2013).

Seaborne, Malcolm, *Victorian and Later Stained Glass Windows in Flintshire Churches* (Mold: Privately published, 1996).

Seaborne, Malcolm, 'Victorian and later stained glass in Flintshire Churches', *The Journal of the Flintshire Historical Society*, vol. 35 (1999), pp. 115–142.

Sewter, Albert Charles, *The Stained Glass of William Morris and his Circle* (New Haven/London: Yale University Press, 1974), two volumes.

Shepherd, Stanley A., *The Stained Glass of A.W.N. Pugin* (Reading: Spire Books, 2009).

Sowers, Robert, *The Lost Art: A Survey of one thousand years of stained glass* (London: Lund Humphries, 1954).

Taylor, Richard, *How to Read a Church (Pocket Guide)* (Rider Books, 2007).

Waters, William, *Angels & Icons: Pre-Raphaelite Stained Glass 1850–1870* (Abbots Morton: Seraphim Press, 2012).

Whall, Christopher, W., *Stained Glass Work: A text book for students and workers in glass* (Bristol: Morris & Juliet Venables, 1999, first published 1905).

Readers are also encouraged to explore relevant online links available on the 'Stained Glass in Wales' catalogue: http://stainedglass.llgc.org.uk. The site also has a much longer bibliography.

Chapter One

Medieval Stained Glass

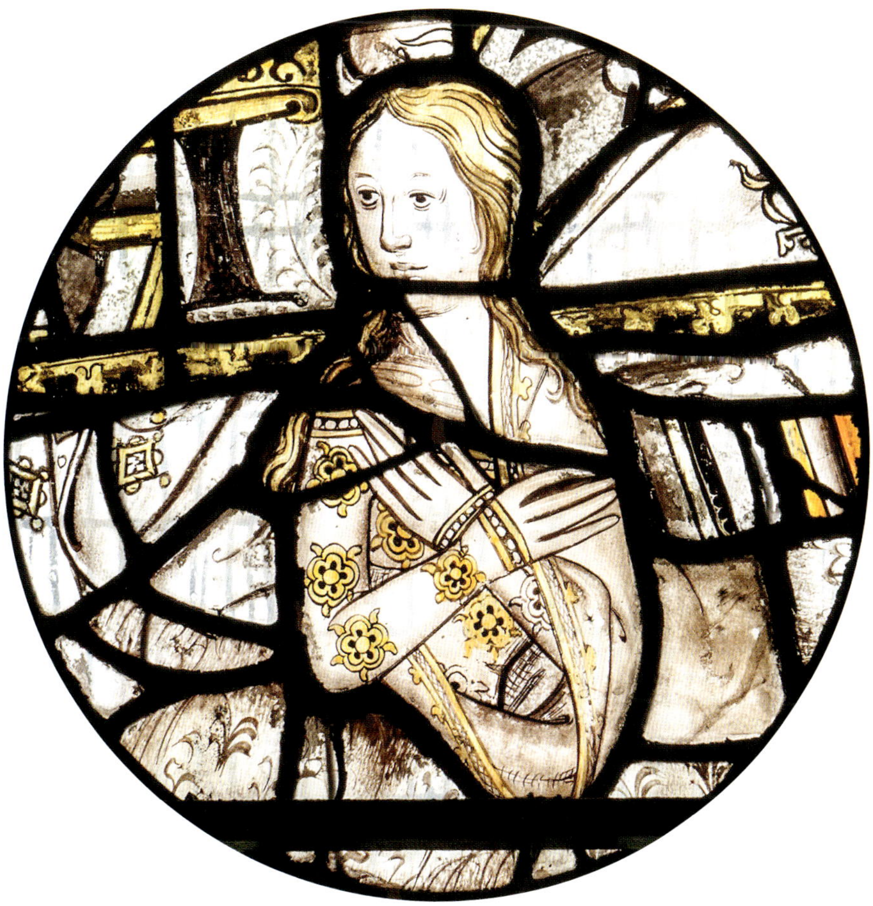

It is not known when church windows began to be glazed in Wales, nor when colour and imagery were introduced into these windows. Glass was an expensive commodity in the Middle Ages, and when it was possible to afford window glass for churches, much of it would have been plain and leaded together in diamond or square quarries. These quarries could also be ornamented with glass paint and with silver stain, as a simple floreate pattern or perhaps with small heraldic or religious symbols, such as the instruments of the Passion, which were a series of emblems relating to aspects of Christ's suffering and crucifixion. The use of coloured glass was an additional luxury and could cost more than twice as much as white glass, partly because it had to be imported from the continent.

The earliest evidence for the use of stained glass in Welsh churches comes from monastic sites, and according to William of Worcester the arms of Roger Bigod, Earl of Norfolk, were placed in the east window of Tintern Abbey, probably in the late thirteenth century.[1] Archaeological excavation has also recovered evidence of stained glass at monastic sites, most significantly at Greyfriars, Carmarthen, where sufficient glass was discovered to indicate the design of a heraldic panel.[2]

Window glass at Cwmhir Abbey was found when the site was cleared in about 1837 and excavations by Stephen Williams in the late 1880s and early 1890s at the Cistercian abbeys of Strata Florida and Strata Marcella recovered fragments of grisaille glass of uncertain date.[3] The Cistercian rule forbade the use of figurative art, but this austerity was waning by the fourteenth century as monastic houses grew in wealth and influence. Poems in praise of the abbots of the Cistercian houses of Valle Crucis and Strata Florida by Guto'r Glyn and Dafydd Nanmor in the mid-fifteenth century refer to glazed windows including the

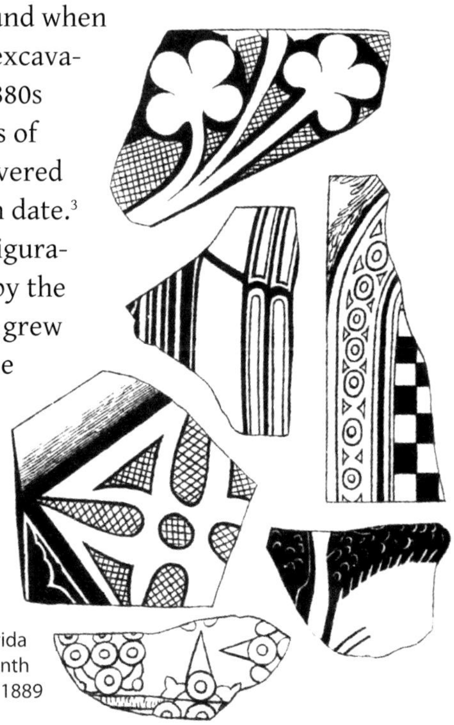

54. Excavated fragments from Strata Florida Abbey, probably fourteenth or fifteenth century, drawn by Telfer Smith, 1889

1 The window at Tintern is the first known use of coloured glass in a Cistercian house in Britain. Richard Marks, 'Cistercian window glass in England and Wales', in Christopher Norton and David Park (eds.), *Cistercian Art and Architecture in the British Isles* (Cambridge: Cambridge University Press, 1986), p. 218.

2 Susan Lloyd-Fern, 'A 13th Century Stained Glass Window from Carmarthen', in *Journal of the Pembrokeshire Historical Society*, vol. 1 (1985), p. 53. Initially thought to be from the later thirteenth century, it has since been reconsidered as late fourteenth century. However, if the red enamel paint is original, it would be much later. Andrew Renton, 'Discovering Pre-1700 Stained Glass in South Wales' in *Vidimus*, vol. 34 (November 2009), <http://vidimus.org/issues/issue-34/feature>

3 Stephen W. Williams, 'The Cistercian Abbey of Cwmhir', in *Montgomeryshire Collections*, vol. xxiv (1890), p. 413. Some of the window glass at Strata Florida was coloured, and the location and condition of some of the fragments suggested that it could have been thirteenth-century glass destroyed by Edward I. Stephen W. Williams, 'On Further Excavations at Strata Florida Abbey', *Archaeologia Cambrensis*, fifth series, vol. vi (1889), pp. 42, 267; Stephen W. Williams, 'Excavations on the Site of Strata Marcella Abbey', *Montgomeryshire Collections*, vol. xxv (1891), pp. 163, 173, 185–6, plate xiv.

53. (Title page) The Virgin Mary, probably from a scene of the Annunciati
late fourteenth century, Church of St Mary, Treuddyn, sanctuary a

55. (right) Medieval and later fragments, Church of St Michael, Caerwys, chancel

56. (far right) Medieval fragments, probably late fifteenth or early sixteenth century, Church of St Mary, Llanfair Kilgeddin, chancel

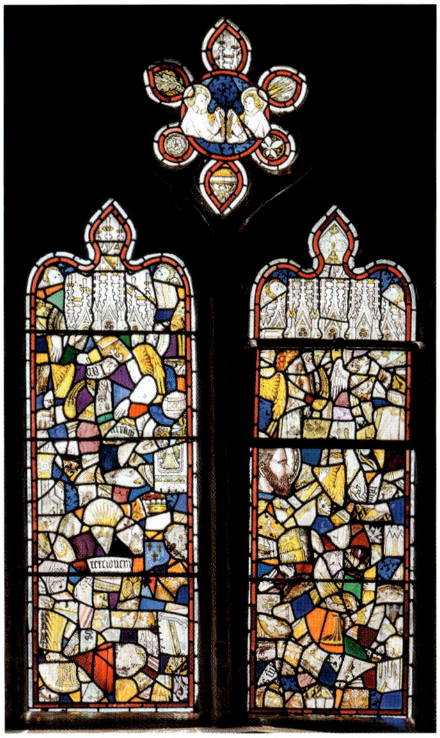

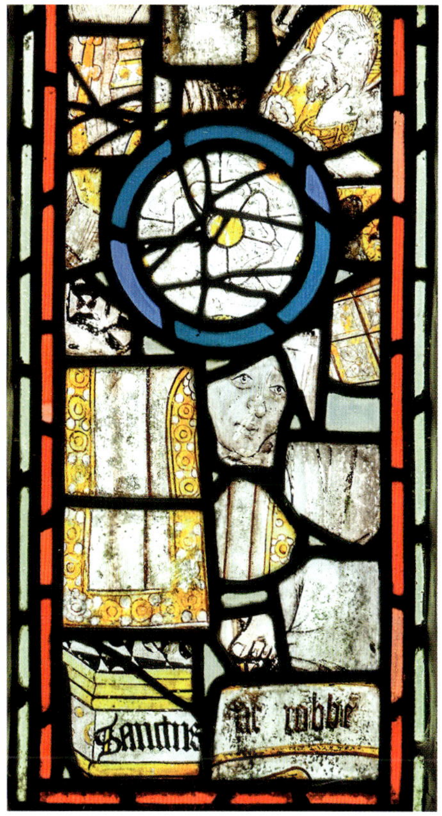

'gyfrestri gwydr ffenestri' (rows of glass windows) ornamenting the chancel of Strata Florida.[4] Excavations at Cardiff Greyfriars and Blackfriars found grisaille painted glass and coloured fragments, while Lewis Morgannwg praised windows with armorial bearings at Neath Abbey in about 1520.[5]

Not much of the medieval glass extant in Welsh churches remains in its original context. Subject to destruction, decay and disinterest, surviving fragments of medieval glass were often relocated in different windows, making it difficult to understand adequately their subject matter and original design. The present arrangement of most medieval glass in Welsh churches was largely determined when they were restored, altered and rebuilt in the latter half of the nineteenth century: early glass was also lost at this time, while preservation followed different approaches. Sometimes fragments were collected together as an abstract mosaic, and in other cases new compositions with nineteenth-century glass were made to contain the surviving pieces, based on suppositions of what the original scenes were thought to have been. Some surviving figures and scenes were completed or identified with modern inscriptions, and in other cases simply set within plain glass surrounds.

The fate of the medieval glass at the Church of St Mary at Treuddyn was raised in a letter to the Church Restoration Building Committee when the church was demolished and a new church built in 1875. The writer, the architect George Vialls, explains that 'The old work is chiefly made up of odd pieces, but there are some parts of figures that are tolerably perfect'. Insufficient glass remained to fill the apse windows, although he pointed out that the cost, £6.10.0, could be deducted from the cost of ordinary glazing, and the medieval glass 'would by this means be preserved, & a very good effect of colour at the East end

4 Guto'r Glyn, 'Ode in praise of Abbot Rhys ap Dafydd of Strata Florida' (8: 57–8), and 'In praise of Abbot Dafydd ab Ieuan of Valle Crucis', <http://www.gutorglyn.net>; Dafydd Nanmor 'I abad Ystrad Fflur' (to the abbot of Strata Florida). Thomas Roberts and Ifor Williams (eds.), *The Poetical Works of Dafydd Nanmor* (Cardiff: University of Wales Press, 1923), p. 73. Glass from Valle Crucis was said to have been dug up by Lady Eleanor Butler and Sarah Ponsonby, the Ladies of Llangollen, who assembled an eclectic collection of glass in the windows of their house at Plas Newydd. They also appropriated the font from Valle Crucis.

5 Some of the glass at Neath survived into the late seventeenth century. Andrew Renton, 'Discovering Pre-1700 Stained Glass in South Wales' in *Vidimus*, vol. 34 (November 2009), <http://vidimus.org/issues/issue-34/feature>.

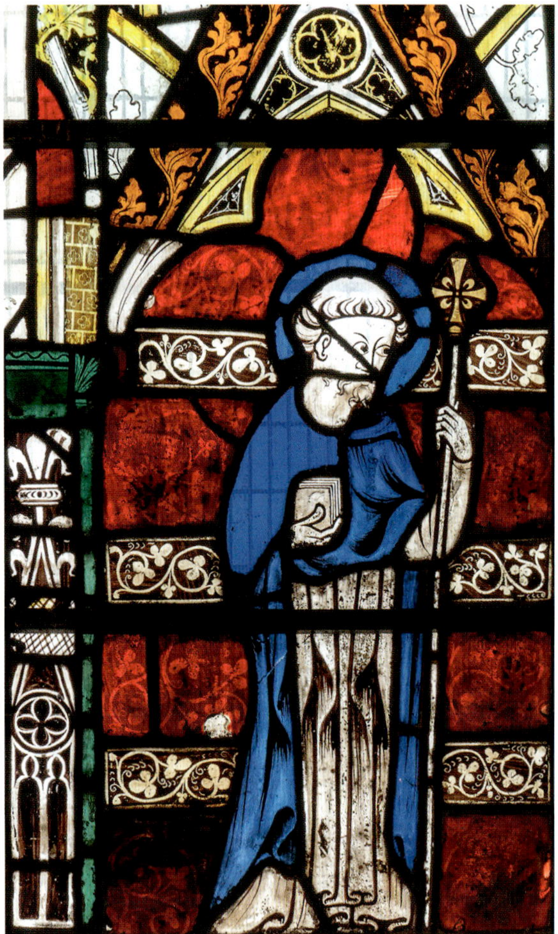

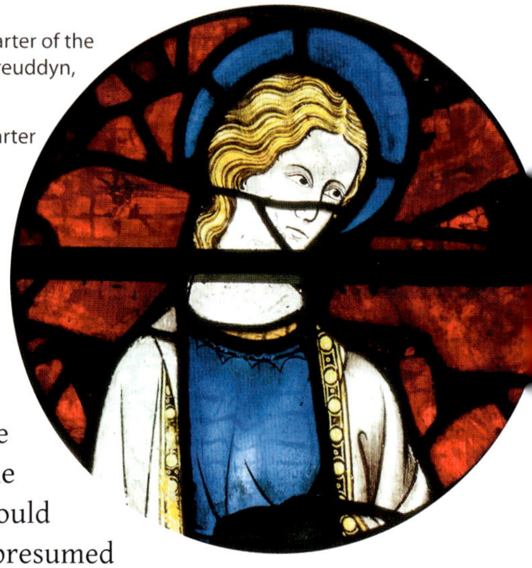

57. Unknown saint, probably second quarter of the fourteenth century, Church of St Mary, Treuddyn, sanctuary apse

58. Head of a Saint, probably second quarter of the fourteenth century, Church of St Mary, Treuddyn, sanctuary apse

would be gained, though the actual pattern would be for the most part irregular & undecided.'[6] He concludes the letter by suggesting that if the glass was not to be used, it would be sent back, and it must be presumed that in other cases glass that was not used could have remained in glaziers' workshops or was returned and subsequently lost or destroyed.

The two figures and half-length figure in the upper roundel in the northernmost chancel window at Treuddyn have similarities with glass of the 1330s at Grappenhall, Cheshire, which dates the glass to the early fourteenth century. Some of the glass in the other window, including a female figure thought to be Mary from an Annunciation scene, has been dated as later in the fourteenth century, but very little other stained glass and no other surviving figures in Wales can be securely dated before the fifteenth century.[7]

Most of the surviving medieval stained glass in Wales was made between the mid-fifteenth century and the 1530s, and within this timeframe it is possible to establish a more precise chronology. In some instances dates have been preserved in medieval inscriptions, such as at the Church of St Mary, Llanfair Dyffryn Clwyd, where the date of 1503 survives upside-down among the fragments.[8] At the Church of All Saints, Gresford, the east window of the Lady Chapel includes scenes from the Life of the Virgin Mary and retains a date of 1498 with details of its donation. A date of 1453 was identified among the fragments of glass at the Church of St Mary, Llanllugan, perhaps dating the figure of the crucified Christ, but not necessarily all of the glass in the window.[9]

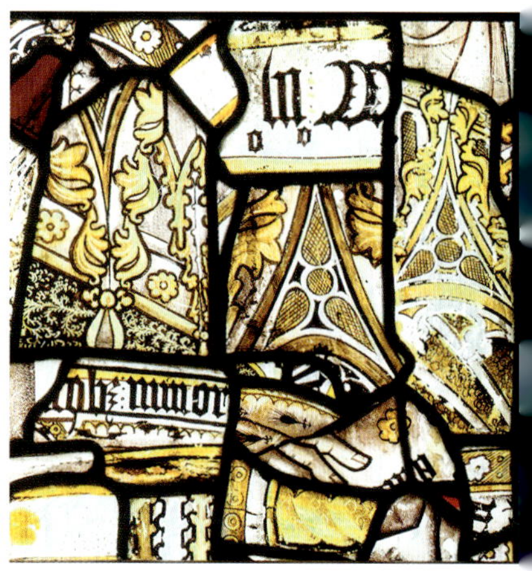

59. Medieval fragments, most probably 1503, Church of St Mary, Llanfair Dyffryn Clwyd, south nave

6 T.W. Pritchard, *Notes on the History of Treuddyn Parish Church of Saint Mary* (church publication, 1975), pp. 3–4.

7 Mostyn Lewis, *Stained Glass in North Wales up to 1850* (Altrincham: John Sherratt and Son Ltd, 1970), p. 4.

8 The date is incomplete and could be interpreted as 1403, but that would be inconsistent with the style of the glass. Mostyn Lewis, *Stained Glass in North Wales up to 1850*, p. 61.

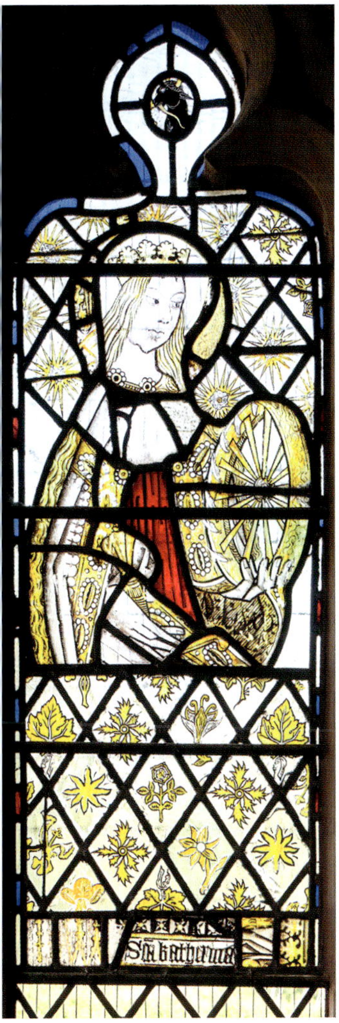

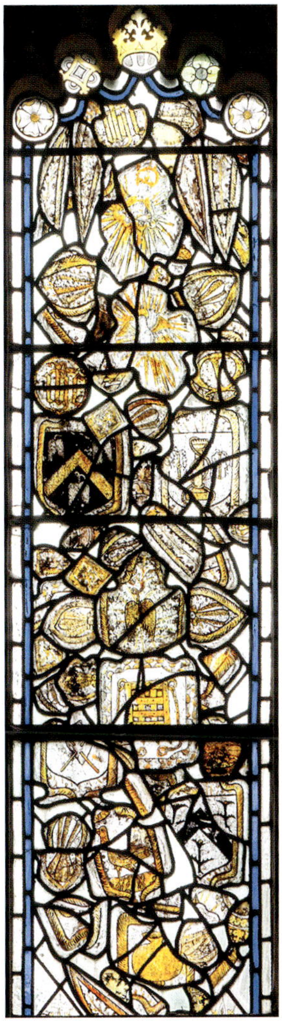

60. (far left) St Catherine, *c.* 1461–83, Church of St Stephen, Old Radnor, vestry

61. (left) Medieval fragments, probably late fifteenth or early sixteenth century, Church of St Tewdric, Mathern, south aisle

Royal badges and heraldry can also help to date glass. The white rose of York is found among fragments at the Church of St Michael, Caerwys, and at the Church of St Stephen, Old Radnor, the white rose *en soleil* and the black bull in a roundel above are badges of the Yorkist king Edward IV, dating the glass to his reign between 1461 and 1483.[10] The rose *en soleil* is also present in the rectangular quarries at the Church of St Ust and St Dyfrig, Llanwrin, and was copied extensively in the lower lights by the restorer. A lion and boar, symbols of Edward's brother Richard III, are found in the east window at the Church of St Mary, Nercwys, which incorporates medieval fragments in the five-light window of the Crucifixion with Mary, John and saints.[11] Little surviving medieval glass can be found in south Wales, but among the fragments at the Church of St Tewdrig, Mathern, heraldic motifs associate the glass with both Bishop John Marshall and John Arnold, suggesting late fifteenth and early sixteenth century dates.[12]

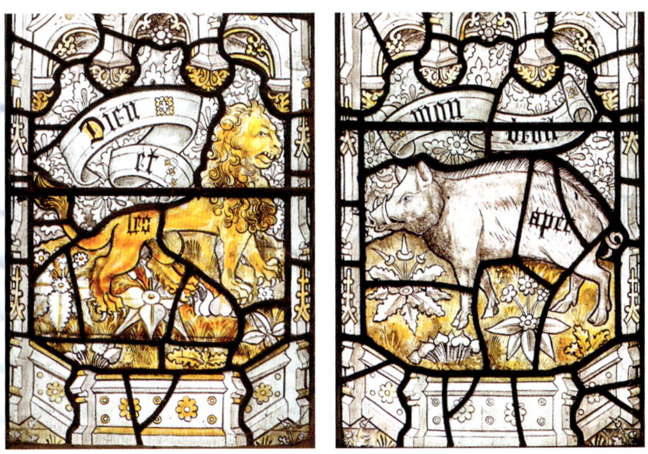

62–3. Lion and Boar, probably 1485–5, restored by Burlison & Grylls, 1883, Church of St Mary, Nercwys, east window

9 Mostyn Lewis surmised that the date should have read 1553. Mostyn Lewis, *Stained Glass in North Wales up to 1850* (Altrincham: John Sherratt and Son Ltd, 1970), pp. 68–9, and see also note 50 in this chapter. By the late 1530s, the religious house was 'a veri litle poore nunneri', making it unlikely that stained glass was commissioned there in the mid-sixteenth century; Lucy Toulmin Smith (ed.), *The Itinerary in Wales of John Leland* (George Bell & Sons: London, 1906), p. 55.

10 The rose *en soleil* (a rose with the rays of the sun behind it) is prominent behind the kneeling figure of Edward IV in the north-west transept window at Canterbury Cathedral, made in the later fifteenth century. M.A. Michael, *Stained Glass of Canterbury Cathedral* (London: Scala, 2004), p. 176.

11 Mostyn Lewis believed that the lion and hind part of the boar were medieval: Mostyn Lewis, *Stained Glass in North Wales up to 1850*, p. 86. Some of the Victorian glass could be copies of poorly surviving medieval glass.

12 Gerald Vaughan-Hughes dated the glass to 1480 when building work by John Marshall, bishop of Llandaff 1478–96, was undertaken and stained glass was added: 'Church of St Tewdrig, Mathern', *Proceedings of the Monmouthshire & Caerleon Antiquarian Association* (1924), p. 11. I am also grateful to Madeleine Gray who has identified a heraldic motif in the glass belonging to John Arnold, who held the manor of Mathern and Moynes Court in the early sixteenth century.

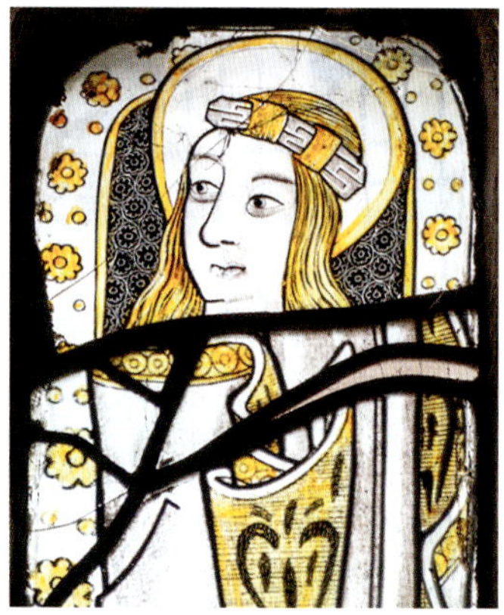

64. Angel, *c.* 1500–10, Church of All Saints, Gresford, Lady Chapel (north aisle)

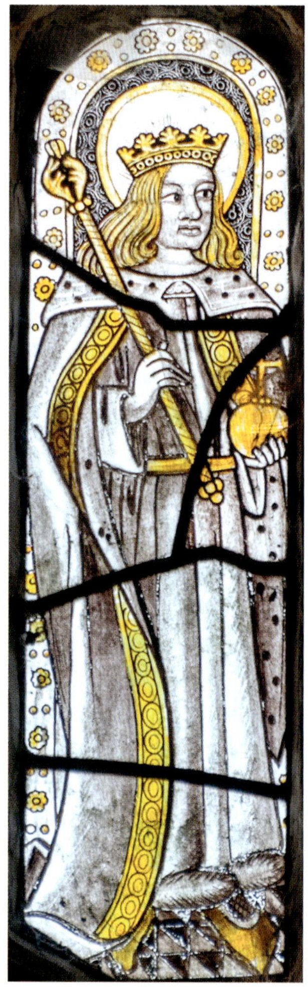

65. Crowned Saint, late fifteenth or early sixteenth century, Church of St Mary, Llanllugan, east window

Manuscript sources and early books have provided dates both for surviving and lost glass. At Gresford the dates and donors of two of the east windows and several of those in the north and south walls of the aisles were recorded by a visitor to the church in 1574.[13] John Davies of Rhiwlas, who published his book *A Display of Herauldry* in 1716, refers to a window of around 1400, destroyed during the Civil War, at the Church of St Silin, Llansilin.

Stained glass can also be dated by comparison with fragments that have been dated by other methods. In particular, techniques or painterly styles that resemble characteristics from medieval glass at Gresford are instructive in providing approximate dates for stained glass in churches at Llandyrnog, Hope, Dyserth, Gwyddelwern and further south at Llanllugan. The two saints in the tracery lights of the east window at Llanllugan bear close similarities to figures now in several windows at Gresford, suggesting a date nearer 1500 than 1453.

Fragmentary inscriptions can identify lost subjects as well as providing dates. Inscriptions at the Church of St Elidan, Llanelidan, indicate that the apostles James and Thomas were present, and at Llanfair Dyffryn Clwyd names including PETRUS (Peter) and [JA]COB MINOR (James the Less) can be identified.[14] Further fragmentary inscriptions at Llanfair Dyffryn Clwyd are from the Apostles' Creed, and it was common to depict all of the apostles with the line from the creed with which they were associated. The presence of fragments of the creed indicate that sets of apostles were present at the Church of Corpus Christi, Tremeirchion, the Church of St Michael, Caerwys, the Church of St Mary, Llanfair Kilgeddin, and the Church of St Matthew, Llandefalle, even though no figures survive.[15]

13 Full details of the windows, from British Library Harleian MS 473, are given in D.R. Thomas, *The History of the Diocese of St Asaph* (Oswestry: Caxton Press, 1913), vol. iii, p. 247. The identity of the visitor was thought to be the historian Sampson Erdeswicke, but was subsequently identified as the writer Dr John Dee in F. Noble, 'The identification of Dr. John Dee as the author of Harleian MS. 473 from its Radnorshire references', *The Transactions of the Radnorshire Society*, vol. xxvi (1956), pp. 40–2.

14 Stephen Glynne also recorded the names of Catherine and Elizabeth, as well as the remains of 'large figures of saints under enriched canopies' that occupied both east windows of the church in 1849. S.R. Glynne, 'Notes on the older churches in the four Welsh dioceses', *Archaeologia Cambrensis*, fifth series, vol. i (1884), p. 173.

15 The amount of medieval glass now at Llandefalle is much less than that mentioned in the second quarter of the nineteenth century. Samuel Lewis, *A Topographical Dictionary of Wales* (London: S. Lewis & Co., 1834), vol. ii, no pagination.

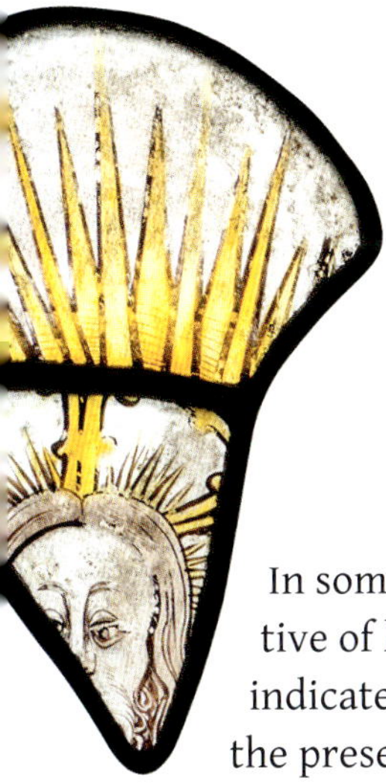

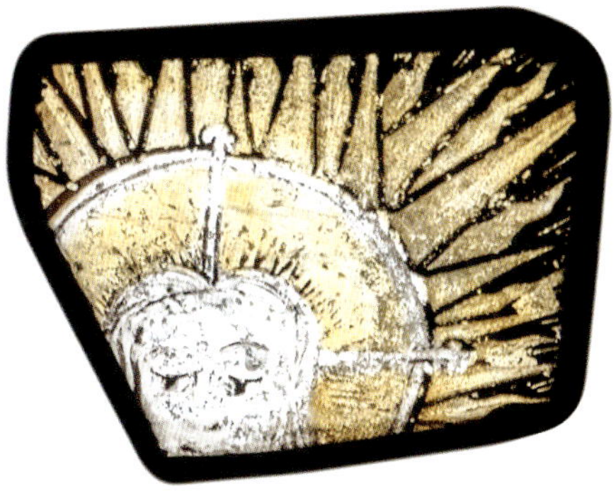

66. (far left) Head of Christ, probably *c.* 1500, Church of St Michael, Caerwys, chancel

67. (left) Head of Christ, late fifteenth or early sixteenth century, Church of St Pedrog, Llanbedrog, west window

68. (right) The Infant Christ, *c.* 1512, Church of St Gwyddelan, Dolwyddelan, east window

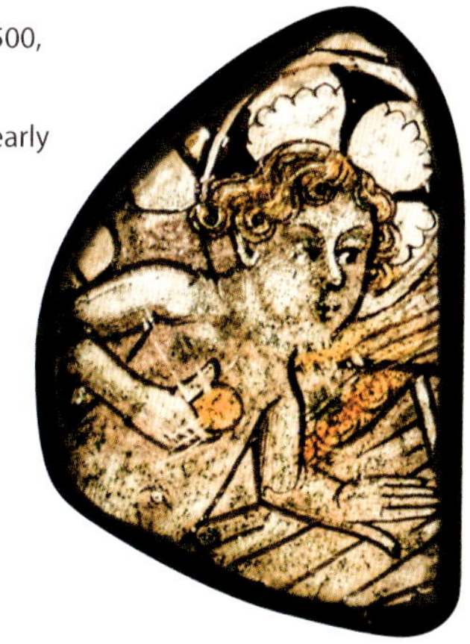

In some cases individual surviving fragments can be suggestive of lost subject matter in medieval windows. Nimbed heads indicate saints or angels, and angels can also be inferred by the presence of feathered wings. A fragment of a demon at Tremeirchion could either be from a scene of the Last Judgement or perhaps a depiction of the Archangel Michael weighing souls, in which demons were often shown upsetting the balance.

A cruciform halo denotes the head of Christ, as at Caerwys and at the Church of St Pedrog, Llanbedrog, where a single fragment shows part of the face with rays of light emanating from the halo, suggestive of a figure of the risen Christ, or perhaps Christ in Majesty. A seated figure of Christ in Majesty in stained glass was recorded at the Church of St Dyfnog, Llanrhaeadr-yng-Nghinmeirch, although it is no longer recognisable among the surviving fragments in the west window of the north nave.[16] At Dolwyddelan a young half-length naked figure may be identified as the young Christ by his crossed nimbus, although the original scene and the nature of the yellow item that he holds is unclear. At the same church there is also a fragment with part of a male head with closed eyes wearing what looks like a twisted crown of thorns. This is also probably the head of Christ, perhaps from a Crucifixion scene or a depiction of Christ as the Man of Sorrows.A further fragment at Dolwyddelan includes a dice and a ladder, two of the Instruments of the Passion of Christ. Further examples of the Instruments of the Passion can be identified at Llanelidan and a set are found at the Church of St Asaph and St Cynderyn, Llanasa, where they remain associated with the scene of the Crucifixion. This sacred heraldry is also among the fragments at Mathern, which includes the portcullis badge of Lady Margaret Beaufort, the mother of Henry VII, who helped to popularise the devotion.

16 A page of drawings of glass from the windows of the church at Llanrhaeadr-yng-Nghinmeirch was inserted into an extra-illustrated copy of Thomas Pennant, *A Tour in Wales* (vol. ii, *The Journey to Snowdon*), at the end of the eighteenth century or perhaps beginning of the nineteenth century. National Library of Wales PD 9872, p. 58/1. The present window of fragments was said to have incorporated glass found in a chest in 1830, and does contain some pieces of glass shown in the drawings, including the mitre and halo of a bishop and part of some of the inscriptions.

71. The Five Wounds of Christ, late fifteenth or early sixteenth century, Church of St Elidan, Llanelidan, north chancel

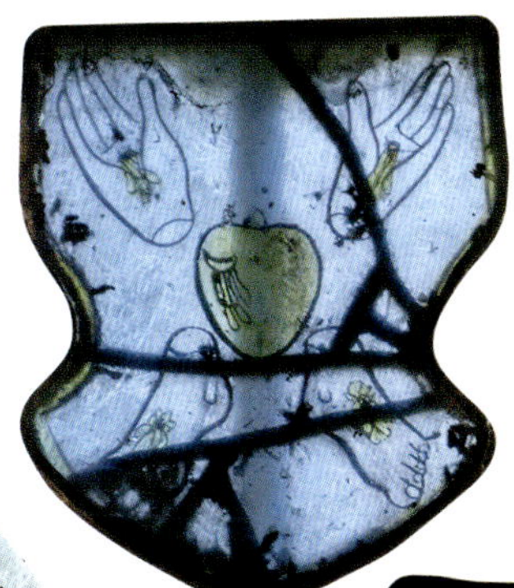

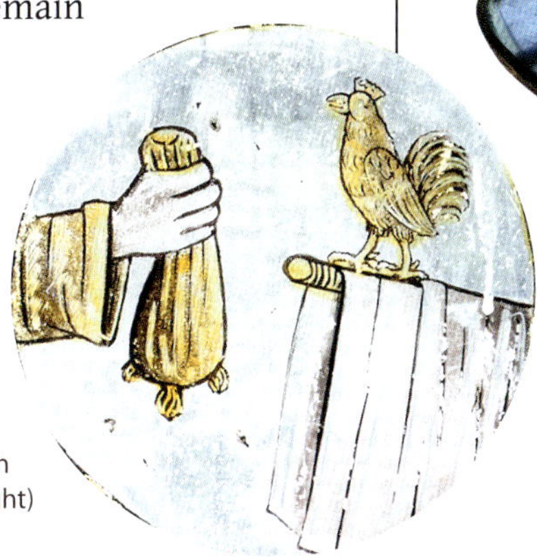

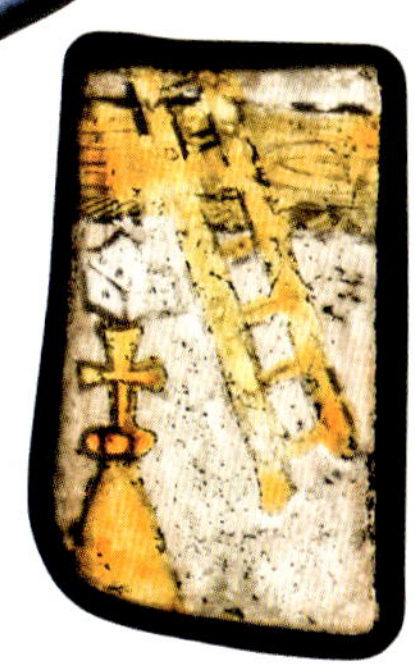

69–70. Instruments of the Passion: Money Bag and Cock, early sixteenth century, Church of St Asaph and St Cynderyn, Llanasa, south chancel (right); Dice and Ladder, *c.* 1512, Church of St Gwyddelan, Dolwyddelan, east window (far right)

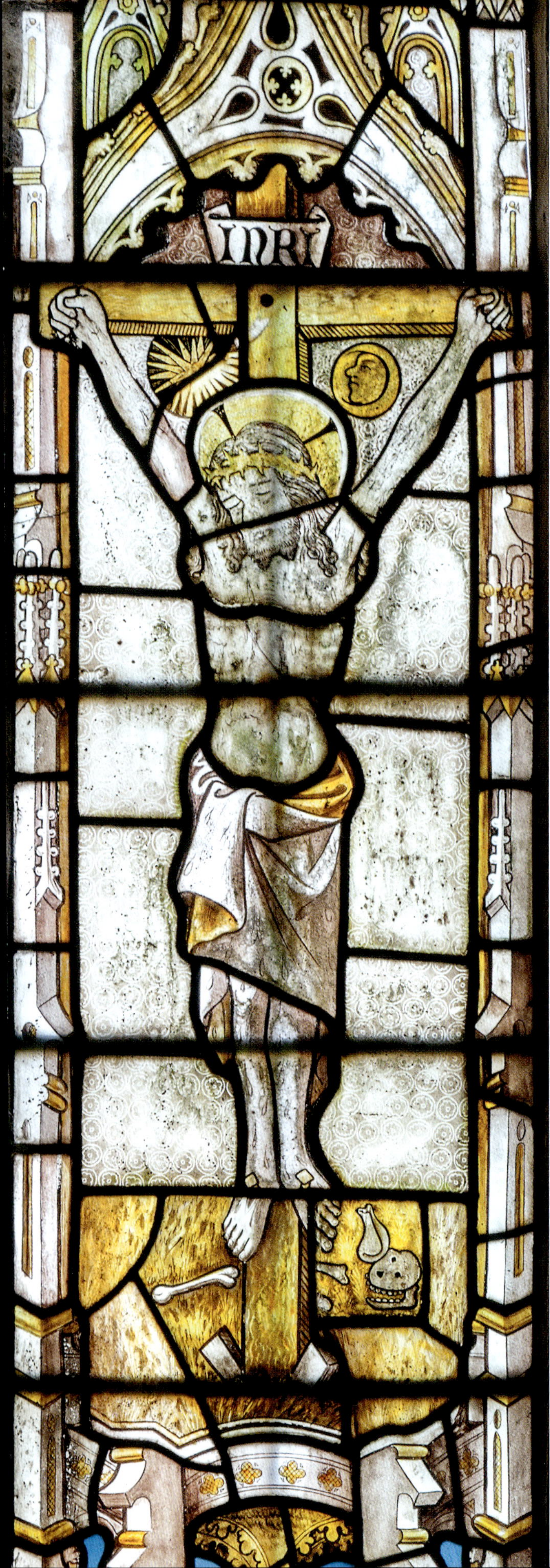

72. The Crucified Christ, possibly 1453, Church of St Mary, Llanllugan, east window

The image of the crucified Christ is the most commonly identified subject in medieval stained glass, partly because a single fragment of glass can sometimes identify the theme. Single hands or feet nailed to the cross can imply that a Crucifixion was present, as they do in fragments from churches at Caerwys, Llanfair Dyffryn Clwyd, Llanelidan and Clocaenog. Enough of Christ's head and upper body are depicted in fragments at Buttington to indicate clearly a Crucifixion, in which he wears the crown of thorns.

Some figures of the crucified Christ are more complete and have additional iconography. Crucifixion scenes often show bones and a skull at the foot of the cross, signifying the bones of Adam buried at Golgotha, whose meaning is interpreted as 'the place of a skull' in the gospels of Matthew, Mark and John. These bones are preserved in the churches at Llanllugan, Tremeirchion, Llandefalle, Llanwrin, Trefdraeth, Llandyrnog and Cilcain, and they were drawn by Thomas Dineley in 1684 at the Church of St Chad, Hanmer, although the glass no longer survives.[17] The sun and the moon were shown at either side of the cross signifying the darkness over the land that accompanied Christ's hours on the cross, and they survive in churches at Llanllugan, Nercwys and Llandyrnog, while the sun alone survives at the Church of St Beuno, Trefdraeth.

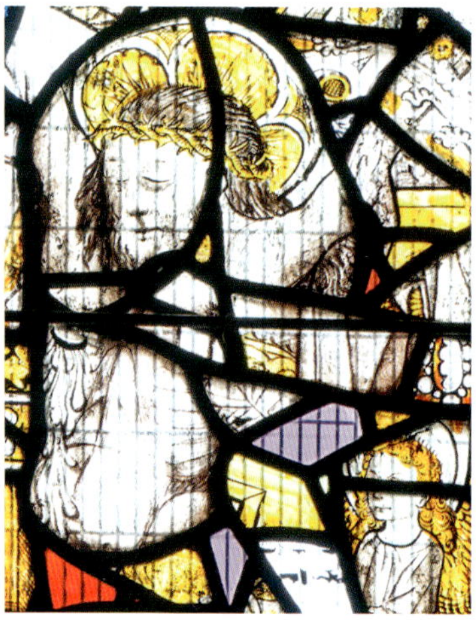

73. Part of the Crucified Christ, late fifteenth or early sixteenth century, Church of All Saints, Buttington, west window

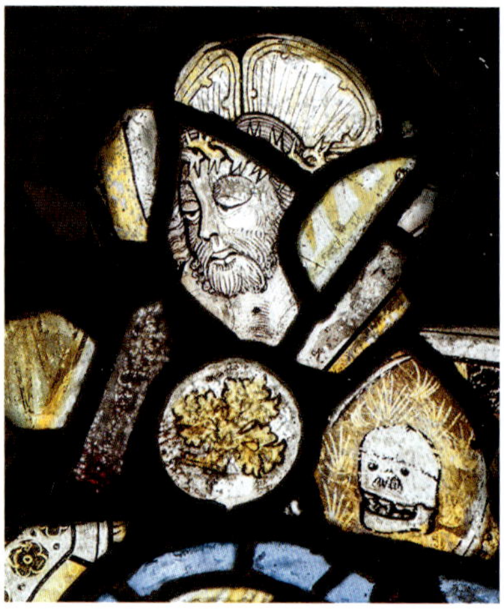

74. Part of the Crucified Christ, probably *c.* 1500, Church of St Beuno, Trefdraeth, chancel

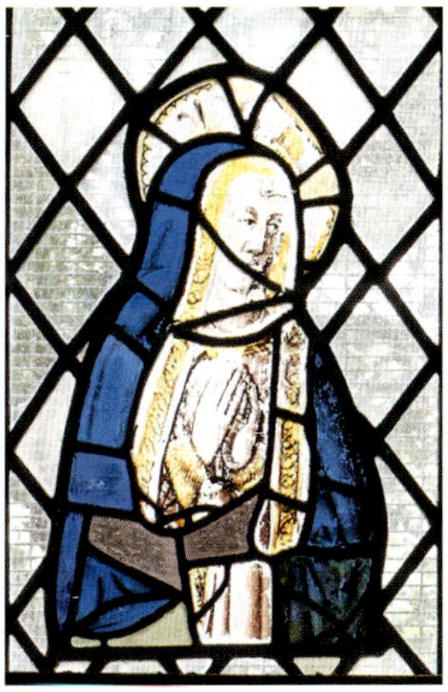

75. (above) The Virgin Mary, probably from a scene of the Crucifixion, late fifteenth or early sixteenth century, Church of St Mary and St Nicholas, Beaumaris, chancel

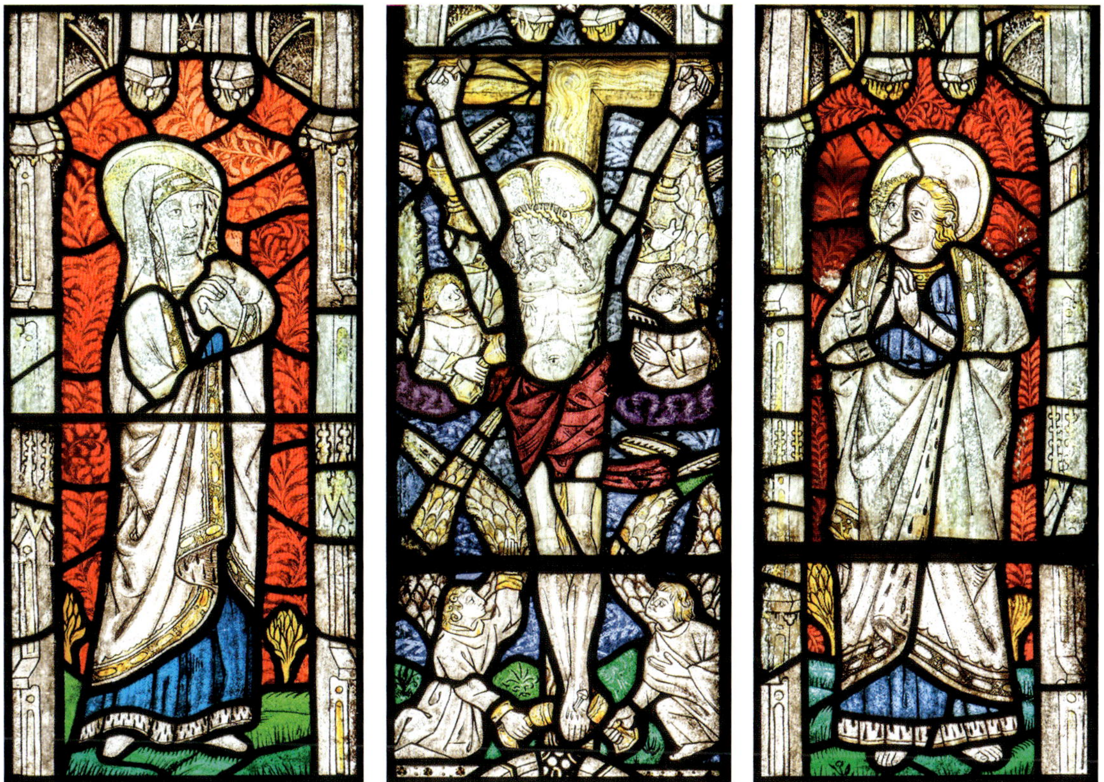

76. The Crucifixion with the Virgin Mary and St John, *c.* 1490–5, Church of St Cadwaladr, Llangadwaladr, east window

Christ was often shown on the cross between the figures of his mother Mary and his disciple John, and these figures (or parts of them) survive at Llangadwaladr, Llanrhychwyn, Llanasa, and Cilcain, where Mary is in tears. A female figure at the Church of St Mary and St Nicholas, Beaumaris, suggests the attitude of Mary at the side of the cross, although other indicators of a medieval Crucifixion scene are absent. The figures of John in the almost entirely reconstructed Crucifixion scenes at Nercwys and Mamhilad both appear to have medieval heads, but the remainder of the figure at Nercwys is nineteenth century.[18] Some Crucifixion scenes are theologically sophisticated. At the Church of St Ust and St Dyfrig, Llanwrin, angels collect blood from the wounds of Christ in chalices, as they also do at Llangadwaladr and Llandyrnog, but the black halo of one of the angels identifies it as an 'angel of the abyss'.[19]

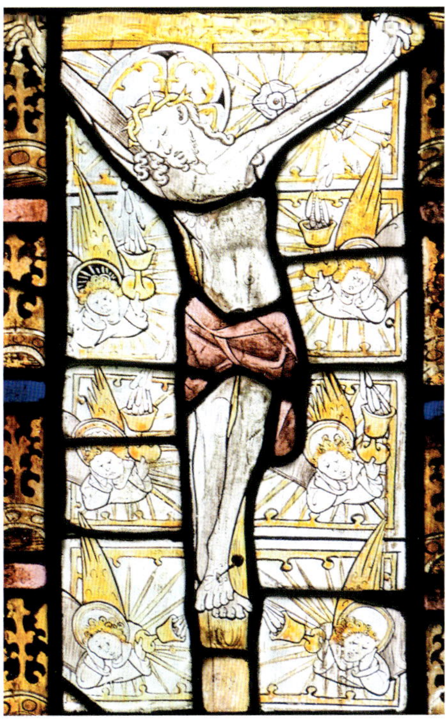

77. The Crucified Christ, *c.* 1461–83, Church of St Ust and St Dyfrig, Llanwrin, east window

17 A drawing of the east window of the north aisle at Llanrhychwyn includes a skull at the foot of the cross, although the elliptical piece of glass now in its place has lost its paint. The illustration is inserted as a supplementary plate into an extra-illustrated copy of Thomas Pennant, *A Tour in Wales* (vol. ii, *The Journey to Snowdon*), National Library of Wales PD 9872, p. 191/10.

18 It is difficult to distinguish which parts of the scene at the Church of St Illtud, Mamhilad, are medieval. The slightly contorted drawing of the face of John was copied in reverse for the face of Mary.

19 Peter Lord, *The Visual Culture of Wales: Medieval Vision* (Cardiff: University of Wales Press, 2003), p. 178.

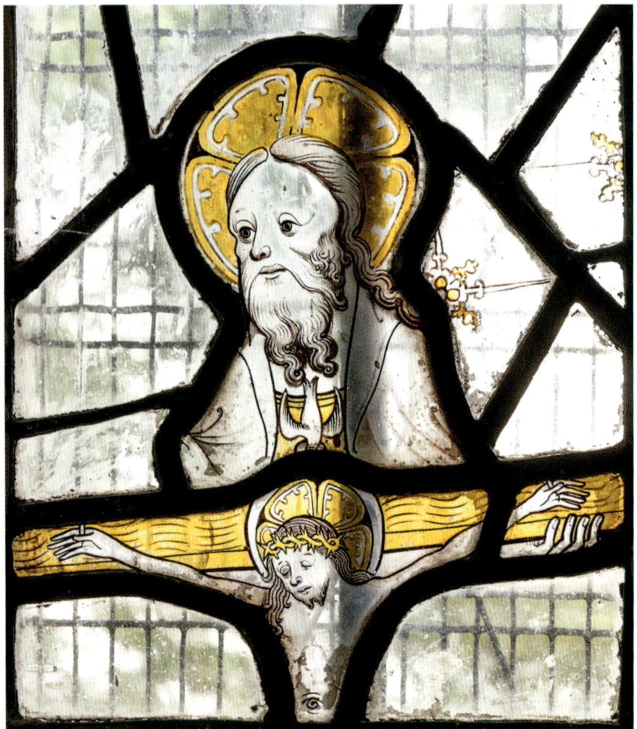

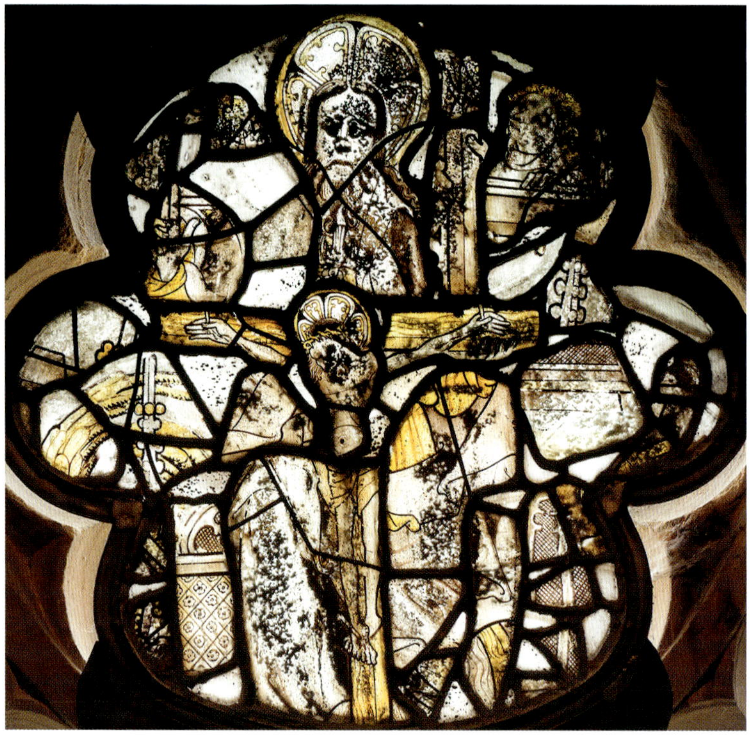

78. (above) The Holy Trinity, *c.* 1460, Church of St Rhychwyn, Llanrhychwyn, south chancel

79. (above right) The Holy Trinity, probably *c.* 1460, Church of St Mechell, Llanfechell, north transept

Small images of the crucified Christ were not always part of Crucifixion scenes. At Llanrhychwyn and the Church of St Mechell, Llanfechell, Christ is shown on the cross with God the Father and the dove of the Holy Spirit above as a depiction of the Trinity. At Gresford, the three persons of the Trinity are among the seven large figures in the east window of the chancel, depicted with triple crowns, long hair and curly beards. God the Father stands at the centre of the window, flanked by seated figures of the Son and Holy Spirit, who seat Mary and the dove of the Holy Spirit in their laps.[20]

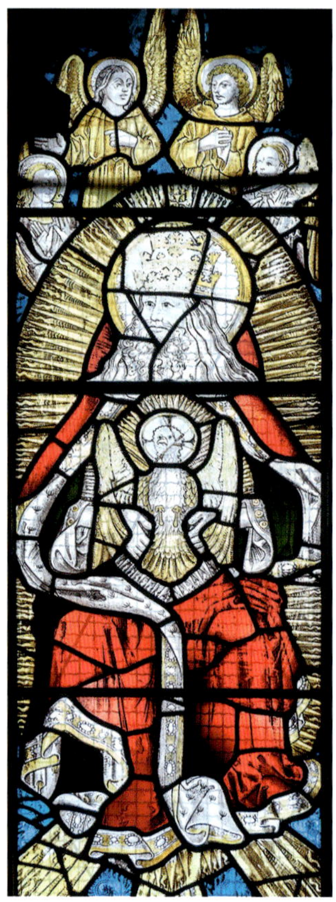

80. God the Holy Spirit, 1500, Church of All Saints, Gresford, east window

As well as images of Mary at the side of the cross, a few images of her holding the Infant Christ survive in stained glass in Welsh churches, with perhaps the most complete being at Llanwrin. An image of the Virgin and Child also survives at the Church of St Michael, Abergele, and at Llanrhychwyn two depictions of the Infant Christ survive. One of these is just a head,

20 A further depiction of the Father and Son together in the north wall of the Lady Chapel at Gresford may also have represented the Trinity, since the dove of the Holy Spirit might have been originally shown above. At Mathern a crowned figure, which may perhaps be Christ or God the Father, is shown radiating light and is very similar to a depiction of a dove, suggesting that they could also have been part of a representation of the Trinity. Carved depictions in stone of the Trinity are also found at St Bride's Wentloog, Holyhead, Llanddyfnan, and on a brass at Beaumaris; see Peter Lord, *The Visual Culture of Wales: Medieval Vision* (Cardiff: University of Wales Press, 2003), pp. 180–3.

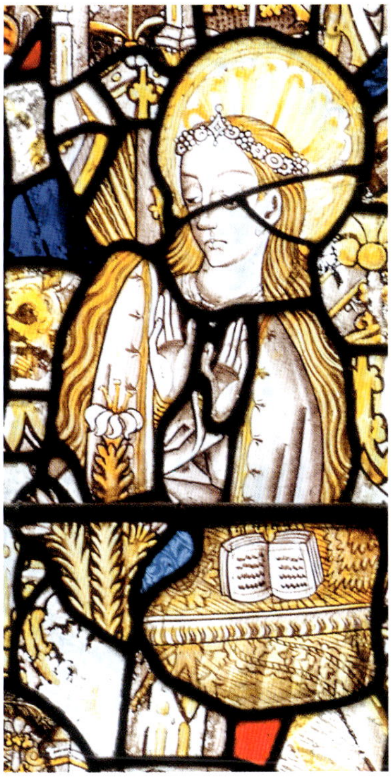

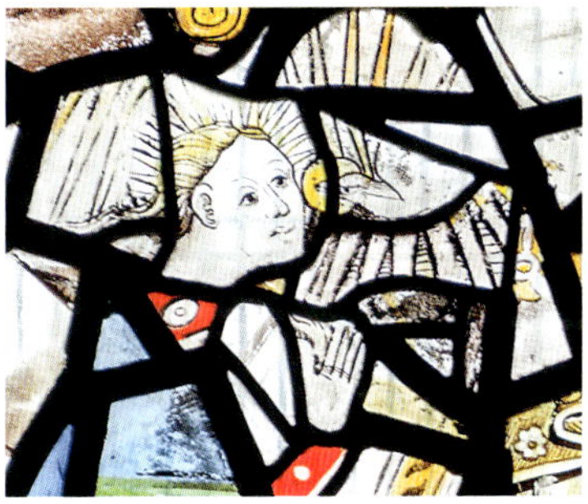

81–2. The Virgin Mary, probably from scenes of the Annunciation, late fifteenth or early sixteenth century, Church of St Dyfnog, Llanrhaeadr-yng-Nghinmeirch, west wall (left); Church of St Mary, Mold, south aisle (above)

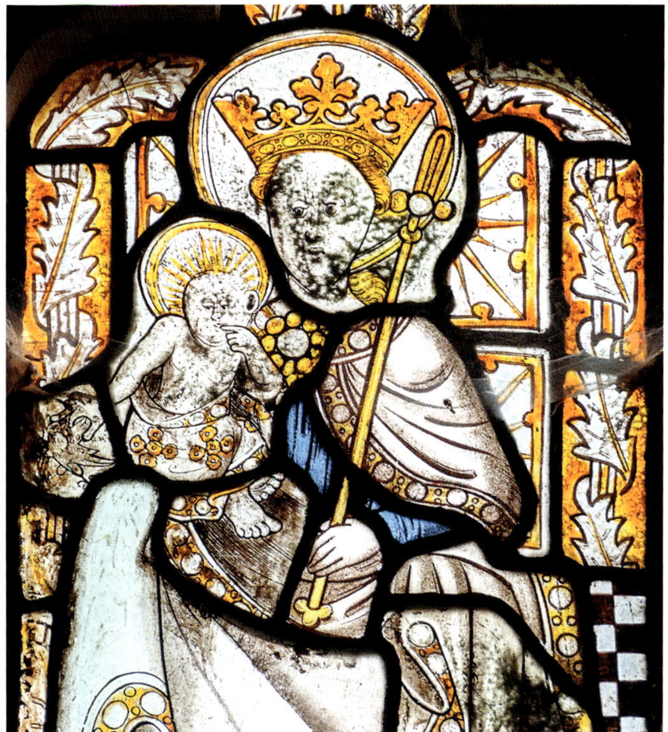

83. (right) The Virgin and Child, *c*. 1461–83, Church of St Ust and St Dyfrig, Llanwrin, east window

84–5. Fragments of the Virgin and Child, *c*. 1460, Church of St Rhychwyn, Llanrhychwyn, south chancel (below right); *c*. 1500, Church of St Michael, Abergele, south nave (below far right)

while the other is more complete with what is presumably the hand of Mary. Two full-length figures of Mary at Gresford accompany the three persons of the Trinity in the east window of the chancel at Gresford. That on the right is paired with Gabriel, suggestive of the Annunciation, and the figures of Mary and Gabriel in the tracery of the east window at the Church of St Tyrnog, Llandyrnog, are part of a more complete Annunciation scene that was originally part of a series of scenes of the Life of Mary.[21] The figures of Mary and Gabriel in the tracery lights at Llandyrnog form an Annunciation scene and female figures at the Church of St Dyfnog, Llanrhaeadr-yng-Nghinmeirch, the Church of St Mary, Mold, and from the lower part of the east window of the Trevor Chapel at Gresford, also seem to have been portrayals of Mary at the Annunciation.

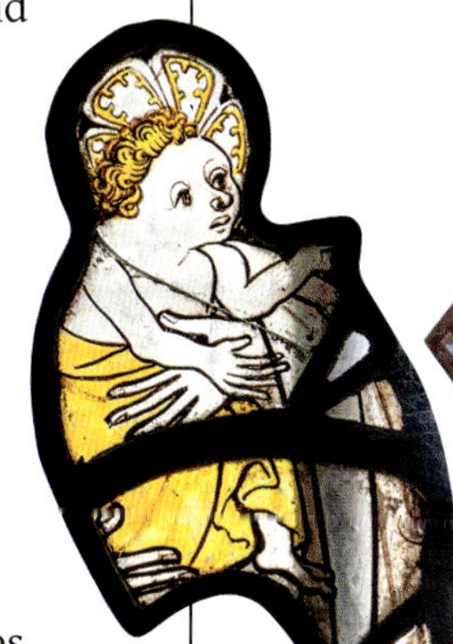

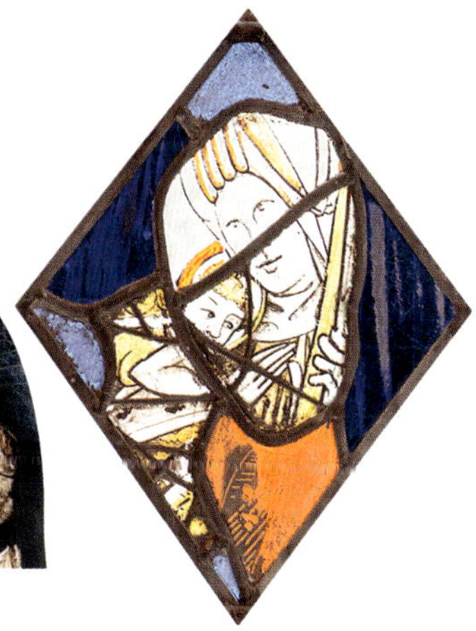

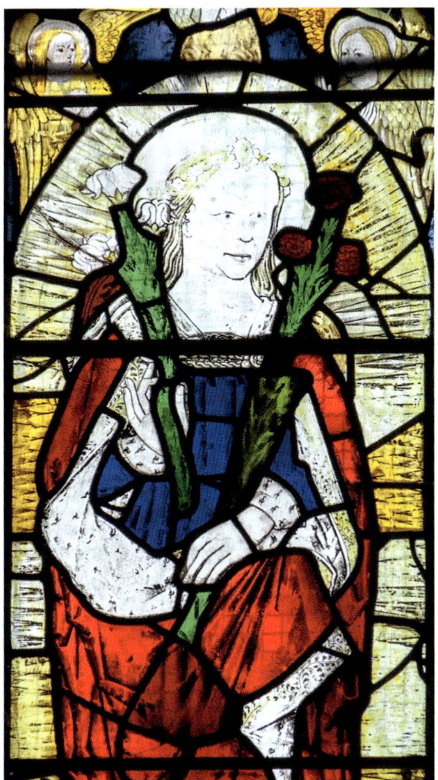

86. The Virgin Mary, 1500, Church of All Saints, Gresford, east window

21 The large figure of Gabriel at Gresford appears to be mainly nineteenth century, and the second figure of Mary with Gabriel was given a new head at the time of the window's restoration in 1867. The stained glass at Llandyrnog was recorded by Stephen Glynne in 1847. S.R. Glynne, 'Notes on the older churches in the four Welsh dioceses', *Archaeologia Cambrensis*, fifth series, vol. 1 (1884), p. 173.

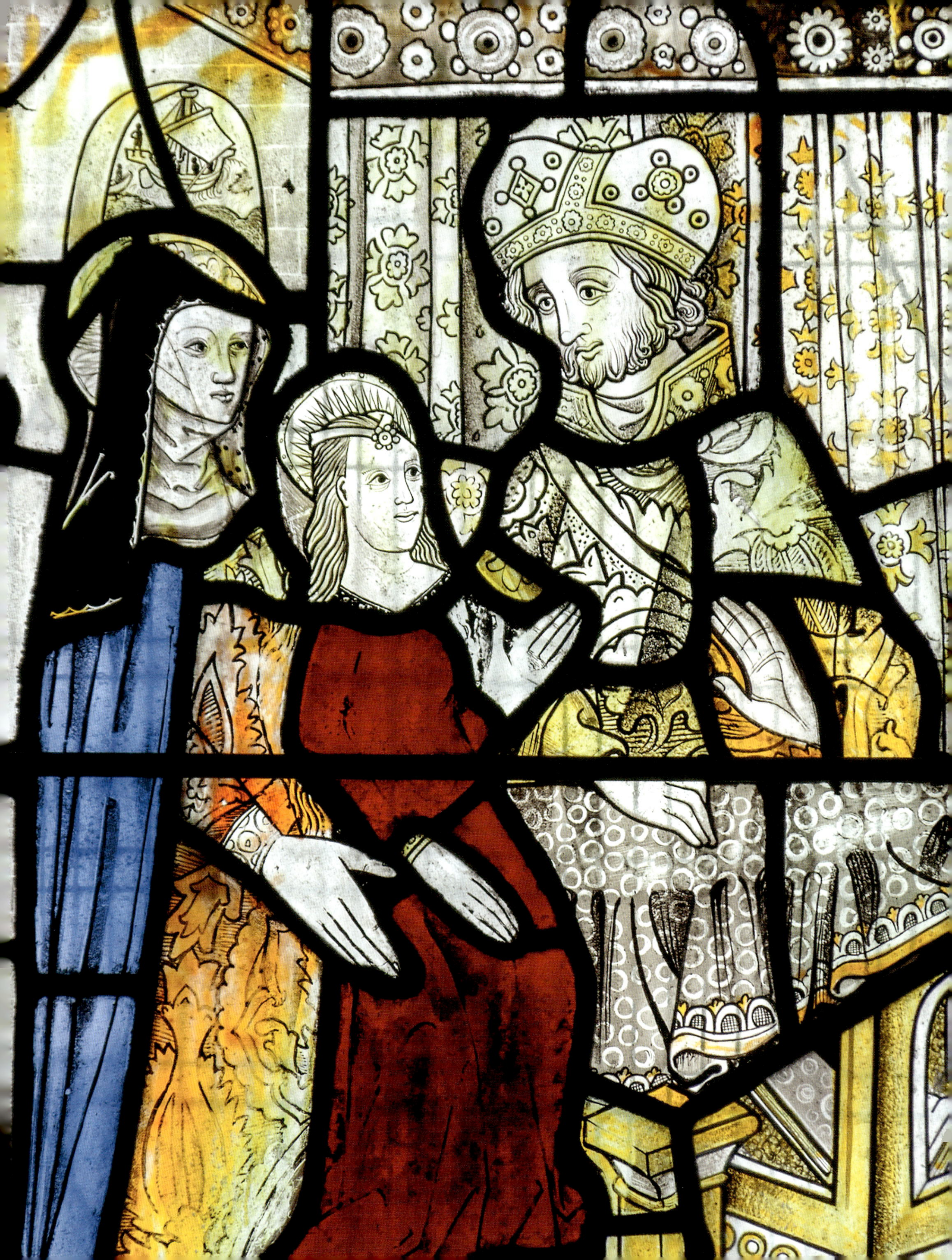

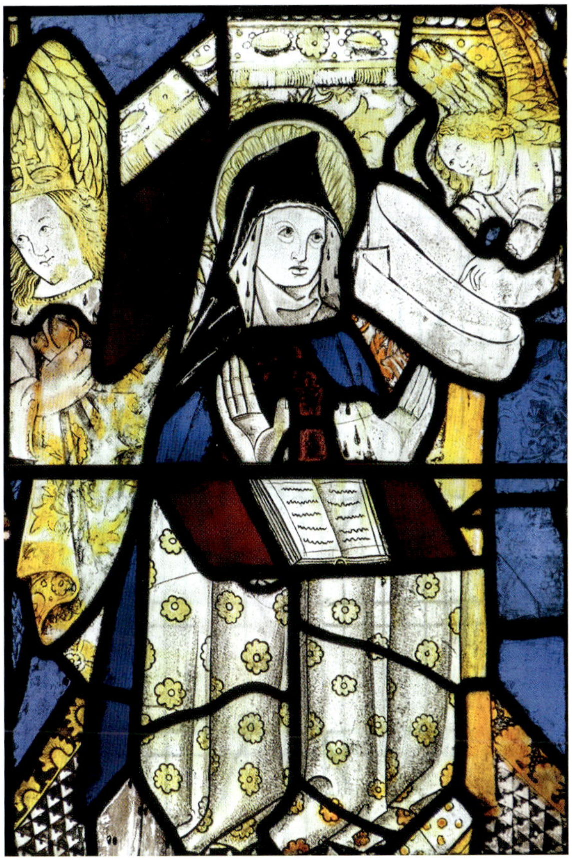

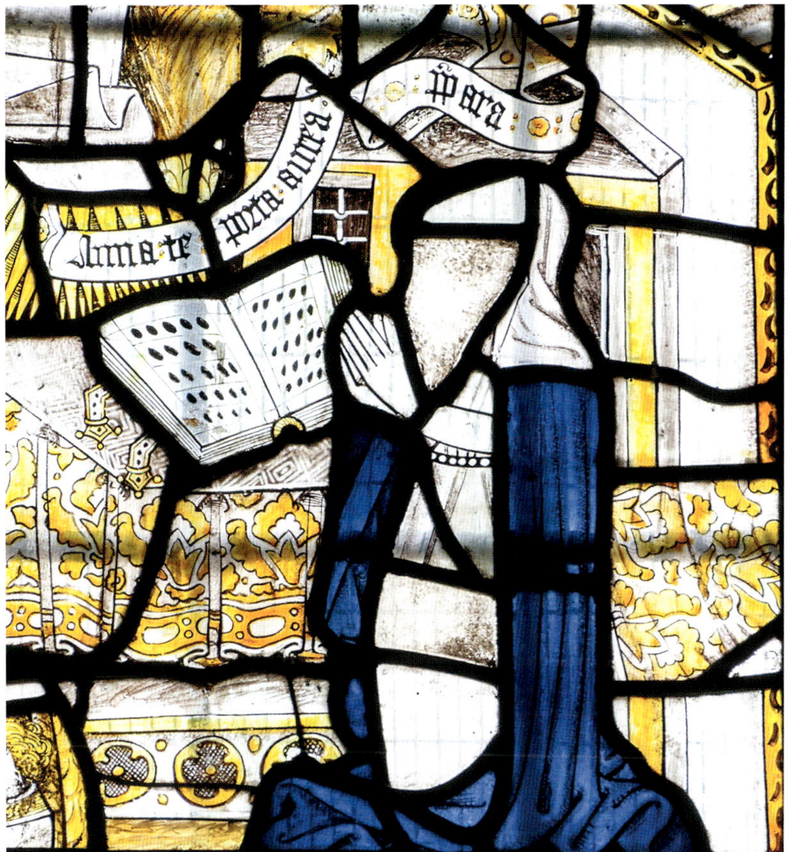

88. (above left) The Annunciation to St Anne, 1498, Church of All Saints, Gresford, Lady Chapel (north aisle)

89. (above) The Annunciation to St Anne, *c.* 1500, Church of St Cyngar, Hope, east window

Parts of an Annunciation scene also remain in the east window of the Lady Chapel at Gresford, among a series of panels illustrating Marian subjects. The series begins with five scenes drawn from the 'Protoevangelium of St James' concerning the birth of Mary and her parents Joachim and Anne. Some panels are virtually complete, such as that of the Presentation of Mary in the Temple, while others such as the Annunciation were completed with new glass by the restorers Clayton & Bell in 1872. A complete set of original Latin inscriptions allowed the two lost scenes at the bottom of the window to be correctly replaced with the Nativity and the Flight into Egypt.

Fragments of some of the same subjects survive at the Church of St Cyngar, Hope. The scenes with Joachim and Anne are identifiable by the presence of inscriptions rather than imagery, although the kneeling figure of Anne praying in the garden survives with the instruction by the angel 'ANNA TE PORTA AUREA' (Anne be ready at the Golden Gate) given above. Although a similar painterly style suggests that both sets may be the work of the same workshop, the composition of the two cognate scenes is quite different.[22]

22 Both scenes of Anne at prayer, when an angel brings her the news that she will soon be with child, echo the usual depiction of Mary at prayer when Gabriel brings her the news that she will have a son. The angel tells Anne to go and meet her husband Joachim at the Golden Gate in Jerusalem.

. The Presentation of the Virgin Mary in the
nple, 1498, Church of All Saints, Gresford,
dy Chapel (north aisle)

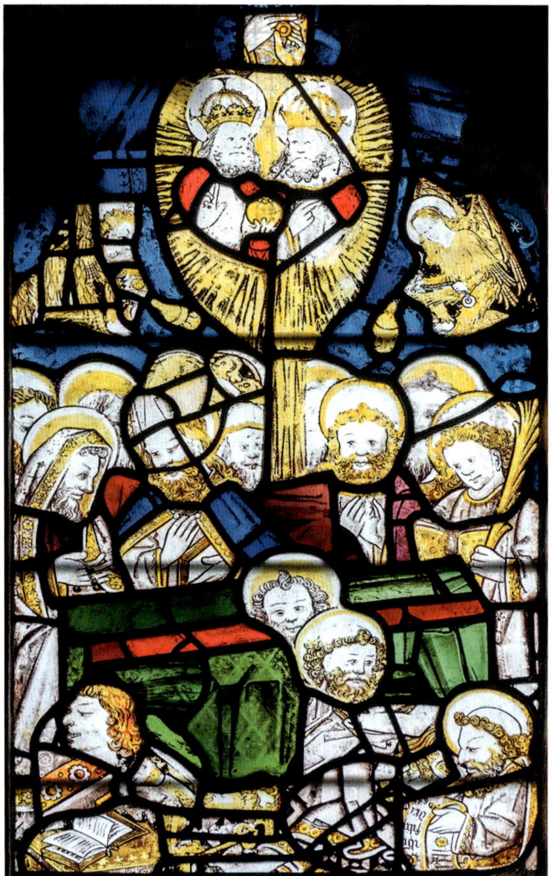

90. The Funeral of the Virgin, probably early sixteenth century, Church of All Saints, Gresford, Lady Chapel (north aisle)

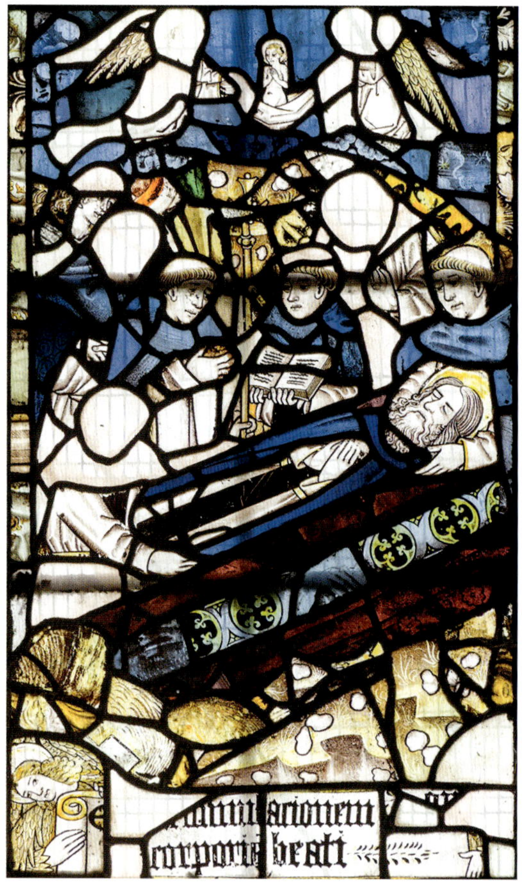

91. The Burial of St Anthony, 1510, Church of All Saints, Gresford, Trevor Chapel (north aisle)

Four scenes now in the north wall of the Lady Chapel at Gresford depict the Funeral, Burial, Assumption and Coronation of Mary. The window includes the unusual episode in the narrative of the funeral of Mary from the fifth-century apocryphal text 'De Transitu Beatae Mariae' (The Passing of Blessed Mary) when a disbelieving Jew attempts to overturn the coffin but finds that his hands are stuck to it and are torn from his body.[23] The scene of the Assumption of Mary has been restored as a complete scene, while the adjacent panel with parts of the Coronation scene is patched with fragments from elsewhere.

The reglazing of the east window of the Trevor Chapel at Gresford in 1915–16 placed the remains of four scenes across the centre of the window. Two panels depict the execution of John the Baptist and his head being brought to the feast by Salome, alongside scenes of Anthony entering religious life, and his burial. A window with scenes from the life of Anthony, given in 1510 by the vicar William Rodon, was formerly on the south side of the church. It seems likely that these four surviving scenes, all of which have inscriptions below, were originally part of a series of more comprehensive scenes from the lives of both saints.[24] The restoration of the glass follows a more conservative approach to that used in the 1872 restoration of the scenes from the Life of Mary, and the heads of figures have been left blank in preference to being completed with new painted glass.[25]

23 The Jew is subsequently converted and then healed by Peter. Other examples of the scene may be found in the late thirteenth-century glass at Stanton St John in Oxfordshire, in a more similar composition at the Church of St Peter Mancroft, Norwich, and in the sixteenth-century glass at King's College, Cambridge.

24 D.R. Thomas, *The History of the Diocese of St Asaph* (Oswestry: Caxton Press, 1913), vol. iii, p. 247.

25 A proper appreciation of the glass is hampered by the inexpert cleaning of the windows in the 1960s, which caused considerable damage to some of them. However, some of the nineteenth-century glass suffered most.

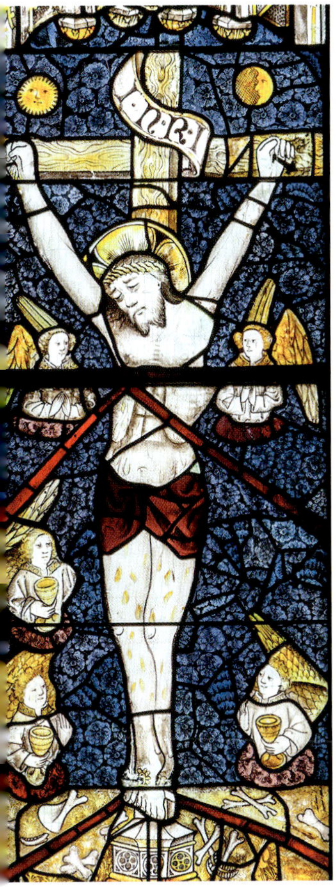

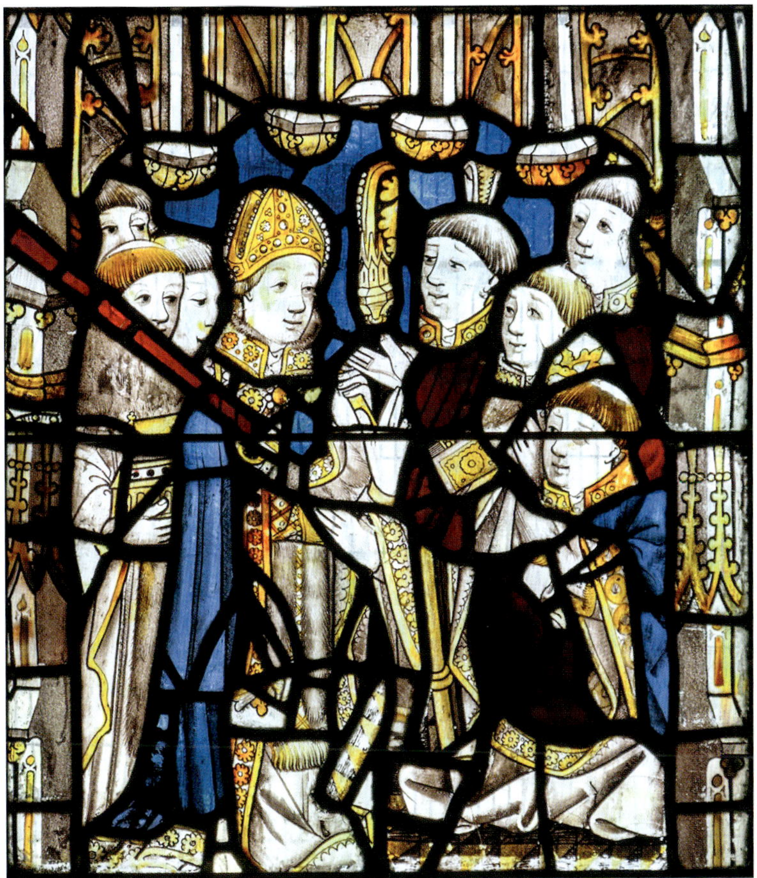

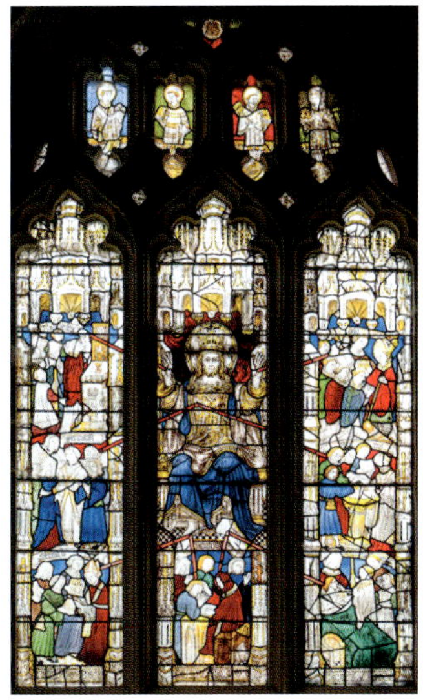

92–3. Ordination (left) and the Crucified Christ (far left), from the Seven Sacraments, late fifteenth or early sixteenth century, Church of St Tyrnog, Llandyrnog, east window

94. (above) The Seven Sacraments, *c*. 1480, restored with a new central figure of Christ by Clayton & Bell, 1877, Church of St Michael, Doddiscombleigh, Devon, north aisle

The panels from the Life of Anthony appear to be by the same hand as the surviving panels depicting the Seven Sacraments at Llandyrnog. Devotion to the Seven Sacraments became popular in the second half of the fifteenth century and the subject survives in whole or in part elsewhere in English churches with a similar pattern of the sacraments arranged around the figure of Christ, such as at the Church of All Saints, Crudwell, in Wiltshire, and the Church of St Michael, Doddiscombleigh, in Devon.[26] Only three of the sacraments are discernible at Llandyrnog, with those of Marriage and Ordination being the best preserved. At Doddiscombleigh all of the seven scenes are well-preserved in their original locations. Although the central seated figure of Christ is not original, the window shows the connection between each of the sacraments with the five wounds of Christ by lines of blood. This helps to explain the four shafts of red glass that radiate from the crucified Christ at Llandyrnog, one of which connects correctly with the panel of Ordination in the adjacent light, which is shown in the same relative position in the window at Doddiscombleigh.[27]

26 A single panel of Ordination also survives at Melbury Bubb in Dorset.

27 The restoration of the window at Doddiscombsleigh by Clayton & Bell in 1877 provides a further comparison with their work on the medieval glass at Gresford. David Evans, Rachel Thomas and Roger Rosewell, 'Medieval and Modern at Doddiscombsleigh', <http://vidimus.org/issues/issue-10/feature>, accessed 19 December 2013. The article gives further examples of the subject in other churches, and notes that standing figures of Christ are found in examples from the southern part of England, while the crucified Christ is at the centre of the scene further north, as at Llandyrnog and the Church of St Andrew, Cartmel Fell, Lancashire.

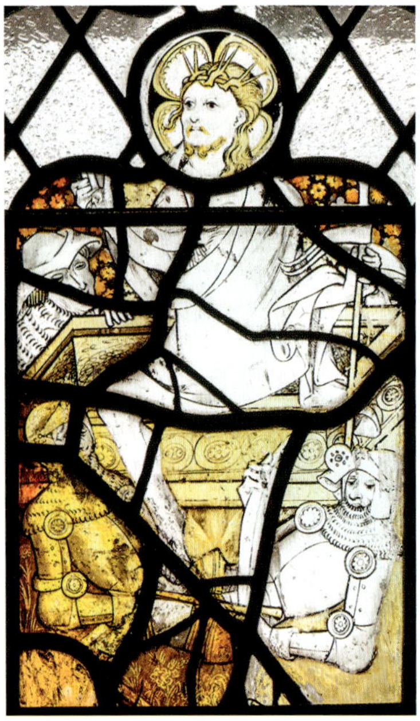

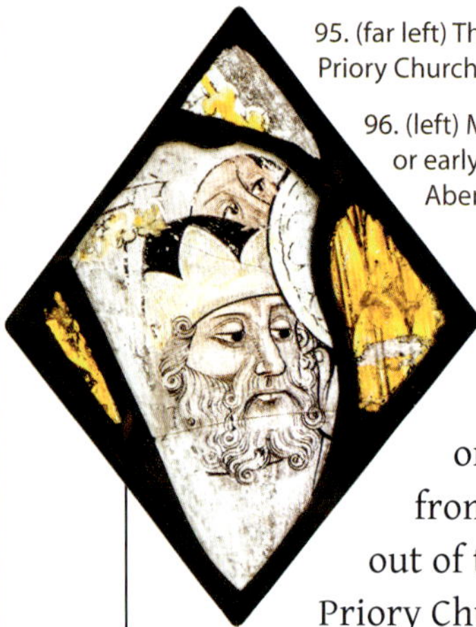

95. (far left) The Resurrection, probably fifteenth century, Priory Church of St David, Swansea, north aisle

96. (left) Medieval fragments, probably late fifteenth or early sixteenth century, Church of St Michael, Abergele, south nave

The panels at Gresford and Llandyrnog are almost the only fairly complete narrative scenes in stained glass from medieval Welsh churches. The risen Christ stepping out of the tomb with soldiers below at the Roman Catholic Priory Church of St David, Swansea, was given to the church in the nineteenth century, and was thought to have originated in the west of England.[28] Only the suggestions of other lost narrative scenes survive elsewhere, such as the small group of heads shown together at Abergele. Among the fragments in the north wall of the Lady Chapel at Gresford, a boy carrying a bundle of sticks could represent Isaac as he assists his father Abraham prior to his own sacrifice (pre-empted by the angel), but no other Old Testament scenes have been identified in the stained glass of Welsh medieval churches.[29]

Old Testament kings and prophets were included in depictions of the Tree of Jesse, in which the genealogy of Christ is visually traced back though the kings of Judah to David and Jesse.[30] The subject was re-created in the tracery lights of the east window of the chancel at Gresford in 1867, although only parts of nine or ten of twenty-seven figures are likely to be from the original window of 1500. A pair of mirror image kings on the opposite sides of the central six lights makes it possible that the subject may be original, and both figures are conceivably in their original position.[31]

Two remarkably well-preserved late medieval portrayals of the Tree of Jesse survive at Llanrhaeadr-yng-Nghinmeirch and the Church of St Bridget, Dyserth. Both are dated to 1533, and demonstrate the continental influence on British glass painting brought by Flemish craftsmen in the later fifteenth century.

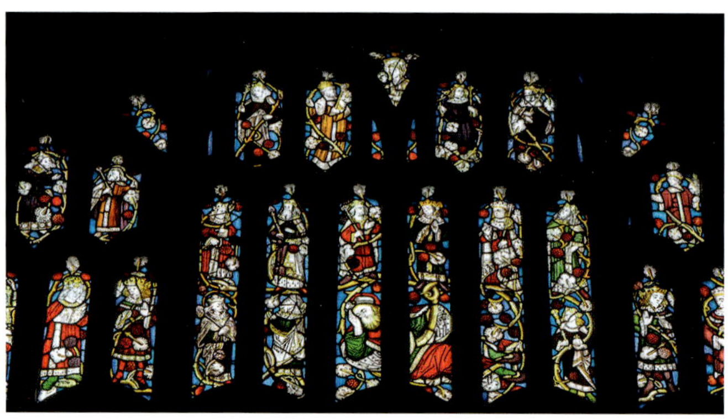

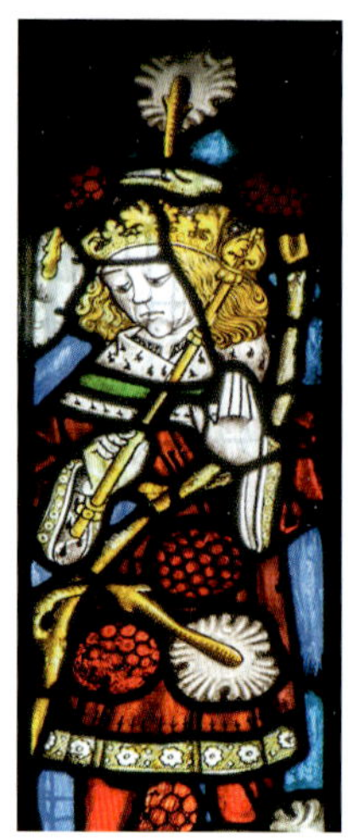

97–8. Clayton & Bell, The Tree of Jesse, 1867, incorporating glass of *c.* 1500 (right), including Crowned King, 1500 (far right), Church of All Saints, Gresford, east window

28 A figure of Christ displaying his wounds at the tomb, according to the vision of Gregory, survives in a fragment from the Church of St Cystennin, Llangystennin, see Peter Lord, *The Visual Culture of Wales: Medieval Vision* (Cardiff: University of Wales Press, 2003), p. 187.

29 This interpretation may be supported by a Latin inscription, and a further fragment that remains in the porch. Mostyn Lewis, *Stained Glass in North Wales up to 1850* (Altrincham: John Sherratt and Son Ltd, 1970), p. 40.

30 The Tree of Jesse was a long-lived subject in medieval stained glass, dating back to the twelfth century at York Minster. The subject is found in stone and wood carving elsewhere in Wales, the most remarkable example being the giant recumbent figure of Jesse at the Priory Church of St Mary, Abergavenny. See Peter Lord, *The Visual Culture of Wales: Medieval Vision*, pp. 203–7.

31 The Virgin and Child at the apex of the window is also medieval, but the recumbent Jesse below is not. Mostyn Lewis, *Stained Glass in North Wales up to 1850*, p. 38.

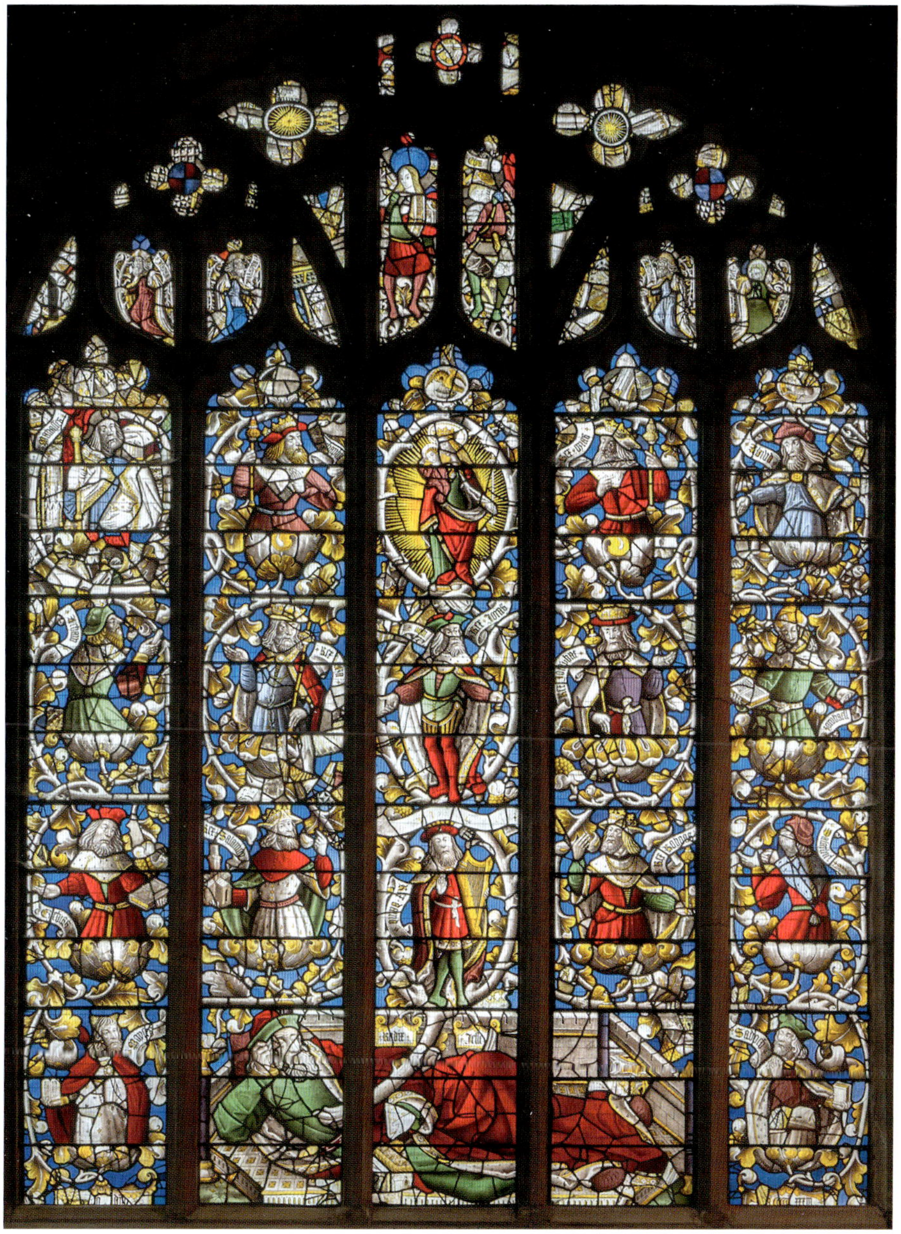

99–100. The Tree of Jesse (left), including the Virgin and Child (below), 1533, Church of St Dyfnog, Llanrhaeadr-yng-Nghinmeirch, north chancel

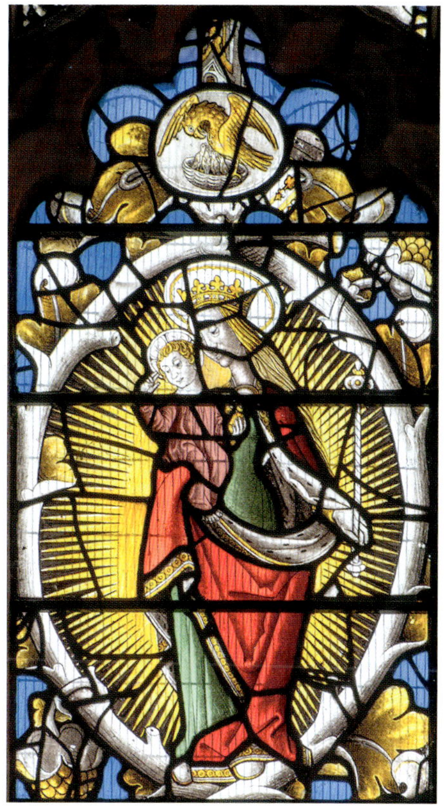

The larger of these two windows is at Llanrhaeadr-yng-Nghinmeirch, and is a rare example of the survival of a whole medieval window in Wales. The figure of Jesse lies at the bottom of the window with a full-length figure of David above him, and the Virgin and Child at the top of the central light. King Jehoram stands between David and the Virgin and Child and fourteen other half-figures appear to 'flower' from the calyces on the vine, a French innovation in the arrangement of the subject during the early sixteenth century. The reclining Jesse also has close parallels with a French woodcut from a book of hours printed in 1498.[32]

32 Bernard Rackham & C.W. Baty, 'The Jesse Window at Llanrhaiadr, Denbighshire–I', *The Burlington Magazine*, vol. 80, no. 468 (March 1942), pp. 62–6. A full description of the window was also published in a booklet by E. Gwynne Matthews, *The Llanrhaeadr Jesse Window: its meaning and history* (2000). A French panel of Ezekiel of about 1500–15, now in the Albright-Knox Art Gallery, Buffalo, New York, is so similar to the depiction of Hezekiah at Llanrhaeadr-yng-Nghinmeirch that it has been suggested that the panel was a forgery based on an illustration of the figure at Llanrhaeadr, published by Charles Winston in 1865. Meredith Parsons Lillich, *Stained Glass Before 1700 in Upstate New York* (London/ Tournhout: Harvey Miller Publishers, 2004), pp. 48–53.

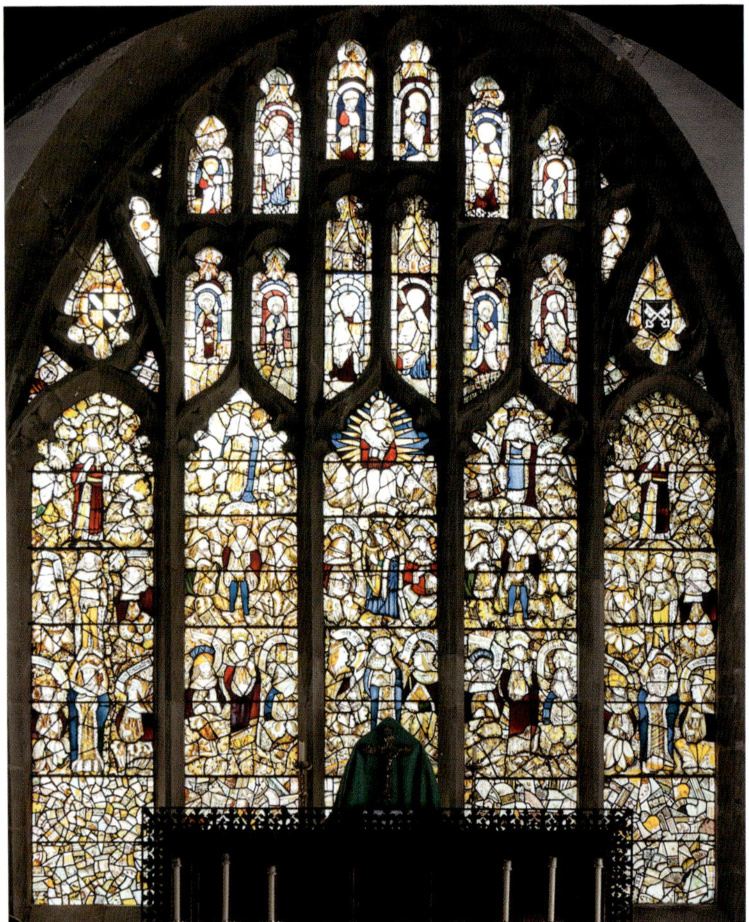

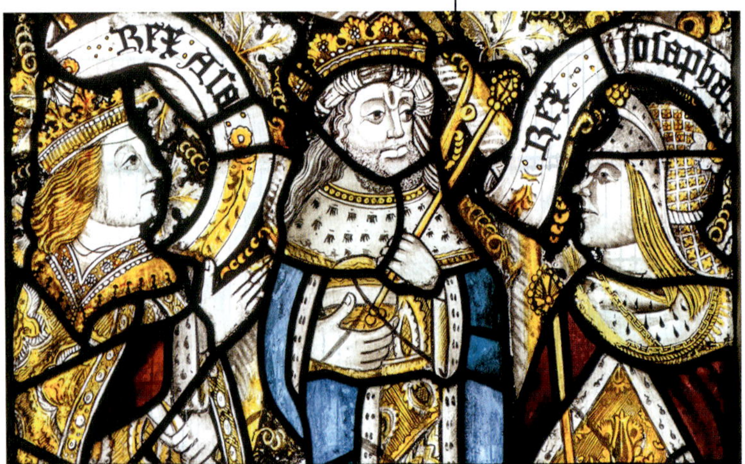

101–2. The Tree of Jesse (left), including Old Testament kings Asa and Jehosaphat (below left), 1533, Church of St Bridget, Dyserth, east window

Moses is included among the figures to the left of Jesse in addition to those from the genealogy, and four further Old Testament prophets, Isaiah, Zechariah, Obadiah and Joel, appear in the tracery lights.

The Tree of Jesse at Dyserth also appears to be largely complete, although the lower panels have been lost, and no traces of the figure of Jesse remain. The window depicts kings and further male figures who are not crowned, nearly all of whom are arranged in threes, the central one standing between half-length figures emerging from the petals. Prophets are not included among the figures, although some ancestors preceding Jesse are present, such as Salmon and Obed, the grandfather and father of Jesse.

The main lights of the east window at Dyserth were commissioned by Archdeacon Peter Conwey, and above them the set of apostles with their lines from the Apostles' Creed is the most complete in Wales. The figures are placed in twelve tracery lights and are probably in their original positions, but are stylistically close to the four evangelists in the east window of the Lady Chapel at Gresford, given in 1498. The remains of four apostles with lines from the creed are found at Llandyrnog, where the texts from the creeds arch over the figures in a similar way to those at Dyserth. The terminals of the scrolls and the decoration between the words suggests a common workshop, although the painting of the Llandyrnog figures is not of the same standard as at Dyserth or Gresford.[33]

33 Other details, such as the inscriptions, are similar in both the tracery and main lights at Dyserth, which could suggest that the same workshop might have been involved in both commissions.

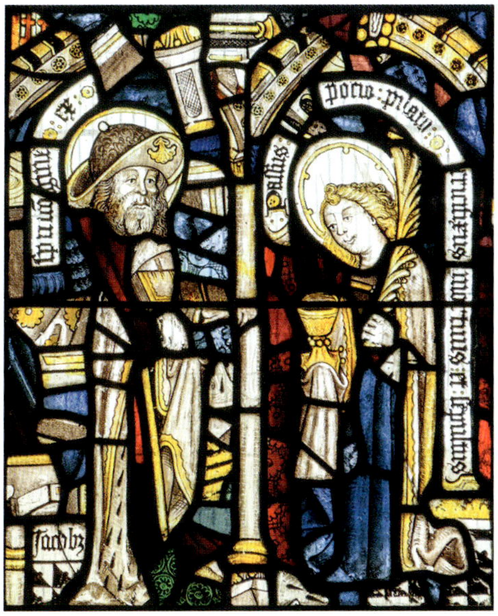

103. St James and St John, late fifteenth or early sixteenth century, Church of St Tyrnog, Llandyrnog, east window

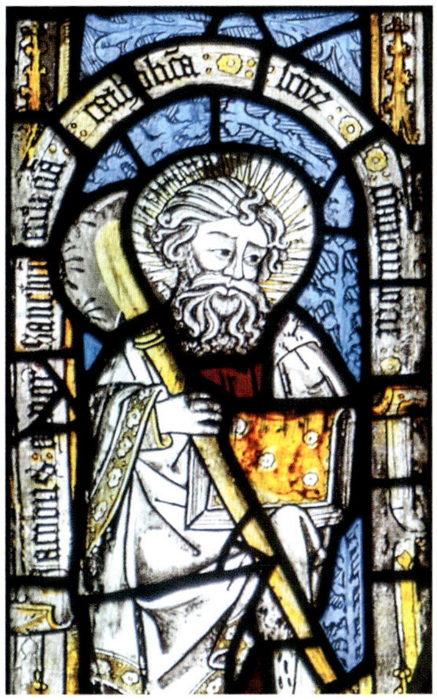

104. St James, *c.* 1500, Church of St Bridget, Dyserth, east window

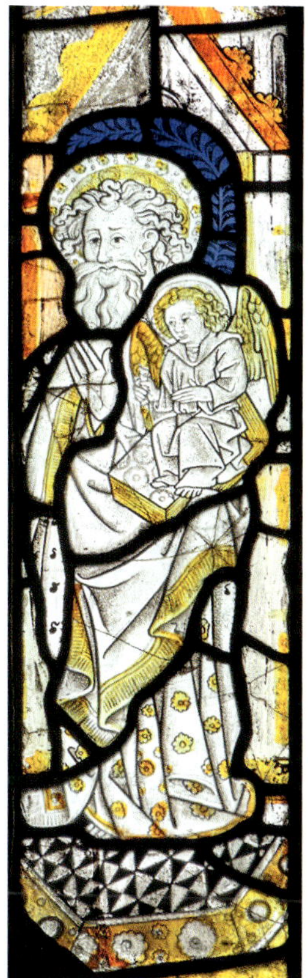

105. (right) St Matthew the Evangelist, 1498, Church of All Saints, Gresford, Lady Chapel (north aisle)

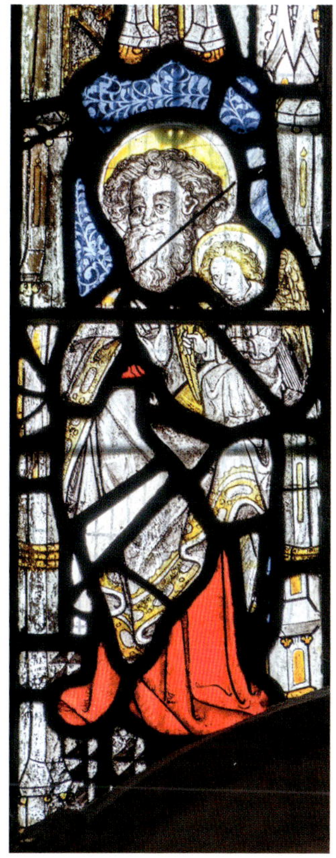

106. (far right) St Matthew the Evangelist, late fifteenth or early sixteenth century, Church of St Cyngar, Hope, east window

Individual apostles survive elsewhere such as the figures of Peter at Cilcain and another formerly at the Church of St Cystennin, Llangystennin (now kept at Llandudno Museum), with his usual attribute of the keys of heaven, a reference to Matthew 16: 19. James is one of the two figures, the other unidentified, at the Church of Tysilio, Llantysilio, where he is dressed as a pilgrim. James is also among the figures at Llanasa where he carries a pilgrim's staff, and both figures of James hold a book, a symbol of his authorship of a text in the New Testament.[34]

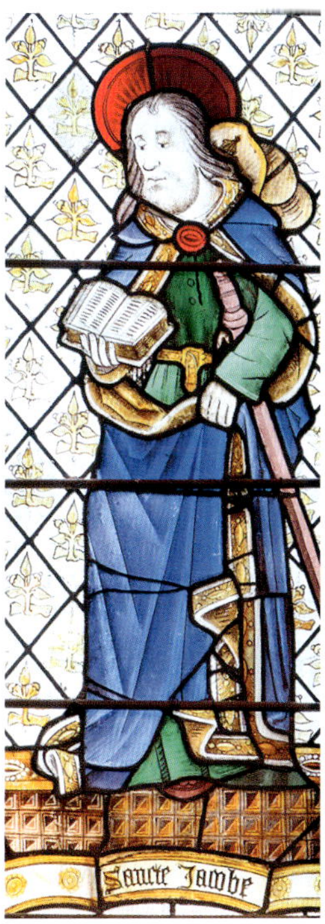

107. St James, early sixteenth century, Church of St Asaph and St Cynderyn, Llanasa, south chancel

The apostle John is also found as part of Crucifixion scenes as well as among sets of the four evangelists, the authors of the gospels. A set of evangelists holding their symbols, inspired by Revelation 4, are found in the east window of the Lady Chapel at Gresford and at Hope.[35] The symbol of John the Evangelist is an eagle, but he is also shown holding a chalice with a serpent when beside the cross or among groups of apostles.[36]

34 The drawing of the face of James is similar to both a head at Gwyddelwern and others at Llanrhychwyn. The restoration of the glass by Joseph Bell of Bristol has made it difficult to ascertain how much of the glass is medieval and it is possible that the head is in fact the restorer's copy of one of those at either Gwyddelwern or Llanrhychwyn, although neither church is very close to Llanasa.

35 The figure of Mark at Hope is incomplete and the head, beardless and tonsured with a stone on it, is probably that of the first Christian martyr Stephen, who was stoned.

36 The symbol is from an apocryphal legend in which John was handed a poisoned cup of wine, and, after John blessed the cup, the poison rose out of it in the form of a serpent. Unlike most other male saints, John is distinguished as a beardless, and sometimes rather effeminate, young man.

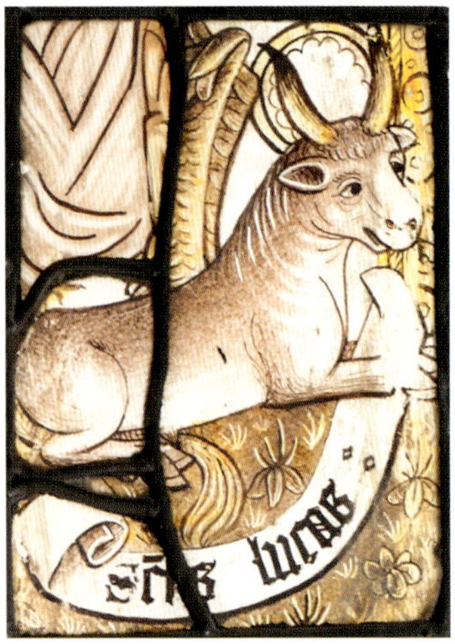

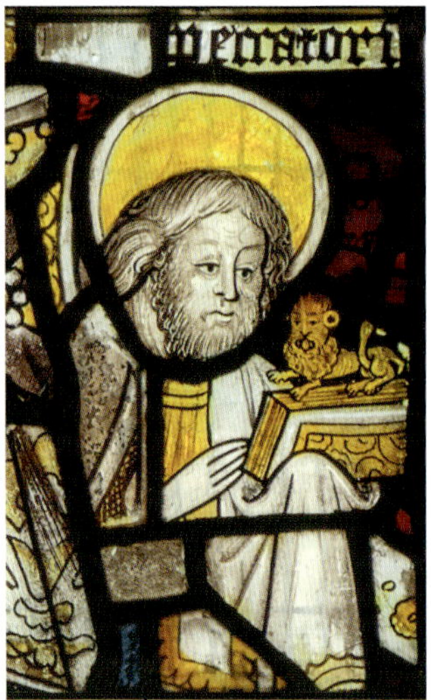

108. (far left) Winged Ox, Symbol of St Luke the Evangelist, late fifteenth or early sixteenth century, Church of St Elidan, Llanelidan, vestry screen

109. (left) St Mark the Evangelist, late fifteenth or early sixteenth century, Church of St Tyrnog, Llandyrnog, east window

110. (below left) Winged Ox, Symbol of St Luke the Evangelist, early sixteenth century, Church of All Saints, Gresford, Trevor Chapel (north aisle)

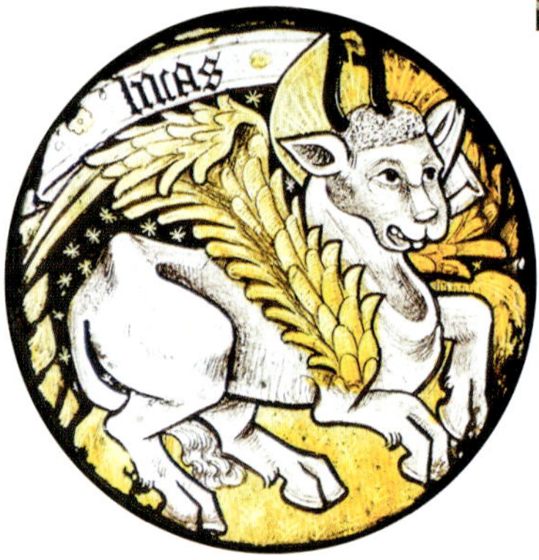

A set of symbols of the evangelists without figures are found at Gresford in the east window of the Trevor Chapel and the symbols of Luke and Mark survive in the tracery of a further south aisle window, while the winged ox, the symbol of St Luke, is well-preserved at Llanelidan. A figure at Llandyrnog can be identified as Mark the Evangelist as he holds a book and is shown with his symbol, a winged lion, and a similarly drawn head in the same panel of fragments is perhaps also an evangelist.

Few other figures from the New Testament have been recognised among medieval glass in Wales. Part of a figure with a sword at Llanwrin could be the apostle Paul, while John the Baptist survives at Llansantffraid Glan Conwy, and the lower half of his body clothed in animal skins is identifiable at Llanllugan. Without inscriptions or symbols it is impossible to know who the many figures or parts of figures still extant were intended to portray.[37]

In addition to biblical saints, many other saints were venerated in Wales during the late Middle Ages, and were depicted in glass, on wall paintings and as carved figures. The identification of these figures is often problematic in the absence of inscriptions, but iconographic conventions can sometimes identify saints. Several surviving depictions of saints such as Catherine of Alexandria, Christopher and George are known in medieval Welsh stained glass and parallel their survival as carved figures and wall paintings, indicating the strength of their cults in late medieval

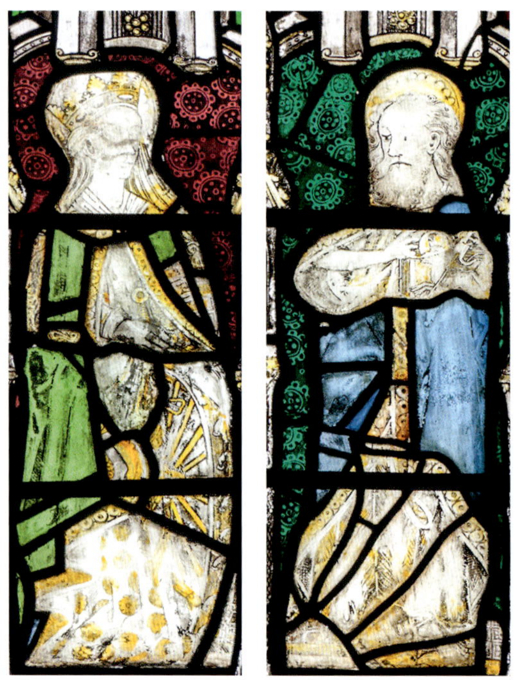

111. St Catherine and St John the Baptist, *c.* 1500, Church of St Ffraid, Llansantffraid Glan Conwy, west window

37 A female figure at Tremeirchion has been thought to be that of Anne, the mother of Mary, because of its similarity with another figure at the Church of All Saints, York. Mostyn Lewis, *Stained Glass in North Wales up to 1850* (Altrincham: John Sherratt and Son Ltd, 1970), p. 93. However the similarity is tenuous and even if the figures had been drawn from the same cartoon, it might not have represented the same saint.

38 It is tempting to suggest that fragments of wheels at Tremeirchion and Llanfair Dyffryn Clwyd could indicate her presence, although they could easily be from carts.

39 The illustration was inserted as a supplementary plate into an extra-illustrated copy of Thomas Pennant, *A Tour in Wales (vol. ii, The Journey to Snowdon)*, National Library of Wales PD 9872, p. 191/10.

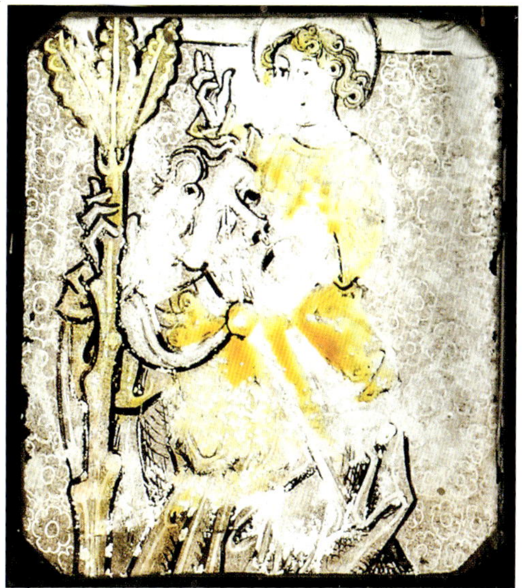

112. (right) St Christopher Carrying the Infant Christ, *c.* 1512, Church of St Gwyddelan, Dolwyddelan, chancel

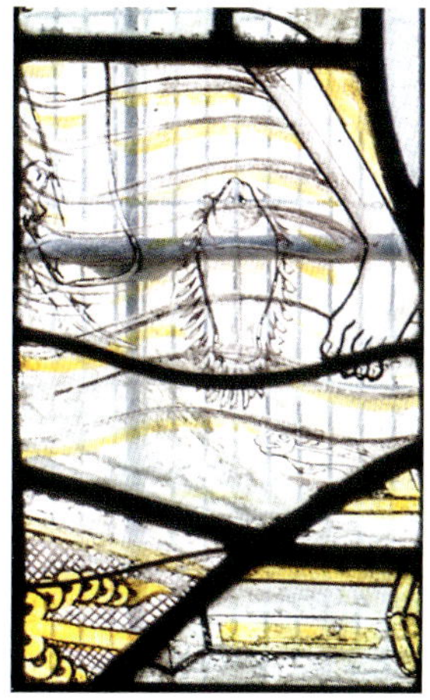

113. (below right) Probably part of St Christopher, late fifteenth or early sixteenth century, Church of St Cyngar, Hope, east window

Wales. Catherine is known by her wheel on which she was tortured, but not finally executed.[38] Christopher is usually shown carrying the Infant Christ across a river, and either the Infant Christ or a figure walking through water helps to identify the saint at Dolwyddelan, Gresford, Hope, Penmon, and possibly at Treuddyn.

The figure of George fighting with the dragon has been discovered in several medieval wall paintings in Welsh churches, such as at the churches dedicated to Cadog at Llangattock Lingoed, Llanmaes and Llancarfan. A particularly animated portrayal of George on horseback is among the figures from Llangystennin, and a further example is in the east window of the Trevor Chapel at Gresford. The Archangel Michael was often depicted weighing souls in medieval times, but in other instances was also shown fighting a dragon, as for example at Cilcain, and in a now lost figure at Llanrhychwyn that was recorded in an illustration of the east window of the north aisle in about 1800.[39]

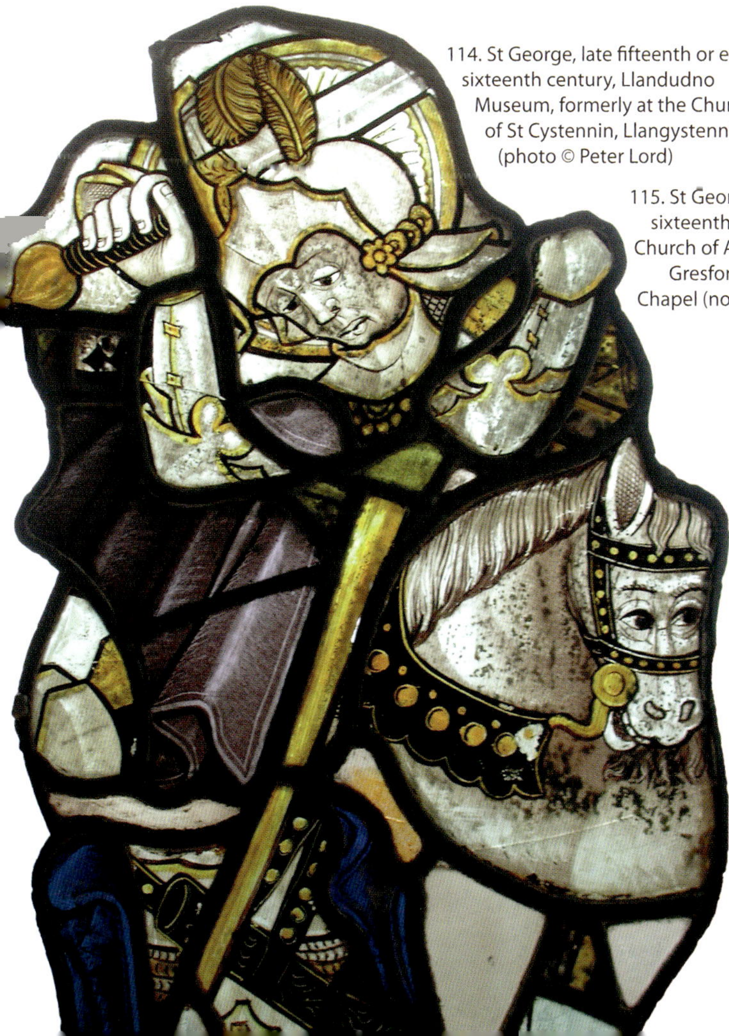

114. St George, late fifteenth or early sixteenth century, Llandudno Museum, formerly at the Church of St Cystennin, Llangystennin, (photo © Peter Lord)

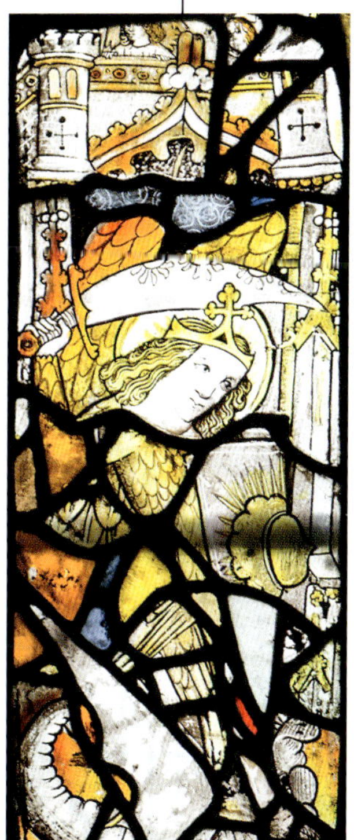

115. St George, early sixteenth century, Church of All Saints, Gresford, Trevor Chapel (north aisle)

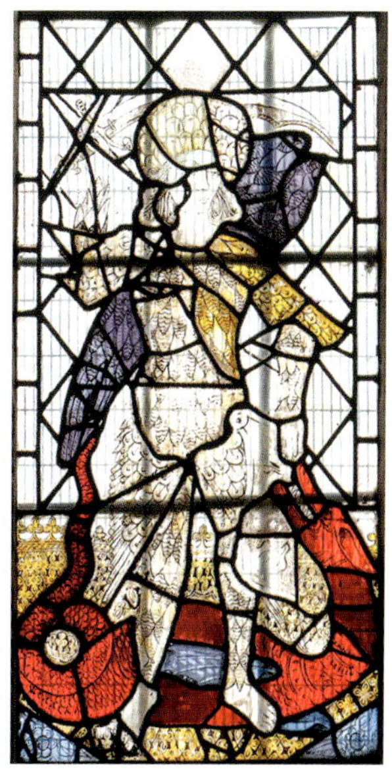

116. St Michael, 1546, Church of St Mary, Cilcain, east window

At Gresford and Hope groups of saints were assembled in a representation of the 'Te Deum Laudamus', an early Christian hymn ascribed to Ambrose that offers praise to God from apostles, prophets, martyrs and the church throughout the world. The subject may have been imposed on the figures brought together by the restorers of the east window of the chancel at Gresford, where figures were completed with new glass and additional figures in 1867.[40] Some of them can be identified by their attributes, such as Barbara, Catherine of Alexandria and Dorothy among a group of five saints, although it is difficult to distinguish which of the fragments are medieval and which are of 1867. A further virgin martyr, Apollonia, is also found among the figures of the 'Te Deum', and although the figure appears to be modern, medieval depictions of the saint are found in the east windows of the Lady Chapel and the Trevor Chapel. She holds a pair of pincers, having had her teeth extracted during her martyrdom, and it has been suggested that it was an image of this saint at the church that made it a centre of pilgrimage in the fifteenth and early sixteenth centuries.[41]

40 The window is described and the restoration discussed in E.A. Fishbourne, 'Notes on the East Window of the Church of All Saints, Gresford', *Archaeologia Cambrensis*, sixth series, vol. vii (1907), pp. 352–7. See also Mostyn Lewis, *Stained Glass in North Wales up to 1850* (Altrincham: John Sherratt and Son Ltd, 1970), pp. 38–9.

41 Mostyn Lewis, *Stained Glass in North Wales up to 1850* (Altrincham: John Sherratt and Son Ltd, 1970), pp. 5–6.

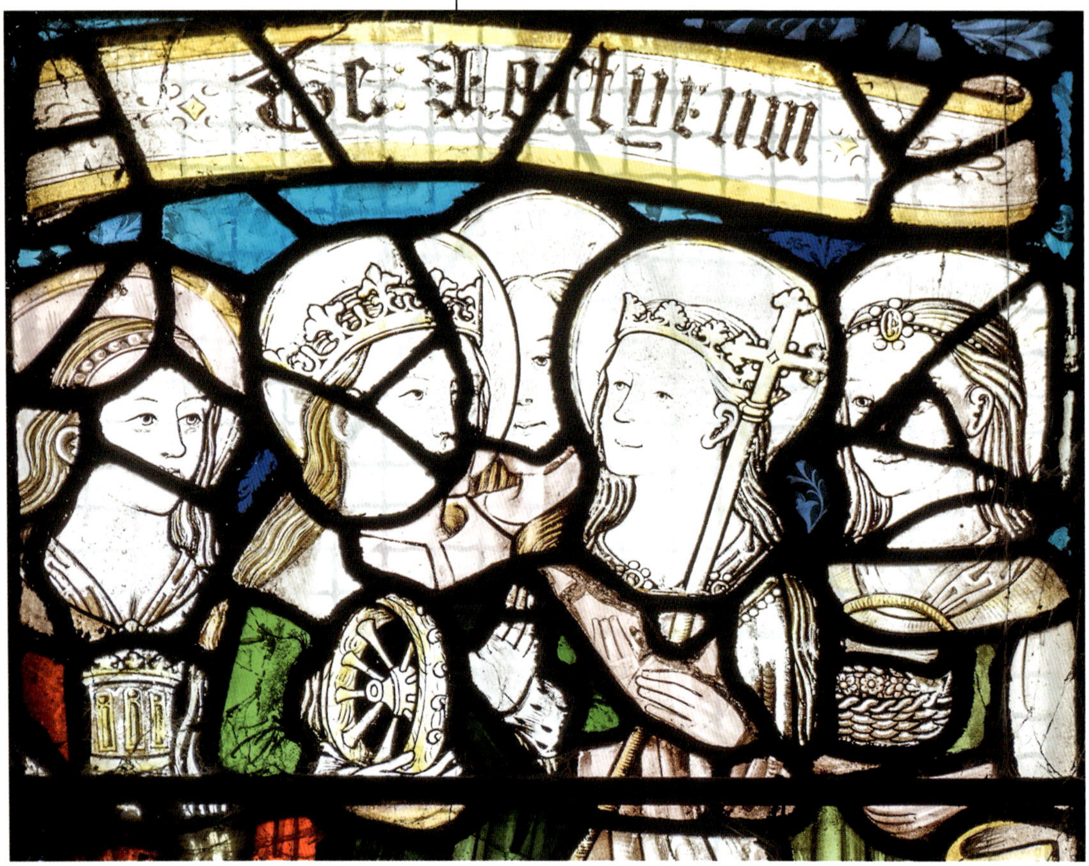

117. (below) Female Saints including St Barbara (left), St Catherine (second left) and St Dorothy (right), probably 1500, Church of All Saints, Gresford, east window

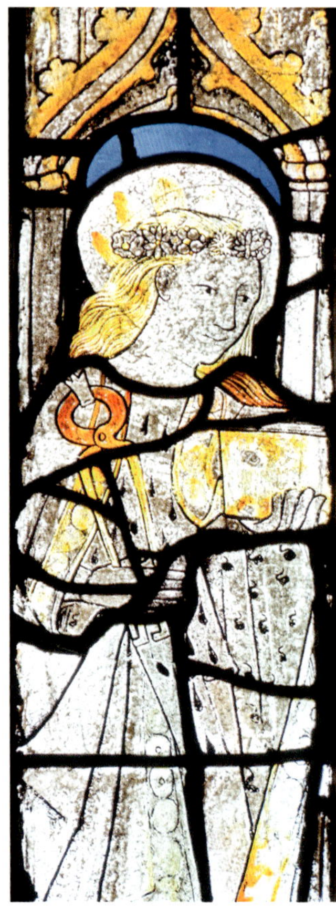

118. (below right) St Appolonia, 1498, Church of All Saints, Gresford, Lady Chapel (north aisle)

Local saints without established iconographic symbols are harder to recognise. Saints in the tracery at Llandyrnog survive with inscriptions, identifying Catherine and Frideswide in the company of the Welsh saints, Asaph and Deiniol, both dressed as bishops, with Winifred and Marchell.[42] Lost inscriptions identify figures at Llanrhychwyn as David and Rhychwyn, recorded in the drawing of the window in about 1800, and are corroborated early in the nineteenth century by Gwallter Mechain.[43] The author also recorded a lost inscription at the Church of St Gwynog, Llanwnog that names the patron of the church as the saint depicted, lending support to the possibility that unnamed saints elsewhere could be the patron saint of the church.[44]

42 Deiniol is spelled Daniel, and wears the mitre of a Metropolitan Archbishop, which he was not, and if he represents a Welsh saint he must be David. I am grateful to John Morgan-Guy for this observation. Unlike the scenes and fragments below, the figures in the tracery lights are largely complete and appear to be in their original positions. The four female saints are drawn from only two cartoons, with the figure of Winifred reversed from the figure of Catherine, whose wheel is replaced with a book, while both hold swords.

43 S. Baring-Gould & John Fisher, *The Lives of the British Saints* (London: The Honourable Society of Cymmrodorion, 1913), vol. iv, p. 113.

44 'Sanctus Gwinocus, cujus animæ propitietur Deus. Amen.' Rev. D. Silvan Evans (ed.) *The English Works of the Rev. Walter Davies, M.A.* (Carmarthen: William Spurrell and London: Simpkin, Marshall & Co., 1868), p. 76.

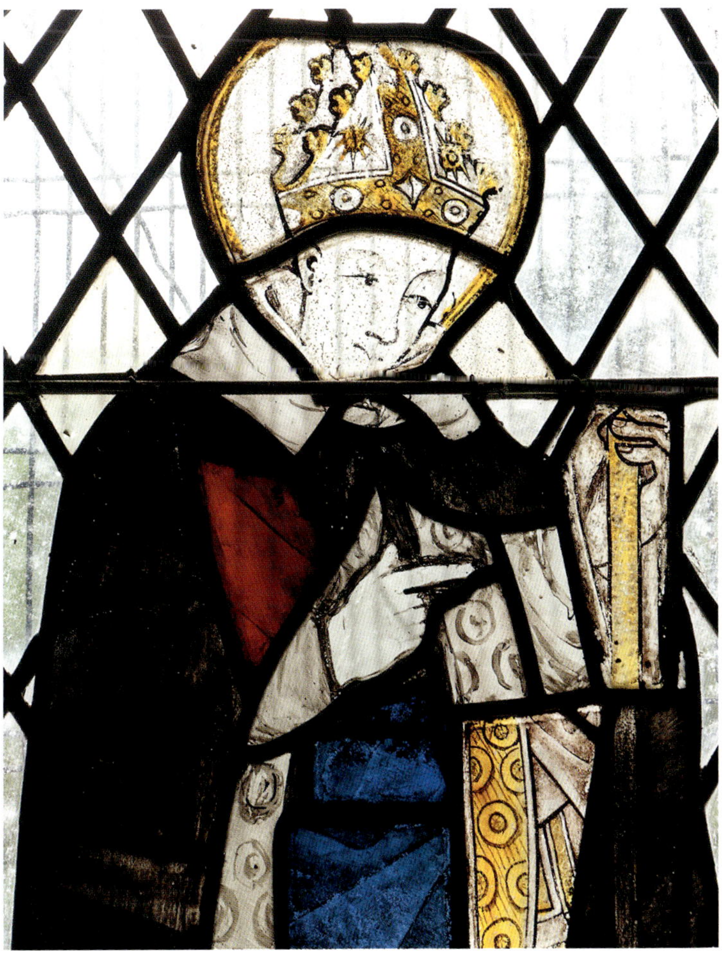

119. Perhaps St Deiniol, perhaps 1500–10, Church of St Deiniol, Penmorfa, west window

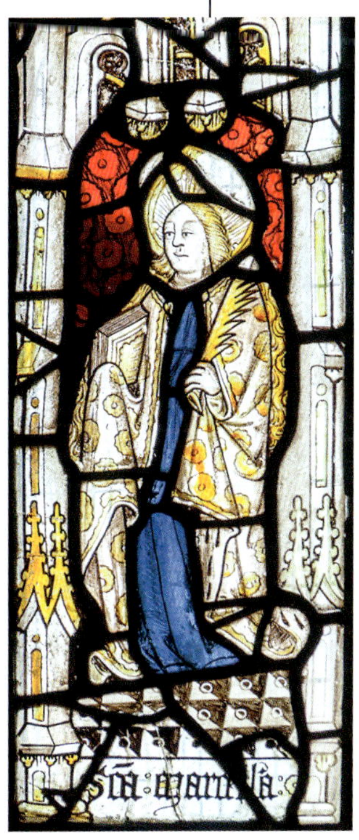

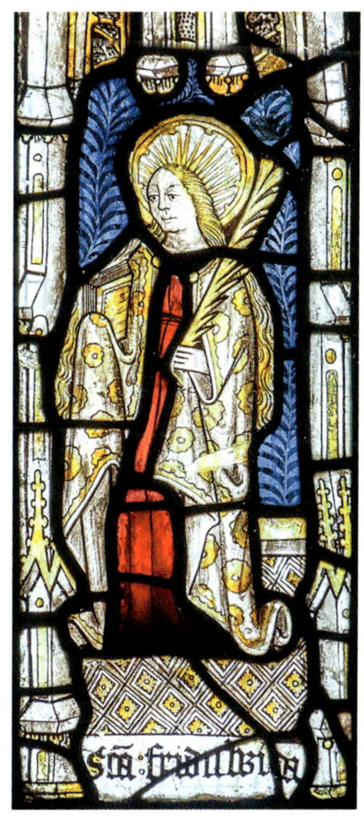

120–21. St Marchell (right) and St Frideswide (far right), late fifteenth or early sixteenth century, Church of St Tyrnog, Llandyrnog, east window

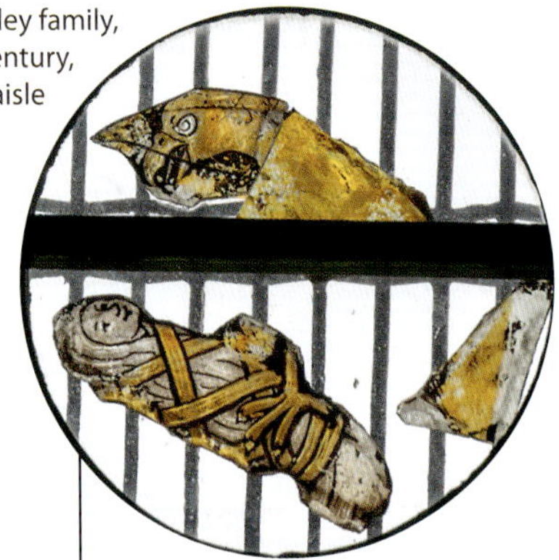

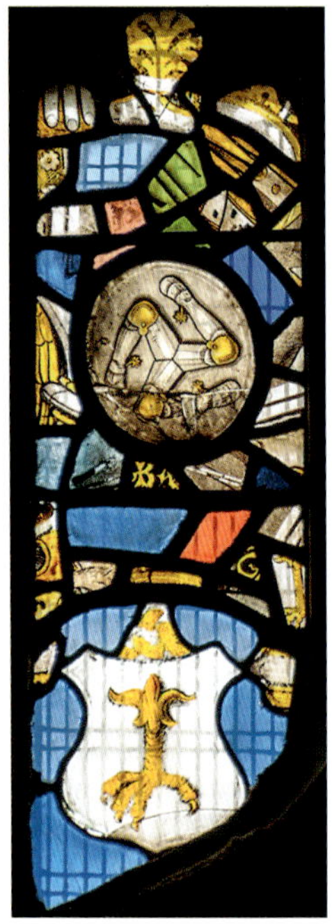

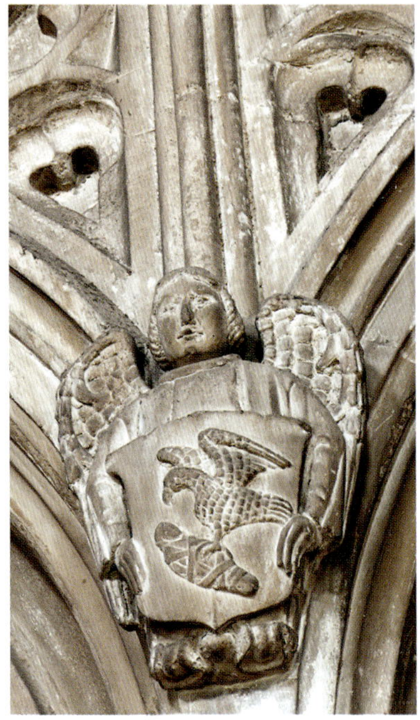

122–4. Emblems of the Stanley family, late fifteenth or sixteenth century, Church of St Mary, Mold, north aisle

The expense of commissioning stained glass necessitated the collective patronage of either guilds or other groups of parishioners, or more commonly clergy and members of local landowning families. The patrons of stained glass windows at Gresford between 1498 and 1510 were individuals including a former mayor of Chester, the rector of the parish, and Thomas Stanley, first earl of Derby, who gave the east window in 1500.[45] Thomas Stanley married Margaret Beaufort, and effectively assisted her son, Henry Tudor, to become king in 1485.

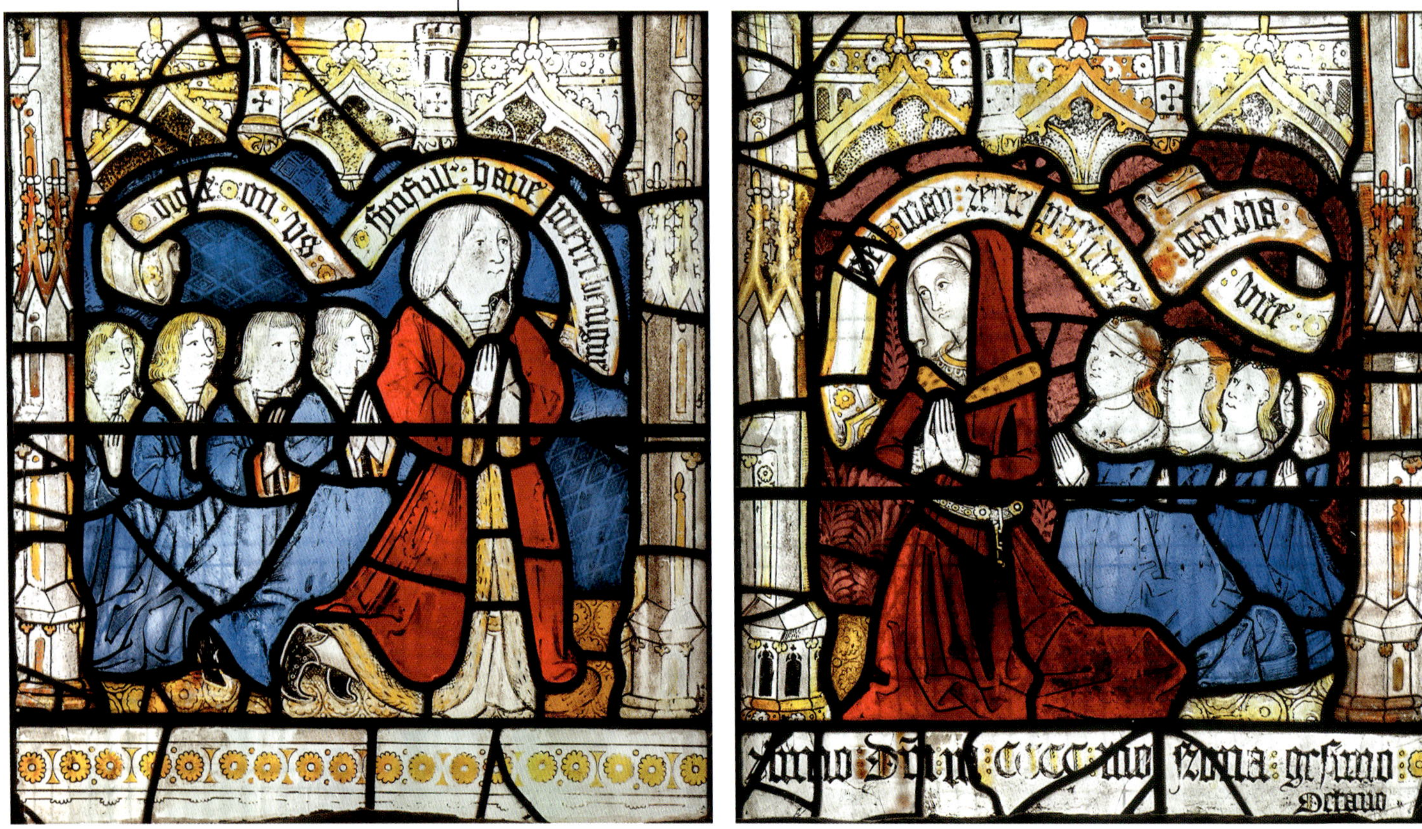

125. John ap Madog Vaughan, his Wife Margaret, and their Sons and Daughters, 1498, Church of All Saints, Gresford, Lady Chapel (north aisle)

45 D.R. Thomas, *The History of the Diocese of St Asaph* (Oswestry: Caxton Press, 1913), vol. iii, p. 247.

46 William Stanley's patronage was shorter-lived. He was executed in 1495 for his part in the rebellion against Henry VII.

The church at Gresford was one of a number in the area that was extensively rebuilt under their patronage in the late fifteenth century, along with others under the patronage of Stanley's brother, William.[46] Stanley's grandson, also Thomas, and second earl of Derby, gave a further window on the south side of the church in 1507. The patronage of the first earl is seen most clearly at the Church of St Mary, Mold, where family badges can be seen on shields held by angels along the nave arcades, and in the fragmentary remains of the stained glass.

These patrons were sometimes visually represented in windows. At Gresford kneeling figures of the donor John ap Madog Vaughan, his wife Margaret and their children are found at the base of the east window of the Lady Chapel. A group of heads in the lower left-hand light of the east window of the Trevor Chapel are also perhaps the sons of a donor. Fragments of donor portraits at Llangadwaladr, dating from about 1490, were reconstructed in about 1850. Meurig ap Llywelyn ap Hwlcyn is shown kneeling with his wife, Marged ferch Ifan Fychan, and it is possible that they gave the window glass in thanksgiving for the safe return of their son Owain ap Meurig from the Battle of Bosworth. Owain is depicted opposite in full armour, with his wife, Elin ferch Robert, and the figures are identified in the partially restored inscriptions given below the figures.[47] A lost donor figure at the Church of St Eleri and St Mary, Llanrhos was drawn by Moses Griffith for Thomas Pennant, and identified as Howel ap Tudor of Mostyn, the donor of the window.[48]

47 Richard B. White, 'The Llangadwaladr East Window – an Examination of the Inscription and its Personae', *Transactions of the Anglesey Antiquarian Society and Field Club* (1969–70), pp. 89–93.

48 The drawing is inserted in Thomas Pennant's own extra-illustrated copy of *A Tour in North Wales* NLW PD9870, after page 327.

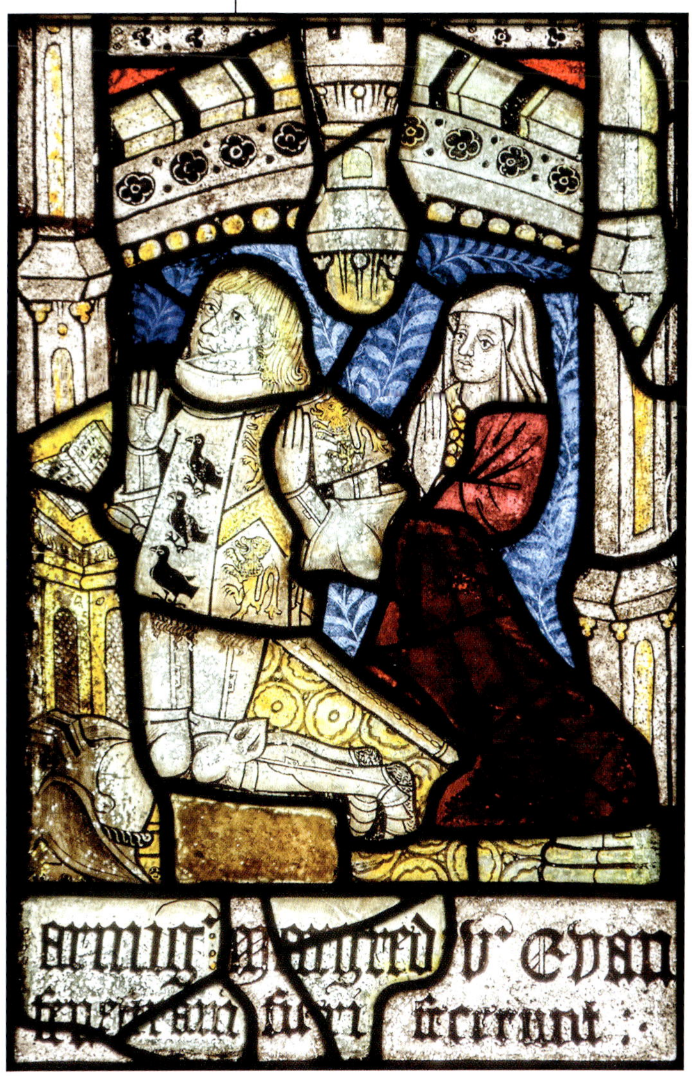

127. Owain ap Meurig and his wife Elin ferch Robert, *c.* 1490–5, Church of St Cadwaladr, Llangadwaladr, chancel

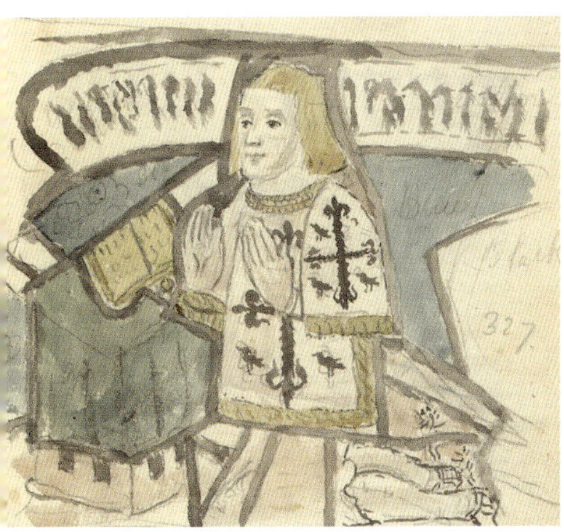

126. Moses Griffith, Drawing of Howel ap Tudor, Church of St Eleri and St Mary, Llanrhos, 1770s

(image courtesy of the National Library of Wales)

128. Probably an Abbess, late fifteenth or early sixteenth century, Church of St Mary, Llanllugan, east window

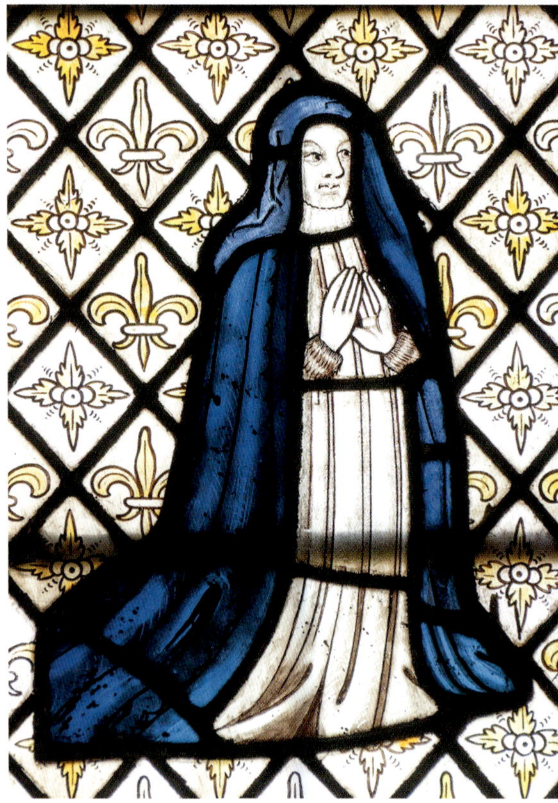

A kneeling figure of a nun now in the east window at Llanllugan may be a donor figure, although there are examples of similar portraits that are not donors.[49]

The arms of the Order of the Garter in the right-hand light at Llanllugan are probably those of Richard, Duke of York, and patronage was frequently indicated through the use of heraldry rather than portraiture, as it was at Mold.[50] Rows of angels in the tracery lights of windows in the north and south aisle at Gresford hold shields with heraldic devices executed with only glass paint and silver stain, and similar angelic figures appear in other windows at the church. Many further examples of heraldry in stained glass were recorded in 1645 by Richard Symonds, who accompanied Royalist forces during the Civil War, and in many cases these windows were of medieval date. The diary is a valuable record of early stained glass at Llandaff and St Asaph cathedrals, parish churches at Knighton, Presteigne, Chirk, Ruthin and particularly of the numerous windows at the Priory Church of St Mary, Abergavenny.[51] The diarist adds hardly any details of any other imagery in the windows, if present, adding only that the Church of St Hilary, Denbigh, had shields with emblems of Christ's wounds and Instruments of the Passion. How much this omission was due to his lack of interest in matters beyond the heraldic, or to the earlier loss or destruction of other subject matter cannot now be known.

49 Madeleine Gray and John Morgan-Guy, ' 'A better and frugal life': Llanllugan and the Cistercian women's houses in Wales', *Archaeologia Cambrensis*, vol. 154 (2007), p. 106.

50 Richard of York was the father of Edward VI and Richard III. For the identification of the arms see Madeleine Gray and John Morgan-Guy, ' 'A better and frugal life': Llanllugan and the Cistercian women's houses in Wales', pp. 100, 104. Mostyn Lewis preferred a later date for the garter arms, as he believed that red enamel, now faded, was used on the glass, which would make it no earlier than the second quarter of the sixteenth century. Mostyn Lewis, *Stained Glass in North Wales up to 1850* (Altrincham: John Sherratt and Son Ltd, 1970), p. 68.

51 Charles Edward Long (ed.), *Diary of the Marches of the Royal Army During the Great Civil War kept by Richard Symonds* (Camden Society, 1859), pp. 208–62.

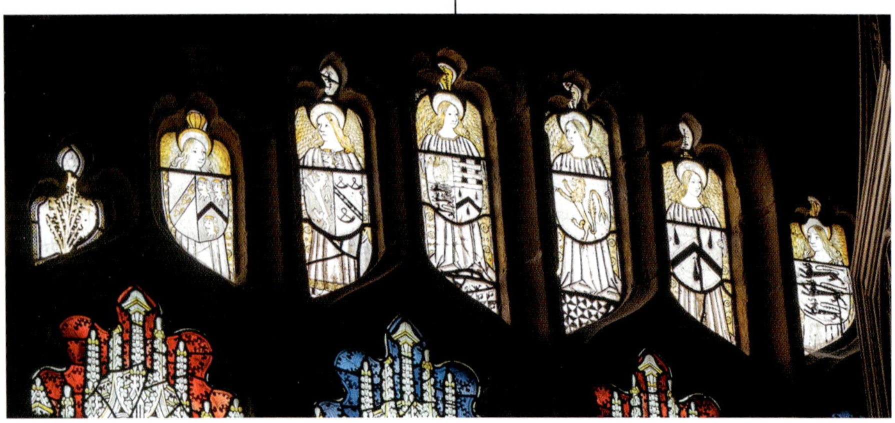

129. Angels with Heraldry, early sixteenth century, Church of All Saints, Gresford, north aisle

Chapter Two

Stained Glass After the Reformation and Continental Stained Glass

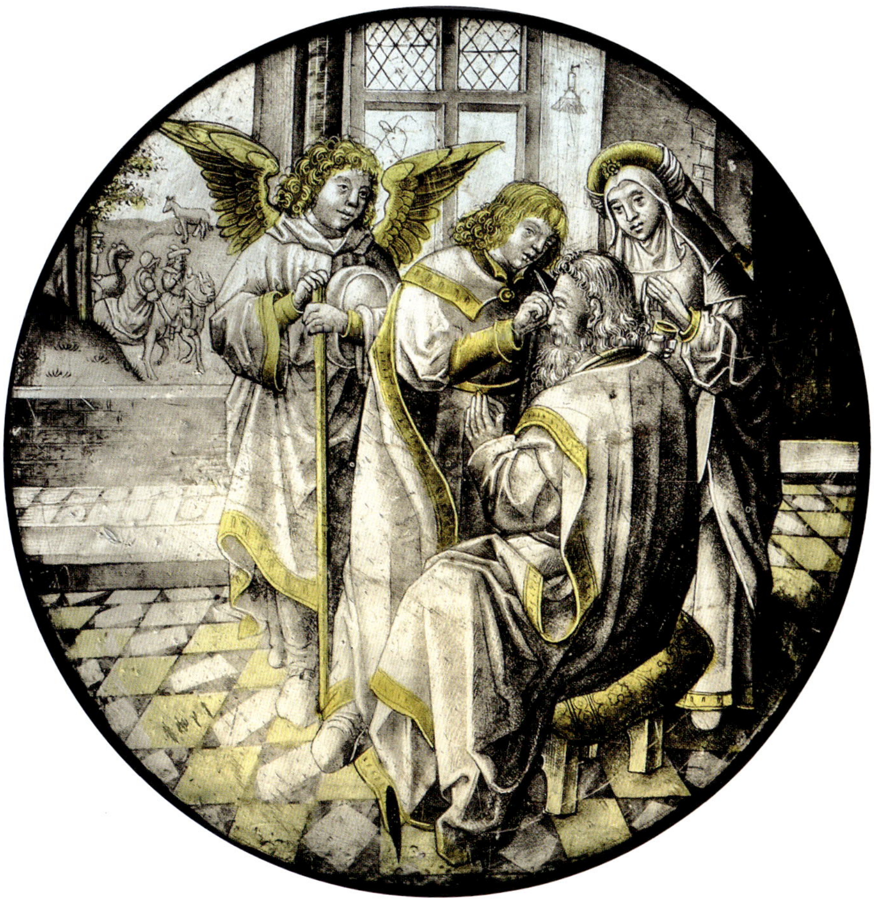

Stained glass depicting biblical scenes and saints became vulnerable to attacks by Protestant reformers from the 1530s. The break with the Church in Rome, and the Act of Supremacy in 1534 that made Henry VIII the head of the Church of England, created the freedom for reformist preachers to denounce the veneration of saints and encourage the destruction of images. This iconoclasm was probably stronger in areas of the south and east of England than elsewhere in England and Wales, but devotional images and relics were removed from parish churches and places of pilgrimage in Wales and destroyed. The first major losses of medieval stained glass were a result of the dissolution of the monasteries from 1536, and in some cases the fabric of former monastic buildings was systematically dismantled for reuse as building material. At the Cistercian abbey of Strata Marcella, bells, the organ, stone and lead gutters were sold, and window glass and lead was removed, along with plate and vestments.[1] The dispersal of monastic architectural fabric and fittings subsequently gave rise to traditions that surviving medieval stained glass came from monastic houses. According to Samuel Lewis' *A Topographical Dictionary of Wales*, the late medieval figures at Llanasa, as well as both of the Jesse windows at Dyserth and Llanrhaeadr-yng-Nghinmeirch, were all said to have come from Basingwerk Abbey.[2]

The Act of the Six Articles of 1539 stayed the force of reformist destruction until the accession of Edward VI in 1547, when the act was repealed and an order to destroy religious images was explicitly extended to windows. The extent of the loss of stained glass in Wales is uncertain. Instead of destroying whole windows, reformers may have only smashed or whitewashed the faces of saints, and in some cases windows could have been made more acceptable by simply altering the inscription. There is evidence for this at Llanrhaeadr-yng-Nghinmeirch, where the appeal for prayers for the soul of the donor on the Jesse window was removed.[3] As an essential part of the fabric of the building, and costly to replace with plain glass, stained glass may have survived while carved figures were defaced or removed; vestments, plate and books sold off and neighbouring walls whitewashed. Valuables were returned or replaced during the reign of Mary, and

1 This included the sale of 'the glass in 8 or 9 great windows in the church and other places in the house, with the lead' sometime before 1547. E.A. Lewis & J. Conway Davies (eds.), *Records of the Court of Augmentations Relating to Wales and Monmouthshire* (Cardiff: University of Wales Press, 1954), pp. 152–3.

2 Samuel Lewis, *A Topographical Dictionary of Wales* (London: S. Lewis & Co., 1833), two vols, no pagination. In the case of Llanasa, the removal is supported by the tradition that the glass was presented by Harry ab Harry, a native of the parish, who purchased the site of Basingwerk after the dissolution. Glass from the east window at Gresford was also said to have come from the abbey, E.A. Fishbourne, 'Notes on the East Window of the Church of All Saints, Gresford', *Archaeologia Cambrensis*, sixth series, vol. vii (1907), p. 354. Similarly, Mostyn Lewis has suggested that medieval glass at Trevor Hall Chapel, near Llangollen, came from Valle Crucis: *Stained Glass in North Wales up to 1850* (Altrincham: John Sherratt and Son Ltd, 1970), p. 93.

3 E. Gwynne Matthews, *The Llanrhaeadr Jesse Window: its meaning and history* (2000), pp. 11–12.

4 The background to the period is described by Eamon Duffy, *The Stripping of the Altars: Traditional Religion in England 1400–1580* (New Haven: Yale University Press, 2005, second edition), pp. 379–593. A summary of the effect of the Reformation on stained glass in England is provided in Richard Marks, *Stained Glass in England in the Middle Ages* (London: Routledge, 1993), pp. 229–34.

130. (Title page) Tobias Restores his Father's Sight, probably ea
sixteenth century, Church of St Bride, St Bride's-super-Ely, east wind

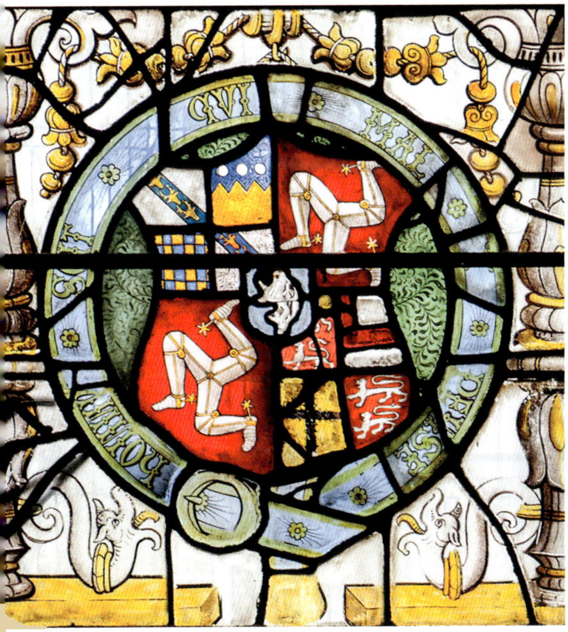

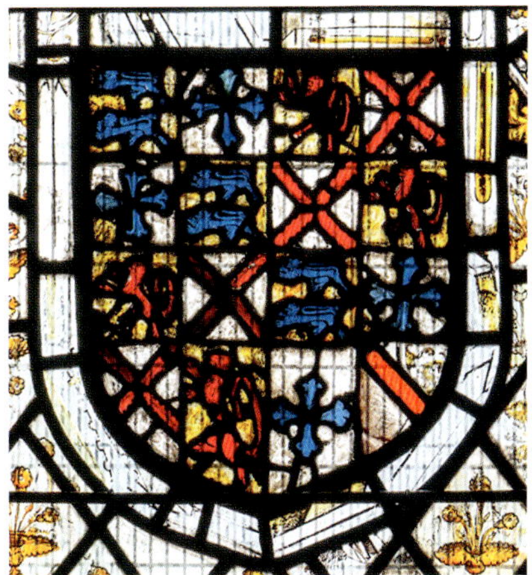

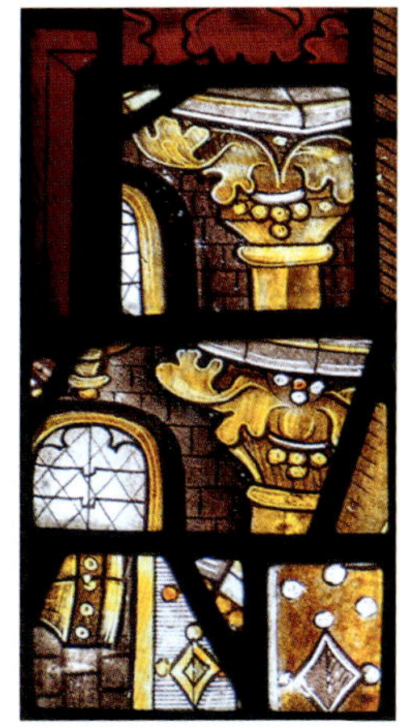

133. Architectural fragments, probably 1538, Church of St Foddhyd, Clocaenog, east window

131. (left) The Arms of Edward Stanley, 3rd Earl of Derby, probably 1570s, Church of St Mary, Mold, north aisle

132. (above) Heraldic Shield, probably late sixteenth century, Church of All Saints, Buttington, west wall

expunged again with greater reforming zeal after the restoration of Protestant practices following the accession of Elizabeth I in 1558.[4]

Little new stained glass in Welsh churches can be securely dated between the 1540s and the beginning of the nineteenth century, and the collapse in demand for ecclesiastical stained glass brought financial hardship to glass painters.[5] Heraldic display, rather than religious figures or narrative scenes, was probably the subject of most new commissions, both for private houses and for differentiating private spaces in churches, such as burial chapels and family pews. Examples survive at the Church of All Saints, Buttington, thought to date from the end of the sixteenth century, and at the Church of St Mary, Mold.[6] The glass at Mold commemorates a vicar who died in 1576 and Edward Stanley, the third earl of Derby, who died in 1572, and it is surprising that the inscriptions below request prayers for both men at so late a date, suggesting a deeply held adherence to the Catholic faith at variance with the times.[7]

The Renaissance character of the detailing around the coats of arms at Mold reflects the Flemish influence on glass painting found in England from the end of the fifteenth century. Continental influence on earlier windows is most apparent in the Jesse windows at Dyserth and Llanrhaeadr-yng-Nghinmeirch, but Renaissance capitals of 1538 survive among the fragments at Clocaenog. Similarly, Renaissance-style ornament was also found in early sixteenth-century wood carving in

5 Richard Marks, *Stained Glass in England in the Middle Ages* (London: Routledge, 1993), p. 234.

6 A possible identification of the owner of the arms at Buttington suggests a late sixteenth-century date. Mostyn Lewis, *Stained Glass in North Wales up to 1850* (Altrincham: John Sherratt and Son Ltd, 1970), p. 30. The medieval glass at Mold is discussed by Mostyn Lewis on pp. 82–3. Domestic heraldic work was commissioned by the Mostyn family for Gloddaeth Hall at Llanrhos in the third quarter of the sixteenth century and for Mostyn Hall in the seventeenth century. See Mostyn Lewis, *Stained Glass in North Wales up to 1850*, pp. 108, 113. The subjects of the windows listed in Thomas Pennant, *The History of the Parishes of Whiteford, and Holywell* (B. & J. White, 1796), pp. 70–2.

7 Penny Hebgin-Barnes makes a convincing claim that the Reformation was slow to establish itself in Cheshire and Lancashire in the mid-sixteenth century, acknowledging the religious conservatism of the earls of Derby, the most powerful magnates in the region, which lasted until the death of Edward Stanley in 1572. Penny Hebgin-Barnes, *The Medieval Stained Glass of Cheshire* (Oxford: Oxford University Press, 2010), pp. lxx–lxxviii.

Wales, now known from panels in the Church of St John the Baptist, Cardiff, the Raglan Castle frieze and the nave roof of St Davids Cathedral.[8]

Flemish glass-painting workshops flourished in the cities of the Burgundian Netherlands, such as Amsterdam, Leiden and Antwerp, from the late fifteenth and into the mid-sixteenth centuries. These workshops produced painted and stained glass for churches and monasteries, but also made small finely-painted roundels (which could be rectangular as well as elliptical) for domestic use.[9] Although there is no extant Flemish stained glass commissioned by Welsh patrons from the fifteenth century or early sixteenth century, it may have been commissioned by powerful Welsh patrons such as Charles Somerset, the earl of Worcester, at Raglan, or Sir Rhys ap Thomas at Carew.[10] Later in the sixteenth century Richard Clough of Denbigh worked in Antwerp and through his mercantile connections commissioned a set of heraldic roundels in 1567, probably for his house Bachegraig, which was built in a modern Dutch style.[11]

The presence of sixteenth-century Flemish glass painting in Welsh churches is not a legacy of sixteenth-century Welsh patrons but of the fashion for collecting the art in England and Wales from the late eighteenth century. The finest group of Flemish panels in Wales was given to the Church of St Gwenllwyfo, Llanwenllwyfo (near Dulas in northern Anglesey), by Sir Arundel Neave in 1877, from the collection of his grandfather Sir Thomas Neave at Dagnam Park, Essex.[12] The glass is of various dates and is mounted internally across the nave windows, but set into the windows of the chancel. Scenes have been reset with formerly unrelated panels from other scenes placed above and below, and the panels inserted into the stonework of the chancel windows are likely to have been cut down to fit. For example, a set of half-figures, probably representing prophets, have been added above many of the scenes.

The east window contains panels from at least three different styles and dates. The upper cinquefoil contains the Emperor Charles V with Pope Adrian VI surrounded by courtiers, martyrs, angels and eleven disciples, and came from the memorial chapel to Adrian VI at the Charterhouse of St Mary Magdalene at Louvain. The Carthusian monastery was founded

8 See Peter Lord, *The Visual Culture of Wales: Medieval Vision* (Cardiff: University of Wales Press, 2003), p. 271.

9 The same workshops executed the exquisite illuminated manuscripts, tapestries and paintings that attracted the patronage of Welsh patrons such as Sir John Dwnn of Kidwelly and Sir William Herbert of Raglan in the fifteenth century. Peter Lord, *The Visual Culture of Wales: Medieval Vision*, pp. 252–62.

10 Peter Lord, *The Visual Culture of Wales: Medieval Vision*, pp. 266–72. Richard Symonds recorded heraldic glass in the hall of Raglan Castle in 1645. Charles Edward Long (ed.), *Diary of the Marches of the Royal Army During the Great Civil War kept by Richard Symonds* (Camden Society, 1859), p. 208.

11 Mostyn Lewis, *Stained Glass in North Wales up to 1850* (Altrincham: John Sherratt and Son Ltd, 1970), pp. 106–108, and see also *Imaging the Nation*, pp. 17, 26–8. The panels are now at Glasfryn, Llangybi (Caernarfonshire), but were seen by Thomas Pennant at Bachegraig in the 1770s.

12 The glass is described in J.O. Hughes, *A Short Guide to the Early 16th Century Glass of Llanwenllwyfo Church Isle of Anglesey* (1995). For the collection of Thomas Neave see Yvette Vanden Bemden & Jill Kerr, 'A group of 16th century panels from the Low Countries now in British Churches', *The Journal of Stained Glass*, vol. xviii, no. 1 (1983–4), pp. 32–3.

134. Perhaps the St Gregory Master, Abraham Greeting the Three Angels, probably 1520s, Church of St Gwenllwyfo, Llanwenllwyfo, nave

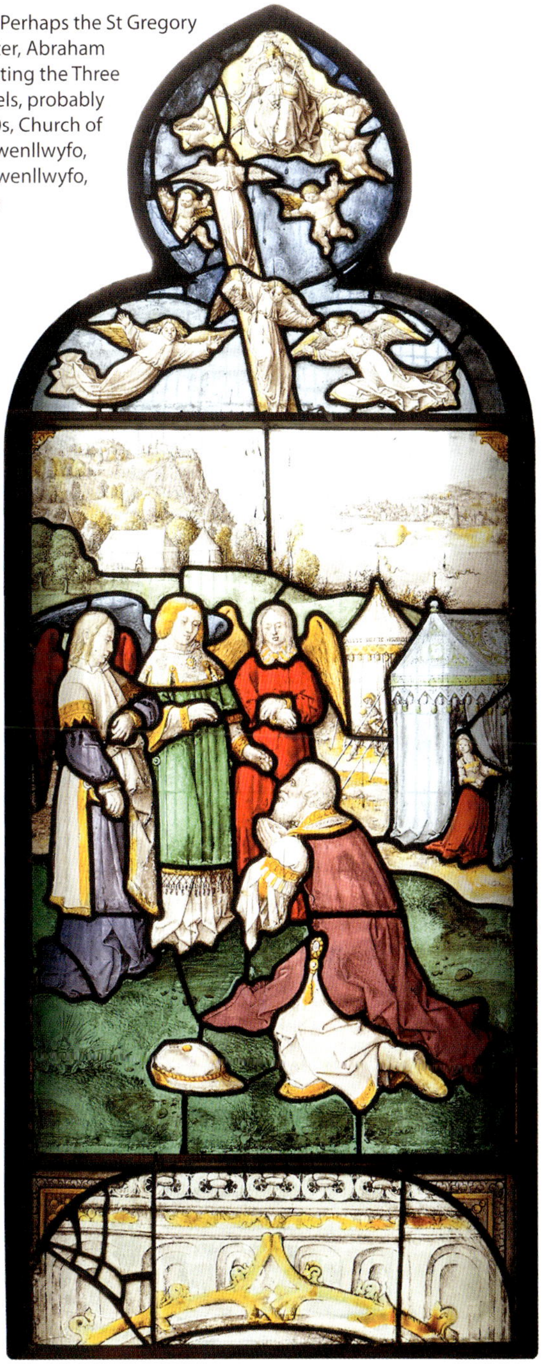

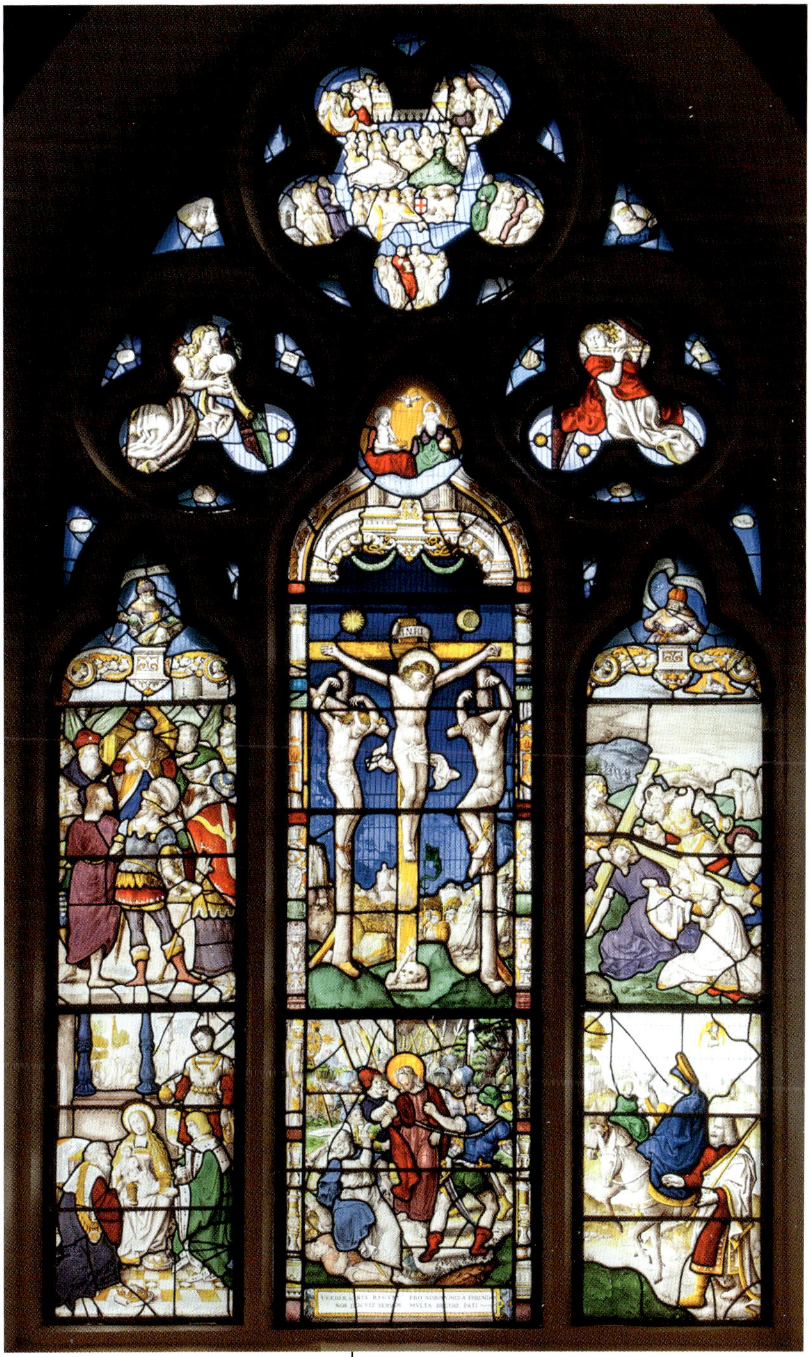

by the Dukes of Burgundy at the end of the fifteenth century, and the chapel was endowed by the young Charles V in memory of his former tutor.[13] Similarities in style suggest that other panels could have come from the monastery, and these and panels elsewhere, originally from Thomas Neave's collection, have

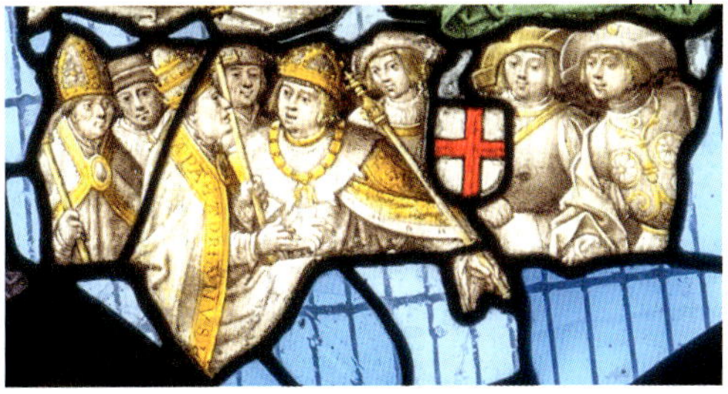

13 Adrian Florenszoon Boeyens was a native of Utrecht. He taught at the Catholic University of Louvain, where Erasmus was one of his pupils. He later became chancellor and then rector at the University.

135–6. (above) East Window with scenes of various sixteenth-century dates, including, perhaps Peter van den Houte, Charles V with Pope Adrian VI and courtiers, probably *c.* 1523 (left, detail of the upper cinquefoil), Church of St Gwenllwyfo, Llanwenllwyfo

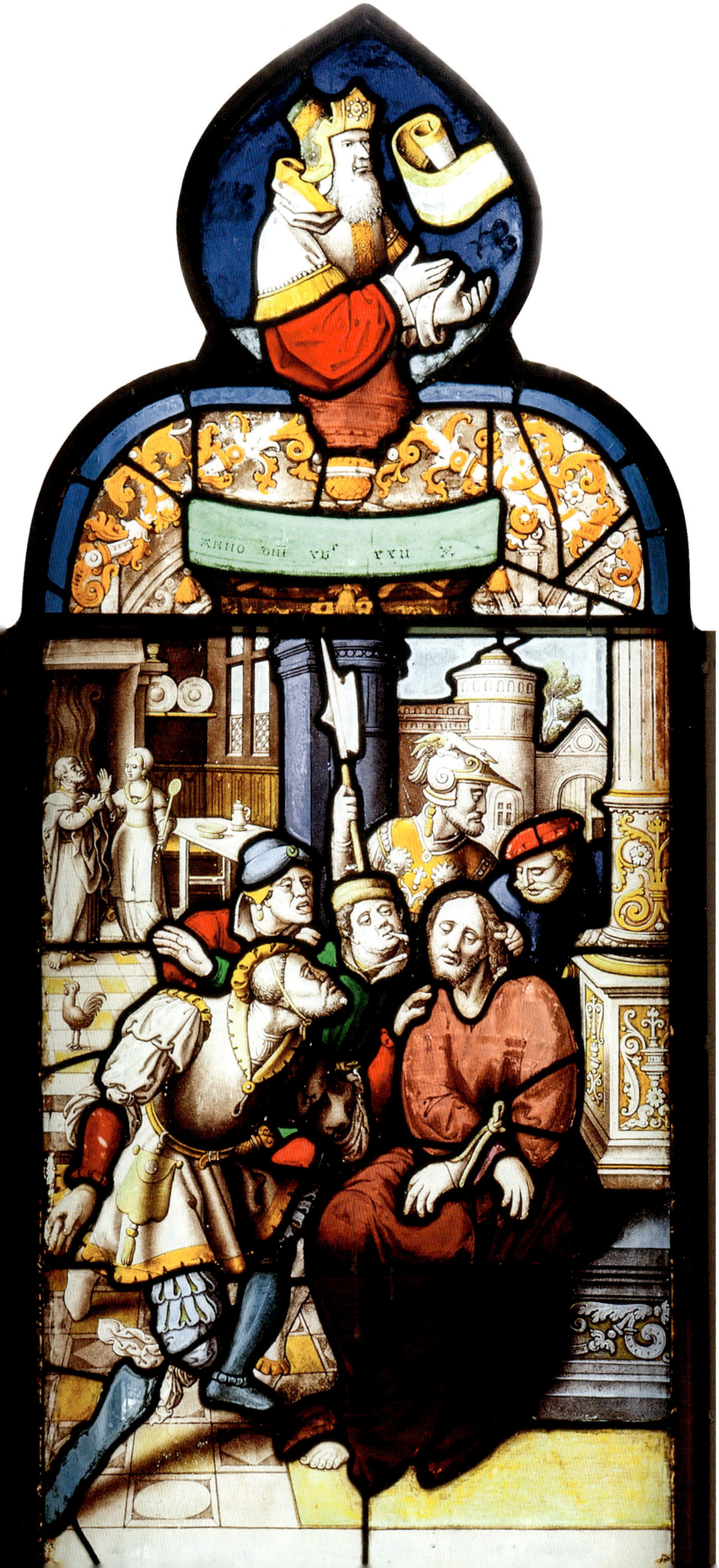
ANNO DNI VC XXII

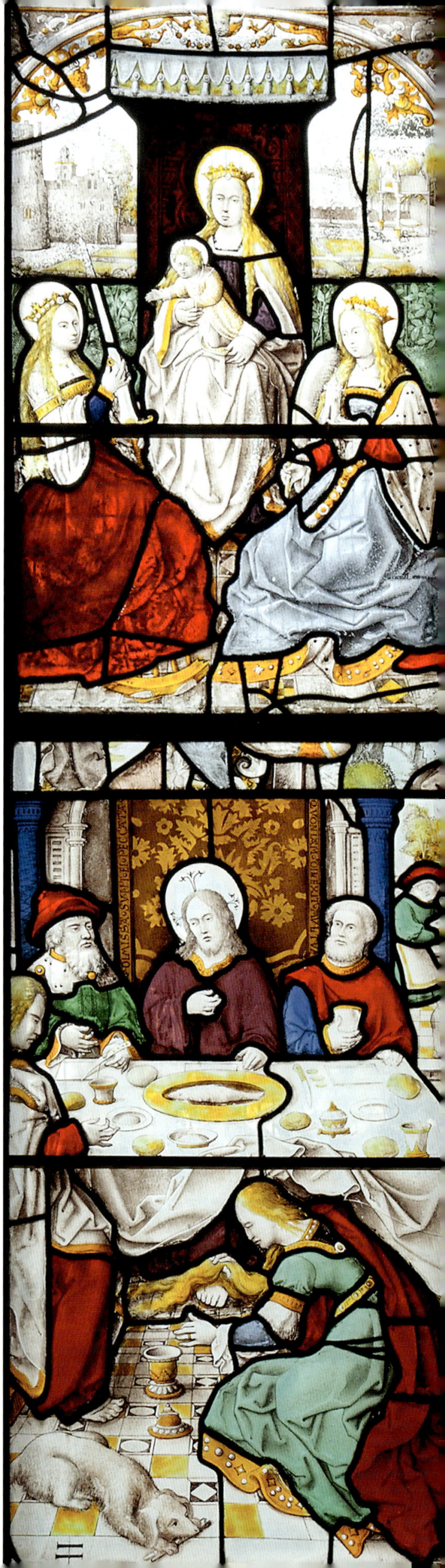

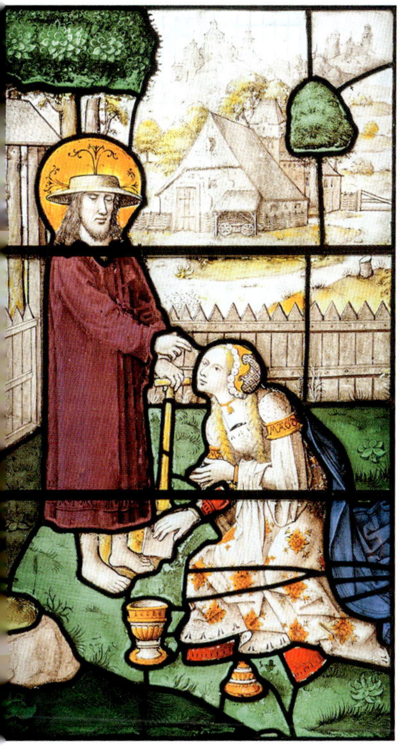

139. Perhaps the St Gregory Master, The Risen Christ Appearing to St Mary Magdalene, probably 1520s, Church of St Gwenllwyfo, Llanwenllwyfo, chancel

been identified as the 'Anglesey group'.[14] Adrian VI died in 1523 and the group probably dates to the 1520s, particularly as the date of 1522 survives above the scene depicting the Mocking of Christ, although it does not belong with this panel.[15]

Workshops of the period often executed the designs of other artists, a collaboration facilitated by the circulation of drawings and prints on paper. Analysis of panels related to the style of the 'Anglesey group' by Hilary Wayment has given us the names of artists and workshops to which some panels can be tentatively attributed, including the Master of the Mass of St Gregory, his followers, and Peter van den Houte.[16] A few of the scenes at Llanwenllwyfo share similarities with designs by the workshop of Valentijn van Orley in Brussels, which could date the design for Christ healing Peter's mother-in-law, and perhaps Christ being anointed at the house of Simon the Pharisee, some years earlier than the 1520s.[17] The wealthiest patrons were able to afford designs for stained glass by the leading artists of the northern Renaissance, such as Albrecht Dürer and Barent van Orley, the son of Valentijn, whose drawing of the scene of Christ being mocked prior to his crucifixion still survives.[18]

Some of the panels have delicately-painted backgrounds with added narrative detail, such as Peter's denial behind the scene of Christ being mocked, and Moses praying on a hill behind the scene of his meeting with Aaron and Miriam. In other panels the background is simply a landscape setting, such as the house and hilltop castles behind the meeting of the risen Christ with Mary Magdalene. In addition to the biblical scenes, other panels portray saints and donors. In the panel of the Mystic Marriage of St Catherine, the saint is shown with Barbara and the Virgin and Child, and Catherine holds a ring given to her by the infant Christ in a dream.

. (far left) Perhaps the workshop of Peter Coecke, The cking of Christ, designed by Barent van Orley, probably 0s, Church of St Gwenllwyfo, Llanwenllwyfo, nave

. (left) Perhaps the St Gregory Master, The Mystic riage of St Catherine, probably 1520s (above); probably workshop of the St Gregory Master, Christ in the House imon the Pharisee, *c.* 1519–22 (below), Church of wenllwyfo, Llanwenllwyfo, chancel

14 Yvette Vanden Bemden & Jill Kerr, 'A group of 16th century panels from the Low Countries now in British Churches', *The Journal of Stained Glass*, vol. xviii, no. 1 (1983–4), pp. 36–7.

15 Hilary Wayment and J.O. Hughes match the dated portion of the top of the brown hanging behind Christ in the scene at the house of Simon the Pharisee, now in the chancel of St Gwenllwyfo. Hilary Wayment, 'The Master of the Mass of Saint Gregory Roundel', *Oud Holland*, vol. 103, issue 2 (1989), p. 83. J.O. Hughes, *A Short Guide to the Early 16th Century Glass of Llanwenllwyfo Church Isle of Anglesey* (1995), p. 12. However, the sections are not continuous and the upper part has no extension of the architectural features at either side of the hanging. The inscription could however date the eight demi-figures, probably prophets, which appear above many of the panels.

16 Hilary Wayment, 'The Master of the Mass of Saint Gregory Roundel', 1989.

17 A date of around 1500 was suggested by Timothy B. Husband, *The Luminous Image: Painted Glass Roundels in the Lowlands, 1480–1560* (New York: The Metropolitan Museum of Art, 1995), p. 136. A date after 1519 is probably more likely for the execution of the window, when a new glazier was employed to make windows for the monastery, perhaps using earlier designs. Hilary Wayment, 'The Master of the Mass of Saint Gregory Roundel', pp. 78–81.

18 J.O. Hughes, *A Short Guide to the Early 16th Century Glass of Llanwenllwyfo Church Isle of Anglesey*, p. 12. The panel was perhaps made by the workshop of Peter Coeke. Hilary Wayment, *King's College Chapel Cambridge: the Side-Chapel Glass* (Cambridge: The Cambridge Antiquarian Society and the Provost and Scholars of King's College, 1988), p. 60.

19 The glass may have been presented by William Herbert, third son of John Jones of Llanarth, who 'formed a very remarkable collection of pictures, statuary, and other art treasures'. *The Tablet*, 30 May 1885, p. 862.

20 Andrew Renton, 'Discovering Pre-1700 Stained Glass in South Wales' in *Vidimus*, vol. 34 (November 2009), <http://vidimus.org/issues/issue-34/feature>.

The sixteenth-century glass now at the Roman Catholic Church of St Mary and St Michael, Llanarth (Monmouthshire), was acquired by a descendent of the Herbert family and presented to the church, which stands in the grounds of their former house at Llanarth Court.[19] The church was probably the first Roman Catholic church built in Wales after the Reformation, constructed secretly in 1750 by Philip Jones, from a senior branch of the Herbert family. A set of half-length portraits of Christ and the apostles James and John appear to date from the 1510s and have been attributed to a Cologne workshop.[20]

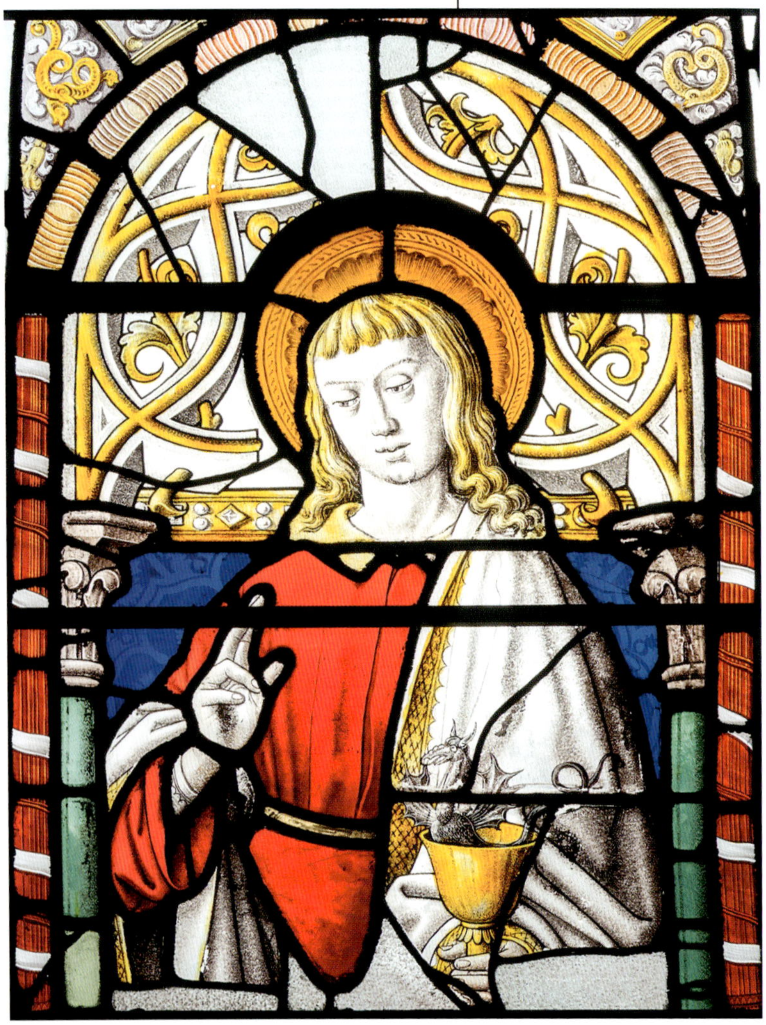

140. St John the Evangelist, *c.* 1510–20, Church of St Mary and St Michael, Llanarth, nave

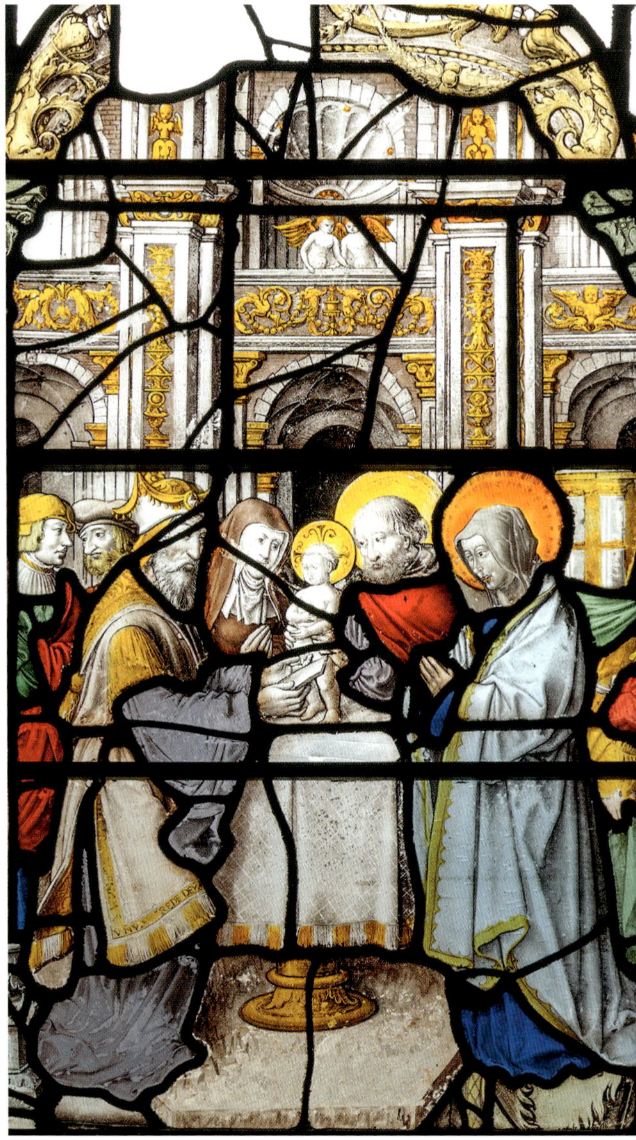

141. The Circumcision of Christ, 1522–6, Church of St Mary and St Michael, Llanarth, nave

A fourth large panel in the collection at Llanarth has been identified as among the dispersed stained glass from the cloister of Steinfeld Abbey in Germany and dates from around 1522–6. The Steinfeld cloister glazing scheme consisted of 27 windows made from about 1522 to 1558, all of which were removed in 1785 and sold in 1802. The glass was bought and subsequently sold on by John Christopher Hampp of Norwich, the dealer who also sold the Flemish glass to Thomas Neave. The scene of the Circumcision of Christ at Llanarth was originally part of a three-light window at the abbey accompanying the Nativity and the journey to Bethlehem.[21]

In addition to the panel at Llanarth, four panels from Steinfeld are now at the Church of St Cadoc at Aberpergwm. Each of the panels represent abbots or brothers kneeling before saints, or being presented by saints. Originally placed in the lower part of the windows below biblical scenes, they were designed to be placed alongside other panels at the base of a two-light or three-light window. For example, the panel showing Abbot John IV being presented by Potentinus originally depicted the abbot adoring the figure of Christ as the Man of Sorrows.[22]

142–3. Abbot John IV being presented by St Potentinus, 1531 (below), Virgin and Child with Abbot John V von Münstereiful and St Chrysanthus, 1531–2 (below right), Church of St Cadoc, Aberpergwm, east window

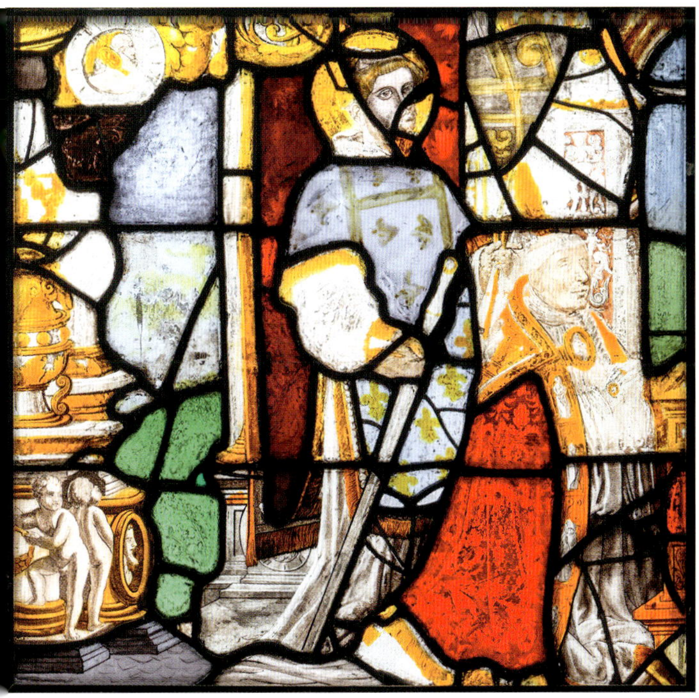

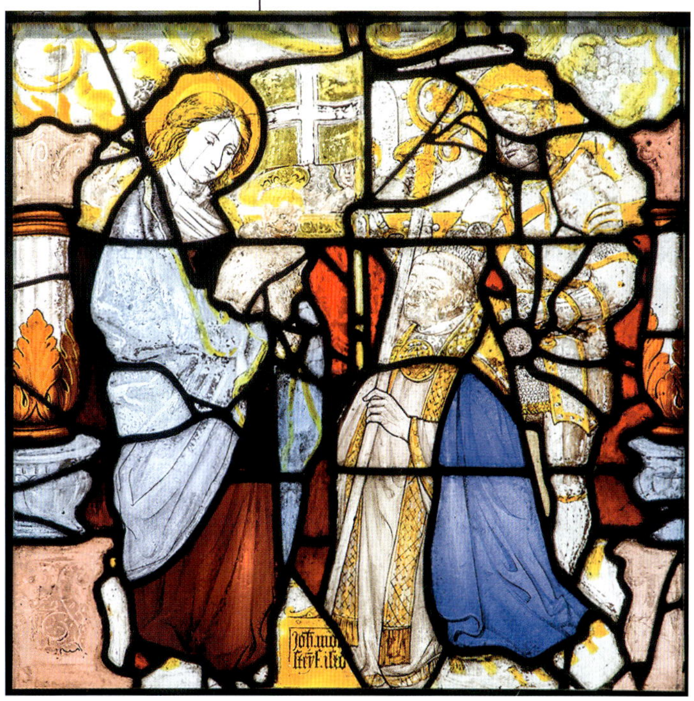

21 The scenes were designed to read from right to left around the cloister. The Nativity scene survives at Blickling Hall, Norfolk, where the head of Joseph is very similar to that in this panel. Panels from the abbey have been dispersed across collections in south and east England and Cheshire, while examples are on display in London at the Victoria and Albert Museum, as well as three museums in New York and Harvard University. Some of the glass has since been returned for display at the Abbey in Westphalia. David King and Roger Rosewell, 'New Steinfeld Discoveries: Special Supplement' in *Vidimus*, vol. 35 (December 2009), <http://vidimus.org/issues/issue-35/features>.

22 Potentinus was a patron of the abbey and his relics were venerated there. The saint was also depicted in another panel with the Virgin and Child, now at the Church of St Botolph, Hevingham, Norfolk. David King and Roger Rosewell, 'New Steinfeld Discoveries'.

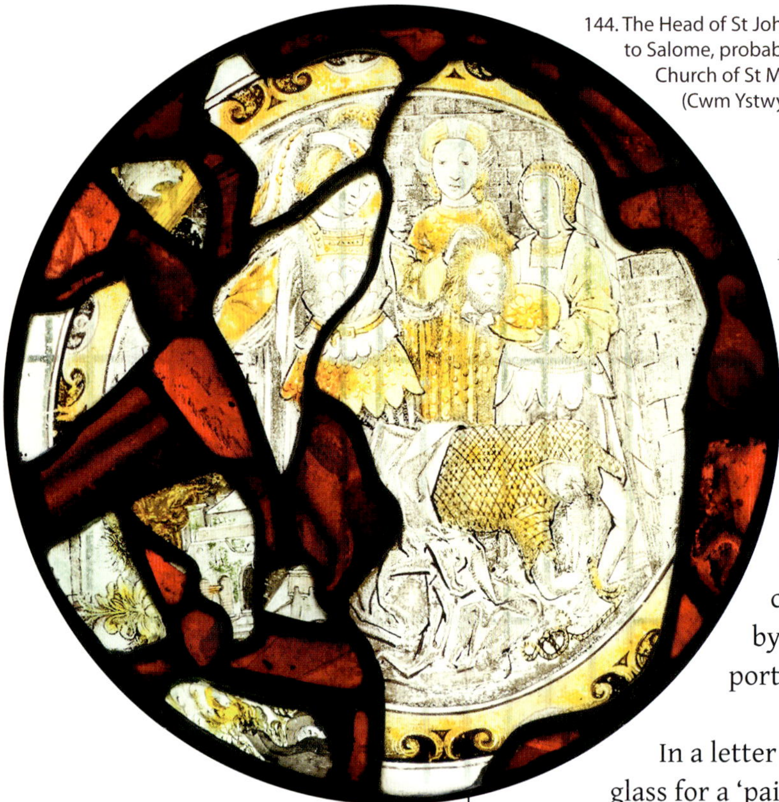

144. The Head of St John the Baptist Presented to Salome, probably sixteenth century, Church of St Michael, Eglwys Newydd (Cwm Ystwyth), chancel

A dazzling collection of continental glass was assembled by the connoisseur Thomas Johnes at Hafod, his house in the Ystwyth valley, Ceredigion, although the provenance of the glass is uncertain. A list of artworks at the house from 1807 includes painted glass in the ante-library brought from a German convent after its suppression by Emperor Joseph II in the 1780s. The list suggests that a portrait of a cardinal in the collection may have been designed by Holbein and engraved by Dürer, and other portraits or scenes were also after Dürer.[23]

In a letter of 1806 Johnes remarked that he had sufficient glass for a 'painted Window in my Church & for those at the end of my painted gallery upstairs'. In 1805 he gave stained glass for the east window of Eglwys Newydd, his estate church rebuilt to the design of James Wyatt in 1803.[24] This glass therefore escaped the conflagration at Johnes mansion at Hafod in 1807, but not the fire in the church of 1932. The north-west window was described by Samuel Rush Meyrick in 1808, when it contained nine panels of New Testament scenes with fourteen roundels above them.[25]

The remains are now collected together in diamonds and roundels. As well as pieces of faces and figures, a couple of scenes are partially discernible. These include an armoured man transfixed by a spear wielded by another standing man in armour, and supported by a female figure; a saint baptising in a river and the head of John the Baptist being placed on Salome's platter by the executioner.

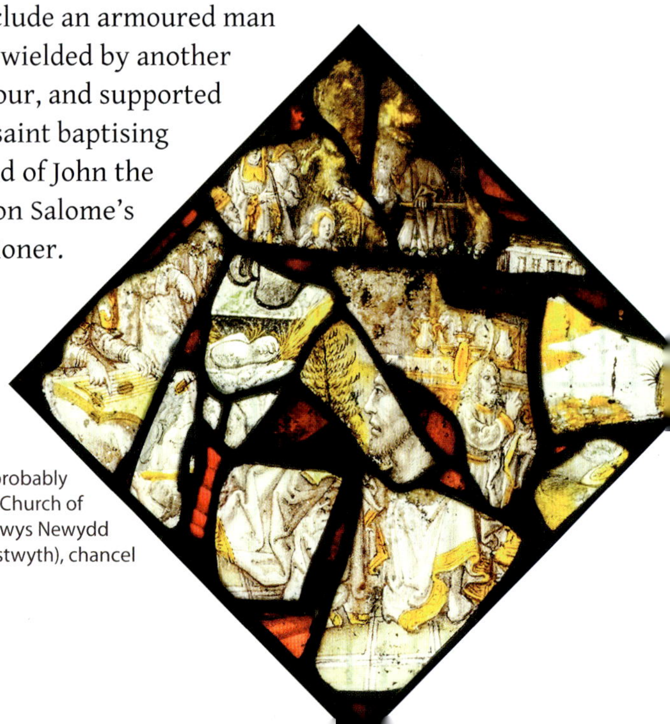

145. Fragments, probably sixteenth century, Church of St Michael, Eglwys Newydd (Cwm Ystwyth), chancel

23 Ceredigion Record Office, Friends of Hafod Collection, FOH. A/05/14. The writer Benjamin Heath Malkin visited Hafod in 1803, and records a large window with 'an uncommonly fine portrait of a cardinal, kneeling with his tutelary saint', which he attributes to Holbein, with the arms of the cardinal on the covering of the reading desk. *The Scenery, Antiquities, and Biography, of South Wales* (London: T.N. Longman & O. Rees, 1804), p. 358.

24 Richard J. Moore-Collier (ed.), *A Land of Pure Delight: selections from the letters of Thomas Johnes of Hafod, Cardiganshire (1743–1816)* (Llandysul: Gomer, 1992), pp. 198, 206.

25 Samuel Rush Meyrick, *The History and Antiquities of the County of Cardigan* (Rhayader: Stephen Collard, 2000, reprint of 1907 edition), p. 289.

The collection at Llanwenllwyfo demonstrates the development in the use of enamels for painting on glass in the sixteenth century. While the 1520s glass demonstrates beautiful detailing using only brown glass paint and silver stain, the background of the scene showing the kneeling governor of the Netherlands with his patron saint, John the Evangelist, uses green and blue enamel pigments.[26] This dates the panel to the last quarter of the sixteenth century, which accords with the dress of the governor, and a panel now set in the east window depicting the arrest of Christ in the garden of Gethsemane is of a similar style and technique. The latest glass in the collection, the seventeenth-century panels depicting the story of Joseph and one of the two scenes of the visit of the three angels to Abraham and Sarah, shows how the sophisticated use of enamels dispensed with the need for leading coloured glass. In these panels the leading interrupts the design, partly delineating the figures and partly creating a simple horizontal or vertical grid for rectangular pieces of glass.[27]

26 The introduction of red enamel to Wales in the sixteenth century may be seen at Llanrhaeadr-yng-Nghinmeirch, where the lips of King David were painted in red. Blue enamel was used on the arms of Edward Stanley at Mold.

27 Some of these rectangular pieces have been broken and re-leaded in earlier restorations, which partially disguises their original appearance.

146. (below left) The Governor of the Netherlands with St John, late sixteenth century, Church of St Gwenllwyfo, Llanwenllwyfo, nave

147. (below) Joseph Sold to Potiphar, probably early seventeenth century, Church of St Gwenllwyfo, Llanwenllwyfo, nave

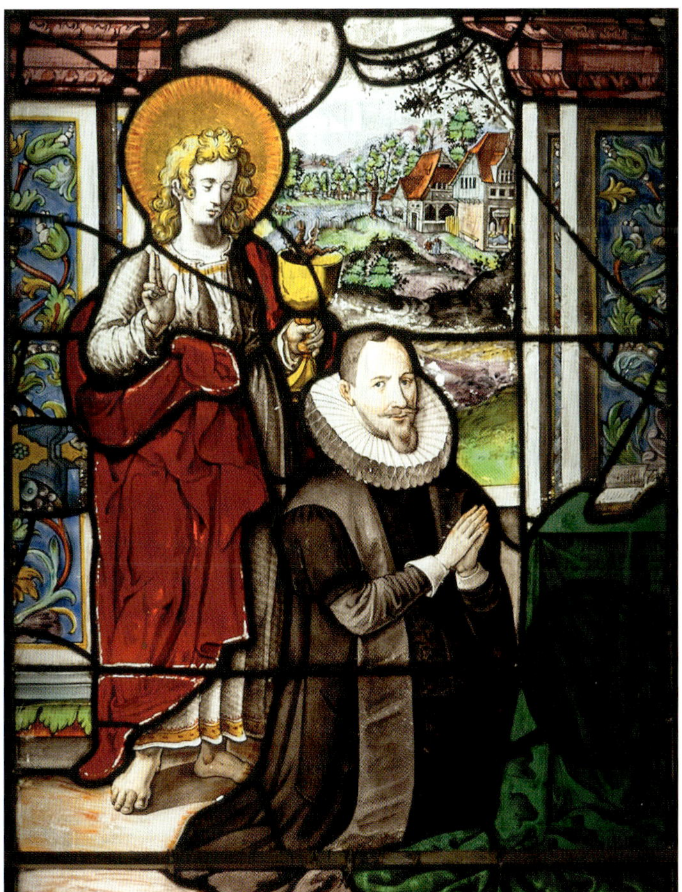

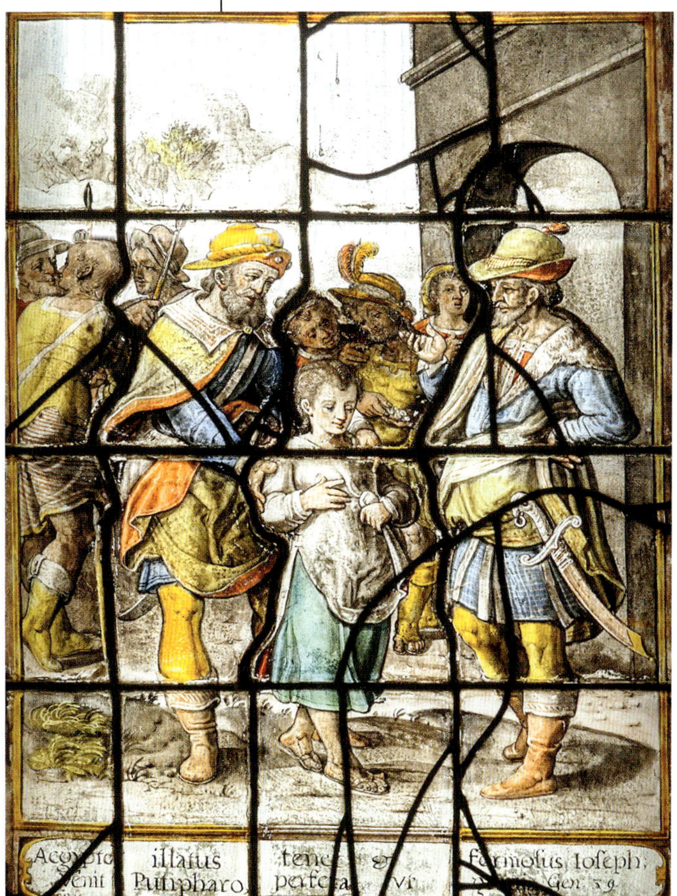

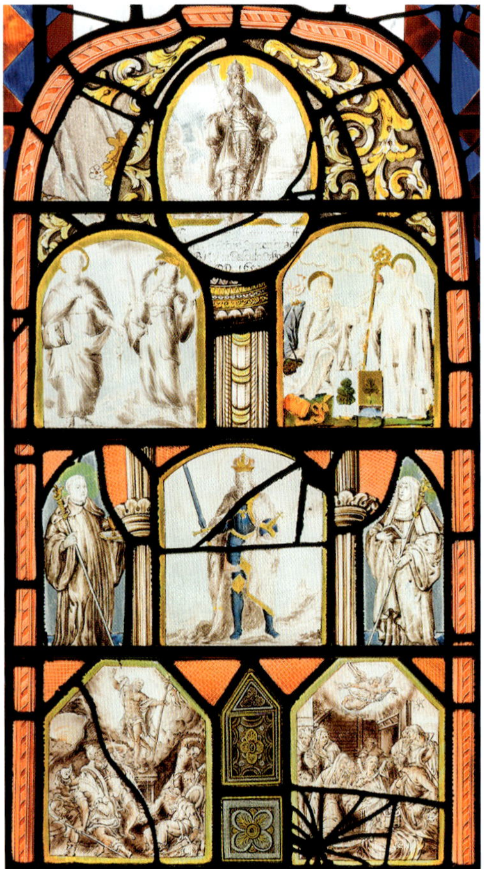

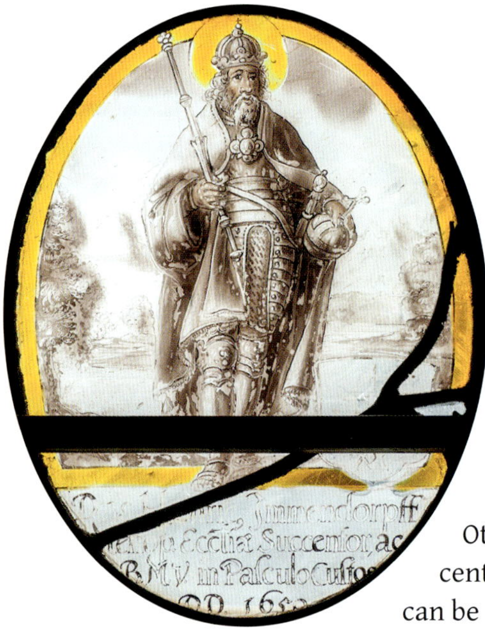

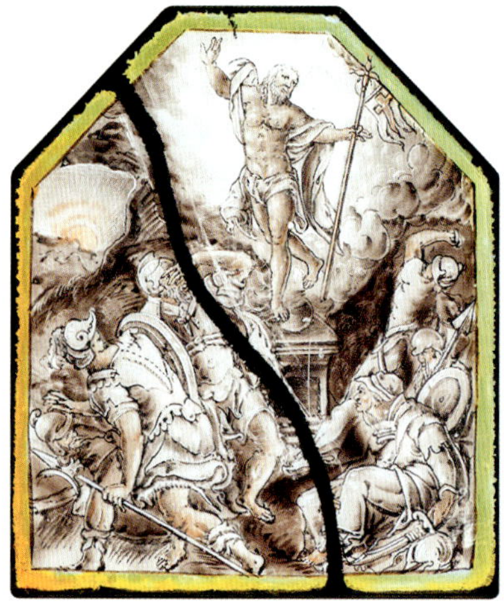

148–50. Collection of seventeenth-century roundels, including an unidentified Saint, 1650 (above centre); The Resurrection, probably seventeenth century (above right), Church of St Michael, Llanarth (Monmouthshire), nave

Other examples of seventeenth-century continental glass painting can be found in Welsh churches. A further window in the south wall of the Church of St Mary and St Michael at Llanarth Court is composed of several small scenes and figures, each of which were painted on a single piece of glass. One of these roundels, an oval depicting a standing crowned figure, has an inscription dating the piece to 1650, although this does not necessarily date other fragments, most of which have different styles of glass painting. As well as the standing figures, two scenes in a similar style depict Christ rising from the tomb and the shepherds adoring the Virgin and Child. Two small roundels reset in the north wall of the chancel in the Church of St Mary, Newport (Pembrokeshire), are of uncertain provenance, although one is dated 1631. This roundel depicts three musical angels while the other depicts John the Evangelist standing in a landscape.[28]

A complex assortment of fragments have been gathered together in two three-light windows in the south wall of the nave of the Church of St Beuno, Bettws Cedewain. The glass was given to the church in the nineteenth century by the

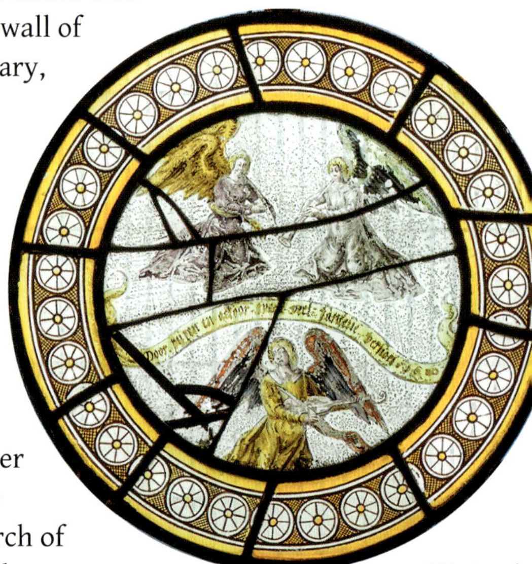

151. Angels, 1631, Church of St Mary, Newport (Pembrokeshire), chancel

28 A third roundel of the Nativity has also been given an early date, but is probably nineteenth century.

29 Charles Hanbury-Tracy, first Lord Sudeley, was the third son of the Pontypool ironmaster John Hanbury. He accumulated an extensive collection of Flemish stained glass roundels at Toddington Manor in Gloucestershire, which were subsequently dispersed and some of which was sold at auction in Munich in 1911.

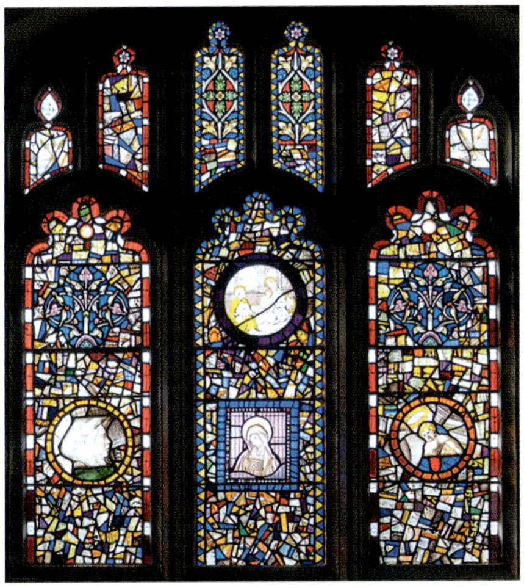

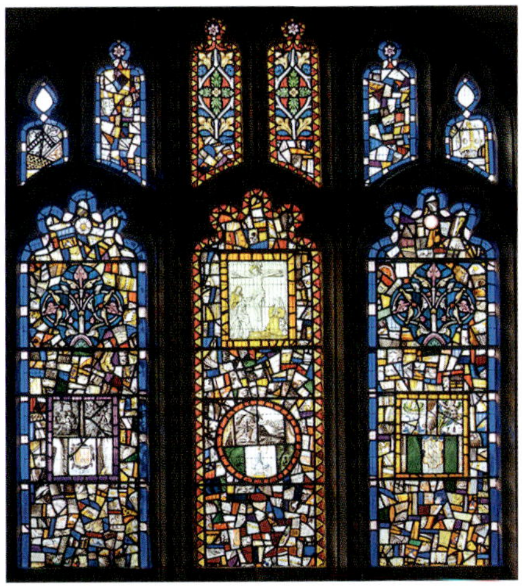

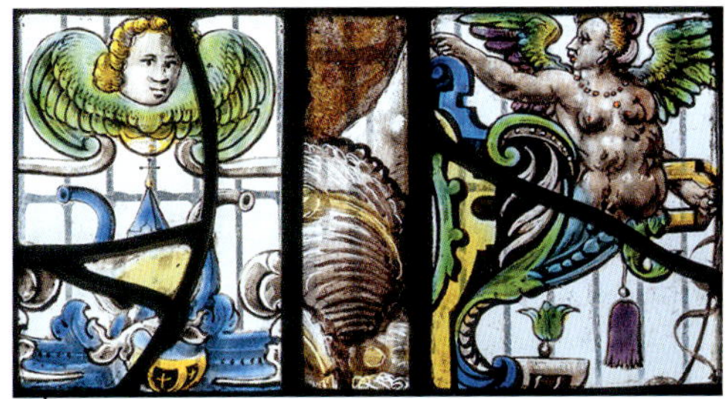

152–3. (left) Two windows with an assortment of late medieval and early modern fragments, Church of St Beuno, Bettws Cedewain, nave

154. (below left) Grisaille panels, probably mid-seventeenth century, Church of St Beuno, Bettws Cedewain, nave

155. (above) Painted fragments, seventeenth or eighteenth century, Church of St Beuno, Bettws Cedewain, nave

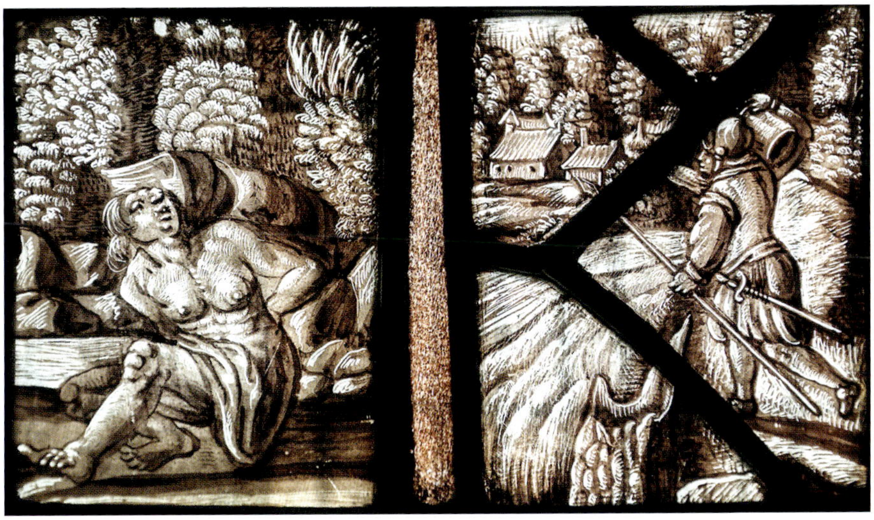

Hanbury-Tracy family who owned nearby Gregynog Hall at the time.[29] A roundel of the Nativity and a rectangular panel of the Crucifixion are in the style of the sixteenth century, but most of the surrounding mosaic of small fragments, including parts of figures and several small scenes, are probably of the seventeenth century or later.

Native medieval stained glass that survived into the seventeenth century was less vulnerable to iconoclasm during the early years of the seventeenth century. A revival in stained glass during the reign of Charles I was encouraged during the Anglican counter-reformation led by Archbishop William Laud, although new windows are not known to have been made for churches in Wales.[30] It was at this time that the windows at Gresford were repaired at the expense of Anthony Lewis of Burton in 1634, and the head of John among the large row of figures in the east window could have been added at this date.[31]

30 Graham Parry, *Glory, Laud and Honour: The Arts of the Anglican Counter-Reformation* (Woodbridge: Boydell, 2006), p. 100–5.

31 Mostyn Lewis, *Stained Glass in North Wales up to 1850* (Altrincham: John Sherratt and Son Ltd, 1970), p. 38. The bequest of Anthony Lewis is quoted in D.R. Thomas, *The History of the Diocese of St Asaph* (Oswestry: The Caxton Press, 1913), vol. iii, p. 248: 'I give and bequeath to mende and make cleane the fayre and curious painted glasse windows in Gresford Church that I sawe was falling in decaye the somme of one hundred poundes to be mended neatly with coullored glass, where a head, arm, body, legg or Coate of the Personages be broken or inscripcion gone to mende them art like in shape and proper coullor.' He also paid for the floor to be raised and paved, and the church was partly reordered in accordance with Laudian principles.

32 William Bell Jones 'Ancient stained and painted glass in Flintshire', *Flintshire Historical Society Journal*, xi (1925), p. 70. J. Wyn Evans, 'The Reformation and St. David's Cathedral', *The Journal of Welsh Ecclesiastical History*, vol. 7 (1990), p. 13. Armorial glass in St Davids Cathedral was described in a transcript of a late sixteenth-century manuscript included in Browne Willis, *A Survey of the Cathedral Church of St David's and the edifices belonging to it, as they stood in the year 1715* (London: R. Gosling, 1717), pp. 74–87. 'The old painted Windows', the text adds, 'were demolish'd in the Great Rebellion', p. 88.

33 Glass was brought from Normandy and installed after the church was rebuilt in 1472, indicating that the windows probably used coloured glass. Samuel Lewis, *A Topographical Dictionary of Wales* (London: S. Lewis & Co., 1848), vol. ii, p. 439.

Three seventeenth-century miniature portraits at the Church of Corpus Christi, Tremeirchion, are perhaps of British origin, although nothing regarding their original commissioning is known. The small panels depict James I and Archbishop John Williams, within decorative surrounds, while a further partial figure of Charles I is on a plain background. These portraits were brought from the old vicarage at the instigation of Canon Maurice Ridgway, probably in the 1940s, although their earlier provenance is uncertain.

The violence and iconoclasm of the Civil War and the Puritan sympathies of Parliamentarian troops in Wales presented a new threat to figurative glass in medieval churches. For example, at Hawarden, faces in windows were smashed in 1643, leaving the remainder of the figures; and in 1648 soldiers destroyed windows at St Davids Cathedral, where heraldic stained glass was plentiful in the late sixteenth century.[32] The survival of the Jesse window at Llanrhaeadr-yng-Nghinmeirch has been attributed to the tradition that it was removed in advance of the arrival of Parliamentarian troops in the area in 1646. At the Church of St Giles, Wrexham, the church building was used by Parliamentarian troops as a prison and a stable after 1643, which may have seen the destruction of any surviving stained glass.[33]

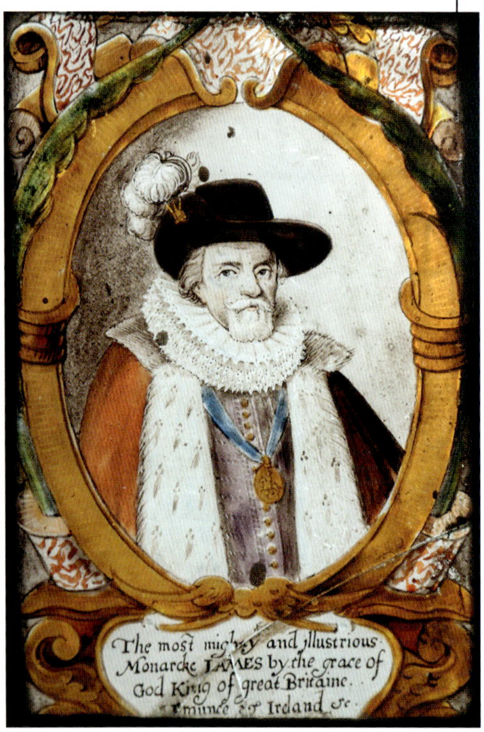

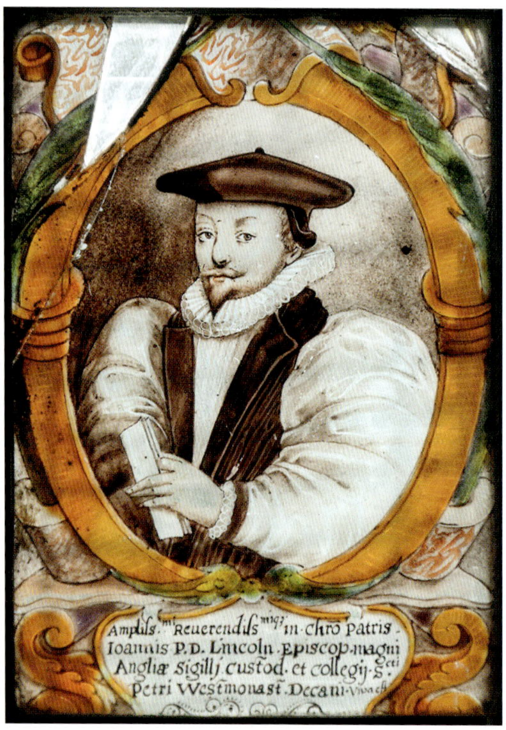

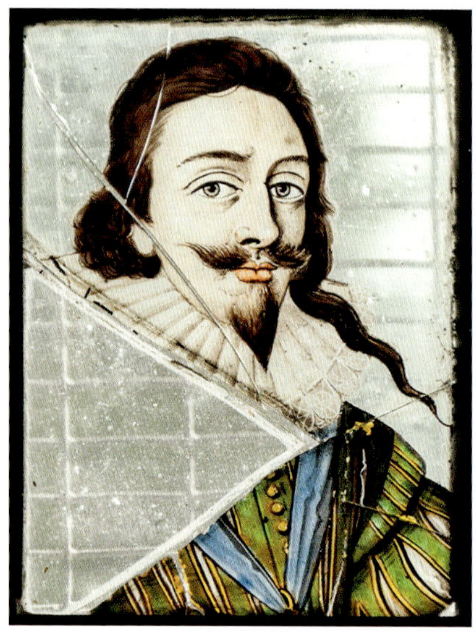

156–8. (left to right) James I, Archbishop John Williams (after an engraving published by Thomas Jenner, *c.* 1621–5), Charles I, probably seventeenth century, Church of Corpus Christi, Tremeirchion, nave

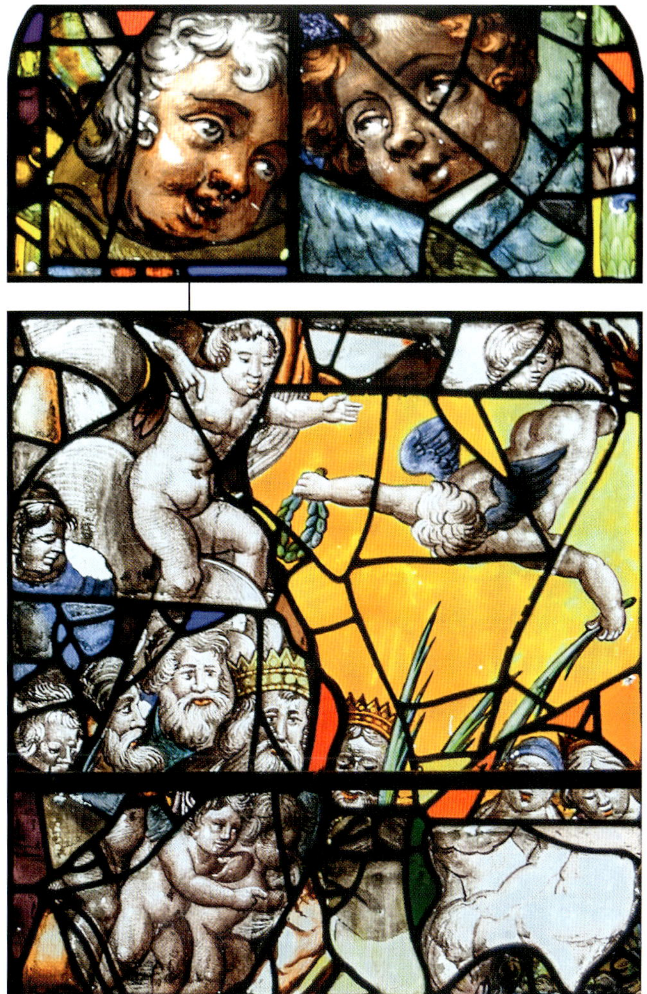

159. Coloured fragments, probably seventeenth or early eighteenth century, Church of All Saints, Gresford, north porch

As well as having the richest collection of native medieval glass in Wales, in amongst some of the assemblages in the north and south walls of the chapels at the Church of All Saints, Gresford, are fragments dating from the eighteenth century. Some of this material may have been part of a collection of Italian glass, originally given to the church in the eighteenth century by Mr Tudor, a merchant born in the parish.[34] Glass from this collection, formerly in the north wall of the church, was brought together in the south porch as a First World War memorial, commemorating two brothers who died in 1917 and 1918. The partial scenes and fragments contain numerous cherubs as well as some crowned heads, and are painted with coloured enamels.

A collection of small panels in the east window of the Church of St Basil, Bassaleg, were probably given by the Morgan family of nearby Tredegar House, now on the outskirts of the city of Newport. Probably of eighteenth-century German origin, they include a number of scenes from the life of Christ including the Nativity, the Rest on the Flight into Egypt, the Deposition, and the appearance of the risen Christ to Thomas, as well as Peter escaping from prison from the Book of the Acts of the Apostles. Painted in black and brown enamels with yellow silver stain, some of the panels still demonstrate a strong chiaroscuro effect, although many are in need of conservation, having suffered considerable paint loss.

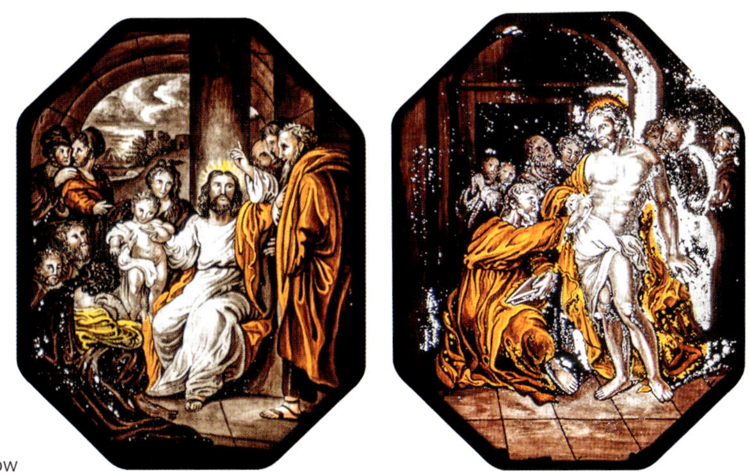

160–1. Christ with Disciples and a Child (right), and Christ Appearing to St Thomas (far right), probably eighteenth century, Church of St Basil, Bassaleg, east window

34 There is some confusion over the date of the bequest and the identity of the donor. Mostyn Lewis states that it was a Mr Trevor who gave the glass in the early nineteenth century, *Stained Glass in North Wales up to 1850* (Altrincham: John Sherratt and Son Ltd, 1970), p. 37, but the inscription in the window states that Mr Tudor, a native of the parish, gave it in the eighteenth century, but it was afterwards removed. According to *The Ecclesiologist*, a gift of Italian glass by Mr. Tudor in the early eighteenth century was 'not graciously received'. *The Ecclesiologist*, vol. iv (1845), pp. 182–3. The glass was presumably accepted, or otherwise acquired, at a later date, before being assembled in its current location in about 1918.

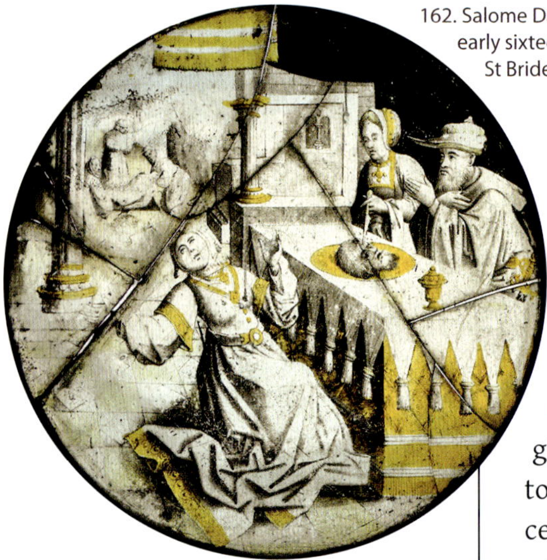

162. Salome Dancing Before Herod, probably early sixteenth century, Church of St Bride, St Bride's-super-Ely, east window

The gifts of continental glass to churches in the nineteenth century were stimulated by the desire of wealthy benefactors to add imagery to churches as a conscious revival of medieval practice, sometimes alongside the commissioning of new stained glass in medieval styles. In other cases stained glass, paintings and other furnishings were given to churches by descendants of collectors who found them surplus to requirements. More recent gifts have brought pre-nineteenth century glass to Welsh churches, such as the roundels given for the east window of the Church of St Bride, St Bride's-super-Ely in 1956.[35] Eight panels, thought to be French sixteenth-century work, were given for the Welch Regimental Chapel at Llandaff Cathedral in memory of two brothers by their sister Margaret Prothero, together with Lady Florence Bradney and Evelyn Clarke. These panels contrast with the rectangular quarries of flowers and animals of the seventeenth century, but of uncertain provenance, which came from Hale Hall in Lancashire, and were given by the Friends of Llandaff Cathedral in 1955.[36]

35 The roundels were installed under the supervision of the York architect George Pace, and the presence of a roundel of William of York and what appears to be a fifteenth-century York-type angel suggests a Yorkshire provenance.

36 Nevil A. James, 'The Stained Glass of Llandaff Cathedral' in Nick Lambert (ed.), *Llandaff Cathedral* (Bridgend: Seren, 2010), p. 197. See also Penny Hebgin-Barnes, *The Medieval Stained Glass of Cheshire* (Oxford: Oxford University Press, 2010), p. cxliv.

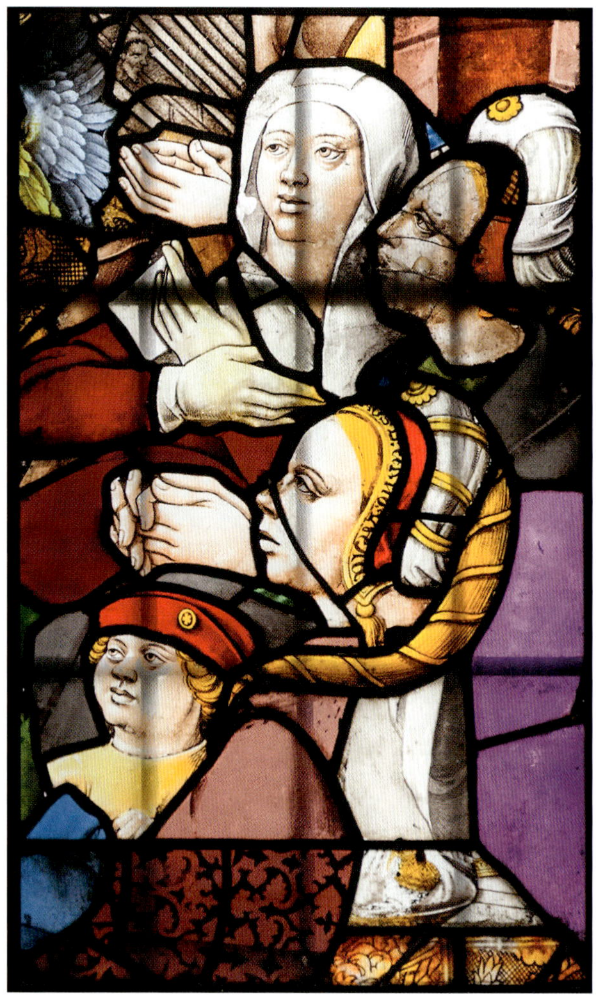

165. (right) Heads from an Unknown Scene, probably sixteenth century, Llandaff Cathedral, Welch Regimental Chapel

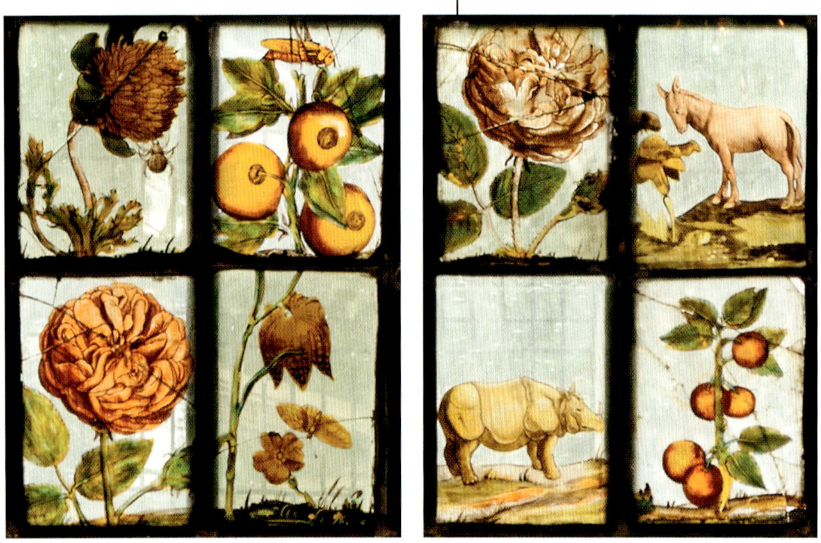

163–4. Flowers and Animals, probably *c.* 1620–1640, Llandaff Cathedral, south aisle

Chapter Three

A Revival of Gothic

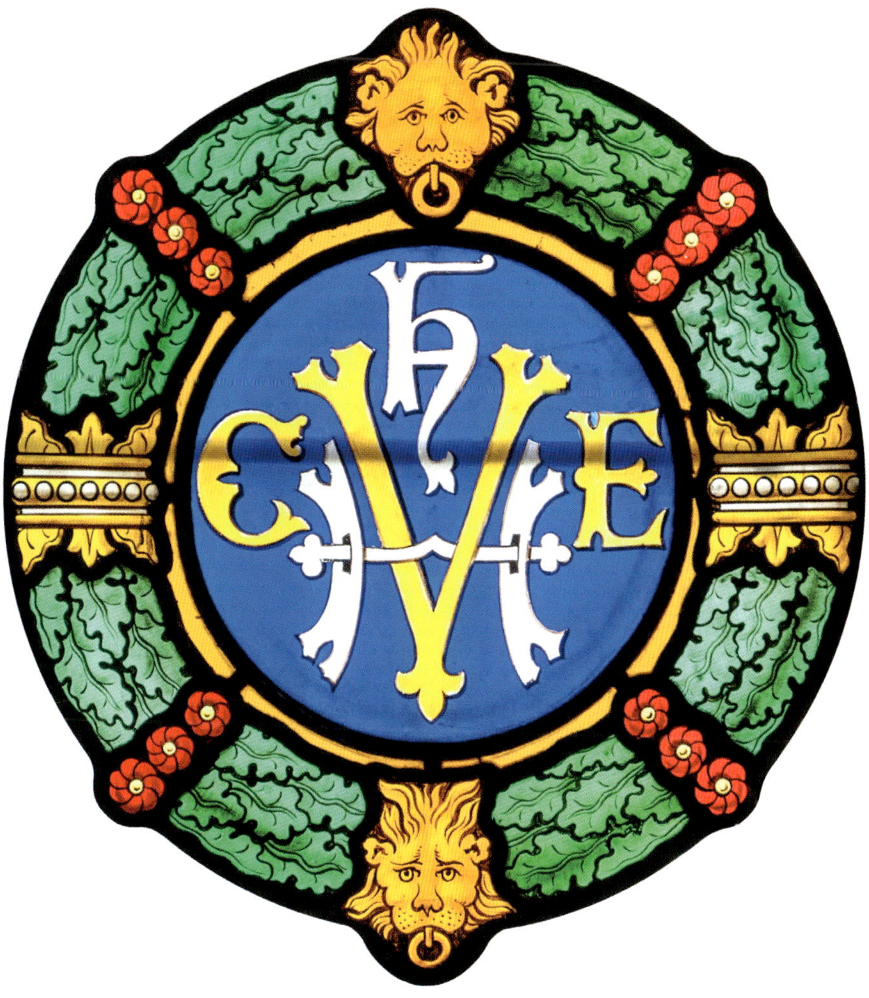

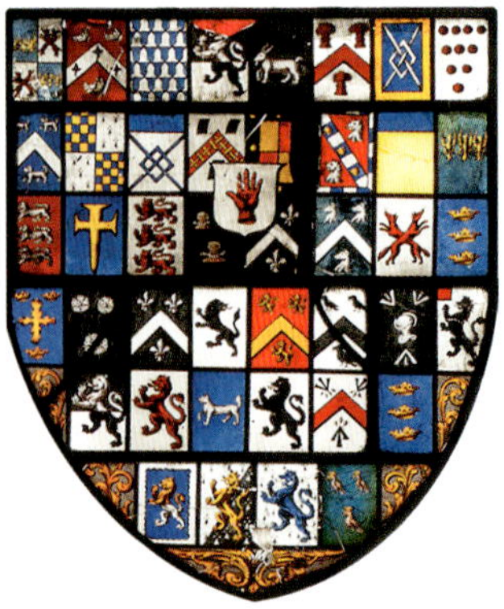

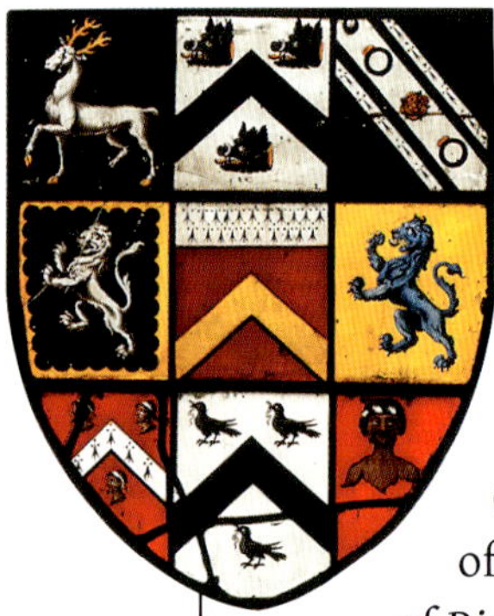

167–8. (above) Francis Eginton, Arms of Sir Watcyn Williams-Wynn, fifth baronet (left) and of John Lloyd of Hafodunos (right), *c.* 1800, St Asaph Cathedral, south transept (from the former east window)

169. Drawing of the tracery of the east window of St Asaph Cathedral, probably *c.* 1800, inserted in an extra-illustrated copy of Thomas Pennant, *A Tour in Wales* (vol. ii, *The Journey to Snowdon*), NLW PD9872, after p. 18
(image courtesy of the National Library of Wales)

170. (right) Francis Eginton, Christ Contemplating his Crucifixion, *c.* 1800, Church of St Tegla, Llandegla, east window (from the former east window of St Asaph Cathedral)

In 1800 new painted glass was commissioned for the east window of the choir at St Asaph Cathedral. A series of heraldic shields surrounded three central lights depicting the young Christ contemplating his Crucifixion, in a curiously morbid scene with cherubs toying with the instruments of the Passion.[1] The window was painted by Francis Eginton of Birmingham using coloured enamels on rectangular pieces of glass, which emulated the painting of oil on canvas. The technique was famously employed in the west window of New College, Oxford, executed from 1775 to 1785 by Thomas Jervais after designs by Joshua Reynolds. Eginton also made other windows in a similar style based on paintings and designs by Benjamin West and Joshua Reynolds for cathedrals, churches and gentry patrons.[2]

Further heraldic glass of an earlier date by the artist may be found in north-east Wales at the Church of St Deiniol and Marcella, Marchwiel, with heraldry mainly relating to the Yorke family of nearby Erddig Hall.[3] Made in 1788, Eginton's technique owed little to the medieval craft of

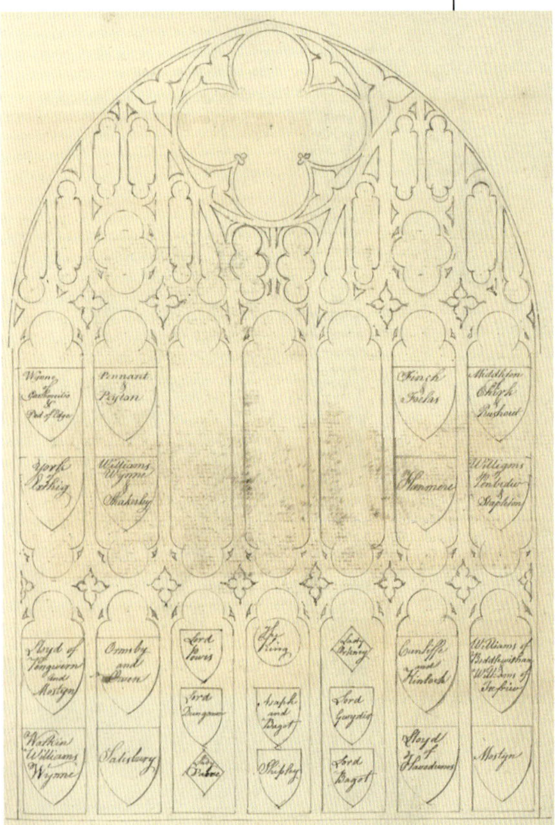

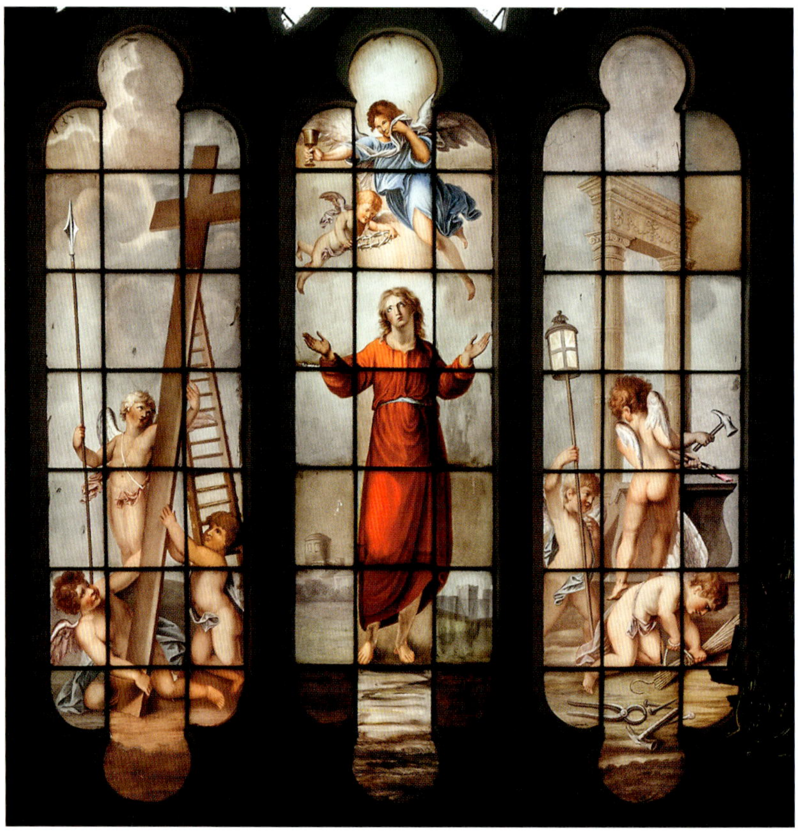

166. (Title page) Thomas Willement, Monogram of the Vivi
Family, *c.* 1850, Church of St Paul, Sketty, chanc

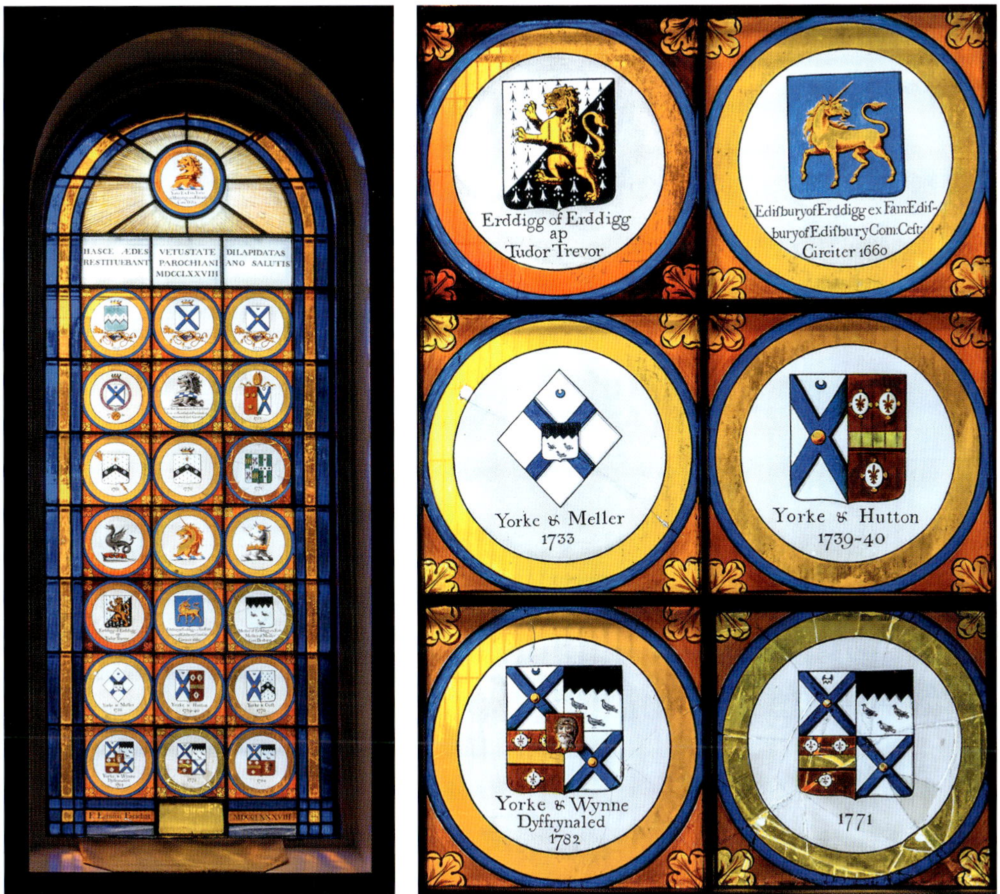

171–2. Francis Eginton, Heraldic Panels, 1788, Church of St Deiniol and St Marcella, Marchwiel, nave

stained glass. Rather than using shaped pieces of coloured pot-metal glass leaded together as a mosaic, silver stain is used to create yellow, orange and red on square glass panels, with additional blue enamel paint.

The use of family heraldry reflected the growing fashion for medievalism among the gentry classes, and increasingly from Industrialist families. The industrialisation of the country was accompanied by a growth of medieval romanticism, and as 'Britain prospered, crenellations were constructed, disused armour was polished and displayed, and family coats of arms were carved on walls and installed in stained glass windows.'[4] Interest in medieval glass was also motivated by opportunities for collecting examples brought from the continent in the 1790s in the wake of the French Revolution, which ultimately brought stained glass from the Charterhouse at Louvain and Steinfeld Abbey to Wales. English enthusiasts for Gothic such as Horace Walpole and William Beckford, as well as collectors in Wales such as Thomas Johnes at Hafod,

1 The heraldic shields are collected together at St Asaph in a transept window, while the scene of the young Christ is now at the Church of St Tegla, Llandegla.

2 Many of these windows have since been replaced and lost. A window in a similar style of 1795 survives at the Church of St Alkmund, Shrewsbury: a copy of *The Assumption of the Virgin* by Guido Reni. The scene painted for St Asaph is a copy of a work by Albinus, see 'Glass Painters of Birmingham, Francis Eginton, 1737–1805', *Journal of the British Society of Master Glass-Painters*, vol. ii, no. 2 (October 1927), p. 69.

3 Phillip Yorke, first earl of Hardwick, also commissioned stained glass for his house at Wimpole Court and its church in Cambridgeshire during the mid-eighteenth century, some of which was subsequently moved to the chapel at Erddig Hall. Mostyn Lewis, *Stained Glass in North Wales up to 1850* (Altrincham: John Sherratt and Son Ltd, 1970), pp. 105–6; see also Geoffrey Lane, ' 'A Fine Window at Price's': Sanderson Miller, William Price the Younger and the Uses of Stained Glass in the Mid-Eighteenth Century', *The Journal of Stained Glass*, vol. xxxvi (2012), pp. 10–12.

4 Michael Alexander, *Medievalism: the Middle Ages in Modern England* (New Haven and London: Yale University Press, 2007), p. 109.

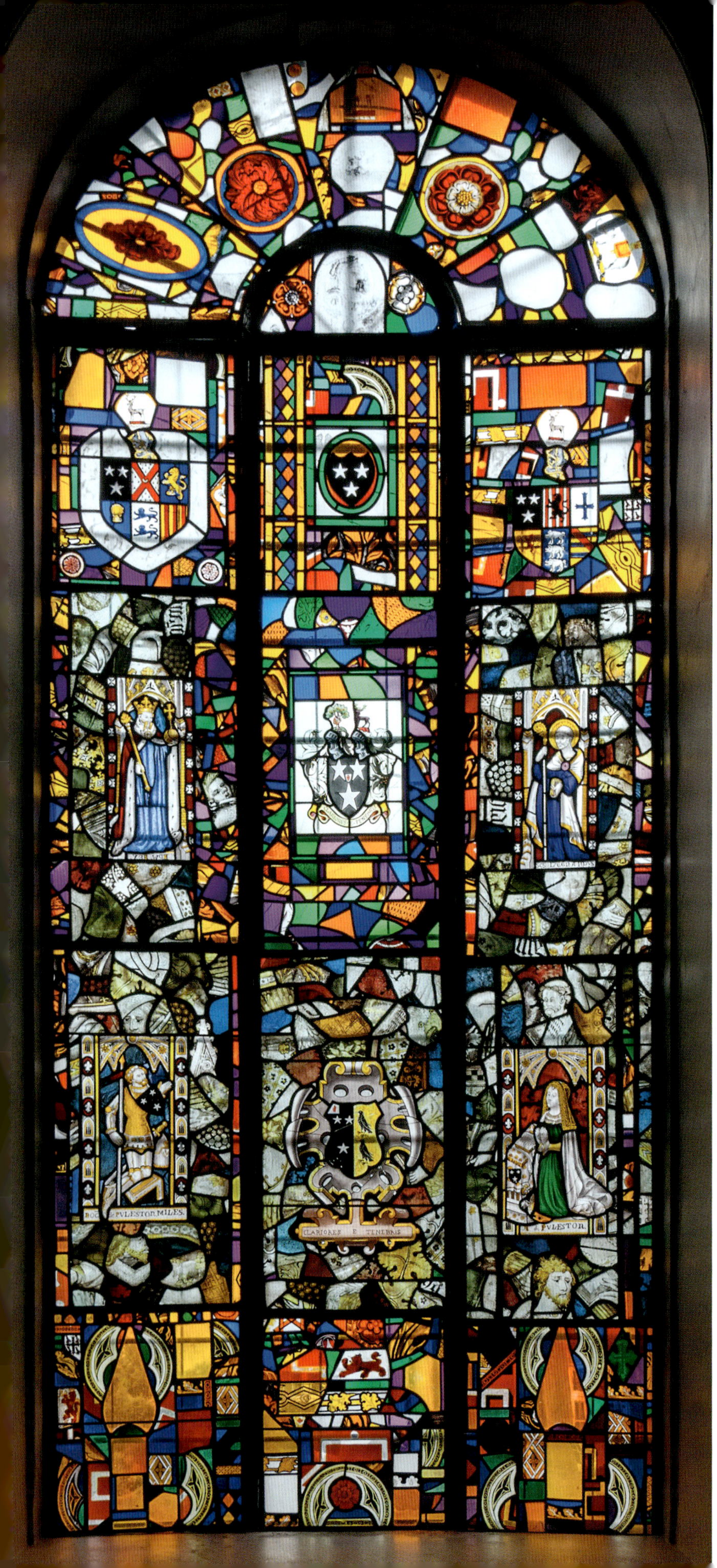

introduced what must have been an exotic coloured light into the opulent Gothic Revival houses that they had built in the second half of the eighteenth century.[5]

Few glass painters would have been at work in Wales during the eighteenth century. However, glaziers were needed to keep out the wind and the rain and surviving medieval glass in churches was sometimes re-leaded and retained in situ. At the Church of St Cyngar, Hope, a piece of graffito among the medieval glass fragments records 'John Bird plumber and glazier new leaded these lights March 26 1766'; and only a few miles away at Treuddyn, Charles Bill re-leaded the medieval glass in 1763 and 1775, an event also recorded in graffito. The most skilled of these artisans would have been called upon to install the expensive acquisitions of the gentry, thereby gaining first-hand knowledge of medieval glass.

The understanding of restoration in the early nineteenth century was not one that would be recognised today. In 1822 the studio of Betton & Evans of Shrewsbury removed the late fourteenth-century glass from the east window of Winchester College Chapel and inserted close copies in their place, having been unable to clean the medieval glass satisfactorily. Betton & Evans made

173. Betton & Evans, East Window, 1823, Church of St Deiniol, Worthenbury

use of these medieval fragments elsewhere, such as in their east window for the Puleston family made for the Church of St Deiniol, Worthenbury, in 1823. Fragments from Winchester College Chapel were set among an assemblage of further medieval fragments and other glass said to have come from Emral Hall, near Worthenbury, which had been demolished in 1775. These fragments are in a fourteenth-century style and surround figures of Edward I, St Leonard, and Sir Roger Puleston and his wife Agnes Puleston with further family heraldry.[6]

The younger of the partners, David Evans, was born at Llanllwchaiarn near Newtown in 1793 and worked with Sir John Betton of Shrewsbury from 1815. Betton retired soon after the completion of the Worthenbury window, and Evans assumed full control of the studio in 1825 and continued to work until his death in 1861. The firm was responsible for many restorations, and copies of old glass as well as new windows across England and Wales. Most of Evans' new work in Wales is found in the northern half of the country, but he also undertook heraldic work at Margam Castle in the 1830s and made the decorative east window for the cemetery chapel at Tenby.[7] Some of his work for churches was also heraldic, and a series of armorial shields survive at the Church of St Tysilio and St Mary, Meifod, initially made for the east window of the north aisle in 1838.[8]

A list of windows made by Thomas Willement was published in 1840, and demonstrates that the majority of his commissions were for private houses, although the number of commissions for churches increased

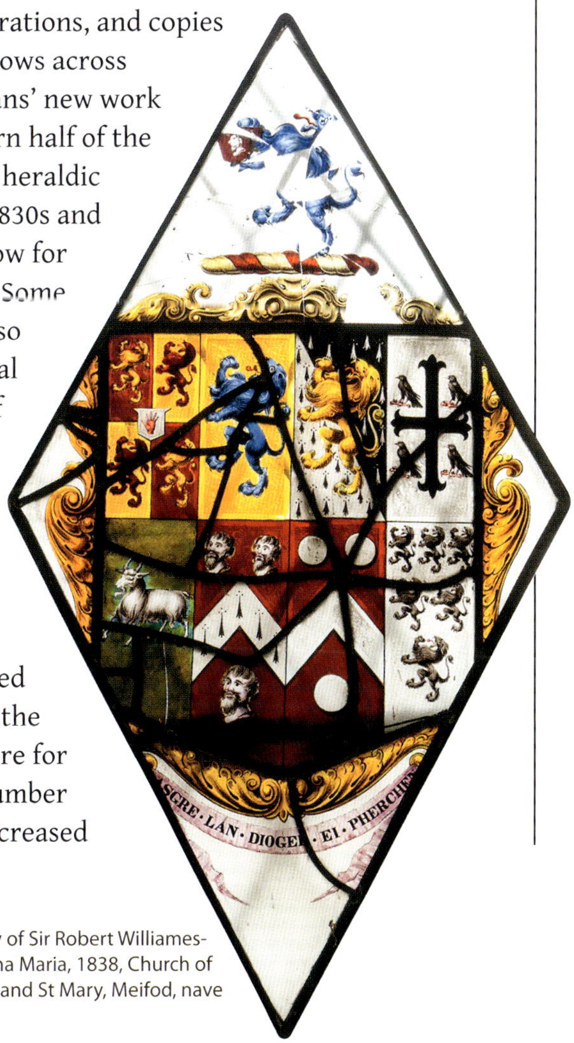

174. David Evans, Heraldry of Sir Robert Williames-Vaughan and his wife Anna Maria, 1838, Church of St Tysilio and St Mary, Meifod, nave

5 The use of Gothic Revival styles for domestic architecture in the eighteenth and nineteenth centuries is described in Megan Aldrich, *Gothic Revival* (London: Phaidon, 1994). For the acquisition of continental glass by English collectors see William Cole, *A Catalogue of Netherlandish and North European Roundels in Britain*, CVMA Summary Catalogue 1 (Oxford: Oxford University Press, 1993); none are listed in Wales.

6 Edward I granted Emral Hall to his favourite, Sir Roger Puleston, in about 1282. The window is discussed in detail by Mostyn Lewis, *Stained Glass in North Wales up to 1850* (Altrincham: John Sherratt and Son Ltd, 1970), pp. 95–7.

7 For the work of David Evans at Margam see Alun Adams, 'Stained and Painted Glass at Margam', *Port Talbot Historian* (Transactions of the Port Talbot Historical Society), vol. iv, no. 2 (2000), pp. 35–6.

8 Mostyn Lewis gives a detailed description of the heraldry in *Stained Glass in North Wales up to 1850* (Altrincham: John Sherratt and Son Ltd, 1970), pp. 80–2.

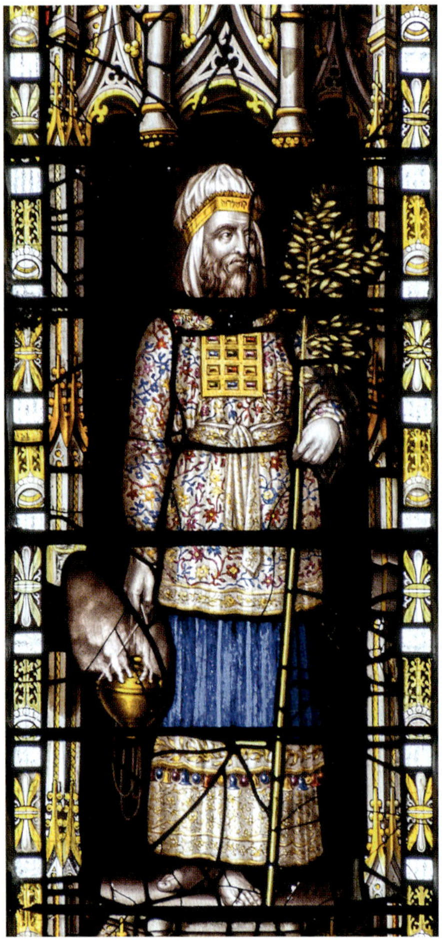

175. David Evans, Aaron, 1838, Bangor Cathedral, west window (from the former east window)

during the course of the 1830s.[9] In 1828 Willement made an armorial window for Hussey Vivian in Swansea, and Thomas Hopper, the architect of the Gothic revival residence for George Hay Dawkins-Pennant at Penrhyn Castle, employed Willement to provide a number of windows for the castle in north Wales near Bangor. These included two large windows for the Great Hall containing roundels depicting the months of the year and the signs of the zodiac, made in 1835 in a thirteenth-century style.

Thomas Willement worked as a heraldic artist for George IV and for Queen Victoria after her accession in 1837. He may have planned the scheme of heraldic glass for Penrhyn Castle, but some of these windows, as well as the figurative windows in the chapel, were made by David Evans. Shortly after the completion of the glass at the castle, in 1838 David Evans was employed nearby at Bangor Cathedral to provide figures for the east window given in thanksgiving of the long service of the vicar and precentor of the cathedral, James Henry Cotton, on his appointment as Dean.

The technical versatility and variety of artistic influences adopted by David Evans during the period is impressive. His standing figures for Bangor Cathedral in 1838 are placed under white glass Gothic canopies heightened with silver stain, the figures painted with considerable detail and plenty of dark paint to give a three-dimensional chiaroscuro effect. These figures contrast with the three scenes in the chancel apse of Christ Church, Welshpool, where his Transfiguration is a copy of the painting by Raphael.[10] His east window at the Church of St Chad, Shrewsbury, is a copy of *The Descent from the Cross*, the central panel of Peter Paul Rubens' altarpiece of 1612–14 for the Cathedral of Our Lady, Antwerp, Belgium. The right-hand panel of the triptych, depicting the Presentation of Christ in the Temple, was also copied by Evans at Llangollen, although much of the dark paint is this window has been lost. In contrast, his small medallions formerly in the east window of the Church of St Giles, Wrexham, use silver stain with blue enamel in a sixteenth-century Flemish style.[11]

9 See *A concise account of the principal works in stained glass that have been executed by Thomas Willement* (London, 1840).

10 Raphael's *The Transfiguration*, 1518–20, is at the Pinacoteca, Vatican. The scene below shows the possessed boy being brought to the disciples. Martin Harrison noted that Raphael's scene of the Transfiguration was adapted in stained glass more than any other Renaissance painting during the first half of the nineteenth century: *Victorian Stained Glass* (London: Barrie & Jenkins, 1980), p. 17.

11 Among the small scenes at Wrexham are further copies of Rubens' *The Descent from the Cross* and Raphael's Christ from *The Transfiguration*.

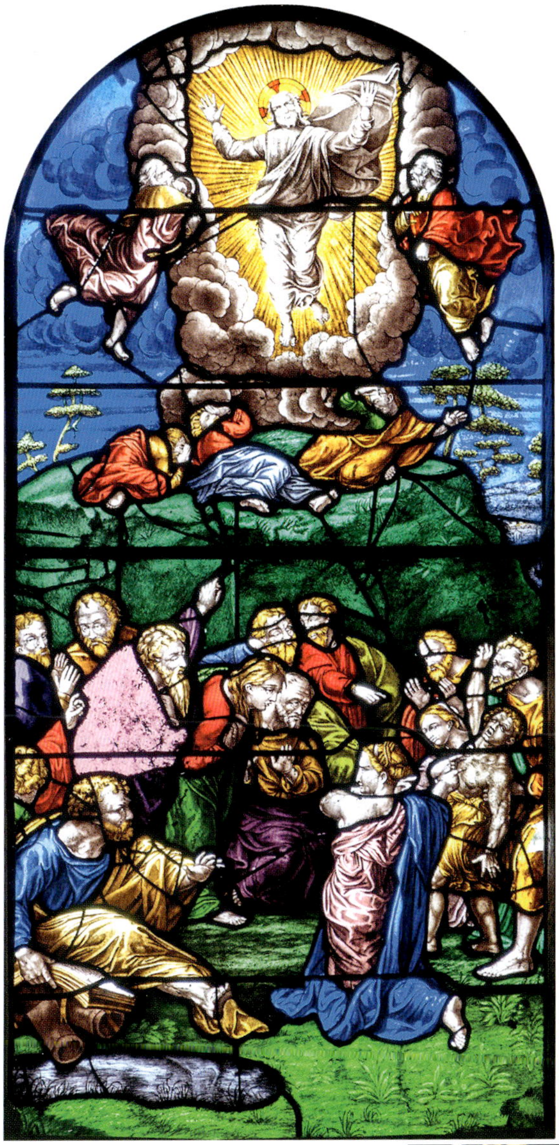

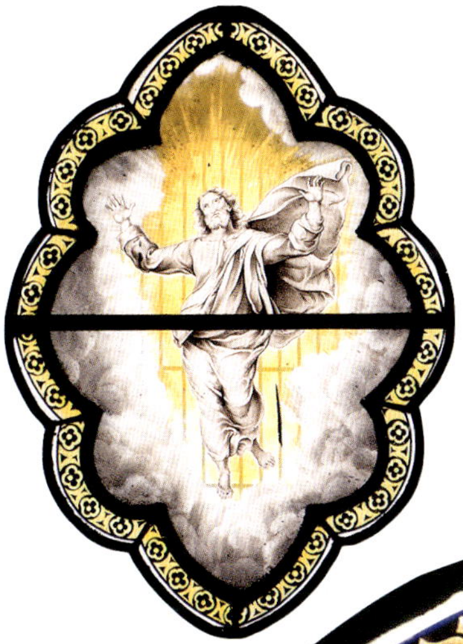

176. (far left) David Evans, The Transfiguration (after Raphael), probably 1844, Christ Church, Welshpool, chancel apse
(Building now in private ownership but accessible to the public, courtesy Karl Meredith and Natalie Bass)

177–8. David Evans, The Transfiguration (after Raphael) (left), and Christ with the Woman of Samaria (below), 1841, Church of St Giles, Wrexham, chancel (from the former east window)

179. (bottom left) David Evans, The Presentation of Christ in the Temple (after Rubens), 1833, Church of St Collen, Llangollen, tower

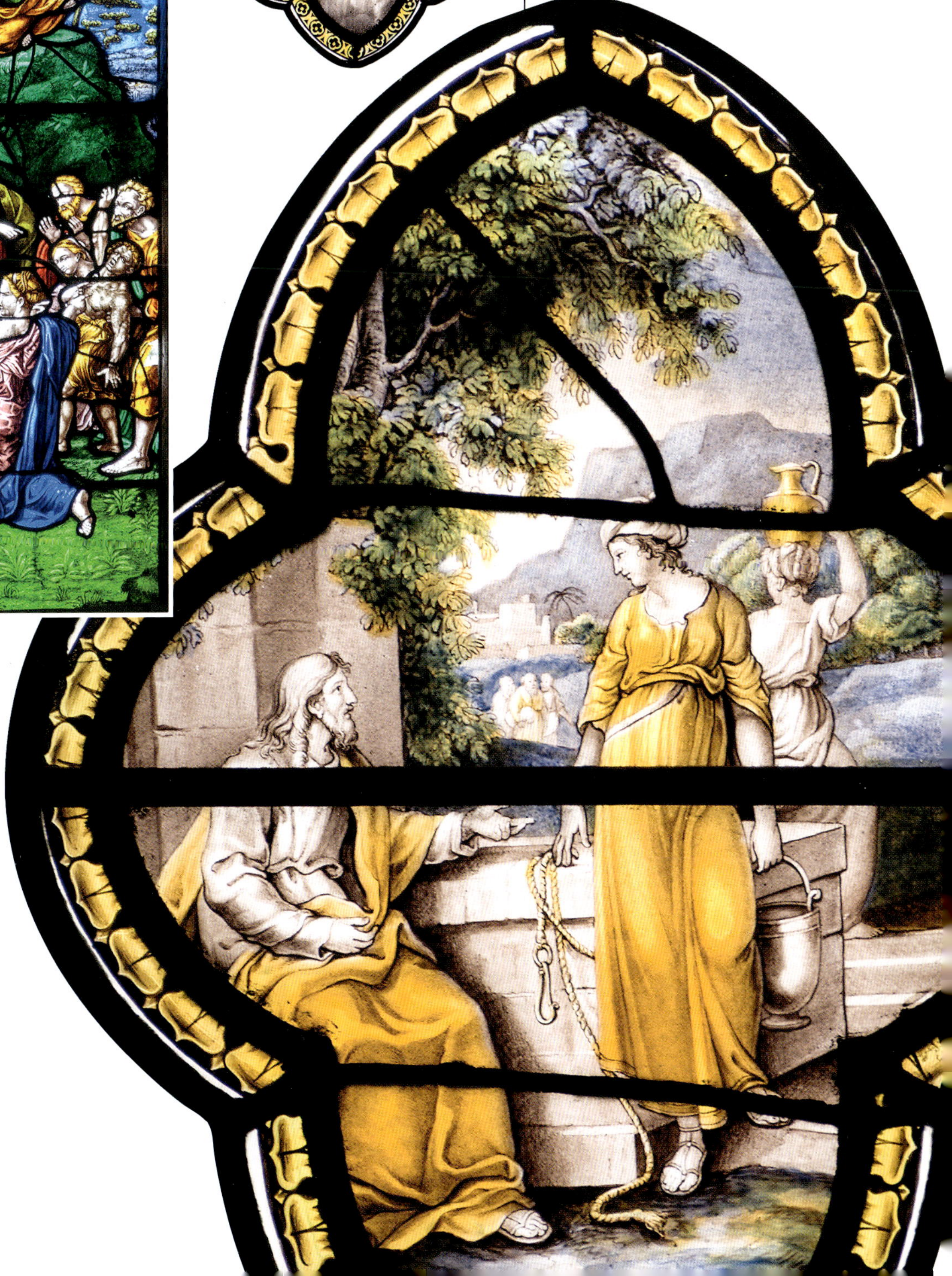

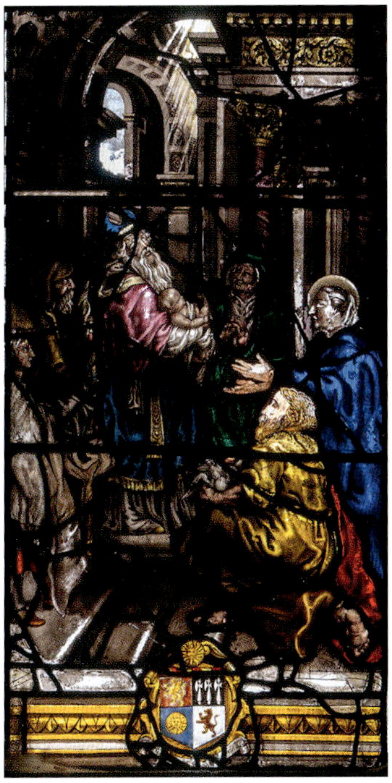

The painterly style of David Evans is paralleled in the contemporary windows of Charles Clutterbuck. Based in Stratford in Essex, his work is well represented in north Wales through his connection with Archdeacon Hugh Chambres Jones, the Rector of West Ham (then an industrial Essex village east of London) who kept a house at Bryn Eisteddfod, near Conwy. Although many more windows by Clutterbuck were made for churches in London and East Anglia, his east window at Llangernyw, if correctly dated to the early 1830s, would be his earliest known work.[12] Chambres Jones funded the rebuilding of the new church at Llansanffraid Glan Conwy in 1839, and commissioned the east window from Clutterbuck, depicting the Magi with Joseph and the Virgin and Child. The patron is reputedly depicted as one of the Magi in the richly

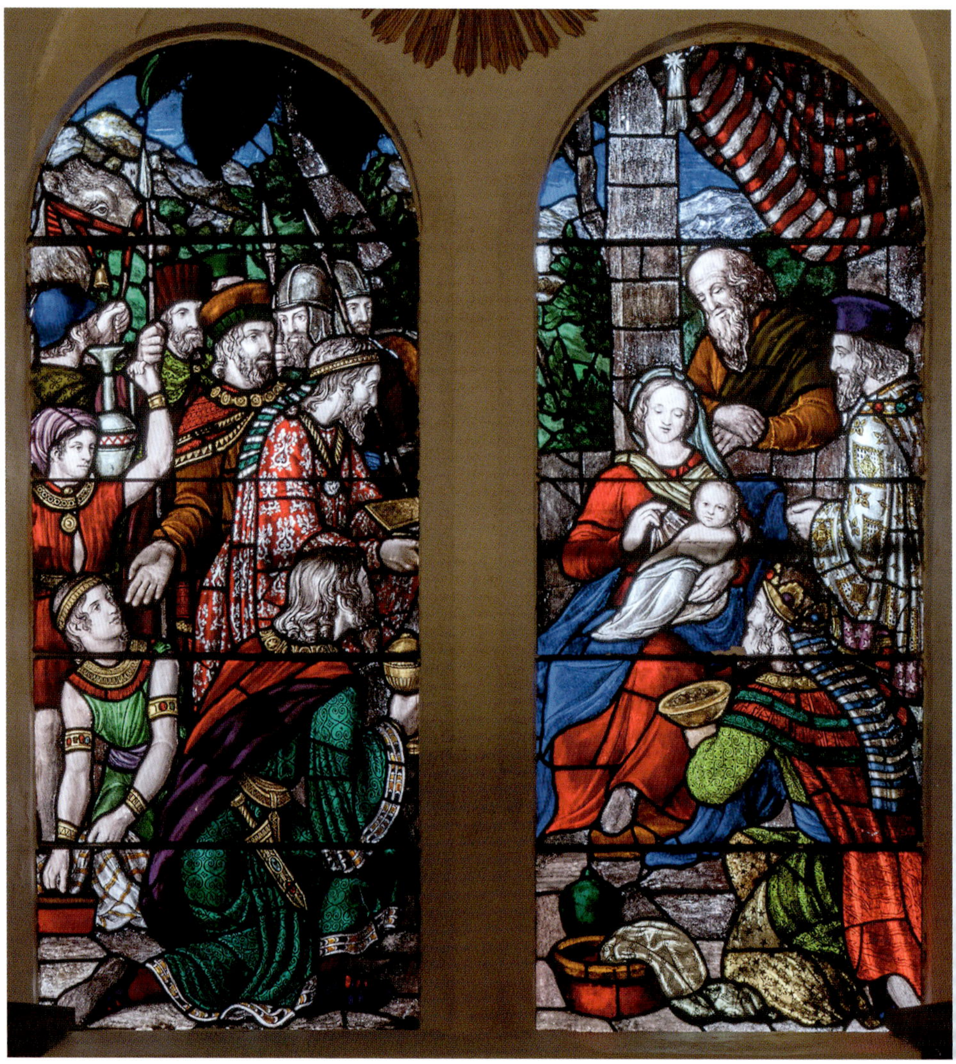

180. Charles Clutterbuck, The Adoration of the Magi, 1839, Church of St Ffraid, Llansanffraid Glan Conwy, east window

12 Mostyn Lewis dates the work according to the assumption that the window was given to the church by the donors before they left their house at Hafodunos in 1830, *Stained Glass in North Wales up to 1850* (Altrincham: John Sherratt and Son Ltd, 1970), p. 64; in fact the house was probably sold in 1833, see Mark Baker, *Hafodunos Hall, Llangernyw, Triumph of the Martyr* (Privately published, 2005), pp. 22–3. The window certainly pre-dates the restoration of the church in 1849, as it was seen by Stephen Glynne in 1847: Stephen Richard Glynne, 'Notes on the Older Churches in the Four Welsh Dioceses', *Archaeologia Cambrensis*, fifth series, vol. i (1884), p. 101. For biographical details of Charles Clutterbuck see Birkin Haward, *Nineteenth Century Suffolk Stained Glass* (Woodbridge: The Boydell Press, 1989), p. 155. Clutterbuck also exhibited versatility in style. For example his work for Ely Cathedral and the Church of St Andrew and St Mary, Watton-at-Stone, Hertfordshire, demonstrates his abilities in a sixteenth-century Flemish style.

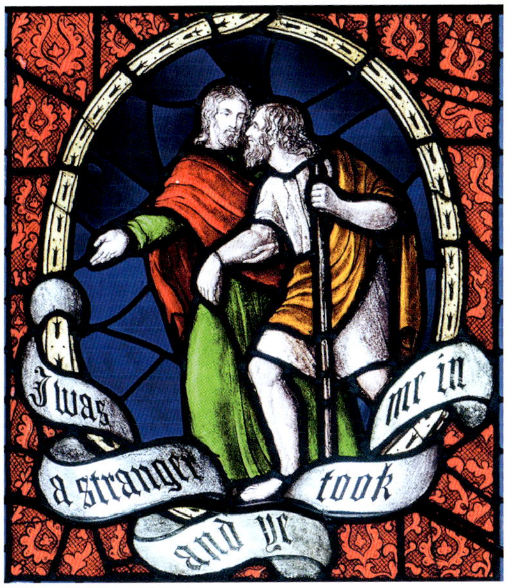

181. Charles Clutterbuck, Sheltering the Stranger, *c.* 1830–3, Church of St Digain, Llangernyw, east window

detailed composition, along with family and servants, and the view of Snowdonia from the patron's house at Bryn Eisteddfod.

Figures of the evangelists of uncertain date at Carmarthen and Haverfordwest are examples of late-Georgian glass painting. At the Church of St Mary, Haverfordwest, small figures of the four evangelists originally adorned the east window, and three are now located in the vestry. At Heol Awst, an Independent Chapel in Carmarthen, two figures depict John and probably Matthew, suggesting that this too was a set of the four evangelists.

Amateur artists from gentry families also painted windows for churches on or near their estates. At the Church of St Mary, Llanwern, small scenes of about 1840 survive in the south chancel window painted by Sarah Salusbury, the daughter of Sir Robert Salusbury. Her east window at the church depicted her brother, the Revd Sir Charles Salusbury, rector of the parish from 1818–68, as Abraham with scenes from the Old Testament, but the window has been lost. The scene with Christ blessing the bread and wine in the south chancel window at Llanwern is similar to a panel by David Evans at the Church of St Mary, Llanfair-yng-Nghornwy, and both are based on the painting by Carlo Dolci of 1670, which was widely reproduced in engravings.[13]

13 The scene is also among the small panels at the Church of St Basil, Bassaleg, thought to be eighteenth-century German work. For the early glass at Llanwern see Joseph Bradney, *A History of Monmouthshire* (Chesterfield: Merton Priory Press, 1994, originally published in twelve parts between 1904 and 1933), vol. 4, part 2, p. 254.

182. (below left) St Matthew, probably second quarter of the nineteenth century, Church of St Mary, Haverfordwest, vestry (from the former east window)

183–4. (below) St Matthew the Evangelist and St John the Evangelist, perhaps *c.* 1826, Heol Awst, Carmarthen, vestibule

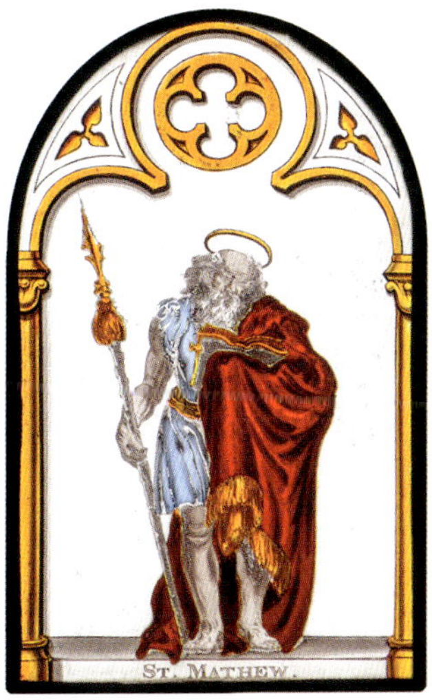

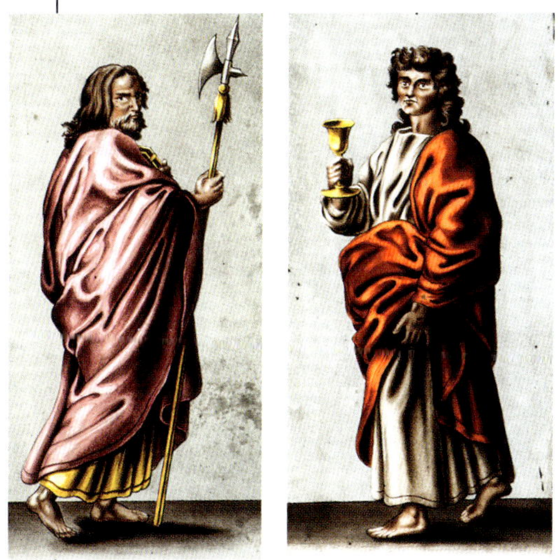

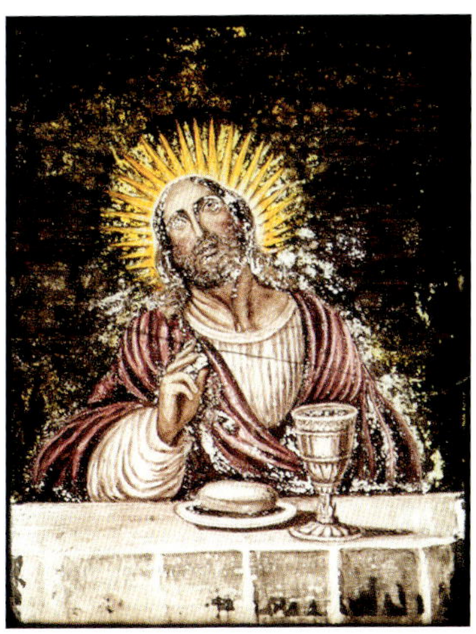

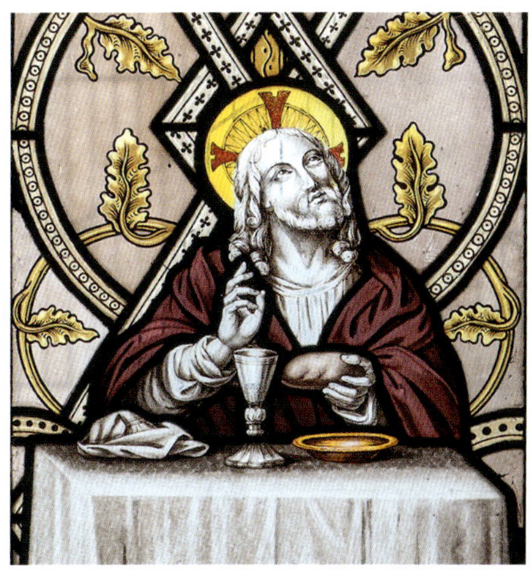

185. (right) Sarah Salusbury, Christ Blessing the Sacrament, *c.* 1840 (after Carlo Dolci), Church of St Mary, Llanwern, chancel

86. (far right) David Evans, Christ Blessing the Sacrament, 1850 (after arlo Dolci), Church of St Mary, Llanfair-yng-Nghornwy, east window

14 See for example the similarity with one of Pugin's examples of 'Revived Sepulchral Brasses', plate vi, *An Apology for the Revival of Christian Architecture in England* (London: John Weale, 1843). The figure in Pugin's design for the brass memorial is depicted kneeling in prayer, rather than as a recumbent effigy.

At the church of St Peter, St Pierre, a window in the sanctuary depicts a recumbent woman holding a child. Fanny Susan Williams died on 22 March 1843 aged 24, and a few weeks later her four-month-old son, Henry Wynne Williams, also died. The mother and child are depicted as effigies on a tomb chest, with a dog at the mother's feet, delineated with dark enamel and a little silver stain. Around them are angels holding texts from the creed: 'I believe in the Communion of Saints' and from the Beatitudes 'Blessed are the pure in heart for they shall see God' (Matthew 5: 8), an expression of faith and hope in the resurrection in the face of tragedy. The depiction of a recumbent effigy in stained glass betrays an emphatic medievalism, in contrast to the numerous wall tablet memorials of the eighteenth and early nineteenth centuries throughout the church. The design is set under crocketed canopies using colours typical of the early fourteenth century, and together with the form of the angels, strongly suggests the influence of A.W.N. Pugin.[14]

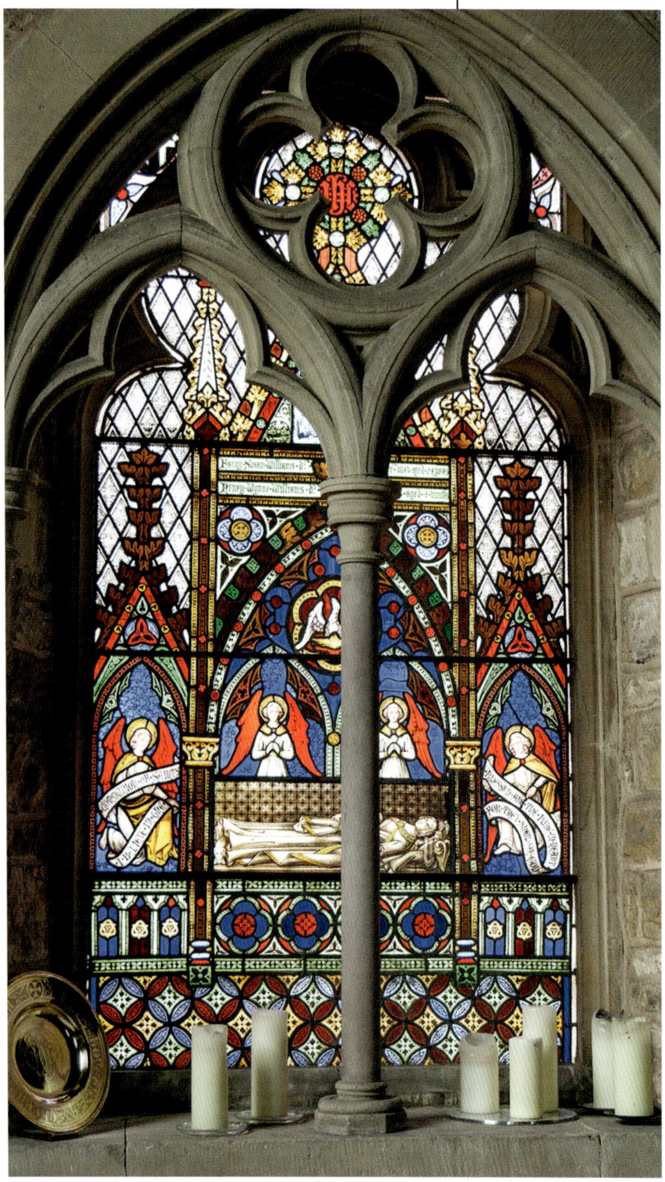

187. Memorial to Fanny Williams, *c.* 1843, Church of St Peter, St Pierre, chancel

By 1843 the Houses of Parliament were being built in a Gothic style, with architectural details and fittings designed by Pugin, and the building did much to popularise the Gothic Revival. A more scholarly approach to Gothic architectural styles had been made possible with the establishment of a better chronology of medieval architectural styles, primarily through the work of the antiquary and architect Thomas Rickman, whose *An Attempt to Discriminate the Styles of English Architecture from the Conquest to the Reformation* was in its fourth edition.[15] Pugin promoted 'pointed' (Early English and Decorated Gothic) architecture as a national style, 'an architecture whose beauties we may claim as our own' and adoption of this Christian architecture amounted to the recovery of England's 'ancient dignity'.[16] In churches this was to be accompanied by sacred symbols and the representation of biblical scenes as well as scenes from the lives of the saints.[17] Pugin's design was at variance

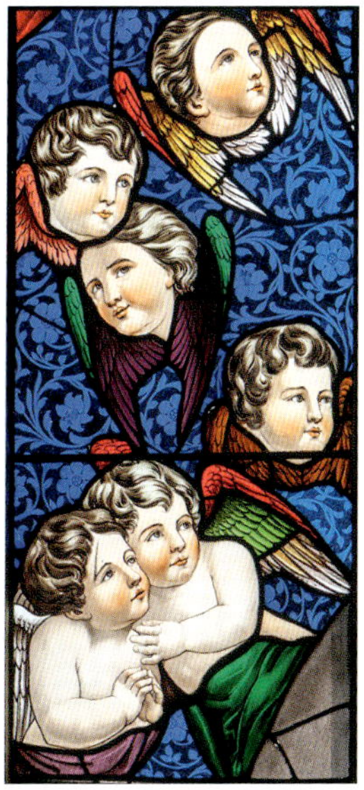

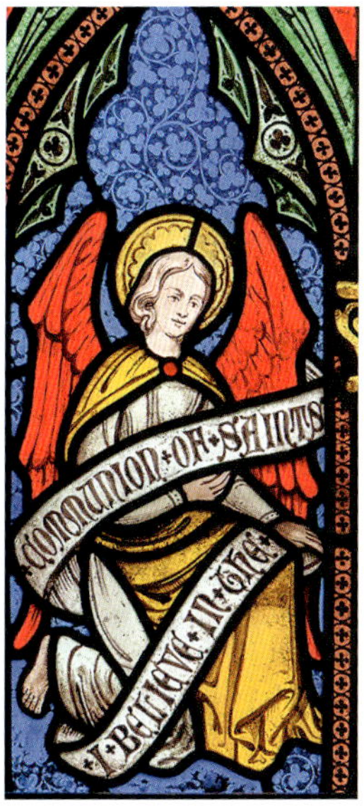

188. Angels, probably second quarter of the nineteenth century, Church of St Mary (Roman Catholic), Monmouth, nave

189. Angel (from Memorial to Fanny Williams), c. 1843, Church of St Peter, St Pierre, chancel

with the prevailing late-Georgian style of religious art, and the dignified angels in the St Pierre window contrast with what Pugin described as 'revived Pagan' cherubs found in a window at the Roman Catholic Church of St Mary, Monmouth. This pre-Reformation Catholic imagery resonated with the efforts of the Oxford Movement to reform the Anglican church in the 1830s and 40s and rediscover its Catholic past. The movement was led by John Henry Newman and Edward Pusey, who, with others including John Keble, published a series of wide-ranging 'Tracts for the Times' and proponents of the Oxford Movement became known as Tractarians.

The interest in medieval liturgy and architecture was also taken up by the Cambridge Camden Society, formed in 1839. The Society did much to shape the taste of patrons and the design of new and restored churches, particularly through its journal *The Ecclesiologist*, whose first issue appeared in November 1841. Complete with pronouncements and diktats on the proper forms for church architecture and fittings, the journal first offered its remarks on stained glass in 1843. The recent works of Thomas Willement and his former pupil William Warrington were commended as 'equal in all respects to the best works of antiquity', while the recent window by David Evans at Ely Cathedral was singled out for criticism.[18] Pugin expressed a preference for the architecture based on the principles of the thirteenth and fourteenth centuries, and churches in this style required stained glass whose form was appropriate to the architecture, complete with images of saints and biblical scenes. Through its journal, the Society expressed its preference for the Middle Pointed or Decorated Gothic style of Thomas Rickman's classification, which had the advantage of being less tainted by the late-medieval excesses of the Catholic church that had given rise to the Reformation.

15 Charles Hanbury-Tracy, first Lord Sudeley, was among the first to adopt a scholarly use of Gothic for the design of his house at Toddington. He also chaired the Commissioners who judged the designs submitted for the new Houses of Parliament in 1835, and remained influential on its design after the commission was awarded to Charles Barry. Megan Aldrich, *Gothic Revival* (London: Phaidon, 1994), pp. 130–8. For Toddington Manor, built 1819–35, see David Verey and Alan Brooks, *The Buildings of England, Gloucestershire 2: The Vale and The Forest of Dean* (London/New Haven: Yale University Press, 2002), p. 767. In contrast, Charles Hanbury-Tracy's house at Gregynog was built in a Tudor Revival style in 1840.

16 A. Welby Pugin, *An Apology for the Revival of Christian Architecture in England* (London: John Weale, 1843), pp. 6, 51.

17 A. Welby Pugin, *An Apology*, p. 29.

18 *The Ecclesiologist*, vol. ii (1843), pp. 16–17. David Evans was evidently aware of their criticism, and wrote to the journal correcting the complaint that the window cost 'the enormous sum of £500', pointing out that it cost only £310, published in *The Ecclesiologist*, vol. iv (1845), p. 292.

The 1840s saw an increase in the study and appreciation of medieval styles of stained glass. The publication of Charles Winston's *An Inquiry into the Difference of Style Observable in Ancient Glass Paintings* in 1847 classified stained glass styles and periods. In the work he broadly followed Thomas Rickman's classification of medieval architecture, dividing the styles as Early English (to 1280), Decorated (1280–1380), Perpendicular (1380–1530), Cinque Cento (1500–1550) and Intermediate (after 1550). Winston was a barrister who had taken a keen interest in stained glass, drawing medieval examples and gaining practical knowledge from the glass painters Joseph Hale Miller and Thomas Ward. He advised Joseph Bell of Bristol on the restoration of the medieval glass at Bristol Cathedral, and designed windows made by the studio of Thomas Ward & James Henry Nixon from about 1836. Sometime during the 1840s he collaborated with Ward & Nixon on a finely-executed heraldic window for the Church of St Sadwrn, Henllan (Denbighshire).[19]

19 Charles Winston promoted the work of George Hedgeland after 1853, but still regarded Ward & Nixon highly in 1856: 'Ward stands supreme as a master of ornamental detail, and he has an assistant who draws well.' Letter to C.H. Wilson, 21 March 1856, published in *Memoirs illustrative of the Art of Glass-Painting* (London: John Murray, 1865), p. 18. Winston and his father are commemorated in a window in the Church of St Thomas, Rhyl, by, appropriately enough, Henry Hughes, who was probably the assistant to whom Winston referred. Hughes became a partner of Thomas Ward by 1857, and remained the principal artist of the firm until Hughes' death in 1883. Winston also worked with Ward, Nixon and Hughes in their restorations of medieval glass, using the new antique glass that he had helped James Powell & Sons to manufacture. See A.C. Sewter 'The Place of Charles Winston in the Victorian Revival of the Art of Stained Glass', *Journal of the British Archaeological Association*, vol. 24 (1961), pp. 80–91; Martin Harrison, *Victorian Stained Glass* (London: Barrie & Jenkins, 1980), pp. 37–8.

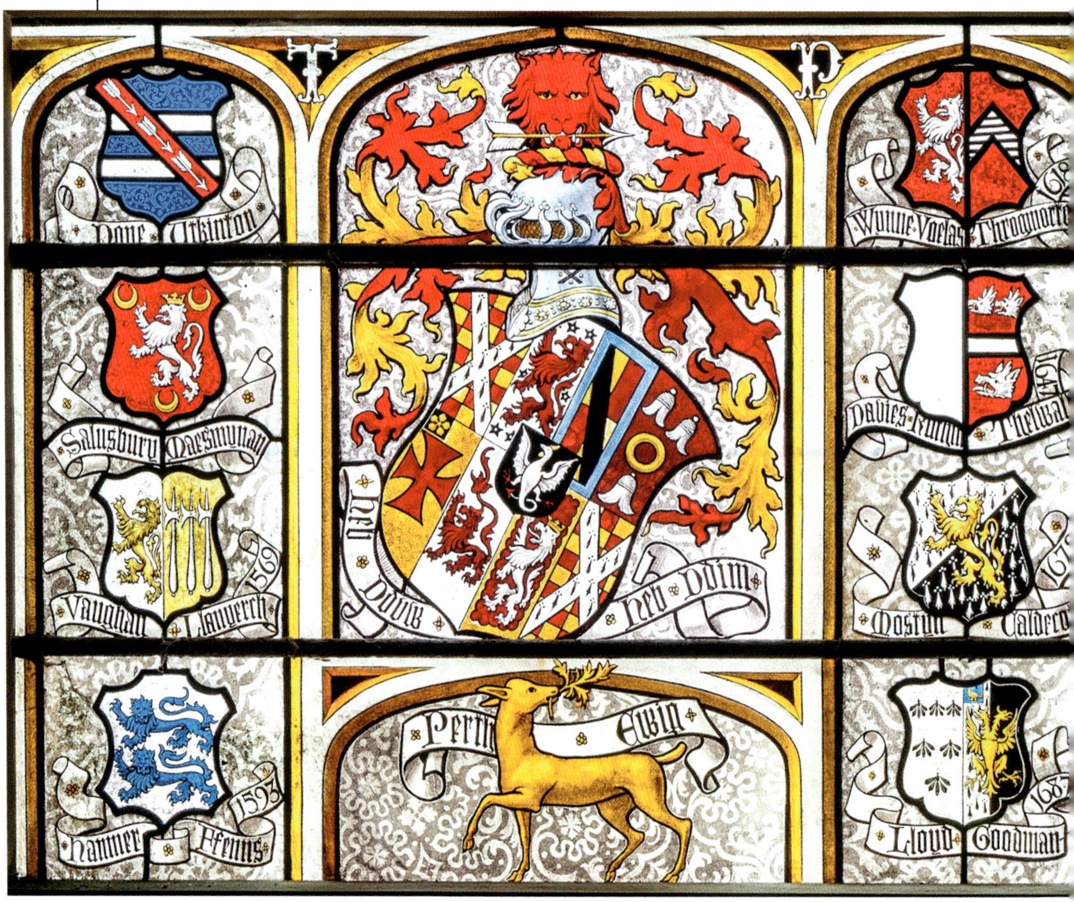

190. Ward & Nixon, Heraldic Window, probably 1840s, designed by Charles Winston, Church of St Sadwrn, Henllan, nave

The antiquary James Heywood Markland recommended the use of stained glass as an alternative to wall tablets for commemorating family members in his influential *Remarks on Sepulchral Monuments*, published in 1842.[20] Markland's criticism of 'the heathen trash' depicted on mural monuments was welcomed in a review of the book in *The Gentleman's Magazine*,[21] and the practice was also encouraged by writers in *The Ecclesiologist* and in the architectural journal *The Builder* as a way of beautifying the church. In a review of some examples of stained glass placed in churches in *The Builder*, the writer comments: 'The erection of these windows affords us an opportunity of suggesting to our readers the desirability of commemorating their deceased friends by memorial windows, instead of the wretched marble monuments (stone placards, as somebody calls them) which disfigure churches, and are really as expensive as painted windows.' The sum of 20/. for a single light, the writer continues, was about the same as a 'dab of marble'.[22] The piety encouraged among the gentry also resulted in the transition from windows displaying family heraldry to those representing biblical themes or saints for memorial windows. At the Church of St Beuno, Aberffraw, the memorial to Owen Roberts of Bwlan, who died in 1849, takes the theme of Faith, Hope and Charity, with Charity represented by the parable of the Good Samaritan.

From 1838 A.W.N. Pugin worked with a number of glass painters who made windows to his design, although the results were not always to his satisfaction. He became frustrated with the interpretation of his designs by William Warrington. 'The glass-painters will shorten my days,' he wrote in 1841, 'they are the greatest plagues I have'. Pugin complained that Warrington had become 'conceited, and got nearly as expensive as Willement'.[23] Warrington and Willement were undercut by new studios such as that established by William Wailes in Newcastle, who made windows for Pugin until 1845, when Pugin persuaded his friend John Hardman of Birmingham to set up a stained glass studio. There are few windows in Welsh churches that are the result of this

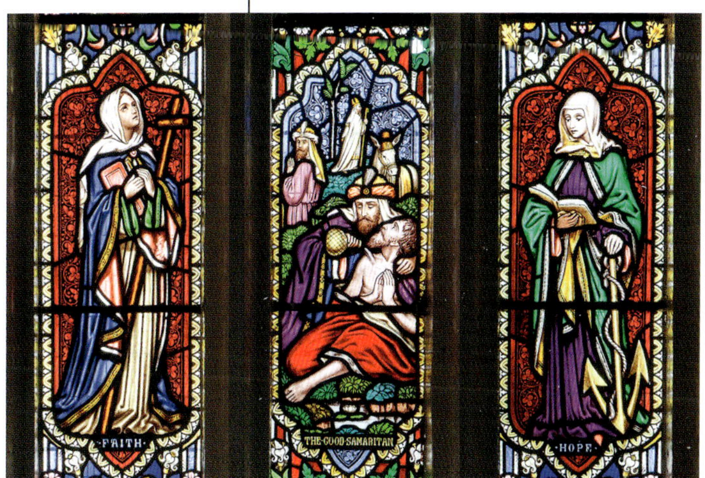

191. Charles Gibbs, Faith, Hope & Charity, *c.* 1850, Church of St Beuno, Aberffraw, north nave

20 In 1859 James Markland gave a window by the firm of Michael & Arthur O'Connor at Llandaff Cathedral, in memory of the dean of the Cathedral, William Daniel Conybeare (1787–1857). Nevil A. James, 'The Stained Glass of Llandaff Cathedral' in Nick Lambert (ed.), *Llandaff Cathedral* (Bridgend: Seren, 2010), p. 173. James states that Markland (1788–1864) was the dean's son-in-law, but the two were near contemporaries, and according to the *Dictionary of National Biography*, Markland's only daughter, Elizabeth Jane, married the Revd Charles R. Conybeare, presumably one of the dean's six children.

21 *The Gentleman's Magazine*, vol. 171 (April 1842), pp. 403–5.

22 *The Builder*, vol. 9 (18 January 1851), p. 44.

23 J. Knowles, 'Glass-Painters 1750–1850', *Journal of the British Society of Master Glass-Painters*, vol. xiii, no. 3 (1961–2), p. 522.

formative collaboration prior to Pugin's early death in 1852, although examples survive in the south wall of the chancel at the Church of St Paul, Bryncoedifor, and the south transept at the Church of St Michael and All Angels, Castlemartin.[24]

Pugin's influence is visible in the independent works by William Wailes, William Warrington and Thomas Willement, and their association with Pugin enhanced their reputations and informed their approach to the design and manufacture of stained glass.[25] For example, the scenes by Willement from the former east window at the Church of St Cadoc, Trevethin, echo Pugin in the sensitive medievalist depictions of five scenes from the Life of Christ.

Willement returned to Swansea to provide fine armorial glass in the Vivian Memorial Chapel of the Church of St Paul, Sketty in about 1850.[26] The architect of the church was Henry Woodyer, who, like his patron Henry Hussey Vivian, was a staunch Anglo-Catholic. Elsewhere Woodyer had commissioned glass from John Hardman, but on this occasion

24 See Stanley A. Shepherd, *The stained glass of A.W.N. Pugin* (Reading: Spire Books, 2009), pp. 390–1.

25 The expanded edition of James Heywood Markland, *Remarks on English Churches and on the expediency of rendering sepulchral memorials subservient to pious and Christian uses* (Oxford: John Henry Parker, 1843), included a list of works by William Wailes, indicating the esteem in which his studio's work was held in the 1840s.

26 The mural scheme that he designed for the chapel is not extant and may not have been executed. John Newman, *The Buildings of Wales: Glamorgan* (London: Penguin Books, 1995), p. 618.

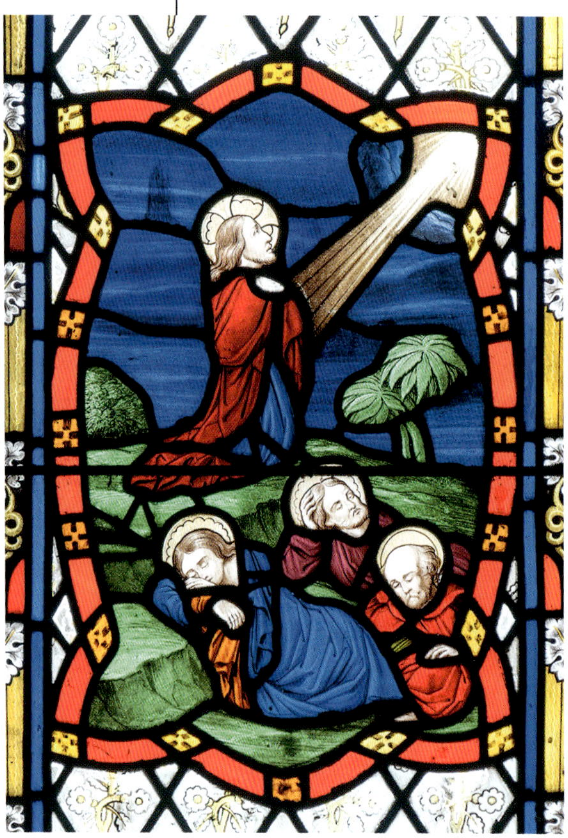

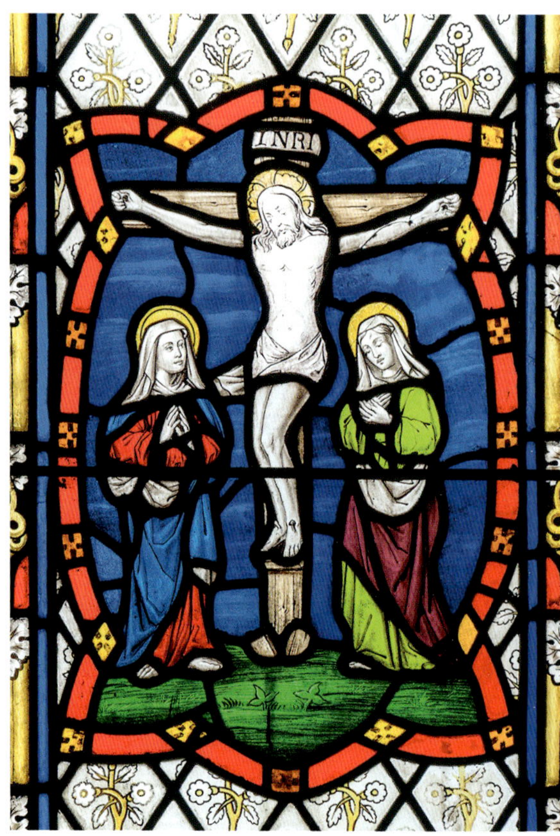

192–3. Thomas Willement, Christ in the Garden of Gethsemane (right) and The Crucifixion (far right), 1847, Church of St Cadoc, Trevethin, south transept (from the former east window)

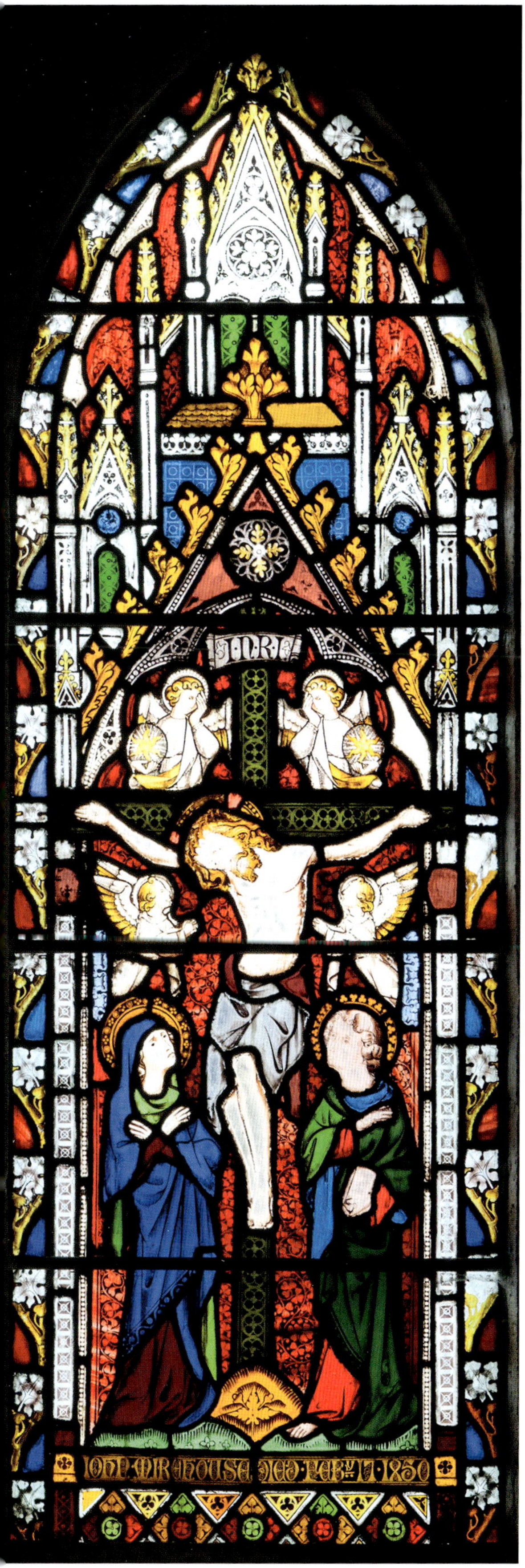

194. John Hardman & Co., The Crucifixion, 1850, designed by A.W.N. Pugin, Church of St Michael and All Angels, Castlemartin, south transept

he turned to William Warrington for the east and west windows. The influence of Pugin in the design and colouration is clear in the surviving window, but the quality of the figure drawing is poor, particularly in comparison with the later window by William Wailes with scenes of the Good Samaritan in the north wall of the chancel, which was given in 1856 in memory of Henry Hussey Vivian's father, John Henry Vivian, by his wife and children.[27]

27 For a full description and discussion of these works see F.G. Cowley, *A History of St. Paul's Church, Sketty, Swansea* (Swansea, 2001), especially pp. 5–8 and Maurice Broady's chapter, 'The Stained Glass Windows and Decorative Art', pp. 86-109. The poor drawing, or medieval 'mannerism' of some windows by William Warrington was attacked by the *Ecclesiologist*, vol. x (1849), p. 91; see also Martin Harrison, *Victorian Stained Glass* (London: Barrie & Jenkins, 1980), p. 22.

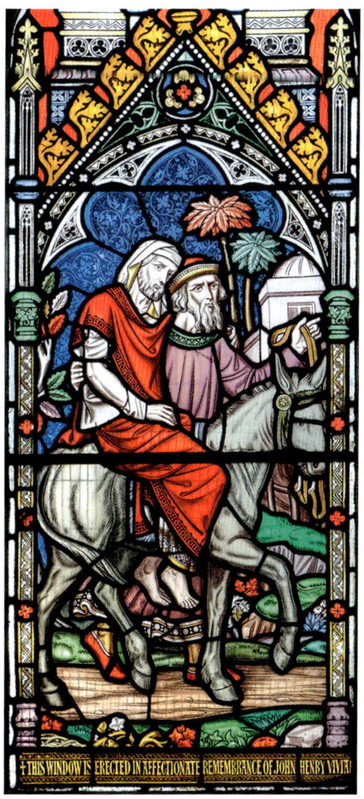

195. (below left) William Wailes, The Good Samaritan, 1856, Church of St Paul, Sketty, chancel

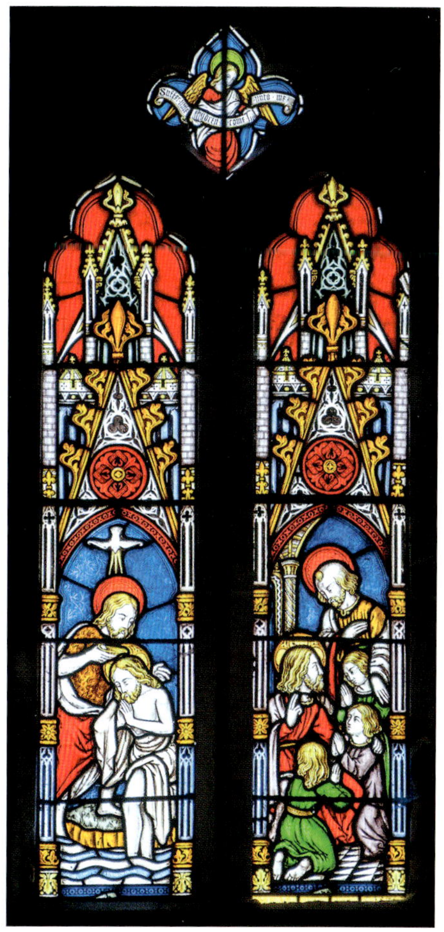

196. (below) William Warrington, The Baptism of Christ and Christ with Children, *c.* 1850, Church of St Paul, Sketty, baptistry (tower)

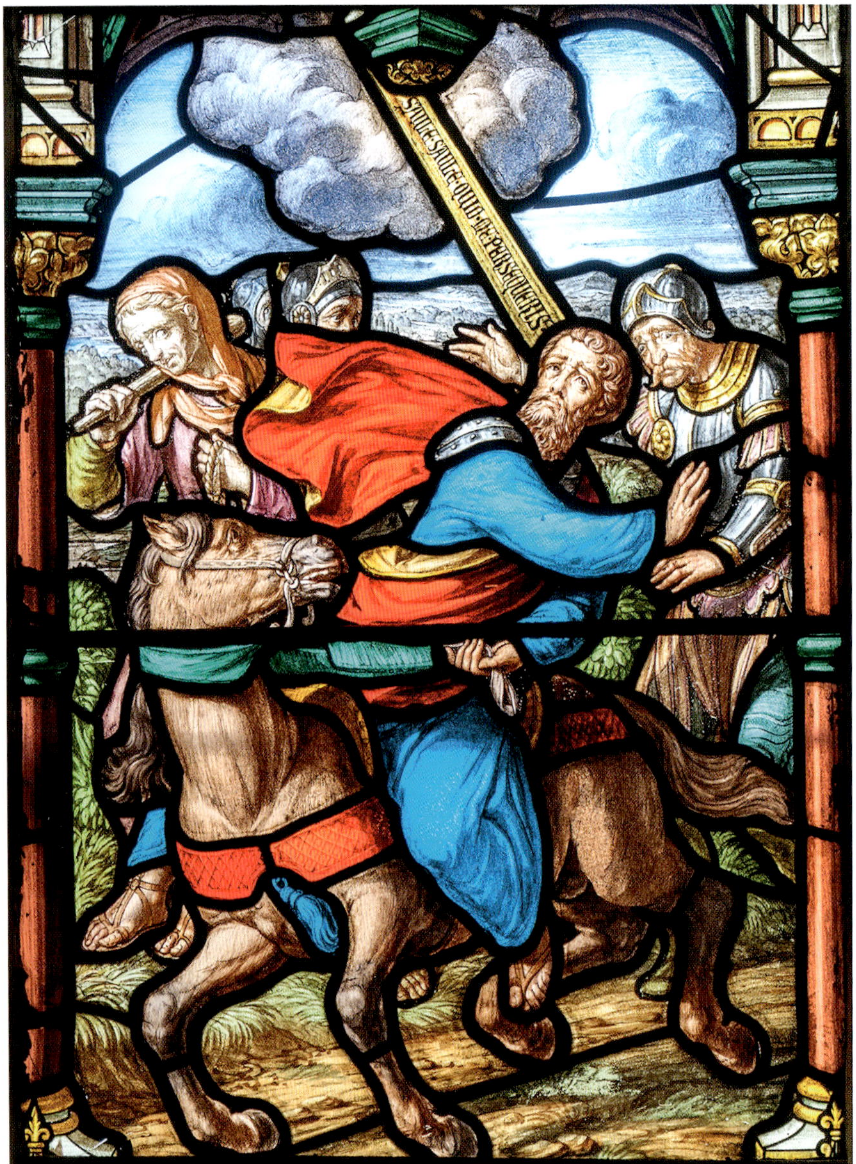

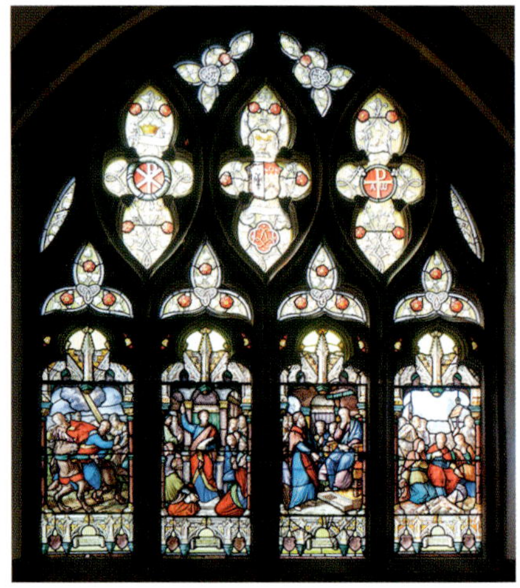

197–8. Gsell-Laurent, Scenes from the Life of St Paul (above right), including The Conversion of St Paul (above), 1853, Church of St Paul, Sketty, south aisle

In a church built according to the 'true principles' of A.W.N. Pugin, with stained glass in an early fourteenth-century style, the four-light window in the nave made in 1853 comes as a surprise. The window was made by the French firm of Gsell-Laurent, and the four biblical scenes from the life of St Paul are painted in an early sixteenth-century style and set under late Gothic canopies.[28] The window undermines the initial visual unity of the stained glass in the church and prefigures a tendency to add stained glass of different styles to churches during successive decades.

As churches were restored and rebuilt in the second half of the nineteenth century, architects were not afraid to dislodge the early Gothic Revival windows. At Sketty, Warrington's east window is no longer extant, probably lost when the chancel was enlarged in 1928. Restorations by Gilbert Scott displaced the east windows by Francis Eginton at St Asaph Cathedral and by David Evans at Bangor Cathedral, where the glass occupied its location in the chancel for only thirty years before it was moved to the west end of the building. Other east windows of the mid-nineteenth century can also be found relocated in other windows. The Crucifixion of 1850 by James Powell & Sons at Bryncoedifor was moved to the vestry in 1895, while Willement's former east window at Trevethin is virtually out of sight in the west wall of the south transept.[29]

28 The window was given by William Jones Loyd, a contemporary of Hussey Vivian at Eton and Trinity College, Cambridge. Maurice Broady, 'The Stained Glass Windows and Decorative Art' in F.G. Cowley, *A History of St. Paul's Church, Sketty, Swansea* (Swansea, 2001), p. 93.

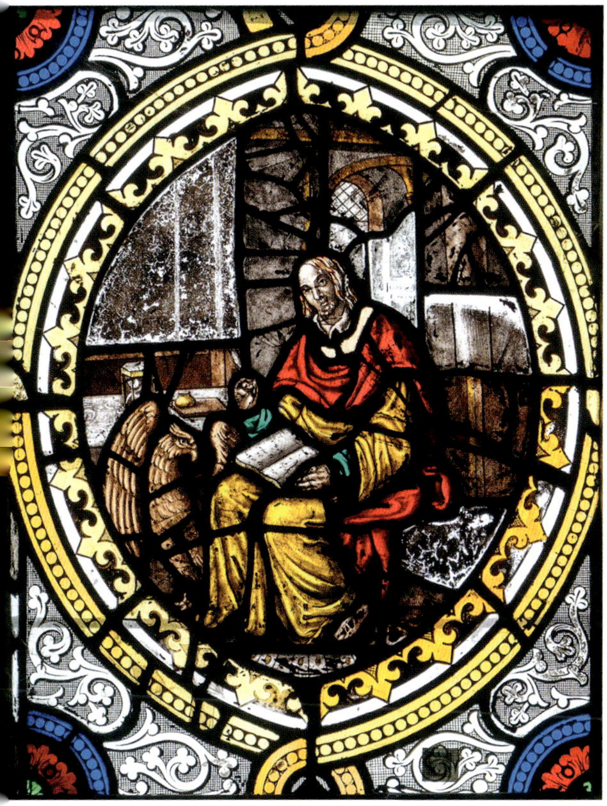

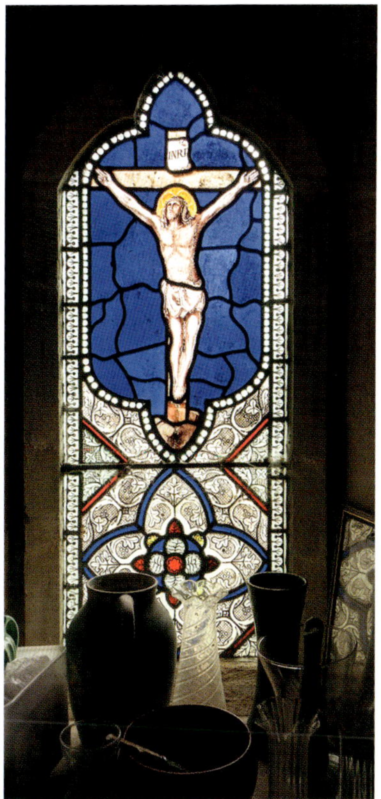

199. (far left) St John the Evangelist, possibly 1830s, Church of St Aidan, Llawhaden, east window

200. (left) James Powell & Sons, The Crucifixion, 1850, Church of St Paul, Bryncoedifor, vestry (from the former east window)

In some instances earlier Victorian glass did survive rebuilding or restoration, such as the roundels of the four evangelists at the Church of St Aidan, Llawhaden. The church was reopened after restoration in 1862 and the scenes, which could date to an earlier restoration in the 1830s, have been incorporated in new decorative glass surrounds.

The displacement of many windows from their intended locations has helped to eclipse the reputations of artists such as David Evans and Charles Clutterbuck. While windows such as Clutterbuck's east window at Llangernyw have been recently restored, other works of the 1830s and 40s have been lost. A further window in Wales by Eginton, a half-length figure of Christ in the east window of the Church of St Collen, Llangollen, was lost during the remodelling in the mid-1860s.[30] The only known work in Wales attributed to Joseph Hale Miller, an artist admired by Charles Winston, was made for the Priory Church of St Mary, Chepstow in 1841 and has since been lost.[31] At Abergele the east window of five lights depicting seven virtues was painted in 1850 by Mrs Jones-Bateman of Pentre Mawr, in memory of her husband, but was replaced and lost in the 1920s, by which time it had become damaged, and was no doubt of a style no longer in keeping with the times.[32]

29 The new glazing scheme at Bryncoedifor left the window designed by Pugin of 1850 in situ in the south wall of the chancel, where it is not even visible from the top of the chancel steps.

30 The window was recorded in Samuel Lewis, *A Topographical Dictionary of Wales* (London: S. Lewis & Co., 1848, third edition), vol. ii, p. 44. It is referred to as a depiction of Christ in the Garden of Gethsemane in 'Glass Painters of Birmingham, Francis Eginton, 1737–1805', *Journal of the British Society of Master Glass-Painters*, vol. ii, no. 2 (October 1927), p. 68.

31 The attribution to Joseph Hale Miller has been questioned by Michael Kerney, who suggests that it may have instead been the work of William Miller, whose relationship with Joseph Hale Miller has not yet been established, but who apparently inherited the studio of the older artist. Michael Kerney, 'Joseph Hale Miller (1777–1842) and the Revival of Gothic Glass Painting', *The Journal of Stained Glass*, vol. xxxiii (2009), p. 73 (footnote 83). The London artist William Miller went on to make several windows in Glamorgan in the 1850s, see chapter four.

32 D.R. Thomas, *The History of the Diocese of St Asaph* (Oswestry: Caxton Press, 1913), vol. iii, p. 191.

At the Church of St Peter and St Eurgain at Northop, the east window by Michael O'Connor of 1850, set within a text-book Geometrical Gothic-traceried window designed by the architect William Butterfield, remains gloriously in situ, while most of the three-light east window of the north aisle painted a few years earlier by Clutterbuck in 1839 has been removed. Clutterbuck's work, as well as that by David Evans, has often suffered from the subsequent loss of the black enamel, which can be seen on two other windows of the 1850s by Clutterbuck at Northop, and glass from another former east window by the artist, at the Church of St Berres, Llanferres. These windows, and others such as his Adoration of the Magi at Llansantffraid Glan Conwy, are now in need of restoration. Not a fan of the Victorian Gothic Revival, Mostyn Lewis described this window, also of 1839, as the most beautiful mid-nineteenth century window in north Wales.[33]

33 Mostyn Lewis, *Stained Glass in North Wales up to 1850* (Altrincham: John Sherratt and Son Ltd, 1970), p. 75.

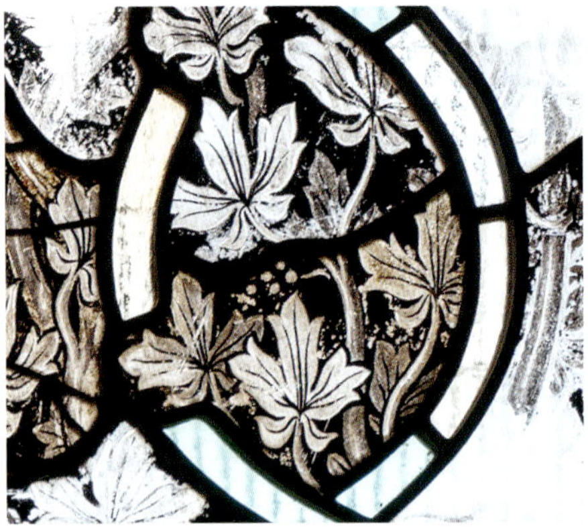

201. Charles Clutterbuck, Detail from the former east window, 1844, Church of St Berres, Llanferres, west wall

202. Charles Clutterbuck, Blind Faith, *c.* 1856, Church of St Peter and St Eurgain, Northop, nave

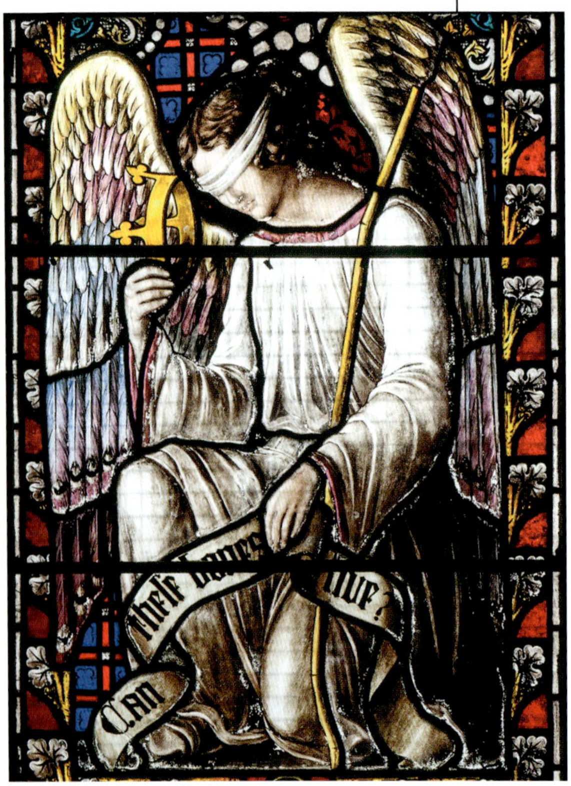

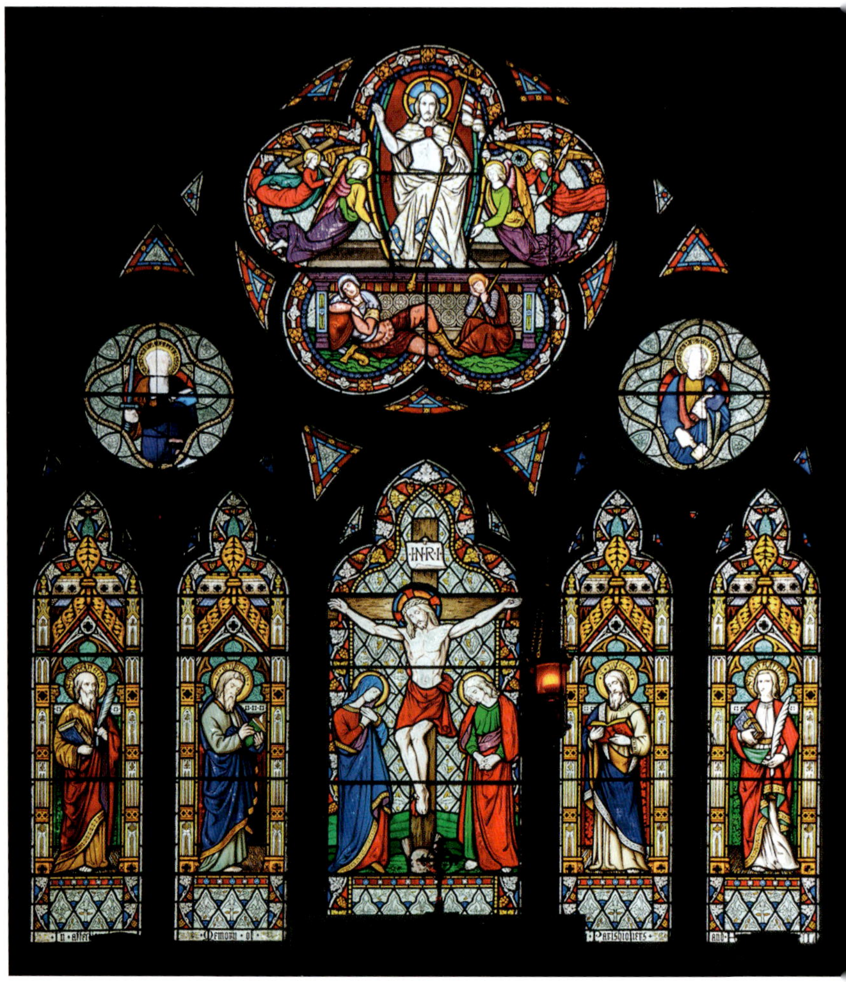

203. Michael O'Connor, The Crucifixion, the Resurrection and the Four Evangelists, 1850, Church of St Peter and St Eurgain, Northop, east window

Chapter Four

Tractarians, Ecclesiologists and the Puginian Vision

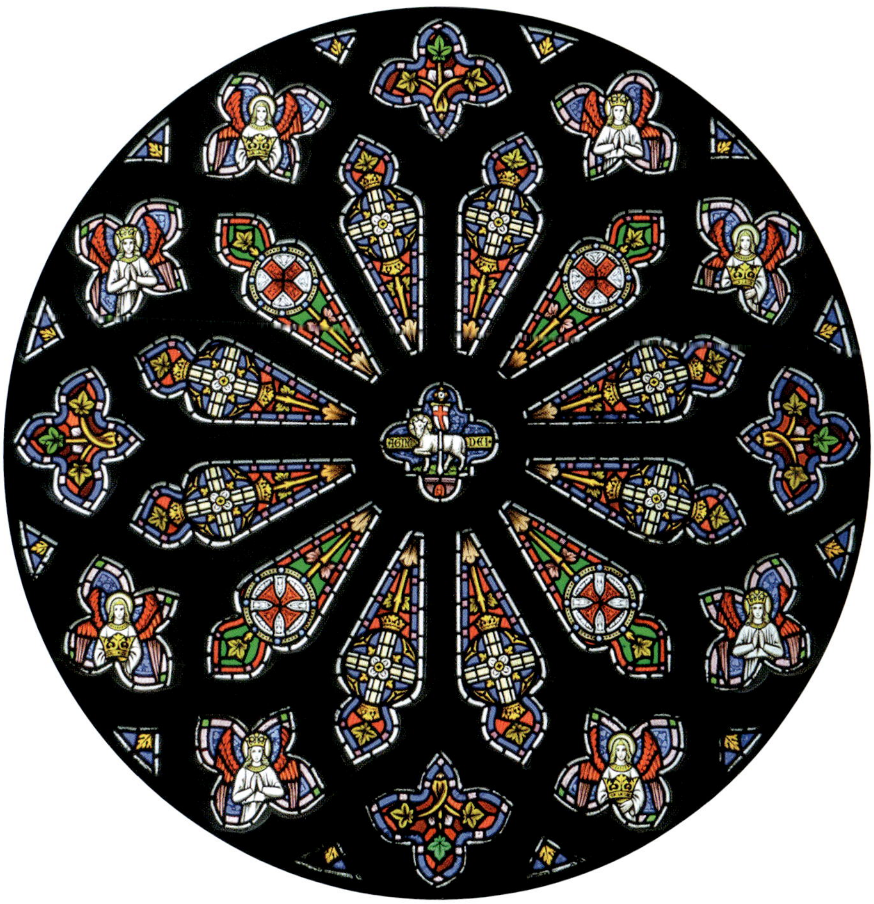

The change in taste that displaced early Gothic Revival windows developed out of a new, medievalist, vision of what churches should look like. A.W.N. Pugin promoted an ideal of a church interior to inspire faith and worship: beautiful and appropriate, mystical and practical:

> It is, indeed, a sacred place; and well does the fabric bespeak its destined purpose: the eye is carried up and lost in the height of the vaulting and the intricacy of the aisles; the rich and varied hues of the stained windows, the modulated light, the gleam of the tapers, the richness of the altars, the venerable images of the departed just,—all alike conspire to fill the mind with veneration for the place, and to make it feel the sublimity of Christian worship.[1]

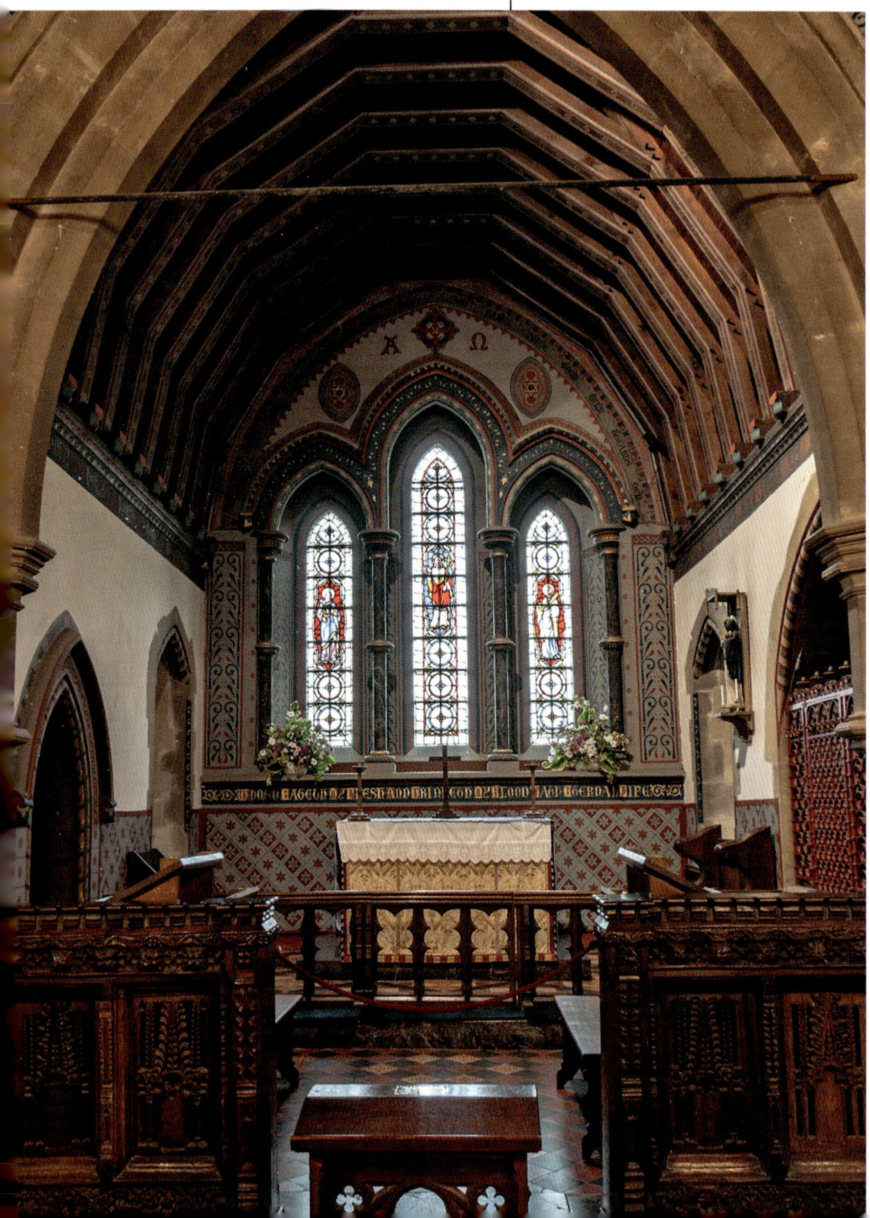

This Puginian vision was taken up enthusiastically by the Tractarians and the Ecclesiological Society during the 1840s and 1850s.[2] It was also adopted at the outset of what became a widespread programme of church building and restoration undertaken across the country, affording architects the opportunity to conceive interiors as an architectural whole, incorporating fittings and furnishings. The manipulation of space, light and colour, through the juxtaposition of architectural sculpture, woodwork and metalwork, ceramic tiles, stained glass, murals and altar cloths, created both splendour and harmony, while communicating the message of salvation.[3]

By the shore of Llangorse Lake, a church built by Robert Raikes at Llangasty Tal-y-llyn in Breconshire was a deliberate attempt to introduce Tractarian liturgical practices into the area. Raikes bought the mansion at Treberfydd in 1848, and entrusted the

205. John Loughborough Pearson, Church of St Gastyn, Llangasty Tal-y-llyn, 1849, stained glass by William Wailes

204. (Title page) Michael & Arthur O'Connor, Rose Window, 18
Church of St Margaret of Antioch, Bodelwyddan, north a

1 A.W.N. Pugin, *Contrasts; or, a parallel between the architecture of the fourteenth and fifteenth centuries, and similar buildings of the present day; shewing the present decay of taste* (Salisbury, 1836), p. 2.

2 The Cambridge Camden Society was renamed the Ecclesiological Society in 1845.

3 A detailed study of two ecclesiological glazing schemes of *c.* 1845 and *c.* 1850, is provided in Jim Cheshire, *Stained glass and the Victorian Gothic Revival* (Manchester: Manchester University Press, 2004), pp. 142–54.

206. (right) William Wailes, The Crucifixion, 1843, Church of All Saints, Llangorwen, east window

207. (far right) William Wailes, Christ with Children, 1849, Church of St Gastyn, Llangasty Tal-y-llyn, tower

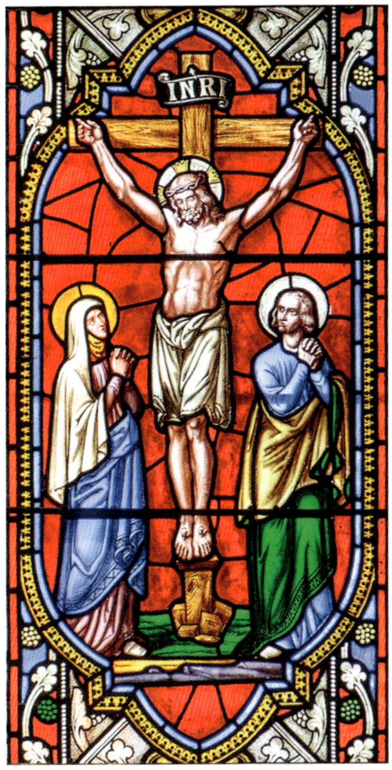

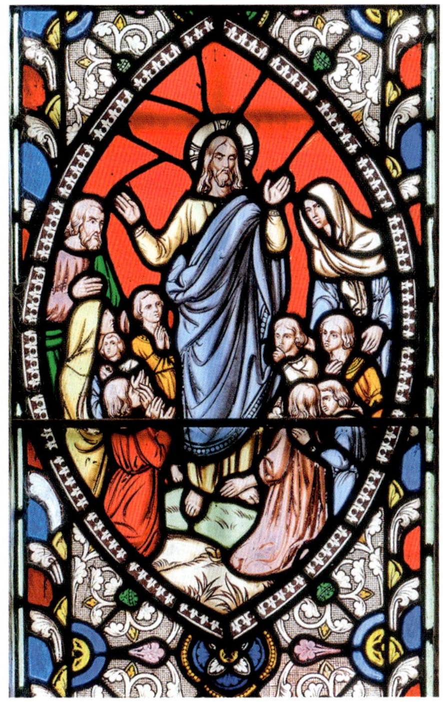

young architect John Loughborough Pearson with the transformation of the eighteenth-century mansion and the rebuilding of the medieval church. Together with a new school and rectory, the church and Treberfydd House demonstrate Pearson's close adherence to the ideals of both Pugin and the Tractarians, following earlier work in the 1840s for Tractarian patrons in Yorkshire.[4] The chancel is decorated with stained glass, patterned tiles and stencilled mural design, and a hint of continuity with the Catholic past was provided by the reuse of parts of the medieval rood screen as a low chancel screen. The three-light east window was made in 1849 by William Wailes, and there are five other single-light windows with figurative glass by the firm. The remaining windows were filled with decorative grisaille panels with geometric designs using some red and blue glass.[5]

In 1842 Wailes made the east window for the Church of All Saints, Llangorwen, where biblical scenes are also enclosed in lozenges amid decorative geometric patterns. The east window here is larger than the windows at Llangasty Tal-y-llyn, with eight subjects from the Gospels and Christ in Majesty at the top of the central light. The church had been designed by Henry Jones Underwood for M.D. Williams of Cwmcynfelin, whose brother was the Tractarian theologian and poet Isaac Williams. Isaac Williams had been John Henry Newman's curate at his church at Littlemore in Oxfordshire, also designed by Underwood, and at Llangorwen the Tractarian inclination is signalled by the presence of what was the first stone altar in Wales since the Reformation.[6] Windows designed by A.W.N. Pugin were being made by Wailes around the time that the Llangorwen window was made, and although it is not his work, Pugin's influence is clear in the adoption of a thirteenth-century Gothic form.

4 For a description of the group of buildings at Treberfydd and Llangasty Tal-y-llyn see Robert Scourfield and Richard Haslam, *The Buildings of Wales: Powys* (New Haven/London: Yale University Press, 2013), pp. 520–3; and Anthony Quiney, *John Loughborough Pearson* (New Haven and London: Yale University Press, 1979), pp. 27–36, who describes the work as a 'Tractarian Utopia', p. 36.

5 Four of these nave windows were subsequently replaced with pictorial stained glass by Clayton & Bell.

6 The church was praised by *The Ecclesiologist* as 'one of the most complete and successful imitations of ancient models that the present age has produced', vol. i (January 1842), p. 47. For the church at Llangorwen and Tractarian activity across Wales see John Morgan-Guy, 'The Oxford Movement and its Effect in Wales', *The Welsh Journal of Religious History*, vol. 6 (2011), pp. 49–68.

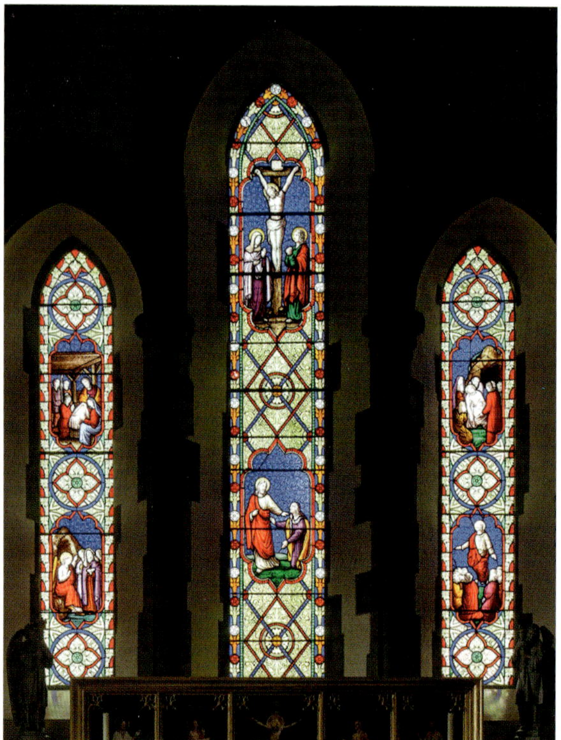

208. Joseph Bell, Scenes from the Life of Christ, 1852, Church of St Thomas, St Dogmaels, east window

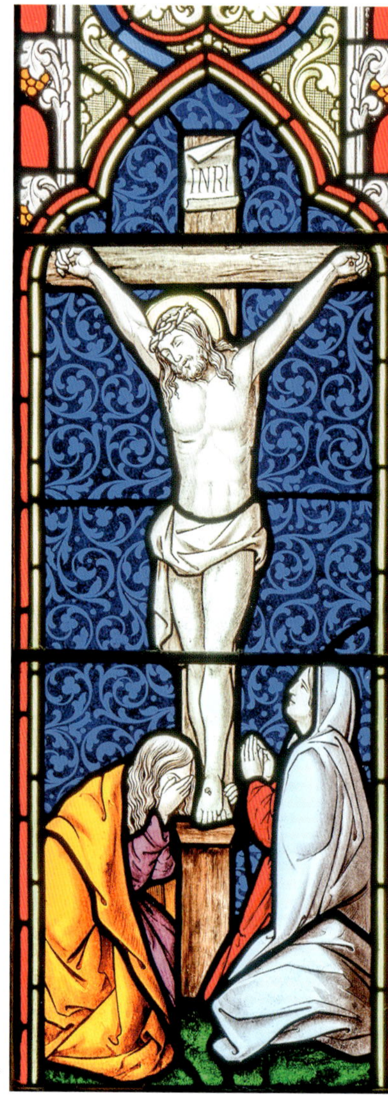

209. Joseph Bell, The Crucifixion, 1849, Church of St Tewdric, Mathern, chancel

A similar arrangement of scenes in medallions surrounded by geometric patterned glass can be found further down the Cardigan Bay coast in Pembrokeshire, at the Church of St Thomas, St Dogmaels. The three-light east window of the chancel was made by Joseph Bell of Bristol for another Tractarian patron and antiquary, the Revd H.J. Vincent, vicar of the parish. Aware of the importance of Tractarian patrons to help with gaining commissions, Bell actively courted them by joining the Bristol and West of England Architectural Society, and turned his attention to a closer modelling on medieval Gothic styles as required by discerning ecclesiologically-minded patrons. Like David Evans, Joseph Bell was capable of working in a number of styles. His restoration of the sixteenth-century glass at the Church of St Asaph and St Cynderyn, Llanasa, is hard to distinguish from the original sixteenth-century painting, while the first of his two windows at the Church of St Tewdric, Mathern, is designed in a fourteenth-century style.[7]

The Church of St John the Baptist at Pentrobin in Flintshire was built in the Early English style at a cost of over £3,000 for Sir Stephen Glynne of Hawarden in 1843. Glynne was an antiquarian and had joined the Cambridge Camden Society, along with his brother-in-law W.E. Gladstone, in 1841. *The Ecclesiologist* did not report on the building of the church, but its views on church architecture were shared by the *North Wales Chronicle*: 'The church is in fact a complete gem; and affords convincing evidence that an impulse has lately been given to

7 The central panel of this window may also be found at Buckland Dinham in Somerset, illustrated in the chapter on Joseph Bell in Jim Cheshire, *Stained glass and the Victorian Gothic Revival* (Manchester: Manchester University Press, 2004), pp. 107-141.

8 *North Wales Chronicle*, 1 August 1843.

9 It is also likely that J.E. Troughton came under the influence of the Cambridge Camden Society while at Corpus Christi College, Cambridge, prior to his appointment in 1843. The windows were memorials to Lavinia Glynne, the wife of the rector of Hawarden, Henry Glynne, who was the brother of Stephen Glynne. T.W. Pritchard, *A History of the Old Parish of Hawarden* (Wrexham: Bridge Books, 2002), p. 166.

10 For further detail on the scheme at Pentrobin see Martin Crampin, 'Biblical Art from Wales: The Mediaeval Influence' in *Biblical Art from Wales* (Sheffield: Sheffield Phoenix Press, 2010), pp. 124–5.

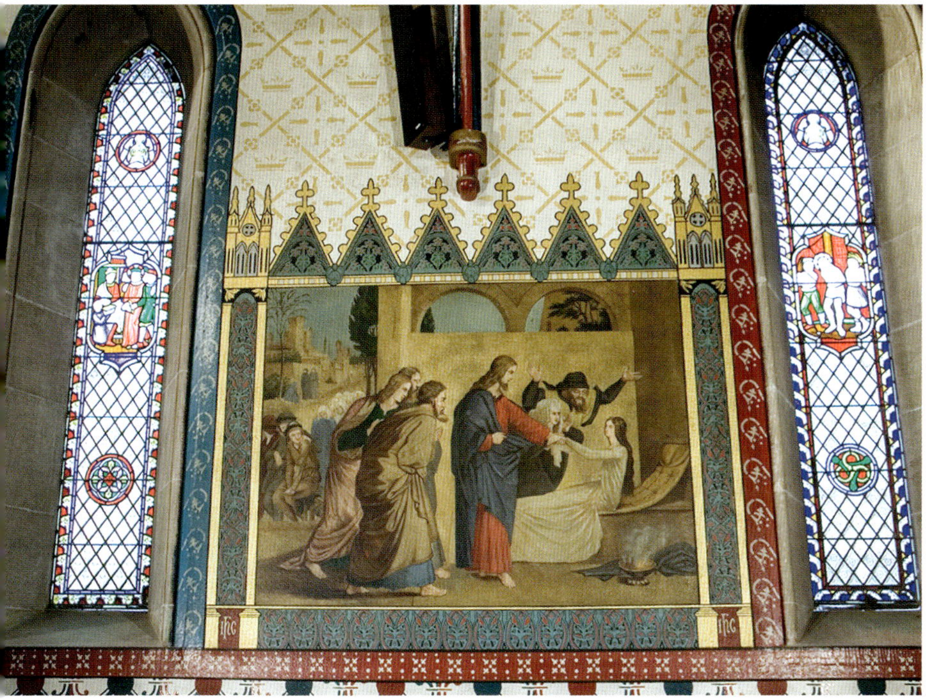

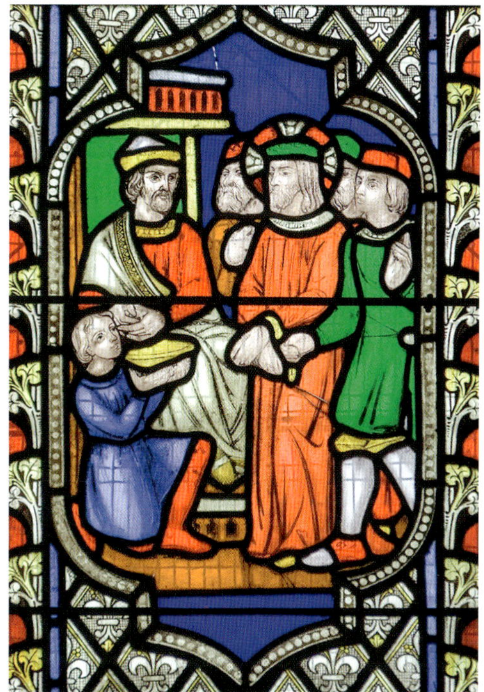

210–11. John Ellis Troughton, Christ Raising Jairus' Daughter (after Johann Friedrich Overbeck) between Christ Before Pilate (above right) and The Mocking of Christ, *c.* 1850, Church of St John the Baptist, Pentrobin, nave

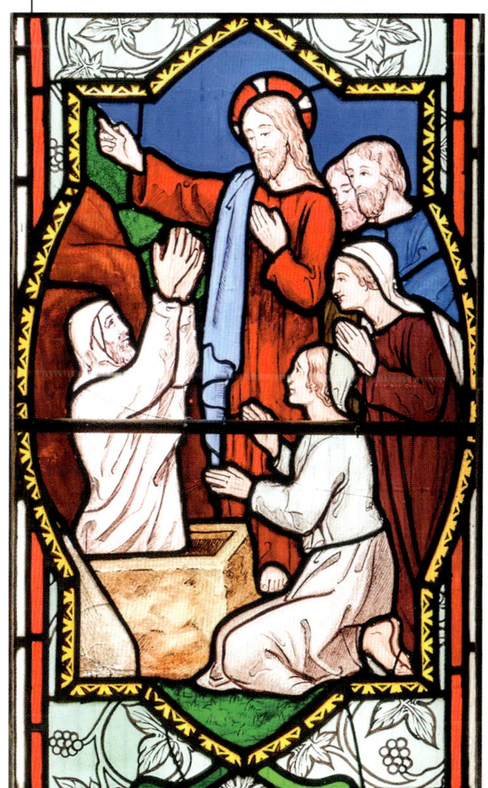

212. (right) Lloyd Sisters of Rhagatt, The Raising of Lazarus, probably 1857, Church of St Ffraid, Carrog, nave (from the former east window)

an improved and improving spirit and taste in matters of ecclesiastical architecture.'[8] A single figure of John the Baptist adorned the east window of the chancel at the time that the church was built, but within ten years a series of ten scenes occupied the centres of the tall lancets along the north and south walls of the nave. The windows were painted and made by the curate J.E. Troughton, and were part of a decorative scheme including murals and carving all undertaken by the artist, probably under the patronage and influence of Glynne.[9] By the time much of the scheme was complete in 1860, the work was lavishly praised in *The Ecclesiologist*, while lamenting that the church was too far from London to be more widely admired.[10]

Members of gentry families were sometimes involved in the production of windows. Some of the daughters of Edward and Frances Lloyd of Rhagatt were responsible for six accomplished painted scenes originally placed in the east window of the restored Church of St Ffraid, Carrog. In Glamorgan, Charlotte Louisa Traherne designed the north window given in memory of the former vicar, the Revd George Traherne, at St Hilary.

The church was rebuilt at her expense as a memorial to her husband, the Glamorgan antiquary, the Revd J.M. Traherne, half-brother of the former vicar.[11] Charlotte Traherne also contributed to other church restorations, sometimes jointly with her brother, C.R.M. Talbot, who had inherited the fortune of his father, the industrialist Thomas Mansel Talbot of Margam. C.R.M. Talbot was a staunch Anglican and restored other churches in the area, as did his daughters Emily and Olive later in the century.[12]

Many of the churches restored by C.R.M. Talbot were entrusted to John Prichard, who began his architectural practice in Glamorgan in the 1840s. Prichard trained with Thomas Walker, who introduced him to A.W.N. Pugin and Benjamin Ferrey, although he had previously worked for T.H. Wyatt at Llandaff Cathedral, where Prichard's father was a vicar choral.[13] Stained glass was provided for the east windows of Prichard's churches of St Mary, Malpas, built 1849–50, and the Church of St Michael, Cwmafan (formerly Michaelstone-super-Avon), built 1850–1. At Malpas the church was faithfully rebuilt in a Romanesque style to replicate features of the demolished twelfth-century priory church. Three windows in the east wall of the chancel have a series of roundels set within decorative foliate borders and were painted by George Rogers of Worcester.[14] Rogers had worked with the Worcester architect and

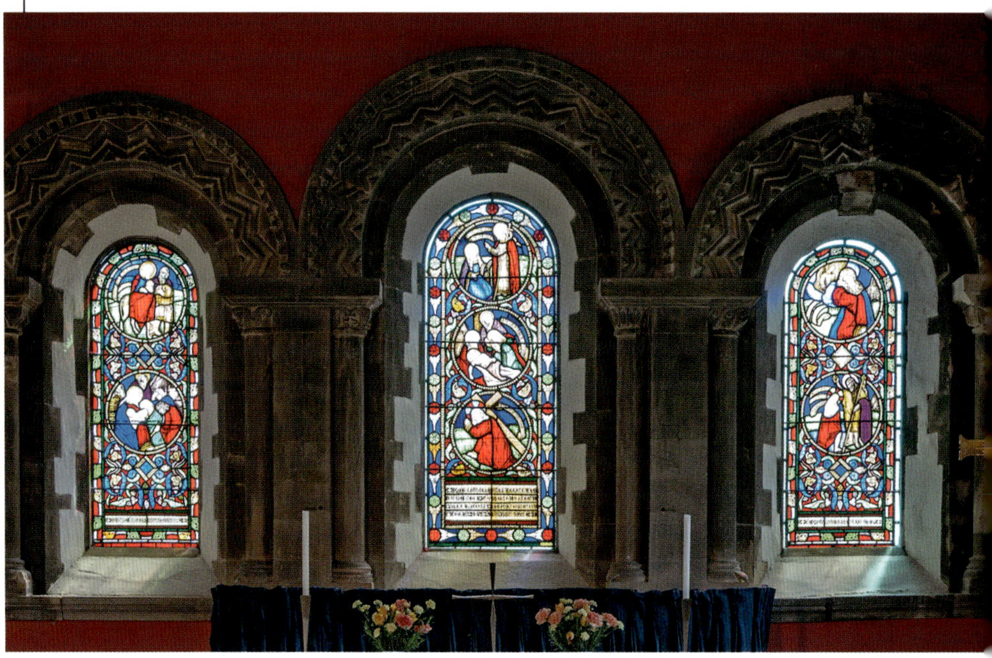

213–4. George Rogers, Scenes from the Life of Christ, includin
Christ in the Garden of Gethsemane and the Baptism of Chris
(right), 1850, Church of St Mary, Malpas, east windo

11 J.M. Traherne was the son of Llywelyn and Charlotte Traherne, while George Traherne was the son of Llywelyn Traherne by his second wife, Barbara-Maria Manning. Painted heads in the tracery of the east window of the south aisle may be of eighteenth or early nineteenth-century date, as stained glass was recorded in the window prior to 1849, although nothing of the family heraldry present at the time survives now. Samuel Lewis, *A Topographical Dictionary of Wales* (London: S. Lewis & Co., 1848, third edition), p. 414.

12 Emily and Olive Talbot, as well as their brother Theodore, who died aged only 37, all expressed strong Tractarian sympathies and financed the building of further churches in the vicinity of Margam and on the Gower peninsula. See Geoffrey R. Orrin, 'The Role of the Talbot Family in Church Building and Restoration in Victorian Glamorgan, 1837–1901', in *Morgannwg*, vol. xlvi (2002), pp. 57–70. However, few of them were enriched with pictorial stained glass when they were built. The same is true of the Anglo-Catholic pioneer Revd J.D. Davies of Gower, who adorned his churches at Llanmadoc and Cheriton with carved woodwork that he made himself, but not stained glass. Windows by John Hardman & Co. and William Miller were installed nearby at Reynoldston, where Davies had lived when his father John Davies was rector there. Two of these windows were given in the late 1860s by Richard Meux Benson, half-brother of Starling Benson of Fairyhill, Gower, who founded the Anglican monastic order, the Society of St John the Evangelist (the 'Cowley Fathers').

designer Frederick Preedy from about 1849, although within a few years Preedy became dissatisfied with the quality of Rogers' work, and began to paint his own glass. Preedy designed the east window for the Church of St Teilo, Merthyr Mawr in 1850, although the maker is unknown.[15]

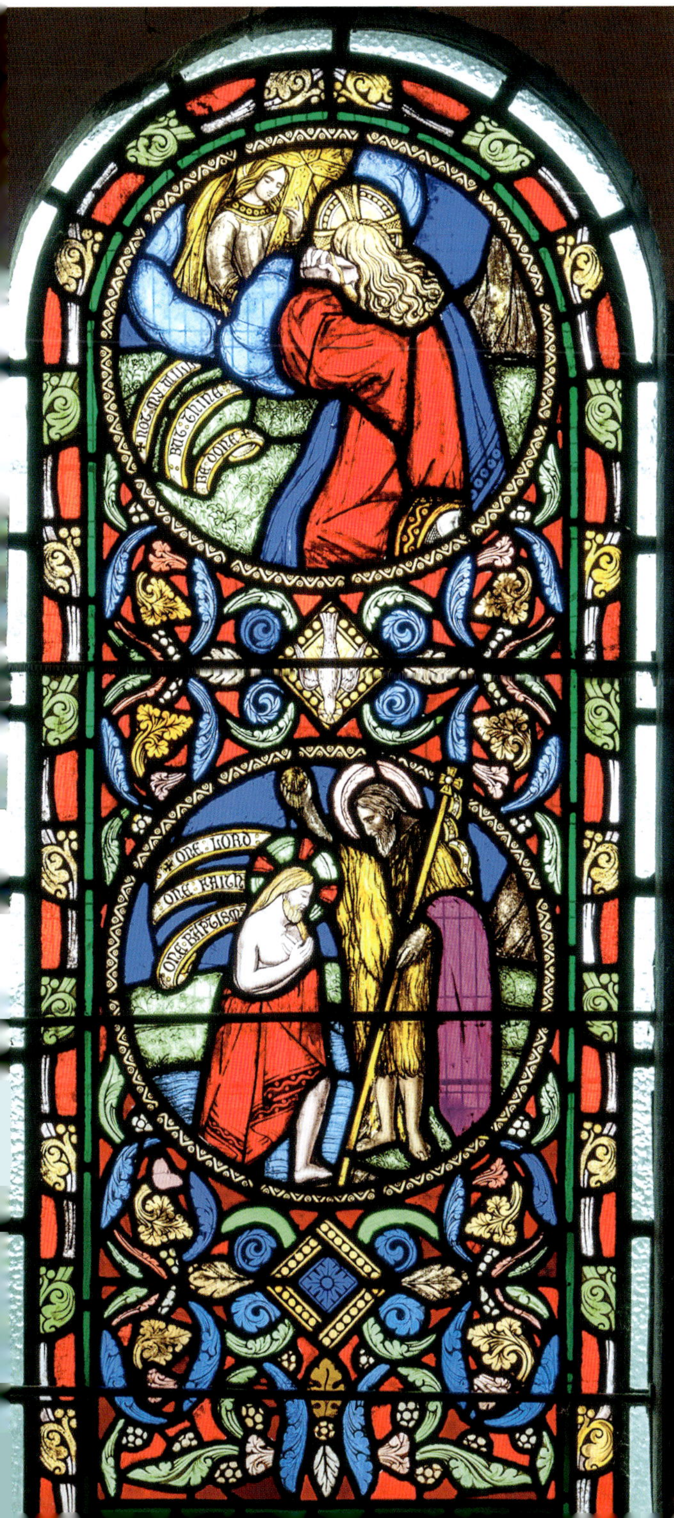

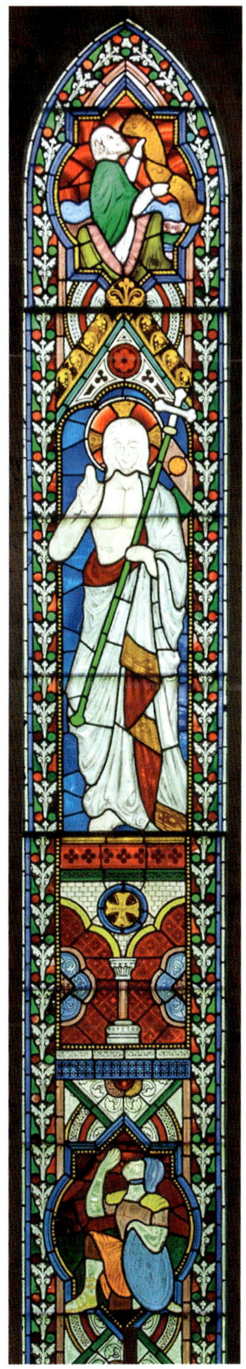

215. The Risen Christ, *c.* 1851, designed by Frederick Preedy, perhaps made by George Rogers, Church of St Teilo, Merthyr Mawr, east window

13 An outline of the life and work of John Prichard is given in John Newman, *The Buildings of Wales: Glamorgan* (London: Penguin Books, 1995), pp. 91–4.

14 Rogers provided further stained glass for the church, and a window for the Church of All Saints, Llanfrechfa. At Llanfrechfa the window was retained from the old church when it was rebuilt by John Loughborough Pearson in 1872–4. The primitive Gothic Revival style of Rogers' work would have made his windows vulnerable to loss in similar circumstances.

15 Olwen Jenkins' attribution of the chancel windows to William Wailes, noted in John Newman, *The Buildings of Wales: Glamorgan* (London: Penguin Books, 1995), p. 432, is unlikely on stylistic grounds. The north and south chancel windows, probably of a similar date, are attributable to William Miller. The church was designed by Benjamin Ferrey, but he was assisted by John Prichard, see Geoffrey Orrin, *Church Building and Restoration in Victorian Glamorgan* (Cardiff: University of Wales Press, 2004), pp. 102–3. The window dates from the time of Preedy's collaboration with George Rogers, but does not look like his work at Malpas; Preedy also had windows made by John Hardman & Co. For the work of Frederick Preedy, see Michael Kerney, *The Stained Glass of Frederick Preedy (1820–1898)* (London: The Ecclesiological Society, 2001).

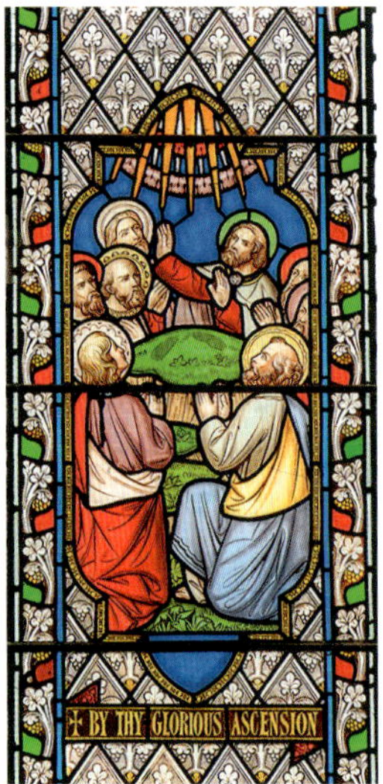

216. (right) William Wailes, The Ascension, *c.* 1860, Church of St Mark, Connah's Quay, nave (from the former east window)

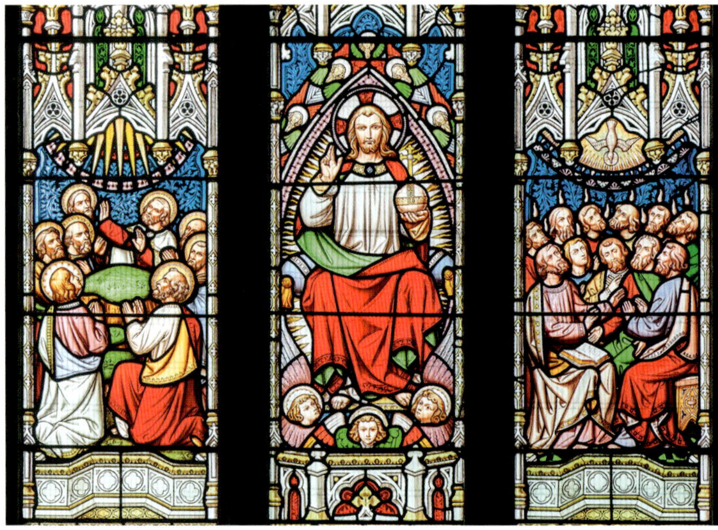

217. (far right) William Wailes, Christ in Majesty with the Ascension and Pentecost, *c.* 1856, Church of St Mary, Mold, sanctuary apse

Few windows were made by William Wailes for the Llandaff diocese in south-east Wales, and the firm found more commissions in the north-east and the west of Wales.[16] For example, Wailes made the east window of about 1851 for David Brandon's restoration of the Church of St Nicholas, Penally, in Pembrokeshire, and the large east window for the same architect's restoration of the Church of St Mary, Tenby, in 1856. In the north, four windows were made for the Church of St Deiniol, Hawarden, in the 1850s, as well as the east windows for the churches nearby at Gwersyllt, Ruthin, Trefnant, Mold and Bylchau.[17] Demand for work by the firm inevitably led to the reuse of their designs in other windows. The four scenes in the outer lights of the east window at the Church of the Holy Trinity, Trefnant, were all used two years later in the apse windows for the Church of St Mary, Mold, in both instances for the architect George Gilbert Scott. Designs for the three main panels for the east window at Connah's Quay in about 1860 were also previously used at Mold.[18] Windows in a very similar style were made by Francis Wilson Oliphant, who designed for both William Wailes and John Hardman. While designing for Hardmans he worked for a time with A.W.N. Pugin, whose influence is clear in his east window at Pentrefoelas, another church for which Scott was the architect.

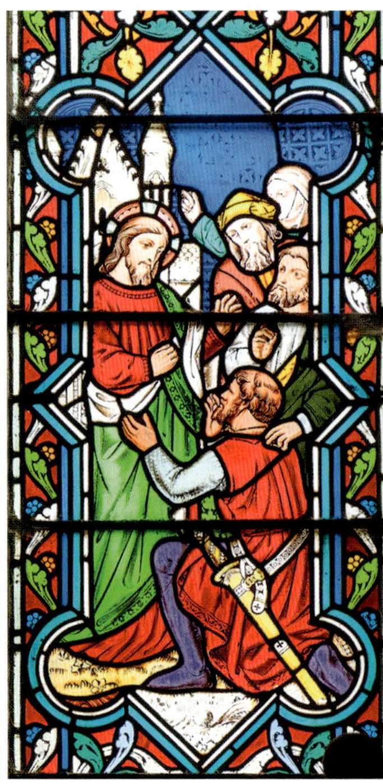

218. Francis Wilson Oliphant, The Centurion Kneeling Before Christ, 1858, Pentrefoelas Church, Pentrefoelas, east window

With stained glass still relatively novel in the 1850s, most churches were built or restored

16 William Wailes made grisaille windows with heraldic shields for the Church of St John the Baptist, Cardiff, and although they were praised in the *Cardiff and Merthyr Guardian* as 'a very perfect work' (18 March 1854), the commission caused consternation to the patron, Lady Sophia Crichton-Stuart, the marchioness of Bute. I am grateful to Alison Rennie for providing notes on the correspondence regarding the commission. This might have proved to be a setback to their progress in the diocese. The firm did however make the east window at the Church of St David, Rhymney, probably shortly afterwards in the 1850s, and a five-light east window at Troedyrhiw in 1863, but in neither instance does it seem that the diocesan architect John Prichard was involved.

17 Two of the windows in the Whitley (south) chancel at Hawarden were given in memory of members of Stephen Glynne's family and survived the disastrous fire at the church in 1857. The east window of the south chancel was added after the fire in 1859, the restoration having been entrusted to Gilbert Scott. The east window at Ruthin was for the architect R.K. Penson, who also used Wailes in the 1850s and 60s for his churches in west Wales at Angle and (extensively) at Laugharne.

18 The three lights that constituted the east window at Connah's Quay have been moved to the nave.

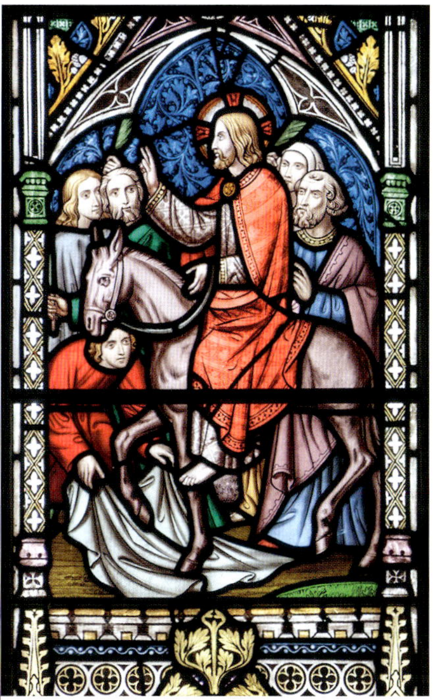

219. William Wailes, The Entry into Jerusalem, 1855, Church of St Peter and St Meugan, Ruthin, east window

with only the east wall of the chancel being furnished with stained glass, giving emphasis to the sacrament of Holy Communion. The east window was sometimes balanced by a west window, or perhaps a baptistry window (the surviving window at Sketty by Willam Warrington is both), and some chancels were further adorned with stained glass in the north or south walls. Other windows were sometimes filled with patterned glass, as at Llangasty Tal-y-llyn, although here and in other churches these windows have been replaced by later figurative windows.

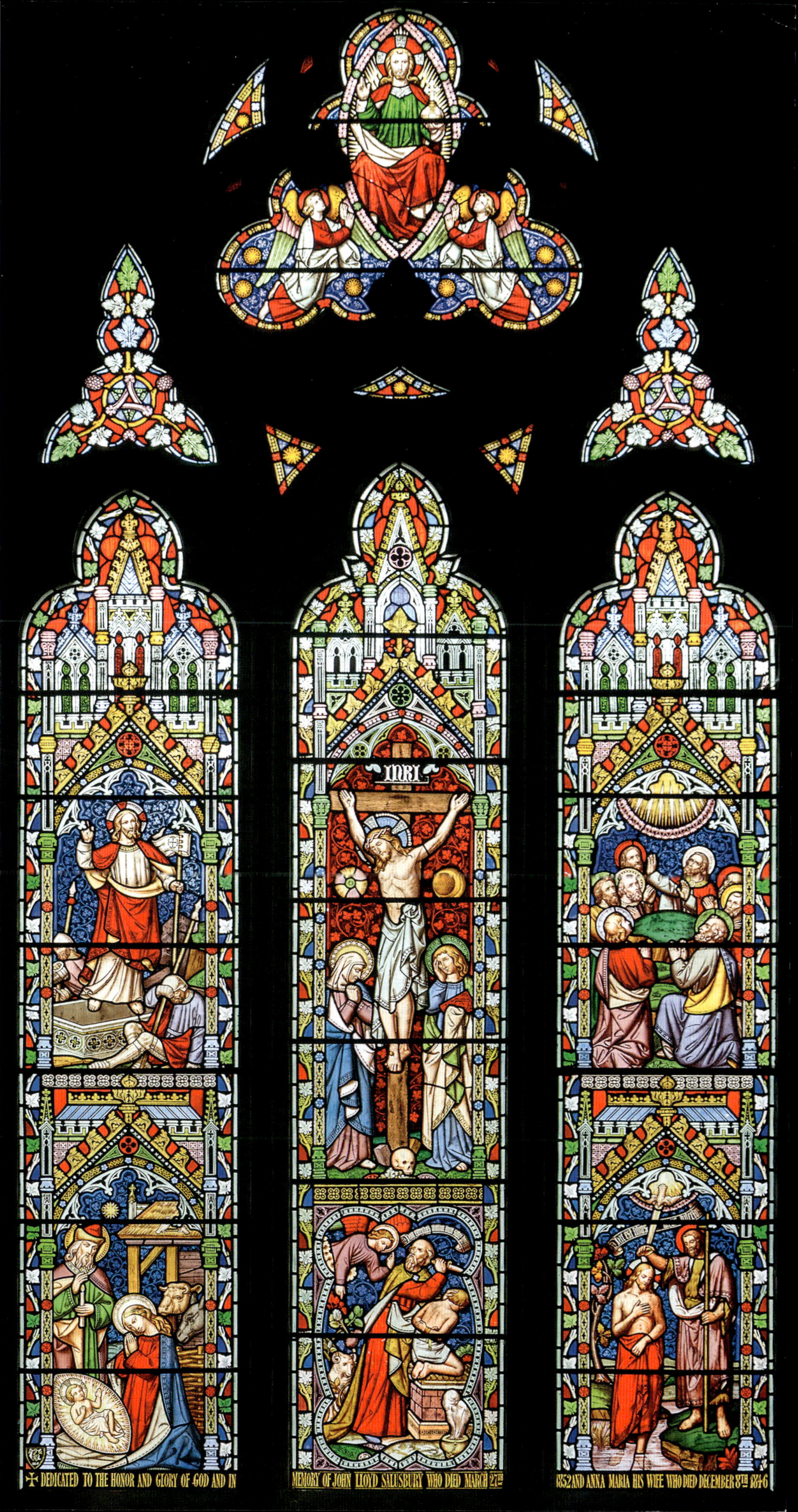

220. William Wailes, Scenes from the Life of Christ with the Sacrifice of Isaac, 1854, Church of the Holy Trinity, Trefnant, east window

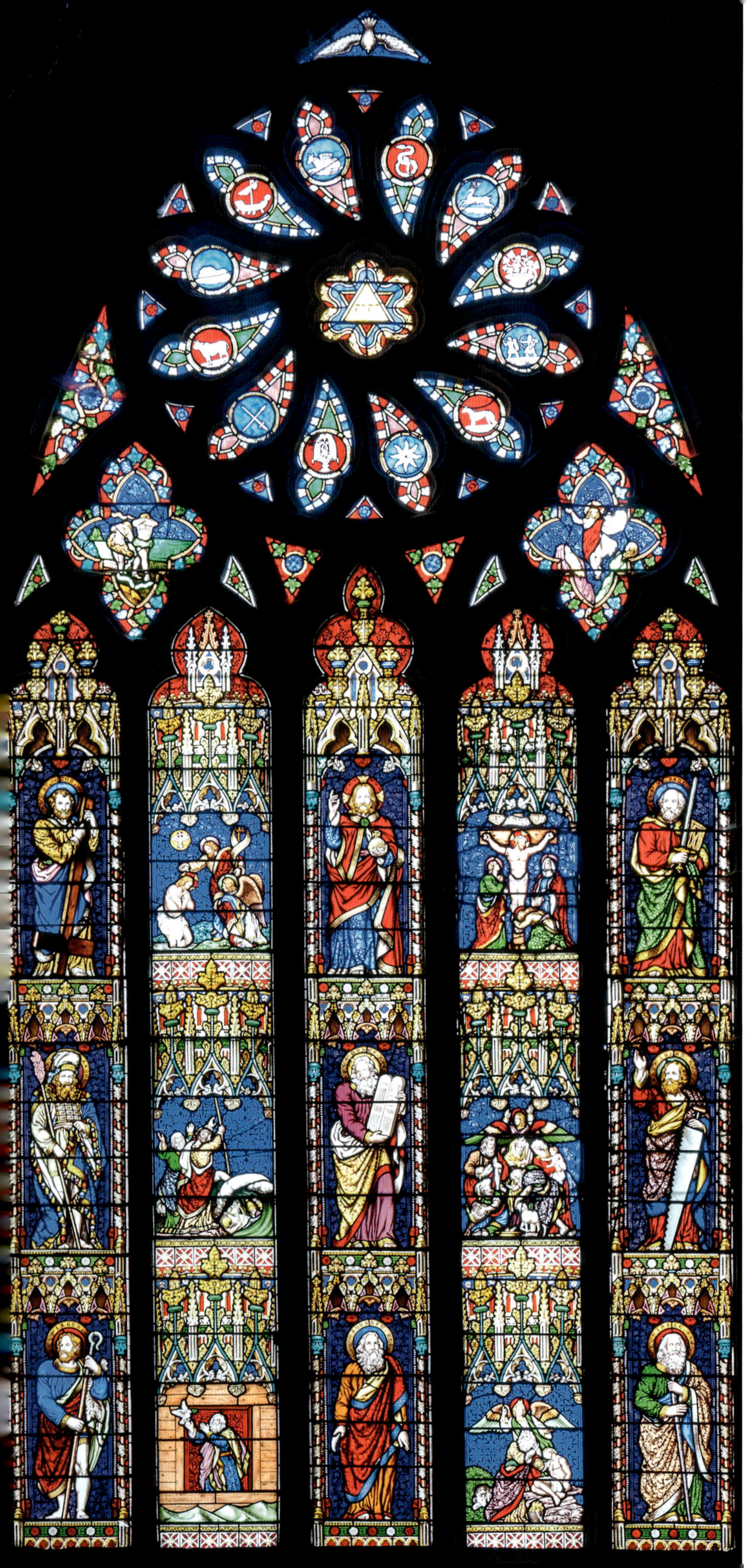

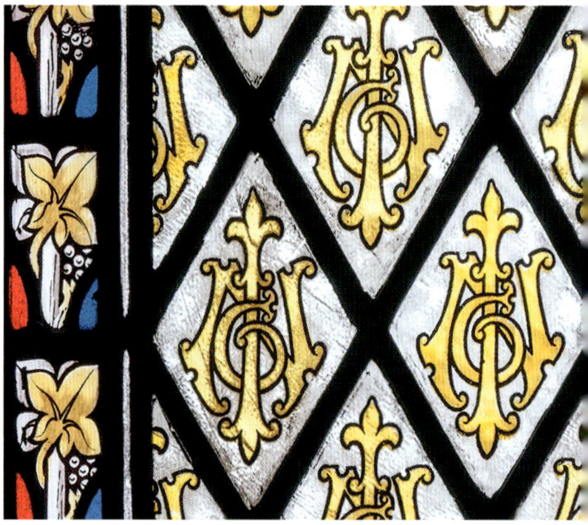

221. (left) Forrest & Bromley, West Window, 1853, Church of the Holy Trinity, Leighton

222. (above) Forrest & Bromley, Detail of Family Monogram, 1853, Church of the Holy Trinity, Leighton, nave

223. (below) Forrest & Bromley, St Peter, *c.* 1858, Church of St Rhuddlad, Llanrhuddlad, east window

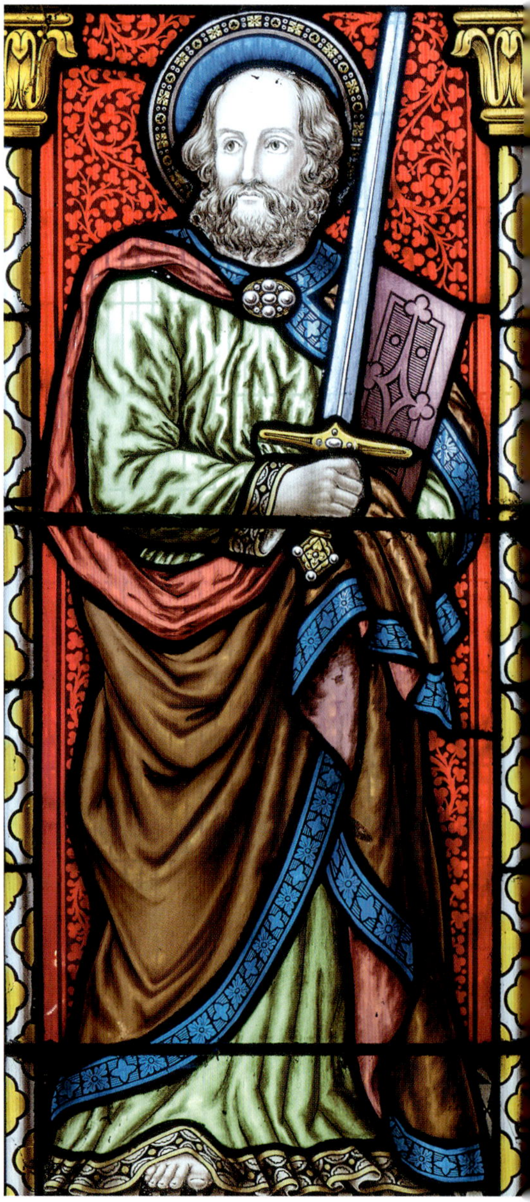

The glazing scheme of 1853 for John and Georgina Naylor's estate church at Leighton, near Welshpool, survives in its entirety. The Naylors employed the Liverpool architect W.H. Gee to design the church in Decorated Gothic, or Middle Pointed, which was advocated by the Ecclesiologists as the best style for churches. The windows were executed by Forrest & Bromley of Liverpool, which included the five-light east window depicting Christ with the four evangelists and the still larger six-light west window with figures from the Old and New Testaments together with typological scenes. Each of the aisle windows, which all remain in situ, bear the monograms of the patrons painted on each quarry, and further grisaille glass is to be found in the Naylor mausoleum.[19] To the north of Welshpool east windows by David Evans and Charles Clutterbuck were commissioned in the 1850s at Meifod and Llanfyllin, and Forrest & Bromley's figures have a solidity reminiscent of those made by David Evans in 1855 for the Church of St Tysilio and St Mary, Meifod.

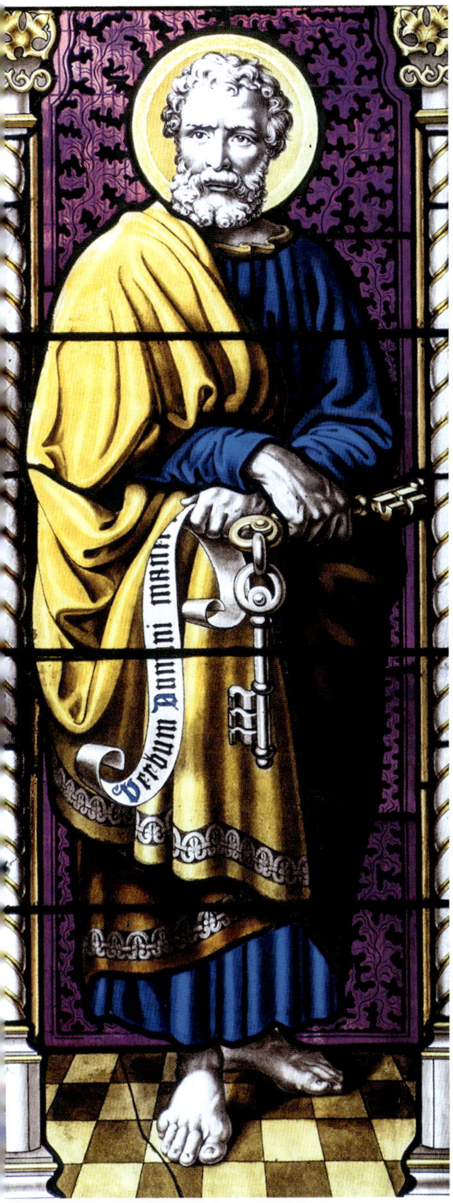

224. David Evans, St Peter, *c.* 1856, Church of St Tysilio and St Mary, Meifod, south aisle

In the Bangor diocese, churches designed in the 1850s by the diocesan architect Henry Kennedy often lacked the funds for the introduction of stained glass.[20] One of his earliest churches, at Llanllechid, has an east window of about 1844 by Clutterbuck, replacing medieval glass recorded there in about 1800.[21] Further windows by David Evans were also installed in the region during the 1850s. East and west windows for Kennedy's church at Llanrhuddlad on Anglesey were made by Forrest & Bromley in about 1858, where the

19 The architect also designed their home, Leighton Hall, in a mix of Gothic styles with interiors to the design of A.W.N. Pugin as well as further stained glass probably also by Forrest & Bromley. Robert Scourfield and Richard Haslam, *The Buildings of Wales: Powys* (New Haven/London: Yale University Press, 2013), pp. 130–4

20 *The Ecclesiologist* was scathing of the state of churches in the region in 1849, vol. x (October 1849), p. 163.

21 An illustration of the medieval glass at Llanllechid is inserted after p. 299 in an extra-illustrated copy of Thomas Pennant, *A Tour in North Wales*, NLW PD9870.

225. Charles Clutterbuck, The Resurrection, 1857, Church of St Myllin, Llanfyllin, east window

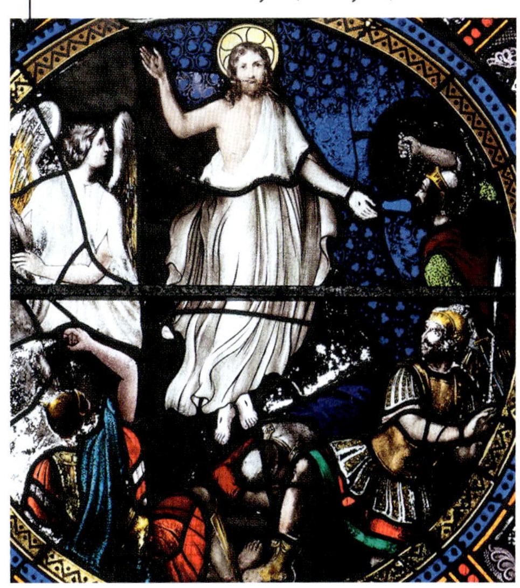

same figures of Peter and Paul from the great west window at Leighton were used again. Another estate church at Llandwrog afforded Kennedy the opportunity to add stained glass at one of his churches, under the patronage of the third baron Newborough, Spencer Bulkeley Wynn, built between 1858 and 1864. Here the large five-light east window and further windows in the church are by the London glass-painter William Miller.

Little is known about William Miller. He made the east window for the Church of St John the Baptist, Cardiff, in 1852 and three windows in the east wall of the chancel at St Mary Church in the Vale of Glamorgan for Prichard and Seddon's restoration in 1862.[22] This has enabled further identification of his work at Merthyr Mawr, possibly St Hilary, and at Llandwrog. At both Llandwrog and St Mary Church, Miller uses a particular depiction of the Nativity that he used elsewhere, such as at the Church of St James the Great, Aston Abbotts in Buckinghamshire. The scene was also used by the Lloyd sisters at Carrog; in a roundel from Church of St Mary, Newport (Pembrokeshire), of unknown date and perhaps also an amateur work that was reset in 1879; as well as in an illuminated Book of Collects, made in 1854 and given to the Cathedral Library of St Davids in 1928. At the Church of St Meugan, St Maughans, the same scene fills the tall central light of a three-light window, with additional attendant figures in the two outer lights. The close similarity of these images by disparate artists suggests that the image, which is close to late fifteenth-century paintings by Sandro Botticelli, Domenico Ghirlandaio and Fra Bartolomeo Della Porta, was known from an engraving or an early pictorial Bible.

22 Prichard had taken John Pollard Seddon into partnership in the 1850s and together they embarked on the restoration of Llandaff Cathedral, as well as working on other churches in the Llandaff diocese. For their partnership, and the attribution of William Miller at St Mary Church, see Olwen Jenkins, 'Illustrative examples of the effect on medieval and later parish church fabric in the post-1844 Archdeaconry of Llandaff of restoration work by John Prichard and John Pollard Seddon' (unpublished diploma thesis, Architectural Association, London, 1985), NLW ex 839. Two more windows by Miller were made for the Church of St Sadwrn, Henllan, after 1855. D.R. Thomas, *The History of the Diocese of St Asaph* (Oswestry: Caxton Press, 1911), vol. ii, pp. 32–3. This attribution has enabled the identification of another window by him on the Gower at the Church of St George, Reynoldston, of about 1867.

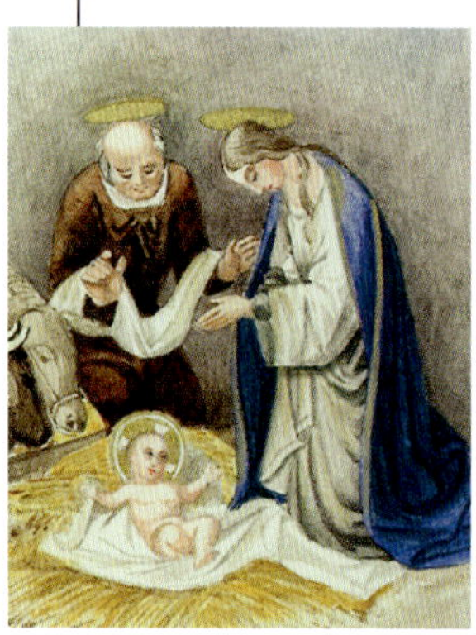

226. (right) The Nativity, 1854, from an Illuminated Book of Collects, St Davids Cathedral Library (reproduced courtesy of the Sub-Librarian)

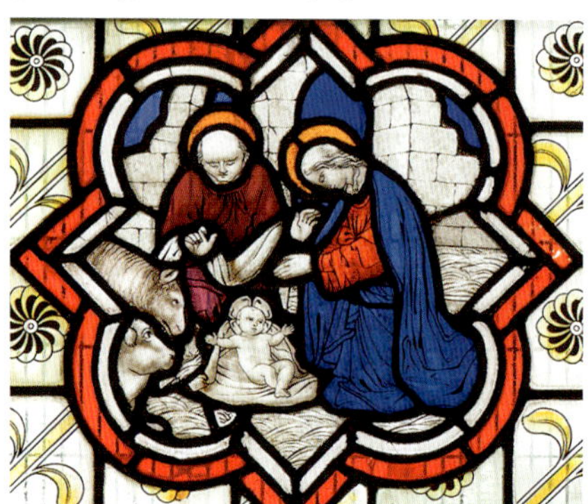

227. (centre right) The Nativity, probably *c.* 1850, Church of St Mary, Newport (Pembrokeshire), chancel

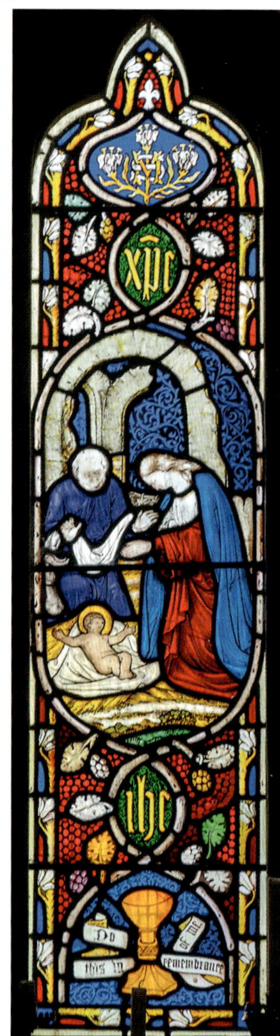

228. (far right) William Miller, The Nativity, 1862, Church of St Mary, St Mary Church, east window

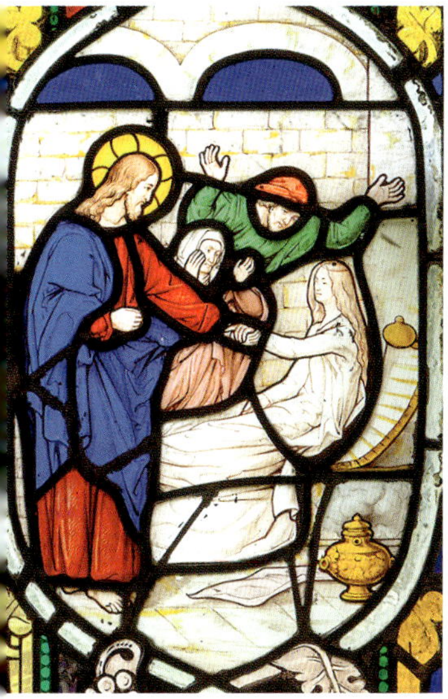

229. William Miller, Christ Raising Jairus' Daughter, *c.* 1851, Church of St Teilo, Merthyr Mawr, chancel

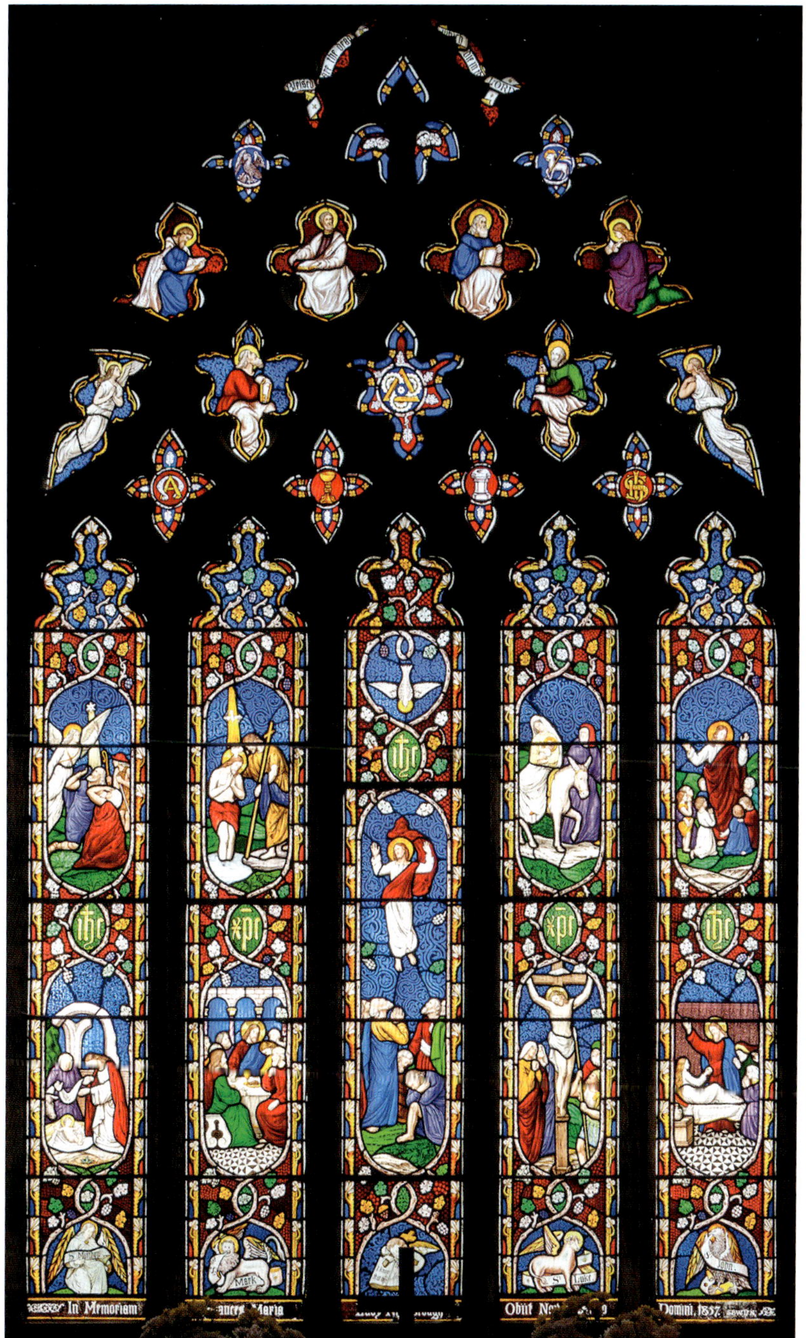

230. William Miller, Scenes from the Life of Christ, *c.* 1857, Church of St Twrog, Llandwrog, east window

As well as fifteenth-century painting, the work of the German painters working in Rome, who became known as the Nazarenes, was also imitated in stained glass. The Nazarenes were admired by A.W.N. Pugin and the ecclesiologists for their rejection of the Renaissance painting that evolved after Raphael in favour of earlier Italian and Northern Renaissance painting. Stained glass designers in Munich adapted their work as early as the 1820s, and one of the chancel windows at Merthyr Mawr is a version of Johann Friedrich Overbeck's painting of Christ raising the daughter of Jairus. The scene was also copied by J.E. Troughton in one of his murals at Pentrobin, where he also drew on the work of Peter Cornelius, another Nazarene painter.[23]

Architects such as A.W.N. Pugin and William Butterfield sought greater control over the design and manufacture of stained glass to ensure that it matched their vision of the completed interior. Pugin realised that when glass painters failed to interpret his designs correctly it could dramatically alter the effect of the stained glass on the character of his buildings. Furthermore he found it difficult to give exact instructions due to the inconstancy of the medium: 'I cannot see the effect in a cartoon not even a coloured

23 For the influence of the Nazarene artists on stained glass designers, especially in Germany, see Virginia Chieffo Raguin, 'Revivals, Revivalists, and Architectural Stained Glass', *Journal of the Society of Architectural Historians,* vol. 49, no. 3 (September 1990), p. 323.

231–2. John Hardman & Co., Viscount and Louisa Feilding, *c.* 1853, designed by John Hardman Powell, Church of St David, Pantasaph, chancel

233. (opposite, left) Michael & Arthur O'Connor, Scenes from the Life of Christ, 1855, Church of St David, Pantasaph, east window

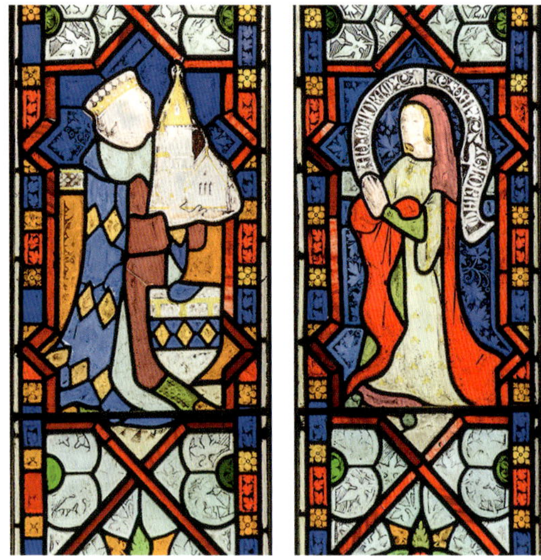

one the transparent light changes the effect & deceives me altogether.'[24] After the frustration of having his designs poorly interpreted, Pugin supervised the drawing of the cartoons for his windows at his house in Ramsgate, before they were sent to John Hardman's studio in Birmingham to be made.

Pugin's most trusted pupil, John Hardman Powell, was the nephew of John Hardman, and he married Pugin's daughter in 1850. He became the chief designer of stained glass for Hardman after Pugin's death in 1852 and his designs for the north and south chancel windows of 1853 at the Church of St David, Pantasaph, are therefore close in spirit to other furnishings designed by Pugin for the church. The church was originally built for the Diocese of St Asaph, but given to the Roman Catholic Capuchin Friars after the donor, the Viscount Feilding, converted to the Roman Catholic church in 1850. The event caused considerable controversy, particularly in the context of the restoration of the Roman Catholic hierarchy in 1850 and the ensuing anti-Catholic protests of 1851. Pugin and Hardman, both Roman Catholics, supplied fittings for the church, although the five-light east window was supplied in about 1855 by another firm, Michael and Arthur O'Connor, perhaps the most admired English stained glass studio of the 1850s.[25]

The strength of the Roman Catholic Church was transformed in south Wales with the influx of Irish immigrant workers, and new churches were founded, initially near the two old recusant centres around Holywell in north Wales, and in Monmouthshire. Stained glass was placed in the east window of the new Gothic church at Newport prior to its opening in 1840, while further west at Carmarthen the Church of St Mary was furnished with stained glass in the chancel when the

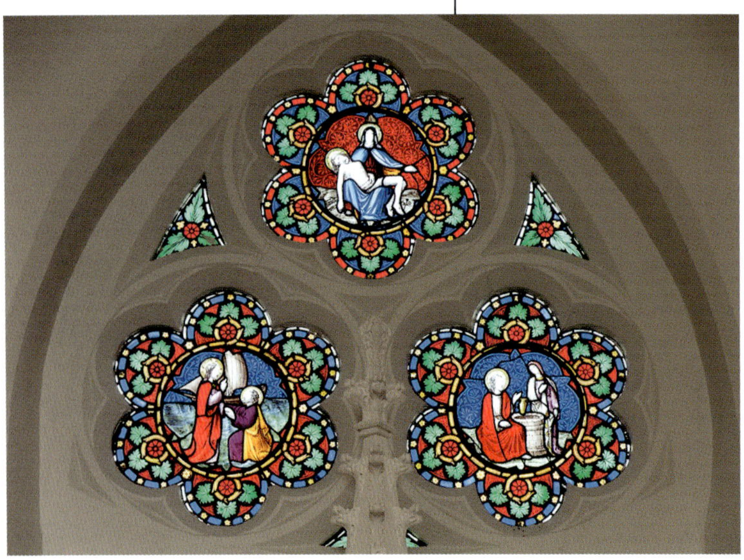

234. Scenes from the Life of Christ, 1852, Church of St Mary, Carmarthen, east window

24 Letter to John Hardman, about 1849, quoted in Stanley A. Shepherd, 'Stained Glass' in Paul Atterbury and Clive Wainwright, *Pugin: A Gothic Passion* (New Haven/London: Yale University Press, 1994), p. 198.

25 Michael O'Connor was a Catholic who was born in Dublin, had trained with Thomas Willement and also worked with Pugin. His son Arthur became a partner in the firm in about 1851. The employment of these Catholic artists became problematic for Anglican patrons, typified by the controversy over the design of the memorial window for Queen Adelaide at Worcester Cathedral. Michael O'Connor and the firm of John Hardman were discounted on the grounds that they were Catholic and the commission passing to the safely Protestant local architect Frederick Preedy, whose design was painted by George Rogers. See Michael Kerney, *The Stained Glass of Frederick Preedy (1820–1898): A Catalogue of Designs* (London: The Ecclesiological Society, 2001), p. 8, and Jim Cheshire, *Stained glass and the Victorian Gothic Revival* (Manchester: Manchester University Press, 2004), p. 128.

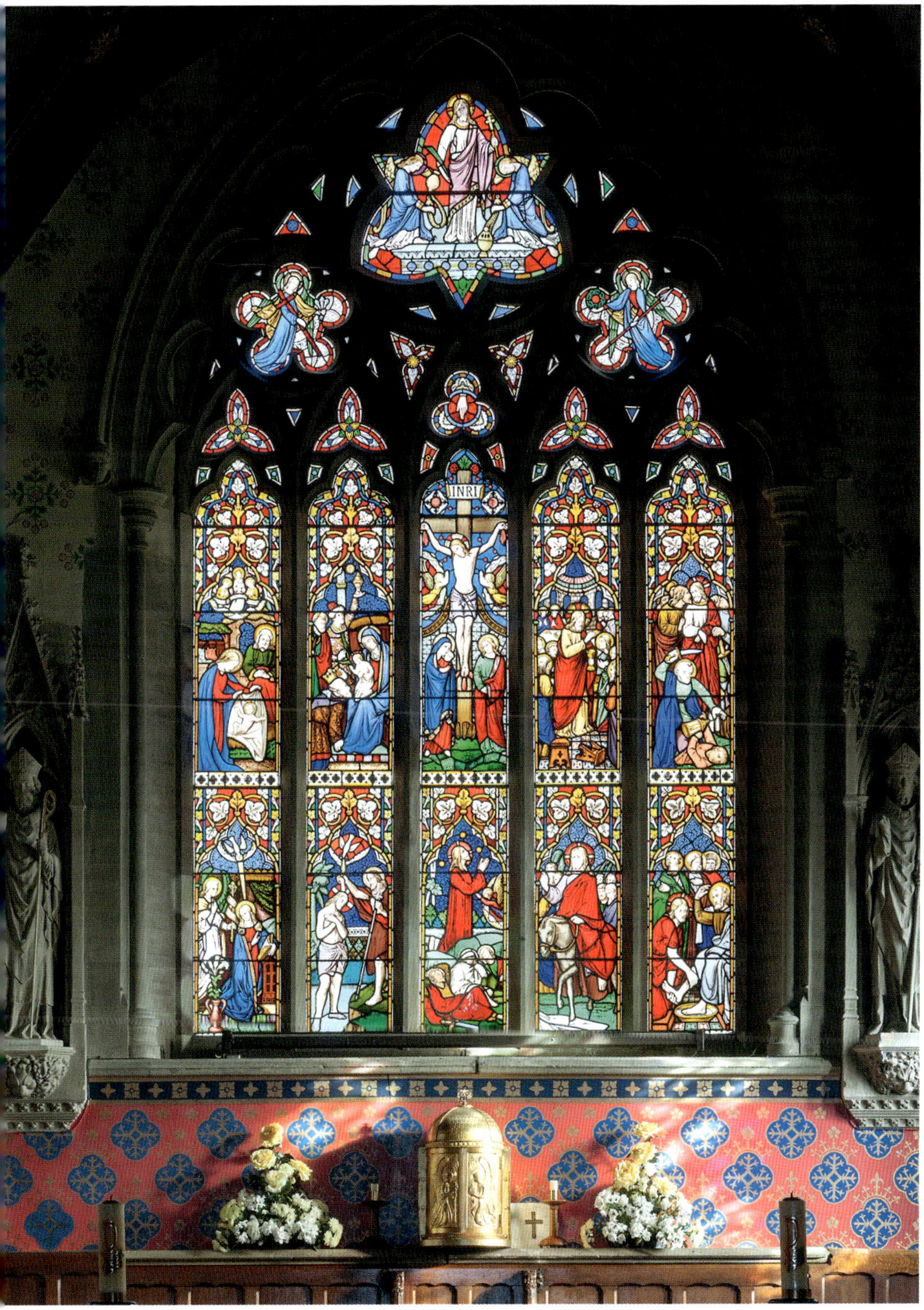

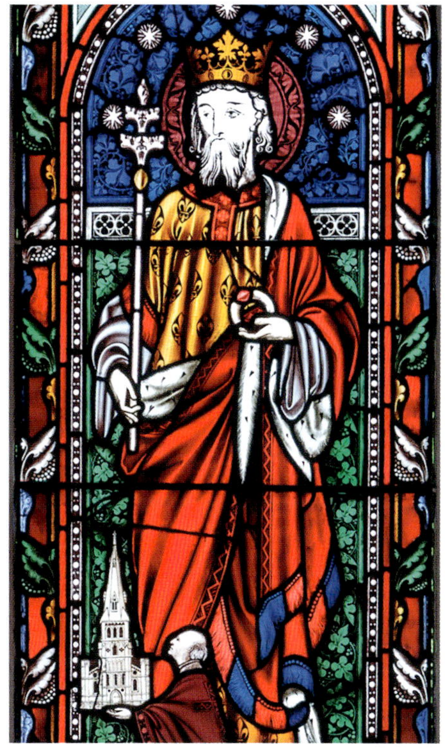

235. John Hardman & Co, St Edward the Confessor, 1859, Church of St Mary, Newport, chancel

building was opened in 1852.[26] Stained glass made by John Hardman & Co. was installed at the Roman Catholic churches in Newport and Usk in the 1850s. The saints John the Evangelist and Edward the Confessor flanked the original three-light window at Newport, with the figure of the Revd Edward Metcalfe, holding the original design for the church, complete with tower, below Edward the Confessor.[27] At the Church of

26 The church at Newport replaced an earlier modest chapel on the site. The three figures from the east window, Mary and the conspicuously Welsh saints David and Woolos (Gwynllyw), were re-sited in the south wall of the south aisle after a new east window was added, by John Hardman & Co., in 1911. A detailed description of the original east window was given in the *Monmouthshire Merlin*, 3 October 1840.

27 The cost of the window was met by public subscription and commemorates the Revd Edward Metcalfe, who built the church. The window depicting John was paid for by John Arthur Herbert of Llanarth Court. Formerly John Arthur Jones, he was descended from a senior branch of the Herbert family, who had remained Catholic throughout the seventeenth and eighteenth centuries. I am grateful to Tony Corten for information on the glass at the Church of St Mary, Newport.

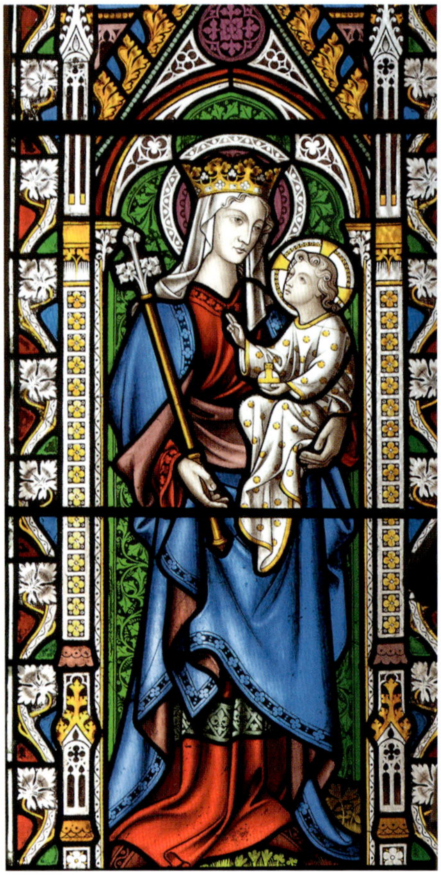

236. G.B. Maycock, Virgin and Child, 1860, Church of Our Lady and St Michael, Abergavenny, north aisle

237. Clayton & Bell, St Benedict, 1861, Church of Our Lady and St Michael, Abergavenny, chantry chapel

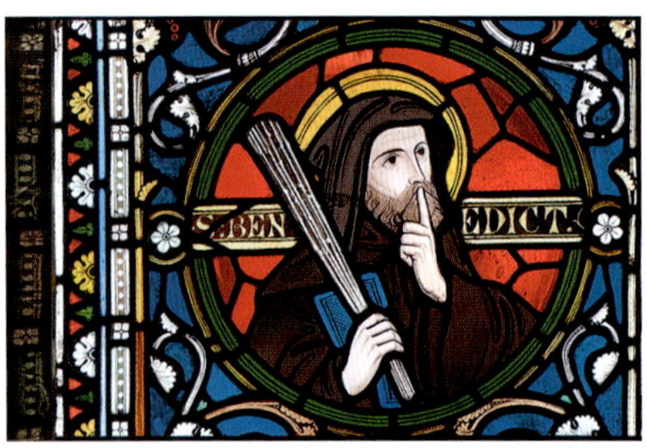

238. (right) William Wailes, The Holy Family in the Carpenter's Workshop, 1852, Chapel of the Jesuit College, Tremeirchion

239. (far right) The Virgin Mary, 1861, Church of St Winifrede, Holywell, nave

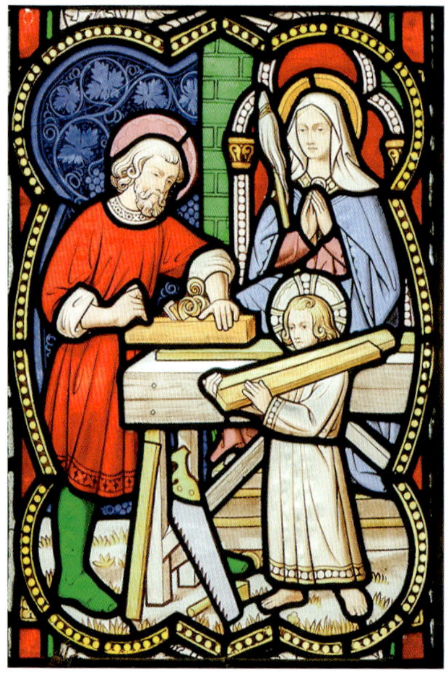

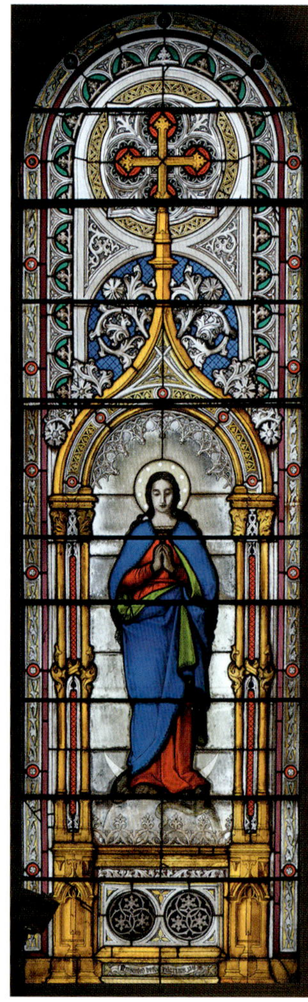

Our Lady and St Michael, Abergavenny, the first stained glass windows were provided by G.B. Maycock in 1860 and Clayton & Bell in 1861 for Benjamin Bucknall's Decorated Gothic church, and work by Hardman's was to follow.

In north Wales eight windows were installed in the chapel of the Jesuit College at Tremeirchion in 1852, while stained glass was also gradually added to the large Classical Roman Catholic Church nearby at Holywell, originally built in 1832–3. A window given by pilgrims to the shrine of Winifred at Holywell in 1860 was made by Hardman's depicting scenes from the life of Winifred, while the window given by the pilgrims of the following year is perhaps of Italian origin.[28]

Once the Anti-Catholic sentiment of the early 1850s had subsided, both John Hardman & Co. and Michael & Arthur O'Connor found favour with Anglican Tractarian patrons in Wales. The leading architects of the 1850s, such as George Gilbert Scott, William Butterfield, George Edward Street and John Loughborough Pearson, were mostly sympathetic to High Church practices, and all employed stained glass in their churches. Hardman's made stained glass for G.E. Street's acclaimed restoration of St Fagans under the generous patronage of Baroness Windsor, and their east window at the Church of St Beuno, Berriew, is one of their best early works in Wales.

28 The provenance was suggested by Malcolm Seaborne, 'Victorian and Later Stained Glass in Flintshire Churches', *The Journal of the Flintshire Historical Society*, vol. 35 (1999), p. 128. Sculpture in the church also originated from Italy.

240. John Hardman & C
The Transfiguration, 18
Church of St Beuno, Berrie
east windc

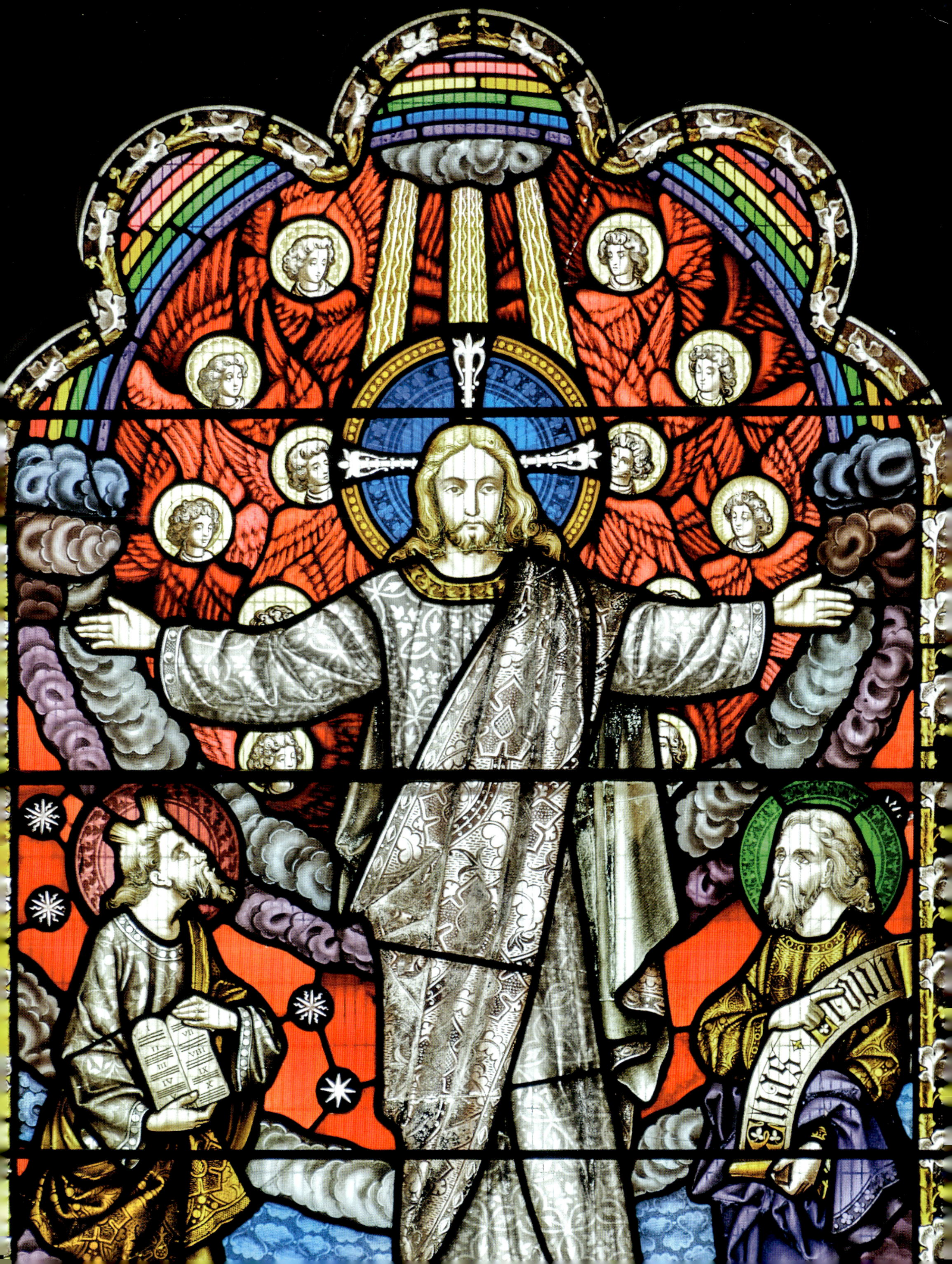

The architect John Gibson had the benefit of Lady Willoughby de Broke's greater riches at the Church of St Margaret of Antioch, Bodelwyddan, where numerous windows were made by O'Connor's.[29] Gibson was a pupil of the architect Charles Barry at the time when Barry and Pugin were working on the Houses of Parliament, and while Gibson's classical buildings for financial institutions in Glasgow and London owed little to A.W.N. Pugin, his design for Bodelwyddan certainly did. Built at a cost of £60,000, the church uses an impressive combination of stained glass, flamboyant stonecarving and the famous marble pillars and panelling for dazzling effect. The use of coloured windows for lavish display, while emphatically providing a liturgical focus true to Pugin's vision of the church, demonstrates the rapid ascent of the Gothic for church architecture less than twenty years since the first small Welsh Tractarian country churches of the 1840s.

29 This included stained glass for the east window, windows in the north and south walls of the chancel, east windows of the north and south aisles and west rose window. The nave windows are edged with coloured glass and have patterns in their tracery lights.

241. John Gibson, Church of St Margaret of Antioch, Bodelwyddan, 1856–60, stained glass by Michael & Arthur O'Connor, 1859

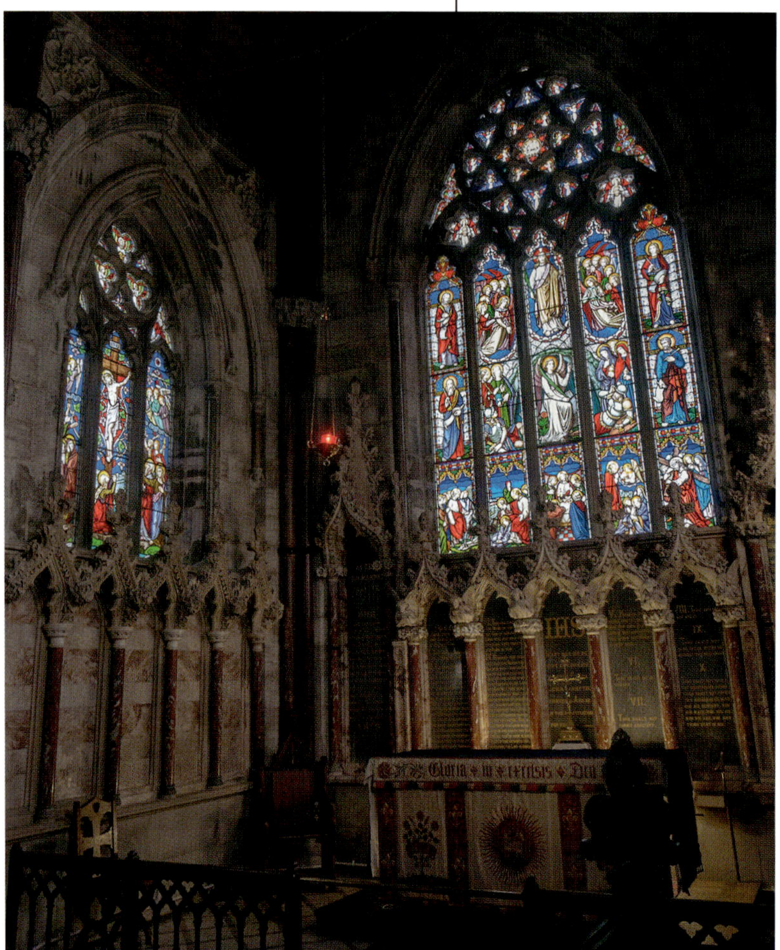

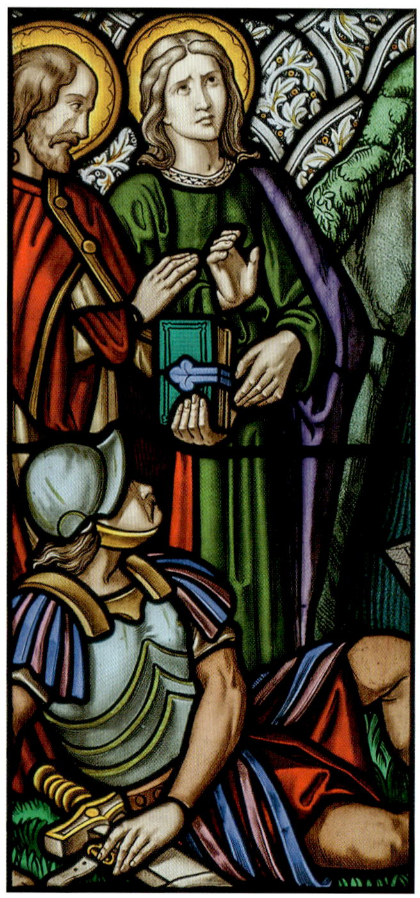

242. Michael & Arthur O'Connor, Figures from the scene of the Resurrection, 1859, Church of St Margaret of Antioch, Bodelwyddan, east window

Chapter Five

Victorian Stained Glass Firms

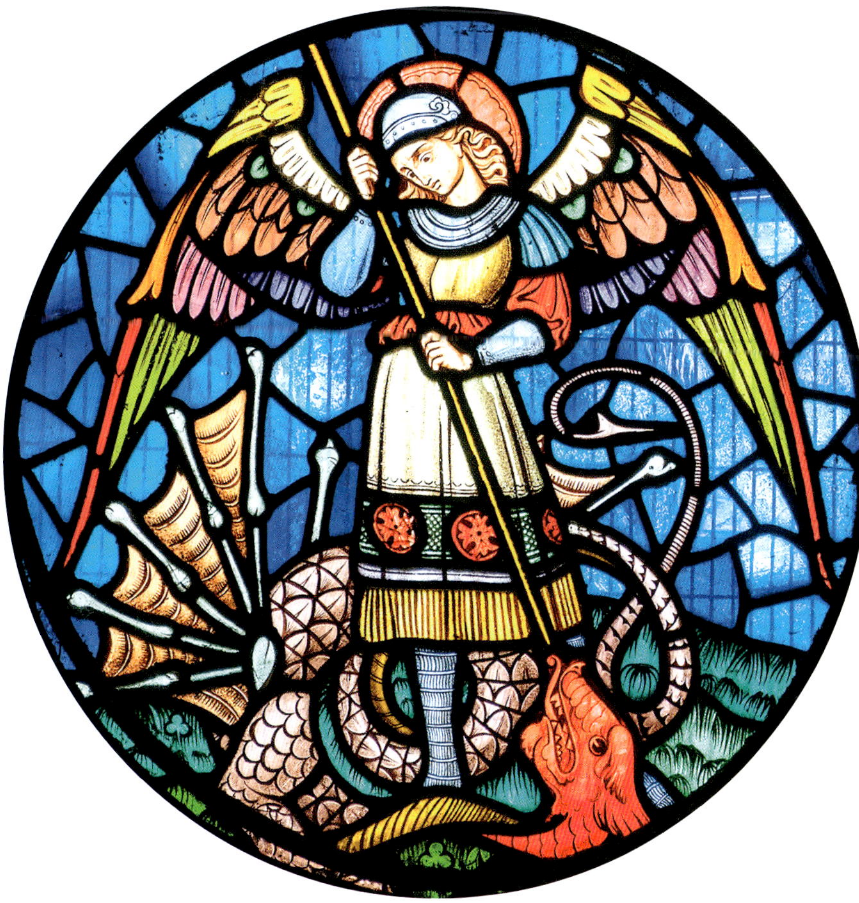

245. Probably John G. How
St Mark the Evangelist, *c.* 185
Church of St Llawddog, Cilgerra
chanc

1 Quoted in Stanley A. Shepherd, *The Stained Glass of A.W.N. Pugin* (Reading: Spire Books, 2009), p. 81–2.

2 For the exhibiting of stained glass at the Great Exhibition see Jim Cheshire, *Stained glass and the Victorian Gothic Revival* (Manchester: Manchester University Press, 2004), pp. 155–9; the fittings for Pantasaph are discussed, together with edited correspondence between Pugin and the patron, in Rosemary Hill, 'A.W.N. Pugin and Viscount Feilding', *True Principles*, vol. iii, no. 5 (2008), pp. 25–31.

3 See Martin Harrison, *Victorian Stained Glass* (London: Barrie & Jenkins, 1980), p. 24.

The efforts of the ecclesiologists to beautify the church in combination with generous private patronage created many opportunities for the makers of stained glass during the middle years of the nineteenth century. In the early 1840s there were relatively few glass painters that A.W.N. Pugin was able to call upon to translate his designs into glass. By the time of his death in 1852, the firms that he worked with, such as those of John Hardman, William Wailes and Michael O'Connor, were well established and were to prosper in the following decades. As early as 1847, William Wailes remarked in a letter to John Hardman that 'there is plenty work for us all'.[1]

As the names suggest, these firms were often established by individual glass painters or glaziers who took on assistants to increase their capacity. The renewed interest in furnishing the church was also furthered by the Great Exhibition of 1851. The Medieval Court of the Great Exhibition, designed by Pugin, displayed work in stained glass made by John Hardman & Co. in the context of other ecclesiastical furnishings, including interior fittings made for the Church of St David, Pantasaph, and did much to popularise medieval taste.[2] Most of the stained glass at the Great Exhibition was displayed separately from Pugin's Medieval Court, and brought other firms making stained glass to the attention of a wider public. Alongside well-established makers such as William Wailes, Ballantine & Allan, and Michael & Arthur O'Connor, exhibitors included firms who had their own glassworks, such as Chance Brothers and James Powell & Sons, and others such as Edward Baillie and John G. Howe, of whom little is now known, as well as exhibitors from the continent.

These exhibitors demonstrated considerable variety and were not restricted to ecclesiastical work. William Holland of Warwick presented windows in a range of styles from the twelfth to the late sixteenth century to display his studio's capacity to suit different architectural settings.[3] Others worked in a less medievalist style, such as Ballantine & Allan, who, according to *The Ecclesiologist*, did 'not keep up their reputation'. Of others the journal remarked darkly 'We fear we could not say much to their advantage.'[4] Their views on stained glass were

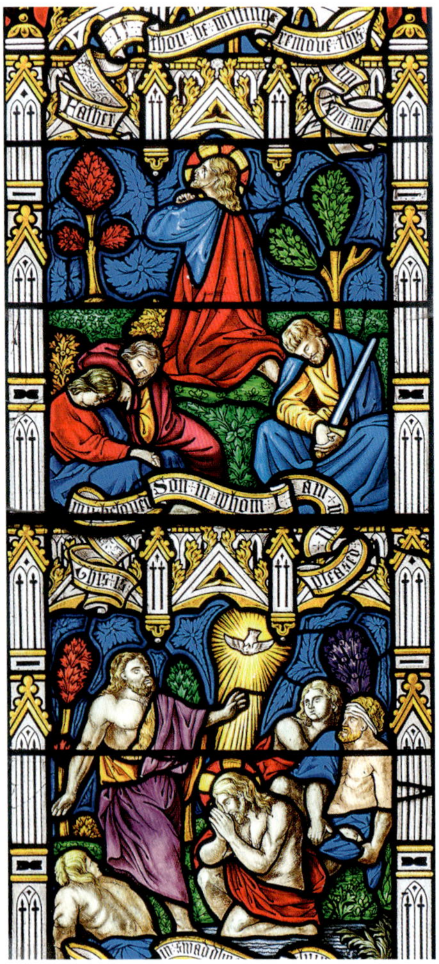

244. William Holland, Christ in the Garden of Gethsemane and the Baptism of Christ, 1849, Church of St Collen, Llangollen, north aisle

243. (Title page) Heaton & Butler, St Michael, 185
Church of St Michael, Michaelston-super-Ely, east windo

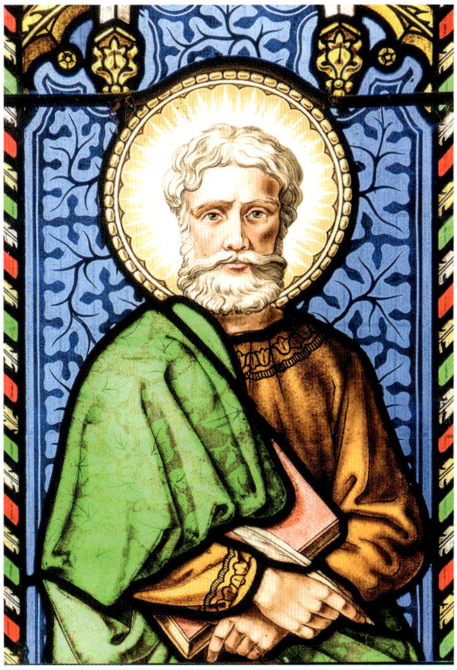

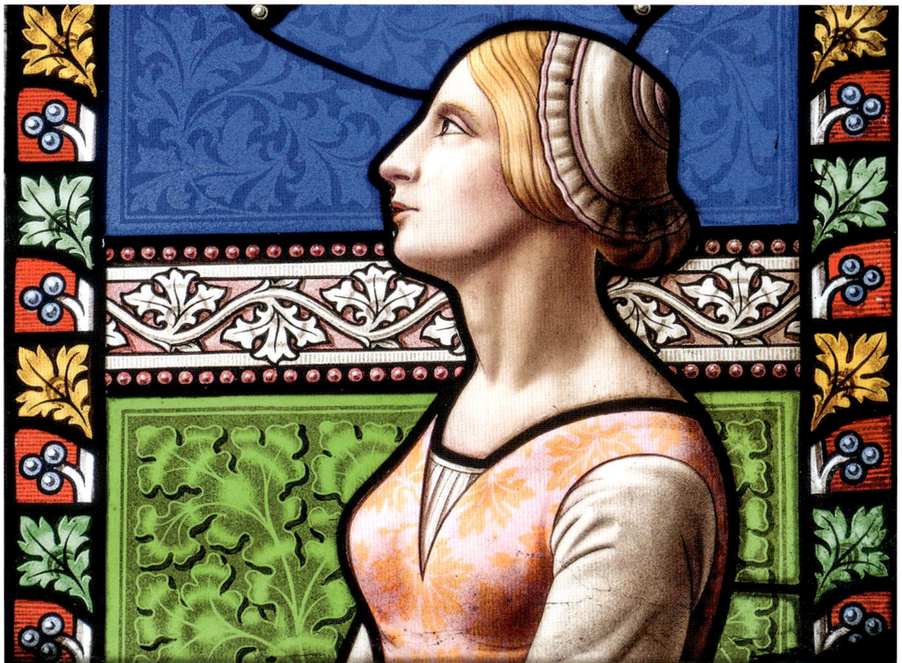

246. (above right) James Ballantine, Female Figure from Faith, Hope, Charity and Brotherly Kindness, *c.* 1853, Church of St Digain, Llangernyw, south transept

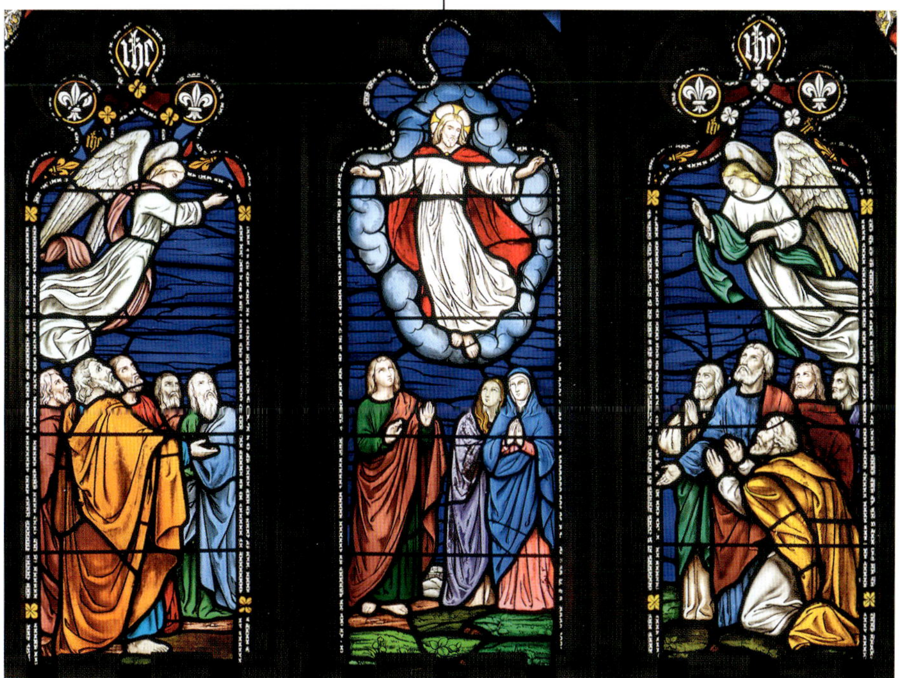

247. (right) James Powell & Sons, The Ascension, 1855, Church of St Andrew, Presteigne, east window

not shared by Charles Winston, whose report was influential on the jurors who awarded medals for glass painting. Winston endorsed the pictorial style developed in the first half of the sixteenth century, with scenes designed across the window lights and the use of light and shade.[5] As a result most of the medals did not reward those who worked in thirteenth and fourteenth-century styles. The English studios generally failed to impress the jury and four of the five medal winners were from the continent: the French makers Alfred Gérente and Maréchal & Guynon, S. Kellner of Bavaria and G. Bertini of Austria. Notwithstanding Winston's influence, A.W.N. Pugin was among the jury, and John Hardman & Co., whose work Pugin had designed, was the only English firm to be awarded a medal for stained glass.

4 *The Ecclesiologist*, vol. xii (1851), p. 184.

5 His view was criticised by the review of his *An Inquiry into the Difference of Style Observable in Ancient Glass Paintings* in *The Ecclesiologist*, vol. x (1849), pp. 92–97.

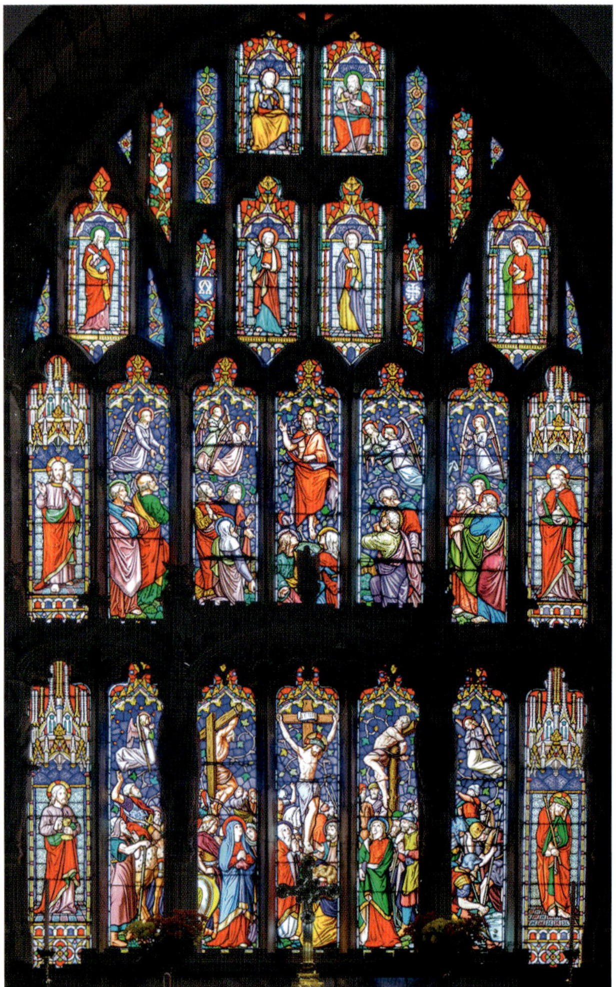

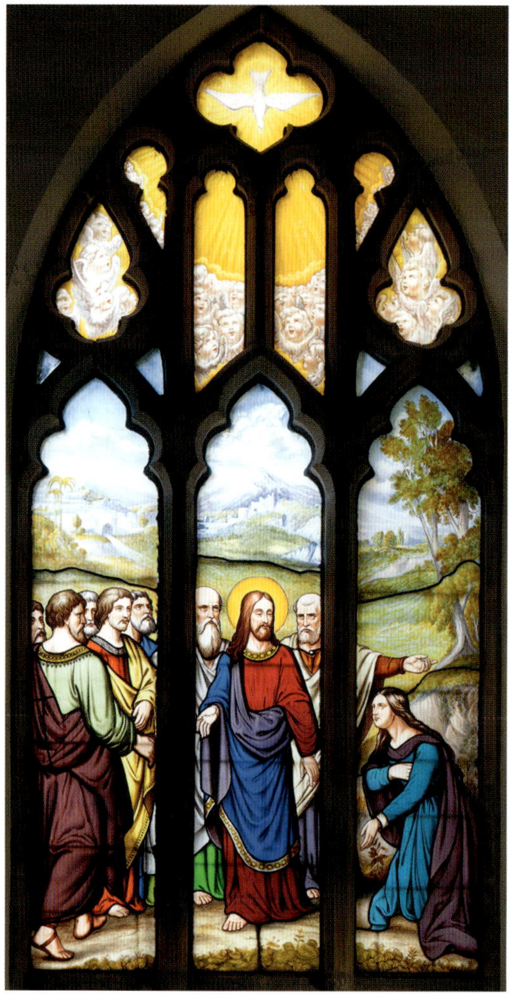

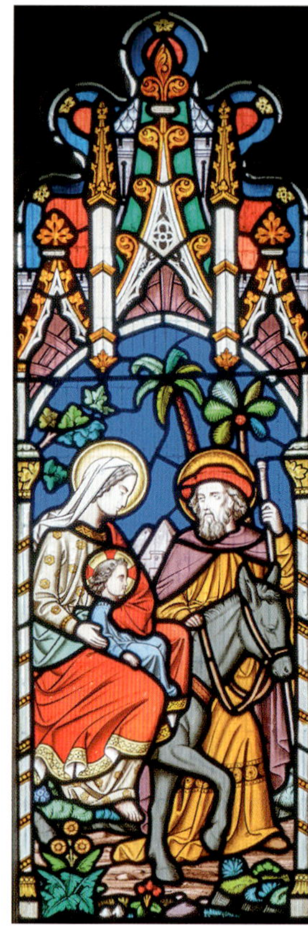

250. (above) Thomas Baillie, The Flight to Egypt, *c.* 1855–67, Church of the Holy Cross, Cowbridge, east window

248. (above left) Thomas Baillie, The Ascension and the Crucifixion, 1859, Church of St Nicholas, Montgomery, east window

249. (above centre) Thomas Baillie, Christ with the Woman who Touched the Hem of His Garment, *c.* 1857, Church of St Gwynog, Aberhafesp, east window

Edward Baillie took exception to the medal awarded to Hardman's and to the imitation of medieval styles in stained glass.[6] His ecclesiastical furnishing firm was taken over by his brother Thomas Baillie, after his death in 1856, and the firm's stained glass shows considerable variety in style. Their large five-light east window for the Church of St Nicholas, Montgomery, features a scene of the Crucifixion across the lower three central lights of the window, placed on blue grounds reminiscent of the stained glass of the late twelfth or thirteenth century. Yet one of the crucified figures is clearly derived from Rubens' *Le Coup de Lance* of 1620, and the scene has further parallels with the version of the painting in stained glass in the east window at Peterhouse College Chapel, Cambridge, made in about 1632.[7] Not far from Montgomery, the firm made two windows for the Church of St Gwynog, Aberhafesp, probably in about 1857, and also carved oak frames for the altar. The nave window has decorative floreate borders around an angel leading

6 His letter of complaint was reproduced in part in *The Builder*, vol. ix (6 December 1851), p. 774, and quotes Charles Winston extensively. Earlier in the year he had complained of the tendency to imitate poor medieval drawing and antiquate glass, *The Builder*, vol. ix (29 March 1851), p. 208.

7 The Peterhouse College Chapel window is described in detail by Jasmine Allen in *Vidimus*, 33, 2009 <http://vidimus.org/issues/issue-33/panel-of-the-month>.

a young woman to heaven, set on a patterned blue ground, the two figures divided by the central mullion of the two-light window. In contrast, the east window is in a thoroughly pictorial style, also spread across the whole width of the three-light window, with finely-painted flesh tones and detailed backgrounds. Other work by the studio, such as their east window for the Church of Holy Cross, Cowbridge, of an uncertain although roughly contemporary date, is in a late thirteenth or fourteenth-century Gothic style. In this window small scenes are confined within the window lights and painted with a medievalism typical of the work of Michael & Arthur O'Connor or William Wailes.

As well as showing versatility, the east window at Aberhafesp may still have been an exceptional commission. The tracery lights, with the descending dove of the Holy Spirit and cherubs, and a finely painted landscape in the upper main lights, were dated to about 1795 and attributed to Francis Eginton by Mostyn Lewis.[8] While the main scene of the late eighteenth-century window has clearly been supplanted, the inserted figures, and perhaps some of the background, effectively match the earlier work.

A group of painterly works in a similar style by Ballantine & Allan, also in the Diocese of St Asaph, but in the north of Denbighshire, can be found in the churches at Tremeirchion, Abergele and Llanelian-yn-Rhos.[9] The detailed modelling of the figures and skilfully-painted backgrounds are reminiscent of the pictorial style promoted by Charles Winston, and the comparatively high number of these works in this part of Wales may be attributable to Winston's family connections in north Wales at Rhyl. While the windows by Ballantine & Allan still demonstrate allusions to medieval stained glass design and coloration,

8 Mostyn Lewis, *Stained Glass in North Wales up to 1850* (Altrincham: John Sherratt and Son Ltd, 1970), p. 26.

9 Further windows by Ballantine & Allan can be found at the Church of St Llawddog, Cilgerran, where a more painterly approach to stained glass seems to have prevailed in the 1850s and 60s.

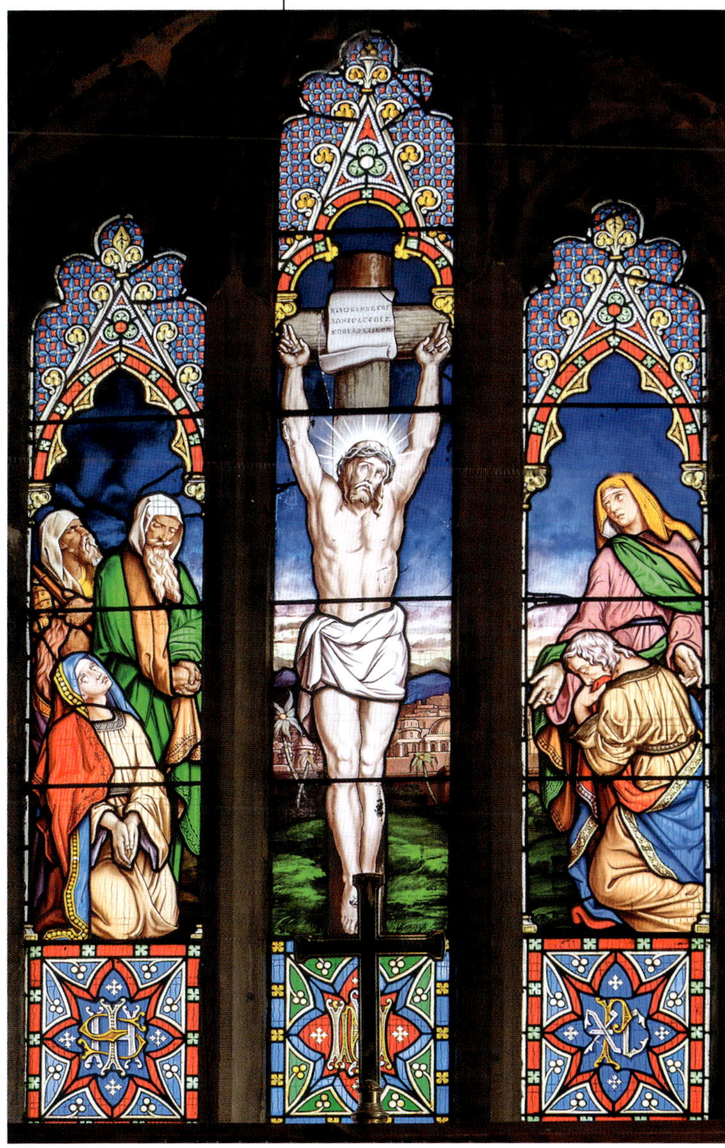

251. Ballantine & Allan, The Crucifixion, Church of St Elian, Llanelian-yn-Rhos, *c.* 1862, south chancel

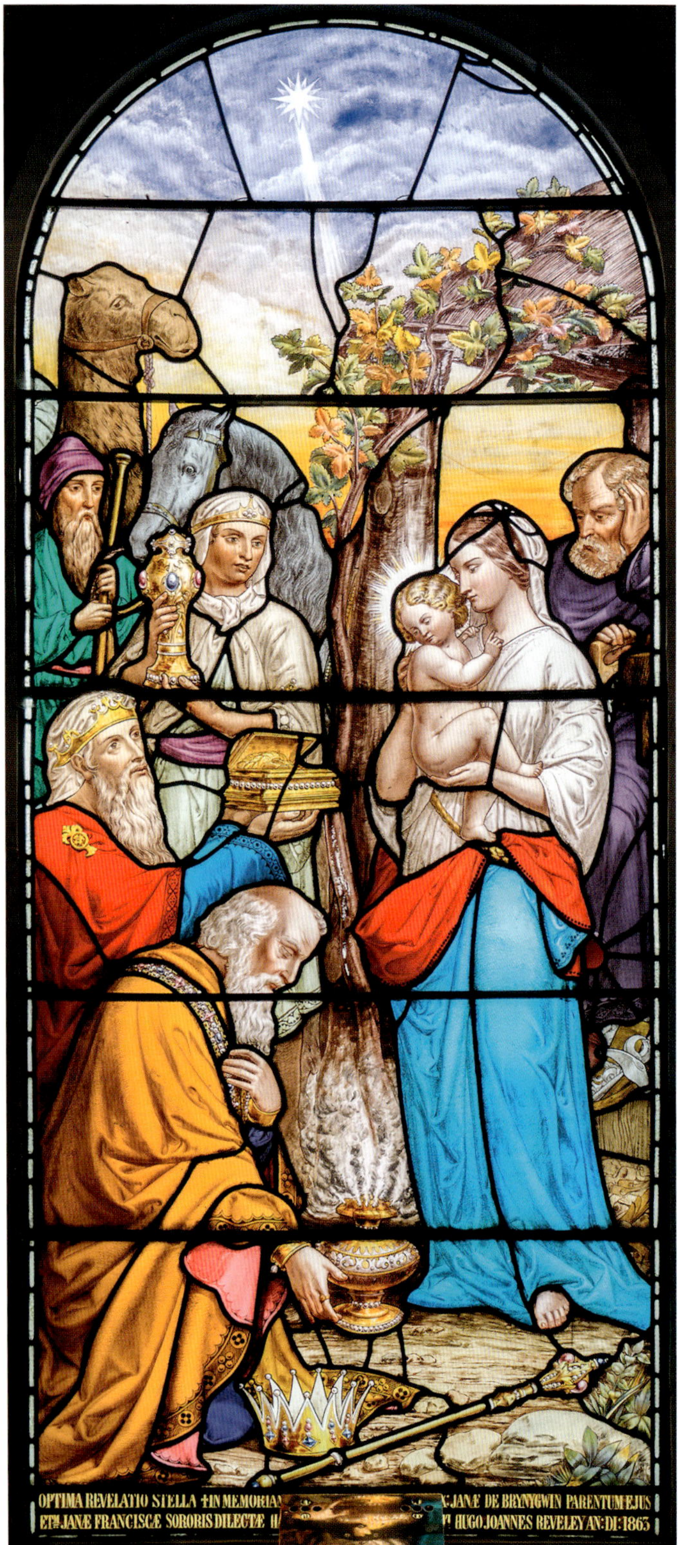

252. The Adoration of the Magi, probably 1860s, Church of St Mary, Dolgellau, sanctuary apse

a few windows of the period did not. For example, the window depicting the Adoration of the Magi at the Church of St Mary, Dolgellau, probably made in the mid-1860s, uses leading to delineate the figures in combination with coloured enamels for detailed paintwork.

The work of Jim Cheshire has shed considerable light on our understanding of the efforts of glass painters to establish their reputations in the west of England in the mid-nineteenth century. In the early stages of his career Joseph Bell of Bristol sometimes painted pictorial panels that were then installed by other studios, perhaps set in stock geometric patterns. Jealous of his own reputation, he sometimes signed these panels, as he did at Mathern, in an effort to stop other studios passing off his work as their own.[10] Lesser studios were able to supply stock decorative glass that did not require the work of a skilled glass painter. For example, at the Church of St Cadoc, Raglan, a large four-light window was installed by Mark Bowden & Co. of Bristol, a cut-glass works whose advertisement listed products including 'richly-cut and engraved crystal table-glass,

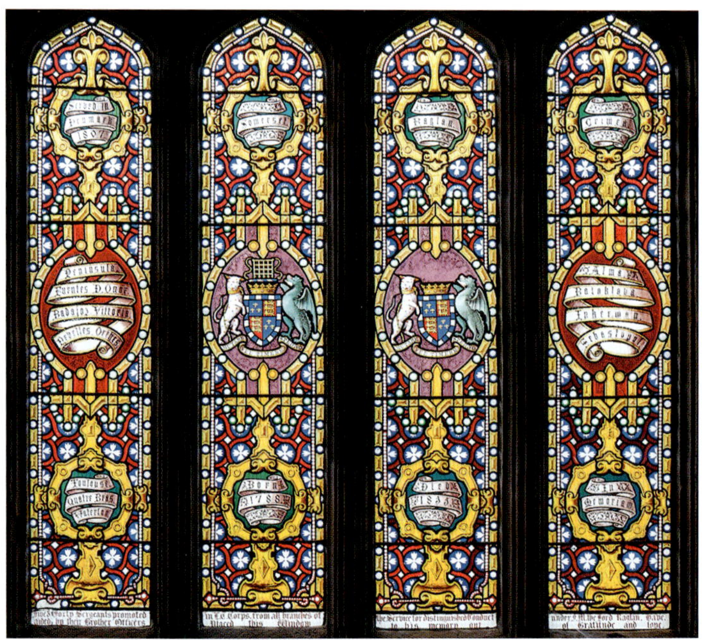

253. Mark Bowden & Co., Memorial Window, 1858, Church of St Cadoc, Raglan, north wall

cheval, toilet, and gilt chimney glasses' as well as 'brilliant-cut ornamental window glass'. The window was placed in memory of FitzRoy James Henry Somerset, the first Lord Raglan, and contains heraldry and the names of places where Lord Raglan had served during his career in the army, but is devoid of other imagery.

Success in winning commissions brought its own difficulties. The Great Exhibition arguably had a detrimental effect on makers, as their windows were perceived not as a creative process – a collaboration between patron, designer and maker – but as a range of commodities.[11] In response, and to compete on cost, firms recycled designs and adopted a production line approach to the design and manufacture of windows. Often known (usually disparagingly) as 'the trade', these stained glass studios increasingly became commercial, rather than artistic, enterprises, producing windows to suit a range of predefined architectural styles.

In this context, glass painters such as Joseph Bell found it difficult to be accepted as a creative artist. William Warrington and Francis Wilson Oliphant argued that the best stained glass could equal the art of oil painting in their books *The History of Stained Glass* (1848) and *A Plea for Stained Glass* (1855), and even *The Ecclesiologist* saw the need for skilled artists in the medium: 'a glass-painter who shall be himself an artist: no mere copyist, no mere chemist for the tinctures, no mere executor of another's designs;—but an artist whose particular medium is glass.'[12] In practice, artistic freedom was restricted by the controlling influence of the leading Gothic Revival architects, and *The Ecclesiologist* itself, whose editorial stance demanded adherence to its preferred medieval forms. Writing in *The Ecclesiologist* in 1852, the young G.E. Street refuted the claim that stained glass could be a 'high art', contending that it was merely an architectural craft that should be 'schemed out by the architect'.[13]

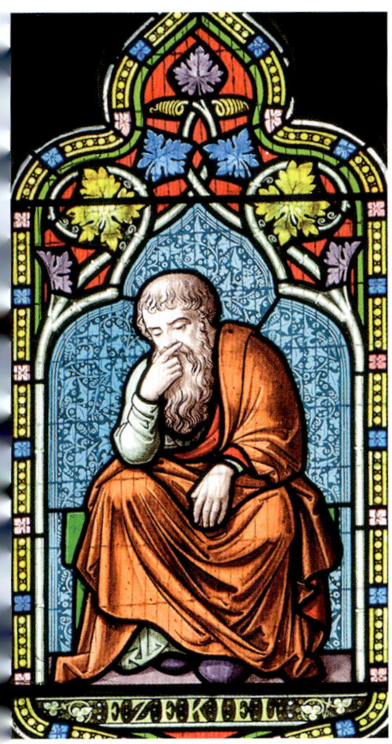

254. Joseph Bell, Ezekiel, 1864, Church of St Peter, Carmarthen, south aisle chapel

10 Jim Cheshire, *Stained glass and the Victorian Gothic Revival* (Manchester: Manchester University Press, 2004), pp. 111–13.

11 Jim Cheshire, *Stained glass and the Victorian Gothic Revival* (Manchester: Manchester University Press, 2004), pp. 157–8.

12 *The Ecclesiologist*, vol. x (1849), p. 97. Few artists in the medium could satisfactorily fit this description until the advent of the Arts and Crafts Movement at the end of the nineteenth century.

13 Furthermore, Street maintained that stained glass was only 'a vehicle for architectural decoration, and not primarily for the introduction of religious pictures into churches', something that should be done with murals. *The Ecclesiologist*, vol. x (1852) p. 241. In contrast, Edward Baillie quoted Charles Winston's contention that glass painting was 'as capable of high artistic development as a fresco painting', and that the 'display of high art depends not on the nature of the materials employed, but on the mode of employing them.' *The Builder*, vol. 9 (6 December 1851), p. 774.

With many commissions to be won for new and restored churches, the success of stained glass makers was enhanced by good working relationships with architects. Architects' studios also proved to be an important place for designers and artists to meet. Alfred Bell entered the studio of George Gilbert Scott in 1847, at the same time that George Edmund Street and George Frederick Bodley were working for Scott, both of whom became successful architects in their own right. It was during his brief period in the office of G.E. Street that the young William Morris met Philip Webb in 1856, forming a relationship that proved formative for the foundation of Morris, Marshall, Faulkner & Co. in 1861.[14]

Alfred Bell designed windows for Nathaniel Wood Lavers from 1855 to 1857, including the east windows for R.J. Withers' churches at Aberporth and Llanfair Nant-Gwyn. Bell also designed for James Powell & Sons from 1854 until 1871, but his collaboration with John Richard Clayton from 1856 led to the formation of one of the most successful stained glass firms in Britain. Initially their windows were made by Clement Heaton and James Butler, who had formed a partnership in 1855, but within fifteen years the firm of Clayton & Bell had more than 300 employees working at their own workshops in Regent Street, London.[15]

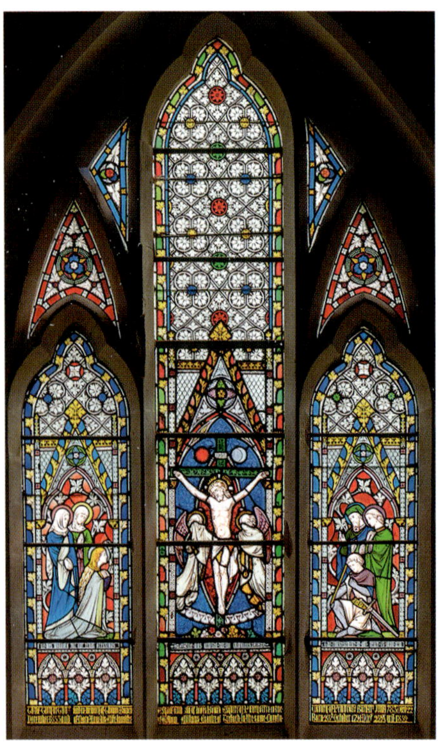

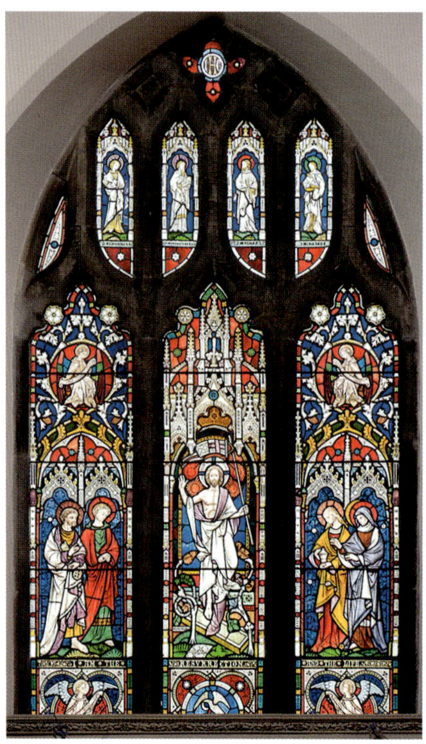

In 1860 John Hardman & Co. and William Wailes were the two largest studios making stained glass in England. But high output brought inconsistency: 'Why is it that Mr Wailes's work is always a lottery?' asked the *Ecclesiologist* in 1852.[16] Architects such as John Loughborough Pearson and Gilbert Scott, who had used Wailes for their buildings in the 1850s, increasingly went to other firms, notably Hardman's and the newly established Clayton & Bell. The east

255. (far left) N.W. Lavers, The Crucifixion, 1857, designed by Alfred Bell, Church of St Mary, Llanfair Nant-Gwyn, east window

256. (left) Clayton & Bell, The Resurrection, *c.* 1866, Church of St Catwg, Llangattock

14 Morris abandoned his intention to enter the Church in 1855 and decided, along with his close friend Edward Jones (later Burne-Jones), to pursue an artistic vocation. Morris approached Street to take him as a pupil, although the arrangement was short-lived. See Fiona MacCarthy, *William Morris: A Life for Our Time* (London: Faber and Faber, 1994), pp. 102–5.

15 Peter Larkworthy, *Clayton & Bell, Stained Glass Artists and Decorators* (London: The Ecclesiological Society, 1984), pp. 7–15. For additional detail on the early work of J.R. Clayton and Alfred Bell, see Martin Harrison, *Victorian Stained Glass* (London: Barrie & Jenkins, 1980), pp. 30–2, and William Waters, *Angels & Icons: Pre-Raphaelite Stained Glass 1850–1870* (Abbots Morton: Seraphim Press, 2012), pp. 41–65.

16 *The Ecclesiologist*, vol. xiii (1852), pp. 409–12.

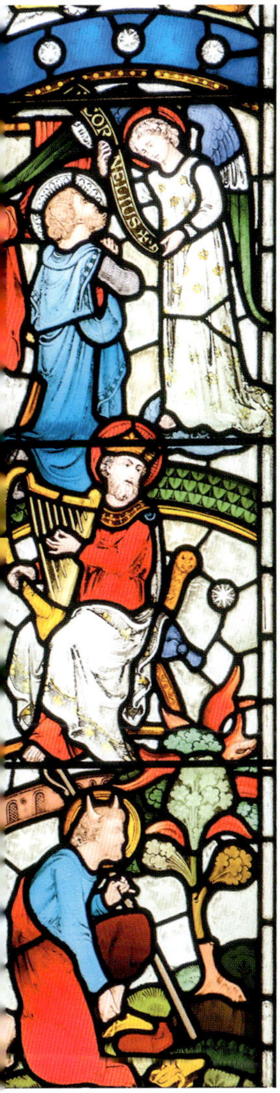

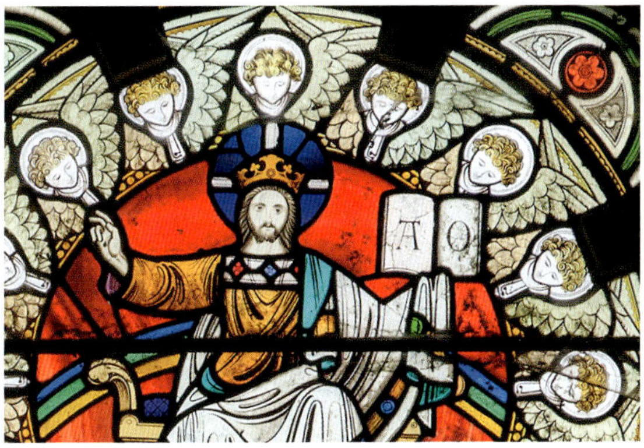

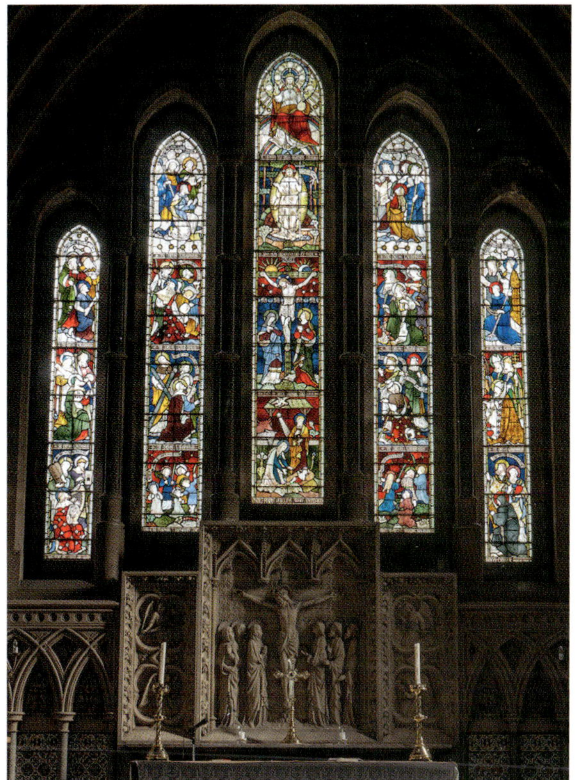

257. (left) Clayton & Bell, Cornelius, David and Moses from the 'Te Deum', 1868, Eglwys Oen Duw (Church of the Lamb of God), Beulah, west window

258. (above) Clayton & Bell, Christ in Majesty, *c.* 1865, Church of St Llonio, Llandinam, east window

259. (right) Clayton & Bell, 'Te Deum', *c.* 1877, Church of All Saints, Llanelli, east window

window for the Church of St Mary, Towyn (Denbighshire), was made by Hardman's to Street's design, where the architect's important collection of buildings were commissioned by the Tractarian Robert Bamford-Hesketh.[17] Street worked with Clayton & Bell at numerous churches in Wales in the 1860s and 70s. Clayton & Bell provided the east windows for his restored church at Llandinam in 1864–5, his new chancel at Carrog in 1867 and his new church at Bettisfield in 1874.[18] Street himself designed the east window that the firm made for the Church of St Tysilio, Llandysilio, built in 1867 and during the same year Clayton & Bell were responsible for the restoration of the medieval glass in the seven-light east window of the chancel at Gresford under Street.[19] Another notable collaboration with Street in the 1870s is the east window by the firm at Street's new Church of All Saints, Llanelli, which is part of an impressive east end boasting a large carved reredos designed by Street. In the 1860s Clayton & Bell were responsible for the sanctuary apse windows at the Church of St David, Neath, and the east and west windows at Eglwys Oen Duw (Church of the Lamb of God), Beulah, both important buildings in Wales designed by John Norton.

The early stained glass by Clayton & Bell shows considerable originality, although it soon became conventional in the 1860s, as its popularity

17 John Hardman & Co. continued to specialise in metalwork, Hardman's original business, and provided the altar plate and four coronae of twenty-four lights. D.R. Thomas, *The History of the Diocese of St Asaph* (Oswestry: Caxton Press, 1913), vol. iii, p. 231.

18 Clayton & Bell also made a three-light window for the south wall at Carrog in 1863 in memory of Edward and Frances Lloyd. The painted panels by the Misses Lloyd of Rhagatt from the former east window were reset in the nave windows when the new chancel was added in 1867, at the expense of Gertrude Jane Mary Lloyd, in memory of her husband, the artist's brother, John.

19 In 1872 Clayton & Bell restored the Lady Chapel east window at Gresford, with scenes from the life of Mary. Clayton & Bell also provided further new windows for the church.

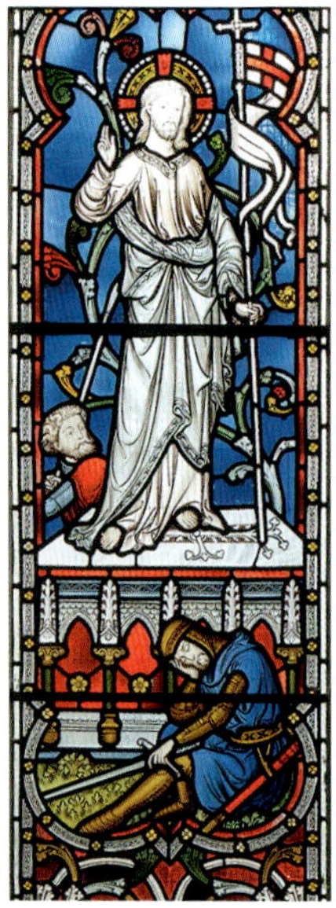

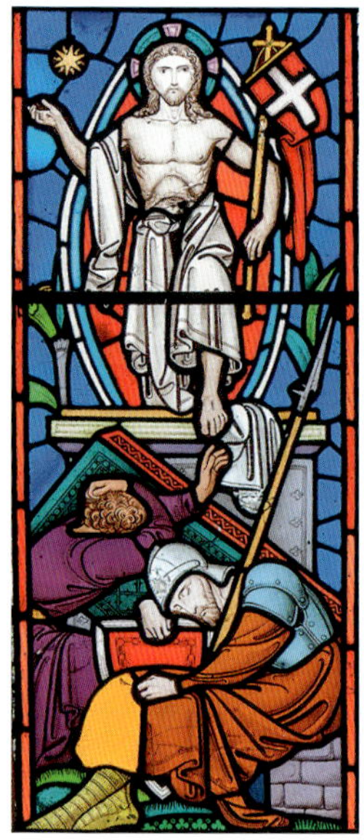

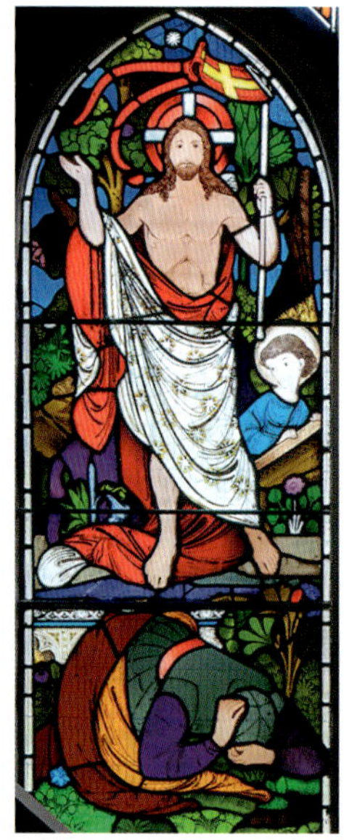

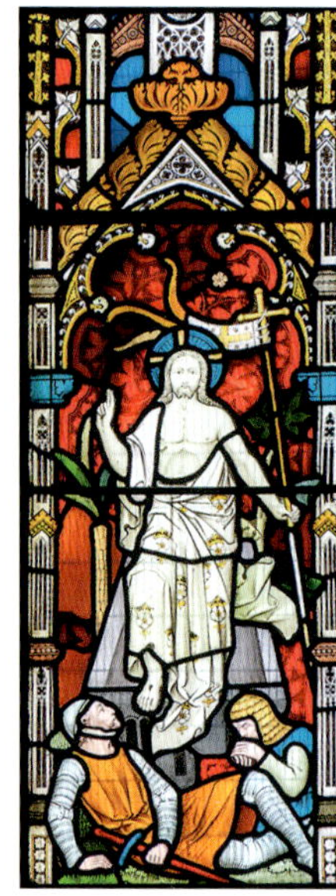

260–3. Scenes of the Resurrection (left to right): John Hardman & Co., 1872, Church of St Llawddog, Cenarth, sanctuary apse; Heaton, Butler & Bayne, 1863, Church of St Barnabas, Felindre (Carmarthenshire), sanctuary apse; Heaton, Butler & Bayne, 1866, Church of St Mary the Virgin, Abbey Cwm-hir, east window; Clayton & Bell, *c.* 1865, Church of St David, Neath; sanctuary apse

and output increased. Despite their successful, if no doubt subordinate, collaboration with architects such as G.E. Street, both J.R. Clayton and Alfred Bell still took their artistic abilities seriously, also expressing it in other media. Bell was a prolific watercolourist and exhibited at the Royal Academy, while Clayton worked as a sculptor and was a friend of Dante Gabriel Rossetti and a member of the Hogarth Club, an exhibition society founded by members of the Pre-Raphaelite Brotherhood.[20]

One of Clayton's pupils, Robert Bayne, joined the firm of Heaton & Butler in 1862. His designs reflect the liveliness of Clayton & Bell's earliest work such as those used in the sanctuary of the Church of St Barnabas, Felindre (Carmarthenshire). Their colouration, which derives from late twelfth to thirteenth-century glass, was also similar to early work by Clayton & Bell and often employed by other firms such as John Hardman & Co. and Lavers & Barraud in the 1850s and 60s. The set of windows designed by Robert Bayne at Abbey Cwm-hir demonstrates the work of the firm at its most inventive. The scene of the resurrection in the east window depicts Christ in a conventional medieval pose, although the overall design is much more original, as is the depiction of the Baptism of Christ and Christ in the Garden of Gethsemane, all of which make full use of the window lights without borders or canopies. They also demonstrate a slightly subtler palette, employing a greater use of green, brown and ochre glass, colours which were more associated with the fourteenth century. In the 1860s Clayton & Bell also made windows in a style closer to that of the fourteenth century, often making more use of architectural canopies.[21]

20 The case for J.R. Clayton to be considered among the Pre-Raphaelite Brotherhood is put convincingly in William Waters, *Angels & Icons: Pre-Raphaelite Stained Glass 1850–1870* (Abbots Morton: Seraphim Press, 2012), pp. 41–60.

21 The use of canopies and decorative surrounds also had the advantage of facilitating the reuse of cartoons for different sized windows, streamlining production to meet demand.

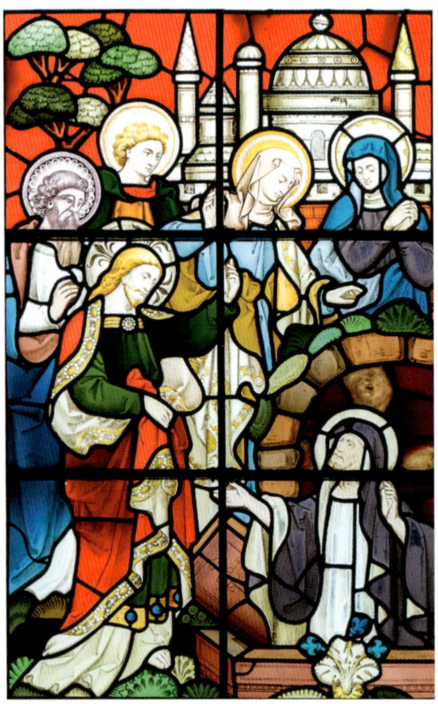

264. Clayton & Bell, The Raising of Lazarus, *c.* 1865, Church of St Mary, Dolgellau, south aisle

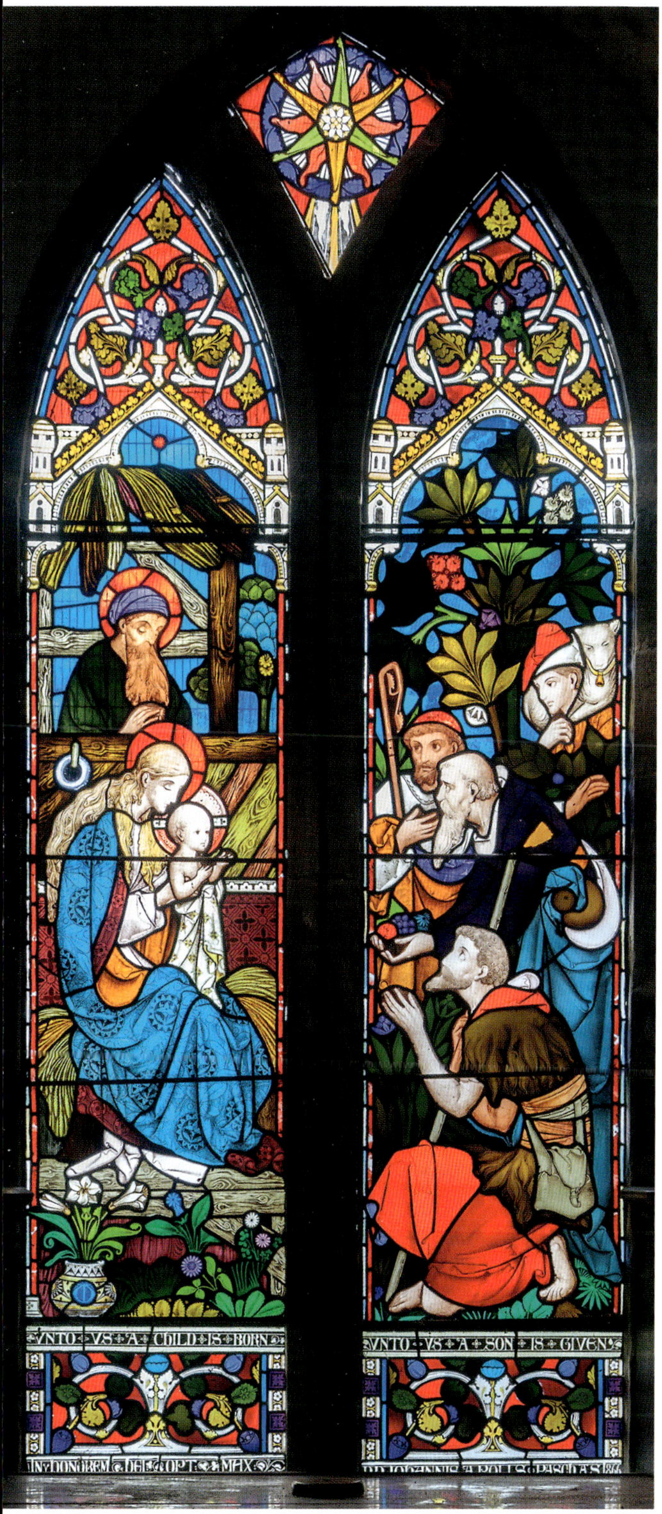

265. Heaton, Butler & Bayne, 1866, Church of St Meugan, St Maughans, east window

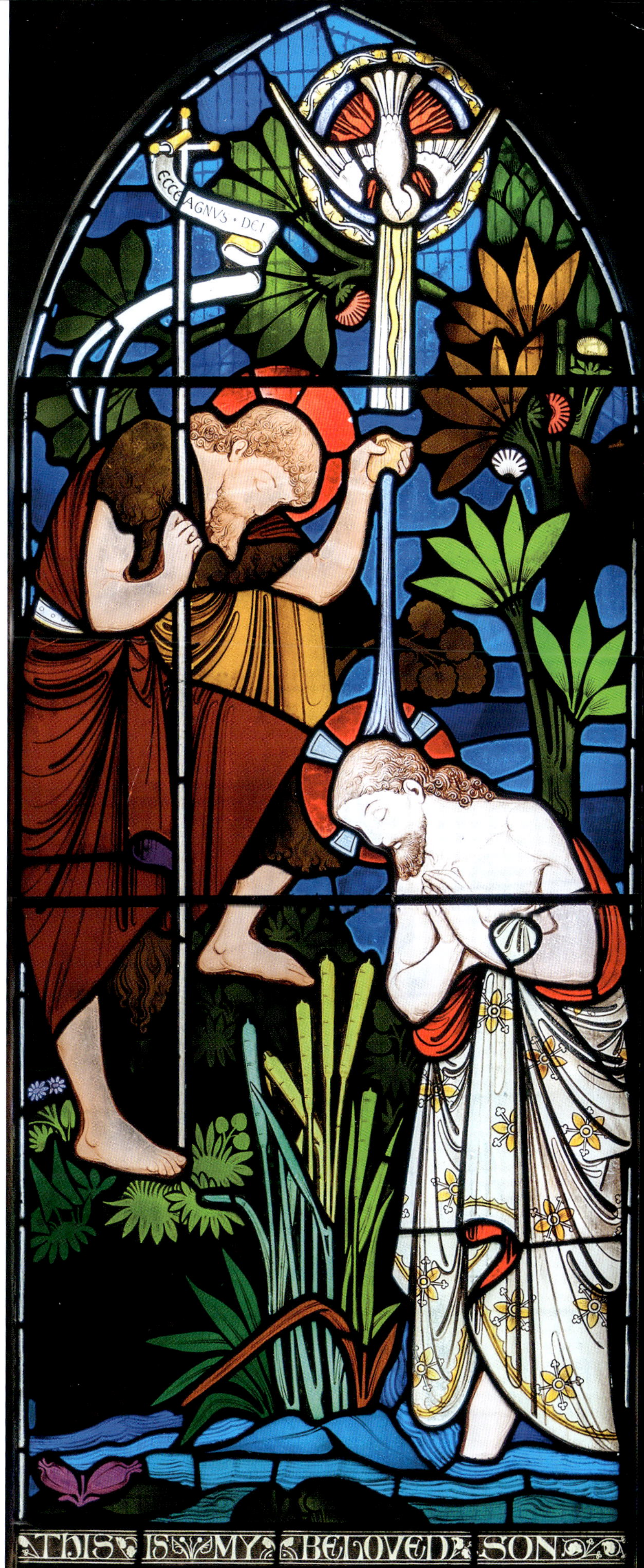

266. Heaton, Butler & Bayne, The Baptism of Christ, 1866, Church of St Mary the Virgin, Abbey Cwm-hir, chancel

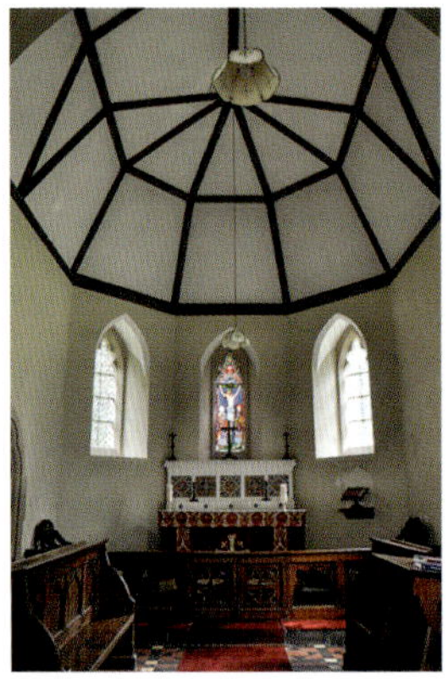

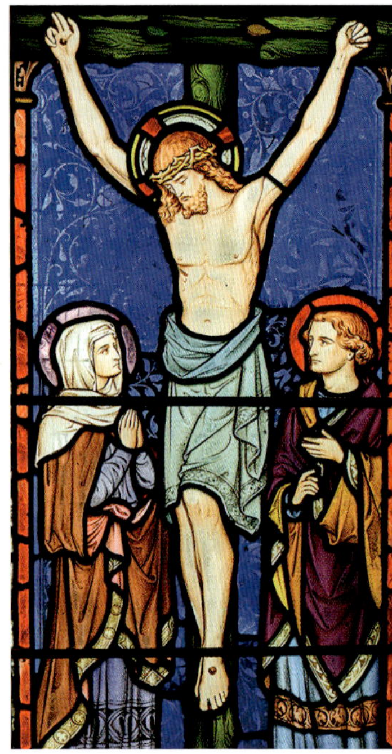

267–8. R.J. Withers, Church of St Dogmael, Meline, 1865 (right), with stained glass by Lavers & Barraud, The Crucifixion (far right)

In 1858 N.W. Lavers entered into a partnership with Francis Barraud and enjoyed a fruitful association with the architect R.J. Withers. Withers was a member of the Ecclesiological Society and unusually busy in west Wales for a London architect. He consistently used stained glass made by Lavers & Barraud for windows installed in the churches that he built or restored. Withers' concern for the provision of stained glass was clear in his gift of stained glass for his church at Llandygwydd in 1862, where a window was also given by Lavers.[22] Many of these churches were relatively modest, and a lone chancel window often effectively sets off the interior of otherwise simple churches, such as at the Church of St Dogmael, Meline, Pembrokeshire.[23] Other contemporary work by Lavers & Barraud for churches designed by Withers in the 1860s include their chancel windows at Nevern, Blaenporth and Llangoedmor, although the architect's main work in the region, the Church of St Peter, Lampeter, has stained glass by Bell & Almond.[24] Some work by Lavers & Barraud was designed by Barraud, while other windows made by the firm were designed by John Milner Allen, and Nathaniel Westlake, who later became a partner in the firm.

While architects such as Withers worked with one or two firms quite regularly, some took longer to establish a satisfactory relationship. William Butterfield worked with Michael O'Connor until his eyesight began to fail in the mid-1850s, after which the firm's work was supervised by his son Arthur. Butterfield also worked with other firms and artists including William Wailes, John Hardman & Co., Joseph Bell and Frederick Preedy.

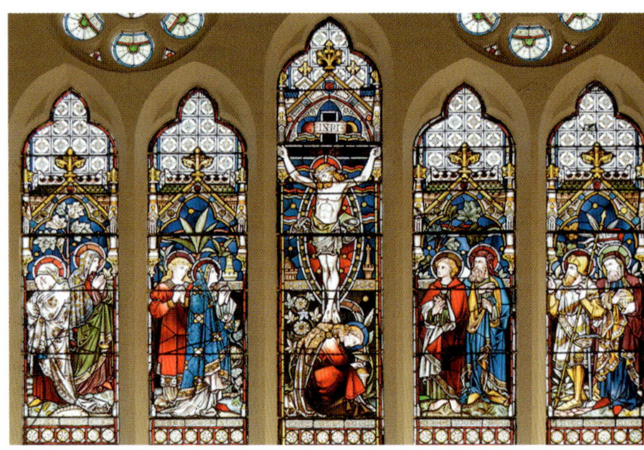

269. Bell & Almond, The Crucifixion, 1875, Church of St Peter, Lampeter, east window

22 See Gwynfor Rees, '"The new and very satisfying church of Llandygwydd": The transient glory of a flawed edifice', *Ceredigion*, vol. xiv, no. 4 (2004), p. 31. Other architects gave windows for churches in Wales. In north Wales Thomas Penson gave windows during the 1850s for the church that he designed at Gwersyllt, near Wrexham, where he lived, and the Chester architect John Douglas provided the east window of 1867 for his church at Sealand, made by John Hardman & Co.

23 The scene of the Crucifixion with Mary and John by Lavers & Barraud, in the sanctuary apse at Meline, was made from the same cartoon as the central scene of the three-light window depicting scenes from the Passion and Resurrection at Caerwent. The latter was moved to Caerwent from Angersleigh in Somerset and inserted as a First World War memorial, but both were independently dated 1865. The design was also used as the central light of the east window at Raglan, completed in about 1868, the year in which the designer of the panel, Nathaniel Westlake, became a partner of the firm.

24 Daniel Bell trained with his brother's firm Clayton & Bell. He worked with Richard Almond until 1875, the date of the east window at Lampeter. This was inserted five years after the building of the church, although two windows on the south side of the church seem to have been added in 1870. The window by Lavers & Barraud of 1864 at the Church of St Brynach, Nevern, inserted at the time of the building of the church, was also placed in the south side of the chancel, but the east window was not filled with stained glass until about 1879, probably by Clayton & Bell.

270. Lavers & Barraud, The Angel of the Resurrection, from the Three Marys Visit the Empty Tomb, 1865, Church of St Eleri and St Mary, Llanrhos, east winc

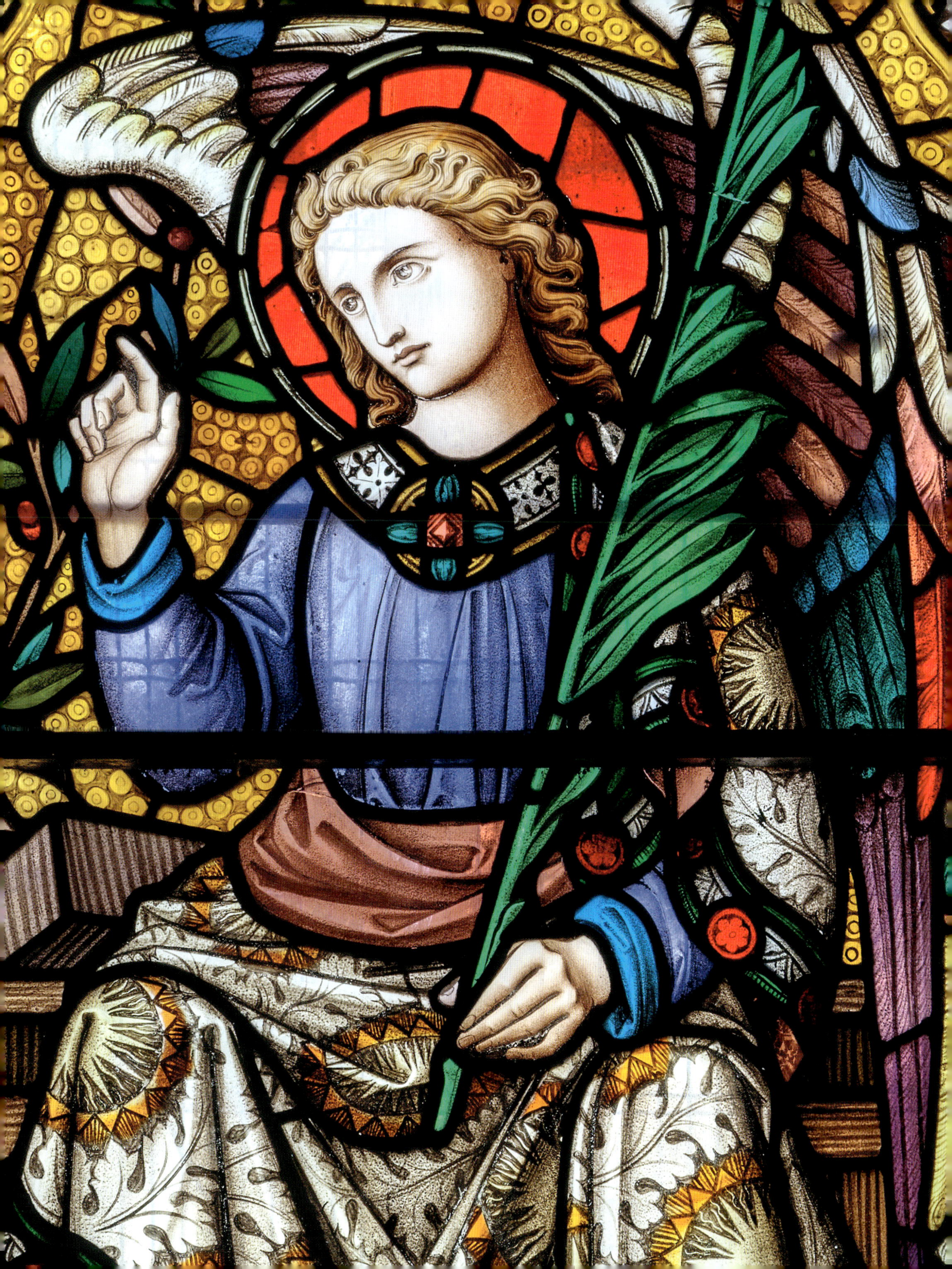

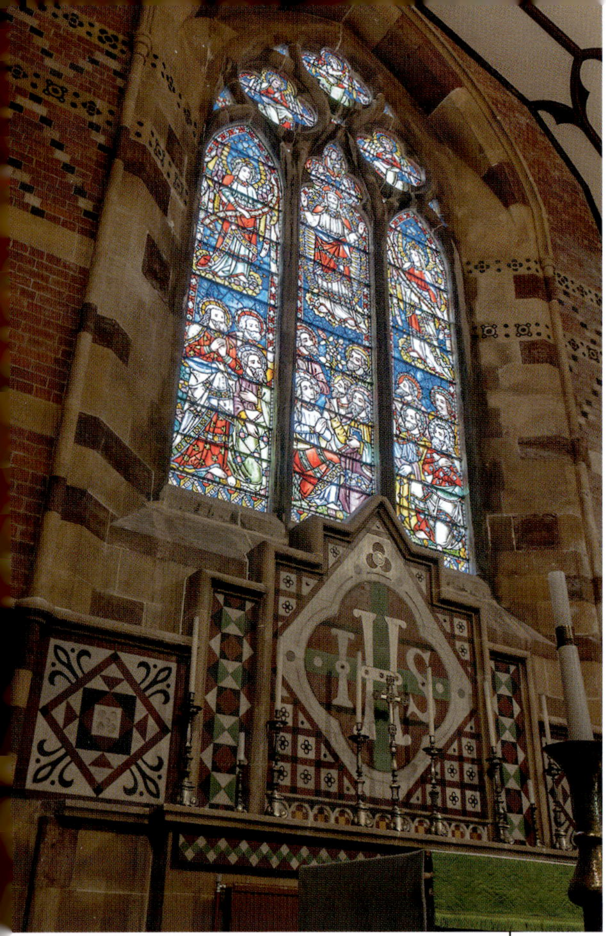

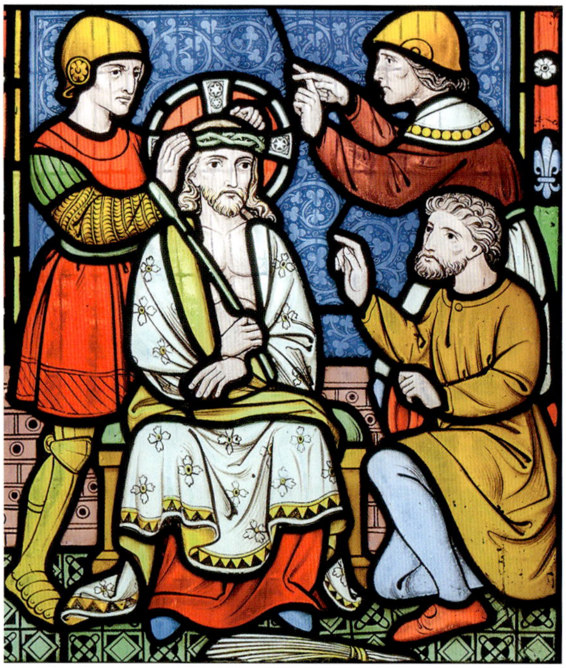

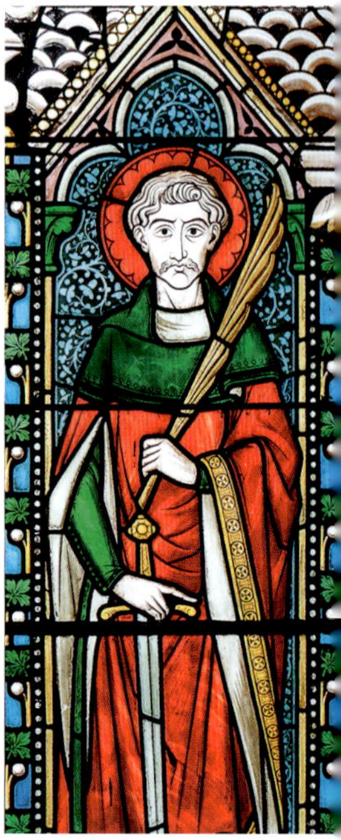

271. (left) Alexander Gibbs, The Ascension, 1866, Church of St Augustine, Penarth, east window

272. (above) Alexander Gibbs, The Mocking of Christ, 1868, Church of St Peter, Elerch, east window

273. Alfred Gérente, St Alban, 1857, Llanfrechfa Grange (from the south aisle of the Church of All Saints, Margaret Street, London)

Butterfield quarrelled with John Hardman and his leading designer John Hardman Powell, and eventually embarked on a longer lasting relationship with Alexander Gibbs, who made the east windows for his churches at Penarth and Elerch. The Church of St Augustine, Penarth, was generously funded by Baroness Windsor, who had been the main benefactor at the Church of St Mary, St Fagans, while at Elerch, the Revd Lewis Gilbertson, the Tractarian vicar of Llangorwen, was the patron.[25] Gibbs had provided the replacement glass for Butterfield's most influential church, the Church of All Saints, Margaret Street, in London, where the original glass by Alfred Gérente did not suit the architect's polychromatic interior and was taken out. Some of these panels were acquired for Llanfrechfa Grange, now on the edge of modern Cwmbrân.[26]

Alexander Gibbs was the son of the glass painter Isaac Gibbs, and his brothers Charles and Isaac also made stained glass. Charles Gibbs made windows for a number of churches in Wales, while Alexander Gibbs and his firm made further windows for Welsh churches independently of his collaborations with Butterfield. His large five-light east windows for the Church of St Dunawd, Bangor-on-Dee, in 1868 and at the Church of

25 See John Morgan-Guy, 'Glass by Alexander Gibbs at Elerch: An exploration of the heart of the Christian faith from the Gothic Revival', 2009 <http://www.imagingthebible.org/wales/research/essays/elerch.html>. For Butterfield's dealings with stained glass practitioners see Paul Thompson, *William Butterfield* (London: Routledge & Kegan Paul, 1971), pp. 461–8; and Martin Harrison, *Victorian Stained Glass* (London: Barrie & Jenkins, 1980), pp. 26–9. For his work with Frederick Preedy see Michael Kerney, *The Stained Glass of Frederick Preedy (1820–1898)* (London: The Ecclesiological Society, 2001), pp. 14–17; for his early collaboration with Joseph Bell in 1845 see Jim Cheshire, *Stained glass and the Victorian Gothic Revival* (Manchester: Manchester University Press, 2004), pp. 114–15.

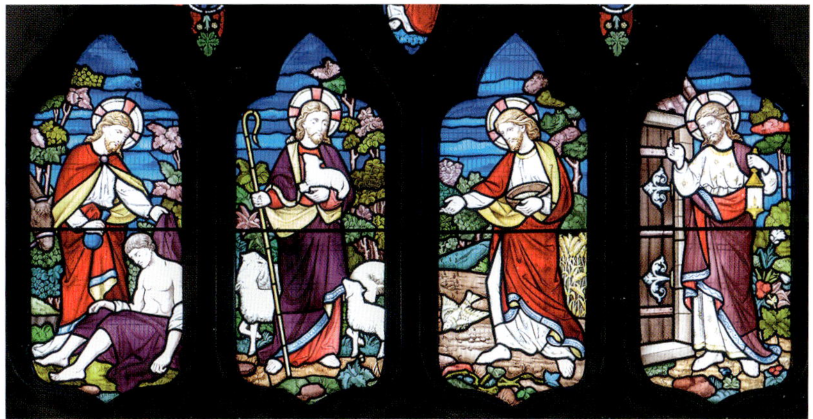

274. Alexander Gibbs, Christ as the Good Samaritan, the Good Shepherd, the Sower and the Light of the World, 1873, Church of St Peter, Carmarthen, east window

St Peter, Carmarthen, are both confident works with a similar use of strong colour. Both also employ a more natural figurative style with background landscapes, compared to the awkward Byzantine figures on patterned blue grounds prescribed by Butterfield at Penarth. Butterfield's designs also dispense with architectural or ornamental borders around the pictorial scenes used by Gibbs and other designers of the period, although Butterfield's influence is perhaps seen in the four depictions of Christ in the large tracery lights at Carmarthen, where the scenes completely fill the openings.

26 See Michael Kerney, 'All Saints, Margaret Street: a glazing history', *The Journal of Stained Glass*, vol. xxv, 2001, pp. 27–52.

The architect John Pollard Seddon took a particularly close interest in fittings and furnishings, including the stained glass, both for his own churches and those designed or restored in collaboration with the Llandaff diocesan architect John Prichard. Seddon worked with a number of makers, including Lavers & Barraud, who made a window to his design at Dixton in 1862, and Clayton & Bell, who interpreted his unusual design for the large east window at Christ's College Chapel, Brecon, in 1865, using much patterned white glass. In the same year, Seddon employed the Smethwick firm of Chance Brothers to make the east window to his design for the Church of St John the Evangelist, Maindee, Newport.

Through his brother, the painter Thomas Seddon, J.P. Seddon was introduced to the work of the circle of Dante Gabriel Rossetti and William Morris, and in 1863 Morris, Marshall, Faulkner & Co. made the east window for Prichard and Seddon's church at Coity. The most important work by the partnership of

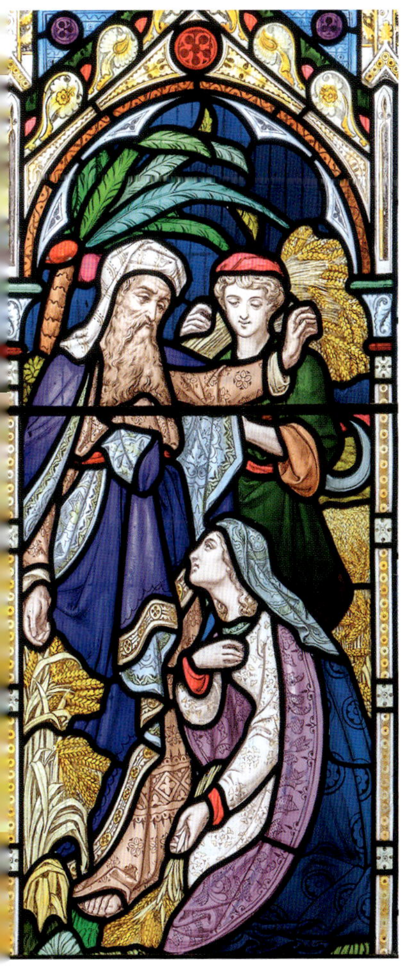

275. Charles A. Gibbs, Ruth and Boaz, *c.* 1872, Church of St Faith, Llanfoist, nave

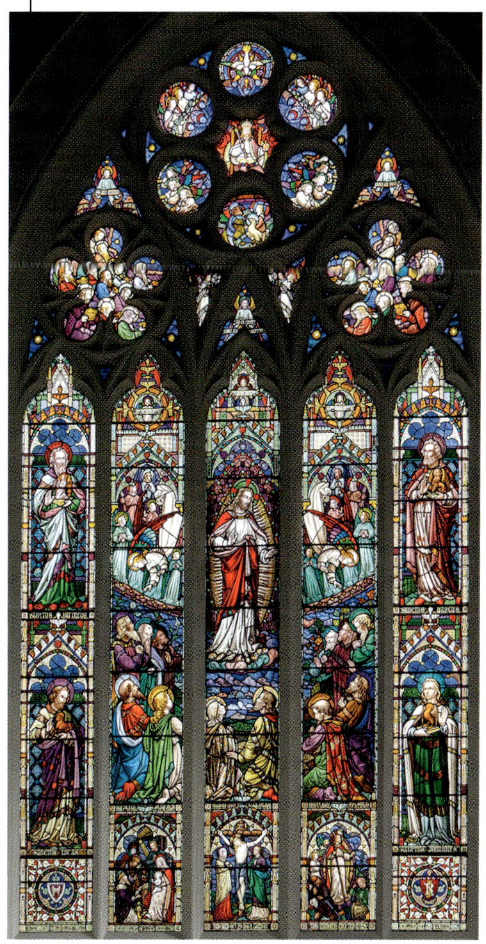

276. Chance Brothers, The Ascension, 1865, Church of St John the Evangelist, Maindee, Newport, east window

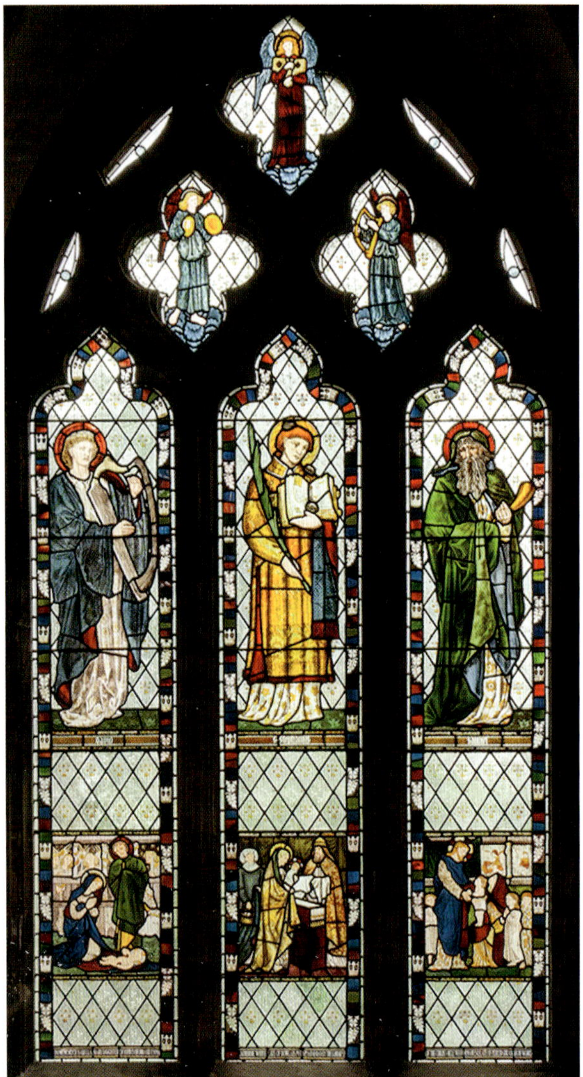

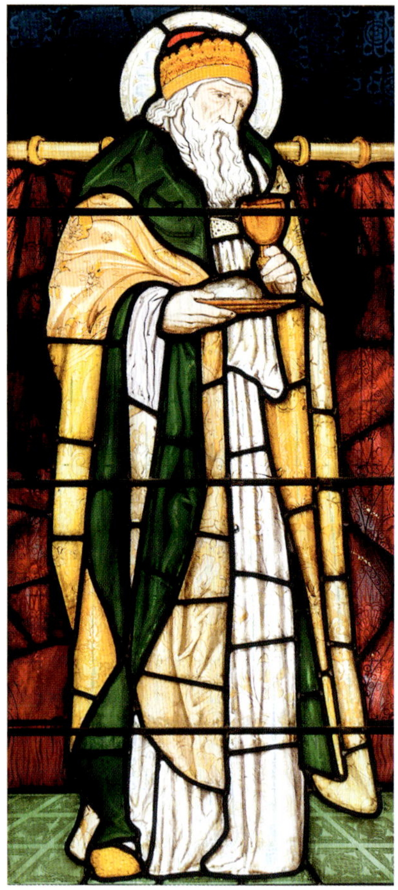

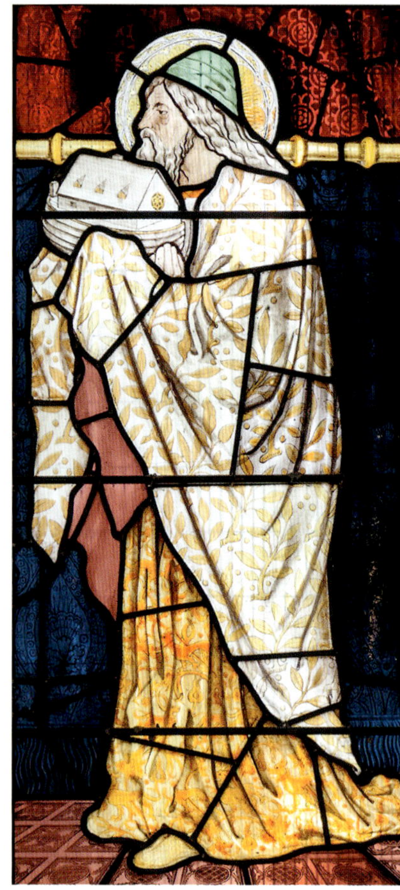

277. (left) Morris, Marshall, Faulkner & Co., St Stephen with David and Samuel, 1869, figures and scenes designed by Edward Burne-Jones, except the Presentation in the Temple, by William Morris, Llandaff Cathedral, south aisle

278–9. (above) Morris, Marshall, Faulkner & Co., Melchizedek, designed by Edward Burne-Jones (left), and Noah, designed by Ford Madox Brown (right), 1869, Church of St John the Baptist, Cardiff, north wall

Prichard & Seddon was the restoration of Llandaff Cathedral during the 1860s, and Clayton & Bell and Lavers & Barraud made windows to Seddon's design in 1861 and 1864. Morris' firm produced five windows for the cathedral between 1866 and 1874, with figures and scenes by a number of designers, placed on delicately-patterned quarries.[27]

The success of the firm's early stained glass built on the previous experience of Edward Burne-Jones and Ford Madox Brown as designers for the medium and the recruitment of experienced craftsmen such as George Campfield, who had worked as a glass painter for Heaton & Butler.[28] The firm received further commissions from the Llandaff diocese, such as at the Church of St John the Baptist, Cardiff, in 1869, and churches at Margam and Newton Nottage in the 1870s. Morris saw their work

27 The windows by Clayton & Bell and Lavers & Barraud did not survive the destruction of the Cathedral by a land mine in 1941, whereas the Morris, Marshall, Faulkner & Co. windows had been taken out for safe-keeping. For the glass at Llandaff see Nevil A. James, 'The Stained Glass of Llandaff Cathedral' in Nick Lambert (ed.), *Llandaff Cathedral* (Bridgend: Seren, 2010), pp. 171–98. The work of the Pre-Raphaelite artists at Llandaff Cathedral is discussed in David Jasper, 'Pre-Raphaelite Biblical Art in Wales' in *Biblical Art from Wales* (Sheffield: Sheffield Phoenix Press, 2010), pp. 147–9.

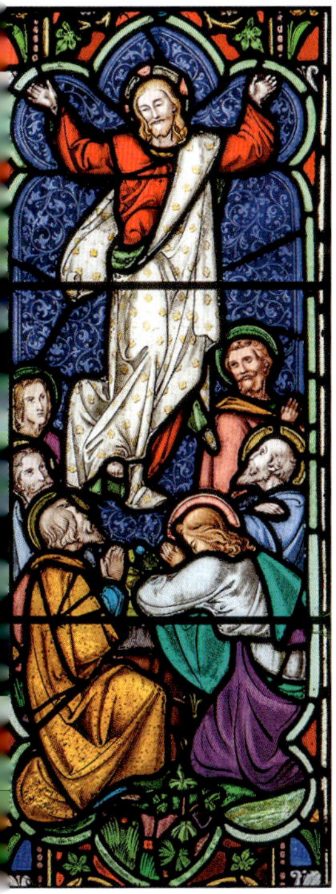

280. Cox & Sons, The Ascension, *c.* 1868, Church of St Thomas á Becket, Haverfordwest, south wall

as distinct from other major firms such as Ward & Hughes and Clayton & Bell, and was particularly dismissive of windows made by the 'curious nondescript mixture of clerical tailor and decorator that flourishes in Southampton Street, Strand.'[29]

Thomas Cox was a clerical tailor who was making stained glass by 1862 on Maiden Lane and moved nearby to Southampton Street as Cox & Son by 1878. As well as furniture, metalwork and soft furnishing, their windows were designed by 'eminent church designers', according to their catalogue of 1870.[30] Cox & Sons' Crucifixion and Ascension of about 1868, made for the Church of St Thomas á Becket, Haverfordwest, sets the two scenes on a patterned blue ground with decorative surrounds in a loosely thirteenth-century style. In comparison with windows by Morris, Marshall, Faulkner & Co., Cox & Sons' figures appear mannered and their full-coloured compositions conventional and unsophisticated. In contrast, Morris bought the best antique glass from James Powell & Sons and his colours, which he personally supervised, are muted.[31] Two of their windows at Llandaff have compact and detailed scenes below the figures; those by Ford Madox Brown beneath the saints Simon, Peter and Jude are especially lively in comparison to the earlier, more awkward, lower panels beneath the psalmist David, Stephen and Samuel by Edward Burne-Jones.[32]

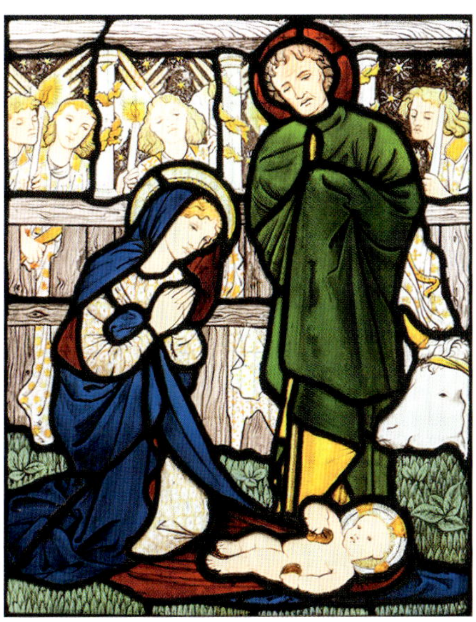

281. Morris, Marshall, Faulkner & Co., The Nativity with Angels, 1869, designed by Edward Burne-Jones, Llandaff Cathedral, south aisle

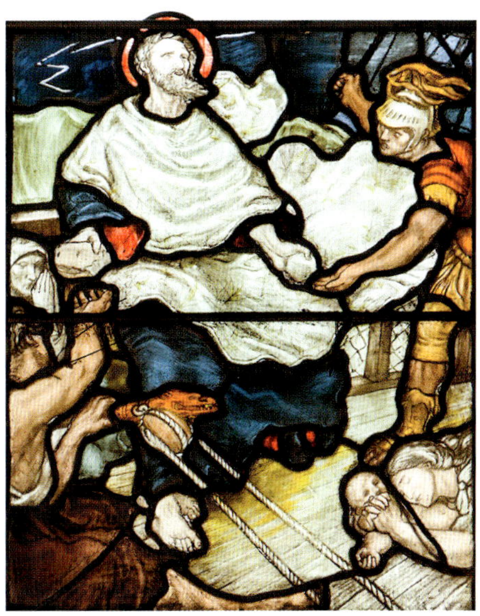

282. Morris, Marshall, Faulkner & Co., Paul Breaking Bread during the Storm at Sea, 1874, designed by Ford Madox Brown, Llandaff Cathedral, north aisle

28 For George Campfield see Tony Beynon, 'Stained glass workers employed by James Powell & Sons and by Morris, Marshall, Faulkner & Company and Morris & Company: a biographical listing', *The Journal of Stained Glass*, vol. xxxv (2011), pp. 245–6.

29 Quoted in Fiona MacCarthy, *William Morris: A Life for Our Time* (London: Faber and Faber, 1994), p. 176.

30 'Cox and Son', *Mapping the Practice and Profession of Sculpture in Britain and Ireland 1851–1951*, University of Glasgow History of Art and HATII, online database 2011 <http://sculpture.gla.ac.uk/view/organization.php?id=msib3_1218441946, accessed 16 January 2014>. Lavers & Barraud were also located in large premises on Southampton Street.

31 Charles Winston experimented with Powell's to manufacture glass of a similar character to medieval glass, which went into production after 1853. A.C. Sewter 'The Place of Charles Winston in the Revival of the Art of Stained Glass', *Journal of the British Archaeological Association*, vol. 24 (1961), pp. 84–5. William Edward Chance of Smethwick was also producing antique glass by 1863; see Albert Charles Sewter, *The Stained Glass of William Morris and his Circle* (New Haven/London: Yale University Press, 1974), vol. i, p. 9.

32 The idea of figures with scenes below was inspired by windows William Morris and Edward Burne-Jones had seen at Chartres in 1855. Fiona MacCarthy, *William Morris: A Life for Our Time* (London: Faber and Faber, 1994), p. 88.

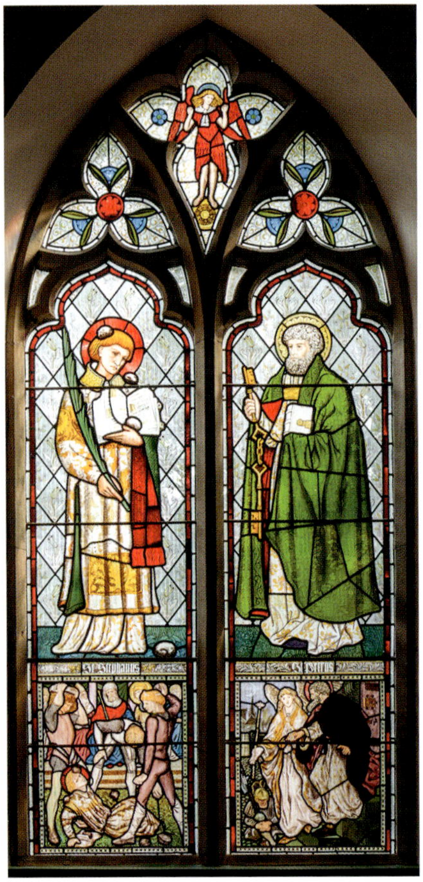

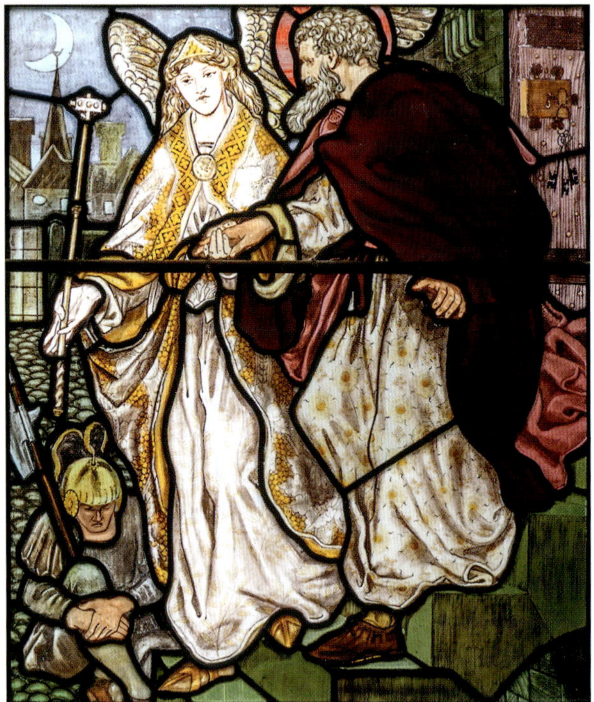

283–4. Morris, Marshall, Faulkner & Co., St Stephen and St Peter, including Peter being Released from Prison by an Angel, designed by Ford Madox Brown (above right), *c.* 1870, Church of St Llwchaiarn, Llanllwchaiarn, nave

The figure of Stephen, designed by Edward Burne-Jones and first used at Bradford Cathedral in 1864, was also used in the following year at the Church of St Llwchaiarn, Llanllwchaiarn. However the scene below the adjacent standing figure of Peter, in which he is being led from prison by an angel, may be the only surviving example of this particular design.[33] Their window at Forden, installed in 1873, is the firm's most colourful window of the period in Wales. Although the window comprises an amalgam of unrelated cartoons from other windows, the scenes demonstrate compositional inventiveness, the designs filling the panels with minimal borders. In contrast, the figures designed by Burne-Jones at Margam Abbey, also of 1873, are set on lightly patterned quarries, two of which were designed especially for the commission.[34]

In a lecture in 1859 Charles Winston denounced the state of glass painting in England as 'worse than it has ever been at any other time or in any other country' due to the suffocating influence of medieval romanticism. This had discouraged the best artists of the period from designing stained glass as they 'left the archaeology and the details to be done by draughtsmen'.[35] He was fiercely critical of the imitation of medieval styles by glass painters, 'mere tradesmen', who 'cannot even copy correctly, but have set up a style of their own, which resembles the old work only in its defects.'[36] Winston's insistence that the best contemporary artists should design stained glass free from medieval convention was taken up instinctively by William Morris, Edward Burne-Jones and other designers of windows made by Morris, Marshall, Faulkner & Co. The firm was initially courted by Gothic Revival architects such as G.E. Street, G.F. Bodley and William Burges, partly because

33 The other known use of this cartoon, by Ford Madox Brown, was in the same year (1870) at the Church of St Peter, Stepney, but the window was lost in the bombing of London's Docklands in 1940. A.C. Sewter's study of the work of the windows of Morris and his circle, published in 1974, remains unmatched as anything approaching a comprehensive survey of a major Victorian stained glass studio, and together with subsequent additions it is possible to trace designs and variants of the same cartoons in a way that remains impossible for any other firm.

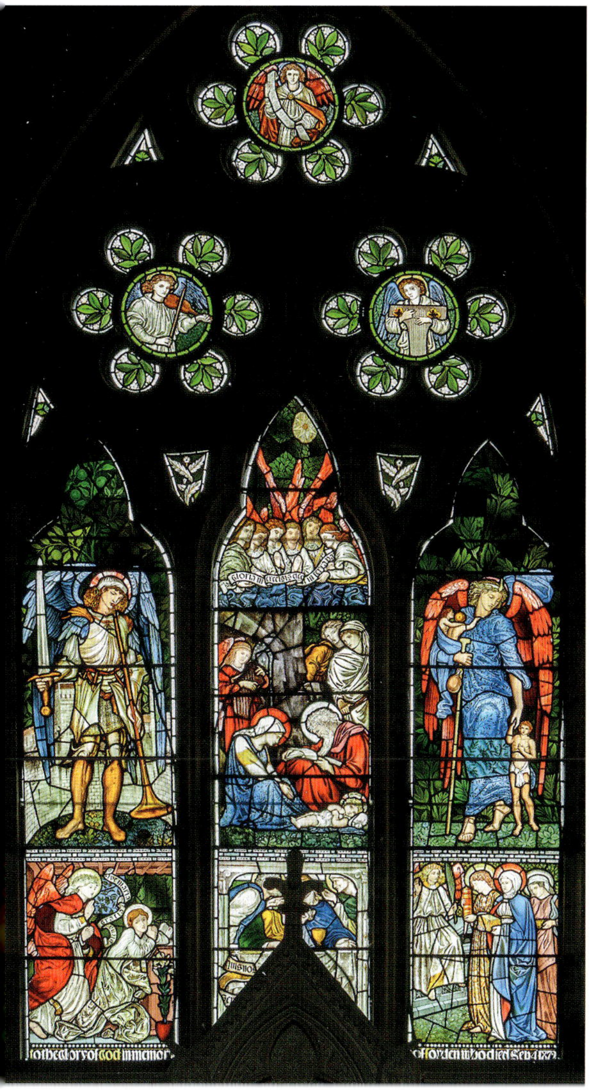

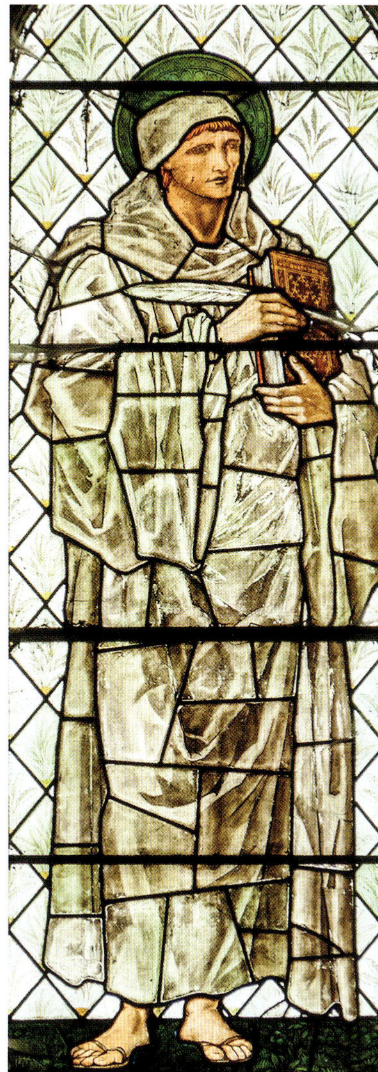

285. (far left) Morris, Marshall, Faulkner & Co., Scenes from the Gospels with Archangels, 1873, figures and scenes designed by Edward Burne-Jones, Church of St Michael, Forden, east window

286. (left) Morris, Marshall, Faulkner & Co., St Bernard, 1873, designed by Edward Burne-Jones, Abbey Church of St Mary, Margam, west wall

of the antiquarian interests of Morris and Burne-Jones. Nevertheless, their work was derided at the 1862 International Exhibition in London. *The Ecclesiologist* regarded it as the worst on display, while *The Builder* was puzzled that the firm won a medal with glass that was 'irredeemably bad'. Despite these poor reviews there was praise from other quarters, and the exhibition did much to launch the firm and generated new commissions.[37]

Designers followed Morris and Burne-Jones by producing original designs for ecclesiastical stained glass, more in keeping with contemporary painting than medieval models. James Powell & Sons were particularly responsive to new directions in stained glass design, employing freelance artists to provide designs for their windows, rather than

34 The artist described these new figures as 'of colossal size and excellence', Douglas E. Schoenherr, 'Burne-Jones's Account Books with Morris & Company (1861–1900)', *The Journal of Stained Glass*, vol. xxxv (2011), p. 142. Both cartoons are now at the Whitworth Art Gallery, University of Manchester.

35 Published in a collection of the writings of Charles Winston published in the year after his death, *Memoirs illustrative of the Art of Glass-Painting* (London: John Murray, 1865), pp. 253–4.

36 Letter from Charles Winston to C.H. Wilson, 21 March 1856, published in *Memoirs illustrative of the Art of Glass-Painting* (London: John Murray, 1865), p. 18. The names of those who were criticised were dutifully removed by the editor.

37 In many cases these commissions were not for churches. For the reaction to their work at the 1862 exhibition see Jim Cheshire, *Stained glass and the Victorian Gothic Revival* (Manchester: Manchester University Press, 2004), pp. 172–3; Fiona MacCarthy, *William Morris: A Life for Our Time* (London: Faber and Faber, 1994), pp. 179–81.

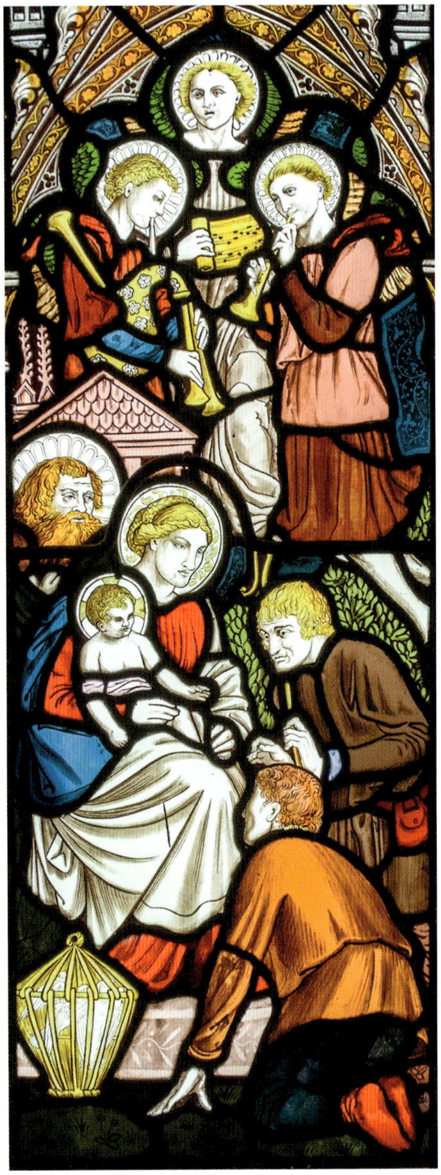

287. James Powell & Sons, The Nativity, 1869, designed by H.E. Wooldridge, Church of St Mary, Derwen, chancel

in-house designers. This provided a useful source of income for aspiring artists at the outset of their careers such as Edward Burne-Jones, Edward Poynter, Henry Holiday and Harry Ellis Wooldridge. Burne-Jones designed his first windows for James Powell & Sons in 1857 and also designed for N.W. Lavers before the formation of Morris, Marshall, Faulkner & Co.[38] Poynter, later Director of the National Gallery, had designed for William Wailes and Heaton & Butler in the 1850s and early 1860s, and his interpretation of Raphael's figure of the ascended Christ may be seen in a window by Powell's over figures of the four evangelists by Henry Casolani in a four-light window at Llansilin.

The painter Henry Holiday was one of the most influential designers for the firm and was outspoken in his criticism of medievalism in stained glass design. Holiday drew inspiration from the windows by Morris' firm, as well as frescoes by the Italian Renaissance artists Giotto and Masaccio. Free from Gothic canopies and decorative surrounds, and with a detailed and naturalistic drawing

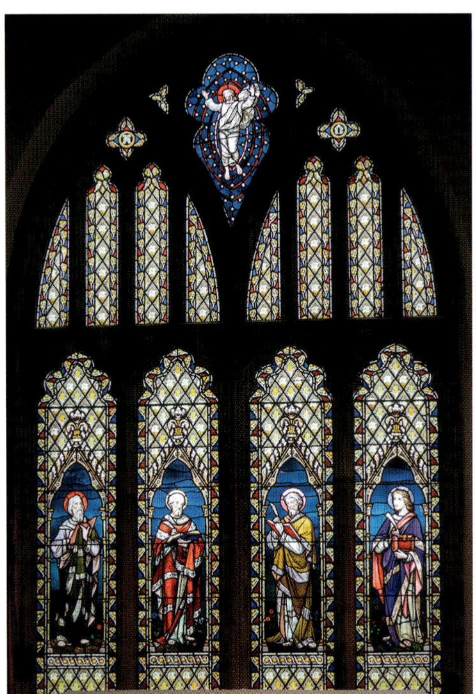

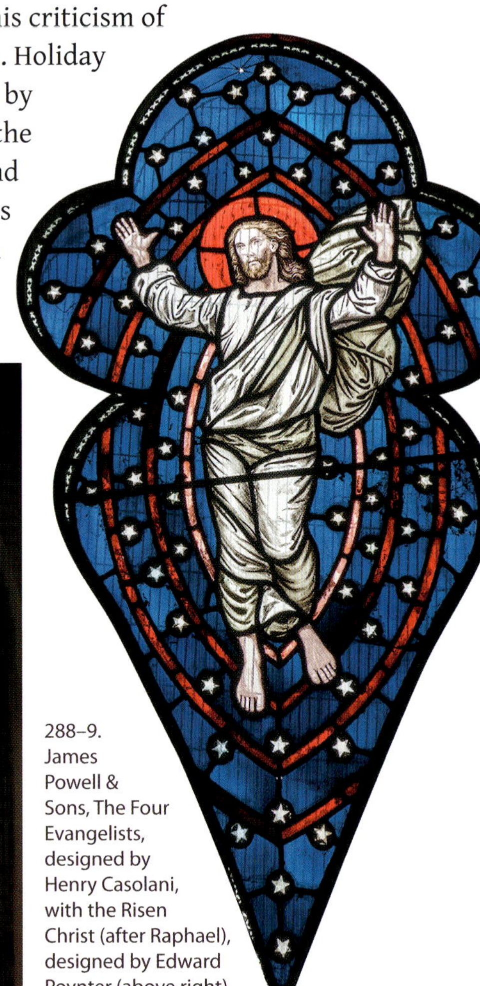

288–9. James Powell & Sons, The Four Evangelists, designed by Henry Casolani, with the Risen Christ (after Raphael), designed by Edward Poynter (above right), 1866, the Church of St Silin, Llansilin, east window

38 See Albert Charles Sewter, *The Stained Glass of William Morris and his Circle* (New Haven/London: Yale University Press, 1974), vol. i, pp. 13–15, and Fiona MacCarthy, *The Last Pre-Raphaelite: Edward Burne-Jones and the Victorian Imagination* (London: Faber and Faber, 2011), p. 77–8. H.E. Wooldridge enjoyed a successful career as a painter, as well as working as a muralist and designer of stained glass, many of his windows being made by James Powell & Sons.

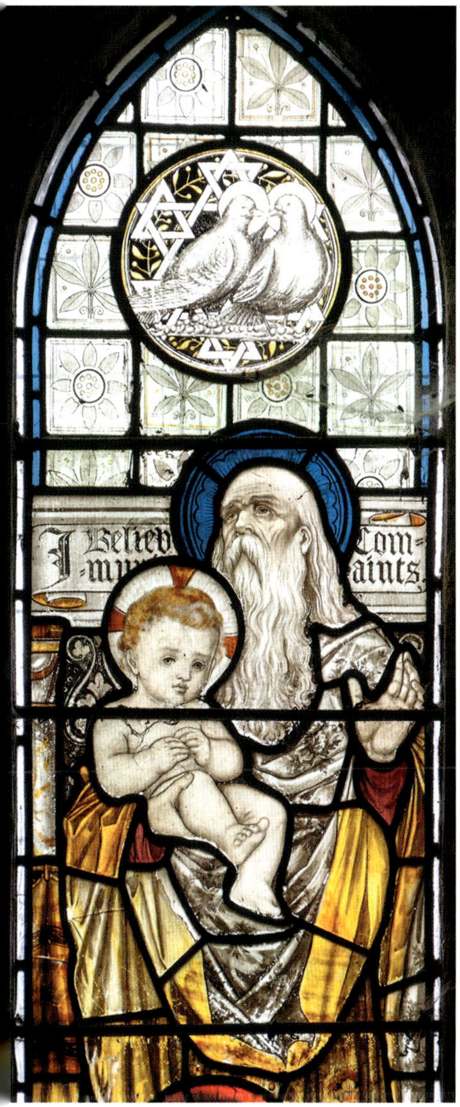

290. James Powell & Sons, Simeon with the Christ Child, 1877, designed by J.W. Brown, Christ Church, Bwlch-y-Cibau, west window

291. James Powell & Sons, Christ with Mary and Martha, designed by Henry Holiday, 1870, Church of St Mary the Virgin, Caldicot, west window

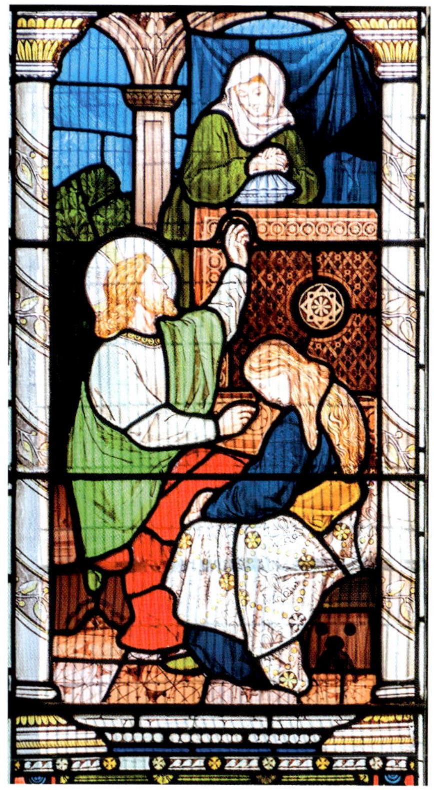

of the figures and drapery colouration, his windows were influential on the work of his assistants and other designers at Powell's, such as H.E. Wooldridge, J.W. Brown and the Swedish artist Carl Almquist, as well as Arthur Hunt, who worked for Heaton, Butler & Bayne at the time when Holiday had windows made by the firm in the late 1860s.[39] J.W. Brown was also influenced by the work of Burne-Jones, and worked at Morris' firm before joining Powell's, initially as a glass painter and eventually succeeding Holiday as their senior designer.[40] His three windows at the west end of Christ Church, Bwlch-y-cibau, with their subdued colouring and natural poses, could scarcely be more different from the full-coloured sanctuary apse windows made only four years earlier by William Wailes.

The rejection of medieval forms and conventions did not meet with the approval of many Gothic Revival architects. Those who commissioned Morris, Marshall, Faulkner & Co. in its early days, such as G.F. Bodley, Gilbert Scott and G.E. Street increasingly realised that their work, in its rejection of Gothic forms, did not complement their buildings. More seriously, architects were becoming increasingly wary of independently-minded artists. While it may have been desirable for the best artists of the period to design and make stained glass, these same artists valued their own artistic integrity and were less inclined to be dictated to by architects.[41] Neither did William Morris help the cause of his firm by the stand taken against the destructive restoration of medieval churches by these architects. His position, formative in the

39 Arthur Hunt took control of the Lancaster firm Hudson & Shrigley in 1874 and appointed Carl Almquist as chief designer, forming a firm that proved to be long-lived and made many windows throughout Wales.

40 Giles Gilbert Scott described J.W. Brown as 'a disciple of Burne-Jones' who was influential on his successor at James Powell & Sons, James Hogan. Obituary to J.H. Hogan, *Journal of the British Society of Master Glass-Painters*, vol. x, no. 1 (1947–8), p. 50.

41 This was true of larger studios as well as individual artists and was exemplified by the argument between John Hardman and William Butterfield in 1860. Paul Thompson points out that in John Hardman's defence of his firm's 'artistic credit' he argued for a recognisable personal style that 'was undermining the gothic ideal of architecture as the mother of the arts.' Paul Thompson, *William Butterfield* (London: Routledge & Kegan Paul, 1971) p. 466.

292. Morris, Marshall, Faulkner & Co., The Crucifixion with the Virgin Mary and St John, 1874, figures designed by Edward Burne-Jones, Church of Illtyd, Gwynno and Dyfodwg, Llantrisant (Glamorgan), east window

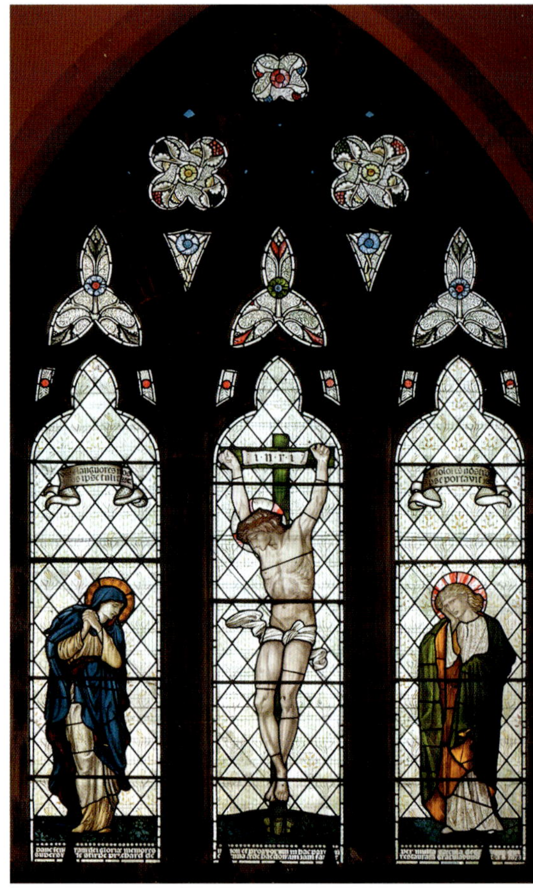

foundation of the Society for the Protection of Ancient Buildings, brought him into sharp conflict with both his former employer G.E. Street, and J.P. Seddon, with whom he had worked at Llandaff Cathedral.[42]

It is therefore all the more remarkable that J.P. Seddon's former partner and committed Gothicist, John Prichard, continued to work with Morris' firm in the 1870s and 1880s. The firm provided the east window for Prichard's restoration at Llantrisant (Glamorgan) in 1874, given by the architect himself in memory of his family who were associated with the area, some of whom were buried at the church, and must infer his personal liking of their work.[43] The window depicts the Crucifixion with Mary and John, and the same figure of Christ, designed by Burne-Jones, was used at the Church of St Catherine, Baglan, built for Prichard's cousin Griffith Llewellyn of Baglan Hall between 1875 and 1882 at the considerable cost of £17,000.[44]

Apart from figurative east windows, John Prichard seems to have maintained a preference for patterned quarries in enamel and silver stain. This is clearly suggested at Baglan, where the east window is placed over an elaborate reredos by Henry Armstead in the east wall of the sumptuous polychrome chancel. A further three-light window by Morris & Co. is discretely placed in the south transept, while each of the nave windows were filled with delicately-foliated quarries within brown foliate borders, suggesting that Prichard chose to use patterned glass even where funds might have permitted a more liberal use of figurative painted glass.[45]

42 In 1878 a bitter exchange took place with J.P. Seddon over his restoration of the nave of Llanbadarn Fawr, near Aberystwyth, summarised by Martin Harrison, *Victorian Stained Glass* (London: Barrie & Jenkins, 1980), pp. 58–9.

43 The window is dated 1873, but A.C. Sewter gives a date of 1874, Albert Charles Sewter, *The Stained Glass of William Morris and his Circle* (New Haven/London: Yale University Press, 1974), vol. ii, p. 74.

44 Geoffrey Orrin, *Church Building and Restoration in Victorian Glamorgan* (Cardiff: University of Wales Press, 2004), p. 12. The densely foliated east window at Baglan has suffered considerable paint loss. The cartoon of Christ on the cross was reused elsewhere on numerous occasions. For example, the figure was used in 1881 at the Church of St James, Staveley, Cumbria, and set against a deep blue sky with stars, in marked contrast to the subtly patterned quarries, typical of Prichard's patterned glass, against which the figures are set at Llantrisant.

45 The firm of Morris, Marshall, Faulkner & Co. was reconstituted as Morris & Co. in 1875, when William Morris took full control of the firm. The south transept window uses principal figures by Burne-Jones, famously used at Christ Church Cathedral, Oxford, in 1874, where the figures were robed in white and set against dark foliated backgrounds.

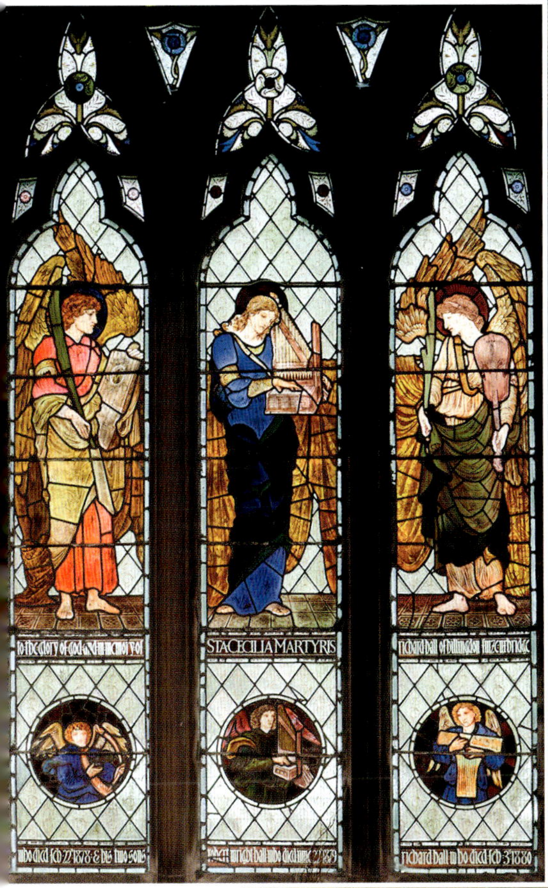

293–5. Morris & Co., ·
St Cecilia with Angels,
:igures designed by
3urne-Jones, Church
of St Catherine, Baglan
(above); perhaps Morris
& Co., Nave Windows
(below); John Prichard,
Chancel of the Church
of St Catherine, Baglan,
completed 1882, stained
glass by Morris & Co.
(right)

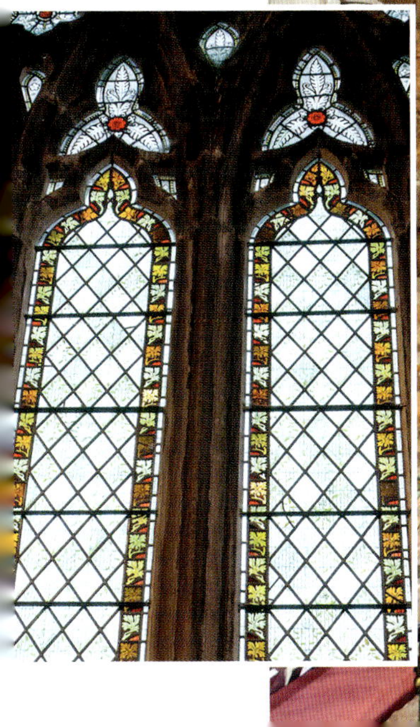

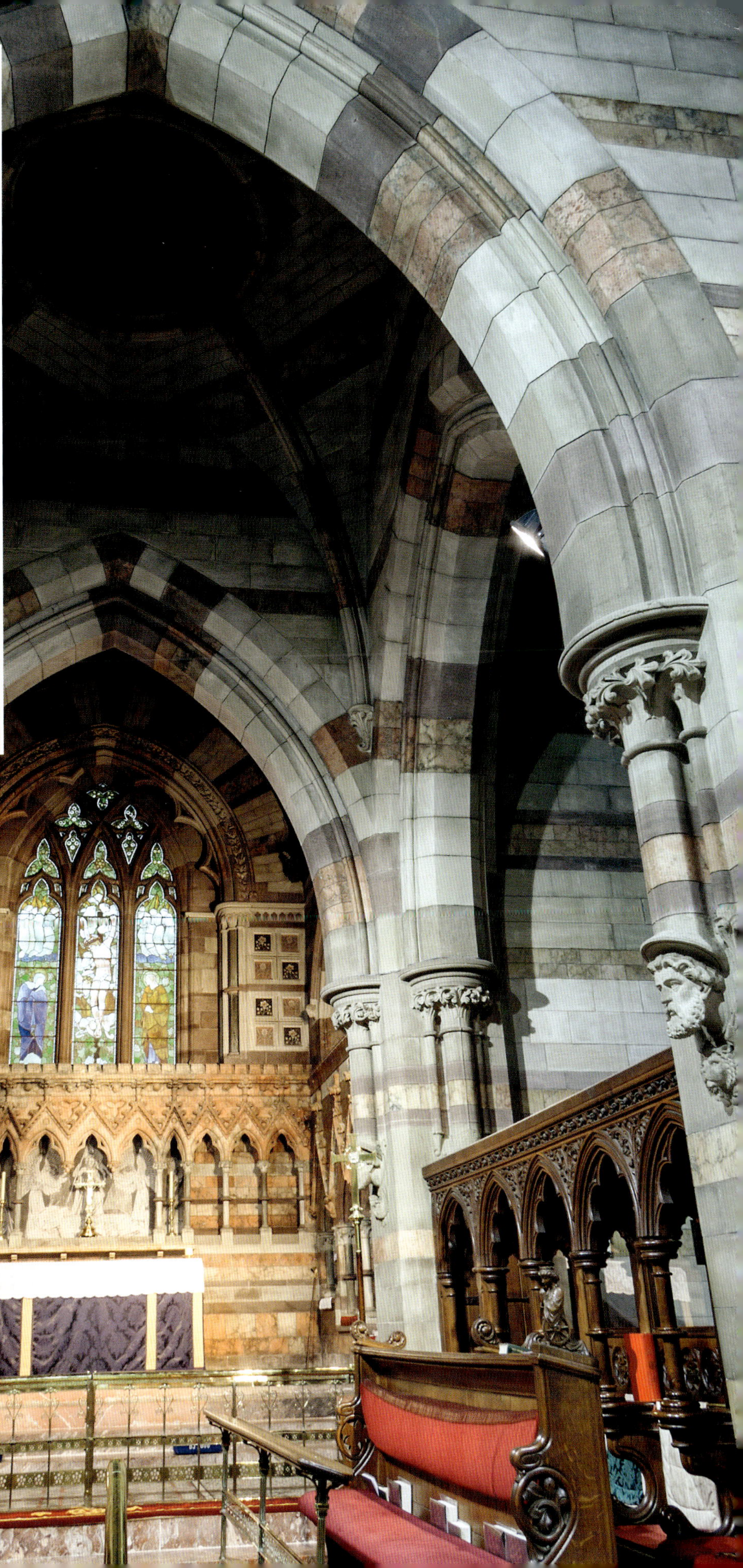

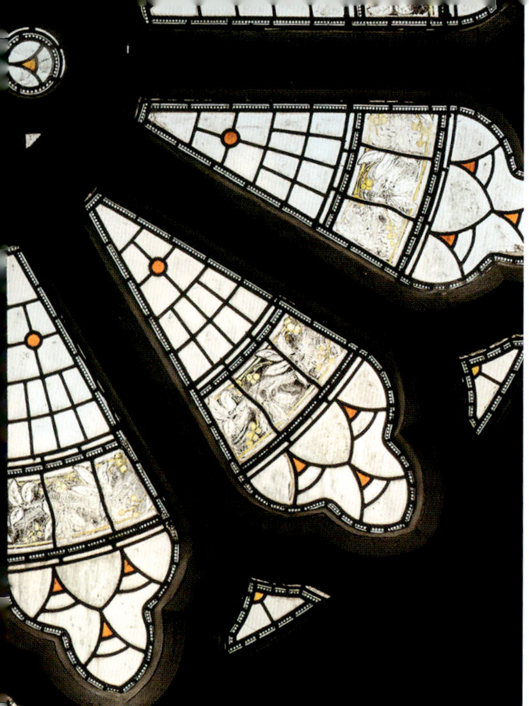

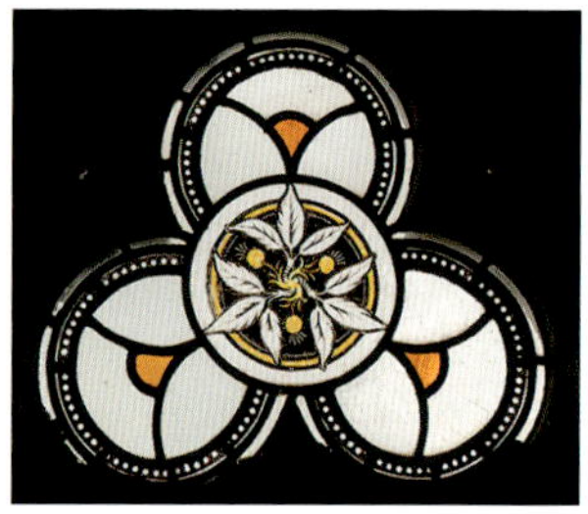

296–7. Ward & Hughes, West rose window (above) and trefoil of south nave window (above right), 1877, Church of St Cadfarch, Penegoes

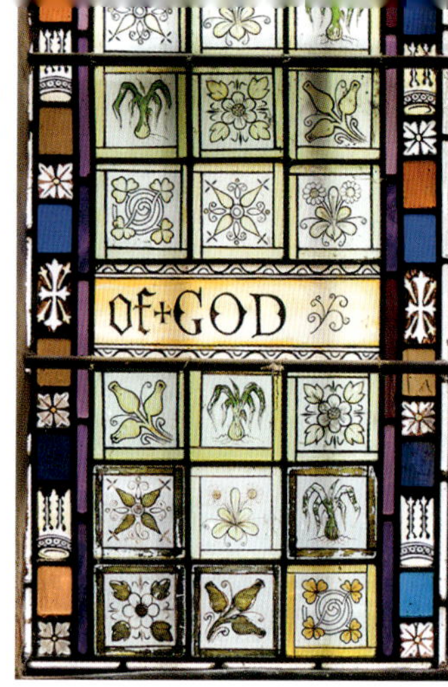

298. Probably Holland & Holt, Patterned Quarries, *c.* 1873, Church of St Madoc, Llanbadoc, north aisle

John Prichard employed a number of firms to provide the patterned quarries for the naves of his churches, many of which have been replaced by later figurative stained glass. Prichard's church in Roath built for John Patrick Crichton Stuart, the third marquis of Bute, dedicated to St Margaret of Antioch, has since lost nearly all of its original glazing of 1870 by Saunders & Co.[46] Clayton & Bell made the nave windows at St Mary Church in 1862, Holland & Holt were used at Llanbadoc in 1872–3, and Ward & Hughes at Mitchel Troy in 1873 and, away from the majority of his churches in south-east Wales, at Penegoes, near Machynlleth, in 1877. In these churches, and at Llandaff Cathedral, patterned quarries were based on medieval examples illustrated by Augustus Wollaston Franks in his *Book of Ornamental Glazing Quarries*, published in 1849.[47] At Penegoes most of the decorative glass that complements the pictorial windows in the chancel by Ward & Hughes survives, although two later windows, probably by Heaton, Butler & Bayne, were substituted for two windows in the north wall. Smaller rural churches have sometimes escaped later intrusions and retained their original patterned glass, for example at Prichard's church at Ystradowen, where each of the patterned windows made by Thomas Baillie remain in place.[48] At Llanbadoc, a window depicting Christ holding a child is similar in style to the work of the Manchester firm of Ralph Bolton Edmundson, and the firm was responsible for the entire glazing scheme that remains in place at the little church built at Talsarnau under the patronage of Lord Harlech. Figures of Christ and John within decorative borders in the sanctuary apse were complemented by patterned glass windows in the nave.

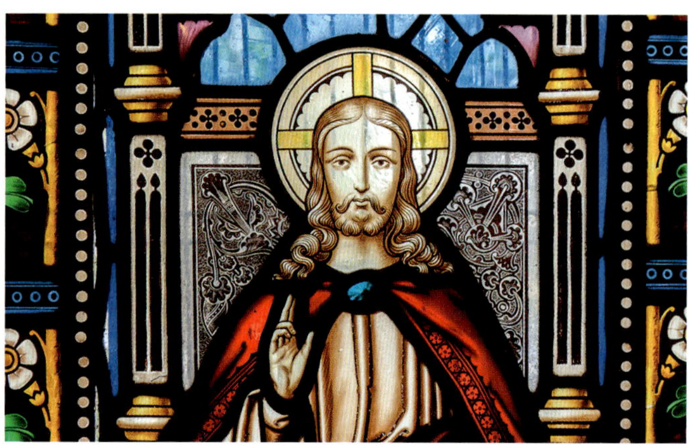

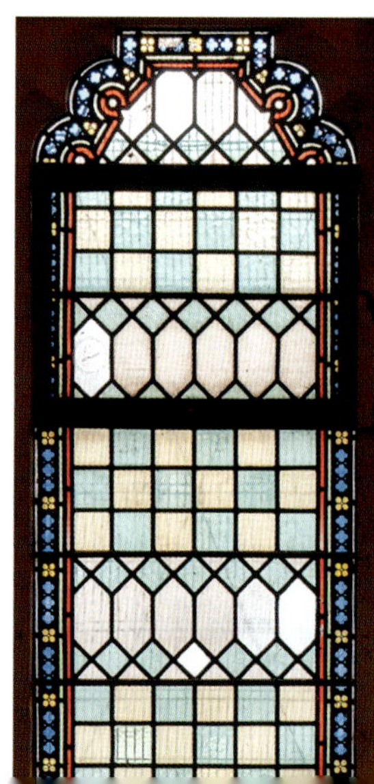

299–300. R.B. Edmundson, Nave window and Figure of Christ (chancel), 1871, Christ Church, Talsarnau

46 The firm later made stained glass for William Burges at Cardiff Castle for the third marquis.

47 Augustus Woolaston Franks, *A Book of Ornamental Glazing Quarries, collected and arranged from ancient examples* (London: J.H. Parker, 1849). Specific examples are discussed in Olwen Jenkins, 'Illustrative examples of the effect on medieval and later parish church fabric in the post-1844 Archdeaconry of Llandaff of restoration work by John Prichard and John Pollard Seddon' (unpublished diploma thesis, Architectural Association, London, 1985), NLW ex 839. The thesis also provides the attribution of the makers at St Mary Church, p. 53.

48 Red discs were placed at the centre of each light to pick out the colours of his polychromatic walls, but here the effect has been lost as the interior has been whitewashed. John Newman, *The Buildings of Wales: Glamorgan* (London: Penguin Books, 1995), p. 651.

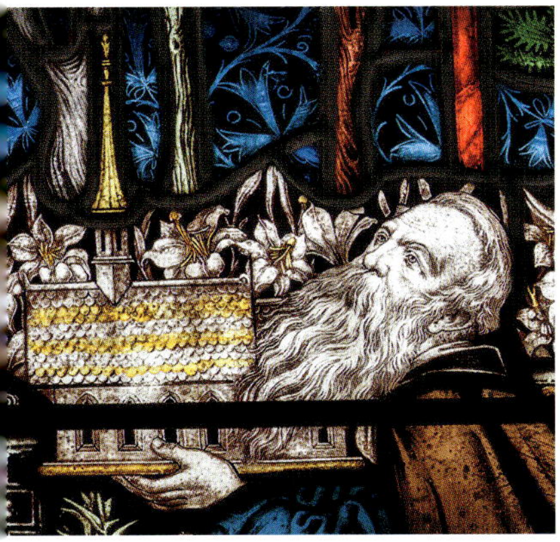

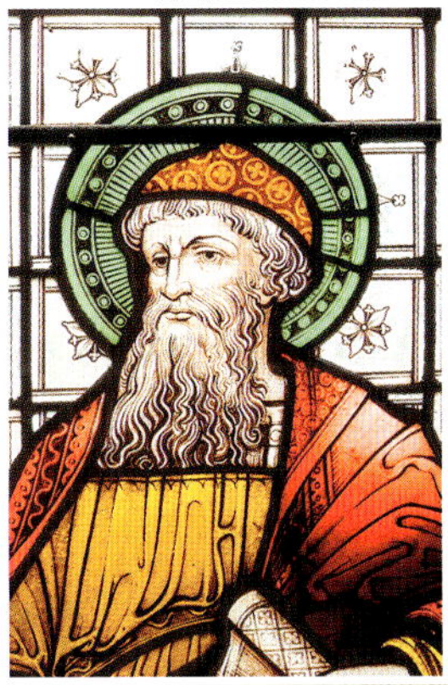

301. (above left) Clayton & Bell, Henry Bath, *c.* 1870, Church of the Holy Trinity, Pont-ar-gothi, west window

302. (above right) Clayton & Bell, Isaiah, *c.* 1870, Church of the Holy Trinity, Pont-ar-gothi, nave

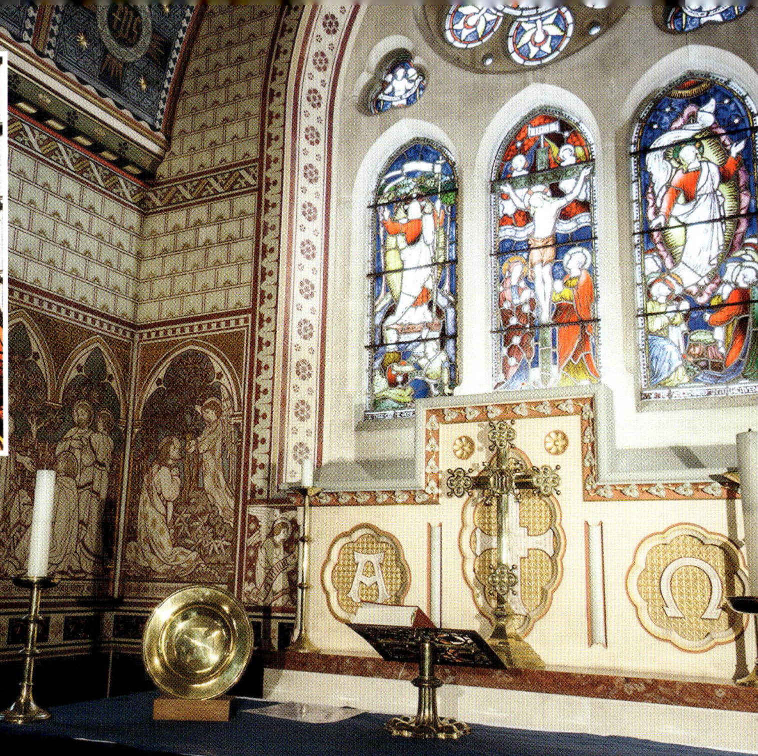

303. Benjamin Bucknall, Sanctuary of the Church of the Holy Trinity, Pont-ar-gothi, *c.* 1865–70, stained glass by Clayton & Bell, murals by Alfred Stansell

Sometimes the patronage extended to a complete series of figurative windows for the chancel and the nave, and even more lavish decorative schemes integrating windows with other interior decoration such as murals or sculpture. At the Church of the Holy Trinity, Pont-ar-gothi, Clayton & Bell provided fourteen windows for the church, which was designed by Benjamin Bucknall for the industrialist Henry Bath in about 1870. The windows were conceived in combination with murals and stencilling throughout the church by Alfred Stansell. The east and west windows depict New Testament scenes, while two sets of four standing figures in the nave depict the four evangelists and the Old Testament prophets Isaiah, Ezekiel, Jeremiah, and Daniel. The patron of the church and his wife are depicted in medieval fashion in the west window, with Henry Bath shown presenting the church as an offering.[49]

Stained glass firms such as Clayton & Bell also undertook mural painting and other forms of church decoration. Mosaic work by Clayton & Bell depicting prophets and evangelists at the Church of St Nicholas, Montgomery, was probably contemporary at the time of G.E. Street's restoration in 1878, and the firm also made the Christ in Majesty for the Bute Mausoleum, at the Church of St Margaret, Roath, Cardiff, in the 1880s, although they did not receive commissions for stained glass in either church. Heaton, Butler & Bayne made two windows at Gresford in the 1870s, and also supplied the painted reredos for the chancel beneath the medieval east window that had been restored by Clayton & Bell.

49 The faces of some of the prophets and evangelists were modelled on family members, see interview with Revd Philip Johnes, 'The Bible and the Welsh Landscape: The People of Wales', in Martin Crampin and John Morgan-Guy, *Imaging the Bible in Wales* (DVD-ROM) (Sheffield: Sheffield Phoenix Press, 2010).

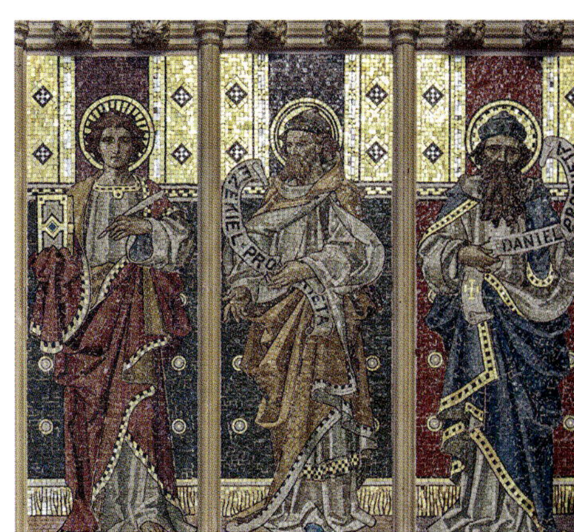

304. Clayton & Bell, St John the Evangelist, Ezekiel and Daniel, 1890, Church of St Nicholas, Montgomery, east wall

The expansion of these firms to meet demand brought criticism from architects. In 1867 the architect G.F. Bodley had a low opinion of Heaton, Butler & Bayne, regarded the windows of John Hardman & Co. as 'getting worse & worse', and felt that Clayton & Bell were usually too busy to give proper attention to their work.[50] As a result of this, and in the interests of having an acquiescent firm producing high quality ecclesiastical work, Bodley and his architectural partner Thomas Garner helped to establish Burlison & Grylls in 1868. John Burlison and Thomas John Grylls had trained with Clayton & Bell, and although examples of Bodley's own collaboration with Burlison & Grylls are not found in Wales until the 1890s, their work can be found in Welsh churches from the 1870s.

Burlison & Grylls were recommended by the architect Gilbert Scott for the production of both the windows and mural decoration at the time of the restoration of the Church of St Curig, Llangurig. Scott felt able to entrust the work to their judgement, and he intervened only to ensure that the chancel windows would admit as much light as possible.[51] The church was restored at the expense of Chevalier J.Y.W. Lloyd, although ultimately his money did not extend to include the proposed mural scheme as the cost of the restoration increased to almost three times the initial estimate. The windows illustrate aspects of the *History of Powys Fadog* and Lloyd's adopted family heraldry, although many are now faded having used paint made with water-soluble borax, a problem that has afflicted many windows of the period. The work of the firm adopts a sixteenth-century style and colouration in its figures and scenes that consciously departs from the earlier medieval styles usually favoured in the 1850s and 60s.

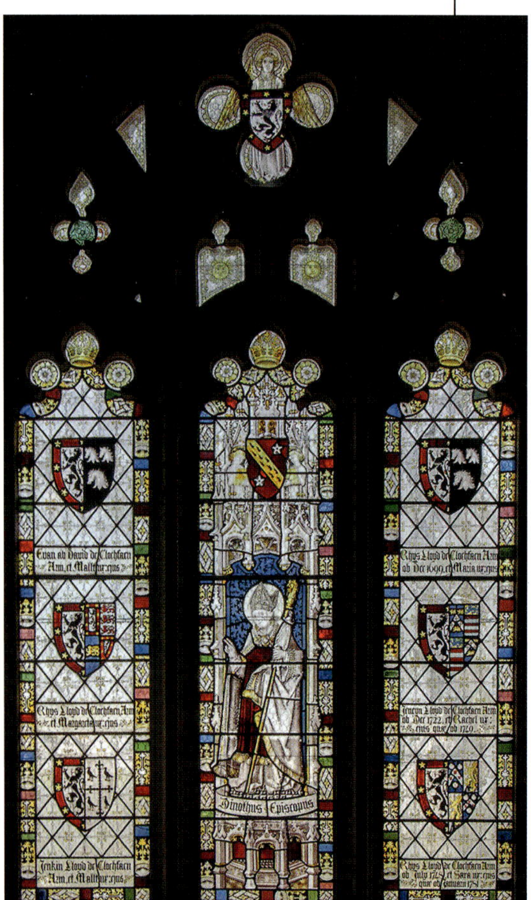

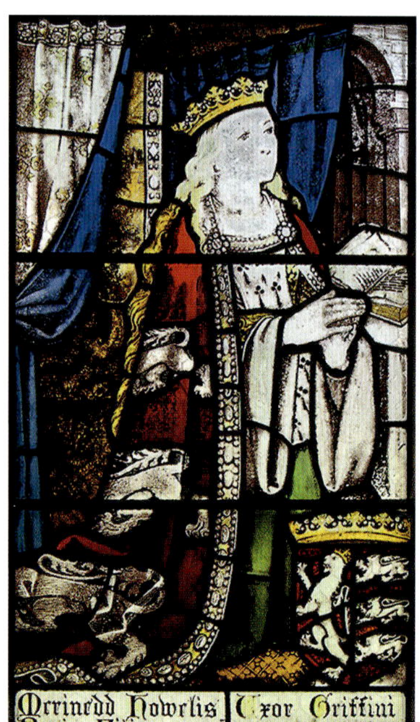

305. (far left) Burlison & Grylls, St Dinothus (Dunawd) with Heraldry of the Clochfaen Family, 1878, Church of St Curig, Llangurig, nave

306. (left) Burlison & Grylls, Merinedd, Daughter of Gruffudd ap Cynan, 1879, Church of St Curig, Llangurig, north aisle

50 Stanley Shepherd, *The Stained Glass of A.W.N. Pugin* (Reading: Spire Books, 2009), p. 190.

51 J.R. Stirk, 'Chevalier J.Y.W. Lloyd, Burlison & Grylls and the windows of Llangurig Church: The Relationship of Patron and Manufacturer in Victorian Ecclesiastical Art', *Montgomeryshire Collections*, vol. 77 (1989), p. 146. The article discusses the commission and production of these windows in detail with the help of the archive now at the National Library of Wales, NLW MSS 20693, which includes sketches by Lloyd and designs by Burlison & Grylls. The firm had a further personal link with Scott as John Burlison's father, also John, worked for Scott for more than twenty-five years.

Gilbert Scott used the firm of his former pupil Alfred Bell for the east window at Bangor Cathedral and at smaller churches in Wales, such as the Church of St Andrew, Norton.[52] For other major commissions in north Wales he used Ward & Hughes. They provided the chancel windows for the restoration of St Asaph Cathedral from 1864 as well as for his church at Rhyl from 1867. Although provided for by numerous donors, all of the stained glass in the church is by the firm and dates from 1867 until 1905. While there was always stylistic variation in the output of large firms producing hundreds of windows for churches in Britain and across the British Empire, changes of ownership and the recruitment of new designers introduced changes in style. At the Church of St Thomas in Rhyl the windows at the west end of the north and south aisles were inserted after 1883, by which time Henry Hughes had died and Thomas Figgis Curtis had taken over the firm, effecting a marked change of style. A further complete glazing scheme by Ward & Hughes was made for the Church of St John, Clydach. The windows at the western end of the church consist of patterned quarries and simpler designs with angels and biblical texts, and similar windows were probably replaced by the later pictorial windows made by the same firm as new donors came forward.

Stained glass firms responded not only to architects, but also patrons and clergy, for the design of their windows, and sometimes showed sensitivity to the surrounding architectural style and existing stained glass.

52 In Glamorgan Scott approved the design by Clayton & Bell for the east window of the chancel at St Hilary, which he had restored in 1861–2.

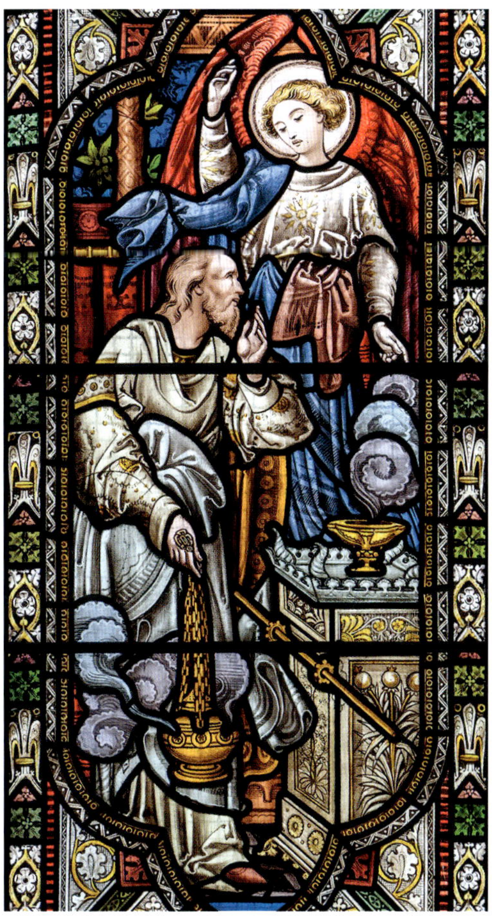

307. Ward & Hughes, The Annunciation to Zechariah, *c.* 1872, Church of St Thomas, Rhyl, south aisle

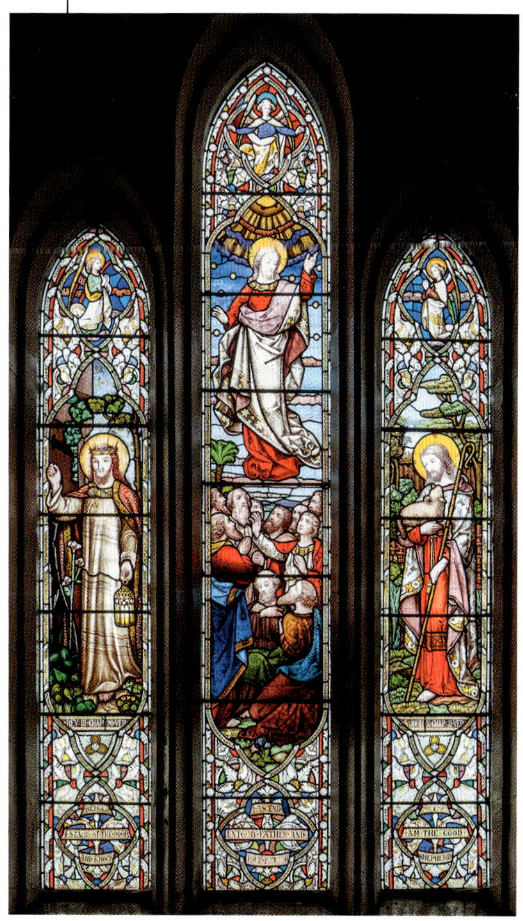

308. Ward & Hughes, The Ascension with Christ as the Light of the World and the Good Shepherd, *c.* 1870, Church of St John, Clydach, east window

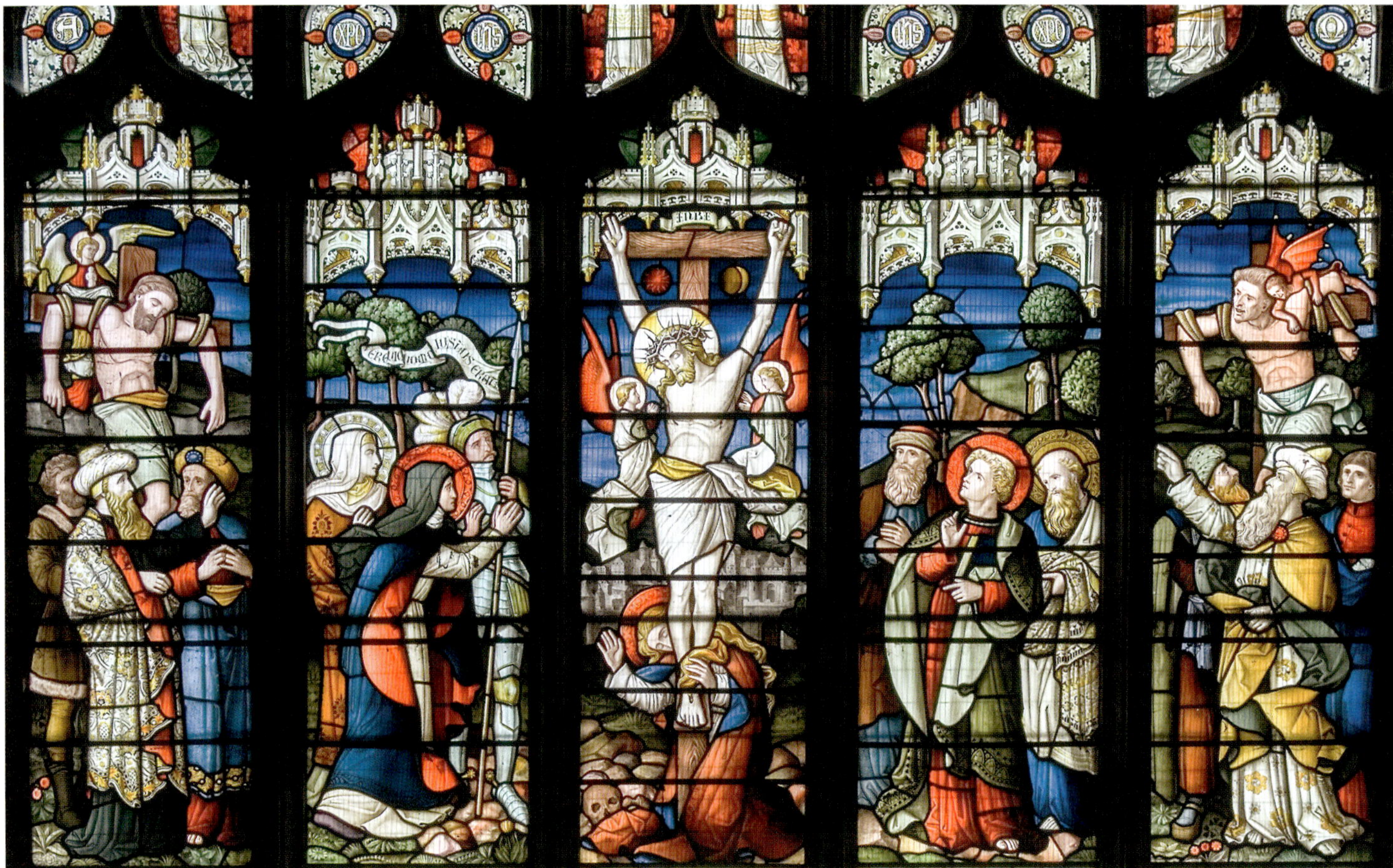

309. Lavers, Barraud & Westlake, The Crucifixion, 1872, Church of St Cynfarch and St Mary, Llanfair Dyffryn Clwyd, north chancel

Many firms continued to demonstrate versatility across a range of styles, and illustrative of this are windows by Lavers, Barraud & Westlake of a similar date for churches at Llanfair Dyffryn Clwyd and Llanfor. The three chancel windows of 1875 at the Church of St Mor and St Deiniol, Llanfor, are of late twelfth to early thirteenth-century character with scenes and figures in medallions contained within the window lights with decorative surrounds. However, their window, probably made a few years earlier at Llanfair Dyffryn Clwyd, spreads a busy scene of the Crucifixion above a depiction of the Last Supper, across all five lights of the larger east window. It was made at the time of the restoration of the church by John Dando Sedding, and is more expertly painted with a detailed landscape in the background and architectural canopies above and below, reminiscent of early sixteenth-century stained glass. As a further variation, two windows by the firm of 1877 at the Priory Church of St Mary, Chepstow, depict the scenes of the Wedding at Cana and Christ feeding the multitude and are set in Renaissance framing, complementing the round-headed Romanesque windows of the nave.

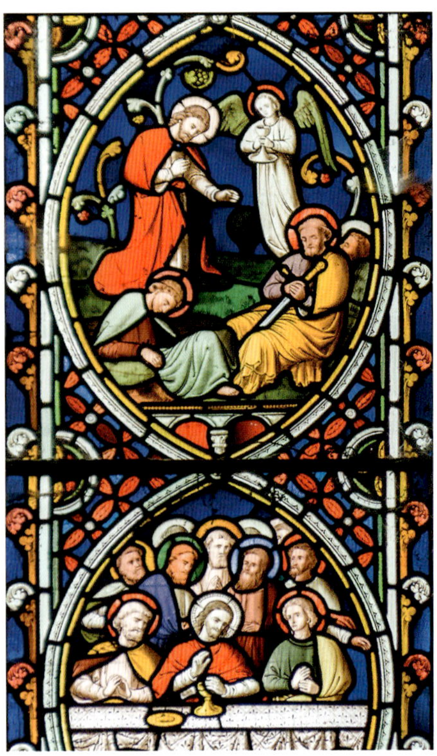

310. Lavers, Barraud & Westlake, Scenes from the New Testament, 1875, Church of St Mor and St Deiniol, Llanfor, east window

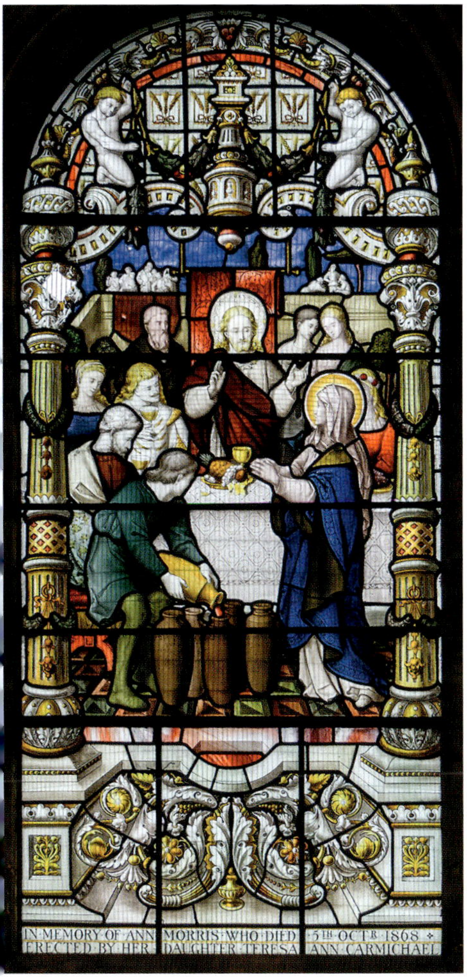

311. Lavers, Barraud & Westlake, The Wedding at Cana, 1877, Priory Church of St Mary, Chepstow, nave

Nathaniel Westlake published *A History of Design in Painted Glass* in four volumes between 1881 and 1894, and other leading stained glass designers drew and studied medieval glass, which influenced their own work and enabled them to restore medieval glass effectively. Clayton & Bell successfully imitated the stained glass of about 1500 at the Church of All Saints, Gresford, when they restored the medieval glass and added lost figures and scenes for G.E. Street in 1867 and 1872. Their new windows commissioned for the church after 1868 adopt the character of the surviving medieval glass in the church, with small scenes and figures placed under canopies within the bounds of the window lights. The restoration of the medieval glass in the east window of the Church of St Tyrnog, Llandyrnog, is an early work in Wales by Charles Eamer Kempe, who travelled widely in northern Europe studying and drawing medieval glass. His restored figure of the crucified Christ at Llandyrnog is similar to many figures included in later windows made by his studio.

The stained glass of many firms during the 1880s was also a reflection of the changing fashions of the later nineteenth century. The bright primary colours of much early Gothic Revival glass were replaced by more subdued tones and the imitation of medieval draughtsmanship gave way to more naturalistic figure drawing and backgrounds.[53] This was accompanied by a greater use of white glass in architectural canopies, typical of late medieval stained glass, and the large firms of Clayton & Bell, Burlison & Grylls and Lavers, Barraud & Westlake settled into a style that they perpetuated well into the twentieth century.

53 Just as Gilbert Scott removed the early Gothic Revival windows of 1838 by David Evans in 1873, so also windows of the 1850s and 60s began to be replaced in the latter nineteenth century. However, these replacement windows were not always purely a response to changing fashion. At the Church of St Elvan, Aberdare, the large north transept window of 1868 was replaced in 1905, after independent reports by Robert Newbery and Clayton & Bell stated that it was bulging, cracking and suffering from serious paint loss. Newbery added, no doubt speculatively, that it was 'a bad specimen of stained glass work and colouring' while Clayton & Bell were more to the point, offering 'one of our very best works at the lowest possible cost.' The correspondence is among the National Library of Wales Records of the Church in Wales: Diocese of Llandaff, LL/F/23.

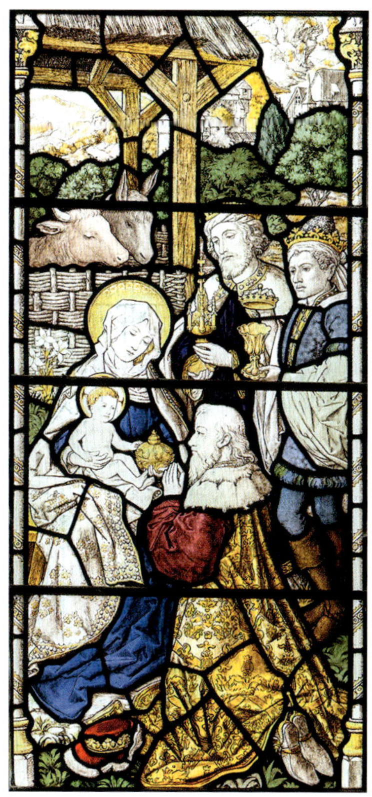

312. Burlison & Grylls, The Adoration of the Magi, 1878, Eglwys Oen Duw (Church of the Lamb of God), Beulah, chancel

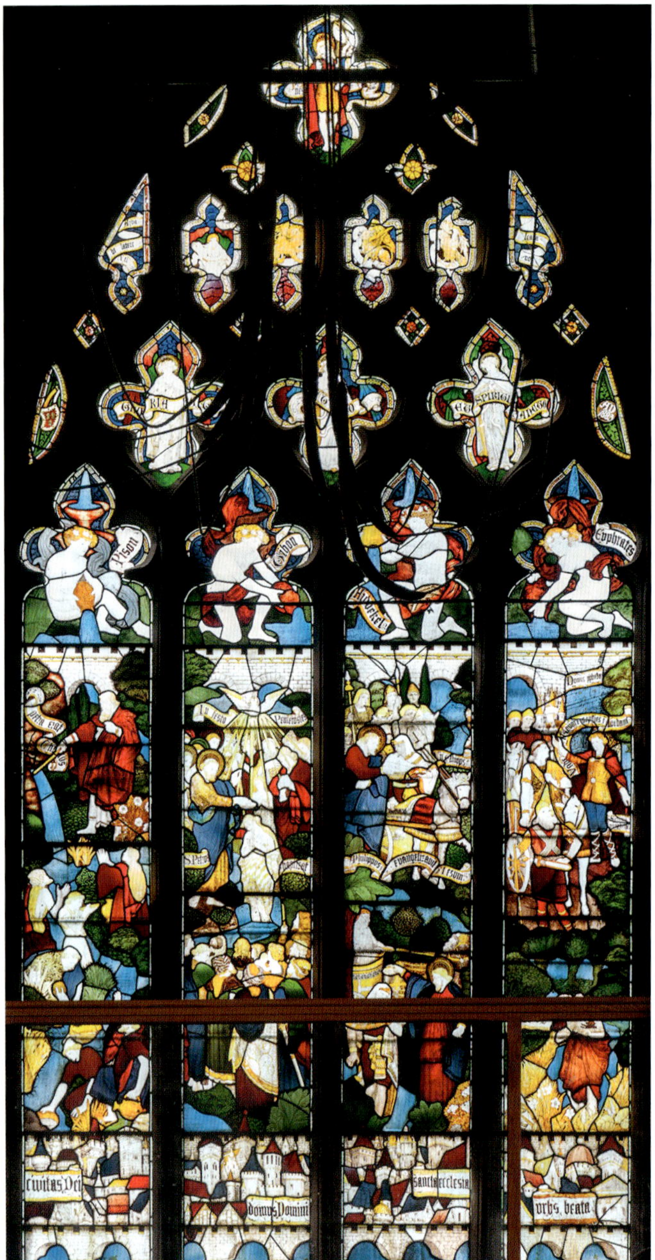

313. C.E. Kempe, The Four Rivers, 1883, Priory Church of St Mary, Monmouth, tower

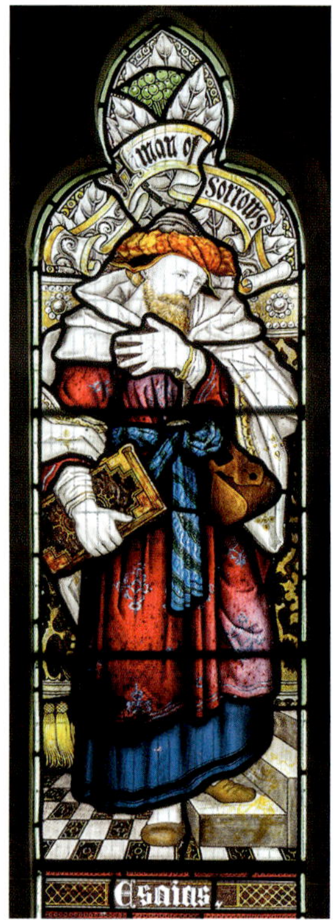

314. C.E. Kempe, Isaiah, 1883, Church of All Saints, Newbridge-on-Wye, sanctuary apse

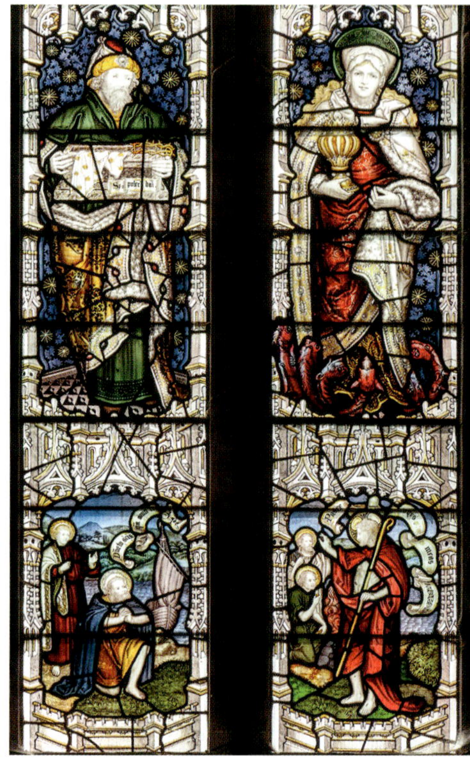

315. C.E. Kempe, Joseph of Arimathea, St Mary Magdalene and the Commission to Peter, 1872, Church of St John the Divine, Barmouth, chancel

Windows by C.E. Kempe are often richly detailed with similarities to late fifteenth-century English stained glass as well as continental work of the earlier sixteenth century. The reasons for his studio's success are evident at Newbridge-on-Wye, where the series of standing figures in the chancel apse demonstrate a mastery of the use of silver stain and flashed glass. By the later 1880s the firm of C.E. Kempe was producing hundreds of windows in a style that changed little until the firm closed in 1934, but a few of his earlier windows in Wales demonstrate more invention. In particular, his window at the Priory Church of St Mary, Monmouth, represents the four rivers of paradise, Pishon, Gihon, Tigris, and the Euphrates, flowing down each of the four lights.

John Hardman & Co. continued to appeal to a wide range of patrons from both Anglican and Roman Catholic churches and often retained a distinctive medievalism in their figures and scenes. These were usually set within a variety of decorative or Gothic architectural surrounds, but

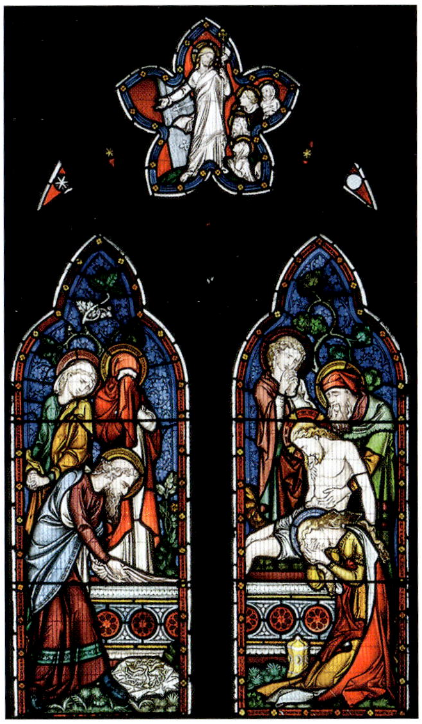

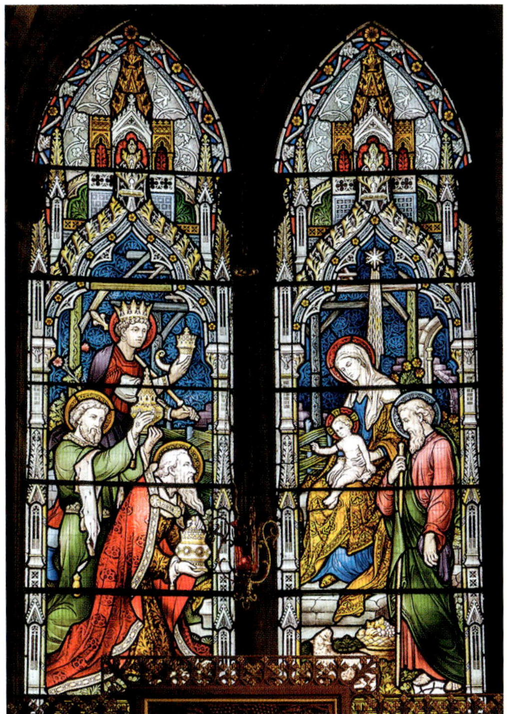

316. (far left) John Hardman & Co., The Entombment, *c.* 1870, Cathedral Church of Our Lady Of Sorrows, Wrexham, south aisle

317. (left) John Hardman & Co., The Adoration of the Magi, 1880s, designed by J.H. Powell, Church of the Holy Trinity, Llandudno, sanctuary apse

sometimes filled the windows, as in the depiction of the Entombment rendered in the colours and figurative style of the thirteenth century at the Cathedral Church of Our Lady of Sorrows, Wrexham.[54]

54 John Hardman's association with A.W.N. Pugin ensured that his firm continued to be favoured by Roman Catholic patrons, for example at Wrexham, where Pugin's son Edward Welby Pugin had been the architect, the Church of Our Lady and St Michael, Abergavenny, and at both the Church of St Mary and of St Michael in Newport.

The acquisition of the studio of Ward & Hughes in 1883 by T.F. Curtis soon initiated a new artistic direction in the work of the firm, while changes in style took time to develop in other firms. In 1873 W.G. Taylor joined the firm established by the Irish artist Michael O'Connor and subsequently took over the firm in 1877. Windows of the 1880s at Brecon Cathedral by Taylor show signs of the break from the medievalism of the O'Connors, while their windows at the cathedral of the late 1890s are further subdued in colour, with an aestheticism more typical of the late nineteenth century, under elaborate white Gothic canopies. Other Victorian firms followed similar trends but demonstrated little artistry. Ownership of the firm of William Wailes passed to his son-in-law, Thomas Rankine Strang, after 1881, but the firm's late work lacks the vigour of their earlier windows, a transition that is especially evident at the Church of St Martin, Laugharne, where the firm also made windows in the 1850s, 60s and 70s.

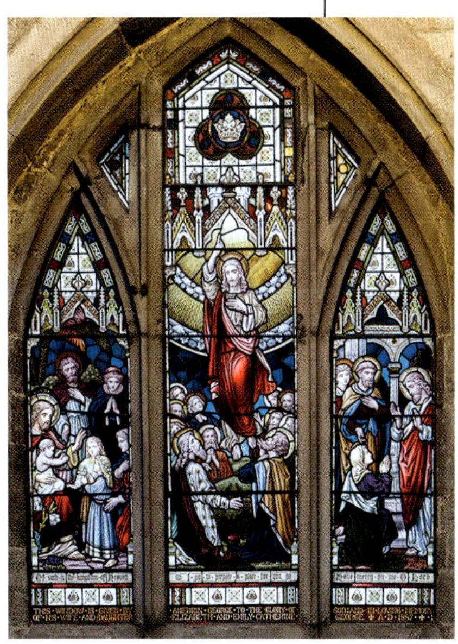

318. Taylor & O'Connor, Scenes from the Gospels, 1887, Brecon Cathedral, north aisle

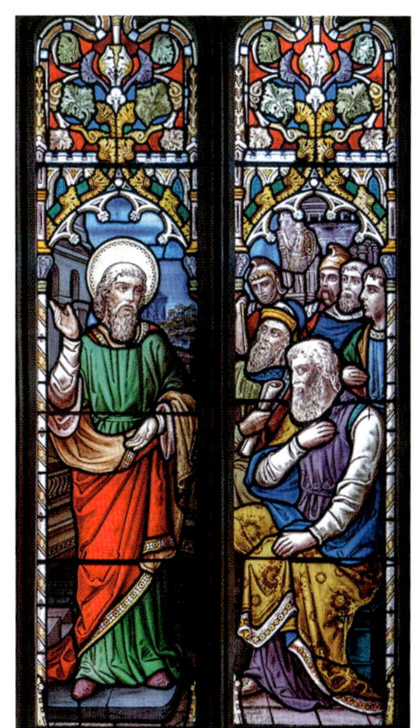

319. Wailes, Son & Strang, Paul Preaching in Athens, 1888, Church of St Martin, Laugharne, south transept

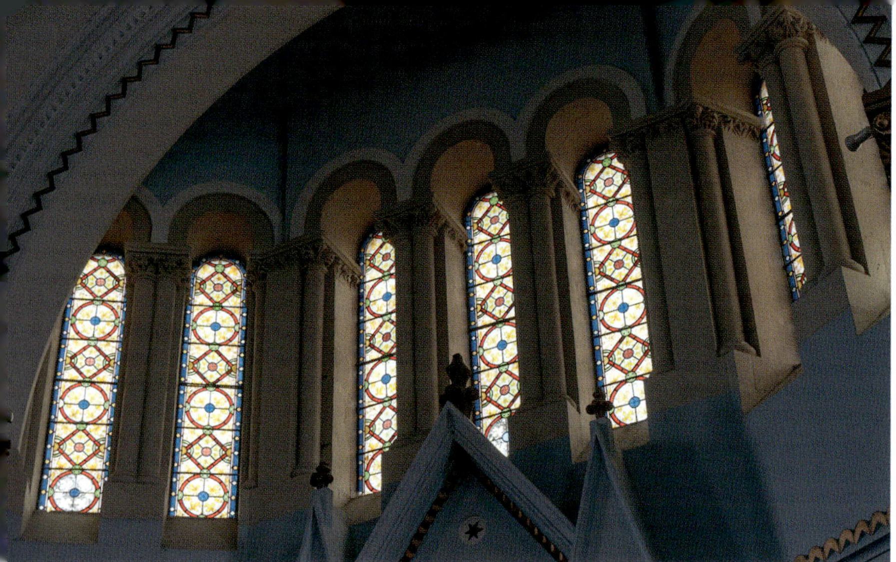

320. Cox & Son, Apse windows, 1878, Bethesda Baptist Church, Haverfordwest

The demand for stained glass for places of worship, as well as for the civic and domestic market, created opportunities for stained glass studios far beyond the artistic circles inhabited by the high Victorian architects and artists such as J.R. Clayton, William Morris and C.E. Kempe. Decorative glass sometimes used for nave windows and Nonconformist chapels was made and installed without the need for an artistic designer and in many instances was probably provided by the local building contractor or a local glazier. The increased use of stained glass for civic and domestic architecture, as well as Nonconformist churches from the 1880s, also helped to broaden the market and create new opportunities for an increasing number of stained glass studios.

321. Memorial Windows, 1874, Castle Street Independent Chapel, Abergavenny, front wall

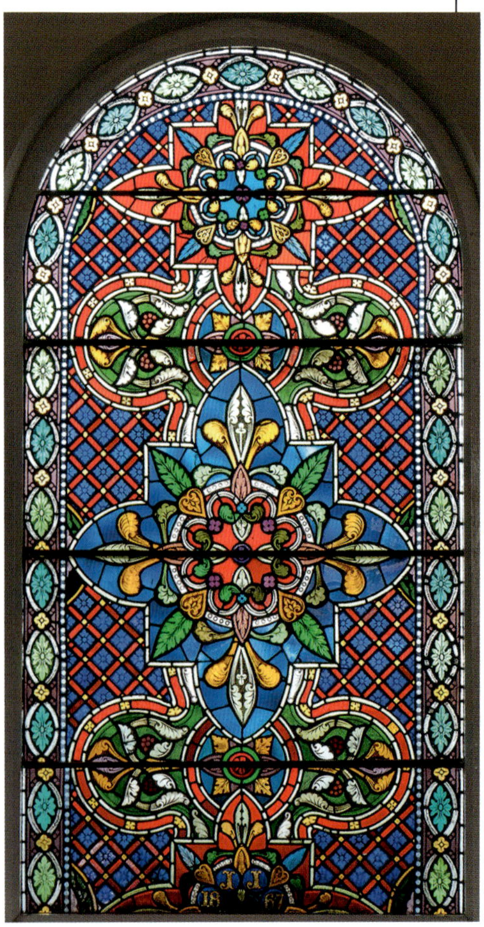

Little figurative stained glass was commissioned for Nonconformist places of worship in the nineteenth century. In some cases this represented a deliberate distancing from Anglican and particularly Roman Catholic practice, but also, as in the case of many Anglican churches, the additional funds for the provision of stained glass were simply not available. Nevertheless, some chapels were sumptuously decorated, and the addition of colour and pattern to interiors through window glass proved highly effective. Avoiding figurative imagery, some chapels made use of biblical texts within decorative panels. The rose of Sharon and the lily of the valley are the theme of two pairs of windows above the upper

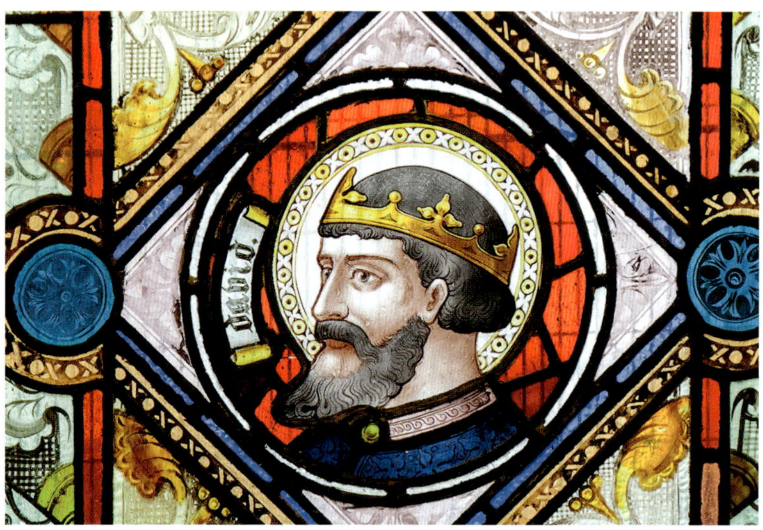

322. King David, *c.* 1880, Tredegarville Baptist Church, Cardiff, side wall

323. Probably Swaine Bourne, Rose Window, *c.* 1889, Bethel Welsh Baptist Church, Aberystwyth, front wall

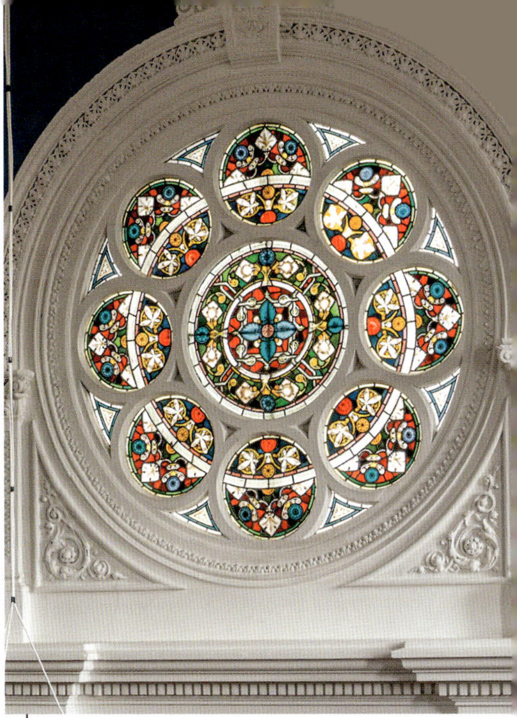

gallery at Heol Dŵr Calvinistic Methodist Chapel in Carmarthen, which carry the same biblical texts in Welsh and in English. Biblical texts and Christian symbols amid flowers filled the three windows of the eastern apse of the Wesleyan Methodist Church of St John, Colwyn Bay, built in 1887–8, while the large window in the west end of the church also consisted of flowers and texts. A biblical scene depicting the return of the Prodigal Son was placed over the pulpit at the English Presbyterian (Calvinistic Methodist) Chapel dedicated to St Andrew, Pembroke Dock, between two windows with texts in 1882, and roundels of the four evangelists with Moses, Abraham, David and Daniel and were made for Tredegarville English Baptist Church, Cardiff.

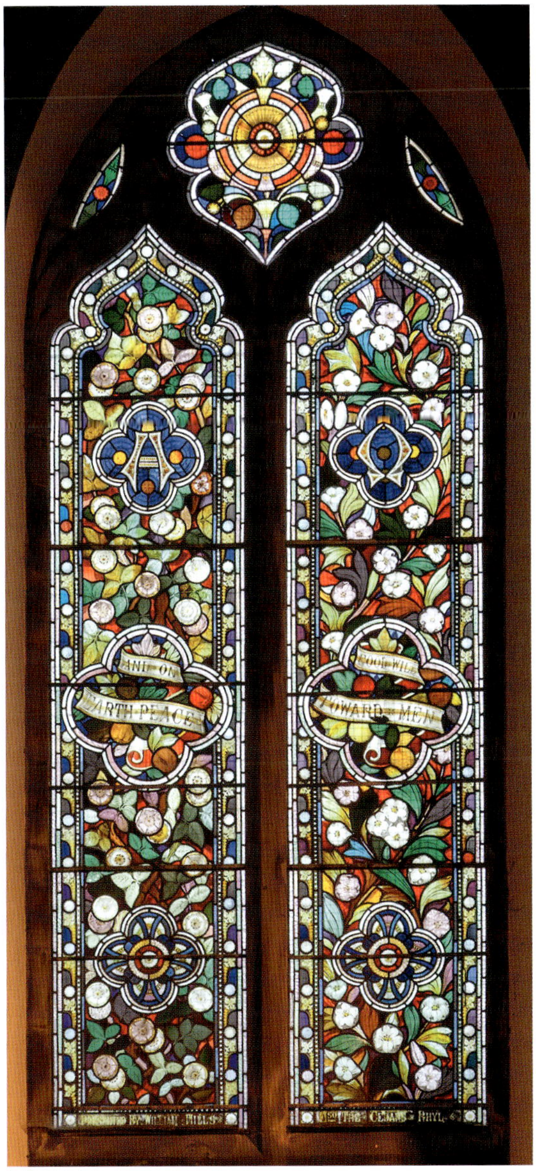

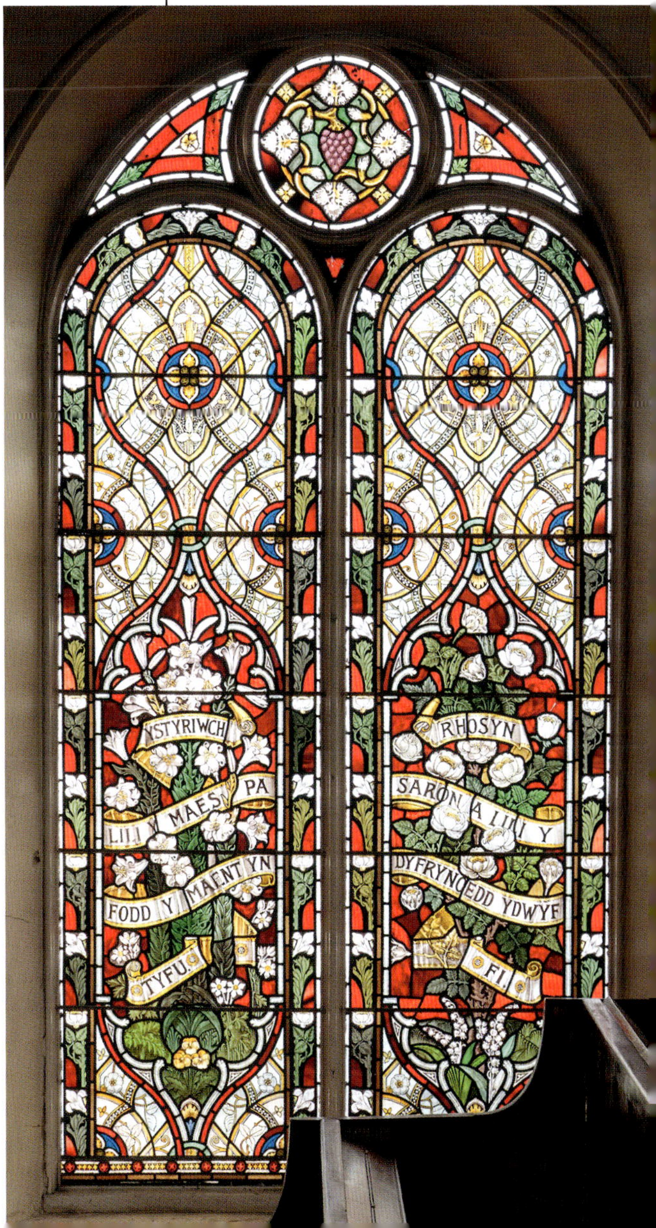

324. (right) Decorative window with flowers, texts and the Alpha and Omega, *c.* 1887–8, Wesleyan Methodist Church of St John, Colwyn Bay, apse

325. (far right) Farmiloe & Son, Decorative window with flowers and texts, 1892, Heol Dŵr Calvinistic Methodist Chapel, Carmarthen, gallery

326. S. Belham & Co., The Annunciation, 1877, Church of St Jerome, Llangwm Uchaf, east window

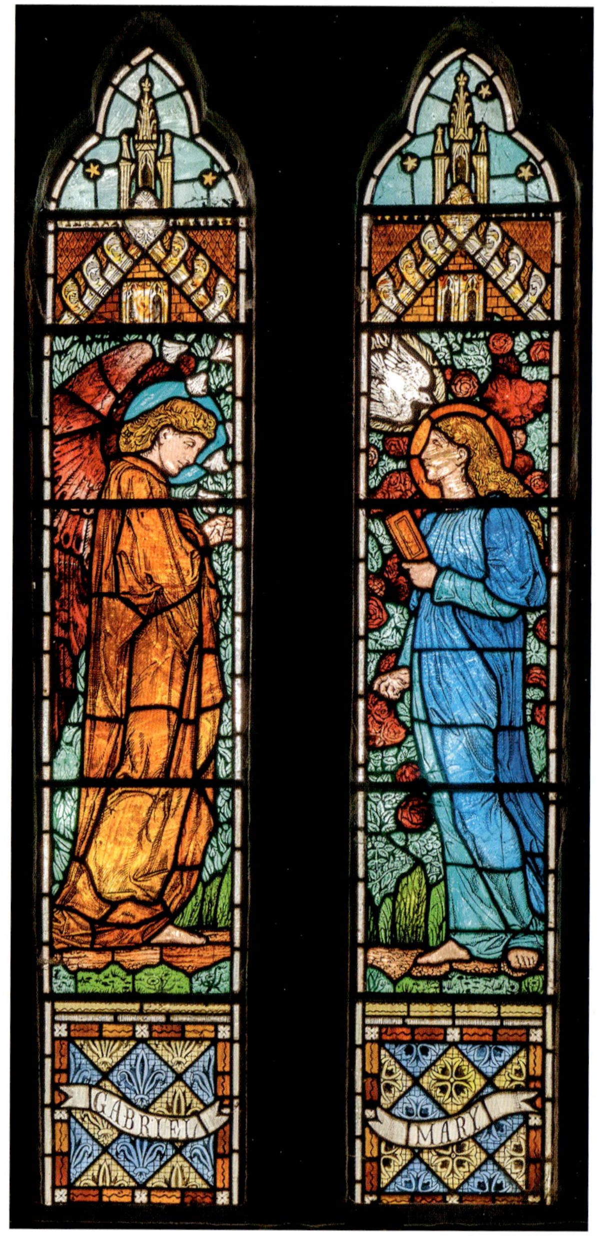

One building firm that set up its own stained glass studio to provide windows for the projects on which they were contracted was that established by Stephen Belham. S. Belham & Co. was originally established in 1865 on Buckingham Palace Road in London as a building firm, and worked on several projects with the architect J.P. Seddon. S. Belham & Co. made the east window to his design for his restoration of the church at Llangwm Uchaf, and the manufacture of their own glass, under the supervision of Jesse Rust, was instrumental in attracting Seddon to work with the firm. [55]

S. Belham & Co. built what is now the Old College of Aberystwyth University, a major work by Seddon, where they also provided patterned stained glass. Seddon had connections locally following his controversial restoration of the Church of St Padarn, Llanbadarn Fawr, in the 1870s, and he subsequently restored the chancel in 1884. At Llanbadarn Fawr, S. Belham & Co. made the east window as well as four or five further windows at the church, added at the time of Seddon's involvement. The firm also undertook murals and other church decoration, and here they were responsible for the decorative reredos and tiling for the east wall of the chancel.[56]

55 The window was cartooned by one of the firm's designers, H.A. Kennedy. John Newman, *The Buildings of Wales: Gwent/Monmouthshire* (London: Penguin Books, 2000), p. 317.

56 Seddon's design for the east window at Llanbadarn Fawr was modified by Frederic Shields, and Shields designed at least one of the other windows in the church made by S. Belham & Co. for Seddon, depicting Jonathan, David and Samuel, using Rust's antique glass. The attribution of the design of this window is given in *The Manchester Weekly Times*, 6 September 1884, and brought to my attention by Michael Belham, who also provided further information concerning the firm of S. Belham & Co. Shields was a painter and engraver, as well as a designer of stained glass, and provides a further link between Seddon and the later Pre-Raphaelite circle as he was a friend of Dante Gabriel Rossetti. Both Rossetti and John Ruskin helped him to establish himself as a painter, and he was responsible for the design of the stained glass memorial to Rossetti at Birchington, Kent. P. G. Konody, 'Shields, Frederic James (1833–1911)', Revd Vivien Allen, *Oxford Dictionary of National Biography* (Oxford: Oxford University Press, 2004; online edn, Jan 2008), <http://www.oxforddnb.com/view/article/36067>.

327. S. Belham & Co., The Transfiguratio
1884, Church of St Padarn, Llanbadarn Fav
(Ceredigion), east windo

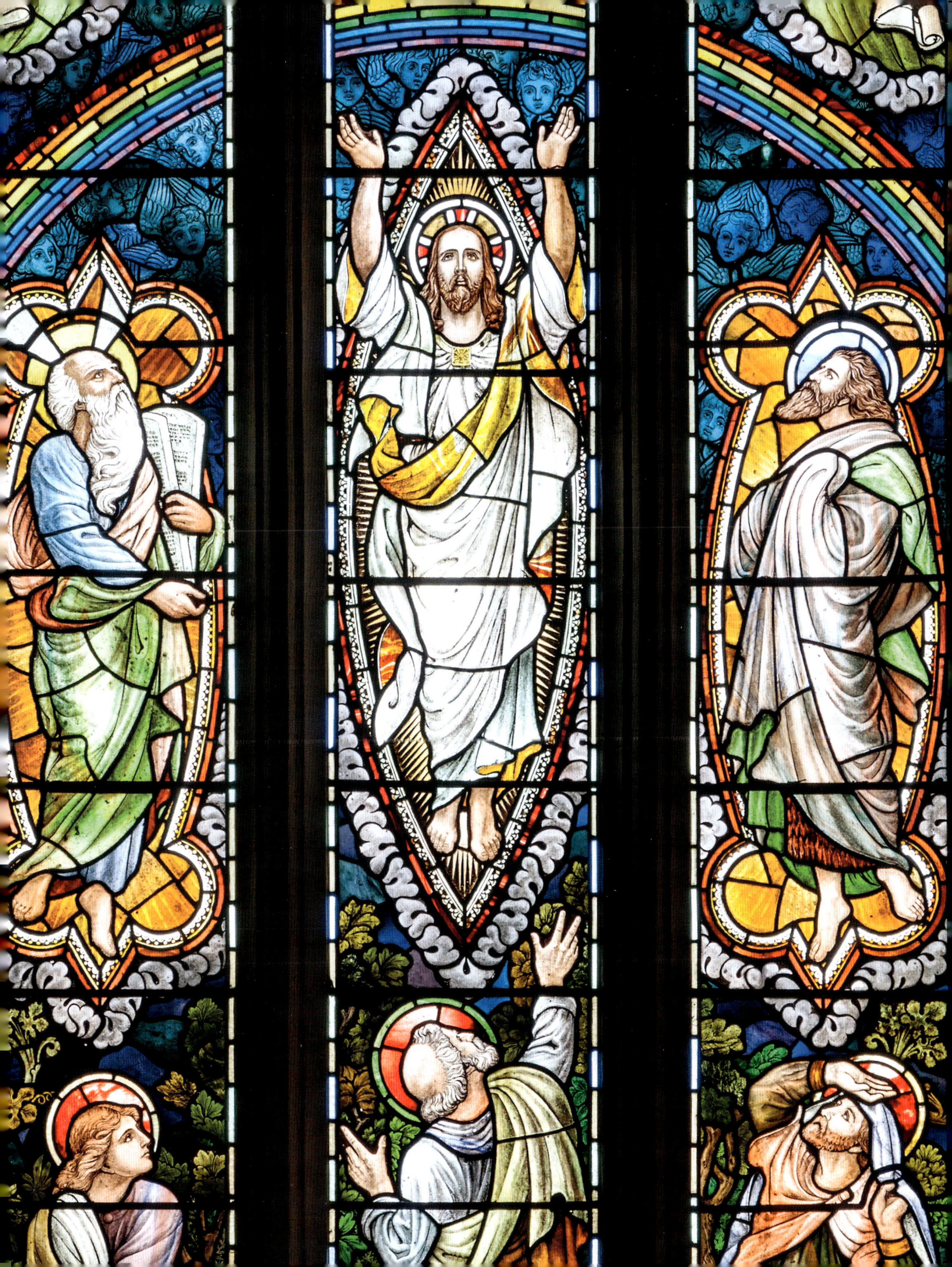

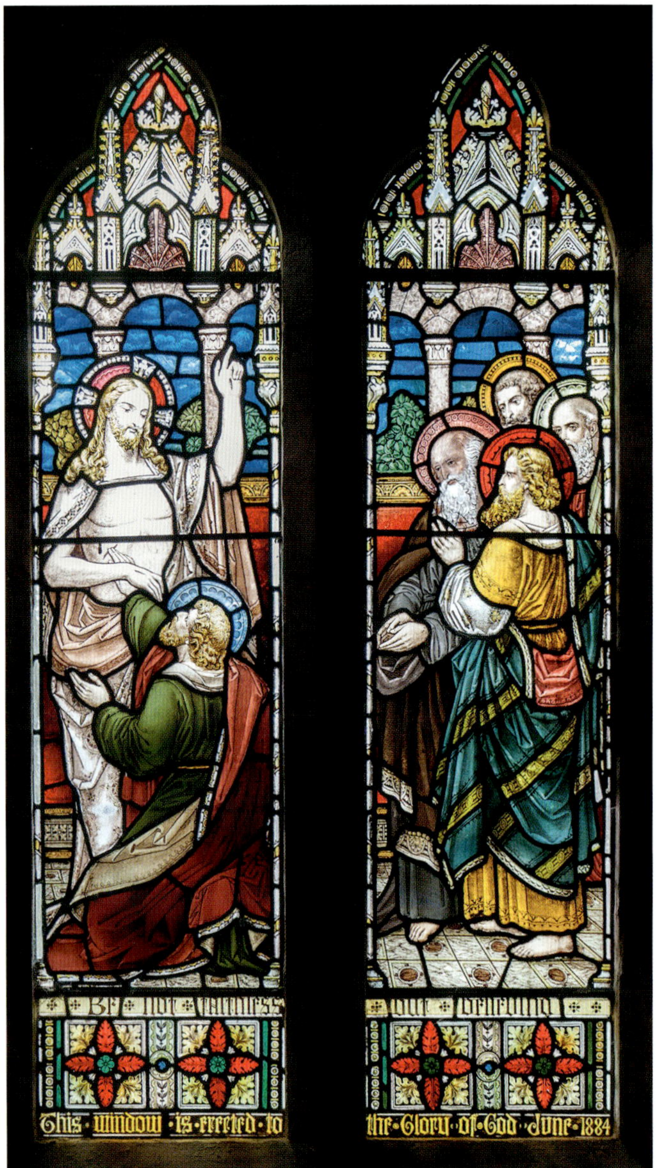

328. A.L. Moore, The Risen Christ Appearing to his Disciples, 1884, Church of St Nicholas, Penally, nave

Church furnishing firms that included stained glass among their products continued to flourish, develop and change hands. Cox & Sons merged with Buckley & Co. in 1881, before being taken under the ownership of Curtis, Ward & Hughes in 1893. Jones & Willis Ltd of Birmingham provided altar rails at Llanbadarn Fawr in 1884, and in the same year the firm refitted the interior of the Church of St Nicholas, Penally. The six new windows at Penally were all made by A.L. Moore, although they were perhaps supplied through Jones & Willis, and by the 1890s Jones & Willis had established their own stained glass studio.

Arthur Louis Moore was one of a number of artists who established successful studios in the closing decades of the nineteenth century. Many were begun as aspiring artists – designers, glass painters and studio managers – left larger firms to establish their own studios and partnerships. Former employees of Clayton & Bell were notable in this respect. Robert Bayne, John Burlison, Thomas Grylls and C.E. Kempe left the firm in the 1860s, and subsequently W.F. Dixon, A.O. Hemming, Edward Frampton and Horace Wilkinson established successful new workshops. By the 1880s architects and individual patrons wishing to commission stained glass could therefore call upon a vast array of large and small firms and studios, as well as individual artist-designers, for the design and manufacture of stained glass for churches in Wales.

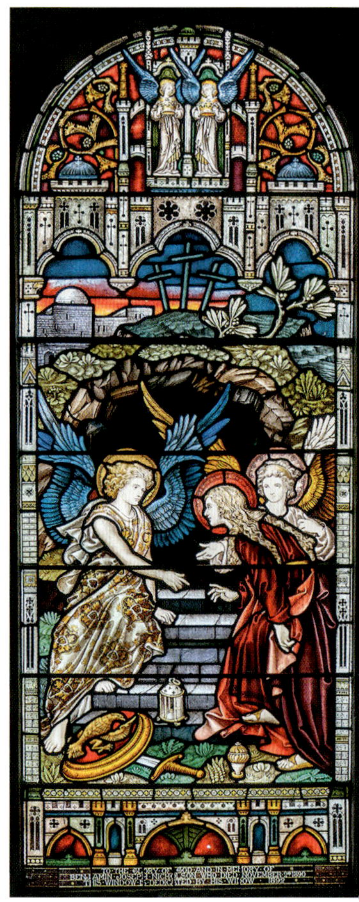

329. A.O. Hemming, Angels with Mary Magdalene at the Empty Tomb, 1892, Christ Church, Welshpool, north aisle

(Building now in private ownership but accessible to the public, courtesy Karl Meredith and Natalie Bass)

Chapter Six

Stained Glass Memorials

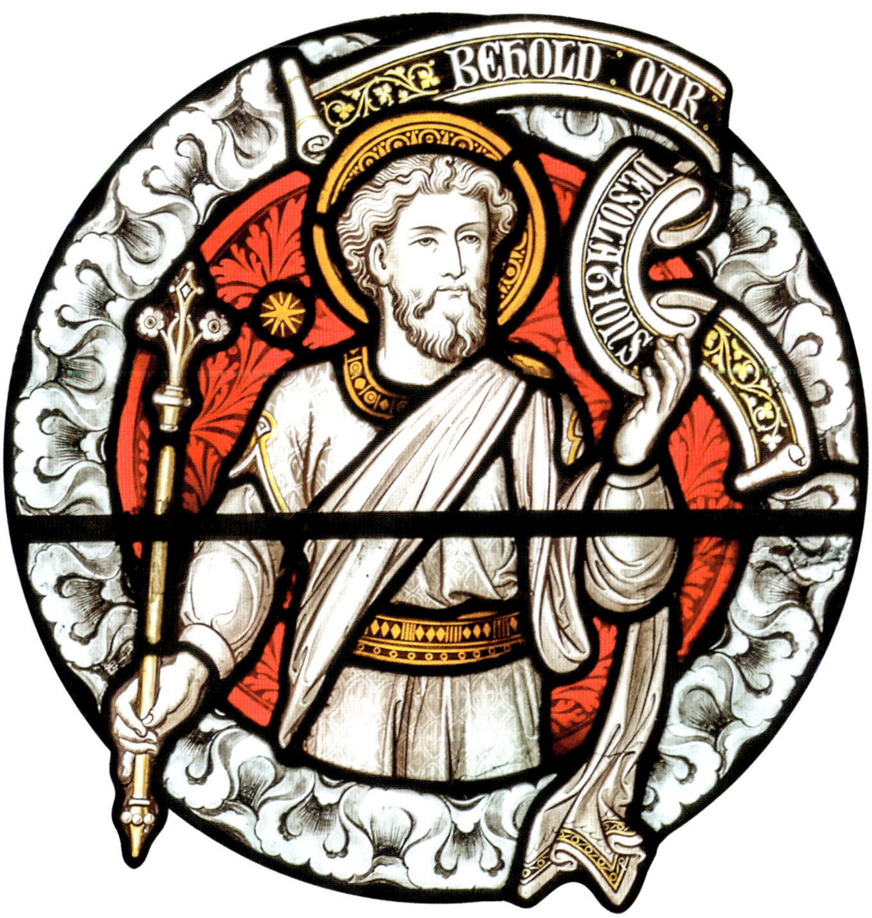

The majority of church building and restoration in the nineteenth and early twentieth centuries was privately funded. Wealthy members of the congregation gave stained glass, memorial windows and other furnishings to add splendour to the church, sometimes as thank-offerings by the living, but usually commemorating family members who had died. The giving of windows was both an act of piety and a public display of benefaction in buildings used by a large section of the community, often located at its very centre.

In medieval times wealthy patrons depicted themselves and their family heraldry in murals and stained glass, and in death were memorialised in relief on graveslabs and in brasses, and as effigies on tomb chests until the seventeenth century. By the eighteenth century the majority of memorials were in the form of wall tablets. Many were plain or with simple ornamentation, but some were spectacular and continued to incorporate portrait sculpture, such as those commissioned for the Williams-Wynn family of Wynnstay at the Church of St Mary, Ruabon. The transition to the commissioning of stained glass windows for family memorials can be seen at the church following its restoration in 1870–2 by Benjamin Ferrey, at the expense of Sir Watkin Williams-Wynn (sixth baronet). In 1872 a chancel window was given by his wife Marie Emily Williams-Wynn in memory of her brothers Grenville and Arthur, the latter having died in Crimea in 1854. In 1884 the five-light east window was given in memory of their daughter Marie Nesta Williams-Wynn with the three central lights depicting a Crucifixion scene. The biblical scenes in the outer lights include the raising of Jairus' daughter: an appropriate expression of faith in the resurrection, as Marie Nesta was only fourteen when she died. Marie Emily gave a window in memory of Watkin Williams-Wynn in 1888.

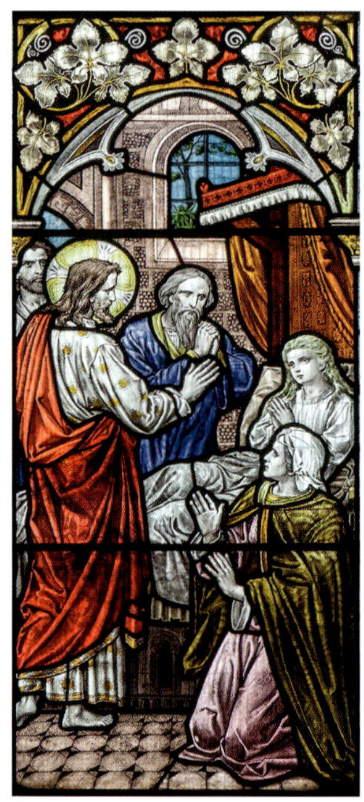

331. Ward & Hughes, Christ Raising the Daughter of Jairus, 1884, Church of St Mary, Ruabon, east window

1 Sir John Trevor cited the presence of his family's coat of arms in the south window as evidence of this right. D.R. Thomas, *The History of the Diocese of St Asaph* (Oswestry: Caxton Press, 1911), vol. ii, pp. 271–3. This heraldic stained glass has since been lost.

2 The Tottenham family of Plas Berwyn also provided all four of the windows, each from different makers, at the Church of St Thomas, Glyndyfrdwy, from 1895 to 1938. The architect, S. Pountney Smith of Shrewsbury, was surely instrumental in bringing in the local studio of William Done and John Davies, pupils of David Evans of Shrewsbury, for the commission.

3 The reredos was dedicated in 1878, given by Robert Bamford-Hesketh of Gwyrch Castle, the benefactor of several other new churches and church restorations in the area. The most important of these was the church and school at Towyn, designed by G.E. Street. Bamford-Hesketh's antecedents, the Lloyd family, are also commemorated in a five-light east window of 1857 at Abergele, vividly interpreting Guido Reni's *St Michael Slaying Lucifer* (1636) in glass.

4 The scenes are now in the east window of the south aisle chapel.

330. (Title page) John Hardman & Co., Daniel, 18
Church of St Martin, Caerphilly, east wind

332. Done & Davies, Christ with the Four Evangelists and Prophets, *c.* 1867, Church of St Collen, Llangollen, east window

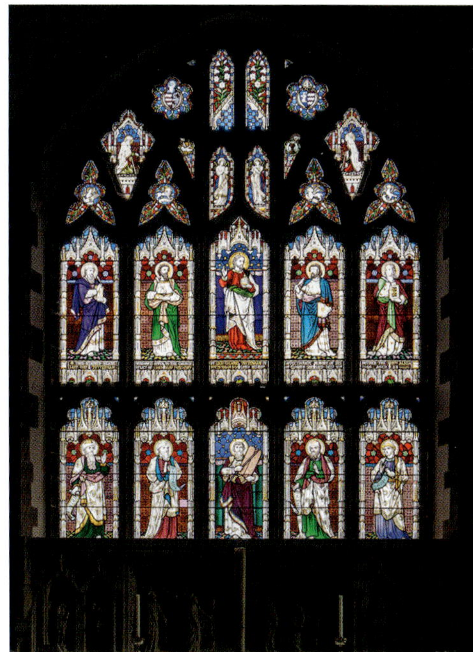

Competition between families can sometimes be inferred, as at the Church of St Mary, Chirk, where rivalry between the dominant Myddleton family and the Trevors resulted in a dispute over the rights to sit in the south chancel during the seventeenth century.[1] A window in memory of Robert Myddleton-Biddulph fills the east window of the north chancel, while a later window in the east window of the south aisle, in memory of Moyra Hill Trevor, is flanked by two earlier wall tablets to members of the Myddleton family. Nearby at Llangollen, the Tottenham family provided the east window of the chancel at the Church of St Collen in about 1867 made by Done & Davies.[2] Colonel Charles John Tottenham subsequently opposed the erection of a reredos, on the grounds that it would partly obscure the window, and an agreement was reached so that the height would not interfere with the visibility of the lower lights of the window.[3] The window is filled with the standing figures of Christ, the four evangelists and Old Testament prophets, and the inclusion of Patrick, opposite David in the tracery, is with reference to the marriage of Colonel Tottenham's mother, Alicia, to Lord Robert Ponsonby Tottenham, the Irish bishop of Clogher. Family heraldry is also discreetly included in the upper tracery lights.

333. Joseph Bell, Christ Walking on the Water, 1881, St Julian's Chapel, Tenby, nave

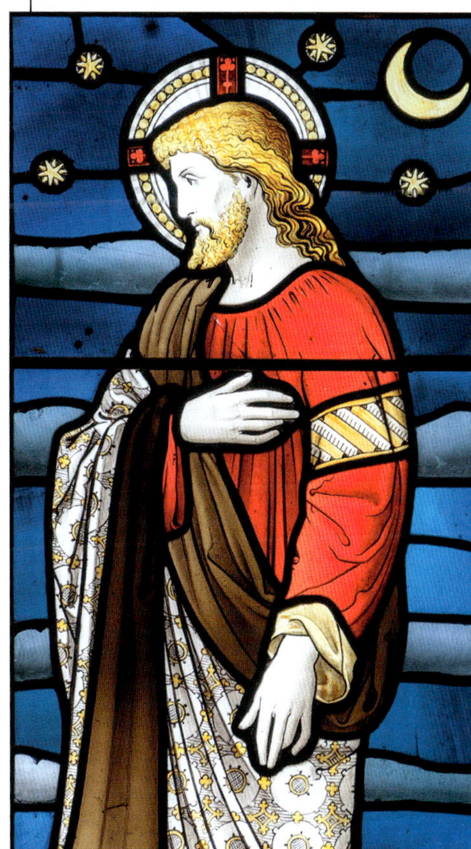

Some windows bear witness to stories of tragedy and loss. Thirty-one victims of the Llanddulas railway disaster of 20 August 1868 are buried in the churchyard at Abergele, including the Revd Sir Nicholas Chinnery, 3rd Baronet Chinnery, of Flintfield, Co. Cork, and his wife, who were returning to Ireland. Although they had no other connection with the church, they are commemorated in a window by Clayton & Bell depicting figures of Christ carrying the cross, crucified, and risen. During the previous month six choristers from Christ Church, Prestatyn, were drowned while bathing, and stained glass given in their memory was originally set in the chancel. Panels by Lavers & Barraud show scenes of Christ with children, the boy Christ disputing with the Doctors of the Law in the temple, and, poignantly, Christ in a boat calming the storm.[4] Three men who lost their lives near Caldey Island, including a father and son, are remembered in a window at the Fishermen's Chapel in Tenby, where a scene of Christ walking on the water was made by Joseph Bell & Son. In the south Wales coalfield 181 victims of two

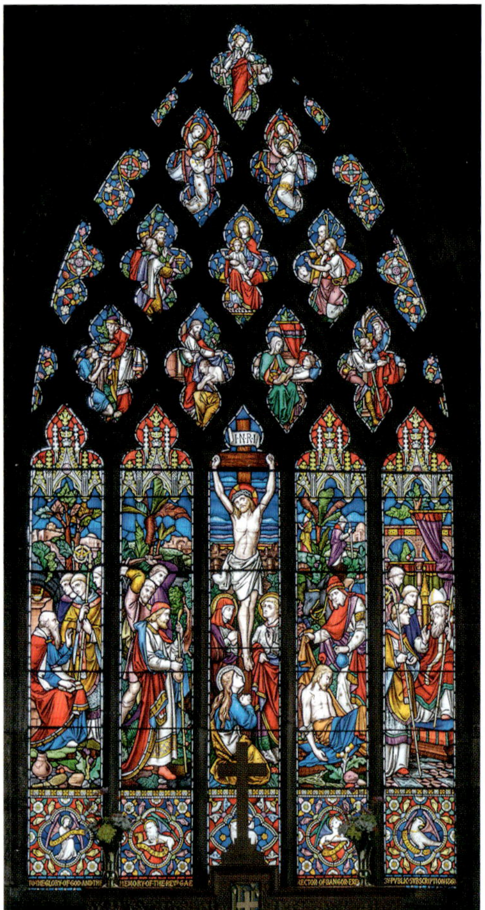

334. Alexander Gibbs, Scenes from the New Testament, 1868, Church of St Dunawd, Bangor-on-Dee, east window

mining disasters in 1890 are commemorated in the east window at the Church of St Cadoc, Trevethin, given by the Pontypool Fire Brigade and replacing the earlier window by Thomas Willement.

Windows funded by subscription allowed a wider range of individuals to participate in the provision of stained glass. Employees of industrial entrepreneurs contributed to windows in memory of their masters, as did their associates, while tenants of large estates gave windows in memory of some of the more generous landowners. As well as windows given by the Williams-Wynns of Wynnstay and other families at Ruabon, a window was given by subscription for William Jones of Plas Newydd, a former agent of the Wynnstay estate, and another in memory of Ebenezer Wood Edwards, who was vicar for 36 years, and his wife Charlotte Eva. This window, by T.F. Curtis, Ward & Hughes, depicts figures bearing crosses as the vicar walked with the aid of a crutch towards the end of his life. Funds for windows in memory of former incumbents were often commemorated by public subscription, and in the five-light east window by Alexander Gibbs at Bangor-on-Dee the face of the Good Samaritan bears the portrait of G.A.E. Marsh, who was rector of the parish for 32 years.[5]

Where stained glass windows were inserted as part of the original design or at the time of a restoration, the most prominent (usually the east) window often commemorated family members of the main benefactors of the church. For example, when the Church of St Llwchaiarn was rebuilt in 1878–80 at Llanychaearn, near Aberystwyth, the east window was given in memory of Emma Davies of nearby Plas Tanybwlch, who had died in 1872, by her son Matthew Lewis Vaughan Davies, later first baron Ystwyth. Sometimes memorial windows were given by families when new

5 The achievement of some more ambitious projects involving stained glass was also undertaken collectively. For example the sum of over £5,000 raised for the restoration of the chancel and choir of St Asaph Cathedral included donations from wealthy individuals around the diocese who paid for other church building and restoration projects, such as Sir Watkin Williams-Wynn, Sir Stephen Glynne, Lord Sudeley, Lady Willoughby de Broke and Mrs Lloyd of Rhagatt. Robert Bamford-Hesketh and his wife gave the reredos, while nieces of William Carey, bishop of St Asaph from 1830–46, gave the east window in his memory and that of his wife. D.R. Thomas, *The History of the Diocese of St Asaph* (Oswestry: Caxton Press, 1908), vol. i, p. 310.

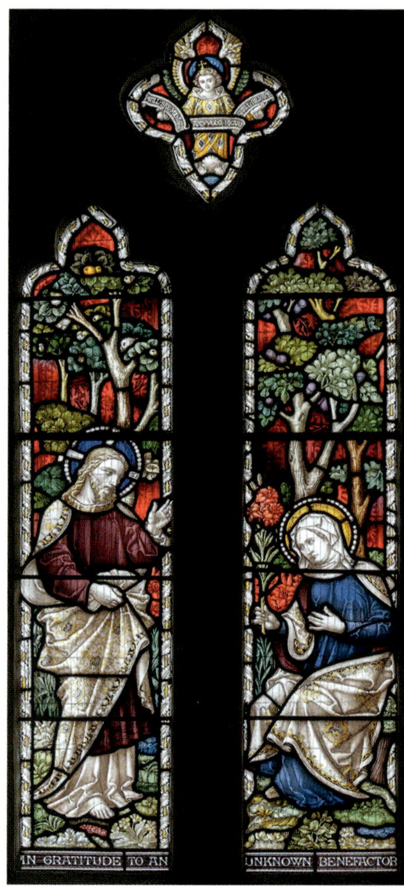

335. Clayton & Bell, The Risen Christ Appearing to the Virgin Mary, 1887, Church of St Mary, Begelly, east window

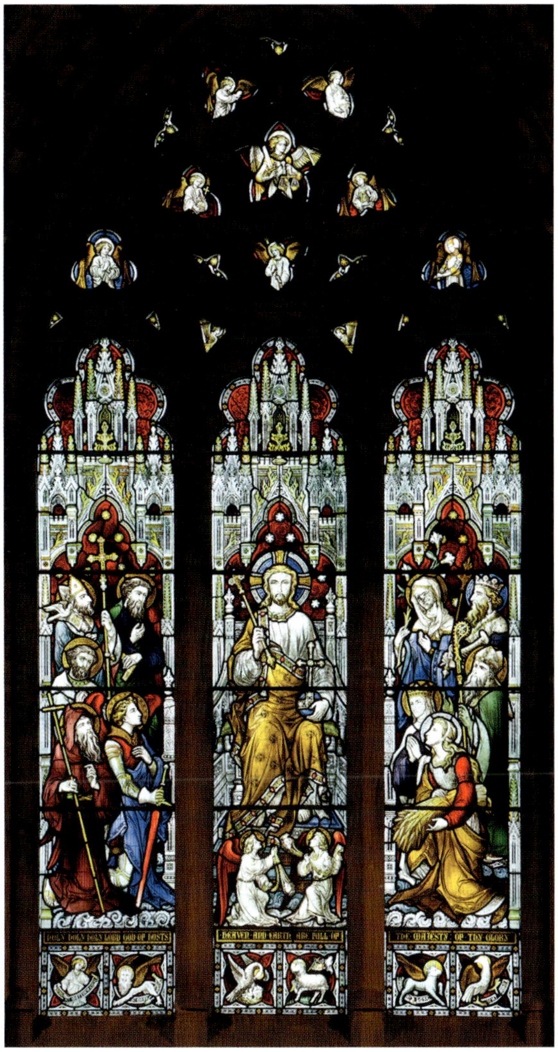

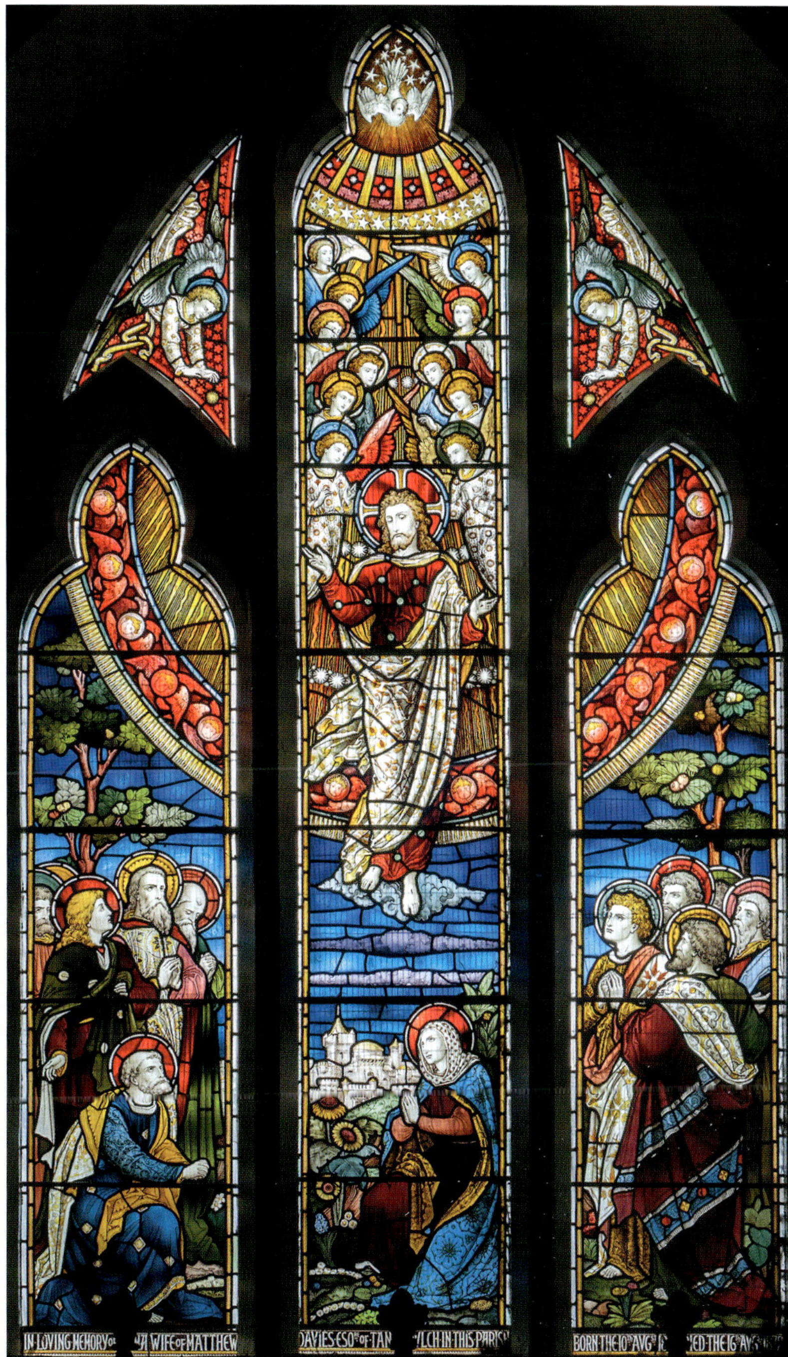

chancels or aisles were built. At the Church of St Catherine, Llanfaes (Anglesey), the Williams-Bulkeley family built the north aisle to seat the family in 1885 and two windows in memory of the tenth and eleventh baronets were added by Mary Emily Williams-Bulkeley. No stained glass was added at the time of the sumptuous decoration of the new Church of St Cynllo, Llangynllo, but after the death in 1877 of the primary patron of the church, Sir Thomas Lloyd, the window in the east wall of the chancel by John Hardman & Co. was given in his memory. An unknown patron is commemorated in the east window at the Church of St Mary, Begelly, whose gift of funds for the restoration of the church in 1887 was made anonymously.

336. (above left) John Hardman & Co., Christ in Majesty with Saints and Angels, *c.* 1877, Church of St Cynllo, Llangynllo (Ceredigion), east window

337. (above right) Heaton, Butler & Bayne, The Ascension, *c.* 1880, Church of St Llwchaiarn, Llanychaearn, east window

6 J.T. Micklethwaite, *Modern Parish Churches: Their Plan, Design, and Furniture* (London: Henry S. King & Co., 1874), pp. 246–7.

7 John Piper, *Stained Glass: Art or Anti-Art* (London: Studio Vista, 1968), pp. 34–7.

8 These windows probably date to the 1880s, except for one of the five windows that is dated 1964.

The plain glass and grisaille quarry patterns inserted in the windows of new and restored churches did not always survive very long. The gradual addition of new windows frequently led to a loss of uniformity and harmony in the overall design of a church. In his parody of Victorian ecclesiastical taste, the architect J.T. Micklethwaite described the appearance of the windows of the imaginary St Simeon's in musical terms: 'here one bellows "God save the Queen" on a "Prince Consort memorial", mostly pink and blue; there one of a newer school chants a *Te Deum*, all in green and yellow. On one side a worthy churchwarden feebly sounds the Jews' harp in a medley of subjects from the Old Testament, whilst on the other the squire of the parish blows his own trumpet with a lot of crudely-coloured heraldry, most likely from the Apocrypha. And so on, all through the windows, each trying to outroar the rest.'[6] Almost one hundred years later John Piper was similarly critical of churches that had become 'imitation art galleries, with odd and hopelessly divergent examples of different personalities in the windows – not placed as a gallery is hung, in helpful relation one to another, but arbitrarily, in the mere order of commissioning.'[7]

338. I.A. Gibbs & Howard, The Good Shepherd, *c.* 1890, Church of St Catherine, Llanfaes (Anglesey), south aisle

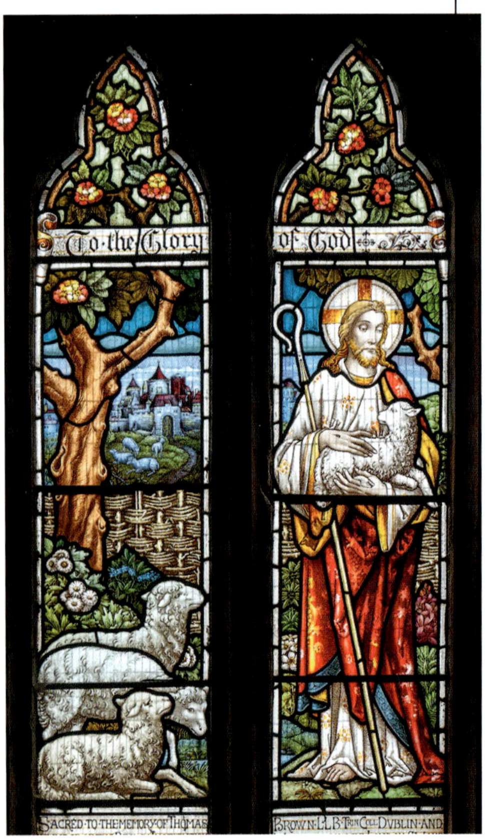

The uncoordinated addition of stained glass windows over decades probably troubled nineteenth-century architects and those of a mid-twentieth century modernist outlook more than it does for those used to the eclecticism that emerged at the end of the twentieth century. At the Church of St Paul, Sketty, the process had begun in the early 1850s, and the windows by Thomas Willement, William Warrington, William Wailes and Gsell-Laurent were joined by examples by Clayton & Bell and Burlison & Grylls by the end of the century, most of which were commissioned by the Vivian family. At Llanfaes, the Williams-Bulkeley family sat in the north aisle surrounded by family memorials in glass and stone, while the south aisle has further stained glass memorials to members of other local families, all of which appear to be by different makers.[8] At the Church of St Mary, Marshfield, the chancel boasts five windows by three different makers dating from the 1880s and 90s. The east window is by Edwin Horwood, a maker from Somerset, and representations of the virtues by Cox, Sons, Buckley & Co., Heaton Butler & Bayne and Horwood fill the windows of the north and south walls of the chancel.

339. (right) Cox, Sons, Buckley & Co., Charity, 1887, Church of St Mary, Marshfield, chancel

340. (centre right) Heaton, Butler & Bayne, Meekness, 1888, Church of St Mary, Marshfield, chancel

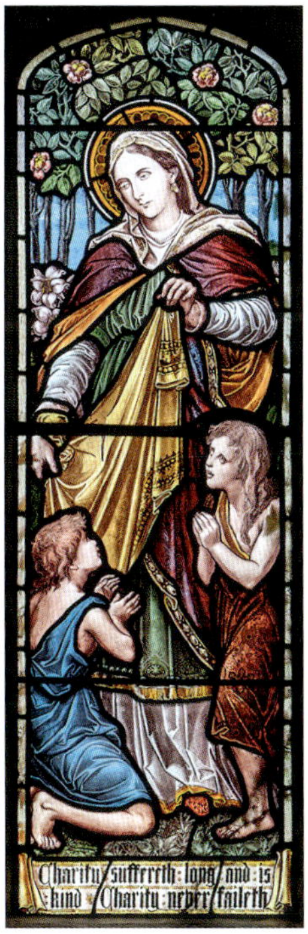

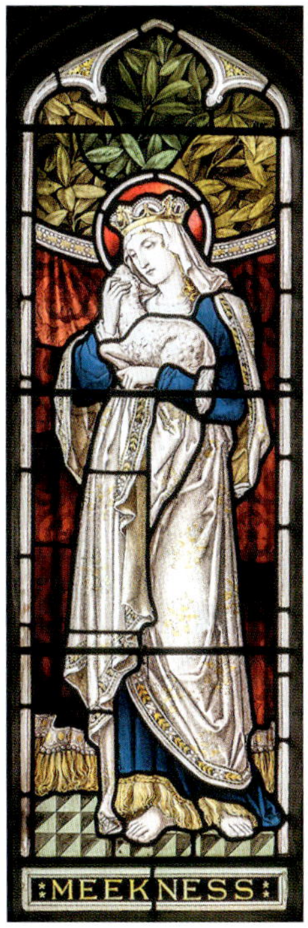

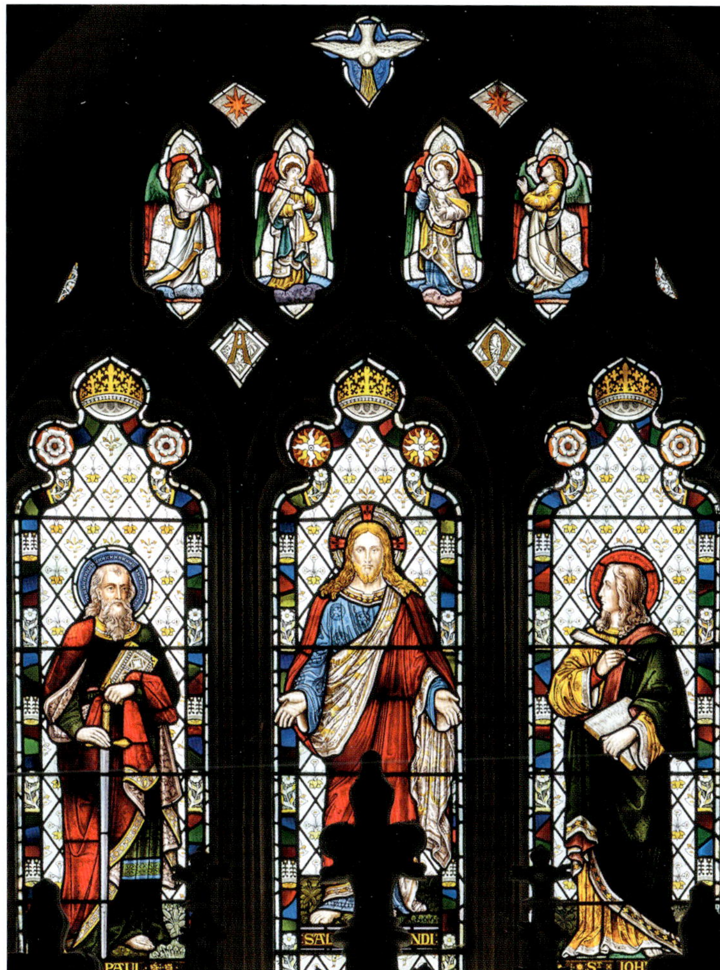

341. Edwin Horwood, Christ with St Paul and St John the Evangelist, 1883, Church of St Mary, Marshfield, east window

In other churches a unity of style prevailed. At Dwygyfylchi a set of six Welsh saints in the north and south nave windows of the Church of St Gwynan were given by separate donors, but seemingly as a single commission undertaken by Heaton, Butler & Bayne in about 1889. The firm also made the east and west windows of the church at around the same time and this complete scheme still survives. Other churches, large and small, have a number of windows filled over time by the same firm. John Hardman & Co. supplied memorials in stained glass for Baroness Windsor's church at St Fagans from 1859 until 1891, and were favoured by the family to make the east window given in her memory at the Church of St Martin, Caerphilly, in 1879. The firm of C.E. Kempe made all of the nine stained glass windows for the Church of St David, Barmouth, from 1872 until 1911, and twelve for the Priory Church of St Mary, Monmouth, from 1882 until 1923.

Memorials sometimes consisted of sets of windows. At the Church of St Michael, Aberystwyth, three of the six windows by A.O. Hemming were a single memorial to a former vicar and archdeacon of Cardigan.

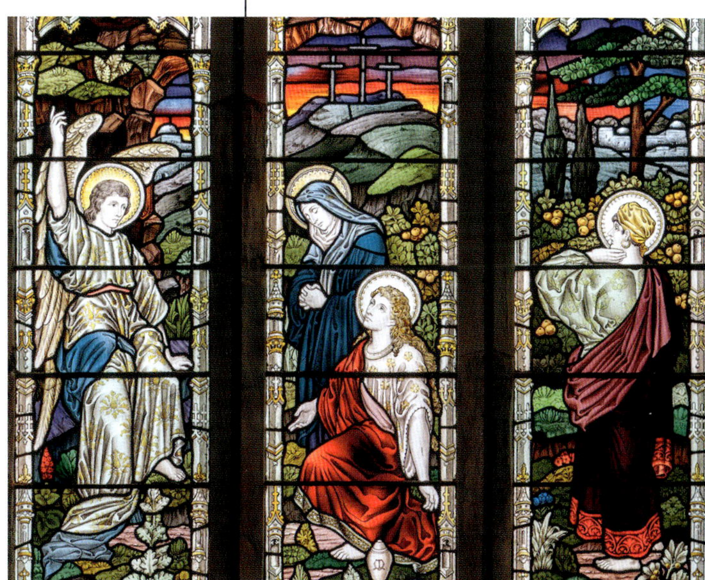

342. A.O. Hemming, An Angel Greets the Three Marys at the Empty Tomb, 1903, Church of St Michael, Aberystwyth, south aisle

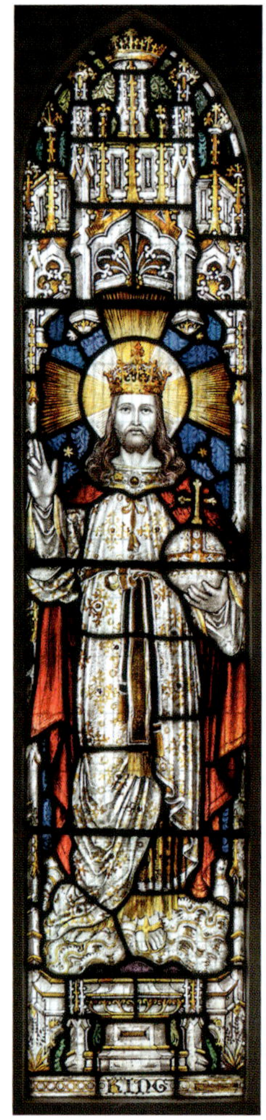

343. (right) Herbert Davis, Christ the King, 1901, Church of St Bridget, St Brides, nave

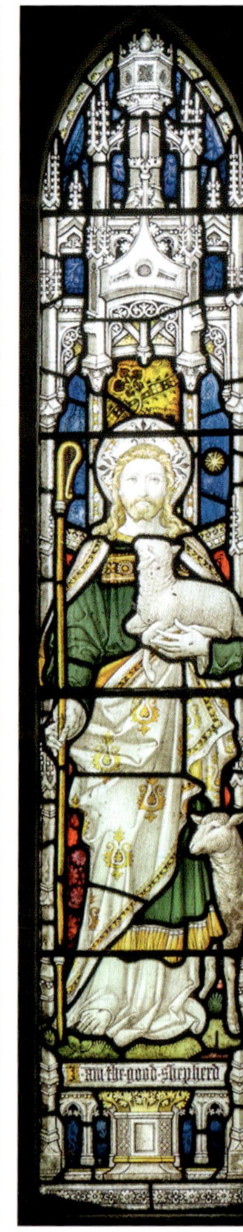

344. (far right) Clayton & Bell, The Good Shepherd, 1900, Church of St Machreth, Llanfachreth, nave

At the Church of St Bridget, St Brides, where earlier windows by makers including Clayton & Bell, and Cox, Sons, Buckley & Co. had been installed in the chancel, north transept and west wall, all of the six nave windows were filled with stained glass by Herbert Davis in 1901 as a single commission.[9] The chancel decoration commissioned by the Revd Martin Ricketts, vicar of the parish, in memory of his wife Susan, at the Church of St Edward, Knighton, in 1900 included five chancel windows as well as murals by T.F. Curtis, Ward & Hughes.[10] The Church of St Nicholas, Nicholaston, was itself a memorial, built by Olive Talbot in memory of her father C.R.M. Talbot. With the luxury of Olive Talbot's wealth at his disposal, the architect G.E. Halliday forewent his usual preference for plain glass in favour of exquisite stained glass by Burlison & Grylls in each window, to furnish the small church at Nicholaston in 1894.[11]

The continuation of patronage at a particular church sometimes also provided the circumstances for churches to be filled with the work of a single maker. This can be seen at churches located on large private estates, and built for the convenience of the family, their household and tenants. These churches, reflecting the interests of their patrons, accumulated family memorials that sometimes took the form of stained glass windows. For example, the Church of All Saints, Glasbury, was built by the de Winton family in 1883 within the gates of their estate at Maesllwch Castle, where windows and other

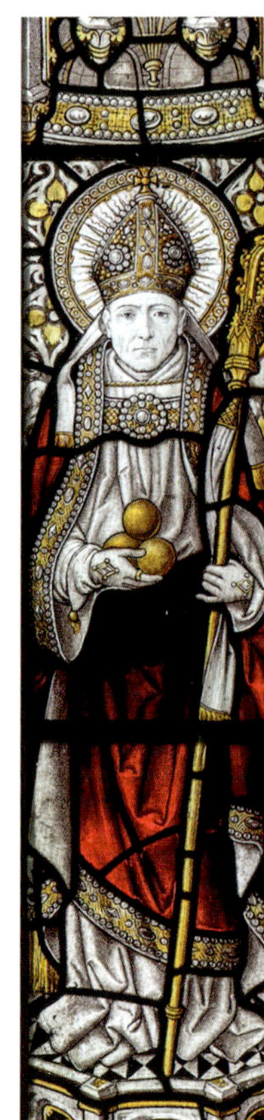

345. Burlison & Grylls, St Nicholas, 1894, Church of St Nicholas, Nicholaston, west window

9 The windows were given in memory of William Edwardes, fourth baron Kensington and his son, also William, the fifth baron, who lived nearby, and the six windows contained representations of Christ as the True Vine, the Light of the World and the Good Shepherd, and as Prophet, Priest and King.

10 The three-light east window, also by T.F. Curtis, Ward & Hughes had been added in 1897 when the chancel was rebuilt. All of the windows in the south aisle were also by the firm, and include a memorial to Martin Ricketts himself, who died in 1901.

11 Few of the churches built under the patronage of Olive or her sister Emily Talbot included stained glass as part of the original design. Stained glass by Clayton & Bell at the large and elegant church of St Theodore, Port Talbot, built in memory of their brother Theodore Talbot to the design of J.L. Pearson, is only found in the apse of the Lady Chapel.

12 The use of a single firm over time occasionally exposes a loss of quality and originality in their work. For example, none of the later windows at Llanychaearn, all by Heaton, Butler & Bayne and for members of the same family, match the colour and vigour of their east window depicting the Ascension of 1879.

furnishings were given in memory of family members, in addition to numerous wall tablet memorials. Similarly, local gentry largely appropriated rural churches, expressing their dominance through the commissioning of family memorials, a practice that sometimes extended back for centuries.[12] Some memorials were given by employees and tenants as a mark of esteem for their masters, such as the window of the Good Shepherd given for John Vaughan of Nannau at the Church of St Machreth, Llanfachreth, near Dolgellau.[13]

The church of Eglwys Oen Duw, Beulah, was built by Clara Thomas near her house, Llwynmadoc, to the design of John Norton in 1867–8. Stained glass for the east and west windows was made by Clayton & Bell, but the windows given in memory of Clara Thomas herself in 1878 were made by Burlison & Grylls. The firm also provided stained glass for the east and west windows at another church endowed by her daughter, also Clara Thomas, at Cwmbach Llechryd, where all of the windows were filled by the firm from 1886 until the 1950s, when the firm closed. Built at a cost of about £12,000, the church was intended for the new railway community at Builth Road, but was also conveniently located about half way between the family houses of Pencerrig and Cae'r Unon.[14]

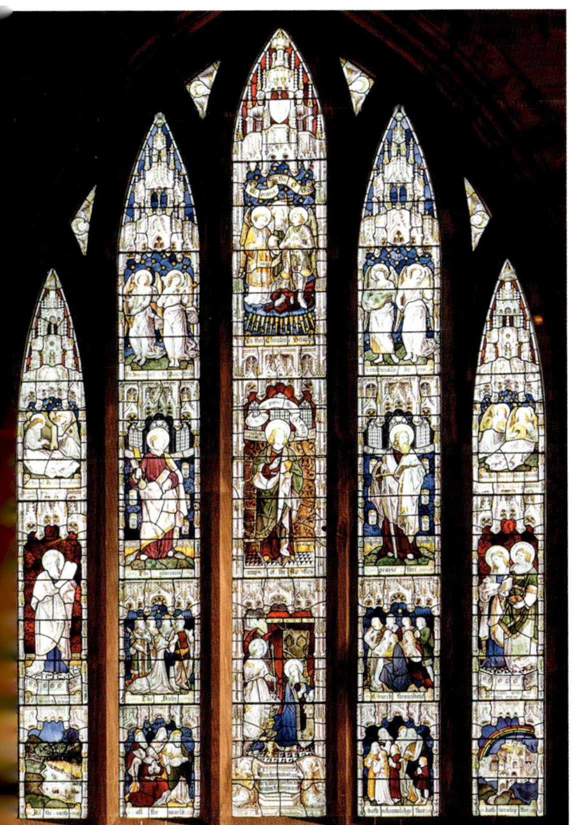

346. Burlison & Grylls, 'Te Deum', *c.* 1887, Church of St John the Divine, Cwmbach Llechryd, west wall

The east window of the Church of St John the Divine, Cwmbach Llechryd, is filled with much white glass above and below the three main coloured scenes, and these panels depict groups of figures, angels, and, above, Christ in Majesty, using only glass paint and silver stain. The increased use of white or lightly tinted glass in stained glass design enabled more windows

13 John Vaughan had continued the improvements to the estate undertaken by Robert Williams Vaughan, the second baronet, earlier in the century. Other windows, also by Clayton & Bell, were given around the same time in the church, including a window given in memory of John Vaughan by his daughter and son-in-law. Clayton & Bell were also commissioned to add a contemporary set of windows in the neighboring parish of Bryncoedifor, at the Church of St Paul, probably all part of an interior refitting of about 1895 commissioned by the Owens of Hengwrt Uchaf, Rhydymain.

14 Clara Thomas also contributed to the repair of the Church of St Mary, Builth Wells, and gave the stained glass for the east wall of the chancel in memory of her mother, made by C.E. Kempe in 1903. The family's wealth, inherited by Clara Thomas after her brother's sudden death when she was only twenty-two, derived from the mineral wealth beneath the family estates at Llanbradach and Pontypridd. R.G.B. Oliver, 'Pencerrig: House at the top of the rocks', *Radnorshire Society Transactions*, vol. 39 (1969), pp. 43–4. Her patronage also extended to Cardiff, and the stained glass for her family memorial at Llandaff Cathedral is the only work by Burlison & Grylls in the cathedral, replacing an earlier family memorial in memory of Henry Thomas by the firm of Michael & Arthur O'Connor. Nevil A. James, 'The Stained Glass of Llandaff Cathedral' in Nick Lambert (ed.), *Llandaff Cathedral* (Bridgend: Seren, 2010), p. 182.

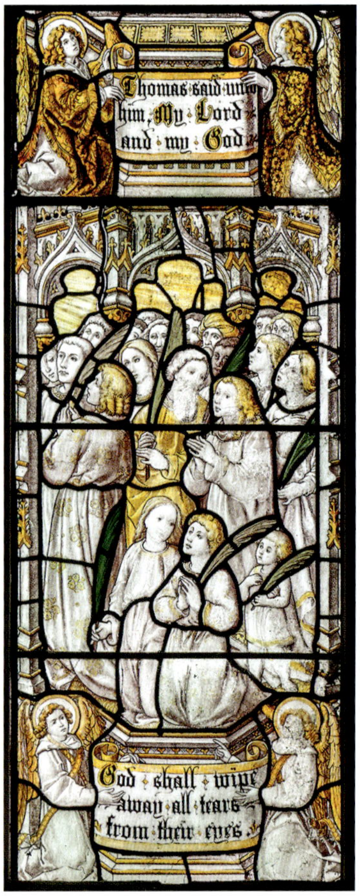

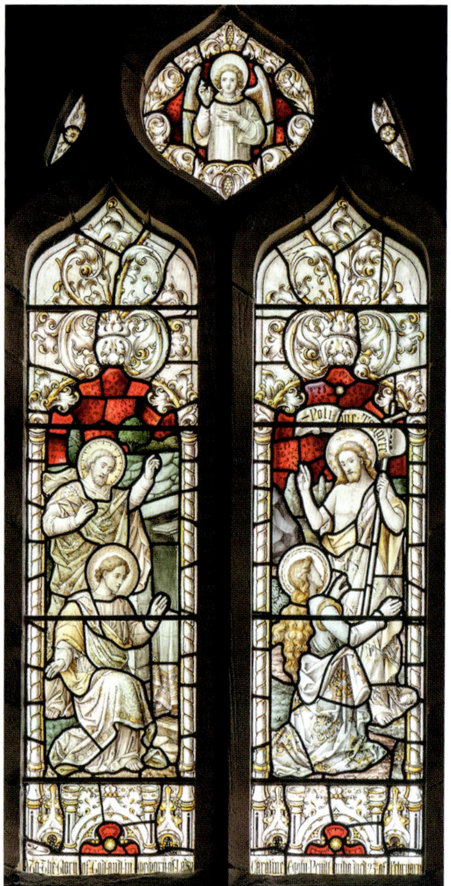

347. (far left) Burlison & Grylls, Martyrs Before the Throne of God, 1887, Church of St John the Divine, Cwmbach Llechryd, east window

348. (left) Lavers, Barraud & Westlake, Peter, John and Mary Magdalene with the Risen Christ, *c.* 1899, Church of All Saints, Deganwy, chancel

to be filled without darkening church interiors significantly. At the Church of All Saints, Deganwy, built by Lady Henrietta Augusta Mostyn in 1897–9 as a memorial to her parents, the Earl and Countess of Abergavenny, the chancel and nave windows by Lavers, Barraud & Westlake use very little coloured glass in their depiction of biblical scenes and figures of the four evangelists.

Following the decline in the use of heraldry in windows during the course of the nineteenth century, memorial windows were personalised in other ways. This was sometimes expressed in the choice of biblical subject matter. For example, clergy were often commemorated with an image of the Good Shepherd or Christ's commission to Peter to care for his sheep; doctors or surgeons with Luke, the author of one of the gospels and the physician from the Acts of the Apostles; while Sunday school teachers or headmasters might be remembered with scenes of instruction, such as the Sermon on the Mount, Anne teaching Mary to read or Paul with Timothy. Children were often remembered with the most common scene in Victorian and Edwardian stained glass, that of Christ blessing the children brought to him. The Good Wife, as described in the last chapter of the book of Proverbs, as well as Dorcas performing acts of charity, were popular subjects with widowers commemorating their wives and sometimes children commemorating their mothers.

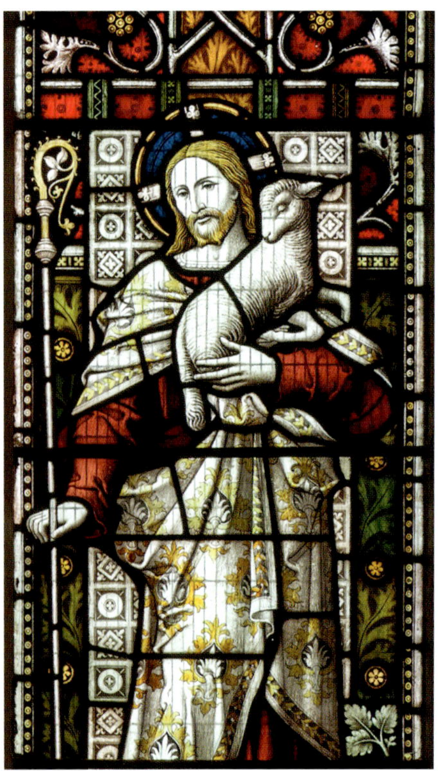

349. Clayton & Bell, The Good Shepherd, *c.* 1883 Church of St Egwad, Llanegwad, east window

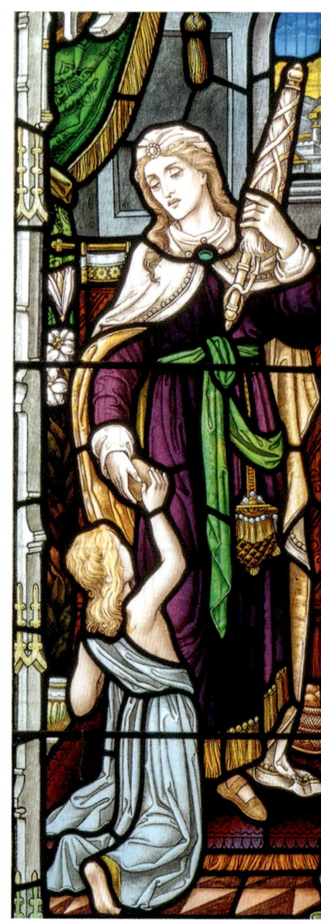

350. J.A. Campbell, The Good Wife, 1907, Church of St Thomas, Glyndyfydwy, nave

At the Church of St Tydecho, Cemaes (Powys), Thomas, John and Morgan Hughes gave a two-light window for the west wall of the nave in memory of their parents, John and Margaret Hughes. John Hughes had been the parish priest from 1827–58, and the left-hand light depicts Christ with Peter among sheep, with the text below 'He saith unto him feed my lambs' (John 21: 15). In the right-hand light Mary Magdalene is shown drying the feet of Christ with her hair, together with the text 'She hath done what she could' found in Mark 14: 8. The text is from the passage where a woman anoints Christ's head, but implies that Margaret Hughes also did what she could in the faithful service of Christ, whether by good works or pious devotion. In a similar way windows depicting figures performing the Acts of Mercy described in Matthew 25, or symbolic figures representing, Faith, Hope, Charity (from 1 Corinthians 13: 13) and other virtues, emphasised the goodness and generosity of deceased family members and friends.

Other subjects were chosen for less spiritual reasons. The four scenes in the window commemorating John Kirk at the Church of St Mary, Brecon, all illustrate the story of the birth of Christ, as he was born on Christmas

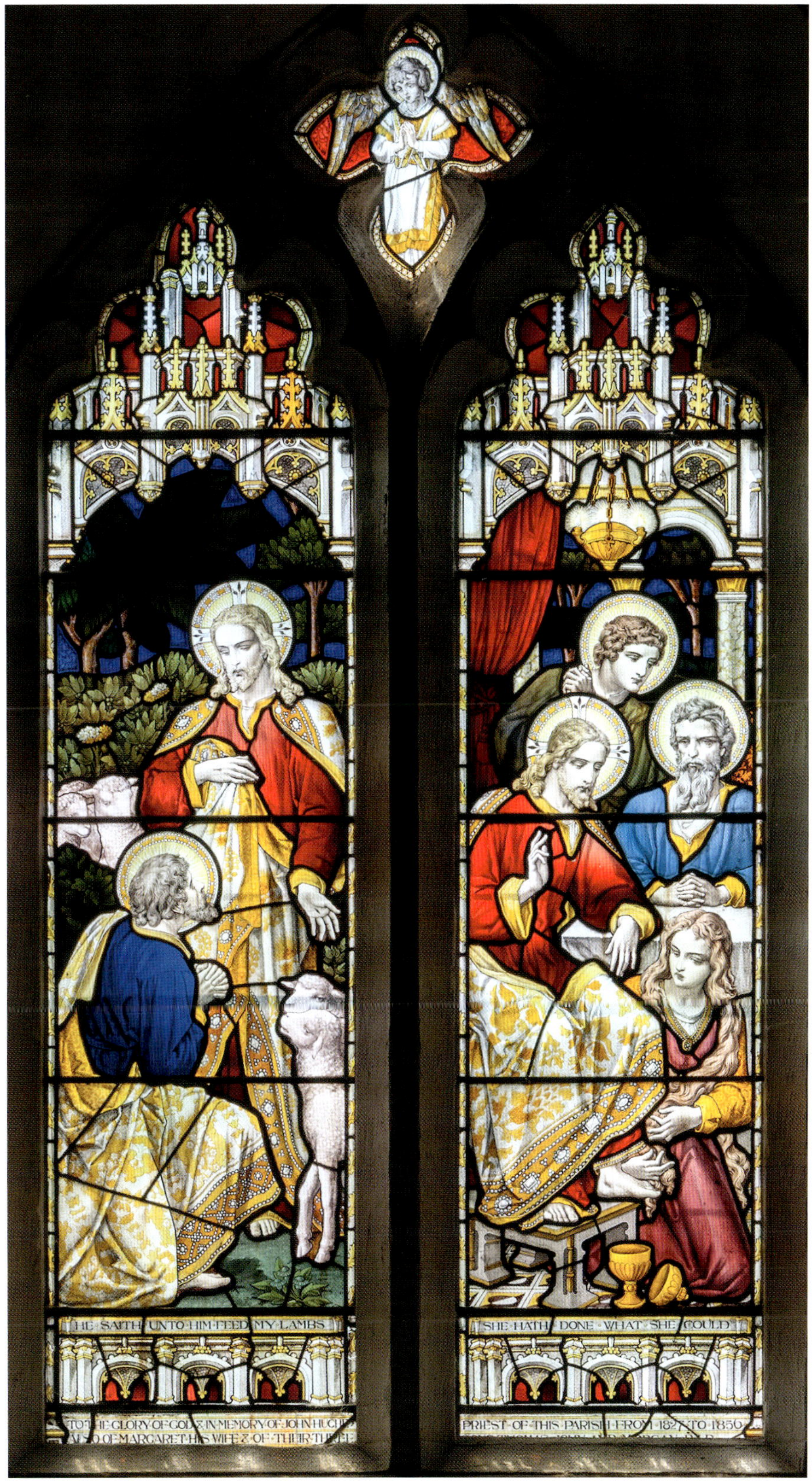

351. T.F. Curtis, Ward & Hughes, The Commission to Peter and Christ Anointed at the House of Simon the Pharisee, 1889, Church of St Tydecho, Cemaes (Powys), west wall

352. W.F. Dixon, St Gertrude of Nivelles, St John the Divine and St Emily, *c.* 1881–6, Church of St Margaret, Roath, Cardiff, Bute Mausoleum

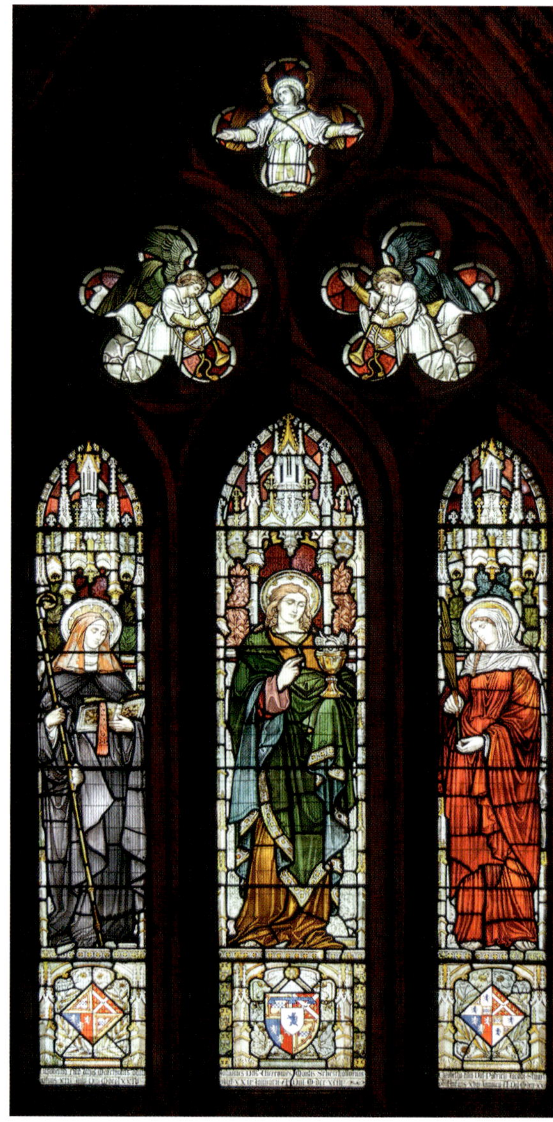

Day in 1818. The window given by Florentia Maria Crawshay in memory of her parents at the Church of St George, Reynoldston, features Barnabas in the central light because her own birthday fell on his feast day, 11 June. Saints were frequently chosen in memory of those who shared their Christian names, which sometimes introduced some more unusual subjects. The saints chosen for the Bute Mausoleum, built on the north side of the Church of St Margaret, Roath, Cardiff, for the third marquis of Bute, included Elizabeth of Hungary, the Holy Roman Emperor Henry II, Gertrude of Nivelles and Emily, representing members of the family buried there and indicative of the Roman Catholic faith of the marquis. The mausoleum was housed in an Anglican church, and a further window paid for by the marquis depicted Christ the Good Shepherd with John the Baptist and John the Evangelist at the Church of St John the Baptist in central Cardiff, with panels below depicting angels holding family heraldry.[15] Bute's great wealth enabled his patronage of both Anglican and Roman Catholic churches in the Cardiff area, and he was also among the donors of the sanctuary glass at the Church of St Peter in Roath. Installed in 1882, the windows were the work of Mayer of Munich, a firm that, like John Hardman & Co. was much in demand for Roman Catholic churches.[16]

15 The window was designed by N.H.J. Westlake, a friend of the marquis who had designed the windows for his bedroom at Cardiff Castle, as well as executing the painted decoration for Cardiff Castle Chapel. A further window by his firm was made for the church, depicting two scenes from the life of John the Baptist.

16 Mayer & Co. of Munich opened their London showroom soon after in 1865 at 70 Grosvenor Street. Sets of memorial windows by Mayer & Co. can also be found at Roman Catholic churches elsewhere in Wales, such as the Church of St Michael, Newport, the Cathedral Church of St Joseph, Swansea, and the Church of St David, Pantasaph. John Hardman & Co. had previously undertaken the decoration of the interior, including painting and gilding the altar, at the expense of the marquis of Bute in 1869. Michael Fisher, *Hardman of Birmingham, Goldsmith and Glasspainter* (Ashbourne: Landmark Publishing, 2008), p. 163.

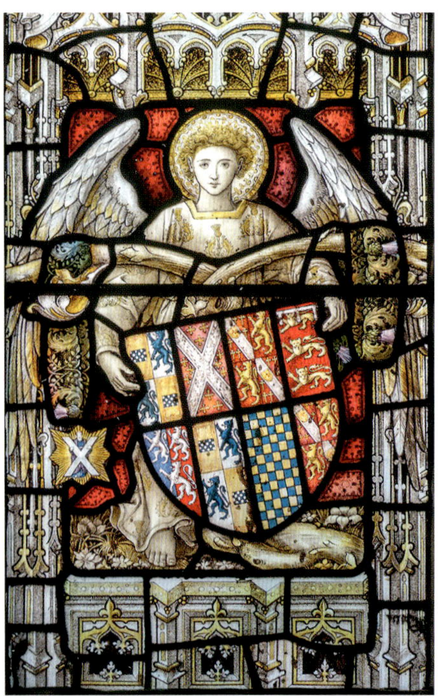

353. Lavers, Barraud & Westlake, Angel with the Arms of the Bute Family, *c.* 1890, Church of St John the Baptist, Cardiff, Lady Chapel

354. Mayer & Co., Sanctuary Wind
1882, Church of St Peter, Ca

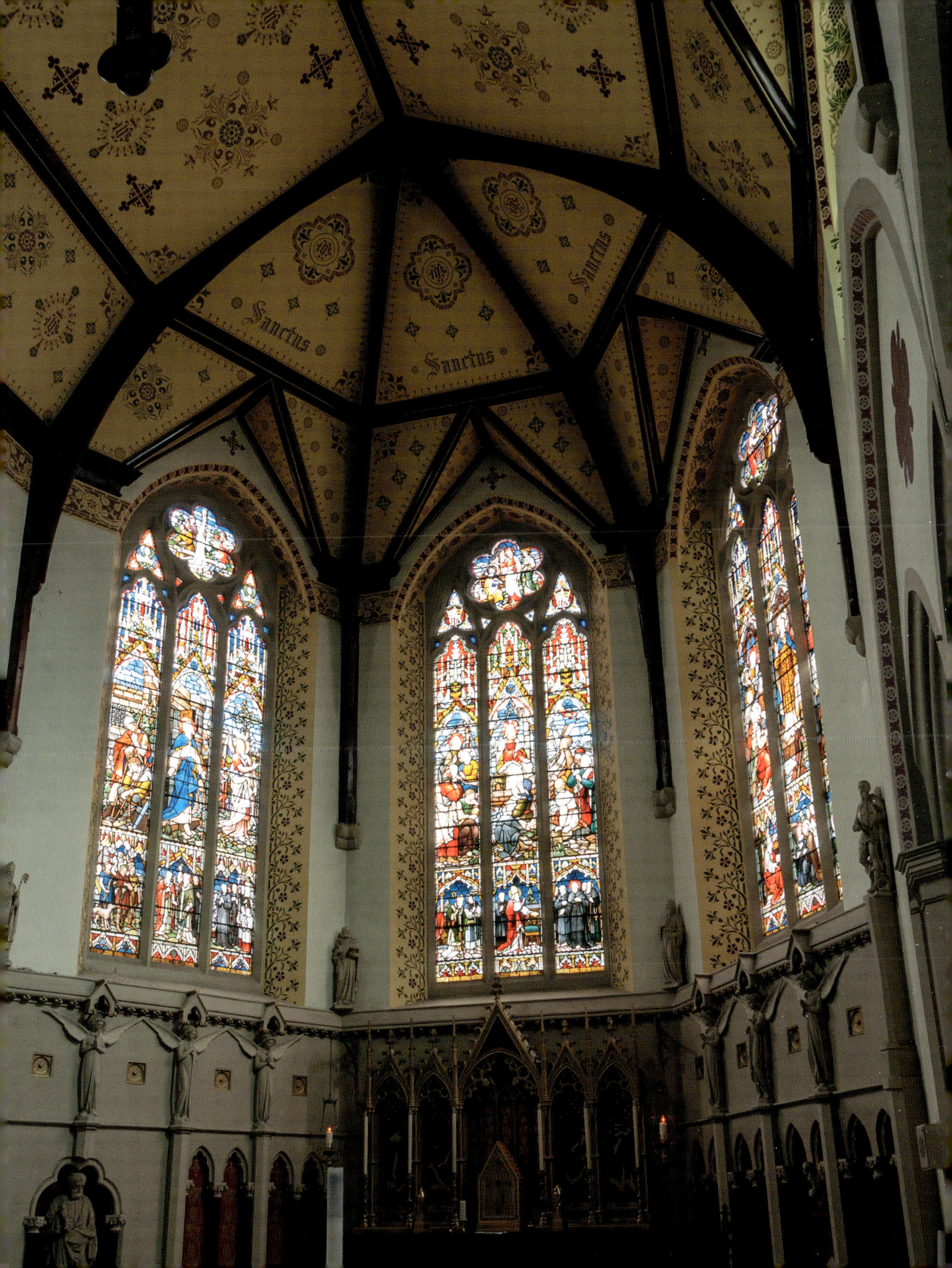
Sanctus
Sanctus
Sanctus

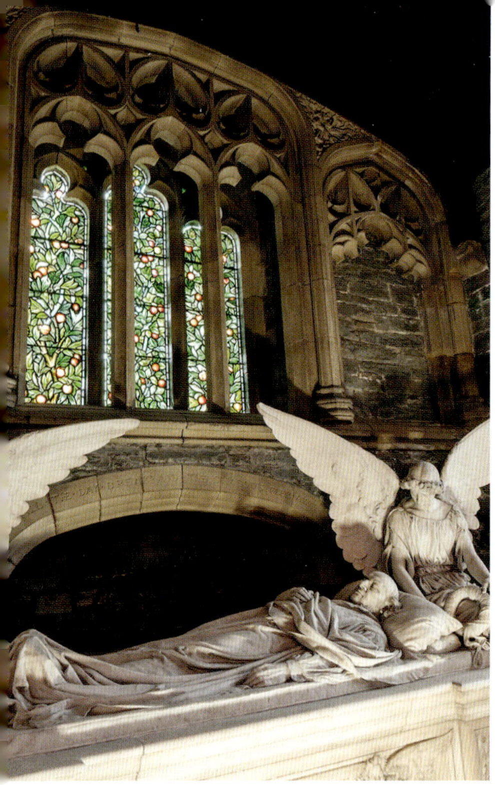

355. Memorial to William Owen Stanley, stained glass by Morris & Co., tomb by Hamo Thornycroft, 1897, Church of St Cybi, Holyhead, south chapel

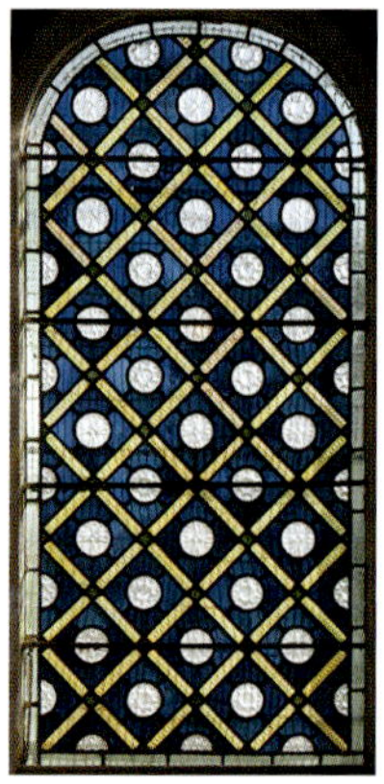

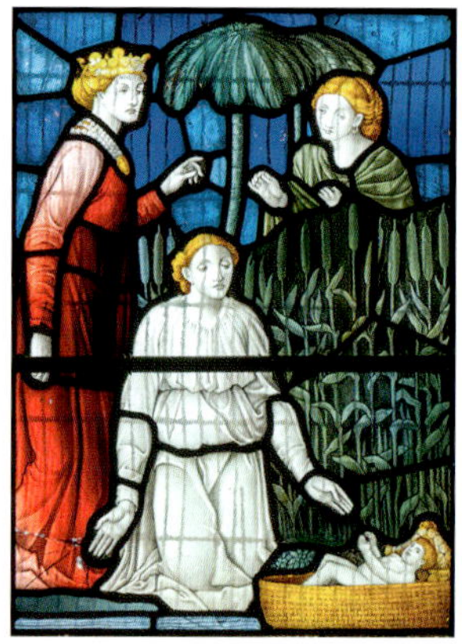

356. (centre left) James Powell & Sons, Nave Window, *c.* 1895, Church of St Mary, Bodewryd

357. (left) James Powell & Sons, The Finding of Moses in the Bulrushes, 1880, designed by H.E. Wooldridge, Church of St Peter, Newborough, east window

On Anglesey the religious faith of Henry Stanley, third Baron Stanley of Alderley, exerted an unusual influence on the glass made for the church restorations that he financed. His conversion to Islam in 1862 did not deter him from funding the restoration of several Anglican churches on the island, and James Powell & Sons, who had made a range of windows extending from patterned grisaille work to pictorial windows since the 1840s, made abstract leaded windows and pressed glass for churches at Llanbadrig, Bodewryd and Newborough. Biblical scenes were depicted in the east window for the Church of St Peter, Newborough, but unusually were all chosen from the Old Testament. His uncle, William Owen Stanley of Penrhos, also restored churches on the island, including the Church of St Cybi, Holyhead, where he is buried in an elaborate tomb beneath a three-light window by Morris & Co. filled with the branches of a tree bearing fruit as a representation of the Tree of Life.[17]

Patrons first began to reappear in Victorian stained glass as small donor portraits reminiscent of medieval windows, and were subsequently occasionally included as part of the biblical scenes depicted, or as charitable benefactors. A window given in memory of George Vane-Tempest, fifth marquis of Londonderry, by his 'Welsh friends and neighbours' depicts not only Lord and Lady Londonderry performing Acts of Mercy, but also a scene with the text 'For he loveth our nation, and he hath built us a synagogue' (Luke 7: 5), in reference to the Roman centurion whose faith so impressed Christ. Lord Londonderry lived with his wife at her house at Plas Machynlleth, and is commemorated as a 'foreign', but generous, benefactor of the Church of St Peter, Machynlleth.[18]

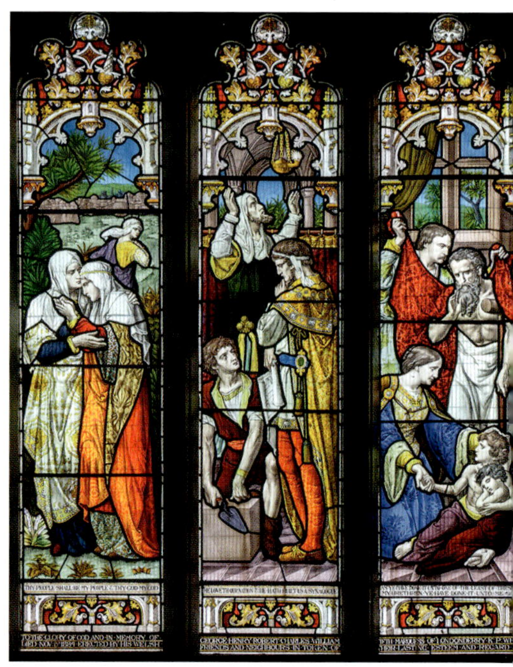

358. T.F. Curtis, Ward & Hughes, Ruth and Naomi, The Building of the Temple with Works of Charity, 1886, Church of St Peter, Machynlleth, chancel

17 Henry Stanley's sister, Rosalind Howard, and her husband, the artist George Howard, ninth earl of Carlisle, were close friends of William Morris and Edward Burne-Jones, and important patrons of Morris & Co. The Church of St Patrick, Llanbadrig, does feature a mosaic of Christ as the Good Shepherd with tiles of Islamic character also by James Powell & Sons. James Powell & Sons also made windows for the Church of St Michael, Valley, where windows were given in memory of William Owen Stanley.

18 His wife, Mary Cornelia (née Edwards), is depicted here as well as in her own memorial window in the church, where she is thought to have been the first female churchwarden in a Welsh diocese. The personalisation of the window did not prevent the cartoon being adapted at the Church of St Thomas, Rhyl, for another memorial window in 1890.

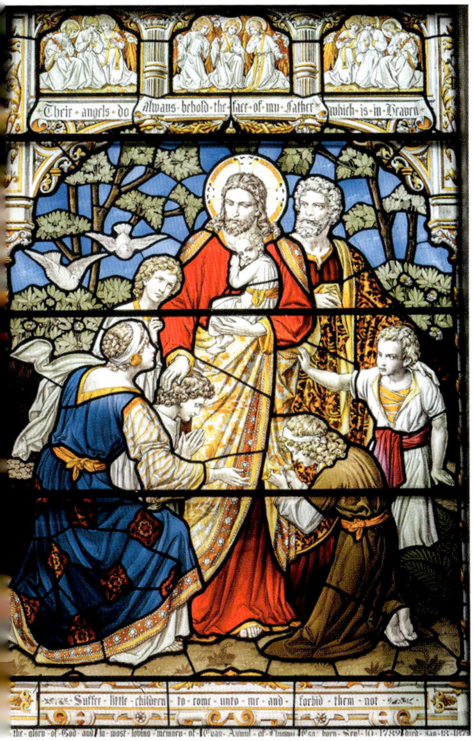

359. T.F. Curtis, Ward & Hughes, Christ with a Family Group, 1893, Church of St Peter ad Vincula, Pennal, nave

A window in a church nearby at Pennal by the same firm, T.F. Curtis, Ward & Hughes, appears to be a conventional depiction of the popular theme 'Suffer little children to come unto me'. Unusually, the biblical text is interpreted as a family group, with Christ at the centre. Often one or more of Christ's male disciples are depicted as part of the scene, showing their disapproval of Christ's interest in the children, but the male figure here has his hand on the shoulder of one of the children, as if to gently bring the child into the group. As only one mother is shown, this is clearly a family group with five children gathered around the central figure of Christ.

T.F. Curtis, Ward & Hughes stand out as a firm that made use of portraits drawn from photographs, such as at the Church of St Margaret of Antioch, Bodelwyddan, where Ellinor Harriet Williams (née Sitwell) is depicted as the Good Wife in a family group with other portraits.[19] A window by the firm at Oystermouth depicts several members of the family of Sir John Jones Jenkins (later Baron Glantawe) in a memorial to his wife Katherine Prudence as the virtues Gentleness, Love and Patience, making them the personification of the virtues that they depict.[20]

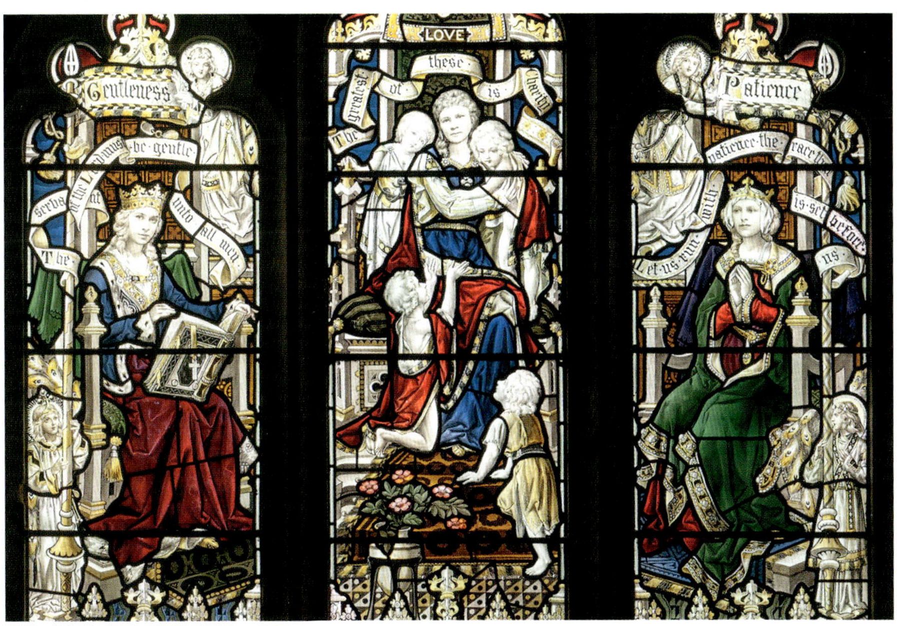

19 The church itself is included in the right-hand light. Margaret Williams, Lady Willoughby de Broke, had the church built in memory of her husband Henry Peyto-Verney, Lord Willoughby de Broke, after his death in 1852. The couple were childless and the estate passed to her brother Hugh Williams, whose son William Grenville Williams lost his wife Ellinor, who was twenty years his junior, when she was twenty-nine.

20 Lord Glantawe is himself in a window given by his daughters, depicted as the Good Soldier of Christ wearing the whole armour of God. Placed in 1920, his portrait is taken from a photograph of the early 1880s. I am grateful to Edward Llewellyn-Jones for further information on these windows.

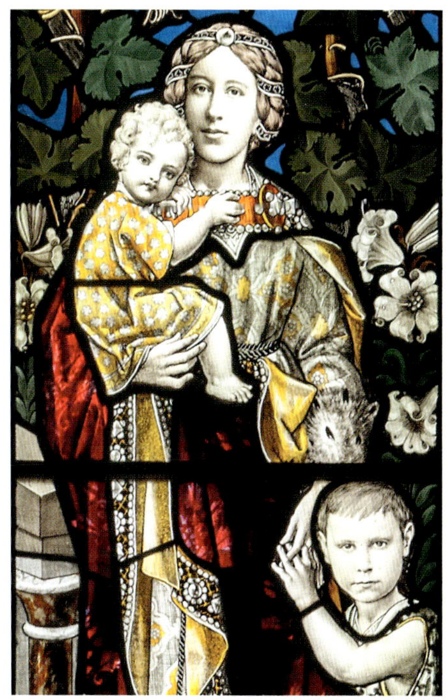

360. T.F. Curtis, Ward & Hughes, Ellinor Harriet Williams as the Good Wife, 1896, Church of St Margaret, Bodelwyddan, south aisle

361. T.F. Curtis, Ward & Hughes, Love with Gentleness and Patience, *c.* 1900, Church of All Saints, Oystermouth, south aisle

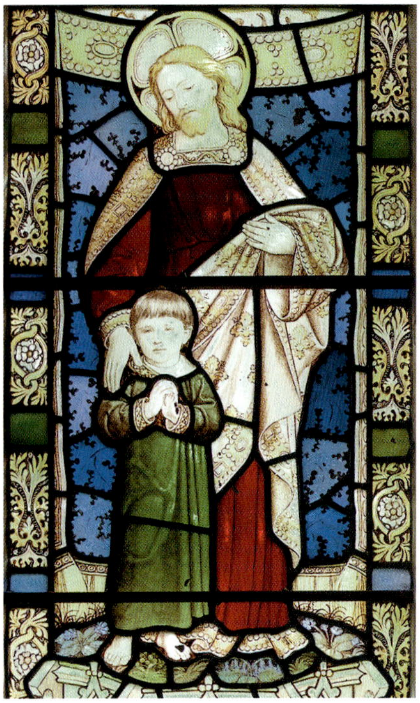

362. Burlison & Grylls, Christ with a Child, *c.* 1896, Church of St Tysilio, Bryneglwys, south aisle chapel

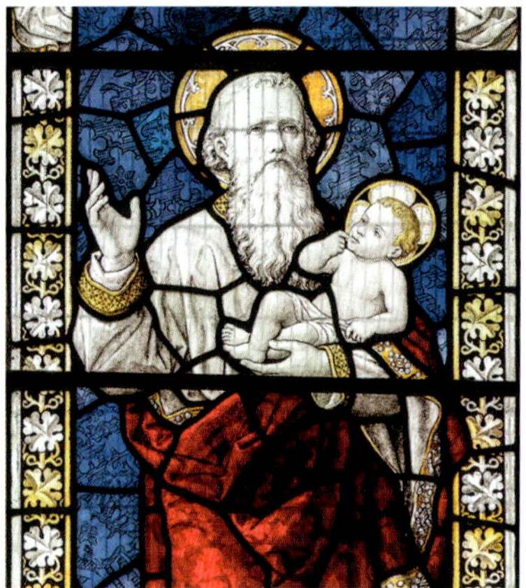

363. Burlison & Grylls, Robert Blezard as Simeon, from the Presentation in the Temple, 1907, Church of St Mwrog and St Mary, Llanfwrog, north chancel

Windows by Burlison & Grylls also include family portraits. At the Church of St Tysilio, Bryneglwys, a two-light window was given in memory of John Edward Ivor Yale by his parents. The left-hand light depicts Christ with their son as a child, the face surely a portrait, even though John Yale was in his thirties when he died, far away in Port Elizabeth, South Africa. Portraits sometimes appear among the bystanders in biblical scenes, and a further window in the style of the firm, at the Priory Church of St Seiriol, Penmon, depicts Henry Owen and Sarah Williams of Tre Castell as bystanders in two separate scenes in the east window given by their children in 1912. Some of those memorialised are depicted in the guise of biblical characters. Another window by Burlison & Grylls at the Church of St Mwrog and St Mary, Llanfwrog, depicts Robert Blezard as Simeon holding the infant Christ in the scene of the Presentation of Christ in the Temple, and the face of the prophetess Anna could be that of his wife.

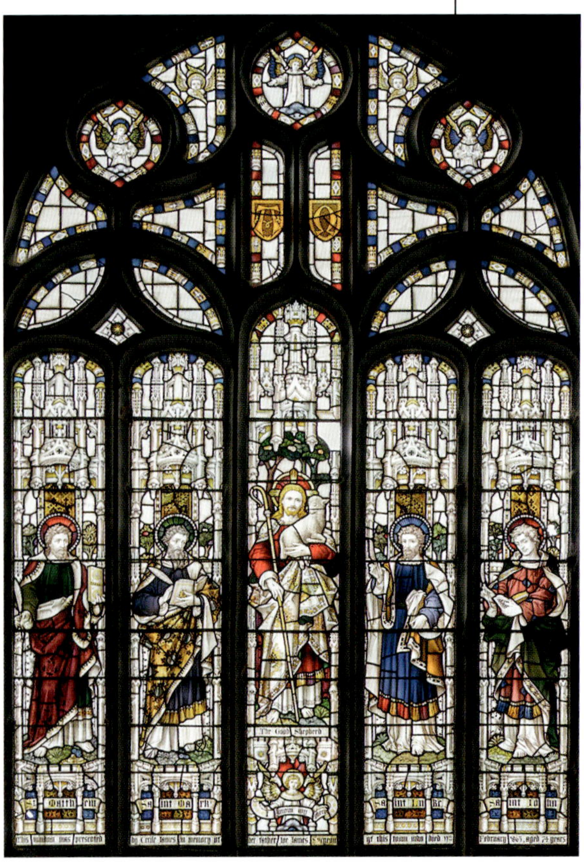

Although pictorial stained glass is more common in Anglican and Roman Catholic churches, members of Nonconformist chapels also commissioned pictorial windows. For example, the Unitarian church in Merthyr Tydfil was rebuilt in an Art Nouveau Gothic style in 1901, and a large five-light window was commissioned and given in memory of a surgeon of the town and his wife, although he had died in 1863. Some of the leading industrialist families in south Wales were Nonconformists, including members of the two Cory families who were coal transporters and owners, some of whom were prominent Baptists and Wesleyan Methodists. At St Julians Methodist Church, Newport, a window given in memory of Minnie Cory by her daughter Ethel Firbank, includes the unusual detail of a Roman mosaic pavement, no doubt a reference to the nearby Roman fortress of Caerleon.

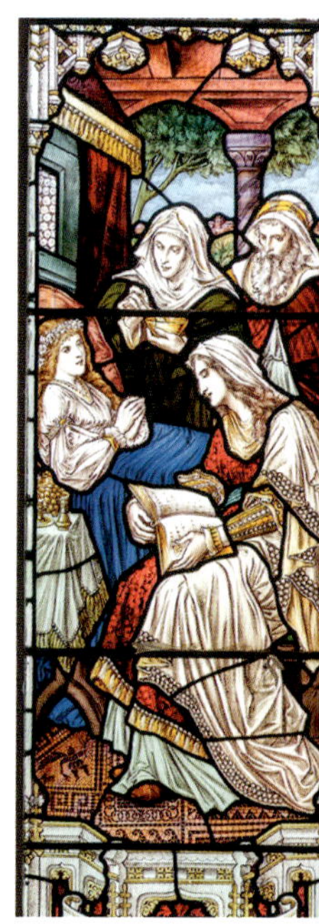

364. Probably Clayton & Bell, Christ with the Four Evangelists, *c.* 1901, Church of St Margaret, Merthyr Tydfil, rear wall

365. Jones & Willis, Visiting the Sick, 1907, St Julian's Methodist Church, Newport, side wall

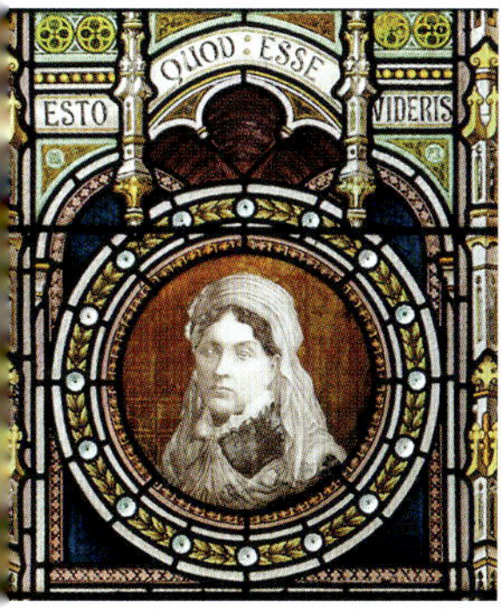

66. Katherine Lever, *c.* 1887–8, esleyan Methodist Church of t John, Colwyn Bay, west wall

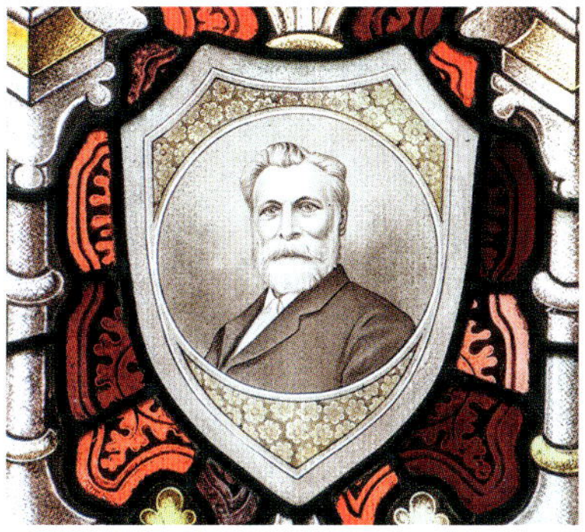

367–8. Swaine Bourne, Christ with Mary and Martha, and Christ with Women and Children, including portrait of William Sandbrook (above), 1904, Mount Pleasant Congregational Church, Pontypool, front wall

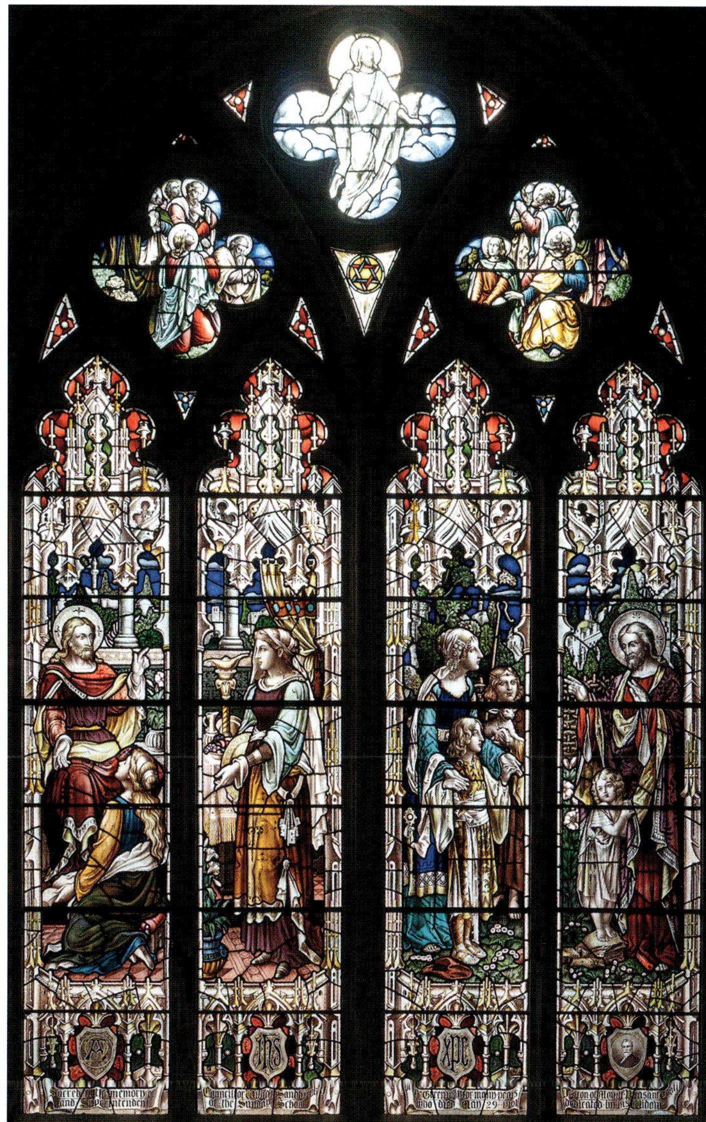

Some of these windows included portraits of donors or those commemorated in the windows. The west window of the Wesleyan Methodist Church of St John, Colwyn Bay, has a portrait of Katherine, the wife of Ellis Lever, who had moved to the seaside town in 1888.[21] The large window consists of climbing flowers and the text from the Parable of the Talents in Matthew 25. Figurative glass was first introduced in the church when a memorial window to Thomas George Osborn, the foundng headmaster of Rydal School, displaced the original central two lights of the apse in 1912.

At Mount Pleasant Congregational Church in Pontypool a large window depicts scenes of Christ with Martha and Mary, and with women and children, across four-lights. The window was made by the firm of Swaine Bourne & Son in 1904 and given by the widow of Councillor William Sandbrook, a deacon of the church and superintendent of the Sunday school. His portrait was added in the lower right-hand light of the window.

Some of these portraits were controversial. The east window at the Church of St Margaret, Mountain Ash, included a small inset portrait of the mining engineer and coalowner John Nixon, and was given by his wife. This was reputedly the cause of a further gift to the church, when Henry Bruce, second Baron Aberdare, commissioned a reredos in 1904 to be installed in front of the window to obscure the portrait.[22]

21 Ellis Lever was the son of a collier who became a successful corn merchant and lived in the wealthy parish of Bowdon, near Manchester. I am grateful to Helen Watt for her help with establishing the identity of the couple.

22 Information provided by Brian Davies, see 'The Bible and the Welsh Landscape: The People of Wales', in Martin Crampin and John Morgan-Guy, *Imaging the Bible in Wales* (DVD-ROM) (Sheffield: Sheffield Phoenix Press, 2010).

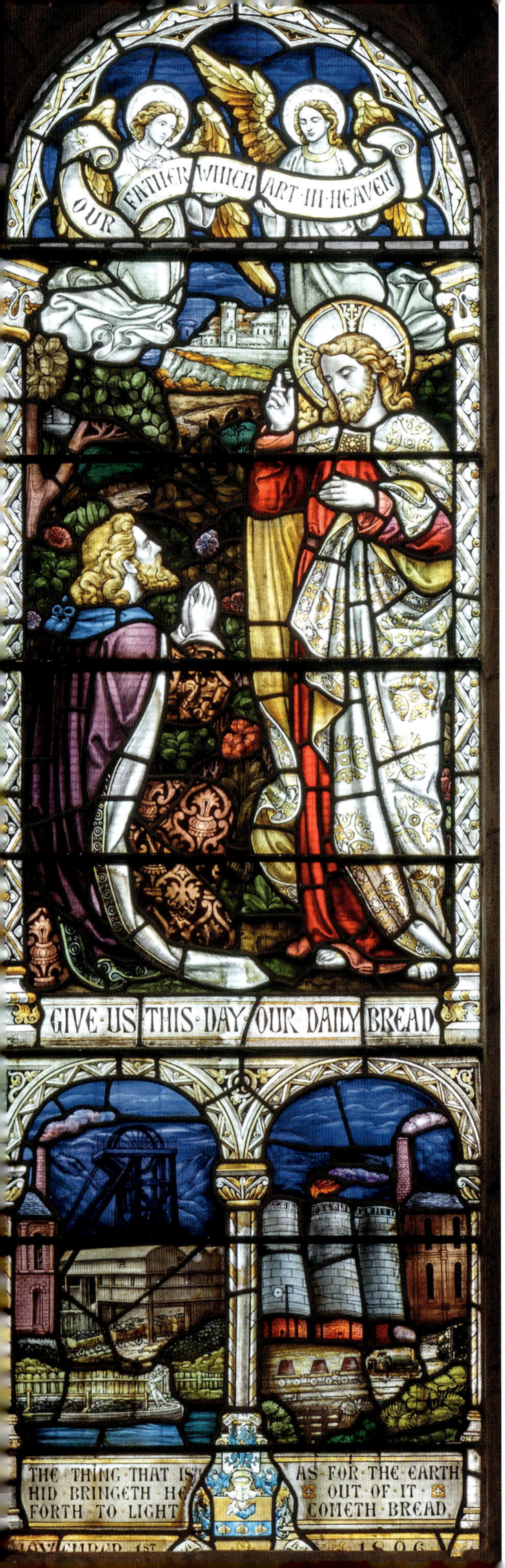

370. Thomas Brock, W.T. Lewis, 1913, Aberdare Park

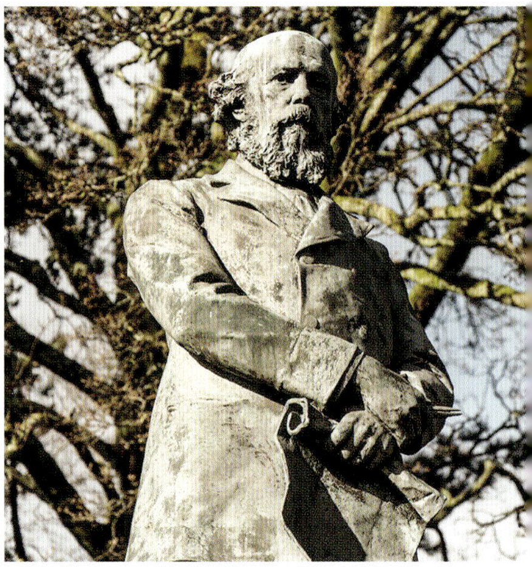

The window was designed by Robert Newbery, who was established in London, but had family connections in Pembrokeshire. This may help to account for the large number of his works being found across southern Wales from Monmouthshire to Pembrokeshire.[23] An early work in Wales by his studio was the window on the subject of creation at the Church of St John, Dowlais, in 1896. Sir William T. Lewis, later created first baron Merthyr of Senghenydd, was sufficiently impressed by it to commission a window by Newbery in the same year commemorating the 'Captains of Industry' at the Church of St Tydfil, Merthyr Tydfil. Where the Dowlais window had contained a depiction of miners, that at Merthyr Tydfil depicted a pithead and blast furnace beneath the figure of Christ and a kneeling figure.[24]

W.T. Lewis was a churchwarden at the Church of St John, Aberdare, and commissioned memorial windows by Robert Newbery for the Church of St Elvan, Aberdare, in the early 1900s.[25] This included a window dedicated to the 'Captains of Industry' in 1913 that included the late John Nixon among those 'who were associated with him in developing the Aberdare Valley minerals'. In 1911 he had added a window in thanksgiving for 'numerous blessings' and in particular his marriage to Anne Rees, in which she is depicted as Hannah holding the infant Samuel. She had died in 1902 at Hean Castle, their residence overlooking Saundersfoot Bay in Pembrokeshire, and windows in her memory were given by Lewis at Aberdare and the Church of St Issell, St Issells, near Hean Castle. Both were designed by Robert Newbery and include her portrait in small roundels by the dedication at the bottom of the window.

369. Robert Newbery, 'Give us this day our daily bread', 1896, Church of St Tydfil, Merthyr Tydfil, west window

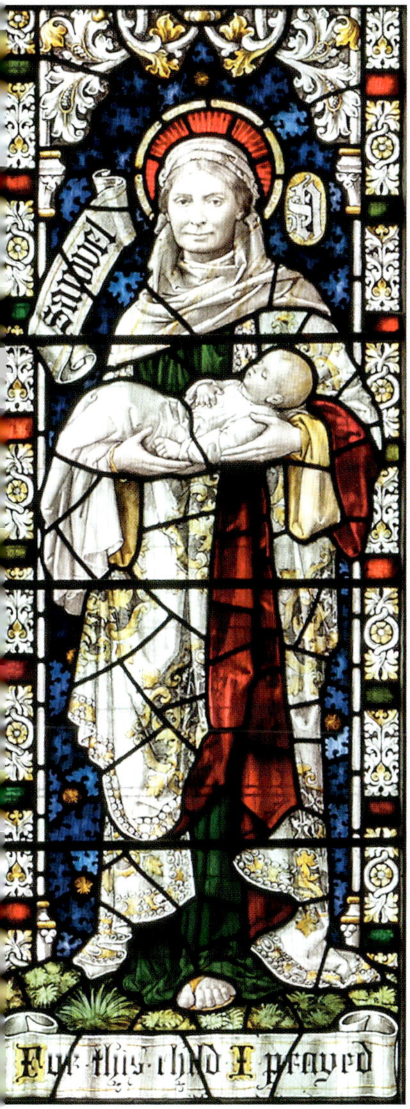

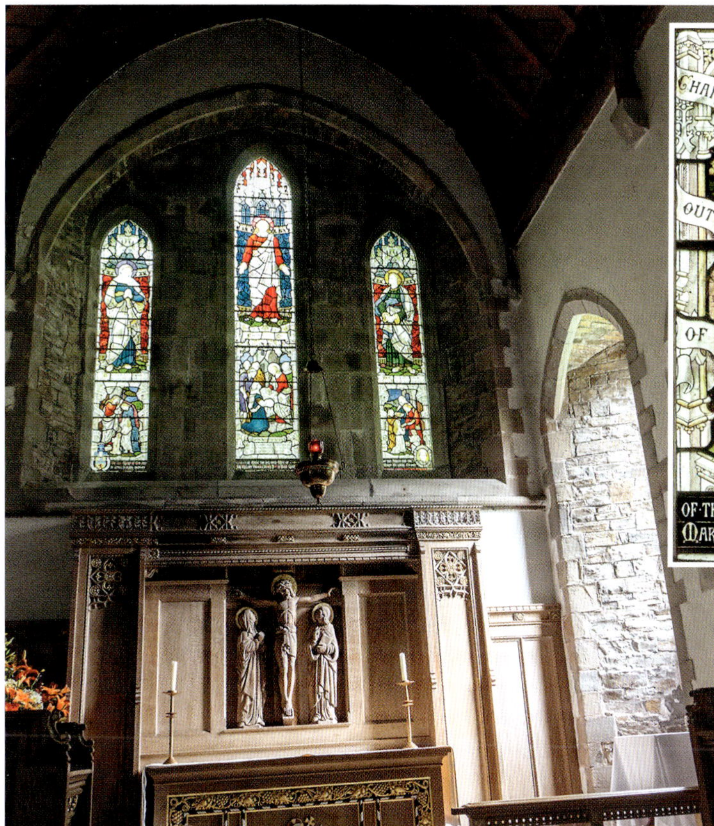

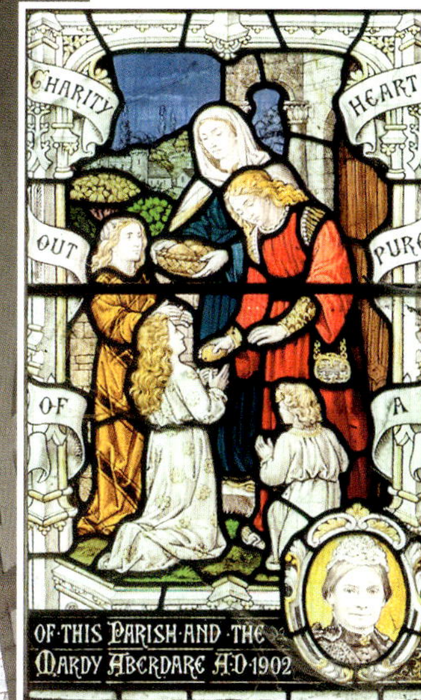

373–4. Robert Newbery, Christ with the Virgin Mary and St John, including Works of Charity (above) 1902, Church of St Issell, St Issells, east window

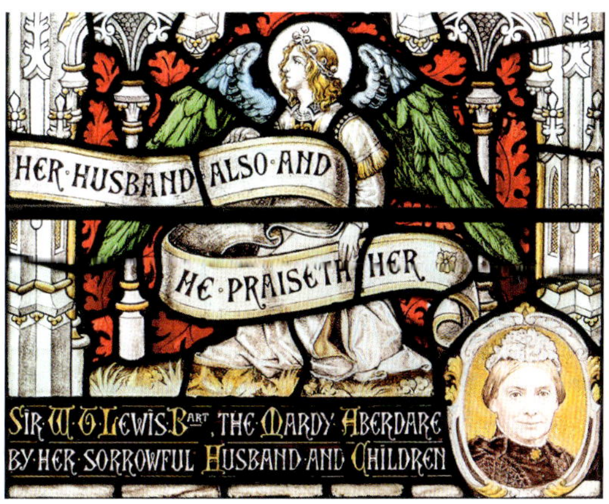

71–2. Robert Newbery, Hannah with the Infant amuel, 1911, south aisle (above); lower panel f memorial window to Anne Rees, *c.* 1902, orth aisle (right), Church of St Elvan, Aberdare

Some of the windows commissioned by W.T. Lewis and his family at Merthyr Tydfil, Aberdare and St Issells were conspicuous in their depiction of Welsh saints and legendary British history. Such subject matter was not always welcome. W.T Lewis commissioned another window in memory of his wife for Llandaff Cathedral depicting Welsh saints, but when the Dean and Chapter refused permission for its installation in the nave it was confined to the north choir aisle (Dyfrig Chapel).[26]

23 Robert Newbery married the sister of John Bland of Haverfordwest although his only known work in the town was for Tabernacle English Congregational Church. A window nearby at the Church of St Ishmael, Uzmaston, was given in 1908 in memory of his wife's parents.

24 W.T. Lewis gave two further windows by Newbery to the church in 1900 and 1910.

25 Lewis had also commissioned at least one window at the Church of St John, giving a window in 1888.

26 Information provided by Brian Davies. A further window in memory of Lord Merthyr was given by his children and dedicated in 1920, depicting the kings Arthur, Tewdrig and Cadwaladr. See Nevil A. James, 'The Stained Glass of Llandaff Cathedral' in Nick Lambert (ed.), *Llandaff Cathedral* (Bridgend: Seren, 2010), pp. 182–3.

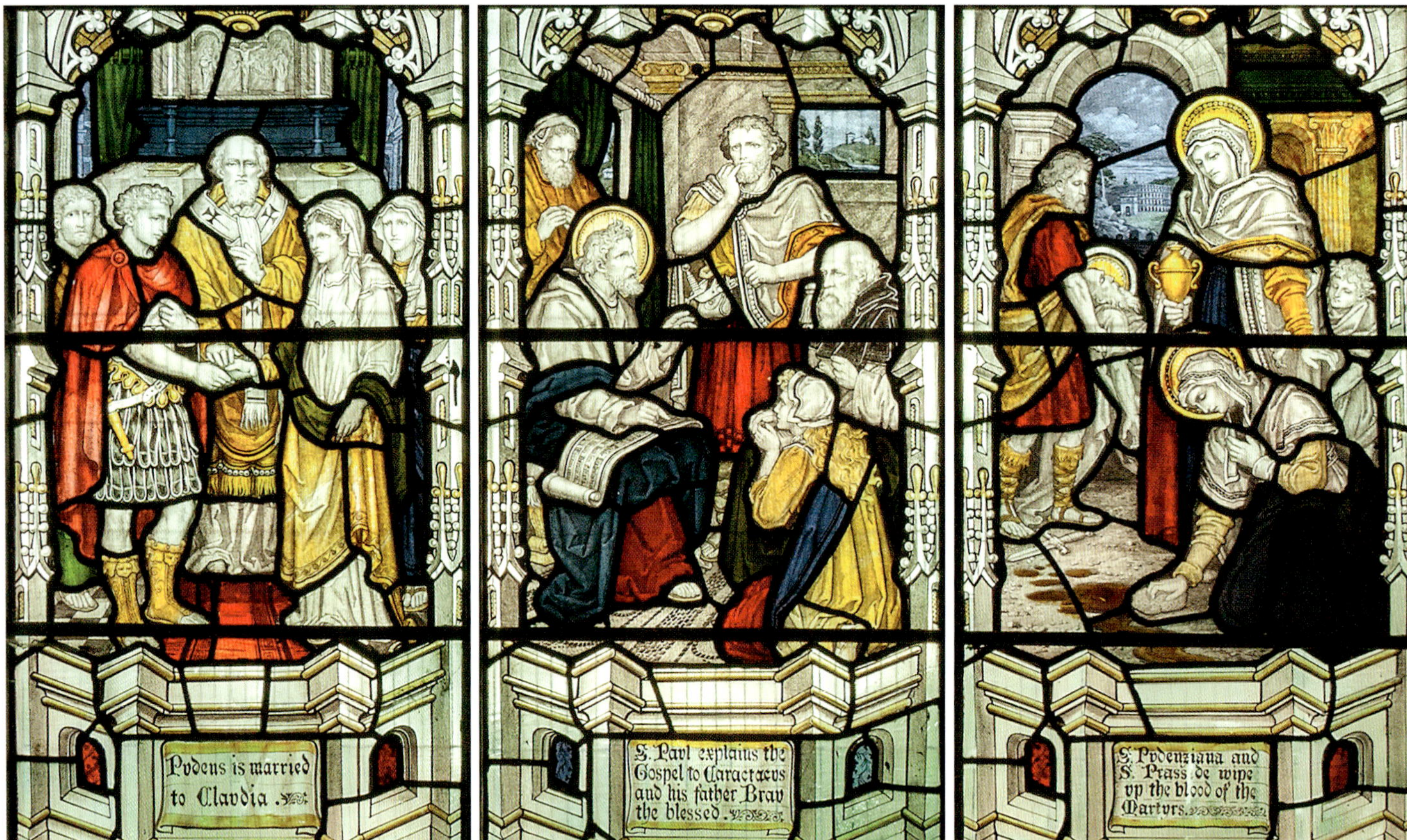

375. C.E. Tute, Scenes Pertaining to the Family of Caractacus in Rome, 1897, Church of St Llonio, Llandinam, south chapel

Other patrons occasionally expressed their interests in legendary British history. Ellen Powell, who lived near London in Upper Norwood, gave a window for the Church of St Llonio, Llandinam, with subjects relating to the family of Caractacus in Rome including a scene of Paul explaining the Gospel to Caractacus and Bendigeidfran. The window was given in memory of her parents Richard and Elinor Powell of Trewythen, near Llandinam, and she took the trouble of writing a detailed description of the window, with her reasons for the choice of subject, to the bishop of Bangor as she was concerned that he would be unfamiliar with the scenes depicted. In her letter she hoped that the window would be not only acceptable to the parishioners, but might also 'lead, perhaps, to some one else placing another window more fully representing Arwystli, who first introduced Christianity into the district. And likewise commemorating St Llonio – who, in later years, founded the Church.'[27]

In Cardiff, windows with Welsh saints by Burlison & Grylls were given by the architect E.M. Bruce Vaughan for the sanctuary apse of the Church of St James, which he had designed in 1892–3.[28] Welsh saints can

27 National Library of Wales, Records of the Church in Wales: Diocese of Bangor, B/F/252. Letter dated 28 June 1897. In the event the only windows subsequently installed in the church, in about 1900, depicted the Resurrection and Ascension.

28 Subsequent gifts filled the remainder of the apse windows, completing a set of standing figures of Tydfil, Illtud, David, Dyfrig, Teilo and Asaph, at either side of the figure of Christ.

376–7. Clayton & Bell, Royal Welsh Fusiliers Memorial Window (far right), including the Battle of Poitiers (right), 1895, Church of St Giles, Wrexham, west window

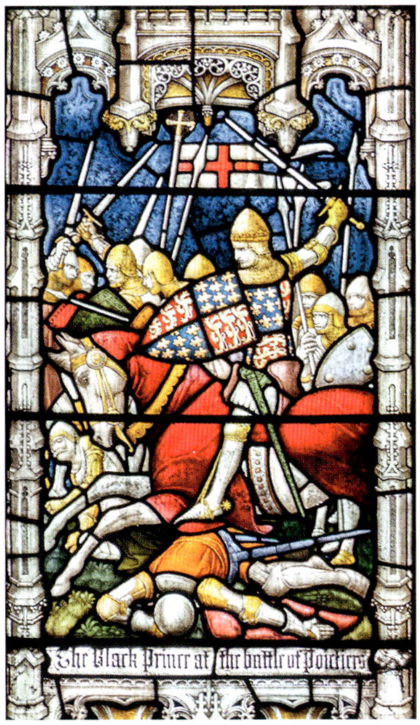

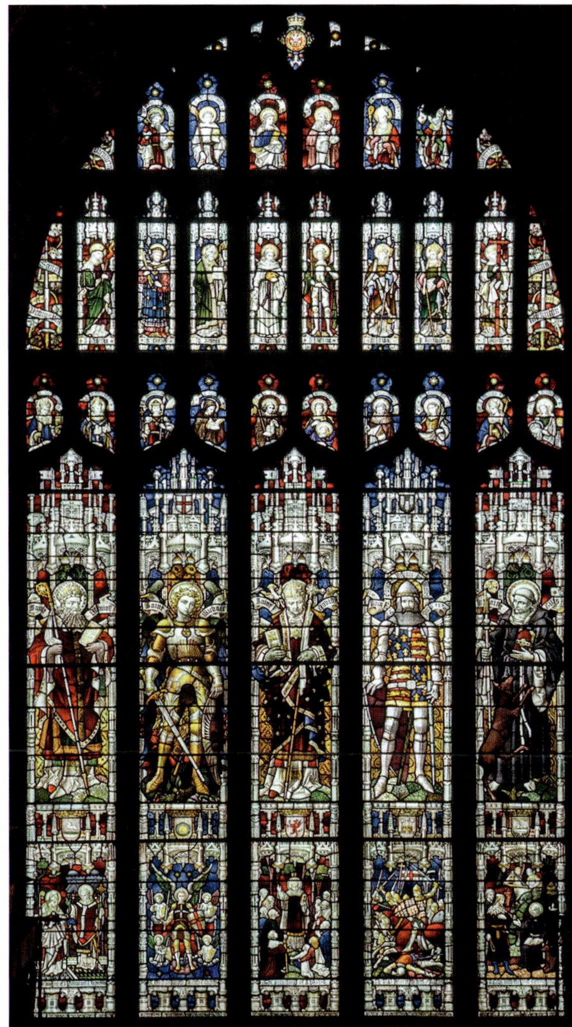

also be found in the five-light west window at the Church of St Giles, Wrexham, given by the Royal Welsh Fusiliers in memory of those who served with them. In the tracery lights are numerous saints either associated with Wales or with names of places where battles were fought by the Fusiliers; below are the Archangel Michael and the saints Deiniol, David and Giles, but also Edward the Black Prince, created Prince of Wales in 1343, with a scene from his victory at the Battle of Poitiers.[29]

Some patrons looked beyond Wales for their choice of saints. No images of David were commissioned for the family memorials at the Church of St David, Capel Dewi, by the Stewart family of Alltyrodyn, whose house overlooks the site. Above the east window, a copy of Gustave Doré's *Christ Leaving the Praetorium*, are four English saints: Chad, Augustine, Alban and Wilfred. Two other stained glass windows depict the four evangelists, and a fourth, of the soldier Martin dividing his cloak to clothe a beggar, commemorates James Logan Stewart of the 7th Hussars.[30] The regiment served in Africa in the year of his death in 1898, and returned to that continent to fight in the Boer War in 1901. The loss of life during the Second Boer War of 1899–1902 introduced further military saints into the stained glass of Welsh churches.

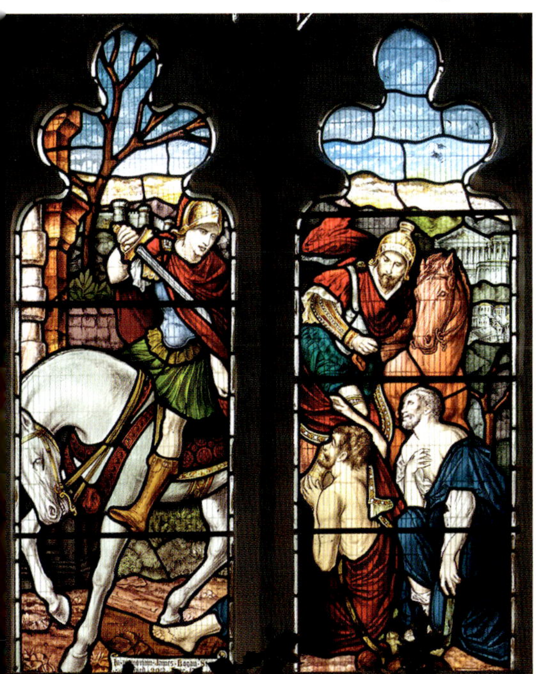

378. Jones & Willis, St Martin Dividing his Cloak, 1904, Church of St David, Capel Dewi, chancel

29 The window is located in the west wall of the tower, the former location of the Royal Welsh Fusiliers Chapel. This chapel is now located in the north aisle, where a window by Joseph Nuttgens commemorates the tercentenary of the Royal Welsh (or Welch) Fusiliers in 1989. Welsh saints were also prominently placed in the two windows either side of the east window in the sanctuary apse in 1914. Welsh saints were also prominently placed in the two windows either side of the east window in the sanctuary apse in 1914.

30 This window is based on a painting of the scene by Anthony van Dyck of about 1620 and in the Royal Collection.

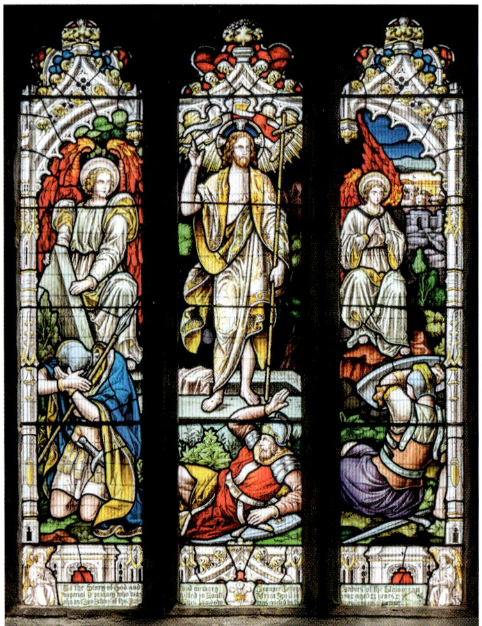

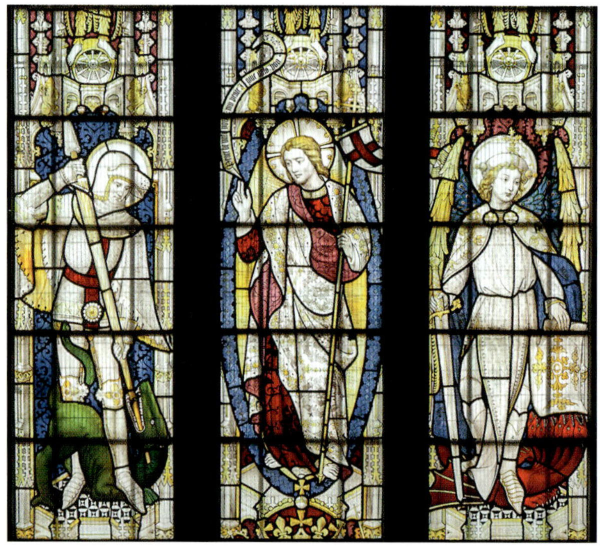

379. (above) H.W. Lloyd, The Resurrection, 1902, Church of St Augustine, Rumney, Cardiff, nave

380. (above centre) Ninian Comper, Christ with St George and St Michael, 1902, Church of St John the Baptist, Newport, south aisle

The risen Christ is depicted with George and the Archangel Michael in an early window in Wales designed by the architect Ninian Comper, given for the Church of St John the Baptist, Newport, in thanksgiving for the safe return of a son from the war. Others were not so fortunate. At the Church of St Martin, Flimston (near Castlemartin), the church was restored by the Lt Col. Francis Lambton and his wife Lady Victoria Lambton as a memorial to their three sons who all died between December 1899 and September 1901, two of whom were killed while serving in South Africa.[31] A set of figures by Heaton, Butler & Bayne filled the windows with the military saints Longinus, Eustace, Martin, Maurice, George and the Archangel Michael.[32] Some Boer War memorials depict biblical subjects, such as the Resurrection scene by H.W. Lloyd at the Church of St Augustine, Rumney, Cardiff. The Boer War memorial window at the Priory Church of St Mary, Monmouth, with its patriotic and local imagery including George and Henry V standing by the Monnow Bridge, contrasts with a glimpse of modern warfare at the Church of St Rhystud, Llanrhystud, where George is depicted with an angel and a cannon.

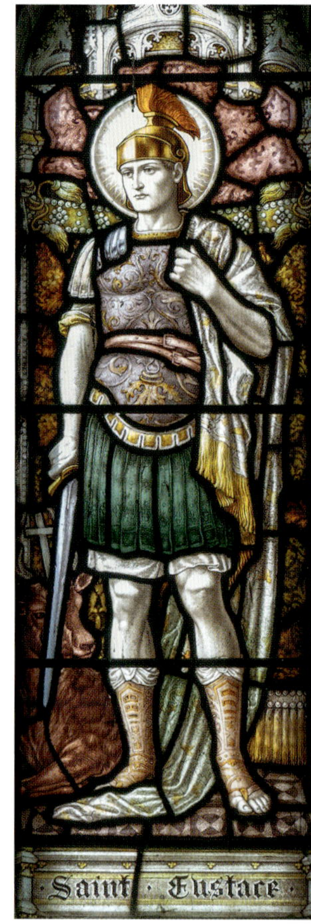

381. Heaton, Butler & Bayne, St Eustace, *c.* 1903, Church of St Martin, Flimston, sanctuary

31 Their oldest son, William Francis Lambton, died in Santiago, Chile, in December 1900 aged 32.

32 No Welsh saints were depicted, but room was found for Cuthbert, while the east window depicted the risen Christ with the apostles James and Andrew.

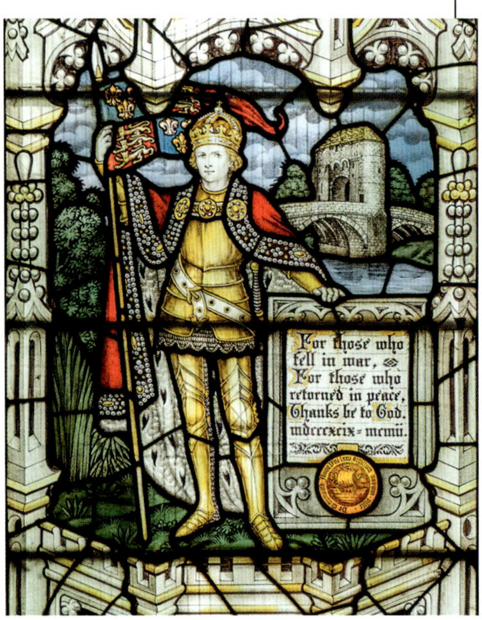

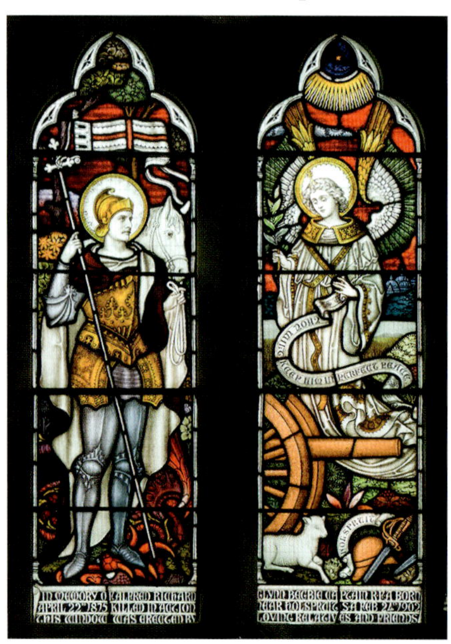

382. (far left) C.E. Kempe, Henry V, 1904, Priory Church of St Mary, Monmouth, south aisle

383. (left) Clayton & Bell, St George with an Angel, *c.* 1902, Church of St Rhystud, Llanrhystud, nave

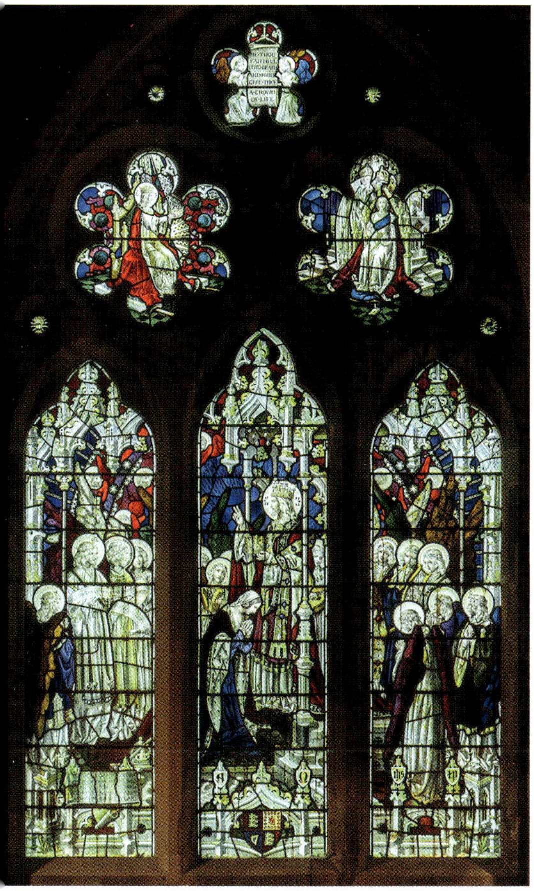

384. T.F. Curtis, Ward & Hughes, Queen Victoria Memorial Window, *c.* 1901 Church of St Seiriol, Penmaenmawr, west window

At the Church of St Peter, Glasbury, the Boer War volunteer William Jones is depicted as a kneeling knight in armour receiving the crown of life from Christ himself in a window by Robert Newbery. The depiction of a knight in armour receiving the crown of life prefigures similar windows that were given in memory of those who died in the First World War, but the crown of life was also a theme used for other memorial windows. The west window of the Church of St Seiriol, Penmaenmawr, is an example of a number of windows in Welsh churches given in memory of Queen Victoria following her death in 1901.[33] The main scene depicts Queen Victoria kneeling before Christ and surrounded by angels, while Christ holds the crown of life in a sexfoil above, opposite an image of the earthly coronation of Queen Victoria. The text from Revelation 2: 10 is given in the cinquefoil at the apex of the window: 'Be thou faithful unto death and I will give thee a crown of life.' A further memorial to the late Queen at the Priory Church of St Mary, Monmouth, depicts national figures representing each country of the British Isles: Alfred the Great and the saints Margaret of Scotland, David and Patrick. The window was given in 1905 by the people of the town, and a further royal memorial window was given in 1911 by John Allan Rolls, Lord Llangattock, following the death of Edward VII.[34] This window depicts four royal, and English, Edwards: Edward the Confessor, Edward I, Edward the Black Prince and Edward VII himself. The visit of Edward with Queen Alexandra and Princess Victoria to Pembrokeshire in 1902 was commemorated in the large east window at Monkton Priory, although in this case the imagery is of the Crucifixion and the birth and youth of Christ.[35]

33 Other windows placed in memory of Queen Victoria include the five-light east window by James Powell & Sons at the Church of St David, Newtown. Windows had also been erected to mark her Diamond Jubilee in 1897, such as that by E.R. Suffling at Christ Church, Cyfarthfa, given by parishioners and other inhabitants of Cyfarthfa.

34 John Allan Rolls was responsible for the introduction of many windows by C.E. Kempe in churches near his home at the Hendre, near Monmouth. A further, monumental, depiction of Edward VII, along with his mother Queen Victoria and his wife Alexandra, was commissiond by Isaac and Mary Butler for the west windows of the Church of St Hilda, Griffithstown, as a thank-offering for their fiftieth wedding anniversary in 1911, and made by Jones & Willis.

35 The enterprising vicar raised funds for the window through the sales of lithographed copies of the royal autographs in the visitor's book at 1s. 6d. *Weekly Mail*, 11 October 1902.

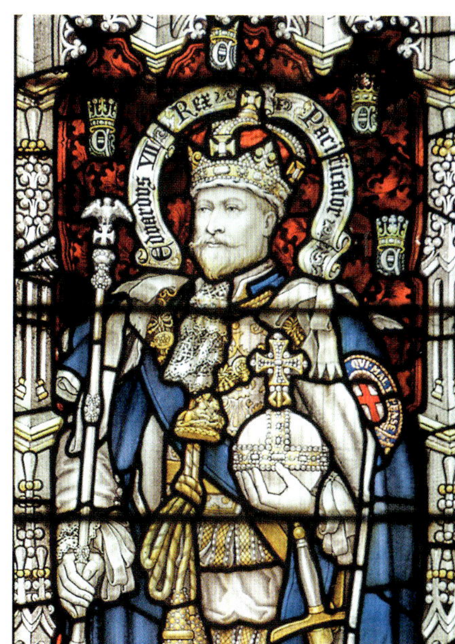

385. C.E. Kempe & Co., Edward VII, Priory Church of St Mary, Monmouth, south aisle

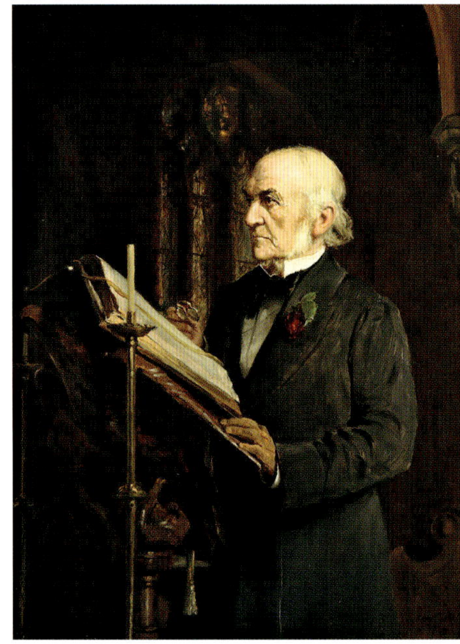

386. Sydney Prior Hall, *Gladstone Reading the Lesson in Hawarden Church*, 1892, Lady Lever Art Gallery, Port Sunlight (image by Public Catalogue Foundation, supplied courtesy of National Museums Liverpool)

Unusual saints by an even more unusual patron are found among the numerous memorials to the former Prime Minister William Ewart Gladstone, his wife Catherine, and their family in the area around Hawarden. A window by Edward Frampton at the Church of St Deiniol, Hawarden, depicts standing figures of Bartholemew and Gregory the Illuminator and carries the dedication: 'To the glory of God and in memory of the Armenians in Turkey who have suffered for the faith, and in undying gratitude for the inspiring example of William Ewart Gladstone, dedicated by Arakel Zadouroff of Baju, Russia in 1897.'[36] Frampton made four other memorial windows in the church, the first of which was for his first wife, Rosie, who died in childbirth in 1885.[37] The artist was also responsible for the windows in the west wall of the Church of St Ethelwold, Shotton, given in memory of Catherine Gladstone, as well as the apse windows at the east end of the church. The west windows were given by Catherine's grandchildren who were the children of her daughter Agnes and son-in-law E.C. Wickham, the dean of Lincoln, which explains the presence of Hugh of Lincoln (accompanied by his swan) among the figures.[38]

The most celebrated window commemorating Gladstone is the four-light west window at Hawarden, which was designed by his friend Edward Burne-Jones. This and other memorial windows at the church, and nearby at Buckley, made by Morris & Co., Henry Holiday and James Powell & Sons, form a group representing the work of some of the most influential stained glass designers of the emergent Arts and Crafts Movement.

36 According to various traditions, both saints were traditionally responsible for the conversion of Armenia.

37 Rosie Frampton was a member of the Boydell family, the most famous of whom was the artist and publisher John Boydell, who became the Lord Mayor of London in 1790, and further memorials to family members are nearby.

38 W.E. Gladstone had made the initial donation of £1,000 towards the new church shortly before his death, although the cost eventually rose to £7,000. T.W. Pritchard, *A History of the Old Parish of Hawarden* (Wrexham: Bridge Books, 2002), pp. 248–9.

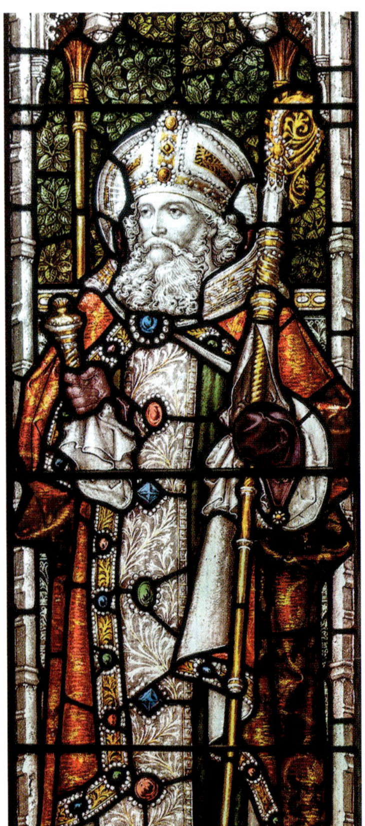

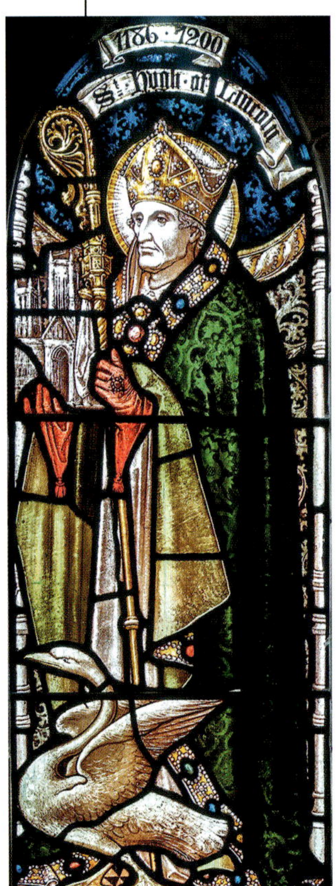

387. (far left) Edward Frampton, St Gregory the Illuminator, 1897, Church of St Deiniol, Hawarden, north aisle

388. (left) Edward Frampton, St Hugh of Lincoln, *c.* 1901. Church of St Ethelwold, Shotton, west wall

Chapter Seven

The Arts and Crafts Movement

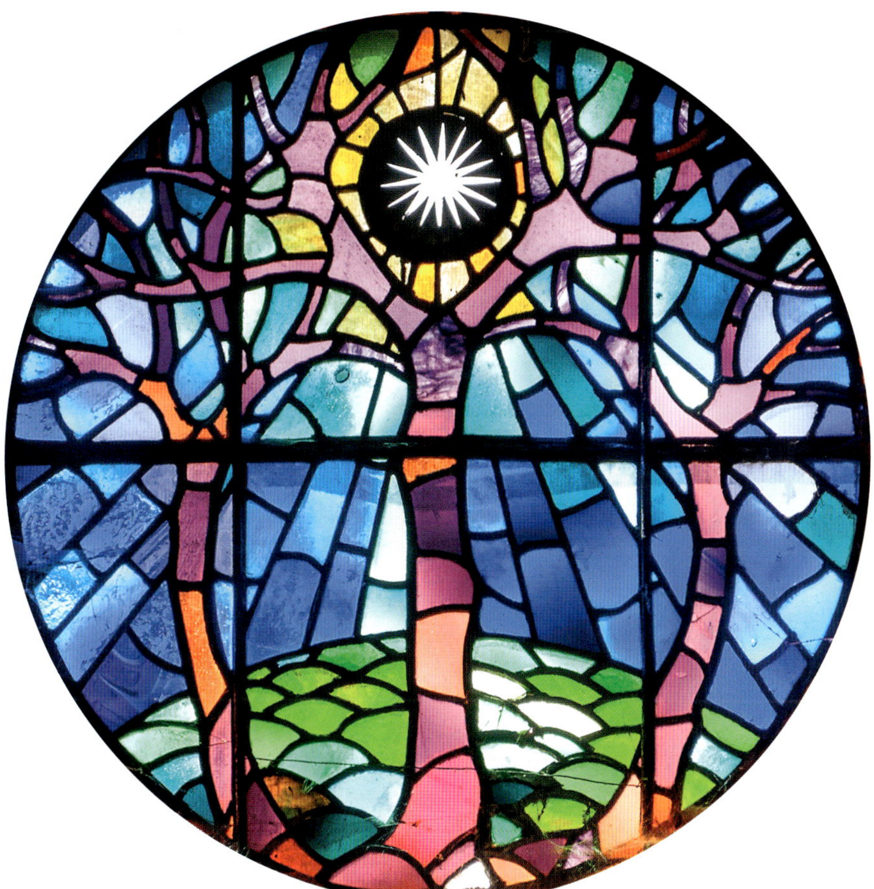

1 1904 catalogue. The catalogue does not include any stock designs for stained glass, and potential clients were encouraged to see work in hand at their studios, or completed pieces that they had made in churches, suggesting that this aspect of their business was more bespoke than the standard designs for pulpits, altar crosses and banners.

2 A paper read by Holiday in 1871, quoted in Peter Cormack, *Henry Holiday 1839–1927*, Exhibition Catalogue, William Morris Gallery, London, 1989, p. 1.

3 Henry Holiday, *Stained Glass as an Art* (London: Macmillan & Co. Ltd, 1896), pp. 4–5. Holiday's book draws on his own work, as well as that of his friends Edward Burne-Jones and William Blake Richmond, for illustrations exemplifying the best work of his time.

The dramatic rise in demand for ecclesiastical stained glass in the nineteenth century brought commercial success and the adoption of a production-line approach to the largest Victorian stained glass firms. Those such as Clayton & Bell; Heaton, Butler & Bayne and C.E. Kempe were all established with strong artistic credentials, but were forced to streamline their production as orders came in from across Britain, its Empire and the United States. Windows were also produced in great numbers by church furnishers such as Cox, Buckley & Son and Jones & Willis, and their catalogues included examples of their work in stained glass alongside painted mural decoration and stock designs for fonts, pulpits, pews, lecterns, lamps, vestments and banners. A 1904 catalogue produced by Jones & Willis prices their windows from 25/- to 50/- per square foot, indicating that the quality of their windows varied according to the funds available for the window.[1]

The work of these firms was often technically sophisticated, beautifully painted, but artistically dull. Designs and cartoons were reused over the years and painted and manufactured by craftsmen, and occasionally women, who had little or no input in the concept or artistic intention of the window. As early as the 1870s Henry Holiday observed that 'The great advantage of this system was, that it was not necessary that an artist should come near the windows.'[2] As a designer of many windows for James Powell & Sons he observed that the vast majority of stained glass windows made for churches were 'trade and not art', and 'produced for profit' rather than as 'original conceptions of artists'.[3]

The separation of the design and production was also a product of the social division between designer and maker. John Ruskin challenged the assumption that 'one man's thoughts can be, or ought to be, executed by another man's hands', and thought it better that workmen should also be thinking, and that the thinker should also be working, 'and both should be gentlemen, in the best sense.'[4] This division had governed the relationships between architects and makers of stained glass, and as it did with stained glass

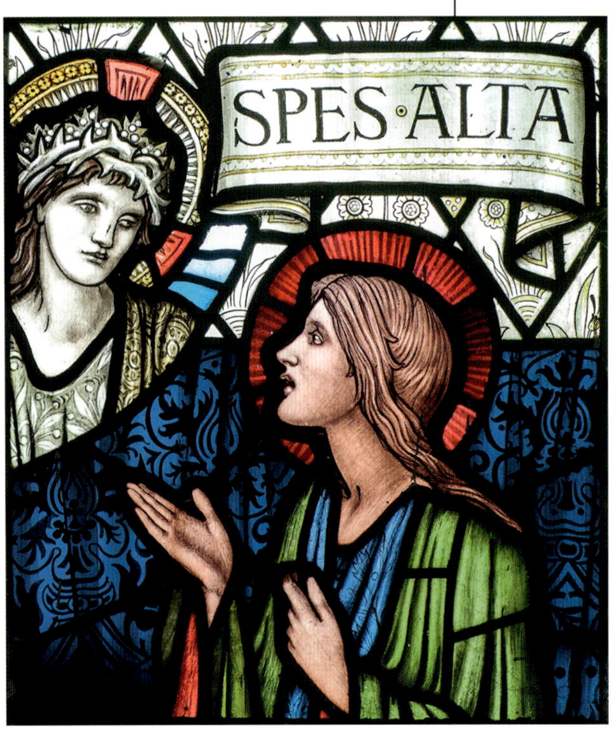

390. Morris & Co., Faith, 1895, designed by Edward Burne-Jones, Church of St Maelog, Llandyfaelog, east window

389. (Title page) Theodore Baily, Tree of Life, *c.* 1922
Church of St David, Caldey Island, west w

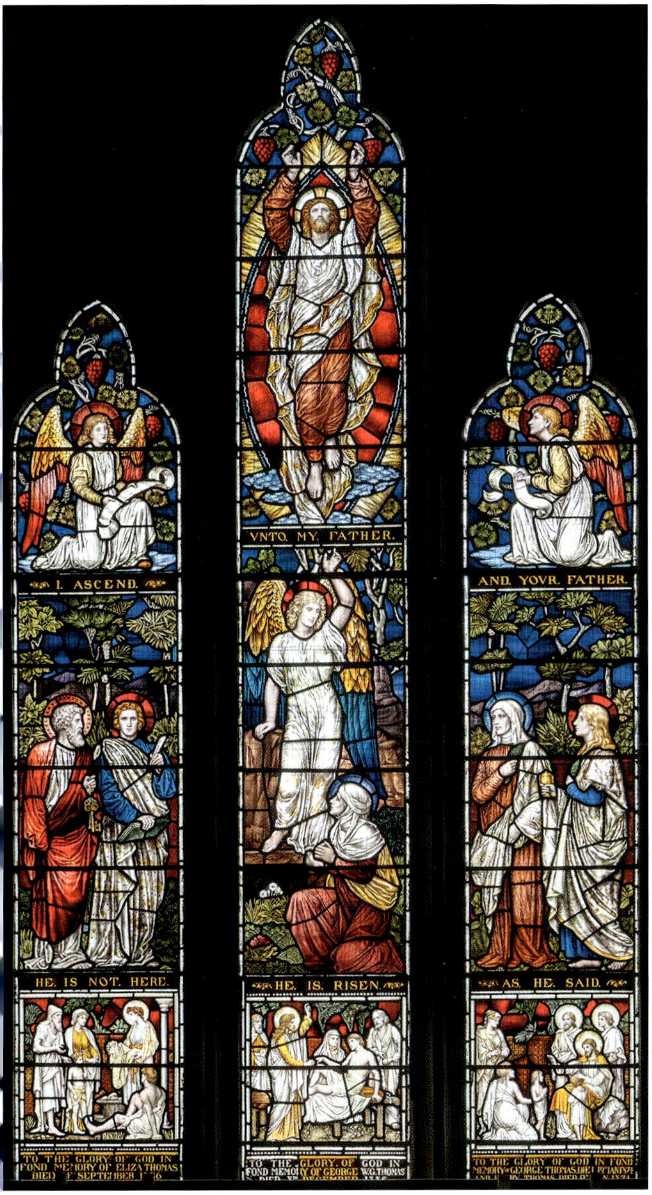

391. James Powell & Sons, The Resurrection, 1888, designed by Henry Holiday, Church of the Holy Trinity, Ystrad Mynach, east window

designers-turned-proprietors and their workers. Influenced by Ruskin, William Morris transgressed his status among the educated classes by engaging himself in handwork and mastered an impressive range of craft processes. Through his practical knowledge of processes and materials, Morris pioneered the notion of the designer-maker and artist-craftsman that contributed to the revival of interest in traditional craft skills and artistic engagement in the decorative arts during in the 1880s.[5]

The Art Workers' Guild was formed in 1884 to promote craftsmanship and raise the status of decorative arts. Founding members of the Art Workers' Guild worked in the office of the architect Norman Shaw, and they were joined by other architects, such as John Dando Sedding and his pupil Henry Wilson, as well as a number of English Italianate painters including Henry Holiday, Walter Crane and William Blake Richmond.[6] Some of its members went on to found the Arts and Crafts Exhibition Society in 1887, and following their influential exhibitions of decorative arts in the 1890s, which included work by Morris & Co., the society gave its name to the Arts and Crafts Movement.

4 John Ruskin, *The Stones of Venice* (London: Smith, Elder & Co., 1853), vol. ii, pp. 168–9.

5 Fiona MacCarthy, *William Morris: A Life for Our Time* (London: Faber and Faber, 1994), pp. 175, 590–2. A weaver, embroiderer and calligrapher, William Morris is not known to have painted glass or played any part in the manufacture of windows for Morris & Co. Paul Thompson goes as far as describing the firm's production of stained glass as 'an extreme example of the division of labour'. *The Work of William Morris* (Oxford: Oxford University Press, third edition, 1993), p. 139. Morris supervised the making of the windows, and especially the colour of the glass, in the 1860s and 70s, but largely left this to John Henry Dearle in the 1880s, when Morris' interests were taken up with the socialist cause. Dearle became responsible for the artistic direction of the firm after Morris' death in 1896.

6 These painters, known as the Etruscan School, identified with the Aesthetic Movement and the work of Dante Gabriel Rossetti and Edward Burne-Jones; they also shared an interest in designing for the decorative arts. Considerable weight was lent to the Art Workers' Guild by the eventual involvement of William Morris himself, who was master in 1892, and Burne-Jones who was a member from 1891–3.

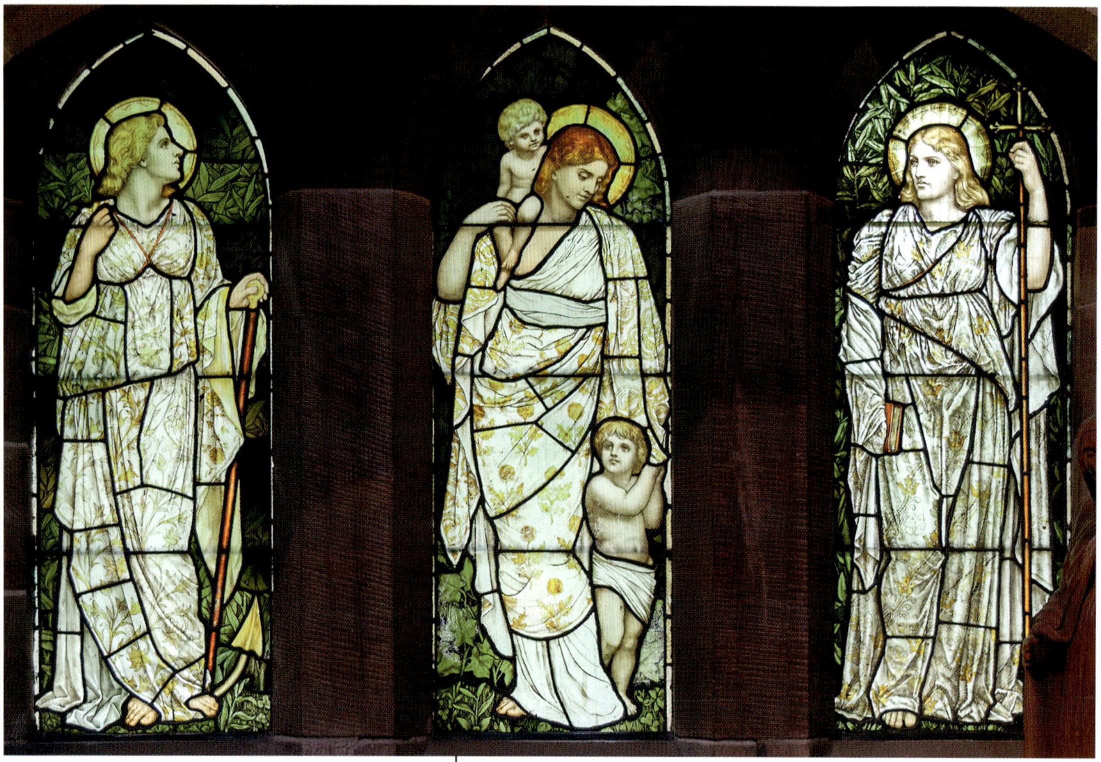

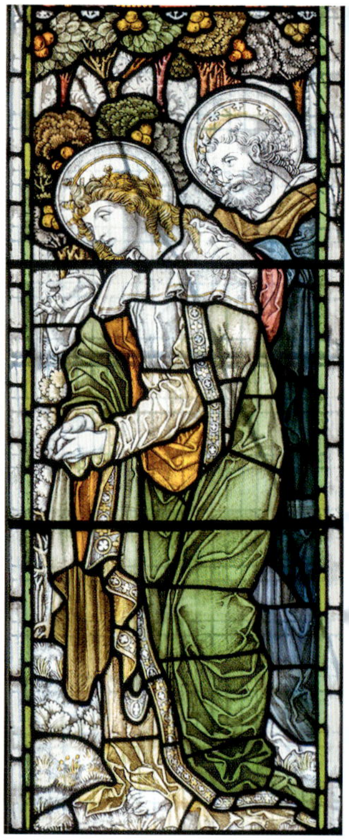

392. (above) James Powell & Sons, Faith Hope and Charity, 1880, designed by Henry Holiday, Church of St Mary, Betws-y-Coed, north aisle

393. (above right) W.F. Dixon, Peter and John from the Resurrection, 1884, Church of St Cadfan, Tywyn, east window

Henry Holiday was a founder member of both the Art Workers' Guild and the Arts and Crafts Exhibition Society. The influence of Edward Burne-Jones and the Aesthetic Movement, as well as the green-yellow palette characteristic of William Morris, is clear in the three lights designed by Holiday and given by the artist to the Church of St Mary, Betws-y-Coed.[7] A similar Aestheticism is sometimes found in the allegorical female figures representing Faith, Hope and Charity made by Clayton & Bell, Burlison & Grylls and Lavers & Westlake. The influence of Burne-Jones' drawing of drapery and the colours of Morris & Co. can also be seen in the work of W.F. Dixon, whose windows were used in the later churches designed by John Prichard and his successor as Llandaff diocesan architect, F.R. Kempson. Two windows depicting female figures by Dixon were commissioned by James Harvey Insole, in memory of his wife, for both Llandaff Cathedral and the small church at Pendoylan in the Vale of Glamorgan. These and other windows by the artist demonstrate the influence of Burne-Jones and Dante Gabriel Rossetti in the figures and scenes and employ Art Nouveau detailing at the base of the windows.

Similar influences can be seen in the work of the Lancaster firm Shrigley & Hunt, where Holiday's former assistant, Carl Almquist, was the senior designer. A complete scheme of 1886–7 was made by Shrigley & Hunt for

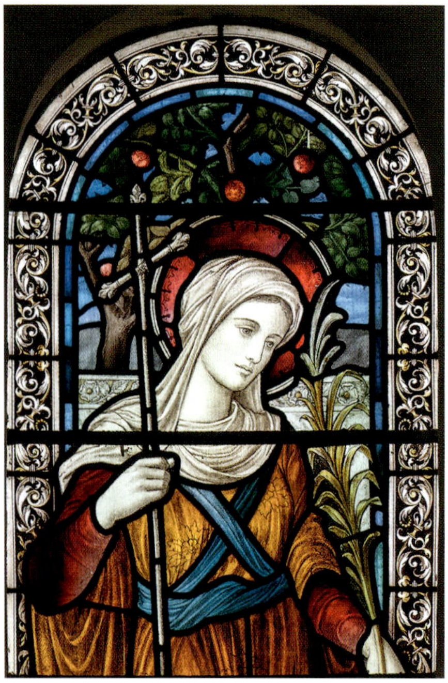

394. Lavers & Westlake, Faith, 1899, Church of St Gwyndaf, Llanwnda, sanctuary apse

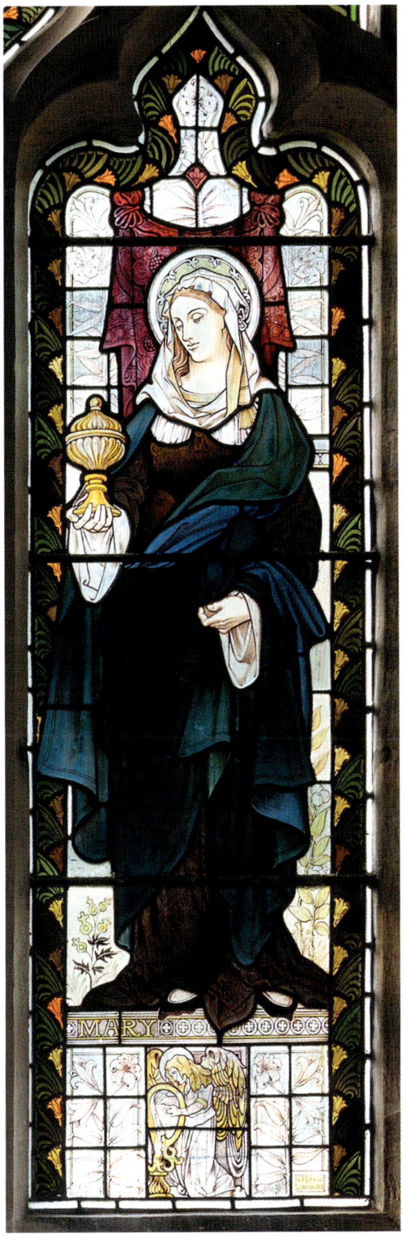

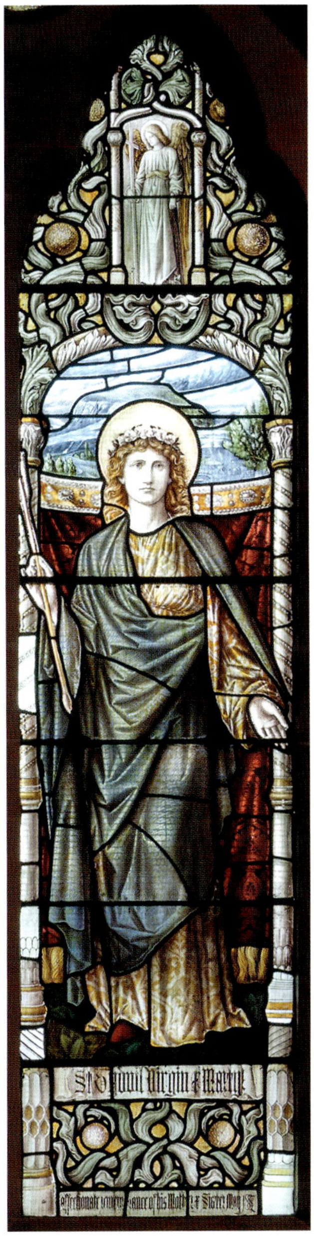

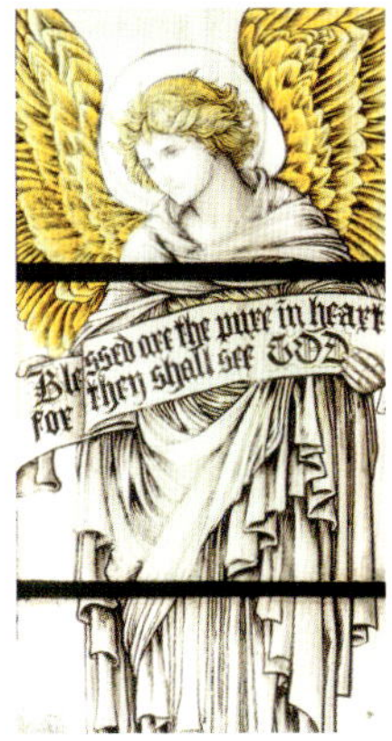

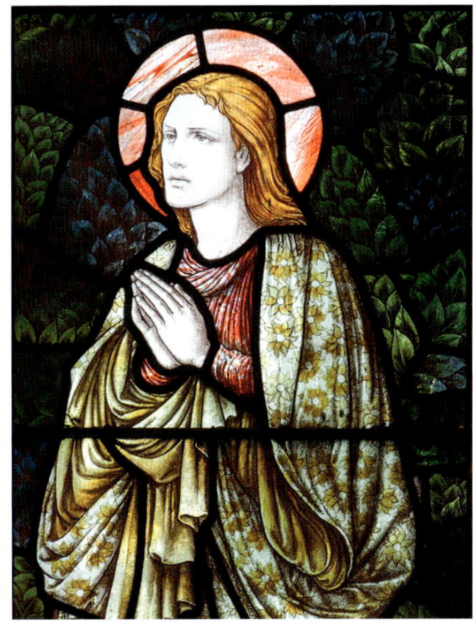

397–8. Shrigley & Hunt, Angel holding text from the Beatitudes, nave (above); St John, from the Crucifixion with the Virgin Mary and St John, east window (right), *c.* 1887, Church of St Bledrws, Betws Bledrws

395. (far left) W.F. Dixon, St Mary Magdalene, 1884, Church of St Cadoc, Pendoylan, nave

396. (left) Shrigley & Hunt, St Tydfil, 1887, cartooned by Carl Almquist from designs by Henry Wilson, Church of St David, Merthyr Tydfil, south aisle

the Church of St Bledrws, Betws Bledrws, where east and west windows are complemented by a set of angels in the nave windows with the words of the Beatitudes. Carl Almquist also worked with Henry Wilson who had trained with the architect J.D. Sedding, and the figures of David and Tydfil at the Church of St David, Merthyr Tydfil, were made from cartoons prepared by Almquist but based on Wilson's 'colour, layout & poses'.[8] Shrigley & Hunt's windows are often richly coloured with dark foliate backgrounds that are reminiscent of work by Morris & Co. For example, beneath a colourful array of angels in the west window at the

7 Holiday visited the town regularly between 1856 and 1864, then at the height of its fame as an artists' colony, and married Catherine (Kate) Raven in the church in 1864. Peter Cormack, *Henry Holiday 1839–1927*, Exhibition Catalogue, William Morris Gallery, London (1989), pp. 3, 7. According to the plaque in the church, the window was in memory of his wife's brother, the landscape painter John Raven, who drowned at Harlech in 1877. However, according to Dennis and Joan Hadley, the window was given in memory of Kate and John's parents. 'Henry Holiday, 1839-1927', *The Journal of Stained Glass*, vol. xix, no. 1 (1989–90), p. 57.

8 William Waters, *Stained Glass from Shrigley & Hunt of Lancaster and London* (Lancaster: Centre for North-West Regional Studies University of Lancaster, 2003), p. 85. The window was commissioned by W.T. Lewis, later Lord Merthyr, before his patronage of the firm of Robert Newbery. Henry Wilson's most important work in Wales was for J.D. Sedding's Church of St Dyfrig, Cardiff (now demolished, although fittings survive in other churches), and the furnishing of the church built to his own design at Brithdir, near Dolgellau.

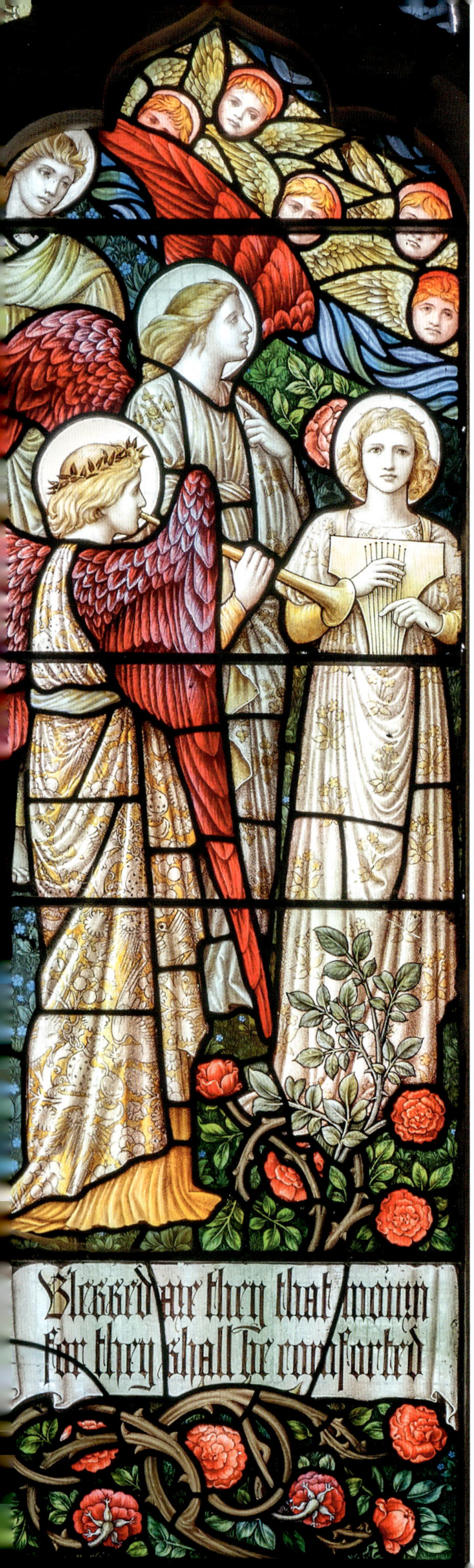

399. (far left) Shrigley & Hunt, Angels, *c.* 1890, Church of St Tysilio, Llantysilio, west wall

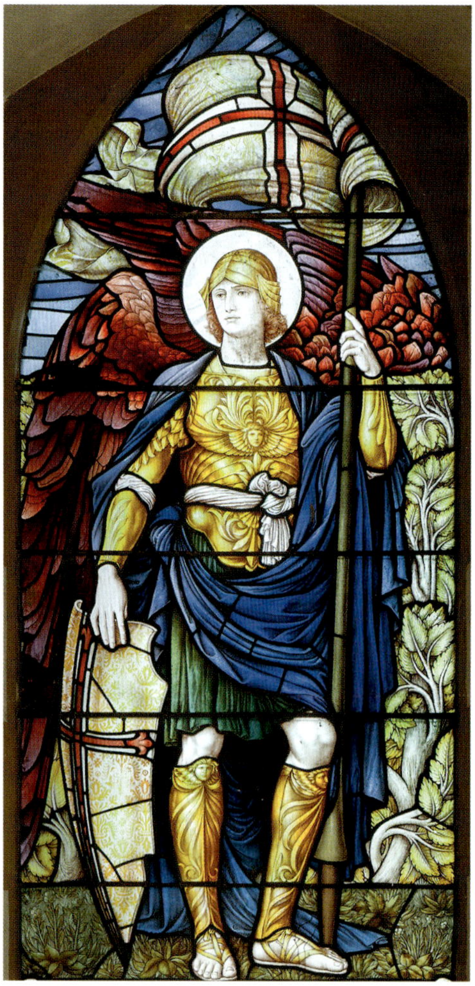

400. (left) Shrigley & Hunt, St Michael, *c.* 1887, Church of St Bledrws, Betws Bledrws, west wall

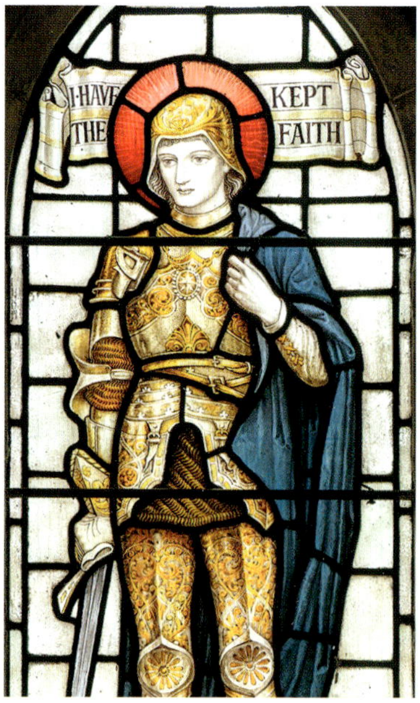

401. (above) Heaton, Butler & Bayne, The Good Soldier of Christ, *c.* 1904, Church of St Hilda, Griffithstown, north aisle

402. (below) Shrigley & Hunt, The Good Shepherd, 1898, Church of St Peter, Llanbedr Dyffryn Clwyd, nave

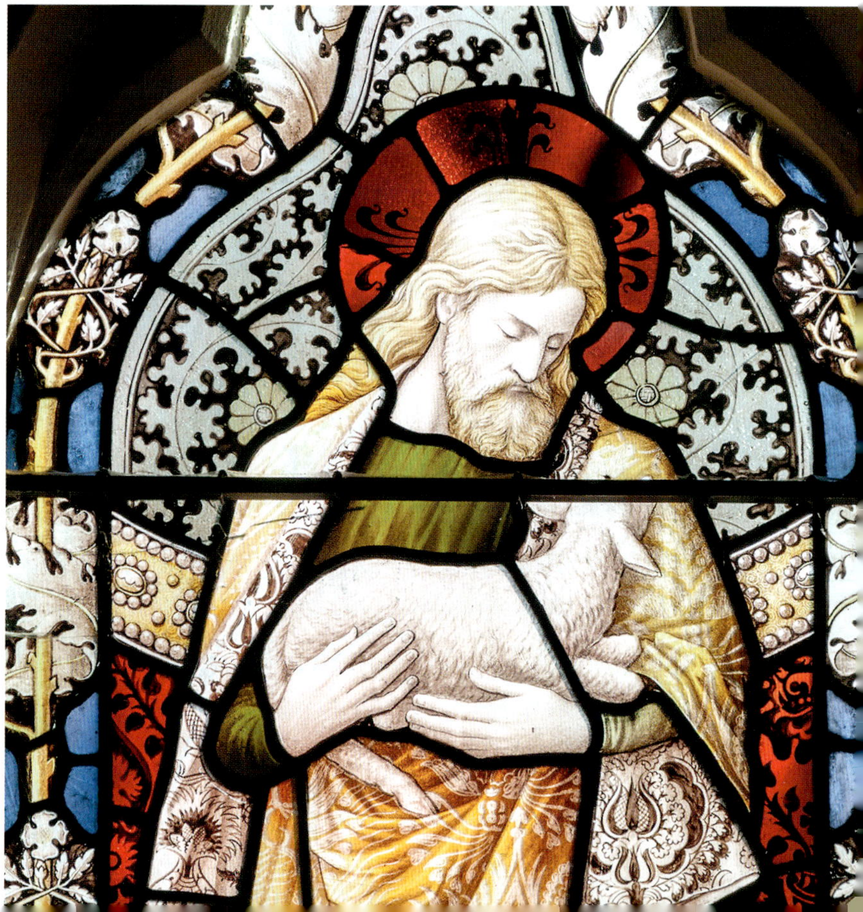

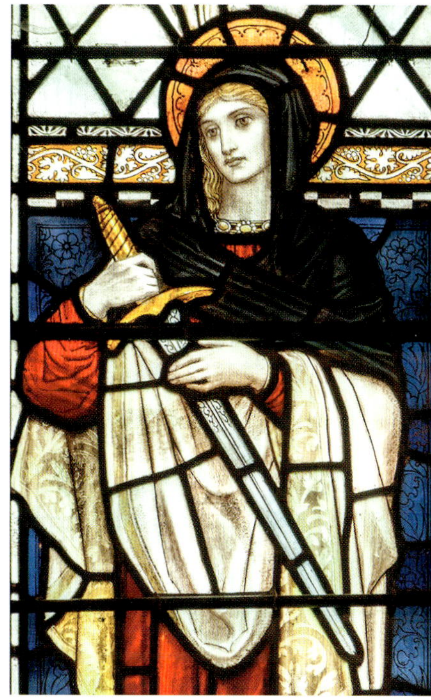

403. James Powell & Sons, St Winifred, 1911, designed by James Hogan, Bangor Cathedral, north aisle

Church of St Tysilio, Llantysilio, the tangled flowers and foliage are suggestive of wallpaper designs by William Morris.

The stained glass design of Edward Burne-Jones and Henry Holiday remained visible in the work of successive designers at James Powell & Sons, such as J.W. Brown, William Aikman, Ernest Penwarden and James Hogan, and a recognisably Pre-Raphaelite strain of figure drawing permeates the stained glass of Morris & Co, James Powell & Sons, Shrigley & Hunt and Heaton, Butler and Bayne well into the twentieth century, and remains almost synonymous with popular perceptions of the Arts and Crafts Movement. This is something of an irony as these firms made little attempt to engage designers with the process of making stained glass, which lay at the heart of Arts and Crafts philosophy, although several designers who had worked for Powell's led the way by establishing their own stained glass studios.

Henry Holiday established his own workshop in 1891, where he was able to supervise production, and the studio even made its own glass by about 1900.[9] Here, Holiday painted some of the glass himself, and he employed his favoured glass painter at Powell's, William Glasby, as his foreman and chief glass painter.[10] A group of windows by Henry Holiday from this period in his career are among the memorials to William Ewart Gladstone, his wife Catherine, and her family, the Glynnes of Hawarden. The Gladstones' son-in-law, Harry Drew, was the vicar of Buckley and oversaw the rebuilding and ornament of the Church of St Matthew, Buckley, between 1897 and 1904, when he was made rector of Hawarden.[11] A fine depiction of the Good Shepherd by Henry Holiday was given in his memory after his death in 1910, but Holiday had already designed windows during Harry Drew's incumbency.

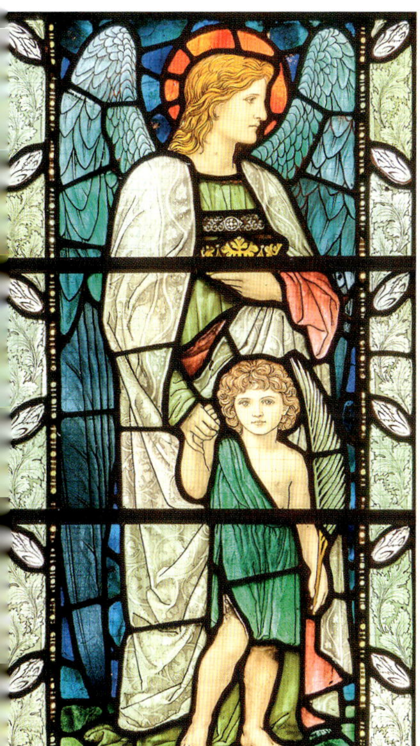

404. Henry Holiday, Child with Guardian Angel, 1902, Church of St Matthew, Buckley, baptistry

9 Henry Holiday had been dissatisfied with the way in which the painters and craftsmen at James Powell & Sons interpreted his cartoons as early as the 1860s, when he had entrusted the manufacture of some of his windows to Heaton, Butler & Bayne. See Martin Harrison, *Victorian Stained Glass* (London: Barrie & Jenkins, 1980), pp. 45-6.

10 Donald Green, Dennis Hadley and Joan Hadley, 'The life and work of William Glasby (1863–1941)', *Journal of Stained Glass*, vol. xxxii (2008), pp. 92–5.

11 The chancel was rebuilt in memory of W.E. Gladstone in 1900. J. Clifford Jones, *Buckley Parish Church 1822–1972* (Buckley: Buckley St Matthew's Churchwardens and Parochial Church Council, 1974), pp. 24–31. It was financed by Harry Drew's wife Mary and her sister Helen, daughters of W.E. and Catherine Gladstone, assisted by the publication of letters written to Mary Drew by John Ruskin. T.W. Pritchard, *A History of the Old Parish of Hawarden* (Wrexham: Bridge Books, 2002), p. 112.

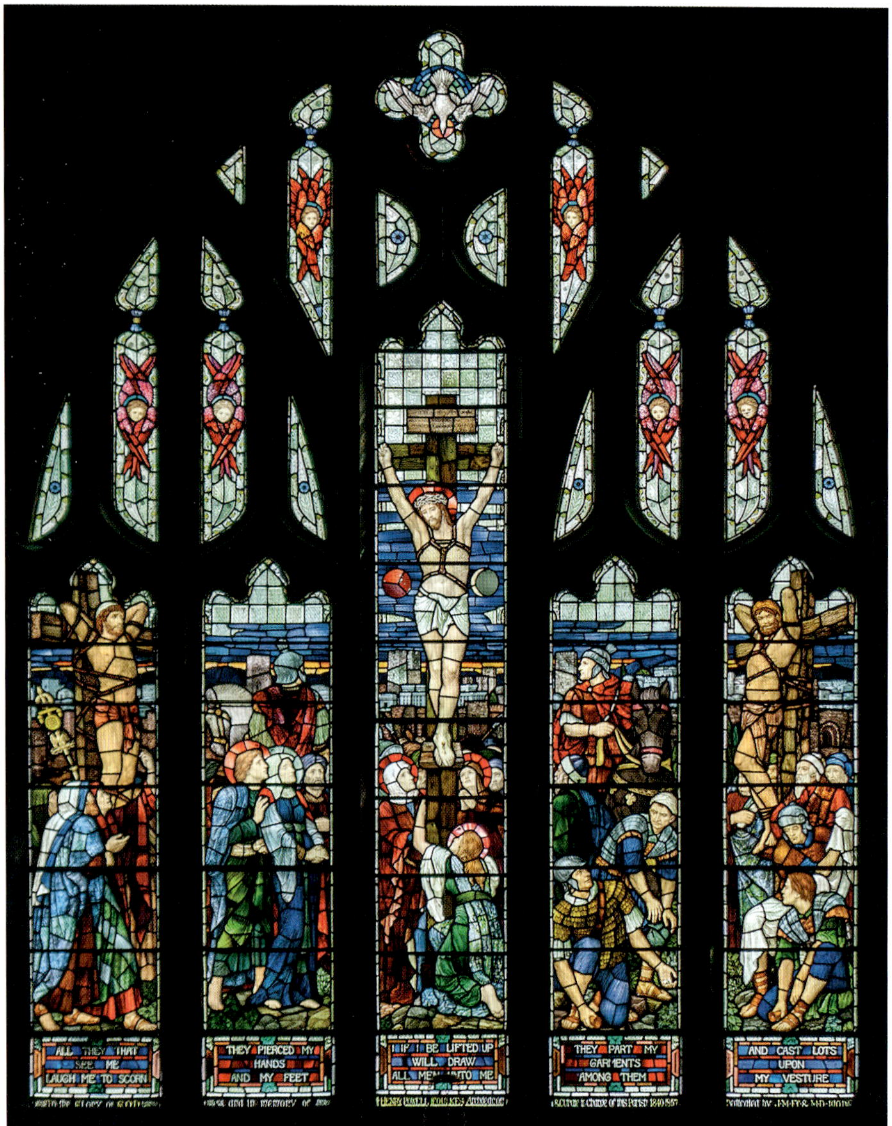

405. Henry Holiday, The Crucifixion, 1901, Church of St Matthew, Buckley, east window

He designed a pair of lights in the baptistry, given in memory of Catherine Gladstone, as well as the scene of the Crucifixion spread across the five-light chancel east window in 1901. At either side of the east window, a pair of two-light windows with allegorical female figures representing Righteousness, Truth, Faith and Love was also given in memory of William and Catherine Gladstone. One of the two-light windows was given by Henry Holiday and his wife Kate, and the other was given by Mary Drew.

A single window by Henry Holiday is among the numerous windows given by the Gladstones and their family at Hawarden, depicting Agnes and Catherine.[12] The west window of the nave was the last window designed by Edward Burne-Jones in the year of his death, and given in thanksgiving for the lives of William and Catherine Gladstone by their children, who knew the artist.[13] This major work by Morris & Co. was accompanied by later works commissioned from the firm for the church after the death of both William Morris and Burne-Jones. Made between 1907 and 1913, these windows do not match the attention to detail in Holiday's windows and demonstrate the continued use of cartoons by Burne-Jones, who had been the firm's main designer since the 1870s. This length of time separating the windows of Morris & Co. in the twentieth century and their design by Burne-Jones in the previous century was increasingly at odds with the Arts and Crafts concern with the unity of design and production of stained glass. Burne-Jones' design for the Gladstone memorial window was used again at other churches including the Church of St Elli, Llanelli, where additional

12 The window was given by E.C. Wickham, dean of Lincoln, in thanksgiving for his marriage to Agnes, a daughter of William and Catherine Gladstone.

13 In a letter to Henry Dearle, Burne-Jones expressed his reluctance to draw new angels for the window, complaining that 'I must have by now designed enough to fill Europe.' Albert Charles Sewter, *The Stained Glass of William Morris and his Circle* (New Haven/London: Yale University Press, 1974), vol. ii, p. 91.

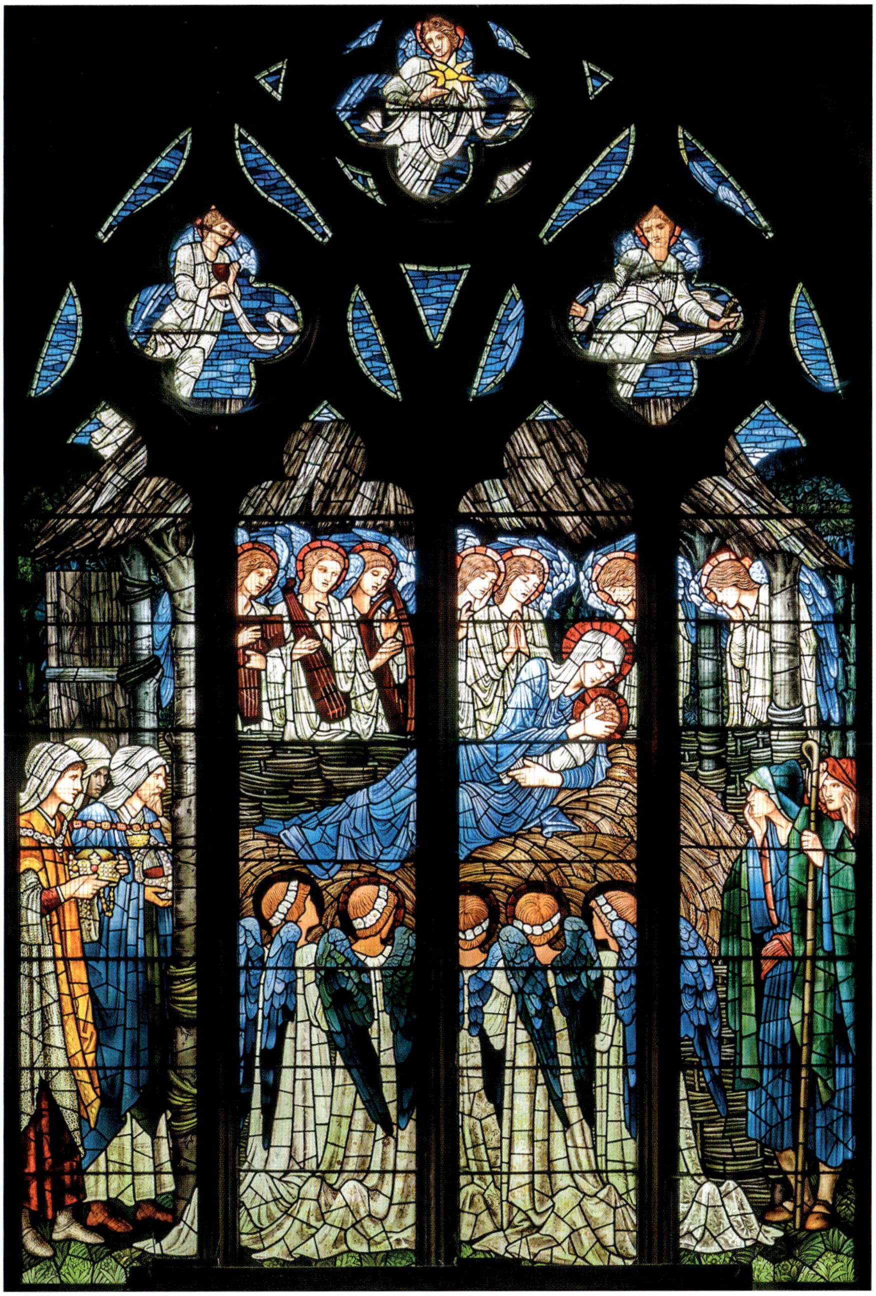

406. Morris & Co., The Adoration of the Shepherds and the Magi, 1898, designed by Edward Burne-Jones, Church of St Deiniol, Hawarden, west window

14 The outer figures of the Welsh saints David and Elli were from other designs by Burne-Jones from the 1890s. The use of stock designs was something that William Morris had sought to avoid at the time of the establishment of Morris, Marshall, Faulkner & Co. in 1861, which he had hoped would operate along artistic rather than commercial lines. Demand for their work meant that by the time they were producing their first windows for Prichard & Seddon at Llandaff Cathedral, many scenes and figures were being reused from previous commissions. The firm's early idealism also belied any real appreciation of economic reality, as the firm only began to return a profit, rather than relying on Morris' family fortune, after it was reorganised under Morris' own control in 1875, by which time their stock of designs had accumulated for reuse. Several other figures designed by Burne-Jones can be found at two or three churches in Wales alone, making the firm just as repetitive as other large Victorian firms.

decorative work occupies the additional space in the lower part of the south transept window. The standing figure of John used in the east window at Hawarden had also been used many times before, including in the right-hand light of the east window at Baglan in 1880. It was first used in another Crucifixion scene with Mary and John designed by Burne-Jones in 1877 for a window in the Church of St Michael, Torquay, and all three figures form the centrepiece of the impressive five-light window made in 1911 for Llanelli.[14]

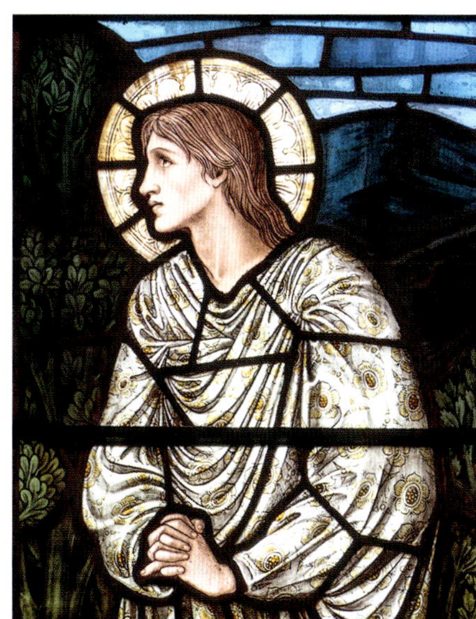

407. Morris & Co. St John, from the Crucifixion with Saints, 1911, designed by Edward Burne-Jones, Church of St Elli, Llanelli, east window

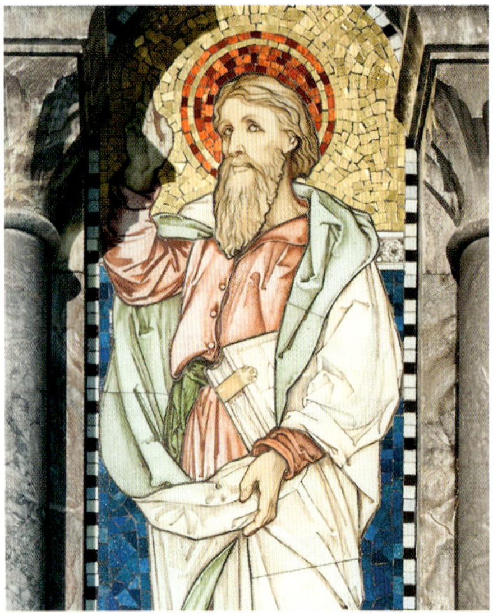

408. James Powell & Sons, St Paul (opus sectile), 1889, Church of St Oudoceus, Llandogo, chancel

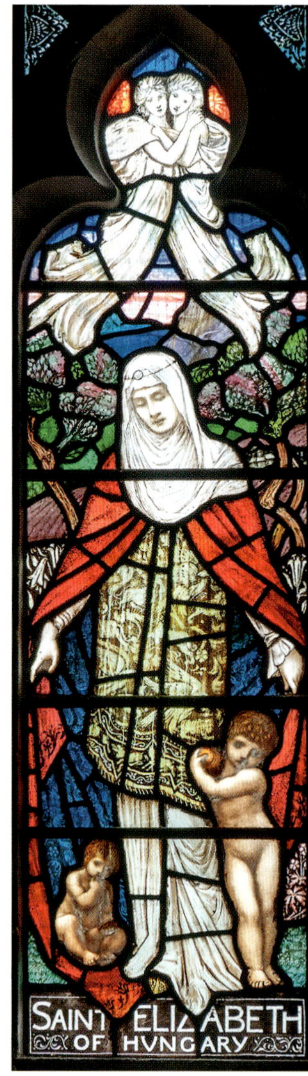

409. James Powell & Sons, St Elizabeth of Hungary, *c.* 1906, designed by William Blake Richmond, Church of St Deiniol, Hawarden, Gladstone Memorial Chapel

The Gladstone memorial chapel at Hawarden contains a set of four windows depicting saints, prophets and an Annunciation scene, designed by William Blake Richmond and made by James Powell & Sons.[15] Richmond was master of the Art Workers' Guild in 1891 and provided designs for the decoration of St Paul's Cathedral in London, also made by Powell's in stained glass and mosaic, from 1891–1908.[16] As manufacturers of glass Powell's were well-placed to produce glass mosaic and opus sectile, and examples of their mosaic work in Wales include sections for the Christ in Majesty for the chancel arch at the Church of St Mary, Llanfair Kilgeddin, designed by Heywood Sumner in 1888, and the reredos for the Church of St Peter, Glasbury. The opus sectile figures of Moses and Paul, from designs by H.E. Wooldridge and Frank Mann for the decorative scheme of 1889 by J.P. Seddon and John Coates Carter in the chancel at the Church of St Oudoceus, Llandogo, were also interpreted in stained glass elsewhere.[17]

The association of Powell's with an artist of the calibre of William Richmond, knighted in 1896, and professor of painting at the Royal Academy, suggests the status of the firm at the time, and windows made from the work of their own designers could be of considerable quality and originality. An expensive work by the firm was commissioned in 1904 by Emily Talbot for the east window of what was, until 1913, the family's private chapel at Margam Abbey. Probably designed by William Aikman, who had assisted William

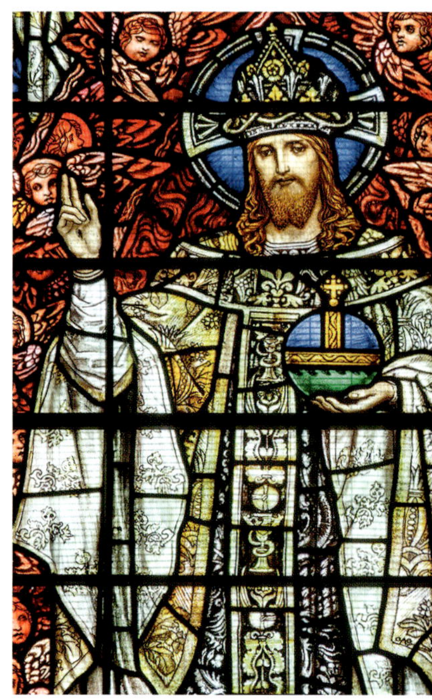

410. James Powell & Sons, Christ in Majesty, 1904, probably designed by William Aikman, Abbey Church of St Mary, Margam, east window

15 William Richmond was a successful portrait painter and also designed the stone monument in the centre of the chapel with effigies of W.E. and Catherine Gladstone 'lying in the boat of life', T.W. Pritchard, *A History of the Old Parish of Hawarden* (Wrexham: Bridge Books, 2002), p. 109.

16 Richmond designed glass for J.D. Sedding's Church of the Holy Trinity, Sloane Street, a masterpiece of the Arts and Crafts Movement that was completed by Henry Wilson after Sedding's death in 1891. The church features stained glass by Morris & Co. and Christopher Whall and sculpture by H.H. Armstead. Armstead had worked for Prichard & Seddon at Llandaff Cathedral and painted the reredos for Prichard's church at Baglan.

17 The firm increasingly specialised in opus sectile memorial tablets, such as those at Flimston and Knighton, although the stained glass in these churches was made by Heaton, Butler & Bayne and T.F. Curtis, Ward & Hughes. Opus sectile panels are more akin to the manufacture of stained glass, as the shape of each piece contributes to the design, whereas mosaic uses very small pieces of stone or glass.

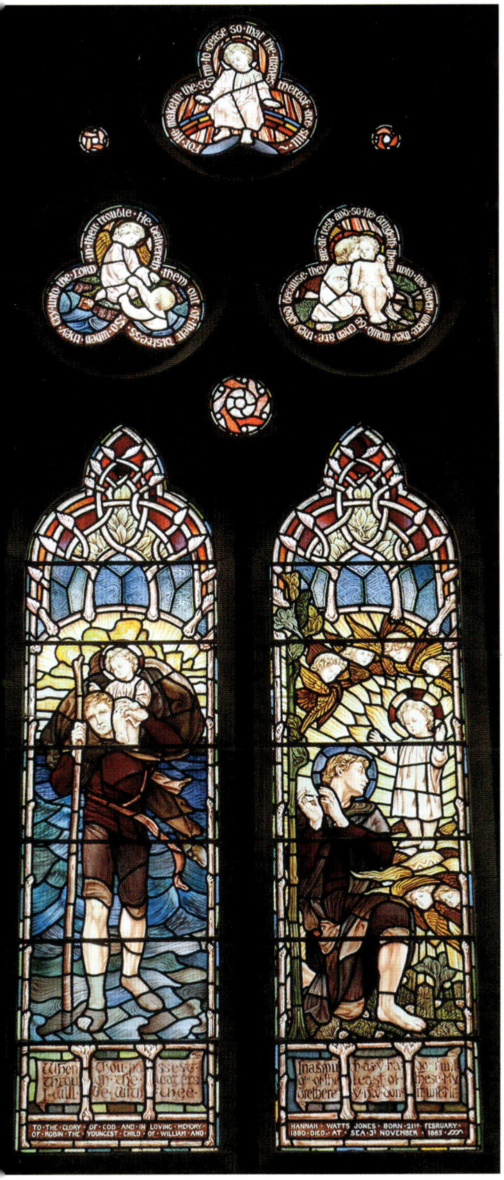

411–12. James Powell & Sons, The Infant Christ with St Christopher (left) and Seated on a Rainbow (right), 1889, designed by Christopher Whall, Church of St Seiriol, Penmaenmawr, north chapel

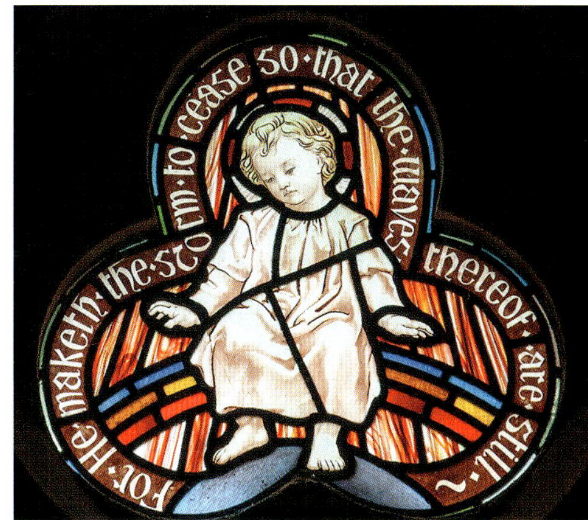

Richmond with the mosaics for St Paul's, the window demonstrates the sumptuous colours and rich detailing that the firm was capable of producing for the sum of about £550.[18]

Two windows made by James Powell & Sons for churches in north Wales were to the design of Christopher Whall, who was to become the most influential stained glass designer of the Arts and Crafts Movement. His memorial window of 1889 at the Church of St Seiriol, Penmaenmawr, is an imaginative response to the tragedy of a child who died at sea with scenes of the infant Christ with Christopher, the patron saint of children, and with child angels. The window has an organic, rather than architectural, framework and fine lettering for the carefully chosen texts.[19] A smaller work designed in 1893 by Whall was made for the Church of St Cynfarch and St Mary, Llanfair Dyffryn Clwyd, a church that had been restored in 1871–2 by J.D. Sedding.

In 1889 Whall was elected to the Art Workers' Guild, by which time he had already begun to learn each of the craft processes required to make stained glass windows. Rather than accepting the rigid division of labour between designers, cartoonists, painters, cutters and lead-workers found in commercial studios, Whall taught that those who carried out each stage of the design and manufacture of stained glass should know how to carry out the other processes.

18 See Alun Adams, 'Stained and painted Glass at Margam', *Transactions of the Port Talbot Historical Society*, vol. iv, no. 2 (2000), p. 31. Figures from more ambitious windows such as this were often also used as components of other works of varying quality and price. For example, the figure of Michael in the left-hand light of the east window at Margam may be found repeated among the figures representing the 'Te Deum' in their five windows for the north aisle of Bangor Cathedral and in the east window at the Church of St Gwendoline, Llyswen.

19 Cartoons for Christopher Whall's figures for James Powell & Sons entered the stock-in-trade of the firm. For example, his figure of Christopher carrying the infant Christ was reused in a window for Great St Mary, Cambridge, in 1920, the design supervised by James Hogan, a pupil of Whall. Similarly, figures by Holiday were reproduced in a window of 1890 by the firm in the Church of St Peter, Pwllheli, within elaborate Gothic canopies that ran totally contrary to Holiday's approach to stained glass design.

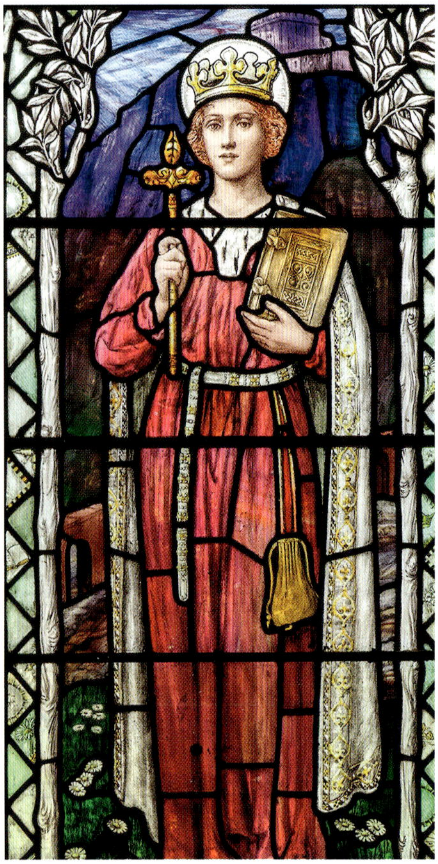

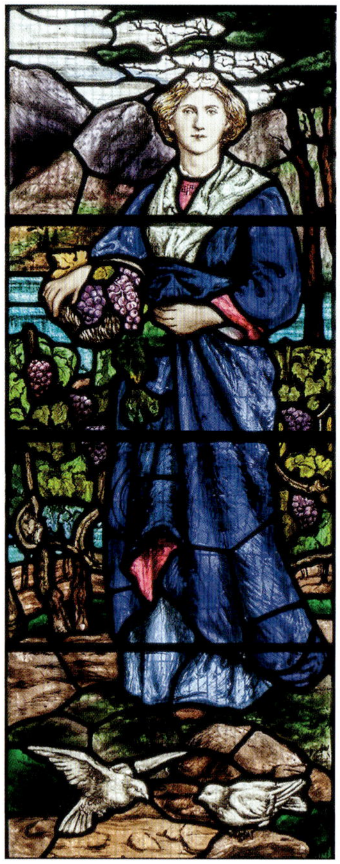

413. (far left) Mary Lowndes, St Margaret, 1917, Church of St Margaret, Mountain Ash, north transept

414. (left) Mary Lowndes, Lady Londonderry as the Good Wife, 1908, Church of St Peter, Machynlleth, nave

After 1897, Whall's windows were made at the studio established by Mary Lowndes and Alfred Drury in 1897 in Chelsea. Mary Lowndes had been a pupil of Henry Holiday and also designed for James Powell & Sons. She received commissions from several Welsh churches in the first quarter of the twentieth century, and among the earliest are a single-light window of Melangell at the Church of St Tydecho, Cemaes (Powys), and a three-light window depicting the Good Wife nearby at the Church of St Peter, Machynlleth. The Church of St Margaret, Mountain Ash, has two windows by Lowndes that, typically, use organic rather than architectural framing devices, echoing the work of Christopher Whall.[20]

After 1907 the facilities provided by Lowndes & Drury at the Glass House in Fulham enabled numerous artists to make, or supervise the manufacture of, their own windows, drawing on the expertise of the craftsmen of the studios as required. The enterprise enabled artists to remain independent, without incurring the expense of setting up a large studio of their own. Henry Holiday moved his studio there in 1906, and other artists whose windows were made at the Glass House included Hugh Arnold and Karl Parsons, both pupils and former assistants of Christopher Whall.[21] Parsons succeeded Whall as the principal teacher of stained glass at the Central School of Arts and Crafts in 1906, the year in which Whall set up his own studio in Hammersmith.

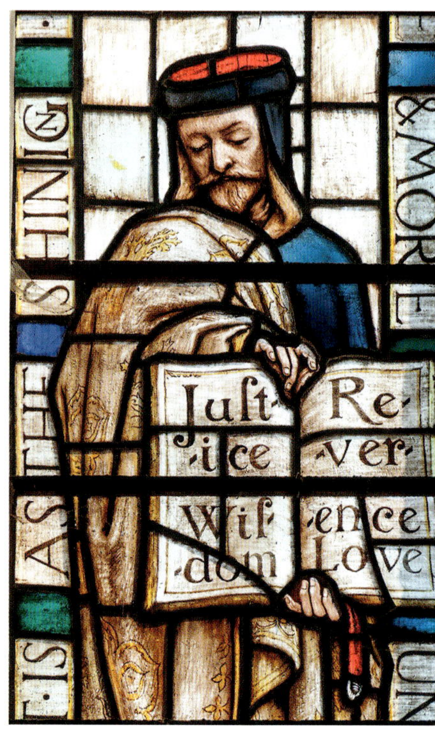

415. Hugh Arnold, Memorial Window, 1904, Church of St Padarn, Llanbadarn Fawr (Ceredigion), nave

20 For a list of her windows see the article by Ann O'Donoghue, 'Mary Lowndes – a brief overview of her work', *The Journal of Stained Glass*, vol. xxiv (2000–1), pp. 38–53. The Good Wife is a portrait of Mary Cornelia, marchioness of Londonderry, for whom see also p. 154 of this volume.

21 Hugh Arnold was killed at Gallipoli in 1915. Parsons rented his own studio at the Glass House and other artists who were based at the Glass House included Caroline Townsend, who took Joan Howson as a pupil, and Wilhelmina Geddes.

22 Arnold Robinson was assisted at the firm by Edward Woore, who had also worked as an assistant to Whall, and Rachel Tancock.

23 I am grateful to Alison Rennie for the attribution of the Clement Skilbeck window at the Church of St John the Baptist, Cardiff.

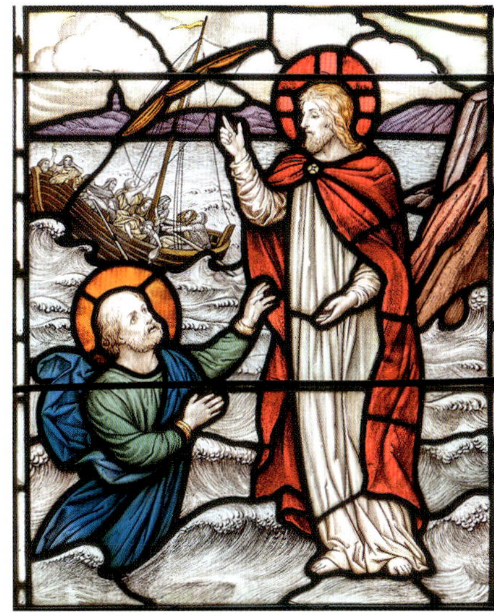

416. James Powell & Sons, Christ Walking on the Water with St Peter, *c.* 1912, designed by James Hogan, Church of St Gwenfaen, Rhoscolyn, east window

Christopher Whall's philosophy influenced some of the larger stained glass firms through his pupils. For example, James Hogan worked at James Powell & Sons, where he sustained the quality and originality of the firm's work as both managing director and chief designer from 1923 until his death in 1948. Another of Whall's pupils, Arnold Robinson, who had also worked at the Glass House, designed for Joseph Bell & Son and bought the firm in 1923.[22]

Many of the stained glass artists who worked with Christopher Whall can be contrasted with others who were closely associated with the Arts and Crafts Movement, such as Walter Crane and William Richmond, as well as Edward Burne-Jones before them, who were less concerned with involving themselves in the processes of cutting, painting, leading and firing of their windows. Nevertheless, the independence of artists such as Gerald Moira and Clement Skilbeck (both members of the Art Workers' Guild and exhibitors with the Arts and Crafts Exhibition Society) resulted in the creation of windows that were often much more distinctive and original than the usual fare of larger commercial studios.[23]

The painter and illustrator Walter Crane was a friend of William Morris, a founding member of

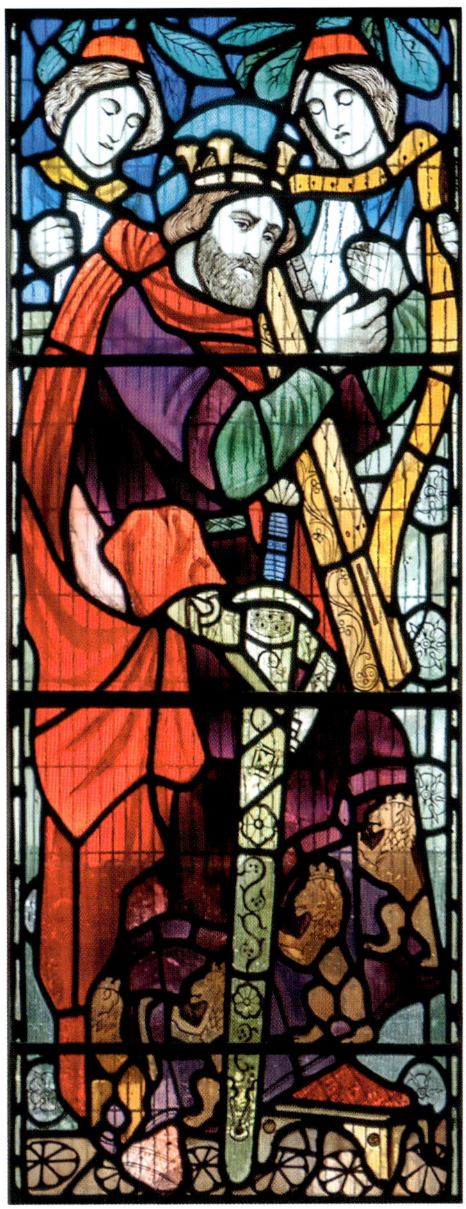

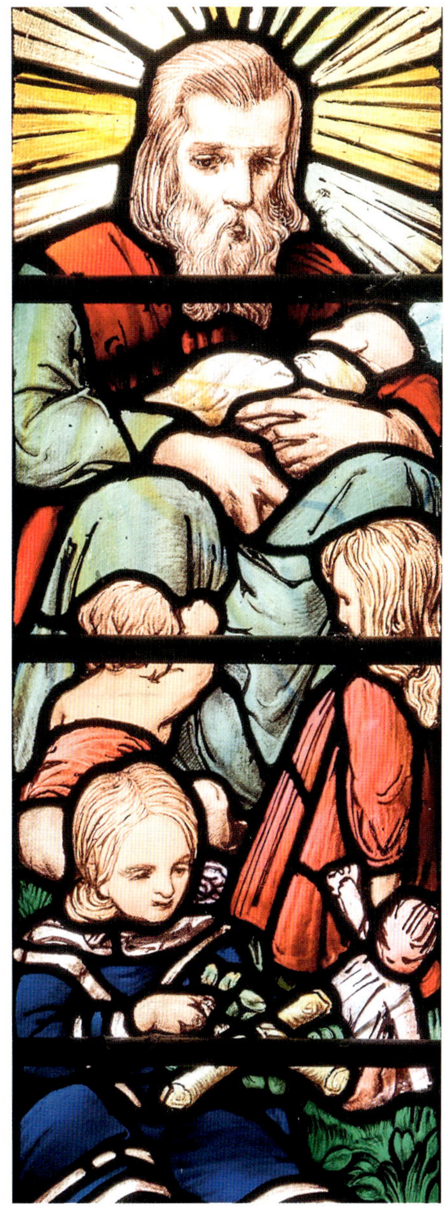

417. (right) Clement Skilbeck, King David, 1900, Church of St John the Baptist, Cardiff, north aisle

418. (far right) Gerald Moira, The Good Shepherd with Children, 1910, Church of St Madoc, Llanbadoc, nave

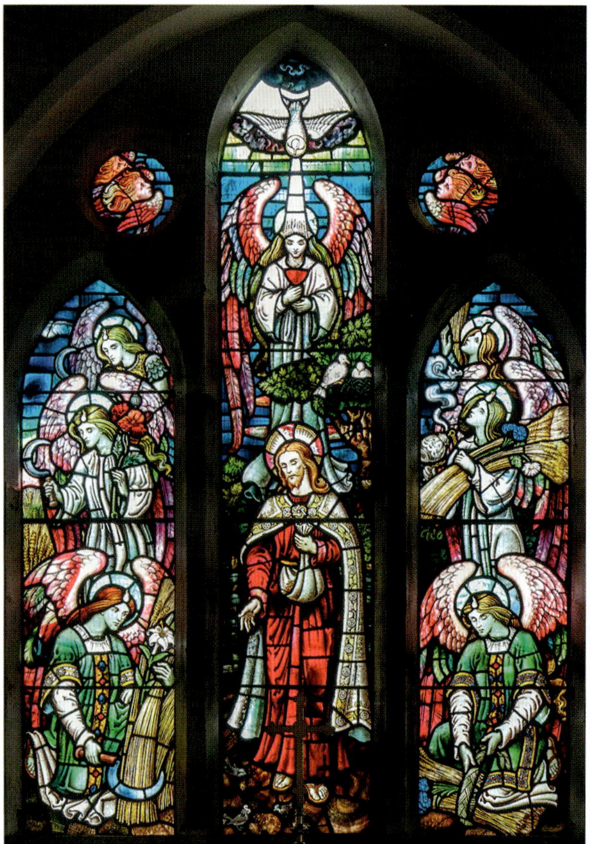

419. Sylvester Sparrow, Christ with Angels Gathering the Harvest, 1902, Church of St Michael, Lledrod, east window

the Art Workers' Guild, and the founding president of the Arts and Crafts Exhibition Society in 1887. He designed for a wide variety of media, including wallpapers, tiles and stained glass, but his windows were made by others including James Sylvester Sparrow.[24] Sparrow also made windows to his own design and was one of several artists who experimented with plating glass by layering it together with wide leads, producing intense and unusual colours. Sparrow's window of 1906 for Llandaff Cathedral is a conventional arrangement of Mary, John, Mary Magdalene and the crucified Christ, and has a rich dark palette made with plenty of streaky glass. The east window by Sparrow at the Church of St Michael, Lledrod, is a more unusual subject, depicting angels gathering the harvest with sickles, drawing on the text of Revelation 14: 17–19. Christ is shown sowing seeds in the central light, which is being set upon by three sparrows below. One of the sparrows holds the letter S, representing the artist's signature.[25]

The plating of layers of glass was used extensively by the foremost practitioners in stained glass in the United States, John La Farge and Louis Comfort Tiffany. La Farge also experimented extensively with opalescent glass, which became fashionable in America from the 1880s until the 1920s, and Tiffany exploited its possibilities on an industrial scale. In Britain, one of the few artists to experiment with opalescent glass was the painter James Eadie-Reid, a pupil of William Richmond who also worked briefly with the designer

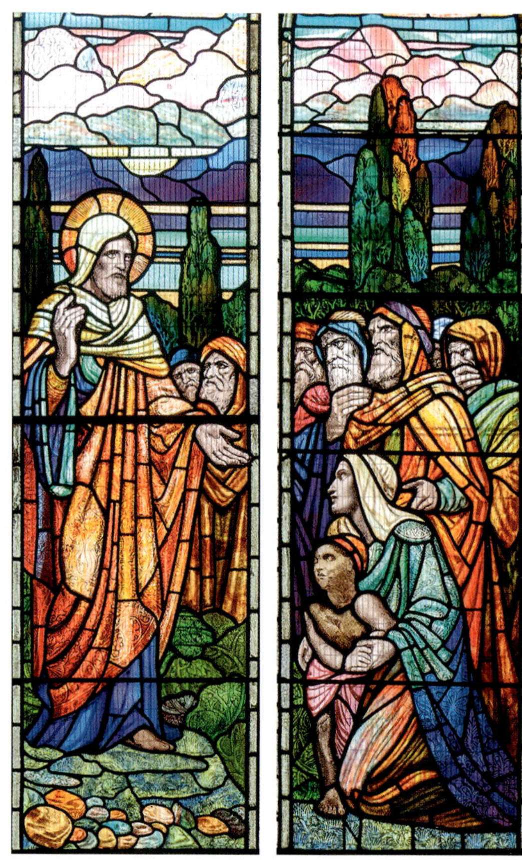

420. Gateshead Stained Glass Company, Christ with Disciples Beside a Lake, *c.* 1902, designed by James Eadie-Reid, Church of St Giles, Wrexham, north aisle

24 Isobel Spencer, *Walter Crane* (London: Studio Vista, 1975), pp. 119–22.

25 A two-light window on the same theme by John Jennings was made in about 1912 for the Church of St Mark, Connah's Quay.

26 Walter Crane invited Sylvester Sparrow to teach at the Royal College of Art and following Crane's attempt to introduce Arts and Crafts ideals to the college, Gerald Moira was appointed as Professor of Painting in 1900. Isobel Spencer, *Walter Crane* (London: Studio Vista, 1975), p. 167.

27 H.G. Hiller also worked with the Liverpool architect T. Taliesin Rees to produce a window for the Ceiriog Memorial Institute depicting Welsh poets. I am also grateful to Peter Jones for bringing more of the artist's work in Wales to my attention.

28 For the history of the teaching of stained glass at Birmingham School of Art see Roy Albutt, *Stained Glass Window Makers of Birmingham School of Art* (Pershore: Privately published, 2013).

C.R. Ashbee. Eadie-Reid designed for the stained glass firm Gateshead Stained Glass Company for a short period from 1900 until 1908, and an example of this collaboration can be found in Wales at the Church of St Giles, Wrexham. The window depicts Christ teaching by the lakeside across four lights with Old Testament figures in the panels below, making use of an unusually gaudy palette of oranges, purples and pinks.

Walter Crane became the director of design at Manchester School of Art from 1893 until his brief tenure as principal of the Royal College of Art in 1898.[26] One of his students in Manchester was Henry Gustave Hiller, who established his own studio in Liverpool in about 1904. Hiller produced stained glass, metalwork and painted panels for churches across north-west England and north Wales for the next thirty years, and early examples of his work can be found at the Church of St Peter, Llanbedr-y-cennin, and the Church of St Sannan, Llansannan. His large five-light window was installed in 1918 at the Church of St Marcella, Llanfarchell (near Denbigh), with scenes depicting the empty tomb and the appearances of Christ to his disciples after the Resurrection.[27]

Studios motivated by the Arts and Crafts Movement continued to develop in cities outside of London. The Birmingham Municipal School of Art developed a distinctive Arts and Crafts ethos during the 1890s and the teaching and manufacture of stained glass began under Henry Payne in 1901 following a brief period of study with Christopher Whall.[28] Some of his pupils established themselves locally, such as Florence and Walter Camm and Kendrick Swaine Bourne, who returned to their family firms in Smethwick and Sandwell. Among the most influential of Payne's students was A.J. Davies, who in 1906 moved to Bromsgrove and established his studio at the premises of the Bromsgrove Guild, on the invitation of its founder, the sculptor Walter Gilbert. He was joined there by more of Payne's students who worked as his assistants, including Henry John Hodgetts, who remained at

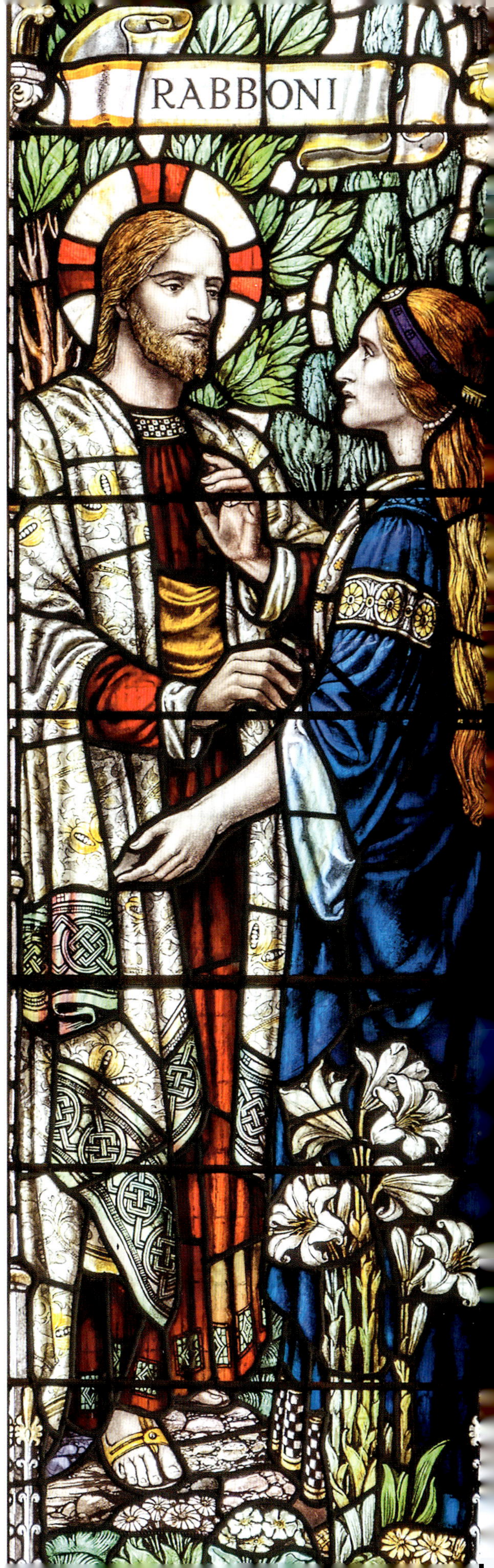

421. H.G. Hiller, The Risen Christ Appearing to Mary Magdalene, 1918, Church of St Marcella, Llanfarchell, east window

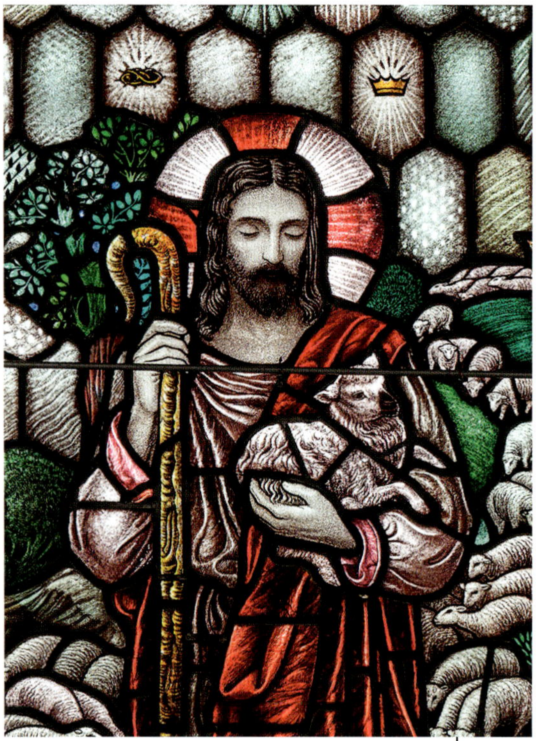

422. A.J. Davies, The Good Shepherd, 1917, Church of St Tydfil, Bryn, reset in the sanctuary of the new church

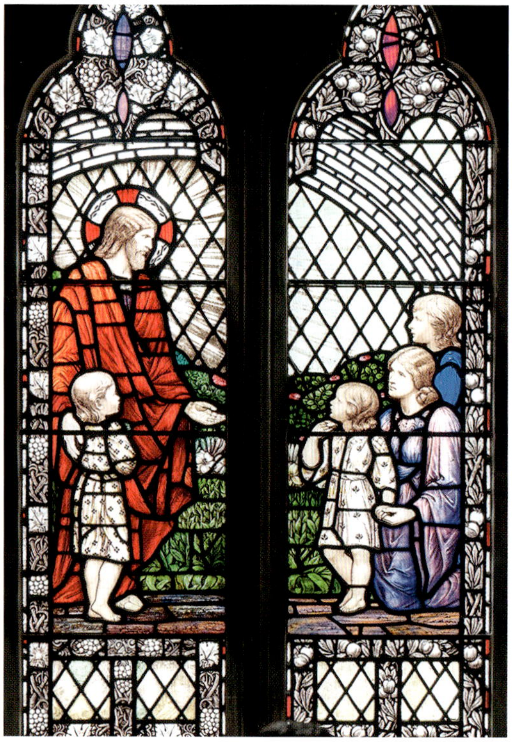

423. H.H. Martyn & Co. Christ with Children, 1923, designed by Sidney Meteyard, Church of St John the Evangelist, Canton, Cardiff, north aisle

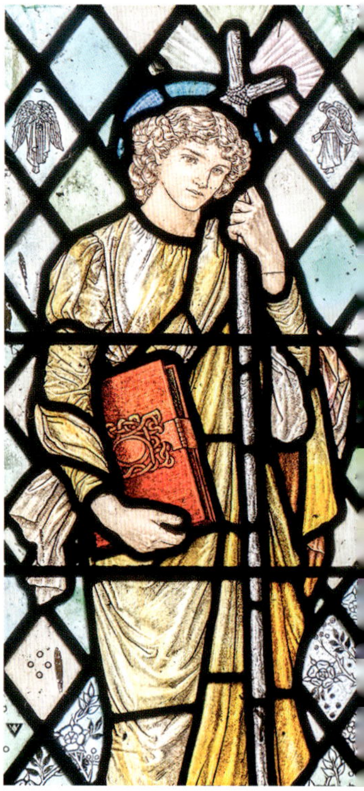

424. T.W. Camm & Co., Faith, designed by Florence Camm, 1915, Church of St Cathen, Llangathen, north nave

the studio until Davies' death in 1953, and A.E. Lemmon.[29] After the First World War, Walter Gilbert left the Guild and became assistant manager at H.H. Martyn & Co. of Cheltenham, which, by contrast, had over a thousand employees in 1920. Initially founded as stone, marble and wood carvers, the firm made ecclesiastical furnishings and in the 1920s had a stained glass department, whose principal designer, Sidney H. Meteyard, had been taught by Payne at Birmingham School of Art and had worked at the Bromsgrove Guild. The window by the firm at the Church of St John the Evangelist, Canton, Cardiff, echoes the work of A.J. Davies in its delicate drawing of natural forms and fine white lettering on a black ground.[30] Other former students taught by Payne went to work elsewhere, and the east window by the Lancaster firm Abbott & Co. of 1913 at the Church of St Brynach, Dinas Cross, suggests the influence of Joseph Sanders, who had assisted both Henry Payne and A.J. Davies in their studios before moving to Lancaster in about 1912.[31]

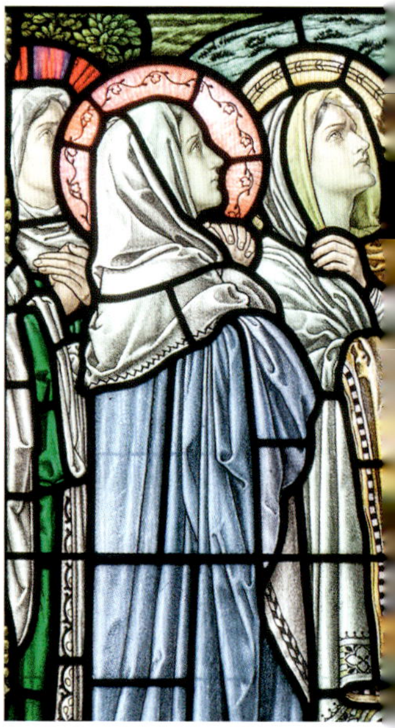

425. Abbott & Co., Women at the Crucifixion, 1913, Church of St Brynach, Dinas Cross, east window

29 Roy Albutt, *The Stained Glass Windows of A J Davies of the Bromsgrove Guild Worcestershire* (Pershore: Privately published, 2005).

30 Although the stained glass studio seems to have been small, the firm's work also included joinery, wrought iron work and bronze casting. H.H. Martyn began building aircraft during the First World War, and was the largest employer in Cheltenham for many years.

31 For Joseph Sanders see Roy Albutt, *Stained Glass Window Makers of Birmingham School of Art* (Pershore: Privately published, 2013), pp. 88–9.

Another former pupil of Christopher Whall came to Wales in 1909 following his appointment as principal of Swansea School of Art. William Grant Murray had first encountered the ideals of the Arts and Crafts Movement when he was still a student in Edinburgh, before training for two years at the Royal College of Art in London where he was taught by Christopher Whall, and had ambitions to establish a Welsh School of Arts and Crafts at Swansea. However, although he was joined by the jeweller Harry Hall, and nurtured a number of young local painters, stained glass was not taught until the 1930s.[32]

In the 1920s a stained glass studio was established on Caldey Island as part of the attempts by Abbot Aelred Carlyle to establish a School of Arts and Crafts among the Benedictine community.[33] Dom Theodore Baily joined the community in 1920 and continued to work as an artist and designer in a wide variety of media throughout his life. In 1922 he went to Paris to train with Georges Desvallières and Maurice Denis, both of whom designed stained glass, and after he returned in 1923 he made a number of stained glass windows and panels for the churches and abbey buildings on Caldey.

A roundel by Theodore Baily at the east end of the chancel of the Church of the Holy Name in Fishguard is perhaps his only work on the Welsh mainland. The seated figure of Christ uses only a little paint to detail the face, crown of thorns and hands, as well as a little detail of the foliage below. A roundel depicting the Tree of Life at the Church of St David on Caldey Island relies solely on the lead lines and colour of the glass for the design, with paint only used to delineate the sunburst at the top of the window.

32 Despite listing stained glass as the craft in which he was most proficient when applying for the post of principal in 1909, no windows are known to have been made by Grant Murray or made to his design. Maurice Broady, 'Stained and Architectural Glass in the School and Institute', in Kirstine Brander Dunthorne (ed.), *Drawn From Wales: a School of Art in Swansea 1853–2003* (Cardiff: Welsh Academic Press, 2003), p. 43.
A gifted but conservative painter, his support of more radical ideas among his students and ex-students was demonstrated in his orchestration of the Swansea National Eisteddfod of 1926. See chapter four of Peter Lord, *The Visual Culture of Wales: Industrial Society* (Cardiff: University of Wales Press, 1998) and 'The Swansea School' (Visual Journeys), in Peter Lord, *The Visual Culture of Wales: Industrial Society* (CD-ROM) (Cardiff: University of Wales Press, 2000).

33 The community at Caldey and its relationship with Eric Gill's community at Capel-y-Ffin is described in Eric Rowan and Carolyn Stewart, *An Elusive Tradition* (Cardiff: University of Wales Press, 2002), pp. 155–84.

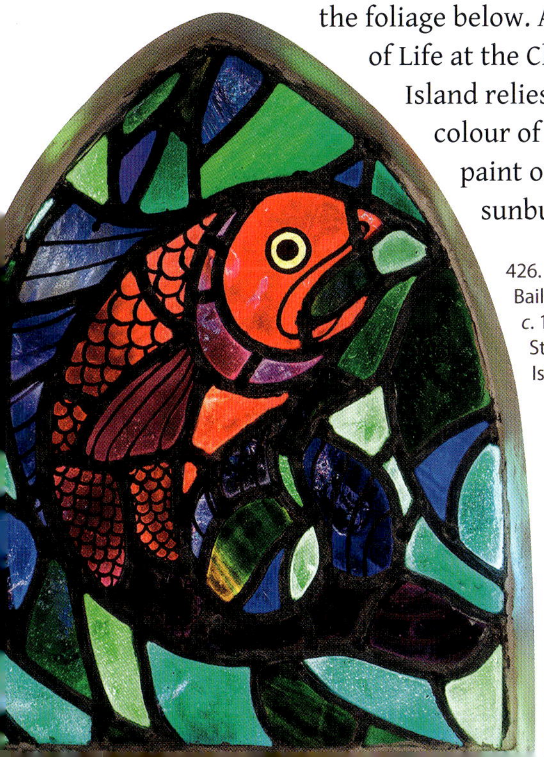

426. (left) Theodore Baily, Fish Window, *c.* 1922–8, Church of St David, Caldey Island, chancel

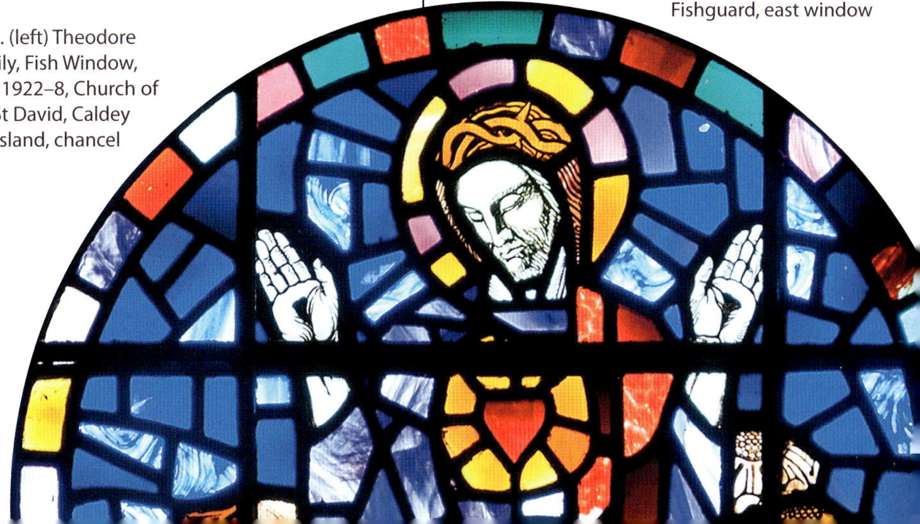

427. Theodore Baily, Sacred Heart of Christ, *c.* 1922–8, Church of the Holy Name, Fishguard, east window

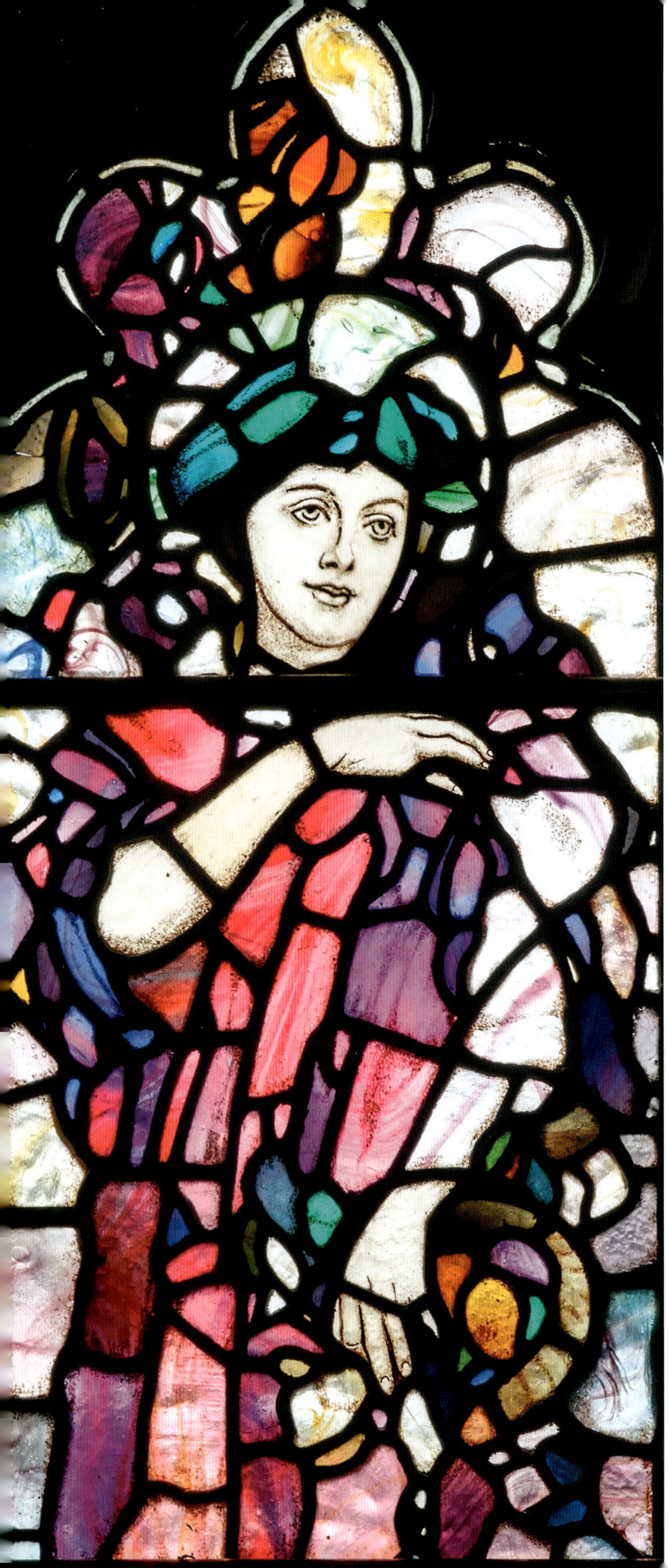

429. Wil
Glasby, The G
Shepherd, 1
Church of All Sa
Ffynnongr
south a

A similar technique was employed by Leonard Walker, whose windows depicting standing figures are found in churches at Tregynon, Llandingat and Llanwrthwl in Wales. In these works paint is used sparingly, mainly to detail facial features, hands and feet, while the remainder of the window is characterised by pieces of streaky slab glass of uneven thicknesses. The glass that he used was made by James Powell & Sons, and he also designed windows made by the firm.

Although the windows by Leonard Walker appear quite different to the work of artists such as Christopher Whall or Mary Lowndes, Peter Cormack recognises that the 'use of slab glass exemplifies one of the underlying principles of the Arts and Crafts philosophy: the primacy of materials in determining both style and workmanship.'[34] In windows by Whall, Walker and Baily, the texture and character of the glass itself is an important feature of the design and manufacture, rather than simply being a surface onto which the design was painted. This underlying approach illustrates the difficulty in identifying a common visual style among artists of the Arts and Crafts Movement, although there was frequent recourse to the Pre-Raphaelite style of Edward Burne-Jones and Henry Holiday.[35]

Stylistic similarities, such as the painterly style used for faces or the use of densely foliated borders and backgrounds, were sometimes the result of individual designers and employees moving between different firms.

428. Leonard Walker, St Dorothy, 1922, Church of St Cynon, Tregynon, chancel

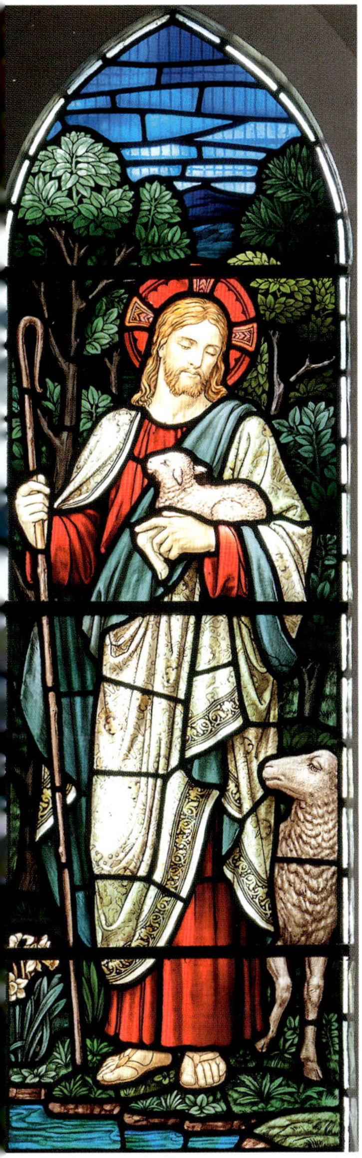

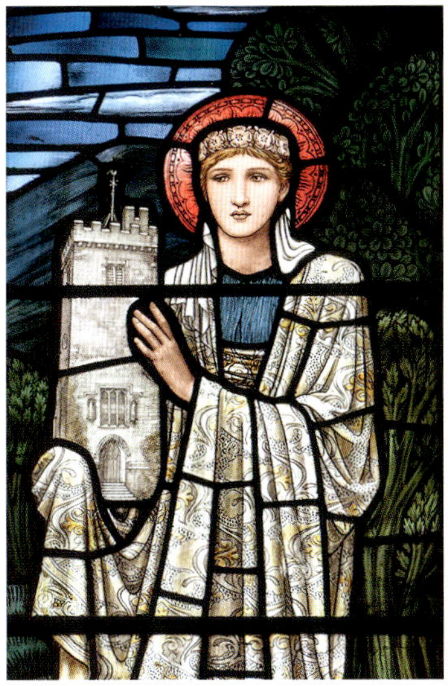

430. (above) Morris & Co., St Elli, from the Crucifixion with Saints, 1911, figure designed by Edward Burne-Jones, painted by William Glasby, Church of St Elli, Llanelli, east window

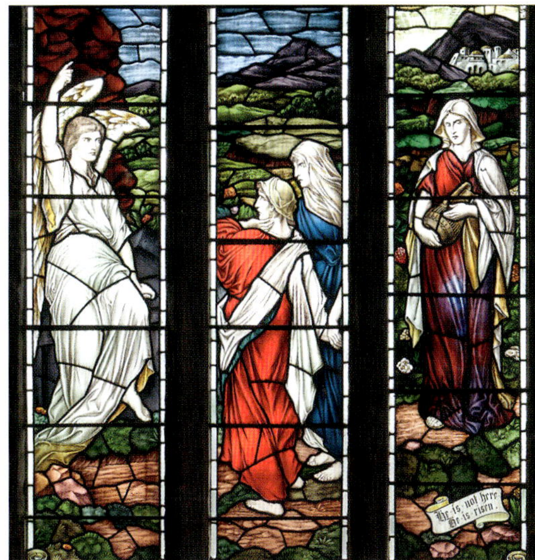

431. Jones & Willis, An Angel Greets the Three Women at the Empty Tomb, 1923, Church of St Mary, Gladestry, chancel

For example, the artist William Glasby was a senior glass painter for Powell's before leaving to work for Henry Holiday from 1891 until 1906, and he was then employed as a glass painter for Morris & Co. from 1909 until 1923. Glasby established his own studio in 1919, and the character of his windows betrays the influence of his former collaborators. Glass painters and glaziers working at Lowndes & Drury's Glass House probably also added a little visual homogeneity to the windows of a number of artists whose windows were made there. Work in stained glass by artists associated with the Arts and Crafts Movement was also characterised by the use of natural rather than architectural borders; detailed depictions of birds and flowers; incidental and whimsical details; fine lettering; and the use of pure white and streaky Norman slab glass.

In time all of these visual characteristics were increasingly imitated by larger stained glass studios and church furnishers. For example, the depiction of the visit of the three Marys to the empty tomb by Jones & Willis at the Church of St Mary, Gladestry, has similarities in the treatment of the landscape with work by Morris & Co. and William Glasby.[36]

34 Peter Cormack, *The Stained Glass Work of Christopher Whall 1849–1924 'Aglow with Brave Resplendent Colour'* (Boston: Trustees of the Public Library of the City of Boston, 1999), p. 15.

35 In the *Journal of the British Society of Master Glass-Painters* Henry Holiday was described in his obituary as the last survivor of the Pre-Raphaelite group, 'and his work and opinions reflected the association', vol. ii, no. 2 (1927), p. 105.

36 Two of the four figures share the poses of figures in the same scene by Shrigley & Hunt nearby at Old Radnor, made nearly ten years earlier in 1914. If the Jones & Willis window at Gladestry is partly inspired by the earlier Shrigley & Hunt window at Old Radnor it is something of an irony, since Shrigley & Hunt had very recently made five windows for the church, including east windows for the chancel and north aisle chapel. Jones & Willis made four windows for the church, resulting in the addition of nine windows in the space of about ten years. The composition of both windows is probably inspired by a common source, as other depictions of the same scene before and after this date also share the poses of the three women and the Angel of the Resurrection.

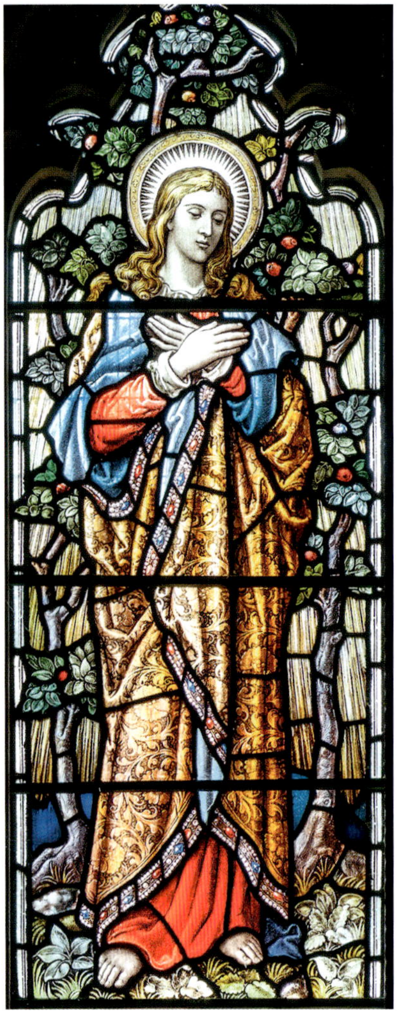

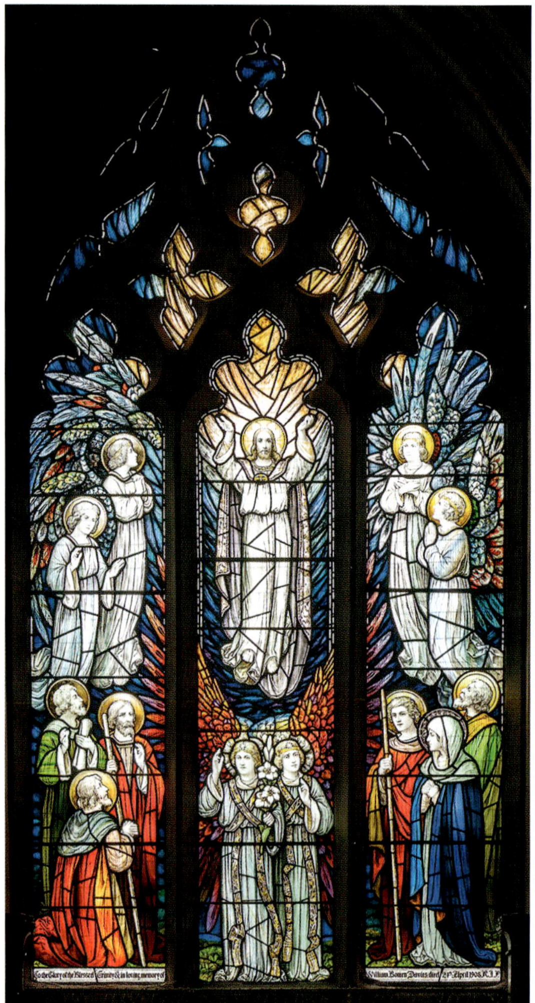

432. (far left) John Jennings, Faith, 1906, Church of St Faith, Llanfoist, west window

433. (left) William Pearce, The Ascension, *c.* 1908, Church of the Holy Trinity, Llandrindod Wells, north chancel

A pair of angels in glowing colours by John Jennings at Connah's Quay resemble the colouring of some of William Glasby's work, with beautifully painted detail. These and other works by the artist at Holyhead and Llanfair Kilgeddin are framed with Gothic canopies and borders, but his three-light window for the Church of St Faith, Llanfoist, dispenses with these architectural features, borrowing natural backgrounds from the visual vocabulary of the Arts and Crafts Movement. The availability of streaky glass was used to good advantage by many studios such as William Pearce of Birmingham for the wings of the angels in their Ascension window at the Church of the Holy Trinity, Llandrindod Wells.[37]

Other artists associated with the Arts and Crafts Movement remained close to the spirit of the Gothic Revival as interpreted by G.F. Bodley and Ninian Comper. Frederick Charles Eden was a contemporary of Comper and a fellow pupil of Bodley. He set up his own stained glass studio in 1910 out of frustration with the quality of the stained glass made to his design, and, unlike Comper, he showed a greater interest in the ideals of the Arts and Crafts Movement and joined the Art Workers' Guild in 1915.[38] Eden's finely crafted windows at Eglwys Cymun demonstrate fine detail while admitting plenty of light into the small dark medieval church.[39] The windows were added between 1906 and 1917, and therefore span the period before and after he set up his own stained glass studio.

37 I am grateful to Alan Brooks for help with the attribution of this window.

38 Both Eden and Comper inherited an interest in fittings for their churches from Bodley and also designed stained glass for their churches. Comper worked with Burlison & Grylls, the stained glass studio that Bodley had helped to establish, but dissatisfaction with their work persuaded Comper to also set up his own stained glass studio. However, he employed assistants to manufacture his windows and did not involve himself in the process, or indeed those of the other decorative arts made for his new churches or restorations.

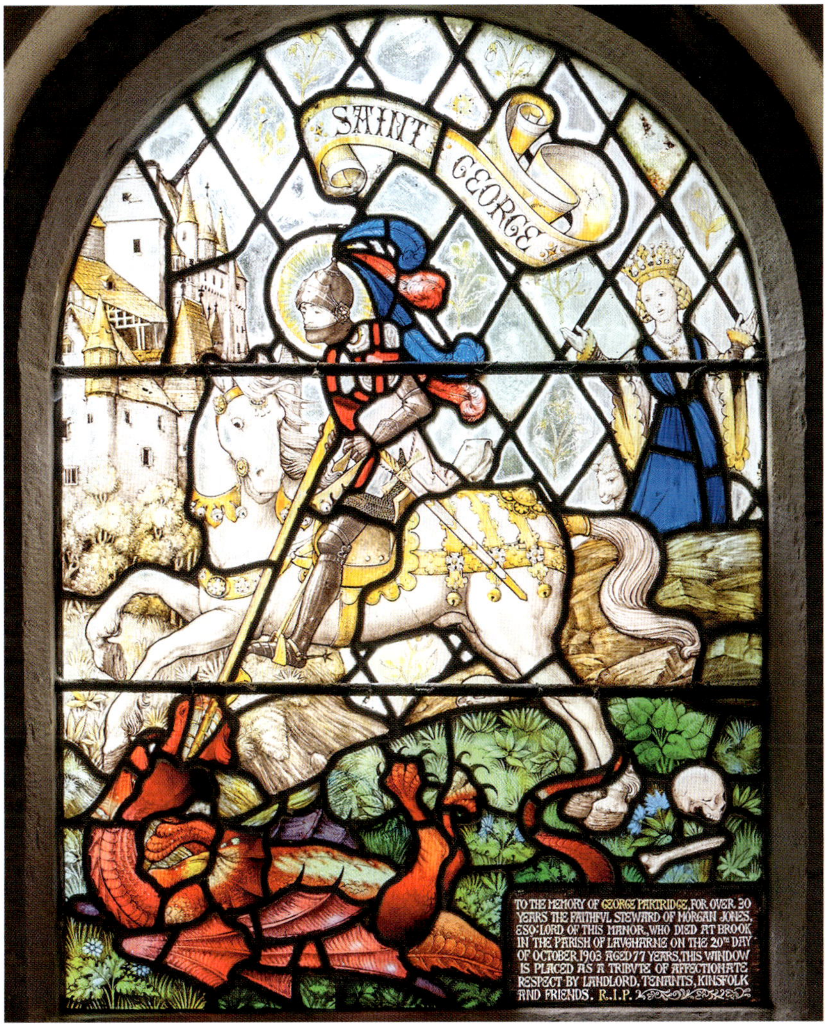

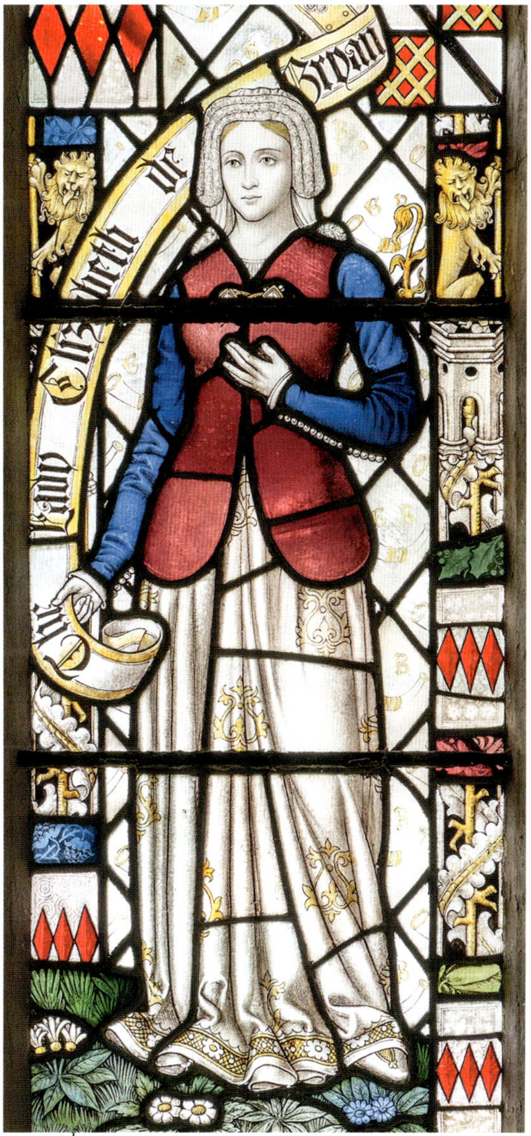

434–5. Frederick Eden, St George and the Dragon, 1907, nave (above left); Lady Elizabeth de Bryan, 1913, west wall (above), Church of St Margaret, Eglwys Cymun

Another Arts and Crafts architect who worked at both churches and cathedrals in Wales was William Douglas Caröe, who was elected to the Art Workers' Guild in 1889. His work was Gothic in spirit and form, and he often used stained glass by Horace Wilkinson, for example at Brecon Cathedral, Cardigan, Llangammarch Wells and Newcastle Emlyn. Wilkinson had worked with Edward Frampton and with Clayton & Bell, and his use of Gothic surrounds in white glass, and dark colouring for scenes and figures, is close to fifteenth-century English stained glass.

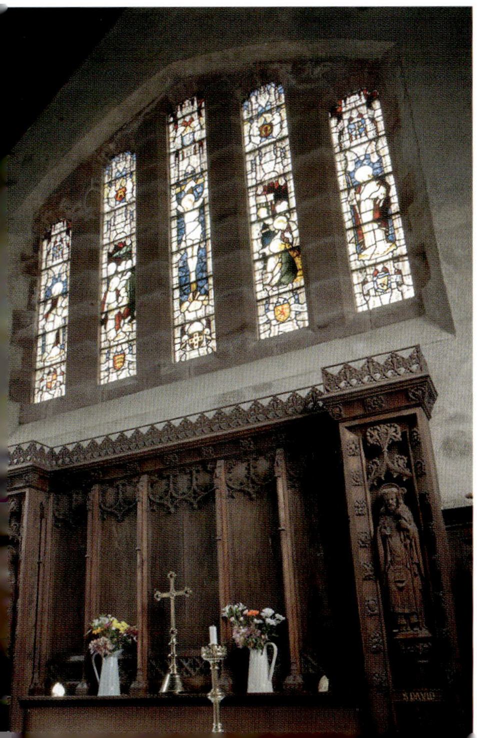

436. W.D. Caröe, Church of St Cadmarch, Llangammarch Wells, *c.* 1916, stained glass by Horace Wilkinson

39 The church's own Arts and Crafts architectural credentials arise from the careful restoration of the porch and nave by William Weir, under the supervision of Philip Webb. Thomas Lloyd, Julian Orbach and Robert Scourfield, *The Buildings of Wales: Carmarthenshire and Ceredigion* (New Haven/London: Yale University Press, 2006), pp. 189–90.

The Arts and Crafts Movement, and in particular its mediation through the teaching of Christopher Whall and his book *Stained Glass Work*, published in 1905, was to have a lasting impact on much stained glass production throughout the twentieth century. He encouraged artists working in stained glass to respect the tradition and craft of the medium, and summarised his philosophy towards the making of stained glass as four essential things: that designers should not direct what they could not practise and should personally supervise the making of their windows; that apprentices should be encouraged to become masters; and that sacrifices of profit should be made 'for the sake of the Art, should the interests of the two clash'.[40] The demand that stimulated the semi-industrial production of stained glass windows in the second half of the nineteenth century was already waning by the end of the century, and as the size of the largest studios decreased, the opportunities for stained glass designers to participate in the making of their windows increased. Sacrifices for the sake of art were more difficult to sustain, and designs and cartoons continued to be reused by large and small makers. For example, Whall's figure of Michael at the Church of All Saints, Glasbury, closely resembles his figure of the archangel in his 1902 window for Canterbury Cathedral, and, within Wales, A.J. Davies' design for the appearance of the risen Christ to Mary Magdalene at Corwen was also used at the Church of St Margaret, Mountain Ash.

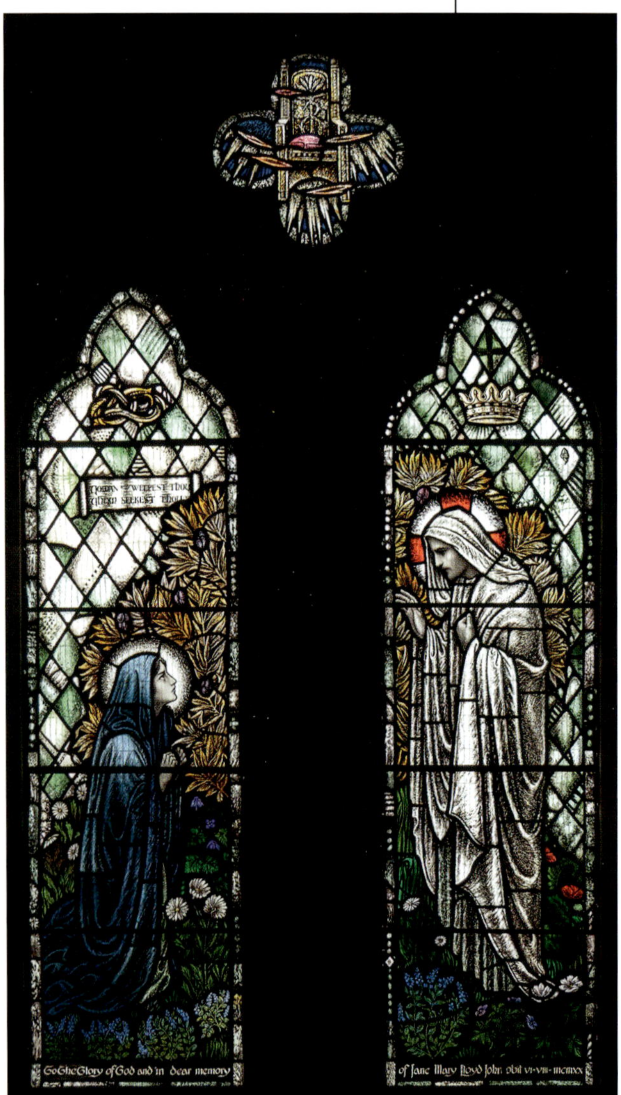

437. A.J. Davies, The Risen Christ Appearing to Mary Magdalene, *c.* 1920, Church of St Sulien, Corwen, nave

The practice and teaching of Christopher Whall, Karl Parsons and Henry Payne encouraged a new seriousness in the medium and provided the basis for greater originality in design and innovation in technique. The dull convention of the representation of the Good Shepherd by firms working in the tradition of the Gothic Revival are in marked contrast to the distinct personalities of windows in churches depicting the same subject by Henry Holiday at Buckley, A.J. Davies at Bryn, Edward Woore at Cwrt Henri, and Mary Lowndes at Nantgwyllt, near Rhayader. Even the adaptation

40 C.W. Whall, *Stained Glass Work: A text book for students and workers in glass* (Bristol: Morris & Juliet Venables, 1999, first published 1905), pp. 268–9.

41 An admiration of the work of Albrecht Dürer, whose designs were interpreted in stained glass during the sixteenth century, is more commonly associated with the work of Burlison & Grylls and C.E. Kempe.

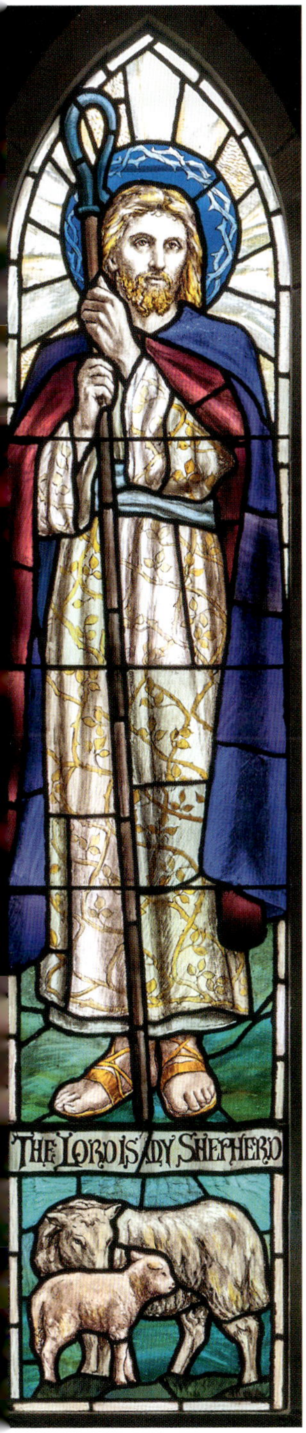

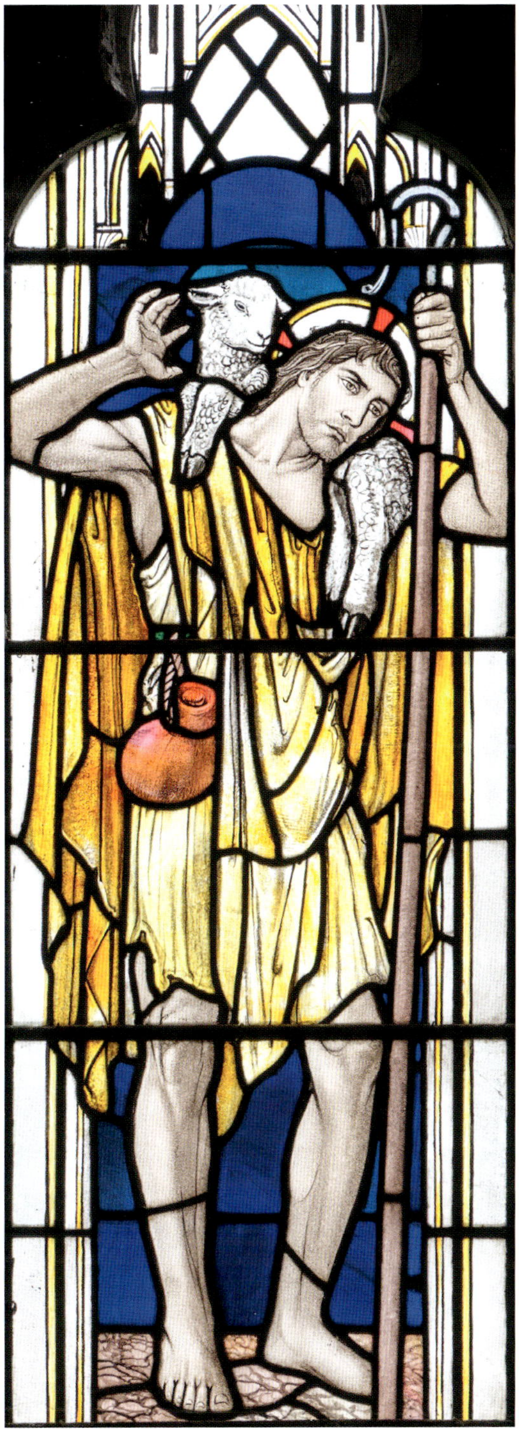

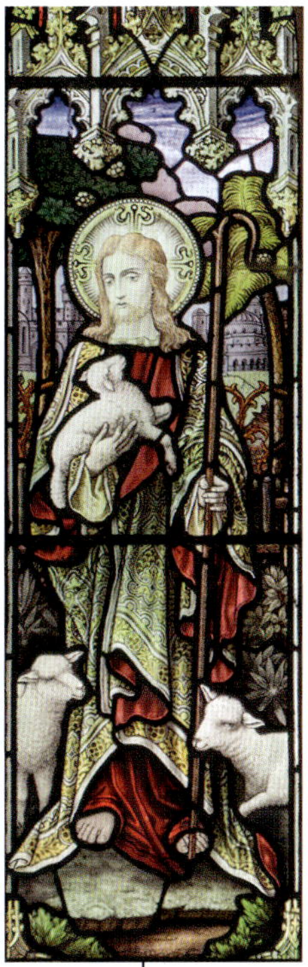

438. (far left) Mary Lowndes, The Good Shepherd, early twentieth century, Nantgwillt Church, Elan Valley, east window

439. (centre left) Edward Woore, The Good Shepherd, 1926, Church of St Mary, Cwrt Henri, south transept

440. (left) A. Seward & Co., The Good Shepherd, *c.* 1923, Church of St Mor and St Deiniol, Llanfor, nave

of art historical models shows a strong personal style, such as A.J. Davies' distinctly Düreresque depiction of the risen Christ at Glyndyfydwy, which is accompanied by a contemplative angel of the resurrection and carefully drawn flowers and birds below.[41]

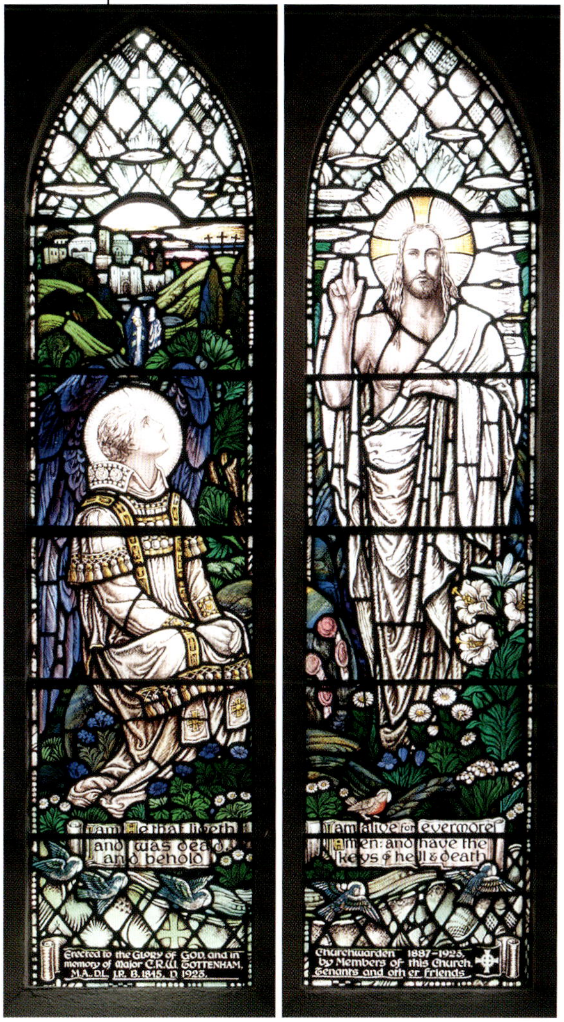

441. A.J. Davies, The Resurrection, 1924, Church of St Thomas, Glyndyfydwy, nave

Artistic innovation in stained glass was not always welcome. Richard Stubington, an artist who had been trained by Henry Payne and who succeeded him as teacher of stained glass at Birmingham School of Art in 1909, was commissioned to make a memorial window for the Church of St Mary, Denbigh, and submitted a design for consideration in 1925. Archbishop Edwards and the diocesan chancellor were both reported to be 'of opinion that neither the design nor the colouring' were suitable for the church, and, in response, the solicitors, replying on behalf of the donor rejoined that 'A great deal of trouble has been taken to set something better than anything which is in the church already.' Although the artist made modifications, its use of pattern, colour and abstracted form sets it apart from the preceding windows made for the church, as well as the later work placed opposite by Veronica Whall in 1933. Although the use of red and blue grounds is reminiscent of medieval work of the twelfth and thirteenth century, as well as some of the best work of the 1860s, the window remained one of the most visually innovative and modernist of all stained glass windows made for a Welsh church until the late 1950s.[42]

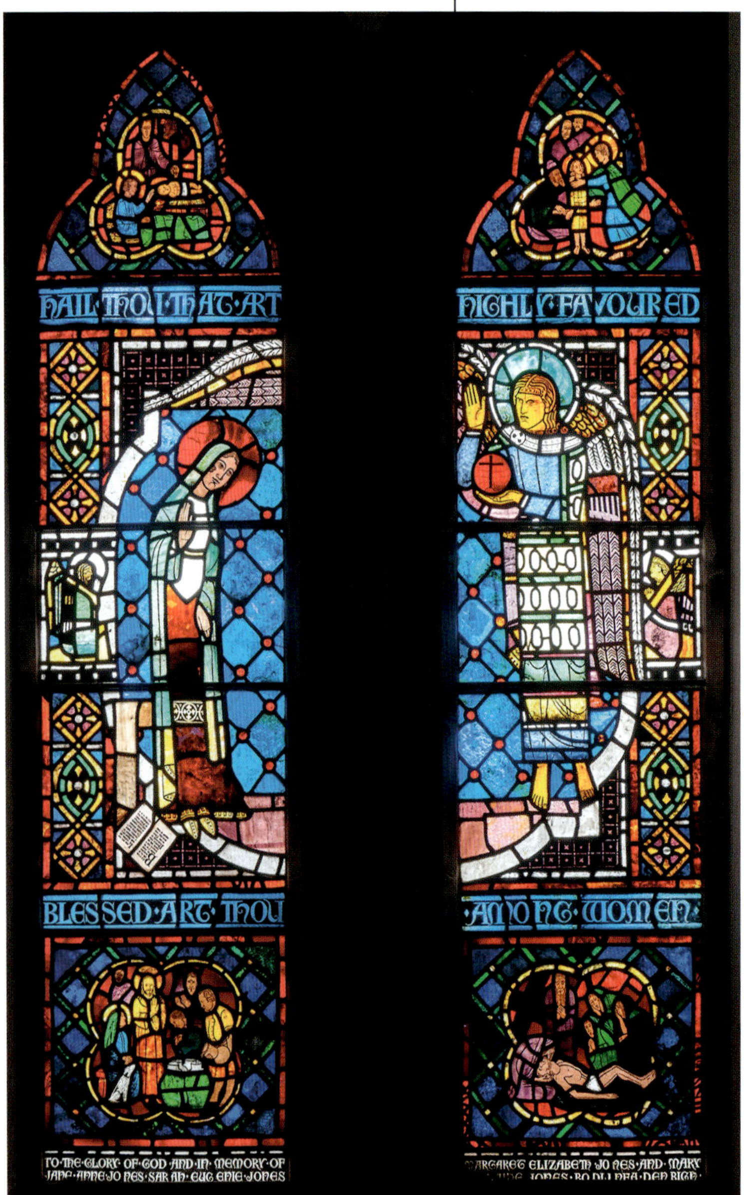

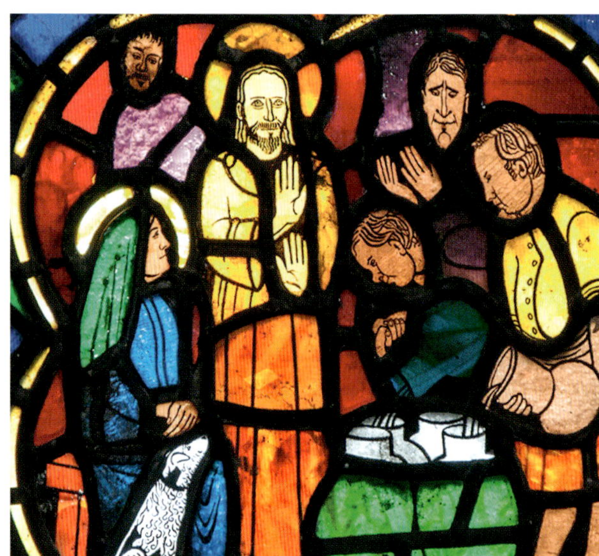

442–3. Richard Stubington, The Annunciation, including Christ at the Wedding at Cana (above), 1926, Church of St Mary, Denbigh, (liturgical) north aisle

42 There was also opposition to the use of the words "Hail Mary blessed among women", which was revised to read "Hail thou that art highly favoured, blessed art thou among women", as found in the Authorised Version of the Bible. Correspondence concerning the window is found in National Library of Wales, Records of the Church in Wales: Diocese of St Asaph, SA/RF 41/17.

Chapter Eight

First World War Memorials

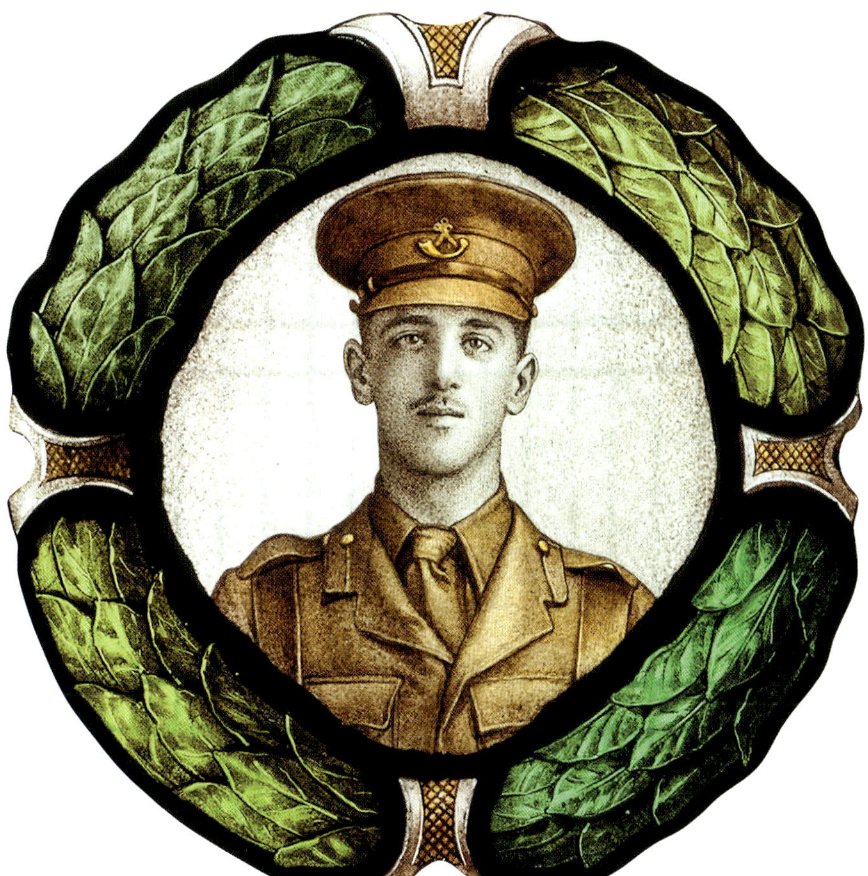

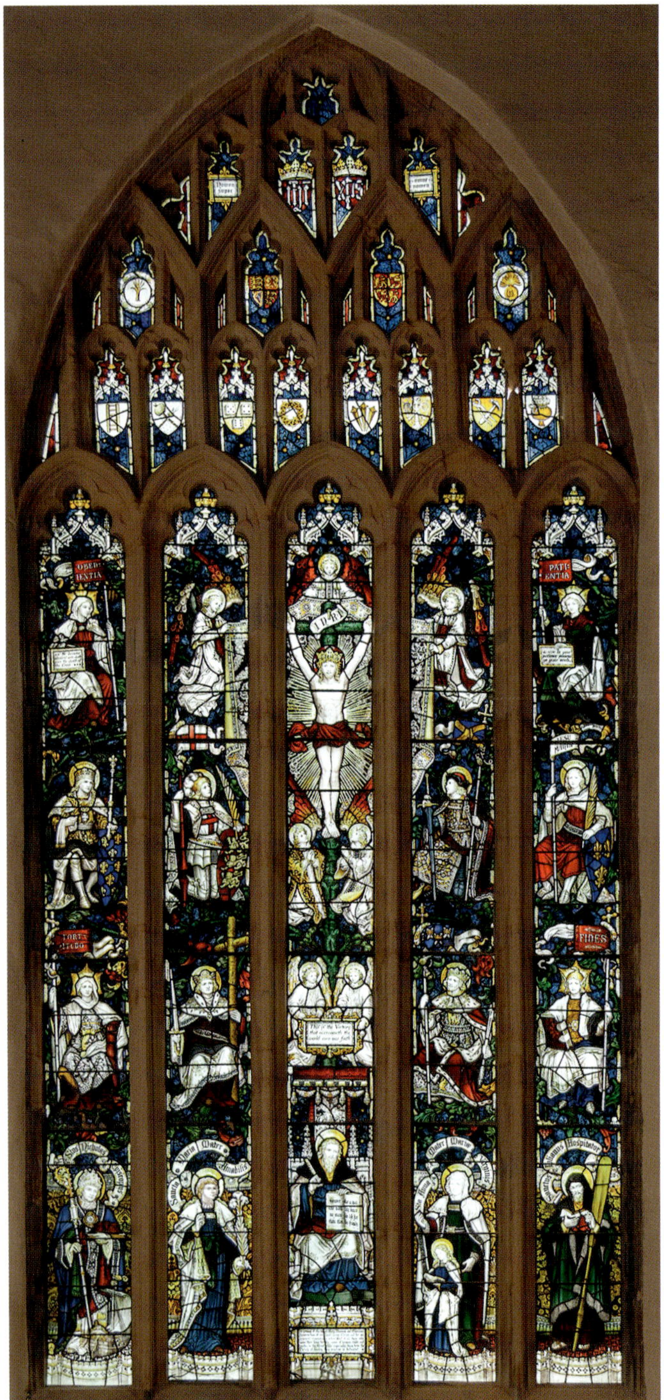

445. C.E. Kempe & Co., The Crucifixion with Soldier Saints, 1920, Church of St Mary, Tenby, south aisle

A spate of commissions for stained glass in churches followed the First World War, as an expression both of the tragic loss of those who died, and the relief brought about by the peace.[1] Many windows were made by large established firms such as C.E. Kempe & Co., Burlison & Grylls and James Powell & Sons, but smaller studios also enjoyed a busy few years following the armistice in 1918. Some of the best windows in Wales by the artists of the Arts and Crafts Movement were war memorial windows.

War memorials in churches were usually given either by congregations in memory of all of those from the church or parish who lost their lives, or by individual families in memory of their lost sons and brothers. In some churches both kinds may be found, such as at the Church of St Mary, Tenby. A four-light memorial window by Karl Parsons was given by the family of Lieut Col. H.M. Henderson, while a larger five-light window by C.E. Kempe & Co. was furnished with stained glass in memory 'of all those who gave their lives for the cause of human right and justice in the Great War especially those from the Parish of Tenby'. Both windows are complex, although the rows of figures in the public memorial is much more conventional and less personal than Parsons' window of H.M. Henderson receiving the crown of life from an angel, in the presence of the risen Christ. The Kempe & Co. window is a confident, triumphal work, showing Christ reigning from the cross, with figures representing Obedience and Patience, and military saints including Louis of France, George, Edmund, Joan of Arc, Alban and Oswald.

At the Church of St Pedrog, Llanbedrog, war memorial windows of both kinds were made by William Aikman: one in memory of all of the men of the parish, and another for an individual, David Henry George Manley,

1 We are accustomed to calling these windows, as well as the other monuments commemorating the First World War, war memorials, but many were given in thanksgiving for the coming of peace.

444. (Title page) Percy Bacon Brothers, Paul Chancourt Gira
c. 1915, Church of St Peter, Carmarthen,

446. Karl Parsons, Receiving the Crown of Life, 1917, Church of St Mary the Virgin, Tenby, north aisle

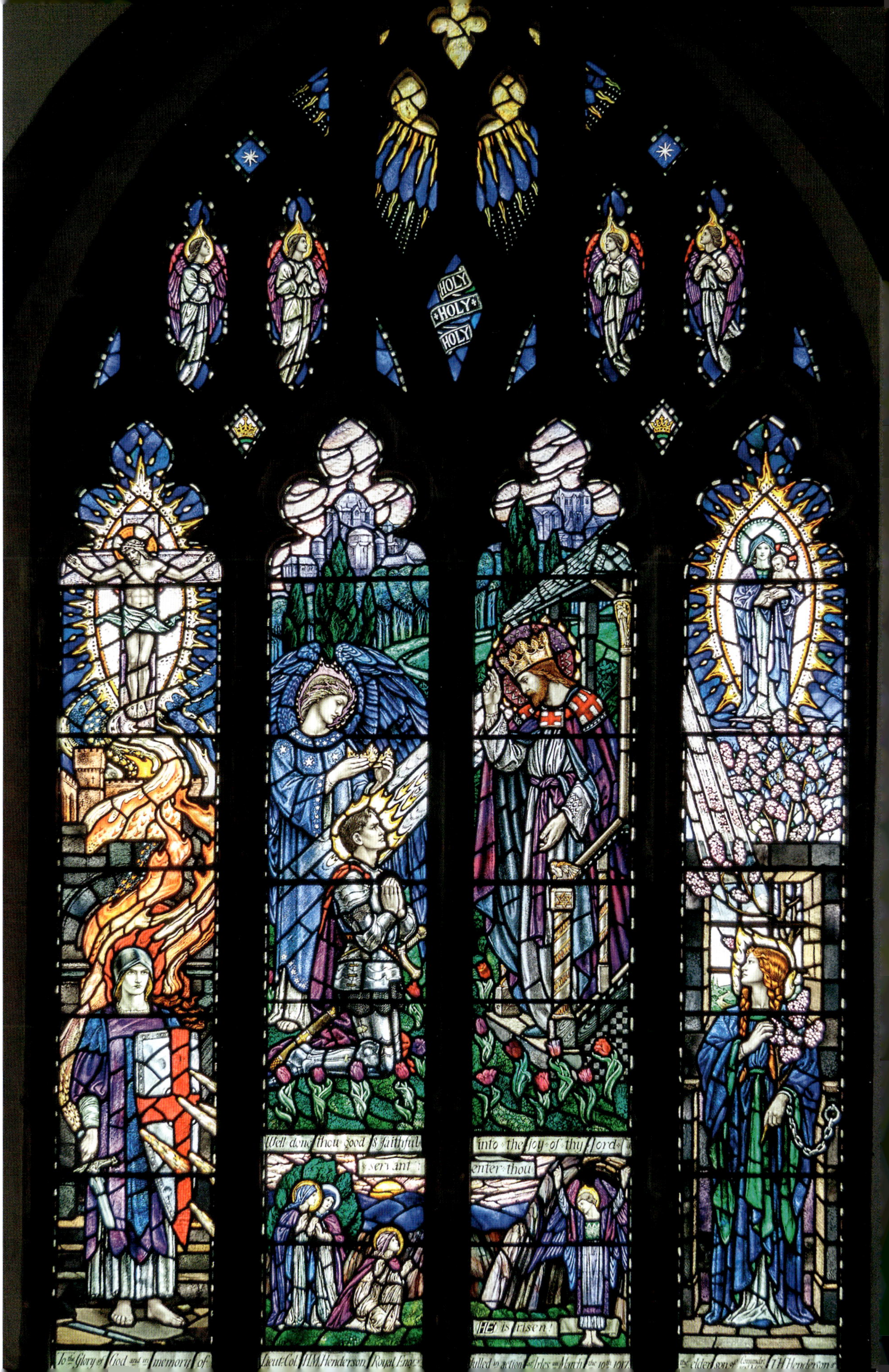

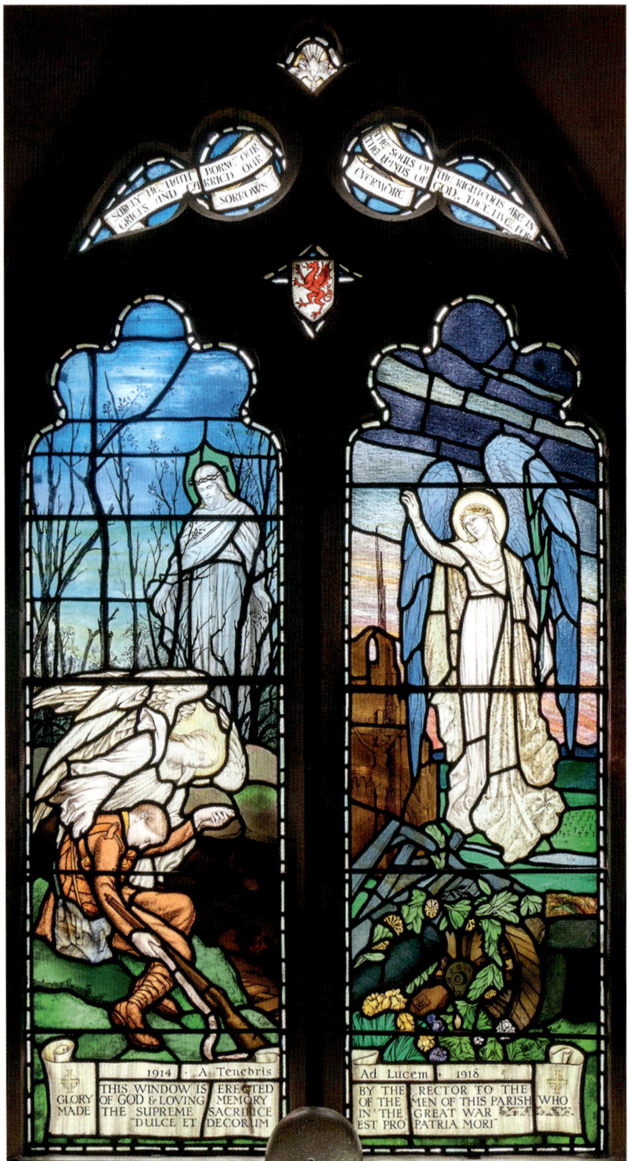

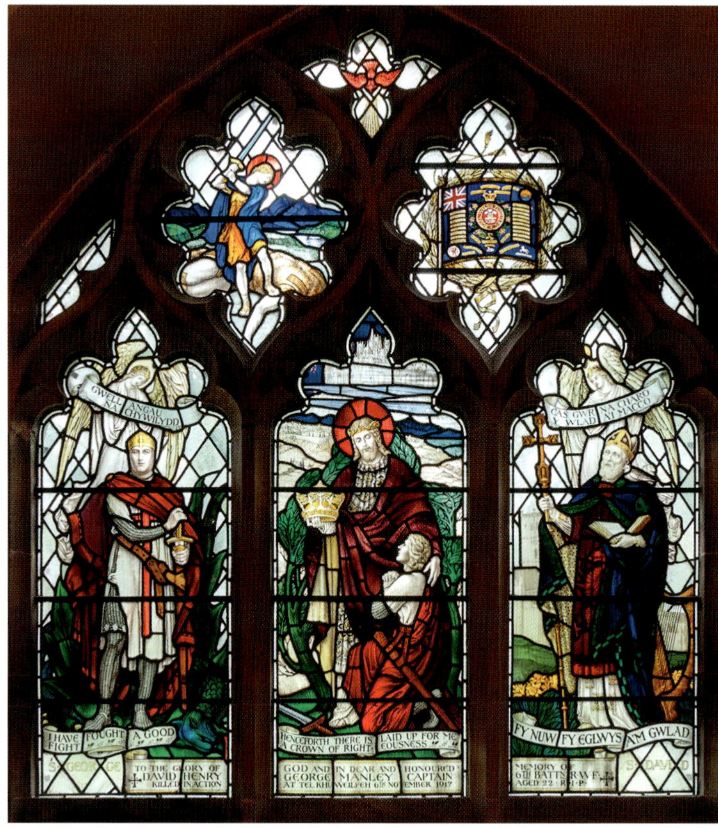

447–8. William Aikman, A Fallen Soldier with Christ and Angels (above); Receiving the Crown of Life with St George and St David (above right), *c.* 1918, Church of St Pedrog, Llanbedrog, nave

killed at Tel Khuweilfeh in Palestine, in 1917.[2] Aikman's windows also demonstrate different approaches for the two purposes, although it is the family war memorial that is more conventional. Manley is shown receiving the crown of life, this time from Christ himself, flanked by standing figures of the saints George and David. The name of the soldier is also reflected above with the depiction of the biblical David overcoming Goliath. The smaller window in the church was given by the rector in memory of the men of the parish 'who made the supreme sacrifice'. A ghostly figure of Christ looks on as an angel lifts a fallen soldier, the leafless skeletons of trees forming a sombre and reflective backdrop to the scene, which shares none of the sumptuous display of the C.E. Kempe & Co. memorial window at Tenby.

Other war memorial windows by Kempe's firm make use of the romantic military imagery of soldier-saints.[3] At the Church of St Mary, Haverfordwest, George and Michael stand in armour over their vanquished dragons, with the English kings Oswald and Edmund in the

2 William Aikman set up his own studio in 1913, after a period as chief designer for James Powell & Sons.

3 C.E. Kempe died in 1907, and his firm continued as C.E. Kempe & Co. under the direction of his nephew Walter Tower.

outer lights. Among the firm's numerous windows at Monmouth, that commemorating the First World War depicts Oswald and Alban, the first British martyr who was usually depicted as a Roman soldier, together with the Old Testament warriors David and Joshua. David and Joshua are joined by two further soldier figures from the Old Testament, Jonathan and Gideon, in the large west window by Clayton & Bell made for the Church of St Augustine, Penarth, which commemorates two men from the same family who were killed in action in 1915 and 1918.

Other military saints were natural choices for war memorials, notably Martin. He is usually depicted as a Roman soldier or a medieval armoured knight, but is dressed as a royal figure and paired with George in Christopher Whall's window at the Church of St Peblig, Llanbeblig.[4] A set of six saints representing England, France and Belgium were made for three two-light windows in the south aisle at the Church of St Catherine, Canton, Cardiff. The windows were among eight windows, all made by Daniells & Fricker for the church between 1916 and 1920, five of which were war memorials. George and Alban were chosen to represent England, Louis of France and Joan of Arc for France, with the crusader Baldwin I of Jerusalem and the seventh-century missionary Amandus being chosen for Belgium. The windows are further distinguished by the small roundels of historic buildings representing each country beneath each figure.

4 Christopher Whall's image of George at Llanbeblig is a close copy of a painting by Andrea Mantegna of about 1460, now in the Gallerie dell'Accademia, Venice. Whall admired fifteenth-century Italian painting, as did members of the Pre-Raphaelite Brotherhood and Edward Burne-Jones. The figure of George by Mantegna was used by another studio for a war memorial window at Christ Church, Welshpool.

below, left to right:

449. C.E. Kempe & Co. St Edmund, 1919, Church of St Mary, Haverfordwest, west window

450. Christopher Whall, St George and St Martin, *c.* 1916, Church of St Peblig, Llanbeblig, nave

451. A.L. Moore & Son, St Martin, *c.* 1917, Church of St Cynllo, Llangynllo (Ceredigion), west window

452. Daniells & Fricker, King Baldwin I of Jerusalem, 1918, Church of St Catherine, Canton, Cardiff, nave

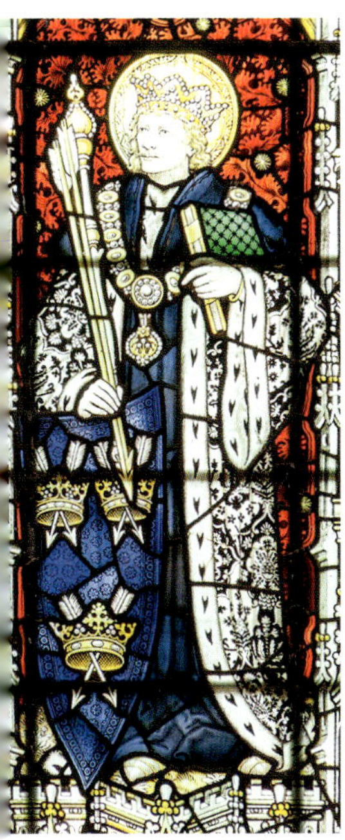

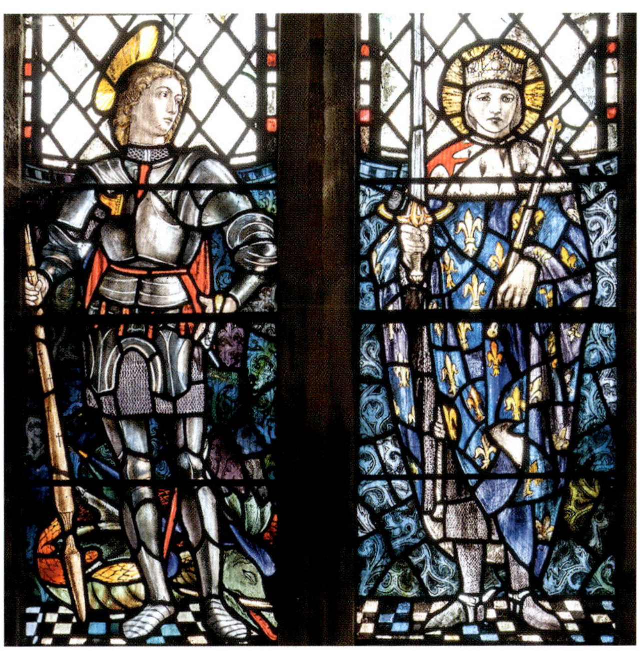

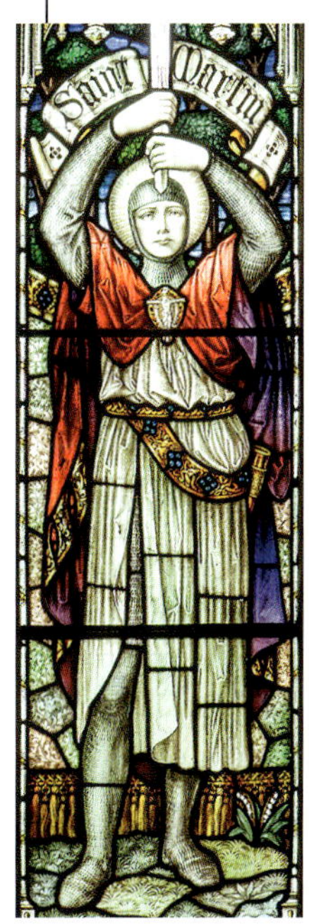

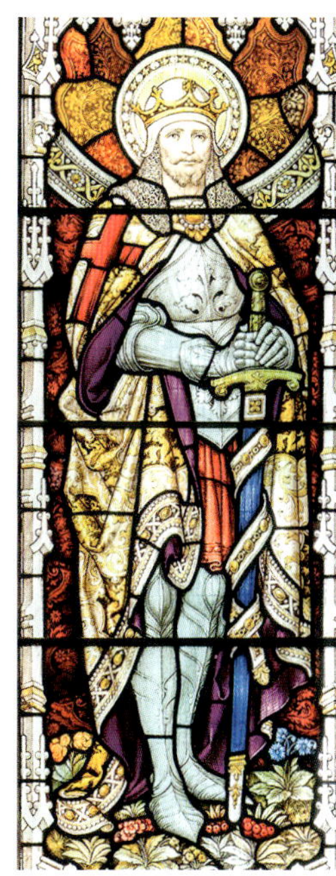

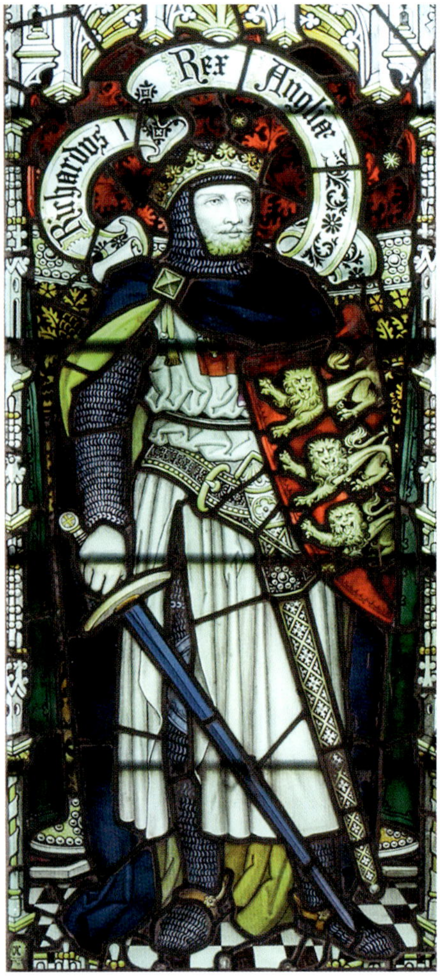

453. C.E. Kempe & Co., King Richard I, 1919, Church of St Michael, Pembroke, nave

454. N.D. Spooner, St George, 1923, Church of St David, Glanadda, Bangor, south chapel

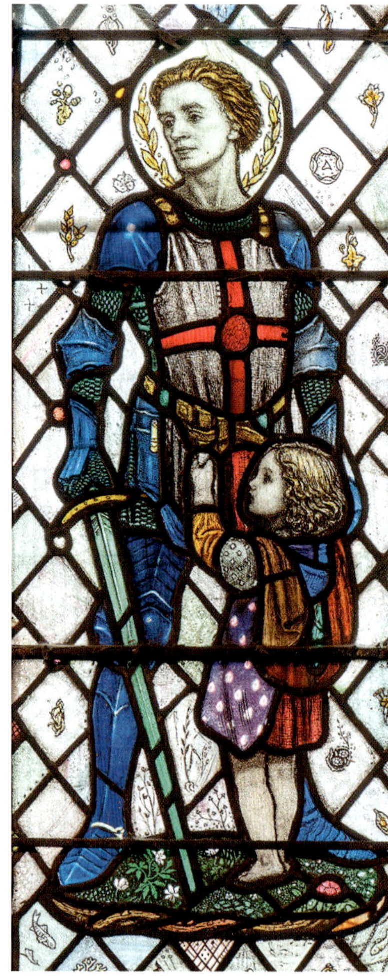

Of all of the military saints, George and the Archangel Michael are most common. Both are usually shown with the defeated dragon at their feet, symbolising the overcoming of evil. The well-known tradition of George slaying the dragon had been popular in England since the twelfth century, and the patron saint of England was also regarded as a suitable national figure across Wales. The choice of David as a national figure representing Wales is less common, although he is found paired with other English national figures including George, Alban, and, more unusually, with Richard the Lionheart at the Church of St Michael, Pembroke.[5] The two windows made for the east wall of the Lady Chapel of the Church of St David, Glanadda, Bangor, depict David and George, and in a rare piece of iconography George stands with a child at his side.

In three-light windows David is sometimes shown opposite George. They are placed at either side of the figure of Christ in the east window by Shrigley & Hunt at the Church of St Caron, Tregaron, and in the west windows of the nave at St Davids Cathedral, beneath archangels. Michael is the central figure between George and David at the Church of St Basil, Bassaleg, in a window distinguished by delicate glass painting, and possibly the work of a former pupil of C.E. Kempe, J.C.N. Bewsey.[6] George and David appear at either side of the soldier receiving the crown of life in William Aikman's window at Llanbedrog, and elsewhere at the Church of Illtud, Gwynno and Dyfodwg, Llantrisant, in a window by Robert Newbery. George and David also stand at each side of the crucified Christ in the war memorial window by Newbery made for the Church of St David, Ton Pentre, and the crucified Christ with the kneeling armoured knight was also used by the firm at Bishopston,

5 The window commemorates Frederick James Mansel Bryant, of the fourth Welsh Regiment, who was killed in action in Palestine during 1917, where Richard I had fought during the Third Crusade.

6 I am grateful to Alan Brooks for help with attributing this window. A further signed window by J.C.N. Bewsey can be found at the Church of St Mary and St Nicholas, Beaumaris. The trio of Michael with David and George seems to be intended in a window by Morris & Co. at the Church of St Maelog, Llandyfaelog, although the figure that stands under the name David is a medieval soldier with sword and shield, with no iconographic connection to David.

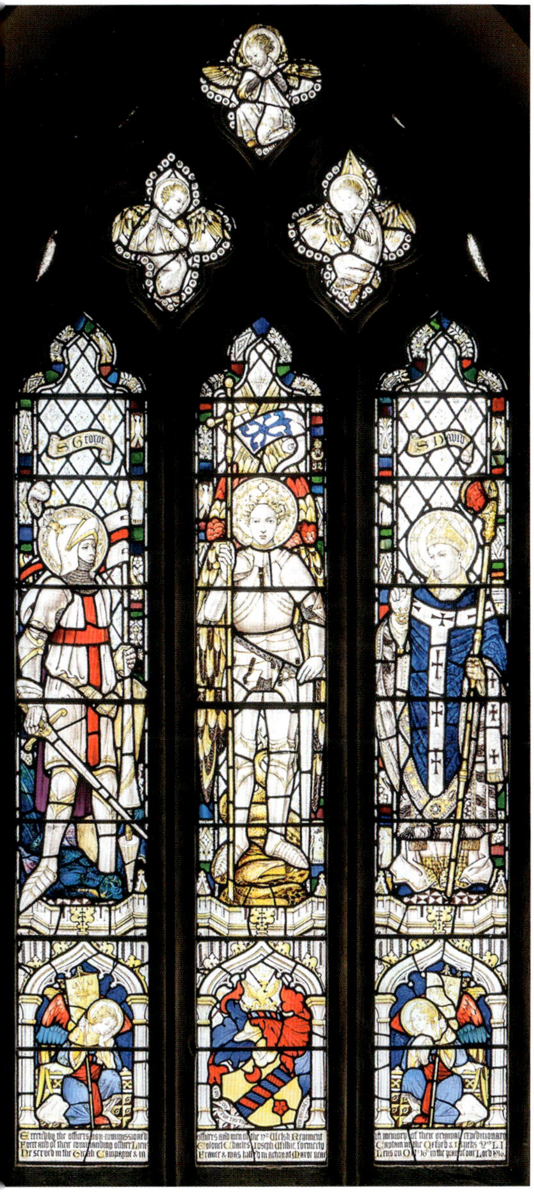

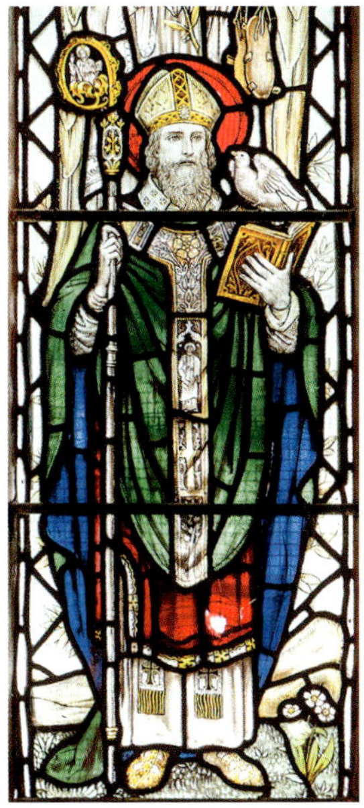

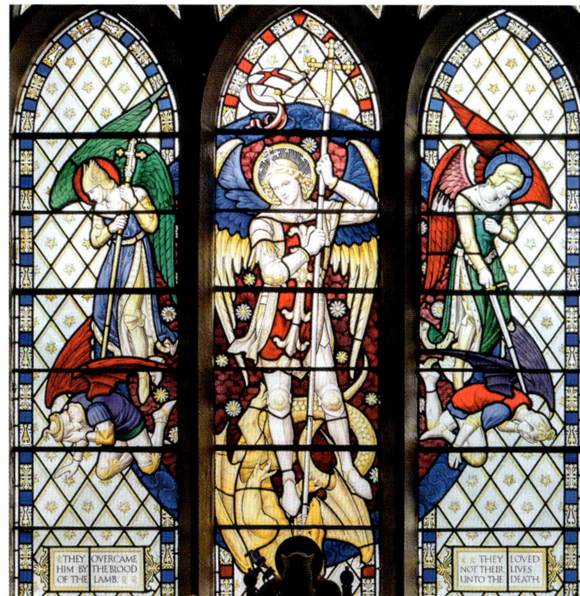

455. (left) Possibly J.C.N. Bewsey, St Michael with St George and St David, 1918, Church of St Basil, Bassaleg, north aisle

456. (above left) James Powell & Sons, St David, 1919, Church of St Cawrdaf, Llangoed, east window

457. (above) Christopher Webb, St Michael Fighting the Dragon, 1923, Church of the Holy Trinity, Esclusham, south transept

where David is paired with the patron of the church, Teilo.[7] It is more unusual to find David as the central figure, as at the Church of St Illtyd, Llantwit Fardre, where he is depicted between the soldier-saints Illtud and Martin in a window by G.A. Rowson of Shrewsbury, or at Llangoed on Anglesey, with the Old Testament judges Joshua and Gideon.[8]

The Archangel Michael's association with the dragon is a reference to Revelation 12, in which he and his angels fight against the dragon, 'that ancient serpent, who is called the Devil and Satan' (Revelation 12: 9). Although the passage makes it clear that the dragon is defeated, he is thrown to earth and continues to fight there, so the figure of Michael overcoming, but not killing, the dragon is a reminder that good will triumph over evil.[9] In some cases the dragon is more anthropomorphic. At the Church of St Mary, Fishguard, the figure of Michael, as 'Justitia' (Justice), stands with the sword and scales of justice, while at his feet a bearded figure clings wearily to a cliff edge, the other hand clasping

7 The window at Ton Pentre is now at the Church of St John the Baptist, in the parish of Ystradyfodwg. I am grateful to Susan Jenkins for information on this and other windows at Ton Pentre.

8 Further English saints were also chosen for war memorials. Alban is paired with Chad in a window at the Church of St Isan, Llanishen (Cardiff), where four war memorial windows are all by different makers. At Manorbier a window commissioned by two Red Cross men who returned from service in France and Italy depicts Alfred the Great and Hugh Paganis (Hugh de Payns), first superior of the Knights Templar.

9 For the imagery associated with this theme see 'The Victory of Good Over Evil: St Michael the Archangel', in Martin Crampin and John Morgan-Guy, *Imaging the Bible in Wales* (DVD-ROM) (Sheffield: Sheffield Phoenix Press, 2010).

458. (right) Morris & Co., St Michael and Fortitude, 1920, designed by Henry Dearle, Church of St Gwenfaen, Rhoscolyn, nave

459. (far right) James Powell & Sons, 'Justitia' (St Michael), 1920, Church of St Mary, Fishguard, nave

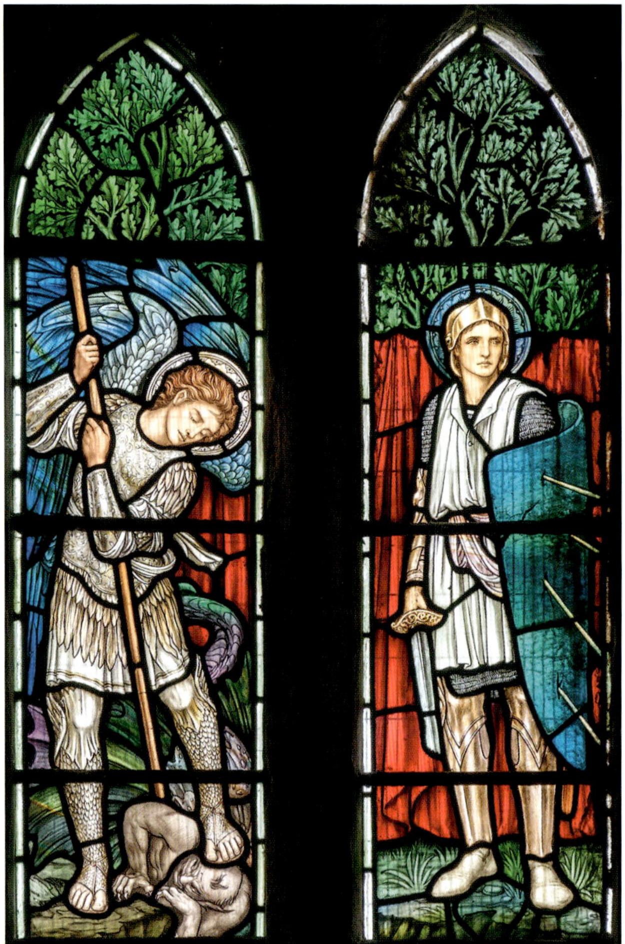

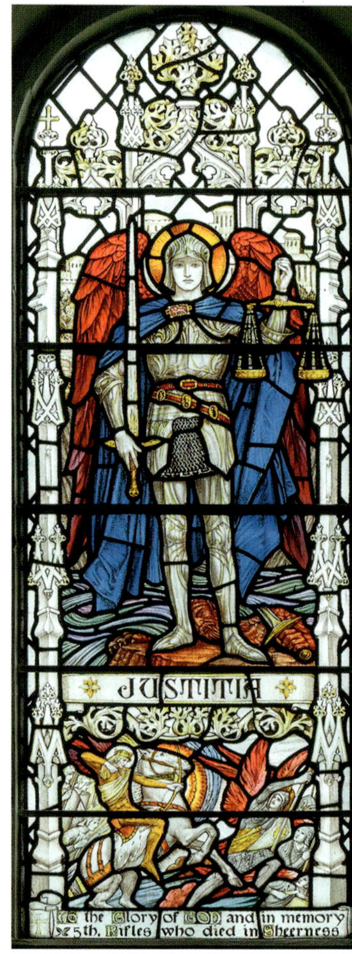

the hilt of a broken sword. The scene below depicts war in heaven and the rider on the white horse described in Revelation 19: 11. The other light depicts George, but represents 'Fortitudo' (Fortitude), and George is shown below contending with a scaly purple dragon. Two war memorial windows by Morris & Co. for churches on Anglesey draw upon Guido Reni's painting of Michael overcoming Satan of 1636 in a design by Henry Dearle. Hardly a Pre-Raphaelite image, Satan's very human torso is winged with a dark tail snaking into the brooding background. At Holyhead, the figure is flanked by two musical angels from designs by Edward Burne-Jones, while nearby at Rhoscolyn the same design of Michael overcoming Satan is reversed and, as at Fishguard, paired with a figure representing Fortitude.[10] The depiction of Michael recalls the figure in the left-hand light of Karl Parsons' Henderson memorial at Tenby, who stands holding a broken sword and a shield to repel the 'fiery darts', a reference to Paul's description of the armour of God in his letter to the Ephesians (6: 16).

10 Another war memorial by Morris & Co. at Rhoscolyn depicts standing figures of George and Michael with figures originally designed by Edward Burne-Jones.

11 The figure of Christ as the Prince of Peace is a reminder that many of these public memorials, in stained glass and in other media, were intended to commemorate the coming of peace at the end of the First World War, rather than the war itself. A further three-light window above the entrance of the chapel was given in memory of a single soldier, William Henry Seager, Second Lieutenant of the Tenth South Wales Borderers.

12 The main figure at Rhuddlan was also used at the Church of St James, Churchill, Worcestershire, in about 1920. The image is surely influenced by *The Attainment: the Vision of the Holy Grail to Sir Galahad, Sir Bors and Sir Percival*, from the Grail tapestry designed by Edward Burne-Jones and first made by Morris & Co. between 1891 and 1894. The imagery of the grail legends for war memorial windows is discussed in 'The Victory of Good Over Evil: The Christian Warrior', in Martin Crampin and John Morgan-Guy, *Imaging the Bible in Wales* (DVD-ROM) (Sheffield: Sheffield Phoenix Press, 2010). The scene was also depicted by the larger firms, such as that across four lights by Clayton & Bell at the Church of St Isan, Llanishen (Cardiff).

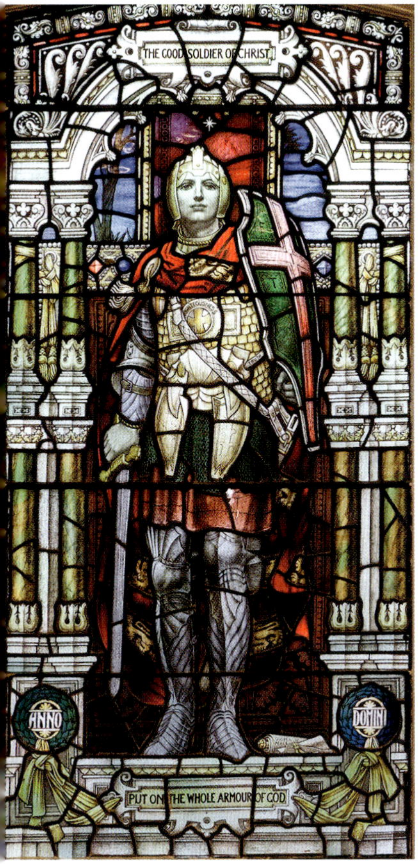

460. Possibly H.J. Salisbury, 'The Good Soldier of Christ', probably 1920s, Conway Road Methodist Church, Canton, Cardiff, vestibule

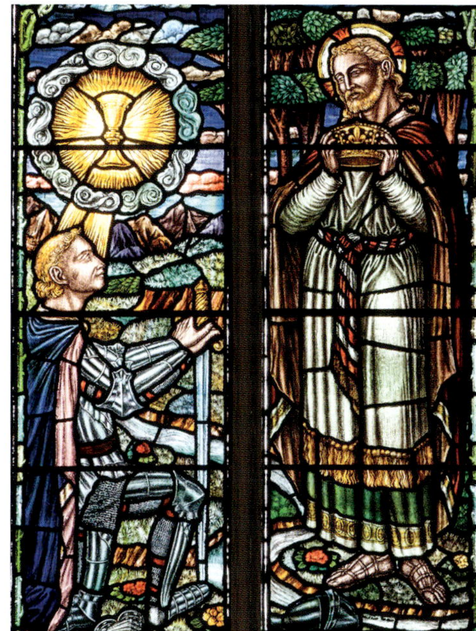

461. Camm & Co., Receiving the Crown of Life, 1922, Tabernacl Independent Chapel, Morriston, front wall (gallery)

The theme of the armour of God is taken up explicitly in a window at Conway Road Wesleyan Methodist Church in Canton, Cardiff. The figure, one of a pair with the figure of Christ as the Prince of Peace, depicts an armoured figure with each item from Paul's description of the armour of God labelled.[11] Another example of the theme in a Welsh chapel is that by Camm & Co. at Tabernacl, Morriston, where a medieval knight is being armed by a woman with the text 'Gwisgwch holl arfogaeth Duw' (Put on the whole armour of God, Ephesians 6: 11). The Arthurian strain of the chivalric knight is clearly implied in the two windows at Tabernacl, and runs through many war memorials in which so many of the military figures are depicted in medieval armour. The partner window depicts a knight receiving the crown of life from Christ, with the light of the Holy Grail shining on him from above.

The imagery of the grail is prominent in war memorial windows by A.J. Davies, such as his memorial at Rhuddlan to Geoffrey Seymour Rowley Conwy, who was killed in action at Gallipoli. Here a young man in armour kneels at an altar before a depiction of Christ as Light of the World, while the chalice is shown above. Davies made other versions of the scene, suggestive of Galahad's quest for the Holy Grail, including a two-light window at the Church of St Margaret, Mountain Ash, which, although not a First World War memorial, commemorated a Colonel in the Fifth Welsh Regiment.[12] A further window by Davies at the Church of St Teilo, Merthyr Mawr, depicts a kneeling soldier receiving the chalice from Paulinus. In this window the medievalism is interrupted by the soldier being depicted in modern dress, a significant departure as the window is not a memorial to a fallen soldier, but a thanksgiving for his return.

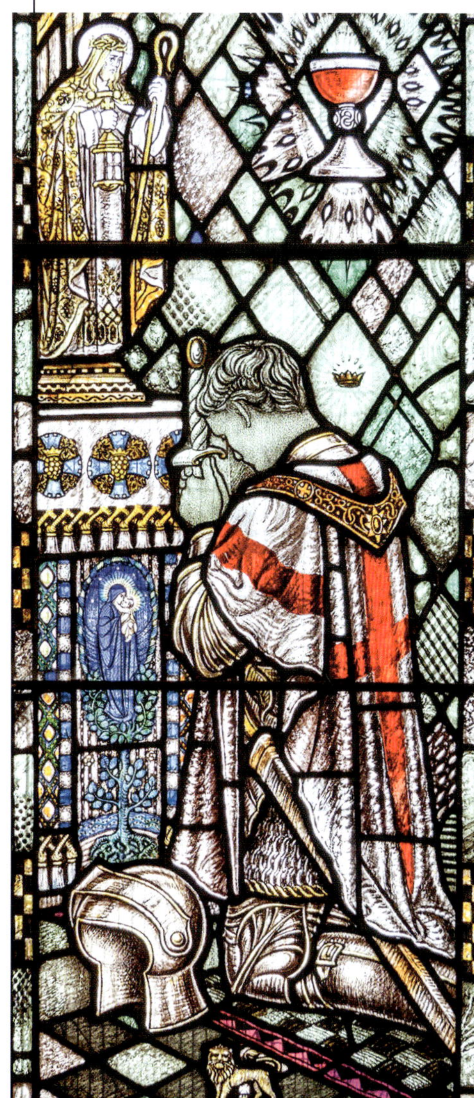

462. A.J. Davies, Sir Galahad, 1919, Church of St Mary, Rhuddlan, chancel

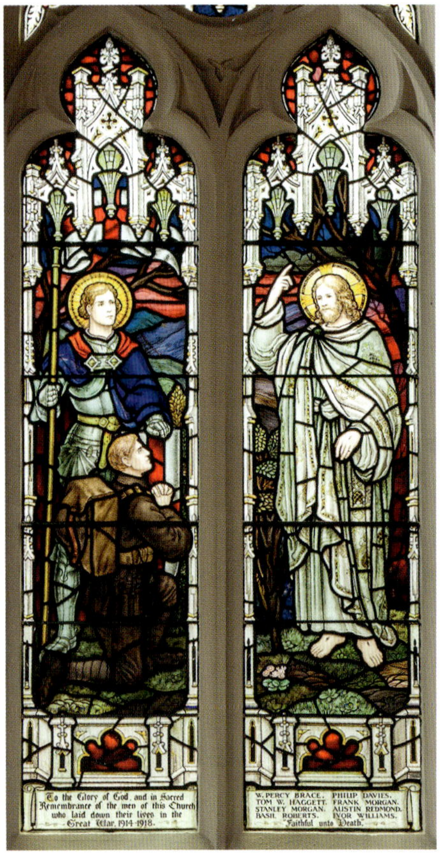

463. W. Pearce & E. Cutler, A Soldier Presented to Christ by St George, *c.* 1920, former Llanthewy Road Baptist Church, Newport, side wall

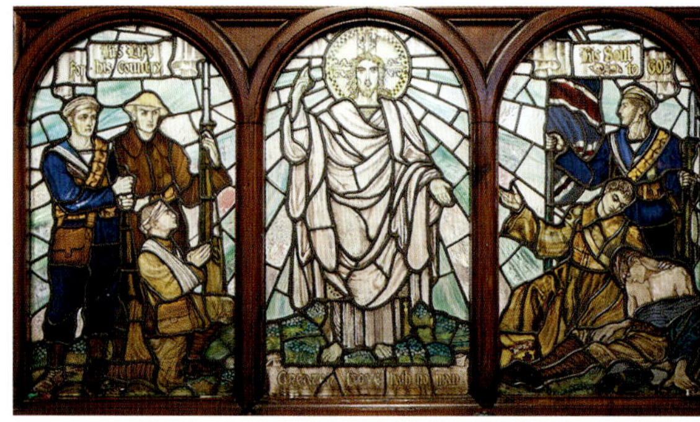

464. Christ with Servicemen, *c.* 1920, Tabernacle Congregational Church, Haverfordwest, vestibule

The depiction of soldiers in contemporary dress is found in other war memorial windows. A single soldier is shown kneeling before the risen Christ at Llanthewy Road Baptist Church, Newport, his contemporary uniform contrasting with the standing figure behind him of George, who is dressed in medieval armour and a cloak. At the Church of St Peter, Carmarthen, the lower portion of a memorial window includes a roundel with a portrait of the dead soldier drawn from a recent photograph in military uniform, beneath the heavily armoured allegorical figures of Courage and Victory.[13]

Unusually, standing figures representing servicemen from Canada, Australia and South Africa form the principal imagery of a war memorial window by Jones & Willis at the Church of the Holy Trinity, Llandrindod Wells, but servicemen, and occasionally women, are more common as supporting figures. Members of the armed forces are shown at either side of the figure of Christ in the foyer window of Tabernacle English Congregational Church, Haverfordwest, and two further war memorial windows by Burlison & Grylls, also in Pembrokeshire, depict soldiers in contemporary uniform. At the Church of St Mary, Fishguard, servicemen and a female nurse are shown surrounding the risen Christ in a lower panel of a window depicting Cecilia with Anne teaching the Virgin Mary to read.[14] The dull brown colouring of this window contrasts with a much brighter work by the firm, probably designed by Harry Grylls, at Manorbier. Here a nurse once again joins servicemen in uniform flanking a Crucifixion scene with Mary and John in the lower part of the window, below standing figures of the crusader, John de Barri, and a contemporary soldier of the Holy Land Expeditionary Force, at either side of the risen Christ.

A large war memorial by the same firm fills the five-light east window of the Church of St Paul, Grangetown. A Crucifixion scene occupies the main part of the three central lights, with saints in the outer lights, but at the base of the window, flanking the dedication, are four war scenes.

13 Paul Chancourt Girardot of the 52nd Oxfordshire and Buckinghamshire Light Infantry, who died aged 18, the only son of the widow Mary Girardot of Trevaughan, Carmarthen. This was not the only window dedicated to him and he is also depicted kneeling in a window by Burlison & Grylls at the Church of the Holy Trinity, Kensington.

14 The window commemorates two sons of Sir Evan Davies Jones who were killed in the war, as well as their mother, the donor's wife, Cecilia.

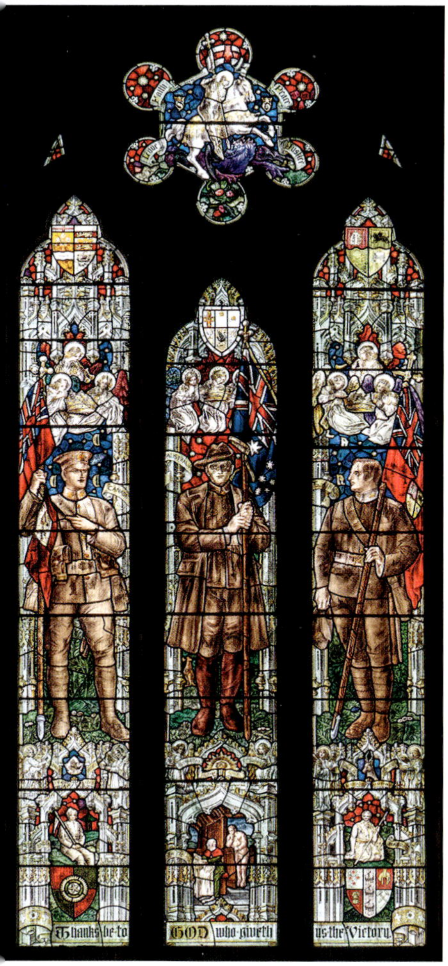

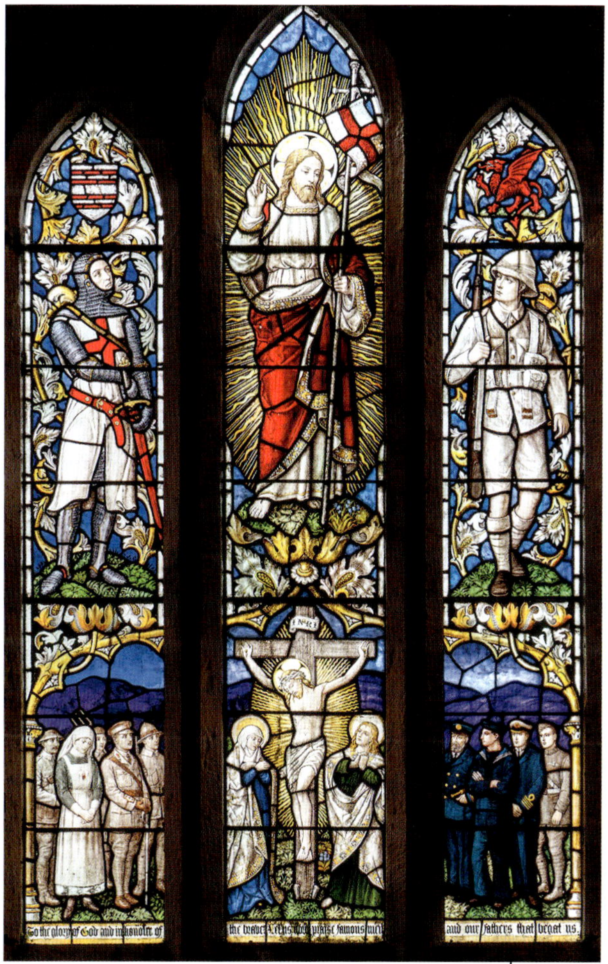

465. (far left) Jones & Willis, First World War Servicemen, *c.* 1920, Church of the Holy Trinity, Llandrindod Wells, west window

466. (left) Burlison & Grylls, The Risen Christ with Soldiers, 1918, probably designed by Harry Grylls, Church of St James, Manorbier, west window

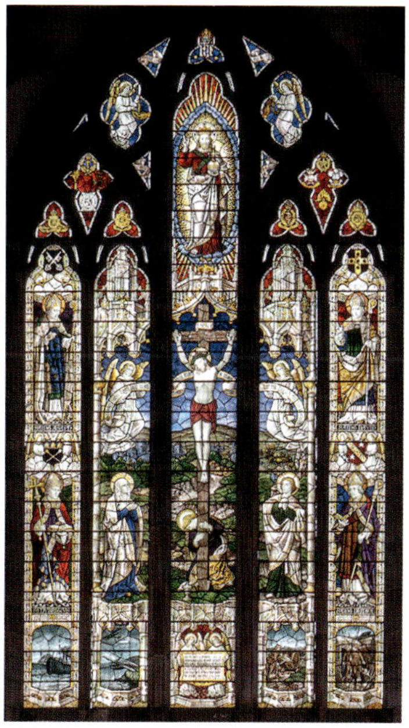

A seascape with warships, early aircraft over the coast, and two army scenes are rare glimpses in ecclesiastical stained glass of the war itself. Depicted in restrained blues, greens and browns, and not easily appreciated from the main body of the large church, these war scenes contrast with the romanticised knights in armour so often used to represent the fallen members of the armed forces.

467–8. Burlison & Grylls, The Crucifixion with the Virgin Mary, St John, St Mary Magdalene and Saints, including scenes from the First World War (below), 1920, Church of St Paul, Grangetown, Cardiff, east window

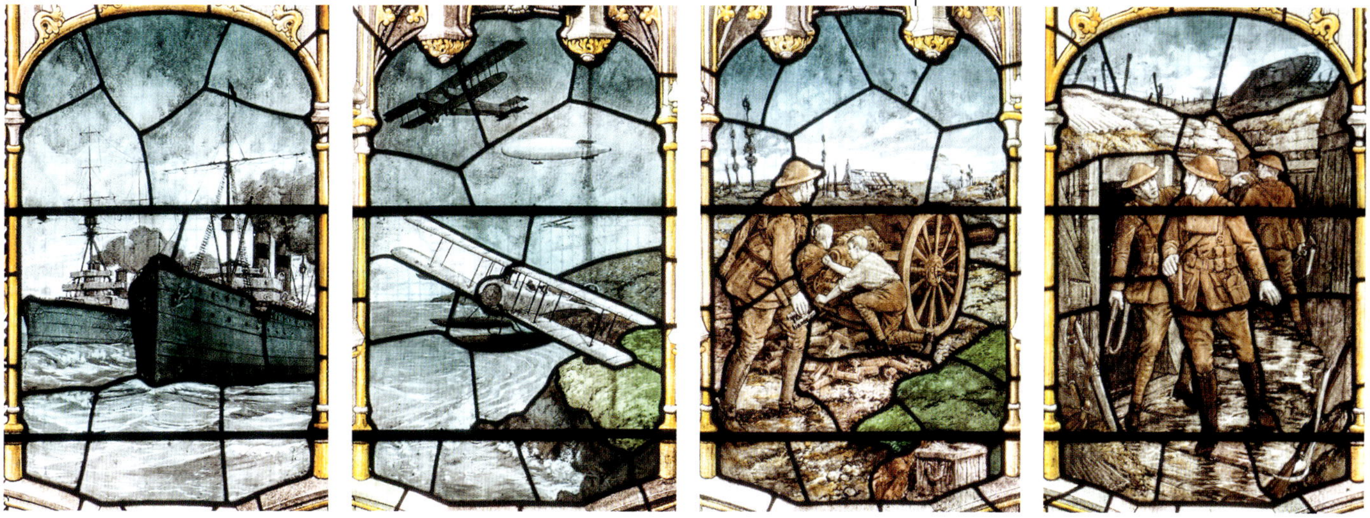

15 Edward Frampton's design for the window is dated 16 April 1919, and survives with the faculty papers. National Library of Wales, Records of the Church in Wales: Diocese of Swansea and Brecon, SD/F/123. The window shows considerable stylistic development from his more conventional Victorian Gothic Revival windows made for churches in north and south Wales around the turn of the century.

Soldiers on the battlefield are the main subject of a window by A.J. Davies at Christ Church, Rossett, and the three central lights of the war memorial at the Church of St Mary, Clydach, in which the Eucharist is being administered with a ruined town in the background.[15]

At the Church of St Margaret, Mountain Ash, a window by James Clark depicts a soldier lying dead on the battlefield with his hand resting on the feet of Christ, nailed to the cross, in the midst of the war scene. This window is a version of the popular painting by the same artist, *The Great Sacrifice*, which was painted in 1914. It became widely reproduced after its publication in *The Graphic*, and was adapted by other stained glass studios, such as Jones & Willis, J. Wippell & Co. and an unknown maker at the little church at Trellech Grange.

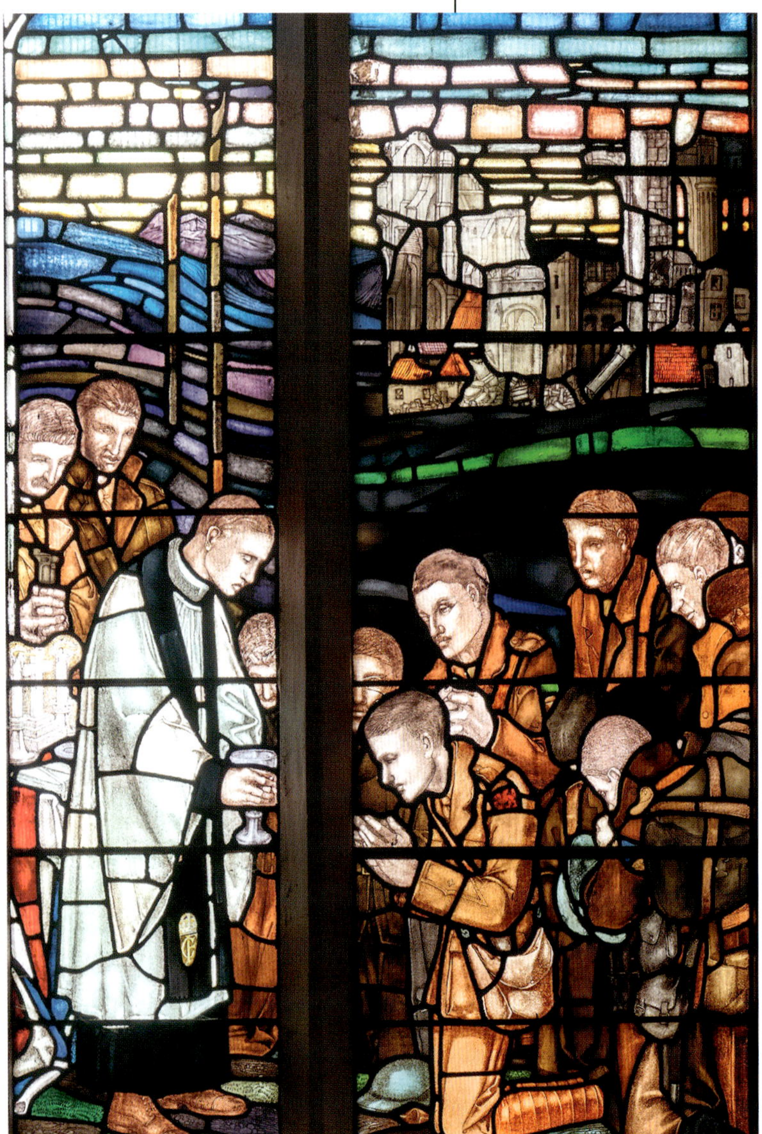

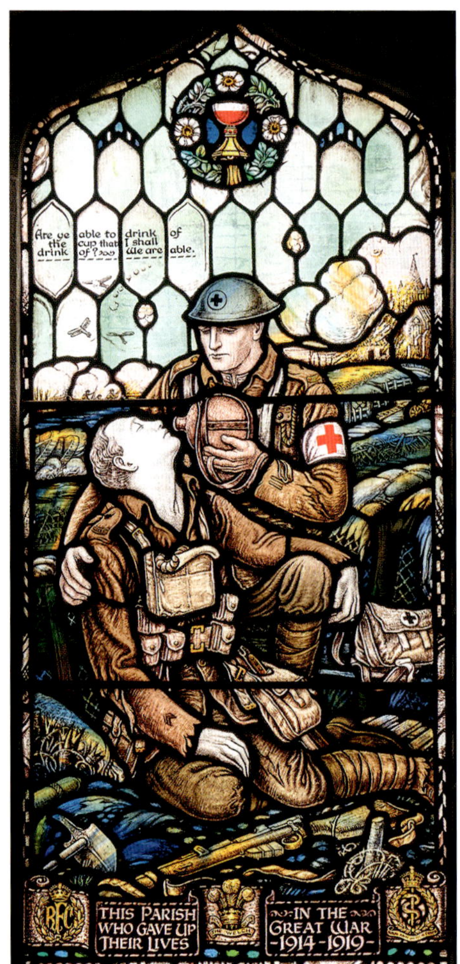

469. Edward Frampton, Soldiers Receiving the Eucharist on the Battlefield, 1919, Church of St Mary, Clydach, west window

470. A.J. Davies, A Wounded Soldier Tended by a Stretcher-Bearer, 1925, Christ Church, Rossett, north aisle

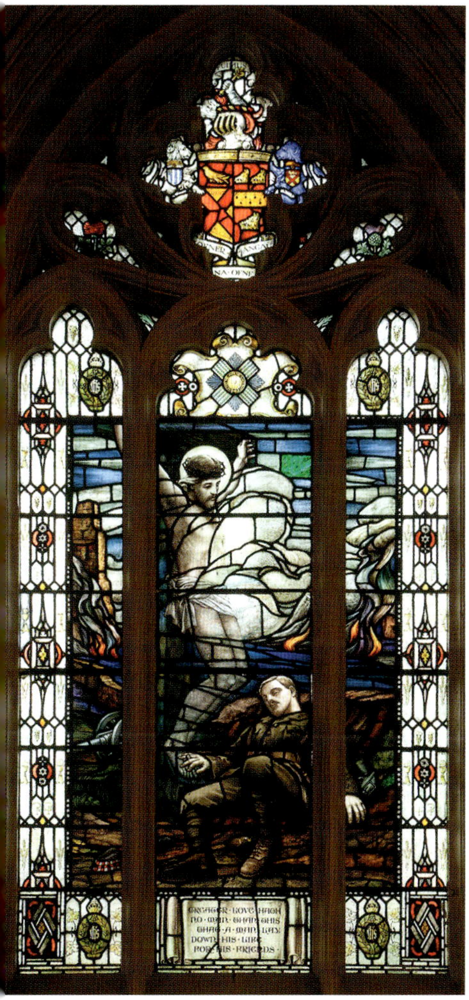

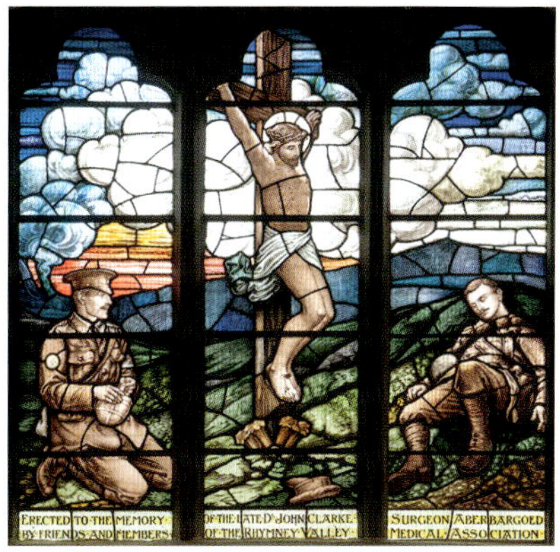

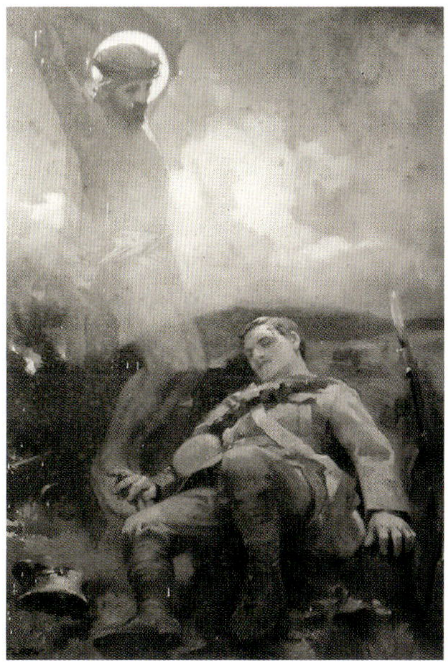

471. (far left) James Clark, *The Great Sacrifice*, Church of St Margaret, Mountain Ash, north aisle

472. (left) J. Wippell & Co., The Crucifixion with Soldiers, 1916, Church of St Sannan, Bedwellty, north aisle

473. (below left) James Clark, *The Great Sacrifice*, print reproduced in *The Graphic*, 1914

This close identification of the sacrifice of life by servicemen in the war for others, and that of Christ for all on the cross, is also made at the Church of St Mary, Spittal, in the east window by Mary Lowndes. Here the soldier being commemorated, Archibald Bellairs Higgon, a major in the Royal Field Artillery, is depicted being presented to Christ by an angel, and Christ is shown carrying the cross on the way to his Crucifixion. The biblical text, 'Greater Love hath no man than this, that a man lay down his life for his friend' (John 15: 13) affirms that Major Higgon has also laid down his life for his friends, following Christ's example.[16] A wounded man is also presented to Christ on the cross by an angel in one of a pair of lights made for Broadway Methodist Church in Cardiff, and paired with a drowning sailor reaching up to Christ who walks on the water.[17] The allusion to the suffering of Christ on the cross and the overwhelming grief of the loss of a son is central to a war memorial window by Christopher

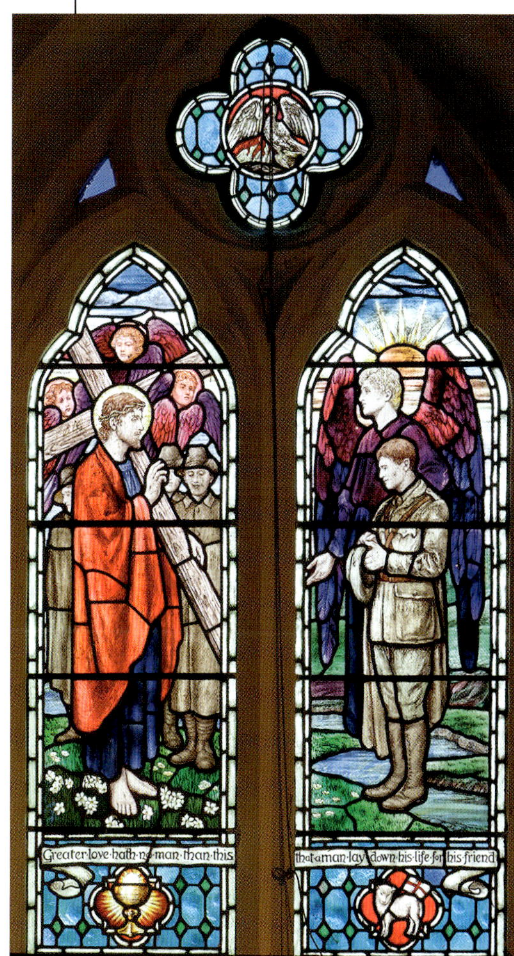

474. Mary Lowndes, An Angel Presenting a Fallen Soldier to the Risen Christ, 1920, Church of St Mary, Spittal, east window

16 The identification of the sacrifice of servicemen with that of Christ's unique giving of his life for all on the cross is theologically problematic, as explored in 'The Victory of Good Over Evil: A Crown of Life', in Martin Crampin and John Morgan-Guy, *Imaging the Bible in Wales* (DVD-ROM) (Sheffield: Sheffield Phoenix Press, 2010). John Morgan-Guy has also pointed out that the window has several references to the hymn by Charles Wesley that begins 'Let saints on earth in concert sing | With those whose work is done'.

17 The war memorial window was moved to the nearby Trinity Methodist Church in 1950.

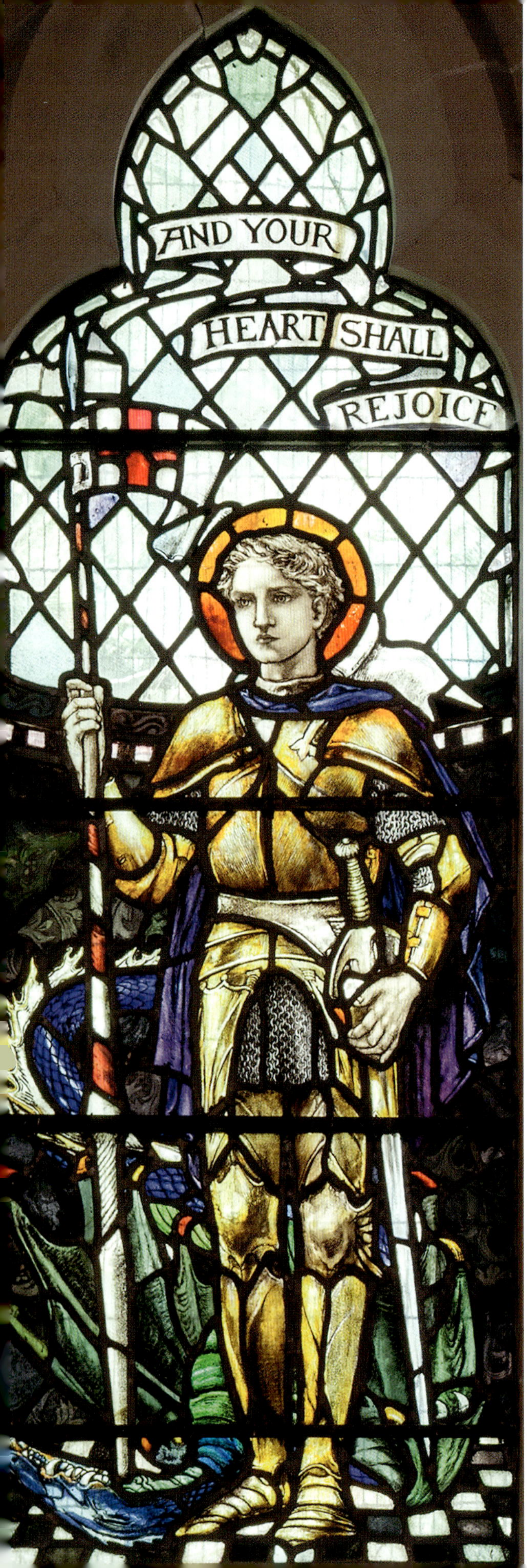

475. Christopher Whall, St George, c. 1915, Church of All Saints, Glasbury, nave

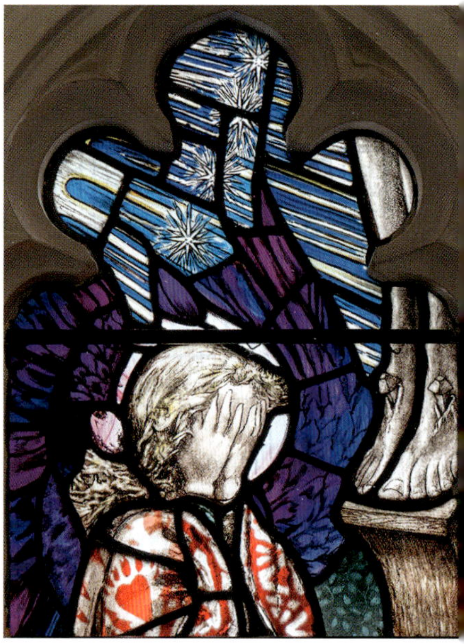

476. Christopher Whall, Angel at the Foot of the Cross, Church of St John the Baptist, Cardiff, south wall

Whall for the Church of St John the Baptist, Cardiff. Devoid of any military imagery, five angels are depicted in this small three-light window, one of whom kneels distraught at the foot of the cross, with only Christ's nailed feet visible at the right of the window.

The biblical texts accompanying the memorials also look forward to the resurrection of the soldiers who fell in the war. The wistful depiction of Michael and George as youths in Christopher Whall's window at the Church of All Saints, Glasbury, is a memorial to Walter de Winton, who was only 22. The text 'I will see you again, and your heart shall rejoice' is from Christ's promise to his disciples after the Last Supper, recorded in John 16: 22, assuring them that they would meet him again after his sacrifice and resurrection. The hope of resurrection is also claimed in a war memorial window at Heol Awst Independent Chapel, Carmarthen, where the text 'Atgyfodir dy frawd drachefn' [your brother will rise again] quotes Christ's words to Martha from John 11: 23.

The text most frequently called upon in commemorating the war dead is Revelation 2: 10: 'be thou faithful unto death, and I will give thee a crown of life.' At the Church of St Teilo, Llandeilo, the text is at the centre of a five-light window, in the east wall of the chancel, beneath a motley band of military biblical characters and saints.[18] The crown of life imagery was used in the

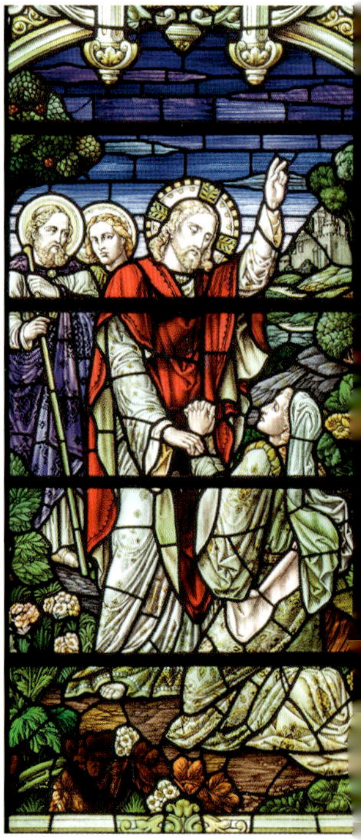

477. Abbott & Co. Ltd, 'Atgyfodir dy Frawd Drachefn', 1922, Heol Awst, Carmarthen, front wall

war memorial window by Robert Newbery at Llantrisant, and the same figure of the kneeling knight receiving the crown of life from Christ is also found at the Church of St Paul, Cwm (near Ebbw Vale). Some windows depict Christ alone holding the crown of life, such as one of the war memorials by Daniells & Fricker in the north aisle chapel of the Church of St Catherine, Canton, Cardiff. Another window by Newbery, commissioned as late as 1932, for the Church of St Dennis, Llanishen (Monmouthshire), adds David in the accompanying light with the text from Revelation running beneath both figures. Further windows by Daniells & Fricker show young men in armour receiving the crown of life from Christ, such as at the Church of St Mary, Aberafan, where the scene is accompanied by saints and angels in the busy four-light west window, and at the former Welsh Independent Chapel, Ebenezer, in central Cardiff.

18 The window at Llandeilo is a compendium of themes used on war memorial windows, including the crown of life in the apex of the window, above the archangels Michael and Gabriel, soldier-saints and military biblical characters, scenes of the Crucifixion and Resurrection of Christ, and biblical scenes representing courage, justice, mercy and peace beneath the saints Nicholas, David, Teilo and Leonard.

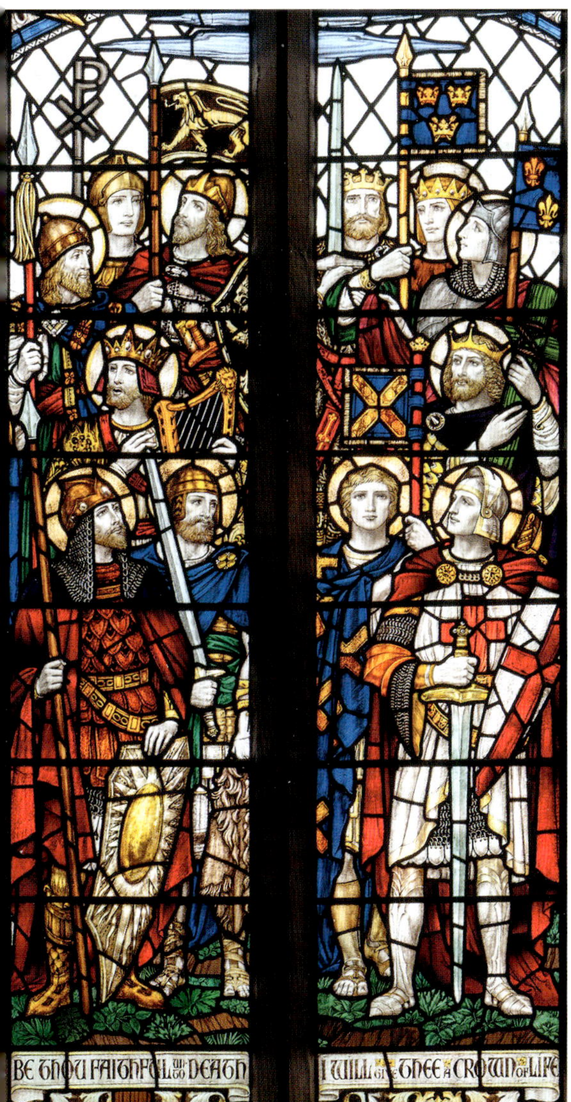

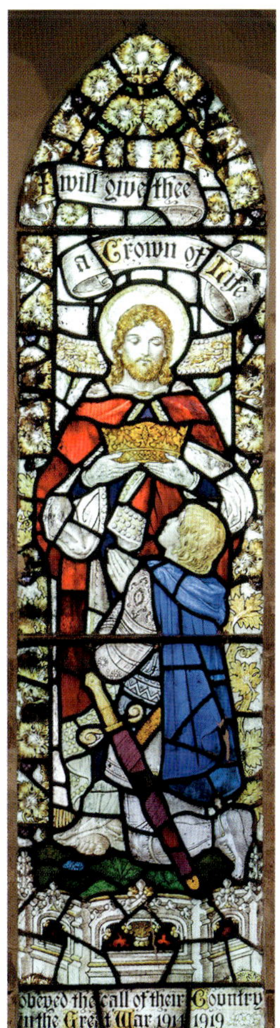

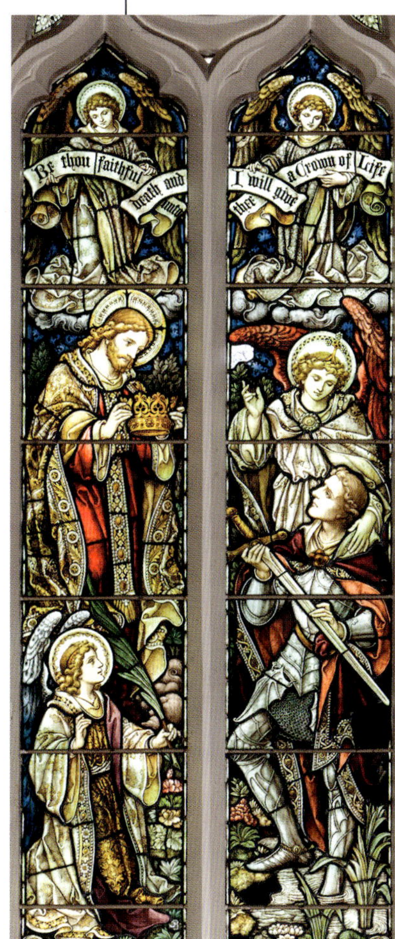

478. (left) James Powell & Sons, Military Biblical Characters and Saints, 1921, Church of St Teilo, Llandeilo, east window

479. (centre left) Robert Newbery, Receiving the Crown of Life, *c.* 1919, Church of St Paul, Cwm, north aisle

480. (left) Daniells & Fricker, Receiving the Crown of Life, *c.* 1920, former Ebenezer Independent Chapel, Cardiff, side wall

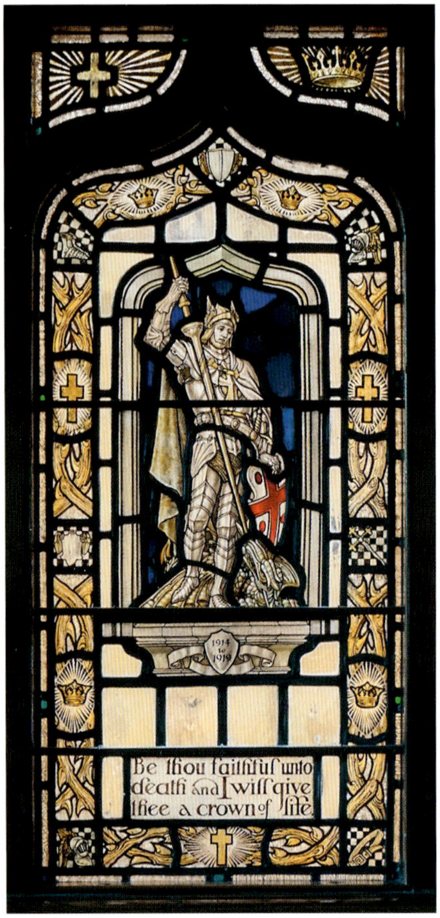

481. T.W. Camm & Co., St George and the Dragon, *c.* 1920, designed by Robert Camm, Tabernacle Baptist Church, Carmarthen, vestibule

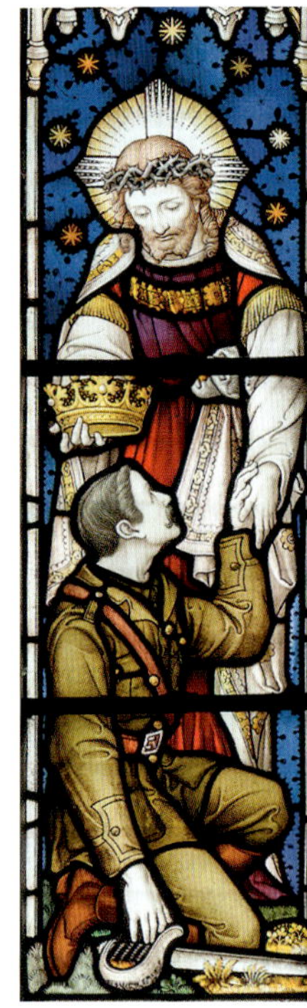

483. Clayton & Bell, Receiving the Crown of Life, *c.* 1916, Church of St Mary, Magor, south aisle

A window by T.W. Camm & Co. at Tabernacle Welsh Baptist Church, Carmarthen, also uses the text from Revelation but places it beneath an image of George slaying the dragon, at the centre of the window between conventional images of Christ as the Light of the World (also derived from the Book of Revelation) and as the Good Shepherd.

The text is also found on memorial windows not associated with the war, and in other memorials the crown of life is sometimes depicted although the text is not quoted. For example the crown of life being presented in the Henderson memorial at Tenby by Karl Parsons shows the soldier receiving the crown of life, although the text accompanying it is from the parable of the talents: ‘Well done thou good and faithful servant ... enter thou into the joy of thy Lord’ (Matthew 25: 21 and 23). In another example, only the first half of the verse from Revelation is used in a window by Clayton & Bell at the Church of St Mary, Magor, in which a soldier in contemporary uniform receives the crown of life from Christ, between the figures of Michael and George.

Some war memorial windows depict biblical scenes. Among those by Daniells & Fricker at Canton is a scene of the mourning over the dead Christ, identifying the sacrifice of those in war with Christ’s own sacrifice. The upper three-light window at Conway Road Methodist Church comprises three main scenes representing the Resurrection, affirming the hope of new life after death. In a window by Henry Holiday for the Church of St John the Baptist, Newton Nottage, a war scene is imaged indirectly through the depiction of the burning of Jerusalem (2 Kings 25: 8–9) in commemoration of the burning of Ypres. Some prominent east windows depicting the Crucifixion were installed as war memorial windows, such as the five-light windows by Burlison & Grylls at Grangetown, and by C.E Kempe & Co. at the Church of St Andrew and St Teilo, also in Cardiff. At the Church of St Mary and St Nicholas, Beaumaris, the bright and assured Crucifixion scene in a sixteenth-century Flemish style by Clayton & Bell was given by Sir Richard and Lady Magdalen Williams-Bulkeley, in memory of their only son who was killed in 1916.

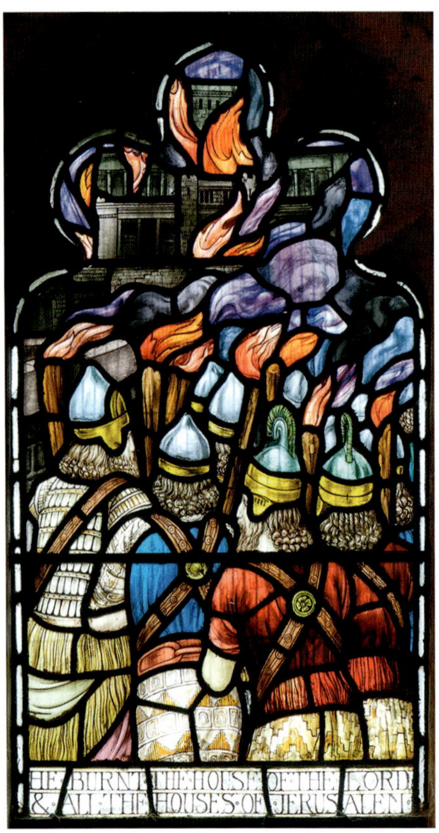

482. Henry Holiday, The Burning of Jerusalem, *c.* 1919, Church of St John the Baptist, Newton Nottage, nave

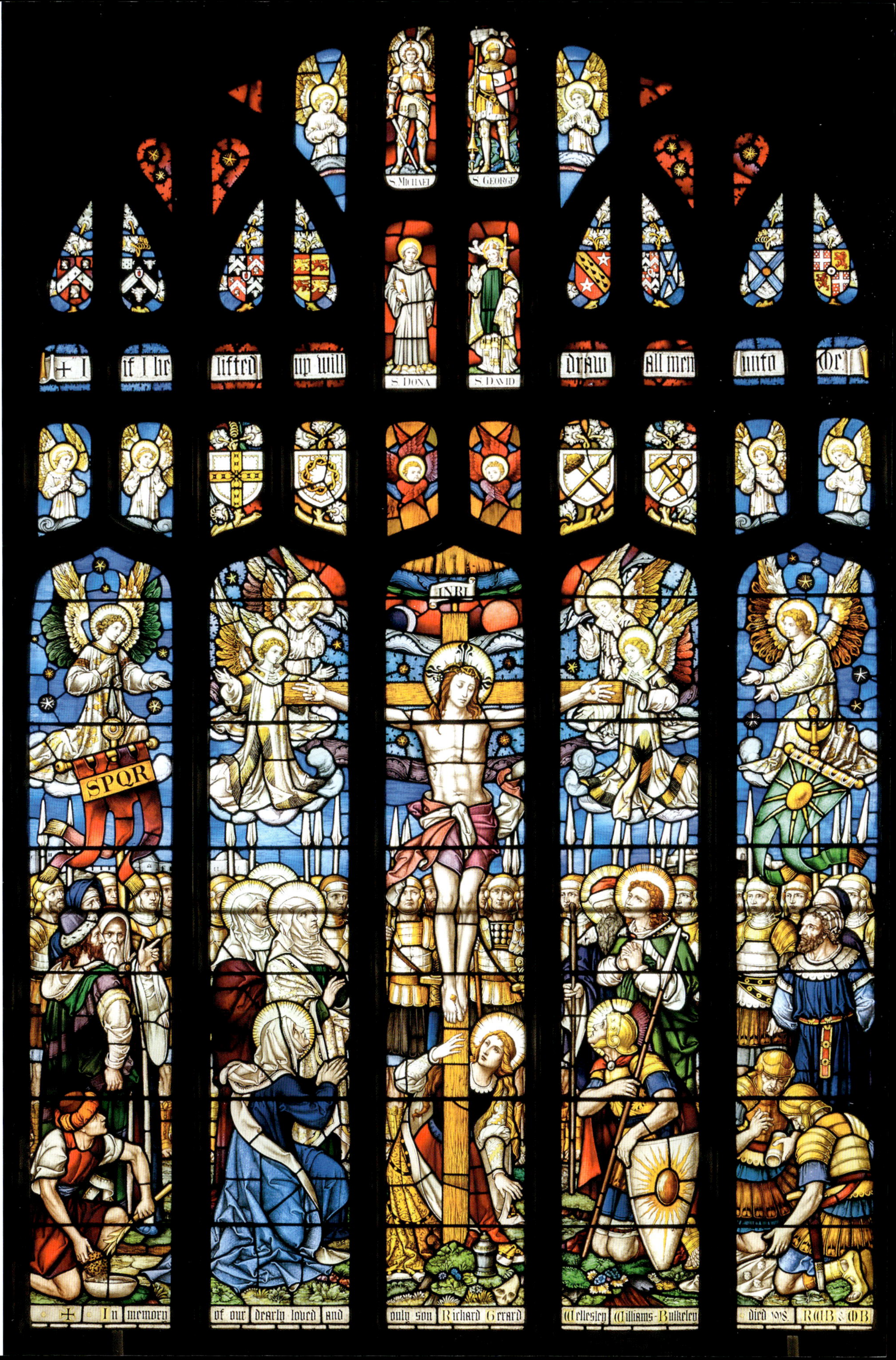

84. Clayton & Bell,
e Crucifixion, 1921,
Church of St Mary
and St Nicholas,
Beaumaris,
east window

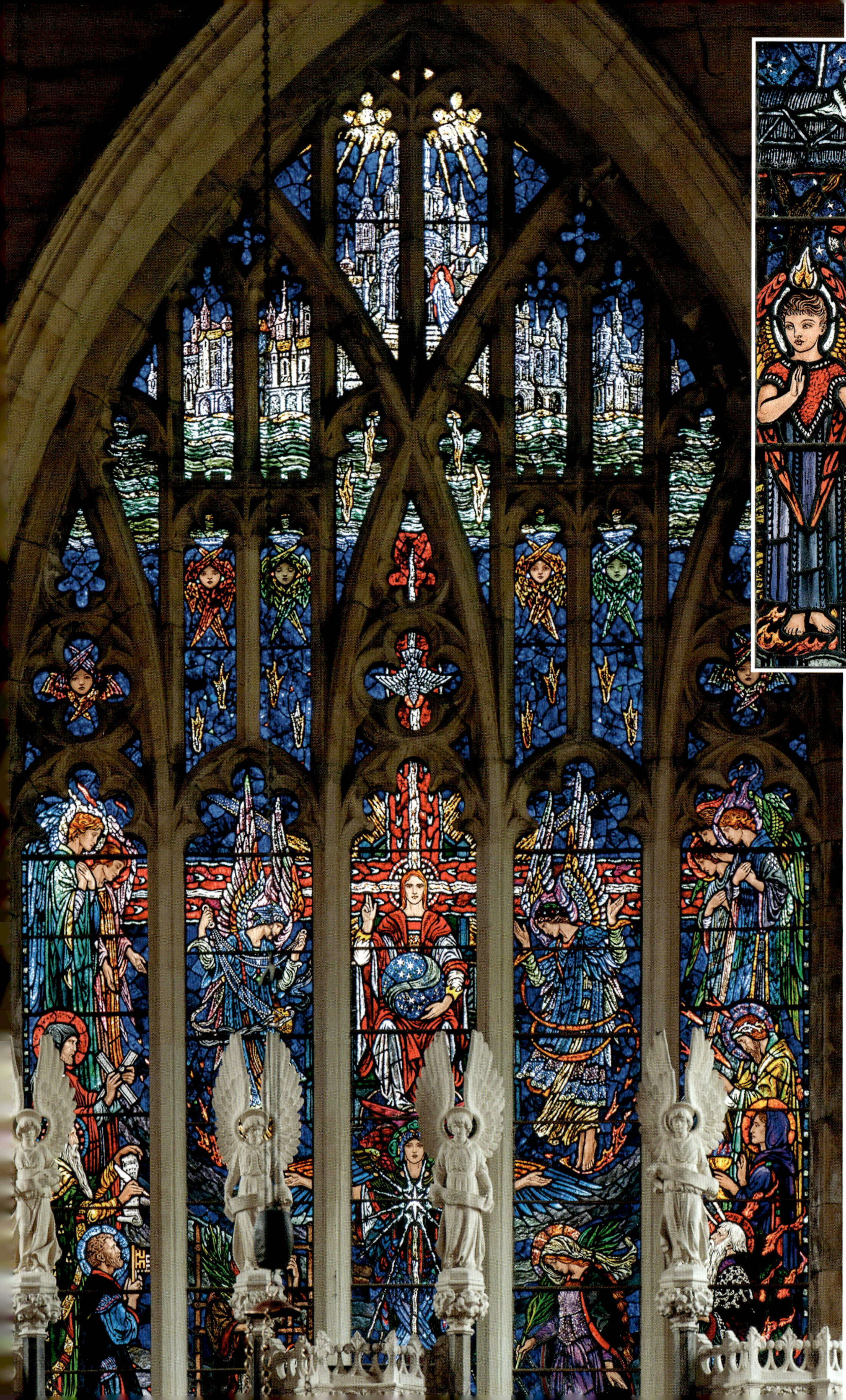

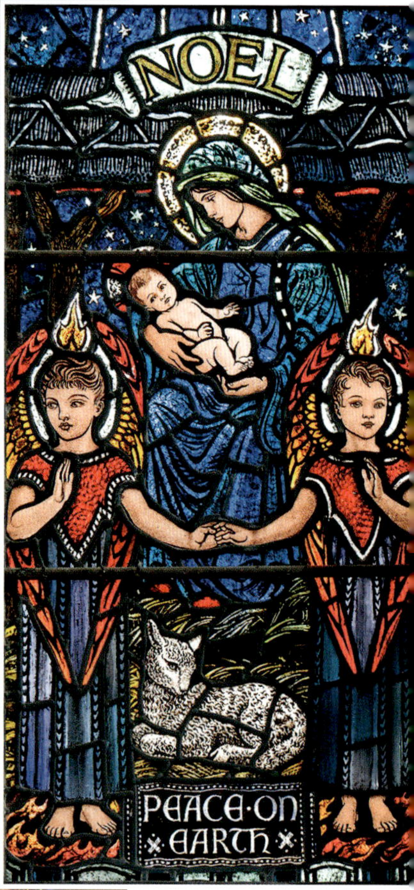

485–6. Karl Parsons, 'Te Deum' (left), Virgin and Child with Angels (above, detail from lower panels behind reredos), 1927, Church of All Saints, Porthcawl, east window

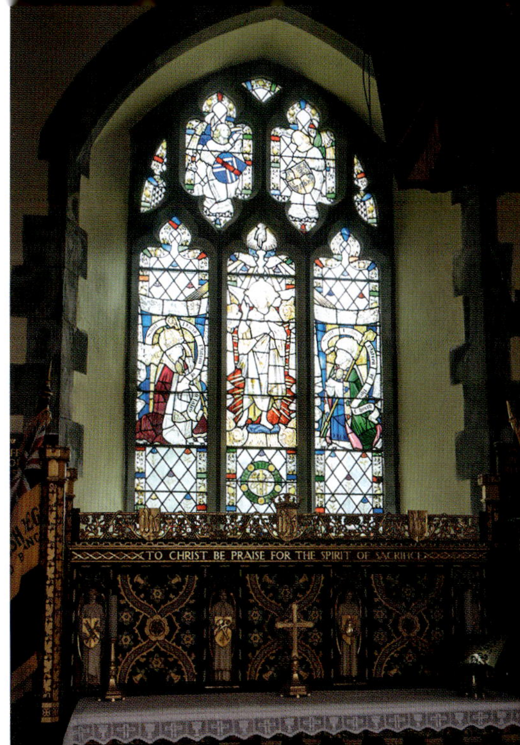

487. War Memorial to the Second Battalion of the Monmouthshire Regiment, 1923, Church of St Cadoc, Trevethin, stained glass by Frederick Eden

A further spectacular war memorial window, also free from military or nationalistic imagery and lavish in expense, is the east window by Karl Parsons for the Church of All Saints, Porthcawl. The window was commissioned by Dora Forsdike (née Williams) for her son Ivor Rees Williams and two other men who had died in active service. Although the lower part of the window is hidden from the body of the church behind a stone reredos, the artist was commissioned to fill the whole window, but with a coherent design that works in isolation from the lower figures and scenes. The window is inspired by the 'Te Deum', and 'represents the linking of Heaven & Earth by the Incarnation.'[19] Christ in Majesty is shown with angels and the new Jerusalem above, while below the Virgin and Child are set between the shepherds and the Magi representing peace on earth, flanked by figures from the Old and New Testaments.[20]

Some war memorials consisted of more than a single window, such as the set of windows in the south aisle at the Church of St Catherine, Canton, Cardiff. Eight figures fill the four pairs of lights in the sanctuary apse of the Church of St Matthew, Maindee, Newport, where Agnes, George, Maurice and Cecilia flank the four evangelists.[21] A war memorial to the Second Battalion of the Monmouthshire Regiment at the Church of St Cadoc, Trevethin, combines a stained glass window with a carved and painted reredos on the eastern side of the south transept. In 1922–3 the Memorial Chapel of the South Wales Borderers was created on the north side of Brecon Cathedral in the area known as the Havard Chapel. Three windows by James Powell & Sons were installed as part of the furnishing of the chapel in the north wall, where

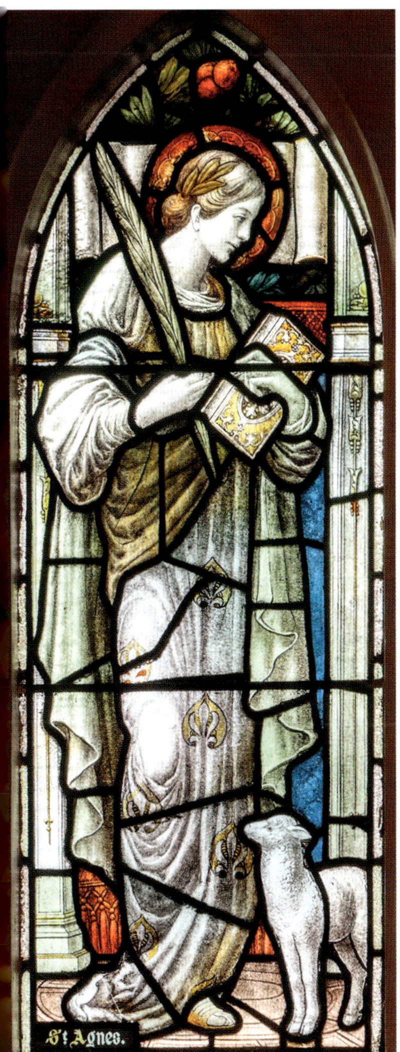

488. Samuel Evans, St Agnes, 1921, Church of St Matthew, Maindee, Newport, sanctuary apse

19 National Library of Wales, Records of the Church in Wales: Diocese of Llandaff, LL/F/607. Letter from Karl Parsons, 8 July 1927. I am grateful to Alun Adams for bringing the correspondence to my attention.

20 Among these figures, Moses holds tablets of the law which in fact carry the detailed signature 'Karl Parsons designed and painted these windows, helped by Leonard Potter, the Glasshouse Lettice Street Fulham in the year 1927.'

21 The windows were given in memory of the members of the congregation who fought in the war, while a separate single window in the nave by the same maker, Samuel Evans of Smethwick, was given 'in grateful thanks-giving for the heroism of our Soldiers and for the inestimable gift of victorious peace' by Samuel Whitmore and his family. Samuel Whitmore himself was commemorated in an adjacent window by the same firm, but in a brighter painterly style, in 1931.

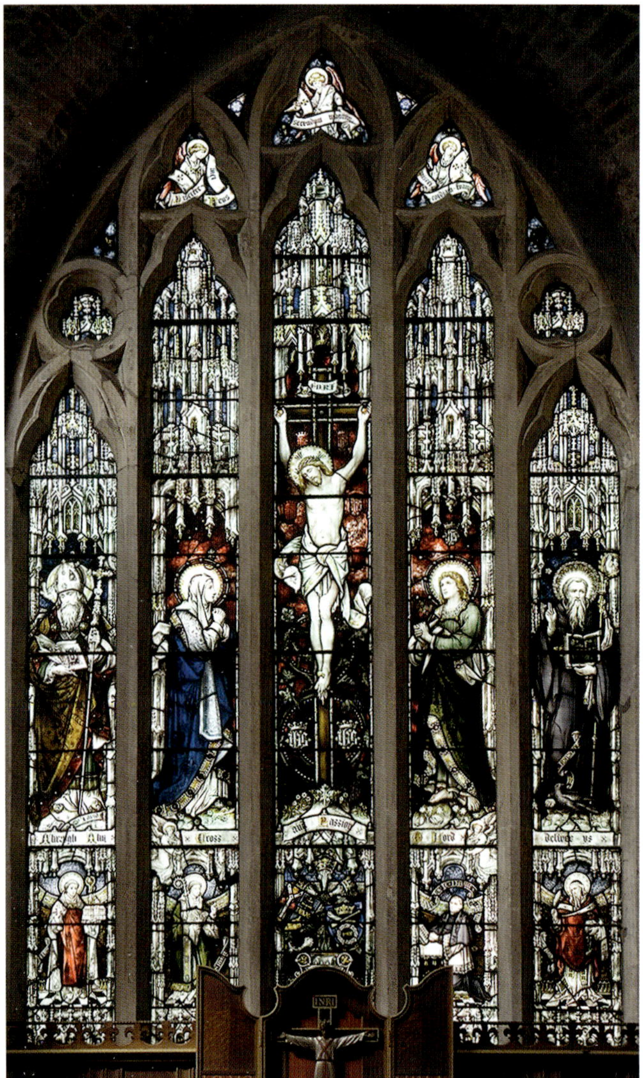

489. John Hardman & Co., The Crucifixion with Saints, 1916, Priory Church of St David, Swansea, east window

the patron saints of Wales, England, Scotland and Ireland stand at either side of a central three-light window depicting the military saints Joan of Arc, Martin and Edmund.

All of the three windows at the east end of the Roman Catholic Priory Church of St David, Swansea, were also filled with stained glass war memorials. The windows, by John Hardman & Co., include one for soldiers and sailors who lost their lives, one in thanksgiving for safe return, while the chancel window was in memory of Canon Gwydir, 'and his heroic death in the cause of his King and Country.'[22] A set of five windows at City United Reformed (formerly Scottish Presbyterian) Church, Cardiff, was placed as a war memorial in 1921, depicting Christ carrying the cross between scenes across two lights of Christ and his disciples on their way to Jerusalem, and Christ calling Peter and Andrew. Here the windows were the first and presently the only stained glass windows added to the church, and are an example of how, by the 1920s, stained glass was adopted across the Christian denominations.

22 Canon Robert Basil Gwydir O.S.B., a naval chaplain, died while trying to save others on the hospital ship *Rohilla* in 1914: *The Tablet*, 19 August 1916. The loss of the ship near Whitby is the subject of Colin Brittain, *Into the Maelstrom: The Wreck of HMHS Rohilla* (Stroud: The History Press, 2014, second edition).

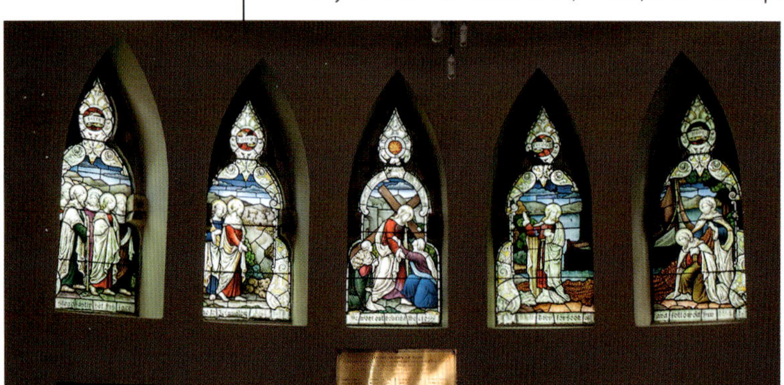

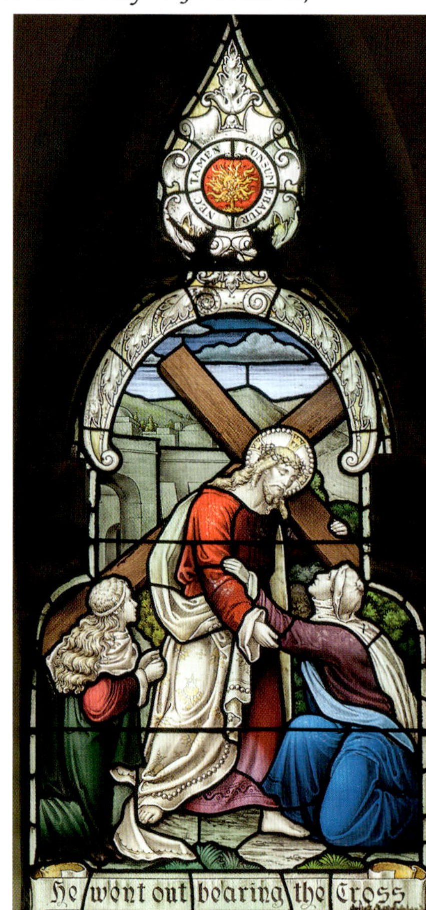

490–1. Joseph Bell & Son, Scenes from the Life of Christ (below), Christ Carrying the Cross (right), 1921, City United Reformed Church, Cardiff, south transept

Chapter Nine

Stained Glass Across the Denominations

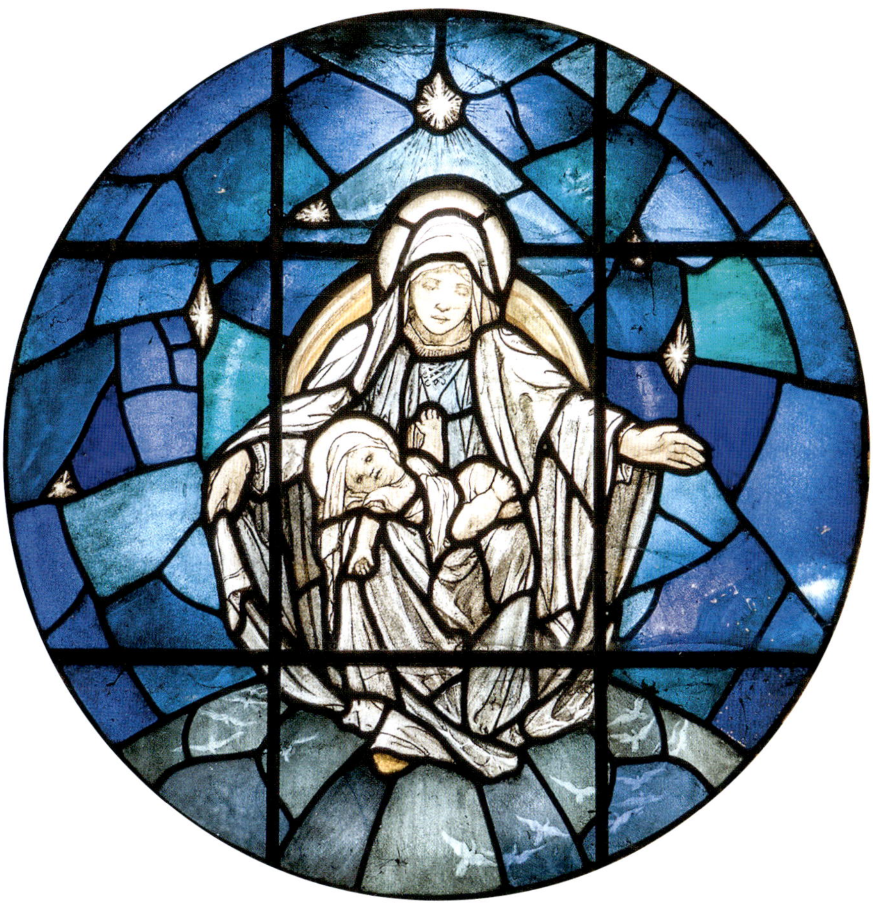

1 *Journal of the British Society of Master Glass-Painters*, vol. i, no. 1 (April 1924), p. 3. Members of Nonconformist churches sometimes contributed to war memorial windows in Anglican churches, such as at the Church of the Holy Trinity, Llandow, where the rector commended the unanimity of both members of the church and local Nonconformists in raising the money for the three-light window. *Glamorgan Gazette*, 3 October 1919.

2 The chapel is now home to a new congregation, and known as Penrallt Baptist Church.

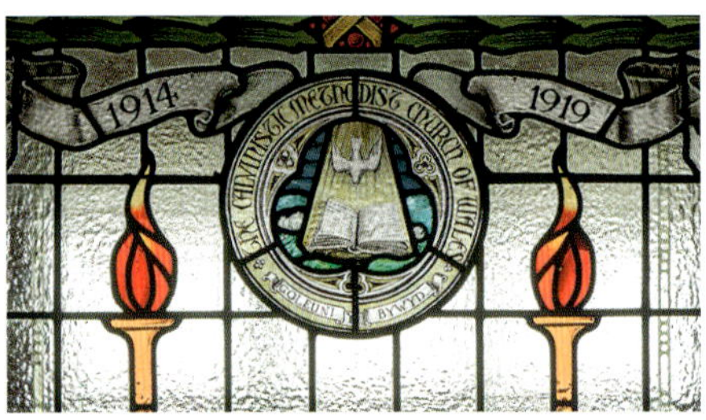

493. War Memorial Window, *c.* 1920, Penrallt Baptist Church, Bangor, vestibule

494. J. Wippell & Co., St John, probably 1920s, Hyfrydle Calvinistic Methodist Chapel, Holyhead, rear wall

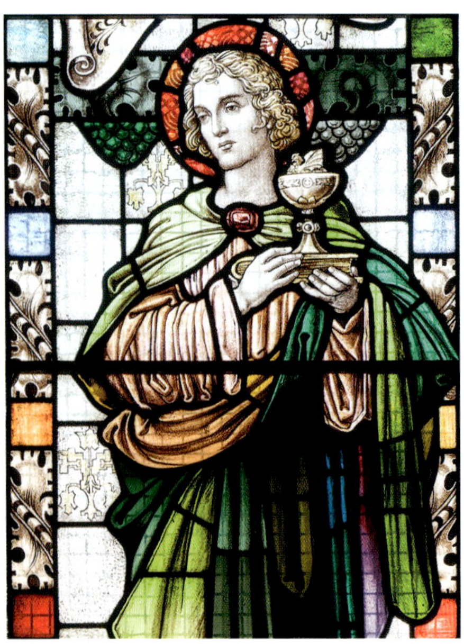

The memorials placed in Methodist, Congregationalist and Baptist chapels after the First World War mark an increasing use of stained glass among Nonconformist denominations. The number of memorials commissioned in the 1920s was the cause of optimism expressed in the first number of the *Journal of the British Society of Master Glass-Painters*, published in April 1924: 'It may be that the enormous number of War Memorial Windows executed during the last four years, windows to which all classes of the community subscribed, have brought the subject home to many people who never concerned themselves with it before.'[1]

Some staunchly Protestant congregations continued to regard the use of representational visual art in their chapels as too Catholic, and in some chapels these war memorials were modest, such as that made for Twr-Gwyn Calvinistic Methodist Chapel in Bangor.[2] The window consists of the badge of the Calvinistic Methodist Church in Wales, between two flames, with the names of the three men who lost their lives below. In contrast, a three-light war memorial window by J. Wippell & Co. at Hyfrydle Welsh Calvinistic Methodist Chapel in Holyhead included standing biblical figures with narrative scenes below. In some cases these first windows lead on to further stained glass. At Conway Road Wesleyan Methodist Church, Canton, Cardiff, the war memorial windows were the first of a number of stained glass windows added during the twentieth century.

In other Nonconformist chapels stained glass had been commissioned before the onset of the First World War. For example, the interior woodwork at Victoria Road Congregational (subsequently United Reformed) Church, Newport, was given in memory of those who died in the war, since so many of the windows had already been filled with biblical scenes in stained glass by two or three makers. The windows are mostly enclosed in Renaissance-style borders, appropriate for the neo-Classical design of the chapel, the style adopted by the majority of Nonconformist places of worship in the nineteenth century. This neo-Classical architecture, which A.W.N. Pugin found incompatible with English Christianity, emphasised the difference between the chapels and the established Anglican Church with their predominantly Gothic

492. (Title page) Theodora Salisbury, Virgin and Child, 1
Church of St Peter, Newchurch (Monmouthshire), east winc

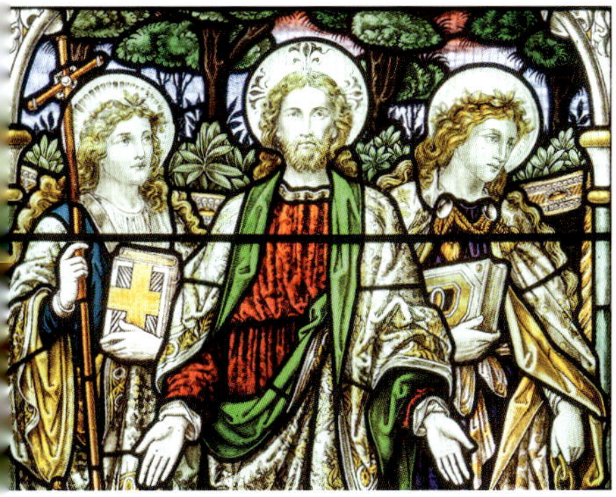

495. Possibly H.J. Salisbury, Christ with Figures of Faith and Hope, *c.* 1910, former Victoria Road Congregational Church, Newport, vestibule

Revival buildings. However, in some cases Gothic styles were used for Nonconformist chapels, often displaying an eclecticism that Pugin also railed against.[3] By the end of the nineteenth century some congregations, particularly from the Wesleyan Methodist Church as well as some from the Independent or Congregational tradition, deliberately adopted Gothic Revival architecture to identify themselves more closely with the established church, or to rival it. These congregations, often English rather than Welsh-speaking, were more likely to add stained or coloured glass, especially where lancet or rose windows invited its use.[4] This can be seen in the set of three two-light windows in the apse and large rose window facing the street at Trinity Methodist Church in Cardiff, and the set of windows by Heaton, Butler & Bayne given by different donors at Christ Church English Congregational Church, Llandudno.

At Penarth, Trinity (Wesleyan) Methodist Church was built in fifteenth-century Decorated Gothic with transepts and a large spired tower, asserting its own Anglicised Nonconformist identity through its rejection of Welsh chapel tradition. The leading families of the church, the Morels, Gibbs and Angels, all derived their wealth from the shipping industry and their children intermarried, while many of the congregation were ship captains and mariners. The earliest windows are the five-light window in the truncated chancel, depicting the Ascension with the four evangelists, given in memory of Thomas and Susanna Morel, and the depiction of the three women at the empty tomb, given in memory of Susan and Annie Gibbs. One of the transept windows is a memorial to John Angel Gibbs, who died while serving in the First World War, although the remaining windows were given by other families, including the opposite transept window given by the widow of Rabjohn Moxey, the general manager for the coal exporters John Cory, in memory of him.[5]

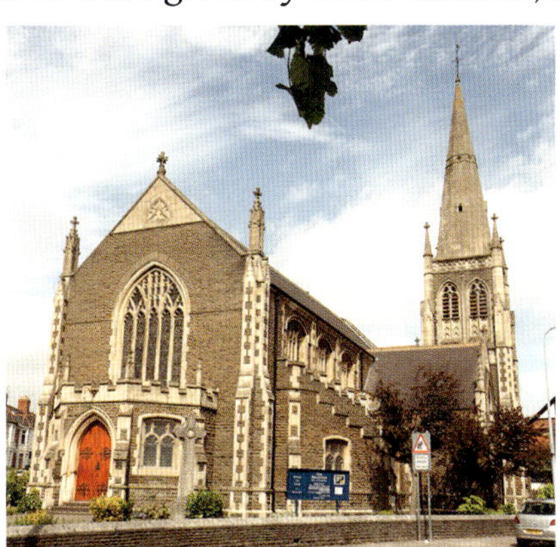

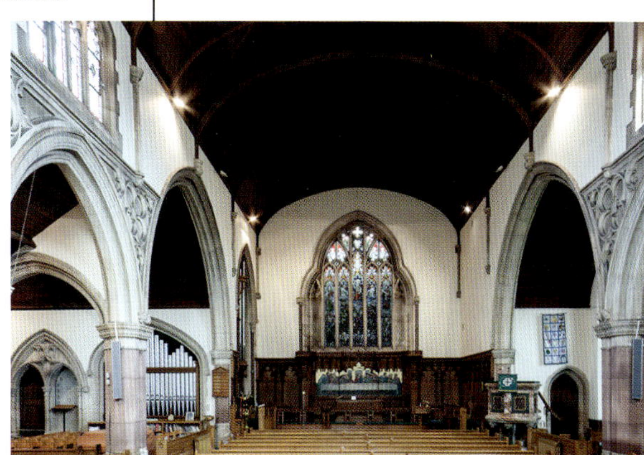

496–7. Henry Budgen, Trinity Methodist Church, Penarth, 1900, stained glass and reredos by H.J. Salisbury (far right)

3 A.W.N. Pugin *An Apology for the Revival of Christian Architecture in England* (London: John Weale, 1843), pp. 4–5.

4 The principal branches of Nonconformism were the Wesleyan Methodist, Calvinistic Methodist, Independent or Congregational and Baptist denominations, although there were sub-branches of each of these groups and many others. The denominations were further subdivided into Welsh and English-speaking congregations, all of which generated a degree of rivalry and a profusion of chapels.

5 Their daughter Kate was the wife of the church's architect, also a Methodist, Henry Budgen, and another daughter married Tom Morel. John Angel Gibbs' only son, John Morel Gibbs, developed an interest in Modernist painting in the 1930s, and later founded the Methodist Collection of Modern Art. By contrast, none of the stained glass in the church has the slightest hint of modernism. Henry Budgen also designed Albert Road Methodist Church in Penarth in a similar style. The five-light stained glass window at the church was removed in 1973 and is now in Bell Street United Church, Ottawa.

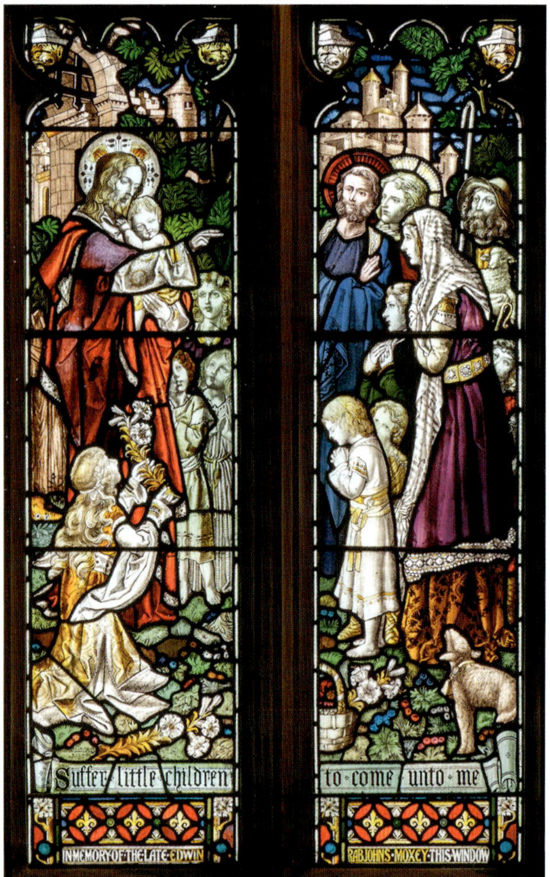

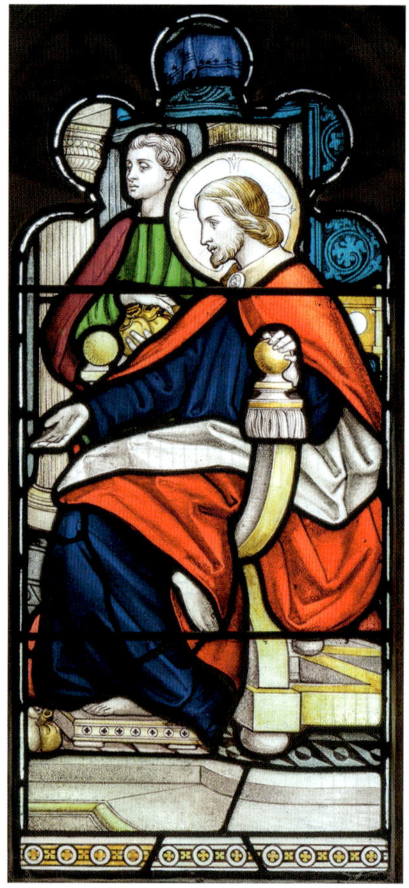

498. (far left) H.J. Salisbury, Christ with Women and Children, *c.* 1920, Trinity Methodist Church, Penarth, north transept

499. (left) Probably H.J. Salisbury, Christ as the Master in the Parable of the Talents, probably 1930s, Trinity Methodist Church, Penarth, aisle

The Methodist artist Henry James Salisbury was chosen to provide the glass, and Salisbury's studio also supplied the painted reredos, a large copy of Leonardo da Vinci's *Last Supper*. In keeping with his religious tradition, his work was scrupulously biblical, depicting scenes from the gospels.[6] Other Nonconformist patrons commissioned stained glass from Swaine Bourne of Birmingham, whose own tradition was Brethren. His studio was responsible for the stained glass at Trinity Methodist Church, Cardiff, and some of the windows at Victoria Road United Reformed Church, Newport.[7]

The church furnishers Jones & Willis made windows before the First World War for Wesleyan Methodist churches in Llandudno and Newport, as well as windows in the 1930s for Tabernacl Welsh Independent Chapel, Barry. Sometimes refurnishing of chapel interiors created an opportunity for the addition of stained glass, such as at Jerwsalem Calvinistic Methodist Chapel, Gwalchmai, where stained glass by A. Seward of Lancaster was installed in 1925. Another Lancaster firm that found favour with Nonconformist patrons was Abbott & Co. and the firm made a pair of windows for Heol Awst, Carmarthen, in 1922. One was a war memorial, while the other, a copy of William Holman Hunt's *Light of the World*, marked the 300th anniversary of the birth of the Revd Stephen Hughes, a Puritan preacher who laid the foundation for many early Nonconformist congregations and chapels in Carmarthenshire.

6 The firm of H.J. Salisbury probably made the later windows in the aisles of the church and may have been responsible for windows at Conway Road Methodist Church in Cardiff, and the central apse window for the Wesleyan Methodist church in Colwyn Bay.

7 Swaine Bourne also made windows for Anglican churches in Wales, as well as a window at the Roman Catholic Church of Our Lady and St Michael, Abergavenny, which is signed and dated 1879.

8 The figure of the Light of the World is probably from the same cartoon as that used at Heol Awst, Carmarthen, and is therefore attributable to Abbott & Co., although the cut lines are placed differently. The two figures by John Hall & Sons at New Siloh were repeated by the firm in windows for Tabernacle Congregational Chapel, Milford Haven.

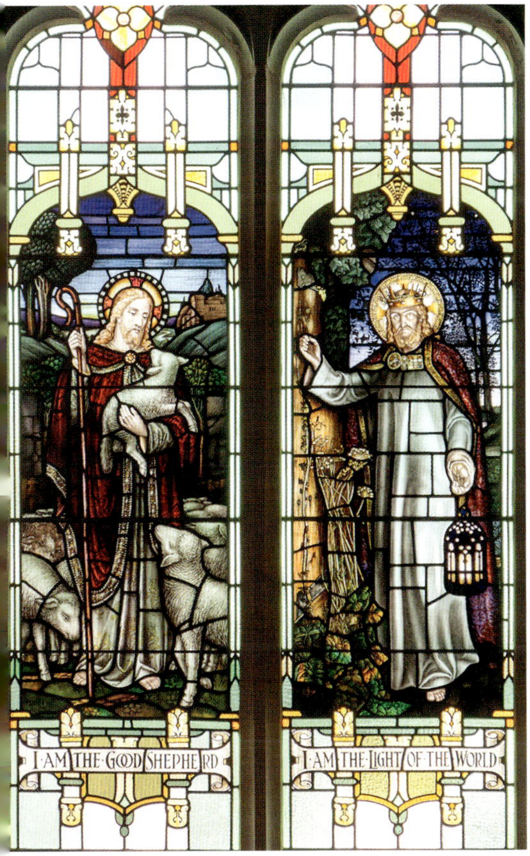

500. (above) Abbott & Co., Christ as the Good Shepherd and the Light of the World, probably 1920s, Gilgal Baptist Church, Porthcawl, rear wall

501. (right) John Hall & Sons, Christ as the Light of the World, 1933, New Siloh Congregational Chapel, Landore, Swansea, front wall (gallery)

The images of Christ as Light of the World and as the Good Shepherd were popular for chapels, both as reproductions hung on the walls as well as in stained glass. The two representations of Christ are placed together at Gilgal Baptist Church, Porthcawl, and at either side of the organ at New Siloh Welsh Congregational Chapel, Landore, Swansea.[8] At New Siloh, Christ as the Light of the World holds a globe of light, departing from the conventional image made famous in the painting by William Holman Hunt.

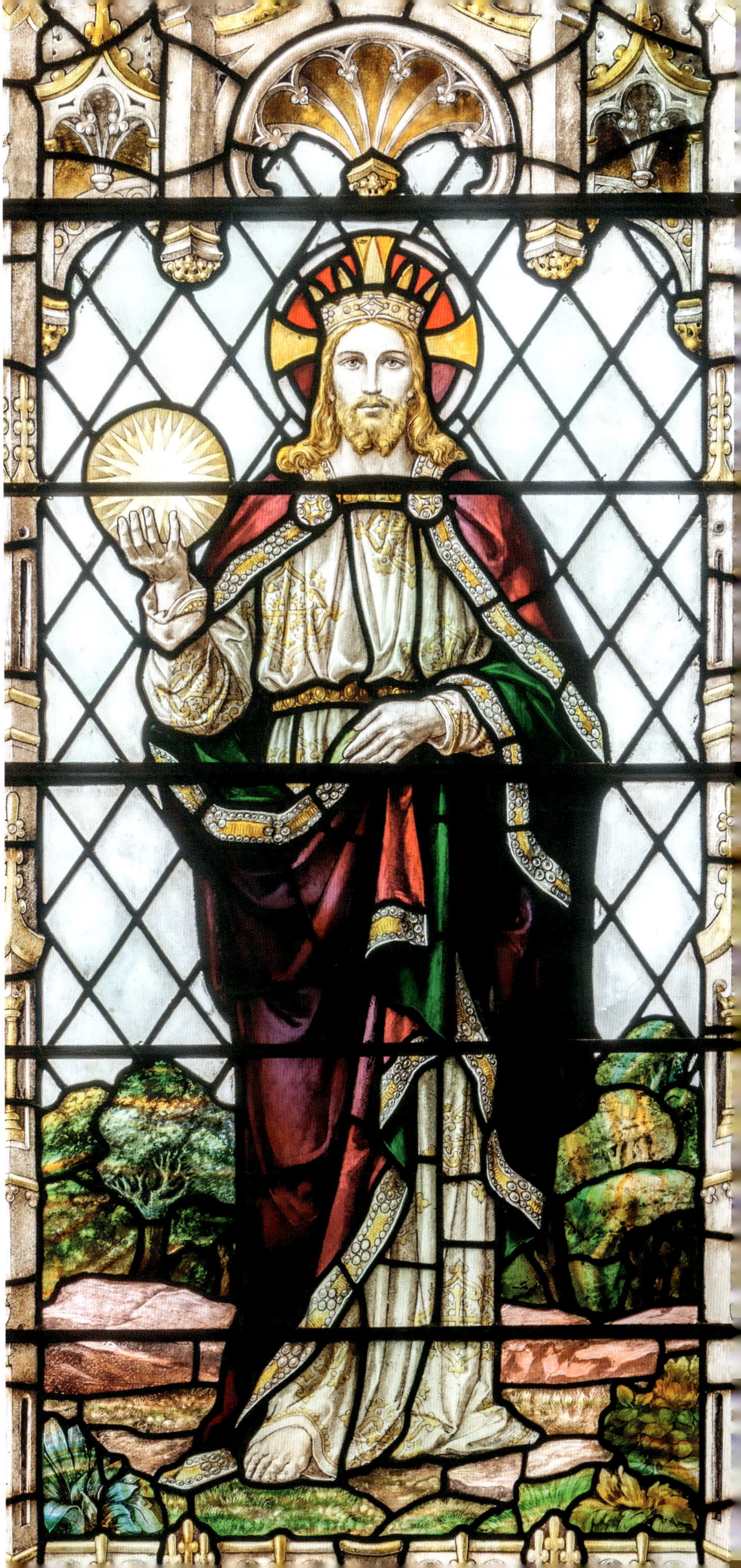

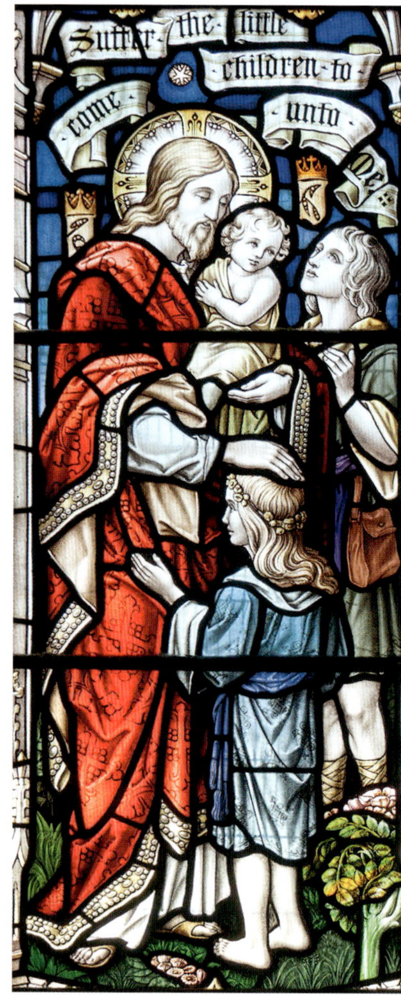

502. Abbott & Co., Christ with Children, *c.* 1925, former Christ Church (Congregational), Llandudno, side wall

A further common image, both in framed reproductions and for stained glass, is the depiction of Christ with children. Abbot & Co. depict the scene in a window at Christ Church, Llandudno, and Powell & Sons' version of the scene in a two-light window at Tredegarville Baptist Church, Cardiff, includes lower panels of women instructing children that suggest depictions of Hannah teaching Samuel to read and the Virgin teaching the young Christ to read.[9]

The Bristol firm John Hall & Sons produced a number of biblical subjects for Nonconformist chapels in Wales. For example, the powerful figure of the apostle Paul for the Unitarian Chapel at Pantdefaid in Ceredigion is placed over a scene of him preaching in Athens, and at Tabernacle Calvinistic Methodist Chapel, New Quay, a single window of 1927 depicts the parable of the Good Samaritan.[10] A later commission of about 1936 for Mount Pleasant Congregational Church, Pontypool, strips away the decorative borders in a smaller window depicting the young Christ with his parents, in a design that departs from late nineteenth-century convention. The young Christ is also the subject of a window at Chester Street English Baptist Church, Wrexham, standing among the doctors of the law in the temple. Two New Testament subjects were depicted in large windows for Tabernacl Welsh Baptist Church, Cardiff, given in memory of the sixth minister, Revd Charles Davies, who died in 1927. The scene of John baptising Christ in the River Jordan, and perhaps also the other depicting the Last Supper, was a version of a painting of the subject by E. Goodwyn Lewis, altered to fit a taller panel.

9 The subjects in the lower panels are not explicit and the depiction of Christ being taught by his mother would be unusual as it is not scriptural. The scene in the upper roundel, only visible above the gallery, shows a pelican feeding her chicks. The late medieval image of 'the pelican in her piety' in which she feeds her young with her blood, symbolises the Real Presence in the Eucharist, and is therefore not characteristic of conventional Baptist teaching.

10 John Hall & Sons use the same design in their window at the Anglican Church of St Peter, Llandevaud, of about the same date, where, unlike the version at New Quay, the window has a Gothic surround. The firm also made windows for other Anglican churches in Wales at Ebbw Vale, Newport and Llanbeblig.

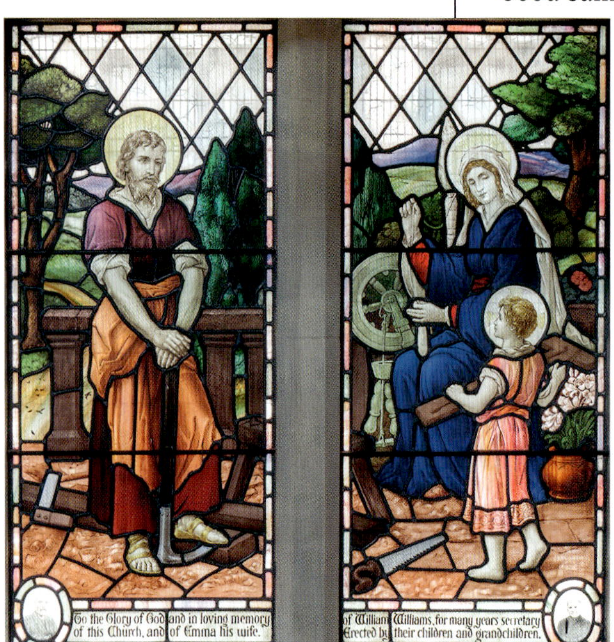

503. John Hall & Sons, The Holy Family, 1936, Mount Pleasant Congregational Church, Pontypool, side wall

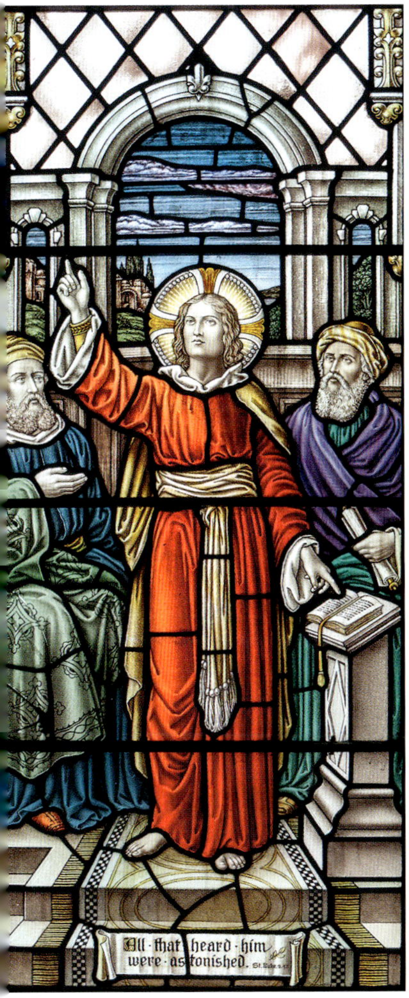

504. Abbott & Co., Christ Among the Doctors, probably 1930s, Chester Street Baptist Church, Wrexham, rear wall

505–6. The Baptism of Christ (right) and the Last Supper (below), 1928, Tabernacl Baptist Church, Cardiff

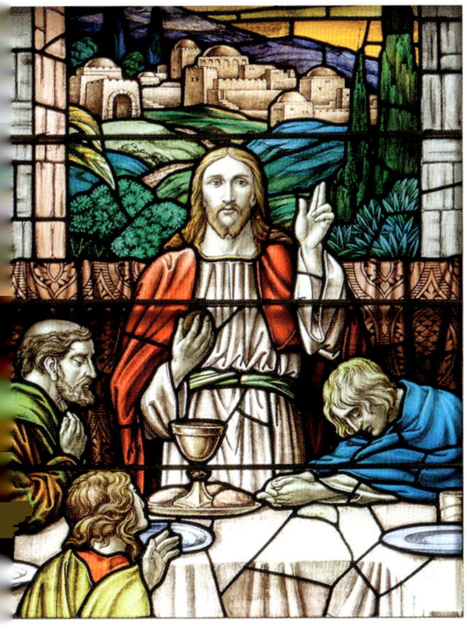

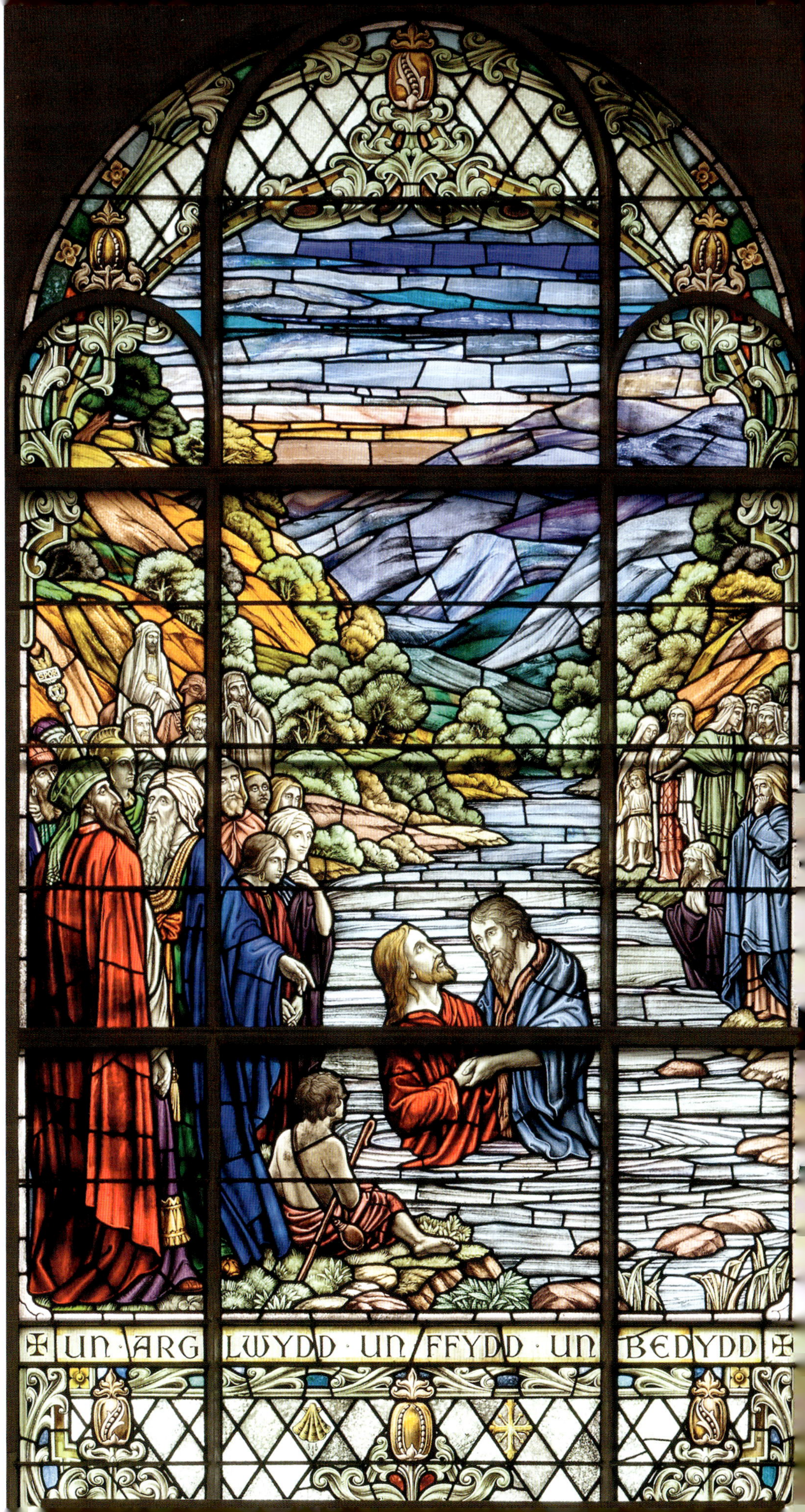

The diversity within the Anglican Communion in Wales had increased during the nineteenth centuries along with the growth of Nonconformity. Figurative stained glass windows were more often commissioned from those churches with stronger Tractarian and Anglo-Catholic traditions than those with an Evangelical tradition, but in the 1920s and 30s the number of Anglican churches with stained glass continued to increase. At the Church of St Mary, Fishguard, an Evangelical tradition prevailed during the nineteenth century, but several windows were inserted from the 1920s, including war memorial windows by Burlison & Grylls and James Powell & Sons, establishing a practice of adding stained glass that continued into the 1980s. At the Church of St Michael, Llanfihangel Genau'r Glyn, the arrival of a new vicar in 1932 led to the commissioning of stained glass that resulted in the gradual replacement of most of the original glazing with pictorial stained glass from 1933 until 1980.

The majority of windows in Anglican churches between the wars depicted Christ and subjects from the New Testament, while Old Testament and Apocryphal scenes and characters were less common than in the nineteenth century. In some cases patrons introduced unusual biblical subjects. For example, the set of three windows given by the Freemasons for the north chancel chapel at Monkton Priory depict the Old Testament characters associated with the building and decoration of the temple: Boaz and Jachin, Hiram King of Tyre, and Solomon.

Alongside these biblical windows a growing number of historical figures and non-biblical saints were depicted in Anglican churches. At the Church of St Mary, Pembroke, the three windows by C.E. Kempe & Co. given in 1907 depict David, patron saint of Wales, as well as the first earl of Pembroke William Marshall, and Henry VII, who was born at the castle. After the First World War, Chad and Oswald were added by the same firm in the chancel as a memorial to officers and men of the third battalion of the King's Shropshire Light Infantry, while alongside, Gerald of Wales, and Archbishop Laud, who was bishop of St Davids from 1621–6, were added in 1918.[11]

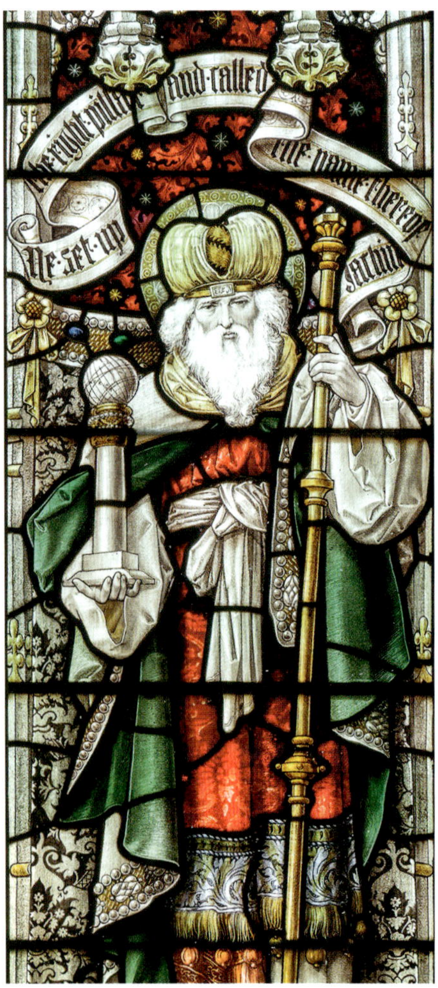

507. Percy Bacon Brothers, Jachin, *c.* 1920, Church of St Nicholas and St John, Monkton Priory, north chancel chapel

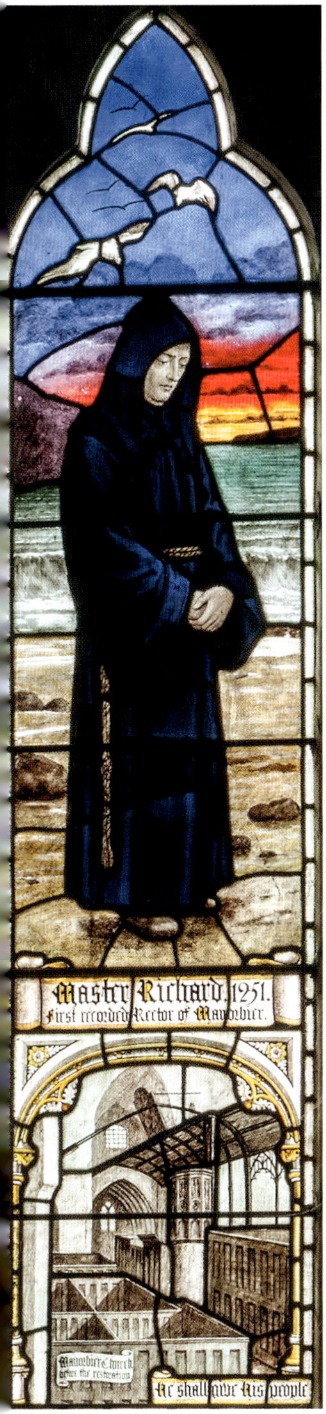

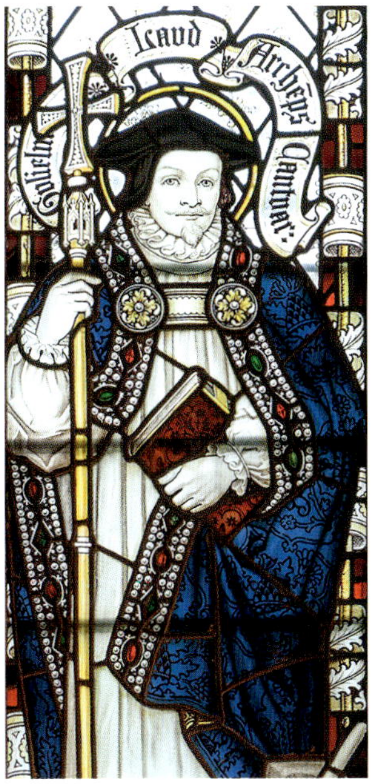

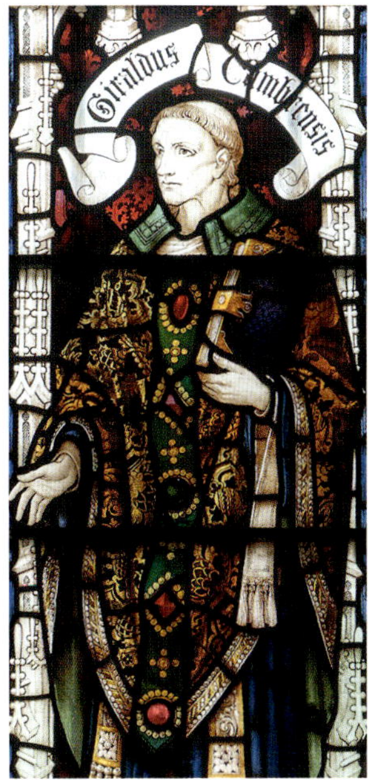

508. (far left) Burlison & Grylls, Master Richard, probably 1920s, Church of St James, Manorbier, north aisle

509. (centre left) C.E. Kempe & Co., Archbishop Laud, 1919, Church of St Mary, Pembroke, chancel

510. (right) Horace Wilkinson, Gerald of Wales, 1924, Priory Church of St Mary, Cardigan, east window

Gerald of Wales and Archbishop Baldwin flank the Crucifixion with Mary and John at the Priory Church of St Mary, Cardigan, a place that they visited in 1188 on their journey through Wales. Gerald of Wales was also depicted with David in another window by C.E. Kempe & Co. at the Church of St James, Manorbier, which stands on high ground opposite the castle where Gerald was born. Here, one of two windows by Burlison & Grylls depicts two further historical figures associated with Manorbier, Master Richard and Lady Margaret Beaufort, the mother of Henry VII. Master Richard, the first recorded rector of Manorbier, stands on the beach with a striking sunset behind him, while the panel below shows the interior of the church with box pews prior to its restoration. Some windows in Anglican churches celebrated significant figures of the Methodist movement in Wales. The Welsh hymnwriter William Williams Pantycelyn is found in the west window at Maentwrog (as the 'Psalmist of Wales') and the east window at Llanfair-ar-y-bryn (where he was born and is buried in the churchyard), while David Jones is depicted in the east window of the Church of St Canna, Llangan, where he was rector from 1768 to 1810.[12]

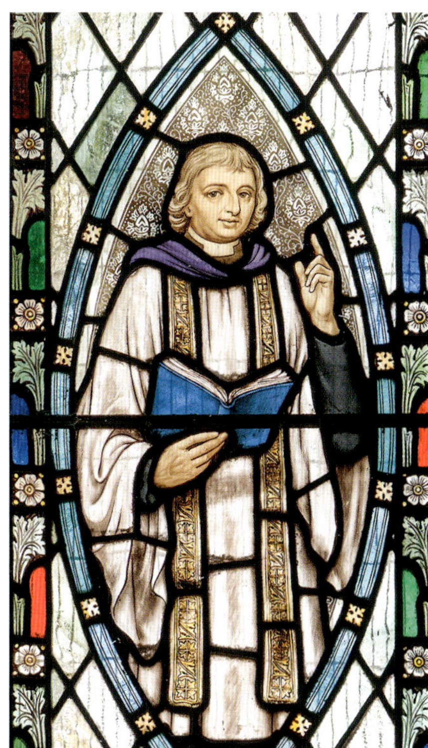

511. William Glasby, David Jones, 1932, Church of St Canna, Llangan, east window

11 Two further windows by the firm depict Welsh saints and George, while the remaining five windows, two more by Kempe & Co. (including the east window) and three earlier windows by Clayton & Bell, were all of biblical subjects.

12 The window was funded by small gifts from people across and beyond Wales, among them David Lloyd George and senior churchmen including the bishop of Llandaff. The Calvinistic Methodist Association also contributed £5 5s. The list of subscribers survives at Glamorgan Archives, P95CW/11/1–2. Historical figures are unusual in Nonconformist churches until the later twentieth century, but portraits of Oliver Cromwell and John Milton, regarded as founding fathers of Nonconformity, were depicted at Christ Church, Llandudno.

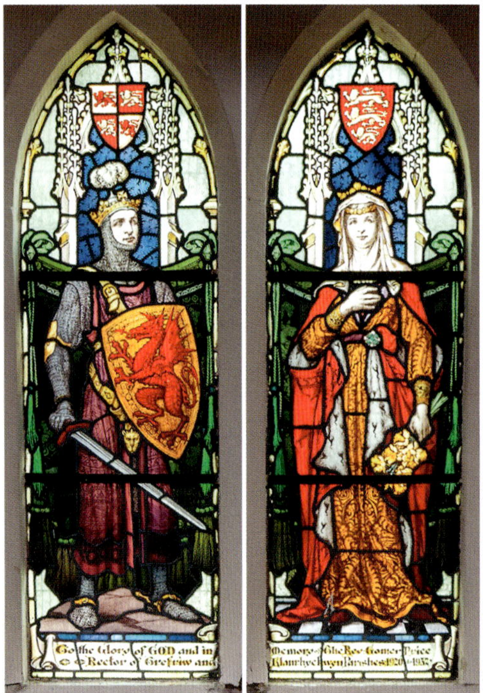

512. A.R. Mowbray & Co., Llywelyn ab Iorwerth and his wife Joan (Siwan), 1933, Church of St Mary, Trefriw, north aisle

513. Probably Burlison & Grylls, William Salesbury, *c.* 1936, Church of St Mary and All Saints, Conwy, south transept

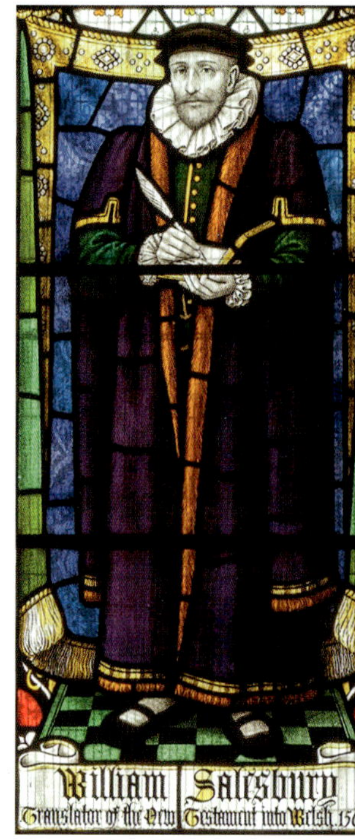

Welsh national figures, apart from saints, rarely feature in the stained glass of Welsh churches, and where present are indicative of local connections. For example, a two-light window at the Church of St Mary, Trefriw, depicts Llywelyn ab Iorwerth (Llywelyn Fawr) and Joan (Siwan) in the church that they reputedly founded in 1230. A window probably by Burlison & Grylls at the Church of St Mary and All Saints, Conwy, depicts the translators of the Welsh Bible, Bishop William Morgan and William Salesbury, on a memorial to Mary Jane Eliza Wood, who was descended from both men through her mother and father.

English military saints, such as Alban, Oswald and Edmund, remained popular for a time after the First World War, even for civilian memorials, such as the standing figures of Martin, George and Alban in military dress at the Church of St Peter, Carmarthen, by Shrigley & Hunt, and a figure of Edmund in medieval armour by Clayton & Bell at the Church of St Mary, Betws-y-Coed. The scene of Galahad kneeling before his vision of the Holy Grail at Wolvesnewton echoes similar windows by A.J. Davies for military memorials, although it is part of the sanctuary furnishing in memory of a mining engineer, William Walker Hood.[13] The free hand frequently given to patrons when commissioning windows continued to add breadth to the saints and subjects

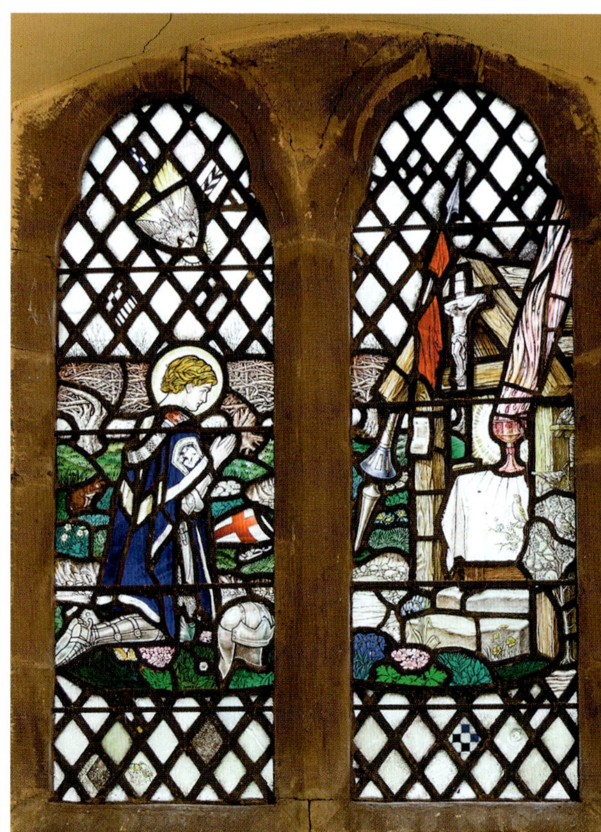

514. T.W. Camm & Co., *Sir Galahad's Vision of the Sancgreal*, 1924, designed by Walter Camm, Church of St Thomas Beckett, Wolvesnewton, chancel

13 The complex iconography of the window includes the tree of the knowledge of Good and Evil; a sitting rabbit, symbolic of peace; and a horse and a dove, symbolic of the sanctity of the place. The subject of the grail was also felt to be appropriate to William Walker Hood's office as churchwarden, and charge of the sacred vessels. The two sanctuary windows and woodwork were all made by T.W. Camm & Co, the Arts and Crafts tradition extending to the use of wooden pegs for the carpentry. According to a privately printed description of the work, *Description Of The Memorial To William Walker Hood Of Tredean, In The Sanctuary Of Wolves Newton Church, Monmouthshire*, the windows were designed by Walter Camm and he made them together with his sister Florence and brother Robert. However, a printed card of the window in the archives of the Welsh School of Architectural Glass, Swansea Metropolitan University, attributes the design to Florence Camm.

515. A.E. Lemmon, St Columba, 1936, Church of St Sulien, Silian, east window

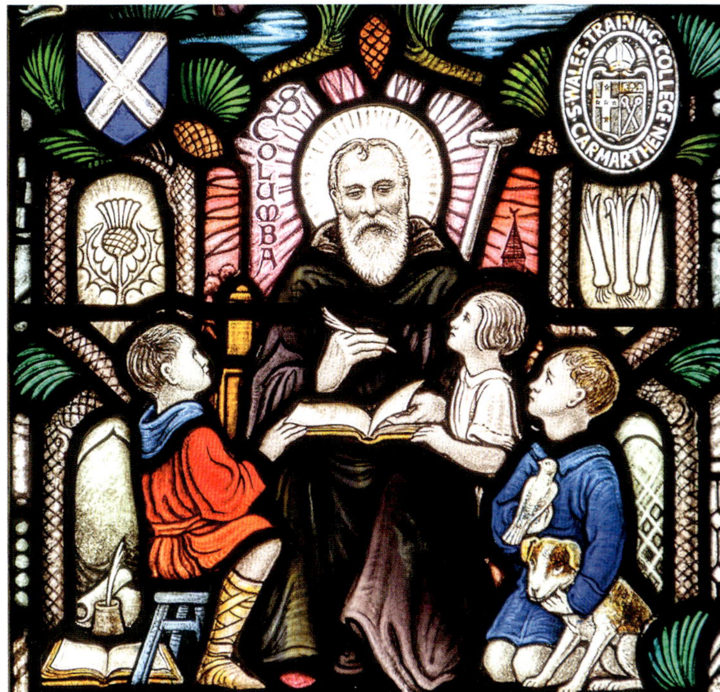

represented. For example, at the Church of St Sulien, Silian, a window by A.E. Lemmon, a pupil of A.J. Davies, includes panels depicting Margaret of Scotland and Columba, since the donors, the Stewart family of Glenview, were from Scotland.[14]

Further English saints, such as Chad and Hugh of Lincoln, are also found in Wales along with international saints such as Cecilia, Christopher and Nicholas. The number of Welsh saints continued to increase during the twentieth century, as an ongoing response to the Welsh national revival of the late nineteenth century and a new interest in the origins of Christianity in Wales. The identification with the founders of the Welsh church was particularly useful after Disestablishment in 1920, as the Church in Wales sought to redefine its identity outside of the Church of England. At the Church of St Michael and All Angels, Bosherston, the transept windows given in memory of David Edward Williams, the incumbent and archdeacon of St Davids until his death in 1920, feature Welsh saints as three of the four figures, including Teilo (his favourite saint), Govan (whose chapel is situated on the coast nearby), and the diocesan patron, David.[15] Teilo is depicted with Justinian at the Church of St Mary, Haverfordwest, in a late work by C.E. Kempe & Co., and these windows reflect the local, rather than national, importance of the saints. The status of the Welsh saints as regional, if not national, figures is emphasised in the nine-light window at the Church of All Saints, Oystermouth, of 1928. Flanking the risen Christ with Mary and John the Baptist, the saints David, Asaph, Deiniol and Woolos (Gwynllyw) stand as patrons of four of the six Welsh dioceses in an impressive full-coloured window by Powell & Sons.[16]

14 Similarly, Robert the Bruce and Margaret of Scotland are found at the Church of St Mechell, Llanfechell, in a window by Shrigley & Hunt.

15 The fourth saint is Michael.

16 John the Evangelist was the patron of the newly-created Diocese of Swansea and Brecon, and Peter and Paul were the patrons of Llandaff, despite the associations of Teilo, Dyfrig and Euddogwy with Llandaff Cathedral.

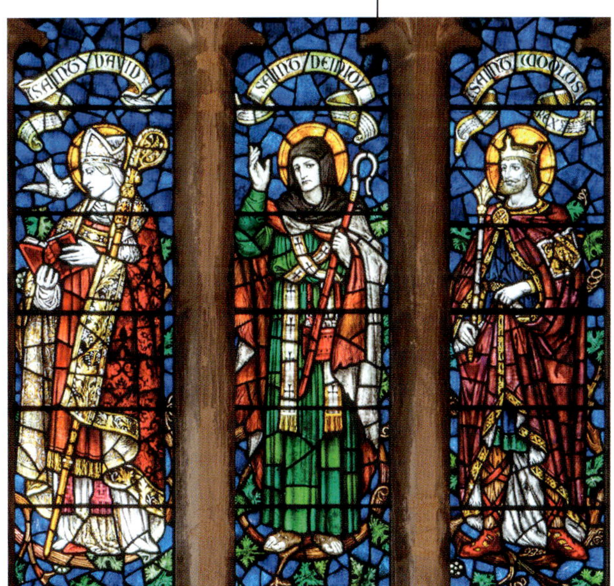

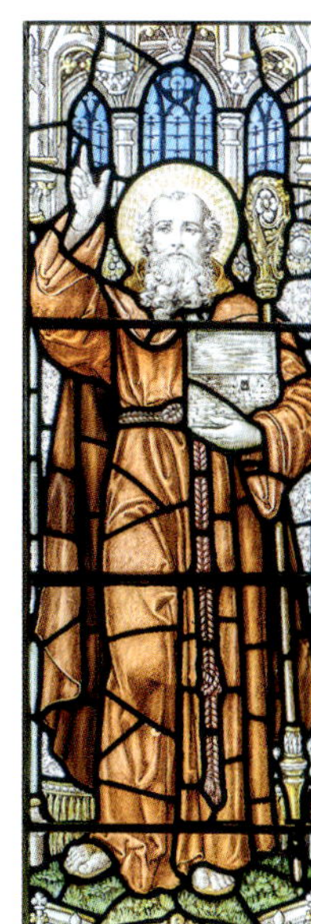

516. (right) James Powell & Sons, St David, St Deiniol and St Woolos (Gwynllyw), 1928, Church of All Saints, Oystermouth, east window

517. (far right) Robert Newbery, St Govan, *c.* 1920, Church of St Michael and All Angels, Bosherston, south transept

518. Burlison & Grylls, Mary and Joseph Finding Christ with the Doctors of the Law, 1920, Church of St Margaret, Roath, west window

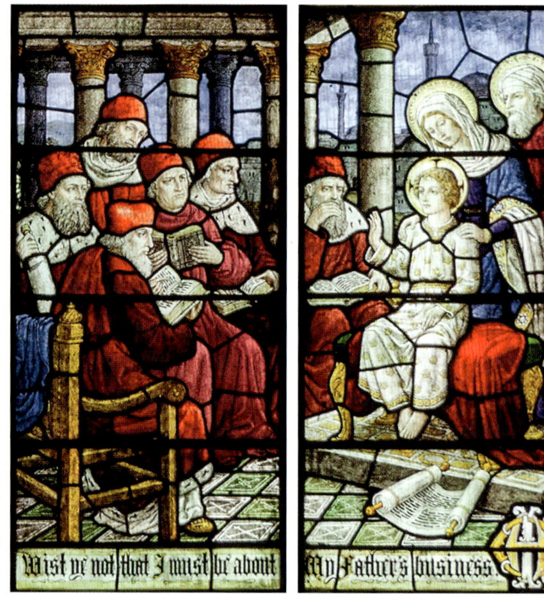

The ornate late Gothic Revival style of Burlison & Grylls, C.E. Kempe & Co., Daniells & Fricker and Robert Newbery was popular with Anglo-Catholic patrons, a tradition that was predominant in the Anglican churches of Cardiff as well as in many other parts of Wales.[17] Inheriting their tradition and reputation from the architect G.F. Bodley, Burlison & Grylls were particularly successful in Anglo-Catholic parishes in Cardiff, having previously made windows for Bodley & Garner's churches, the Church of St German in Roath, and the Church of St Saviour in Splott. They made all of the stained glass for the Church of St James, most of that at the Church of St Margaret, Roath, and a window for the Church of St John the Baptist in central Cardiff. However the firm also made windows for Anglican churches in Cardiff that were not so Catholic in taste, such as the Church of St Paul, Grangetown, and the more evangelical Church of St Stephen, Butetown.[18]

Throughout the 1920s, windows by the large surviving Victorian firms were always skilfully executed, but were often bound by convention and demonstrate little artistic imagination. Many demonstrate a discernible brightening of their late-Victorian palette through the reduced application of glass paint for shading, allowing more light through the glass. The proprietors and designers of these firms, together with some of the artists of the Arts and Crafts Movement, sought to defend the quality of their work through the formation of the British Society of Master Glass-Painters in 1921. The opening editorial of the first number of their journal, having noted the contemporary interest in stained glass, is critical of the 'Clerical Tailors' and 'The Stores' with their 'prettily-printed catalogues': 'they waste no time on artistic discussion of the window or its aesthetic appropriateness, or any stuff of that sort. "Here are our designs" they say, "all tastes catered for at so much per foot." And above all they are cheap.'[19]

17 The evangelical character of the Llandaff diocese was eclipsed both by the Tractarian and ritualist tradition of St Michael's College, Llandaff, endowed by Olive Talbot, and by the appointment of ritualist clergy by the third marquis of Bute. The background to the Anglo-Catholic Revival in nineteenth-century Cardiff, and the visual culture of its churches in Roath, is given in John Morgan-Guy 'The Art and Architecture of the Catholic Revival in Roath', *Roath Local History Society Project Newsletter*, vol. 6, no. 2 (first quarter, 1991), pp. 30–57.

18 G.F. Bodley is credited with the design of windows by the firm at the Church of St Margaret, Roath, and for the two windows at the Church of St Saviour, built to Bodley & Garner's design in 1888. John Newman, *The Buildings of Wales: Glamorgan* (London: Penguin Books, 1995), pp. 300, 312.

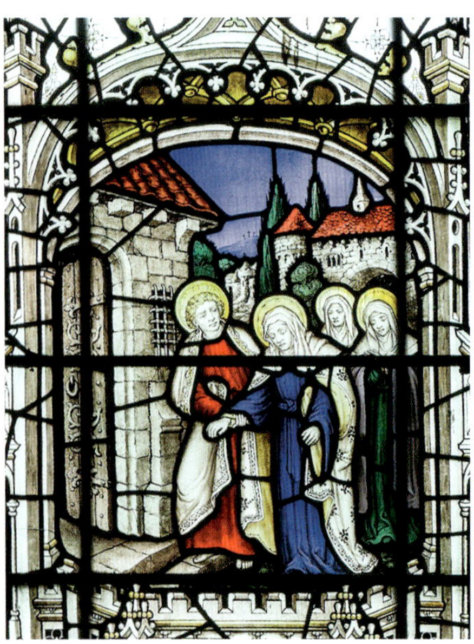

519. C.E. Kempe & Co., John Taking Mary into his Home, 1933, Church of St Mary, Caernarfon, north aisle chapel

520. (right) Burlison & Grylls, Christ with Women and Children, 1927, Christ Church, Prestatyn, south aisle chapel

21. (far right)Burlison & Grylls, Christ with Women and Children, 1888, Church of t Catwg, Llangattock, north aisle

522. (far right, below) rry Grylls, Christ with Women and Children, 927, design for Christ Church, Prestatyn (image courtesy Revd D. entin Bellamy, Vicar of the Parish of Prestatyn)

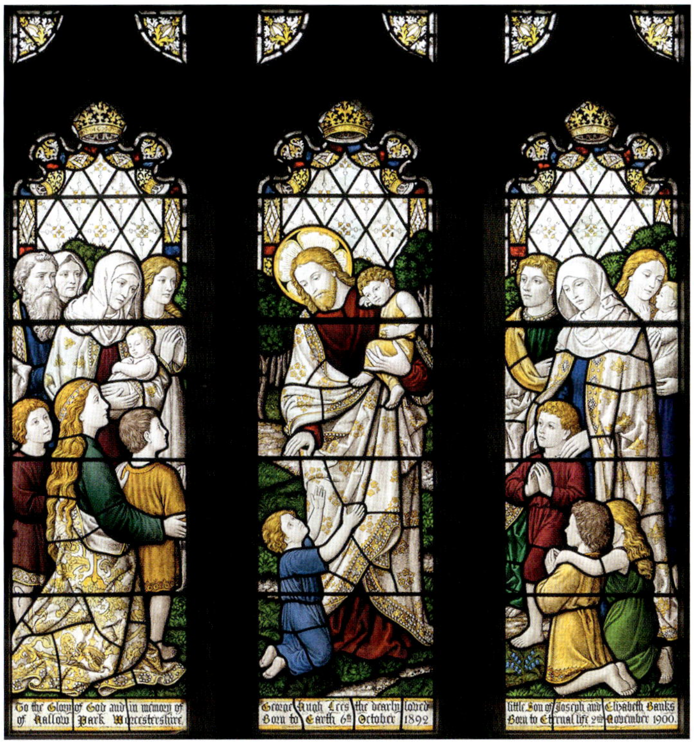

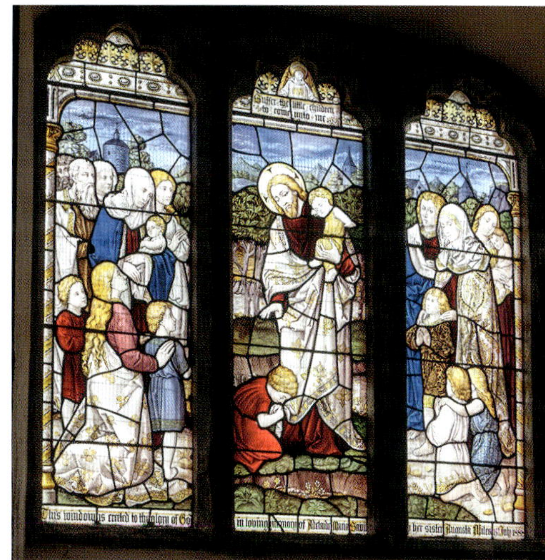

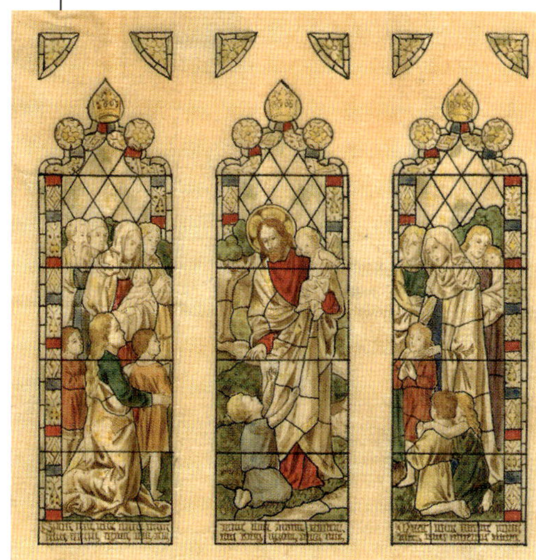

The criticism of their lowlier rivals ignores their own reuse of designs that entrenched convention, and the firms of Walter Tower, who managed C.E. Kempe's studio, as well as Thomas Henry Grylls, continued to make copies of windows they had made forty years previously. For example, the design signed by Grylls and submitted for approval in 1927 for a three-light window at Christ Church, Prestatyn, is in fact a copy of a design used by Burlison & Grylls at Llangattock in 1888.[20] In the case of Clayton & Bell, a small window at the Church of St Andoenus, Mounton, by Reginald Bell, a partner of the firm, is very different from the main output of the firm. Using very little coloured glass, the quarries surrounding the small scene are delicately-patterned with flowers, birds and bells.

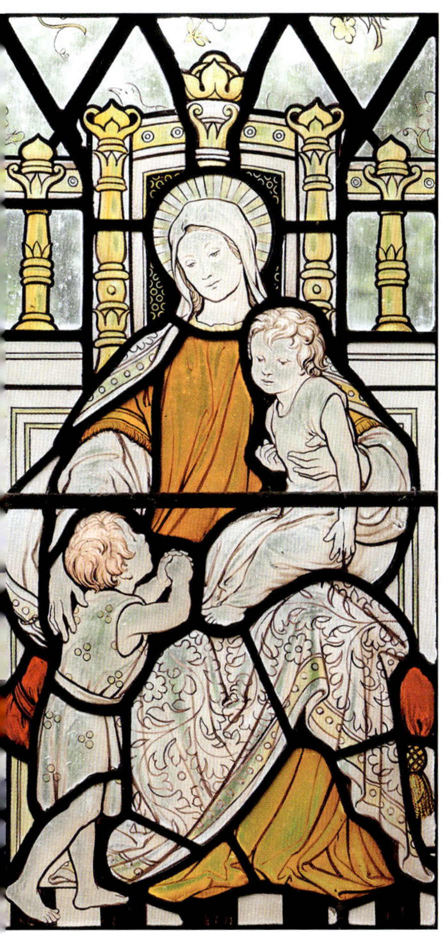

523. Reginald Bell, Female Saint with Children, 1933, Church of St Andoenus, Mounton, nave

19 *Journal of the British Society of Master Glass-Painters*, vol. i, no. 1 (April 1924), p. 3.

20 The differences between the windows are instructive. The finely delineated sixteenth-century turreted landscape and sky are replaced with patterned quarries, an economy perhaps, but simplifying and lightening the window. The drawing of the faces in the later window is more realistic, but the delicate treatment of the background and foreground in the earlier version has been lost, giving a crisper, cleaner effect. I am grateful to Sue Christou for sharing material with me from the archives of Christ Church, Prestatyn.

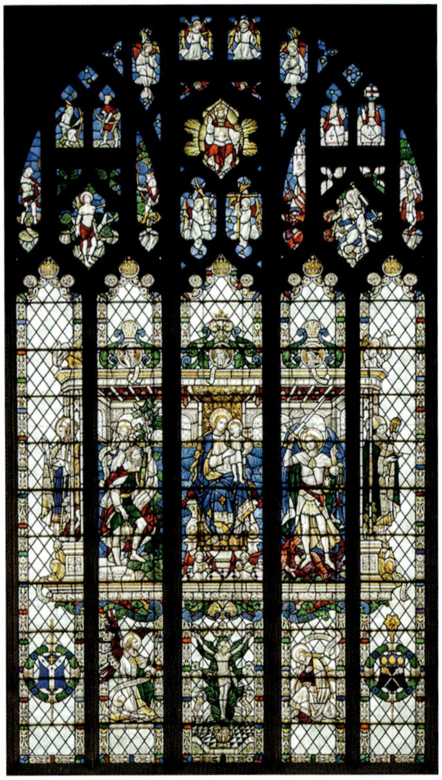

524. Frederick Eden, Virgin and Child with St Christopher and St Michael, 1922, Priory Church of St Mary, Abergavenny, east window

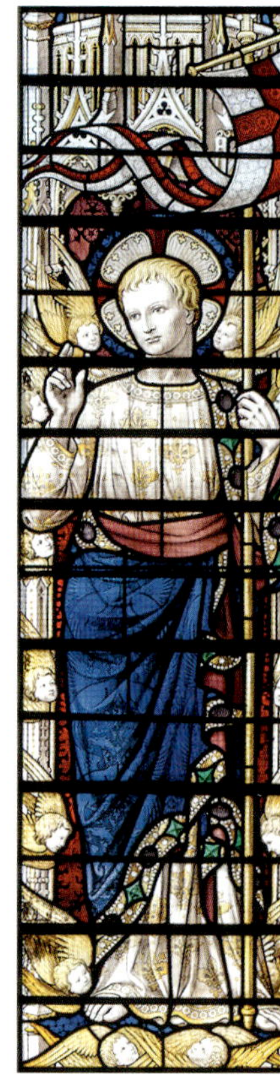

525. Ninian Comper, The Risen Christ, 1917, Church of St John the Baptist, Cardiff, east window

Discerning Anglo-Catholic patrons turned to the studios of a new generation of designers such as Ninian Comper, Geoffrey Webb, Frederick Eden and Horace Wilkinson. Ninian Comper worked in the office of Bodley & Garner and was a voluntary assistant to C.E. Kempe before establishing his own practice in the late 1880s. A devout disciple of Bodley's late Gothic, Comper designed his windows to allow more light into churches, with delicate colours and pure whites. Each of these artists were influenced by fifteenth and early sixteenth-century stained glass, but this medievalism was not without innovation. It is a mark of the general conservatism of the time that, at the unveiling of Comper's east window at the Church of St John the Baptist, Cardiff, in 1917, the speaker anticipated 'some criticism of the unconventional treatment of the central figure', as the figure of Christ was depicted beardless.[21] The beardless Christ is a feature of his other windows, as well as the reredos made to his design for the Church of St Margaret, Roath, Cardiff. Comper's early style is close to that of Burlison & Grylls, favoured by Bodley & Garner and used by Comper until he brought the making of his windows under his own control.[22]

An early work by Geoffrey Webb in Wales at the Church of St Saviour, Splott, Cardiff, is also close to the usual style of Burlison & Grylls and C.E. Kempe, with figures standing in elaborate canopied niches.[23] More characteristic work by Geoffrey Webb can be found in several churches in Wales as well as the Lady Chapel of Llandaff Cathedral, using a distinctive palette of blue, red, mauve and green in combination with lighter patterned quarries, rather than elaborate Gothic canopies. The two windows made for the north wall in 1928 were the first of a scheme of five windows that was eventually completed in 1952, complementing patterned stencilling originally undertaken in 1909. His brother Christopher Webb had worked as a glass painter for Comper, and all three artists share a similar use of colour in the 1920s and 30s, with a delicate and dignified portrayal of figures that has the unfortunate effect of draining them of warmth or depth.

21 C. St. D. Spencer, 'Address at the unveiling of the memorial to the late C.T. Vachell, M.D., on April 14th, 1917', *Reports and Transactions* (Cardiff Naturalists' Society), vol. l [50] (1917), pp. 17–19. Comper's work was almost exclusively ecclesiastical and Gothic, the most notable exception being his classicist war memorial that forms the centrepiece of Cathays Park in Cardiff.

22 Despite their usual adherence to Flemish sixteenth-century stained glass design, the artistic influences of Comper and Burlison & Grylls were much wider, indicated by their copies of Renaissance paintings of the Virgin and Child by Bellini at Christ Church, Welshpool (Burlison & Grylls), and Pentrefoelas Church (Ninian Comper).

23 Webb worked for C.E. Kempe and then briefly with another former employee of Kempe, Herbert Bryans, before establishing his own studio in 1914.

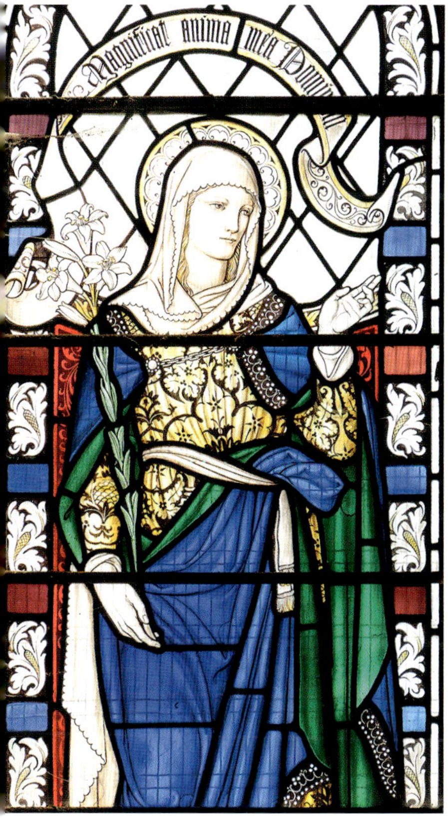

26. Christopher Webb, The Virgin Mary, 1928, hurch of St Caranog, Llangrannog, east window

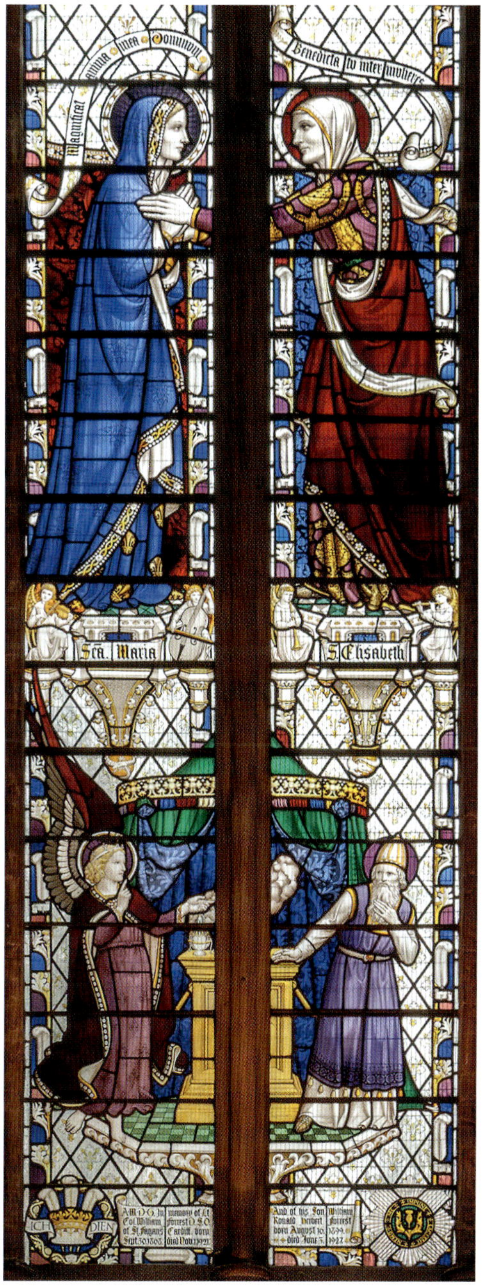

527. (right) Geoffrey Webb, The Visitation and the Annunciation to Zechariah, 1928, Llandaff Cathedral, Lady Chapel

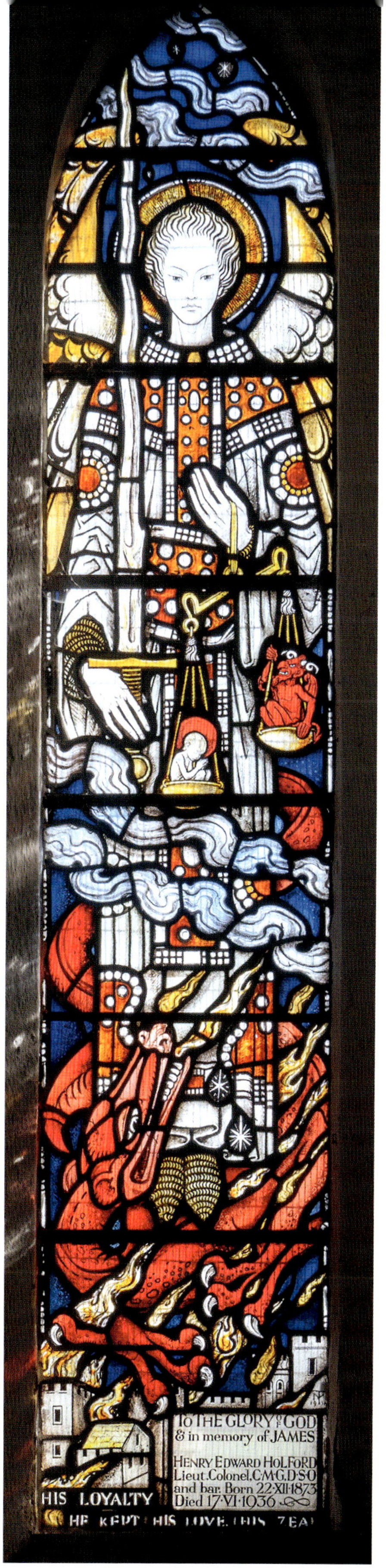

528. (far right) Martin Travers, St Michael, 1938, Church of St Cynfelyn, Llangynfelyn, nave

Other stained glass artists of the period courted by Anglo-Catholic patrons included Martin Travers and A.K. Nicholson, whose work was more rooted in the Arts and Crafts Movement. Travers trained with Christopher Whall and then with Ninian Comper before the First World War, and became influential through his teaching of stained glass at the Royal College of Art from 1925 until 1948. His static depiction of the saints Nicholas and Oswald, made in 1921 for the Church of St Stephen, Butetown, Cardiff, lacks the fiery vitality of his later window depicting Michael at the Church of St Cynfelyn, Llangynfelyn. The studio of A. K. Nicholson received several commissions in the Swansea area,

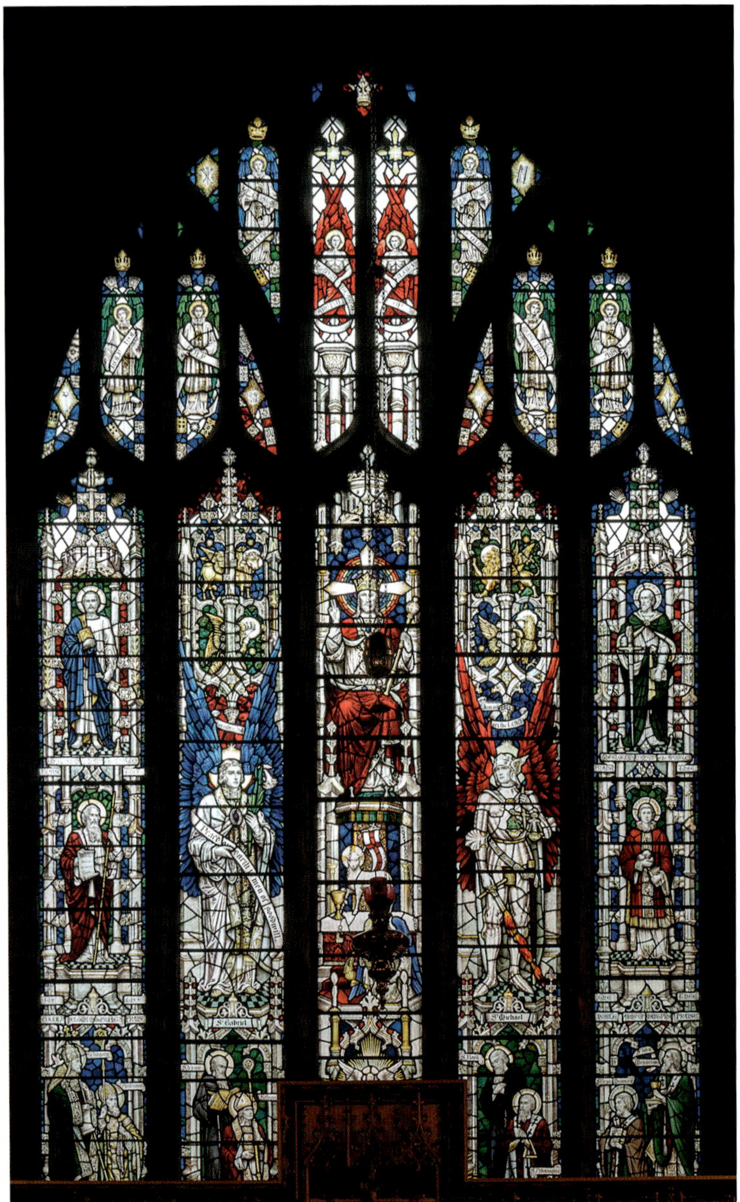

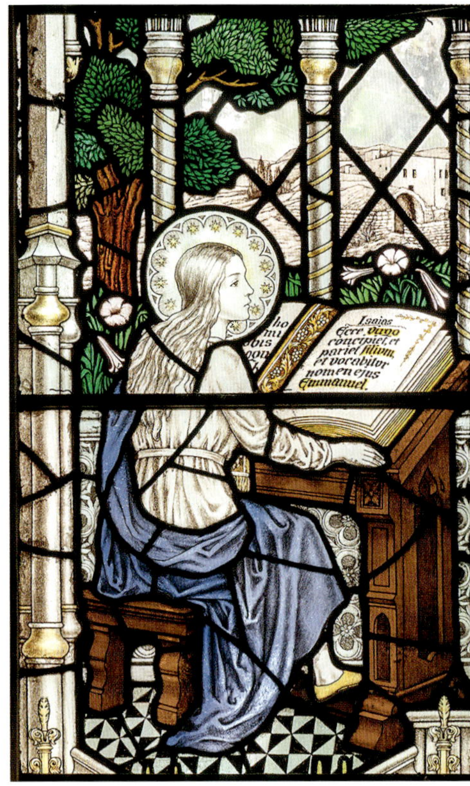

529. (left) A.K Nicholson, Christ with Archangels and the Four Evangelists, 1925, Church of St Gabriel, Uplands, Swansea, east window.

530. (above) A.K. Nicholson, The Instruction of the Virgin Mary, 1926, Church of St Gabriel, Uplands, Swansea, Lady Chapel

notably for the chancel and Lady Chapel of the Anglo-Catholic Church of St Gabriel, Uplands. His chancel east window of 1925 was followed by three two-light windows made in 1926 for the Lady Chapel, depicting the expulsion of Eve, Mary being instructed by her mother, Anne, and, in the east window, the Annunciation.[24]

Windows by the firm of C.E. Kempe remained popular in Wales until the firm closed in 1934. The demand for canopied windows with scenes reminiscent of early sixteenth-century German and Flemish artists provided numerous commissions for Christopher Charles Powell into the 1950s. He learned the craft of stained glass from his father, Charles Powell, and had also worked with C.E. Kempe, and his work shows strong continuity both with the work of the family firm and late windows by Kempe's studio.[25] In 1938 he designed the only window not made by Kempe's firm for the Priory Church of St Mary, Monmouth,

24 Two more windows depicting Catherine and Helen were also made for the chancel. The Marian subjects are indicative of the Anglo-Catholic inclinations of the church, and in the lower panels of the east window biblical or Welsh saints are eschewed for the Latin fathers Gregory, Ambrose, Jerome and Augustine of Hippo, opposite the Eastern fathers Basil, Athanasius, Gregory Nazianzen and John Chrysostom.

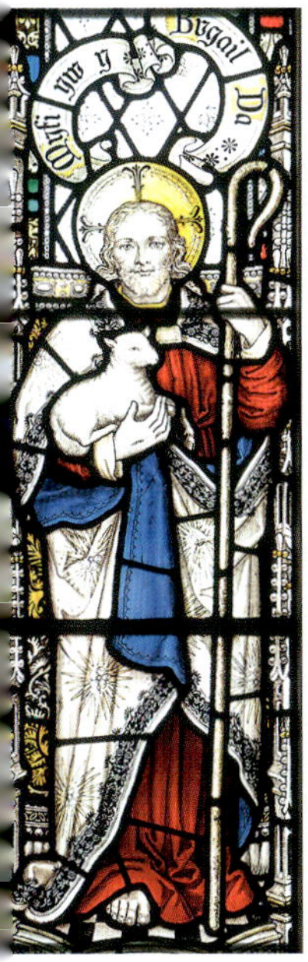

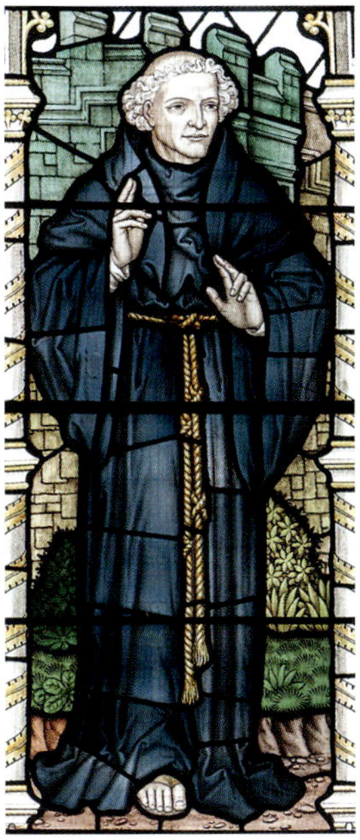

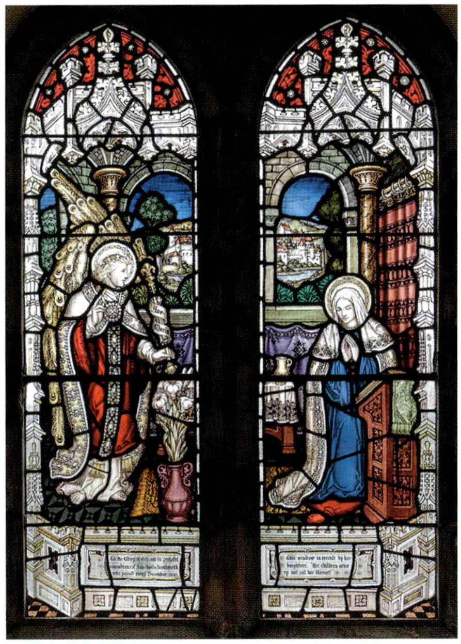

533. (centre left) Christopher Charles Powell, Geoffrey of Monmouth, 1938, Priory Church of St Mary, Monmouth, south aisle

534. (left) Christopher Charles Powell, The Annunciation, *c.* 1941, Church of St Ffraid, Trearddur Bay, nave

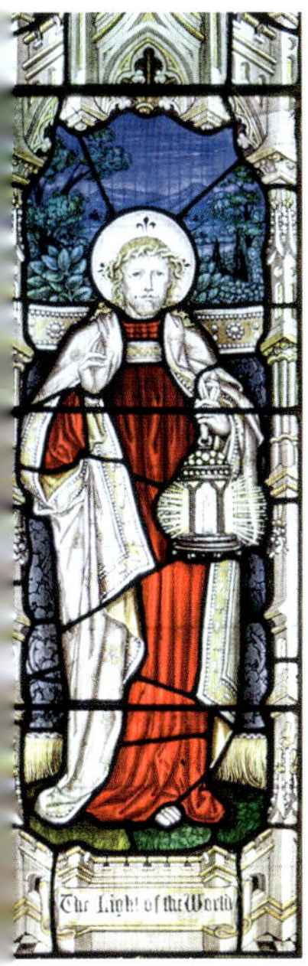

531. (above left) C.E. Kempe & Co., Christ the Good Shepherd, 1927, Church of St Barnabas, Felindre (Carmarthenshire), chancel

532. (left) Charles Powell, Christ the Light of the World, *c.* 1914–26, Priory Church of St Mary Magdalene, St Clears, chancel

with standing figures of the founder of the church, Wihenoc; the writer Geoffrey of Monmouth; and the architects Francis Smith of Warwick and G.E. Street.[26] The number of windows made by Powell for Welsh churches suggests not only the continuing popularity of this style in some circles, but perhaps also his Welsh connections through his membership of the London Welsh Honourable Society of Cymmrodorion. His links with the Welsh ecclesiastical establishment probably brought him commissions such as the figures of David and Archbishop Edwards in the west window of St Asaph Cathedral.[27]

The work of C.C. Powell is conservative in design and composition, but also demonstrates the trend towards more translucent windows with purer colours typical of stained glass during the 1930s. In a few windows, Powell sets aside late Gothic forms, such as his large east window at the Church of St Mary, Kidwelly. Devoid of his usual Gothic architectural framework, the main scene of the Transfiguration, with surrounding figures and angels, floats uncomfortably amid plain diamond quarries. His depiction of interiors, such as the window

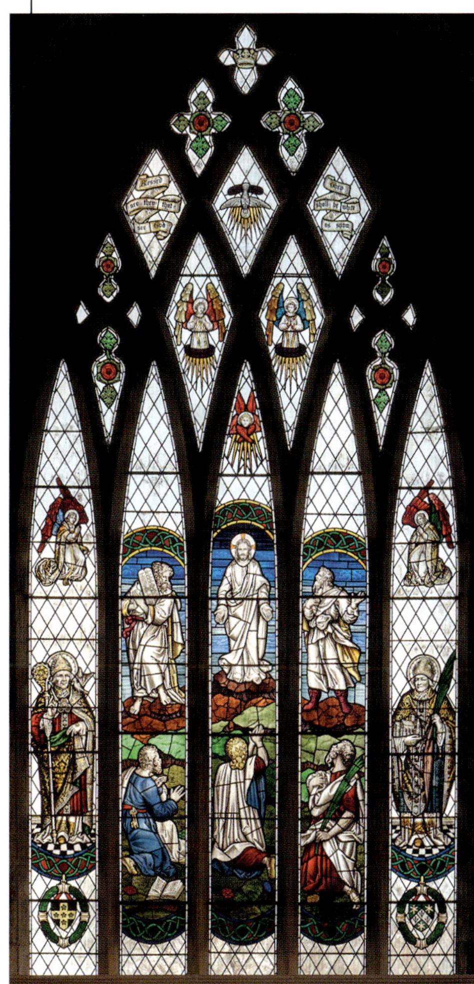

535. Christopher Charles Powell, The Transfiguration, 1936, Church of St Mary, Kidwelly, east window

25 Such is the close continuity of style, C.C. Powell was no doubt responsible for many windows by the family firm made in the 1920s and 30s, such as the group of windows at St Clears.

26 The window was devised by the architectural historian Basil F.L. Clarke when he was a curate at the church. The artist was also commissioned to make two further windows for Christ Church, Swansea, in the 1930s, where there were already four windows by Kempe's studio, dating from 1897 to 1918.

27 He also reminded his potential clients on his address labels that he had been 'Artist in stained glass to H.M. King Edward VII'.

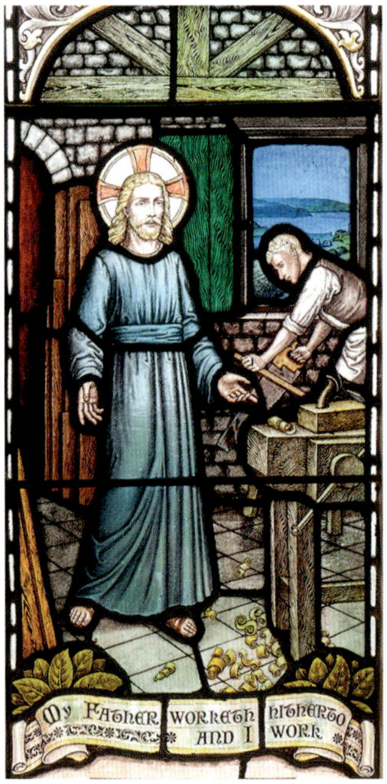

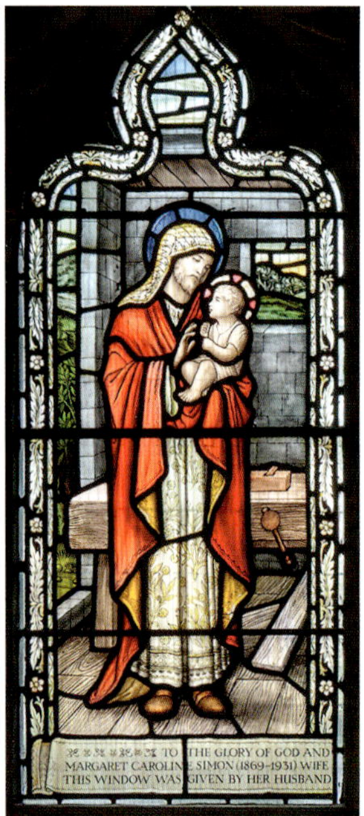

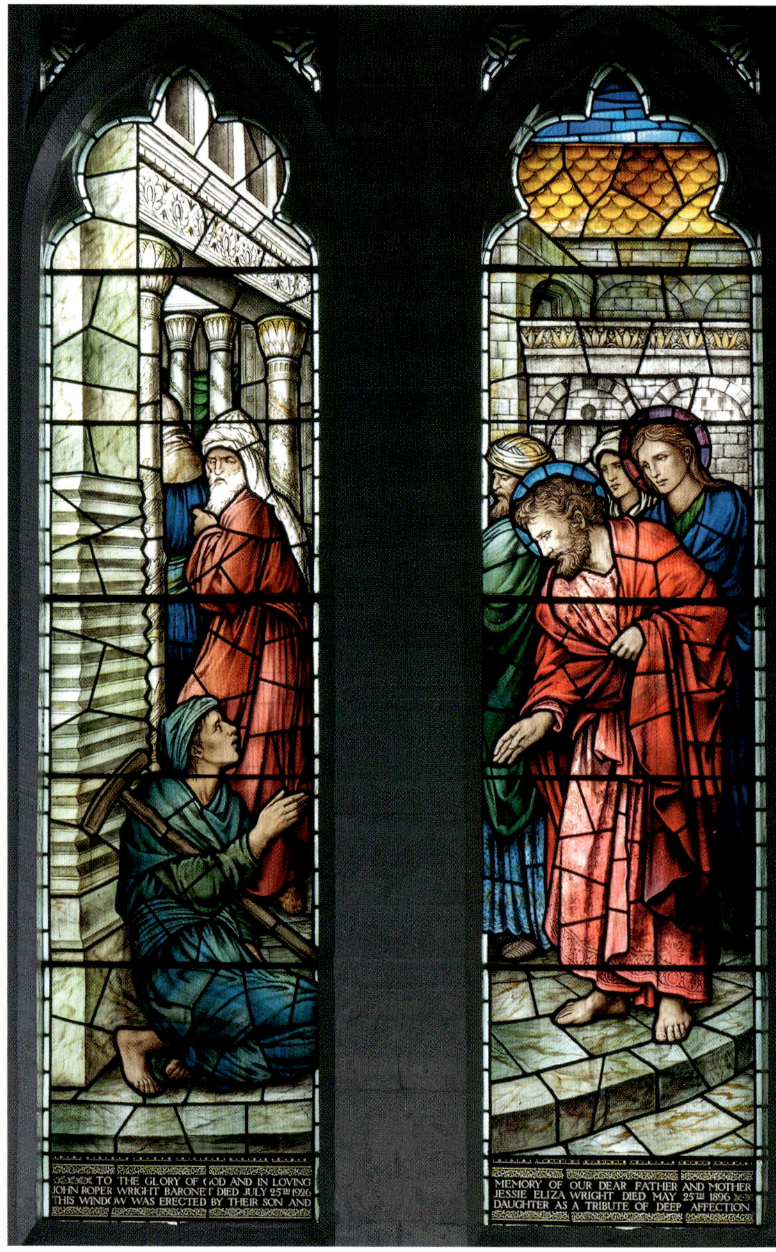

536. (above) Christopher Charles Powell, Christ Appearing in a Carpenter's Workshop, 1936, Church of St Madoc of Ferns, Haroldston West, nave

537. (above right) Morris & Co., Joseph with the Infant Christ, 1935, designed by W.H. Knight, Church of St David, Llanfaes, Brecon, north aisle

538. (right) Morris & Co., Peter and John Healing the Lame Beggar at the Beautiful Gate, 1928, designed by Henry Dearle, Church of St John the Evangelist, Gowerton, nave

depicting Paul in prison at the Priory Church of St Mary, St Clears, and the rather incongruous appearance of Christ in a carpenters' workshop at the Church of St Madoc of Ferns, Haroldston West, is akin to contemporary work of a firm with a very different tradition, Morris & Co. New designs by Henry Dearle and W.H. Knight gradually replaced the use of old cartoons by Edward Burne-Jones, sometimes in intimate scenes such as the Visitation at the Church of St Michael, Caerwys, and the Holy Family at the Church of St David, Llanfaes, Brecon, but also on a more monumental scale at the Church of St John, Gowerton.[28]

28 The depiction of the Christ child in the arms of Joseph at the Church of St David, Llanfaes, is an original design by W.H. Knight and is used in a two-light window opposite the figure of Mary, a design by Henry Dearle from an earlier window, which originally depicted Naomi. A.C. Sewter, *The Stained Glass of William Morris and his Circle* (New Haven/London: Yale University Press, 1974), vol. ii, p. 31.

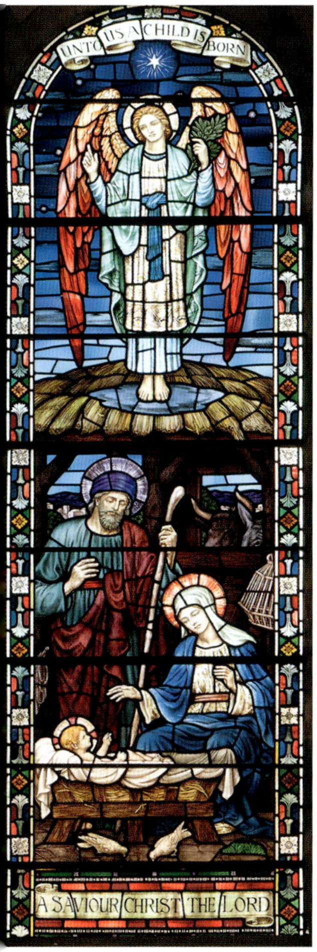

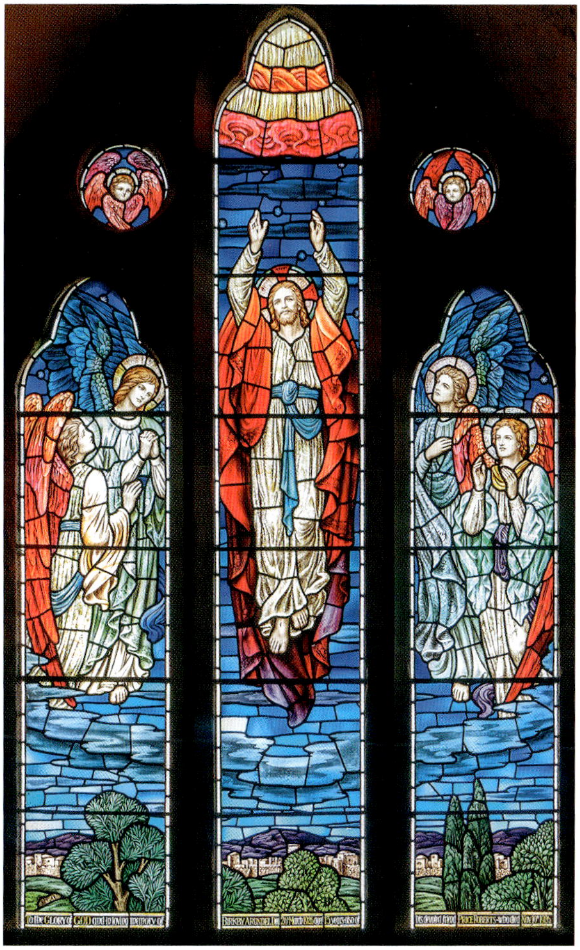

539. (far left) William Glasby, The Nativity, 1929, Ewenny Priory, west window

540. (left) William Glasby, The Ascension, 1927, Church of St Garmon, Llanarmon-yn-Iâl, east window

The colours used by Morris & Co. are often muted in comparison to those chosen by their former painter, William Glasby, whose windows of the 1920s and 30s retain a recognisable Pre-Raphaelite sensibility. Glasby's many windows for churches in north and south Wales include the numinous Ascension with angels at the Church of St Garmon, Llanarmon-yn-Iâl, and his Nativity scene at Ewenny Priory.[29]

At Christ Church, Prestatyn, the strong blue sky in the Annunciation scene by Shrigley & Hunt lifts the range of their usual earthy palette of the period, and the Lancaster firm remained popular throughout Wales. Further east windows of the 1920s and 30s at Abergele, Hanmer and Killay contrast with other windows of the 1930s and 40s that demonstrate a variability of quality and draughtsmanship.

29 The artist made 24 windows for Welsh churches, although two were made for the Church of St Luke, Newport, now demolished. The central light at Llanarmon-yn-Iâl is repeated in Glasby's east window at Llangan, and they are also similar to Henry Holiday's ascending Christ for James Powell & Son at the Church of the Holy Trinity, Ystrad Mynach. For a list of works and biographical information see Donald Green, Dennis Hadley and Joan Hadley, 'The life and work of William Glasby (1863–1941)', *The Journal of Stained Glass*, vol. xxxii (2008), pp. 91–106.

541. Shrigley & Hunt, The Ascension, 1935, Christ Church, Prestatyn, east window

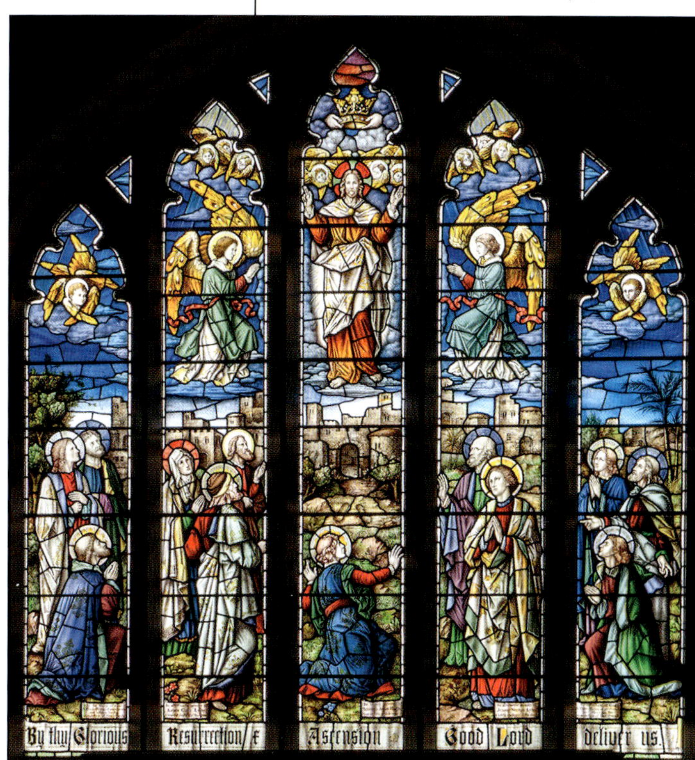

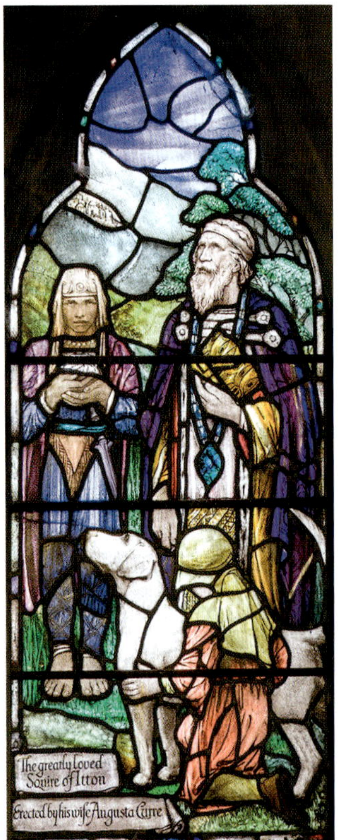

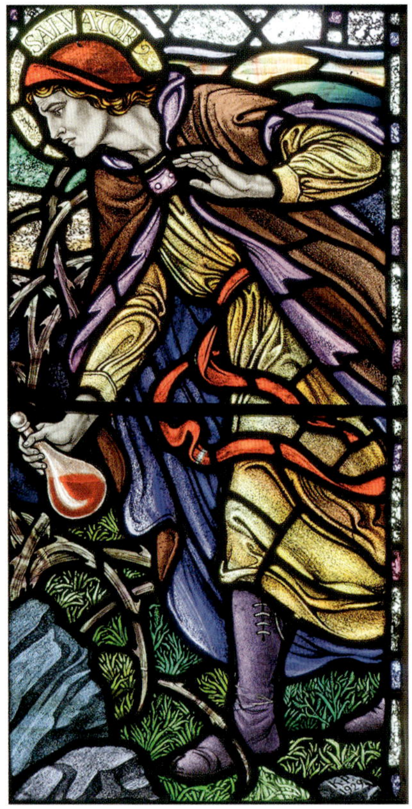

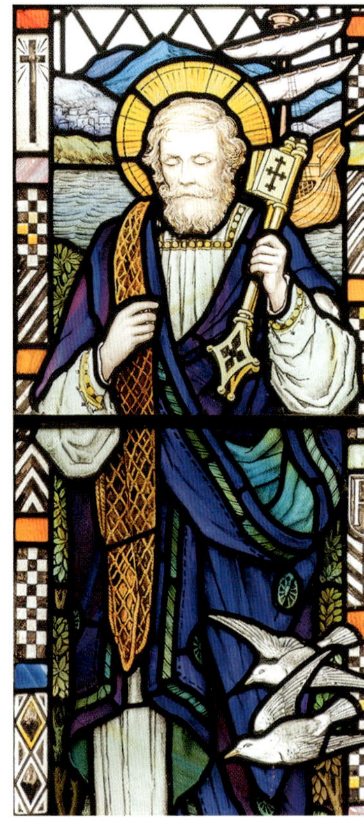

542. (right) Theodora Salusbury, Figures from the Adoration of the Magi, 1931, Church of St Peter, Newchurch (Monmouthshire), east window

543. (centre right) Karl Parsons, The Good Samaritan, 1929, Church of St James, Pyle, nave

544. (far right) W. Pearce & E. Cutler, St Peter, probably 1920s or 30s, Church of St Gwrthwl, Llanwrthwl, nave

The quality and originality of work by the artists connected with the Arts and Crafts Movement was more consistent. Karl Parsons' window at the Church of St James, Pyle, features a handsome depiction of Christ as the Good Samaritan, coming to the aid of the wounded traveller left caught in the briars by the two passers-by. Two former pupils of Parsons made only one window for churches in Wales. Theodora Salusbury designed an unusual portrayal of the Adoration of the Magi for the Church of St Peter, Newchurch (Monmouthshire), with the Virgin and Child in a roundel above and the Magi and their attendants in the two lights below.[30] The window by Joan Fulleylove at the Church of St Andrew, Narberth, is a compact design with standing figures of the saints John and David, with painted scenes on pale tinted glass below.[31]

The darkening effect of the rich colours available to artists in the 1920s and 30s was sometimes offset by the use of white glass as part of the design or in the surrounds. Churches at Caerwys and Llanllwchaiarn have late works by H.G. Hiller, the former displaying an arresting use of orange in combination with the blue of Mary's dress and the purple of Gabriel's cloak in the scene of the Annunciation.

30 With the Magi is a white foxhound, a favourite of Sir William Edward Carne Curre, in whose memory the window was given by his wife. The standing figure on the right is perhaps Sir William. The window is interpreted in an article written by John Morgan-Guy for the Imaging the Bible in Wales website, <http://www.imagingthebible.org/wales/research/essays/newchurch_adoration.html>.

31 The commission came from Lady Margaret Davies, as a memorial to her father William Evans, rector of Narberth and Robeston Wathen and canon of St Davids. At Robeston Wathen, her husband, the composer Sir Walford Davies had commissioned a small reredos from Fulleylove in thanksgiving for his marriage in 1924. See John Morgan-Guy, 'Biblical Art from Wales: Setting the Scene' in Martin O'Kane and John Morgan-Guy, *Biblical Art from Wales* (Sheffield: Sheffield Phoenix Press, 2010), pp. 34–7.

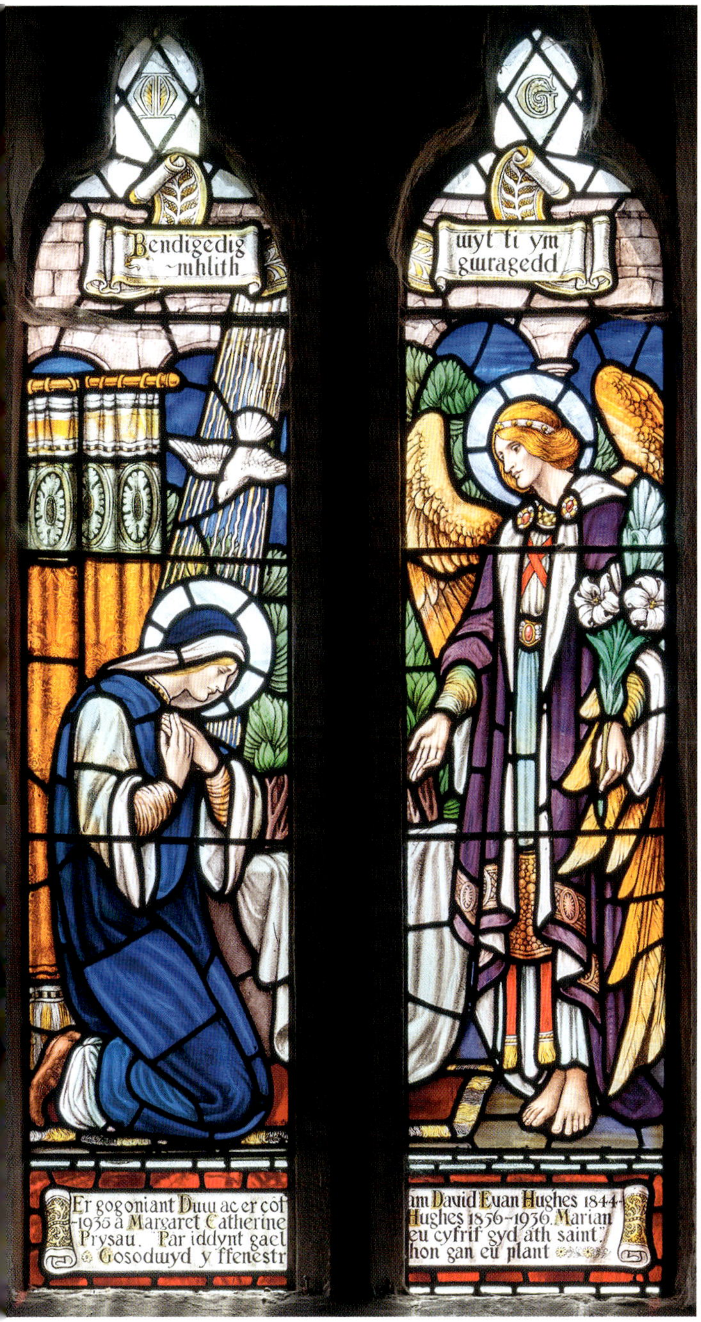

45. H.G. Hiller, The Annunciation, *c.* 1937,
hurch of St Michael, Caerwys, nave

A similar colouration can be found in the figure of Peter in a two-light window by Pearce & Cutler at the Church of St Gwrthwl, Llanwrthwl, a window without the Gothic canopies and dark backgrounds found in some of their other windows of the period.

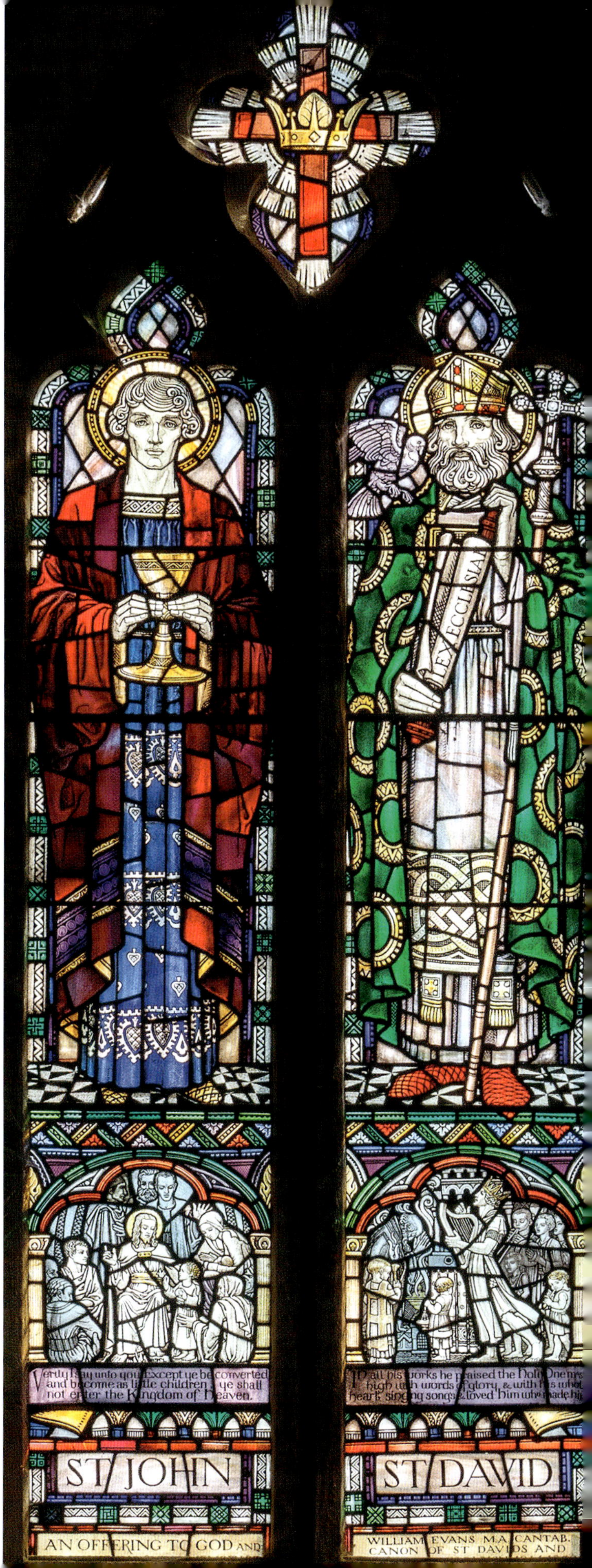

546. Joan Fulleylove, St John and St David, 1932, Church of St Andrew, Narberth, nave

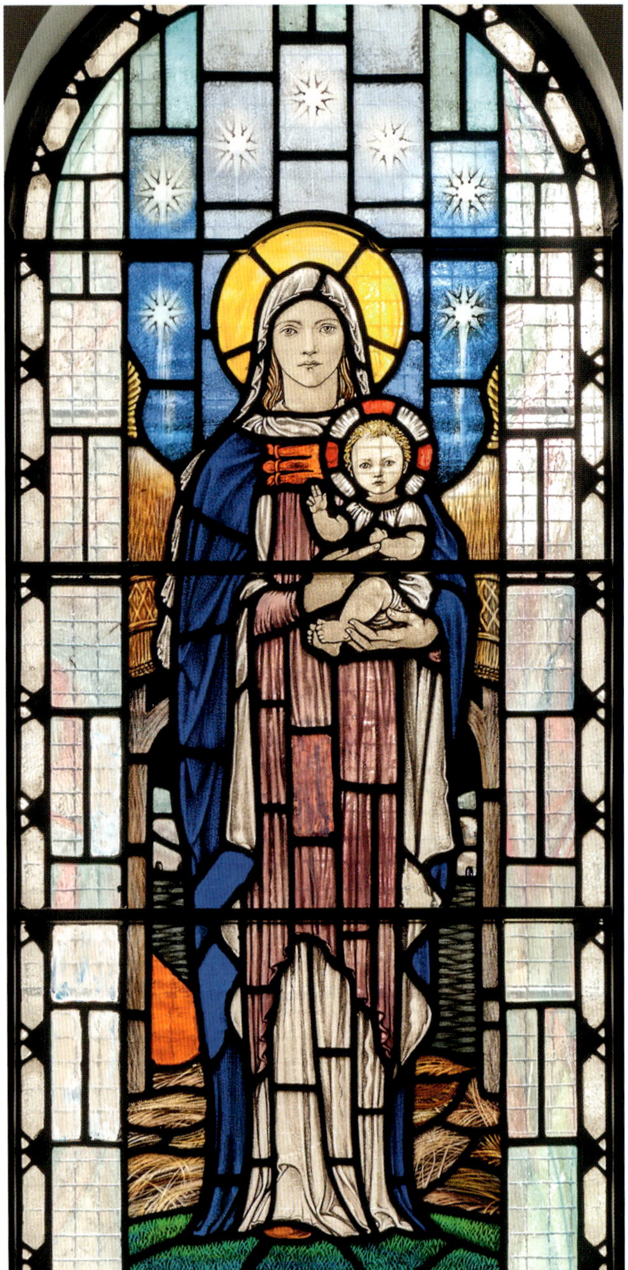

547. (left) Veronica Whall, Virgin and Child, 1934, Church of the Resurrection, Ely, Cardiff, Lady Chapel

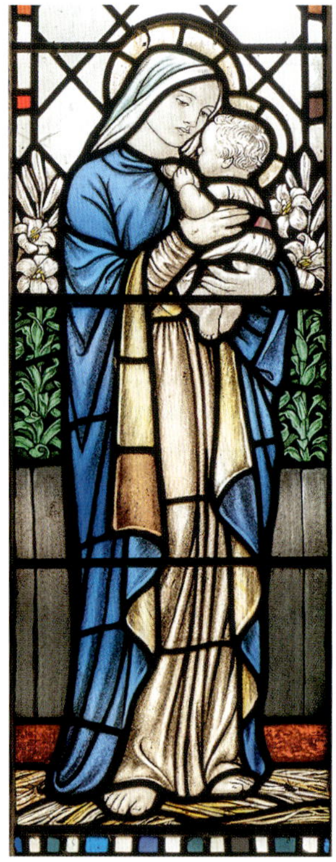

548. (above) Arnold Robinson, Virgin and Child, 1929, Church of St Mary, Rogiet, east window

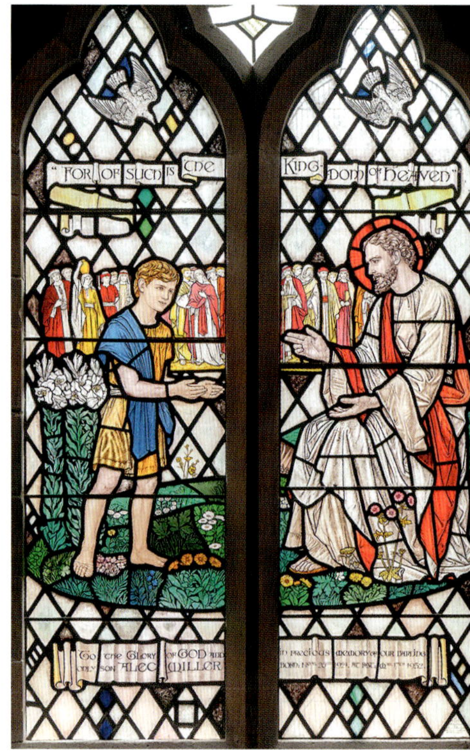

549. Florence Camm, Christ with a Child, c. 1932, Church of the Holy Trinity, Llandrindod Wells, nave

Three windows by Veronica Whall at the Church of the Resurrection, Ely, Cardiff, allow light into the otherwise dark area of the Lady Chapel through the rectangular sections of streaky Norman slab glass around the standing figures.[32] Her work, as well as that by two other pupils and assistants of Christopher Whall who worked together, Arnold Wathen Robinson and Edward Woore, exemplifies what Lawrence Lee later identified as the 'silvery pastoral lyricism unique to the English vision'.[33] Robinson's delicate Virgin and Child, between Christ as the Sower and as the Good Shepherd, at the Church of St Mary, Rogiet, are restricted to a narrow palette with white glass quarries above and below to light the chancel. At the Church of the Holy Trinity, Llandrindod Wells, Florence Camm made use of white glass within the main scene as well as in diamond quarries around it, which were enlivened by the small irregular pieces of coloured glass and painted detail.

Church furnishing firms continued to change and flourish between the wars, such as Jones & Willis and J. Wippell & Co. Ltd, who followed the

32 A fourth window near the chapel by the artist is a scene with Christ in a boat out fishing with his disciples.

33 Lawrence Lee, *The Appreciation of Stained Glass* (London: Oxford University Press, 1977), p. 110.

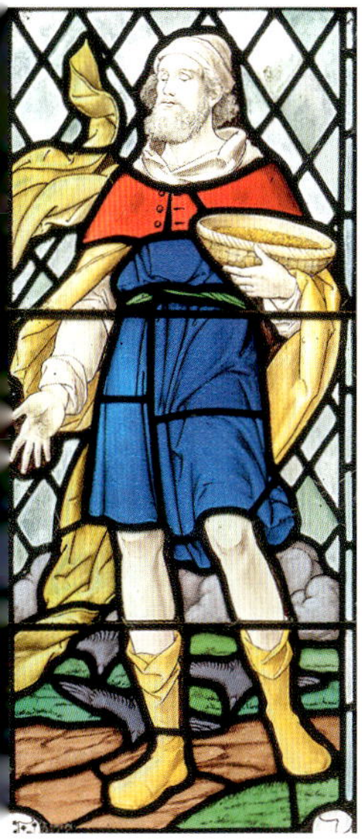

550. Jones & Willis, The Sower, 1939, Church of St Tysoi, Llansoy, nave

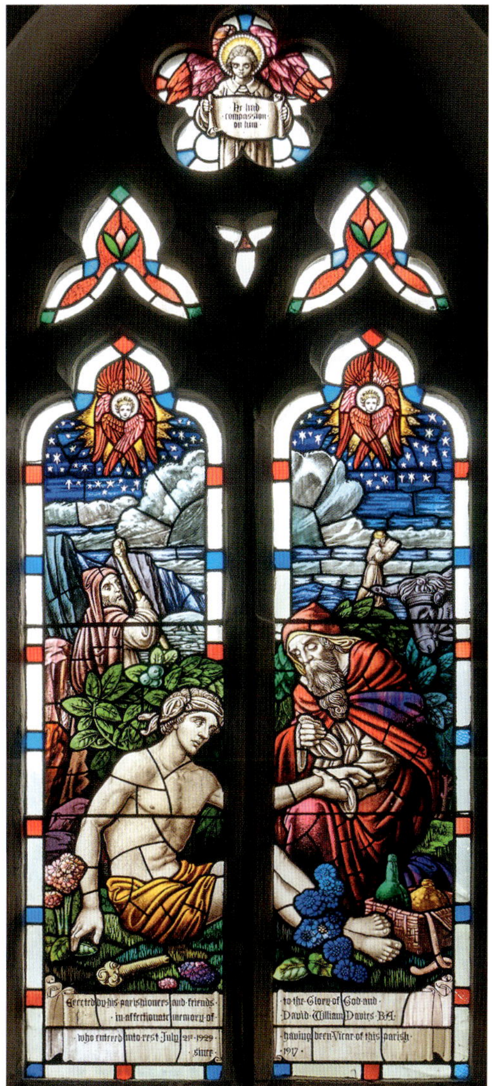

551. J. Wippell & Co., The Good Samaritan, 1931, Church of St Mary, Aberafan, south aisle

fashion for purer and stronger colour in the 1930s. Based in Birmingham with an office in London, Jones & Willis expanded into north Wales from their office in Liverpool, while the stained glass studio of the clerical tailors Wippell's, based in Exeter, but with offices in London and Manchester, also made work for Welsh churches. The colour of windows by Wippell's in the 1920s and 30s is bright and strong in their biblical scenes for the Church of St Hilda, Griffithstown, and the Church of St Mary, Aberafan, as well as the sets of figures designed by George Cooper-Abbs for the east windows at the Church of St Mary, Llanfair Discoed, and the Church of St Bartholomew, Llanover.

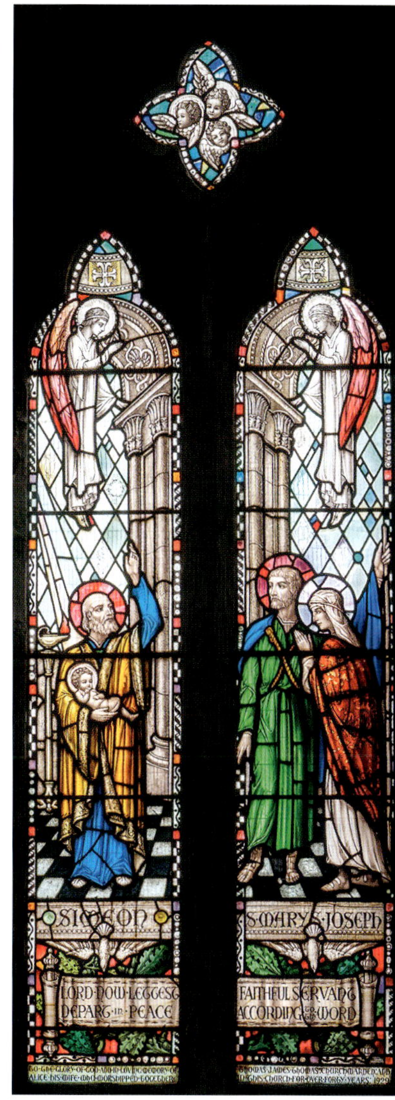

552. William Morris & Co. Westminster, The Presentation in the Temple, 1929, Christ Church, Ebbw Vale, south aisle

A two-light window by the firm depicting Christ with women and children, also designed by Cooper-Abbs, is among a group of good windows installed at Christchurch, Ebbw Vale, between the wars. As well as a two-light window with standing figures of centurions by John Hall & Sons, strong colouring and original design can be found in two windows by William Morris & Co., Westminster. The composition of the scenes of the Transfiguration and the Presentation in the Temple across two lights contrast with their more conventional windows between the wars, such as those for the churches at Montgomery, Llanbadarn Fawr (Ceredigion), Narberth, Fairbourne and Marshfield.[34]

34 The firm was also known as William Morris Studios to distinguish the firm from the more famous Morris & Co. Ruth Cooke, 'The other William Morris', *The Journal of Stained Glass*, vol. xxiv (2000), pp. 53–9. They gained commissions across the denominational spectrum in Wales during the 1930s, making windows for the Roman Catholic Chapel of St Non, and at the Calvinistic Methodist Chapels at Llanreath, Pembroke Dock and Penmorfa, near New Quay.

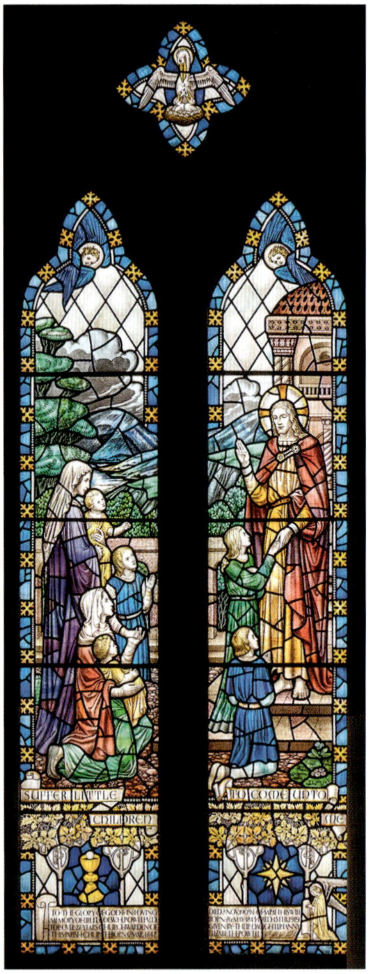

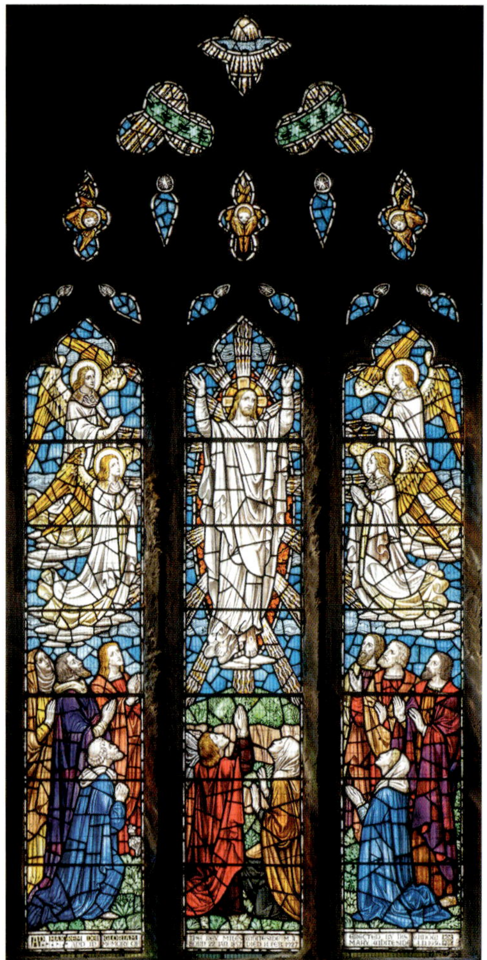

553. (above) J. Wippell & Co., Christ with Women and Children, 1936, designed by G. Cooper-Abbs, Christ Church, Ebbw Vale, north aisle

554. (above right) Powell & Sons, The Ascension, 1936, designed by James Hogan, Church of St Tathan, St Athan, west window

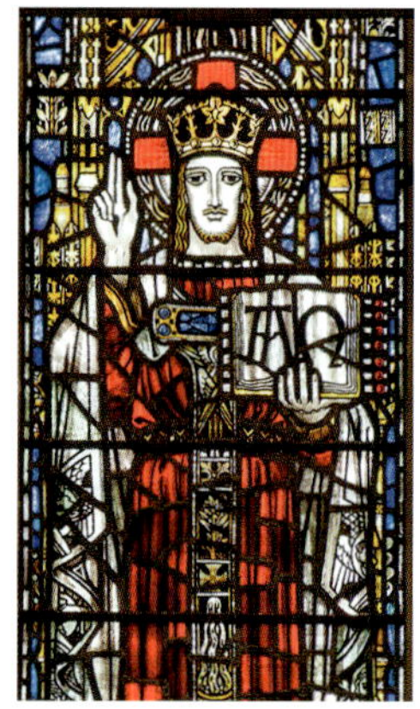

555. Powell & Sons, Christ in Majesty, 1934, designed by A.F. Erridge, Church of the Holy Trinity, Aberystwyth, east window

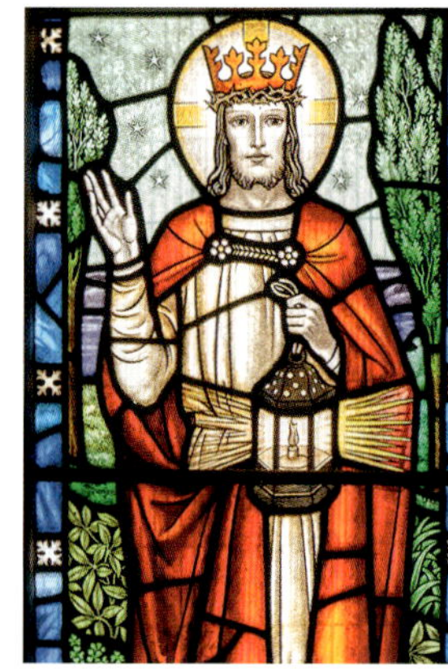

556. J. Wippell & Co., Christ the Light of the World, 1935, probably designed by G. Cooper-Abbs, Church of St Mary, Llanfair Discoed, east window

George Cooper-Abbs had been trained at Whitefriars by Powell & Sons, and some of his work for Wippell's is similar to contemporary work by Powell's, which can be found at many churches around Wales.[35] Under the direction of James Hogan the studio gradually loosened its Pre-Raphaelite style, based on the work of Henry Holiday and J.W. Brown, and some of their windows of the 1930s demonstrate a degree of modernism in their strength of colour and draughtsmanship, such as at the Church of the Holy Trinity, Aberystwyth, and the two windows nearby at Llanfihangel Genau'r Glyn. Powell's had the advantage of making glass themselves, offering their designers the opportunity to utilise the fullest possible range of colour, texture and thickness in the glass employed. In their 1935 booklet *The Art of Stained Glass*, Powell's welcomed the 'check to the commercialisation of ecclesiastical craft-work' effected by the introduction of Diocesan Advisory Committees in the 1920s, and were confident that the quality of their work proved 'that the finest tradition of Stained Glass has been truly rediscovered and is once more a living Art that can compare with the finest medieval work'.

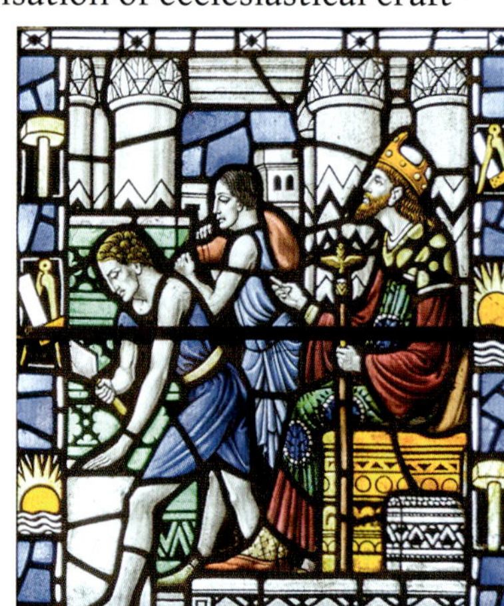

557. Powell & Sons, The Building of the Temple, 1939, designed by James Hogan, Church of St Peter, Lampeter, chancel

35 From 1919 James Powell & Sons altered its name to James Powell & Sons (Whitefriars) Ltd, and was often known thereafter as simply Powell & Sons or as Whitefriars Stained Glass Studios, adopting a makers' mark of a cowled friar.

The breadth of subjects and styles found in Anglican churches can also be found in Roman Catholic churches between the wars, despite the fact that in 1921 there were only 133 churches in the Diocese of Menevia and the newly-created Archdiocese of Cardiff.[36] In the nineteenth century new Roman Catholic churches had sometimes been provided with stained glass when funds were available, but fewer received subsequent gifts of memorial windows from the wealthy local landowners who facilitated much of the church building and restoration of Anglican churches at the time. Most new windows for Roman Catholic churches were made by John Hardman & Co. and Mayer of Munich until the outbreak of the First World War, after which Hardman's enjoyed the bulk of the market.[37] Other artists with Catholic credentials were sometimes preferred. Arthur Orr, who had worked at Hardman's and designed for the Dublin firm of Joshua Clarke, designed chancel windows for the Church of St Mary of the Angels, Canton, Cardiff.

At what is now the Cathedral Church of St Joseph, Swansea, three aisle windows by Hardman's were all given in memory of clergy who served in the parish, rather than wealthy parishioners. The window given in memory of Canon Wulstan Richards, who built the church, includes a kneeling portrait of him offering the church to its patron, Joseph, between his own two patron saints, Wulstan and John. New churches were built after the First World War as the Roman Catholic Church in Wales grew in strength, and Hardman's made the windows given by Archbishop Mostyn for the new church at Neath in 1933, including a rose window in which Joseph is included in four narrative scenes.

36 Figures from D. Densil Morgan, *The Span of the Cross* (Cardiff: University of Wales Press, 2011, second edition), p. 95. The Archdiocese of Cardiff also includes churches in Herefordshire.

37 Hardman's were also popular throughout the nineteenth century for Anglican churches, and increasingly signalled Anglo-Catholic sympathies among patrons. Fewer Anglican patrons commissioned windows from the firm after the First World War, even in Cardiff where the Anglo-Catholic tradition was strong, and this may suggest a distancing of Anglican patrons from the firm.

559. John Hardman & Co., St Joseph with St Wulstan and St John, *c.* 1923, Cathedral Church of St Joseph, Swansea, south aisle

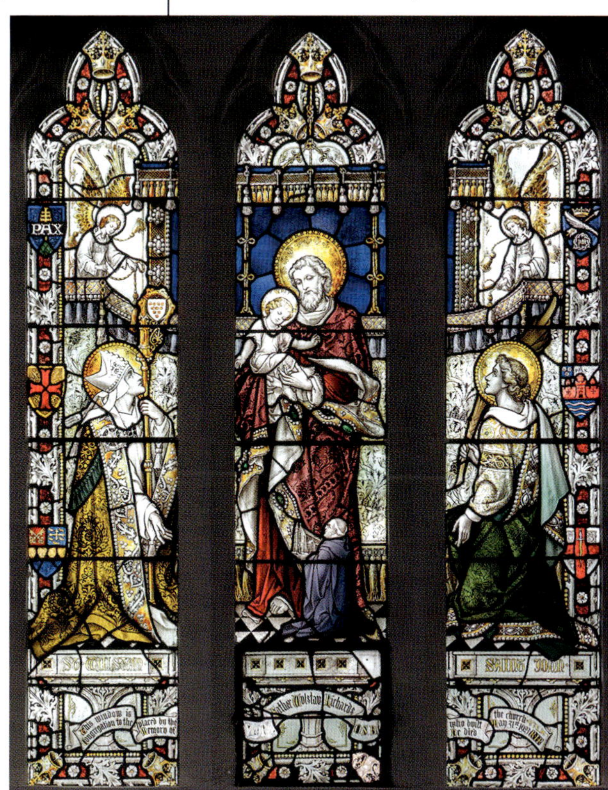

558. John Hardman & Co., St Joseph with Scenes from the Life of St Joseph, 1933, Church of St Joseph, Neath, west window

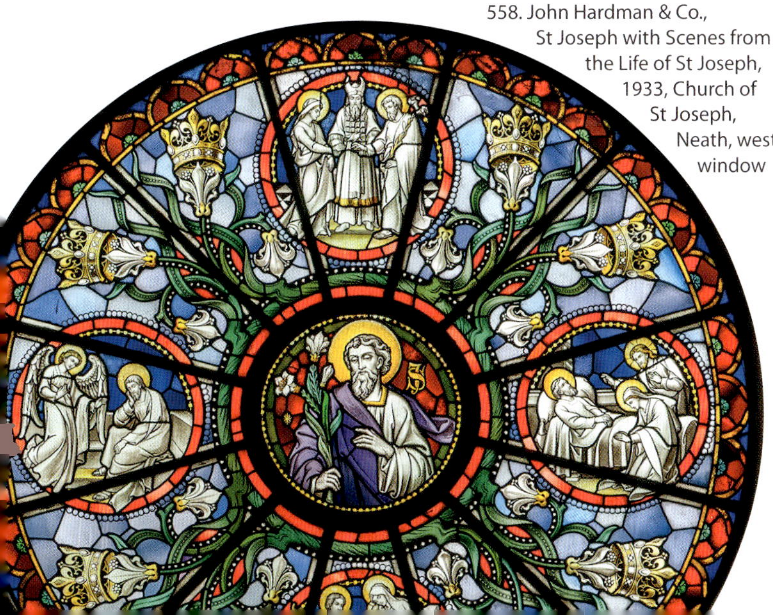

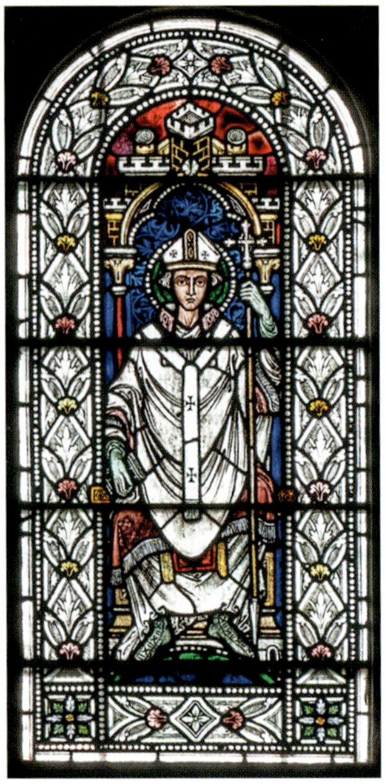

560. St Elphege, probably 1920s, Church of St Mary of the Angels, Canton, Cardiff, nave clerestory

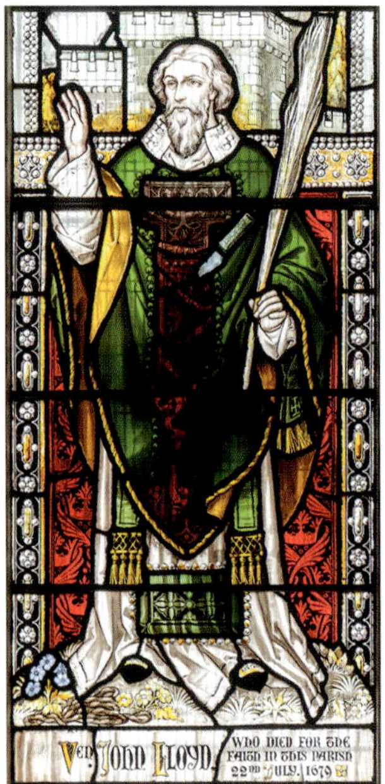

561. John Hardman & Co., John Lloyd, 1926, designed by Dunstan Powell, Church of St Peter, Cardiff, west wall (vestibule)

The patron saints of churches were sometimes the subject of east windows, as at the Church of St Alban in Splott, Cardiff, where the martyrdom of Alban is depicted across the three central lights of the five-light east window. The saints depicted in the nave windows of the church include a wider range of non-biblical saints than are commonly found in Anglican churches, such as Cuthbert, Monica, Charles Borromeo, John Bosco and Joan of Arc.[38] At the Church of St Mary of the Angels, Canton, Cardiff, the numerous stained glass windows have no narrative scenes, but are all of saints. The choice of saints reflects the connection of the church with the Benedictine order and in particular with Ampleforth Abbey in Yorkshire (who supplied priests for the parish), which accounts for the presence of two figures of Lawrence, the patron saint of Ampleforth, one of which is placed between two other saints connected with the north of England, Herbert and William of York. Fr Elphege Duggan, under whose leadership the church was built in 1905, is commemorated in the adjacent three-light window that depicts Patrick with Helen and Elphege. While early Welsh saints are absent, the seventeenth-century Welsh Catholic martyrs John Roberts and Philip Powell are found at either side of a representation of Mary as Mother of Monks.[39]

Two further Catholic martyrs, John Lloyd and Philip Evans, were executed in Cardiff in 1679, and were commemorated in a window at the west end of the Church of St Peter, Cardiff. A window in a similar style and also by John Hardman & Co. at the Church of St Winifrede, Holywell, depicts Bishop John Fisher and Lady Margaret Beaufort. The subject is a deliberate reminder of the pre-Reformation Catholic heritage of the Tudor dynasty: Margaret Beaufort, the mother of Henry VII, offers her vows of chastity and obedience to John Fisher, who was executed for treason by her grandson Henry VIII in 1535, having refused to accept Henry as the head of the English church.

In some Catholic churches early Welsh saints were chosen along with patron saints in the 1930s. The contention over the inheritance of the Welsh saints and the rivalry between the Anglican and Roman

38 Unusually, Joan of Arc, standing in armour with a spear and sword, is not a military memorial, but is in memory of a former rector.

39 I am grateful to Richard Watson for information regarding the history of the church. Elphege was archbishop of Canterbury during the late tenth and early eleventh centuries, and his conversion of King Olaf has been traditionally associated with the coming of Christianity to Norway. The window including Mary Mother of Monks, looks to be in a slightly different style and may date from after the Second World War, perhaps from the 1955 anniversary of the church.

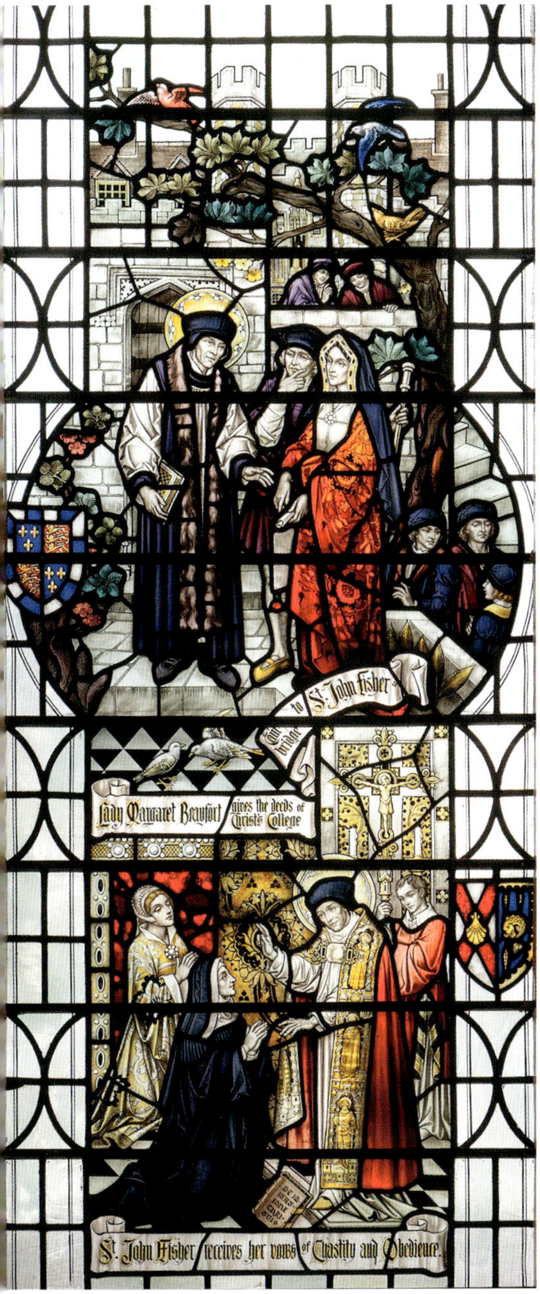

562. John Hardman & Co., Scenes with Bishop John Fisher and Lady Margaret Beaufort, 1936, Church of St Winifrede, Holywell, nave

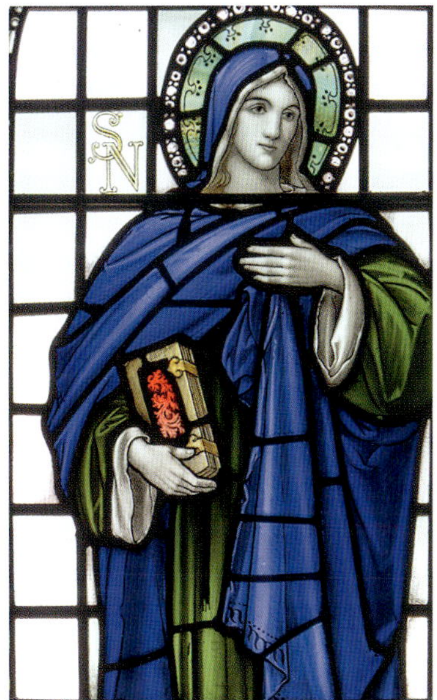

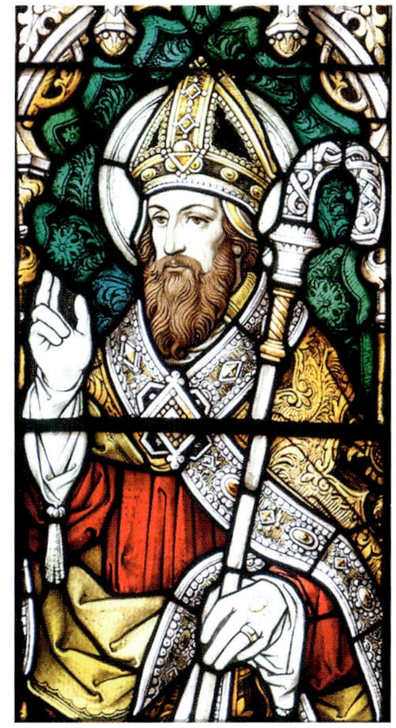

563. (above left) William Morris & Co. Westminster, St Non, 1920, Chapel of St Non, St Non's Bay

564. (above right) St Patrick, *c.* 1930, Church of Our Lady Star of the Sea, Llandudno, east window

Catholic churches after the Disestablishment of the Church in Wales contributed to the building of the retreat house and Chapel of Our Lady and St Non, at St Non's Bay in 1934. This was an attempt to counter the renewed promotion of the Anglican cathedral as a place of pilgrimage to Wales' patron saint, situated at the reputed birthplace of David near St Davids. The east window by William Morris & Co. (Westminster) depicts Non, the mother of David, while the nave windows depict David, Bride, Brychan and Winifred.[40]

Despite the number of depictions of David in Roman Catholic churches, he is probably less common than Patrick, the favourite saint of the Irish communities that were present in Wales and were often instrumental in raising the funds for the building of Roman Catholic churches. At the Church of Our Lady Star of the Sea, Llandudno, Patrick is paired with Thomas of Canterbury in the east window, while in the east window of the Church of St Mary, Pembroke Dock, he is paired with David.[41]

40 The episode is discussed in John Morgan-Guy, 'Shrine and counter-shrine in 1920s and 1930s Dewisland?' in J. Wyn Evans and Jonathan M. Wooding, *St David of Wales: Cult, Church and Nation* (Woodbridge: The Boydell Press, 2007), pp. 286–95. Curiously, the east window is clearly signed and dated 1920, although the chapel was not opened until 1934.

41 While David is written in Welsh (Dewi), Patrick is given in Irish (Padraig), with Ecclesia Dei (the Church of God) in Latin, the language of the Roman Catholic Church.

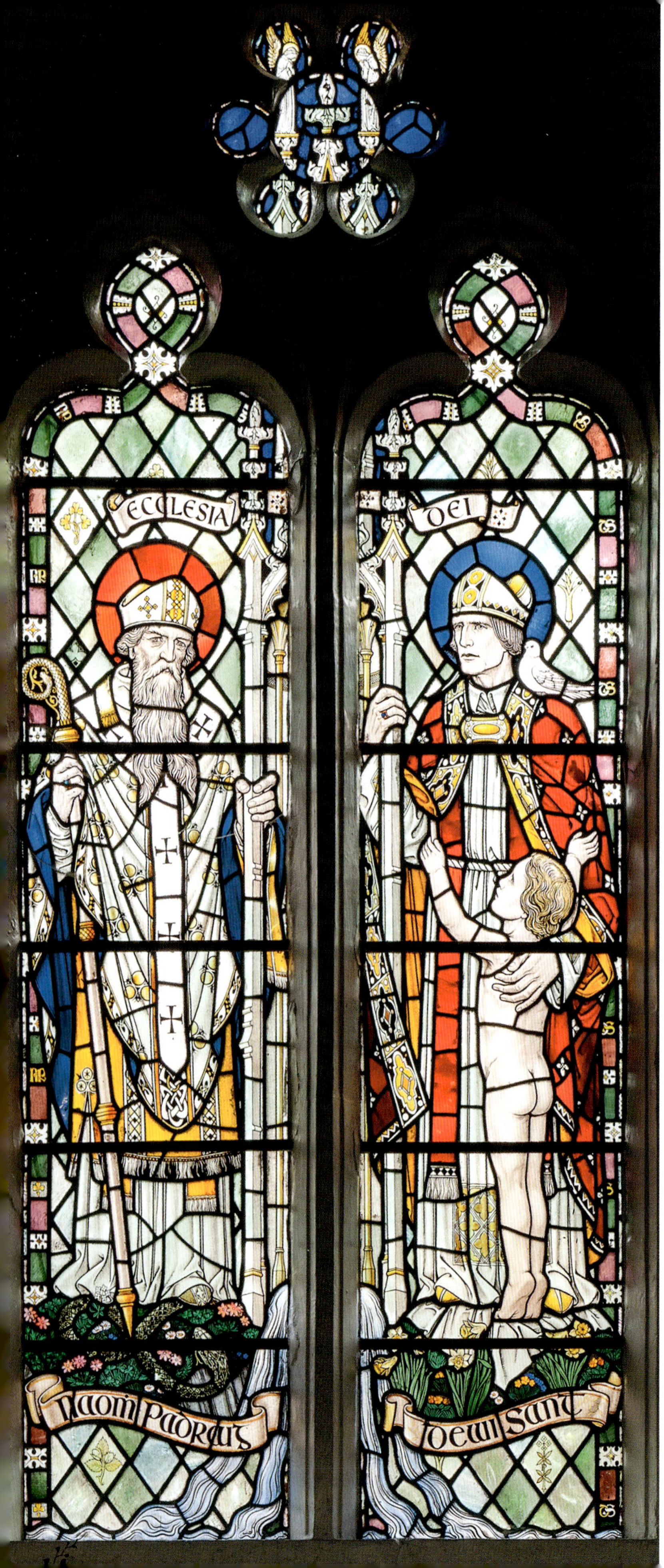

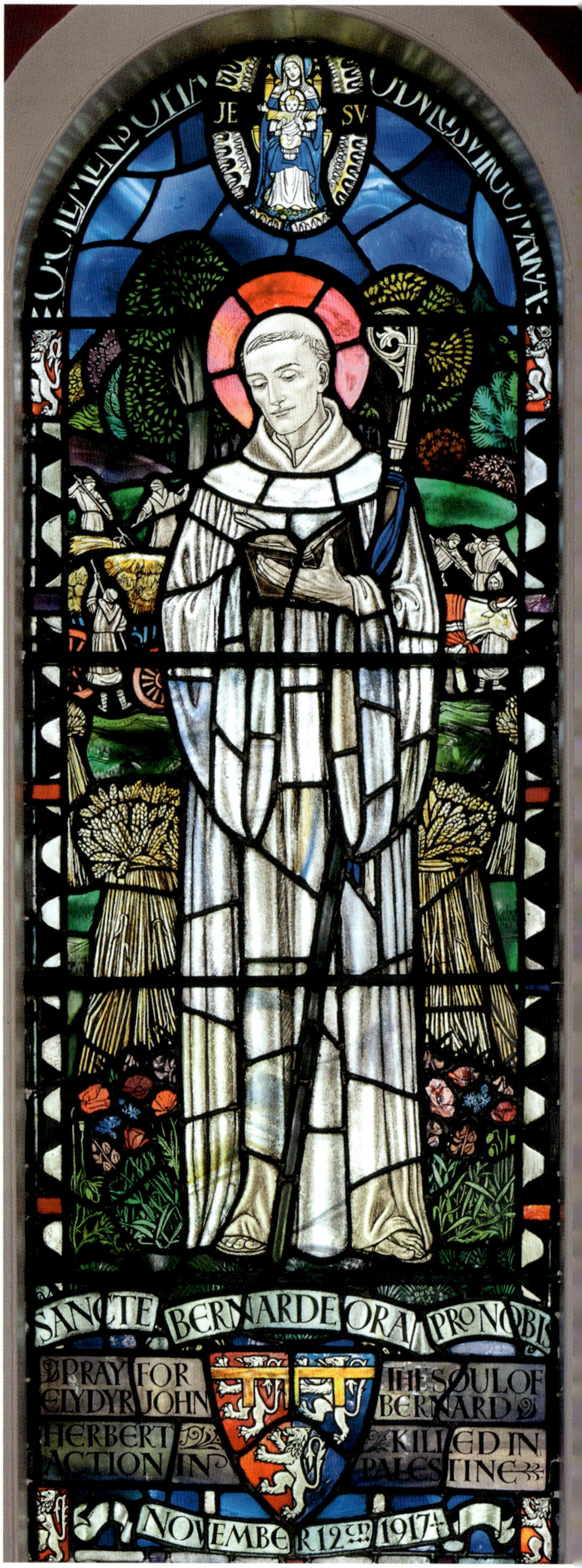

565. (left) Paul Woodroffe, St Patrick and St David, 1929, Church of St Mary, Pembroke Dock, east window

566. (above) Margaret Rope, St Bernard, *c.* 1934, Church of St Mary and St Michael, Llanarth, sanctuary apse

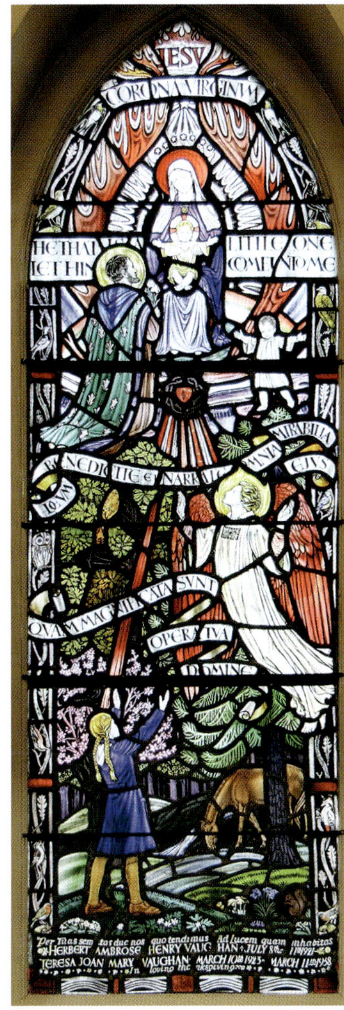

567. Margaret Rope, The Benedicite, *c.* 1938, Church of Our Lady, Llandovery, nave

The window at Pembroke Dock was made by Paul Woodroffe, a devout Roman Catholic and a pupil of Christopher Whall.[42] Woodroffe was a member of the Guild of Catholic Artists, and for other Roman Catholic artists devotion to their faith became a religious vocation. Margaret Agnes Rope trained under Henry Payne at Birmingham, and went to join her cousin, Margaret Edith Aldrich Rope, at Lowndes & Drury's Glass House in Fulham in 1911. She left in 1923 to enter the Carmelite Monastery at Woodbridge in Suffolk, and continued to work in stained glass, her work being fired and leaded up by the craftsmen at the Glass House. Her window at the Church of Our Lady, Llandovery, was given in memory of Teresa and Herbert Vaughan, the niece and nephew of the artist. Both died in childhood and are depicted in the window, Teresa below in a woodland scene and Herbert above in the company of the Virgin and Child and a male figure, perhaps Joseph. A delightful collection of birds borders the window in characteristic Arts and Crafts fashion. Two windows by the artist were made for the apse of the Church of St Mary and St Michael, Llanarth, and birds again are prominent in her depiction of Francis. In the other window, Bernard stands serenely in front of a detailed depiction of labourers in the field collecting the harvest.

In the same church a depiction of another popular Roman Catholic saint, Thérèse of Lisieux, is based on a conventional image and made by John Hardman & Co. Although the upper panel depicts the resurrected Christ holding a banner and standing over the tomb according to medieval convention, the window is otherwise devoid of the Gothicisation almost synonymous with their work up to the 1920s. This lighter style contrasts with the rich dark colours in a contemporary depiction of the same saint at the Church of the Holy Name, Fishguard, made by Harry Clarke Studios of Dublin.

Harry Clarke took over the stained glass studio of his family firm, Joshua Clarke & Sons, in 1921, having been taught by A.E. Child, a pupil of Christopher Whall, at Dublin Metropolitan School of Art.[43] He was also a close friend of Karl Parsons, and although none of his own

42 Christopher Whall also converted to Roman Catholicism, but his windows in Wales are all in Anglican churches.

43 For Harry Clarke see Nicola Gordon Bowe, *Harry Clarke, the Life and Work* (Dublin: The History Press Ireland, 2012). A single window by A.E. Child in Wales can be found at Emmanuel Church, Bistre (Buckley).

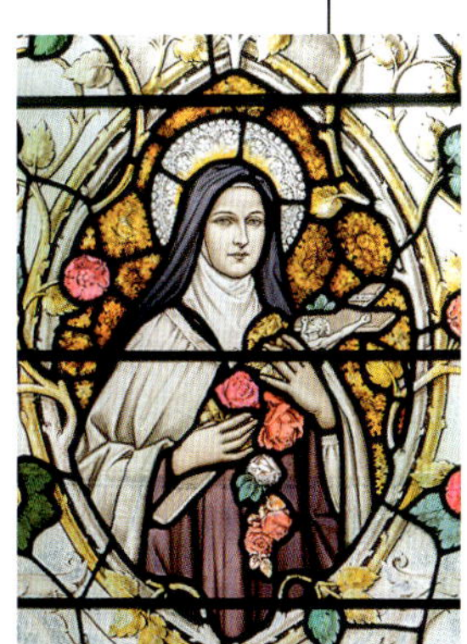

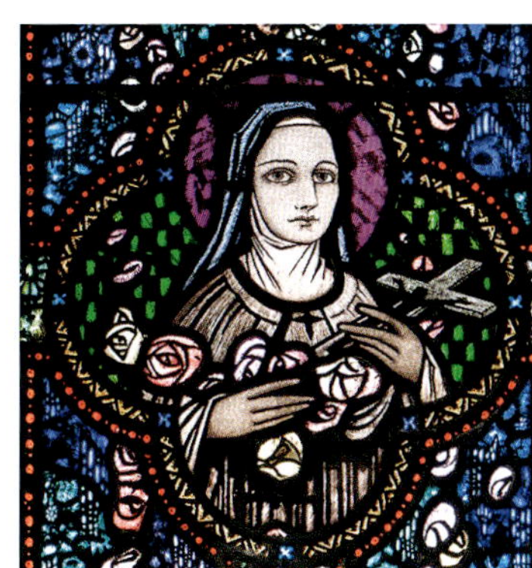

568. (right) John Hardman & Co., St Thérèse of Lisieux, *c.* 1930, Church of St Mary and St Michael, Llanarth, nave

569. (far right) Harry Clarke Stained Glass Studios, St Thérèse of Lisieux, *c.* 1929, Church of the Holy Name, Fishguard, nave

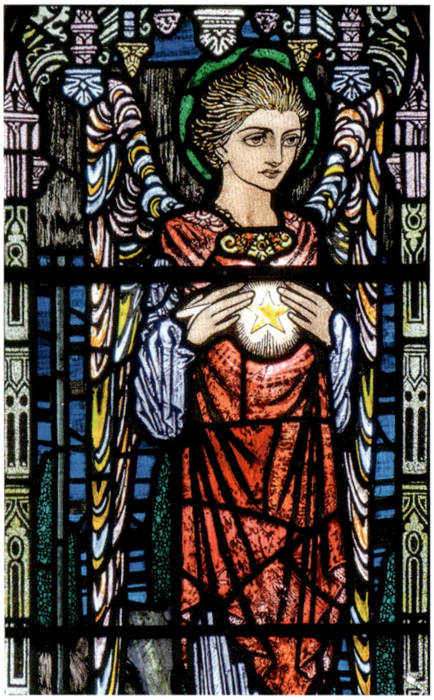

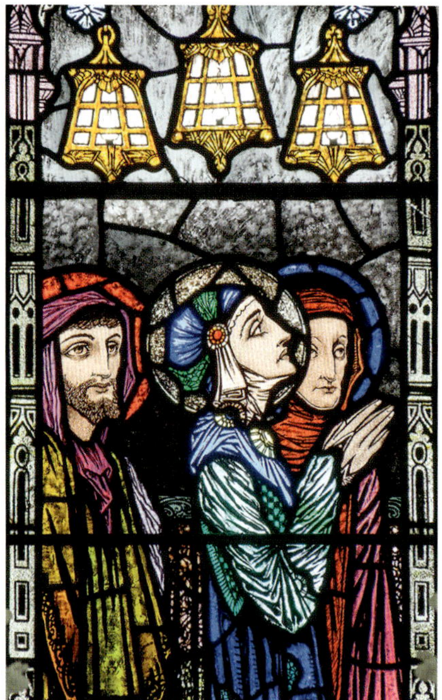

570–1. Joshua Clarke & Sons, Angel from the Nativity (far left); St Joseph, the Virgin Mary and Anna the Prophetess from the Presentation in the Temple (left), *c.* 1925, Church of St Joseph, Colwyn Bay, sanctuary apse

windows survive in Wales, three windows by the firm made for the sanctuary apse of the Church of St Joseph, Colwyn Bay, are similar to his own contemporary windows.[44] The ecclesiastical decorating side of the business, managed by Harry Clarke's brother Walter, also seem to have supplied the stone reredoses, one of which obscures the three windows. Two further windows by Harry Clarke Stained Glass Studios were made for the south-western corner of the Church of St David, Pantasaph, with standing figures of the saints Gregory, Gertrude, Theresa of Avila and Catherine of Siena. The dark figures of Gregory and Gertrude have the characteristic brooding power of Clarke's own windows, while the window with Theresa and Catherine is less densely and intricately painted, demonstrating the variety of work made by the studio in the early 1930s to designs by Richard King and William Dowling.

Few studios worked in a similar style, although a set of windows by Earley Studios, also based in Dublin, made for the Convent of St Winifred in Cardiff, resemble the work of Harry Clarke in design and technique.[45] Trena Cox established a studio in Birkenhead in the 1920s before continuing her long independent career in Chester, and examples of her work can be found at locations across north Wales for both Roman Catholic and Anglican patrons. An early work at the Church of St Winifrede, Holywell, sets the half figure of Christ between heraldry and Christian symbols on a full-coloured abstract background.[46]

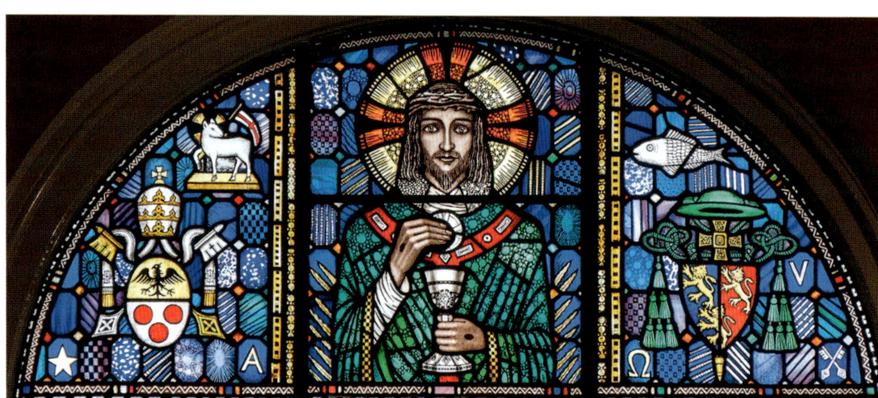

572. Trena Cox, Christ with Chalice and Host, 1931, Church of St Winifrede, Holywell, nave

44 The three two-light windows depict the Nativity, the Presentation in the Temple, and the young Christ with his parents in the carpenter's shop, and share similarities with windows by Harry Clarke for the Church of St Patrick, Kilmaine, County Mayo, and the Convent of Notre Dame, near East Grinstead in Sussex. The only windows made for a Welsh church by Clarke himself were commissioned for one of the Anglican churches in Penarth, and lost to bomb damage in 1941. One of the cartoons is illustrated in Nicola Gordon-Bowe, 'Interpreting the Bible through Painted Glass: The Harry Clarke Studios and Wilhelmina Geddes (1887–1955)' in Martin O'Kane and John Morgan-Guy, *Biblical Art from Wales* (Sheffield: Sheffield Phoenix Press, 2010), p. 208.

45 The windows were removed from the convent and sold in 2010.

46 For Trena Cox see Peter Jones, 'Trena Cox: Emergence of a Stained Glass Artist', *Historic Churches*, 2012, pp. 11–14.

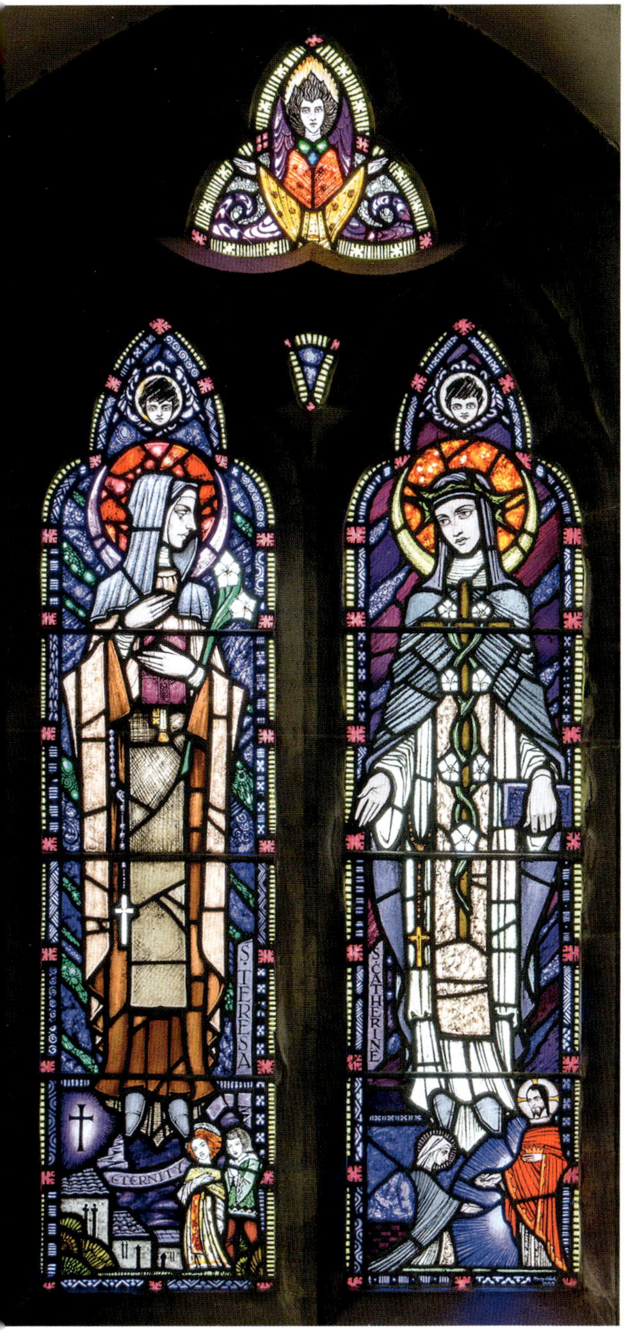

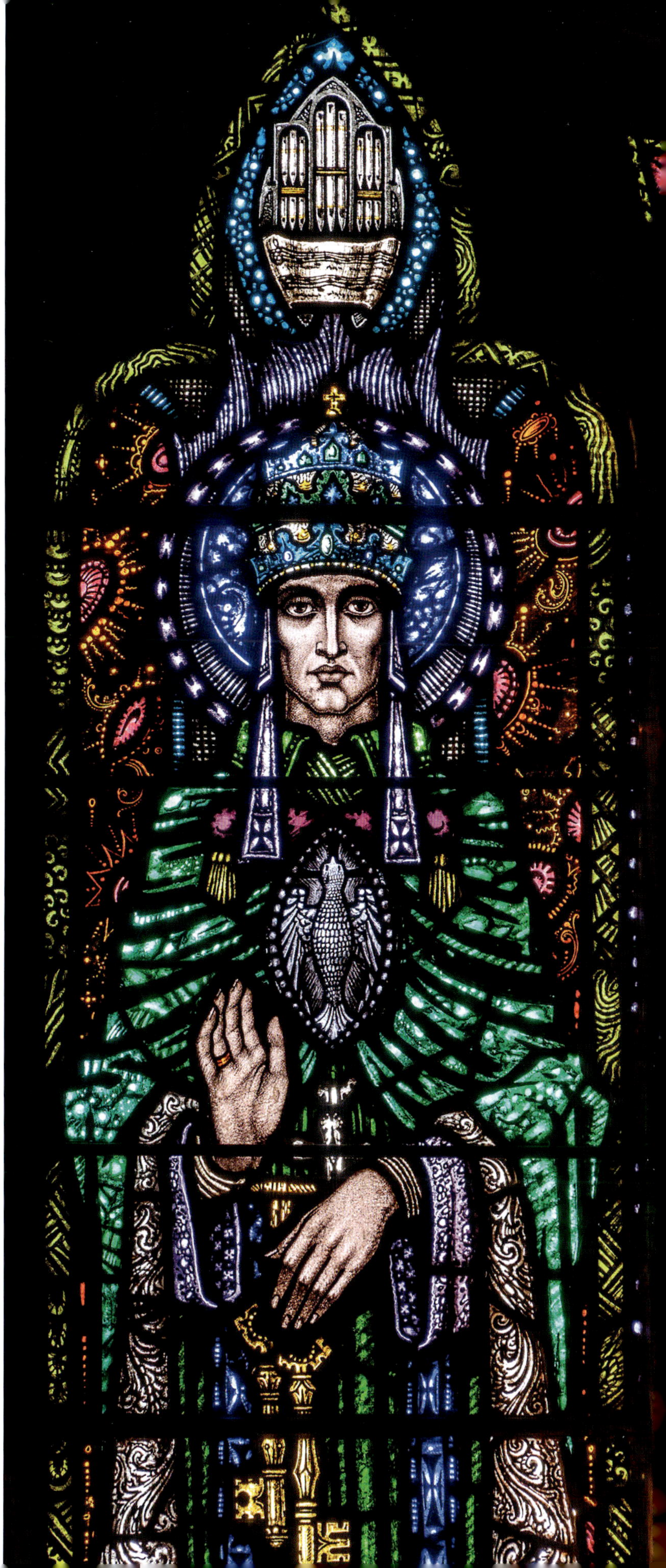

573–4. Harry Clarke Stained Glass Studios, St Theresa and St Catherine, 1933 (above), St Gregory, 1932 (right), Church of St David, Pantasaph, south aisle

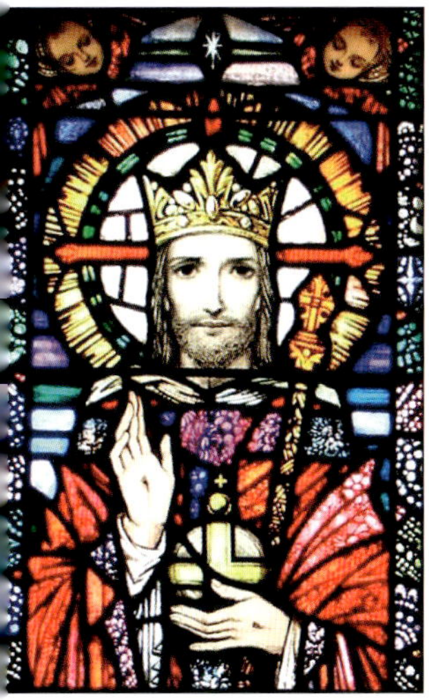

575. Earley Studios, Christ in Majesty, mid-twentieth century, from the former Convent of St Winifred, Cardiff

(photo courtesy Tomkinson Antique Stained Glass Ltd <http://www.vitraux.co.uk>)

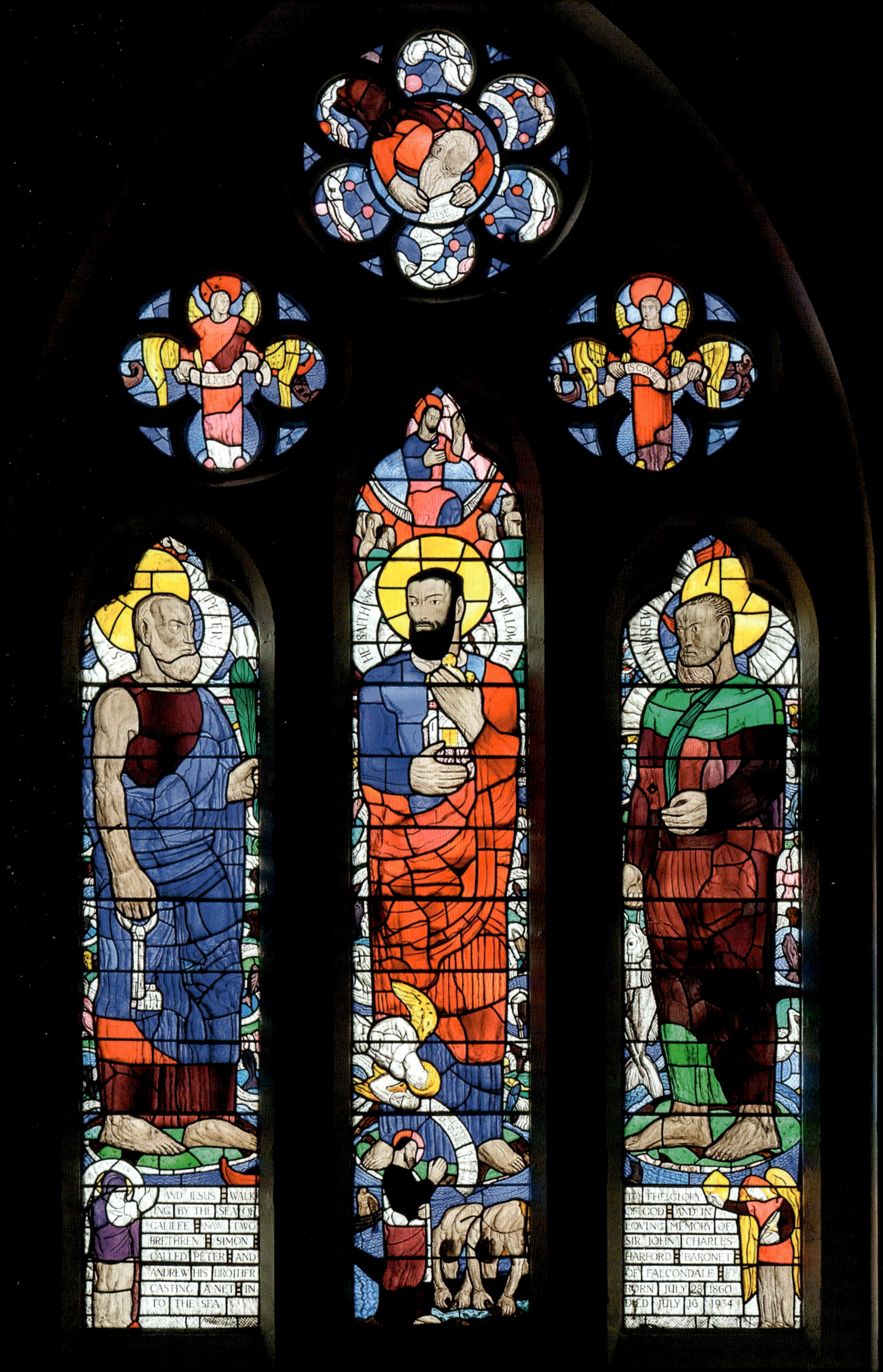

576. Wilhemina Ged-
Christ Calling Peter a
Andrew, 1946, Churc
of St Peter, Lampete
west window

New stained glass windows were still being installed in churches in the summer of 1940, as the first bombs of the Second World War fell on south Wales. Stained glass, old and new, was damaged and destroyed in air raids, particularly in and around Cardiff and Swansea in the latter half of 1940 and 1941. A few windows were made from 1942 onwards, including two of the windows by G. Maile & Son for the Church of St Illtud, Mamhilad, and the window by Edward Woore, far away from docks and factories, at the Church of St Ffraid, Llansantffraid-ym-Mechain, in 1943. Before the end of 1944 a faculty was granted for the replacement of a damaged memorial window, also by Maile's, for the Church of St Margaret, Mountain Ash. In other cases war brought delay and an increase in costs, as in the case of Wilhelmina Geddes' outstanding window for the Church of St Peter, Lampeter, completed in January 1944 but not finally installed until early in 1946. This last major work by Geddes exemplifies a culmination of the finest qualities and achievements of the Arts and Crafts Movement: meticulous attention to detail; apposite (and in this case arresting) use of colour; and an intelligent, rather than imitative, use of art historical precedent (including Assyrian sculpture, Raphael, William Blake, and Aristide Maillol) brought together with striking originality of design.[47]

Church windows that were damaged or destroyed during the war had to be replaced out of necessity, and new stained glass was sometimes funded by the War Damage Commission. The end of the Second World War also brought about a demand for memorial and thanksgiving windows, while other commissions that had been postponed by the war came to fruition. At the Church of St Mary, Builth Wells, the Parish Council resolved to install a large window as soon as 27 May 1945 in thanksgiving for the coming of peace.[48] The renewed demand for stained glass proved to be the catalyst for the work of the Swansea stained glass artist Howard Martin, who was soon to receive commissions for war memorial windows from the local Welsh Baptist chapels Seion Newydd and Calfaria in Morriston.[49] Howard Martin was brought up in an Anglican family in an area of strong Nonconformity, but

47 The window is discussed in Nicola Gordon Bowe, 'Interpreting the Bible through Painted Glass: The Harry Clarke Studios and Wilhelmina Geddes (1887–1955)' in *Biblical Art from Wales* (Sheffield: Sheffield Phoenix Press, 2010), pp. 211–15.

48 National Library of Wales, Records of the Church in Wales: Diocese of Swansea and Brecon, BR/RF19/1–3. Depicting the Annunciation and the Adoration of the Shepherds, the west window of the nave was the first of a succession of three substantial commissions designed by Harry Grylls and made by Burlison & Grylls for the church in 1945–6.

49 The window from Calfaria was inserted internally in Seion Newydd after its closure in 1980.

577. Howard Martin, War Memorial Window, *c.* 1945–8, Seion Newydd Welsh Baptist Chapel, Morriston (formerly at Calfaria, Morriston)

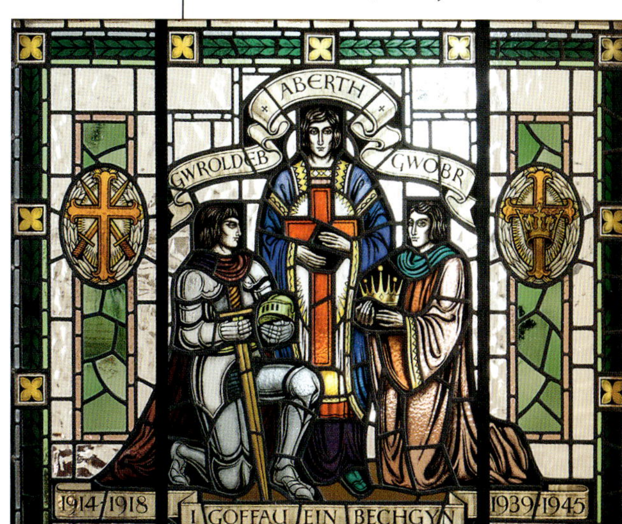

his first ecclesiastical commission, in partnership with his cousin Hubert Thomas, was for four windows for Philadelphia Presbyterian Chapel in their hometown of Morriston, made in 1935–6. After the war, Martin made several windows for Anglican churches and his first major work was the five-light window commissioned for the east wall of the chancel of the Church of St Michael and All Angels, Manselton, situated south of Morriston and close to the centre of Swansea. The window was made with the help of the Swansea painter Kenneth Hancock, who probably secured the commission through his brother, the recently-appointed vicar of Manselton. On the strength of his cousin's success, Hubert Thomas, who had been working for James Hogan at Powell & Sons in London, returned to Wales and in 1948 established the firm Celtic Studios in Swansea with Martin and Hancock.[50]

With his experience gained working with James Hogan, Hubert Thomas became the studio manager of the firm while Howard Martin, who held a full-time position at Swansea School of Art, worked as the firm's chief designer. In contrast to the domestic and commercial commissions undertaken before the war, after the formation of Celtic Studios nearly all of their work was for churches, predominantly Anglican, including a significant number of war memorials.[51]

Celtic Studios entered a market that was growing, but was also competitive and tempered by post-war austerity. Powell & Sons were the most successful firm in attracting commissions for war memorials, with numerous examples made for Anglican churches across south Wales. In north Wales the war memorial window by Powell & Sons at the Church of St David, Blaenau

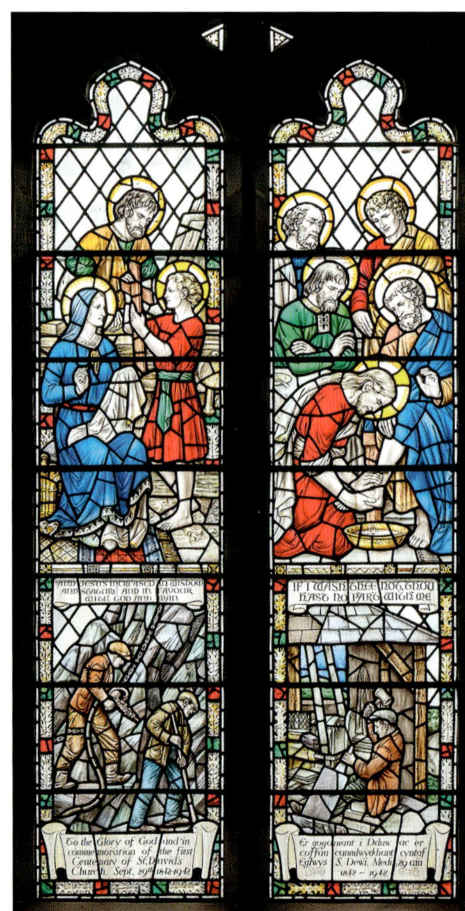

578. Powell & Sons, The Holy Family and Christ Washing his Disciples' Feet, 1948, Church of St David, Blaenau Ffestiniog, chancel

50 For the formation of Celtic Studios and the commission at Manselton see Maurice Broady, *A Vision Fulfilled: The story of Celtic Studios and Swansea's architectural glass tradition* (Swansea: West Glamorgan Archive Service, 2010), pp. 21–2. Kenneth Hancock was appointed principal of Swansea School of Art in 1946 and his association with Celtic Studios was short-lived, as he ceased to design for the firm after 1952, see Maurice Broady, *A Vision Fulfilled*, p. 48.

51 Maurice Broady counted seventeen war memorials made by the firm in their first five years. Maurice Broady, *A Vision Fulfilled*, p. 34.

52 Known locally as the Quarrymen's window, the lower panels have depictions of the slate industry.

53 Still later, John Petts' memorial window at Llanfair-ar-y-bryn, near Llandovery, was installed in 1965 in memory of John Logan Stewart, who died at Dunkirk; see Alison Smith, 'Light, Colour and the Bible: The Stained Glass Windows of John Petts (1914–91)' in Martin O'Kane and John Morgan-Guy, *Biblical Art from Wales* (Sheffield: Sheffield Phoenix Press, 2010), p. 225–6.

54 The diocesan registrar, Geoffrey Stradling, objected to the window because of the number of family memorials already placed in the church, which had been built by the family in 1907, suggesting 'that the Glorification of Mankind is uppermost in the minds of those who wish to put in this stained-glass window.' The bishop also objected, but a faculty was granted in September 1943. The window was designed by Jessie Bayes and made at the studio of William Aikman. Correspondence in National Library of Wales, Records of the Church in Wales: Diocese of Llandaff, uncatalogued papers, faculty 1943/6.

Ffestiniog, faces a window by the firm on the opposite side of the chancel that was also made in 1948 to commemorate the centenary of the church in 1942.[52] Second World War memorials continued to be installed into the 1950s, such as those by Celtic Studios at Briton Ferry, Tregaron and Crynant, and also brought plenty of work in Wales to Alfred Wilkinson, G. Maile & Son, and G.E.R. Smith of A.K. Nicholson Studios. These windows were usually given in memory of all of those from the congregation or whole parish who died in the war, but there were some memorials given for family members, such as the window of the four archangels designed by Ninian Comper at the Church of St Michael, Michaelston-le-Pit, given in memory of Norman Stuart Merrett, killed in August 1940, but not made until 1952.[53] At the Church of St David, Miskin, Sir Rhys Rhys-Williams commemorated his son, Captain Glyn David Rhys-Williams, although the proposal was initially rejected by the diocese who favoured a window that would commemorate all of those who had died in action during the war.[54]

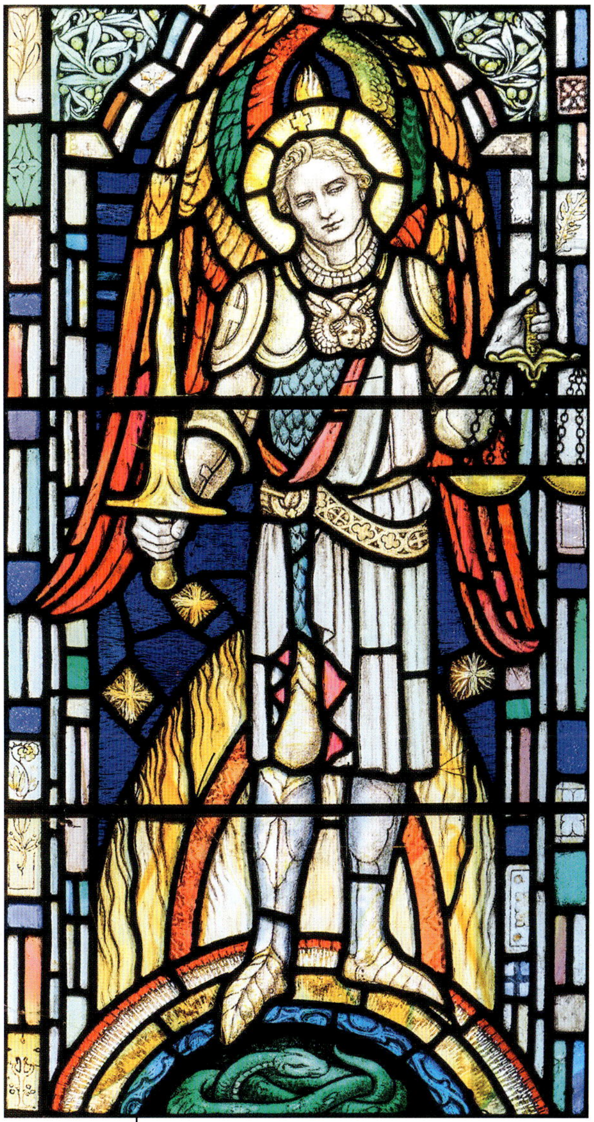

579. Jessie Bayes, St Michael, 1943, Church of St David, Miskin, nave

Many war memorials were images of Christ in Majesty and standing figures of saints, although some included biblical scenes, such as those at Blaenau Ffestiniog, the Priory Church of St Mary, Cardigan, and Llanfair Church, Cwmgors, all of which depicted post-Resurrection scenes.[55] Saints such as George and Michael remained popular, and at the Church of St Andrew, St Andrews Major, a window by Powell & Sons commemorating parishioners who had died in the war used George to represent the Army, Michael for the Air Force and Nicholas for the Navy. War memorial windows were also commissioned for

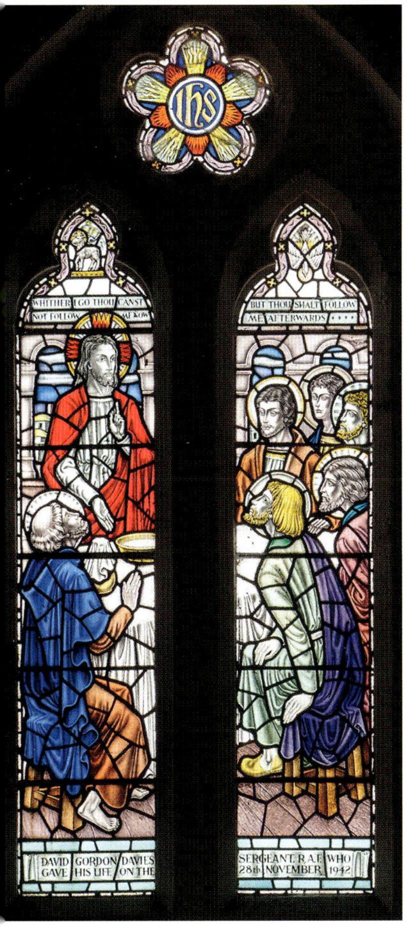

580. Celtic Studios, Christ Announcing His Departure to the Disciples, 1952, Llanfair (Church of St Mary), Cwmgors, west window

55 The west window at Cwmgors, with Christ announcing his departure to his disciples, is one of two war memorial windows in the church by Celtic Studios.

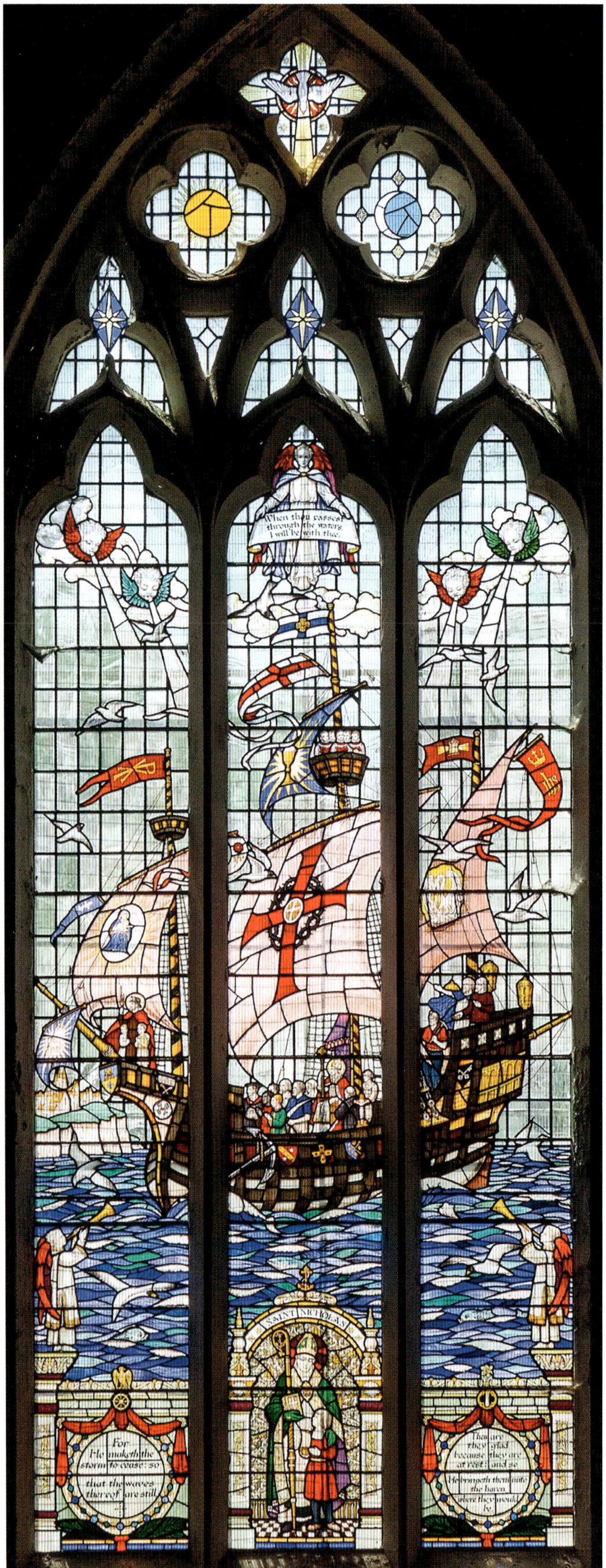

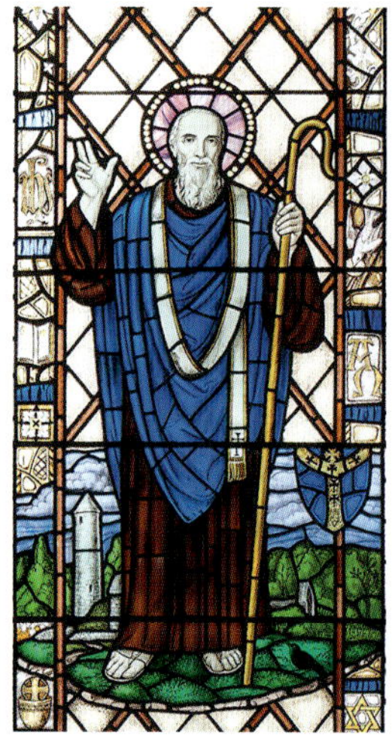

582. St Kevin, *c.* 1945, Church of St Mary, Newport, north chapel

Roman Catholic churches, such as the window depicting the Irish saint Kevin at the Church of St Mary, Newport, that was given in memory of Kevin Francis Moore, killed while serving in the Navy in 1940.

Much of Swansea's town centre had been devastated in 1941 and Howard Martin and Hubert Thomas saw the potential in supplying stained glass for churches that would need to be rebuilt after the war, although many of the more prestigious commissions were awarded to firms from outside Wales. In the mid-1950s money from the War Damage Commission facilitated the commission of large windows for the Church of St James, Uplands, Swansea, where the windows had been lost in the war. Having been temporarily reglazed with plain glass, the windows were made by A.K. Nicholson Stained Glass Studios, and designed by G.E.R Smith. The east window represents the 'Te Deum', while the west window is an unusual depiction of the church as a ship sailing to the new Jerusalem, with David at the prow.[56] When new stained glass for the Church of St Mary in central Swansea was finally commissioned in the late 1950s, after the rebuilding of the church, the windows were made by Powell & Sons.

In Cardiff, the War Damage Commission provided for the new five-light east window made by Powell's for the Church of St Margaret, Roath, in 1952, an important early design for the firm by Rupert Moore. The Church of St Martin, Roath, largely destroyed by bombing in 1941, commissioned two windows from Hugh Easton for the east end. The east window of the chancel, with its depiction of the youthful figure of Christ seated on

581. A.K. Nicholson Stained Glass Studios, The Ship of the Church, *c.* 1955, designed by G.E.R Smith, Church of St James, Uplands, Swansea, west window

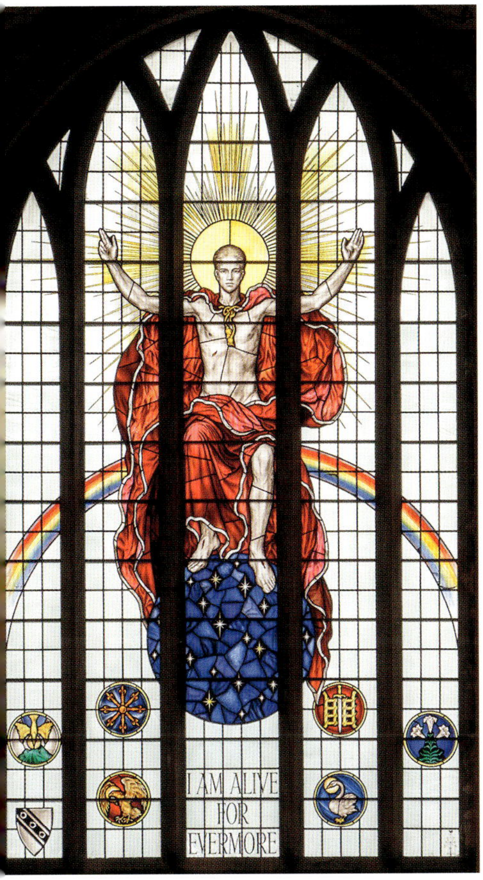

83. Hugh Easton, Christ in Glory, 1955, hurch of St Martin, Roath, Cardiff, east window

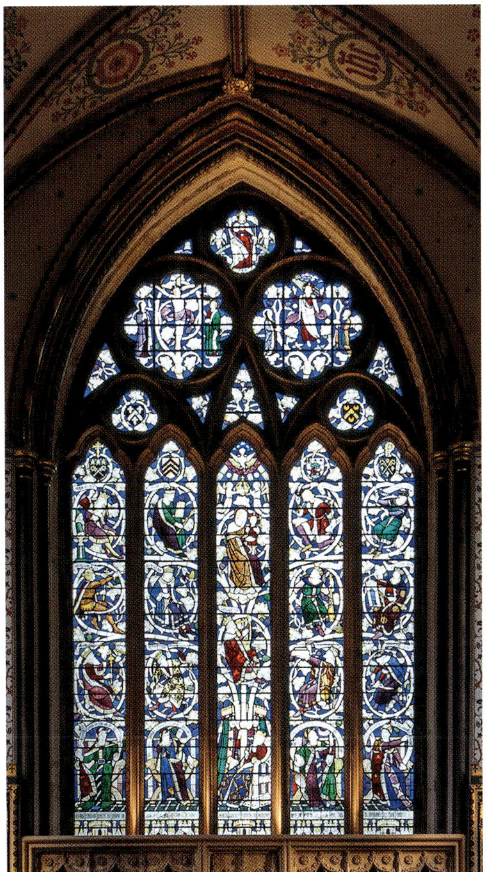

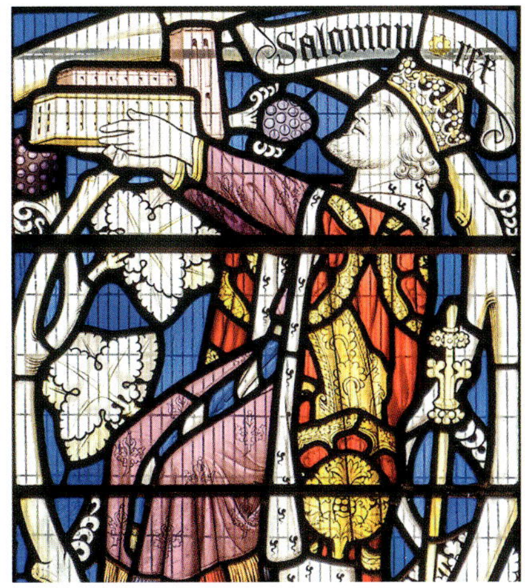

584–5. Geoffrey Webb, The Tree of Jesse, including Solomon (above right), 1951, Llandaff Cathedral, Lady Chapel

the universe, was commended by the Diocesan Advisory Committee and installed prior to the reconsecration of the church in December 1955.[57] Other Anglo-Catholic patrons in the city continued to favour Ninian Comper, whose studio made four north aisle windows for the Church of St Catherine, and windows of the Annunciation and Visitation for the Church of St Luke, both in Canton, in the 1950s.[58] Despite the removal to safety of twelve windows, Llandaff Cathedral lost at least twenty windows when a land mine severely damaged the building in January 1941. Among those saved were Geoffrey Webb's windows and he completed his scheme for the Lady Chapel with the installation of the Tree of Jesse in the east window in 1951, and the two large pairs of lights in the south wall in 1952, demonstrating continuity with his windows of the 1920s.[59]

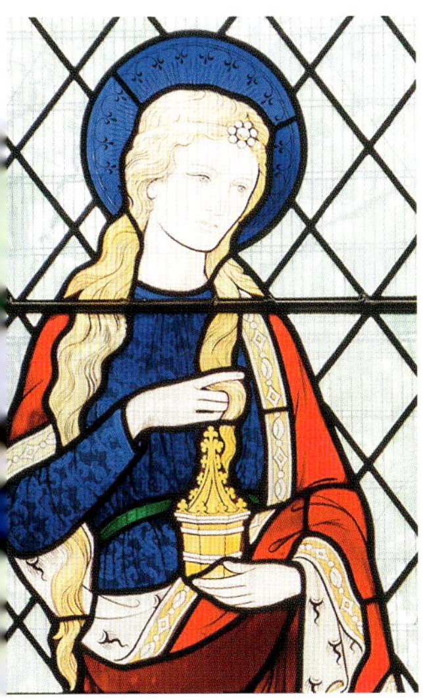

586. Ninian Comper, St Mary Magdalene, 1954, Church of St Catherine, Canton, Cardiff, south aisle

56 Further post-war windows by G.E.R. Smith were made for the Church of St John, Canton, Cardiff, and churches in Maesteg, nearby in Llangeinor, and on the Ceredigion coast at Aberaeron and Aberarth.

57 National Library of Wales, Records of the Church in Wales: Diocese of Llandaff, uncatalogued papers, faculty 1954/48. The figure in the east window at Roath is very similar to that in the upper part of Easton's larger full-coloured west window at Holy Trinity, Coventry, also of 1955 and replacing stained glass lost during the bombing in 1940. The depiction of Christ is also similar to a contemporary work by Goddard & Gibbs at the Church of St Berres, Llanferres.

58 One of the windows at the Church of St Catherine is a war memorial depicting David and Martin, either of which were among the saints included in the numerous First World War memorials.

59 Webb's long association with the cathedral and a detailed description of his windows is provided in Nevil A. James, 'The Stained Glass of Llandaff Cathedral' in Nick Lambert (ed.), *Llandaff Cathedral* (Bridgend: Seren, 2010), pp. 187–95. A devout Roman Catholic, Webb undertook detailed research into the figures of his Jesse window, having suggested the subject himself in 1949.

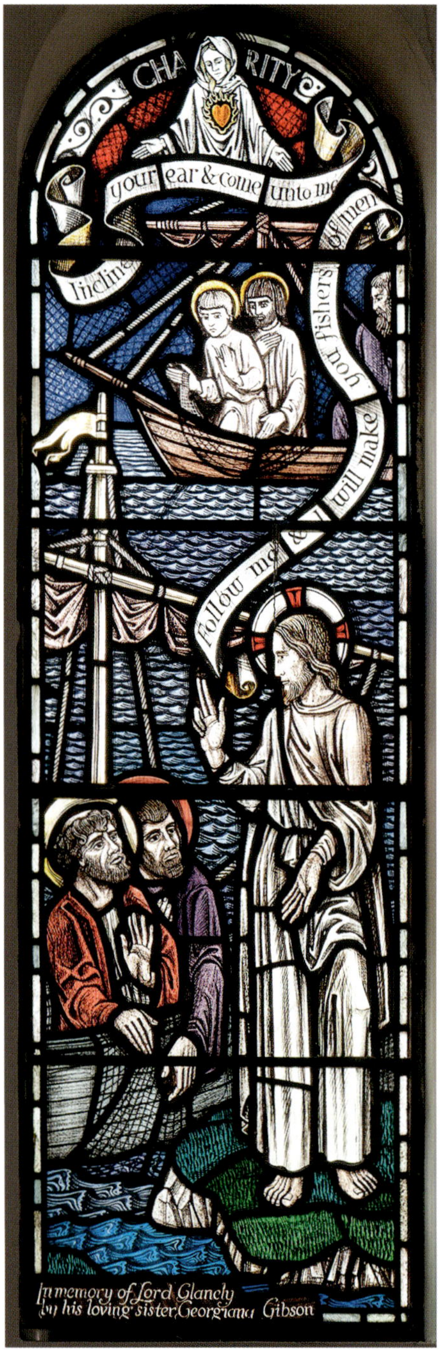

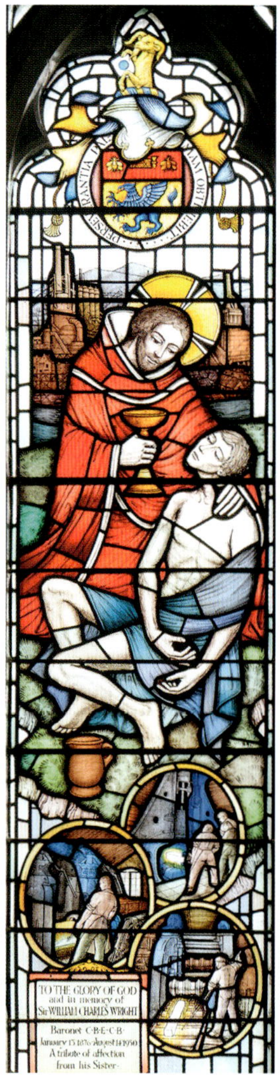

587. (far left) Francis Spear, Christ Calling Fishermen, 1947, Church of the Resurrection, Ely, Cardiff, west wall (baptistry)

588. (left) Lawrence Lee, The Good Samaritan, 1953, Church of St John the Evangelist, Gowerton, nave

589. (right) Francis Stephens, The Lamb of God Standing on the Book with the Seven Seals, 1954, Church of St Peter, Dixton, east window

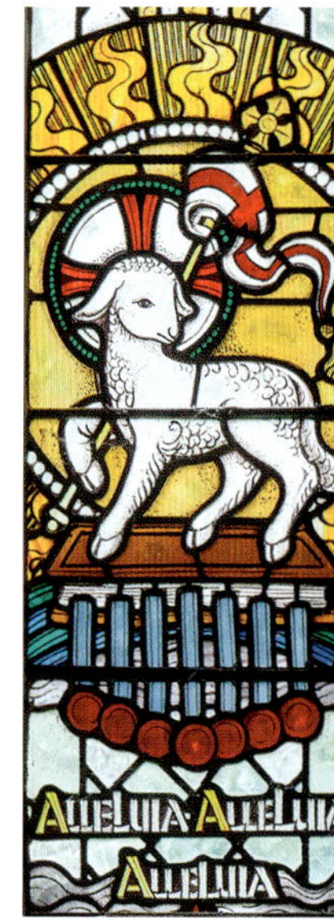

The end of the war made it easier to commission and make family memorial windows, some of which had been delayed during hostilities. William Tatem, Lord Glanely, had died in 1942, and in her will his sister had provided £1,000 for five windows in his memory that were made by Francis Spear for the sanctuary apse of the Church of the Resurrection, Ely, Cardiff. She also gave the three further windows at the west end (baptistry) of the church, also made by Spear and depicting the Nativity, the Baptism of Christ, and Christ calling fishermen.[60] Francis Spear had been a pupil and assistant of Martin Travers, and other former pupils made windows for churches in Wales. Lawrence Lee succeeded Travers as Head of the Stained Glass Department at the Royal College of Art, and completed commissions for windows unfinished at the time of his sudden death in 1948. Lee's window of 1953 for the Church of St John the Evangelist, Gowerton, situates Christ as the Good Samaritan in an industrial landscape, adding scenes from inside a steelworks in the roundels below. Francis Stephens' window of the same date at the Church of St Peter, Dixton, shares similarities with Travers' work in its use of text as part of the design, amid plenty of white glass.

Ninian Comper and Martin Travers adopted clear colours and plain backgrounds as their artistic preference, but it became policy in the Diocese of Llandaff when the Diocesan Advisory Committee recommended the removal of coloured or detailed backgrounds in designs for new windows. When the rector of the Church of All Saints, Barry, sought advice from the DAC regarding the design of a new window, he was advised to suggest to the artist 'that the backgrounds to the figures

60 The Church of the Resurrection had been built in 1934 by William Tatem in memory of his wife. Francis Spear was also commissioned to make a memorial window for him at his birthplace of Appledore, Devon, in 1953. Alan Brooks, *The Stained Glass of Francis Spear* (Privately published, 2012), p. 28.

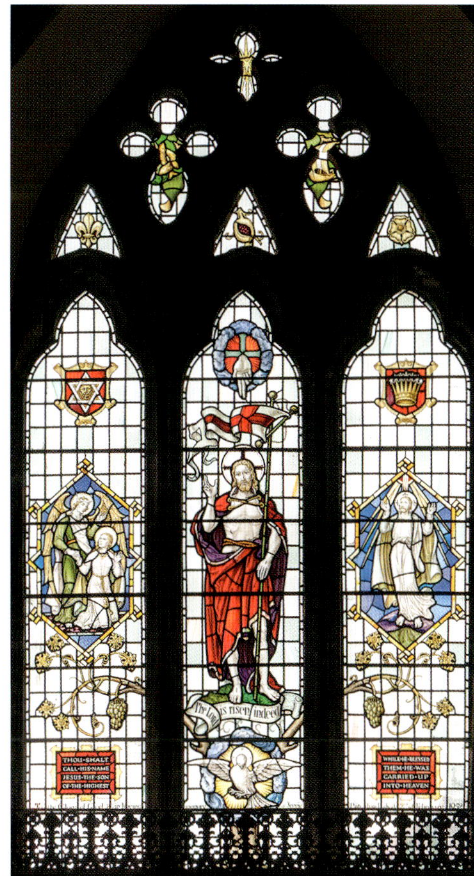

590. A.L. Wilkinson, The Risen Christ with the Annunciation and the Ascension, 1952, Church of St Crallo, Coychurch, east window

and decorations should be white glass as in a Window Mr. Wilkinson has designed for St Donat's Church, Abercynon. This would conserve the light in a dark church and reduces the cost of the work without injury to its artistic quality.'[61] The DAC had previously rejected a design by J. Wippell & Co. and the rector was advised to contact either A.L. Wilkinson or Harry Grylls of Burlison & Grylls. Wilkinson subsequently made six windows for different donors for the church and gained numerous commissions in the diocese. Many of these commissions were of standing figures or groups on plain grounds, and fewer were of narrative scenes, such as those at Barry, and the two three-light scenes at the Church of St Arvan, St Arvans, in the Diocese of Monmouth.

Less work came to Burlison & Grylls from Wales, and the firm closed in 1953 after the death of Harry Grylls. Arthur Walker found plenty of work in the Diocese of Llandaff, and as he had trained with Burlison & Grylls, his designs for G. Maile & Son can be seen as a continuation of their style, albeit stripped of their usual backgrounds and surrounds. He designed a set of windows for the Church of St Matthias, Treharris, before and after the war, as well as several new windows for the rebuilt Church of All Saints, Penarth.

61 National Library of Wales, Records of the Church in Wales: Diocese of Llandaff, uncatalogued papers, faculty 1948/9. Letter dated 15 January 1947.

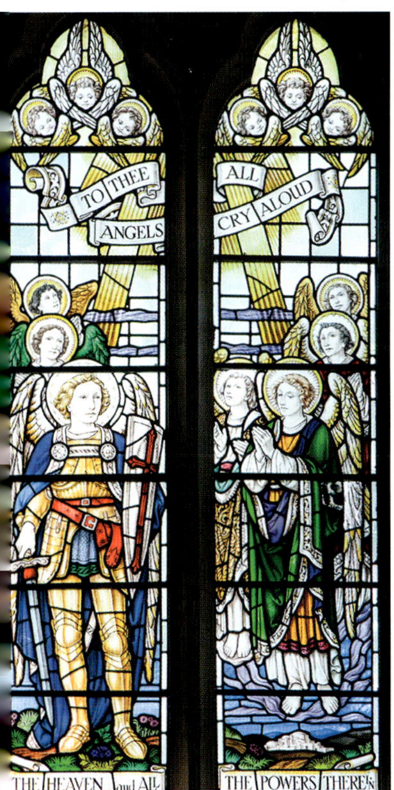

Windows with figures and simple scenes on plain grounds were made for churches in other parts of Wales in the 1950s. In some cases backgrounds were given a little character by the use of pale tinted quarries, such as in the window of the Virgin and Child by Arthur Walker at the Church of St Mary, Hay-on-Wye, or the three saints by Alfred Wilkinson at the Church of St Mary Magdalene, Cerrig-y-Drudion.

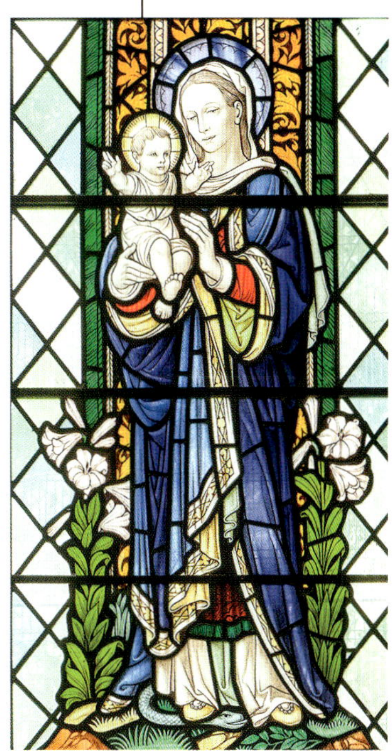

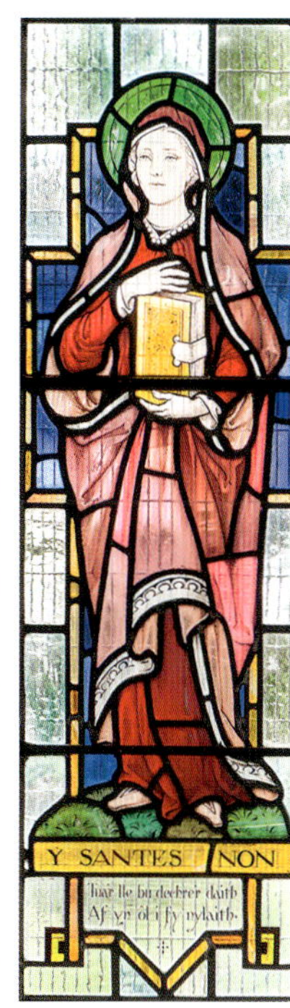

592. (right) G. Maile & Son, Virgin and Child, designed by Arthur Walker, 1956, Church of St Mary, Hay-on-Wye

593. (far right) A.L. Wilkinson, St Non, 1956, Church of St Mary Magdalene, Cerrig-y-Drudion, nave

1. Probably G. Maile & Son ,'To Thee All Angels y Aloud', designed by Arthur Walker, late 1950s, urch of All Saints, Penarth, south aisle

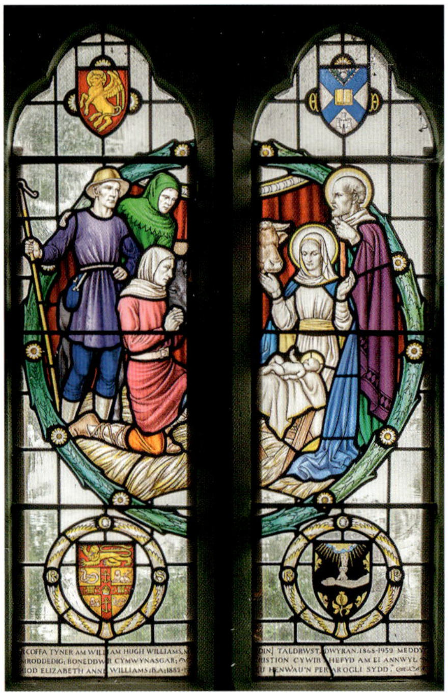

594. Francis Skeat, The Adoration of the Shepherds, 1955, Church of St Mary, Llanfair-yn-y-Cwmwd, east window

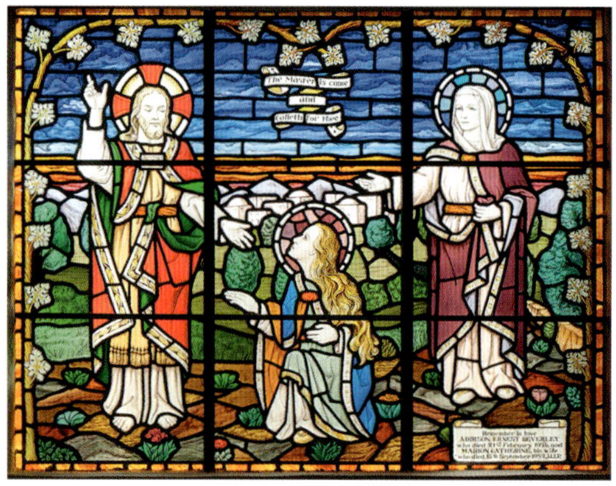

595. Christopher Charles Powell, Christ with Mary and Martha, 1954, Church of St Cadfan, Tywyn, south aisle

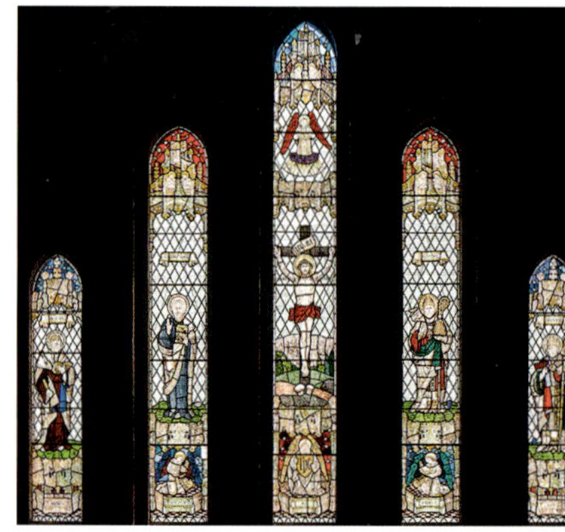

596. Christopher Charles Powell, The Crucified Christ with Saints, *c.* 1950, Church of St David, Penmaenmawr, east window

Working in a similar tradition, Francis Skeat trained with Christopher Webb and designed windows for several churches in Wales. His two-light window at the Church of St Mary, Llanfair-yn-y-Cwmwd, ties the scene of the Adoration of the Shepherds together across the two lights within a roundel defined by a floreate border, while the surrounding heraldry is placed against clear grounds.

White glass Gothic canopies provided framing for scenes or figures in some late works by Burlison & Grylls, Christopher Charles Powell and smaller firms such as J. Drake & Sons of Exeter. These makers, along with Ninian Comper and Geoffrey Webb, remained true to the seriousness of the Gothic Revival that was evidently still popular in Wales, but mainly succeeded in demonstrating its exhaustion into empty convention by the 1950s. The pallid five-light war memorial window by C.C. Powell for the Church of St David, Penmaenmawr, exemplifies this approach, and contrasts with his bolder use of colour in smaller windows such as his Christ with Mary and Martha at the Church of St Cadfan, Tywyn.

The east window by Powell for the Church of St Barnabas, Uplands, Swansea, commissioned at the time that Celtic Studios were gaining a reputation in the area, demonstrates the comparative modernism of Celtic Studios' work. Although they failed to attract Anglican patronage in Cardiff in the 1950s, they found support from a growing number of patrons in Swansea, Gower, and throughout west Wales.[62] At the Church of St Michael, Llanfihangel Genau'r Glyn, chancel windows were commissioned in the 1930s from Powell & Sons and Jones & Willis, but during the course of commissioning a nave window in 1949, the Archdeacon of Carmarthen suggested that a design should be sought from Celtic Studios.

62 The only commissions Celtic Studios received in Cardiff were an early window in the Church of St Mary, Whitchurch, a series of *dalle de verre* windows for Cardiff Reform Synagogue from 1966 until 1977, and windows of 1967 for Park End Presbyterian Church and Christ Church, Radyr.

63 I am grateful for research on the windows at Llanfihangel Genau'r Glyn undertaken by Avril Thomas. The windows are described in Martin Crampin, *Stained Glass Windows in Llanfihangel Genau'r Glyn Church* (Talybont: Wendall Publications, 2013).

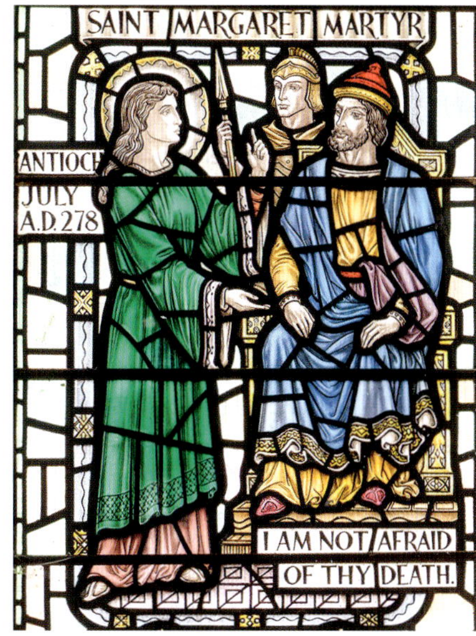

597. Celtic Studios, St Margaret Before the Governor of Antioch, 1952, Church of St Margaret, Crynant, east window

Despite the rise in the cost of the window, this and five further windows were made for the church by Celtic Studios during the next thirty years.[63]

Repeat business underlined the success of Celtic Studios, and a few churches commissioned all of their stained glass from the firm over several decades as a result of early commissions, such as at the Anglican churches in Manselton, Tumble, Crynant and Cwmgors. Of these churches, Crynant is particularly significant. The church had originally approached Carl Edwards, who succeeded James Hogan as chief designer at Powell & Sons in 1948, concerning a war memorial for the east window, but after the priest-in-charge, the Revd Dewi Caradog Davies, met Hubert Thomas, the commission went to Celtic Studios. The proposal soon developed into plans for an ambitious scheme of windows, with windows installed between 1951 and 1966. The windows along the south aisle depict scenes from the early life of Christ, while those in the north wall of the nave portray scenes from Christ's ministry, death and resurrection, intended to 'illustrate how the church was founded and some of the practical acts that were needed for it to become active in the secular world'.[64] The coherence of the scheme was assured in the active participation of Dewi Caradog Davies in determining the subjects to be included.[65]

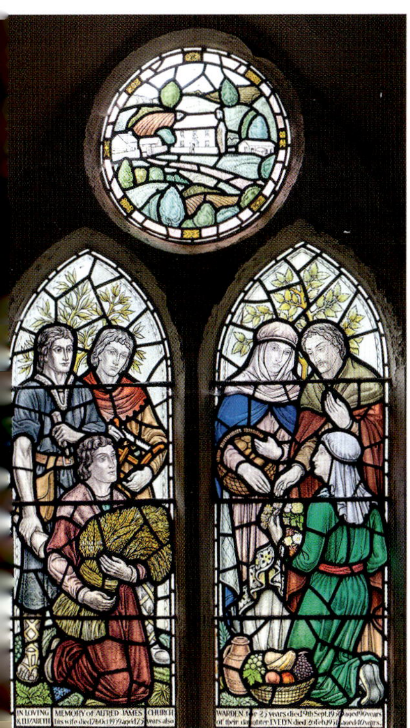

598. Celtic Studios, Family with the Harvest, 1954, Church of St Elidyr, Crunwere, nave

Few windows by Celtic Studios made for churches in Wales went beyond the usual biblical scenes and saints. In their east window at the Church of St Madoc, Llanmadoc, the harvest is presented to Christ, and at the Church of St Elidyr, Crunwere, another window, also given by a farming family, depicts a family group with the fruits of the harvest. Welsh saints were common subjects, but few historical figures and scenes were commissioned for churches, making the west window of 1959 at the Church of St Michael, Caerwys, depicting the Eisteddfod held at the town in 1523, exceptional.

64 Maurice Broady, 'The Secret of the Dulais Valley: the stained glass windows in St Margaret's, Crynant', *Morgannwg*, vol. 32 (1993), p. 84.

65 The series of windows depicting the life of Christ is unusual in that the Passion of Christ is almost absent, an omission that would have been unthinkable in the nineteenth century. A scene depicting the mourning over the dead Christ, with the three empty crosses in the background, is placed between a depiction of Christ with his disciples, and the journey to Emmaus. It is an example of how, by the 1950s, the suffering of Christ was no longer seen as a subject suited to commemorating family members. Neither were images depicting Christ's suffering common for memorials to those who died in the Second World War. At Crynant the east window's theme of sacrifice and martyrdom is depicted through scenes associated with (but not depicting) the martyrdom of James and Margaret of Antioch.

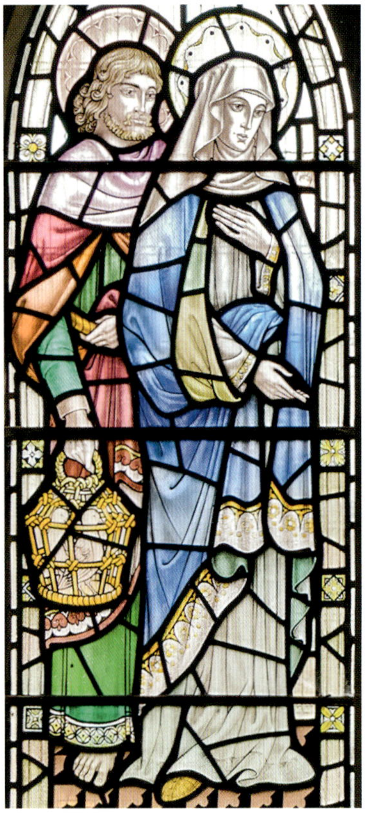

599. Celtic Studios, Joseph and Mary from the Presentation in the Temple, 1951, Church of St Margaret, Crynant, south aisle

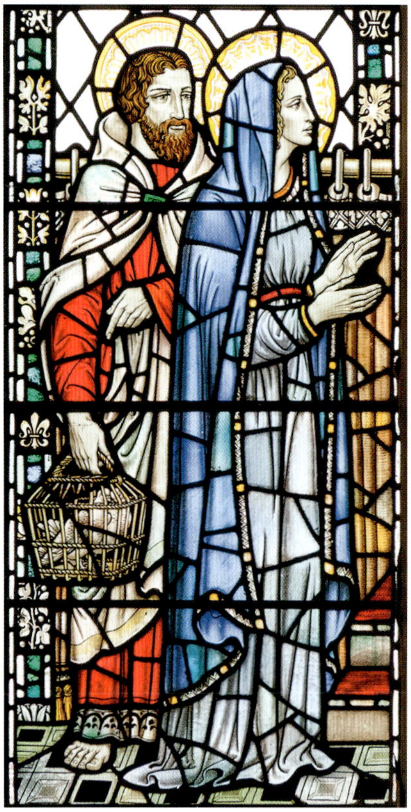

600. Powell & Sons, Joseph and Mary from the Presentation in the Temple, 1949, Church of the Holy Trinity, Aberystwyth, west wall

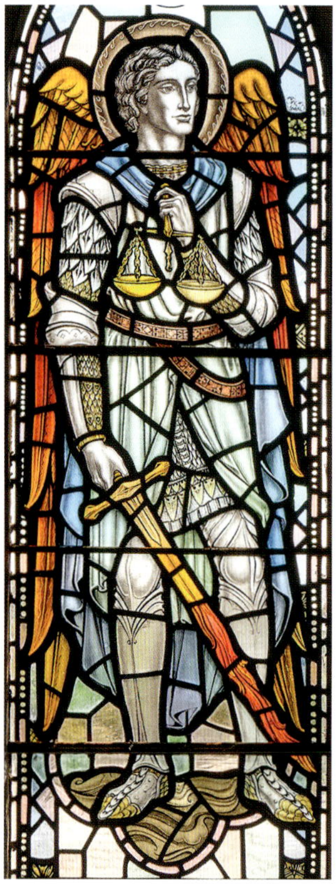

601. Celtic Studios, St Michael, 1952, Church of St Caron, Tregaron, nave

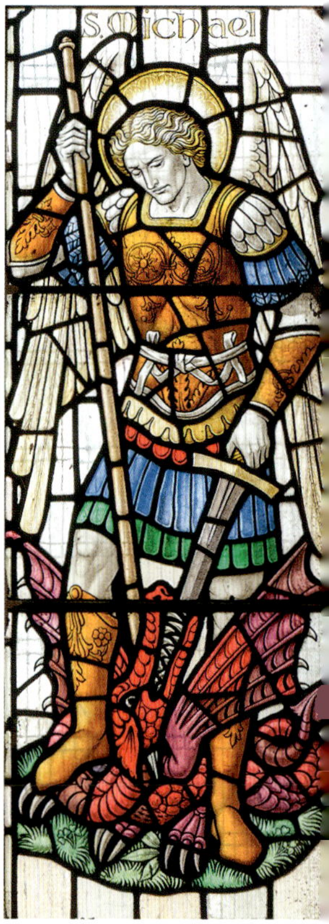

602. Powell & Sons, St Michael, 1948, designed by J. Blackford, Church of St Mary, Pennard, nave

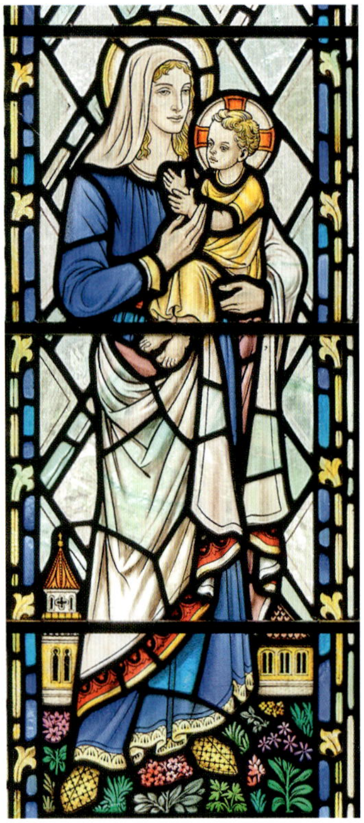

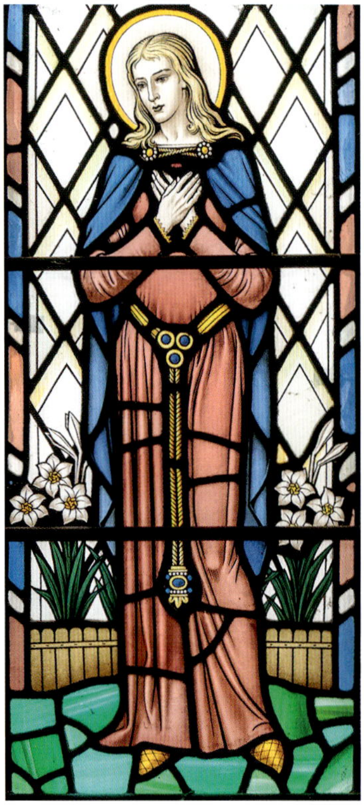

The design of their windows was predominantly the work of Howard Martin and his former pupil, Bryan Tobias Evans, although Hubert Thomas designed windows as well as introducing details and techniques from the windows of his former employers, Powell & Sons. For example, the patterned borders, often with small floral motifs, used on many of their early windows, can also be found on windows in the 1930s, 40s and 50s by Powell's. Compositional similarities may stem from the conventional models that they shared, although the colours of Celtic Studios' windows were usually muted in comparison with most work by Powell's until the later 1950s. This cooler palette was usually matched by their rather static figures. For example, the figure of the Archangel Michael that stands calmly beside the

603. (far left) Powell & Sons: Virgin and Child, 1957, Church of St Mary, Herbrandston, chancel

604. (left) J. Wippell & Co., The Virgin Mary, 1951, Church of St Paul, Newbridge, north aisle

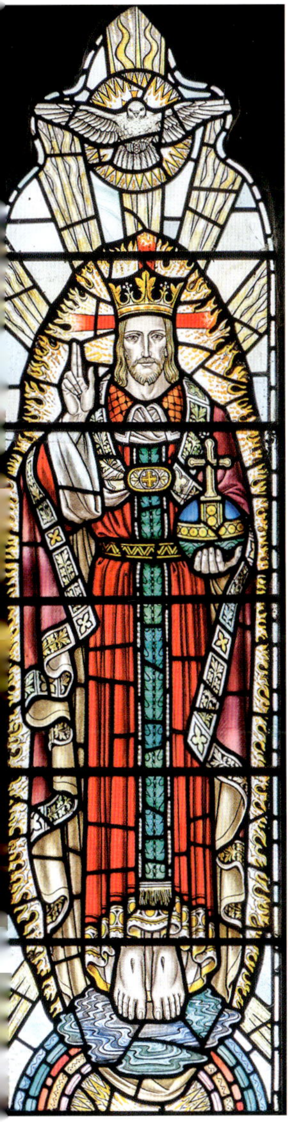

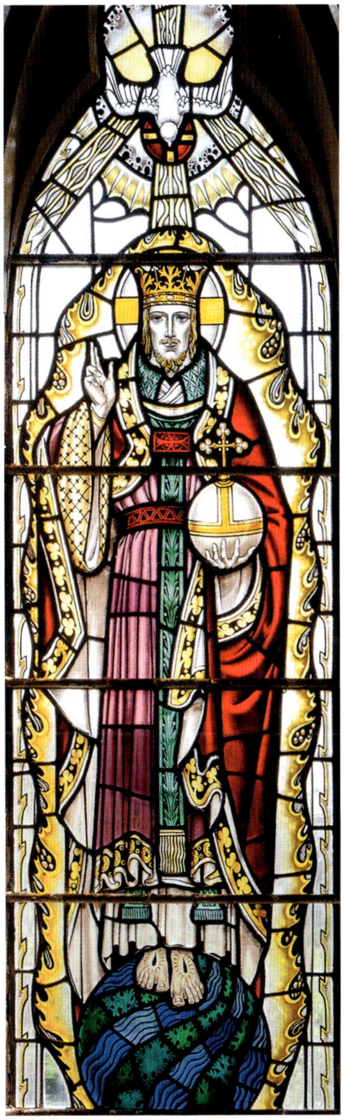

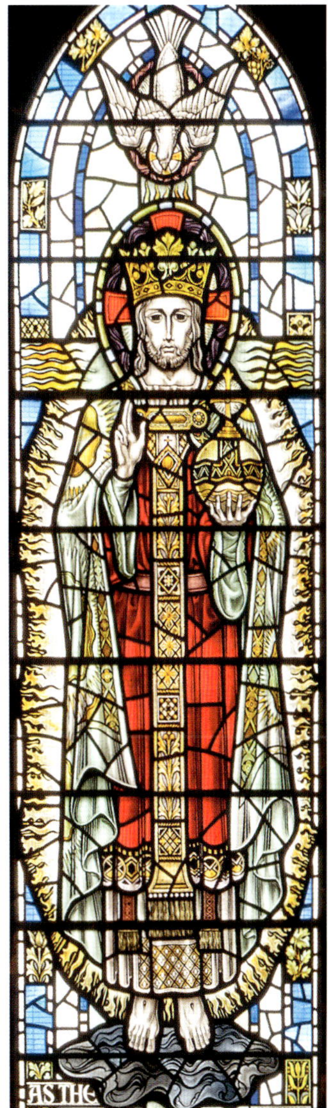

605. (far left) Powell & Sons, Christ in Majesty, 1949, Church of St Michael, Beguildy, east window

606. (centre left) A.F. Erridge, Christ in Majesty, 1952, Church of St Non, Llanerchaeron, east window

607. (left) Celtic Studios, Christ in Majesty, 1950, Church of St Agnes, Port Talbot, east window

figure of Christ at the Church of St Caron, Tregaron, is paler and lacks the energy of the same figure designed by J. Blackford for Powell's at the Church of St Mary, Pennard, who stands with a pink dragon at his feet.[66]

Similarities can also be found in windows by J. Wippell & Co. of the 1950s, and more routine work by all three firms broadly followed the fashion for plain grounds behind figures. The style of Powell & Sons continued in the work of A.F. Erridge, who was a painter at the firm until 1950, after which he designed for Wippell's and made windows to his own design. His depiction of Christ in Majesty in the east window at the Church of St Non, Llanerchaeron, is suggestive of the same influence on the contemporary Christ in Majesty figures made by Celtic Studios.[67]

66 Naturally there was some variation in their design, particularly as Howard Martin and Hubert Thomas sought to identify themselves with the ideals of the Arts and Crafts Movement, designing each window for specific individual settings, see Maurice Broady, *A Vision Fulfilled: The story of Celtic Studios and Swansea's architectural glass tradition* (Swansea: West Glamorgan Archive Service, 2010), p. 24. In the 1950s Celtic Studios' output averaged at about 20 windows per year, although their success in gaining commissions in Canada meant that by the latter half of the decade, about a third of these windows were exported. Maurice Broady, *A Vision Fulfilled*, appendix 1, p. 103.

67 A.F. Erridge also designed windows for J. Wippell & Co, continuing the influence of Powell's on the work of Wippell's that can be seen in designs for the firm by G. Cooper-Abbs before and after the war.

Relatively few windows seem to have been commissioned in the post-war period for Roman Catholic churches, preceding a time of church building and creativity in the 1960s. The fortunes of John Hardman & Co., who produced other decorative ecclesiastical furnishings as well as stained glass, are illustrative of this. The firm completed an average of 120 jobs each year around 1900, but between the period of 1945 and 1961 there was an average of only nine new commissions each year.[68] Perhaps their most significant commission for a Welsh church in the period was a set of eight lights made by the firm for the Church of Our Lady Queen of Peace in Llanelli between 1949 and 1952, although the building was demolished in 1985.[69]

In addition to the war memorials that were commissioned, many windows were repaired or replaced at the Cathedral Church of St David, Cardiff, in the 1950s when the building was rebuilt following an air raid in March 1941. The aftermath of the war was remembered in a different way at Conwy, where Italian Prisoners of War contributed towards the east window at the Church of St Michael and All Angels, Conwy. Some windows of the period followed the fashion for figures on plain quarries such as the single figure of Mary, representing the Annunciation, in the south wall of the Church of St Mary, Carmarthen. Made in 1955 by H.R. Keedy, the window contrasts strongly with the war memorial window placed in the church a few years previously, with its detailed backgrounds framed with Gothic canopies.

68 Michael Fisher, *Hardman of Birmingham, Goldsmith and Glasspainter* (Ashbourne: Landmark Publishing, 2008), p. 166.

69 The west window, designed by Patrick Feeny, was awarded second prize at the annual exhibition of the British Society of Master Glass-Painters and illustrated in the *Journal of the British Society of Master Glass-Painters*, vol. x, no. 4 (1950–1).

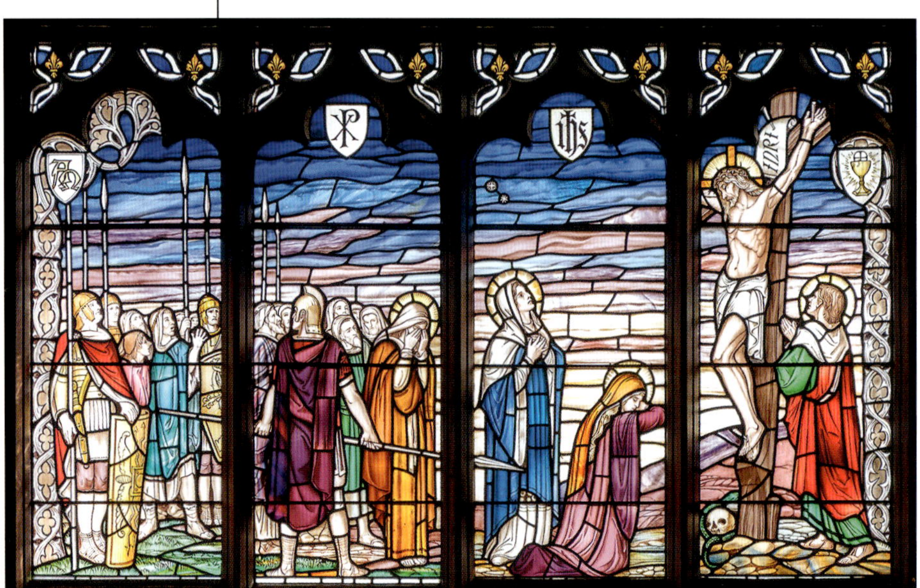

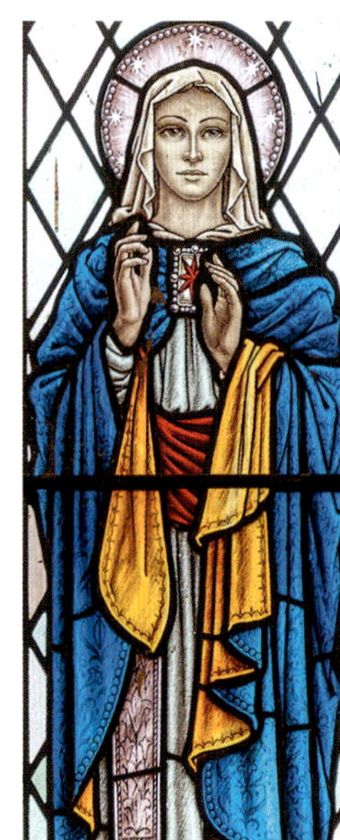

608. (right) The Crucifixion, *c.* 1950, Church of St Michael and All Angels, Conwy, east window

609. (far right) H.R. Keedy, The Virgin Mary, 1955, Church of St Mary, Carmarthen, nave

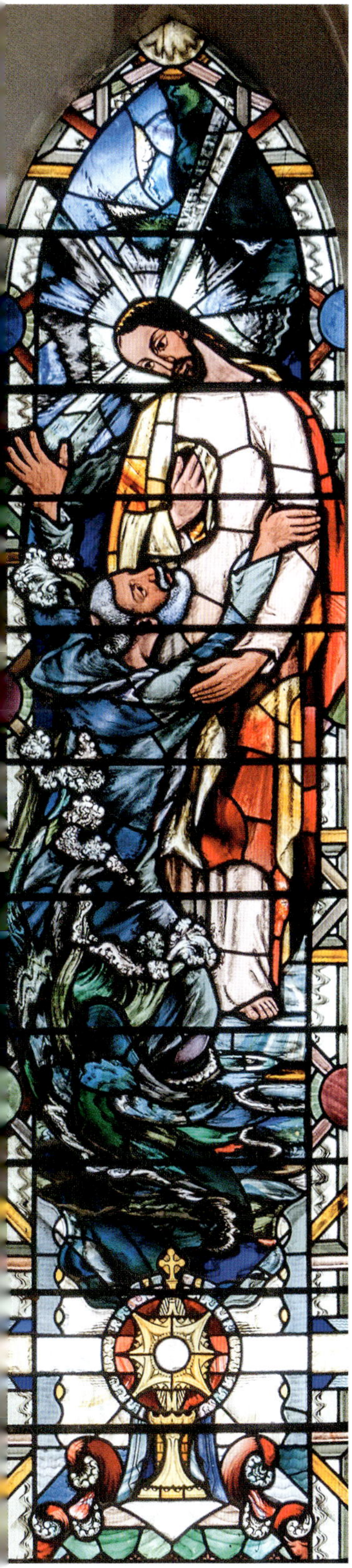

611. Joseph Edward Nuttgens, St Peter and St Paul, 1953, Church of All Saints, Ebbw Vale, west wall

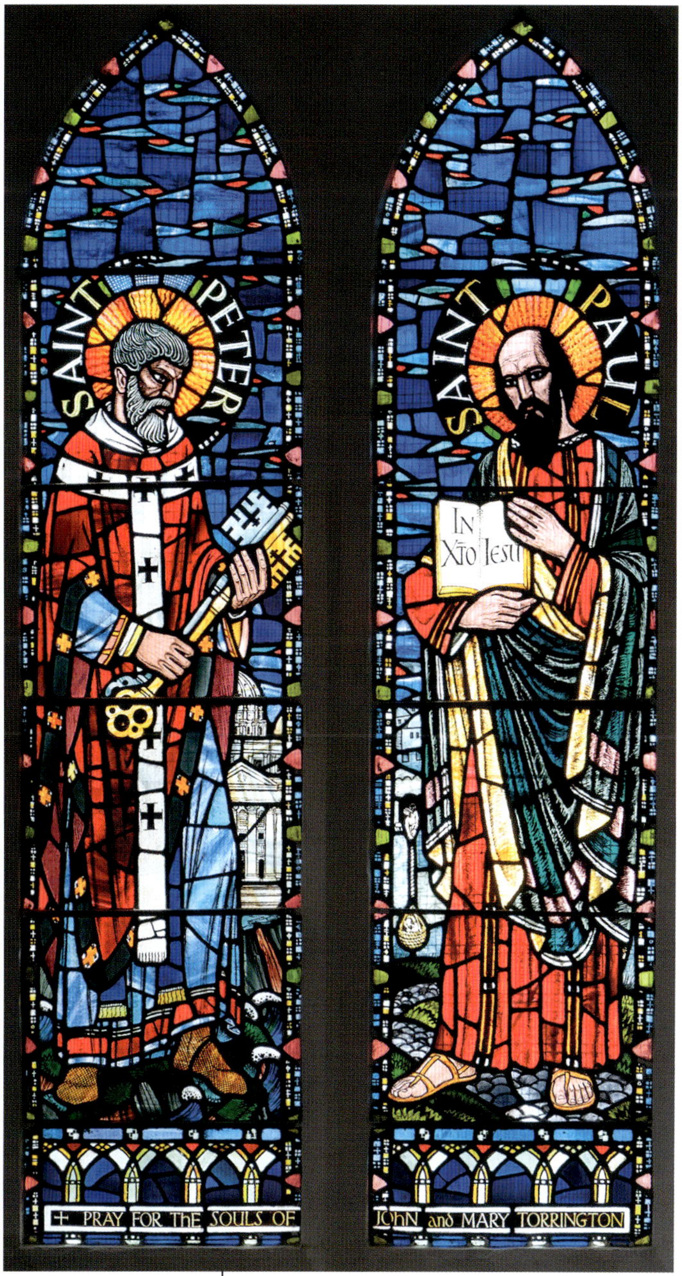

A full-coloured window depicting the vision of Bernadette, probably dating from the late 1940s, was made by Harry Clarke Stained Glass Studios for the Church of the Holy Name, Fishguard, adapting a design found across the Irish Sea in a two-light window in the Church of the Assumption, Wexford. Two windows by the Catholic artist Joseph Edward Nuttgens can be found at the Church of All Saints, Ebbw Vale, both of which show two figures in two-light windows. The earlier window of 1948 depicts the Baptism of Christ, while the second window of 1953 is of greater intensity, depicting Peter and Paul against an abstract blue ground.[70] Charles Blakeman worked with Nuttgens at the studio of Paul Woodroffe in the 1920s, and Blakeman subsequently joined Nuttgens at his studio at Piggotts Hill in Buckinghamshire. In the early 1950s he was working with Wilhelmina Geddes in the few years before her death in 1955, and an example of his expressive style can be found in the Church of St Mary, Newport.

70 After a period studying under Karl Parsons, Nuttgens worked with Martin Travers and Paul Woodroffe. In the 1930s he moved to Pigotts Hill in Buckinghamshire, where his house and studio was a Catholic enclave, close to Eric Gill's community. Late examples of Nuttgens' work can be found in the Roman Catholic Church of Our Lady, Llandovery, and the Anglican Church of the Holy Trinity, Gwersyllt.

0. Charles Blakeman, Christ Saving Peter om Drowning, 1951, Church of St Mary, ewport, north aisle

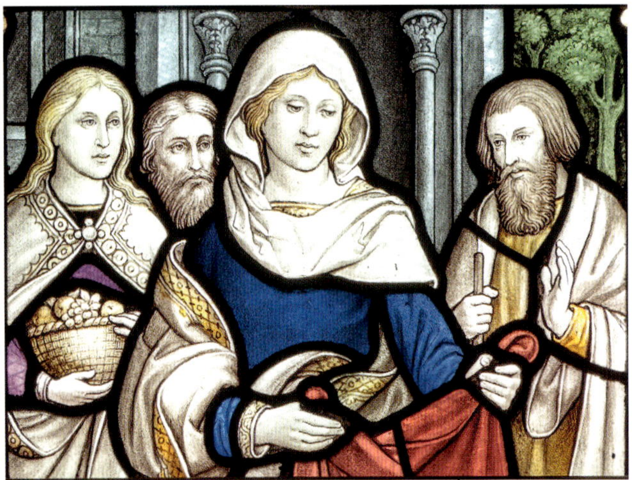

612. Burlison & Grylls, Works of Charity, probably 1940s, Alpha Chapel, Builth Wells, side wall

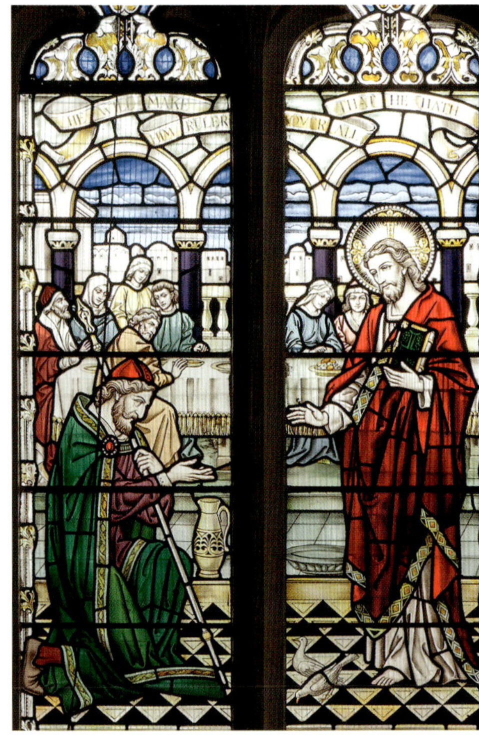

613. John Hardman Studios, Christ and the Faithful Steward, 1953, former Llanthewy Road Baptist Church, Newport, side wall

Stained glass commissioned for Nonconformist chapels after the Second World War sometimes came from a surprising choice of makers. Burlison & Grylls, who had been close to the Anglo-Catholic movement earlier in the century, were responsible for a window given in memory of the minister and his wife in the 1940s at English Presbyterian Alpha Chapel, Builth Wells.[71] The reduction in patronage from their core Roman Catholic market might explain the presence of new windows by John Hardman Studios at Llanthewy Road Baptist Church, Newport, in 1953 and at Christ Church English Congregational Church, Rhyl, in 1954, their centenary year.[72] While the majority of the windows made by Celtic Studios were for Anglican churches, only eight commissions for one or more windows were received from Nonconformist churches in Wales between 1950 and 1960, representing less than a tenth of their output for Welsh Anglican churches during the period.

71 The chapel is situated near the Anglican church where the firm also made three windows in the late 1940s. So the commission probably came about as a result of these other local connections with the firm.

72 Two previous windows were installed after 1937. The firm also continued to provide a small number of windows for Anglican churches in Wales during the 1950s.

73 See for example their listings in the British Society of Master Glass-Painters' *Directory of Stained Glass Windows*, 1966, p. 7–9.

74 Work by Abbott & Co. was made for three other sites in Colwyn Bay between 1949 and 1954: the Anglican Church of St Andrew, Penrhos College, and the Crematorium.

75 The firm made a small window for Bethania Calvinistic Methodist Church in 1967, also designed by R. Moore, as was a single-light window for Ynystawe Moriah Baptist Chapel in Swansea in 1960. A sanctuary window was made by the firm for Old Colwyn Methodist Church in 1955.

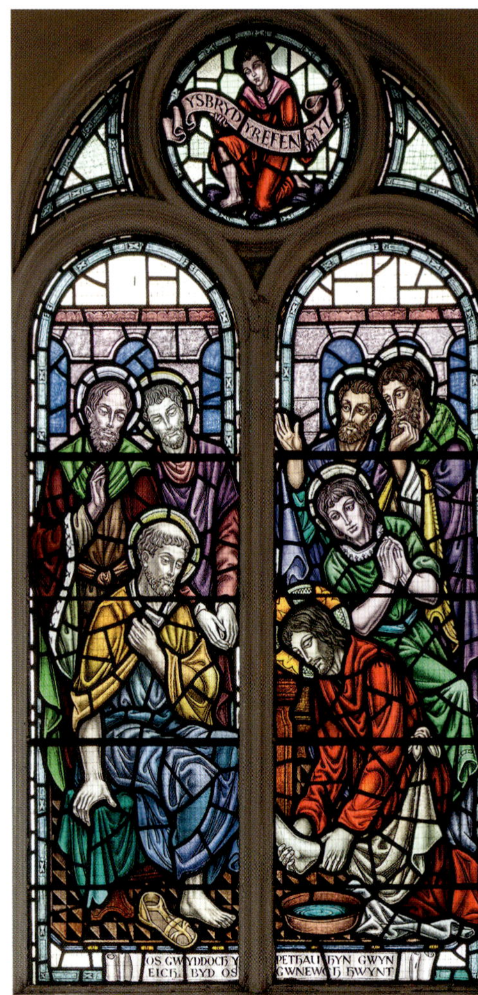

614. Celtic Studios, Christ Washing Peter's Feet, 1957, Bethania Calvinistic Methodist Chapel, Morriston, front wall (gallery)

615. Powell & Sons, Christ's Commission to His Disciples, 1961, designed by Rupert Moore, Tabernacle Baptist Church, Carmarthen, side wall

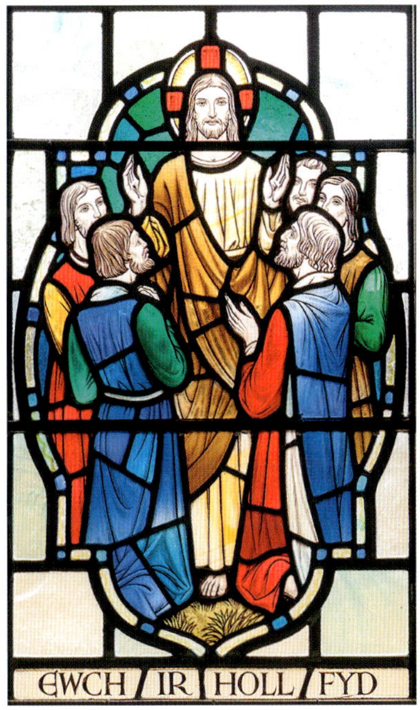

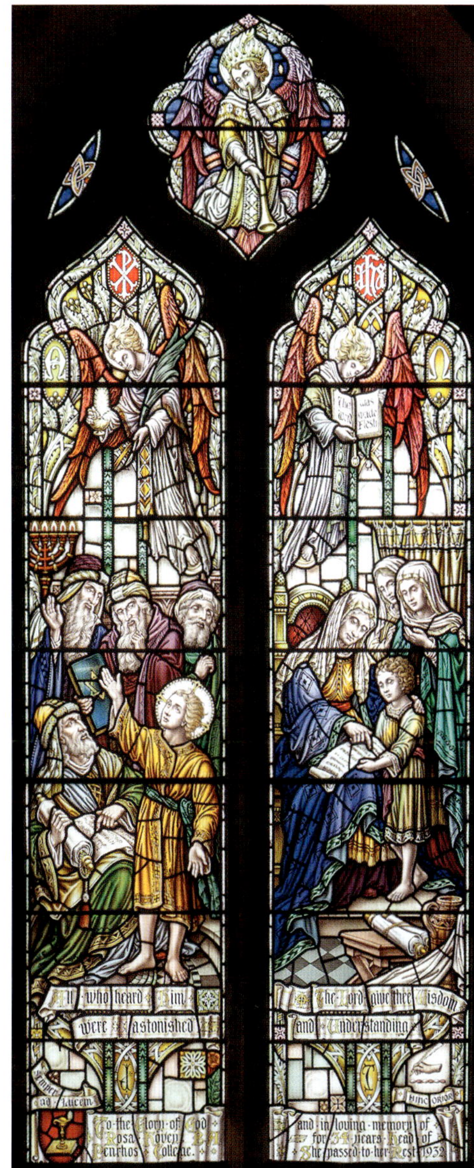

616. Abbott & Co., Christ with the Doctors of the Law and the Virgin Mary Teaching Christ to Read, 1945, Wesleyan Methodist Church of St John, Colwyn Bay, north transept

In contrast, Abbot & Co. of Lancaster produced work more evenly across the Protestant denominations. During the 1950s and 60s about half of their windows were supplied to Nonconformist churches, many of which were Methodist.[73] Methodist churches in Wales with post-Second World War windows by the firm include Roath Park, Cardiff; Chirk, where the window is a war memorial; and the Church of St John, Colwyn Bay.[74] Abbott & Co. provided a further window for Heol Awst in Carmarthen, where they had made two windows in 1922, and a further small entrance lobby window for the Welsh Independent Chapel, Eglwys y Priordy, also in the town. Powell & Sons also made windows for two chapels in Carmarthen, including a series of five scenes for Tabernacl Welsh Baptist Church depicting New Testament scenes, some of which were designed by Rupert Moore.[75] John Hall & Sons made a window of Christ as the Good Shepherd for Nazareth Chapel, Treorchy, and added further windows at Tabernacle Congregational Chapel, Milford Haven.[76]

These windows, and others at Tredegarville English Baptist Church, Cardiff, all depicted biblical figures and scenes. This makes the window made in 1949 by J. Wippell & Co. for Park Street Congregational Church, Llanelli, most unusual. The Victorian founder of the church, David Rees, is commemorated in the window, kneeling before Christ and presenting the church in the fashion of a medieval donor figure, assuming imagery more characteristic of the Roman Catholic Church.

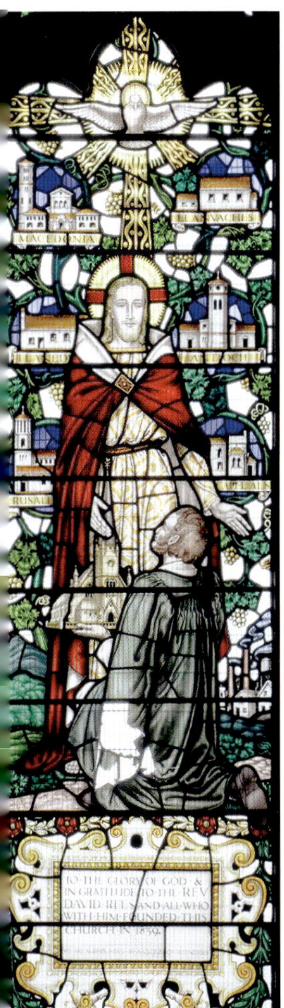

617. J. Wippell & Co., Christ with David Rees, 1949, Park Street Congregational Church, Llanelli, south aisle

76 Two windows at Milford Haven depicted Christ in the house of his parents, one of which is a copy of John Everett Millais's *Christ in the House of His Parents ('The Carpenter's Shop')*, painted in 1849–50.

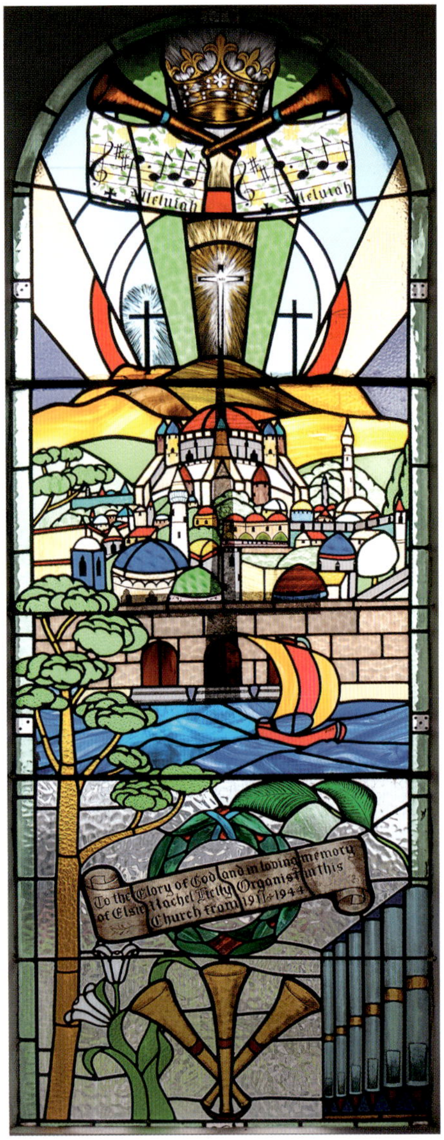

618. Memorial Window, designed by Donald Kelly, 1950s, former Castleton Baptist Church, Castleton, side wall (gallery)

In contrast, a window at Castleton Baptist Church has no figures at all in its representation of the dawn of Easter morning with complex, but not always obvious, symbolism.[77] The window was commissioned in memory of Rachel Kelly, who was the organist at the church, and was designed by Donald Kelly. The lack of painted glass could point to its execution by a local maker.

A set of windows by Williams & Watson of Liverpool at Ruthin English Presbyterian Church include a three-light east window and single north window with the monogram of the designer Arthur Holloway, and were followed by three further side windows between 1961 and 1964 in a similar style. The windows juxtapose figures and biblical texts (and in the case of the Good Shepherd, a line from a popular hymn) on plain quarries, and although they are delineated with a bold clarity of line characteristic of more modern stained glass in Welsh churches in the 1950s and 60s, hints of Modernism in the stained glass of Nonconformist places of worship are rare until the 1980s and 90s.

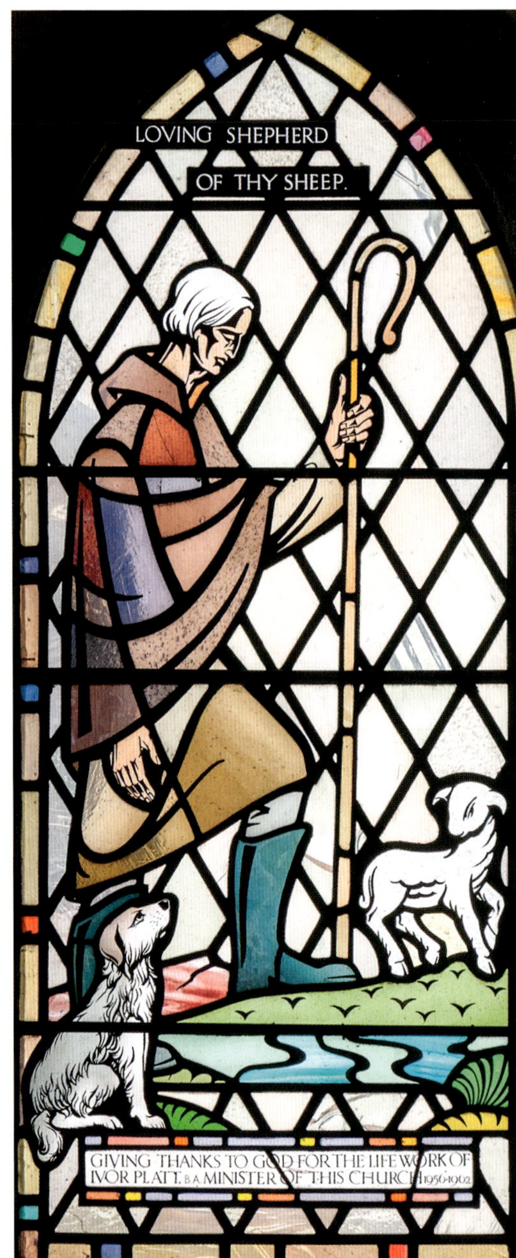

619. Williams & Watson, The Good Shepherd, 1961–4, Ruthin Presbyterian Church, side wall

77 For example, the walls of the city with its locked and closed doors, symbolise the closed minds of its inhabitants, and the broken nimbus in different colours around the crosses symbolise the brotherhood of all, regardless of colour. The church has now been converted to offices.

CHAPTER TEN

MODERNISM IN STAINED GLASS

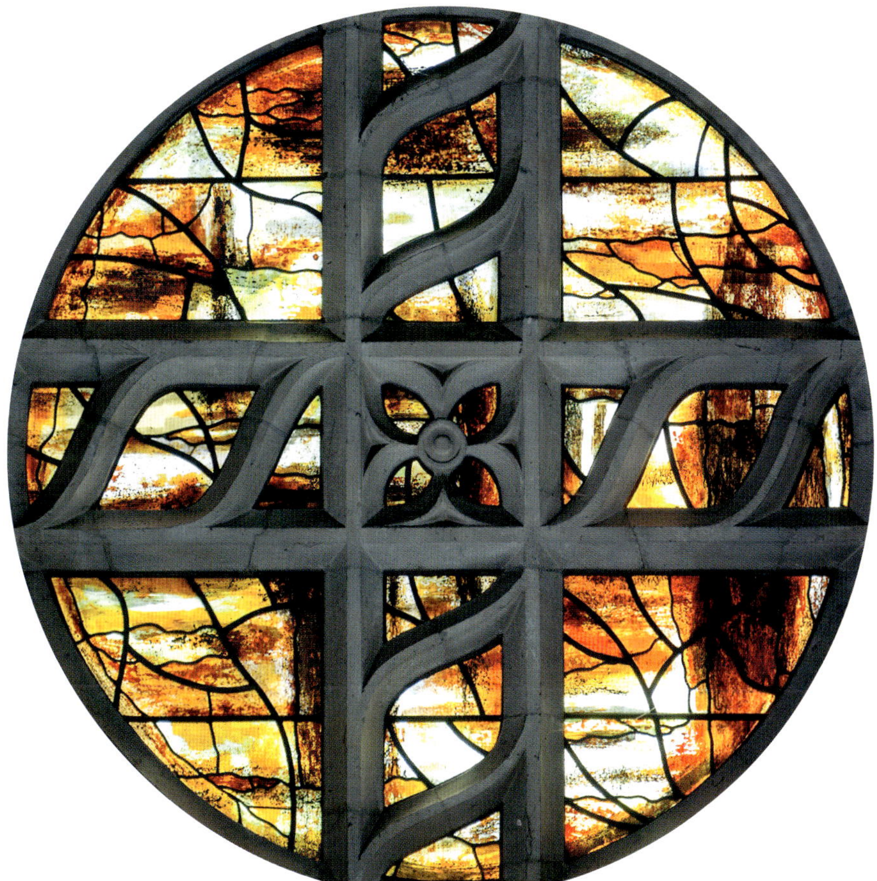

Until the 1960s, stained glass in Wales was largely unaffected by the transformation of the visual arts in Western Europe during the first half of the twentieth century. The avant-garde art movements of Cubism, Expressionism, Surrealism and Abstraction held little appeal for congregations, or even many of the artists commissioned to produce stained glass.[1] This was not the case overseas, and in 1954 an influential book on stained glass by Robert Sowers juxtaposed contemporary experimental work in glass from Europe and America with both abstract painting and medieval stained glass. Sowers presented a range of new possibilities in design and technique, including works designed by the painters Henri Matisse and Fernand Léger, as a rediscovery of the essentials of stained glass. In his introduction, Herbert Read, the historian of applied arts and supporter of British abstract artists, anticipated the obstacles to such innovation:

> ... there still exists a powerful opposition to this revival, which comes partly from a mistaken and reactionary interpretation of tradition (inspired to some extent by 'vested interests' – 'church furnishers' who are unable to adapt themselves to the true tradition) and partly from the modern architectural worship of bland aqueous light. The modern architect is usually afraid of colour, especially of intense colour, and rather than use it would condemn people to worship God in a white glare of antiseptic austerity.[2]

The preference for clear glass backgrounds behind figures and scenes to allow in light certainly contributed to some particularly bland stained glass being made for Anglican churches in the 1950s.[3] The 'antiseptic austerity' of interiors reflected a genuine concern to lighten the interior of churches and in some Anglican dioceses a question on the standard form for a petition for a faculty to install a new stained glass window asked whether it would darken the interior. As a consequence, most of the ecclesiastical stained glass of the 1950s lacked the originality of artists such as Leonard Walker, Richard Stubington and Theodore Baily, who had all explored both the materiality of glass and abstraction in their windows during the 1920s. Neither did it take on the breadth of artistic influences that Wilhelmina Geddes, and her pupil Evie Hone, brought to their work.[4]

1 In 1932 the *Journal of the Society of Master Glass-Painters* recommended a book on contemporary German glass to 'those who are not afraid of knowing what is happening on the Continent'. The journal was conscious of the different ideas on stained and painted glass in England from the modernist approaches in France and Germany, but recognised that there was advantage for its members in promoting the use of the medium in secular buildings. *Journal of the Society of Master Glass-Painters*, vol. iv, no. 3 (1932), p. 107.

2 Robert Sowers, *The Lost Art: A Survey of one thousand years of stained glass* (London: Lund Humphries, 1954), p. 8.

3 Artists such as Howard Martin and Hubert Thomas, who had been receptive to continental innovation before the war, found themselves constrained by traditionalist patrons and the repetition of common biblical subjects. They had visited the Paris Exposition in 1937, and their secular work of the late 1930s suggests their enthusiasm to innovate. See Maurice Broady, *A Vision Fulfilled: The story of Celtic Studios and Swansea's architectural glass tradition* (Swansea: West Glamorgan Archive Service, 2010), pp. 50–1.

4 Evie Hone had also been a pupil of the Cubist painters Albert Gleizes and André Lhote in Paris. Her work, and particularly her east window for Eton College Chapel of 1948 has been regarded by many as marking the beginning of modern stained glass in England. See for example Patrick Reyntiens, *The Beauty of Stained* Glass (London: The Herbert Press, 1990), p. 192.

620. (Title page) Patrick Reyntiens, East Window, 1
designed by John Piper, 1965, St Woolos Cathedral, New

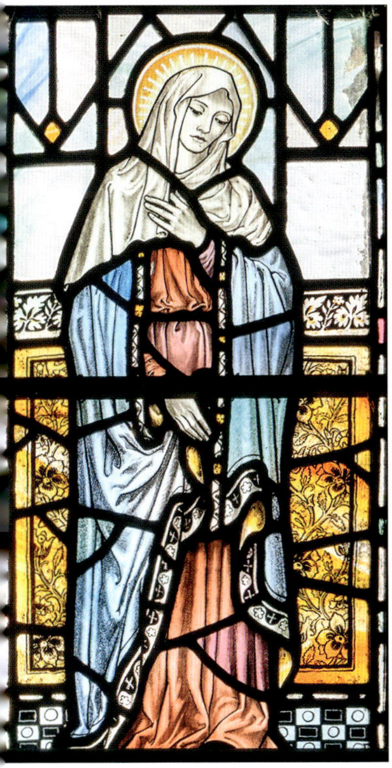

621. Carl Edwards, St Gwendoline, 1959, Church of St Gwendoline, Llyswen, chancel

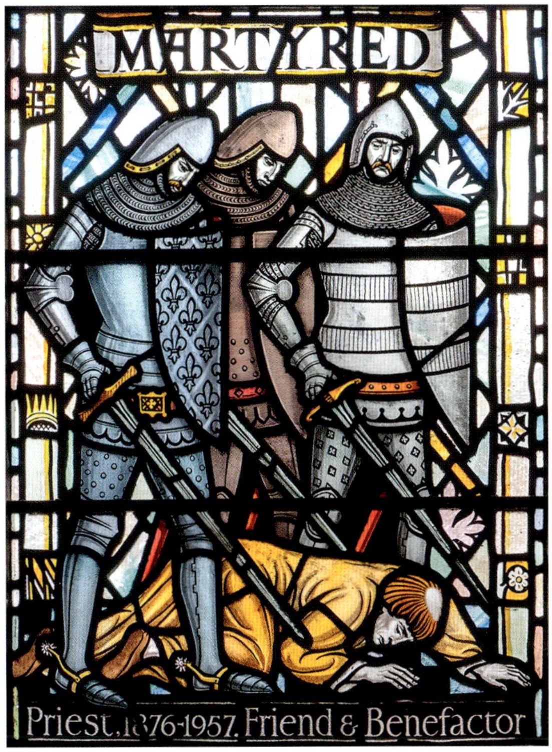

622. Carl Edwards, The Martyrdom of St Thomas Becket, 1958, St Davids Cathedral, Chapel of St Thomas Becket

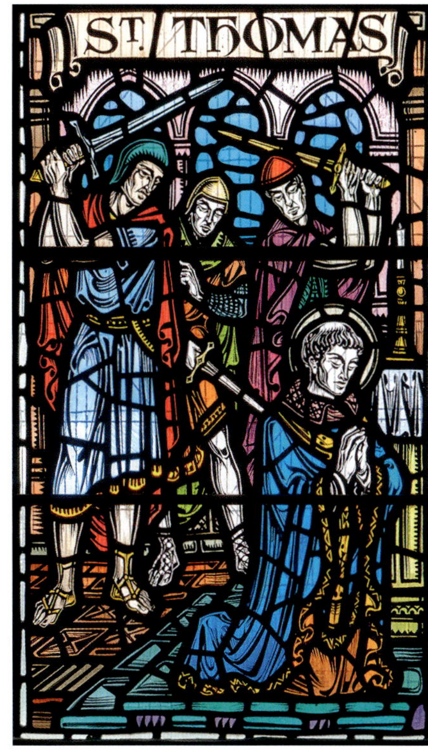

623. Celtic Studios, The Martyrdom of St Thomas Becket, 1957, Church of St Thomas, Overmonnow, east window

By the late 1950s a growing number of studios demonstrated a slightly tentative, and often fairly traditional, modernism, perceptible in the reduction and slight abstraction of the painted detail, a preference for line rather than tone, and in the return to full-coloured designs. Among the larger firms, Powell & Sons stand out in their attempts to modernise their style, a process that had started under James Hogan in the 1920s and was perceptible in designs by Carl Edwards and E. Liddall Armitage. The trend continued in the independent work of former designers and cartoonists, such as Carl Edwards and Kenneth Bunton.[5] The boldness of some of Edwards' work for Powell's is less perceptible in his windows of the 1950s at St Davids Cathedral and the Church of St Gwendoline, Llyswen, the latter exhibiting a delicacy of colour and painted detail.[6] Edwards' scene of the martyrdom of Thomas Becket makes an informative comparison with a similar scene designed by Hogan's Welsh pupil Hubert Thomas, and made by Celtic Studios for the east window at the Church of St Thomas, Overmonnow. Also a lower panel, Thomas' design is more colourful and dynamic, using less white glass and executed with a linear, painterly style for detailing features and drapery.

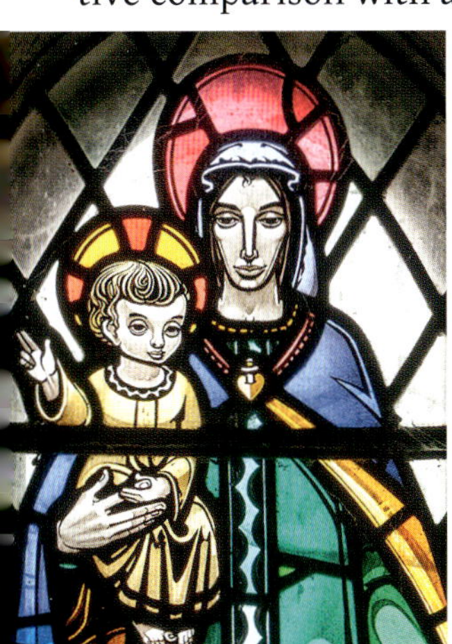

624. Kenneth Bunton, Virgin and Child, 1964, Church of St Martin, Flimston, vestry

5 After a short spell as the successor to James Hogan, Carl Edwards established his own studio early in the 1950s, initially with Hugh Powell, who left his family firm. An example of Hugh Powell's original approach can be seen at the Church of St Arvan, St Arvans, where his two-light window illustrates an unusual biblical verse (Matthew 13: 52) and incorporates the text as a main part of the overall design. Kenneth Bunton was a cartoonist at the firm who also worked for J. Wippell & Co.

6 A fourth window at Llyswen by the artist was added in 1974, and he was probably responsible for a fifth, in a very similar style, made in about 1980. The east window is a First World War memorial by his former employers, Powell's.

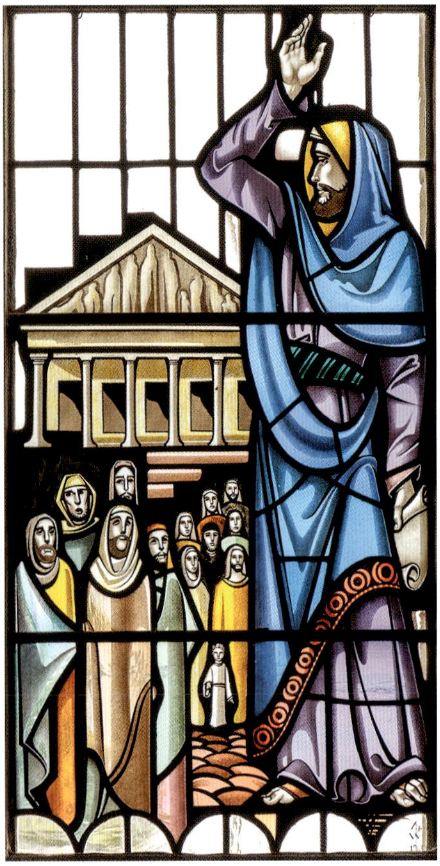

625. J. Wippell & Co., Paul Preaching in Athens, 1963, Church of St John the Baptist, Ystrad Meurig, east window

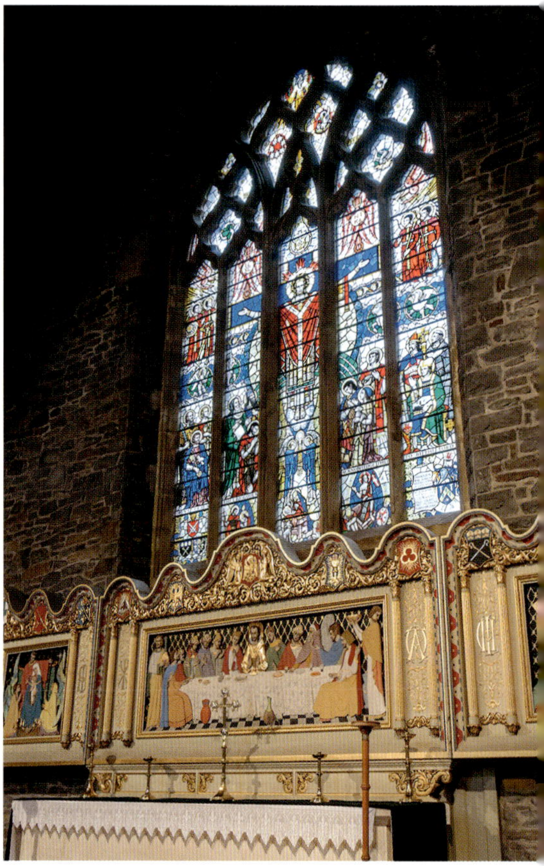

626. J. Wippell & Co., East Window and Reredos, 1959–60, Church of St Paul, Newbridge, window designed G. Cooper-Abbs, reredos designed by G. Miller

A similar simplification of paintwork can be seen in the work of J. Wippell & Co., who made a series of windows for the Church of St Paul, Newbridge, including the east window and a large painted reredos made in 1959–60. Two of the four later three-light nave windows at the church have compact scenes surrounding the central figures of Paul and Christ in Majesty, and scenes against plain grounds across five lights can also be seen at the Church of St John the Baptist, Ystrad Meurig, where their east window is a collection of subjects from the New Testament.[7] Similarly stylised and compacted scenes can be seen in the south transept window by Goddard & Gibbs at the Church of St Berres, Llanferres. Here, the five scenes depicting the parable of the Good Samaritan are connected by a central roundel containing the Samaritan tending to the wounded man, the scene most commonly used to represent the parable.

Goddard & Gibbs also made windows by freelance designers such as the South African painter Maud Sumner, who had studied to be a teacher in London and at Oxford University, but subsequently went to Paris to train as an artist before the war. Her three windows made by the firm from 1958 to about 1962 for the Church of St Michael, Abergele, and Christ Church, Prestatyn, demonstrate a more radical modernism with expressive drawing and bright colouring.

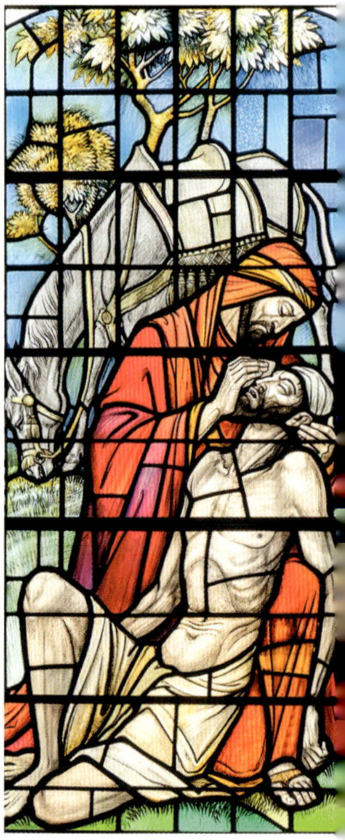

627. Goddard & Gibbs, The Good Samaritan, 1966, Church of St Berres, Llanferres, south transept

7 An additional scene depicted the schoolmaster John Jones, who had the church built and was the priest and schoolmaster for 46 years prior to his death in 1915.

8 The date of the window at Killay is uncertain but it is after 1954 and probably pre-dates the five windows by Celtic Studios, the first of which was made in 1965. The figure of the risen Christ is the same as that used by the firm in 1966 for one of their three windows at the Church of Emmanuel, Bistre (Buckley).

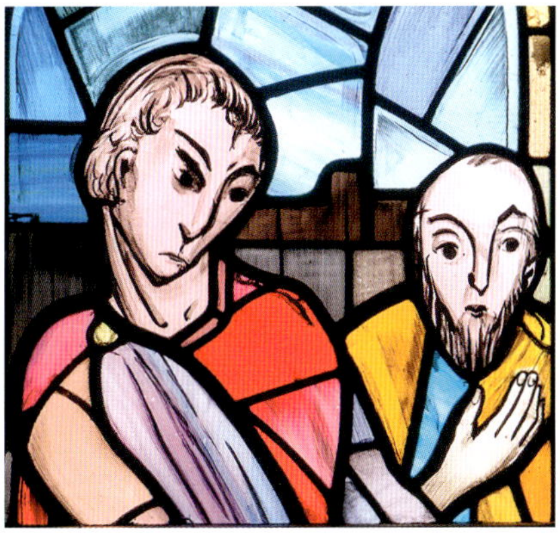

628. Goddard & Gibbs, Figures from the Healing of Blind artimaeus, 1962, signed by Maud Sumner, Christ hurch, Prestatyn, south aisle

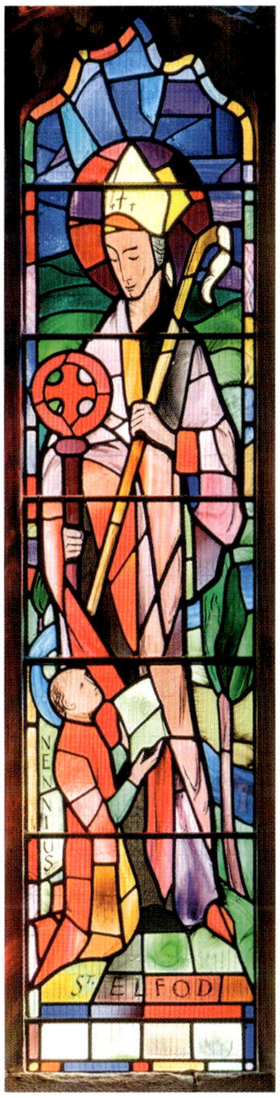

629. (right) Goddard & Gibbs, 1958, designed by Maud Sumner, St Elfod and Nennius, Church of St Michael, Abergele, sanctuary

The design of windows by Shrigley & Hunt was also modernised by Joseph Fisher in the 1950s, with the help of freelance designers such as John Blyth and Harry Harvey. The bright reds and mauves of the firm's window for the Church of St Hilary, Killay, contrasts sharply with the drab late Arts and Crafts style used for their previous windows made for the church.[8]

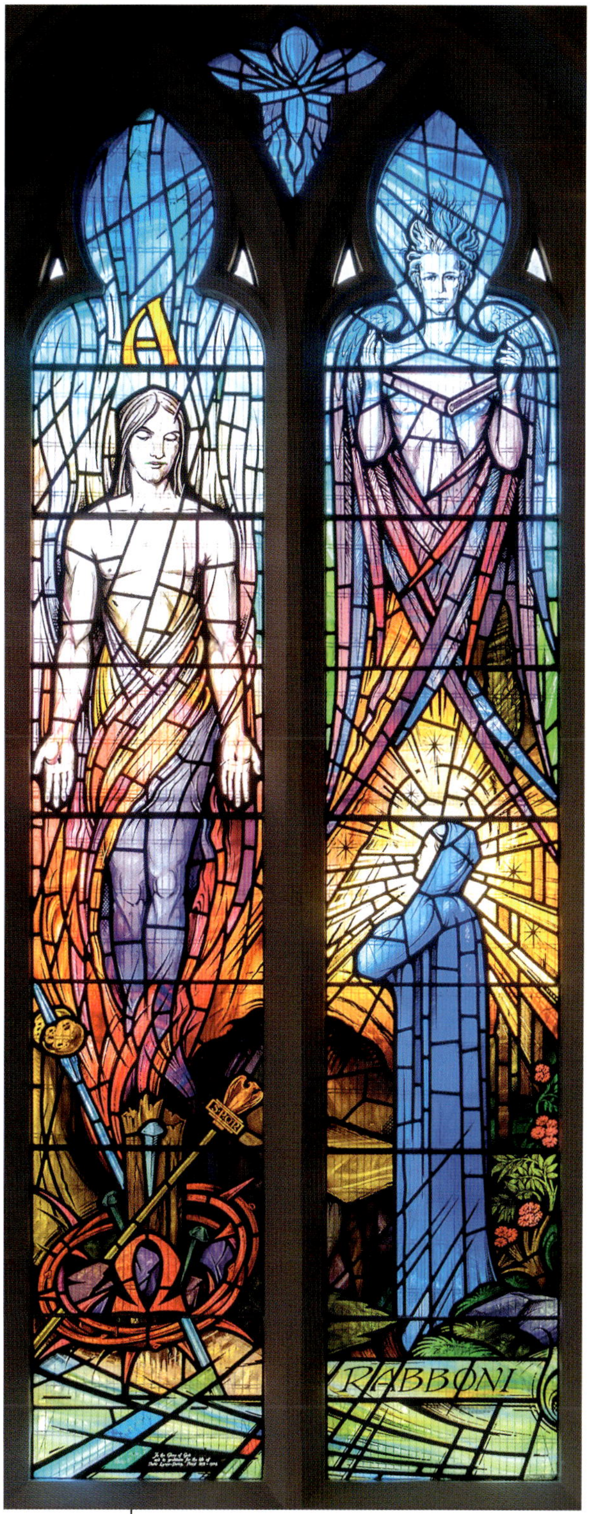

630. Shrigley & Hunt, The Risen Christ Appearing to Mary Magdalene, probably 1950s, Church of St Hilary, Killay, nave

The fashion for plain glass backgrounds and surrounds in the 1950s increasingly gave way to full-coloured designs by the end of the decade. For example Celtic Studios' 1954 scene of the Adoration of the Shepherds and the Magi at the old church outside Llandrindod Wells fills the night sky with blue glass, and similar treatments of the same subject by Celtic Studios in 1957 for the Church of St Mary, Llanwern, and in 1959 for the Church of the Holy Trinity, Newcastle Emlyn, are more tightly packed full-coloured designs.

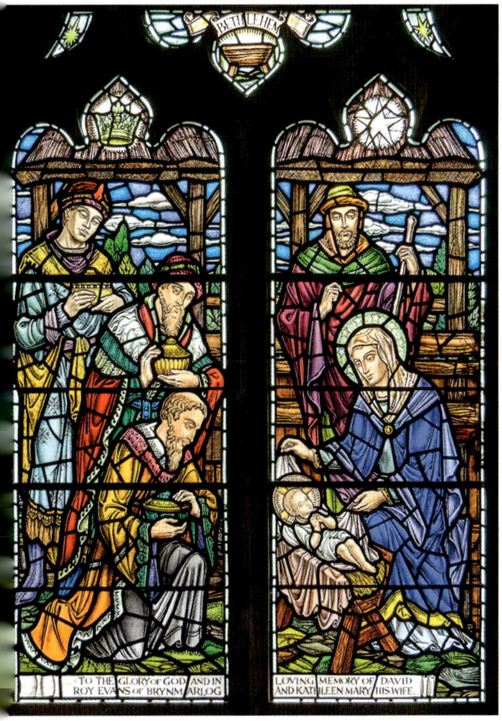

631. Celtic Studios, The Adoration of the Magi, 1959, Church of the Holy Trinity, Newcastle Emlyn, chancel

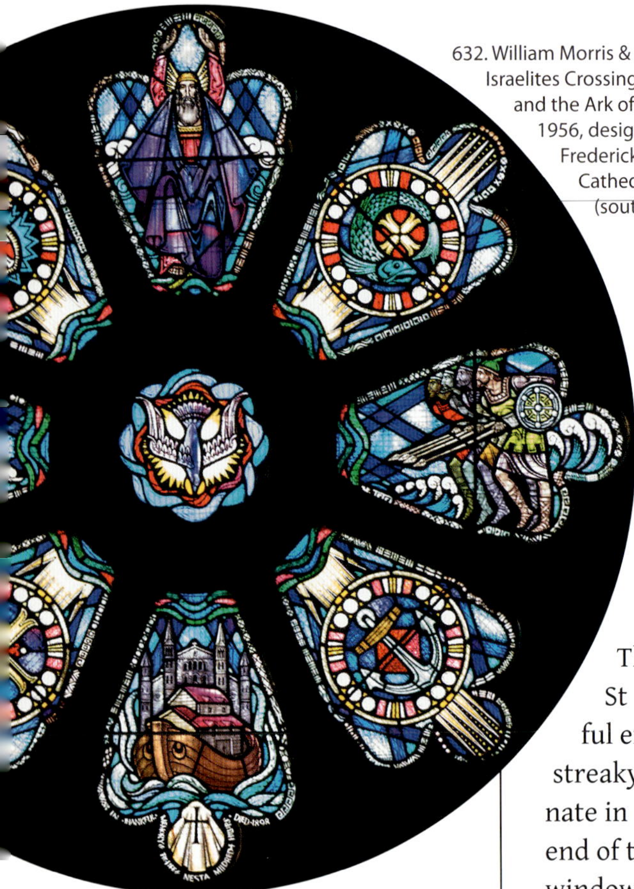

632. William Morris & Co., The Israelites Crossing the Red Sea and the Ark of the Church, 1956, designed by Frederick Cole, St Davids Cathedral, baptistry (south aisle)

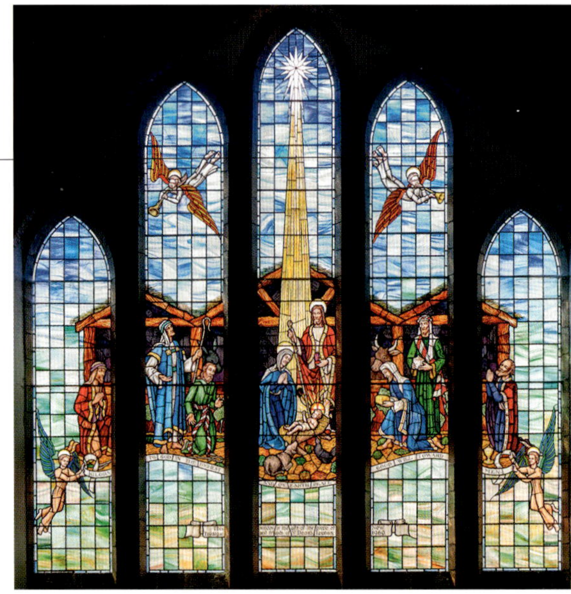

633. Luxford Studios, The Adoration of the Shepherds and the Magi, 1960, Church of St Dingat, New Tredegar, west window

The scene also occupies the west window of the Church of St Dingat, New Tredegar, where Luxford Studios achieved a colourful effect by filling the background of the large five-light window with streaky blue and green rectangular quarries.[9] Intense blues predominate in the pair of rose windows designed by Frederick Cole for the west end of the aisles of St Davids Cathedral.[10] The baptistry (south aisle) window includes scenes representing the crossing of the Red Sea in rich blue and purple glass lightened with yellow, while the west window of the north aisle illustrates symbols from the book of Revelation, which is similar in effect, but substituting purple glass for green.

The simplification of line and use of full-coloured windows was also characteristic of independent artists. Both features can be seen in the work of Trena Cox as early as the 1930s, although some of her windows, such as the two narrow windows with scenes from the birth and early life of Christ at the Church of Emmanuel, Bistre (Buckley), use small amounts of white quarries as backgrounds. In windows by Joan Howson at the Church of St Twrog, Maentwrog, and the Church of St Teilo, Pontarddulais, subtly-coloured streaky Norman slab glass is used as rectangular quarries, while her slightly later window of 1958 restricts white glass to the rays of light emanating from the figure of Christ in the east window of the Church of St Michael, Llanfihangel-y-traethau.[11] Harcourt Doyle, a former student and assistant of Martin Travers, sets his lively graphic figures on clear glass backgrounds in the two-light memorial to Mary Gwendoline and Bertie Cunynghame Dwyer-Hampton at the Church of St Catherine, Llanfaes (Anglesey).[12]

9 Unfortunately, the window is marred by poor draughtsmanship that is not in evidence in the smaller adjacent window by the same firm made in only the previous year.

10 F.W. Cole re-established the firm of William Morris & Co. of Westminster after the Second World War, and successfully modernised their style until its closure in 1958, after which he briefly designed for J. Wippell & Co.

11 Joan Howson was born at Overton in Flintshire in 1885 and was based in London after 1913. She brought twenty-three evacuee babies to Plas Tan-y-Bwlch, Maentwrog, in October 1940, and brought further homeless children to rented accommodation nearby. She died at her studio near Porthmadog in 1964. M.E. De Putron, 'Joan Howson', *Journal of the British Society of Master Glass-Painters*, vol. xvi, no. 1 (1976–7), pp. 46–54.

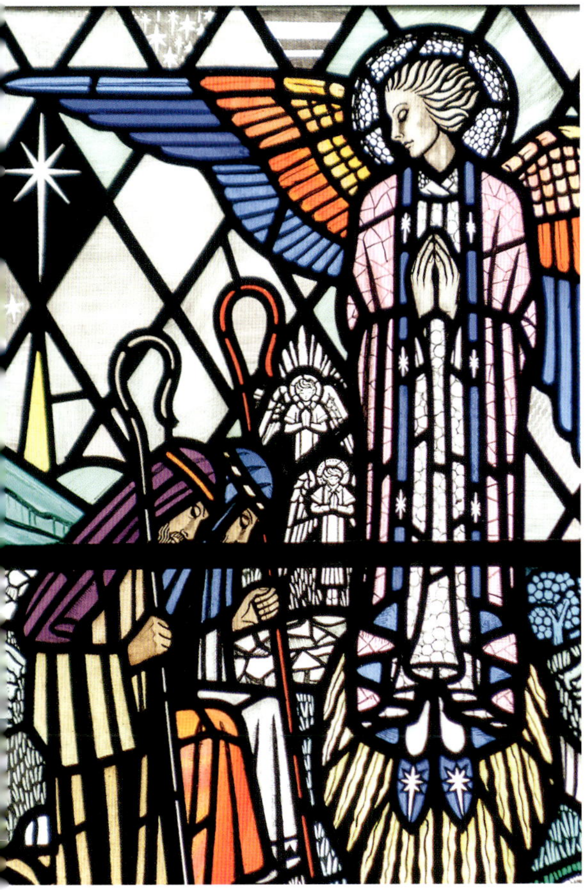

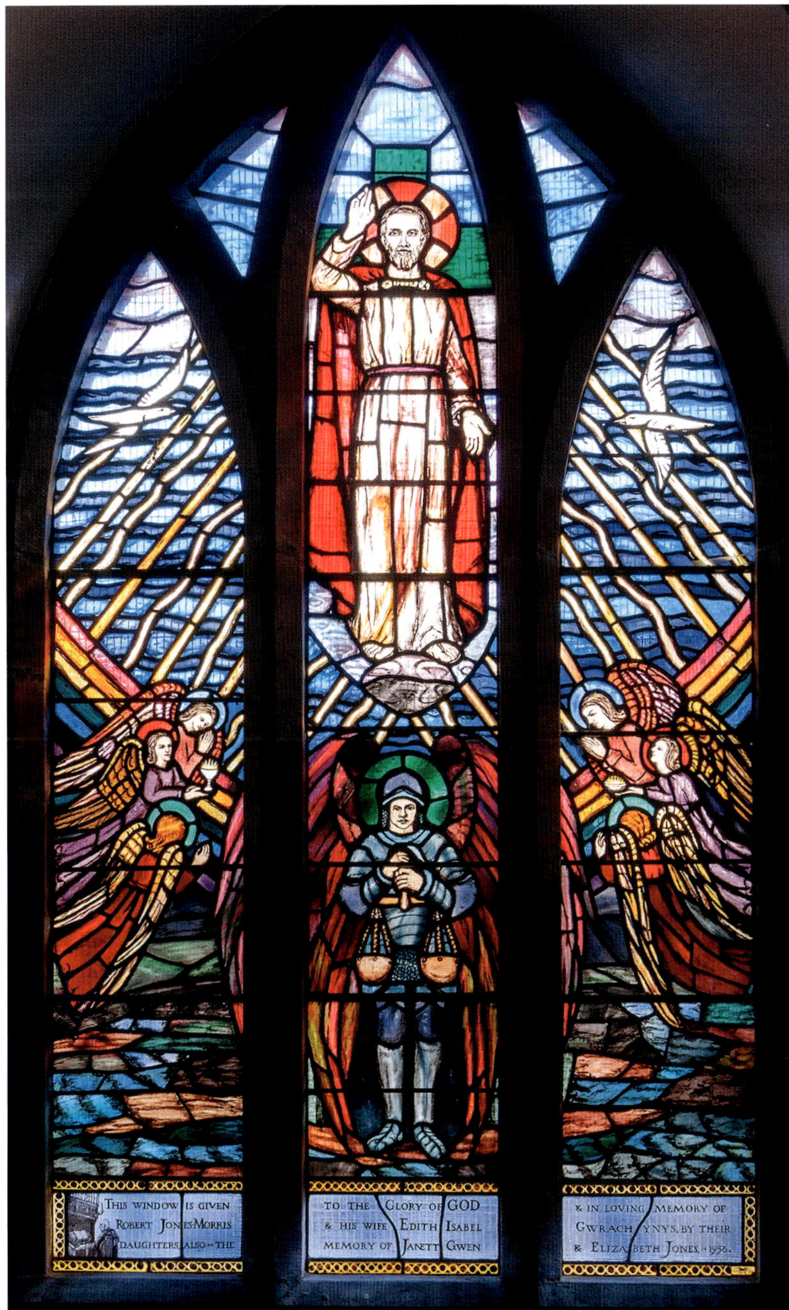

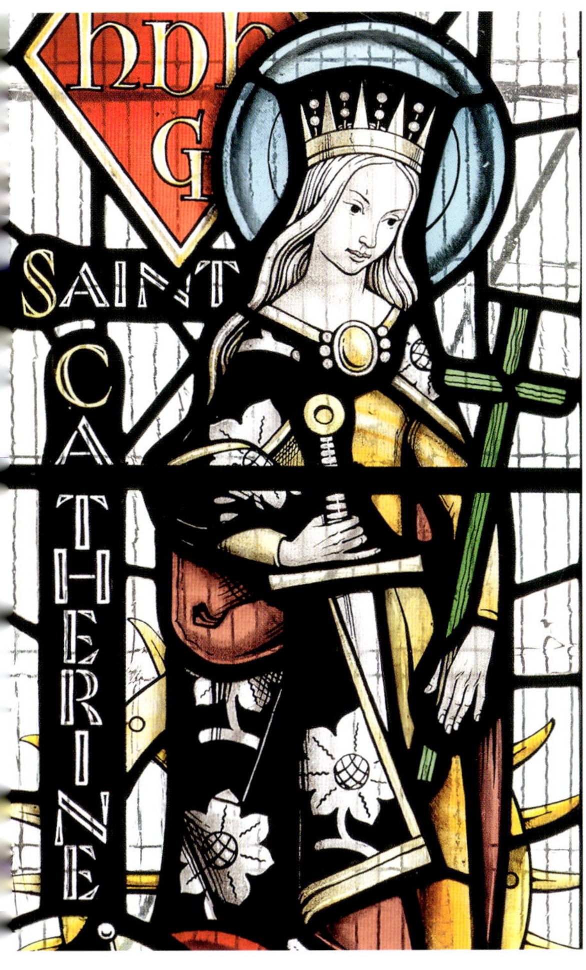

634. (above left) Trena Cox, The Annunciation to the Shepherds, 1954, Emmanuel Church, Bistre, nave

635. (above) Joan Howson, Christ with St Michael and Angels, 1958, Church of St Michael, Llanfihangel-y-traethau, east window

636. (left) H.M. Doyle, St Catherine, 1964, Church of St Catherine, Llanfaes (Anglesey), south aisle

12 Harcourt Medhurst Doyle established his studio in Liverpool in the late 1950s, but moved to Llanrhos, near Llandudno, in 1966. Many of his windows are found in north-west England, and he seems to have made only one window for a Welsh church. For his obituary, see *The Journal of Stained Glass*, vol. xxv (2001), pp. 192–5.

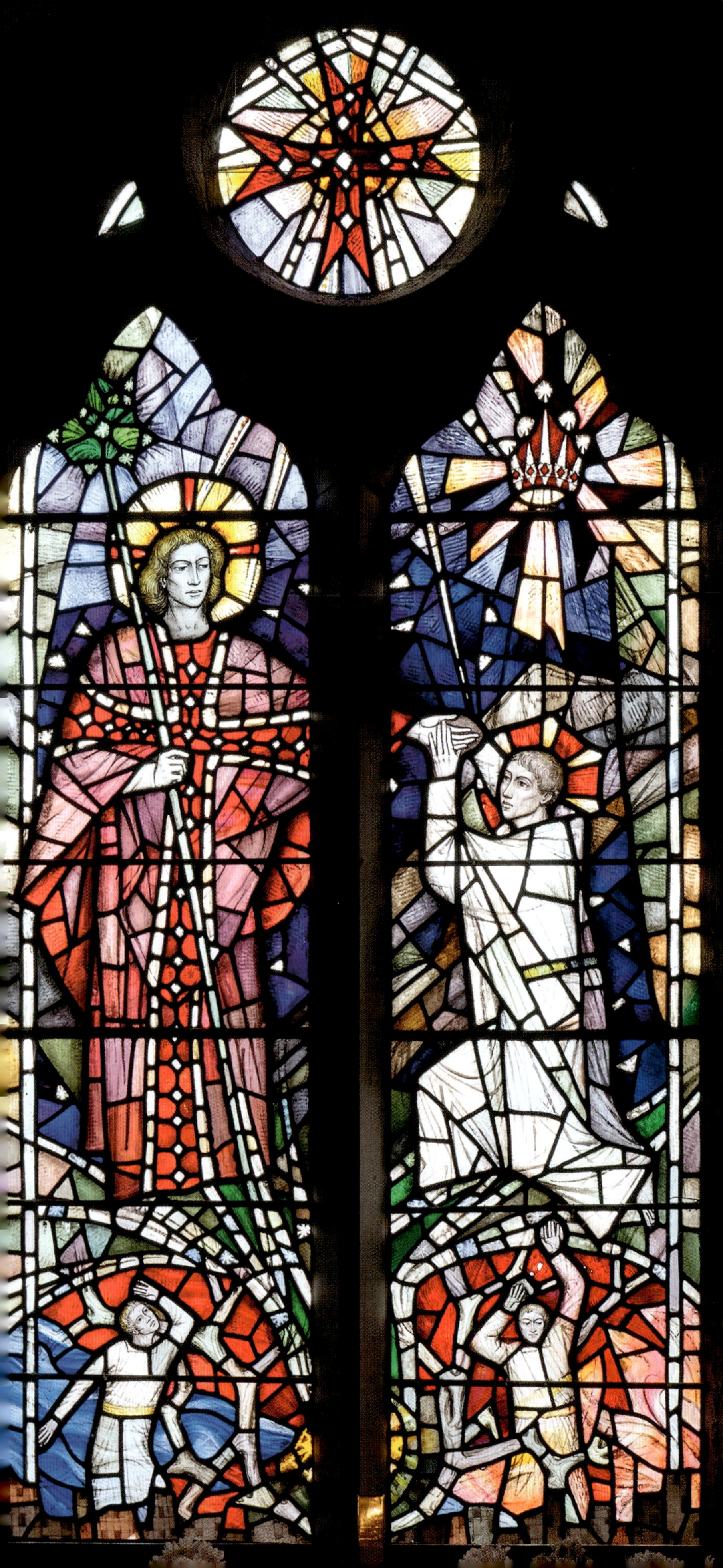

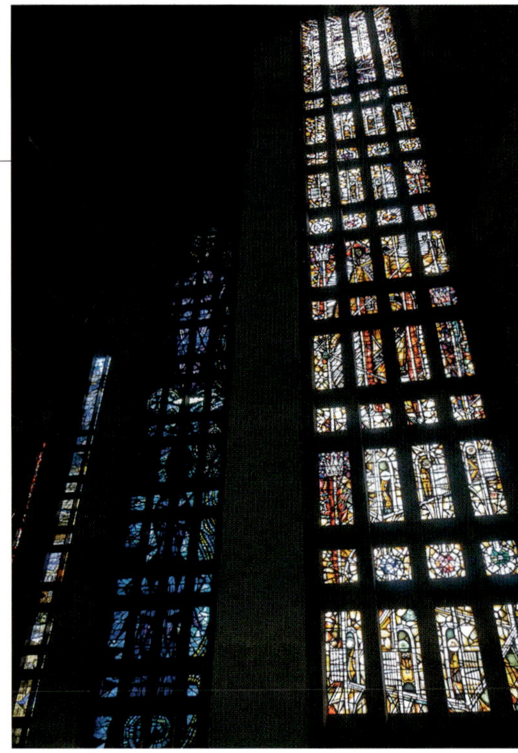

637. (left) Lawrence Lee, 'Guide Me O Thou Great Jehovah', 1960, Church of St David, Betws (Carmarthenshire), east window

638. (above) Nave Windows with Golden Window by Lawrence Lee ('Man' side) foremost, representing Resurrection, *c.* 1954–8, Coventry Cathedral

At the Royal College of Art, Lawrence Lee took an interest in the continental innovation in architectural stained glass and his work as an artist and teacher was profoundly influential on the artists that trained at the college in the 1950s and 60s. In 1952 the architect Basil Spence was sufficiently impressed by the work of his students Keith New and Geoffrey Clarke that he approached Lee to oversee the production of the nave windows for his new cathedral at Coventry, which were designed by the three artists and made at the College assisted by students.

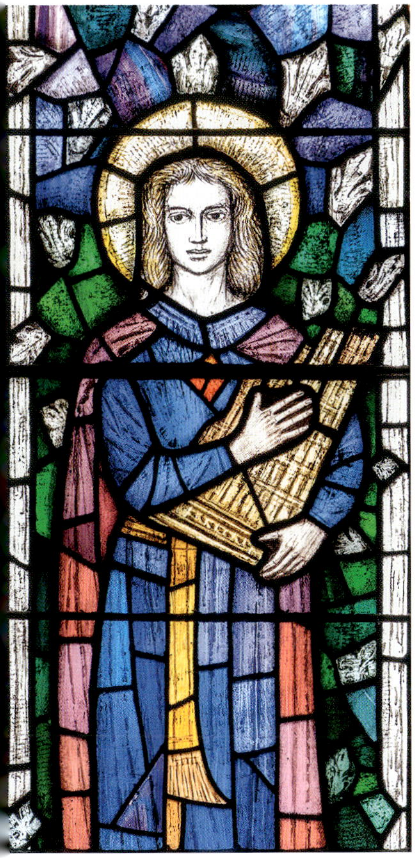

639. Lawrence Lee, St Cecilia, 1962, Church of St Michael, Aberystwyth, north chapel

These towering walls of colour with abstract figures and symbols were utterly foreign to church commissions in both Wales and England. Lee's own windows for Coventry Cathedral were the least abstract and his three windows for churches in Wales were reassuringly representational. After his window at Gowerton in 1953, in 1960 he designed the east window for the Church of St David, Betws, near Ammanford, and a two-light window with figures of Francis and Cecilia for the Church of St Michael, Aberystwyth. The east window at Betws takes the popular Welsh hymn 'Guide Me O Thou Great Jehovah' as its subject, with Christ as the 'strong deliverer' reaching out his 'powerful hand' to the kneeling pilgrim, who can also be seen below making his way through the 'barren land'.

A similar modernist-figurative style can be found in the work of John Hayward, who was deeply impressed by the nave windows at Coventry. Hayward worked as an assistant to Francis Stephens at Faithcraft Studios in St Albans, where he designed a wide range of church furnishings. The risen Christ emerges from a mosaic of pattern and brilliant colour in Hayward's window at the Church of St Llawddog, Llanllawddog, accompanied with the text 'I Am the Way, the Truth, and the Life'.

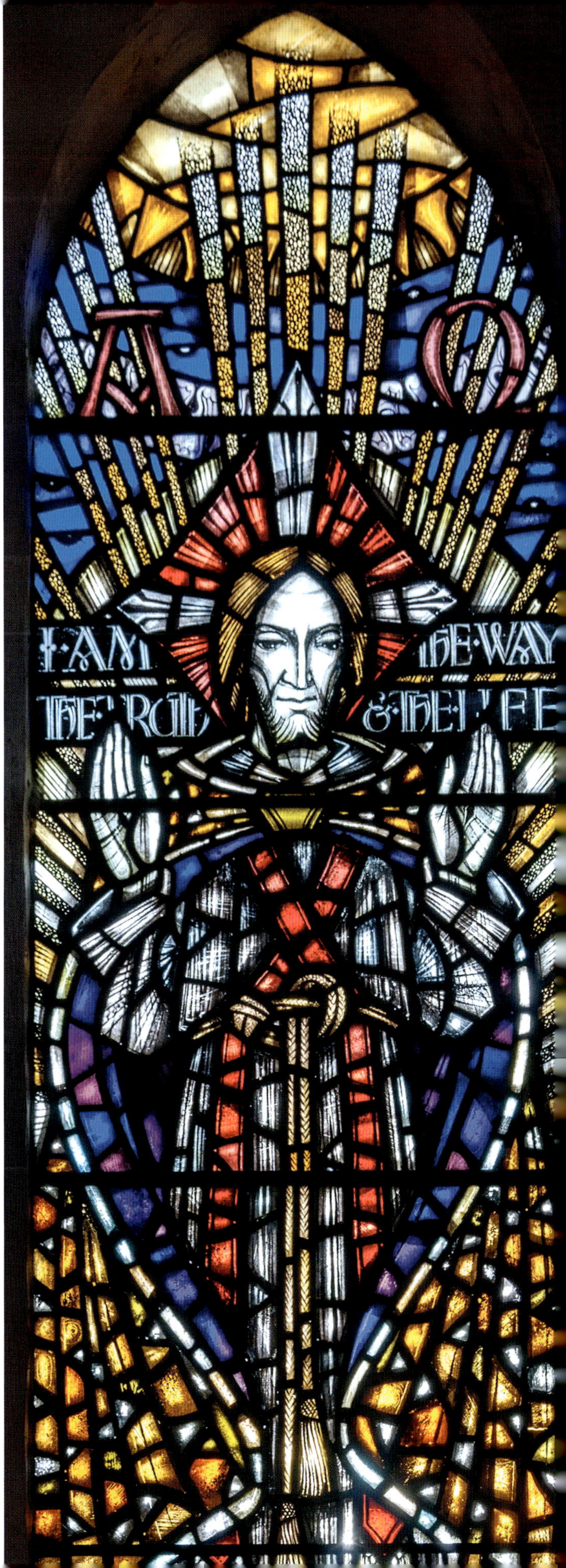

640. John Hayward, 'I Am the Way, the Truth, and the Life', 1958, Church of St Llawddog, Llanllawddog, nave

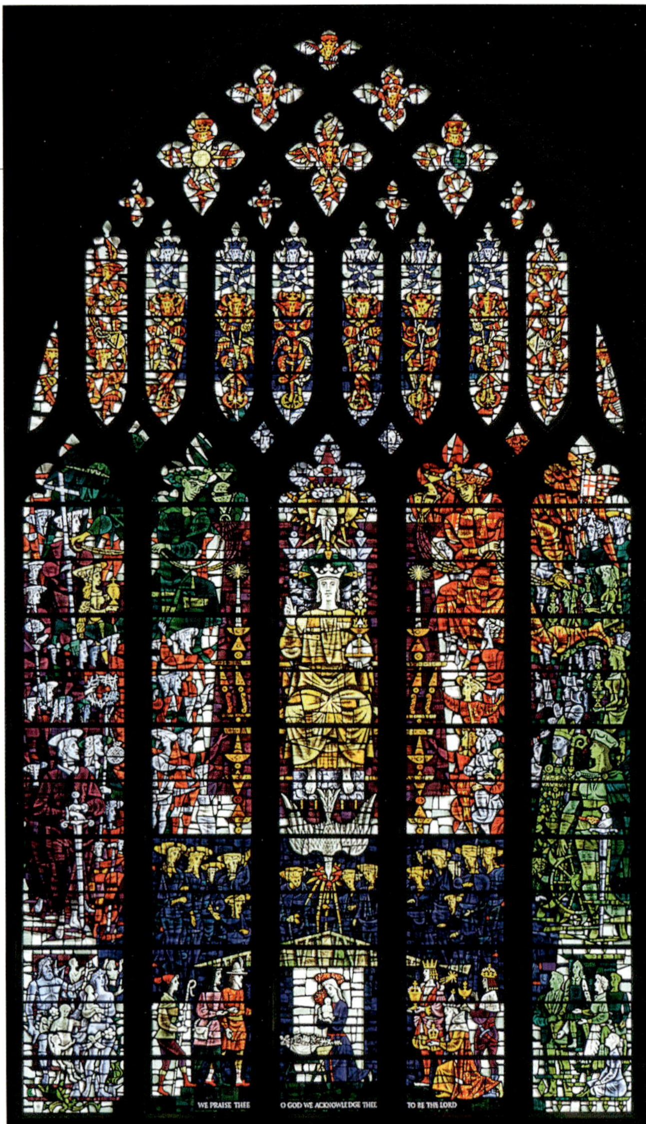

641. (left) Harry Stammers, 'Te Deum', 1959, Holy Trinity, Christchurch, east window

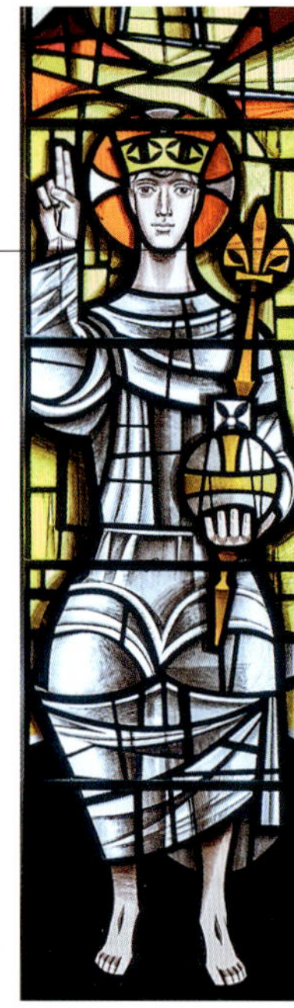

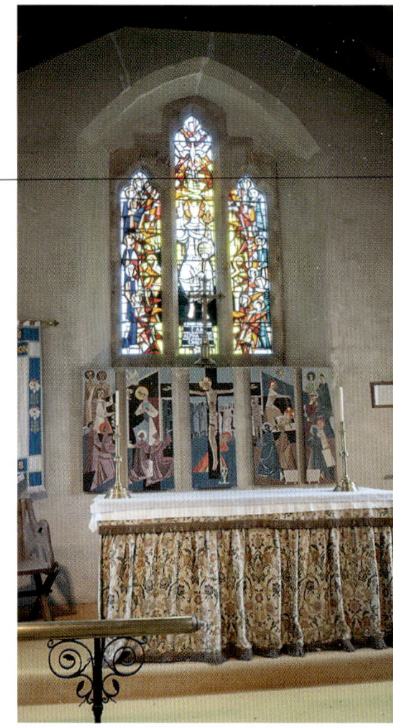

642–3. (right) Harry Harvey, East Window and Reredos, with detail of the central light (Christ in Majesty), 1963, Church of St David, Maesmynys

The war memorial window of 1953 by Harry Stammers at the Church of St Matthew, Buckley, was one of the few to display any hint of the modernism that was adopted for post-war rebuilding and public sculpture. The aftermath of the Second World War saw an increasing adoption of modernist architecture and design, which found favour with town planners and architects, but was not always well-received by the public. The physical attacks on modernist public sculpture provide the context for the distaste which greeted Jacob Epstein's *Majestas* in Llandaff Cathedral, installed in 1957. The architect of the reconstruction of the Cathedral was George Pace, and his restoration of the interior of Holy Trinity, Christchurch, situated on the edge of Newport, in 1953–5, was followed by the introduction of modern windows by Harry Stammers and Harry Harvey.[13]

Harry Harvey was a pupil of Stammers and worked with George Pace again at the Church of St David, Maesmynys, in 1963, where he designed the east window and painted the reredos.[14] At Llandaff Cathedral the only new stained glass commissioned at the time of Pace's association with the Cathedral was the three-light window and an upper roundel over the high altar, designed by John Piper. As an established painter and designer, John Piper became the best-known artist associated with modern stained glass in Britain during the 1950s and 60s. Most of his

13 Harry Stammers' move towards Modernism began with his work as a cartoonist for James Hogan at Powell's in the late 1920s and 30s, although this is scarcely appreciable in his design for a window at the Church of St Isan, Llanishen, of 1935.

14 Both Harry Stammers and Harry Harvey worked in other media. Stammers created the extraordinary sculpture of Christ with the symbols of the evangelists that is suspended in Pace's chapel for St Michael's College, Llandaff, built 1957–9.

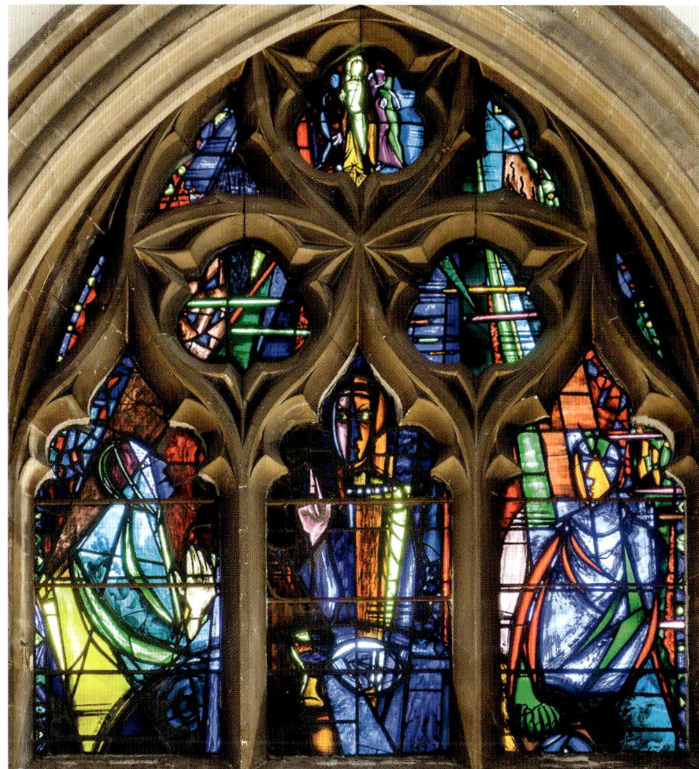

644. Patrick Reyntiens, The Supper at Emmaus, 1959, designed by John Piper, Llandaff Cathedral, chancel

designs for stained glass were interpreted by Patrick Reyntiens, and their collaboration, which originated in the studio of J.E. Nuttgens in 1953, was responsible for some of the most celebrated British stained glass of the twentieth century.

A further commission for John Piper arose at St Woolos Cathedral, Newport, where the chancel of the former parish church was enlarged and a circular window opened in the new east wall. Piper proposed an entirely abstract design for the rose window above a painting with a marbled effect extending to the ground. The scheme was commended by the archbishop of Wales and bishop of Monmouth, Edwin Morris, who embraced the abstract symbolism of the concept and conceded 'I am not a lover of abstract art, much of which seems to be rubbish. It is with some surprise, therefore, that I react so favourably to this abstract scheme.'[15]

Some of the commissions for stained glass taken on by John Piper, such as those in Coventry and Plymouth, were part of restoration or rebuilding after war damage. His work for Llandaff Cathedral and the Church of St Mary, Swansea, also followed bomb damage to the buildings in 1941.[16] John Piper was first approached to fill the Trinity Chapel windows at Swansea in 1963, before he had completed the commission at St Woolos Cathedral, but demand for his work ensured that they were not completed until 1965. These abstract works are also associated with a central dorsal painting designed by the artist.

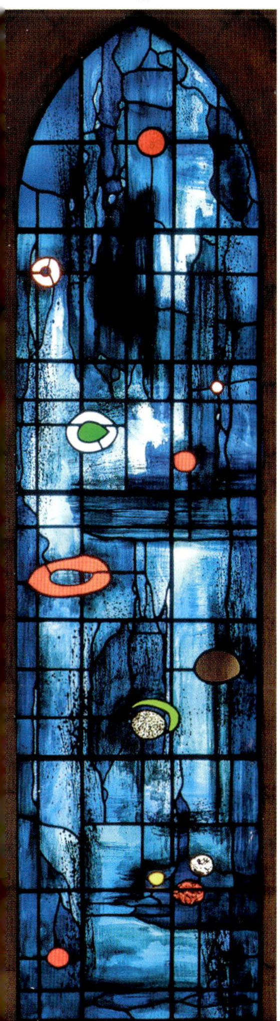

645. (left) Patrick Reyntiens, Trinity Chapel Window, 1965, designed by John Piper, Church of St Mary, Swansea

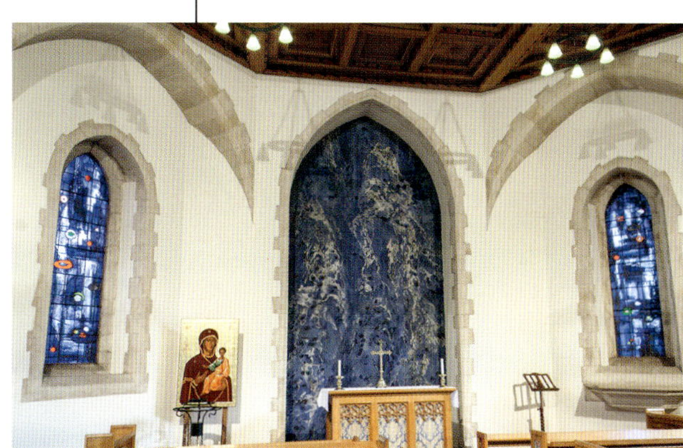

646. (right) John Piper, Windows and Dorsal Painting, 1965, Church of St Mary, Swansea, Trinity Chapel

15 Quoted in Tony Corten's account of the commission, 'John Piper and St Woolos Cathedral, Newport', *The Journal of Stained Glass*, vol. xxxvi (2013), p. 82. The design, wrote the architect A.D.R. Caroe, had 'symbolical suggestions of aspiration' and linked 'the finite expression of the Godhead within the building on the Altar to Infinity visualised through the circular window', quoted by Tony Corten, p. 86.

16 The Piper/Reyntiens glass at Llandaff Cathedral replaced work by Michael O'Connor, and was dedicated 4 October 1959.

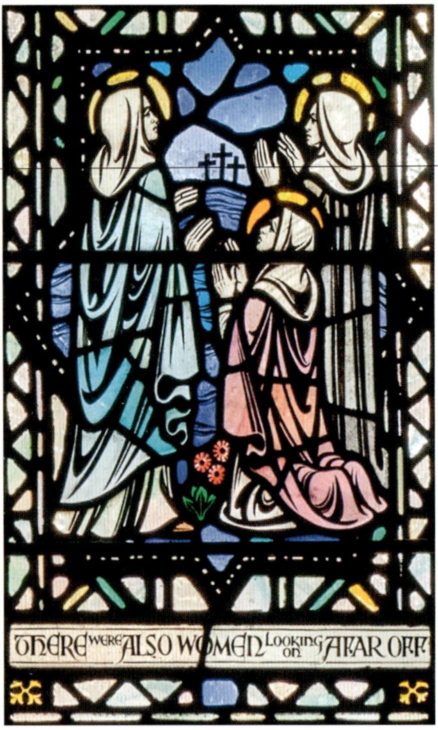

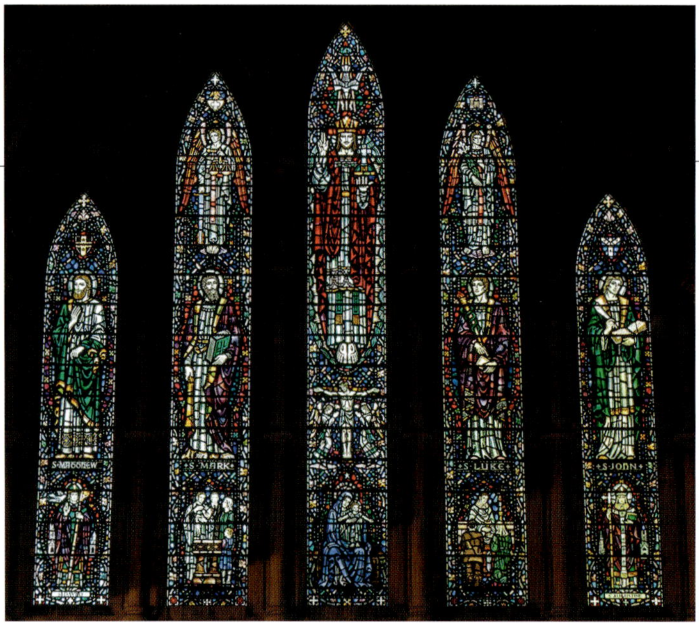

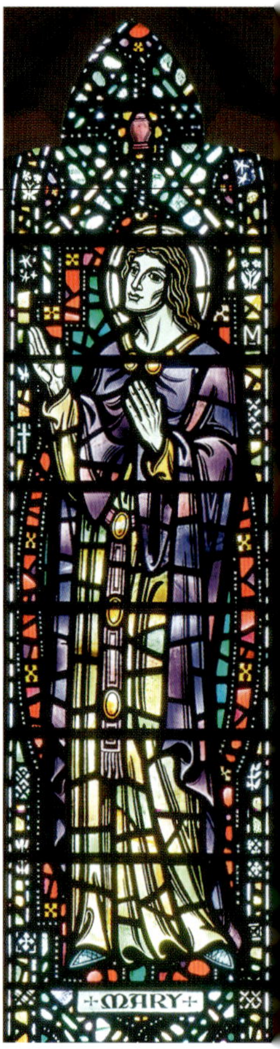

647. (left) Powell & Sons, The Three Marys, 1960, designed by E. Liddall Armitage, Church of St Mary, Swansea, St Anne's Chapel

648–9. Powell & Sons, Christ with the Four Evangelists, east window (above); St Mary Magdalene, chancel (right), 1958–60, designed by E. Liddall Armitage, Church of St Mary, Swansea

Among the windows that were lost in 1941 at the Church of St Mary, Swansea, were four windows by James Powell & Sons, and when new windows were commissioned for the chancel and Lady Chapel in the late 1950s, the work again went to Powell's.[17] Although the windows were designed by E. Liddall Armitage, they were not devoid of Welsh involvement. The chancel windows were cartooned by Colwyn Morris and the St Anne's Chapel windows were cartooned by Marjorie Walters, both of whom worked in London for Powell's but were born locally and returned to Wales to teach at Swansea College of Art.[18] The chancel windows use wide leading without any gradation in the use of black paint, the dense black outlines partly abstracting the figures and small scenes, but also darkening the windows.[19] The small scenes in the Lady Chapel window are relieved by much paler glass surrounds.

Celtic Studios had not been invited to tender for the chancel windows even though they received commissions from many other churches in and around Swansea.[20] While their work was widely admired in the dioceses of St Davids and Monmouth, they found less work in the Llandaff diocese. In the late 1950s the Llandaff Diocesan Advisory Committee, chaired by Rollo Charles, in a remarkable reversal, actively

17 Other windows lost included aisle windows by Clayton & Bell and a west window by A.K. Nicholson made in 1937.

18 Marjorie Walters was briefly married to the Swansea painter Evan Walters, and she returned to Swansea to become the first assistant to Howard Martin in the Stained Glass Department in 1961.

19 E. Liddall Armitage used a similar style, with patterned backgrounds and borders composed of small pieces of glass in his east window for the Church of St David, Llanddewi Brefi, in 1961. The differences between the chancel windows and the Lady Chapel window at Swansea are illustrative of the role of the cartoonist as an interpreter of designs by the same artist, and Armitage illustrates examples of work by cartoonists who worked for Powell's including Colwyn Morris and Marjorie Walters in his book *Stained Glass: History, Technology and Practice* (London: Leonard Hill, 1960).

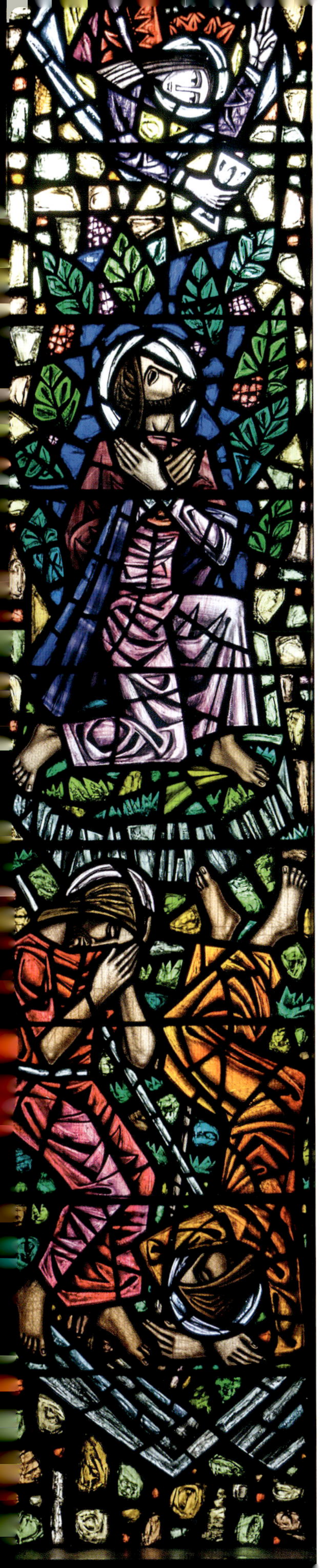

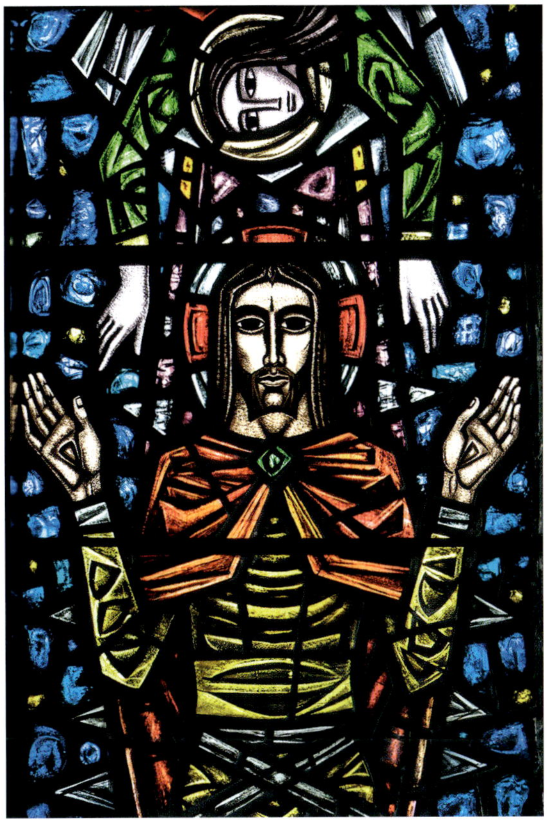

650–1. Celtic Studios, Christ in the Garden of Gethsemane (far left), and the Ascension (left), 1961, designed, cartooned and painted by John Edwards, Church of St Mary and Holy Innocents, Merthyr Vale, rear wall

encouraged more modern design in stained glass.[21] The challenge to modernise their work was taken up by Howard Martin. In 1959, at the request of the DAC, he modified the figures, initially designed by Bryan Evans, to fill the narrow lancets at St George-super-Ely without the use of plain quarries above and below, enlivening the figures and the associated heraldry below.[22] John Edwards, who had joined Celtic Studios as a glass painter in 1954, designed several impressive modern windows for the firm and cartooned and painted these windows himself. His work was chosen for the commissions at the Church of St Mary, Seven Sisters, in 1959 and in 1961 he was responsible for the four windows at the modern Church of St Mary and Holy Innocents, Merthyr Vale. These tightly-packed vertical scenes create a

20 Criticism of this decision may have prompted a request for Celtic Studios to tender for the Trinity Chapel windows. Maurice Broady, *A Vision Fulfilled: The story of Celtic Studios and Swansea's architectural glass tradition* (Swansea: West Glamorgan Archive Service, 2010), pp. 58–9. Hubert Thomas was still hopeful of winning the commission in May 1963, although John Piper had been approached during the preceding month. Correspondence regarding the Holy Trinity Chapel windows by John Piper, West Glamorgan Archive Service, P/123/CW/554.

21 Rollo Charles, Keeper of Art at the National Museum in Cardiff, was a supporter of the 56 Group, a group of painters founded in Wales in 1956 with an explicitly Modernist agenda. The modernism that the dean of Llandaff, Glyn Simon, had initiated in the refurnishing of Llandaff Cathedral, before he was appointed bishop of Swansea and Brecon in 1954, was increasingly visible with the unveiling of Jacob Epstein's *Majestas* in 1957 and the Piper/Reyntiens window of 1959. The shock to the system must have been considerable in the wake of the exceptionally conservative policy on stained glass adopted by the Llandaff Diocesan Advisory Committee since the late 1940s, with its endorsement of conservative artists such as Alfred Wilkinson and Arthur Walker.

22 The story of the adaptation of these windows, with illustrations of the design by Bryan Evans and of the finished window, is found in Maurice Broady, *A Vision Fulfilled*, pp. 56–7.

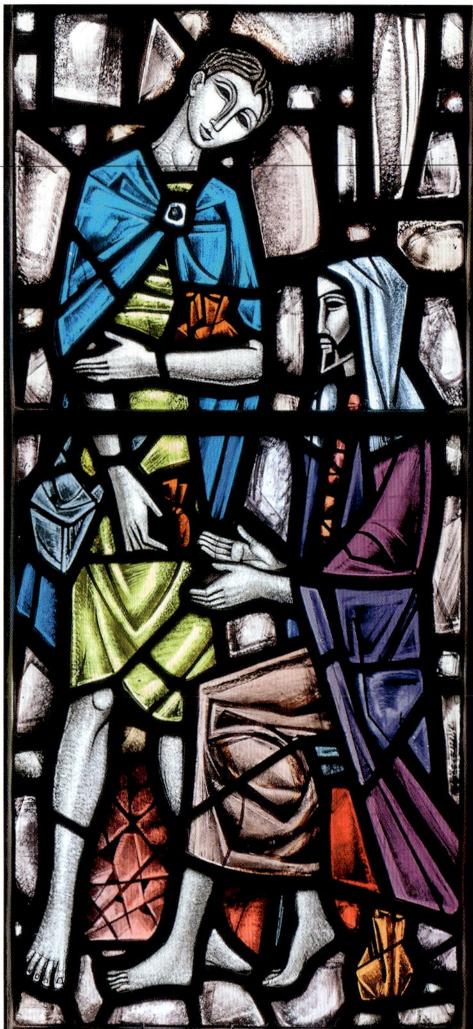

652. Celtic Studios, The Parable of the Talents, 1964, designed by John Edwards, Church of St Michael, Cwmafan, chancel

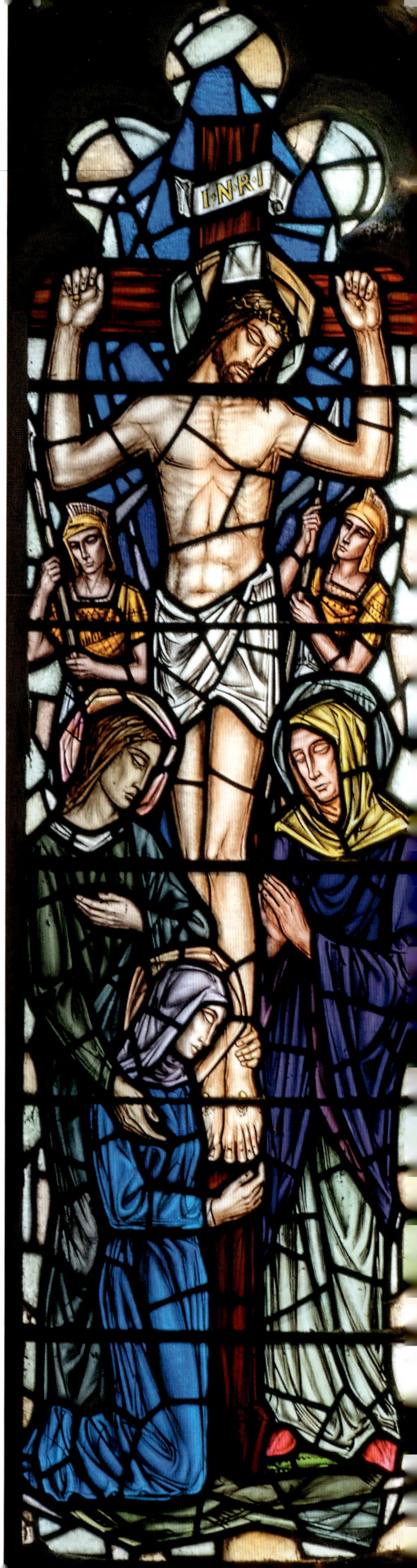

dramatic effect through the use of heavily-leaded outlines, and the small pieces of coloured glass are given the impression of texture through the application of black paint.[23] The faces in the windows by Edwards in this period have a distinct Byzantine simplicity, as can also be seen in his depictions of the parable of the talents at the Church of St John the Baptist, Skewen, and at the Church of St Michael, Cwmafan.

Such innovation was not restricted to commissions in the Llandaff diocese, and similarly compacted scenes were designed by Howard Martin for the main lights of the west window at Kidwelly, also making use of more vivid colours.[24] As the 1960s progressed, Celtic Studios made a greater use of black, as wide leads and additional paint on glass, often with a more fluid use of leading in the design of their best work. At the Church of St Mary, Briton Ferry, the design for the single-light window depicting the shepherds crowded behind the holy family has a dynamic symmetry, while, on a larger scale, the visit of both the shepherds and

653. Celtic Studios, The Crucifixion, 1960, designed by Howard Martin, Church of St Mary, Kidwelly, west window

23 Unusually, the signature of the firm includes John Edwards' name as designer. Maurice Broady records that the designs were chosen over those submitted by J. Wippell & Co., Maurice Broady, *A Vision Fulfilled: The story of Celtic Studios and Swansea's architectural glass tradition* (Swansea: West Glamorgan Archive Service, 2010), pp. 59–60. The windows are further constrained by the loss of their lancet tops after they were re-sited in the new church in 1970.

24 The window was cartooned and painted by John Edwards.

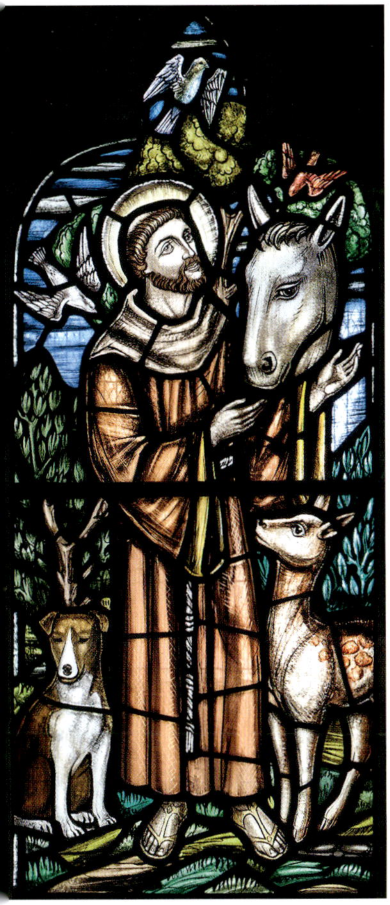

654. Celtic Studios, St Francis, 1963, designed by Howard Martin, Church of St John, Garndiffaith, nave

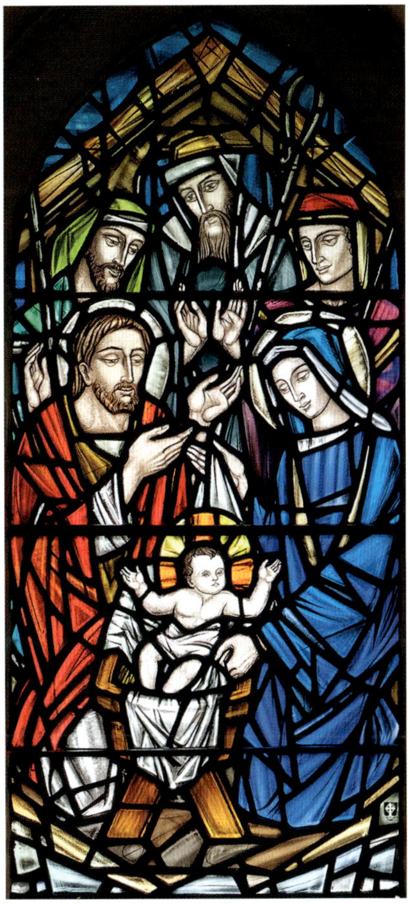

655. Celtic Studios, The Nativity, 1966, Church of St Mary, Briton Ferry, north aisle

the Magi across three large lights in the west window of the Church of St Agnes, Port Talbot, has a more chaotic expressive energy. A design by Howard Martin for the Church of St John, Garndiffaith, is gentler in terms of colour and leading, but retains the strong black outlines in the depiction of Francis and Dorcas clothing the poor.

While Bryan Evans and John Edwards had trained at Swansea and found work at Celtic Studios, another student of Howard Martin, Roy Lewis, studied at the Royal College of Art in London under Lawrence Lee at the time that the windows for Coventry Cathedral were being made. His windows in west Wales, made in the early 1960s, demonstrate a bold and confident style, his Ascension at Llanfihangel Genau'r Glyn (Llandre) using a restricted palette of blues with white glass.

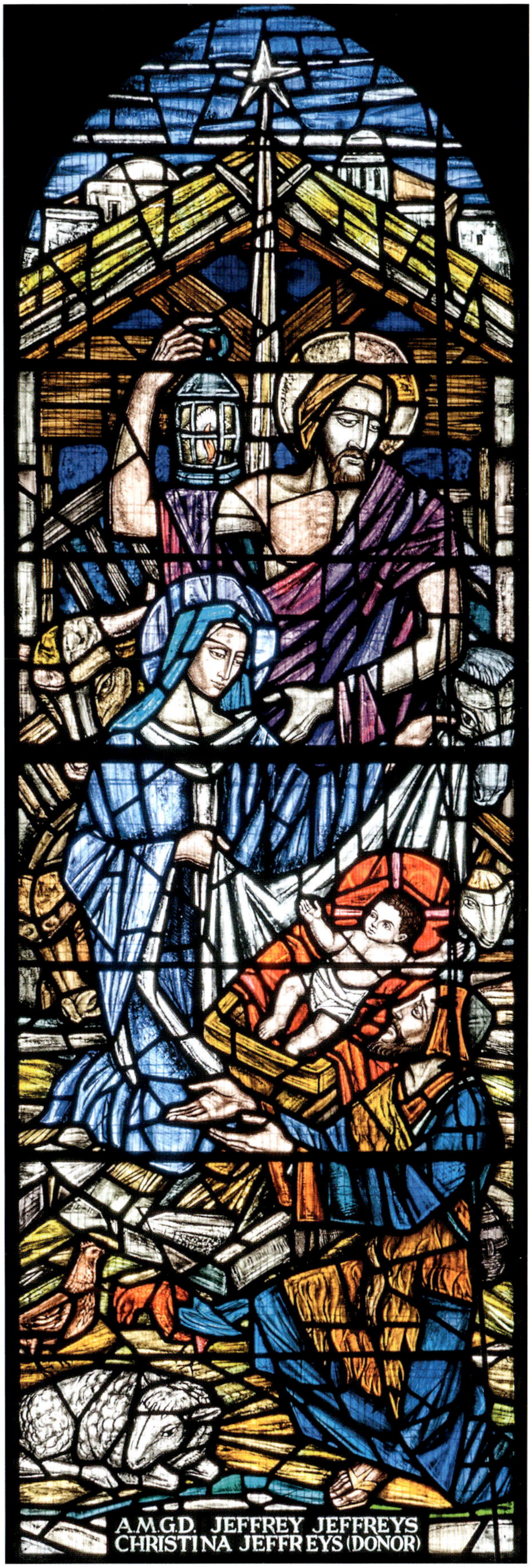

656. Celtic Studios, The Holy Family, from the Adoration of the Shepherds and the Magi 1966, Church of St Agnes, Port Talbot, west window

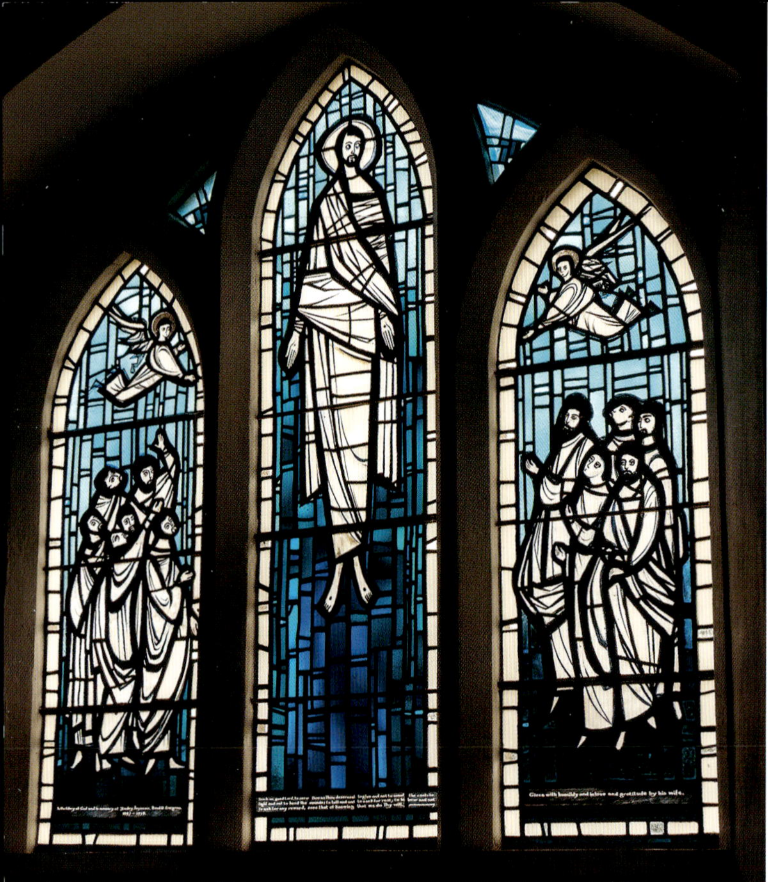

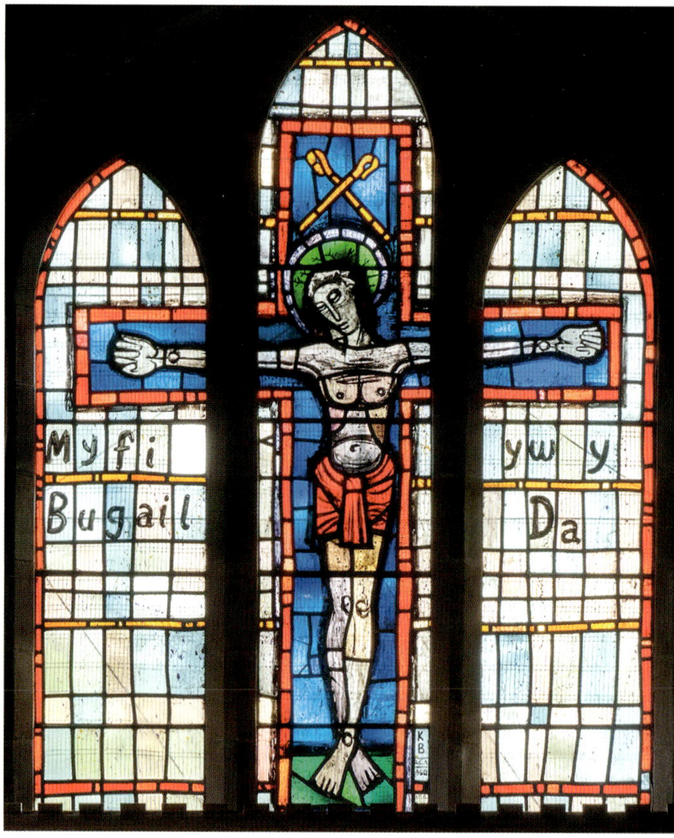

657. (above left) Roy Lewis, The Ascension, 1962, Church of St Michael, Llanfihangel Genau'r Glyn, nave

658. (above right) Kenneth Baynes, The Crucifixion, 1960, Church of St David, Talybont (Ceredigion), east window

In contrast to the encouragement of modern design in the Llandaff diocese, the delays in granting a faculty by the St Davids Diocesan Advisory Committee suggests its discomfort with the design. The application for a faculty was submitted in October 1960, but it was not installed until 1963. The DAC had recommended alterations, but Lewis refused, complaining that it 'would bear resemblance to all the other windows of the Ascension scattered about the British Isles', and insisting that the patron, Mrs Joynson, did not want the window to lose 'its originality and distinction'.[25]

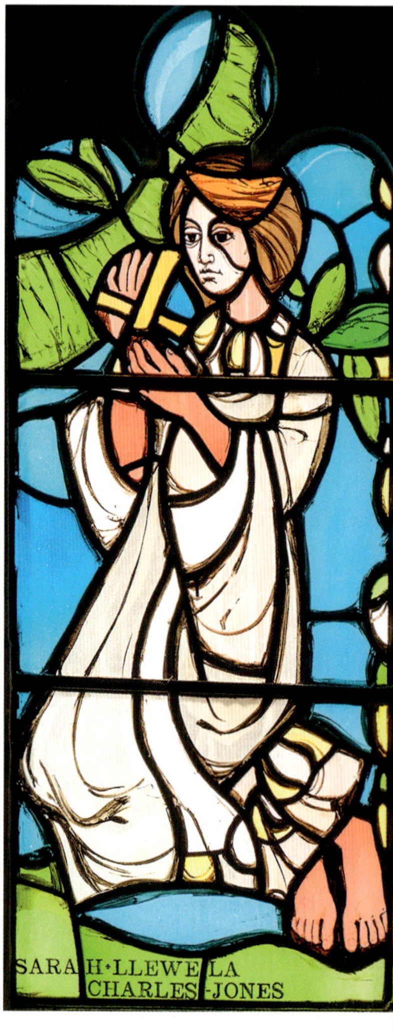

659. Christine Edwards (née Bodycombe) and Christopher Edwards, Faith, 1967, Church of St Barnabas, Uplands, Swansea, nave

25 National Library of Wales, Records of the Church in Wales: Diocese of St Davids, uncatalogued papers, 213/D2618. Letter from Roy Lewis, 16 January 1961. Lewis continued: 'I have a reputation – in London, The Midlands & the Continent for good design which I do not wish to mar by producing what is known in the freelance design world as "Commercialism".' At the time of the dedication of his second window in the church (26 May 1963), the artist is described as 'Mr Roy Lewis, A.T.D., A.R.C.A., a native of Aberystwyth, a young man who has already made a name for himself in the world of art.' I am grateful to Avril Thomas for making me aware of this correspondence. A further window by the artist is found nearby at the Church of St Padarn, Llanbadarn Fawr, and he also made the east window at the Church of St Peter, Little Newcastle. He emigrated to Australia in the 1960s.

660. (right) Tim Lewis, St Luke, 1963, Church of St David and St Cyfelach, Llangyfelach, nave

661. (far right) Tim Lewis, Christian Symbols, 1968, Church of St Luke, Cwmdare, east window

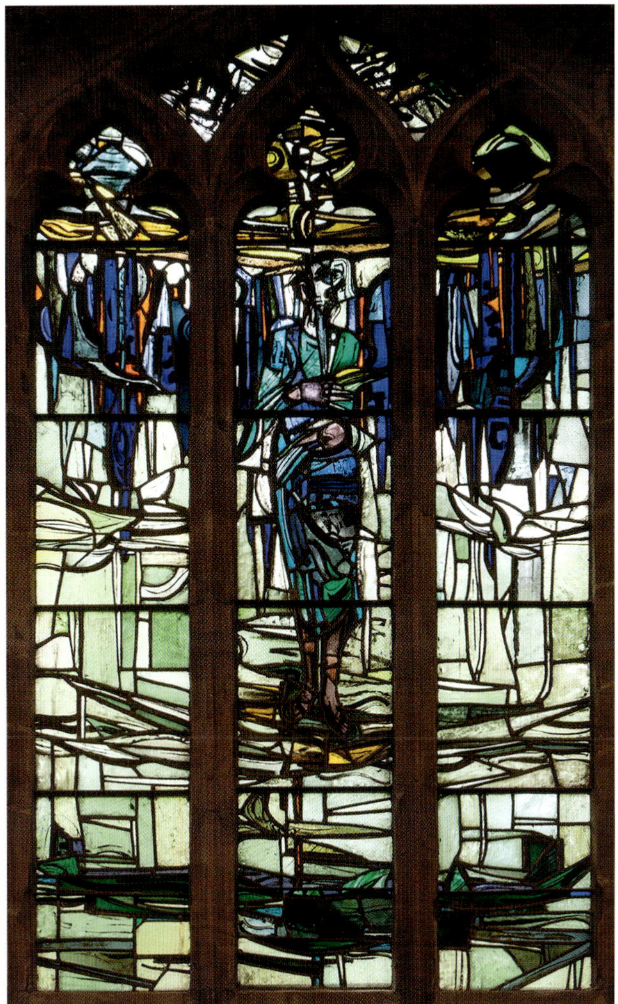

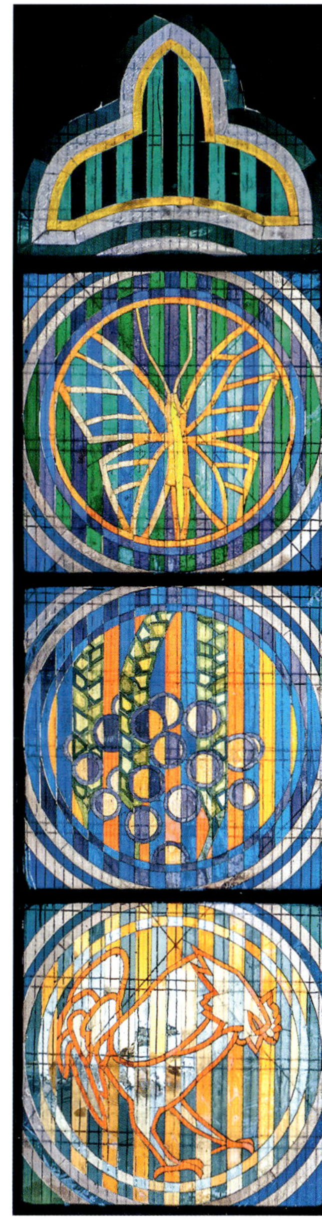

Such conservatism on the part of the St Davids DAC had not prevented the installation of another bold modern design for the east window at the Church of St David, Talybont, only a couple of miles away, a few years earlier. The depiction of the Crucifixion by Kenneth Baynes suggests the influence of Roualt, a painter who had worked in a stained glass studio in his youth, and whose thick black outlines are suggestive of lead lines.

Other students encouraged by Howard Martin in the late 1950s included Tim Lewis and Christine Bodycombe. Bodycombe went on to work in the studio of Patrick Reyntiens on commissions including John Piper's baptistry window at Coventry Cathedral. Following her marriage to Christopher Edwards she collaborated with him on a window representing Faith, Hope and Charity at the Church of St Barnabas, Uplands, Swansea, but died in 1968.[26] Tim Lewis was a King's Scholar at the Royal College of Art before returning to Swansea to teach on the course with Howard Martin in 1965. While in London he made a largely abstract window including the figure of Luke for the Church of St David and St Cyfelach, Llangyfelach, given in memory of a student from Swansea who had died tragically on the River Wye at Symonds Yat. His second commission for a church in Wales was the east window at the Church of St Luke, Cwmdare, made in 1968. The window is experimental in its use of glass appliqué, instead of lead, to join pieces of coloured glass, and is suggestive of his interest in the work of Bridget Riley, whose painting the artist had encountered in London.

26 The female figures are not attributable by their usual emblems. The central figure holds a pelican, symbolic of the sacrifice of Christ, and emblematic of Love (Charity). The left-hand figure holds a cup, while the right-hand figure holds a small cross, the usual emblem of Faith. The way in which the leading and colouring of the glass breaks up the faces suggests Cubist influence. I am grateful to Alan Figg for information about Christine Edwards née Bodycombe.

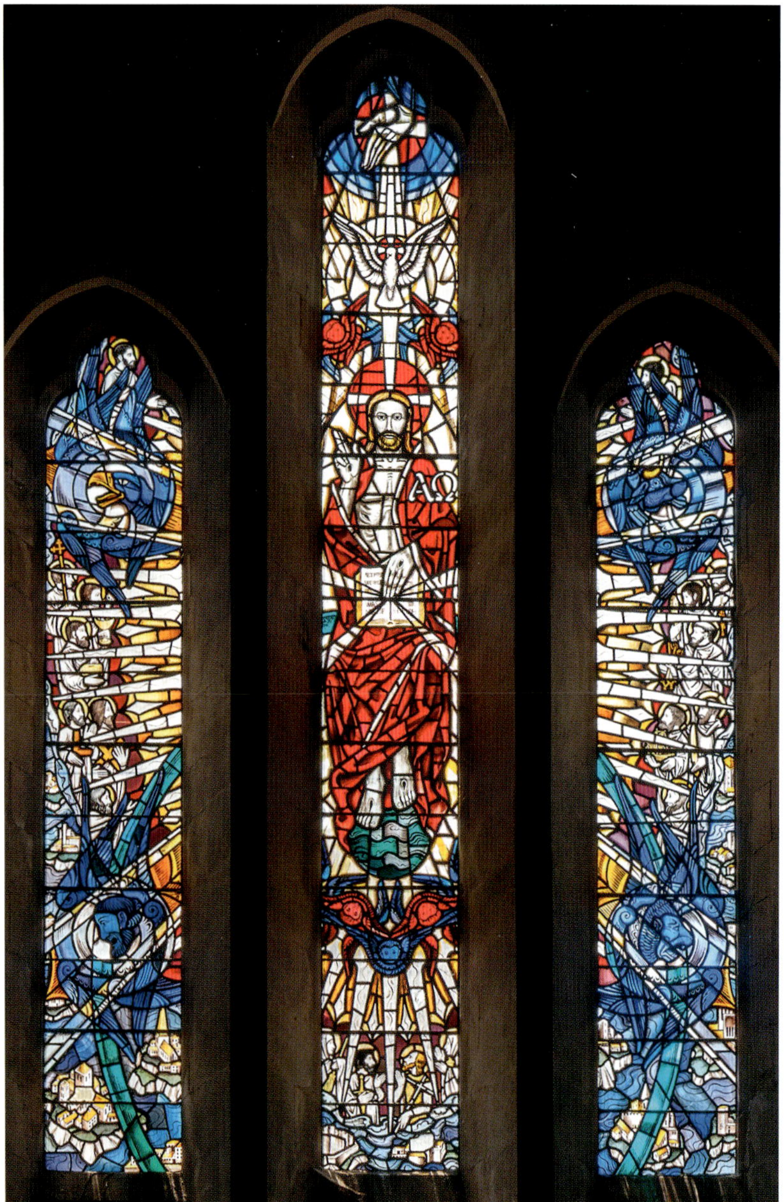

662. Francis Spear, Christ in Majesty with the Symbols of the Four Evangelists, 1962, Church of All Saints, Penarth, west window

The encouragement of modernist work by the Llandaff Diocesan Advisory Committee is especially striking at the Church of All Saints, Penarth, where more modern windows continued to be added after the initial replacement of stained glass designed by Arthur Walker in the 1950s. In 1962 an aisle window designed by E. Liddall Armitage for Powell & Sons has scenes that are similar in style to his windows at Swansea, and Francis Spear added his west window in the same year. The west window, a vision of Christ in Glory with the four winged living creatures as described in Revelation, is a welcome return to the inventiveness of his work after the austerity of the 1950s. The composition seems to exceed its bounds, the light bursting out of the book held by Christ, radiating light throughout the window and beyond.[27]

Another artist who is represented at Penarth is John Petts, whose first north aisle window at the church portrays Michael overcoming Satan.[28] After some success as an artist in a variety of media, Petts taught himself stained glass in order to teach it in his new post as a lecturer in design and crafts at Carmarthen School of Art, having first sought advice from Howard Martin.[29] Rollo Charles encouraged Petts to submit a design for a tall single-light chancel window at the Church of St Cynfelin, Caerau, in 1961, and this led to further commissions at the church and nearby at the Church of St Peter, Nantyfyllon.

27 The window is different in design to both of his sets of windows at Ely (Cardiff) of 1947 and also unlike his two Nativity scenes in Welsh churches, in which the scenes are set within large white borders. One of these was made in 1956 at the Church of St John, Canton, and is an intimate interpretation of the visit of the Magi, while the other was also made for Penarth, in 1963, and depicts the visit of the shepherds, but loses its immediacy on a larger scale.

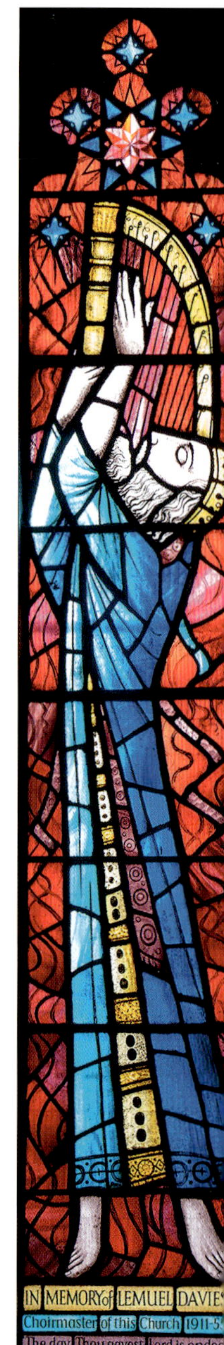

663. John Petts, King David, 1961, Church of St Cynfelin, Caerau, chancel

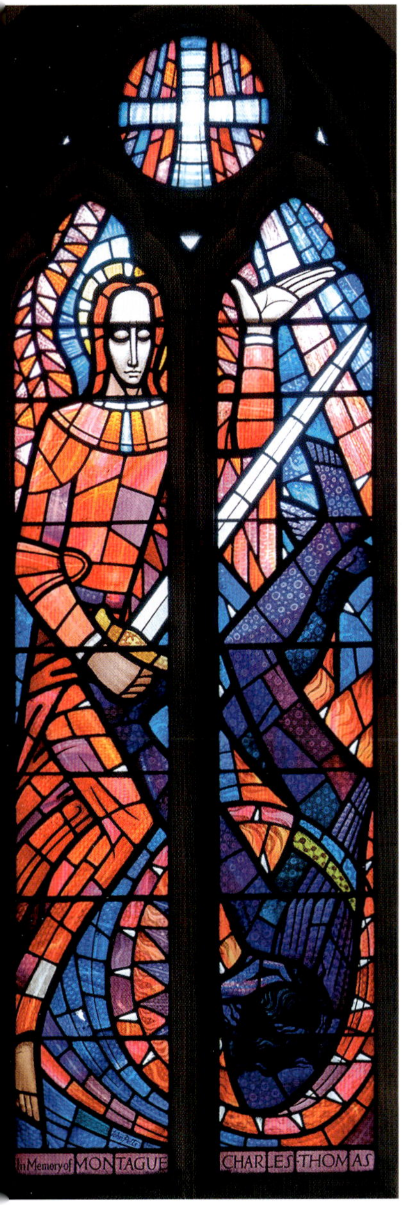

664. John Petts, St Michael Overcoming the Devil, 1966, Church of All Saints, Penarth, nave

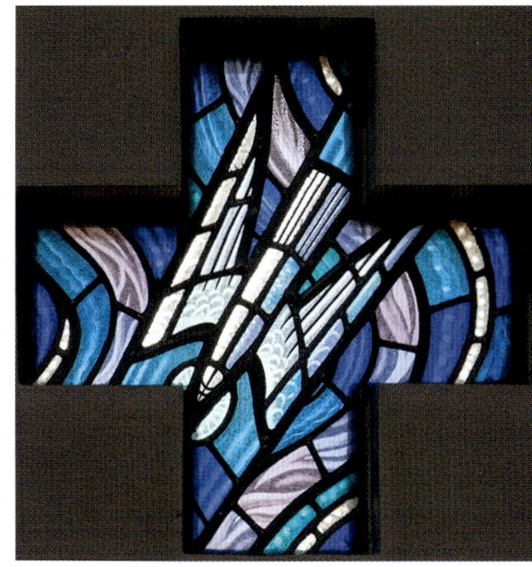

666. John Petts, Dove of the Holy Spirit, 1968, Church of the Blessed Sacrament, Gorseinon, baptistry

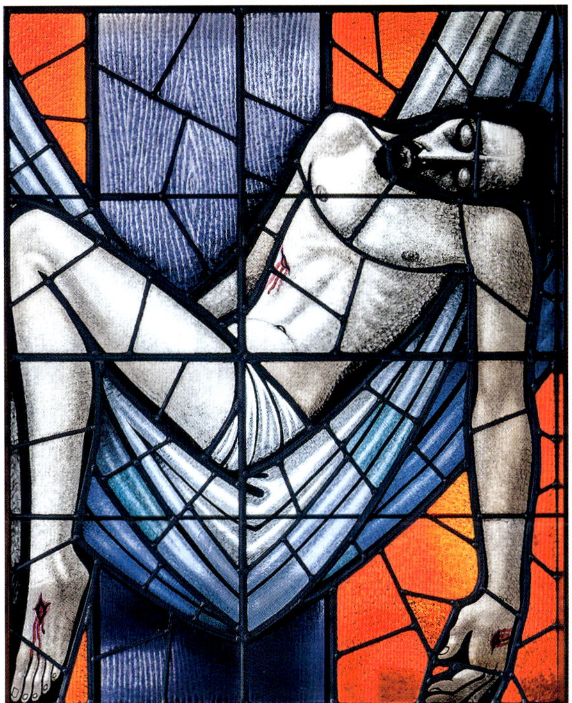

665. (below) John Petts, The Deposition, 1966, Church of Our Lady of the Assumption, Briton Ferry, narthex screen

Petts' work soon found appeal beyond Anglican patrons. In 1966 sixteen panels with scenes from the Passion of Christ were made for the narthex screen of the Church of Our Lady of the Assumption, Briton Ferry. In the following year he began a series of windows for another Roman Catholic church, the Church of the Blessed Sacrament at Gorseinon. Between 1967 and 1981 he made four sets of cruciform windows for the round church in collaboration with Father Gerald Hiscoe, beginning with the red windows for the Blessed Sacrament Chapel. The second set of windows were made for the baptistry chapel in 1968, employing complex symbolism and a blue colour scheme that was used again by the artist in 1969 for two five-light windows at Brighton and Hove New Synagogue.[30] He also provided windows for Nonconformist congregations, such as at Trinity Methodist Church in Glasllwch, Newport.

28 The upper torso of the devil is encircled in the jaws of hell, a reference to the demonic figure in the lower corner of the west window of about 1500 at the Church of St Mary, Fairford, and an example of the wide range of artistic influences absorbed into the personal style of John Petts.

29 John Petts recalled that Howard Martin advised him to 'let your blacks be thick and many'. Alison Smith, 'John Petts: Designer-Craftsman 1914–1991', *The Journal of Stained Glass*, vol. xix, no. 2 (1991–93), p. 219. This advice mirrors changes in style taking place at Celtic Studios at around 1960, and the dark-haired Christ found in windows by Petts has parallels in windows made by Celtic Studios after this date.

30 This was one of two significant works in stained glass by the artist outside of Wales. In 1963 he initiated a campaign to give a commemorative window to 16th Street Baptist Church, Birmingham, Alabama, after it was bombed in a racist attack. The cost of the window was met with donations raised through the *Western Mail*, the artist making no charge for his work. For these windows and further biblical work by the artist see Alison Smith, 'Light, Colour and the Bible: The Stained Glass Windows of John Petts (1914–91)' in Martin O'Kane and John Morgan-Guy, *Biblical Art from Wales* (Sheffield: Sheffield Phoenix Press, 2010), pp. 228–31.

It has been suggested that Celtic Studios exercised a monopoly on ecclesiastical stained glass in the region, and that the Llandaff Diocesan Advisory Committee sought out artists such as John Petts to challenge their dominance.[31] The achievement of Celtic Studios was remarkable, but their success was not always assured and their work is noticeably thin in churches around the Cardiff area. They also continued to face competition for commissions nearer to Swansea. Celtic Studios made a pair of nave windows at the Church of St David, Penllergaer, in 1956, but the next five windows were commissioned from the London artist Eric Dilworth, until a window of the Good Shepherd was made by Celtic Studios for the sanctuary in 1982, the year that Dilworth died. Dilworth was also commissioned to make three windows in the 1960s for the Church of St Peter, Pontardawe, where Celtic Studios had already made two windows and Francis Skeat had been approached to make a window. A few miles away, both up and down the valley, at the Anglican churches in Ystalyfera and Trebanos, Celtic Studios were more consistently successful, making eleven windows in the two churches between 1950 and 1980.

Further competition for commissions in south Wales came from Powell & Sons, J. Wippell & Co., G. Maile & Son and Goddard & Gibbs. The work of all of these firms demonstrates a variety attributable to the specificities of the site and the requirements of the patrons and advisory committees. In some cases simple figurative scenes were set on

31 See Alison Smith, 'Light, Colour and the Bible: The Stained Glass Windows of John Petts (1914–91)' in Martin O'Kane and John Morgan-Guy, *Biblical Art from Wales* (Sheffield: Sheffield Phoenix Press, 2010), p. 221.

32 National Library of Wales, Records of the Church in Wales: Diocese of Swansea and Brecon, BR/RF/100/7. Letter dated 11 August 1965.

33 An earlier use of Christian symbols as subject matter for stained glass is found in the window by Evie Hone for the Church of All Saints, Wellingborough, made in 1955. The windows by Celtic Studios at Prestatyn were followed by two further windows at the parish church and illustrate their success in gaining commissions beyond south and west Wales, not only in north Wales, but also in parts of England and abroad, having established themselves in the Canadian market.

34 From 1970 until 1980, J. Wippell & Co. were associated with A.R. Mowbray of Oxford, after which they took over the Oxford firm.

667. G. Maile & Son, 1964, Christ in Majesty, Monmouth Baptist Church, porch

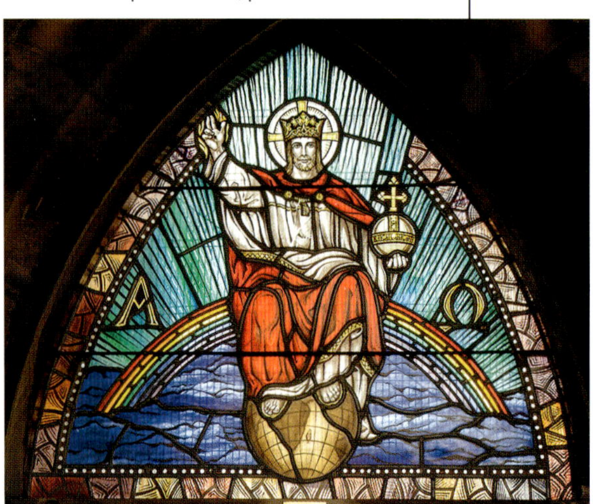

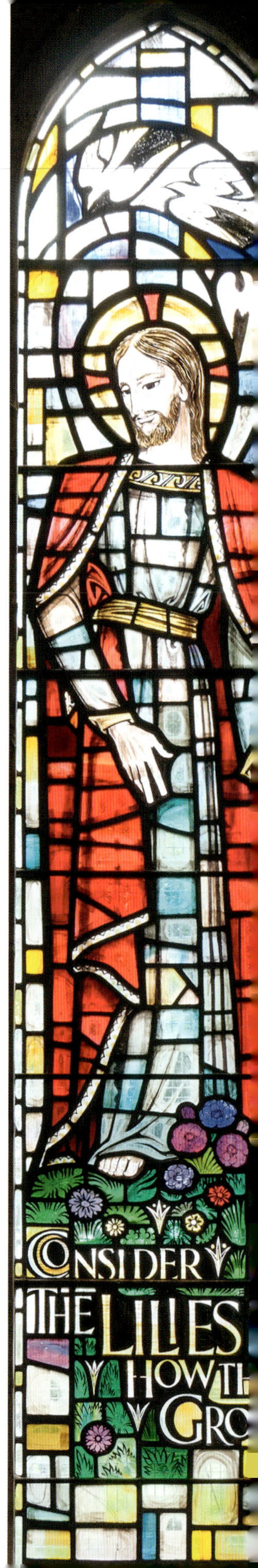

668. Eric Dilworth, 'Consider the Lilies How they Grow', *c.* 1965, Church of St David, Penllergaer, chancel

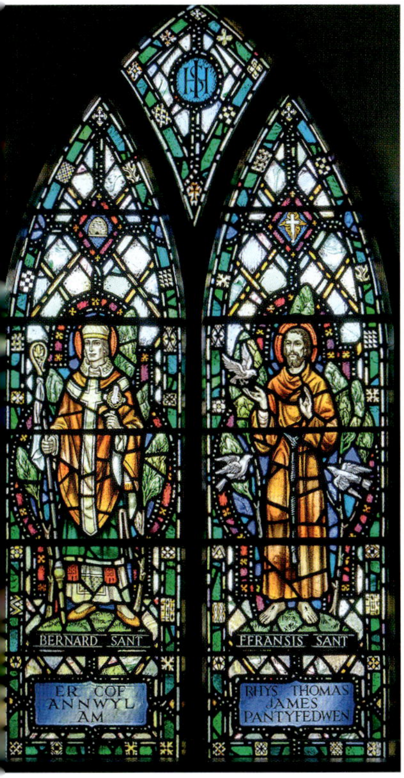

669. Powell & Sons, *c.* 1961, St Bernard and St Francis, Church of St Mary, Strata Florida, nave

plain backgrounds, while others adopted a stronger use of colour. For example, the full-coloured design by Maile's for the porch window for Monmouth Baptist Church contrasts with their large rear window at Arlington Road Presbyterian Church, Porthcawl, with figures on clear grounds. The use of coloured glass throughout a design was not always preferable. Among the correspondence regarding a proposed window by Francis Skeat for the Church of St Peter, Pontardawe, W.D.G. Wilkinson, the archdeacon of Brecon, complained that 'People are too fond of filling every bit and piece with stained glass – and so prevent light coming in.'[32] Of all of these firms, Powell's was usually superior in design and execution, typified by a series of four windows installed in the 1960s at the Church of St Mary, Strata Florida.

A more abstract quality could be achieved in windows that departed from depictions of saints and conventional narrative scenes. A small west window by Celtic Studios at the Church of St Eloi, Llandeloy, is a particularly animated representation of the descending dove of the Holy Spirit, and from the mid-1960s Celtic Studios began to make windows comprising Christian symbols that lent themselves to a more dynamic design. These symbols could also be adapted to fit unusual window sizes, such as the long and thin window that runs across the width of the sanctuary in the modern Church of the Holy Spirit, Prestatyn, and also had the advantage of being cheaper to produce.[33] A similar idea can be seen in a pair of contemporary windows by Wippell-Mowbray for Christ Church, Ebbw Vale, illustrating the sacraments and the six days of creation.[34]

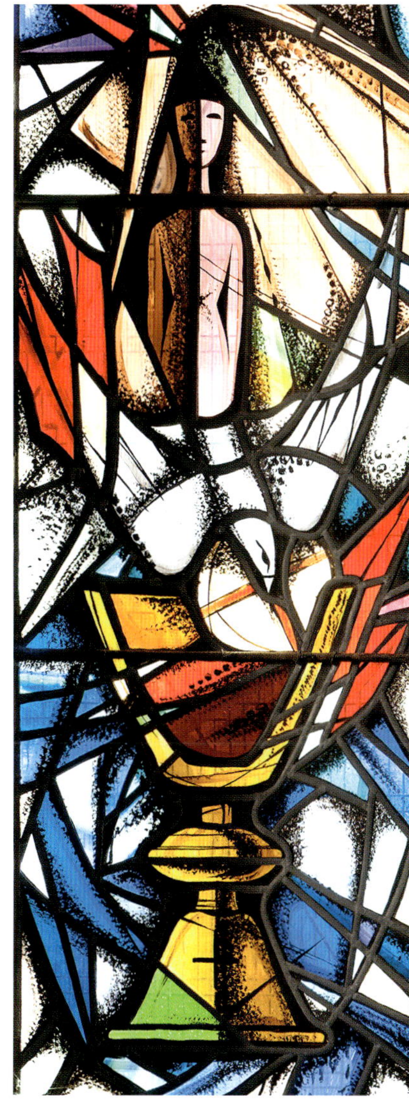

670. Wippell-Mowbray, Dove and Chalice from the Sacraments Window, 1971, Christ Church, Ebbw Vale, south aisle

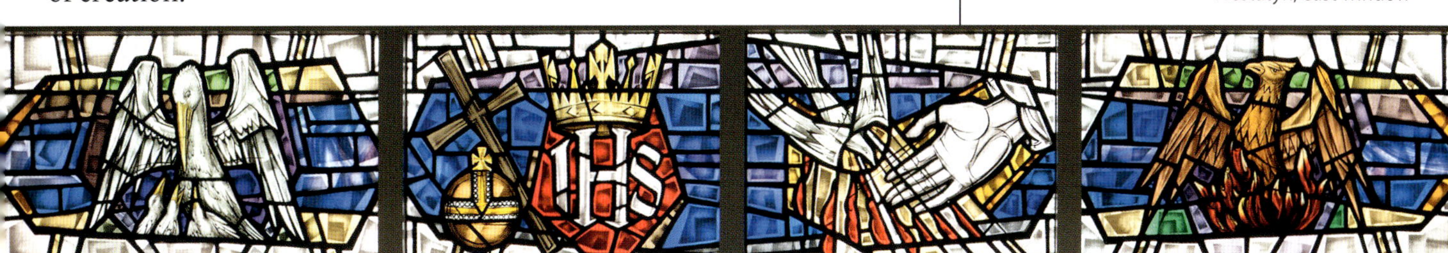

671. Celtic Studios, Christian Symbols, 1970, Church of the Holy Spirit, Prestatyn, east window

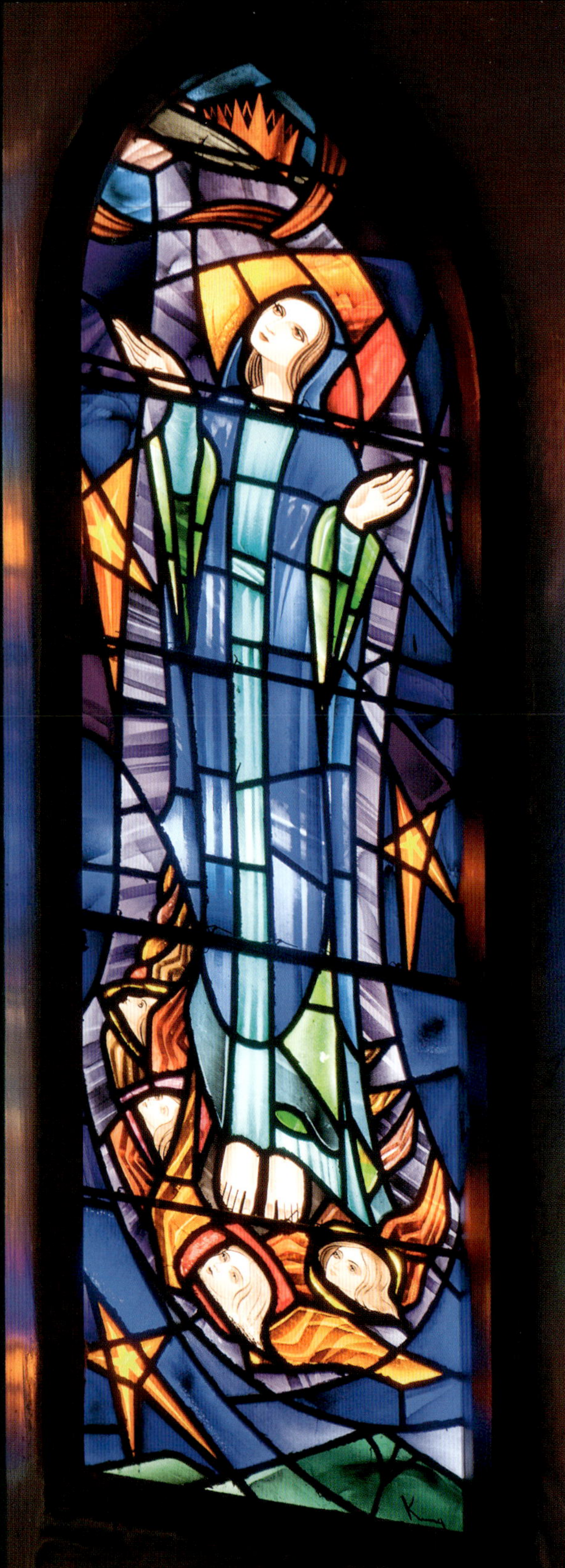

672. Richard King, The Assumption of the Virgin Mary, probably late 1950s or early 1960s, Church of Our Lady of the Angels and St Winifrede, Aberystwyth, east window

During the Second Vatican Council of the Roman Catholic Church in the early 1960s it was decreed that 'The art of our own days, coming from every race and region, shall be given free scope in the Church'.[35] The 'noble simplicity' of the liturgy was soon echoed in the architecture adopted for many new Roman Catholic churches built after the mid-1960s. However some modern work had been commissioned before this, such as the windows by J.E. Nuttgens at Ebbw Vale and the colourful modern windows by Richard King made for Roman Catholic churches in Aberaeron and Aberystwyth.[36] John Hardman Studios demonstrated innovation in some of their windows of the 1960s under the leadership of Patrick Feeny. At the Church Of The Immaculate Conception, Flint, the firm made three windows for the Lady Chapel and baptistry, all demonstrating a clear graphic style and with scenes occupying full-coloured designs. Patrick Feeny also experimented with windows in *dalle de verre*, the technique of setting thick

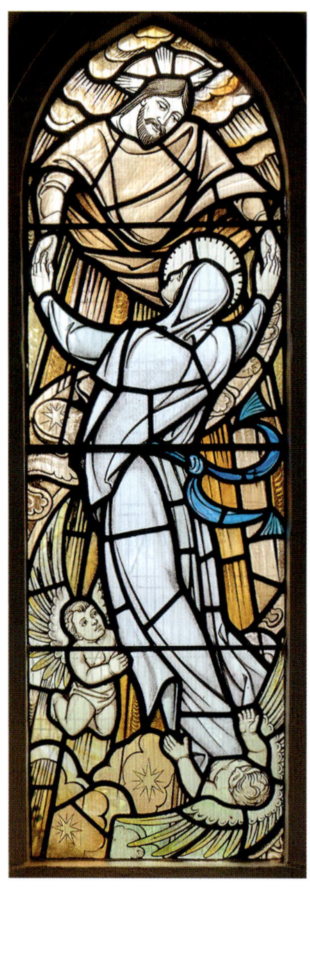

673. John Hardman Studios, The Assumption of the Virgin Mary, 1963–4, Church Of The Immaculate Conception, Flint, Lady Chapel

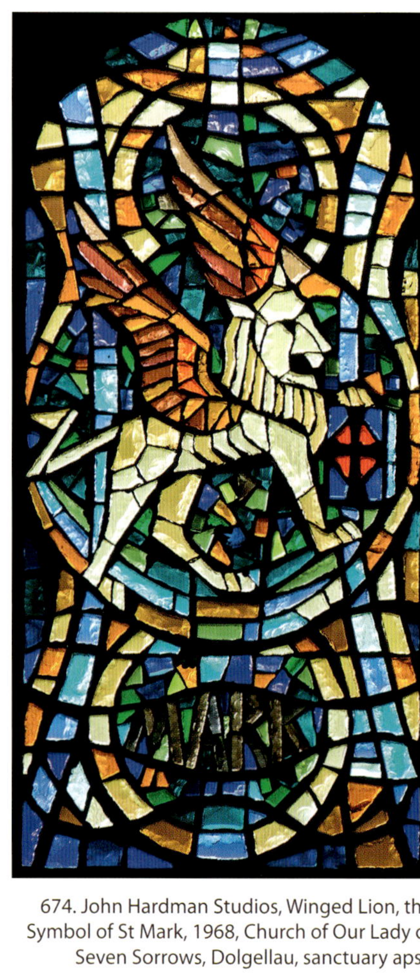

674. John Hardman Studios, Winged Lion, the Symbol of St Mark, 1968, Church of Our Lady of Seven Sorrows, Dolgellau, sanctuary apse

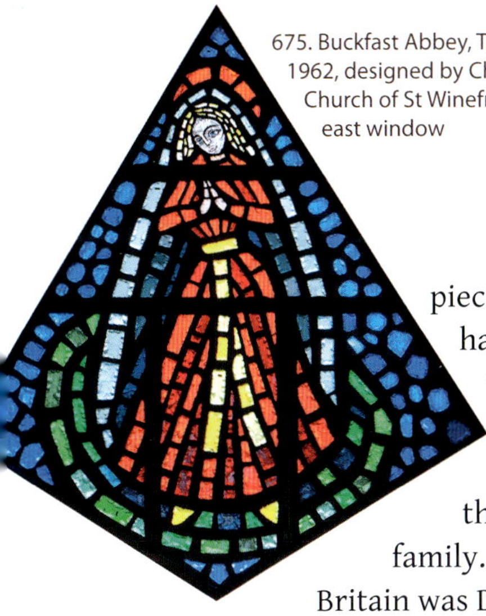

675. Buckfast Abbey, The Virgin Mary, 1962, designed by Charles Norris, Church of St Winefride, Welshpool, east window

pieces of slab glass in resin or concrete that had been pioneered in France before the war. He made five sanctuary windows in this way for the new church built in a Romanesque style at Dolgellau, a place that he visited while on holiday with his family. An early exponent of the technique in Britain was Dom Charles Norris of Buckfast Abbey. He designed the figure of Mary at the Church of St Winefride in Welshpool, and the same figure, with that of Gabriel, are the only figures found in the spectacular abstract scheme made for the Church of Our Lady, Lillington, Warwickshire, which opened in 1963.[37]

The growth and confidence of Roman Catholic congregations in Wales necessitated the building of new churches across Wales in the 1960s. Many of these churches were well suited to the creation of walls of colour or to the intersection of these walls with areas of colour using *dalle de verre*. Powell & Sons were the first English firm to adopt the technique and Colwyn Morris designed the first panel made by the firm in the 1950s. However it was the French designer Pierre Fourmaintreaux who designed works using the technique in Wales for Powell's, at the crematoria at Narberth and Margam, the Convent of the Good Shepherd in Monmouth and above the narthex windows that were soon to be filled by John Petts at the Church of Our Lady, Briton Ferry.[38]

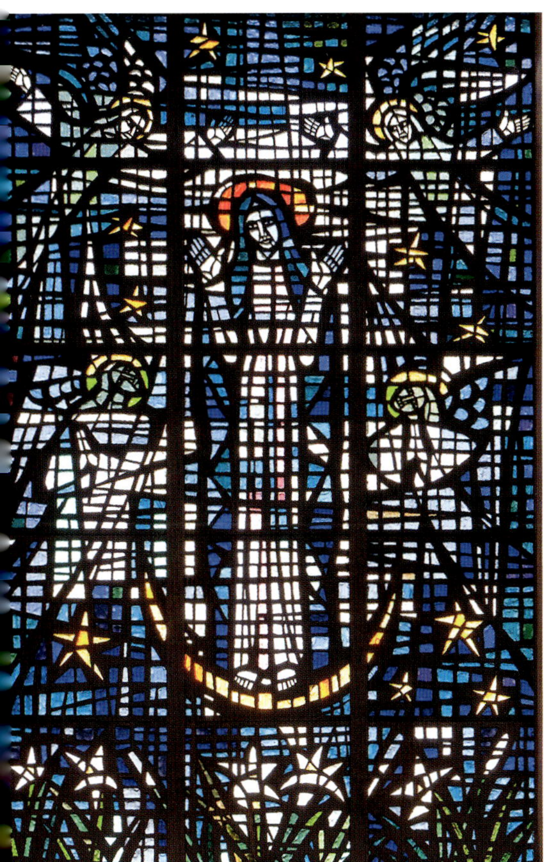

676. Powell & Sons, The Virgin Mary, 1965, designed by Pierre Fourmaintreaux, Church of Our Lady, Briton Ferry, west window

35 Vatican Council II, *Sacrosanctum Concilium*, 4 December 1963.

36 Richard King succeeded Harry Clarke as the chief designer at Harry Clarke Studios in Dublin. The window in Aberaeron was given after 1958 and has the title *Our Lady of Ireland*. The commission may have come through contacts with the Irish Carmelites, since the order were established in Aberystwyth, where they also had oversight of the Church of Our Lady of Mount Carmel in Lampeter. According to some sources on the artist, his window in Aberystwyth has the title *Our Lady of Mount Carmel*, although it seems to depict the Assumption, and suggests part of the dedication of the church (Our Lady of the Angels and St Winifrede). I am grateful to Ruth Sheehy for information on the work of Richard King.

37 Charles Norris was trained at the Royal College of Art and two of his windows using fused glass were included in Robert Sowers' *The Lost Art*. His east window of the Blessed Sacrament Chapel at Buckfast Abbey of 1968 is among the most famous examples of *dalle de verre* glass in Britain. The Lillington windows were not made at Buckfast, but at Prinknash Abbey. Aidan MacRae Thompson, *Warwickshire Churches*, <http://warwickshirechurches.weebly.com/lillington---our-lady.html>.

38 The geometric forms of Margam Crematorium draw on Modernist European architecture, particularly that of Le Corbusier, and it has been described as 'arguably the most dramatic crematorium design in Britain.' Hilary J. Grainger, *Death Redesigned: British Crematoria: History, Architecture and Landscape* (Reading: Spire Books, 2005), p. 253.

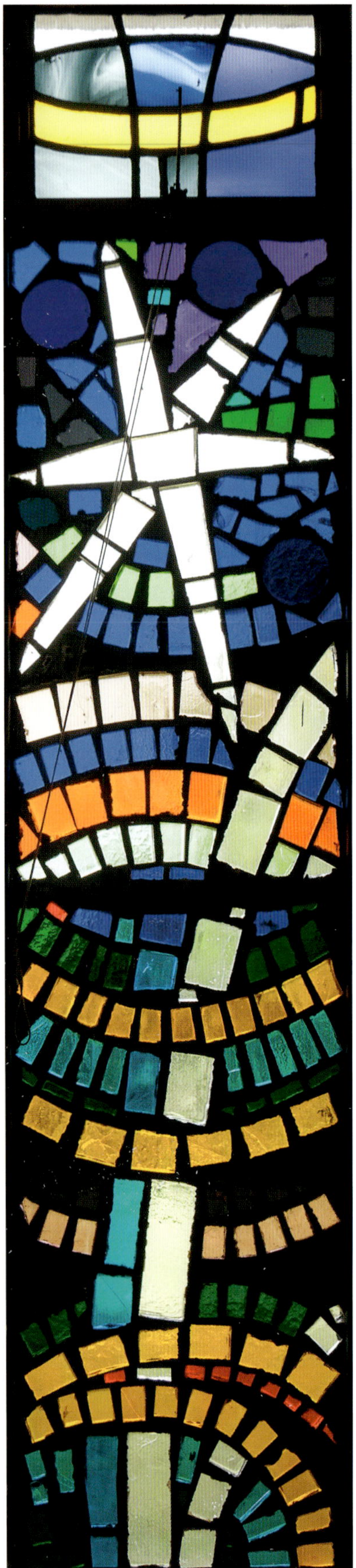

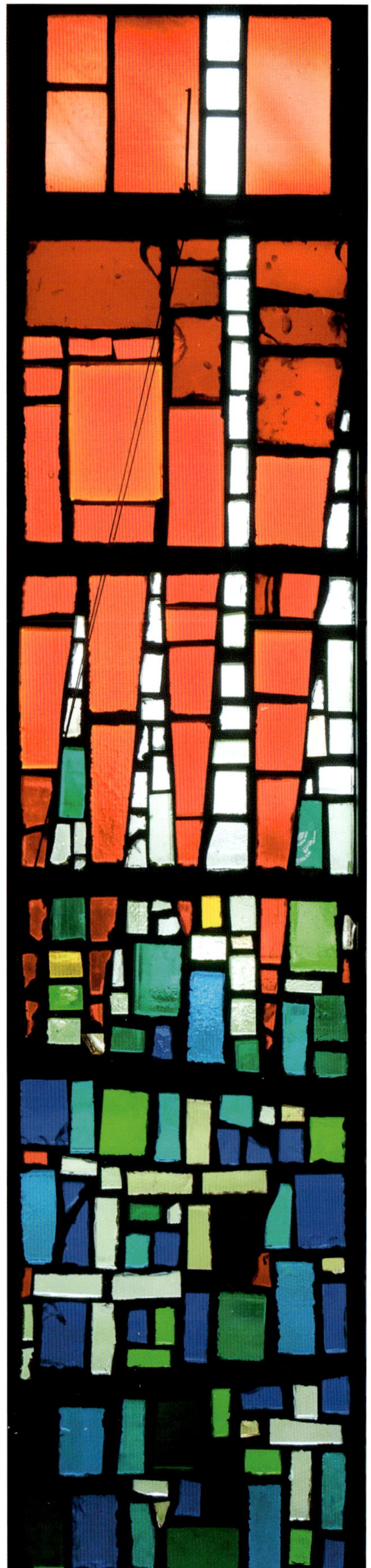

677. Celtic Studios, Christian Symbols, 1965, designed by John Edwards, Church of St Peter, Glasbury, west wall

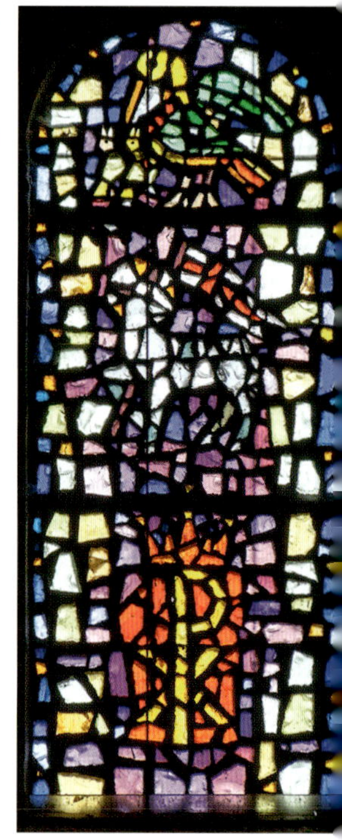

Always keen to keep up with innovations at Powell's, Celtic Studios also experimented with the technique. John Edwards designed two windows for the Church of St Peter, Glasbury, in 1965 and a series of windows for the Reform Synagogue in Cardiff from 1966 until 1977.

The artist Jonah Jones worked as a sculptor in north-west Wales and taught himself the techniques of both traditional stained glass and *dalle de verre*, making work mainly for Roman Catholic churches. His work in *dalle de verre* and other media can be found at both the Church of St Patrick, Newport, and the Church of the Resurrection of Our Saviour, Morfa Nefyn. The ten tall abstract windows around the church at Morfa Nefyn have red glass in the upper half of the windows, symbolising the descending fire of the Holy Spirit, while two further lights in the Lady Chapel demarcate the area with

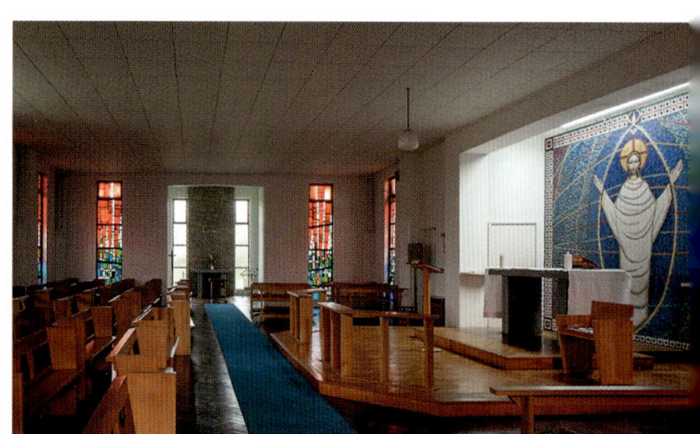

678–80. Jonah Jones, Windows for the Church of the Resurrection of Our Saviour, 1968, Morfa Nefyn

a different use of colour. The technique of *dalle de verre* lends itself to entirely abstract works, but as E. Liddall Armitage wrote in 1960 'some significance is usually expected of the design for a church window.' He observed that the technique could be applied in a haphazard way to good effect, and although there was the precedent of abstract grisaille work of the Middle Ages, such work would 'need all the theories of neo-abstractionism to endow it with any possible significance.'[39]

39 Liddall Armitage also appreciated its 'appeal to those who believe in Herbert Reade's [sic] dictum that the object of Art is to brighten things up a bit.' E. Liddall Armitage, *Stained Glass: History, Technology and Practice* (London: Leonard Hill, 1960), p. 157.

Recognisable figures and narrative scenes were attempted in larger panels and Jonah Jones designed a scene of Christ being baptised for the baptistry of the Church of St Joseph, Denbigh. Elsewhere in the church, other windows were filled with *dalle de verre* and made by Peter Morton, a local artist who had worked at the glass manufacturers Pilkingtons. Some Christian symbols are apparent in the work, but not all of them are easy to discern.

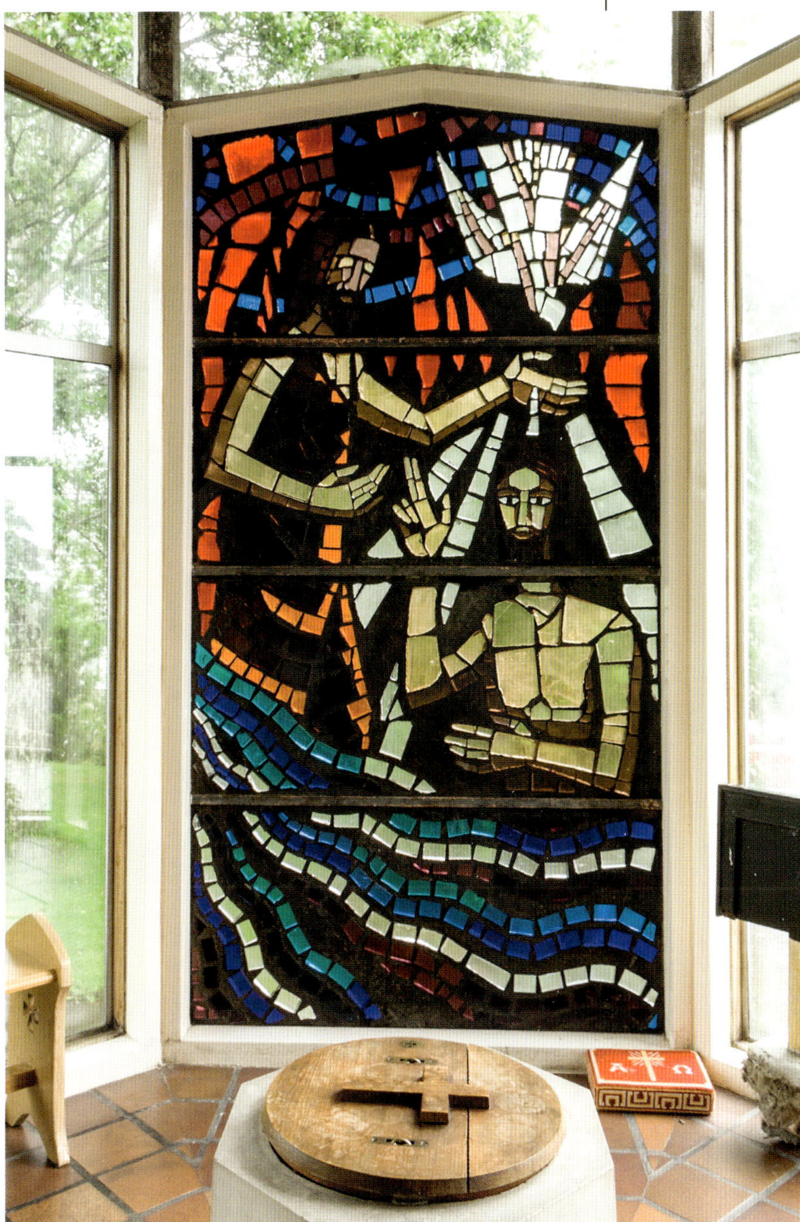

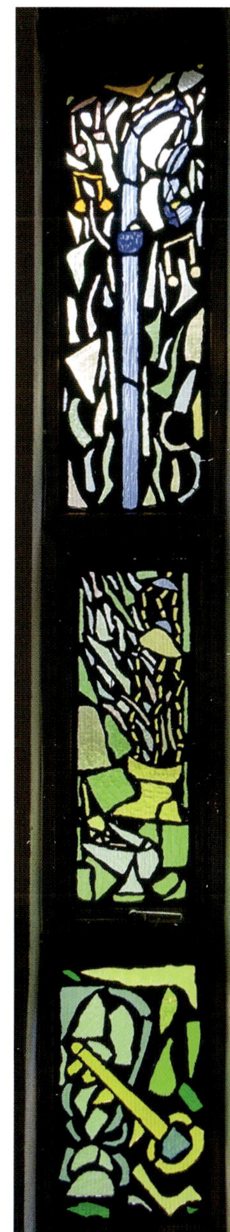

681. (right) Jonah Jones, The Baptism of Christ, *c.* 1970, Church of St Joseph, Denbigh, baptistry

682. (far right) Peter Morton, Christian Symbols, probably 1970s or 80s, Church of St Joseph, Denbigh, east wall

40 The glass studio at Prinknash has its origins in the arrival of monks from Caldey in 1928, no doubt under the supervision of Dom Theodore Baily, before he moved to Farnborough.

Brother Gilbert Taylor also made work in *dalle de verre* at a studio in Prinknash Abbey and was responsible for several windows at the Church of St John Lloyd, Trowbridge, Cardiff, as well as the small east window of symbols at the Church of Our Lady, Llandovery.[40] At Trowbridge, two small sanctuary windows have Eucharistic symbols, while in the body of the church there are three large *dalle de verre* panels, the outer windows predominantly in reds and the central panel predominantly in pinks, with the figure of the patron saint. The imagery in these works is secondary to the abstract architectural and decorative effect of light and colour on the interior of the church.

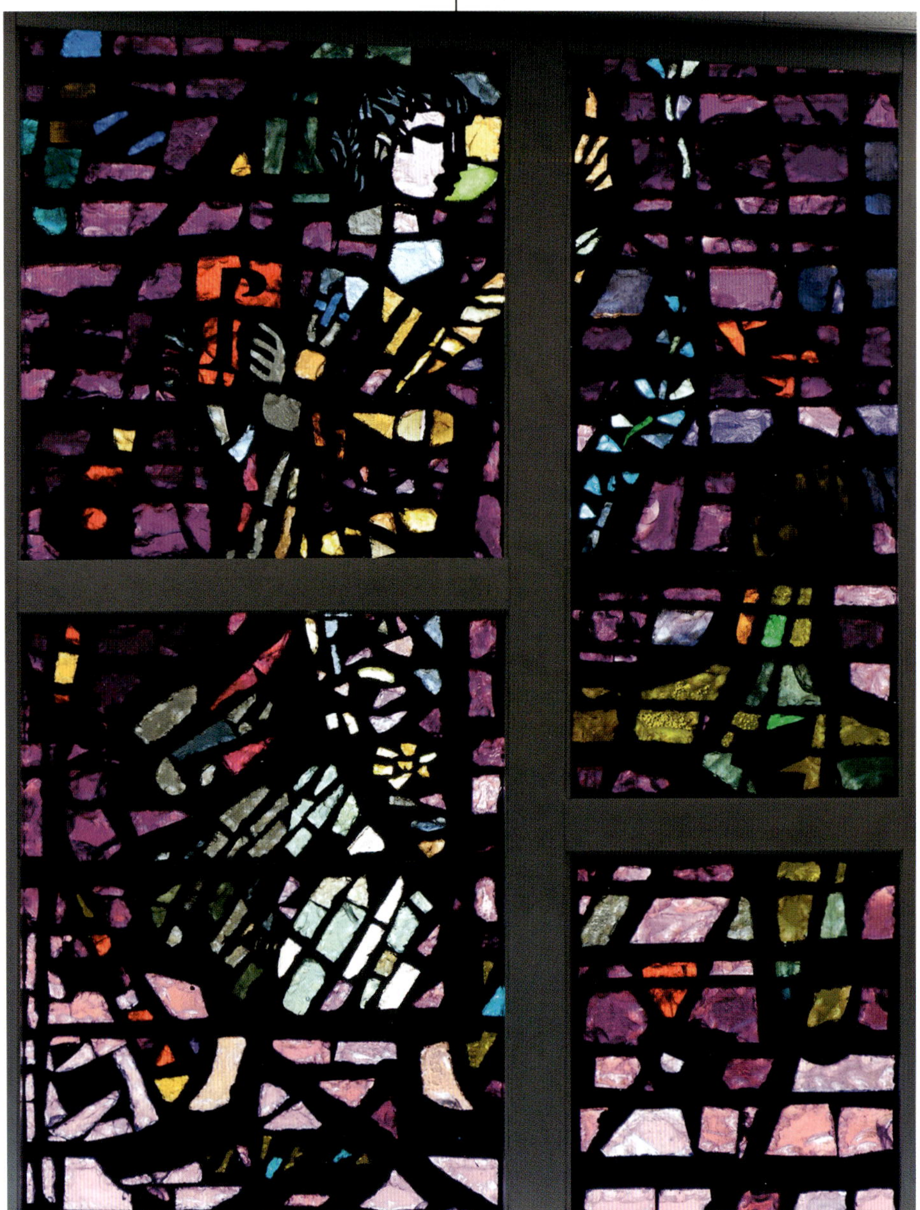

683. Prinknash Abbey, St John Lloyd, 1975, designed by Gilbert Taylor, Church of St John Lloyd, Trowbridge, Cardiff

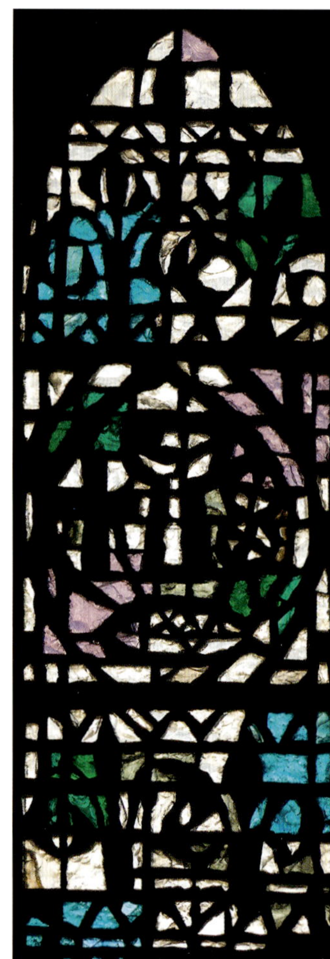

684. Prinknash Abbey, Eucharistic Symbols, *c.* 1980, designed by Gilbert Taylor, Church of Our Lady, Llandovery, east window

CHAPTER ELEVEN

IN SEARCH OF CREATIVE FREEDOM

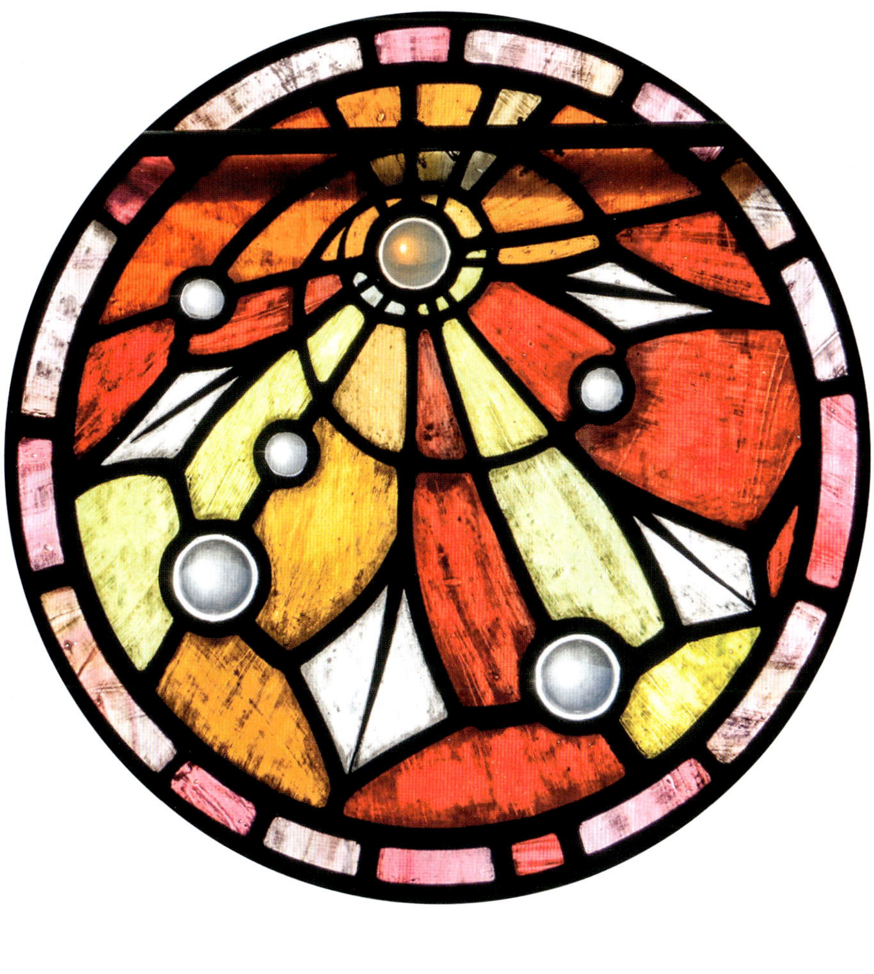

The growing acceptance of modern stained glass brought colourful and inventive work by talented artists into churches in Wales during the 1960s and 70s. These striking windows, successful on their own terms, sometimes sit uneasily with both the architecture around them and earlier stained glass and other furnishings. Self-expression and artistic personality, so integral to contemporary fine art, are not easy companions to the architectural language of the Gothic Revival and the traditions of western Christian iconography.

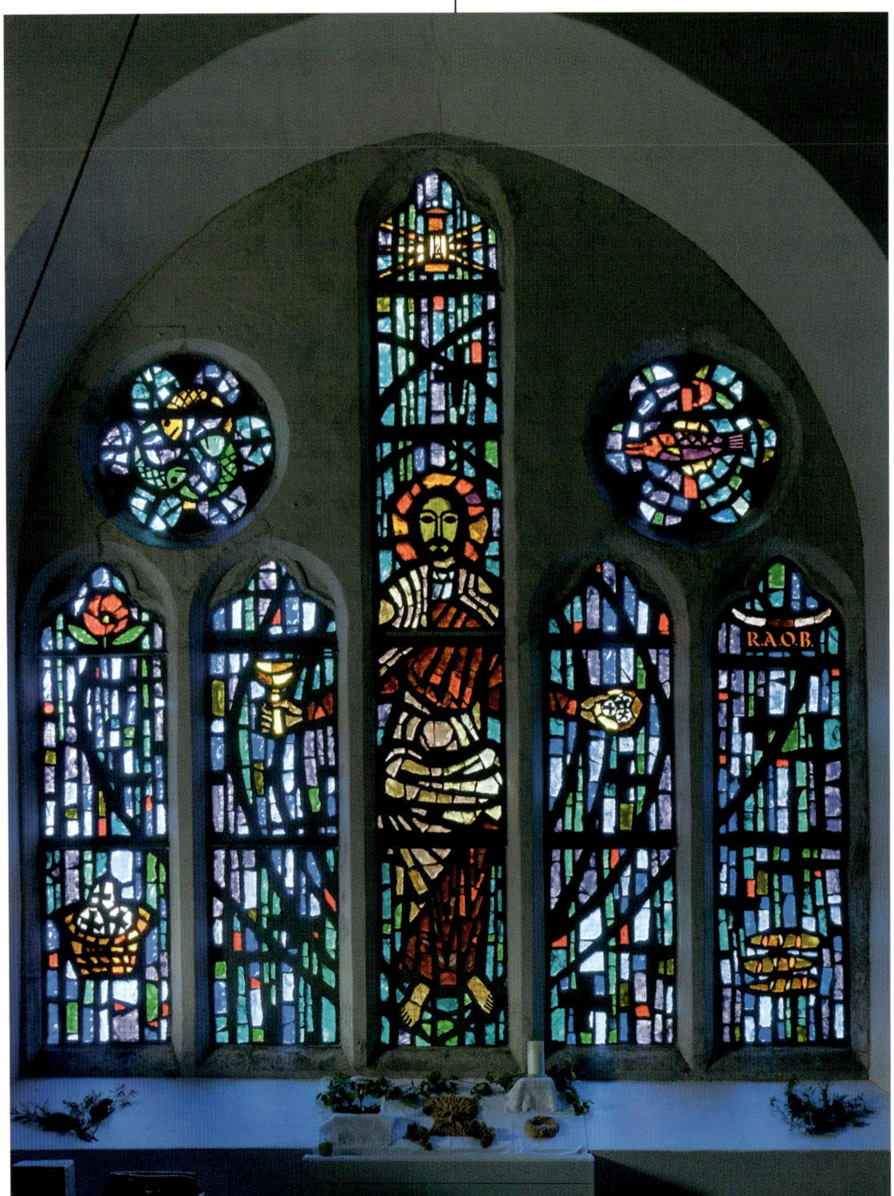

686. Prinknash Abbey, Christ with the Elements of the Eucharist, *c.* 1980, designed by Gilbert Taylor, Church of the Holy Trinity, Tylorstown, west window

Where new windows were commissioned for new buildings a balance could be struck at the outset, just as Gothic Revival architects had tried to do in the nineteenth century. The *dalle de verre* works by Dom. Gilbert Taylor and Jonah Jones work so well in their setting, but would not sit comfortably next to stained glass by Burlison & Grylls or Christopher Whall. In a few cases *dalle de verre* was commissioned for older buildings, and the figure of Christ was designed in this way across a five-light window in the Church of the Holy Trinity, Tylorstown, in the upper Rhondda Fach. The church has no other figurative stained glass for the window to conflict with, and bathes the west end of the church is a rich blue glow.

The windows of the Penarth sculptor Frank Roper are also generally more successful on their own terms, such as the Stations of the Cross that fill all of the windows of the modern Roman Catholic Church of Our Lady Queen of

685. (Title page) Tim Lewis, The Creation of Light, Church of St Luke, Cwmdare, west wi

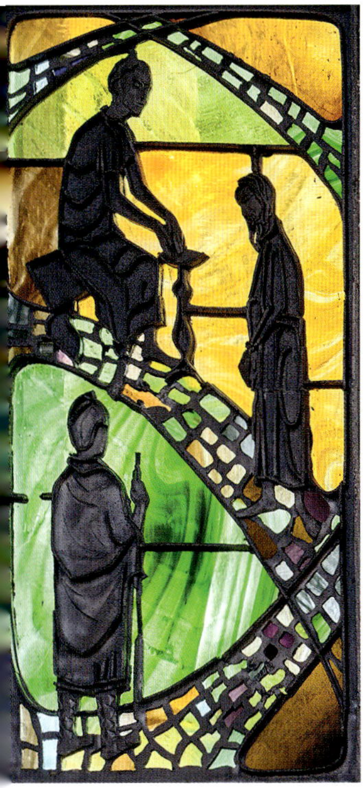

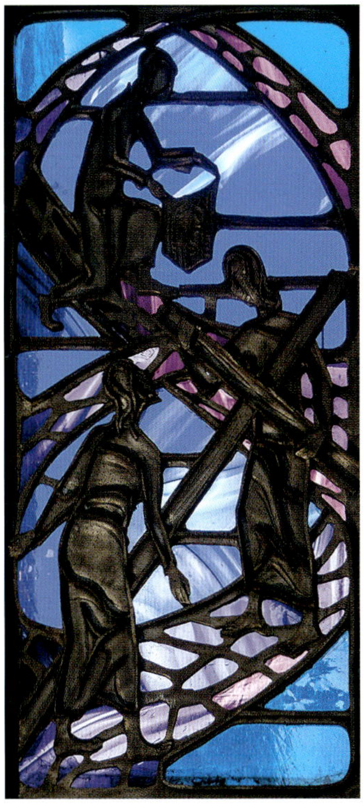

87–8. Frank Roper, Christ Before Pilate, and hrist with Veronica, from the Stations of the ross, 1971, Church of Our Lady Queen of Peace, ewcastle Emlyn, nave

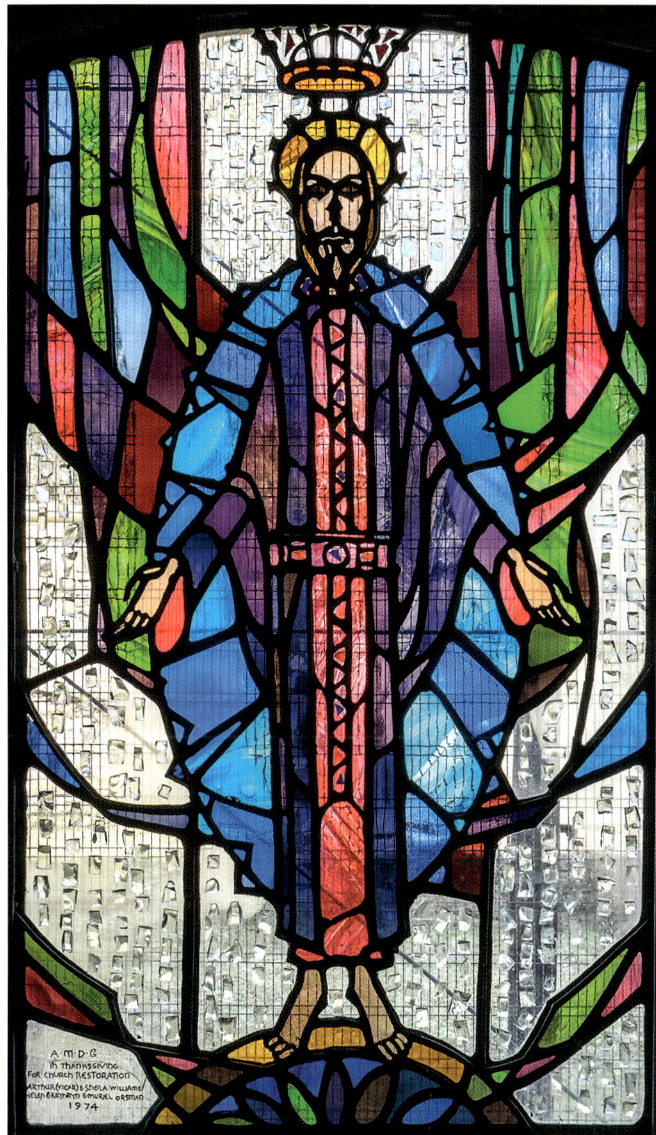

689. Frank Roper, Christ in Majesty, 1974, Church of St Illtyd, Llantwit Fardre, nave

Peace, Newcastle Emlyn, or the set of chancel windows in the Church of St Mary, Talbenny. Roper was experimental with his materials and held the glass together on an aluminium, rather than a lead, framework, using no painted detail, giving the features of his figures a contorted appearance. These glass sculptures were sometimes mounted against the windows internally, and in some cases he affixed small chunks of glass to the surface to catch and disperse sunlight. Roper's work found favour in the Llandaff diocese and he produced a large number of ecclesiastical commissions for metalwork and coloured windows.[1] These windows sometimes appear out of place, even with other modern work, such as at the Church of All Saints, Penarth, where, as John Newman has pointed out, his designs are not always suited to large windows.[2]

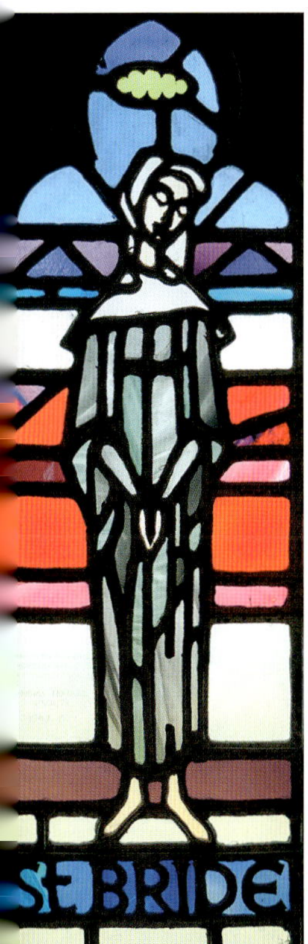

690. Frank Roper, St Bride, 1978, Church of St Mary, Talbenny, chancel

1 Frank Roper's work is not restricted to Wales, as he also received commissions from England. Important works in other media include his sets of the Stations of the Cross at the Church of St Martin, Roath, and the Church of St Saviour, Splott, both in Cardiff, along with several works at Llandaff Cathedral including the Flowers of the Virgin for the reredos of the Lady Chapel, all made in the 1960s.

2 John Newman, *The Buildings of Wales: Glamorgan* (London: Penguin Books, 1995), pp. 171, 491.

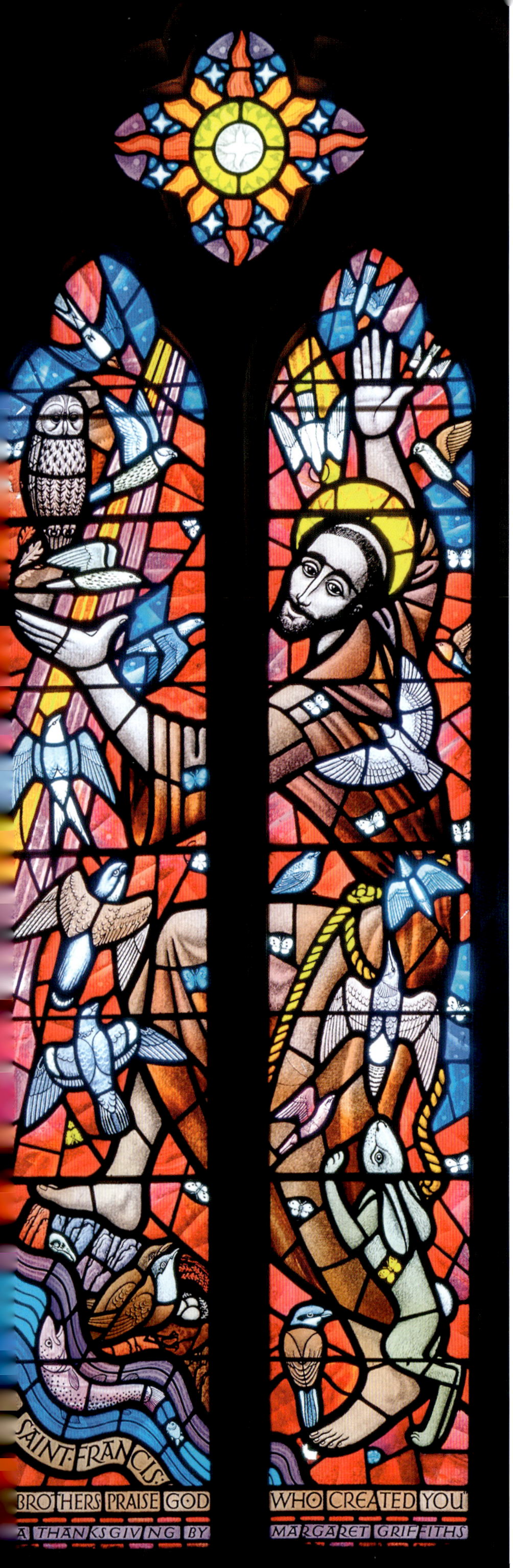

691. John Petts, St Francis, 1978, Church of All Saints, Penarth, north aisle

John Petts added two further windows to the north aisle at Penarth after his first window of 1966. His joyful depiction of Francis dancing, made in 1978 and including twenty-two different species of birds, was joined by an abstract window with a spiral pattern emanating from a cross, made in 1986 using the text 'Thy Light Break Forth'.[3] Although the three windows demonstrate a common approach, their contrasting colour schemes do little to help connect the wide range of different styles of stained glass in the church that begins with the work of Arthur Walker in the 1950s.

At the Church of St David, Betws (near Ammanford), Lawrence Lee's east window of 1960 stands at the head of a set of diverse modern windows by other makers, including two by John Petts.[4] Petts' image of Christ crucified against a tree at Betws prefigures successive windows that use trees as a motif, more often as the Tree of Life, such as those

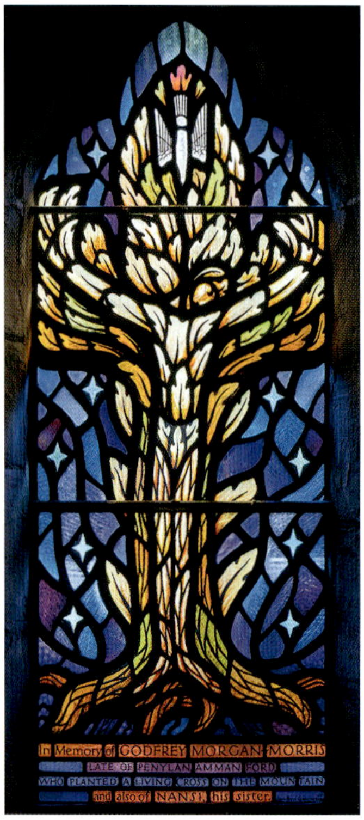

692. John Petts, Christ Crucified on a Tree, 1973, Church of St David, Betws, nave

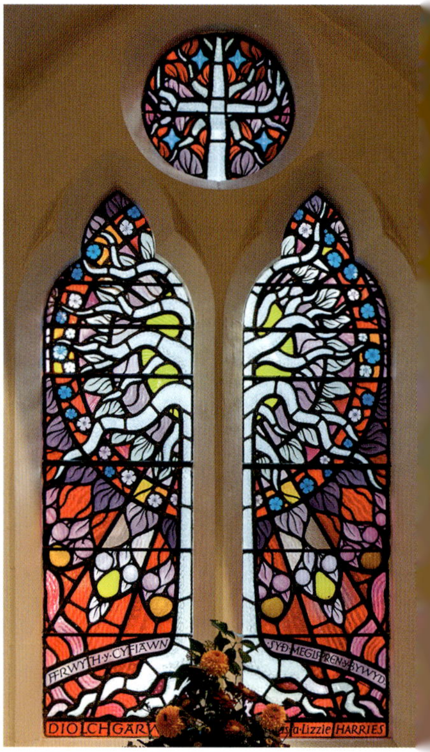

693. John Petts, The Tree of Life, 1979, Church of St Twrog, Llanddarog, nave

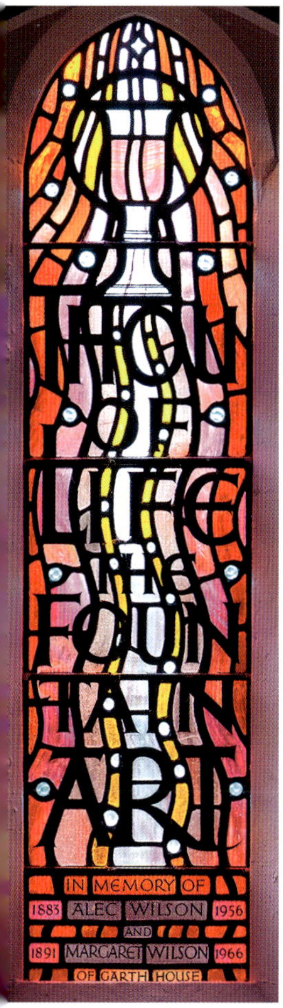

694. John Petts, 'Thou of Life the Fountain Art', 1975, Llanlleonfel Church, sanctuary

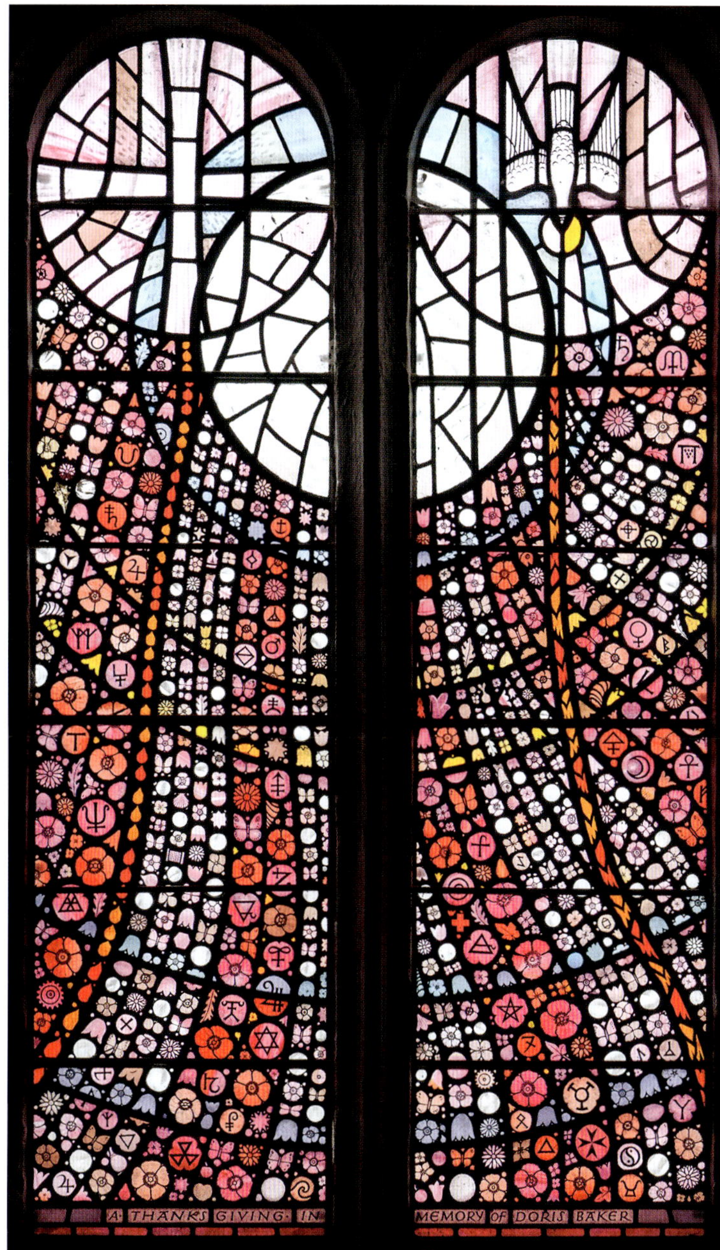

695. John Petts, East Window, 1980, Church of St Stephen, Llansteffan

at the Church of St Twrog, Llanddarog, the Church of St Peter, Carmarthen, and at the Church of St David, Llanddewi Rhydderch, made in 1979, 1987 and 1988 respectively. His second window at Betws is similar in concept and colour to his third window at Penarth, using concentric circles around a central light with orbiting stars and doves, illustrating the text 'The Real Light'. Circles are again in evidence in his east window for the Church of St Stephen, Llansteffan, where three circles symbolising the Trinity are arranged at the head of a two-light window with tiny flowers, butterflies and symbols trailing to the ground in a mesmerising pattern.

Petts also brought an original approach to common subjects. For example, at the Church of St John, Pontyberem, his interpretation of the most common of all biblical subjects (apart from Christ on the cross), Christ in the midst of children, has the Welsh text 'Gadewch i blant bychain ddyfod ataf fi ac na waherddwch iddynt' [Let the little children come to me and forbid them not] flowing around a central cross surrounded by the faces of children, the design divided across a two-light window. The biblical texts used by Petts increasingly became the principal feature of both large and small windows, and the use of scripture in this way proved popular with some Nonconformist patrons who were less inclined towards pictorial windows, but still wanted to introduce stained glass into their buildings.

3 John Petts' race against time to complete the Francis window before the death of the donor is recorded in the *Journal of the British Society of Master Glass-Painters*, vol. xvii, no. 2 (1978–9), p. 55. He sent her a photograph of the completed window when she was in hospital.

4 The others were designed by Bryan Evans for Celtic Studios in 1961, and Janet Hardy in 2000.

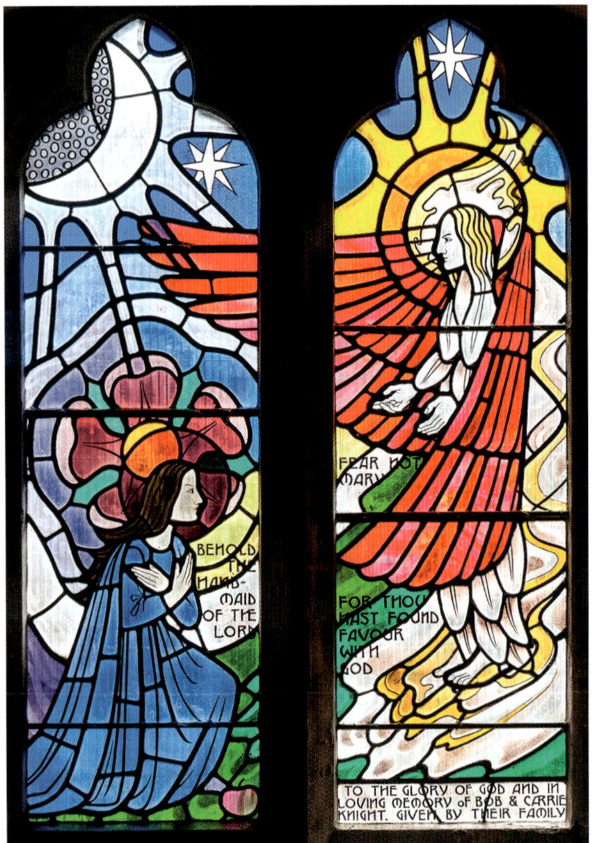

696. Geoffrey Robinson, The Annunciation, 1981, Church of St Mary, Rogiet, north aisle

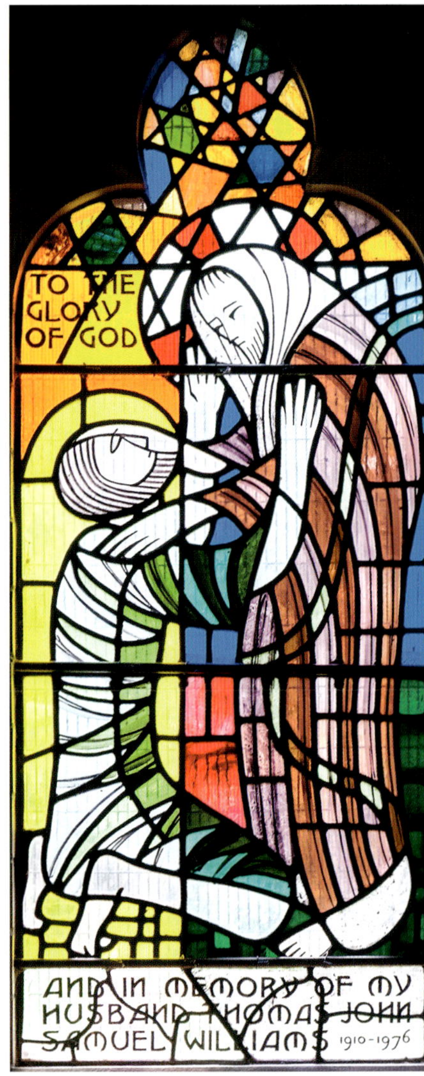

697. Geoffrey Robinson, The Raising of Lazarus, 1976, Church of St David, Beaufort, chancel

Geoffrey Robinson's distinctive modernist-figurative style is found in numerous windows for churches in south Wales, mainly in Monmouthshire and neighbouring parts of Glamorgan.[5] His colourful figures and biblical scenes are designed with a dynamic use of leading and only a little painted detail. Some of his windows are more abstract in character, such as the window at the Church of St John the Evangelist, Canton, Cardiff, and a two-light window with flowers at the Church of St Mary, Llanfair Discoed. In contrast with these modern works, a pair of windows made at his studio for the south aisle at the Church of St Arvan, St Arvans, differ from his usual personal style to complement the adjacent window in the east wall of the aisle by A.L. Wilkinson.

Artists such as Leonard Evetts and Alan Younger applied paint to add abstract detail and texture to the glass, and both artists brought together figurative and abstract elements. Leonard Evetts' windows for three churches in Wales show clear visual continuity over a twenty-year period. As well as his windows of 1964–5 for the Church of All Saints, Porthcawl, and the depiction of Margaret at the Church of St Margaret, Roath, in 1970, four windows were made between 1974–80 for the Church of St Theodore, Port Talbot. These included a pair of figures and a pair of more abstract two-light windows, illustrative of Isaiah 45: 8 and the parable of the wheat and the tares in Matthew 13: 24–30.[6]

5 Geoffrey Robinson took over his father's firm of Joseph Bell & Son in 1959 and made twenty-six windows in south Wales. I am grateful to the artist for supplying a list of these works.

6 Unfortunately the pair of two-light windows have been relocated high in the clerestory windows. They were admired by Tim Lewis for their 'spontaneity and informality that transcended traditional methods where tracing from a finished cartoon was the standard procedure.' Tim Lewis, 'Windows in Wales', in *Leonard Evetts: Master Designer* (Privately printed, 2001), p. 72. Leonard Evetts was born in Newport and went to Newport College of Art before going to the Royal College of Art, where he was a pupil of Martin Travers. He established himself as an artist and teacher in Newcastle, and much of his work is in the north east of England.

698. Leonard Evetts, The Parable of the W and the Tares, *c.* 1977, Church of St Theod Port Talbot, clerestory (formerly in the Chapel and illustrated here in its original f

Celtic Studios' work in the 1970s and 80s became increasingly repetitive, making use of earlier designs for popular biblical subjects, although their work remained much in demand, particularly in churches where they had already made windows. With good colouring and assured execution these were occasionally quite striking, such as their window of Christian symbols made in 1980 for Eglwys Dewi Sant (Church of St David), Tumble. Only a few commissions went beyond the conventional, such as John Edwards' design for a very contemporary image of the Good Shepherd at Bettws Chapel (near Abergavenny) of 1978, and a window commemorating the campaign in Burma at the Church of St Padarn, Llanbadarn Fawr (Ceredigion), made in 1985.[7]

In 1976 Celtic Studios, John Petts and Tim Lewis were invited to produce designs for a window at the Church of All Saints, Oystermouth, commemorating the thirtieth anniversary of the death of the lifeboat

7 A faculty for an intriguing commission for a window for the Church of St Samlet, Llansamlet, was granted in 1976, on the theme of 'Re-Creation' and the text of Revelation 21: 5: 'Behold I make all things new.' Celtic Studios' window was 'designed to reflect the re-creation of the Environment of the Parish through the Lower Swansea Valley Project' but was not installed. National Library of Wales, Records of the Church in Wales: Diocese of Swansea and Brecon, BR/RF/113/2.

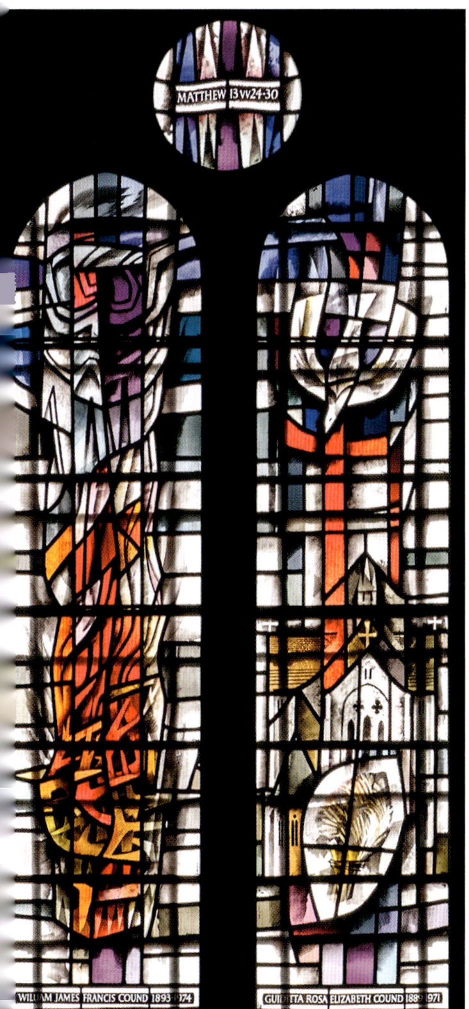

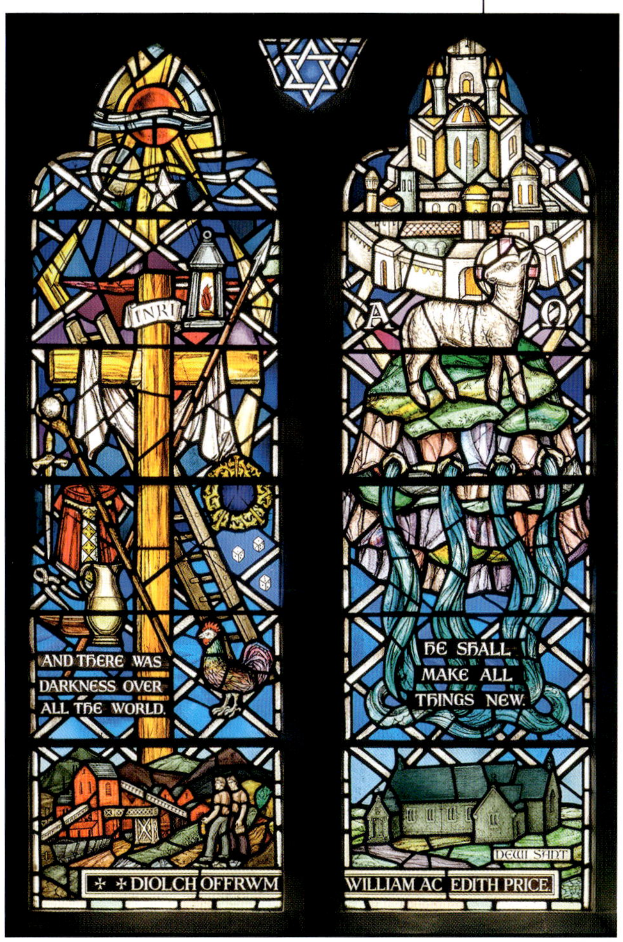

699. (above) Celtic Studios, Christian Symbols, 1980, designed by Hubert Thomas, Eglwys Dewi Sant, Tumble, nave

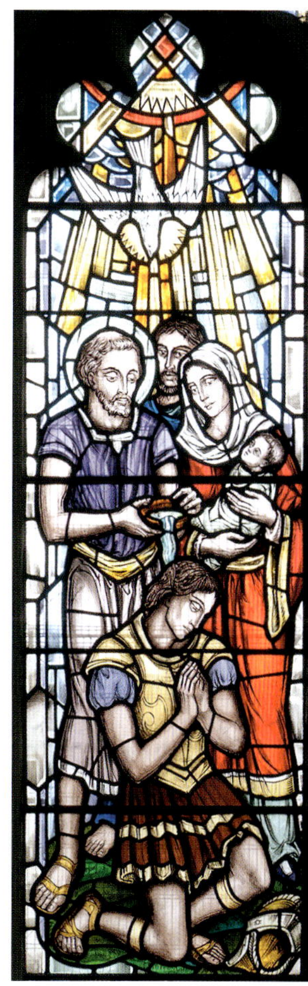

700. Celtic Studios, The Baptism of Cornelius, 1977, Church of St Michael and All Angels, Manselton, south aisle

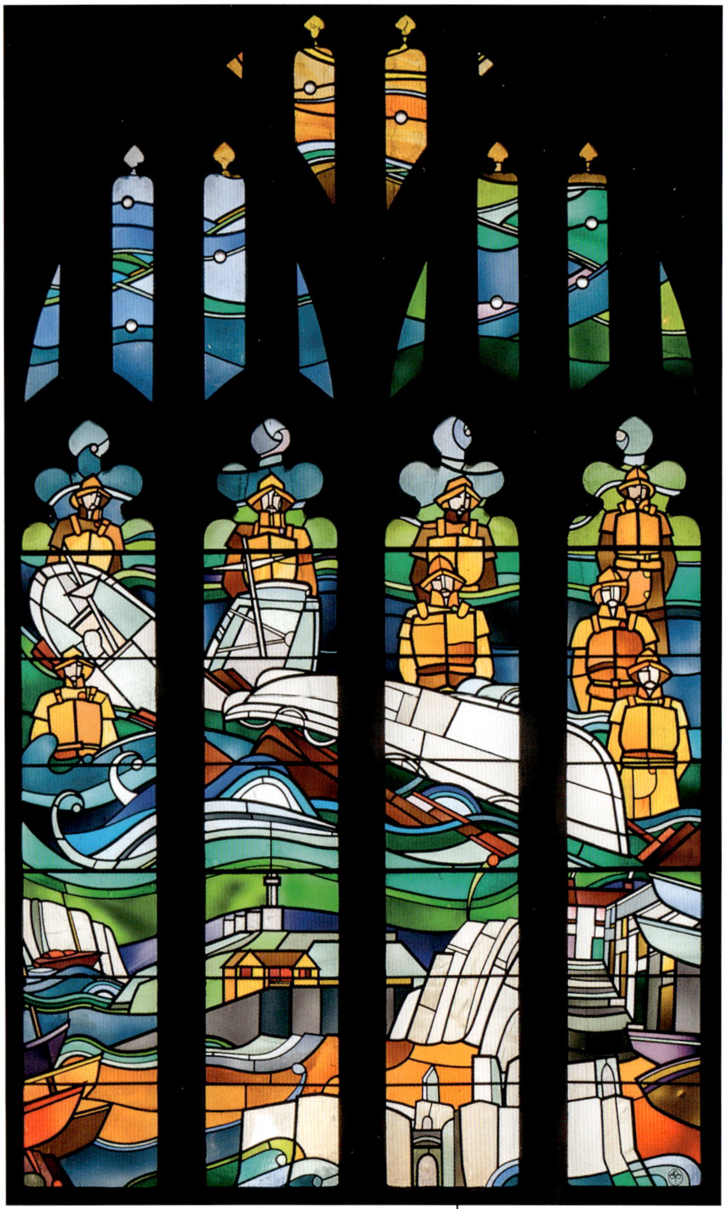

701. Tim Lewis, Lifeboat Window, 1977, Church of All Saints, Oystermouth, north aisle

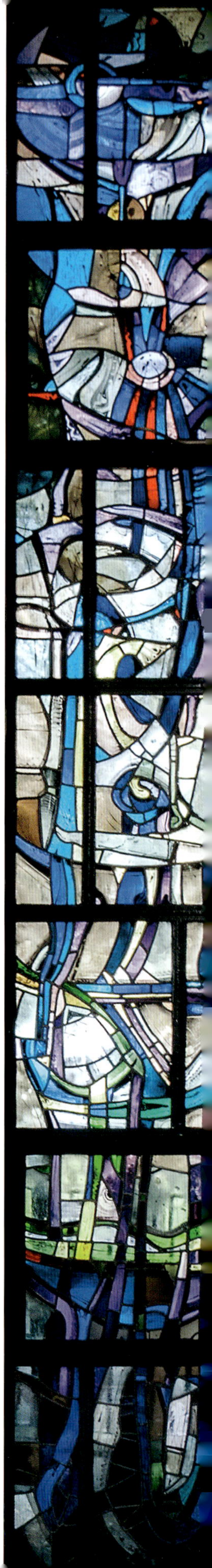

crew who had sought to rescue the crew of the *S.S. Samtampa* in a hurricane-force gale. The commission was won by Tim Lewis, who had succeeded Howard Martin as the head of the Stained Glass Department at Swansea College of Art in 1972, and his design depicts the crew with their upturned boat and the town and seascape of Mumbles below. The window has no painted detail and relies solely on the lead lines and colour of the glass to suggest both the tumult of the storm and the stillness of eternity.

In 1969 the architect Maxwell Fry asked the department to provide windows for the Coychurch Crematorium and a set of four tall abstract windows representing the seasons was designed and made by a student, Roger Hayman, for the Chapel of Remembrance.[8] Howard Martin suggested that windows could be filled with the names of those who had been cremated to fund the addition of further stained glass windows. Tim Lewis was given oversight of this scheme and saw an opportunity for students to gain experience by working on the windows. Thirty-five tall rectangular lights were filled with coloured glass in abstract forms surrounding names for the north wall of the cloister, providing coloured light for the interior without recourse to imagery.

8 By involving local artists the architect hoped to connect the crematorium with its locality. Hilary J. Grainger, *Death Redesigned: British Crematoria: History, Architecture and Landscape* (Reading: Spire Books, 2005), p. 252.

9 Swansea College of Art was renamed West Glamorgan Institute of Higher Education in 1976, and then Swansea Institute of Higher Education after 1992.

.. Roger Hayman,
.dow from the
.apel of the Four
.sons, *c.* 1970,
.church Crematorium

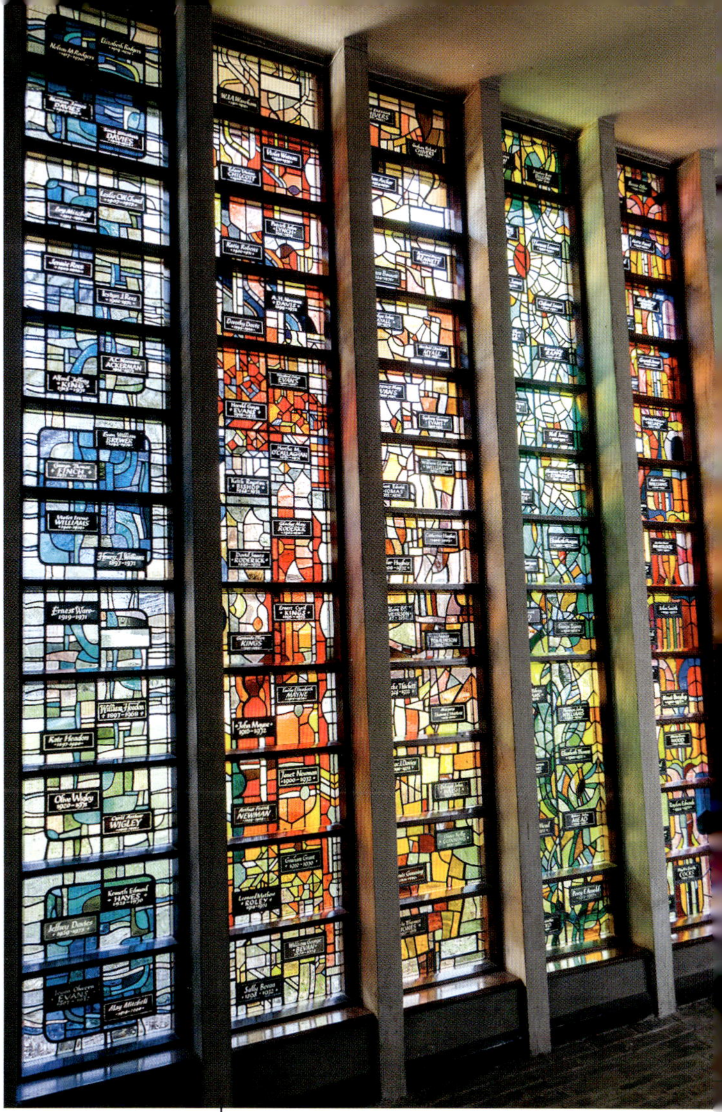

703. Various Artists from Swansea College of Art, Cloister Windows, *c.* 1970–7, Coychurch Crematorium

The windows were designed and made by staff and students, including Amber Hiscott, Mark Angus, Janet Hardy, David Pearl and Lydia Marouf. Despite being the work of so many artists, they form a remarkably coherent group suggesting the guiding hand of Tim Lewis and his colleagues Marjorie Walters, who taught design and pattern; Glenys Cour, who taught colour; and John Edwards and Alan Figg who had both trained at the College with Howard Martin.

A defining influence on many of the students who trained at West Glamorgan Institute in the 1970s was the work of the leading post-war German designers.[9] Tim Lewis had travelled to see their work in Germany and later met Ludwig Schaffrath at the studio of Patrick Reyntiens. A further scheme of four windows for the crematorium designed by Schaffrath, Johannes Schreiter, Jochem Poensgen and Joachim Klos introduced a new abstract visual vocabulary to students at first hand and the artists provided a series of masterclasses while their windows for the cloister were made in the department.

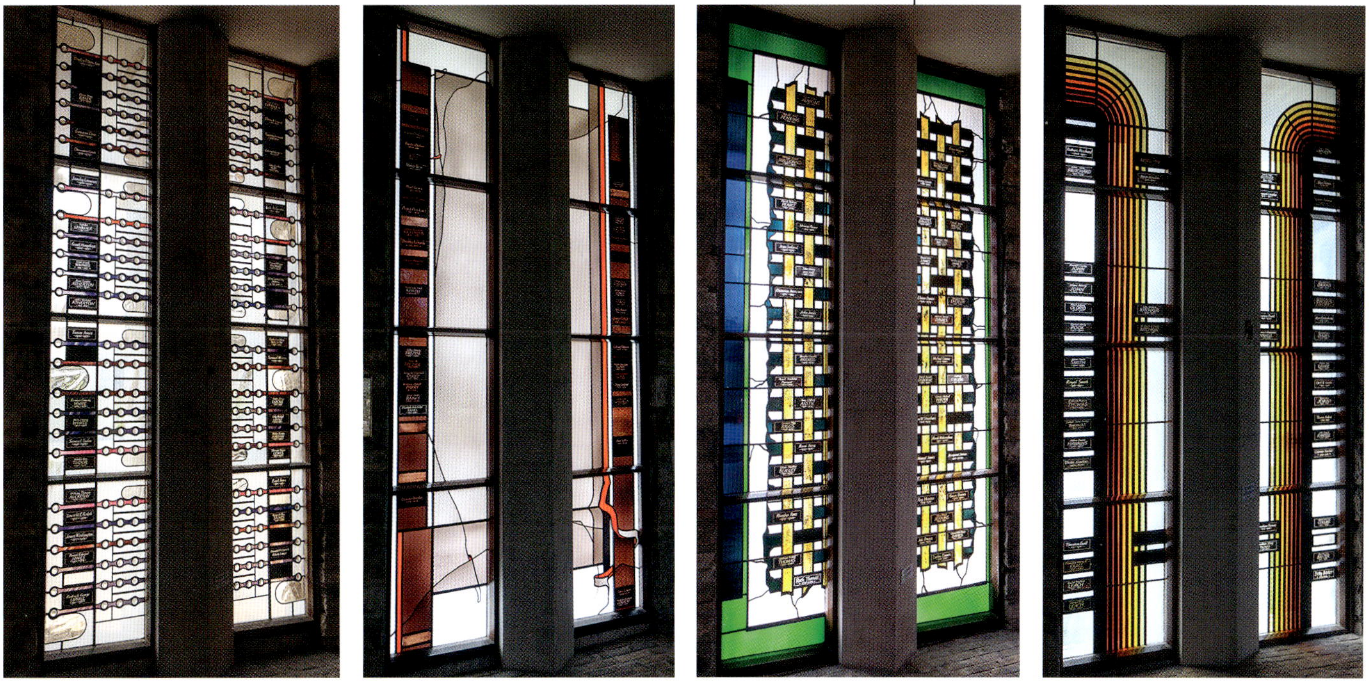

704–7. Cloister Windows at Coychurch Crematorium (left to right): Ludwig Schaffrath, 1979; Johannes Schreiter, 1980; Jochem Poensgen, *c.* 1980–1; Joachim Klos, 1982

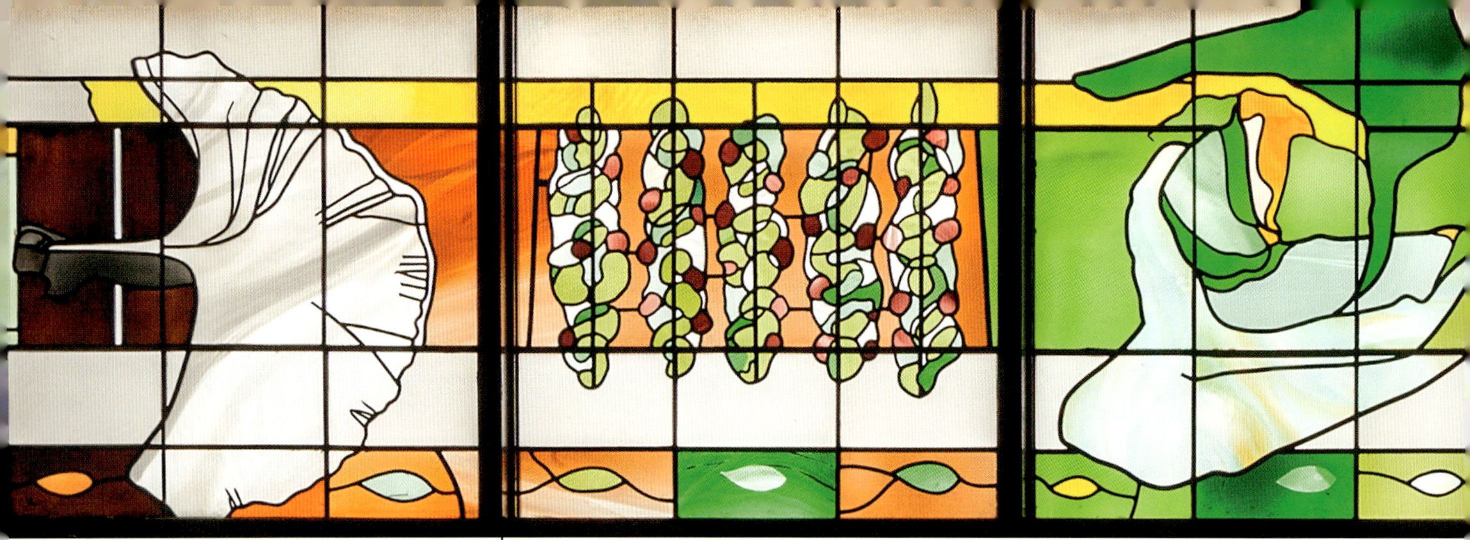

The distinctive use of line, rectilinear pattern and opalescent glass provided inspiration for a number of former students during the late 1970s and 80s. Amber Hiscott had trained at Swansea from 1972–5, and had briefly studied with Ludwig Schaffrath in 1976 before setting up her own studio in Swansea, teaching at the Institute before she moved to Canada for two years in 1979. In glass she found an exciting medium for her own personal expression, and her work was unconnected with the stained glass being made for churches in the period by firms such as Celtic Studios, work that she found unimaginative.[10] Abstraction was rarely popular with parish councils and advisory committees in Anglican churches, and in the 1960s and 70s artists sometimes found it easier to produce innovative windows for Roman Catholic churches where the parish priest alone could sanction the installation of windows. At the Church of Our Lady of the Taper, Cardigan, Hiscott was fortunate to find a stimulating and challenging patron in the form of the parish priest Fr Seamus Cunnane, who encouraged her to produce original symbolism for the theme of the seven sacraments in a series of panels commissioned in 1978. At the time she was also working with David Pearl, who had come from Canada to study at Swansea, and in 1978 he made a pair of two-light abstract windows with a small roundel for the east end of the Roman Catholic Church of St Joseph, Crickhowell.

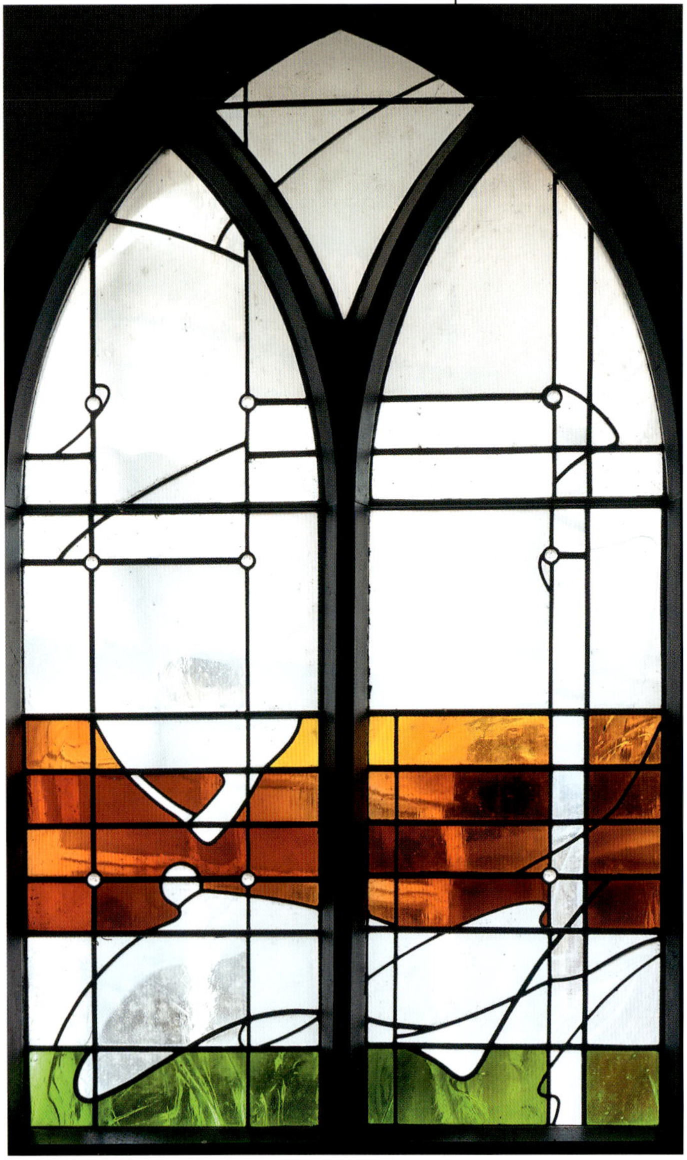

709. David Pearl, Chancel Window, 1978,
Church of St Joseph, Crickhowell

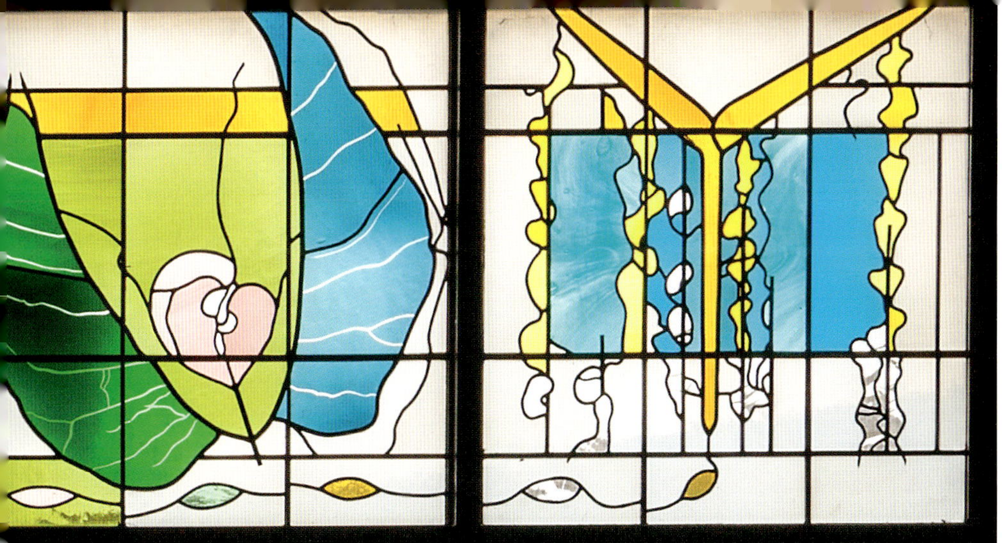

708. Amber Hiscott, Panels from the Seven Sacrament Windows: Eucharist, Confession, Ordination, Sacrament of the Sick, Holy Matrimony, 1978–80, Church of Our Lady of the Taper, Cardigan, rear clerestory

Uncompromising abstract architectural glass met with resistance from Diocesan Advisory Committees in Anglican churches. On the advice of their art advisor, the Swansea and Brecon DAC rejected an abstract design by David La Versha for the Church of St Samlet, Llansamlet, in 1979, as it was thought to be out of keeping with the church. Having recently completed his studies in Swansea, the artist challenged the rejection of his design, complaining that his designs had been 'grossly misunderstood'. Detailed notes subsequently sent by the artist explained how the colours and forms had been chosen to complement the interior and how the glass prisms would add light to the church. The artist also set out the position of contemporary architectural glass artists, explaining that the contribution of the medium to the 'quality and beauty to the space within' necessitated the dispensation with 'the more superficial aspect of symbolism' in order for the windows to be 'part of the overall language of the building'. The artist's defence impressed the diocesan chancellor, and although the lack of easily understandable Christian symbolism denied the design any admiration, it was eventually approved with the concession that the plain glass window that it was to replace had no obvious symbolism either.[11]

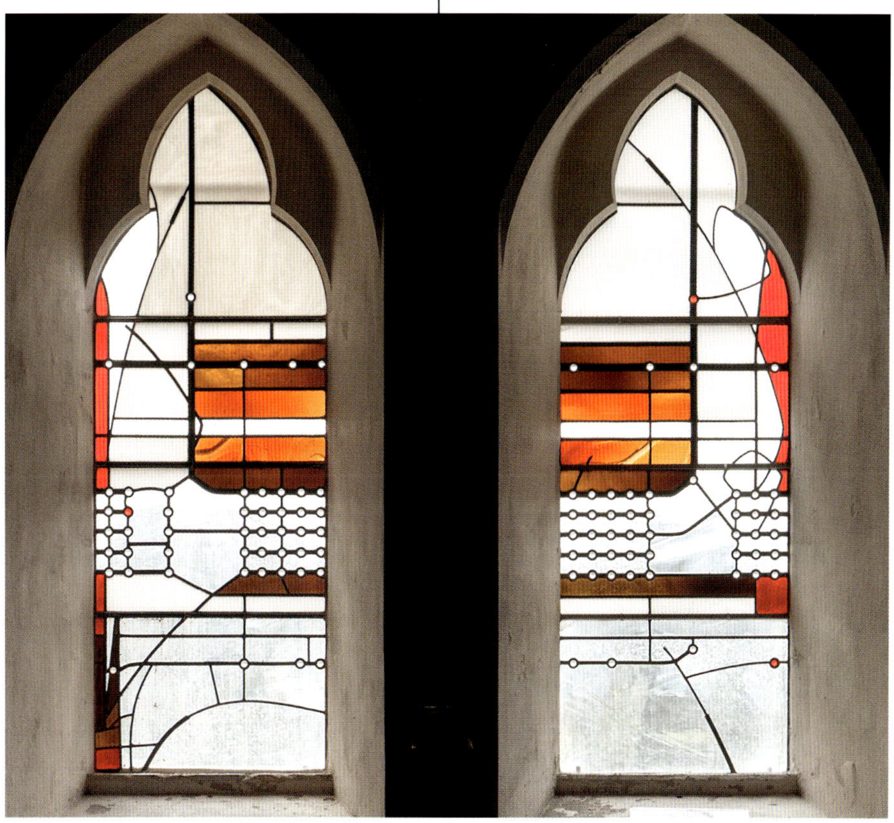

710. David La Versha, Memorial Window, 1979, Church of St Samlet, Llansamlet, nave

10 Interview with Amber Hiscott, 18 August 2008, parts of which were published as part of 'Speaking in Parables: Abstract Expression', in Martin Crampin and John Morgan-Guy, *Imaging the Bible in Wales* (DVD-ROM) (Sheffield: Sheffield Phoenix Press, 2010).

11 The design shows a very direct similarity with the work by Ludwig Schaffrath and Johannes Schreiter, and was contemporary with Schaffrath's window at Coychurch Crematorium. The brown colour symbolised the destruction of the surrounding land through the industrialisation of the area, while the white glass represented the light of the world, and the red the renewal of the Holy Spirit. The correspondence is found in National Library of Wales, Records of the Church in Wales: Diocese of Swansea and Brecon, BR/RF/113/3.

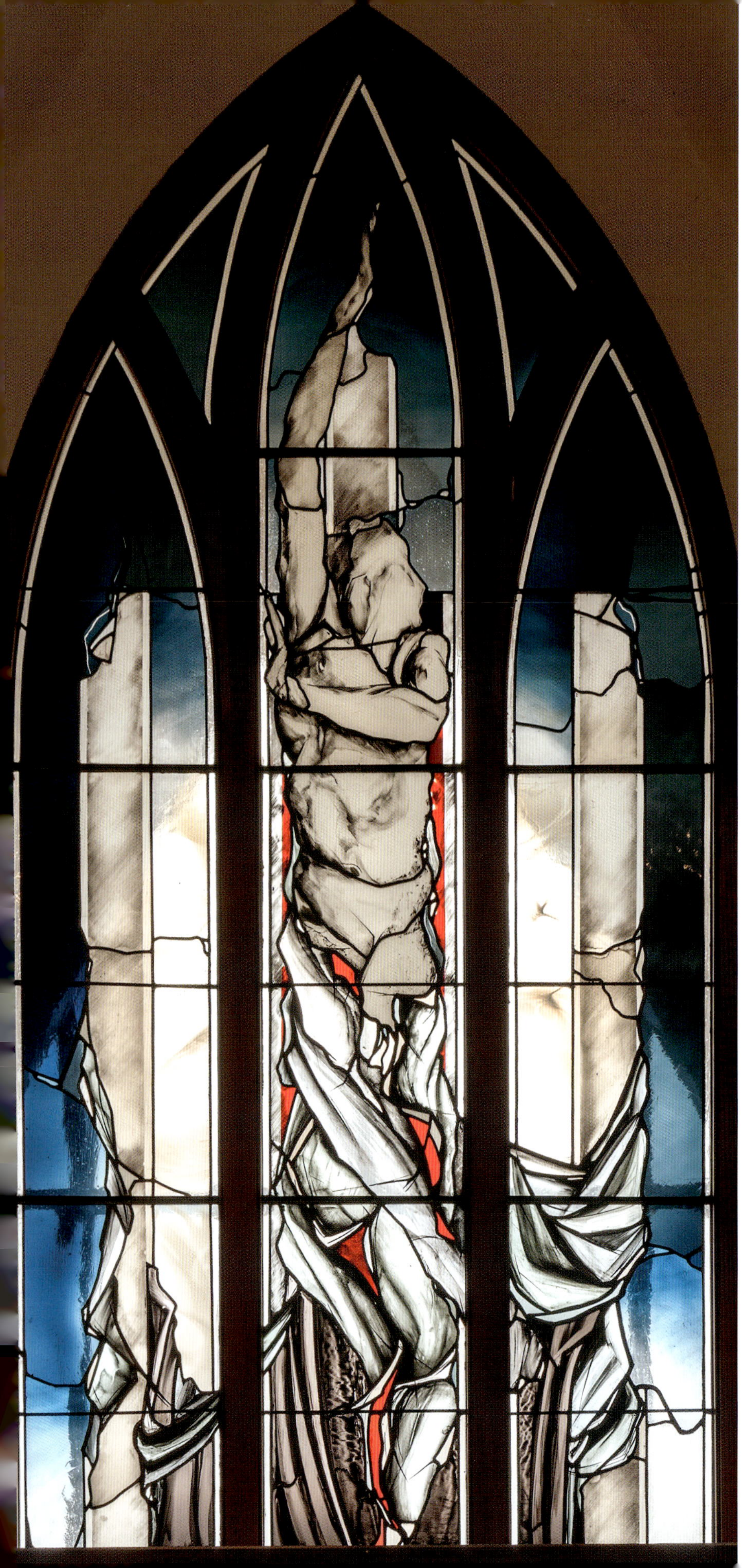

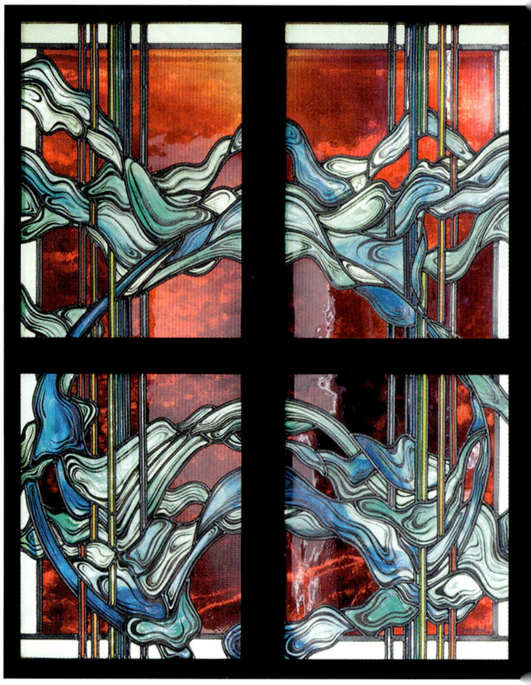

Graham Jones and Lydia Marouf, also students who studied at the College in the late 1970s, were more fortunate in being able to work with an architect who was sympathetic at the Anglican Church of St David, Hendy. Adversity arose from a different source, as a fire at the church required the windows to be altered to fit the modern replacement church. Lydia Marouf's baptistry window was intended to be much taller and the upper panels with orange and golden yellow glass were discarded before the window was installed in 1986. Graham Jones' rising Christ figure, originally made for the east window of the old church, was sited over the entrance on the south side. The figure is given depth through the application of paint to create graded tones, and, combined with expressive leading, adds a dynamic upward force.

711. (left) Graham Jones, The Resurrection, 1980, Church of St David, Hendy, nave

712. (above) Lydia Marouf, Baptistry Window, 1982–3, Church of St David, Hendy, nave

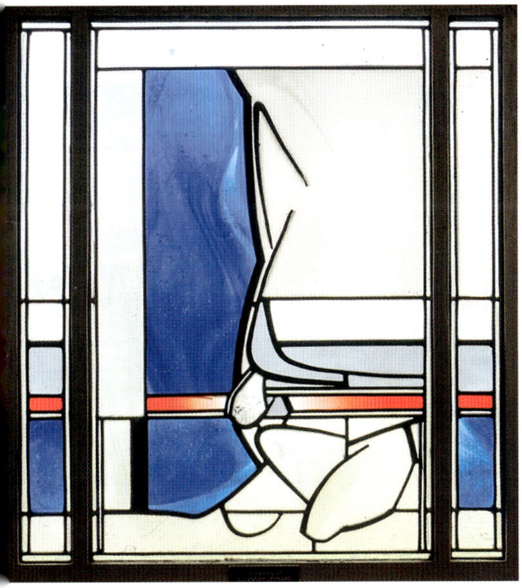

713. Graham Jones, North Chapel Window, *c.* 1980, Church of St Nicholas, Townhill, Swansea

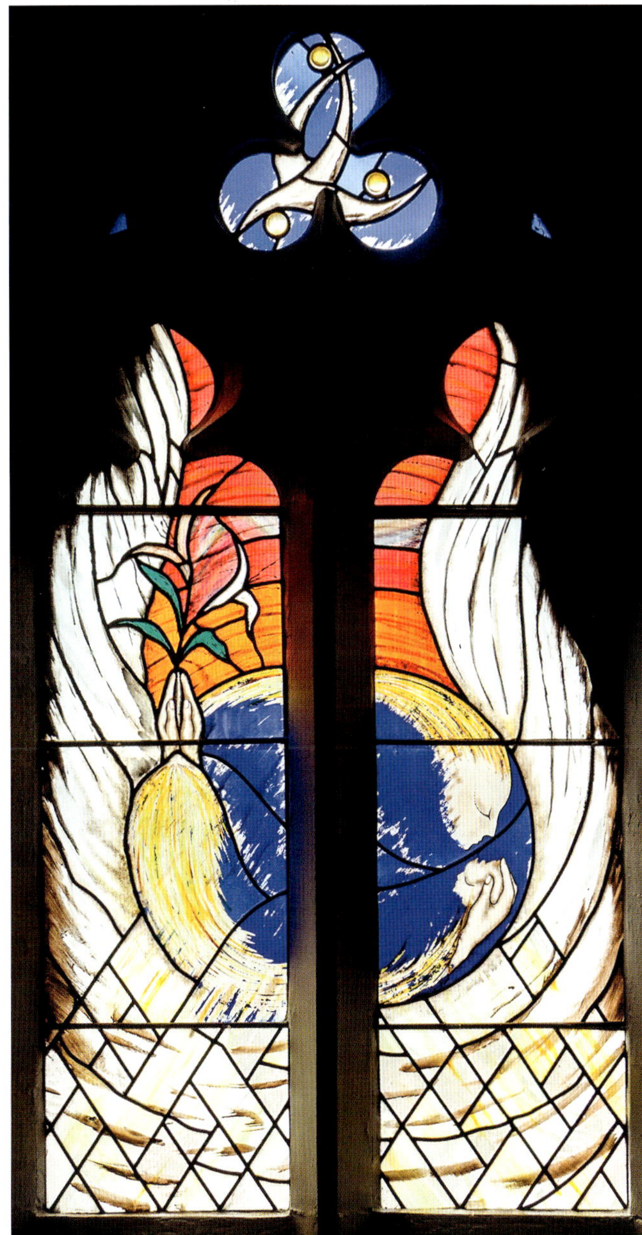

714. Catrin Jones, The Annunciation, 1983, Priory Church of St David, Swansea, north aisle

The Resurrection at Hendy is one of two early works by the artist in Wales, the other being a set of three windows made for the side chapel at the Church of St Nicholas, Townhill, Swansea. These more minimalist windows demonstrate the use of Schreiter's signature wandering lead line, without imagery or apparent symbolism. As with other windows inspired by German design, larger pieces of opalescent glass are used, often cut into rectilinear shapes, with a restricted palette.

Five former students worked together as a collective after completing their studies at the Institute. Glasslight Studios was established in 1982 by Catrin Jones, Lydia Marouf, Elizabeth Edmundson, Jaroslav Mykisa and Krysia Zienkiewicz with the help of the Welsh Arts Council and Swansea City Council. Although the styles of the artists were diverse, their work demonstrated a fresh approach to iconography. In Elizabeth Edmundson's large Annunciation scene, made for the Church of Our Lady of the Rosary, Ammanford, Gabriel points up at Mary, who also looks up at a roundel suggestive of the world with the dove of the Holy Spirit descending upon her. Catrin Jones' window of 1983 for the Priory Church of St David, Swansea, also has a circular effect and combines the Annunciation with a depiction of the Virgin and Child. Mary cradles the infant Christ enfolded by angelic wings that echo an earlier student piece made by the artist for Seion Newydd Welsh Baptist Chapel, Morriston, Swansea.[12]

12 The reality of finding work made it difficult to win the kind of creative commissions that the artists hoped for, and they undertook cutting and leading work for Goddard & Gibbs as well as repair work at the Priory Church of St David, Swansea, which resulted in two commissions for Catrin Jones. Interview with Catrin Jones, 26 May 2010.

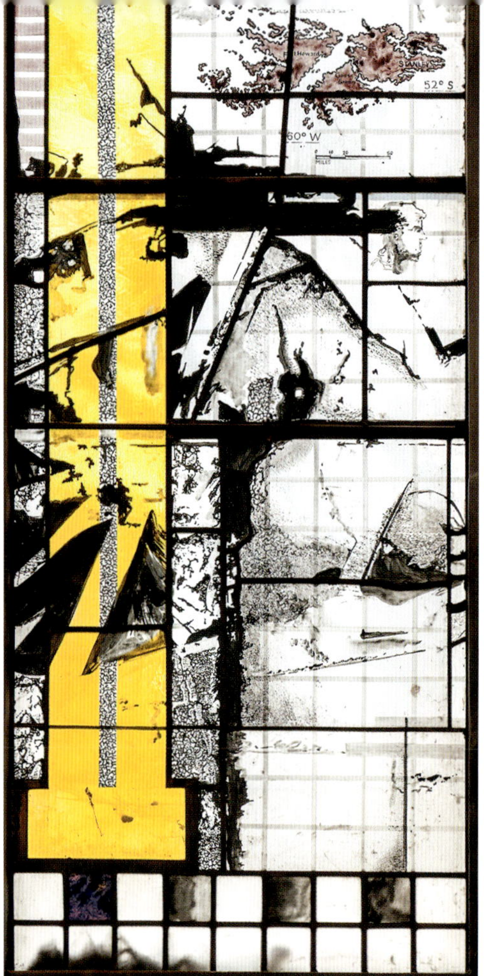

715. Rodney Bender, The Welsh Guards Falklands Memorial Window, made by Hein Derix of Kevelaer, Germany, 1995, Church of St Mary, Swansea, north aisle

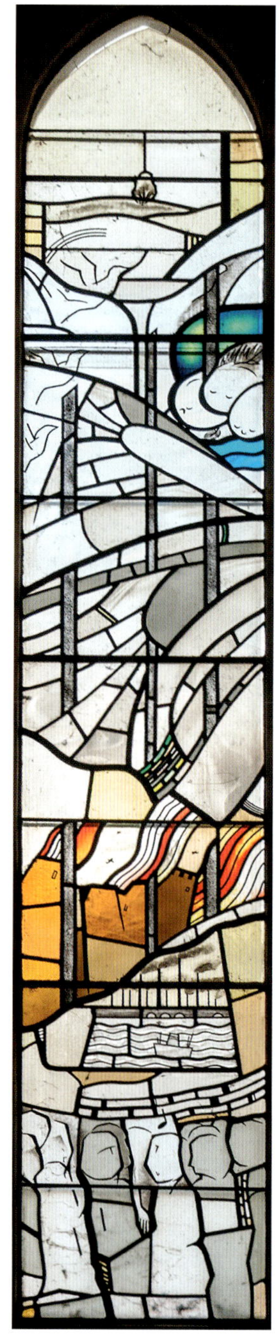

Catrin Jones also received a commission for an Anglican church at the Church of St Mary, Swansea, where Canon Donald Lewis looked for opportunities to add contemporary stained glass to the building. Her two windows of 1982 were made in commemoration of the wedding of Prince Charles and Lady Diana Spencer, and employ complex and mainly abstract symbolism relating to marriage and biblical texts. In the previous year a window by the Japanese artist Kuni Kajiwara commemorated the fortieth anniversary of the destruction of Swansea in the blitz of 1941, when much of the church was badly damaged. Both the destruction by enemy bombers and the rebuilding that followed is represented, overlaid with the wings of a butterfly, a symbol of rebirth.

A sparing use of colour also characterises the stark and uncompromising design by Rodney Bender commemorating the service of the Welsh Guards in the Falklands War. Thirty-two of the regiment died when the troopship *Sir Galahad* was attacked on 8 June 1982, but there is no hint of heroism, only the meticulous planning of military action suggested by the grid pattern underlying the design. Although a skilled maker who had worked on all four of the windows designed by the German artists for Coychurch Crematorium from 1979 to 1982, the artist experimented with having the window made for him by a studio under his supervision, which was common practice in Germany.[13]

The constraints of ecclesiastical commissions proved too frustrating for the creative aspirations for some artists. Catrin Jones was asked to make

13 Before enrolling on the course, Rodney Bender came from Australia to work for Celtic Studios in 1978, and gained valuable experience cutting and leading windows. After completing the course in Architectural Stained Glass, Rodney Bender was the first student to study for an MPhil in the department, researching the collaborations between designers and studios in Germany. Interview with Rodney Bender, 21 July 2011.

14 Andrew Moor's book *Contemporary Stained Glass*, published in 1989, drew attention to the potential of the medium for secular work, featuring work by Alex Beleschenko and Graham Jones, as well as Ludwig Schaffrath and Johannes Schreiter (London: Mitchell Beazley, 1989).

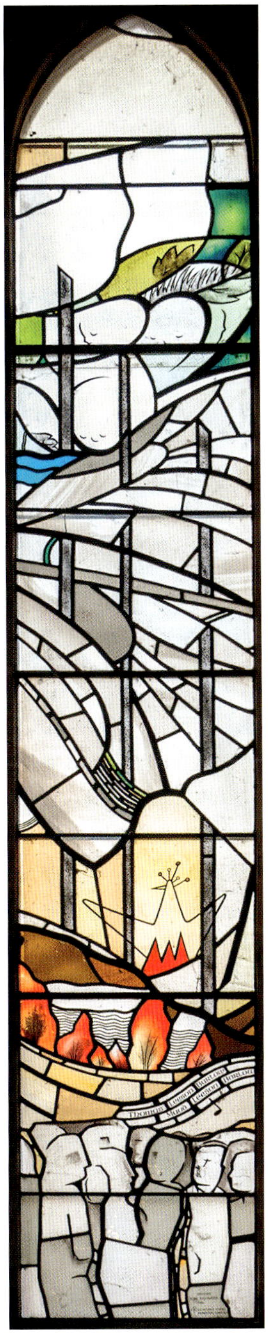

716. Kuni Kajiwara, North Aisle Windows, 1981, made at Glantawe Studios, Church of St Mary, Swansea

a more figurative design for her second window at the Priory Church of St David in Swansea, and after making an abstract-figurative window for the Roman Catholic cathedral in Swansea in 1988, she produced less work for places of worship, and none in Wales. Her reorientation towards other kinds of public spaces – theatres, libraries, schools and hospitals – was in part a recognition that churches were not a natural home for abstraction and innovation in technique.[14] Amber Hiscott's later work at the Shrine Chapel at the Church of Our Lady of the Taper, Cardigan, made in the 1990s, was deliberately more representational, and an acknowledgement that her earlier panels of the seven sacraments were beyond the grasp of many parishioners.[15]

Not all of the former students trained at Swansea in the 1970s and 80s produced primarily abstract work. Alexander Beleschenko was offered a commission for the east window of the Roman Catholic Church in Barry in 1980, employing a rectilinear background behind the conventional arrangement of Mary and John at either side of Christ on the cross.[16] A few years later, a contemporary at the Institute, Graham Pentelow, made a pair of windows for the United Reformed Chapel at Templeton, in which figures are set against a more organic grid of abstract background colour.

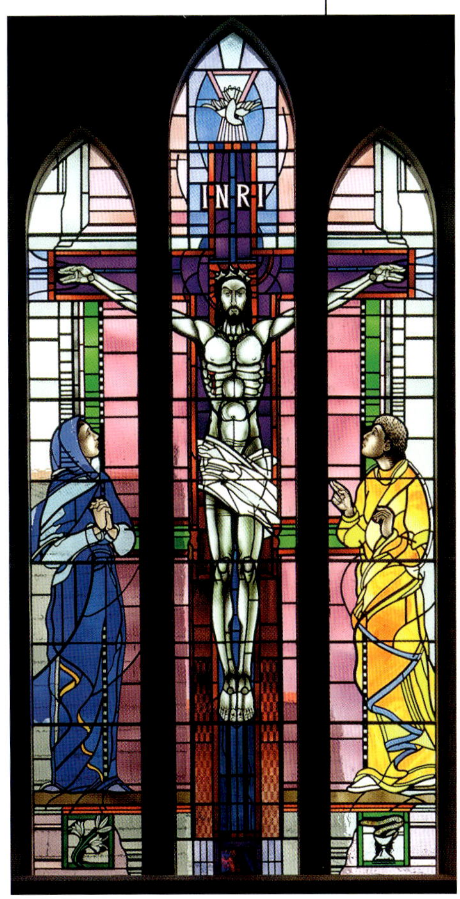

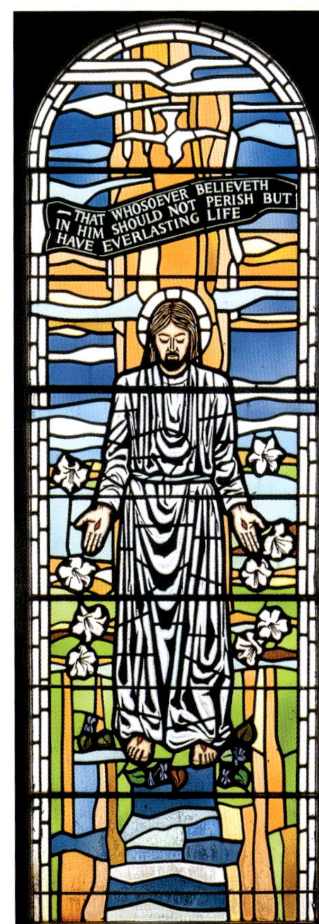

717. (right) Alexander Beleschenko, The Crucifixion with the Virgin Mary and St John, Church of St Helen, Barry

718. (far right) Graham Pentelow, The Risen Christ, 1983, United Reformed Chapel, Templeton, front wall

15 Interview with Amber Hiscott, 18 August 2008, parts of which were published as part of 'Speaking in Parables: Abstract Expression', in Martin Crampin and John Morgan-Guy, *Imaging the Bible in Wales* (DVD-ROM) (Sheffield: Sheffield Phoenix Press, 2010).

16 Alexander Beleschenko trained at several schools of art including the Slade School of Fine Art in London. He worked on cartoons at Celtic Studios while studying for a year at Swansea 1978–9, and then worked as a cartoonist at J. Wippell & Co. in Exeter, where the window for Barry was made. I am grateful to the artist for this information.

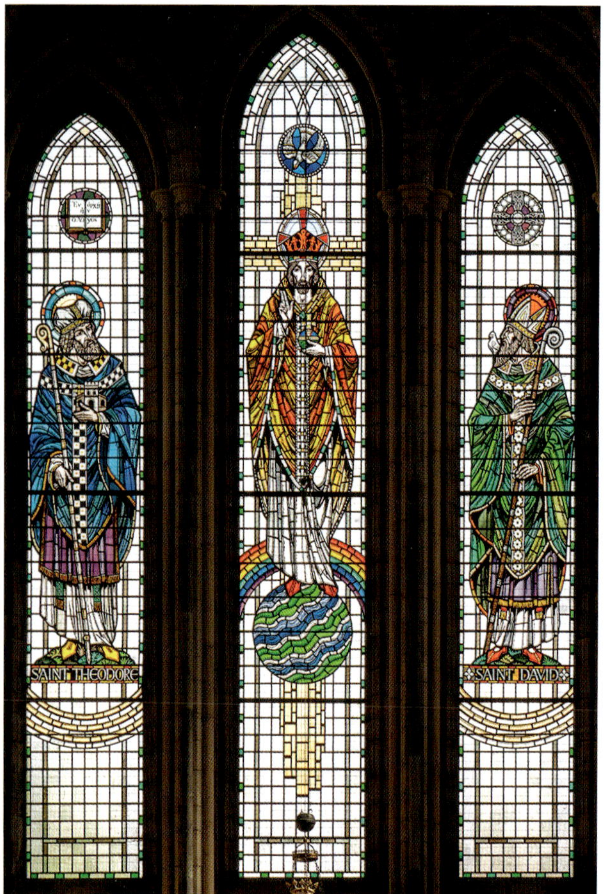

719. Glantawe Studios, Christ with St Theodore and St David, 1983, designed by Colwyn Morris, Church of St Theodore, Port Talbot, east window

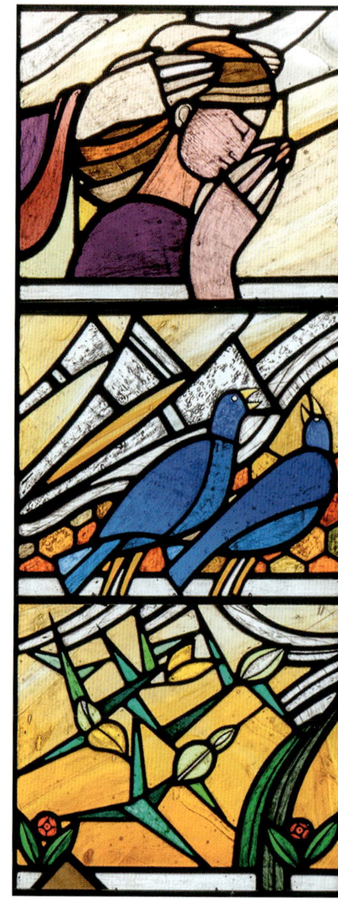

720. Glantawe Studios, Memorial Window, 1986, designed by Tim Lewis, Church of All Saints, Oystermouth, south aisle

Colwyn Morris had returned to Wales and taught at Swansea from 1980, and in 1983 he collaborated with Tim Lewis on the east window for the Church of St Theodore, Port Talbot. The size of the commission necessitated the move of Lewis' Glantawe Studios from his home to new premises in Morriston, and this major work was the first in a series of collaborations between the two artists that would continue for nearly thirty years. Windows designed by Lewis and made at the studio in the 1980s and 90s for churches at Oystermouth, Llansamlet and Hendy all broke away from familiar religious subject matter, reflecting the personal interests of donors or those that the windows commemorated. His second window at Oystermouth, given in memory of the donor's wife, who was a nurse, expresses 'the role of those everyday features that are often taken for granted, namely our senses and the caring love, devotion and companionship of our spouses.'[17] The hands in the upper part of the window are also a feature of other contemporary windows designed by Lewis. At Llansamlet, hands represent touch and the laying on of hands for healing, while another window made for Oystermouth in 1989 is an unusual representation of the Last Supper, viewed from above the table and showing hands making gestures and holding cups.[18]

Some students developed fine glass painting skills, and Caroley Bergman-Birdsall made a largely abstract window for the Church of St Ceinwr, Llangynnwr. Ostensibly on the theme of 'fishers of men', the accent is very much on the beautifully painted fish rather than the biblical context in Matthew and Mark's gospels. Elizabeth Edmundson was capable of working in a range of styles and techniques, collaborating with Peter Lord on sandblasted, etched and enamelled windows,

17 The donor was an ear, nose and throat consultant, and the window therefore reflected his own interest in the senses. Geoffrey R. Orrin, 'Architectural Description of the Church', in Geoffrey R. Orrin and F.G. Cowley, *A History of All Saints' Church Oystermouth* (Llandysul: Gomer, 1990), p. 87.

18 A fourth window designed by Tim Lewis for the Church of All Saints, Oystermouth, in 1990 illustrates aspects of the poem 'Fern Hill' by Dylan Thomas.

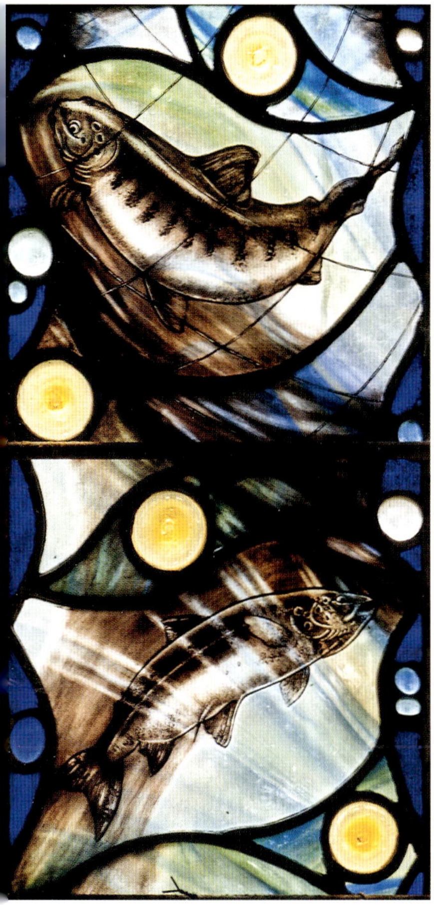

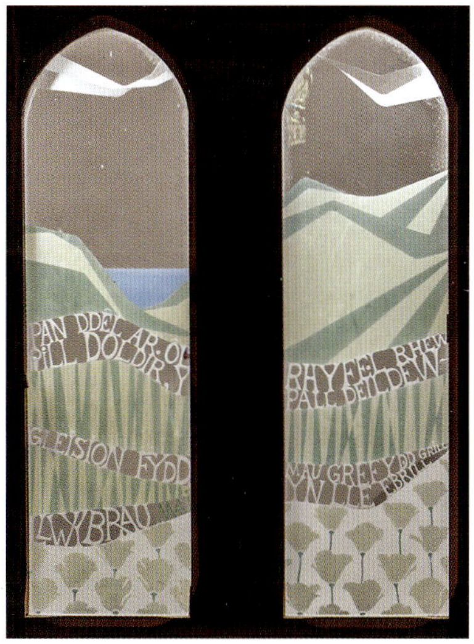

721. (left) Caroley Bergman-Birdsall, 'Fishers of Men', 1993, Church of St Ceinwr, Llangynnwr, south aisle

722. (above) Peter Lord, Four Seasons Windows, 1988, made by Elizabeth Edmundson, Church of St Padarn, Llanbadarn Fawr (Ceredigion), south transept exhibition

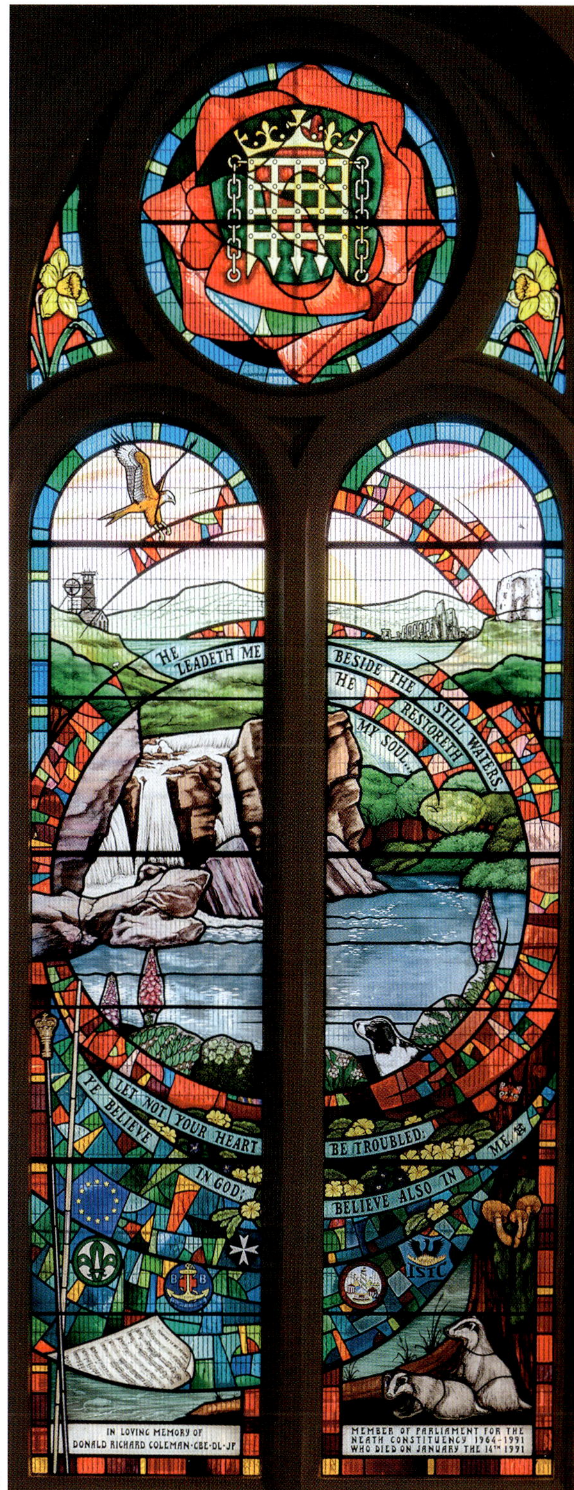

723. Elizabeth Edmundson, Memorial Window, 1992, Church of St Thomas, Neath, north aisle

with poetry by Dafydd ap Gwilym for the south transept exhibition area of the Church of St Padarn, Llanbadarn Fawr (Ceredigion). A window to her own design was also added in the south transept and she made a pair of two-light windows for the Church of St Thomas, Neath, in 1992 and 1994. The first memorial at Neath commemorates Donald Richard Coleman, with local scenes and numerous badges and emblems connected with his life and interests. Among the badges is that of the Showmen's Guild of Great Britain, as he was the only honorary member in Britain. Her second window at the church was commissioned to mark the centenary of the Showmen's Guild, who held their centenary celebrations at the church in 1989, and four roundels depict Christopher (as patron saint of travellers), Julian the Hospitaller (as patron saint of innkeepers and entertainers), a roundabout horse and a scene depicting a fair outside the church in about 1890.

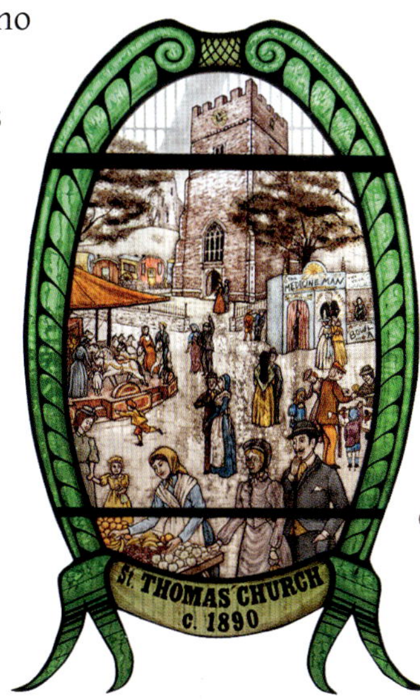

724. Elizabeth Edmundson, Neath Fair, from the Showmen's Window, 1994, Church of St Thomas, Neath, north aisle

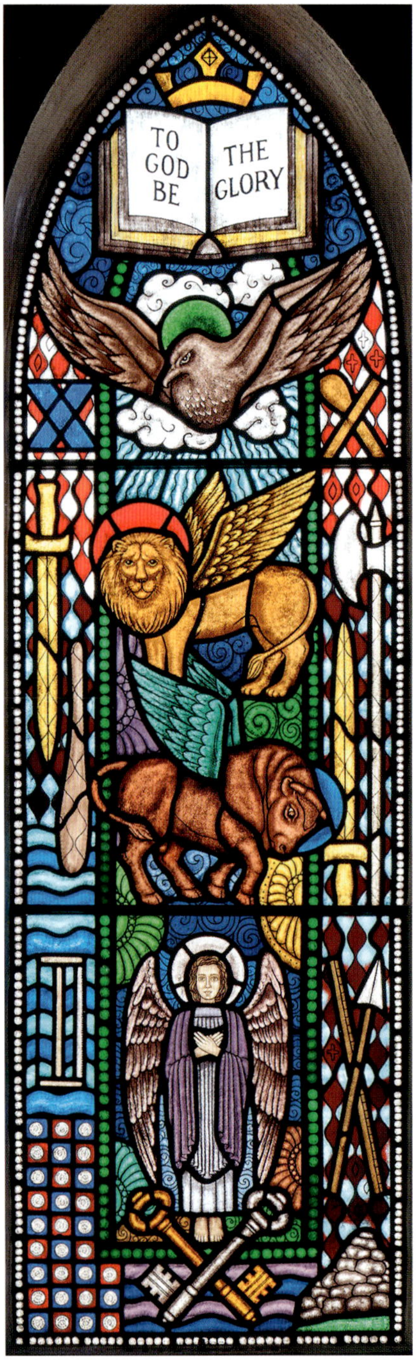

725. Janet Hardy, Symbols of the Four Evangelists, 1994, Church of St Anne, Cross Hands, nave

Janet Hardy trained at Swansea from 1976–9, but was unmoved by German abstraction, and after a period while her children were young, she made her first major window for the Presbyterian Church in Llanelli, where her parents were among the congregation. The four-light window with a view of Llanelli from the Gower was the first of numerous commissions in south and west Wales during the 1990s. A window depicting the patron saint was made for the Church of St Anne, Cross Hands, in 1989 and her second window for the church of 1994 is a more inventive composition in which the symbols of the evangelists are bordered by symbols of the twelve apostles. In the same year she was working on a large four-light west window at the Church of St Twrog, Llanddarog, in which local scenes and Christian symbols are set on a blue chequered background. Two large windows at Cenarth Calvinistic Methodist Chapel also intermingle religious imagery with local themes. Scenes from the gospels connected with water, such as the Baptism of Christ and scenes with fishermen, are included as six panels on a background depicting the river that runs through the village, with buildings (including the chapel) and wildlife.[19]

19 The windows were funded by the Welsh Development Agency, the Prince's Trust and the Welsh Tourist Board, and although the colours can only be appreciated from within the chapel, etched glass was used to make them partially visible from outside.

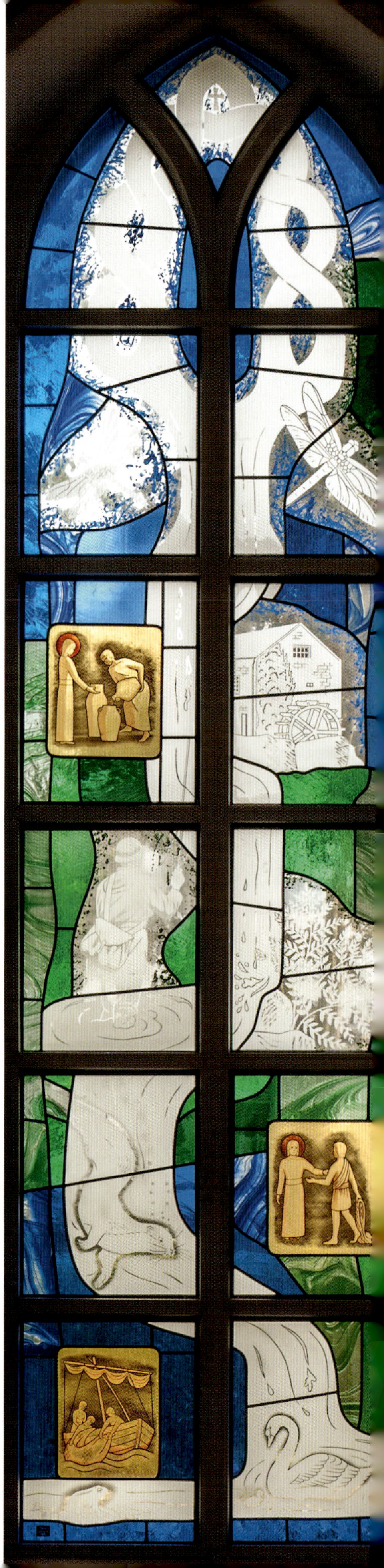

726. Janet Hardy, Window for Cenarth Calvinistic Methodist Chapel, 1997

727. (right) Pandora Hughes, View of the Bay near Manorbier, 1995, Church of St James, Manorbier, west wall

728. (far right) C.G. Toft, Christ as the Sower, 1993, designed by Roy Coomber, Church of St Elidyr, Amroth, west window

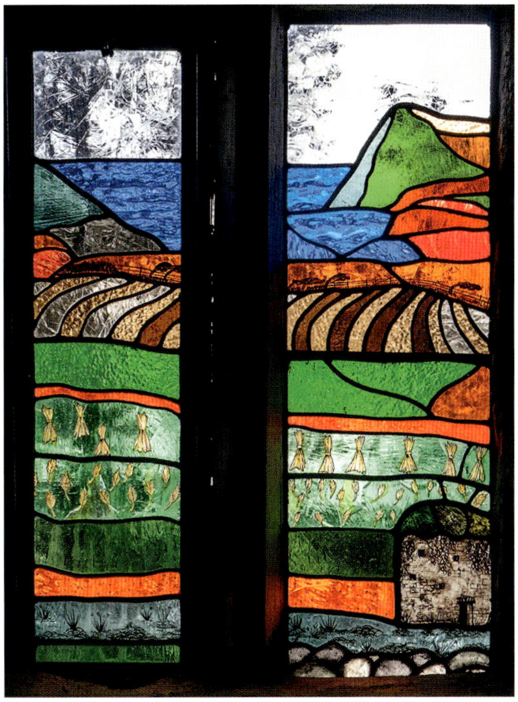

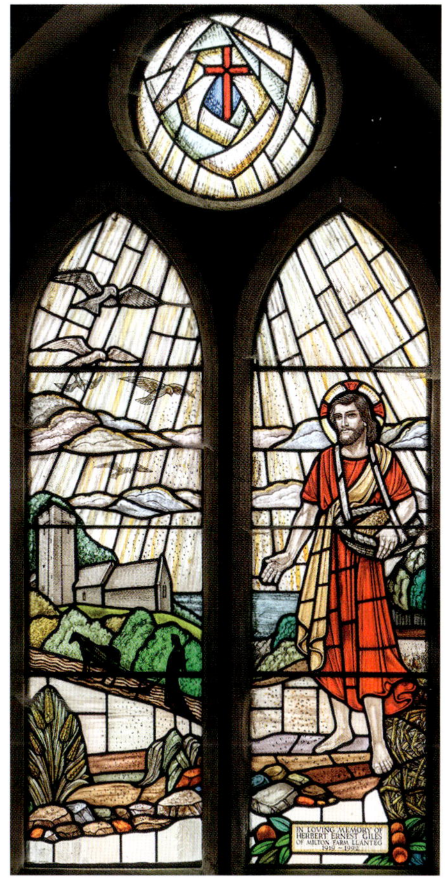

As well as the new students emerging from Swansea Institute in the 1980s, a variety of other local makers based in or near Wales made windows for Welsh churches. In Pembrokeshire a group of three vibrant windows by Pandora Hughes can be found at the Church of St James, Manorbier, all of which reflect the local landscape. John Petts moved from Llansteffan to Abergavenny in the late 1980s and while a cluster of works from that time can be found in the surrounding area, he received numerous commissions from across the southern half of Wales until his death in 1991.[20]

Roy Coomber had designed for J. Wippell & Co in Exeter before establishing his studio in Bristol in 1985. He designed a set of windows made in 1986–9 by Solaglas, also based in Bristol, for the Church of St Illtyd, Llantwit Fardre, while his west window for the Church of St Elidyr, Amroth, was made by C.G. Toft of Swansea in 1993. Geoffrey Robinson continued to make windows for churches in south-east Wales into the 1990s, and also made a pair of windows as far west as Herbrandston in Pembrokeshire in 1992. Michael Lasson worked as his assistant, and also for other artists including Tom Denny, as well as making windows to his own design at his studio at Worship Farm, Lulsgate, near Bristol. His windows in Wales can be found at the Church of St Martin, Caerphilly, the Church of St Lawrence, Marros, the Church of St Dyfan and St Teilo, Merthyr Dyfan, and the Church of St David, Penllergaer, where the west window symbolises resurrection with the tree of life at the centre and a vision of the entry into heaven through an archway of palms.

20 A list of his works is included in Alison Smith, 'John Petts: Designer-Craftsman 1914–1991', *The Journal of Stained Glass*, vol. xix, no. 2 (1991–93), pp. 225–9.

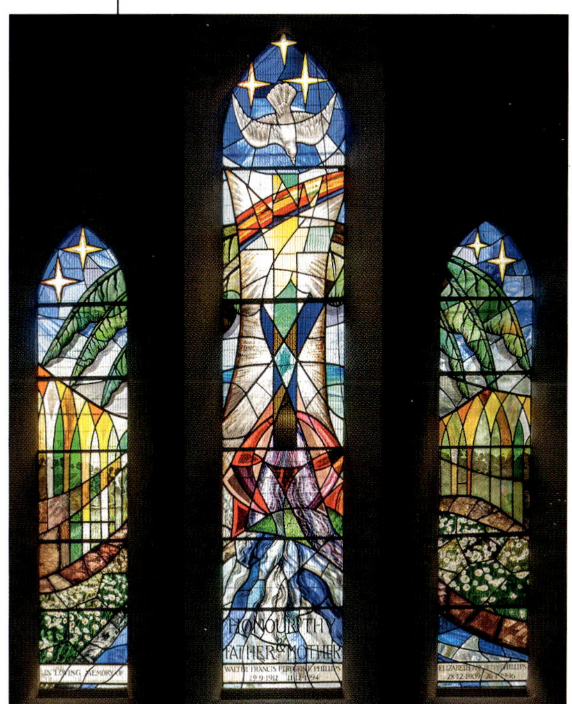

729. Michael G. Lasson, West Window, 1996, Church of St David, Penllergaer

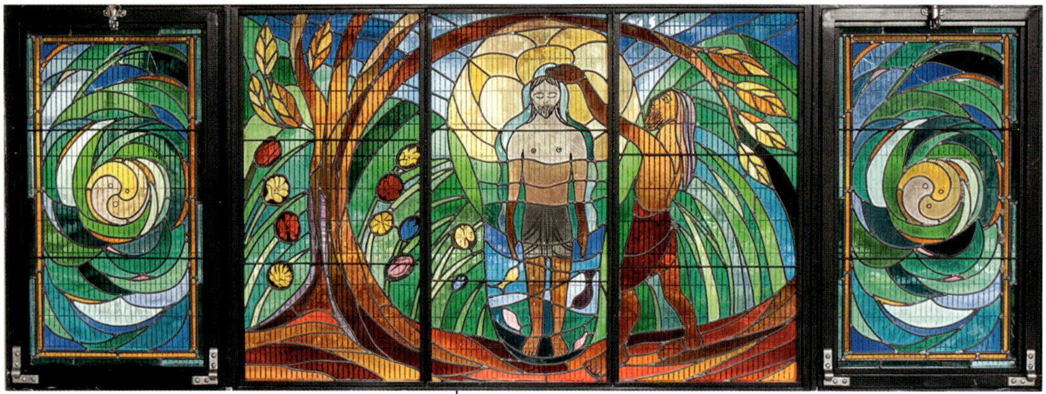

730. (above) Caroline Mackenzie, The Baptism of Christ, 1994, made by Jim Budd, Church of St Anne, Malpas, nave

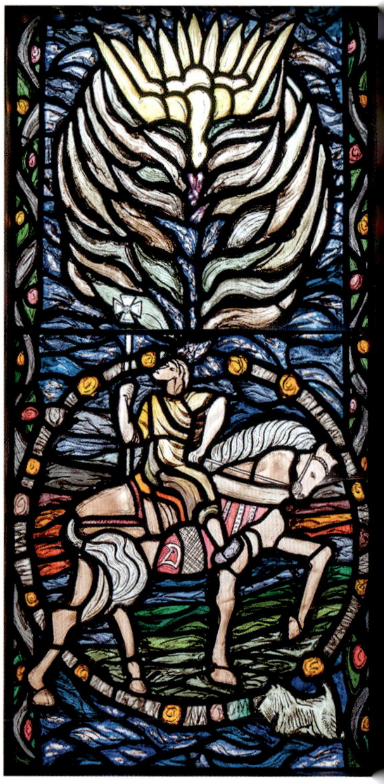

731. (right) Charles Broome, St Andrew, 1990, Church of St Andrew, Norton, nave

At the Church of St Andrew, Norton, the artist Charles Broome of nearby Hereford made a small window of Andrew riding on horseback in 1990.[21] Jim Budd, based near the English border at Gladestry, made a window a little further south at the Church of St Peter, Glasbury, in 1997, where the figure of the local saint Cynidr is enveloped in a swirling pattern of flowers. In 1994 Budd collaborated with the artist Caroline Mackenzie on three windows for the Catholic Church of St Anne, Malpas. These original compositions using bright colours draw on the Hindu influences on her work, also apparent in the sculptures that she carved for another Roman Catholic church, the Church of St Helen, Caerphilly. Further north, the artist Jane Gray, based in Shrawardine near the Welsh border in Shrophire, made the window given in memory of servicemen from the parish for the Church of St Mary, Chirk, in 1994.[22] Her abstract spinning pattern radiates around a cross, with a leek, rose, thistle and shamrock in roundels symbolising the four countries of the British Isles.

In about 1975 Linden Studios was established by Dennis and Linda Robinson, initially based at Ruthin Craft Centre and moving to Cilcain and then Halkyn. A number

21 I am grateful to Melia Cope for the attribution of this window.

22 Jane Gray had worked on Lawrence Lee's windows for Coventry Cathedral at the Royal College of Art in the 1950s and subsequently enjoyed a prolific career making stained glass.

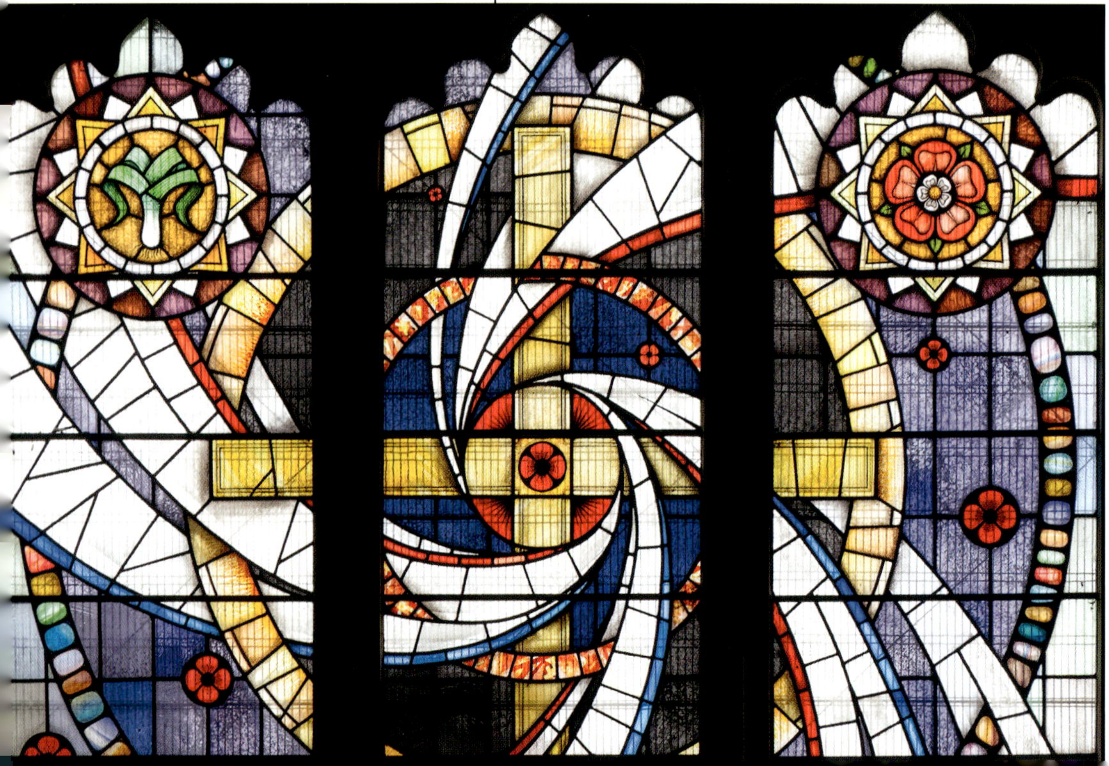

732. Jane Gray, Memorial Window, 1994, Church of St Mary, Chirk, north nave

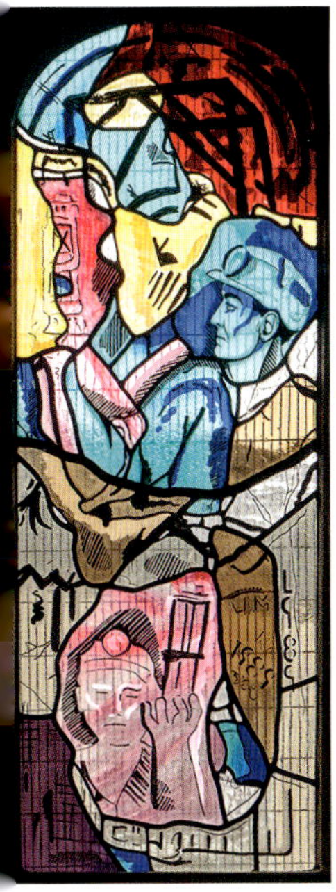

733. Ian Jones, Miners' Window, 1989, Church of St Martin, Llay, north aisle

of windows for churches in north-east Wales were designed and made under Dennis Robinson's direction in the 1980s, including the east window at the Church of St Michael and All Angels, Efenechtyd, an image of Paul at the Church of St Collen, Llangollen, and the Virgin and Child at the Church of St Mary, Treuddyn. Some employees of the studio were former students from the new course in Architectural Glass established by Melvyn Harries at Wrexham College of Art in 1984. Teaching was also provided by artists who had been trained in Swansea, including Chris Bird-Jones and Lydia Marouf.[23] Students from the course provided an abstract window as a memorial to the Catholic martyr Richard Gwyn for Wrexham Cathedral in about 1990, as well as a window for the Church of St Martin, Llay, commemorating the mining industry of the area.

Dennis Robinson changed the name of his studio to L.G.S. Tectonics in an attempt to move into glass import and resale, while still making and restoring stained glass. In the early 1990s Barry Brady was employed as the studio manager and together with Phillip Gough he designed and made a set of windows for the Methodist Church of St John in Llandudno, installed from 1991–2.[24] This substantial commission of three large pictorial windows and plainer nave lights included large scenes in the transept windows depicting the risen Christ by the shore with his disciples and John Wesley preaching in a town square. The more abstract three-light east window shows rays of light emanating from a cross with a flying eagle and dove. Two windows by the firm can also be found at Gorsedd, and a third window of 1996 was designed and made at the studio, which by this time had been bought by Chester Masonry and renamed Linley Glass Studio.[25]

23 Chris Bird-Jones was from Llangollen, and made numerous works for schools, hospitals and other public spaces in the region. She helped to set up the course but left in 1985 to study at the Royal College of Art in London. In 1992 she returned to run the course for a further five years.

24 Both Barry Brady and Phillip Gough were among the first students to study under Melvyn Harries at Wrexham.

25 Chester Masonry moved the studio to Hawarden in 1994, and Dennis Robinson died suddenly shortly afterwards. I am grateful to Geoff and Jamie Moore for information on Linden/Linley Studios. Barry Brady established his own studio as Meridian Stained Glass at St Asaph.

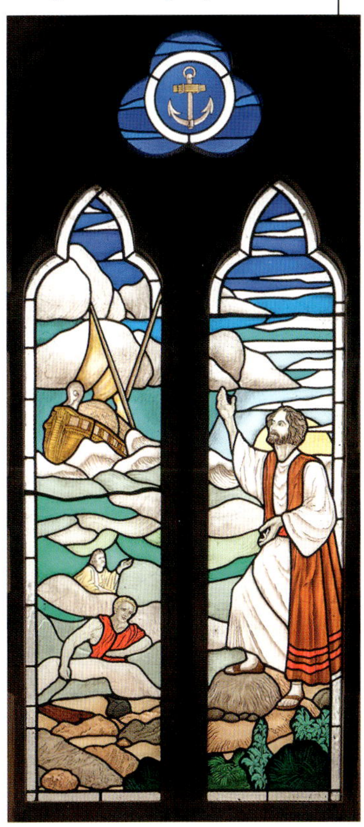

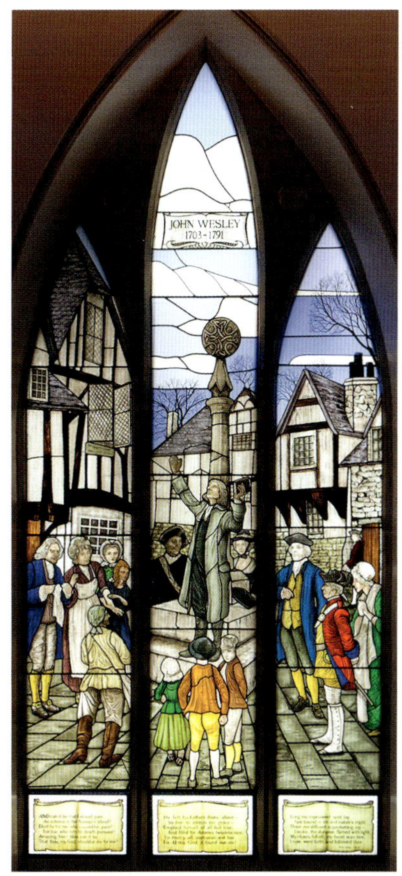

734. (right) L.G.S. Techtonics, Paul Shipwrecked, 1993, Church of St Paul, Gorsedd, nave

735. (far right) L.G.S. Techtonics, John Wesley Preaching, 1991, Church of St John, Llandudno, north transept

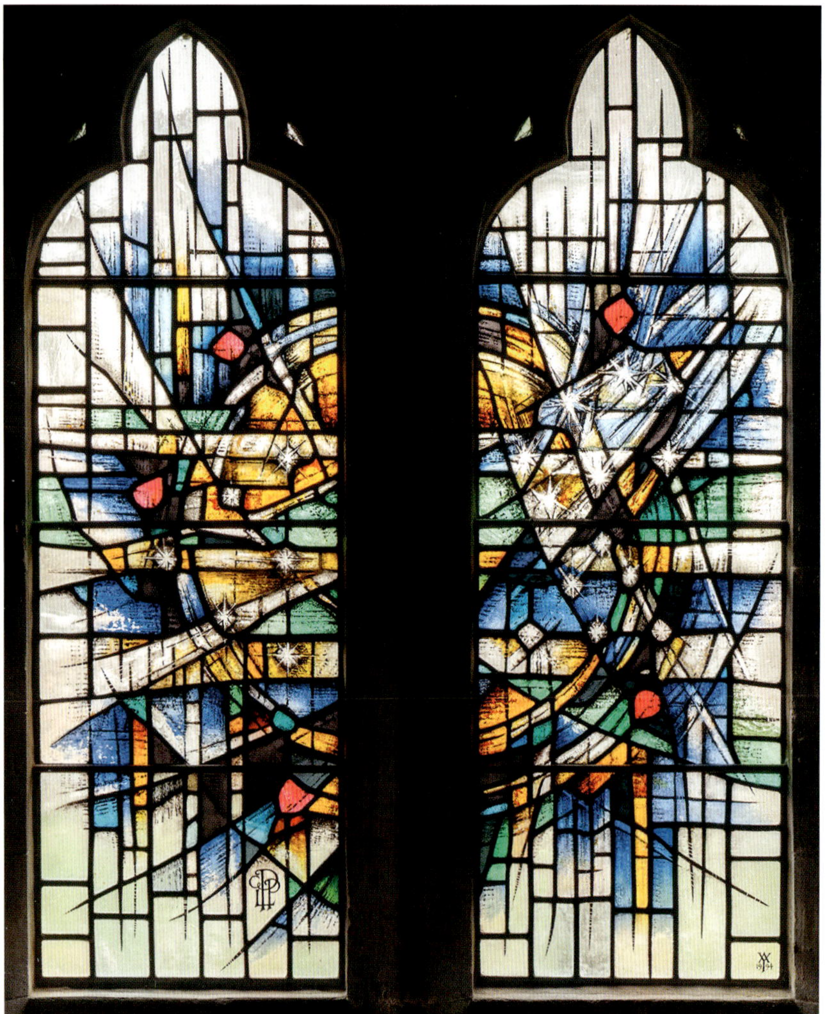

736. Alan Younger, Nave Window, 1994, Church of St Arvan, St Arvans, north aisle

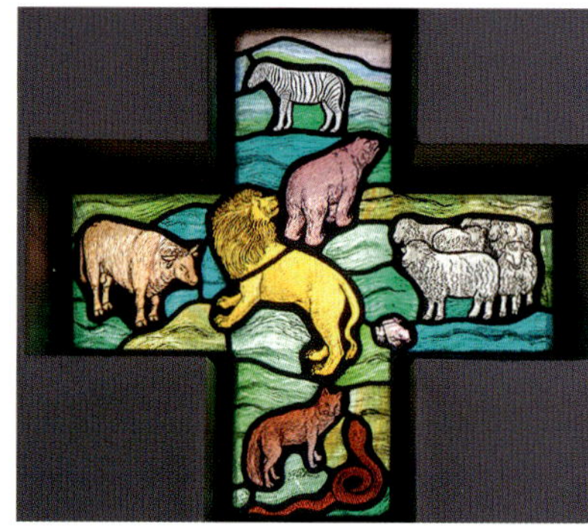

737. Paul Quail, The Creation of the Animals, *c.* 1984, Church of the Blessed Sacrament, Gorseinon, south-west wall

While the 1980s and 90s were characterised by the emergence of a variety of makers trained and based in Wales, churches continued to commission artists and studios outside of Wales to make windows for Welsh churches. Sometimes artists were called upon because of their personal connections with clergy or donors. After four sets of windows were made by John Petts for the Church of the Blessed Sacrament, Gorseinon, the new parish priest commissioned Paul Quail, an artist that he had met through the Claretian Missionaries at Buckden in Cambridgeshire, to make two further sets of cruciform windows based on the days of Creation and scenes from the Book of Exodus.

Alan Younger made a window for the Church of St Mary, Whitchurch, Cardiff, in 1980, as well as three windows before and after this date at the Church of St Basil, Bassaleg. Jeremy Winston was a curate at Bassaleg from 1979, and became vicar at St Arvans from 1983 before moving to Abergavenny in 1993. It seems likely that he was instrumental in approaching Younger, having been aware of the windows in Bassaleg, and the artist made two windows at St Arvans in the 1990s.

At the Church of St Peter, Goetre, Patrick Reyntiens was commissioned to make two pairs of windows for the north and south walls of the chancel, which were installed in 1991 and 1996. The donor of the windows was Peter, Baron Rees of Goytre, who had met the artist when they had served together in the Scots Guards. The windows in the sanctuary depict the saints Joseph and John the Baptist, while the two

26 Although Lord Rees, a former Chief Secretary to the Treasury, died in 2008, his name is yet to be added.

27 Anxious not to be giving work unfairly to a family friend, the vicar, Hugh James, also invited designs from other artists. Susan James and her father, Wynn Garbett Alexander, appear among the many faces in Loire's Prisoners of Conscience window at Salisbury Cathedral. I am grateful for Hugh James for information regarding the commissioning of the window.

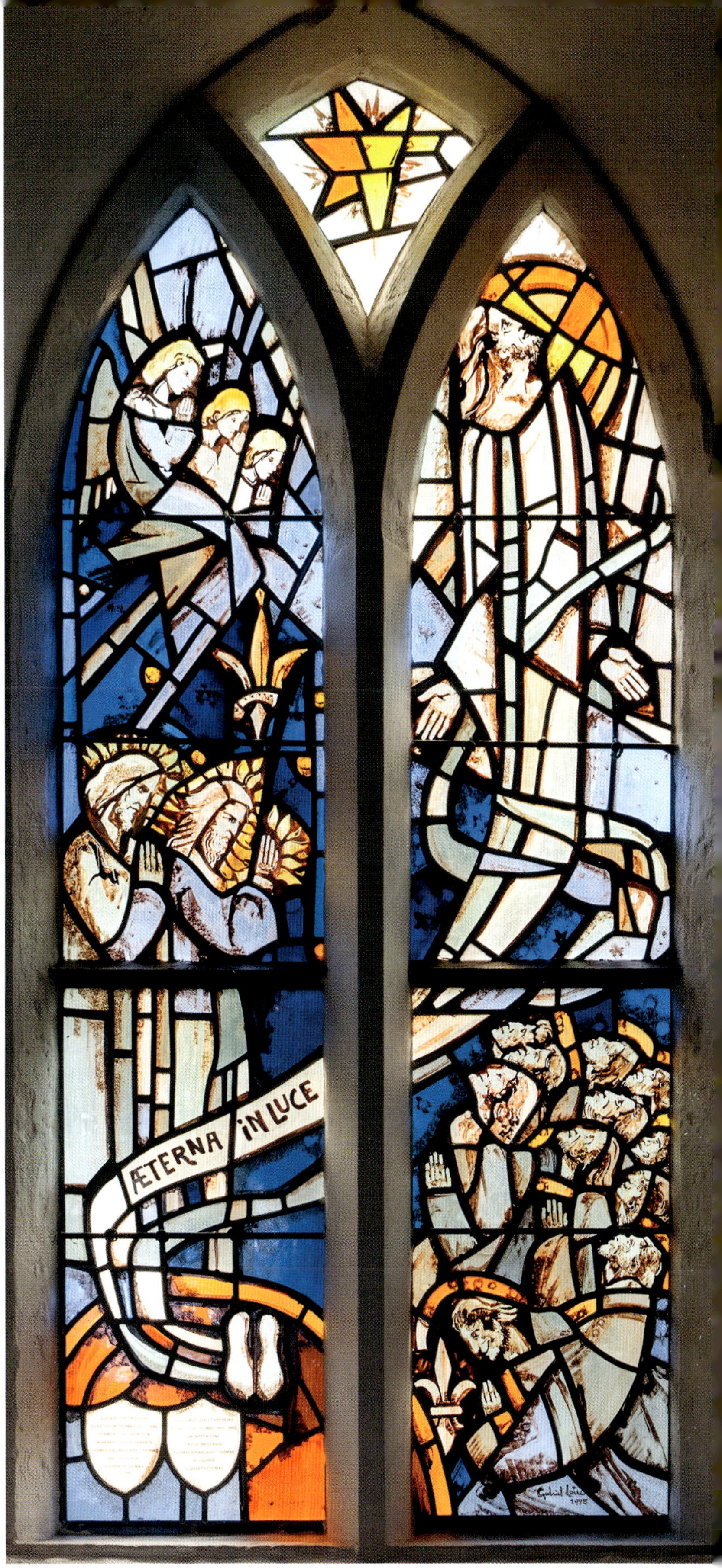

739. Gabriel Loire, The Ascension, 1995, Church of St Michael, Llanfihangel-ar-arth, south aisle

later windows with the saints Caradog and Catherine of Siena have spaces left beneath the figures for the future insertion of inscriptions in memory of the donor and his wife Anthea.[26] Wales is also fortunate to be the home of a late work by Gabriel Loire at the Church of St Michael, Llanfihangel-ar-arth. The artist was approached as he was a friend of the vicar's wife, whose father was an architect and had worked with Loire when he was designing a palace in Saudi Arabia in the late 1970s and early 1980s.[27]

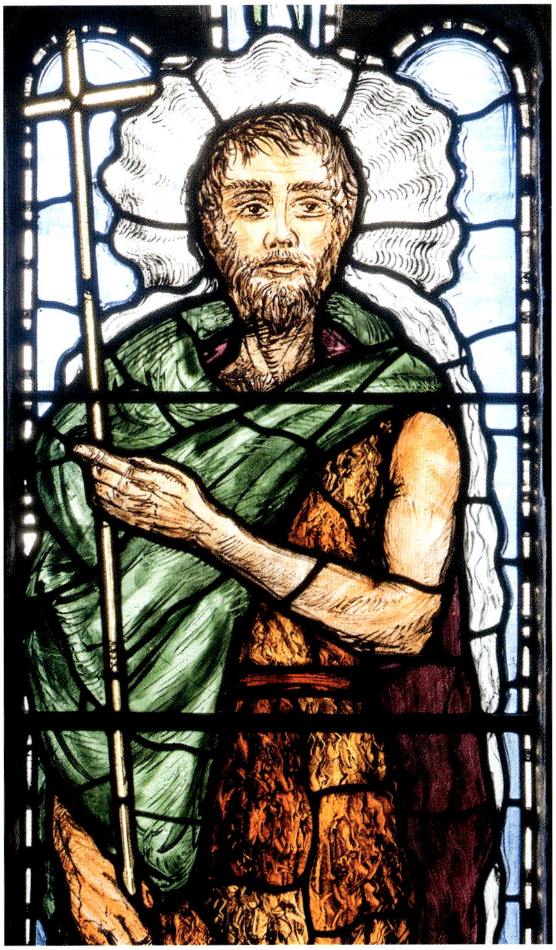

738. Patrick Reyntiens, St John the Baptist, 1992, Church of St Peter, Goetre, sanctuary

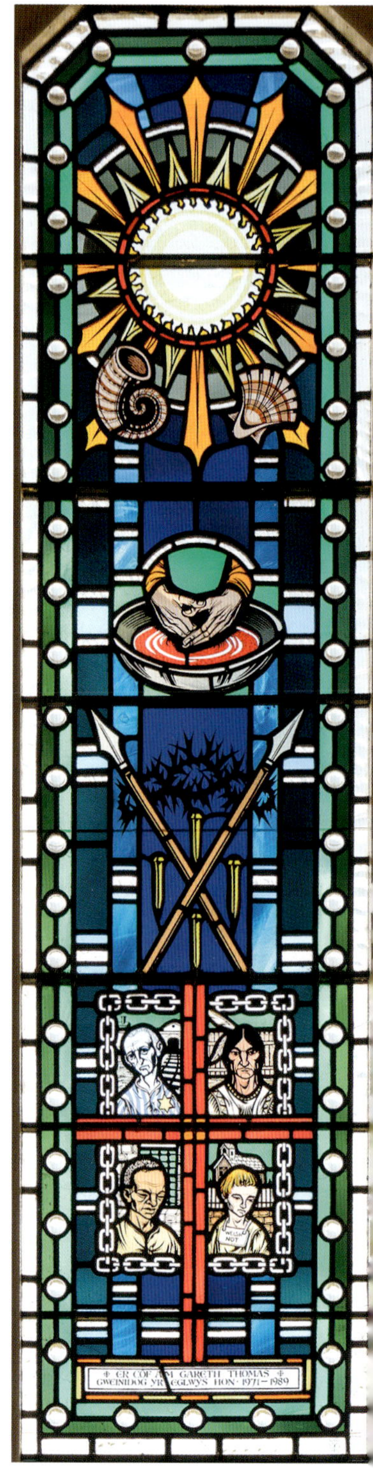

741. Glantawe Studios, Injustice Window, 1991 designed by Colwyn Morris, Capel y Nant, Clydach, stairs (formerly at Hebron Welsh Independent Chapel, Clydach)

Many further windows were made at Glantawe Studios in Morriston during the 1990s for a wide range of churches. Some were designed by Tim Lewis, such as the set of roundels made in 1992 for the Church of St Luke, Cwmdare, although many more were designed by Colwyn Morris, such as those nearby at the Church of St Fagan, Aberdare, the large three-light south transept window for the Church of St David, Neath, in 1993, as well as other Anglican churches in the area around Swansea and Gower. Work for Roman Catholic churches includes the three narthex windows at the Church of St Benedict, Clydach, and a series of windows for the Church of St Joseph, Neath, begun in the 1980s and mostly designed and cartooned by Colwyn Morris. Many of these windows were iconographically traditional and continued the strong modelling of the features and drapery in black glass paint that typified his work for Powell & Sons before the studio closed in 1973.

A more unusual window designed by Morris was made for Hebron Welsh Independent Chapel, Clydach, taking the theme of the Christian's stand against injustice. Below the instruments of the Passion, four symbols of injustice – the persecution of the Jews by Nazi Germany, the treatment of Native American Indians, the apartheid system of South Africa, and the 'Welsh Not' – were depicted around a cross that breaks the surrounding chains.[28]

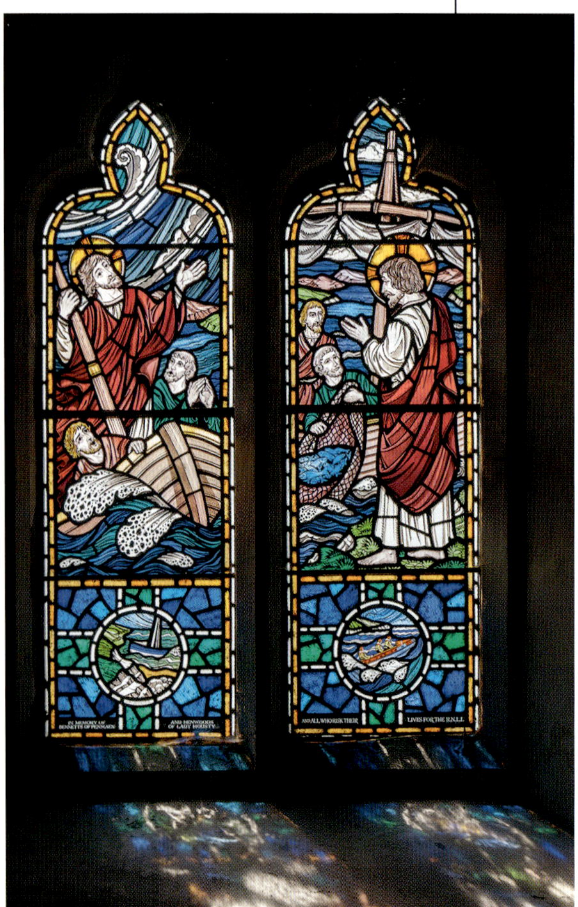

740. Glantawe Studios, Christ Stilling the Storm and Walking on the Water, 1995, designed by Colwyn Morris, Church of St Cattwg, Port Eynon, nave

28 The window has recently been relocated to Capel y Nant, also in Clydach, after the chapel closed. The 'Welsh Not' was used in schools in the nineteenth century to discourage children from speaking Welsh at school. Tim Lewis and Colwyn Morris were both native Welsh speakers.

29 Interview with John Edwards, 21 April 2011.

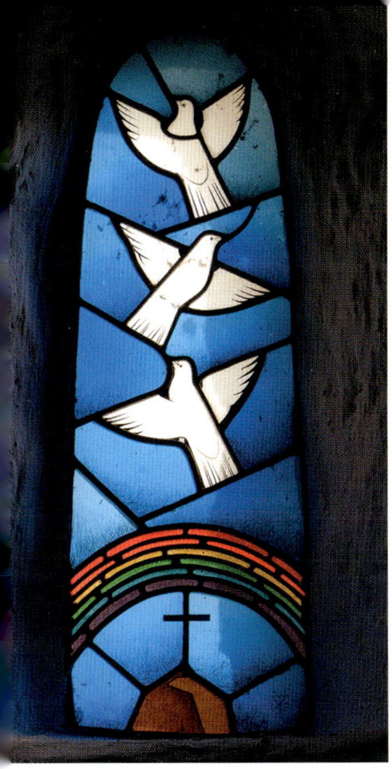

742. Glantawe Studios, Doves and Rainbow, 1995, designed by John Edwards, Church of St Teilo, Bishopston, vestry

John Edwards had sometimes been given a degree of artistic freedom when working for Celtic Studios, and was asked to design windows by Hubert Thomas 'when they wanted something a bit different'.[29] He was also called upon for less traditional commissions by Tim Lewis, with whom he had collaborated on windows for the Church of St Teilo, Bishopston. Edwards made three windows for the church independently, the first in 1969, but after 1988 his windows for the church were made with Tim Lewis and assistants at Glantawe Studios, including the simplest of all the designs, the window with doves and a rainbow, situated in the vestry. This window was made with the assistance of Deborah Lowe, one of several students who gained experience working at Glantawe Studios painting and cutting glass, as well as leading up windows; other students included Ellen and Jane Kharade, Sachiko Yamamoto and Anna Bessant. Several windows designed by Colwyn Morris were painted by Deborah Lowe in the mid-1990s, who had taught her on the Architectural Stained Glass course at Swansea, including those at the Church of St Cattwg, Port Eynon, and the north chancel windows at the Church of St Mary, Swansea.[30]

In 1999 John Edwards designed a window that was made at Glantawe Studios for the children's corner of the Church of St Mary, Swansea. The design is based on stories connected with Nicholas, and the blue glass of the window corresponds with an earlier window, on the corresponding south side of the church, made by Lisa Burkl to commemorate the Mannheim Helicopter Disaster of 1982, which claimed the lives of nine members of the Swansea Skydiving Club. Her imaginative response draws on Jacob's vision of angels ascending and descending a ladder between earth and heaven drawn from Genesis 28: 12, and is unusual in its use of gilded angels that can be seen most clearly from outside the church.[31]

30 Deborah Lowe studied at West Glamorgan Institute between 1991–4 and won the Howard Martin Design Award. Anna Bessant, who was also a student in the department, worked with her on the transept window at Port Eynon in 1996, and both artists subsequently worked independently soon afterwards. The sisters Ellen and Jane Kharade went on to design for other crafts.

31 Lisa Burkl studied at the Institute between 1987 and 1990 and went to work at another local studio, that of Alex Beleschenko, who also taught at the Institute. She joined the teaching staff at the Institute in 1994.

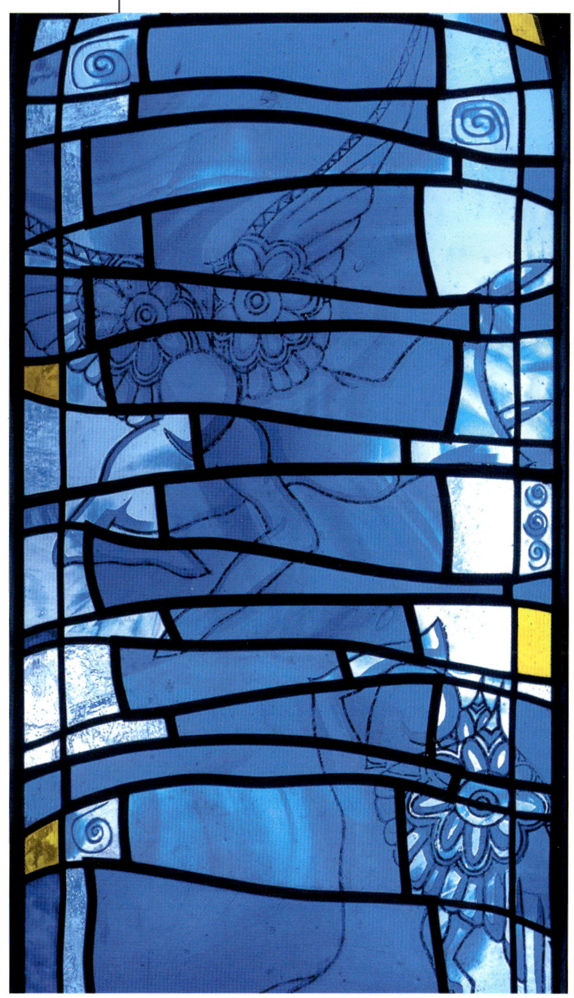

743. Lisa Burkl, Angel from Jacob's Ladder, 1993, Church of St Mary, Swansea, south aisle

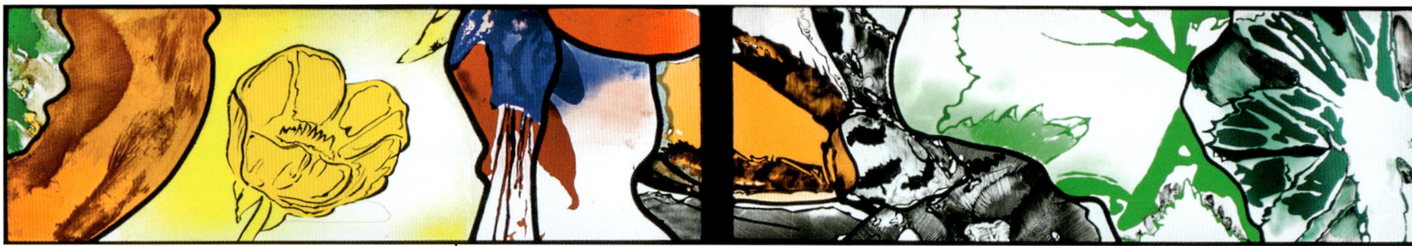

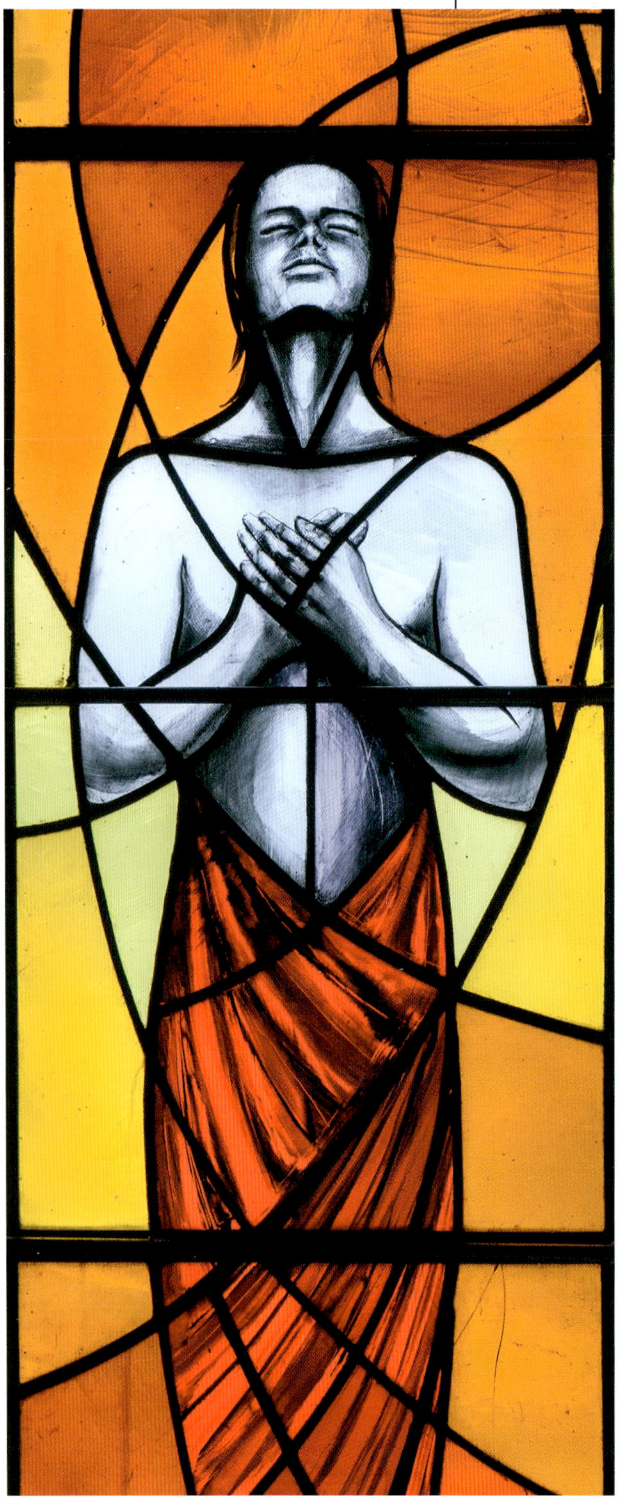

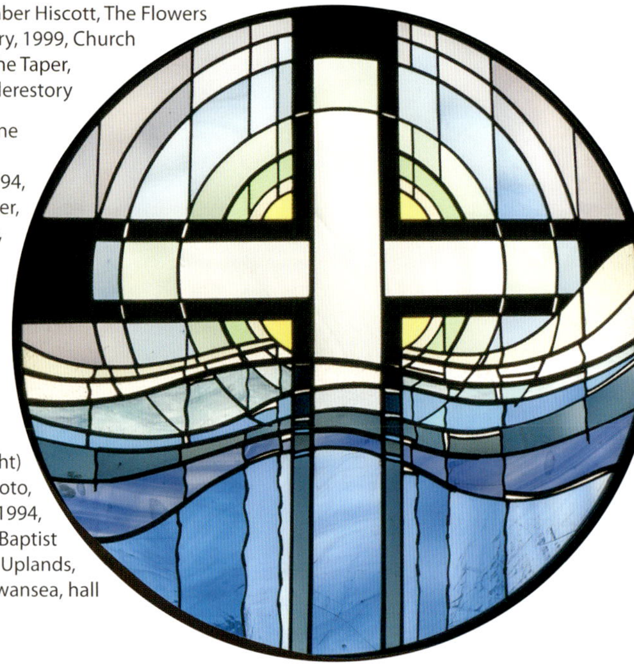

744. (above) Amber Hiscott, The Flowers of the Virgin Mary, 1999, Church of Our Lady of the Taper, Cardigan, side clerestory

745. (left) Caroline Loveys, Christ Ascending, *c.* 1994, Church of St Peter, Little Newcastle, nave

746. (right) Sachiko Yamamoto, Roundel, *c.* 1994, Panygwydr Baptist Church, Uplands, Swansea, hall

Other former students gained commissions for churches in the 1990s. Amber Hiscott made two further sets of windows for the Church of Our Lady of the Taper in Cardigan, and also made two abstract works for the new Roman Catholic Church of All Hallows at Miskin, which opened in 1996. Melanie Howse completed her course in 1992, and in the following year made a pair of tall slender windows for the Roman Catholic Church of St Illtyd, Danygraig, Swansea, the second of four commissions all given to former students at the Institute between 1990 and 2003.[32] Further away in Pembrokeshire, a number of donors from the Church of St Peter, Little Newcastle,

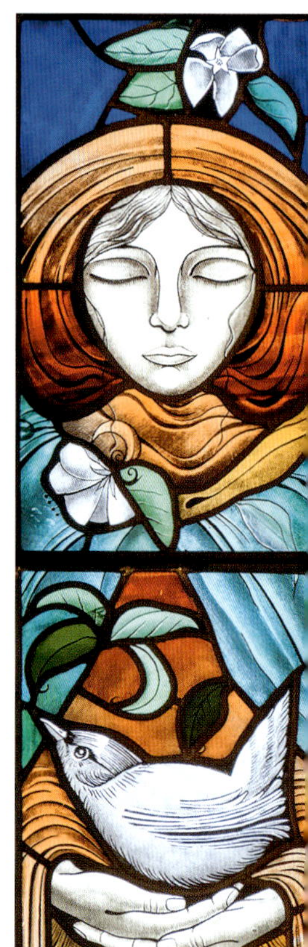

747. Melanie Howse, Eve, from the Sixth Day of Creation (Adam and Eve with Animals), 1993, Church of St Illtyd, Danygraig, Swansea, north aisle

748. Gareth Morgan, 'Deep Calleth Unto Deep', 1991, Church of St John, Pontyberem, nave

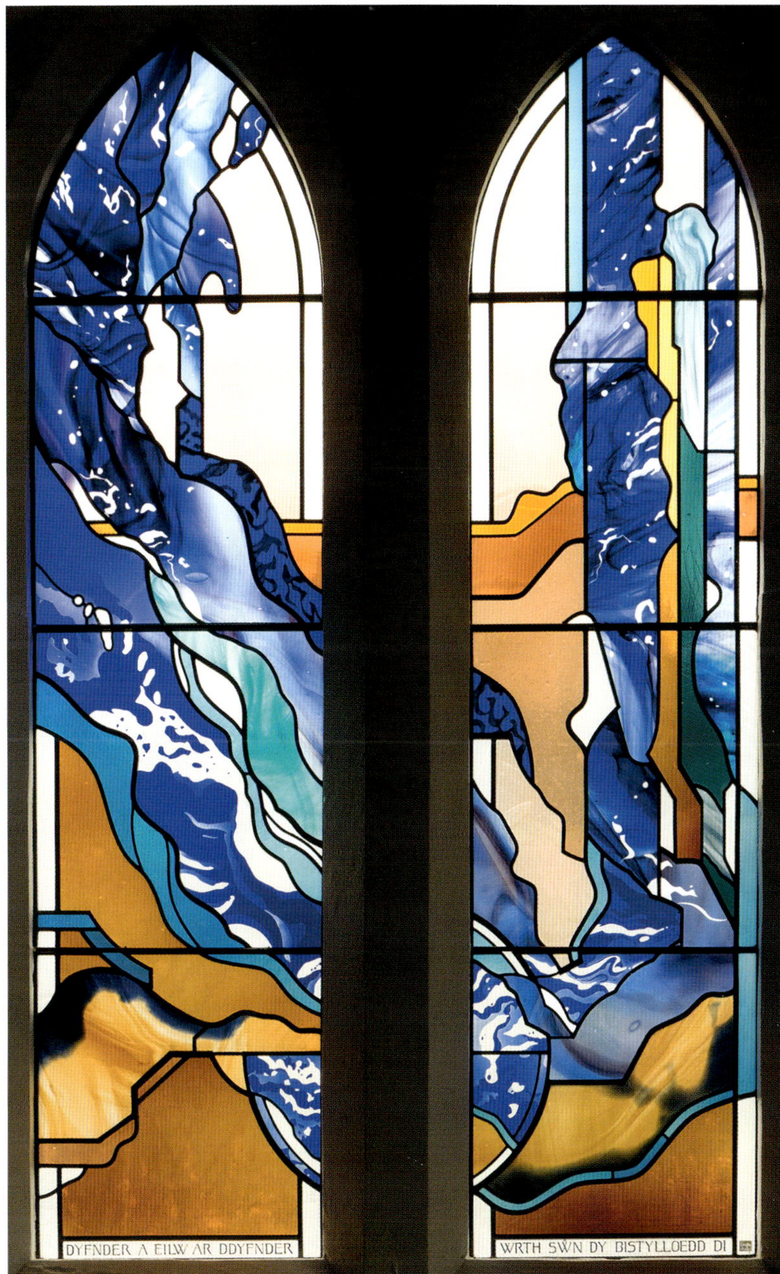

came together to provide funding for a series of works to fill the nave windows and an approach was made to the Institute. The student Caroline Loveys was commissioned to make all five windows, which depicted the Virgin and Child and four figures of Christ representing his Baptism, Crucifixion, Resurrection and Ascension. The course continued to attract students from all over the world and the Japanese artist Sachiko Yamamoto made a roundel for Pantygwydr Baptist Church, Uplands, Swansea.

The simplicity of the forms and subjects of the windows by Caroline Loveys and Sachiko Yamamoto contrast with the complex works of another Swansea graduate, Gareth Morgan, who trained at the Institute from 1985 to 1988. He was deeply impressed with the approach of the German artists and while always designing lead lines that were attractive in their own right, also made use of painted techniques, plating, acid polishing and sandblasting in the execution of his windows. His abstract approach for his first window at the Church of St John, Pontyberem, met with opposition from the St Davids Diocesan Advisory Committee, although its installation was permitted. The window is an interpretation of Psalm 42: 7–8, and, in contrast, a similarly abstract interpretation of Psalm 148 impressed the artistic advisor to the Monmouth DAC when submitted for the Church of the Holy Trinity, Christchurch, Newport.[33]

In other commissions Morgan introduced more pictorial features. The windows for Eglwys y Crwys, Cardiff, and Tabernacl Welsh Independent Chapel, Barry, are redolent of Christian tradition in Wales and include

32 Other windows were made by Colette Vidal in 1990 and Ann Marsh in 2003, and a further set of windows were made by Melanie Howse from 2002 to 2004.

33 Interview with Gareth Morgan, 15 April 2010.

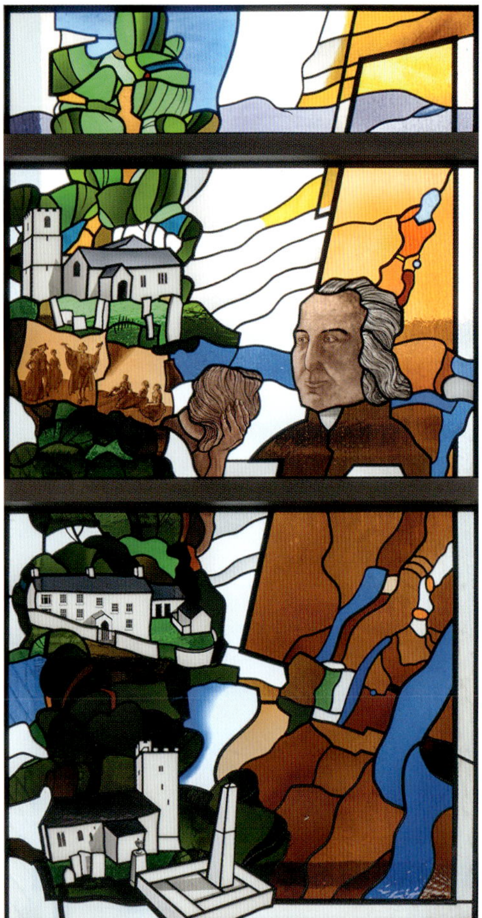

749. Gareth Morgan, Pantycelyn Window, 1991, Eglwys y Crwys, Cardiff, side wall

images of the Welsh hymn writers William Williams Pantycelyn and Ann Griffiths. In a window made for Trinity College Chapel, Carmarthen, the artist combines the theme of the six days of creation with imagery relevant to the Black Book of Carmarthen and the monastic history of the town.

The overall effect of these windows is abstract and at variance with popular expectations of stained glass in churches. Lawrence Lee warned against the 'slavish adherence to a set of rules followed so often by commercial windows that they have degenerated into a dead language'; consequently these windows 'could be classed as good and those of Léger bad—which is nonsense.'[34] However, the adherence to the wavering trends in contemporary visual art, such as those characterised by the Turner Prize-winners, cannot always be appropriate for art made for churches. Addressing the British Society of Master Glass Painters in 2000, the artist Caroline Swash observed that contemporary art 'appears to connect less with assurance than with the *anxieties of society*'.[35] This does not easily accord with the themes of faith and hope that are central to Christian art, and artists who want to engage with Christian themes for churches in a creative and meaningful way often need to work hard to win approval for their ideas. While patrons might demand 'the charm of the recognition of remembered things', stained glass artists need to find ways of designing 'windows that speak well for our time yet which fit within the orchestration of the whole building.'[36] In the hands of the right artists such limitations can be both a guide and an inspiration.

34 Lawrence Lee, *The Appreciation of Stained Glass* (London: Oxford University Press, 1977), p. 50.

35 Caroline Swash, 'On Contemporary Glass', *The Journal of Stained Glass*, vol. xxiii (1999), p. 68.

36 Caroline Swash, 'On Contemporary Glass', p. 71.

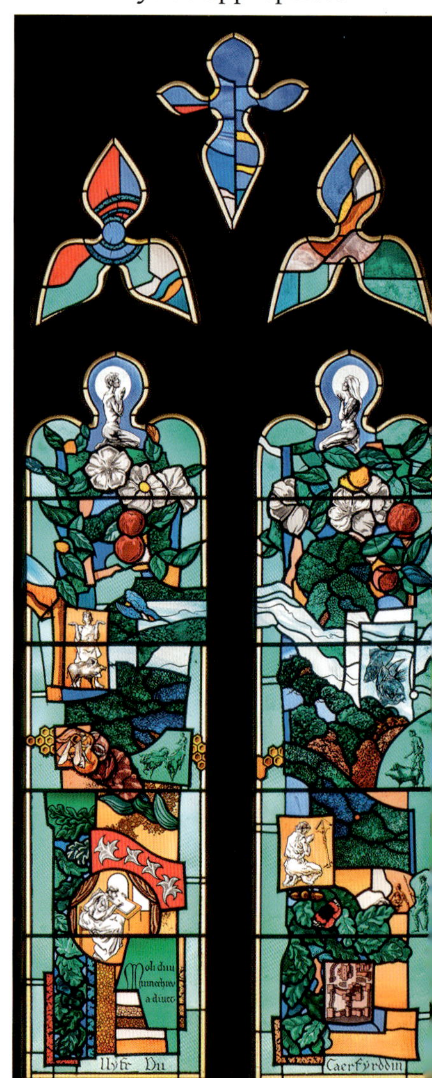

750. Gareth Morgan, Black Book of Carmarthen Window, 1996, Trinity College Chapel, Carmarthen (University of Wales Trinity St David), nave

Chapter Twelve

A New Millennium

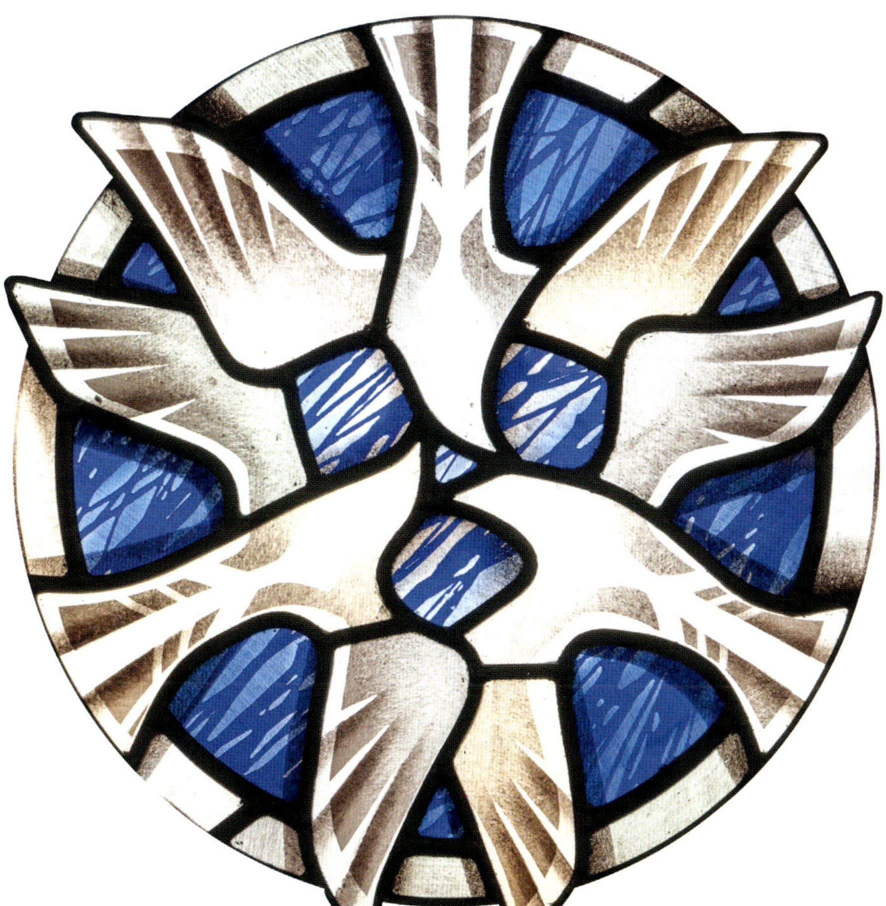

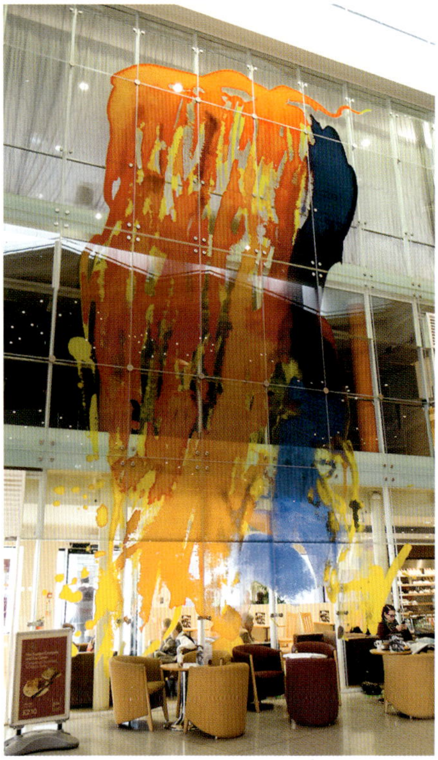

752. Amber Hiscott, *Colourfall*, *c.* 2004, Wales Millennium Centre, Cardiff

By the year 2000 many of the most ambitious and innovative works in architectural glass were for corporate and public spaces rather than places of worship. Swansea-based artists such as Amber Hiscott, David Pearl, Catrin Jones and Alexander Beleschenko were designing site-specific works in glass for new kinds of architectural spaces that had evolved relatively quickly away from the tradition of painted and leaded stained glass as developed in the Middle Ages, revived in the nineteenth century, and in a few cases perfected as an expressive artform in the twentieth century. One of Wales' most distinctive new buildings, the Millennium Centre in Cardiff, which opened in 2004, incorporates large abstract works by Amber Hiscott, and Rodney Bender's studio provided structural glass blocks that were used by the architect Jonathan Adams to light the building.

The celebration of the millennium also brought more new works in architectural and stained glass to churches than any other event since the end of the Second World War. One of the largest commissions was the four-light west window by Martin Donlin for the Church of St Mary, Swansea. The window was made in collaboration with the Architectural Glass Centre at the Swansea Institute of Higher Education, and made possible with a grant from the Millennium Fund. The window is abstract in effect, admitting a rich red glow across the western end of the nave with the assistance of the afternoon sun. This transformation of the light in the church contrasts with the message of the text chosen from Revelation 22: 5: 'They need no light of lamp or sun for the Lord God will be their light and they will reign for ever and ever.'

753. Martin Donlin, 'God will be their light', made at the Architectural Glass Centre, Swansea, 2001, Church of St Mary, Swansea, west window

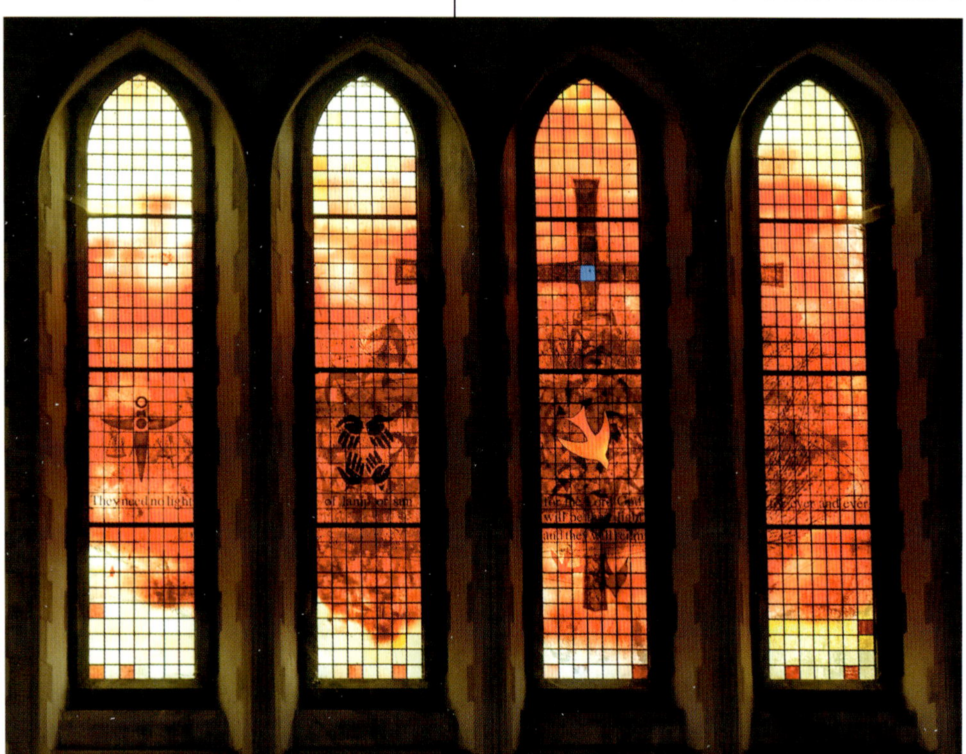

751. (Title page) Alan Davis, Welsh Saints (St D
St Cybi and William Davies), 2004, Church of Our
Help of Christians, Holyhead, (liturgical) south

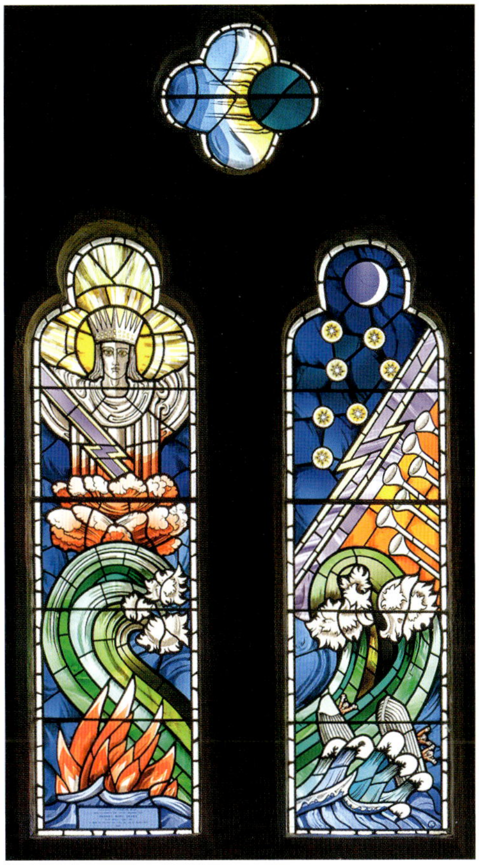

754. Glantawe Studios, The Second Coming, 2001, designed by John Edwards, Church of St Peter, Little Newcastle, west window

Imagery from the book of Revelation and the Gospels relating to the second coming of Christ was drawn upon for the west window commissioned to commemorate the millennium at the Church of St Peter, Little Newcastle. The window was made at Glantawe Studios, and the design by John Edwards contrasts with a less apocalyptic vision expressed in his other millennium windows. At the Church of St Mary, Pennard, an angel releases doves of peace into the first dawn of the new millennium, watched by the Virgin and Child. A rainbow symbolises peace and hope for the future, while the local Gower scenes in roundels below are surrounded by flora and fauna. His millennium window nearby at the Church of St Teilo, Bishopston, links the church, two chapels and the local community centre by a rainbow that flows from a fountain in the centre of the window. The window is an example of an increasing amount of ecclesiastical stained glass that relates to local heritage themes, including a further millennium window designed by John Edwards for the Church of St Nicholas, Montgomery. Here depictions of the church and chapel are also framed with a rainbow, and punctuated by celebratory fireworks.[1] Anniversaries in other churches occasioned the addition of stained glass with local themes. For example, the two-light window at the Church of St Mary, Rhuddlan, depicts the church and castle set in the local landscape, and commemorates the 700th anniversary of the town in

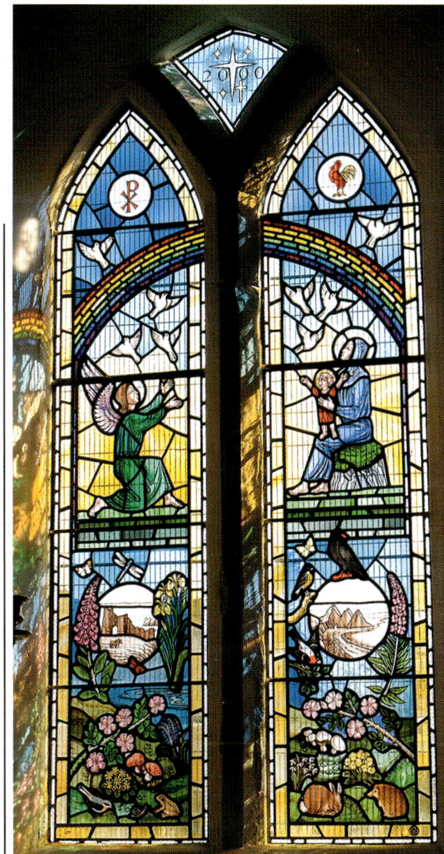

755. Glantawe Studios, Millennium Window, 2000, designed by John Edwards, Church of St Mary, Pennard, nave

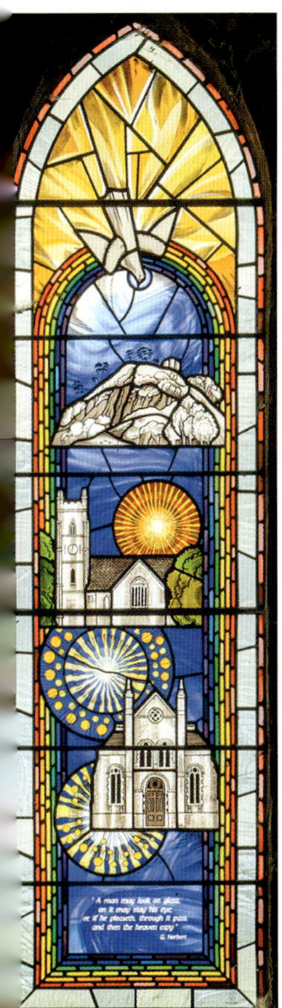

756. Glantawe Studios, Millennium Window, 2002, designed by John Edwards, Church of St Nicholas, Montgomery, south transept

1 The window includes lines by the poet George Herbert, who was born in the town and briefly represented it as a Member of Parliament, lines which play on the nature of the medium, and are from 'The Temple', 1633:

A man may look on glass,
on it may stay his eye:
or, if he pleaseth, through it pass,
and then the heaven espy.

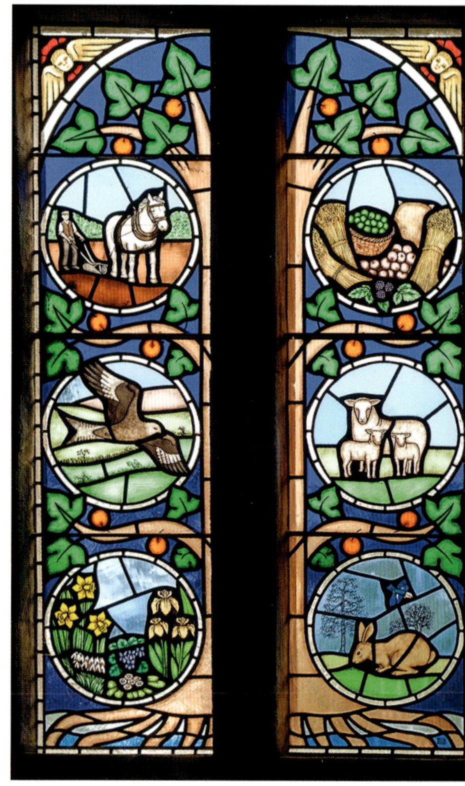

757. Janet Hardy, West Window, 2001, Church of St Michael, Llanfihangel-y-Creuddyn

2001, with a text from the popular hymn: 'Thy hand, O God, has guided/Thy flock from age to age.'

The use of religious poetry and hymns, rather than the biblical text, reflects both the decline in biblical literacy among congregations as well as a move away from less obvious biblical themes since the 1980s. Continuing a trend established in the 1990s, local themes supplant the biblical narrative in several windows by Janet Hardy. At the Church of St Michael, Llanfihangel-y-Creuddyn, a fruiting tree unites a design with six roundels depicting agricultural scenes, flowers and a red kite, an increasingly common bird of prey in this area of Ceredigion, while a window of 2000 at the Church of St David, Betws (near Ammanford), includes references to the agricultural and industrial history of the surrounding area.[2]

2 The Betws window also contains symbolism associated with the patron and diocesan saint, David.

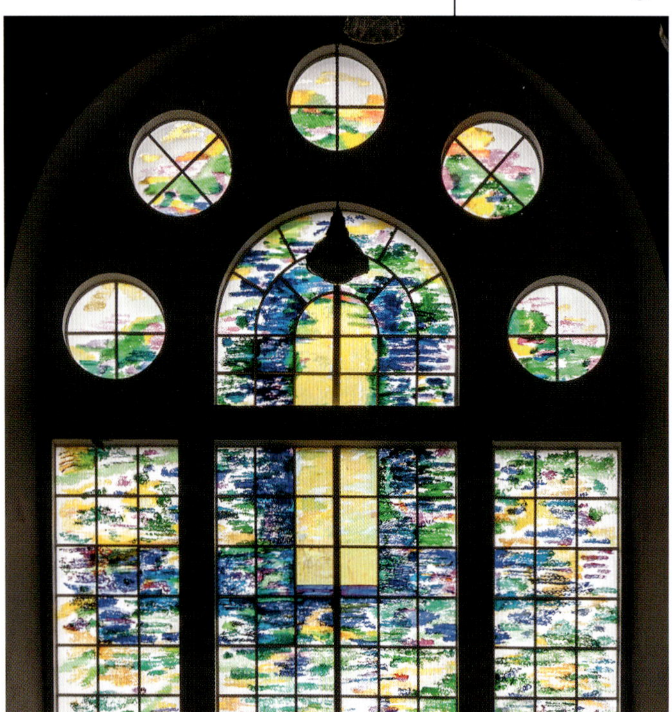

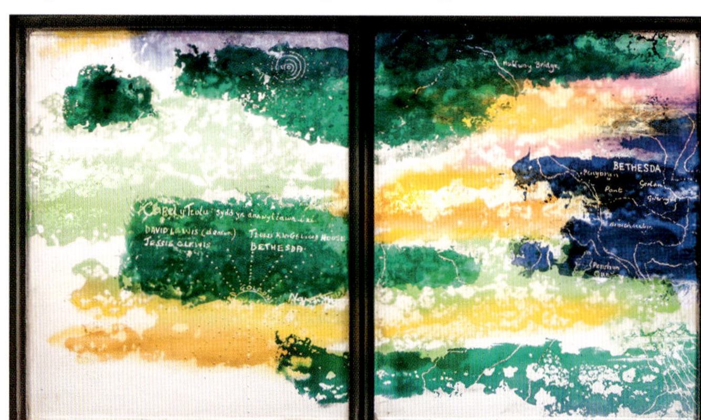

758–9. Chris Bird-Jones, Centenary Window with detail of two panels (below right), *c.* 2003, Bethania Welsh Independent Chapel, Bethesda, rear wall

An imaginative use of local subject matter is found on the window made for Bethania Chapel, Bethesda, by the artist Chris Bird-Jones. The artist made the window as part of her three-year residency that coincided with the centenary of the quarrymen's strike of 1900–3, and members of the local community were invited to engrave text and drawings on the panels of the window

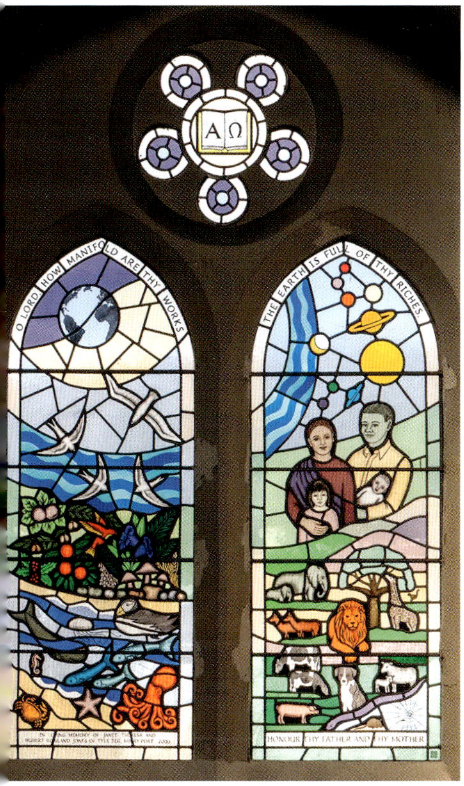

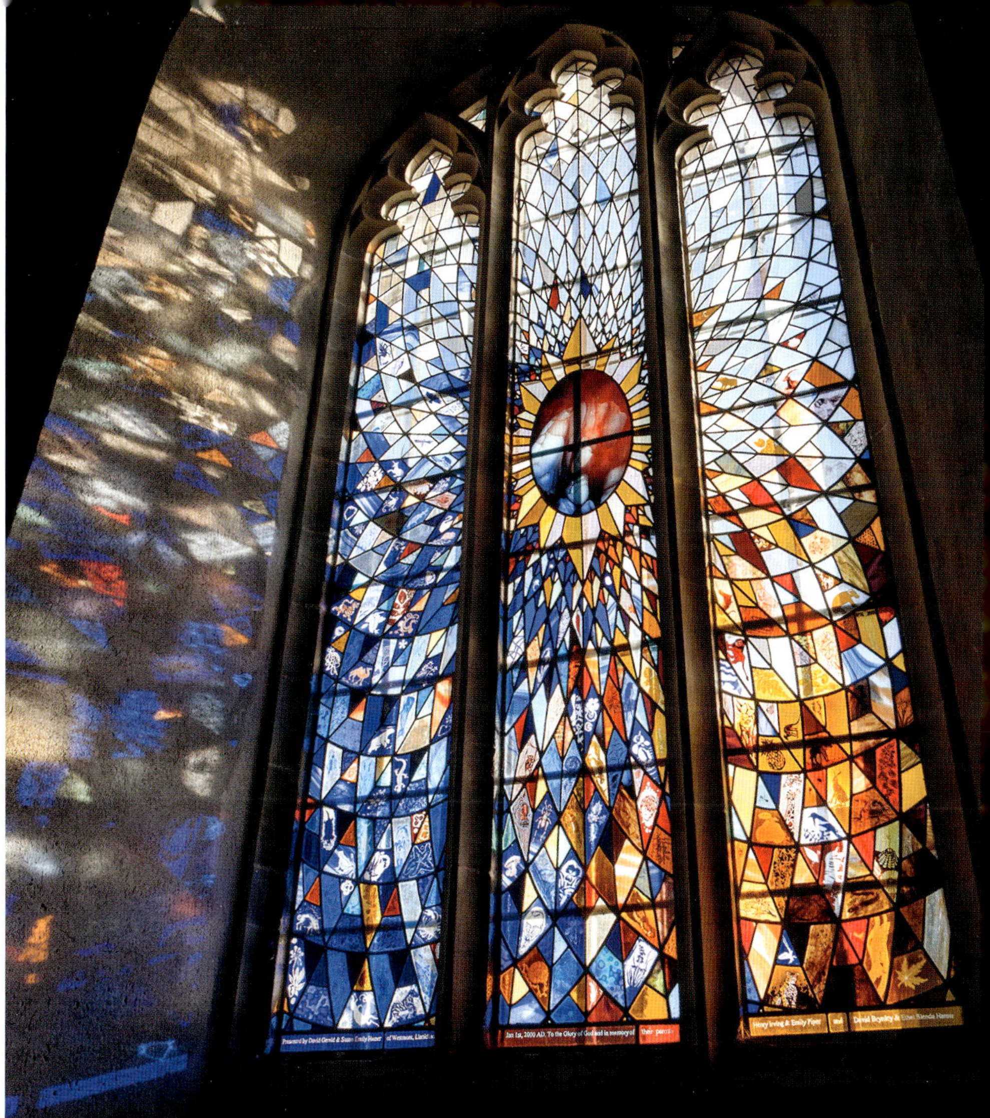

in a way that echoes the graffiti on the wooden pews below. From a distance, the window appears entirely abstract and the details, including maps and lines of poetry and music, can only be appreciated at close hand.

The popularity of natural themes and local flora and fauna for church windows has resulted in a rise in the number of windows taking the theme of creation or using quotations from the Psalms, thereby drawing out the Christian significance of the natural world. Creation was the subject of the millennium window by Bill Bleasdale at the Church of St Idloes, Llanidloes, which includes numerous creatures and plant life emanating from the centre of the window, drawn on small pieces of glass. Like the windows by Chris Bird-Jones at Bethesda, and John Petts at Llansteffan, this gives an overall abstract effect, but proves to be representational on close inspection. Further recent windows representing the days of creation include the two-light memorial windows designed by Janet Hardy for the Church of St Mary, Burry Port, in 2000, and Colwyn Morris in 1999 for the Church of St Samlet, Llansamlet.

760. (above left) Janet Hardy, The Six Days of Creation, 2000, Church of St Mary, Burry Port, north aisle

761. (above) Bill Bleasdale, Millennium Window, 2000, Church of St Idloes, Llanidloes, nave

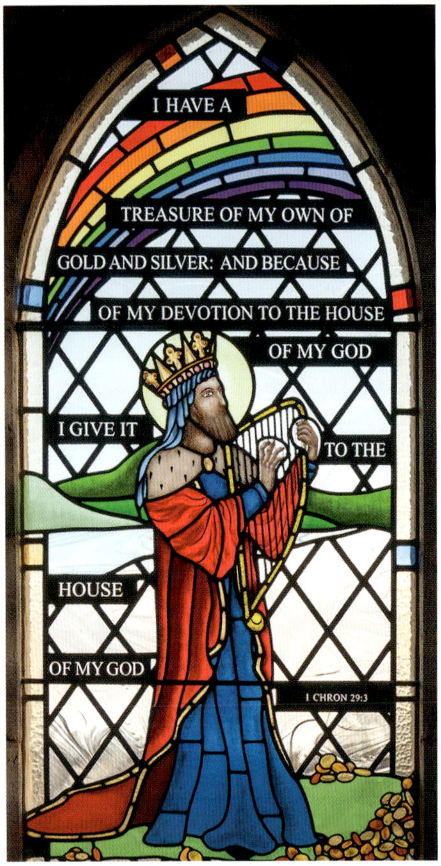

762. Recclesia, King David, 2011, Ruthin English Presbyterian Church, side wall

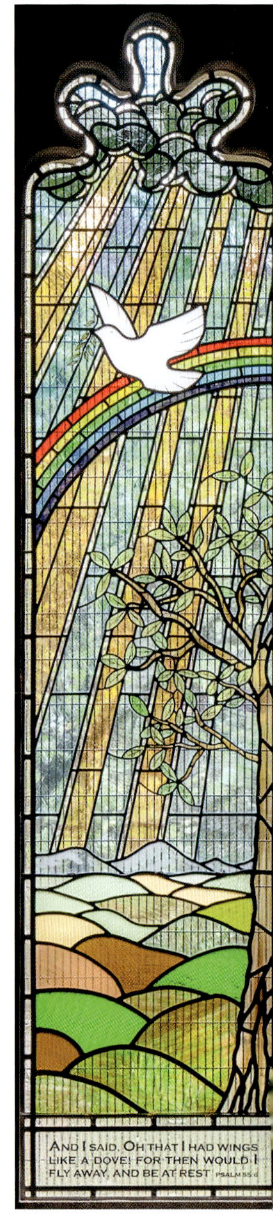

763. Recclesia, Landscape with Dove and Rainbow, 2010, Church of St Asaph and St Cyndeyrn, Llanasa, west wall

John Edwards' millennium windows use rainbows as a main feature and as a framing device, and a rainbow is depicted over the figure of David in a window by Recclesia at Ruthin English Presbyterian Church. The window quotes 1 Chronicles 29: 3, and complements an earlier window by the studio at the church, depicting a landscape and quoting the text Psalm 46: 10 'Be still and know that I am God'.[3] Another natural scene by the studio was designed by Jamie Moore and Garth Evans for the Church of St Asaph and St Cyndeyrn, Llanasa, and was given in memory of a conservationist. The rainbow and the dove flying over the land alludes to God's promise of safety from the story of Noah, although the text quoted: 'Oh that I had wings like a dove!' is from Psalm 55: 6. The companion left-hand light depicts a lively group of fish jumping out of the water, one of which has a ring in its mouth as a reference to the miraclulous recovery of the queen's gold ring that Cyndeyrn finds in a salmon that he catches.[4]

Birds, butterflies and flowers are conspicuous in windows by John Edwards, including his window of 2005 for the Church of St Brynach, Nevern, in which they are the main subject, and by Janet Hardy.[5] Her standing figures of the saints Francis and David at the Church of St Lawrence, Marros, made in 2001, feature daffodils prominently, and they are also a feature of the millennium window by Deanne Mangold at the Church of St Luke, Cwmdare. This window uses the colours of the rainbow to form a border around the left and top of the window, framing a view of a landscape with a pithead, although the last mine at Cwmdare had closed in 1977. Anna Bessant depicted flowers and butterflies in her pair of porch windows for Eglwys Oen Duw, Beulah, made in 1999, and poppies were used in her window commissioned to replace a wooden war memorial that had badly deteriorated in the

3 Both windows closely follow the style of the windows made in the late 1950s and early 1960s by Williams & Watson. The view of the hills with the text of the Psalm was made by Kat Walton and Jamie Moore according to a very precise brief provided by the donor. Interview with Jamie Moore, 10 August 2010.

4 Cyndeyrn, or Kentigern, reputedly founded the monastery at St Asaph when in exile from his bishopric in Strathclyde. He was succeeded by the local saint, Asaph, after his death in 596. Recclesia is based near Chester and was formed in 2009 out of Linley Stained Glass after its parent company, Chester Masonry, went out of business.

5 A memorial window by Janet Hardy of 1995 at Monkton Priory uses butterflies to represent each of the children of the couple who are commemorated in the window.

764. Anna Bessant, War Memorial Window, 2005, Church of St Llŷr, Llanyre, porch

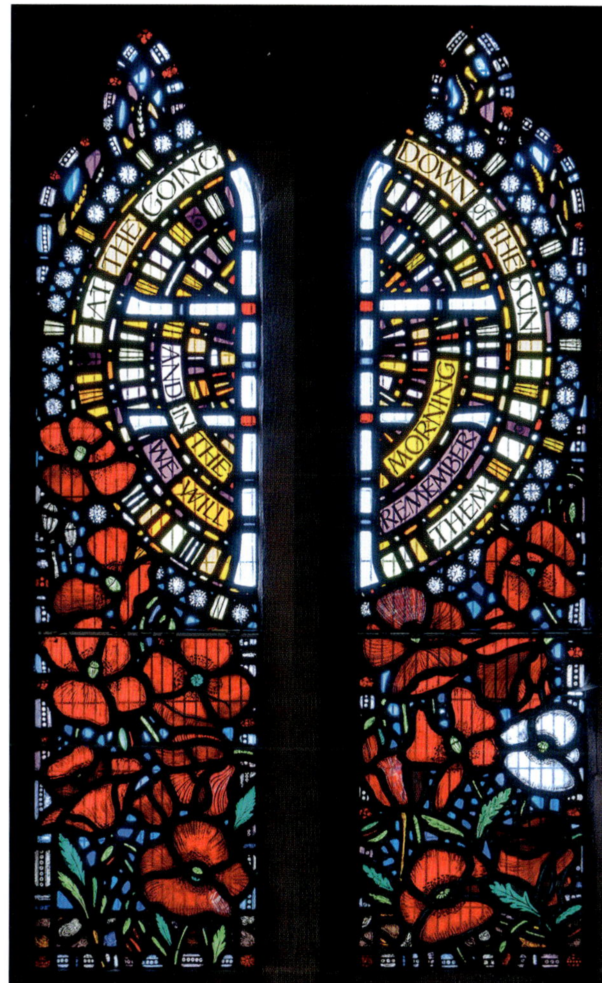

porch of the Church of St Llŷr, Llanyre. Inside the church a further window by the artist includes stars, birds, hares and fish around the text 'All creation will share in the glorious freedom of the children of God' from Romans 8: 21.

Fewer abstract works were commissioned for Anglican churches in the first decade of the new millennium. In 2000 Rachel Walters designed a three-light window for the north chapel at Christ Church, Radyr, with an abstracted Celtic-Christian cross at its centre. The window is an expression of Christ as the Light of the World and draws on the simple colour scheme and small decorative motifs from the original glazing of the nave in 1903–4.[6] Three minimal abstract works by Christian Ryan were installed in the processional walkway in the church, and both works by former students of the Architectural Glass Department were made and installed with the help of the Architectural Glass Centre, established at the Institute in 1999.[7]

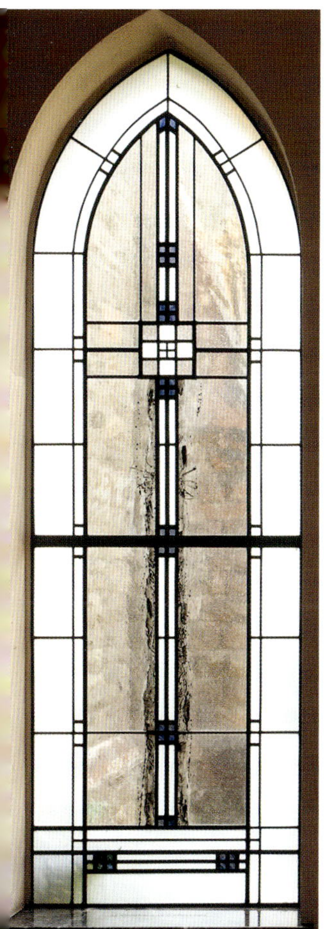

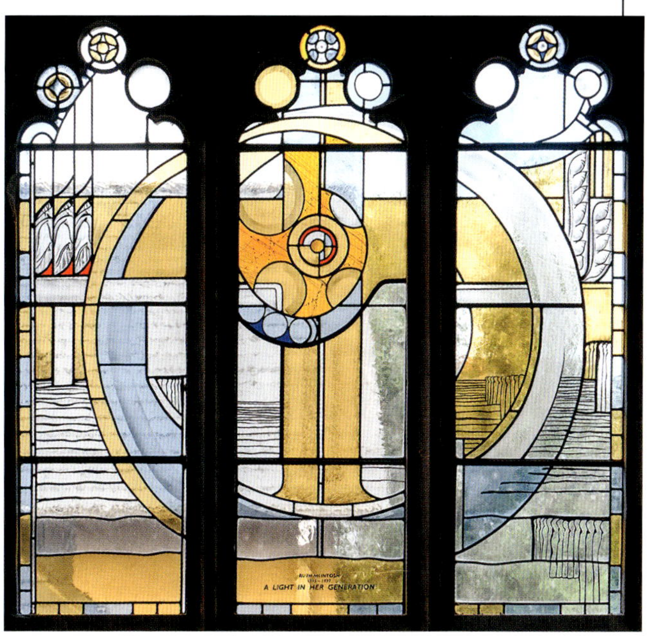

765. (left) Christian Ryan, 'As Kingfishers Catch Fire', 2001, Christ Church, Radyr, processional walkway

766. (above) Rachel Walters, Christ the Light of the World, 2000, Christ Church, Radyr, north chapel

6 Some of these simple decorative windows have been replaced with stained glass by Robert Newbery from about 1912 to the 1930s, while a single window by Celtic Studios was made in 1967. Rachel Walters now works under her married name, Rachel Phillips.

7 The Architectural Glass Centre was established under the direction of Tim Pegler, before Alun Adams was appointed as co-ordinator in 2000. The Centre has overseen numerous commissions across Wales and beyond, many of which have been designed by current and former students from the Swansea School of Architectural Glass. The windows by Christian Ryan are inspired by the work of Gerard Manley Hopkins.

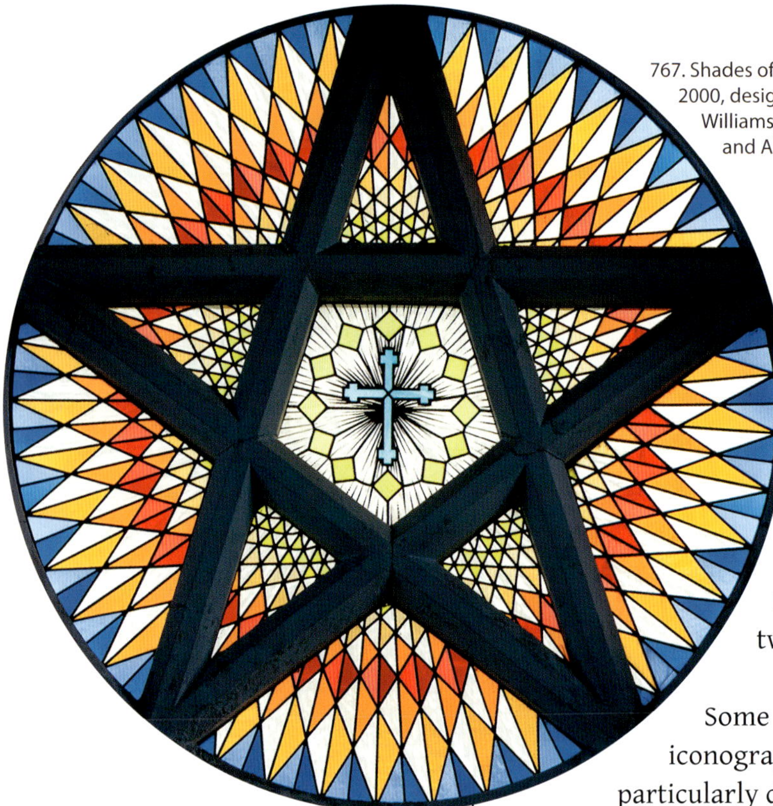

767. Shades of Light, East Window, 2000, designed by Juliet Rhys-Williams, Church of St Michael and All Angels, Beddau

In 2000 three non-representational windows were made for the architecturally unusual Church of St Michael and All Angels, Beddau, at the instigation of the artist Susan Glyn. The circular east window has an unexpected connection with the past as it was designed in 1936 by her mother, Lady Juliet Rhys-Williams. However, the window was not executed in glass until Susan Glyn had it made by the London studio Shades of Light, who also made two pentagonal nave windows with Celtic crosses.[8]

Some windows for Anglican churches remained more iconographically conventional and recognisably biblical, particularly designs by Colwyn Morris and Bryan Evans for Glantawe Studios. Examples by both artists can also be found at the Roman Catholic Church of St Joseph, Neath, and most stained glass commissioned for Roman Catholic churches in the 1990s and 2000s has been more representational and biblical in emphasis.[9] Most of the windows designed by John Edwards and made by Tim Lewis for the Church of St Teilo, Whitchurch, Cardiff, are emblematic of the birth and Passion of Christ. These windows form an unusual arrangement of irregular rectangular openings in the side wall, and also include a single narrow window representing the patron of the church, Teilo, with a bell and an apple tree.

8 The effect of coloured glass in the east window had been imitated with transparent plastic, but the colours had faded. I am grateful to Susan Glyn for information about the windows. The abstract use of colour for window glass is found in the sanctuary windows given by Juliet Rhys-Williams for their church at Miskin in, surprisingly, 1926, containing rich blues, purples and reds in diamond quarries.

9 Bryan Tobias Evans had designed and painted many windows in his long career at Celtic Studios, and also painted and designed windows with Tim Lewis at Glantawe Studios.

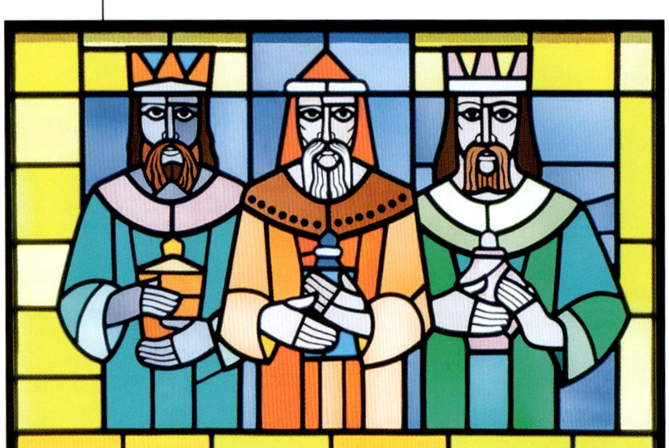

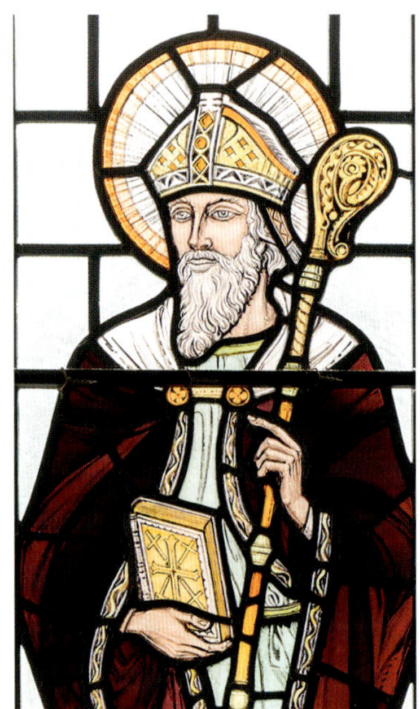

768. (right) Glantawe Studios, The Three Magi, 2004, designed by John Edwards, Church of St Teilo, Whitchurch, Cardiff, south wall

769. (far right) Glantawe Studios, St Augustine, 2005, designed by Bryan Evans, Church of St Joseph, Neath, narthex

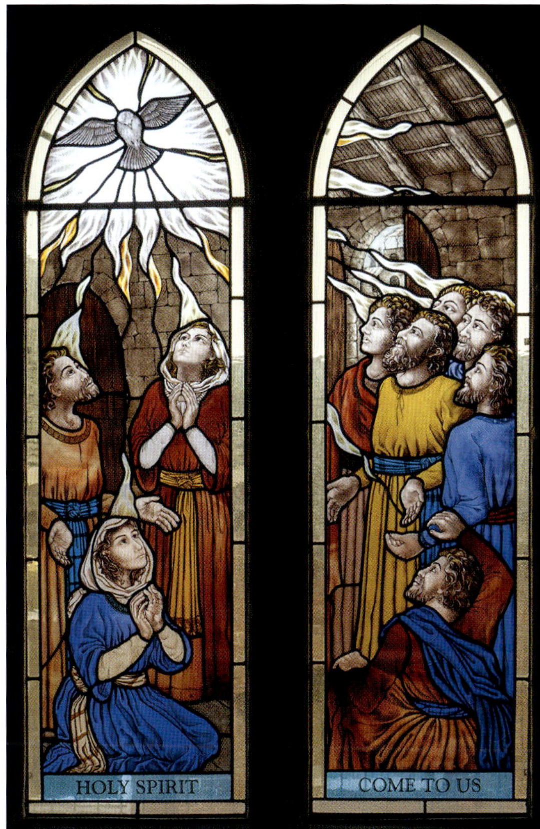

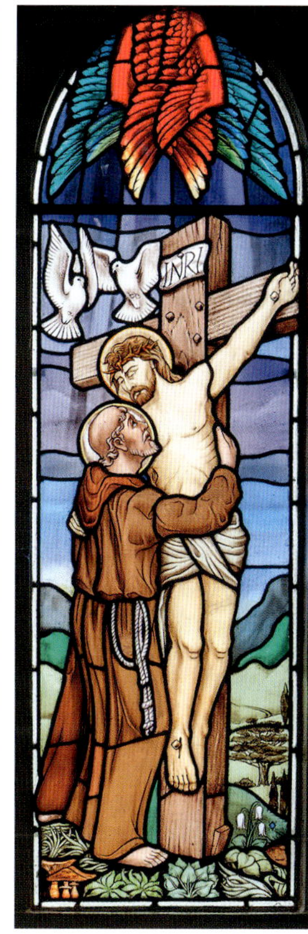

770. (right) Bryony Benwell and Lindsay Abbot, Pentecost, 2005, Church of St Joseph, Colwyn Bay, nave

771. (far right) Bryony Benwell and Petri Anderson, The Crucifixion with St Francis, 2009, Church of the Immaculate Conception, Flint, north aisle

Recent windows by Bryony Benwell at the Catholic church at Colwyn Bay are more traditionally pictorial, depicting the biblical scenes of Pentecost, the women at the empty tomb, Christ appearing to his disciples, as well as Joseph at work as a carpenter, and Bernadette kneeling before Mary as Our Lady of Lourdes in a similar style.[10] These windows were made with the glass painter Lindsay Abbot, while the window for the Church of the Immaculate Conception, Flint, was made by Benwell in collaboration with a former colleague at Chapel Studio in Hertfordshire, the designer and glass painter Petri Anderson, and depicts Christ on the cross embraced by Francis. Francis was among a set of three standing figures designed and made by Gareth Morgan for the Church of Our Lady of the Rosary, Ammanford, together with the Virgin and Child and John the Baptist, who is depicted as the voice crying out to prepare for the coming of the Messiah in Isaiah 40: 3–5. Since 2010 these windows have been augmented by a further six commissions for figures of saints by Janet Hardy.

A set of windows by Rachel Phillips was made in 2005 for the Church of St Benedict, Clydach, as a series of 'Windows of Compassion'. The six windows include portraits of the saints Francis and Vincent de Paul with more recent figures such as Oscar Romero and Pope John Paul II. Occasionally windows have been commissioned for Catholic churches that have been less ostensibly religious, such as the landscape with a river made in 2002 by Simon Howard for the Church of the Blessed Sacrament, Connah's Quay, to a design by J. Ormsby.[11] In contrast with these more modest windows, the muscular figure of the risen Christ by Rachel Phillips for the west window of the Church

10 The Pentecost window was installed for Pentecost Sunday in 2005 and given in 'memory of the spirit given to the world by the life and death of Pope John Paul II'. Bryony Benwell established her studio, The Glass House, in 2000 at Sealand, near Chester.

11 Simon Howard was based in Lancashire when the window was made, but subsequently relocated to Llandeilo.

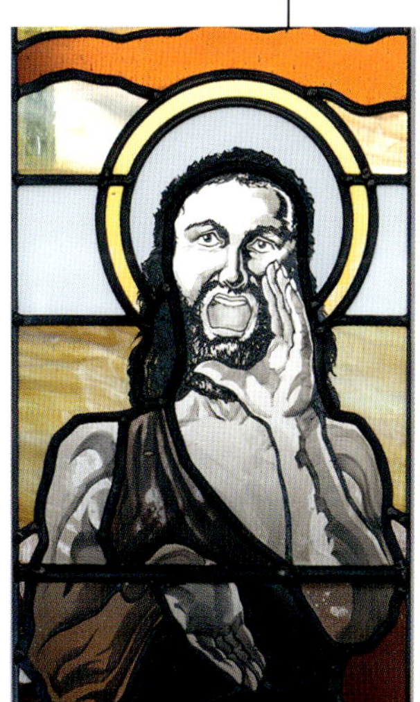

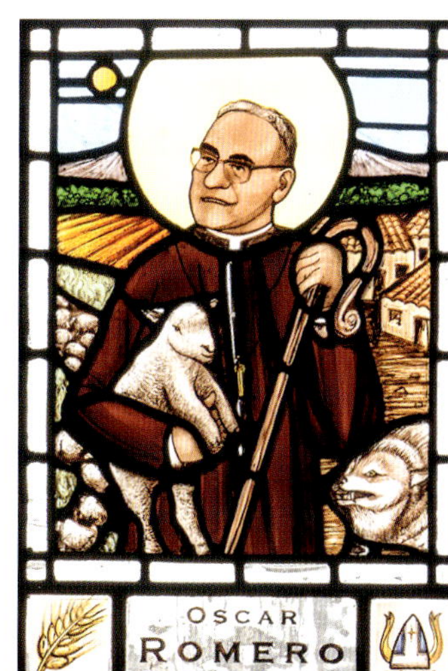

772. (right) Gareth Morgan, St John the Baptist, *c.* 2009, Church of Our Lady of the Rosary, Ammanford, nave

773. (far right) Rachel Phillips, Oscar Romero, 2005, Church of St Benedict, Clydach, nave

776. (right) Deborah Lowe, Memorial Window, mad
Glantawe Studios, 2010, Church of St Joseph, Neath, nart

777. (far right) Melanie Howse, *The Sun and the Moc The Stars Also*, from The Seven Days of Creation, 200
Church of St Illtyd, Danygraig, Swansea, north a

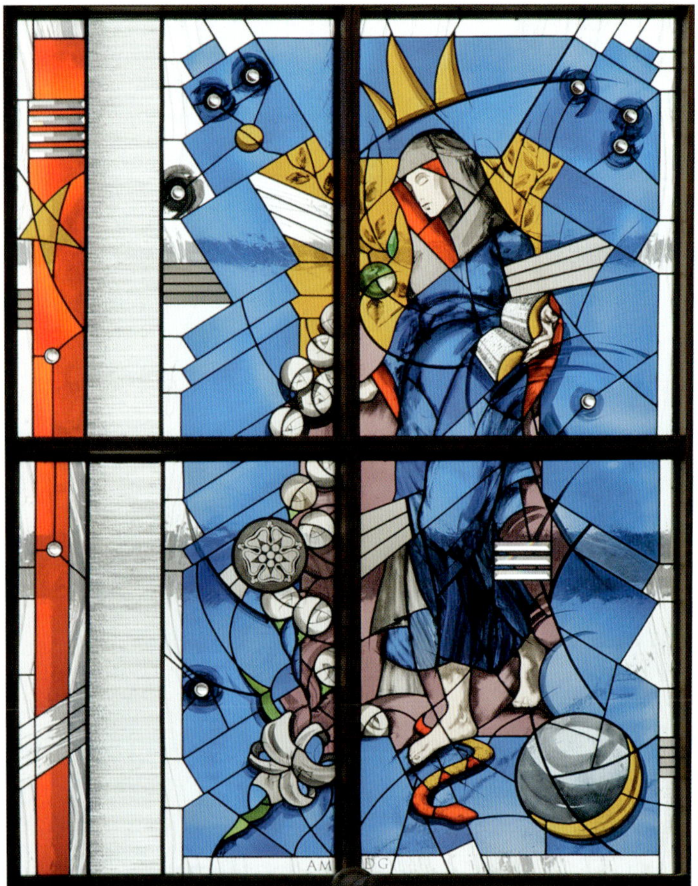

774. Christian Phillips, The Immaculate Conception, 1999, Church of St Mary, Bridgend, narthex screen

of St Helen, Barry, is given force by the surrounding yellow, orange and pink glass. A similarly assertive vision is found in an earlier window by another student at Swansea, Christian Phillips, who was responsible for the representation of the Immaculate Conception of Mary at the Church of St Mary, Bridgend.

Other imaginative designs and interpretations of biblical subjects have been made for Catholic churches in recent years by Swansea graduates. Three small abstract windows representing the Trinity were made by Christian Ryan in 2004 for the Church of St Cadoc, Llanrumney, Cardiff, using enamelling and etching rather than leaded coloured and painted glass. Five pairs of lights representing the first five days of creation by Melanie Howse were more traditional in technique, and follow on from her two windows of 1993 depicting Adam and Eve at the Church of St Illtyd, Danygraig, Swansea. Each contain representational elements in an abstract overall design, and this abstraction is especially appropriate for the first two days of creation as well as the small roundel representing the seventh day, placed high over the two earlier windows representing the sixth day of creation. A window designed and painted by Deborah Lowe in 2010 was commissioned through Tim Lewis for the Church of St Joseph, Neath, and breaks with the pictorialism of the saints and biblical scenes in the numerous preceding windows of the 1930s by John Hardman & Co., and since the 1980s by Glantawe Studios, most of which were designed by Colwyn Morris. A restrained use of paint reveals the qualities of the beautiful English antique glass, with imagery alluding to new life: a bird's nest, Christening candles, the joining of hands young and old, and butterflies symbolising resurrection.[12]

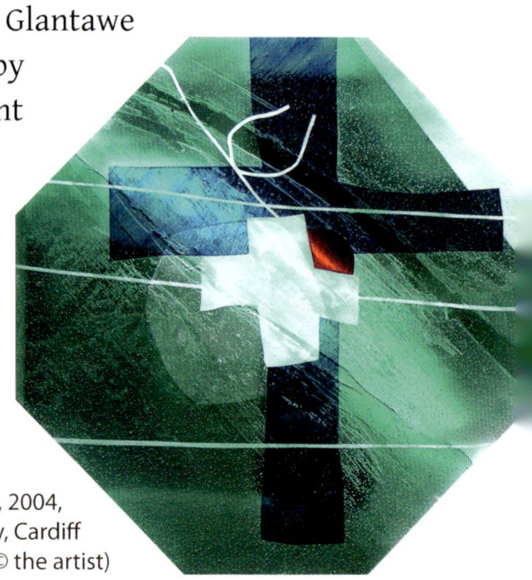

775. Christian Ryan, Trinity, 2004, Church of St Cadoc, Llanrumney, Cardiff (photo © the artist)

12 Other recent examples of the renewed collaboration with Tim Lewis include Deborah Lowe's work on two versions of a design by Colwyn Morris of the Adoration of the Magi for the churches at Llanyre and Llangynnwr before and after his death in 2011. Lowe also designs and paints glass for Pendle Stained Glass, based near her home in Todmorden.

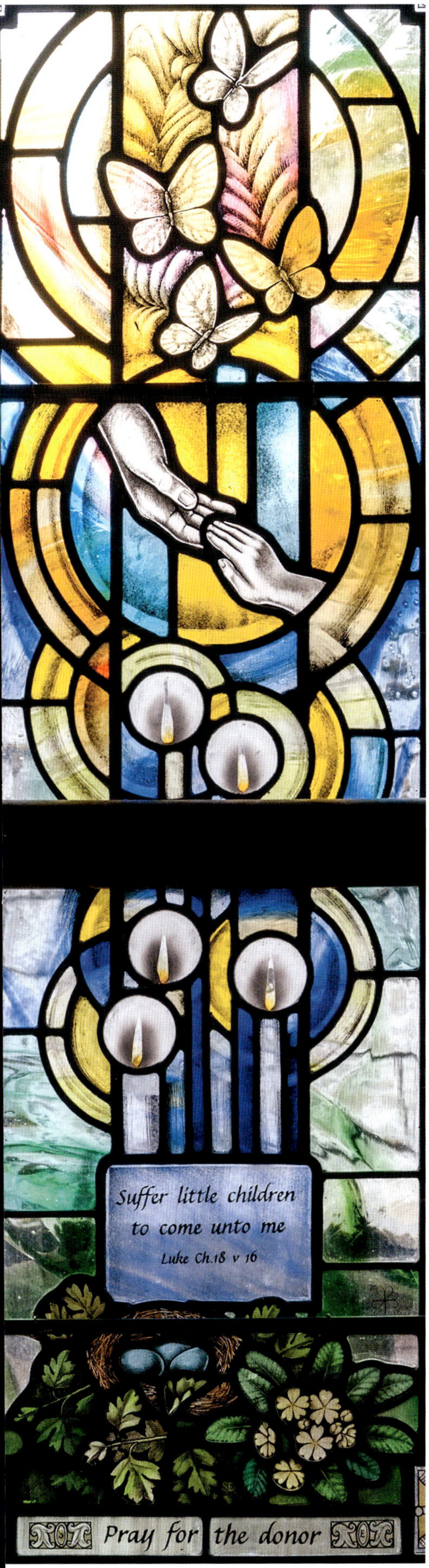
Suffer little children
to come unto me
Luke Ch.18 v 16
Pray for the donor
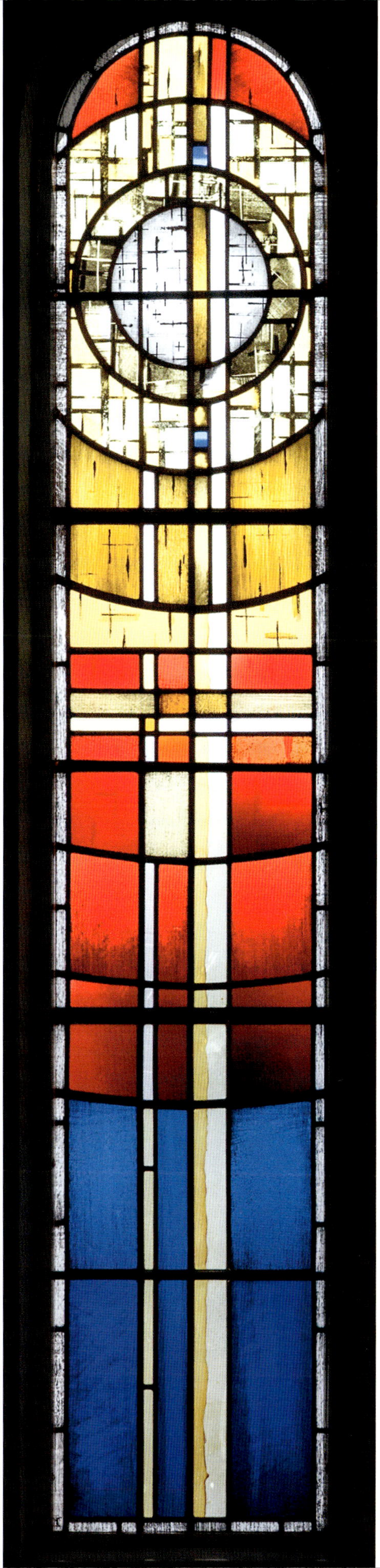
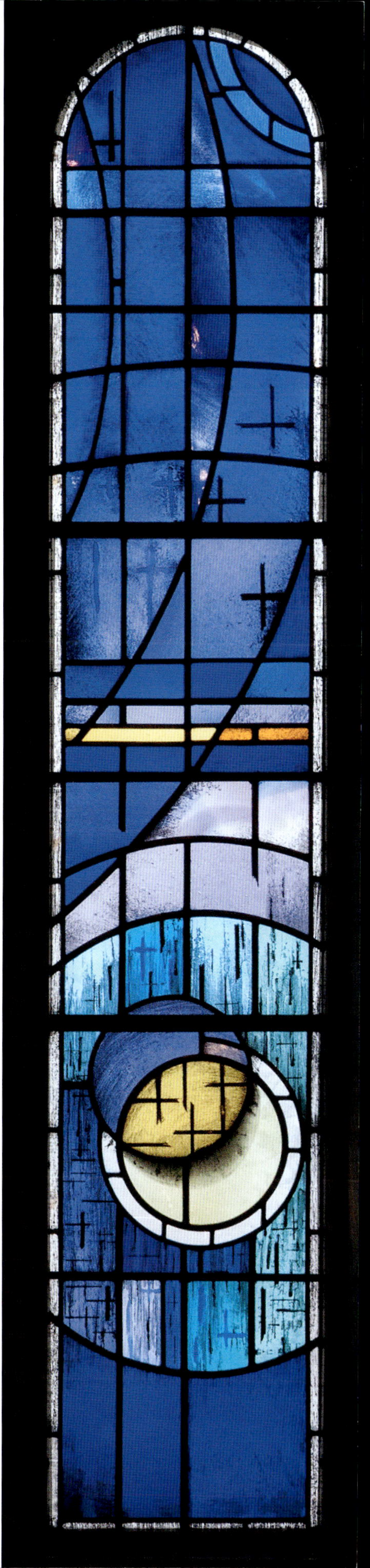

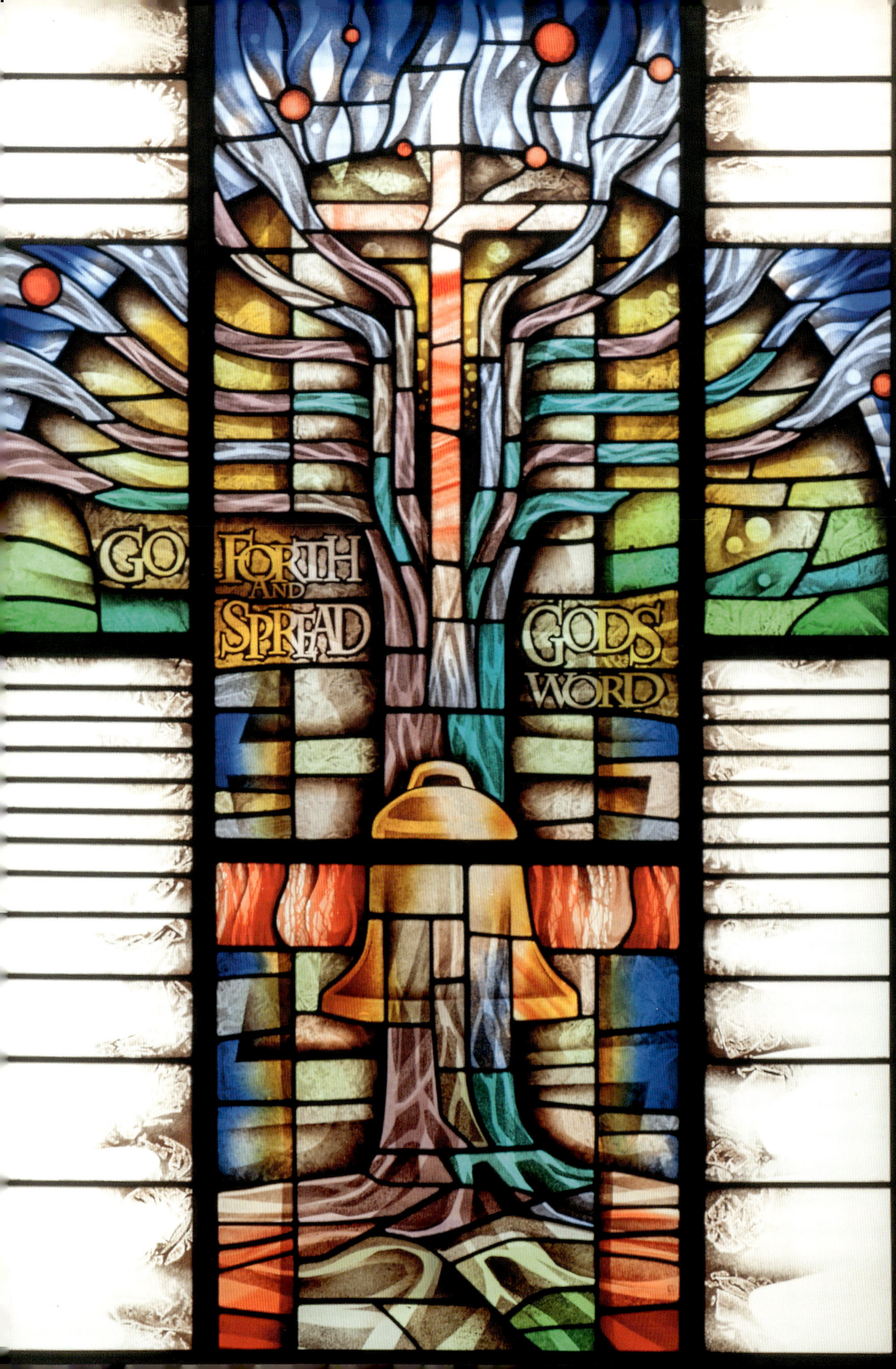

778. Alan Davis,
The Proclamatic
the Kingdom, 2
Church of Our L
Help of Christia
Holyhead, (litur
north aisle

Commissions for a whole set of windows in a church by a single designer have been unusual in recent years, making the series by Alan Davis commissioned for the Church of Our Lady Help of Christians, Holyhead, exceptional. The series of panels were made in 2004–5 for different donors following the removal of earlier works in *dalle de verre* that had deteriorated. Eight large panels are mounted internally across the windows of the north and south walls with smaller windows placed at the end of each aisle, and a further large work was made for the porch in 2007. The series of windows include powerful abstract depictions of biblical scenes such as the Wedding at Cana and the Transfiguration, as well as imaginative interpretations of the Resurrection, the Eucharist and the Proclamation of the Kingdom. This window has a tree as its central motif with twelve branches, representing the disciples, a cross at its centre and leaves and fruit at its extremities, while a bell included below is suggestive of the call to worship.

The figure of Mary standing in the heavens by Christian Phillips at Bridgend is situated over the doors of the narthex screen, through which the church is entered. The screen of the new church also features sand-blasted designs illustrating various titles of Mary in English and Welsh.[13] These works were the first commissions made by Christian Ryan and were part of an initiative to involve local artists in the furnishing of the new church, which was opened in 1999. A commemorative plaque in glass was made by Ryan to record the consecration of the church, and further wall-mounted glass works by the artist were commissioned in 2001 and 2007, depicting symbols of the Eucharist and Mary.[14]

779–81. Christian Ryan, Panels on the narthex screen (below and bottom left); Commemorative Plaque (bottom right), narthex, 1999, Church of St Mary, Bridgend

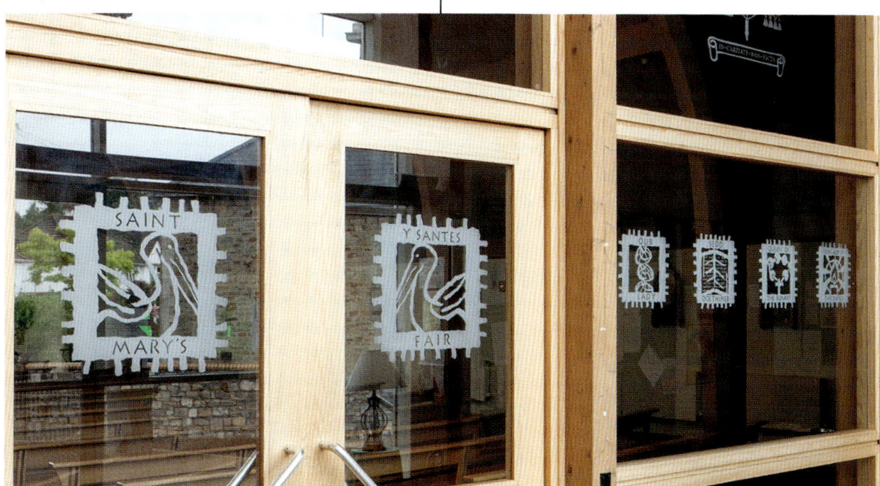

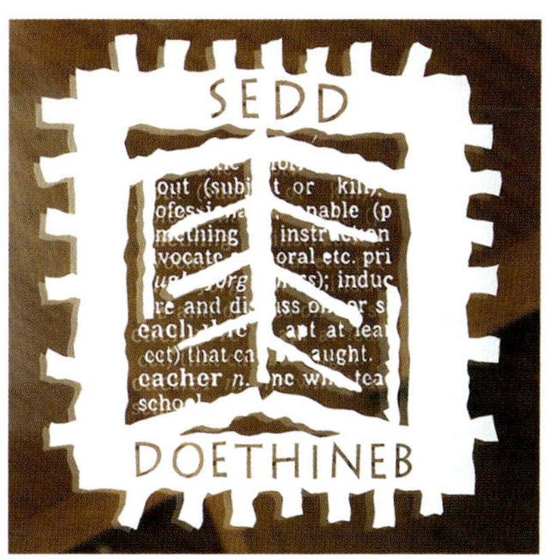

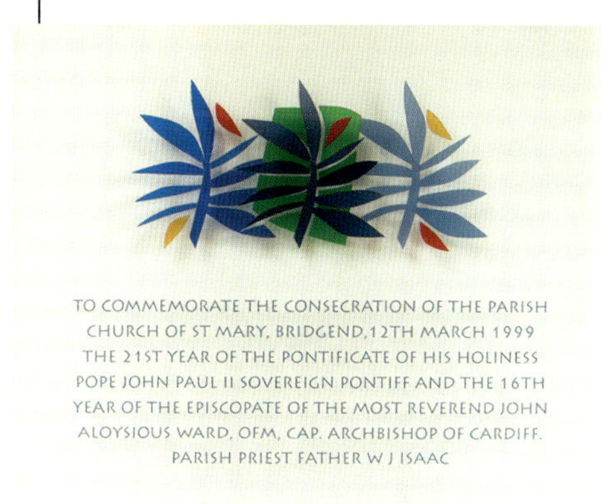

13 These designs include more universal titles such as 'Queen of the Rosary' and 'Queen of Heaven', while others are more specific to Wales, such as 'Our Lady of Penrhys' and 'Our Lady of the Taper', which refer to medieval statues that were the objects of pilgrimage until they were destroyed at the Reformation.

14 Although the new church has reset stained glass from the previous building, neither this nor any of the new commissions are used as exterior windows of the new church.

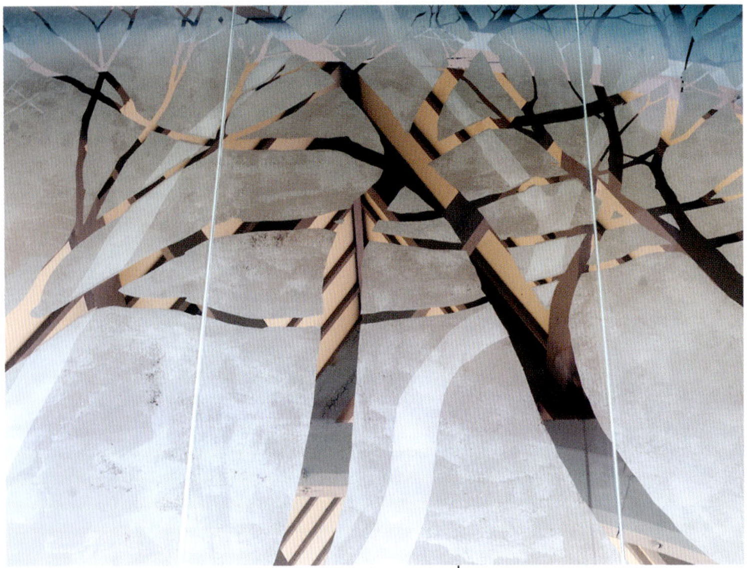

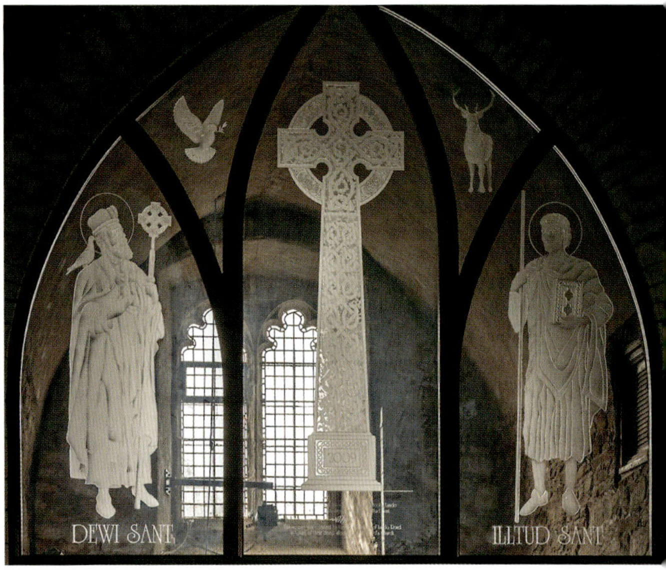

782. Bill Swann, The Tree of Life, 2000, Church of St Maelog, Llanfaelog, first floor screen

783. John Davies, St David and St Illtyd, 2010, Church of St Illtyd, Pembrey, vestry screen

The use of glass within churches as internal screens has increased in recent years as churches have been subdivided and new interior spaces have been created. In 2000 the Church of St Maelog, Llanfaelog, was reordered by the architect Adam Voelcker, shortening the nave and creating an upstairs room at the west end. This room was enclosed with windows overlooking the nave, with a large arched opening above that was glazed with trees etched into the glass by Bill Swann, following a co-ordinated scheme incorporating glass and woodcarving with the theme of the Tree of Life.[15] Etched images of the Welsh saints David and Illtud are set at either side of a large Celtic-Christian cross on the vestry screen at the Church of St Illtyd, Pembrey, and the Lady Chapel at the Church of All Saints, Porthcawl, has been enclosed in a glass screen with designs by the architect Gordon Clarke.[16] In 2006 a memorial panel using more traditional techniques by Anna Bessant was inserted into the glass screen separating the tower room at the Church of St Catwg, Llangattock, with small pieces of coloured glass surrounding a dedication and the text 'I have called you friends' (John 15: 15).

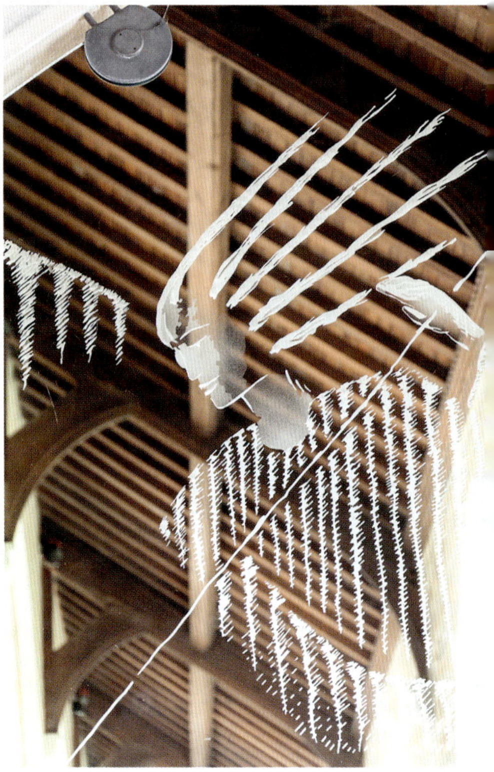

784. Gordon Clarke, Angel, 2007, Church of All Saints, Porthcawl, Lady Chapel

15 As well as the wooden font holder for the medieval font brought from nearby Tal-y-llyn, communion rails, communion table and pulpit by the sculptor Colin Pearce, further glass by Bill Swann was inserted in the door from the new foyer into the church.

16 The engraved and sandblasted figures by John Hutton for the (liturgical) west window of Coventry Cathedral of 1961 are probably the best-known precursor to similar figures achieved by etching and sandblasting glass. Similar engraved figures were designed by Frank Roper in 1963 for the west window of the Church of St Crallo, Coychurch.

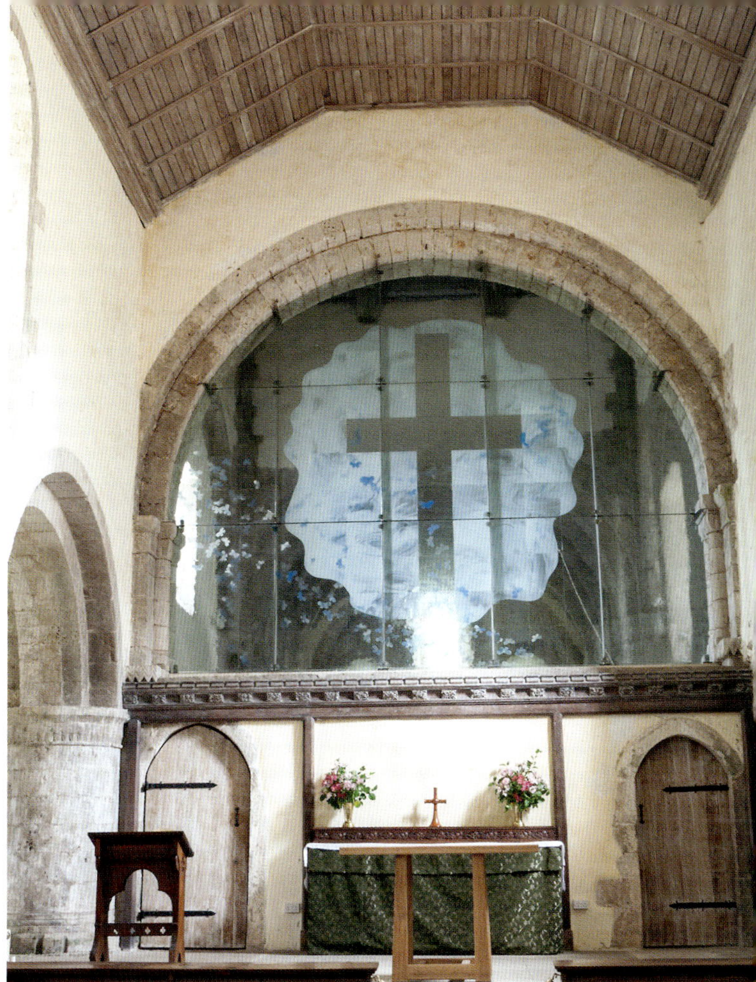

785. Alexander Beleschenko, Pulpitum Screen, made with Rodney Bender, 2006, Priory Church of St Michael and All Angels, Ewenny

Screens dividing internal spaces often require technical innovation in architectural glass that has been developed for other kinds of public and corporate buildings. Perhaps the largest interior screen in a Welsh church was designed by Alexander Beleschenko and installed in 2006 at Ewenny Priory in collaboration with Rodney Bender. The pulpitum screen divides the parish church, in the nave of the former twelfth-century priory, from the crossing and transept, which is in the care of CADW, the Welsh Government body for the historic environment. The artist has placed a cross in the midst of butterflies, which blends rather than dominates its surroundings using soft colours painted on antique glass. This is bonded onto toughened glass plates borne on a stainless steel structural support frame.

The relocation of stained glass from former places of worship that have been demolished or converted for other uses has increased in recent years as financial pressures and declining congregations have accelerated the closure of places of worship. Churches are increasingly making use of windows from other churches that have closed in their external windows, or accommodating them by mounting them internally against external windows. In some places this has been unproblematic, such as at the Church of St Grwst, Llanrwst, a church with only a little early-Victorian stained glass in the chancel, where the three-light east window by William Aikman from the closed church at Capel Garmon was adapted to fit a north wall window. The results have occasionally been convenient for the visiting historian of stained glass. For example, the surviving chapel at Bethlehem, Treorchy (English Calvinistic Methodist), has a collection of stained glass originally from local Nonconformist chapels that have now closed. The re-siting of windows by John Petts and Celtic Studios from the Church of St Peter, Nantyfyllon, alongside others by the same artists at the Church of St Cynfelin, Caerau, has created a varied collection of their work over several decades.[17]

17 All of these windows were quite small and the former east window from Nantyfyllon remains in store.

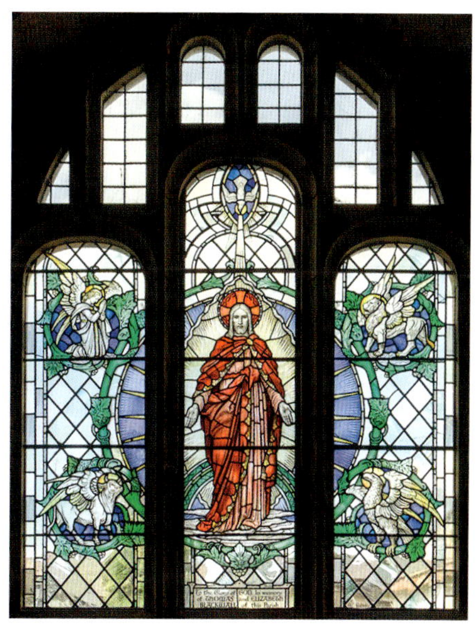

786. William Aikman, Christ with the Four Evangelists, 1939, Church of St Grwst, Llanrwst (formerly at the Church of St Garmon, Capel Garmon, reset by Meridian Stained Glass, 2000)

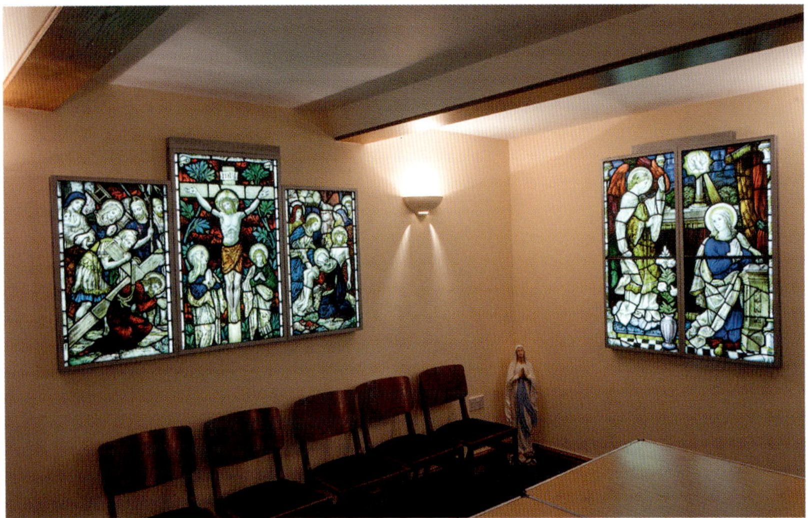

787. Panels by James Powell & Sons, 1897, and probably Burlison & Grylls, early twentieth century, Church of the Holy Trinity, Ystrad Mynach, All Saints Room (formerly at the Church of All Saints, Llanbradach)

In a few cases the addition of new work has been constrained as any plain exterior windows have already been filled with stained glass. Late nineteenth and early twentieth-century windows were saved from the Church of All Saints, Llanbradach, subsequently demolished, and kept in store at the Church of the Holy Trinity, Ystrad Mynach, where all of the windows of the church were unusually narrow and mostly filled with stained glass. Panels from a window by James Powell & Sons and at least one by Burlison & Grylls have now been mounted in lightboxes around the walls of the appropriately named All Saints Room, used for prayer and meetings, situated beneath the church. Lightboxes have also been used to install stained glass by Evelyn Woodcock at the Church of St James, Manorbier, in 2002 and 2011, as the windows of the church were already full of a variety of twentieth-century glass.[18]

Windows have occasionally become detached from the religious purposes that they once served as the result of internal reordering of church interiors. Others remaining in church buildings that have been closed and reused now find themselves in private dwellings,

18 The two works were given to the church by the Bradley-Kidd family, who were related to the artist and had inherited the panels. Evelyn May Woodcock had been a member of the Arts and Crafts Exhibition Society and taught stained glass design at Harrogate School of Art. I am grateful to Gerald Codd for information regarding these panels.

788. (below) Vestibule Window, perhaps 1898, former Noddfa Chapel, Corris (now a private house)

789. (below centre) Ward & Hughes, Angel, c. 1870, Church of St John, Clydach, west end of the church, reordered as a kitchen

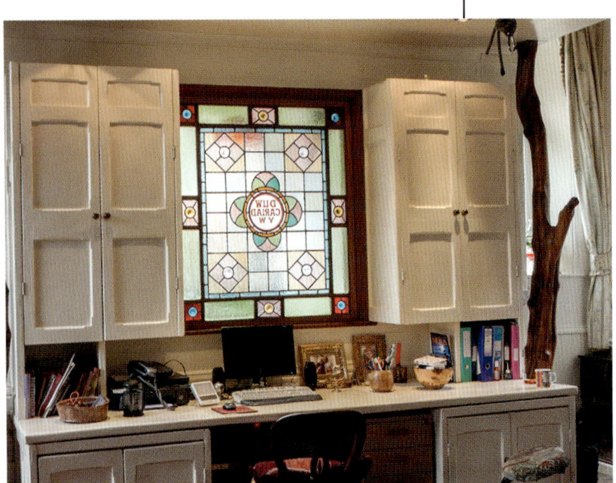

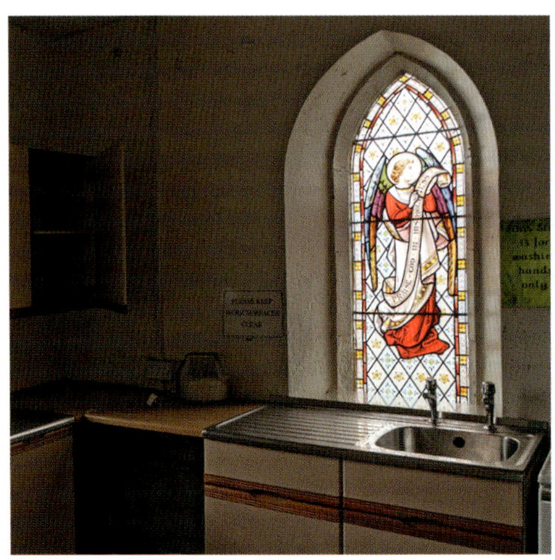

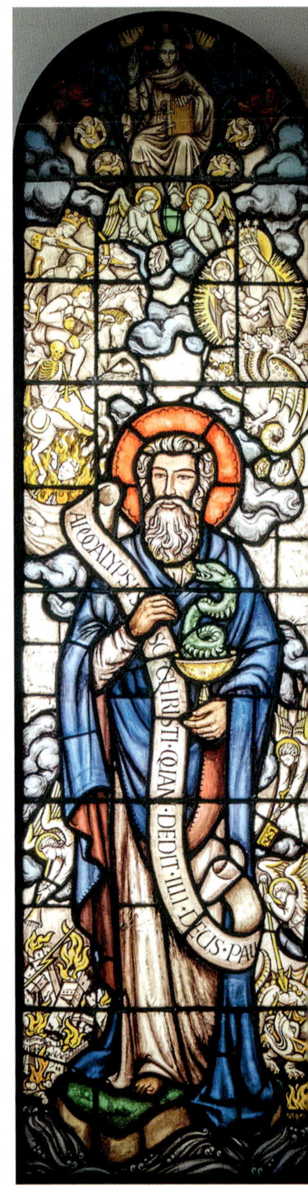

790. Evelyn Woodcock, St Joh probably 1920s, Church of St Jame Manorbier, chanc

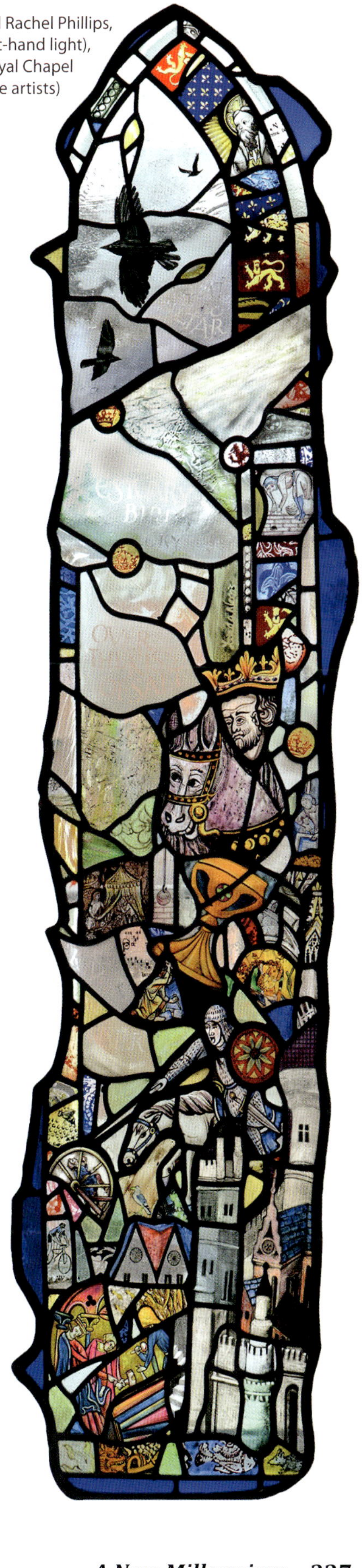

792. Linda Norris and Rachel Phillips, *Garrison of Flowers* (right-hand light), 2012, Conwy Castle, Royal Chapel (photo © the artists)

offices and children's play centres, and carry traces of the meaning of these formerly consecrated buildings. In contrast, new windows with Christian meaning have been placed outside churches but in adjoining buildings, such as Gareth Morgan's window in the ante-chapel at Trinity College, Carmarthen. The window was given in memory of the historian Norah Isaac and expresses the history of Christianity in Wales, including significant figures of the church as well as a Celtic-Christian cross-head and patterns from late medieval rood screens. Three windows by Linda Norris and Rachel Phillips made for the Royal Chapel of Conwy Castle also incorporate medieval imagery, and include copies of surviving medieval stained glass in north Wales. The fragmentary design is reminiscent of the windows put together from unrelated pieces of medieval glass in the nineteenth and early twentieth centuries, and the playful use of fragments of Christian imagery partly re-sanctifies a religious space in the substantial ruins of this popular tourist attraction and World Heritage Site.

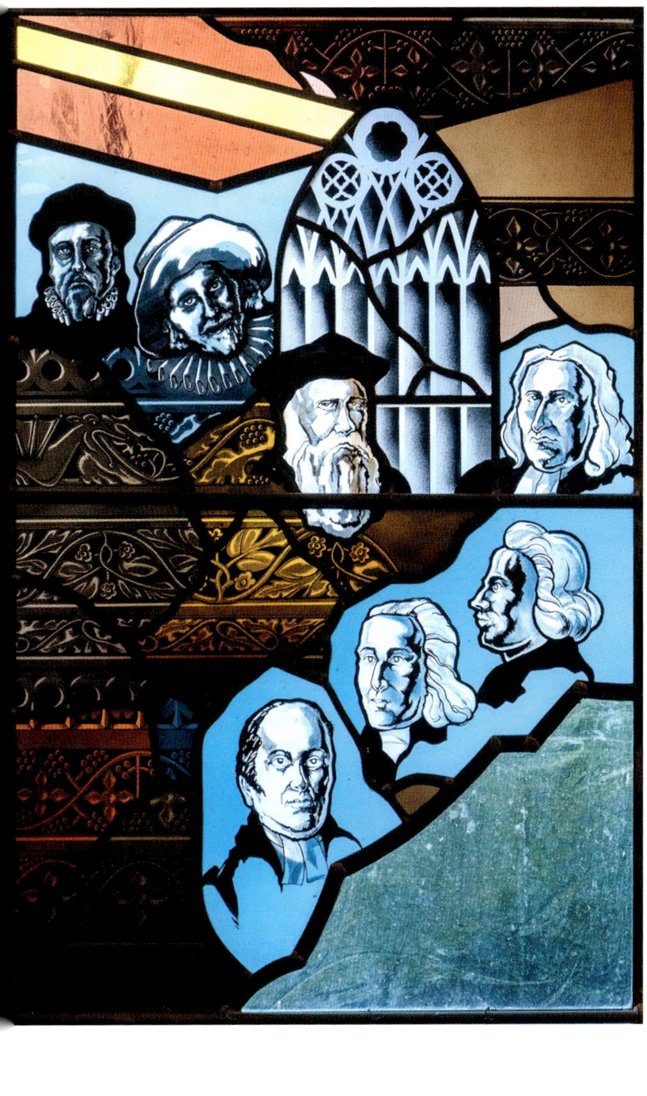

The quotations from the visual culture of the past in these recent examples of stained glass illustrate the irresistible connection of the medium with its medieval past. Rather than being imitative, the artists use tradition in a contemporary way, as does

791. Gareth Morgan, Norah Isaac Memorial Window, 2008, ante-chapel to Trinity College Chapel, University of Wales Trinity St David, Carmarthen

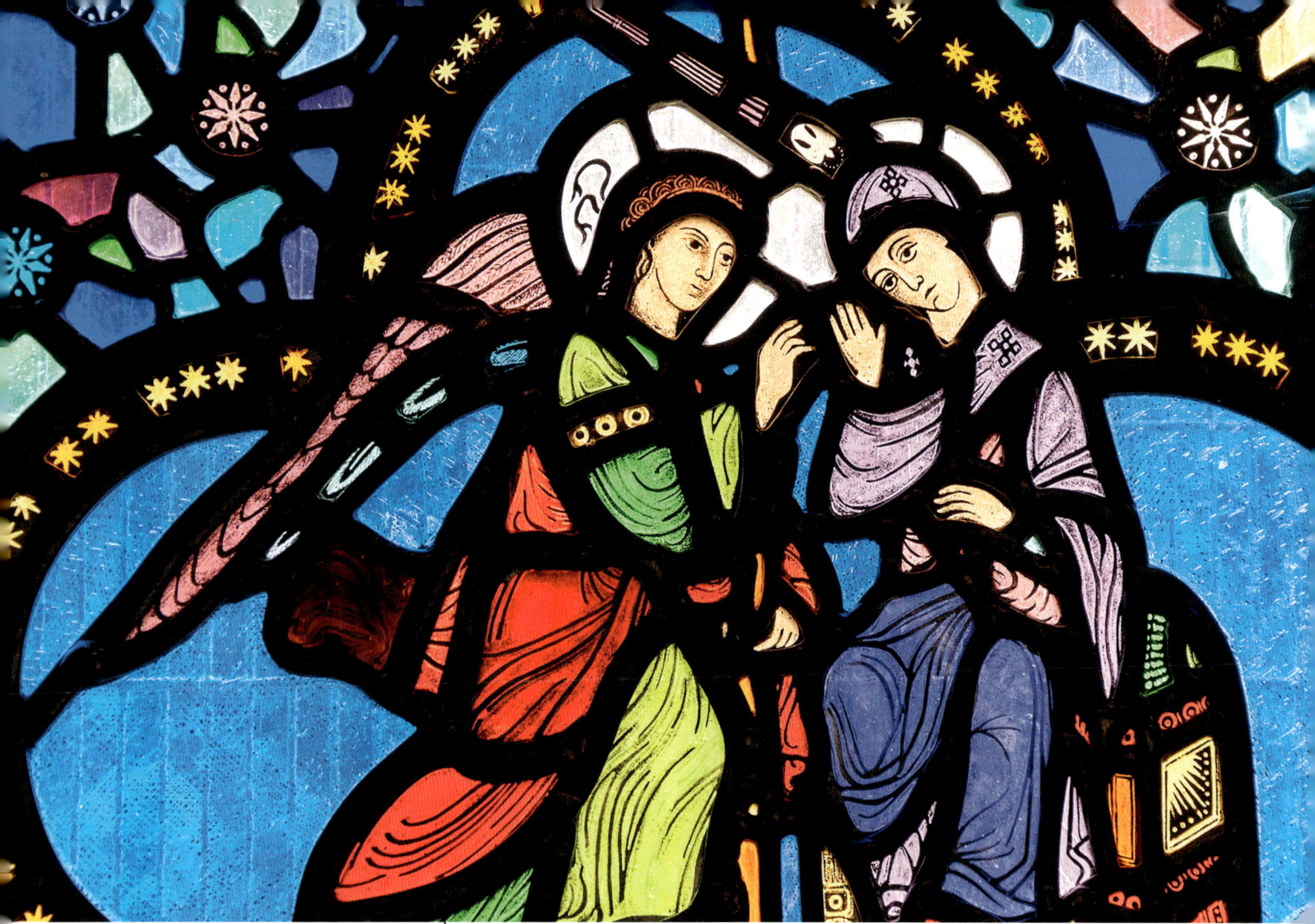

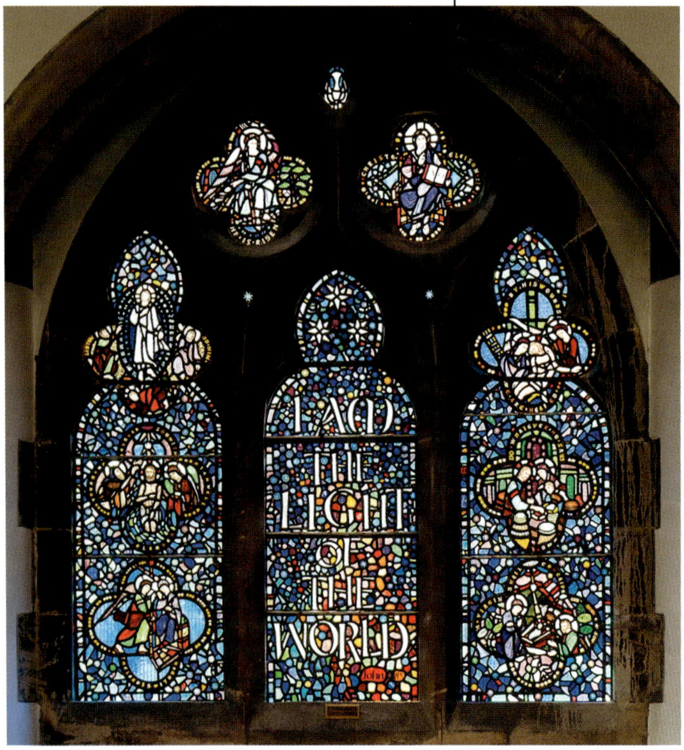

Anna Bessant in her three-light window made in 2010 for the Church of St Martin, Caerphilly. The framing of narrative scenes in medallions, the predominance of blue glass, and use of small pieces are suggestive of late twelfth and early thirteenth-century work, and emphasised by her knowledge of medieval orthodox icons. But the window is a consciously contemporary one. Texts are used to underline the message boldly in the central light and discreetly around the scenes, and the small pieces of glass create abstract patterns around the scenes and figures.

In more expressive painterly works, such as Rachel Phillips' representation of the Good Samaritan at the Church of St Peter, Peterston-super-Ely, the

793–4. Anna Bessant, 'I am the Light of the World', including the Annunciation (above), 2010, Church of St Martin, Caerphilly, north aisle

795. Rachel Phillips, The Good Samaritan, 2013, Church of St Peter, Peterston-super-Ely, chancel

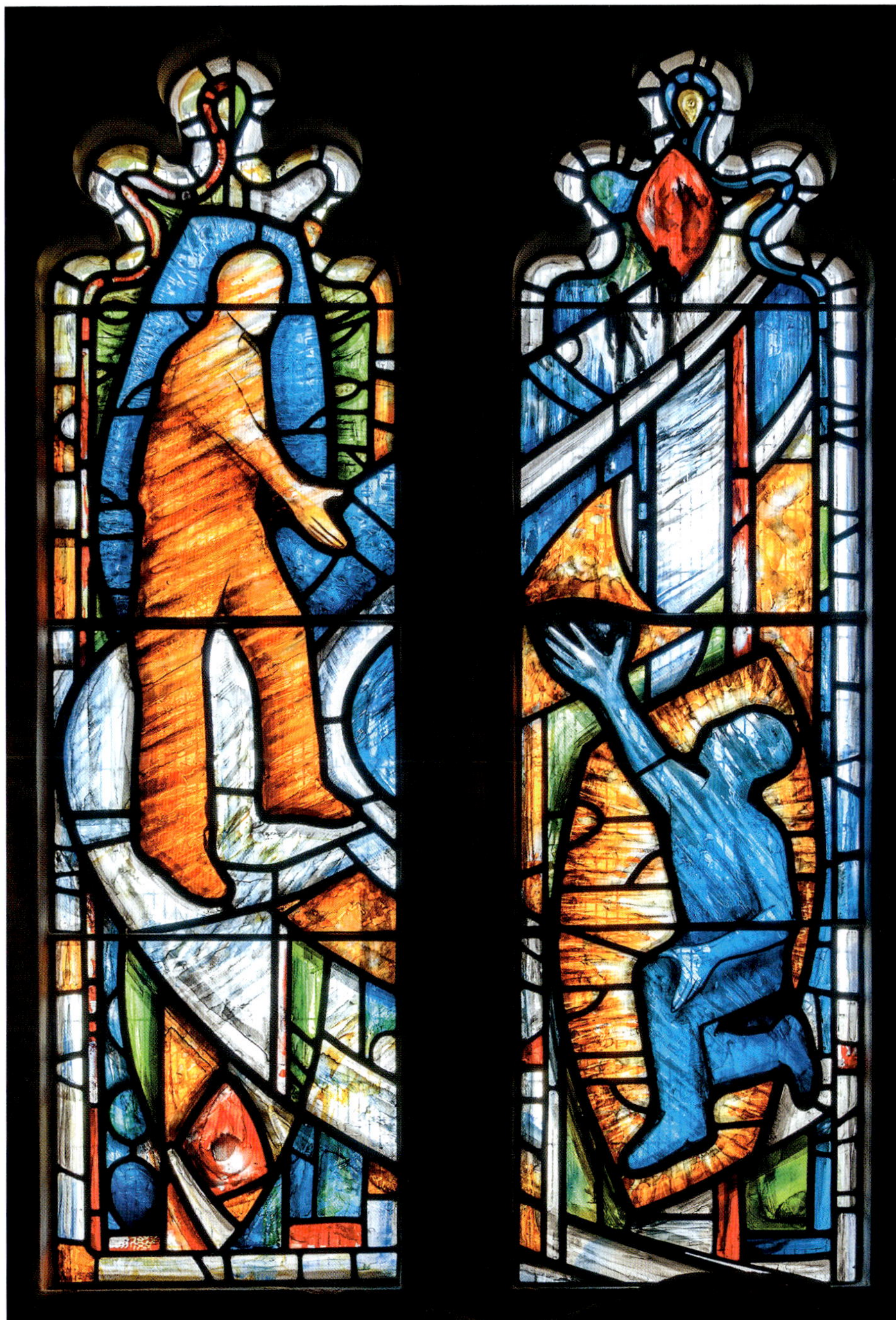

connection with the medieval is less obvious. The glass painting has a modern sophistication and the design also breaks free of the usual representation of the scene, going beyond the biblical narrative to suggest a broader message of a stranger extending a hand to someone in need. Nevertheless, the use of coloured glass leaded together in the medieval mosaic technique remains a feature of the work, along with its biblical subject matter, and the artist acknowledges that medieval tradition is an essential source for her work, along with other artistic influences such as that of post-war artists such as Evie Hone.[19]

The number of new stained glass windows now being commissioned for churches in Wales may be fewer than at any time since the early nineteenth century, with the exception of the lull in production necessitated by the Second World War. Stained glass artists specialising in ecclesiastical work are often busy with restoration in an age that, unlike that which prevailed until the second half of the twentieth century, is more likely to conserve old stained glass than replace it. Artists making new works in architectural glass continue to bring technical innovation to the medium in its widest sense, striking their own balance between tradition and invention in their creative representation of the mysteries of faith.

19 The window, made in 2013 along with another made by Phillips to the design of Delyth Evans, also brings to an end the addition of stained glass to the church, now that each of the windows has been filled with examples from a range of artists and dates since 1891.

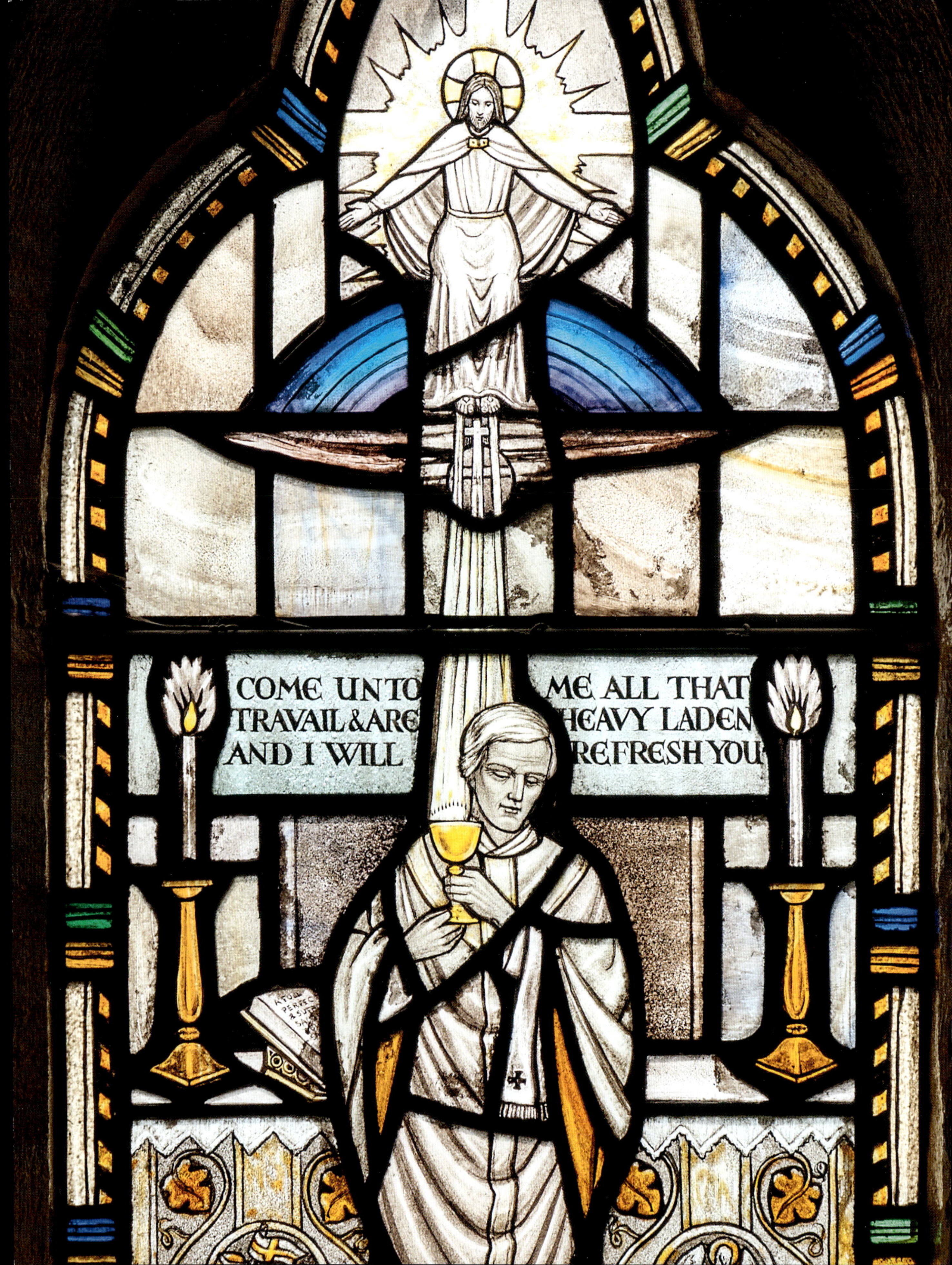
COME UNTO ME ALL THAT
TRAVAIL & ARE HEAVY LADEN
AND I WILL REFRESH YOU

Index

. Aldrich Rope, Priest with the Eucharist, 1950,
rch of the Holy Trinity, Esclusham, south transept

overleaf: Celtic Studios, Dove of the Holy Spirit, 1964, Church of St Eloi, Llandeloy, west window

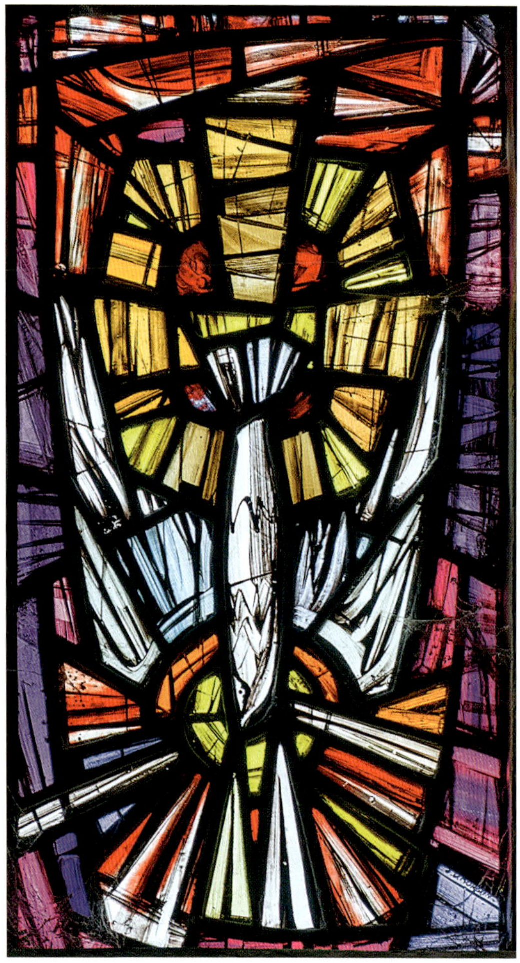